GOVERNMENTS OF CONTINENTAL EUROPE

France

by **R. K. GOOCH**, *University of Virginia*

Italy and Switzerland

by **ARNOLD J. ZURCHER**, *New York University*

Germany

by **KARL LOEWENSTEIN**, *Amherst College*

The USSR

by **MICHAEL T. FLORINSKY**, *Columbia University*

Edited by **JAMES T. SHOTWELL**

President Emeritus, Carnegie Endowment for International Peace

GOVERNMENTS

OF

Continental

Europe

Revised Edition

THE MACMILLAN COMPANY : *New York*

PREFACE

When the first edition of this volume appeared, in September, 1940, the Hitlerian revolution in Europe was already in full swing, challenging at least 300 years of history, practically the whole period of modern state building; but although this movement had, even in its opening phases, wrought far-reaching changes in the polity and way of life of nations which had developed institutions of representative government and liberty, it was much too soon to say what the outcome would be. Nor was this problem clarified throughout the years of World War II when, even more than in World War I, the New World intervened to redress the balance of the Old. In the uneasy and imperfect peace which has followed on the cessation of actual fighting, many questions are still left unanswered, some of them fundamental, but a new state structure has come into being in Europe different in many respects from that described in the first edition of this book. The text has therefore largely been rewritten, although its purpose remains the same: a survey of the political institutions which have withstood the iron pressures of war or which embody the ideals and outlook of Europe today. From an analysis of these studies it is evident that history still furnishes the central clue as to the nature of a nation's choice of the kind of government which it accepts. Even in the stress and strain of war and of its aftermath, national character or need finds an expression either in the acceptance of its political regime or in its protest against it, however futile for the time being.

Although these studies deal with the greatest political creation of modern history, the National State, it takes most of that history for granted, for there is less of the narrative of events in the text than of their outcome as registered in public or constitutional law and administrative structure. This fact explains the absence of discussion of the role of war, not only in these last years, but also in the formation and structure of the national state system of Europe. It was power, symbolized by or embodied in armed might which fashioned that system out of the anarchy of feudalism, from the Hammer of Charles Martel and the swords of medieval kings to Metternich and Bismarck. War as the instrument of national politics cleared the way for the constructive forces of peace. Without security there could be no guarantee of peace or freedom. But the states thus created continued to accept war as a legitimate instrument in their dealings with each other. The "final argument of kings" remained a prerogative of sovereignty. Now two world wars have challenged this historic process in Western Europe. In World War II the Axis powers mobilized the forces of militarism in a joint effort to reconstruct the existing state system by resort to the traditional methods of blood and iron. But in the murky light of the war's aftermath, there are signs that the era of national wars is drawing to a close in that part of the world in which they have been most common in the past. It is at least from this point of view that the foreign policies of Great Britain, France, and Italy are directed today, not by utopian idealists, but by hard-bitten realists with long experience in the responsibilities of government. While no one can say that there will not be a revival of national wars, the prime issue of today is the maintenance of peace. For the first time in history, peace as a technique, has become a major element of practical politics.

It is too soon for the full effect of this revolutionary turn in the instrumentation of politics to be fully registered in terms of government, but its bearing upon the problems of welfare, which are the central interest of the daily life of nations, is as real as upon those of security. These problems of the interplay of national interest and of economic and revolutionary forces are not ignored in this volume, but its discussions stop upon the threshold of the future and do not attempt speculation within its cloudy frontiers. Nevertheless, it would be highly unrealistic if it failed to indicate the impact upon European society and politics of the one most disturbing force in the post-war world—international Communism. The economic doctrines of Marxian Socialism lie too far in the background for description or analysis, but under the guidance of Lenin and Stalin Communism, linked with Russian imperialism, emerged to become a political force consciously disruptive and revolutionary to an even greater extent than the French Revolution, when Jacobinism took on the aspect of a military crusade. The ominous shadow of Moscow is more sinister, because more insidious, than either Fascism or Nazism, but the reaction of Western Europe to Stalinism is awakening a sense of common interests among the nations, with political implications never before seriously entertained by responsible statesmen. Facts like these should be kept in mind in the study of government. It is not a study in statics but in dynamics, for government is strongest when most capable of adjusting itself to changing situations.

As for the method of cooperation by which this composite work was prepared, it should be said that it was, to the fullest extent, that of free association, and that each author is responsible for that section of it which he himself has written, and bears no corporate responsibility for the volume as a whole.

J. T. S.

CONTENTS

PART II. THE GOVERNMENT OF THE FOURTH REPUBLIC

PART III. POLITICS AND PARTIES IN THE FOURTH REPUBLIC

THE GOVERNMENT AND POLITICS OF ITALY
by Arnold J. Zurcher

THE POLITICAL SYSTEM OF SWITZERLAND
by Arnold J. Zurcher

THE GOVERNMENT AND POLITICS OF GERMANY
by Karl Loewenstein

PART I. INTRODUCTION: THE FORMATION
OF THE GERMAN NATION

The Holy Roman Empire of the Germanic Nation (800–1806), 389.
The Reformation, 389. The Rise of Prussia, 390. The Napoleonic Era,
390. The German Bund, 391. The Revolution of 1848, 391. Bismarck and German National Unification, 392. Imperial Germany
(1871–1918), 392.

PART II. THE WEIMAR REPUBLIC (1919–1933)

PART III. THE THIRD REICH (1933–1945)

PART IV. GERMANY SINCE 1945

INTRODUCTION

THE PROBLEM OF GOVERNMENT

by JAMES T. SHOTWELL

1. THE CHALLENGE OF RECENT EVENTS

The world crisis of today is making clearer than ever before the importance of government in the evolution of civilization. Before the Fascist and Nazi autarchies of Central Europe and the Communist Revolutionaries challenged the nature of government as embodied in the National State System of the nineteenth century, students of public affairs were more interested in what political institutions were doing than in what they were.

The process of law-making could, so it seemed, be taken for granted; executive, legislative, judicial organs of government pursued their accustomed routine. The main principles of government were unquestioned in most countries, above all, in the democracies. In the case of the United States the Constitution furnishes an unquestioned framework within which government functions for good or ill. The student of American history has accepted this political structure as inevitable. Similarly, within the British Commonwealth of Nations, that federated group of self-governing countries under the British Crown, the unwritten constitution of the mother country has been regarded as furnishing the essential outlines of a system of guarantees of self-government, embodying indisputable axioms of wisdom. The French have their own tradition of liberty and self-government in a republican framework which has stood seventy years of unparalleled stress and strain, buttressed as it is by the conservatism that is the heritage of history. The smaller European democracies which existed prior to 1914, especially the Scandinavian countries, Switzerland, the Netherlands, and Belgium, likewise have taken their constitutions for granted; and while they, like all the rest, were interested in their maintenance, they concentrated attention more upon social and economic questions than upon the nature of government. In all these countries the structure of government had apparently ceased to be a major question either for practical politics or for academic discussion. Everywhere it was recognized that there was room for betterment, as movements for reform challenged from time to time the complacency of the conservatives. But these were all, or nearly all, in one direction, and that was in the fulfillment of the original plan. Democracies were becoming more democratic, and governments more efficient; the public interest lay in seeing how far this could proceed within the recognized framework of the State. Except for what seemed like a negligible minority, the accent in political debate was upon what the government did, rather than upon what the government was.

The autarchies of Central Europe challenged this way of looking at things, and rejected not only the kinds of government under which they formerly lived but the very reasons for their existence and the purposes they served. Though defeated in World War II, their theories are still held by many of their adherents, who are certain to become articulate when the opportunity arrives for them to speak. In short, the conception of government as power rather than as a living and responsive organ of national life still lives on. This is equally true of the history of the USSR under the Stalinist regime. When movements like these are under way, it is fatal blindness for the citizens of countries not—or not yet—subject to the influence of these attacks upon their institutions to remain indifferent to what is at stake. It may be that the movement will pass into history leaving much less trace than most people think; but it may be that not only our institutions but our fortunes and our lives will be at stake, before the issue as to what is the right form of government will have been fought out. In any case, the situation is one that calls for careful and thoughtful study; for it must be remembered that the national institutions and ideals which we prize were once highly respected by most people in all the countries that have now rejected them. Representative government, for example, was once accepted everywhere, either as a fact or a thing to be desired. Even Czarist Russia paid tribute to the political genius of the English, when it sought to quiet revolution by the establishment of the Duma; and, although war and revolution soon played havoc with liberalism, it was only with the passing of time that the Soviet form of government was to stand revealed as a more important fact than the principles of Communist economics. The Communist State soon modified its collective system for purposes of efficiency, but has been unyielding in its insistence upon absolute power. The Nazi Government, more consistent in its evolution, steadily extended the scope of the authoritarian State. Fascist Italy, having educated a whole generation in its doctrines, claimed utterly to have forgotten the liberalism of Cavour and of Mazzini. Even France, treasuring the tradition of the Revolution, called for a halt in the program of its social reforms and curtailment of political liberty in order to defend the Republic against the menace of a Europe given over to these new political doctrines, and thus did homage to their power.

The student of government should approach these problems not in the spirit of controversy, but with a scientific curiosity as to how the whole evolution has come about. This does not mean that he should be so detached in his outlook as not to have any interest in the ultimate outcome; for this is his world which is here described. The growth of science, with its conquest of time and space, making the world one—forcing interdependence upon nations, even against their will—makes these problems of other peoples his own. Their success or failure, their growth in power or misery, are bound to affect us, even if, happily, they leave untouched the fundamental nature of the American State.

But to understand what has taken place is not easy. It is difficult for those who live within the nations that are engaged upon these great experiments; it is still harder for us who look back across a wholly different history from that of Europe and can view, from what seems the safe distance of the New World, the tragic and hitherto futile struggle to secure an equilibrium. It is therefore important for us to find the best way for setting about the study of these things which are so dominant in Europe today.

2. THE COMPARATIVE STUDY OF GOVERNMENTS

The comparative study of governments is one of the most difficult of subjects. To compare the rules for human conduct in one country with those of another without regard to the differences in tradition, environment, and relation to other nations, or even without regard to the fundamental facts of geography, is more likely to open the door to misunderstanding than to enlightenment. The statistician can measure the output of industry or the extent of the wealth of different countries and produce a relatively reliable balance sheet, but no such balance sheet is possible in the comparison of one country's government with another. The institutions of government which bear the same name can be utterly unlike in their actual functioning. Above all, since government depends to a great degree upon public opinion, or the lack of it, in different countries, the mere study of the framework of institutions may be quite misleading as to their vitality or real importance.

It follows, therefore, that the comparison of externals in the study of government may often prove worse than useless. On the other hand, it is of course necessary in any general study of government to note the outer resemblances which make the history of government in different countries sufficiently similar in purpose at least, so that their general outlines are recognizable everywhere. For instance, to take the most elementary case, the evolution of government tended to bring about a recognition of the necessity of keeping the legislative and the judicial functions separate or carefully defined. This was already evident in the Roman Republic, that supreme experiment in the political development of the antique world—an experiment which was carefully studied by the philosophers who laid the bases for modern political theory. The rigid constitutional separation between executive and legislative functions is of course not to be found in governments of a parliamentary system; it is the peculiar mark of the form of government of the United States and of those countries which have been influenced by its constitutional history. But it is one thing to recognize these three groupings of the powers of government as inherent in the governments of all civilized countries, and it is quite another thing to know the relationship of one to the other and their relative importance. In measuring these facts, or attempting to do so, we must not lose sight of the lesser organs of government in each case and their relation to the sovereign bodies. No country, not even in the centralized systems of autocracy, entrusts all its government to the supreme authority; for government is the management of the nation's business as well as the higher direction of it. Therefore, the administrative systems which extend throughout the whole country must be examined as well as any other special bodies like those which have grown up recently in times of crisis, if we are to have an accurate picture of government as a whole.

It is of interest to point out that the divergencies which seem so striking between the Continental European and the United States forms of government may exist to an equal extent elsewhere. One of the outstanding statesmen of Latin America, who had been and was to be again the President of his country, came to the United States some years ago to study how our government actually worked, because he as a trained jurist had come to the conclusion that the terms which we use to describe government mean different things in different languages. For instance: Liberty does not mean quite the same thing as freedom. Liberty, with its Latin associations, carries the suggestion of escape from tyranny or overexactions of government. This was what the French meant by *liberté* in the French Revolution and in Jacobin philosophy. There it was a revolt against the exactions, mostly feudal, of the Old Regime. It was more a negative than a positive concept. It set bounds to governments and safeguarded the freedom of the individual. Freedom on the other hand has a positive content; it is a normal expression of life itself, something which the individual obtains as a birthright, especially in countries which treasure the common law of England and recognize the inherent regard for human rights, which has become a tradition of the Anglo-Saxon way of living. Even in English, the words liberty and freedom are not entirely synonymous.

The South American statesman, studying the way in which the United States actually governs itself, came to the conclusion that the fundamental concepts of government were different here from what they were in his country, although he used the same language in describing them. For him, government was a synonym for authority, and not for cooperation; the citizen was either on the side of the government or was its political enemy, one whose latent hostility could be taken for granted. The American party system of government, while it divided the nation to some extent on traditional lines and to a greater extent on the issues of the day, was, he said, always subordinate to something which the countries of the Latin tradition found hard to understand, a thing called "public spirit."

It should be evident from this discussion that external comparisons of one government with another have to be used with the utmost care.

3. THE STATE

The fact, which seems obvious to us now, that we must go behind the framework of governments if we are to understand them does not justify the conclusion that the framework is less important than jurists formerly thought it was. On the contrary, as was indicated in the opening sentences of this Introduction, we are becoming more and more aware of the importance of the institutions by which nations act, because they so largely determine the character of the nation. It was, therefore, a contribution of the first order when the political scientists of the nineteenth century traced in such confident outline the place of government in the national State, even if the universal standards which they set up did not always apply. It was something, for example, to have pointed out more clearly than had been done before, the distinction between government and State and to bring to the fore the great issue of the nature of sovereignty.

These were definite gains in the understanding of organized society. The critic of today is too likely to forget what a great advance they represented upon the careless generalizations of earlier writers. But, while appreciating the contributions of these systematizers of political theory, we must at the same time be aware of their limitations.

Among these there was the tendency to think in absolute terms, to erect hard and fast categories into which all the varied data of different national histories would have to fit. We have just seen two examples of this: a touchstone for testing the excellence of governments was rightly held to be the preservation of liberty. Therefore, the country which made provision for it in its constitution had apparently reached a higher stage of development than one which had not. But the logic is misleading, because nations have different ways of doing the same thing and different needs at different times. In times of supreme crisis every nation changes its form of government; but there are varying degrees of emergency all the time, and no one system of government can serve as a rigid universal model for all the world. This is to be borne in mind in the present world crisis.

The study of government, therefore, is but part of a larger problem, that of the nature of the State. The modern State itself might be described as a house for a nation to live in. The older ones often have venerable exteriors and dark or unfrequented rooms within. All of them have brave fronts; for democracies are as susceptible to display and national prestige as monarchies. But most of the nation's activities, those of the day's work of the common man, take place in complete indifference to what is being done in offices of governments. The State is large enough to include both government and the escape from it in the sphere of liberty. Also we must remember that the State, and not merely the government, is the ultimate source of authority, that is to say, sovereignty.

It is an axiom of political theory that only the State can be sovereign; and that sovereignty is the highest expression of power. The German theorists of the nineteenth century, whose teachings molded the thought of American universities at the turn of the century, phrased the concept of sovereignty in more extreme terms. It was absolute power and lay beyond all possibility of question or dispute. One might question its agents or its national embodiment; but sovereignty itself could no more be questioned than life. One might object to this or that living body but life itself is an ultimate that transcends its manifestations. So this ultimate attribute of the State was regarded in theory as unlimited and unqualified power, the exercise and direction of which would depend upon the real needs of the State. "Reasons of State" was the accepted phrase which excused resort to force to attain its ends.

The theory of the absolute sovereignty of States has played an important part in the history of governments, especially in their relations with one another. If sovereignty means that every national State is the judge of its own actions, the consequence is international anarchy. The insistence on the full exercise of such prerogatives is, fortunately, rare; because the process of diplomacy and treaty-making keep the international neighborhood working fairly well under ordinary circumstances. But when major controversies arise, politics of power fall back upon absolute sovereignty. This makes war a potential threat all the time; so long as these conditions last, all talk of permanent peace between nations is utopian. The "balance of power" is an uncertain anchorage for stability.

But over against this assertion of absolute sovereignty, there is also a drift toward a recognition of the conception of the State as a partner with other States in the furtherance of the great ideals of peace and social and political justice. For the attainment of this purpose sovereignty must be relative, not absolute. Just as within the State, it is and always has been limited by habits and morals, so between nations it is—and has been—limited by recognition of common interests. In short, the only political reality is that which can be realized; and it is limited, not absolute, sovereignty.

It is significant that it was in Bismarckian Germany that the idea of absolute sovereignty was given its classic form and that it found lodgment in the United States in the generation that followed the War Between the States. Those who lived through the final process of the making of the States were naturally those who insisted upon its ultimate prerogatives. Since World War I, however, there were two notable movements in the opposite direction, the acceptance by nearly all the world, in principle at least, of the Covenant of the League of Nations and its successor, the Charter of the United Nations, and the recognition of a British Commonwealth of Nations in the Statute of Westminster of 1931. In both cases States surrendered some portion of their sovereignty. The State Members of the League of Nations did not live up to their obligations under the Covenant, it is true, but they all recognized that in not doing so they were making it impossible for the League to fulfill its mission, and that the chief obstacle to any effective League in the future is this question of State sovereignty, a conclusion somewhat obscured but still basic in the history of the United Nations. As for the British Commonwealth of Nations—also in its present form a creation of World War I—the grant of almost complete independence to the Dominions leaves both them and the mother country with incomplete sovereignty as States. This fact is not changed, although it, too, is obscured, by a common allegiance to the Crown of Great Britain. The sovereignty of States is not the same as the sovereignty of kings. Yet one is tempted to wonder if the British, by the device of this symbolism of royalty, may not have found a way to harmonize the sense of unity and stability, which lies in the concept of sovereignty, with that of adjustment to changing circumstance, which is an equally vital need of nations in the dynamic era of science.

4. TRIBAL ORIGINS

The method followed in this volume is the opposite of that which has been described above. Instead of taking the different organs of government in each country and comparing them one by one with those in the other countries of Continental Europe, the institutions of each country are described against their own background, or at least as much of them as is necessary to understand the problems of government today. The final work of comparison is left for the student and the teacher. But the volume supplies the data necessary for a general understanding of the way in which Europe is today consciously experimenting, as perhaps never before in all its history, with the structure and function of the State.

It is not possible in the limited space in this short Introduction to fill out the remoter background of this historical evolution, but some of its more fundamental elements should be kept in mind if we are to have an intelligent picture of the process as a whole; for however widely the institutions of government differ today, they all spring from common origins in the inherent needs of society.

Already in primitive life anthropology shows us some of the elements both of government and social cohesion which still play an important role in the modern world. Excluding as lying outside of history the rather hypothetical groupings of mankind into the semi-animal formations of the horde with no permanent structure or traceable continuity, we strike something definite and stable when the blood-tie becomes the basis of the family, clan, and tribe. But the blood-tie of primitive life was a very different thing from that of today; it was a relationship prescribed and determined by the most ironclad system of law that the world has ever produced—that of taboo. Although it goes without saying that the emotions played their passionate part in kinship relations, those relations themselves were prescribed and could not be violated without incurring death or exile, or at least the loss of membership in the tribe.

Government, apart from the routine of carrying on ordinary activities, might be described as the organization of safety; it was in the hands of those leaders who were recognized as qualified to meet danger and protect the tribe from it. This meant the evolution of two classes of specialists: those who knew how to meet and overcome the dangers of the unknown and the mysterious by the ceremonies of magic or religion (the medicine men or priests); and those who could best lead the war band against the neighboring enemies, but who also would have to know or accept the proper omens or auguries to win supernatural aid. This tribal form of society existed everywhere in Europe at the beginning of history and far along in its annals. In disguised ways some of it has lasted to the present, but until very recently it had ceased to play any important part in social formation, let alone political history. The Jewish people, it is true, when segregated into ghettos, preserved much of the social formation of the tribe on the religious basis, but not having any political embodiment this fact remained unimportant for any but themselves. On the other hand, the growth of nationalism, especially in Germany, fastened on to a racial myth—one that has no scientific validity whatever—that Nordic blood relationship was at least a recognizable qualification for German citizenship. It is because of this fundamental doctrine of the Nazis as to the peculiar quality of Aryan blood that it is necessary for the historian of Continental European governments today to go so far back as this into the tribal origins of settled society. So far as this basis of Nazi philosophy goes, it was only primitive tribalism in modern dress.

5. THE BEGINNINGS OF POLITICS

While the tribe stands in the background of Western history, that history only really begins with the breaking of the blood-tie and the disintegration of the tribe. This fact, that the origin of politics was a revolution—the first and most enduring of all revolutions—is equally true in Greece and Rome as it is in all the countries of Northern Europe. In Greece, the breaking down of the tribe took place in the sixth century B.C. when Cleisthenes reorganized the citizens of Athens according to wealth and situation and so recast the citizenship. From that time on, the management of the affairs of the City-State (Polis) acquired an importance of its own—politics. While never wholly secularized in the antique world, it became a school of human conduct whose leaders were not only the statesmen of Athens, but the philosophers and poets as well. The prime cause for this evolution from tribal life to politics was that Athens was becoming an important seaport, and foreign merchants settling in it brought new problems of law and justice both for themselves and for the native Athenians. The result was registered in the history which stretches from the early rise of capitalism when Solon recast the laws of debt to those of Aristotle who looked back into the history of the Athenian Constitution at the very moment when the long spears of Macedon were making of it only a thing for history.

The early evolution of politics in Rome was almost exactly the parallel of Athens. The traders who nosed their boats up the Tiber to the Seven Hills and spread their wares in their little stalls around the market place (Forum) were destined both to break down the ancient blood-tie of the tribesmen (in the Comitia Curiata) and ultimately to secure the full rights of citizens of Rome. This revolution started back in the days of the kings when Servius Tullius reconstructed both the army and the town meeting (Comitia Centuriata) on the basis of wealth. The process of integration of citizenship was slowly carried forward until at last it embraced all the nations that lived under the Roman sway. Parallel with this extension of citizenship went the other great achievement of Rome—the development of law from tribal custom under the kings, substituting contract for taboo and embracing Greek philosophy and the precepts of Christianity, until it became the noblest expression of the secular ideals of the ancient world and perhaps the most impressive monument of its culture.

The breakdown of the blood-tie north of the Alps was largely brought about through the migrations from Central and Northern Europe. This process had been going on for centuries before the breakdown of the Roman Empire. There were "Gauls" in Rome under the kings and they left their name in "Galatia" in Asia Minor, as well as on the borders of Russia. The Greeks of Homer had come from the north with their steel swords from Danubian smithies. In short, the process of migration which Caesar stopped for four centuries at the bridge of Geneva but which breached the walls of Rome in 410 A.D. was the keynote to both the prehistory and history of those peoples who were to be the ancestors of the French, the British, and the Germans today. The Gauls themselves were Germans, coming as they did not far from Hitler's home to overrun France, conquering the Mediterranean peoples, whose neolithic settlements had stretched up from Corsica to Wales.

While this vast turmoil of peoples, extending over centuries, mingled the blood of conqueror and conquered, it naturally left more of the primitive structure of tribal relationship in Germany than in the countries to the west and south. This is reflected in the history of the early Middle Ages. The German tribesmen, although consolidated into a confederacy called the Holy Roman Empire, maintained a strong feeling of kinship and loyalty to their tribal leaders in the so-called "stem-Duchies." So strongly did this persist that even the creator of the modern German Reich, Bismarck, could write in his memoirs that the German people were unique among Europeans for their attachment to the "stem-Duchies" rather than to the artificial creations of modern statecraft.[1] It was but a step from this to the theory of the Nazis—that German blood was the real cement for the Germanic peoples and that personal loyalty to a chieftain was the supreme test of citizenship.

It is only when we contrast this trend of German history with that of England that we realize how they are worlds apart in the appreciation of political institutions. England, although saved by its surrounding seas from the constant danger of invasion, was overrun by successive floods of invaders in the early Middle Ages, who, however, were not numerous enough wholly to supplant the native inhabitants. Coming by sea, they had been obliged to break their kinship ties to a great extent, and when they settled on the soil of Britain to make it England, their settlements (tuns) became the nuclei of self-government. Thus, little democracies were born which preserved their folk-ways to an astonishing extent throughout the Middle Ages, acting as nurseries of the common law and representative government. From these small units of local management there is an almost unbroken line to the New England town meeting. The body of the English people retained with stubborn tenacity these humble but important rights, recovering them after periods of anarchy or tyranny almost as if they were the expression of a law of nature itself.

6. KINGS, PARLIAMENTS, AND LAW COURTS

The interest of Americans in the history of democratic institutions tends to distort the true perspective of European history; for it was not until modern times that those institutions were really powerful enough to play a dominant political role. Although in the seventeenth century, when the English were

---

[1] It should be added, however, that no other nation has shaken up its tribal residue as fast as Germany in the twentieth century.

maintaining their liberties against the Stuart kings, their historians and lawyers looked back to Magna Carta as having established the fundamental principles of the rights of Englishmen, historians now view it on a less exalted plane as a document that was rather reactionary than progressive, so far as the feudal barons were concerned. Because King John had abused the royal power the barons temporarily resumed the task of State-building, which King John's father, Henry II, had so strongly developed.

But in England no less than on the Continent the dominant fact in the political evolution of the nation from the thirteenth to the seventeenth centuries was the part played by the King in the destruction of feudalism and the realization of national unity.

When under the Plantagenets in the twelfth century, the kingship became the symbol of national union and circuit courts dispensed the King's justice throughout the land, the English people were at least ready for the great experiment of national representative government with the King making the law through Parliament. The growth of the powers of Parliament opens too vast a field to be explored here, but there is one aspect of it that may be kept in mind in judging the institutions of today. At first, no one thought of Parliament as making laws; the King alone was, and still is, in legal theory—acting upon the advice of Parliament—the law-maker of the country. It is the old French formula *le roy le veult* which translates the wishes of Parliament into the laws of the nation. The way this came about is interesting. At first, all that the House of Commons ventured to do was to present a statement of its desire in the shape of a humble petition to His Majesty for redress of grievances, which the King then took into consideration and dealt with as seemed best to him. Then came the Hundred Years' War and the King needed more and more money. Parliament, therefore, became more self-confident, and when Henry IV called it together to vote him money for the continuance of the war, Parliament presented its "bill" in the exact terms in which it wished it to be carried out. In other words, the King was to "sign on the dotted line." Thus a bill of Parliament became an Act of Parliament, and the precedent was established for the procedure of representative government to this day.

This book does not propose to cover the history of the great English experiment to establish a government under liberty which, until recent years, was held everywhere to be a model for the world. It is necessary, however, as we turn back to the Continent, to keep in mind the fact that there is "an English way" of government which is deeply rooted in its own past but exceedingly responsive to the changing influences of time and circumstance. This last fact is perhaps partly due to the absence of a written constitution, a fact which has led the English to put more emphasis upon political and less upon juristic or legal relationships. The nation which holds itself together by contracts that are subject to judicial interpretation is naturally more rigid than one which in theory at least can change its fundamental instruments of government by the enactment of a law. And yet, the unwritten law of England which falls back upon precedent is perhaps as strong a safeguard of conservatism and as great an impediment to oft-times needed reforms as the written constitution which limits such action in countries like the United States. The one thing which the British method has produced to make its government both effective and responsive to the general will is that public spirit of its citizens to which we have made reference above.

The history of France presents the role of kingship in the molding of the State in a clearer outline than does the history of England, because the kings of France had a much harder task. They had no William the Conqueror to look back to, unifying the country under a strict military regime, as had been the case in England; and the territory to be united under the Crown was not only very much larger but more diverse and ruled by feudal lords, whose coalitions might prove as strong as those of the King himself. Royalty in France had three advantages. In the first place, the kings were anointed with sacred oil at their coronation in the cathedral of Rheims; and this marked them off by a kind of eighth sacrament from all other Frenchmen; in the second place, their territories were more strategically placed than those of other feudal lords, being centered in the Ile de France and along the valley of the Seine, with its converging riverways for traffic. The third advantage grew out of the second; the rise of commerce had, by the thirteenth century, created a money economy—the feeble beginnings of modern capitalism—which enabled the wealthy feudal rulers, and especially the King, to purchase services instead of relying upon feudal dues. The thirteenth century, which built the great cathedrals of France and therefore gave the external appearance of religiosity, was erecting institutions of government as outstanding as its churches, when for instance, Louis IX—St. Louis—made over part of his royal palace on the island in the heart of Paris to the lawyers and the law courts, where they still are. The Sainte Chapelle, built by him to enshrine the Crown of Thorns, still holds its miracle of beauty for the lover of art, but the Conciergerie, once the gallery for the guard that watched over the safety of the King, was destined to be the prison of Louis XVI.

The law courts of France thus so highly favored by royalty as an ally in the war on feudalism came in the course of time to serve as a check on royalty itself, from the civil war of the Fronde in the middle of the seventeenth century— which almost synchronized with the Civil War in England—to the French Revolution. The Hundred Years' War and the subsequent anarchy in France had prevented the development of a national French Parliament. The States-General, which had made such a promising beginning in 1302, had never gained control of the purse, meeting only at irregular intervals and never at all from 1614 to 1789. The law courts, especially those known by the confusing title of "parlements," more especially the "parlement de Paris," through the registering of royal decrees paralleled to some extent, though inadequately, the function of the English Parliament, as a check upon the arbitrary rule of the King.

This fact should be kept in mind in the study of the government of France today. As is pointed out in the section of this book dealing with that government, the French still provide not only for the independence of the judiciary by a separation of its powers from interference by the other branches of the government, but give it a somewhat wider field of action. The English courts, it is true, make "case law" by their decisions, but in the interpretation of statutes Parliament leaves little discretion. French laws are for the most part framed in rather general terms, stating clearly the intent and purpose of the law and leaving it to the administrative and judicial organs of the government to give effect to that purpose. Perhaps it should be added that the technique of legal formulation in France shows traces of the heritage of Roman law. Until recently, Acts of Parliament, on the contrary, and still more Acts of Congress of the United States, were frequently drafted to cover every imaginable point raised by the law, and thus to ensure that the purpose would be carried out by prescribing in detail for its application. With the rise of great government departments and an ever-increasing number of public servants, this practice has been changed to allow wide discretionary powers wherever necessary for effective administration. This "delegated legislation," as it is called, "is a natural reflection, in the sphere of constitutional law, of changes in our ideas of government which have resulted from changes in political, social and economic ideas, and of changes in the circumstances of our lives which have resulted from scientific discoveries." [2]

This is but one of many points of difference between the systems of government of France and England, the two great countries of Western Europe in which royalty, having emancipated the nation from feudalism, was in turn obliged to surrender its power to the great institutions of self-government, law-making, and the administration of justice. But there are others that should be noted, which are equally rooted in this parallel but varied history of the two countries. Above all, there is the attitude towards executive or administrative bodies, those whose duty it is to carry the laws into effect. As for France, it is perhaps not too much to say that the country has never wholly recovered from the despotism of the Old Regime, that despotism which was worked out by Richelieu, Mazarin, and Colbert on the foundations laid by Louis XI. It was a ruthless centralizing process which culminated in the "Divine Right of Kings." Thus the reform which substituted royal offices for feudalism, while it united France, failed to recognize the real force which held the country together, that of the rising middle class. Whereas in England, from the Great Revolution of 1688, this class believed, although at times wrongly, that because it held the purse strings of the government, it therefore could identify itself with the officials of the Crown, in prerevolutionary France these officials were the symbols of autocratic rule. The tradition remained, however, after the Revolution and has lasted to this day. The citizen, instead of cooperating readily with the bureaucracy, has felt more or less justified in evading to some extent its demands. French liberalism which found its fullest expression in the doctrine of *laissez faire, laissez aller*—that the best of governments was that which governed least—carried on into the nineteenth and even into the twentieth century the

[2] K. B. Smellie, *A Hundred Years of English Government*, p. 267.

protest against too great administrative interference with private life, a protest which often takes the form of unduly deprecating the competence of the existing government. This is perhaps one explanation—but only one—for the point noted above, that public spirit is less evident in French political life than it is in England, where the citizen feels instinctively that he has a voice in the passing of the budget and therefore must not evade taxation. The Englishman's belief is based upon his confidence in representative government; and even if this confidence may at times be abused, it is one of the greatest assets in securing effective interplay between the government and the citizen. In France, this interplay is lacking to some degree, partly because of French history, and partly because of a different conception of the nature of government to which we must now turn.

7. THE HERITAGE OF ROME

Underlying the whole trend of history that we have been examining, there is something deeper yet which marks off the Continental way of thinking of government from that of the English and American tradition. We have referred to it above in pointing out the contrast between the political ideas of Latin America and of the United States. It is, in a word, the contrast between Rome and Britain. There is no more impressive fact in history than the way in which the splendor of the Roman political achievement lasted on as a memory and an inspiration for those at the close of the Middle Ages who learned over again the lesson of antiquity in the theory and practice of government. It was not by chance that the first great university, that of Bologna in the early twelfth century, which opened its doors to the students of law who flocked down over the Alps from Northern Europe to sit at the feet of Irnerius, was devoted to the study of Roman law. These students of the revival of jurisprudence took back to the courts of the northern rulers the principles of private and public law which had been evolved in ten centuries of experience by a people uniquely endowed with the capacity for political organization. If kingship led in the movement against feudalism, Roman law supplied it with the maxims of government in such colorful expressions as *quod principi placuit legis habet vigorem* ("what the king wishes has the force of law") or even *princeps legibus solutus est* ("the king is not bound by law"). *L'État c'est moi* was already implicit in the maxims of Justinian. We have already seen how the jurists served the cause of monarchy in France. But the rulers of Germany also sought to profit from those who could put their house in order to strengthen their prerogatives. Unfortunately for Germany, there was no one monarch to be served as in France; but electors, dukes, and even bishops rivaled the Hapsburg court in strengthening their sovereignty through the "reception of the Roman Law."

The effect of this systematizing of government should not be overestimated, however. The process of what might be called "modernization by way of antiquity" was ultimately fused with the humanism of the Renaissance and found a lasting place in the cultural as well as the juristic history of Europe. But political progress was blocked by the disastrous series of wars that followed the

Protestant Reformation and the resulting anarchy, especially in Germany. The only lesson in Government that had a chance of being applied was that which emphasized the power of the ruler; as is always the case when wars are imminent. This would probably have been equally the case if the Hapsburgs had won the Thirty Years' War instead of having to surrender so much of the prerogative of empire in the Treaty of Westphalia in 1648. For if the theoretical successor of the Caesars had been the victor, it would have meant the triumph of a reactionary war lord whose power rested on a vast combination of feudal holdings and who had little to gain from the erection of a unified State, with the Diet refurbished into a legislative body with life in it. The Emperor, who was also Duke of Austria, and ruled at the same time a whole series of other duchies as well as the Kingdom of Hungary, was not yet beyond that early stage in the evolution of government which Rome had reached in its policy with peoples not yet within the State—*divide et impera* or rule by keeping the subject peoples apart. Moreover, the exigencies of war, which prevent the growth of civil institutions, would not have been ended by a unification of Germany at the close of the Thirty Years' War. The greatest menace of all, the Turk, was still threatening Vienna, and he besieged that city in 1683. As we shall see below, "the Germanies," as Madame de Stael used to call them, were the homes of frontier peoples, and the precepts of Roman military and bureaucratic rule fitted them better than the peaceful processes of an English parliamentary system.

Nowhere else was the influence of Rome upon theories of government more clearly shown than in the writings of Machiavelli, that realist of the Renaissance who has been termed the schoolmaster of despots. Machiavellism has been the synonym for ruthless and unscrupulous action in which the end justifies the means. The philosophy of government which includes not only force but treachery denies implicitly the principles of Christian morality and bases government both at home and abroad upon the cunning use of intelligence to evade the consequences of ill-doing. While these implications may be found in Machiavelli's manual, *The Prince,* addressed to the ruler of a small Italian State, as practical strategy in a world where such practices were common, Machiavelli's political philosophy had a wider range when taken as a whole. For it was as a student of Livy, upon whose history of the Roman Republic he wrote an extensive commentary, that he sought to apply the lesson of the evolution of that unique creation of antiquity to the problems of the stirring age which was so rapidly turning from Medieval Europe to a new state system—a system the character of which no one at that time, the early sixteenth century, could foretell.

There are at least two outstanding reasons why in spite of his revolt against Christian morality, Machiavelli has exercised such an attraction on the minds of those statesmen who were primarily men of action. In the first place, he was not an abstract thinker but looked to character and the mental caliber of individuals as the motive forces in history. This Roman way of analyzing politics is well brought out in his flat denial of the theory that economic resources can hold their own against armed might. He devotes quite a section of *The Prince* to a warning against what he views as the false theory that the ruler should take as his prime objective the increase of the wealth of his State; because this would only invite envy on the part of others better armed and looking around for plunder. This conclusion naturally rests upon the second of the two ideas which recommended it to the more practically minded statesmen of his day and later. For the whole Machiavellian system of philosophy rests upon the war system as the fundamental basis of sovereignty. This second lesson of antiquity, that war was the prime instrument of politics in the relations of States and rulers with each other, at once shows up the weakness of Machiavelli's historical analysis of what happened to Rome. His chief interest in its history was in that long period of conquest in which for century after century there were always new victims to pay the costs and maintain the splendor of the processes of imperialism. Machiavelli is not to be blamed for having failed to trace this process through to the downfall of the Roman Empire when there was no more tribute to be wrung from the conquered and no adequate means had been worked out for maintaining the vitality of the antique world. It is only now that we are beginning to realize that the fall of Rome was primarily due to the fact that this exhaustion of resources led to an intensification of the very evils from which it was suffering as the army took an ever larger measure of control. As the civil administration lost its initiative, bureaucracy grew both in extent and in inefficiency. In short, the one great lesson which the antique world had to offer to the modern state system, namely that war is the most delusive basis upon which to build the permanent strength of a nation, was never seen by Machiavelli.

8. GOVERNMENT AND LIBERTY; THE MIDDLE CLASS

While Machiavelli was looking back to Rome for the ideals of government and around him in the little sovereignties of Italy for their application, a world event was taking place—the first world event in history—which was to dwarf forever the petty, local politics of Europe. The era of European expansion had begun with the discovery of America and the opening of the sea route to the Far East. The Commercial Revolution which followed swung the center of power from mid-Europe and the Mediterranean to the countries that lie open to the ocean trade. Old Italian cities like Florence, which had played an important part in the origins of modern capitalism, in the techniques of banking and the beginnings of modern commercial associations, situated, as they were, off the track of this trade, were left to dream of their medieval importance and of their splendor in the Renaissance. The thing that Machiavelli rejected as not only secondary to soldiery but a deterrent to princes—money—became the greatest political force in Europe with the influx of gold and silver from the New World and the rise of the middle class, armed for power with new means of banking and credit in what came to be known as modern capitalism. It was this economic fact, and not Machiavelli, which gave the direction to developments in government in the three centuries which followed, although, as we shall see, his influence continued to show itself in those countries where war remained the basic fact of politics.

It is impossible to trace the long process of this revolutionary movement which opened up the modern problems of government, for that would mean passing in review almost the whole political history of all the countries which led in the movement, more especially England, the United States, and France. But that history has generally been written from the standpoint of today and not from that of the time when the events took place. Pride in the achievements of the champions of liberty is justifiable enough, but it should not blind us to the difficulties which royalty, as a survival of the precapitalistic age, had to face in carrying on the functions of government. With the influx from America of more gold and silver than Europe had had in circulation previously, prices went up everywhere several hundred per cent. The cost of government naturally increased proportionately, and the question of taxation became vital. The kings could not govern if they could not meet the ordinary expenses, let alone the cost of such new enterprises as war. Yet it was just at this time, when the business of kingship was becoming most difficult, that it advanced its most extreme claim, that of divine right. There was no answer yet to this claim in France, nor for a century more, when finally royal bankruptcy—partly caused by help to America—brought the triumph of the middle class; for this is the real meaning of the French Revolution. But in England middle-class opposition to royal prerogatives had the advantage of dealing with foreign, that is, Scottish, kings, the Stuarts. James I came to London trained in the Roman ideas which were the product of Scotland's relations with the Continent, especially France. He came to an England which was vibrating with a new sense of nationalism, the spacious age of Elizabeth merging into the stern, self-conscious temper of Puritanism, where the purse strings of government were held by a Parliament doubly aware under rising prices of the burden of taxation. Parliament, therefore, became the leader of the middle class against the King; but the legal bases of its case against royal exactions lay in the revival of old English law which was then taking place. In the conflict between the Roman principles, abstract embodiment of logic, and the common law, concrete embodiment of ways of living, the common law won out not only for England then but for those everywhere who cherish liberty.

The English jurist who thus found in the common law the best defense of English freedom because in its uncodified confusion it never dealt with liberty in the abstract, but with real situations as they arose, was Sir Edward Coke, in whom, to quote Maitland, the historian of English law, "the Common Law had taken flesh." It was the jurists of his day who made Magna Carta a real palladium for the liberties of later days by interpreting it as an active principle of law. The Petition of Right of 1628 made illegal the levying of taxes by the King without the consent of Parliament, or imprisonment for not paying them. The issue was now definitely joined between middle class and royalty; after sixty years of struggle it was finally resolved in the Bill of Rights of 1689, which gave expression to the principles of the Great Revolution of the previous year and almost a century later furnished the inspiration for the leaders in both the American and French Revolutions. Macaulay insisted that this most revolutionary of documents did not make any positive changes in English law; but the system of government which it inaugurated, providing for middle-class rule under a limited monarchy, had other supports than those of Coke's reinterpretation of precedent. It had also, among others, the writings of John Locke, whose *Two Treatises of Government* were published in 1689. Royalty, he said, rests on a contract with the people; and the contract is broken when personal liberty and private property are in danger. The King cannot be a judge of when rights are violated; the people must decide. The way to make secure life, liberty, and property—Jefferson gave a Virginian touch in changing this to "the pursuit of happiness"—would be by separating the powers of the executive, the legislative, and the conduct of international affairs, which he termed the federative function of government. The executive and the judiciary were not separated, and Parliament was to be the supreme power in the land. Locke's arguments are worth recalling not so much for their effect in England as in France and America. For one thing, it was primarily the influence of his thinking upon George Mason of Virginia which resulted in the Bill of Rights, first in the constitution of that state, and then in that of the United States. Then, strangely enough, this recital of the safeguards against the tyranny of governments was the one traceable influence of the American Revolution upon that of France.

9. FRENCH RATIONALISTS AND THE BENEVOLENT DESPOTS

The influence of Locke and the galaxy of English thinkers of the time did not have to await the period of the Revolution, however, to contribute to the current of French thought upon government. It was above all Montesquieu, one of the first to study comparative government by careful researches in foreign countries, who in 1729 found, or thought he found, in England what he had been hunting for, "liberty and equality," a phrase that was to become the slogan of the Revolution. His *Spirit of Laws,* which contained the essence of his philosophy and was especially designed to safeguard the bench against royal encroachment, was destined to have a prodigious effect. Voltaire said of it, "The human race had lost its title deeds; Montesquieu has just found them again." But his study of the English form of government, which he most admired, led him to round out the theory of the separation of the powers, in a formula which implicitly challenged the theory of absolutism, that of the separation of executive, legislative, and judicial organs of government. The simplicity and clarity of this scheme for preserving liberty, while allowing government to function normally, recommended it to the Fathers of the Constitution of the United States, to which it gave the peculiar structure known as the American system. But no government in modern Europe was ever framed on this model.

The other outstanding influence upon the political thinking of prerevolutionary France was, of course, Rousseau. Voltaire's writings bore less upon the structure of government than upon its actual conduct; he was the defender of the persecuted and the opponent of oppressors, but not the revolutionary enemy of the established order. Rousseau went the whole way. The opening sentence of his *Social Contract* rings with a challenge to King and State. "Men are born free and are everywhere in chains." He then proceeded, as others, especially the English thinkers, had done, to develop the idea of society as held together by an implied contract between the ruler and the ruled. But Rousseau presented his thesis as a threat to the established order, because evidently the contract had not been kept by government which no longer made the general welfare its chief concern. We need not linger over this political theory, however, for Rousseau's influence was only revolutionary. It inspired the Jacobin; but it was never used as the foundation for a lasting and stable edifice of State.

Those who put into operation the theories of the French *philosophes* were the benevolent despots and their ministers to whom we now turn. First of all there was France itself. As for Louis XIV, he worked hard and conscientiously at the business of kingship, fitting in his affairs of State with the ceremonies of the Court in the same tireless way that Francis Joseph of Austria did three centuries later. Taking over the task of a Sully, a Richelieu, or a Mazarin was not easy. Fortunately, Louis XIV was well served by such a minister as Colbert, who was a master of detail. The *intendants* in the provinces brought some semblance of royal authority into the confusion of jurisdictions. But the scandals of Louis XV and the incompetence of Louis XVI made the work of enlightened ministers like Malsherbes and Turgot more a foretaste of reforms to come than an achievement of what was needed—a recognition of the rights of the middle class, the Third Estate. It was left for Sièyes in 1789 to formulate the idea that "the Third Estate is the nation," an idea which was put to the test in the transformation of the States-General into the National Assembly. Despotism in the eighteenth century in France was, upon the whole, benevolent in intention, but oppressive in fact; the work of the *philosophes* was less effective in reform than in revolution.

It was different in Central and Eastern Europe. Throughout the eighteenth century the fashions of all courts and capitals were set by the French. The lasting marks of this influence still remain in the museums and the architecture of public buildings throughout Central and even Eastern Europe. But perhaps even more striking than this was the influence of French rationalism upon the rulers of the countries east of the Rhine, especially in Austria, Prussia, and Russia. The idea that a prince should be "the first servant of his people" is centuries older than the writings of the *philosophes,* but they gave it currency and forceful expression. The application of this principle, however, was much more difficult in France, where loyalty itself was so deeply enmeshed in the complications of an outworn feudalism, than in a small country like Prussia, where the military tradition prevailed, or even, so far as externals went, in Czarist Russia, which was accustomed to take orders from an autocratic Czar. The Hapsburgs of Austria, however, were faced with a task even more difficult than that of the Bourbons, and the extent to which Maria Theresa and especially her son Joseph II modernized their ramshackle empire shows what might have been done in France if Louis XVI had been an intelligent and energetic sovereign.

Neither France, in the West, nor Russia, in the East, was destined to embody this idea of benevolent despotism in permanent form; France followed the path of revolution and Russia that of reaction. But in Prussia and Austria the reforms in administration due to the "era of enlightenment" lasted on to the twentieth century. The reasons for this are not to be found, as Machiavelli would have us believe, in the individual capacity or unscrupulous cunning of Hapsburg and Hohenzollern rulers, although these qualities were not lacking in the course of their history, but in the peculiar situation and needs of the countries themselves.

10. THE PROBLEM OF GOVERNMENT IN EAST CENTRAL EUROPE

From the standpoint of Western Europe, both Prussia and Austria-Hungary have always been frontier countries along its eastern borders.[3] Prussia was the spear-point of the age-long thrust of the Germans against the Slavs, from the days of the Saxon emperors in the Middle Ages. Austria was the outpost of the Teutons against the barbarian raiders of the Danube Valley, and then, with Hungary, the joint defender against the most powerful invader that ever attacked Europe, the Ottoman Turk. It was inevitable, therefore, that these dangers of the frontier should affect the form and nature of government of both Hapsburgs and Hohenzollerns. The failure of Slav and German to settle down within agreed limits of territory and live alongside each other as good neighbors did not, it is true, present Europe with the recurring threat of war that came to Southeastern Europe from the failure of the Danubian and Balkan peoples to adjust peaceably the partition of the former empire of the Turks; but in both cases, as happens wherever the frontier is unsettled, the army had first place in the thoughts of both sovereign and people. This situation, which has so much history behind it, much more than the recent sea rivalry between Germany and Great Britain for world empire, has offered the German people the continuing justification for militarism. There is also the "watch on the Rhine" against France, but that danger was no longer real for Germany, after its unification, except as the storm might break—as it did in 1914 and again in 1939—on the southeastern or eastern frontier, and France be drawn in owing to its commitments there. In spite of the confusion in the present relations between Germans and Slavs (both Polish and Russian) the situation in eastern Germany remains fundamentally unchanged, in the matter of security, from what it was in the seventeenth and eighteenth centuries.

The characteristics of government under Hapsburgs and Hohenzollerns were therefore bureaucracy and militarism; for these two go readily together. As for the civilian administration, it will be recalled that in connection with the "reception of Roman Law" at the end of the Middle Ages, the statement was made that German princes profited from the work of the jurists fully as much as, if not

[3] It should be kept in mind that this is not a sketch of Central European history but an explanation of some of its peculiarities of government. Bavaria and the Rhineland had differing political histories and political civilizations. Both Germany and Austria were countries of widely varying outlook and culture. The problem here is what were the dominant trends in government.

more than, the Kings of France. Both in Austria and Brandenburg the profession of the jurist prospered, and these specialists in administration were used to good advantage; and they not only strengthened the civil bureaucracy but furnished an almost hereditary caste to fill its offices. In Prussia, the more businesslike of the two monarchies, these bureaucrats might even reach the highest offices of state; the Chancellor of Imperial Germany at the outbreak of World War I, Bethmann-Hollweg, was a perfect representative of this type of servant of the Crown. It must be said that they justified their position in the State by both their efficiency and their self-effacing loyalty, which accepted without question their social and political subordination as a class to the nobility, while the latter was as a class wise enough not to interfere with the routine business of bureaucratic government.

But any reader of Bismarck's memoirs will recall that, while he pays a fair tribute to the competence of the civil government, he claims that, at least for Prussia, the chief influence in maintaining the high standard of efficiency was not so much its own traditions as those of the army. Nowhere else has such clear light been thrown upon the historical background of Nazi ideas as in these Bismarck memoirs, where he points out the influence upon the Prussian mind of the sense of duty to the sovereign and the State—above all to the dynasty—which is the keynote of Prussian militarism. The unquestioning obedience with which the Prussian soldier accepted the orders of his superiors, even if he knew that they might mean death, was in Bismarck's eyes the greatest and best of all the influences making for stability in the Prussian State. For the Junkers, whose broad acres lay along the Slav frontier, this point of view was not open to question. It was no wonder, therefore, that the Junker who united Germany should look to the sword rather than to a liberal movement of the German people such as that which, in 1848, dreamed of doing what the French people had done for themselves in 1789. The bureaucracy which from the days of the Great Elector —the real founder of Prussia—received recognition along with the army, had no such career of glory as the army of Frederick the Great or that of the War of Liberation. The humdrum task at which it persevered was essential but not dramatic. The Prussian historians and political theorists of the nineteenth century therefore reflected public opinion when they exalted military service for the State as a supreme merit of the citizen. It was but a step from this to their claim, set forth by both historians and statesmen, which is so difficult for any democratic people to understand, that the truest expression of liberty itself is to be found where it is most denied, in the profession of arms. That this is not the mere rhetoric of a paradoxical professor but a summing up of the trend of a nation's attitude is only too clear in the light of recent events. Behind it, however, lies a stretch of history of which the unification of Germany by blood and iron was only one, if the outstanding, episode.

The disappearance of the Hapsburg monarchy from the governments of Europe today makes it unnecessary for us to trace here the history which lies so closely parallel to that of Prussia. As long as it lasted, the army was the symbol of its unity, while the bureaucracy occupied a secondary place, yielding much more to aristocratic influence at court and throughout the country at large; but the concept of government as the embodiment of power was the same in both countries. Parliamentary institutions were only secondary to the efficient management of affairs of State by ministers of the Crown and their subordinates.

A wholly new situation developed in this part of Europe as a result of World War I. The borderland between Eastern Europe and Russia, which we have referred to as the age-long unsettled frontier, then took shape in a whole series of "free nations" from the Arctic Sea to the Mediterranean. Self-determination had loosened the hold of the Hapsburgs and Hohenzollerns upon the non-Germanic peoples, whose most eloquent spokesman was Professor Masaryk, the first President of Czechoslovakia. A close student of the democratic ideals of Thomas Jefferson and of the history of American institutions, he proposed to introduce them as both the expression and the safeguard of the newly won liberties of the smaller nations. Unfortunately, these nations of the Eastern fringe were neither trained by experience to work out compromises, instead of resorting to conflicts, as a first prerequisite of a healthy political life; nor was their idea of the State one that recognized the essential need for compromise, framed as it was on the German concept of absolute sovereignty. Thus their equipment for self-government was weakened at the point that was sure to be tested most at a time of transition; for the political revolutions which had created these States disturbed the conditions of life, and these could not be readily adjusted to their new framework. It was this situation and not any lack of capacity for self-government on the part of the non-Germanic peoples which was responsible for their failure to live fully up to the high standards of Masaryk's democratic ideals and statesmanship.

The judgment on this situation commonly held in Vienna as well as in Berlin, that the non-Germanic peoples were inferior to the Germans in the management of political affairs, has been rendered more than suspect by the renunciation, during the Nazi rule, of political capacity on the part of the Germans themselves. While history has not yet registered its full verdict on the issue of national, or racial, characteristics, it has already shown that the three nations which are furthest from kin to the Germans—the Turks, the Magyars, and the Finns, all of them coming from the heart of Asia—have, each in its own way, remarkable achievements to their credit. There is no more striking chapter in the history of politics than that of the transformation of Turkey in our own time from a quasi-feudal regime, based on the military occupation of conquered territory, to a modern State. The Magyars have another history, that of the easy mastery of one of the most delicate political systems, a combination of diplomacy with oligarchic parliamentary government. A long line of great statesmen has shown that this people can maintain its identity although islanded among others, none of whom can speak its tongue. As for the Finns, cousins of the Magyars, their triumphs in democratic government were as notable as the defense of their country against Stalin was heroic. The Bulgarians, partly Asiatic, partly Slav, have at least produced a Stambulisky, and the Greeks a Venizelos. The Serbs have only now begun to come out of their isolation of the

Middle Ages, where they were kept by the Turk, and the Poles were without any experience in modern self-government; but to judge from these facts that a great people like the Slavs are lacking in political capacity is as absurd as to say that the British lacked it prior to the seventeenth century, or the French prior to the French Revolution.

The problem of racial aptitudes lies outside this study; but in view of the fact that Central Europe is likely to be a laboratory of experimentation in politics in the coming years, it is well to recall that not only is it an area where the mixture of peoples is almost as great as in the United States, but that history rather than biology explains their present situation.

These elements of variety in customs and outlook in the small nations of Eastern Europe have now been submerged in the tidal wave of Soviet power and influence, or at least obscured to Western eyes behind the Iron Curtain. But they were the most real and intimate expression of local freedom. Unfortunately they were not adequately safeguarded by political institutions or experience. All history shows that liberty is an imperishable attribute of life itself; but freedom cannot be treated as a monopoly to be denied to others. It is effective only when it can be shared; and it can be shared only when there is no danger of losing it.

There is only one political system in the world which has for its aim this very interplay of freedom and power, the federal system. It is strange that Continental Europe has never taken it seriously. Outside of Switzerland it is not to be found as an essential basis of the State. The main trend of European history has been toward centralization in government. To some extent centralization was a reaction against the anarchy of small States in feudal times, but the more recent developments have been rather a reflection of the unification of a nation's business under modern conditions, and the rise of new economic and social problems that call for national treatment, as in the United States. In the case of the British Empire, however, the trend has been in the opposite direction, toward a looser federation in the British Commonwealth of self-governing nations. In the eyes of Continental statesmen this is a "ramshackle" State, about to fall to pieces. They fail to see that it is held together by the very liberty which seems to weaken it. No one can tell what hidden strength liberty supplies in bonds of common loyalties. Of one thing the British are sure, however, that the Commonwealth will not break up because it is free.

Now what bearing has this on the problems of government of Eastern Europe? It is fundamental. There are minorities in every State. To secure their loyalty by the recognition of a legitimate opposition, as in England or the United States—or in any genuinely parliamentary system—calls for fair and impartial treatment. As it is difficult to know whether this is the case or not, unless there is a free expression of public opinion, it follows that a federal system functions well only under a regime of liberty. That is why the federal system of Soviet Russia cannot be regarded as a genuine example of federalism in spite of its external framework, as is clearly shown in the description of the Government of the Union of Soviet Socialist Republics. The Communist Party exercises a control in reality which dominates the forms of government. Nevertheless, it must be recognized that Soviet Russia did give a formal expression to federalism in Eastern Europe, especially in its recognition of the rights of nationalities, correcting in this regard the mistakes of its neighbors. It should be added, however, that the recent trend of Stalin's Government has been in the opposite direction, scattering and separating nationalities with ruthless disregard of their wishes or welfare and elevating Great Russia to a position of increasing power.

But it is not merely the internal conditions of a nation which determine whether federalism can flourish there; for the liberty which is the condition of its very life depends as well upon the extent to which a country can rely upon having peace with its neighbors. In proportion as there is danger of war, liberty is curtailed and its institutions wither and die. We are, therefore, brought from the study of internal politics to that of international relations. Here, again, it is now clearly seen by all competent observers that there can be no guarantee of lasting peace without institutions for dealing with international problems and settling disputes. Whether the suppressed liberties of Czechoslovakia, Poland, and the Baltic countries will be restored and coordinated with the interests of their neighbors, are questions for the future to answer. But unless the nations of Eastern Europe learn the lesson Masaryk tried to teach out of American experience, they must inevitably make way for a greater unitary movement.

11. THE ENGLISH MODEL

The new national states which emerged upon the theatre of history in the nineteenth century did not feel themselves fully equipped for government without legislatures modeled more or less consciously on the Parliament of Great Britain.[4] Never was the prestige of the British political genius so high as in the period which saw the unification of Italy and Germany. The Industrial Revolution which brought the middle class definitely to power in Western Europe was spreading with giant strides across the Rhine and down the Danube, creating a new middle class and a new proletariat. Social and economic questions came to the fore; in the discussion of these the people concerned were demanding a part. The unification of Italy also evoked, though in different terms, the ideal of representative government as a symbol of liberation from the reactionary rulers whose overthrow finally brought to Rome Victor Emmanuel as King, with a parliament on the English model.

For half a century and more parliaments were accepted everywhere as fundamental elements in the structure of Continental governments. No one questioned that they had as definite a place as the executive, judiciary, or even the army. In France, after a long and tortuous history, Parliament finally asserted its supremacy over the other branches of the government in 1877, when it forced the hand of the President. Again, ten and twenty years later, in the Boulanger and Dreyfus affairs, it took definite and final control over the army.

[4] It has been impossible in this short introduction to deal with other parliamentary institutions dating from the Middle Ages, as in Spain, Scandinavia, and Hungary.

In recent years, however, this trend has been questioned and opposed. These events are described in detail in the pages which follow; but it is not sufficiently well known that the distrust of "the man on horseback" which finds national expression in the French Parliament made that body a bulwark of "the Rights of Man and the Citizen" in the crisis of World War I in quite the same spirit as was the case with the English Parliament. By September, 1915, that part of France which was not in the direct path of the war itself was given back to civilian administration except for the "exceptional cases" which had to do directly with the military defense of the country. Also, when General Joffre attempted from his headquarters at Chantilly to extend the action of the General Staff from the sphere of war into that of diplomacy, owing to the extension of the battle front beyond French territory, it was the Parliament which forced him back into the strictly military field. In short, France under the Third Republic advanced to the position of a distinctly nonmilitaristic country.[5]

The contrast with Germany in this regard is striking. There it had not been the Prussian Diet or the Reichstag which had kept the military leaders in their place, but Bismarck himself, whose struggles to keep the control of policy in his own hands had been critically challenged after each of his two great wars, that with Austria in 1866 and that with France in 1870. How well he succeeded is an open page of history. But when militarism is embodied in a continuing institution, the Bismarcks capable of standing out against it are few and far between. The limits he set for the General Staff, those of strictly military affairs, were set for the armies and navies of France and England by permanent bodies responsible to the nation, which kept on growing in power with the growth of democratic institutions. It is true that in all four countries, Germany and Austria-Hungary as well as England and France, the military establishment was theoretically subordinate to the civilian government, but the ministers in the Central Powers were the creatures, not of parliaments, but of emperors who were also war lords. Under an impulsive William II or a tired old man like Francis Joseph, a well-meaning bureaucrat like Bethmann-Hollweg, or a reckless gambler for power like Count Berchthold, followed without sufficient thought of the consequences the old tradition of the politics of power.

As in the history of England under the Stuarts, control of the purse was of fundamental importance in the control of policy. In his struggle to secure a military budget free from the criticism as well as the restrictions of the Reichstag, Bismarck succeeded in establishing the constitutional doctrine that the budget presented to the Reichstag was only an "economic plan" (*Wirtschaftsplan*) setting forth the estimates for the year, and while the Reichstag had still the theoretical right to accept or reject it, its rejection would involve a serious paralysis of government. Therefore the Reichstag could not proceed to this extreme step. Thus, the central struggle for power was resolved in Germany in the very opposite way to that in which it was worked out in England.

[5] In the war begun in September, 1939, however, Parliament hardly functioned, having given the Premier *pleins pouvoirs*.

It was only in the Constitution of the German Republic after World War I that the German Parliament recovered its control of the purse.

This subject opens up too large a field, however, for us to deal with fully here—that of the control of foreign affairs. Even in parliamentary countries, this is the branch of government which is least open to public scrutiny. The reasons for this are obvious, such as the need for quiet exploration of difficult subjects, so as not to arouse the prejudices of uninformed public opinion. But, while the actual conduct of negotiations is everywhere more or less handled by bureaucratic methods, the determination of policy tends in parliamentary countries to be less influenced by the military way of looking at things than in countries where popular government is more circumscribed. This has not always been true, for democracies can be belligerent; but where all the other interests of the nation have to be weighed by representative bodies, there is less likelihood of such decisions as Berchthold took in July, 1914, when he led the war party in the Austrian Cabinet. The chief criticism made of the English Foreign Minister, Sir Edward Grey, on that occasion, was that the consciousness of parliamentary control kept him from being wholly frank about the situation in which Great Britain found itself. But this reaction to events already on the march, was a much less serious responsibility than that assumed by one who, with the head of the army egging him on, led the government of Francis Joseph into war.

There is no doubt that times of crises call for special organs of government of the bureaucratic kind.[6] It is in the normal conduct of affairs that we discover the real differences between responsible and nonresponsible governments. They lie as much in the spirit and attitude of mind of statesmen and people, and in political tradition, as in the forms of the constitutions used. Bismarck, for example, never got over his distaste for what he regarded as parliamentary interference in the affairs of the executive branch. Similarly in Austria, the Hapsburg tradition of the concentration of ultimate power in the Emperor was maintained with almost religious devotion to Francis Joseph, in spite of outward concessions to popular demands for parliaments. The result was that both the German Reichstag and the Austrian Reichsrat were in the false position of institutions which voiced public opinion, but were checked and limited when it came to decisions on major policies of State. The consequence of this anomalous position of parliament is best seen in the history of the Austrian Reichsrat. The sense of German discipline and loyalty kept the German Reichstag functioning normally throughout its history, but the Reichsrat was the scene of intermittent rioting between the leaders of the different national groups as well as between Socialists and reactionaries.

In drawing the contrast between parliamentary and bureaucratic governments, we must of course remember that the parliamentary system—which includes the congressional—also depends upon public servants for its effective functioning. There are, upon the whole, approximately as many bureaus and

[6] Professor Lindsay Rogers has analyzed this problem in a most suggestive and informative volume, *Crisis Governments* (New York, 1934).

departments of government and as many civil servants under parliamentary rule as there are in what we call the bureaucratic systems. The difference is one of responsibility and method of government rather than of the number of functionaries employed. This number grows with the extent of government action, and not with regard to the distinction between responsible and autocratic power. For example, the increase in the scope of government in recent years has greatly added to the civil service everywhere. It was in the latter part of the nineteenth century, and more especially in the twentieth, that the civil service became more and more necessary with the growth of government action, and that, in the interests of efficiency, movements for civil service reform became a pressing necessity. Most of the routine and permanent offices of administration ceased to be the spoils of political partisans and were open only to the successful candidates of civil-service examinations. This very important aspect of government should be kept in mind in judging the relative efficiency of the different systems. For the parliamentary system has been able to produce fully as adequate a civil service as has been created in bureaucratic countries. It has long been a byword in Great Britain that the British Civil Service, by correcting the mistakes of politicians and carrying out the purposes of government effectively and well, has done as much as if not more than any other single thing to make the parliamentary system succeed.

As we have seen above, the attempt to reconstruct the governments of the Continental countries by copying the English model was never more than a partial success in the countries east of the Rhine. Bureaucracy dominated within the States, and militarism remained the keynote of diplomacy between nations. But the parliaments themselves were largely to blame for their failures, owing to their not having developed good, practical procedures. The Industrial Revolution, while it exerted its force to widen the electorate, created so many groups of conflicting interests that Continental parliamentary history lacked the simplicity of the English bi-party system. When parliaments are composed of half a dozen parties ranging all the way from the extreme left to the extreme right, there is bound to be confusion and inefficiency. They can and do remedy these conditions partly by coalition, partly by the work of commissions, but they are likely to be slow in reaching results. With all its shortcomings, however, the parliamentary system meant something to the common man throughout Europe; for it was the one part of the government in which the ideals of democracy could at least have a voice.

The role of political parties in government is of course not confined to the part they play in legislative assemblies or, for that matter, in any branch of government. When effectively organized, the party system is the nation in politics, the vital principle, of which the formal organs of government are but the mouthpiece. This, by a strange paradox, is equally true of the new authoritarian States as it has been of those of the parliamentary tradition. The idea of a single party is drawn primarily from the teaching of Marxian Socialism which, while admitting the fact of a bourgeois opposition to the proletariat during the period of transition, taught that ultimately the whole nation would share the single interest of the working class. This identification of the nation—or of all the people—with the proletariat reminds one of the slogan of revolutionary France that "the Third Estate is the whole nation." It was not long before the Third Estate showed as many and fundamental cleavages within itself as had previously existed in the body politic of the Old Regime. Whether that will happen in the case of Communist Russia is a problem for the future. For the present at least, the one-party system is working in governments that have no ideological kinship with Karl Marx. Next to Russia, the country that adopted it most thoroughly was China, where the Government of Chiang Kai-shek fought Communism under the banners of the party of Sun Yat-sen. But it was left for Fascist Italy and Nazi Germany to develop this system with far-reaching effect upon the ideas of government in Europe itself.

To discuss all the implications of this new formation of "the nation in politics" would carry us too far afield. But the more one studies the working of the one-party system, the more one sees that it is not the nation in politics at all, for political vitality depends upon the freedom of the citizen to reach his own conclusions on the issues before him. As policies of State cannot but affect different people differently, many of them must under the one-party system either cease to express these differences or cease to take any real interest in the processes themselves. In short, a one-party system is by the nature of the case a system of acquiescence in despotism. This is best seen in the various "purgings" which have taken place in Soviet Russia. Those who found themselves in opposition to Stalin had no recognized way to make that opposition effective. There was nothing in Moscow like "His Majesty's Loyal Opposition" in the English Parliament, the leader of which receives a salary from the government which he opposes. Instead of this apparently illogical but really most useful method of party government, the opposition in authoritarian States must resort to conspiracy.

We are driven, therefore, to the conclusion that the only forms of party government which are genuine are the bi-party system developed in Great Britain and the United States, and the multi-party system developed in the parliamentary States of Continental Europe. Both depend for their efficiency upon the political maturity of the citizens, the fundamental basis of all self-government.

12. THE CHALLENGE OF DICTATORSHIP

The rest of the story is told in the pages which follow. It is in large part the story of revolutionary movements, reaching farther down into the very foundations of society than any other in European history. The denial of the legitimacy of the things mankind has striven to attain throughout the centuries, personal liberty, security under the law, national and international morality, is now outspoken and unrestrained. The way in which these things have come about is described in detail. Alongside this story stands the description of the structure and functioning of the countries which still cherish institutions of self-government. It is to be hoped that the study of these experiences of other peoples may help to mature our judgment not only with reference to them but with reference to ourselves as well. For, in a time like this there is no safety for any nation that blindly follows its own path, ignorant of the experiences of other peoples. Even from this short sketch, however, it should be clear that the problem of government cannot be solved by any one formula, whether it comes from one's own history or that of others. This is bound to be more and more the case as the scope of government grows with the vastly increasing complexity of society and interdependence of nations. For, after all, the greatest challenge to existing institutions comes not from the improvisation of men in a hurry. It comes from that greatest of all world powers—modern science. Nothing like this ever happened before. At last we are witnessing the most fundamental of all revolutions, that which transfers the day's work from human hands to those of iron and steel, driven by the illimitable forces of nature. Human relationships within the State and within nations are bound to be different from what they were in the quiet, simple days of relatively static life. Science has made the world dynamic, not merely for the few years of its existence hitherto but for all time to come. Therefore, government must achieve both stability and a capacity for adjustment to ever-new situations in the pursuit of social, economic, and political justice.

Among the first to see the epochal significance of applied science was Karl Marx, whose prodigious influence upon political as well as economic thinking should not be ignored in this survey. By temperament and training a philosopher, he turned Hegel's philosophy of history—to use his own figure of speech —the other way round. Instead of viewing ideas as the dominant force in the evolution of civilization, his "economic theory of history" attempted to prove that the methods of economic production have determined not only the structure of society but the direction of thought as well. A resident of England in the mid-nineteenth century, he saw the Industrial Revolution as a world-wide process which was creating a new alignment in history, in which the struggle for control would be no longer between nations but between classes. The working class would unite to transform the State by destroying the institutions of capitalism in a world-wide system of Socialist governments. It is not part of this survey to estimate how much the Socialist movement was responsible for forcing social and economic reforms in the various countries of Europe, but both in wartime and in the post-War years, Socialism yielded to the power of nationalism whenever the State was in danger. Moreover, in the two countries which have been the most outstanding in giving Socialism formal recognition— Germany and Russia—the trend towards nationalism seems all the more intense in proportion as the scope of government has been enlarged to cover almost all the activities of life. This has made for a more closely-knit society, finding expression in only one political party, and a government which, contrary to Marx's idea that it should become responsive to changing opinion with the growth of intelligence, becomes more and more despotic in order to maintain its power.

This interplay of nationalism and Socialism is hard to trace. Even in a country like Soviet Russia, the claim that its Government is based on Marxian philosophy has been more and more challenged by the facts of Stalin's regime. In

Fascist Italy, the problem turned the other way round; protesting nationalist opposition to Socialism, Mussolini became an effective leader of the attack upon free capitalistic institutions. Still more was this the case in Nazi Germany. It is too soon, however, to measure the relative force of the different elements in these totalitarian States because they were revolutionary not only for the immediate period of transition from one form of government to another, but inherently so by their very nature. Recognizing that efficiency in a time like this calls for special measures and special forms of administration, they turned to direct action as a method justified by the needs of the situation, in order to sweep from their path the obstacles presented by institutions dating from quieter times of the past. The resort to direct action implies irresponsible control. Nothing is more difficult than to escape from this trend, as Napoleon III found out when he attempted to establish "the Liberal Empire." To keep the process going effectively, the State must be conceived of as one to which people surrender their individual judgments. The ultimate result, therefore, is that totalitarian States achieve their purpose by the acceptance of a principle of government which is the most ruinous in the history of politics; for the ultimate cost is the sacrifice of the greatest of all assets which a nation possesses—its intelligence.

Democracy, on the other hand, is an embodiment of intelligence itself; for even when its standards are relatively low, its method of trial and error is directed by those who are free to consider all the consequences of the decisions which they make. Its only safety lies, however, in making that freedom work so that it is neither a reliance on ancient ways of doing things because they are the easiest, nor a careless surrender to the appeal of the demagogue. Fortunately, we have more ways now of reaching public opinion than has ever been the case in the past. And while this is by no means a guarantee that people will think right, they are less likely to think wrong than if they were not challenged by press and radio as they are now. Moreover, that challenge is more insistent than it used to be because time will not wait now as it once did for the consequences to be worked out.

This means that we must be free to experiment with the instruments of government as well as with its output. It is no use to accumulate a mass of unenforceable and confusing legislation on the statute books; we need to make surer that there is adequate provision for carrying out the intent and purpose of laws. This cannot be done by improving any one branch of government; the country will react more readily and more critically to legislation if it has confidence that the administration is adequate; and the result will almost inevitably be a greater caution in law-making, because the law will be more of a reality. In all this process, the one guarantee of success remains that mysterious entity of democracy called "public spirit," because the efficient State is that in which government and citizen effectively cooperate.

One final remark. It is a healthy sign that these problems are now receiving so much attention. In the countries of freedom, parliaments are becoming less miscellaneous and therefore less amateurish in their treatment of problems that are bound to grow more and more technical as society develops the intricacies of economic life in the machine age. The Executive is becoming more and more dependent upon the advice of those who have had experience in the management of great affairs. The Judiciary keeps pace—although sometimes with laggard step—with the transformations of human relationships. The task of democracies, as the laboratories of government, will therefore be to keep forever at the conscious, cautious, but fearless process of appraising, rejecting, or applying the proposals of those whose judgment is matured in the study of realities.

These conclusions are not mere speculations. They rise to the surface of all serious thinking on the art and science of government today.

The Government and Politics of

FRANCE

by R. K. GOOCH

INTRODUCTION

CHAPTER I

BASIC ASPECTS OF
THE FRENCH POLITICAL SYSTEM

---

1. THE QUESTION OF REGIME

STANDARDS OF CLASSIFICATION

Working Hypotheses. The American student of political science who undertakes to be introduced to the political system of France will doubtless wish at the outset to have a general characterization of French government. As a matter of fact, the question of what sort of system the French have can be answered through the formulation of several important basic propositions. If the student accepts these propositions as working or guiding principles, he will be able, as he proceeds, to examine and test the principles, and to give fuller meaning to them.

The Republic. The political system of France is *republican* in character. This is certainly the proposition which a large majority of the French themselves would advance if they were asked what kind of governmental regime they possess. Some would say it without enthusiasm, a few would say it with regret, many would say it with pride. The fact is that political democracy has deep roots in France; and the concept of political democracy and the concept of republicanism are for practical purposes to be identified. Yet the student of government knows that in terms of principle, classification of a system as republican is by no means a very significant description of its nature. Such classification necessarily indicates merely that the head of the State has not a title traditionally associated with monarchy. In a deeper sense, a republic is much less a form of government than a complexus of rich historical and doctrinal associations. This is true in especially striking degree of France.

Parliamentary Government. Mr. Winston Churchill, on one occasion in the course of World War II, hinted that the British people, knowing from their own experience that political democracy can develop to a high point in a monarchy, would view with sympathy the restoration of monarchy in France. Mr. Churchill should have known better. The body of the French people feel very differently about this subject; and the important thing in the matter is what they feel rather than what they—or other people—think. They may admire, and even envy, the British political system; but it is in one respect not for them. They know that British government is democratic not because it is monarchical in character but because it is the "classic" model of the *parliamentary system.* The French are aware that this system, characterized by a peculiar form of *ministerial responsibility,* served in Britain the historical purpose of effecting a reconciliation of monarchy and political democracy. However, French history leaves only one logical conclusion as possible from the popular conviction that parliamentary government is democratic government whereas monarchical government is not. Democratic government must be both parliamentary and republican. The student of comparative government must therefore be prepared to assume that in France *political democracy,* the *parliamentary system,* and *republicanism* are, for practical purposes, three interchangeable concepts.

Administrative Structure. In terms of the important matter of the position of smaller political communities within the larger community, French government is in general to be classified as *unitary,* rather than federal. Moreover, the manner and degree of *centralization* in France are exceedingly important, though by no means entirely easy to understand. Hence, the consideration is in this respect particularly pertinent that the preconceptions of the people of one country may easily lead them astray in judging another country. President Roosevelt, before the landings in Normandy, stated that the American military authorities would come to terms with whatever local agencies might prove favorable to the Allies, regardless of the relationship of these agencies to the central regime. The mutual lack of understanding of the situation in the two countries was so great as to cause General de Gaulle to suggest that Mr. Roosevelt apparently desired to re-establish the feudal system in France. The serious American student should be especially slow to apply his own concepts to French administrative structure; and he should be prepared, in an effort at understanding, to find principles and practices that are in many respects so different as to demand much intellectual adjustment and suspended judgment.

2. THE QUESTION OF CONSTITUTION

The Present and Its Background. Much importance attaches, then, to recognizing from the beginning that the French political system is, with peculiar associations attaching to each term, *republican, parliamentary,* and highly *unitary.* The serious American student of government will naturally wish to raise next—indeed, he will probably already have raised in his mind—questions concerning what kind of Constitution France possesses. The simple fact is that at present there prevails in France an elaborate written Constitution. Indeed, the proposition is worth setting down that France, like the United States, is a country of written Constitutions. As a matter of fact, France has had in the course of its history a considerable number of instruments of the kind that an American is accustomed to think of as Constitutions. In the result, the student is presented with a formidable mass of documentary material for study.

CHAPTER II

OUTLINE SKETCH OF FRENCH CONSTITUTIONAL HISTORY

1. THE GOVERNMENTAL SYSTEMS OF FRANCE

The Present System and Its Predecessors. The fact of the existence in France of other governmental systems than that which prevails at present is suggested by the very name of the existing regime. The present Constitution of France is of course the Constitution of the Fourth Republic, a fact which clearly implies the existence not only of three other republics but of other than republican systems. In reality, modern France has, in addition to being a republic on four different occasions, been an absolute monarchy, a constitutional monarchy, and twice an empire. Such names, it is true, in themselves denote little that is necessarily fundamental; but, in specific cases, history associates important connotations with terms of the kind. Some study of the successive governmental systems that have prevailed in France forms an indispensable background for study of the political system of the present day.

Ancient and Modern Periods. Although the division of history into periods is always arbitrary, being at best merely a matter of convenience, a marked tendency nonetheless exists in France to regard history as falling into two almost wholly unrelated periods separated from each other by the French Revolution. The French Revolution, it must be confessed, was an event of such great moment that there is doubtless more justification than in any other case for thinking of the pre-Revolution era and the modern period as being two airtight compartments. Thus, for example, all the many written constitutions that France has possessed belong to the period that began with the Revolution. On the other hand, even in this division of French history as elsewhere, much from the earlier period was carried over into the later.

ANCIEN RÉGIME

The Ancient Constitution. Louis XVI's able minister, Turgot, insisted that France of the *ancien régime* possessed no Constitution. This is reminiscent

37

of the observation made towards the middle of the nineteenth century by de Tocqueville that in modern England no Constitution exists. Both remarks, of course, had in view a specially framed constitutional document. On the other hand, both, in so far as the sum of principles determining the structure and function of a governmental system may properly be regarded as a Constitution, are equally untrue. In that broad but legitimate sense, France of the *ancien régime* undoubtedly possessed a Constitution; and this Constitution, according to the great Burke, was even one of much virtue. Nevertheless, the conditions that prevailed in France towards the end of the eighteenth century were, it is now easy to see, such as to render fundamental change inevitable. In order for what have come to be called modern conditions to exist, a revolution of some kind was necessary.

Absolute Monarchy. The principal causes of the French Revolution have often been recounted. In so far as they were political in character, they were inextricably connected with the phenomenon of *absolutism*. From the constitutional point of view, it is a simple fact that the scheme of government which prevailed under the *ancien régime* was in principle *absolute monarchy*. In general, all concepts that are at present conventionally associated with an abstraction, the State, were associated, in so far as they existed, with a person, the King. This situation, it need scarcely be said, was the result of development extending over centuries.

Consolidation of a Kingdom. In the earlier centuries of the Middle Ages, the unity of governmental authority in France was marred by the prevalence of feudalism. The King was little more than a "first among equals." [1] The "equals" were, of course, the great barons. Though they held their large territories in theory as vassals of the King, they were, in reality, in most respects independent of the royal authority. The Dukes of Normandy are familiar examples. The Church, likewise, possessed much power, and often exercised it at the expense of the King. Finally, towns and cities claimed and established a corporate existence; and, as *Communes,* they enjoyed a large measure of self-government. Royal authority was confined for the most part to a central nucleus of the country, the King's domain. In order for royalty to attain that absolutism which ultimately characterized the *ancien régime,* a first requisite was acquisition by the King of control over the barons. The work was, in fact, accomplished by certain outstanding Kings in the course of the twelfth century, and, more especially, the thirteenth. [2] The great baronial fiefs were annexed to the royal domain, and the privileges of the Church and of the Communes were held in check. In the second place, in order for increased royal authority to be consolidated and maintained against the nobles, the governmental institutions of strong power had to be developed. This work is associated primarily with the names of great royal ministers. Although as early as the thirteenth century

[1] Anointment of the King at Rheims cathedral, it may be noted, meant a great deal to the development of nationalism.
[2] Particularly important in this respect were Philip II (1180–1223), Louis IX (1226–1270), and Philip IV (1285–1314).

financial and administrative advances were brought about, as increasing territory became subject to the real power of the King of France, nevertheless royal
government did not assume its characteristic form until the seventeenth and
eighteenth centuries. More especially, the three renowned seventeenth-century
ministers, Richelieu, Mazarin, and Colbert, developed to a high degree concentration of authority in the hands of central government. They curbed or abolished agents or agencies, central or local, that might pretend to check royal
absolutism. They made particularly effective use of *intendants,* central officials
located in the provinces. These *intendants* were instituted in 1635 by Richelieu;
and, within a short time, they succeeded in exercising, especially in the sphere
of justice, police, and finance, such extensive power as to reduce to practical
impotence the former provincial *governors,* who had, by virtue of being important army men, been abusing their authority. Thus, centralization, according to
de Tocqueville, was "a product of the *ancien régime*" and, moreover, "the only
portion of the political constitution of the *ancien régime* that survived the
Revolution." [3]

Absolutist Theories. The Kings of France, in establishing absolute authority, did not confine themselves to the use of military force and the employment of able ministers. They likewise relied on principles. In creating absolute
monarchy in fact, they asserted a theory of absolute monarchy. This theory
was in part founded on ideas of Roman imperial authority and in part on what
were conceived to be the principles of Frankish monarchy. The Kings insisted
that their rule had been established by divine will. As a consequence, they owed
account to no one except God. This in turn freed them from responsibility to
their subjects. Only the King had political rights; and, these being beyond the
reach of men, any opposition to royal authority was revolutionary and sacri-
legious.

Potential Limitations. The fact that the French King of the *ancien régime*
was absolute ought not to obscure an important consideration. In practice, embryonic forms of the three well known branches of modern government were
developing. The very existence of specialized administrative services with a
highly numerous bureaucracy, of the beginnings of a judicial system, and of an
embryo legislature, in the form of the States-General, constituted potential, and
to a slight extent actual, "checks" on unlimited royal authority. Moreover, reference was at times made to a mythical "Ancient Constitution of the Realm"
and to what were called "Fundamental Laws," with some suggestion that the
King was obligated to adhere to them. Nevertheless, such limitations were of
very restricted efficacy. No genuine development occurred of the idea of contractual relationship; and there was a notable absence of great charters comparable to those that distinguish English constitutional history. The States-
General were abolished in 1614, not to meet again until 1789. In connection
with the more active aspect of government, that is to say, what we should today
call the executive, the work of the great ministers that marked the transition

[3] Cf. de Tocqueville, *L'Ancien régime* (Paris, 1856), Livre II, Ch. II.

from feudalism laid the basis for royal governmental practice which was not only absolute but, as the famous *lettres de cachet* [4] indicate, arbitrary. The greatest difficulty experienced by the King in gathering into his hands complete control of all government was that which was encountered in connection with the judiciary. In the contest between Kings and feudal barons, one of the principal royal aims and one of the most important royal accomplishments was the gradual substitution of royal justice for baronial justice. This was the work of royal jurists and other agents of the King. However, when royal justice had for the most part triumphed over feudal justice, the prestige of the former was so great that the King found it no easy matter to make himself master of those who administered justice in his name. This situation is illustrated especially by the position of the thirteenth-century Parlement of Paris, a body not legislative in character like the assembly of the same name that developed in England but a supreme court. In the course of several centuries, with the disappearance of other agencies, such as that of the States-General in 1614, that were potential checks on royal authority, the Parlement, it is true, added to its judicial power a slight amount of legislative power which at times served as a limitation on the power of the King. This limitation was one that derived from the practice on the part of the Parlement of keeping the official register of laws and of registering in it royal decrees. The power to refuse to register a decree was in effect a veto power on legislation by the King. This position of the Parlement entered into French tradition; and this aspect of tradition has not been without influence in the later judicial history of the country. [5] On the other hand, a minister like Richelieu was able to nullify the power of the Parlement; and, even much earlier, strong Kings had found ways of circumventing it. Later, Louis XV actually abolished the Parlement for a time. However, in each instance, the Parlement succeeded in re-establishing its authority. Intrigues of the Parlement under Louis XVI were among the immediate causes of the Revolution.

Social and Economic Maladjustment. In general, as a distinguished French historian has summarized the royal position at the end of the *ancien régime,* "neither anything nor anyone had got the right or the force to resist the King." [6] At the same time, this political unity that had resulted from the royal triumph over feudalism was not matched by a corresponding social unity. The unity of the nation was yet to be established. In this respect, the most salient characteristic of France at the end of the *ancien régime* was the existence of "Orders," that is, of stratified social classes—the clergy, the nobility, and the "third estate"—each possessed of a different body of rights and privileges. More especially, in the fundamental matter of taxation, inequality was so great as to present highly formidable difficulties. In the circumstances, the conviction grew that reform of abuses was imperative. However, it was here that a regime

---

[4] These were royal letters sealed not with the official seals but with the King's secret or privy seal. Their contents represented a personal decision of the King, and usually contained announcement of a penalty restrictive of liberty, such, for example, as exile or imprisonment in a monastery or fortress.

[5] Cf. Ch. IX, p. 156, *infra.*

[6] E. Lavisse, *Histoire de France illustrée* (Paris, 1911), t. IX, Ière partie, p. 401.

of absolute monarchy was found wanting. No established channel existed through which public opinion could reach the King. Likewise, there was no recognized method of constitutional change. The resulting rigidity goes far to explain the tendency for public opinion, in grappling with reform of a system marked by absolutism, to push to the opposite extreme. The destruction of abuses brought in the end destruction of the regime itself.

CONSTITUTIONAL MONARCHY

King and Nation. The meeting of the States-General in May of 1789, for the first time since 1614, led to the disappearance for all time of royal absolutism. In its stead, there was established a regime of *constitutional monarchy,* destined to prevail at that time for a few short years. Of the two basic elements that must find some kind of equilibrium for limited monarchy to exist, namely, the monarch and the representatives of the nation, the second rapidly gained the ascendancy. The States-General, within approximately a month following its first meeting, became a constitution-making body, the Constituent Assembly. The third estate had a few days previously declared itself a National Assembly; and with it the clergy and nobles gradually became merged. The Constituent Assembly, in the course of a little over two years, during which time the weakness, vacillation, and intrigues of the King and the direct and even violent action of the population, especially in Paris, complicated its task, not only governed France, reorganizing the administrative structure of the country [7] and destroying the last traces of feudalism, but also formulated in August of 1789 the famous *Declaration of the Rights of Man and of the Citizen* and gave to France in September of 1791 a written Constitution.

The Declaration of the Rights of Man. The *Declaration* was a denial of the arbitrary power and a protest against the abuses of the *ancien régime.* Phrased in terms of prevailing eighteenth-century concepts of natural law and the like, it was a manifestation of a strong faith that existed in the efficiency of the clear statement of "fundamental truths." In reality, by no means all the provisions of the *Declaration* were concerned with specific individual rights in the usual sense of the word. Several important and striking provisions were concerned with *equality.* Indeed, the *Declaration* furnishes evidence that its framers were even more concerned with equality than with liberty. And, finally, several provisions clearly proclaimed new principles of public law. For example, sovereignty was declared to reside in the nation, and the separation of powers was asserted to be an imperative requirement.

Potential Parliamentary Government. In the Constitution that was erected on the *Declaration of Rights* as a basis, an attempt was made, with traditional French regard for formal logic, to apply the principles of national sovereignty and of the separation of powers. This, in turn, ensured that the King could not remain in a position of even theoretical irresponsibility. A few mem-

---

[7] The country was divided in 1790 into eighty-three Departments, the old Provinces, their names, and the privileges associated with them being abandoned. The Departments were divided each into several Districts, later called Arrondissements; and each Arrondissement contained a number of Communes. Cf. Ch. VIII, p. 139, *infra.*

bers of the Constituent Assembly, notably Mirabeau, understood that the only way in which monarchy, for which there was at the time general respect and affection, could survive in the presence of development towards political democracy, was for the King to retain in theory his historical position, while a Constitution should arrange matters so that responsibility of the King's ministers to the representatives of the people could develop. In other words, Mirabeau and a few others desired that the English parliamentary system of government across the Channel should be established in France. It is an interesting speculation what French history would have been had such ideas prevailed; but the question belongs to the realm of the hypothetical. The English system was not widely understood in France; it was considered to be characterized principally by corruption, with the result that it was not generally admired; abstract concepts that prevailed in the Assembly and in the country were not favorable; recollection of abuses of arbitrary power was fresh; Mirabeau was distrusted; Louis XVI proved to be far from a strong character; and, in general, events were traveling exceedingly fast.

Failure of Limited Monarchy. Louis XVI's hesitation to accept the new regime, culminating in his unsuccessful attempt to flee the country, caused his position under the Constitution, when he finally appeared to give his adherence to it, to develop under far from favorable auspices. The Legislative Assembly, established by the Constitution of 1791, was a body of no great merit.[8] In less than a year, it felt constrained to summon a sovereign assembly, the Convention. It had a little earlier suspended Louis XVI from the kingship. The unfortunate monarch was imprisoned and subsequently put to death. Constitutional monarchy gave way to the Convention.

THE FIRST REPUBLIC

The Convention. The Convention governed France for three years. The period was one of fateful accomplishments, which history has come to regard as in part glorious and in part horrible.

Soon after the opening of the Convention, the extremist party, the Montagnards,[9] gained ascendancy over the more moderate Girondins.[10] The extremist leaders, who became associated with the Jacobin Club,[11] were characterized by a militant nationalism and by a ruthless determination to guide the Revolution at any cost in the direction which they arbitrarily decided to be in the interests of the people.

---

[8] The Constituent Assembly had, through a curious form of self-denial, made its own members ineligible for election to the Legislative Assembly. As a result, most men of political experience in the country were excluded.

[9] So-called because they occupied the high seats at the back of the chamber in which the Convention met.

[10] This group derived its appellation from the Department of the Gironde, named from the Gironde River, on which Bordeaux is situated. Several outstanding leaders of the group came from that Department.

[11] Political clubs flourished at this time. The Jacobins, originally the Breton Club, were so called because they met in the former monastery of the Jacobin monks. Their official name was, first, *Amis de la constitution* and, later, *Amis de la liberté et de l'égalité.* The Girondins were members in the beginning, but later ceased to attend.

The execution of Louis XVI not only resulted in active hostilities against France on the part of European monarchs but was also followed by civil war, which was, in turn, exacerbated through destruction of the Girondins by the extremists and through subsequent revolt against the Convention on the part of a large number of Departments.[12] The Convention met this formidable situation with the Reign of Terror. In the end, the country was saved. Brilliant victories were scored on the battlefield against the foreign enemy, and internal opposition was ruthlessly crushed. National bankruptcy was overcome and the public debt placed on a basis of firm credit; a system of national education was founded; and other public benefits were realized. The agency through which foreign and internal policies were directed was the famous Committee of Public Safety. This small body of nine members, meeting in secret, exercised dictatorial authority. Its guiding principle was phrased in Marat's contradictory and impossible words, "the despotism of liberty." Concerning the Committee's genuine patriotism there could be no doubt. Nevertheless, success was followed by divisions among the Montagnards. An increasingly uncontrolled development of the Terror culminated in the personal sway of Robespierre. Inevitably, strong reaction within a short time set in. Robespierre was executed; the Terror came to an end; and foreign enemies showed signs of becoming peaceful. The Convention proceeded to set up in 1795, to succeed itself, the system of the Directory.

The Directory. The period of the Directory witnessed the early exploits of Napoleon Bonaparte on the battlefield. The Directory itself, an executive council of five members, failed to distinguish itself. The situation inherited from the Convention was, it must be recognized, far from an easy one. Nevertheless, the members of the Directory were, with little exception, men of mediocre ability. By divisions among themselves they displayed the inherent weakness of a plural executive. Under them, France reached a point where anarchy again threatened within and, Bonaparte being in Egypt, conquest from without. Napoleon, returning to France, decided to take matters into his own hands. The four-year existence of the Directory came to an end in 1799.

The Consulate. The Directory was replaced by a Consulate, a system which derived its name from the fact that executive authority was vested in three Consuls. However, the First Consul possessed even in law a position superior to that of the other Consuls; and, in practice, the First Consul, in the person of Napoleon, exercised transcendent power. France was, with striking rapidity, restored from the unfortunate situation in which it had found itself. Far-reaching achievements in domestic affairs alternated with brilliant military exploits. In the first category, an accomplishment of much lasting importance was establishment of a highly integrated administrative system.[13] On the basis of the new territorial divisions of the country that had been made soon after the outbreak of the Revolution,[14] Napoleon set up a series of co-ordinated local

---

[12] Cf. this Ch., p. 41, n. 7, *supra.*
[13] Cf. Ch. VIII, pp. 150–151, *infra.*
[14] Cf. this Ch., p. 41, n. 7, *supra.*

agents and agencies. In the result, local organization throughout the nation acquired characteristics which resembled in large measure those of the system of central government that was being quickly and effectively developed. Among other nonmilitary achievements were certain financial reforms, such for example as reorganization of the system of accountability and establishment of the Bank of France. Furthermore, secondary and higher education was developed; French law was codified; [15] the Legion of Honor was founded; the Concordat with the Papacy was concluded; and agriculture, industry, and commerce were encouraged.

THE FIRST EMPIRE

Napoleon I. The Consulate lasted until 1804. In that year, Napoleon, who had previously had himself made Consul for life, became Emperor.

Imperial Accomplishments. The period of the First Empire was in most respects merely the further development and the culmination of the period of the Consulate. Napoleon added to the number of his brilliant military achievements and pushed further his accomplishments in the fields of administration, jurisprudence, art, and education.

The Imperial Tradition. The French not unnaturally look back to the Empire with much pride. This fact affects, not least in the political sphere, their outlook and their pattern of thought in many and perhaps sometimes unsuspected ways. In respect of government, the *Bonapartist* tradition involves, in general, regard for and attraction by direct, effective, and authoritative action in time of crisis. The tradition not unnaturally relegates the democratic process to a minor, even though apparently basic, position. More particularly, employment of the *plebiscite,* whereby acceptance or rejection of a regime or its accomplishments is in appearance left to free decision of the voters, is associated with Bonapartism. On the other hand, the same tradition is also influential in a negative sense and direction. The essentially democratic masses in France distrust a single individual possessed of overweening ambition; and though this aspect of the tradition involves more recent examples as well,[16] no small part of it is based on the experience that France has had with emperors.

THE RESTORATION AND THE MONARCHY OF JULY

The Last French Kings. At the end of the Empire in 1815, France of course again became a monarchy. It so remained until 1848. However, inasmuch as history seems never quite to turn back upon itself, what is called the Restoration did not in reality, whatever may have been the wishes or the theories of the first two Kings, re-establish the *ancien régime.* At the same time, the Bourbon family, in the person of Louis XVIII (until 1824) and in the person

---

[15] The famous Napoleonic Codes were five in number: the Civil Code (begun in 1800—though such work had been contemplated as early as the Constituent Assembly—and adopted in 1804); the Code of Civil Procedure (begun in 1802, adopted in 1807); the Criminal Code (begun in 1801, adopted in 1808); the Penal Code (begun in 1808 as a supplement to the Criminal Code, adopted in 1810); and the Commerce Code (begun in 1801, adopted in 1807).

[16] Cf., e.g., Ch. XI, p. 185, *infra.*

of Charles X (until 1830), regained the throne. Monarchy even survived the 1830 Revolution of July, the throne, through parliamentary decision, passing to Louis Philippe of the younger, or Orleanist, line.

Monarchy and Parliamentary Government. Though the earlier part of the period from 1815 to 1848, especially the reign of Charles X (1824–1830), was typified by much that is associated with the Bourbon family and its concept of monarchy, a beginning was made in the development of a parliamentary system of government along English lines. In reality, power was gradually shifting towards Parliament. The accession of the Orleanist King, Louis-Philippe (1830–1848), was striking evidence of this. At the same time, Louis-Philippe was the last French King. Under him, the essentials of parliamentary government were readily accepted; but royal ineptness, partisan squabbles, and shortsighted opposition to extension of the suffrage marred operation of the system. Destiny seemed to will that parliamentary government could not survive in France unless accompanied by republicanism and political democracy.

THE SECOND REPUBLIC

Louis-Napoleon as President. The period of the Second Republic, 1848 to 1852, was at the beginning marked by a Parisian republican revolution. The period saw the introduction—the definitive introduction, as it turned out to be—of universal manhood suffrage. It witnessed successively a provisional government, a short period of rule by a unicameral National Assembly, the election under a republican Constitution of Louis-Napoleon for a four-year term, and, at the end of three years of the term, a second election, through a plebiscite in conditions of authoritarian duress, of this nephew of Napoleon Bonaparte, this time for ten years.

THE SECOND EMPIRE

Napoleon III. Louis-Napoleon, after a year of his second term, became Emperor, with the title Napoleon III. The regime, the Second Empire, was marked in its earlier years by a thoroughgoing absolutism. Though substantial concessions in the direction of parliamentary government were later made, they did not take place early enough to prevent the end of the regime in 1870.

THE THIRD REPUBLIC

Imperial Collapse. The Franco-Prussian War, declared on July 15, 1870, brought the reign of Napoleon III to a close. The Emperor, after a series of overwhelming defeats for France, actually became, in the first week of September, a prisoner of the enemy at Sedan. In the somewhat chaotic political situation that resulted in Paris, leaders of the Republican Party [17] seized the initiative.

---

[17] Towards the end of the Second Empire, open opposition, which had in earlier years been practically nonexistent, became possible. There was formed an anti-imperial coalition made up of Republicans and of the two branches—Orleanist and Legitimist—of the Royalists. In 1869 the opposition polled more than three and a quarter million votes as against somewhat less than four and a half million votes for "official candidates." The Republican members of the Legislative Body numbered thirty.

Provisional Republican Government. On September 4, the Third Republic was proclaimed; and a Government of National Defence was set up. The vigorous attempts of this Government to turn the course of the War in favor of the French were unsuccessful. Paris soon became subjected to a state of siege; and the Government was constrained on January 28, 1871, to sign an armistice. This in turn made possible the election on February 8, 1871, of a National Assembly, to which the Government of National Defence at once turned over its powers.

Definitive Republican Government. The primary issue in the elections to the Assembly having been that of war or peace, the voters, though, on the whole, Republican in sentiment, returned, in their desire for peace, a majority of Monarchist members. When the war with Prussia had been formally concluded, this majority proved itself incapable of establishing at once a definitive governmental system. The Monarchists were divided among themselves; the Bourbon claimant to the throne, though accepted reluctantly by the Orleanist wing of the majority in the interest of harmony, proved hopelessly stubborn and reactionary; and the Republican leanings of the body of the people became increasingly more manifest. In the result, the National Assembly of 1871, after governing France for five years, hesitatingly endowed the country at the end of 1875 with a Republican Constitution. This Constitution was put into effect at the beginning of the following year; and though it was presumed to be merely temporary, it actually had a much longer life than any other French Constitution since the Revolution. The likelihood is that it would be in existence at the present day but for the disastrous defeat of the French at the hands of Nazi Germany in the spring of 1940.

THE VICHY REGIME

Counter-Revolution. The military collapse of France in June of 1940 was followed in July by the establishment at Vichy of a dictatorship. It was headed by the aged Marshal Pétain, and conducted by politicians of somewhat unsavory character. It was modeled on the Fascist systems of Italy and Spain. The regime owed its existence and most of its strength to support by the Nazis, as was demonstrated by the fact that the whole system disappeared along with, and literally even in advance of the disintegration of, the German armies, at the time of the liberation of France.

THE FOURTH REPUBLIC

Return to Freedom. The Vichy regime was supplanted in 1944 by a provisional government under the leadership of General de Gaulle, who, in England and North Africa during the War, had become the symbol of resistance in and out of France. He had from nearly the beginning spoken of a Fourth Republic; and, after free consultation of the nation, such a regime was at the end of 1946 established and launched on an uncertain and fateful career.

The successive regimes in France may be seen in outline in the following table:

To 1789: *Ancien régime*	1830–1848: Monarchy of July: Louis-
1789–1792: Constituent Assembly—	Philippe
Legislative Assembly (1791)	1848–1852: Second Republic
1792–1795: Convention	1852–1870: Second Empire
1795–1799: Directory	1870–1940: Third Republic
1799–1894: Consulate	1940–1944: Vichy Regime
1804–1815: First Empire	1944– : Fourth Republic
1815–1830: Restoration: Louis XVIII	
(to 1824)—Charles X	

2. THE CONSTITUTIONS OF FRANCE

GENERAL ASPECT

Constitutional Longevity. Reference to a tendency towards rapid constitutional change in France applies of course primarily to the series of Constitutions preceding the Constitution of the Third Republic. This Constitution existed for nearly three-quarters of a century. The other Constitutions [18] had much shorter lives. The longest (that of 1852) lasted only eighteen and a half years. One (that of 1793) was voted but never applied; whereas another (that of 1791) had a life of less than a year.

THE FIRST WRITTEN CONSTITUTION

The Basic Law of Limited Monarchy. The monarchical Constitution of 1791 was a long document, containing as a preamble the famous Declaration of the Rights of Man. The form of government that was set up may, without too much violence to the facts, be compared with the traditional American system or with the British government before the establishment of the present cabinet system. It was, as has been mentioned, based deliberately on the twin principles of national sovereignty and of the separation of powers. The King was retained. However, he was in terms of the Constitution no longer King of France, but King of the French. Likewise, interestingly enough, the stipulations dealing with the King were placed after those concerning the legislature. The law-making body took the form of a unicameral Legislative Assembly of 745 members, chosen for two years and distributed amongst the eighty-three Departments according to territory, population, and direct taxes. The suffrage was restricted to French males twenty-five years of age who were not servants, and who were qualified by domicile or military service and by the payment of certain taxes. The method of election was indirect, the electors, who were required to be persons with a considerable property qualification, numbering one out of every hundred voters. To the Legislative Assembly the King was granted entrance, but he was possessed of no initiative. His disallowance of legislation could be overridden by a somewhat difficult process.

[18] The most convenient collection of French Constitutions through the Vichy period is Duguit et Monnier, *Les Constitutions et les principales lois politiques de la France depuis 1789* (6ᵉ éd., Paris, 1943). A subsequent edition can be expected to include more recent documents, including the present Constitution. In English a convenient collection up to the time of publication is F. M. Anderson, *The Constitutions and Other Select Documents Illustrative of the History of France* (2nd ed., Minneapolis, 1908). The text of the Constitution of the Fourth Republic is available in French and English in a variety of editions.

He was deprived of the power of dissolution. The ministers, who could not be members of the Legislative Assembly, were declared to be responsible to the King; but they could be impeached before a High Court. The ordinary judiciary consisted of judges elected at intervals by the voters.

CONSTITUTIONS OF THE FIRST REPUBLIC

The Constitution of 1793. The Convention, having succeeded the Legislative Assembly, abolished the Monarchy. In the early months of 1793, a Constitution known as the Girondin Constitution, which had been drawn up by a committee, was presented to the Convention; but this draft was not voted. In June, the Convention framed the Republican Constitution of 1793, known as the Montagnard Constitution, which, being referred by the Convention to the people, was ratified by a vote of 1,810,910 to 11,910. Though this instrument was destined never to be applied, its general provisions are not without interest. Power was vested in a single assembly, which was to be elected annually by direct universal manhood suffrage. This assembly was empowered to issue decrees and to pass laws, the latter being subject to a kind of optional referendum. The executive was to consist of a Council of Twenty-four, to be chosen, one-half annually, by a complicated process. The voters were to choose electors, who in turn were to nominate candidates from amongst whom the legislative body was to select the actual members of the executive council.[19]

The Constitution of the Directory. The Montagnard Constitution, before it could be applied, was suspended by decree of the Convention. In turn, the Convention, having become an instrument of revolutionary government, presented France, as the result of a conservative reaction, with another Constitution. This was the Constitution of the Directory, usually called the Constitution of the Year III (1795). It is the most elaborate of all French Constitutions, consisting of 377 articles. It is especially notable for having attempted to make a careful application of the principle of the separation of powers and for having introduced for the first time in France a bicameral legislature.[20] In the second respect, the legislature was composed of a Council of Five Hundred and a Council of Elders, the second body containing 250 members. The age limit for the Council of Five Hundred was thirty, that for the Council of Elders forty. The members of both houses were chosen one-third at a time each year. The method of election, which was the same for the two houses, was indirect; and the suffrage was limited in extent. Thus, in the second respect, the vote was given only to adult males, not of the servant class, who were subject to direct taxation, who had been resident for a year in France, who were able to read and write, and who were qualified to practice a trade. The voters chose electors, who were required to be twenty-five years of age and to be possessed of certain property qualifications; and these electors

---

[19] It may be noted that this council would not seem to have a very close resemblance to the Committee of Public Safety.

[20] One of the most important and interesting debates in the Constituent Assembly of 1789 was that which preceded the decision not to establish a bicameral parliament on the English model.

selected the members of the two houses. The Council of Five Hundred had the sole initiative of legislative measures, its proposals being submitted to the Council of Elders for integral acceptance or rejection. The Council of Elders alone possessed the power to propose amendments to the Constitution. This body likewise chose the executive, that is to say, the Directory of five members. The choice of the members of the Directory, for whom the age limit was forty, was made from a list of fifty, prepared by the Council of Five Hundred. One member of the Directory was chosen annually. The power possessed and the functions performed by this plural executive were those commonly regarded as being executive in character. Amongst other things, it chose ministers; but, in accordance with the prevailing interpretation of the doctrine of the separation of powers, neither the ministers nor the members of the Directory were allowed entrance to the houses of the legislature.

The Constitution of the Year VIII. The Constitution of the Year III was replaced in 1799 by the famous Constitution of the Consulate, based on a plan framed by Sieyès, considerably modified in a monarchical direction by Napoleon Bonaparte. The Constitution was put into operation even before the result was announced of a referendum in which it was approved by a vote of 5,111,187 to 1,567. The document, considerably shorter than the Constitutions that had preceded it, consisted of ninety-five articles; and it is notable, among other reasons, in that it contained no declaration of rights. It was to endure for fourteen years. One of the most striking aspects of this Constitution of the Year VIII was its complex system of suffrage and election, based on the maxim of Sieyès that confidence comes from below but power from above. The voters consisted of all males over twenty-one years of age, not in the servant class, who could read and write and who were qualified to practice a trade. These voters chose in each Arrondissement a tenth of their number to form a list known as that of the *Communal Notabilities*. From those persons finding a place on these lists various local officials were chosen by the national executive. Moreover, the persons on these lists chose in each Department a tenth of their number to form a list of *Department Notabilities*. These Department Notabilities furnished from their number certain Department officials, appointed by the national executive, and, in addition, chose a tenth of themselves to form a *National List*. From this List, a Senate chose the important legislative, executive, and judicial agents of national government. The legislature was composed of several different bodies, there being, in addition to the Senate composed of eighty members [21] over forty years of age serving for life, a Legislative Body of three hundred, a Tribunate of one hundred, and a Council of State. Legislative measures were prepared by the executive and submitted to the Council of State, where discussion took place and where amendments might

[21] According to the Constitution of the Year VIII, the Senate was to consist originally of sixty members. The members were to choose two members each year for ten years. The Senate also filled vacancies in its own membership. A member was to be chosen from three candidates nominated respectively by the Legislative Body, the Tribunate, and the First Consul. A majority of the original sixty members was selected by four individuals mentioned in the Constitution (Ducos, Sieyès, Cambacérès, and Lebrun); and the remainder were co-opted.

be adopted. The same measures were also submitted to the Tribunate, which could debate them but could not amend them. The next step consisted of the choice by each of these bodies of three of its members for the purpose of debating the proposals before the Legislative Body. This assembly could take no part in the debate, its function being confined to accepting or rejecting measures as a whole. The Senate, besides its important electoral functions, was guardian of the Constitution, in which capacity it was empowered to annul unconstitutional measures, a power that was construed to recognize the Senate as possessed of constituent authority. This situation was in practice of considerably less moment than might have been expected, owing to the great and increasing power of Napoleon. His position, of course, gave to the system of the Year VIII its distinctive character. The First Consul possessed the real authority; and the other two Consuls, though chosen like him for ten years, had only the power to be consulted. Finally, the members of the judiciary ceased to be elective; and from the Year VIII dates the modern system of courts.

THE IMPERIAL CONSTITUTIONS

The First Empire and Premature Parliamentary Government. The Constitution of the Consulate was fundamentally altered later in several respects by senate-consults. Whether or not a new Napoleonic Constitution can be said to have come into existence after the Year VIII is largely a matter of terminology and of point of view. At all events, the usage was well established of making reference to the *Imperial Constitutions.* Thus, aside from reorganization in the Year X of the system of suffrage and election, an organic senate-consult in the same year revised the whole Constitution in view of a senate-consult which two days earlier made Napoleon Consul for life. Likewise, an organic senate-consult of the Year XII (1804) revised the Constitution so as to establish the First Empire. Moreover, the so-called Imperial Constitutions were materially altered by an Additional Act, which was accepted by Napoleon in 1815 upon his return from Elba. Thus, it and its brief life belong, in strict chronological order, after the Constitutional Charter of 1814, which, after the first abdication of Napoleon, marked the re-establishment of hereditary monarchy—in fact, the Additional Act was in a sense an adaptation to the imperial system of the liberal reforms of the Charter. However, after the Hundred Days, the Constitutional Charter was re-established as the recognized Constitution of France.

MONARCHICAL CHARTERS

The Constitutional Charter of 1814. The Constitutional Charter of 1814 marked the Restoration—in a certain theoretical sense, the restoration of the *ancien régime*. This, of course, does not mean that feudal privileges and the like were restored; but, on the other hand, the personal sovereignty of the King was definitely recognized, both in the manner of the granting of the Charter and in its own express words. This recognition of royal sovereignty is, in French theory, necessarily in all conditions inconsistent with national sovereignty. The King, whose divine right was asserted in the preamble of the Charter, was the personal chief of the executive power; and he possessed alone the initiative in law-making. He, however, naturally delegated certain authority to other agents and organs. Foremost of these, of course, was the legislature, a bicameral assembly consisting of a Chamber of Peers, which could also sit as a High Court in the trial of ministers and of persons accused of an attempt on the life of the State, and of a Chamber of Deputies. The Deputies were required to be forty years of age and to qualify through the payment of 1,000 francs in direct taxes. They were directly elected under a system of suffrage so highly restricted as to reduce the number of voters for the whole of France to 100,000. This restriction of the suffrage was accomplished through provisions confining the vote to those persons who were thirty years of age and who paid direct taxes to the amount of 300 francs. Of the decisions of the legislature the King possessed an absolute veto. Especially worthy of note is the fact that there appeared in this Constitution certain features that are usually associated with the parliamentary type of government. Thus, the Chamber of Deputies could be dissolved by the King and the ministers had entrance to the Chambers. On the other hand, ministerial responsibility, though recognized in a terse general provision of the Charter stipulating that "the ministers shall be responsible," had to be developed gradually in practice.

The Constitutional Charter of 1830. The monarchy of the Restoration was succeeded by the Monarchy of July. Charles X was supplanted by Louis-Philippe; and the Constitutional Charter of 1814 gave way to the Constitutional Charter of 1830. Under this second Charter, there was, in French eyes, no longer a negation of the principle of national sovereignty. The King, who owed his position not to heredity but to action by the representatives of the nation, could lay no claim to divine right. He was declared to be King of the French, instead of King of France. Thus, the principal change was one of basic assumption and of spirit, a change due largely, so far as written provisions were concerned, to fundamental departure in the preamble from the terms of the previous Charter. Though the King entertained definite ambitions of being able himself to direct the policy of government, the principle of political responsibility of the ministers to the Chamber of Deputies became in practice clearly recognized; and the general result was that the parliamentary system became better established in French tradition. On the whole, the framework of government, as well as much of the wording of constitutional provisions, remained the same as under the Charter of 1814. The Chambers, it is true, gained the important power of initiative in legislation. Moreover, the hereditary peerage was abolished; and the position of the Chamber of Deputies was somewhat liberalized. In this second respect, the property qualification for membership was reduced so as to render persons eligible who paid 500 francs in direct taxes; and the number of voters was more than doubled by changes in the suffrage requirements. The vote was granted to males twenty-five years of age who paid direct taxes to the amount of 200 francs. This amount was reduced by another 100 francs for Members of the Institute of France and for certain retired officers. However, unenlightened opposition in respect of further suffrage extension was largely instrumental, it will be recalled,[22] in bringing on the Revolution of 1848.

THE CONSTITUTION OF 1848

Presidential Government. In the Republican Constitution of 1848, legislative power was entrusted to a unicameral Legislative Assembly of 750 members, directly elected for three years; and executive power was vested in a President of the Republic, directly elected for four years. The President was, at the expiration of his term, not again eligible until after an interval of four years. Both Assembly and President, it should be stressed, were elected by male voters for whom the only real qualification was that of being twenty-one years of age. Thus, as things turned out, definite establishment of universal manhood suffrage in France was effected at this time.[23] Though, according to the Constitution of 1848, the ministers were asserted to be responsible to the Assembly, though the President was given no power of dissolution, and though legislative measures initiated by the President had first to be submitted to the Council of State, the characteristic feature of the regime was, in reality, the paramount power of the President of the Republic. The President was as directly representative of the nation as was the legislature—in fact, his constituency, being the whole people, was much larger than that of any individual member of the Assembly. In the result, the President overshadowed the Assembly. The fact that the choice of the people fell on Louis Napoleon accentuated the situation. This nephew of Napoleon Bonaparte was an ardent admirer of the Constitution of the Year VIII; and, after the *coup d'état* by which he acquired dictatorial power, it was essentially the system of the Consulate that he established with the Constitution of January 14, 1852.

THE CONSTITUTION OF 1852 AND THE SECOND EMPIRE

Imperial Dictatorship. The Constitution of January of 1852 maintained at first the republican system. It accomplished this through a simple provision stipulating for a President elected for ten years. However, a senate-consult in November re-established the Empire. The executive power which had belonged to the President was, of course, lodged by the senate-consult in the Emperor. Likewise, the responsibility of the ministers to the President, this relationship having been substituted by the 1852 Constitution for responsibility to the Assembly, was transferred to the Emperor. The Emperor was responsible only to the nation. The initiative in legislation belonged exclusively to him. The legislature was a simplified edition of the legislature of the Consulate.[24] The Council of State, composed of from forty to fifty members named by the Emperor, stood in an advisory capacity for purposes of formulating and discussing proposed legislation. Such proposals were voted by the Legislative Body.

[22] Cf. this Ch., p. 45, *supra.*
[23] Cf. *ibid.*
[24] Cf. *ibid.,* p. 49, *supra.*

This assembly contained something more than 250 members, who were elected for six years by direct universal manhood suffrage. However, during the Second Empire, the theoretically democratic basis of government was in considerable measure stultified through a practice on the part of the executive of recommending to the voters *official candidates*. The Senate of about 150 members was appointed by the Emperor. It was, as under the Consulate, the guardian of the Constitution. As such, it possessed the power of interpreting the Constitution and of annulling legislative acts that were unconstitutional. In agreement with the executive, the Senate could alter the Constitution.

The Constitution of the Liberal Empire. The consular system that was established in 1852 and continued under the Second Empire was at first strengthened by various senate-consults. However, during the last ten years of its existence, that is, from about 1860 to 1870, the authoritarian character of the Empire was, through a series of senate-consults, altered in the direction of what came to be called the Liberal Empire. This tendency culminated in the Constitution of May 21, 1870. According to the provisions of this Constitution, the Senate became purely a legislative second chamber; initiative in legislation was shared between the executive and the two chambers; the ministers, who could belong to the chambers, formed a council or cabinet which, though presided over by the Emperor, was responsible to the legislative branch; and the Emperor was responsible to the nation. In short, the attempt was made to combine an imperial system and parliamentary government. The Constitution was submitted to the people and approved by them. This liberalizing of the Second Empire, however, turned out to have been effected too late. Within two months, the Franco-Prussian War broke out. Within another two, the Second Empire had disappeared. It was replaced by the Third Republic and a more viable parliamentary system.

THE CONSTITUTION OF THE THIRD REPUBLIC

Constitutional "Laws." In the course of the long period of the Third Republic, the usage came to have general acceptance of designating as the Constitution of France three short Acts passed by the National Assembly of 1871 in the form of ordinary statutes—the "Laws" of February 25,[25] February 24,[26] and July 16, 1875.[27] This brief [28] triune Constitution naturally displayed more points of difference from, than of resemblance to, previous French Constitutions. The structure of the document was characterized neither by logic nor by

[25] This Act originally contained nine articles, of which one was subsequently repealed. Its title, Organization of the Public Powers, sufficiently indicates its general content.

[26] This Act originally consisted of eleven articles, of which the last two were of only transitory effect and the first seven were subsequently repealed. It was a special Act, concerned with the Organization of the Senate. It was passed contingent on passage of the Act on the Organization of the Public Powers. As a consequence, they are regularly referred to out of their chronological order.

[27] This Act, which was the only one of the three that had the epithet *Constitutional* in its title, had to do with the Relations of the Public Powers. Its fourteen articles dealt with a variety of matters.

[28] Some French authorities assert, on the basis of the principle that all unrepealed law continues in force, that the Declaration of Rights automatically became a part of the Constitution of the Third Republic.

symmetry. As the result of a number of compromises, it was based on no single or simple principle. Though it was a Constitution republican in character, it was far removed from what the Republicans would have drafted, had they been free to follow their own wishes; and a republican regime was, of course, not what the Monarchists desired. However, each party, though expecting as well as hoping that the Constitution would be soon replaced by a document more to its liking, contributed an important elementary principle—the Monarchists that of unity in ruling power, the Republicans that of a popular, and hence diversified, basis for authority. According to a well-worn French aphorism, only the provisional endures. In any case, combination of the two principles proved successful.

Governmental Structure. For the first time in history, there was established a parliamentary system that was republican in form. Simple constitutional stipulations set up a legislature consisting of a Chamber of Deputies and of a Senate, the former to be elected directly through universal manhood suffrage, the latter to be chosen indirectly. The two chambers were endowed with concurrent legislative authority, but the Chamber of Deputies was recognized to possess priority in respect of money measures. The Senate was established as a high court of justice for trying high officials or hearing cases involving attempts on the life of the State. The position of Chief Executive and of formal head of the State was bestowed on a President of the Republic, to be chosen by a joint session of the two chambers. He was to serve for seven years, and was re-eligible. Associated with the President were the usual powers of heads of State such, for example, as the power of law enforcement, of command over the army and navy, of appointment, of pardon, of dissolution,[29] and the like. The legislature and the head of the State were bound together, in the traditional style of parliamentary government, by a ministry which was required to countersign decisions of the President. The latter was declared to be irresponsible, except in case of high treason. The ministers were granted entrance to both chambers, where upon request they were to be heard. They were specifically declared to be responsible to Parliament.

Amendment. In view of the political situation, Monarchists and Republicans of the Assembly of 1871 quickly agreed on an easy method of amendment—that by the two chambers in joint session. Some alteration of the text of the Constitution took place in this formal way during the course of the Third Republic; but, as is not difficult to understand, much more change was effected by statutory law and, especially, by the growth of custom.

Omissions. Such development, though known everywhere, was particularly natural under so brief a document as the Constitution of the Third Republic. Containing provisions only sufficient to establish the bare outline of a central government, the Constitution was characterized by many omissions. A simple illustration is to be found in the fact that there was complete silence with respect to the judicial system and with respect to the whole system of local government.

[29] Previous consent of the Senate was necessary. Cf. Ch. VII, p. 134, *infra.*

VICHY CONSTITUTIONAL ACTS

Pétain and Constituent Power. At Vichy, in July of 1940, formal use was made of the amending process defined in the Constitution of the Third Republic, in order to vest, through a constitutional "Law," constituent authority in Marshal Pétain. This marked the official end of the Third Republic. The complex attendant circumstances and the question how far the action was legally and morally valid will probably be subject of discussion for many years to come.[30]

"Legal" Dictatorship. Marshal Pétain received authority for the formulation, "through one or more acts, of a new Constitution for the French State." The Constitution was to be "ratified by the nation." Such ratification, however, was indefinitely postponed through Pétain's simple expedient of employing not one but several acts. The constitutional "Acts" numbered a baker's dozen.[31] Through the brief provisions of the first three of these, which followed at once upon the enabling constitutional "Law," Marshal Pétain declared himself Head of the French State, assumed "plenary governmental powers," adjourned until further order the chambers, and repealed all provisions of the Constitution of the Third Republic that were inconsistent with his authoritarian position. Subsequent "Acts" were for the most part designed to strengthen this position, until April of 1942. At this time, pressure from the Nazis caused the establishment, in the eleventh "Act," of the position of Head of the Government, to the end of advancing the fortunes of Pierre Laval. The latter succeeded in drawing the substance of power gradually into his hands. However, he, together with his aged chief and their dictatorial system, gave way, at the time of the Liberation, to the Provisional Government of the French Republic,[32] headed by General de Gaulle.

---

[30] If there is any tentative consensus, it would seem to be that the constitutional "Law" was probably legal in a technical sense, but that the constitutional "Acts" were both legally and morally untenable.

[31] They were numbered one to eleven. No. 4 received through modification no less than six successive forms, of which the last was never made public. No. 11 received two forms.

[32] For detailed analysis of this government, cf. Ch. IV, pp. 64–65, *infra*.

CHAPTER III

THE EVOLUTION OF FRENCH DEMOCRACY

1. INTRODUCTORY

The regime of the Third Republic, it will be recalled, was, at the time of its establishment, regarded as only one more change in the kaleidoscopic development of French political experience. Its Constitution was viewed, with a particularly marked degree of certainty, as destined to be short-lived. However, the event completely belied such expectations. The regime and its Constitution had a much longer life than had any of the others; and though the Third Republic was by no means free from vicissitudes, it weathered formidable storms, especially those of the World War of 1914 and of the period between the Wars.

The long life of the Third Republic raises interesting and important problems of historical interpretation. Unless historical forces are to be regarded as wholly capricious, they must in France have been leading up to a democratic parliamentary republic. Through apparently chaotic events and conditions, advance towards an end, at the time unperceived, must have been in the course of being realized. Some explanation must exist both for the lack of stability in former regimes and for the fact that in some way after 1876 necessary forces became so combined as to produce a desired and desirable equilibrium. Careful search ought to bring to light the elements that made for stability.

2. REPUBLIC AND REVOLUTION

Before the Third Republic. The student of French constitutional history ought constantly to recall the attitude of the French towards democracy and republicanism. He ought always to bear in mind the pronounced tendency in France to identify the one with the other. One of the watchwords of the Revolution, it should be remembered, was *equality*.[1] This, in the circumstances, meant, of course, political equality. But a struggle for political equality is a struggle for political democracy; and, in France, the forces that were set in

[1] Cf. Ch. ii, p. 41, *supra*.

56

motion at the time of the Revolution ultimately brought political democracy to France. For this, however, time was required. Again, the party that undertook direction of the struggle for political equality and democracy, that is to say, the revolutionary party, was, from the nature of the case, antimonarchical, in other words, a republican party. This Republican Party was on several occasions successful in seizing power. Such success, it should be recalled,[2] was in large measure made possible by the extreme centralization of the French administrative system. To seize Paris was, at least temporarily, to secure possession of France. This is precisely what the Republican Party succeeded in accomplishing. However, the Republican Party was, on such occasions, in the minority. The country at large had not yet fully accepted political democracy into its regular habits of thought. Hence, though the Republican Party might establish itself at the centre of the State, it could not, without the support of the country, remain in control. The party was, therefore, on successive occasions driven from power.[3] Thus, the revolutionary and Republican Party succeeded in gaining power in 1792. However, the party was unable so to maintain itself; and it was supplanted and decimated by Napoleon and the Bourbon Restoration. In a new generation, a small Republican Party, which considered itself to be in the revolutionary tradition, brought about in Paris the Revolution of 1830. The party, it is true, was not at the time, nor in successive armed revolts during the next two or three years, able itself to secure power; but the fact remains that the Monarchy of July was a revolutionary monarchy.[4] Again, the Republican Party brought about at Paris the Revolution of 1848. However, the party remained in power only for a very short time; and its subsequent efforts during the period were repulsed. Napoleon III, by means of deportations and expedients of a similar nature, thoroughly disorganized the party. In this way, monarchy of an extreme kind was able to flourish.

Democracy and the Third Republic. On the occasion of earlier Republican successes in France, democracy, it may be repeated, had not become accepted by majority opinion. The Republican Party, that is to say, was not in reality representative of the country. Nevertheless, democracy was making its way slowly but surely. By 1870, it had reached the point of being widely accepted in the country at large, so that predominance of the Republican Party, it can now be seen in retrospect, was to be postponed only for a short time.[5] After the party had, following precedent, brought about the Revolution of September 4, it was temporarily disorganized by the war, the Monarchists being presently returned in a majority [6] to the National Assembly of 1871.

In the same year, the Paris revolutionists were annihilated as a result of the

---

[2] Cf. Ch. I, p. 36, *supra.*
[3] This interpretation is suggested by Ch. Seignobos, *Histoire politique de l'Europe contemporaine* (7e éd., 2 vol., Paris, 1924), t. I, pp. 278 *et seq.*
[4] Cf. Ch. II, p. 45, *supra.*
[5] Cf. Ch. XI, p. 183, *infra.*
[6] Cf. Ch. II, p. 46, *supra.*

defeat of the Commune. On the other hand, the Republican Party was no longer a minority party that followed the lead of Paris. Being by this time in a majority in the country, it repudiated Paris and took its stand on the side of legality. Though at the moment in a minority in the National Assembly, the party was able in a short time, under a republican Constitution established by compromise, to establish itself firmly in power. "Generations of monarchists, who were disappearing little by little, were succeeded by republican generations. From 1876 on, the Republican Party was predominant in the cities. In 1876, it possessed definitive mastery of the regions of the East and the South. This assured to it a majority and power. No further motive pushed it towards revolution. It had only to maintain the Republic, which had become the legal regime, in order little by little to secure control of the West and the North, which were more conservative or more indifferent. Revolutions ceased when the Republican Party, the only one organized for revolution, had no more need of revolution." [7]

3. PARLIAMENTARY GOVERNMENT AND EQUILIBRIUM

ORDER IN APPARENT CHAOS

Extremist Principles and Their Combination. The idea suggests itself that the definitive establishment under the Third Republic of the parliamentary system was the inevitable culminating result of certain forces brought into play at the time of the French Revolution, just as the forces working for political equality ultimately resulted, in some apparently deterministic fashion, in political democracy and republicanism. Indeed, a look backwards will lead to the discovery that no more than in the case of democracy and the republican regime could the parliamentary system have been the immediate outcome of the Revolution.[8] Since parliamentarism is inextricably interconnected with democracy and republicanism, the development leading to its final establishment followed *pari passu* their development. Corresponding to the temporary revolutionary successes of republicanism there existed a form of government in which power was concentrated in a sovereign assembly. When reaction against revolutions that were supported only by minorities brought about the downfall of government by a sovereign assembly, the resulting reactionary form of government was that of executive dictatorship. But each of these two systems, government by sovereign assembly and government by executive dictatorship, contains an element which experience shows to be an important ingredient of good government; and, though experience likewise proves that neither of these elements can long continue to exist alone, they are together capable of reaching an equilibrium that may render a governmental system stable, if the system contains them in combination. This equilibrium is typical of the parliamentary regime. It is, in fact, necessary to the existence of this

[7] Seignobos, *loc. cit.,* p. 280.
[8] Cf. Ch. II, p. 42, *supra.*

system in its true form. In France, this equilibrium was, in reality, temporarily realized in the first quarter of the nineteenth century, in the period following the Restoration.[9] However, the parliamentary system that was established at this time was a monarchical system and was not democratic in its basis. Though in theory nothing prevents such a combination, apparently it cannot prevail in France. Accordingly, the definitive establishment of the parliamentary system had to await the definitive establishment of republicanism and democracy. This took place in the period following 1870.

Historical Consistency. The history of the various French regimes that prevailed from the Revolution to the Third Republic may, on the basis of the foregoing analysis, be regarded as falling into two cycles.[10] The first of these cycles extended from 1789 to 1848. The second has extended from 1848 to contemporary times. Furthermore, each of these cycles falls into three periods, characterized in the first place by government by a sovereign assembly, in the second by executive dictatorship, and in the third by parliamentary government. In the first cycle, the first period extended from 1789 to 1795; the second period from 1795 to 1815; and the third from 1815 to 1848. In the second cycle, the first period extended from 1848 to 1849; the second from 1849 to 1870; and the third was the period of the Third Republic, beginning in 1870.

FIRST CYCLE: 1789–1848

Assembly Omnipotence: 1789–1795. During the period between the meeting of the States-General in May of 1789 for the first time in a century and three-quarters [11] and the end of the Convention in 1795, including the National (Constituent) Assembly and the Legislative Assembly of 1791, governmental power was actually concentrated in the hands of an assembly. That the kingship did not disappear for a few years is only incidental. Furthermore, it is important to bear in mind that government by a sovereign assembly as well as government by one man may assume the character of dictatorship. This was particularly true of the last two years of the period under consideration, when France was without a Constitution and when the basis of the authority of the Convention was wholly revolutionary. French experience appears to demonstrate that in modern conditions neither kind of dictatorship can successfully survive, though each contains in it an element which, taken in combination with a corresponding element of the other, may lead to a durable regime, whether that regime be denominated monarchy, republic, or some other. At the same time, inasmuch as revolutions in France have traditionally been the work of the Republican Party, radical or extreme protagonists of republicanism, as distinguished from what may roughly be called moderate [12] republicans, retain even at the present day a tender regard for government by a

[9] Cf. *ibid.*, p. 45, *supra.*
[10] This account is suggested by M. Hauriou, *Précis de droit constitutionnel* (2e éd., Paris, 1929), pp. 293 *et seq.*
[11] Cf. Ch. ii, p. 40, *supra.*
[12] This term has at present in France definitely reactionary associations.

sovereign assembly. The *régime conventionnel* is considered by these extreme republicans to be the only true republican system.[13]

Executive Dictatorship: 1795–1815. The Directory marked the beginning of reaction towards executive government and its four-year lease on life constituted a transition to executive dictatorship. This dictatorship took the successive forms of the Consulate, the Life Consulate, and the Empire. The dominant will was, of course, that of Napoleon Bonaparte. Nevertheless, even this man of genius was unable to establish a definitive regime. Bonapartism, it is true, possesses even at the present day a strong latent appeal for the French nation; and a tendency towards strong, direct action, which in certain conditions asserts its attractions in all countries, manifests itself in flare-ups from time to time in France.[14] At the same time, no system that is not based on the genuine consent of the people can hope to be stable and definitive in that country. Napoleon's sporadic bids for popular support were of doubtful sincerity. As usually happens, the real will of the ruler was manifested institutionally. Thus, for example, suffrage was for practical purposes abolished.

Parliamentary Government: 1815–1848. The fall of the First Empire was followed by the establishment of a parliamentary system. The system marked a compromise between government by a sovereign assembly and government by executive dictatorship. Whether the regime might have been rendered stable and permanent is a question that might be the subject of interesting reflection; but it belongs to the realm of the hypothetical. "The compromise system set up in 1814 was, with slight alterations in 1830, to last until 1848, a period of thirty-four years. It was in reality a period of relative peace and of national rehabilitation. If it did not last longer, this was no fault of parliamentary monarchy but that of men who did not believe it compatible with universal suffrage and democracy. Indeed . . . it was the obstinate persistence of doctrinaires in retaining a ridiculously restricted suffrage that caused the regime to fall . . ."[15]

SECOND CYCLE: THROUGH THE THIRD REPUBLIC

Historical Repetition. Failure of the compromise between the two extremes characterizing the first two periods of the first cycle necessitated the beginning of a second cycle. This second cycle consisted of the same three periods as the first. There was revolution; there was reaction; and there was a compromise that attempted to find equilibrium in the form of a mean between two extremes.

Assembly Omnipotence: 1848–1849. The first period of the second cycle was short-lived. At the same time, the Revolution of February of 1848 was in several respects a miniature edition of 1789. Similar ideas were expressed in similar language. The forces set in motion extended beyond the confines of France, more especially into Italy and Germany. In France itself, a provisional

---

[13] Cf. Ch. v, pp. 79 *et seq., infra.*
[14] Cf. Ch. ii, p. 44, *supra.*
[15] Hauriou, *op. cit.,* p. 309.

government established universal manhood suffrage. On this basis, a National Constituent Assembly was elected. It convened in May of 1848. It was dissolved in May of 1849. Meantime, it consciously endeavored to follow the tradition of the *régime conventionnel*. However, it had little peaceable opportunity to prove its merits. Political revolution was immediately followed by a social revolutionary movement; and, as a result, reaction set in much sooner than after the Revolution of 1789.

Executive Dictatorship: 1849–1870. Government by the National Assembly was succeeded in May of 1849 by a system of presidential government, based on the Constitution of November 4, 1848. In a very short time, the President, in the person of Louis Napoleon, and the Chamber were in conflict; and this led straight to the *coup d'état* of December of 1851. Thereafter, Louis Napoleon ruled as President with dictatorial power until, with the establishment of the Second Empire in November of 1852, he acquired the title of Emperor.

Parliamentary Government: 1870 through the Third Republic. The third period of the second cycle began in 1870. On the other hand, beginning in 1859, a tendency had manifested itself for executive dictatorship to be somewhat softened. In the course of eleven years, during the period that is known as that of the Liberal Empire, this tendency gathered such momentum as to give rise to the Constitution of the Liberal Empire, adopted in May of 1870.[16] That this year might have in any event marked the beginning of a period of equilibrium, that is to say, the beginning of parliamentary government, is altogether possible; but this again belongs to the realm of the hypothetical. In about two months, war broke out between France and Prussia; and the Second Empire fell.

Following upon catastrophic experiences of the French nation at the time of this war and of the fall of the Empire, the parliamentary system of the Third Republic came into being and began its uniquely long period of existence and development.

SINCE THE THIRD REPUBLIC

The Historical Problem. It is impossible to prove and exceedingly difficult to believe that the Third Republic would have fallen without the blows of unprecedented might which it received from the outside. On the whole, the regime appeared to have become adapted to French needs and to the French character. Nevertheless, the French people, in accordance with what has been called [17] a law of their history, associated the Constitution of the Third Republic with the disastrous defeat of the French armies by the Nazis in 1940; and, after the Liberation, no substantial part of the people favored re-establishment of that Constitution.[18] However unreasoning and in most respects unreasonable

---

[16] Cf. Ch. II, p. 53, *supra*.

[17] J.-J. Chevallier, *Histoire des institutions de la France de 1789 à nos jours: Second cycle: 1870–1945* (Paris, 1950), p. 357. Cf. Jacques Théry, *Le Gouvernement de la IVe République* (Paris, 1949), p. 13.

[18] Cf. Ch. IV, pp. 66–67, *infra*.

this attitude may be, it is a simple fact. Therefore, the Vichy regime and the existence of the Fourth Republic may appear to some students to falsify, or in any case to require modification of, any suggested historical pattern that might be based on the undoubted fact of the long life of the Third Republic.

From Third to Fourth Republic. Cycles of history and similar conceptions being—like historical periods, the seasons, and so on—fundamentally arbitrary in character, they are to be justified, if at all, only by their convenience. If a particular student finds that a particular suggestion is not helpful to him in his thinking and in his attempts at understanding, his simplest procedure is to disregard the suggestion. So far as French political development is concerned, nothing could be more natural, it would seem, than to view it in terms of political democracy, republicanism, and parliamentary government. During the darker days of World War II, some observers, perhaps not unnaturally, allowed their vision to become so narrowed as to predict that France would not in a foreseeable future go back to a regime of political democracy; but there were others who felt that if any prediction about the future could be made with confidence, one was that the French, if free to choose, would choose to re-establish a parliamentary republic. A Frenchman once said [19] that this is the system "to which every civilization turns or returns." In this context, a simple historical hypothesis would take the form of regarding the Vichy regime as an interlude, fundamentally non-French in character and based on foreign armed force, and the Fourth Republic as in its essentials a continuation of the kind of democratic regime the French had developed, and were developing, for themselves.

[19] Paul de Rémusat, *A. Thiers* (Paris, 1889), p. 136.

CHAPTER IV

THE FRAMING OF THE CONSTITUTION
OF THE FOURTH REPUBLIC

1. INTRODUCTORY

The prevailing Constitution of France was submitted to, and ratified by, the voters on October 13, 1946.[1] This and a few other dates and the events connected with them constitute the immediate historical background of the establishment of that Constitution.

2. THE PROVISIONAL GOVERNMENT OF THE FRENCH REPUBLIC

THE RESISTANCE

Composition and Organization. The period between the collapse of France in the summer of 1940 and its Liberation in the summer of 1944 witnessed a number of developments, inside and outside France, that are related to the establishment of the present governmental regime. During the time of the Provisional Government of France under the Vichy regime and of the simultaneous occupation first of part and then of all of the country by the Nazi armies, various forms of opposition to the occupiers and to the existing Government developed at various points in the country. From the nature of the case, such activity, which came to be known as the Resistance, tended to be, espe-

---

[1] It is sometimes referred to as the Constitution of September 28, this being the date on which the document was voted by the Constituent Assembly that formulated it. However, the technically correct date by which to refer to the Constitution is October 27, the day on which the text was officially promulgated by the President of the Provisional Government and thereby given legal status. Cf. J. Laferrière, *Manuel de droit constitutionnel* (2e éd., Paris, 1947), p. 925 n; and G. Vedel, *Manuel élémentaire de droit constitutionnel* (Paris, 1949), pp. 329 *et seq.* The assembly, elected on June 2 is known as the Second National Constituent Assembly, in contrast with a First National Constituent Assembly, elected on April 21, 1945, which on April 19, 1946, adopted a Constitution that was rejected by the voters on May 5. The legal basis for the two assemblies and for their activities consisted of provisions ratified by the voters in October of 1945, at the time of the election of the first assembly. These provisions, in turn, were formulated for submission to the voters by the Provisional Government of the French Republic, under the Presidency of General de Gaulle, which was established in France at the time of the Liberation in 1944.

cially in the beginning, essentially sporadic and largely unorganized. Its effectiveness naturally varied with circumstances. For example, the Communists, after the Nazi attack on the Soviet Union, played a part that was, because of their organization and discipline, so striking as to serve to some extent as a model for other elements.[2] In general, these elements may be said to have been of three kinds. In addition to resistance groups in the literal sense, parts of several political parties of the Third Republic and elements of organized labor became increasingly opposed to Vichy. Various extensions in structure and activity were, with the passing of time, realized. Not the least interesting development was that of clandestine discussion and writing concerning the future political regime of the country. In general, this was animated by the elevated spirit that prevailed in resistance. A renovated France was envisaged that would be characterized by the same spirit. In the course of time, relations on varying scales were established among the elements in the Resistance movement, the culmination being the creation in May of 1943 of a National Council of Resistance. Likewise as time went by, General de Gaulle became the recognized symbol of the Resistance; and the movement within France established on the outside, through the General, contact with elements of resistance abroad.

Leadership. General de Gaulle had been a member of the Ministry of M. Paul Reynaud, which, shortly after the fall of Paris in June of 1940, resigned in favor of Marshal Pétain, whose Ministry arranged the surrender of France. General de Gaulle, in a dramatic radio speech, urged French people everywhere to join him in refusing to accept either defeat or a government which was founded on it. From that time forward, the fortunes of the General were checkered and uncertain. His movement, beginning as a military enterprise, soon became obliged, because of adherence to it by a considerable part of French overseas possessions, to assume a political character and to effect a certain amount of organization centering in London. Following the invasion of North Africa in the fall of 1942 by the Allies, the mysterious presence there of Admiral Darlan and acceptance of him by the Allies as French High Commissioner resulted in a nominal continuity with Vichy. General Giraud having upon the assassination of Darlan succeeded at the end of 1942 to the position of High Commissioner and having about a month later received the title of Civil and Military Commander-in-Chief, he and General de Gaulle became on June 3, 1943, at Algiers Co-Presidents of the French Committee of National Liberation. In the course of about four months, General de Gaulle had established himself as head of the Committee; and, on June 3, 1944, anniversary of the founding of that body, the Committee became the Provisional Government of the French Republic, with General de Gaulle as President. Its members were, according to their own decision, to remain in power until they could surrender their authority to a regularly constituted government.

Consultative Assembly. Meanwhile, there was created at Algiers in September of 1943, in accordance with an intention of General de Gaulle announced as much as two years before, a Provisional Consultative Assembly,

[2] Cf. this Ch., p. 68, *infra.*

representative of various elements of the Resistance both inside and outside France. President, Government, and Assembly were set up in Paris in August of 1944.

LIBERATION

Government on French Soil. Upon the Liberation of France and the establishment of the provisional authorities in Paris, the composition of each of the two agencies underwent some modification. The members of the Government, to whom were added several leaders of the clandestine movement, became known as Ministers, instead of Commissioners. The Assembly was substantially enlarged. The representation of the clandestine elements inside France and that of the Chambers of the Third Republic were tripled; the representatives of the Resistance outside France were slightly increased; and, in June of 1945, a group was added of representatives of persons who had been imprisoned or deported. The size of the Assembly was in the end approximately 300. In November of 1944, a High Court of Justice was established. In general, the Assembly served the purpose of reflecting public opinion as well as possible in abnormal circumstances; and its function, as its title indicates, was to give advice. The Government not only exercised general executive power; it likewise enacted legislation, its acts in this respect being known as *ordonnances.* The High Court of Justice had as its mission the trial of persons connected with government under Vichy whose actions might be proved to have been criminal. In the course of the late summer and early fall of 1945, it convicted and sentenced to death Pétain and Laval.

From the Provisional Towards the Definitive. General de Gaulle and the elements of which he came to be the symbol and the leader had all along asserted that a free consultation of the French people must take place as soon as circumstances should be favorable. Such consultation, in the event, became possible considerably earlier than was at first anticipated. The Liberation of the country and the return of prisoners and of deported persons proceeded rapidly enough for national elections [3] to be held on October 21, 1945.

3. THE FIRST NATIONAL CONSTITUENT ASSEMBLY

CONSULTATION OF THE NATION

Suffrage and Voting. The general elections of October 21, 1945, were the first occasion since 1936 on which the French voters were consulted on a national scale. Woman suffrage had been introduced by an ordinance of the French Committee of National Liberation at Algiers in April of 1944. This decision was confirmed after the Liberation; and the new franchise for women, together with the universal manhood suffrage that prevailed under the Third Republic, ensured that the suffrage should be as liberal as is normally found in modern democratic conditions.[4] The members of a national assembly were

[3] Local elections were held as early as April and May.
[4] Cf. Ch. VI, p. 94, *infra.*

chosen according to a special system of proportional representation, with the Department as the basic constituency.

Political Background. The determination of the Provisional Government of the French Republic to hold national elections was announced in August of 1945. This determination, the nature of the decisions which the voters were asked to make, and the voting and the campaign that preceded it had as a background the intricacies of the political situation that prevailed. In general, a tendency existed for organizations, practices, and doctrines of the Third Republic, naturally modified in varying degrees by the bitter experience through which France had passed, to gain some ascendancy over the hopes and aspirations that characterized the Resistance. Certain questions were put to the voters with the aim of securing from the people solutions of several conflicts of views which divided prevailing opinion. This consultation took the form of two referenda that were held on October 21, 1945, at the same time that the National Assembly was chosen.

First Referendum. The first question submitted to referendum on October 21, 1945, was worded as follows:

Do you wish the Assembly elected this day to be a Constituent Assembly?

In this way, the voters were in a position to choose between a complete break with the Third Republic and a continuation of that regime. It was understood that in the case of a negative decision the Assembly elected would become a Chamber of Deputies under the Constitution of 1875, which could, together with a Senate then required to be arranged for, constitute if desirable a National Assembly with a view to constitutional amendment.[5] Such a negative decision might at first glance be presumed to have been the natural one. The Constitution of the Third Republic had, it will be remembered, had the longest life of any French Constitution. It had become adapted to French needs and to the French character. It was the basis of the regime which the enemies of political democracy in France greatly hated. General de Gaulle and the Resistance had all along repudiated the Vichy system as a usurpation. An *ordonnance* of August 9, 1944, summarized the situation by declaring that "the form of government of France is and remains the Republic, which in law has never ceased to exist." The French Radical Party, a liberal party in the Revolutionary tradition which had been the heart of the principal governing majorities of the Third Republic,[6] vigorously supported, along with a few elements of the Right, the continuance or the re-establishment—depending on juristic niceties—of the Constitution of 1875; and certain public men made a strong case for the intrinsic merits of that document and the system based on it. On the other hand, aside from certain difficulties of law and fact about the thesis of the continuity of the Third Republic, which have continued to be the basis of hairsplitting argument in France, tradition and public opinion were, as has been observed, hostile to a regime under which France had suffered disastrous mili-

[5] Cf. Ch. II, p. 54, *supra.*
[6] Cf. Ch. XII, pp. 202–203, *infra.*

tary defeat. At the end, the Radicals were almost alone in advocating a negative answer to the first referendum question. In the result, the question was answered overwhelmingly in the affirmative (more than 18,500,000 to less than 700,000). This, it would seem, proved nothing about the question of continuity up to that point; but it left no doubt but that a large majority of the voters at the time willed the end of the Third Republic. Moreover, the impressive majority would seem to preclude for all time controversy, like that which is still possible concerning the Convention of 1792 and the Bordeaux Assembly of 1871, about the possession of constituent power by the Assembly elected on October 21, 1945.

Second Referendum. The second question submitted to referendum was worded as follows:

> If the electorate shall have answered "Yes" to the first question, do you approve, until the new constitution shall be put into effect, organization of the public powers in conformity with the bill the text of which appears on the back of the ballot paper?

Here the choice was between what came to be called a "limited" and an "unlimited" assembly. The latter, an assembly free of limitations on its power to govern at will and to formulate a constitution at its pleasure, is in the French tradition—the Convention of 1792 and the Assemblies of 1848 and 1871 being bodies of this kind. On the other hand, a substantial body of moderate opinion was influenced by the view that these very precedents augured badly for a "sovereign" assembly, especially after the difficult years through which France had been passing. General de Gaulle, it has been suggested, might naturally have been expected to prefer avoiding a constituent assembly altogether; but the mere submission to the people of a constitution which their elected representatives had played no part in framing would scarcely have been consistent with proclamations which involved commitments to a free consultation of the Nation. However that may have been, the General was undoubtedly forced to modify procedures which he would himself have preferred. Early in 1945, he seemed favorable to a "presidential"—that is, in general, an American—system of government. He therefore advocated submitting to the voters a scheme for temporary government which would involve choice by the Constituent Assembly of a provisional President who could in the American manner be independent of the representative body. He was apparently reconciled to the calling of a constituent assembly by the hope that such an assembly, with the object lesson of a presidential system before its eyes, would come to favor this regime. However, support of the parliamentary relationship, especially in the Consultative Assembly, compelled formulation for the back of the ballot of a system in which the provisional President and his Ministers would be responsible to the Constituent Assembly. Even this, while regarded as preferable to the presidential system, was less attractive than an "unlimited" assembly to the elements of the extreme Left. These elements were to be found primarily in the Communist and, to a lesser extent, in the Socialist Party. These parties, together with the MRP (*Mouvement Républicain Populaire*), a Christian Socialist Party, which like the Socialists was organized and disciplined in considerable measure on the Communist model,[7] formed the "big three" or the "monolithic" parties of the post-War period.[8] With de Gaulle urging acceptance of the "limited" arrangement and the extreme Left appealing to the voters to answer "No," the outcome of the referendum on the second question was certain to be different from the near unanimity with respect to the first question. As a matter of fact, the affirmative vote, in spite of General de Gaulle's great prestige, was only some 12¾ to 6½ millions.

The Will of the People. On the basis of the two referenda, the will of the French Nation seemed to be clear. The voters, in repudiating by an overwhelming majority the Third Republic, indicated their desire for an entirely new constitution; but they showed themselves at this time, as well as when their representatives set out to draft a fundamental document, much less certain concerning what sort of constitution was desired.

TRANSITIONAL PERIOD

The Act of November 2, 1945. The brief provisions set out on the back of the ballot paper on October 21, 1945, having been approved by a majority of the voters, were promulgated as a law, rather than as an *ordonnance,* by the Provisional Government of the French Republic. The law is known as the Act of November 2, 1945. It is a document of no little interest.[9]

The provisions of the Act of November 2 which relate to the temporary system of government thereby set up are worded as follows:

Art. 1.—The Constituent Assembly shall elect at once, by public ballot and by a majority of the members composing it, the President of the Provisional Government of the Republic. The latter shall form his Government and present it, together with his governmental program, for the approval of the Assembly.

The Government shall be responsible to the Assembly; but the rejection of a measure or of an appropriation item shall not require its resignation. This shall be obligatory only as the result of a distinct vote of a motion of no confidence which shall be brought up at the earliest two days after being placed on the table of the Assembly and shall be adopted by a majority of the members of the Assembly by means of a recorded ballot individually cast.

Art. 4.—The Assembly shall have the power of law-making. It shall have, concurrently with the Government, the initiation of legislation.

Within the period of one month stipulated for the promulgation of laws, the Government shall have the right to request a second reading. If following upon this the first vote shall be confirmed by a majority of the members composing the Assembly, the law shall be promulgated in three days.

Art. 5.—The Assembly shall vote the budget, but it may not initiate expenditures.

The simplest analysis of the essential provisions of this Act will reveal its intention to provide a cure for ministerial instability, regarded as a radical defect of government under the Third Republic. Thus, the effort is manifest to avoid the fall of ministries as the result of "snap" votes; and the provision is particularly interesting which is analogous to the well-known "self-denying ordinance" of

[7] Cf. this Ch., p. 64, *supra.*
[8] Cf. Ch. xii, p. 191, *infra.*
[9] The official text is to be found in *J. O., Ordonnances et Décrets,* 2–3 nov. 1945, p. 7159.

the English House of Commons in respect of financial initiative.[10] On the other hand, several differences, formal or substantial, from the "classical" English model, or even from the system of the Third Republic, are easily to be noted. The most manifest are the absence of a bicameral legislature, the lack of distinction between the head of state and the head of government, and the omission of the power of dissolution.

The Two Assemblies. The Assembly which was elected on October 21, 1945, formulated a constitution, it may be once more noted in anticipation, only to have the draft rejected by the voters. Hence, another Assembly was chosen on June 2, 1946, which was known as the Second National Constituent Assembly, its predecessor becoming retroactively designated as the First National Constituent Assembly. During all this time, the system of government was in operation that was provided for in the Act of November 2, 1945; and this situation was having its influence on the constitution-makers in the two Assemblies. As has been well said,[11] "The Constitution of the Fourth Republic is only the Act of November 2, 1945, twice reviewed and twice corrected."

Assembly Status. The interesting and important fact that each of the two Assemblies of 1945–1946 served not only as a body concerned with formulation of a constitution for France but also in terms of the Act of November 2 as an integral part of the governmental system of the nation assimilated these bodies to all similar French Assemblies but, of course, differentiated them from the Philadelphia and most other American constitutional conventions. The two capacities of the Assemblies were naturally, it should be stressed, closely interrelated; so that, as has been hinted,[12] the daily operation of government and, more particularly, the play of party politics were exceedingly important considerations during the process of constitution-making.

The Provisional President. The Assembly which was elected on October 21, 1945, met on November 6. The Provisional Government of the French Republic surrendered at once its authority [13] into the hands of the chosen representatives of the nation. General de Gaulle a week later was duly elected President, in terms of the Act of November 2. However, in spite of a unanimous vote for the General, the political situation was so acute that somewhat typical crises developed. It was not until November 21 that the President, who because of an apparent impasse between the Communists and himself had meanwhile put his powers back into the hands of the Assembly, was able to form a ministry, and not until the 23rd that the ministry and its platform were, again unanimously, approved by the representatives of the nation.

Political Conflict. The post-War phenomenon of a cabinet in France based on a coalition of the three "monolithic" parties has been called [14] a "sys-

---

[10] Cf. Ch. VI, p. 109, *infra*.

[11] J. Théry, *Le Gouvernement de la IVe République* (Paris, 1949), p. 17.

[12] Cf. this Ch., p. 66, *supra*.

[13] In accordance with regular French practice, it continued temporarily to conduct routine business.

[14] By M. Léo Hamon in "Le Régime parlementaire de la IVe République" and "La Fin du régime de quasi-unanimité," *Politique*, t. IV, no. 24, juin 1947, pp. 385 *et seq.*, no. 25, juillet 1947, pp. 523 *et seq.*

tem of quasi-unanimity." As is not difficult to imagine, such tripartite coalition involved much stress and strain; and unanimity, which not unnaturally proved in the end impossible to maintain, was always difficult to secure. Thus, a kind of personal antagonism between the Communists and General de Gaulle was never far below the surface of things. This, in turn, was merely one element in a complex and deep-running division which displayed most of the character- istics of the traditional opposition between Left and Right.[15] Embedded in the various details, and of course closely interrelated with them, was a constitu- tional issue that can be formulated in fairly simple terms.

The Central Constitutional Issue. Importance attaches to recalling that the French variant of the parliamentary system of government experienced dur- ing the Third Republic a development that took place in the presence of two opposing tendencies. A tendency for the characteristics of the parliamentary system in its classic form to survive in France was modified in a "republican" direction towards a regime in which Parliament tended to become "all-power- ful." In general, the issue of strong executive versus weak executive was in- volved. In the post-War period, political controversy has afforded since the beginning abundant evidence of the Left's support of, and the Right's hostility to, what has long been called in France [16] the Convention System (*régime con- ventionnel*), and what has continued since the War usually to be referred to as Assembly Government (*gouvernement d'assemblée*). This furnishes a simple clue to most political and constitutional developments during the period of constitution-making.

Position of the Left. The intention of General de Gaulle and his principal supporters that the provisions of the Act of November 2, 1945, should estab- lish for the cabinet a more stable position than under the Third Republic [17] was regarded by the principal elements of the Left as literally reactionary in terms of traditional French development in the matter of the relationship between legislature and executive. On the other hand, the Left, as was no doubt natural, was accused by its opponents of stultifying, in accordance with its own pattern, the Act of November 2, which its extreme elements had unsuccessfully opposed at the time of the referendum. The situation was accentuated by the fact that the Constituent Assembly was somewhat further to the Left than was the coun- try itself.[18] One significant political consequence was the elimination of General de Gaulle.

Resignation of de Gaulle. General de Gaulle, at a specially called meet- ing of Ministers on January 19, 1946, bluntly expressed without warning his intention of resigning. Though the political situation, marked by clear signs of Communist-Socialist appeasement, was tense, General de Gaulle had been re- ceiving a number of unanimous votes of support in the Assembly. He had, more particularly, weathered a storm at the end of 1945 that had threatened to wreck his majority, the Socialists and Communists supporting vigorously against his

---

[15] Cf. Ch. x, p. 173, *infra.*
[16] Cf. this Ch., pp. 71–72, *infra,* and Ch. v, p. 79, *infra.*
[17] Cf. this Ch., p. 68, *supra.*
[18] Cf. this Ch., p. 74, *infra,* and Ch. v, p. 78, *infra.*

equally firm opposition a 25 per cent cut in military expenditure. In spite of an apparent solution of this problem, General de Gaulle, during a parliamentary recess of a fortnight, formulated for himself during his vacation reasons for withdrawing from the position of President, reasons which will perhaps always remain obscure and controversial. In general, the Communists and in increasing measure the Socialists, being concerned at the slowness with which internal conditions were improving, were irritated with what they regarded as the General's tendency to remain on too high a plane, too little concerned with the practical problems of the day. This strained situation was a conditioning factor in the crisis over military expenditure. The constitutional implications are of the greatest interest and importance.

Power of the Purse. When the members of a legislative body are limited, whether voluntarily or otherwise, in the matter of initiative of proposals for expenditure, no derogation at all is of course intended of the basic democratic principle that final control of public money should belong to the representatives of the people.[19] Such limitation has its foundation partly in the assumption, based on experience and reason, that a responsible and controlled executive is in a better position than a legislature to know in detail what outlays are necessary and desirable, and partly in the similarly based assumption that in practical politics the representatives of the people are more likely to prove wastrels than to be guardians of the people's money. Serious students of government everywhere are likely to accept the first assumption; and this may be sufficient to cause them to approve limitation of initiative. The second assumption is on the whole congenial to conservatives, who are shown by experience frequently to confuse opposition to waste with opposition to expansion of governmental activity. On the other hand, progressives often tend, because of their sympathy for socialization of the government process, to disapprove limitation, failing to appreciate sufficiently the importance of leadership and responsibility. In some instances, however, the Left and the Right tend in practice to exchange positions. Military expenditure is a natural example. All these considerations may be seen to be connected with the situation which gave rise to the retirement of General de Gaulle.

Assembly Government and the Left. When General de Gaulle in effect insisted that acceptance of his Government's proposals for military expenditure was a question of confidence, a square issue was joined of a kind by no means unknown in the history of parliamentary government. According to the general principles of that system, threat of resignation is a recognized weapon in the hands of the executive. The majority of the legislature must either accept the position of the executive or accept the consequences of resignation by the executive.[20] In the French crisis of December of 1945, the Socialists and Communists insisted that this was not the case, basing their contention on a highly important and interesting interpretation of the terms of the Act of November 2,

---

[19] Cf. Ch. VI, p. 108, *infra*.

[20] Where dissolution is regularly practiced, as it is not in France (cf. this Ch., p. 74, *infra*, and Ch. VII, pp. 133–134, *infra*), the situation is somewhat less simple, but the principle is the same.

1945. Their argument was that the provision of Article 1 according to which "rejection of . . . an appropriation item shall not require . . . resignation" made General de Gaulle's position improper; and they held that the provision according to which resignation should "be obligatory only as the result of a distinct vote of a motion of no confidence" rendered resignation illegitimate in the absence of the voting of such a motion. Though this argument scarcely seems consistent with the simplest principles either of logic or of parliamentary government, the significant thing is that it seems clearly to be based on a belief in the thorough subjection of the executive to the representative Assembly. If the fact that General de Gaulle was by the letter of the law relieved of the necessity of resigning because of the reduction of one of his expenditure proposals should be interpreted as forbidding his resignation, and if the executive should be compelled to remain in office until formally dismissed by the Assembly, the result would undoubtedly be a stultification of parliamentary government. Therefore, the French opinion seems entirely plausible which held at the time, and has since continued to hold, that the Left was contending for a system of assembly government.[21] The crisis attendant on the resignation of General de Gaulle is important precisely because thus early in the history of the Fourth Republic the constitutional issue was so clearly joined.

THE CONSTITUTION OF APRIL 19, 1946

Legal Basis. The provisions of the Act of November 2 which defined the "limited" constituent authority of the elected assembly are phrased as follows:

Art. 2.—The Assembly shall set up a new Constitution.

Art. 3.—The Constitution adopted by the Assembly shall be submitted for the approval of the electorate of French citizens within the month which shall follow its adoption by the Assembly.

Art. 6.—The powers of the Assembly shall expire on the day the new Constitution shall be put into effect and, at the latest, seven months after the first meeting of the Assembly.

Art. 7.—In the event the electorate shall reject the Constitution set up by the Assembly, or in the event that the latter shall not have set up one within the period stipulated in Art. 6, steps shall at once be taken to elect in the same manner a new Constituent Assembly, which shall possess the same powers. It shall meet automatically on the second Tuesday after its election.

Committee on the Constitution. The Assembly elected on October 21, 1945, "The First National Constituent Assembly," attacked without great delay its essential task of framing a Constitution for France. In accordance with traditional practice, the bulk of constructive work fell to a committee. This was the Committee on the Constitution, a body of forty-two elected by the Assembly on November 29. Employment of proportional representation ensured that some three-fourths of the members of the Committee should belong to the "big three" parties, just as election of the Assembly by proportional representation had caused the same fraction of its membership to belong to these "monolithic" organizations.[22] However, inasmuch as no majority was possible except

[21] Cf. this Ch., p. 70, *supra.*
[22] Cf. Ch. vi, p. 97, *infra.*

by a combination of two of the three parties, the necessity of some compromise was clear from the beginning. The Socialists, though somewhat less numerous than the members of the other two parties, found themselves in a strong strategic position.

General Principles. During parts of the next two months, the months of December and January, the meetings of the Committee on the Constitution were in general devoted to discussion of broad principles, without reference to a specific draft text. In this way, the general tendencies of the parties began to manifest themselves. The Socialists, especially after the January vacation and the withdrawal of General de Gaulle, began to lean less towards the MRP and more towards the Communists.

Socialist-Communist Predominance. In the course of the next two months, the months of February and March, the Socialists came to side with the Communists in greater and greater degree, the rift between the MRP and the two Left parties thereby becoming more pronounced. During this period, the President of the Assembly, M. Vincent Auriol, attempted repeatedly and patiently to mediate on the outside between the elements which were manifesting strong tension within the Committee on the Constitution. M. Auriol gave his attention particularly to an effort to find solutions in the matter of the issue between a bicameral and a unicameral legislature and in the matter of the character of the projected position of President of the Republic.[23] In the end, the patience of the members of the MRP gave way. When a point which the MRP felt to have been settled was rejected by the Socialists and Communists in the Committee, M. de Menthon, the MRP member who had been chosen as General Reporter of the Constitution, together with an MRP member entrusted with a special report, resigned.

Formulation of a Text. In spite of continued efforts at mediation and conciliation, the fact became clear during the period following the resignation of M. de Menthon that a Constitution was to be drafted which would prove acceptable only to the Socialist and Communist elements. The position of General Reporter was assumed by M. Pierre Cot, a former Radical who became an ally of the Communists. He guided the draft Constitution through the Constituent Assembly. Meanwhile, in the course of the month of March, the Assembly had adopted, a Socialist serving as Reporter, a *Declaration of the Rights of Man.*[24] This was an elaborate document in which a number of articles on "Social and Economic Rights," regarded as required by modern conditions, were joined to articles on "Liberties," provisions from the famous *Declaration* of 1789, with some significant omissions, being included, sometimes verbatim, sometimes in more or less modified form. Between April 9 and 19, the body of the Constitution, some eighty-odd articles, was voted. Though final drafting of certain sections was necessary, no really important concessions were made by the Communists and Socialists. These parties contained practically all the supporters of the Constitution as finally framed.

[23] Cf. Ch. v, p. 81, *infra.*
[24] Cf. *ibid.*, p. 78, *infra.*

Proposed Governmental System. The principal provisions of the new Constitution outlined a system of government for the Fourth Republic. The legislature was to consist of a single chamber. It was to choose a colorless President of the Republic, the butt of various jokes, and, at the beginning of each legislature and on any occasion of vacancy, a Prime Minister. Other institutions that were provided for included consultative economic and imperial councils and a high court of justice and a judicial council. Ministers were made politically responsible to the Assembly. The controversial matter of dissolution of the Assembly received a form such as practically to render it inoperative. M. Pierre Cot described [25] the system proposed to be established as "representative government founded on a national assembly, involving a constitutional division of powers and characterized by a highly elaborate organization of counterweights and equilibrium." Though obliged to recognize that various differences from traditional parliamentary government were established, he insisted to the end that the system was not one of assembly government. Most serious commentators were not able to agree with this contention of the General Reporter.

Rejection by the Voters. The text of the Constitution of April 19 was given wide distribution.[26] A referendum concerning its adoption was set for May 5. The closeness of the vote in the National Constituent Assembly (309 to 249) was only the earliest indication that approval was doubtful. In the result, there was confirmation of other evidence that the Assembly had been further Left than the voters. The positive vote was some 9,280,000, the negative 10,-450,000. The Constitution thus had the distinction of being the only Constitution ever to be disapproved by the French voters.

4. THE SECOND NATIONAL CONSTITUENT ASSEMBLY

NEW ELECTIONS

Legal Continuity. In accordance with the provision of Article 7 of the Act of November 2, 1945, elections for another assembly were required. The date of June 2, 1946, was set.

Political Complexion. The results of the June elections were in general not greatly different from those of the previous October. There was, it is true, a slight swing to the Right. The MRP, with 160 members as against 141, and the Communists, with 146 as against 148, exchanged first and second places. The Socialists, the other member of the "big three," had 115 as against 134. The MRP was flanked on the Left by the Radicals and their allies, with 48 members, and on the Right by 35 members of the PRL (Republican Party of Liberty). As in the First National Constituent Assembly, a combination of at

[25] V. *Docs., Assemb. Nat. Const.,* no. 885, p. 849.

[26] The draft not having been ratified, the text was never printed in the *Journal officiel* in official form. However, it was distributed through the press and other agencies. A convenient quasi-official text is to be found in Secrétariat d'Etat à la Présidence du Conseil et à l'Information, *Notes Documentaires et Etudes,* no. 209, 3 août 1946, "Les Projets constitutionnels français."

least two of the "big three" was necessary for a majority. As things turned out, all three reached agreement on a draft Constitution. The results of the referendum of May 5 and of the elections of June 2 imposed on the MRP the responsibility of initiative; but the Socialists were clearly still in a key position.

THE CONSTITUTION OF OCTOBER 27

Committee on the Constitution. The Second National Constituent Assembly met on June 11. Eight days later, a Committee on the Constitution was established. It was of the same size and was chosen by the same method as in the previous Assembly. A curious situation presented itself in the fact that, owing to the presence of extreme overseas members in the second Assembly, the members of the Committee were exactly divided, 21 to 21, between those who had supported and those who had opposed the first Constitution. M. André Philip, a Socialist, was again [27] elected President of the Committee. The General Reporter was M. Paul Coste-Floret, a member of the MRP.

Compromise Drafts. The Committee on the Constitution not unnaturally took as the basis of its work the rejected Constitution. The effort was in general to modify it in such a way as to meet what were presumed to be the views of the people that caused a somewhat narrow majority of them to vote against the document in the May 5 referendum. Though the Communists had, soon after this vote, proclaimed the propriety of following the wishes of the people, they held in the end that the text of the Constitution of April 19 represented the extreme limits of their concessions. They prepared and introduced a draft Constitution,[28] which was of no practical importance and which is of interest only as indicating the kind of extreme system they might favor if they could make their views prevail. A Socialist draft,[29] representing the views of that party as to what changes the popular vote required in the Constitution they had previously supported, was the starting point of the Committee's work. The MRP, as the member of the "big three" with which the people had sided on May 5, introduced a draft [30] which modified somewhat further the defeated text. Two additional drafts emanated from Right elements outside the "big three." [31] By the first week of August, the Committee was able to take a vote on the body of a draft the compromise character of which is manifest from the fact that it was an adaptation of the Socialist and MRP drafts, themselves adaptations. The Committee members from those two parties, forming a majority, voted in the affirmative, the remaining elements of the membership abstaining.[32]

---

[27] During the First Assembly, he retired from the position upon becoming Minister of Finance.

[28] The draft was introduced into the First Assembly (v. *Docs., Assemb. Nat. Const.,* no. 20, pp. 25–28), but not formally brought before the second.

[29] V. *Docs., Assemb. Nat. Const.,* no. II–23, pp. 8–12.

[30] V. *ibid.,* no. II–68, pp. 61–63.

[31] V. *ibid.,* no. II–35, pp. 27–31, no. II–166, pp. 162–165. The five drafts are reproduced, together with the Constitution of April 19, in the document cited in this Ch., p. 74, n. 26, *supra.*

[32] The minutes of the Committee on the Constitution in both Assemblies were, on proposal of the President, ordered printed and are readily available. Cf. *J. O., Debs., Assemb. Nat. Const.,* 26 avril 1946, p. 2239, 3 octobre 1946, p. 4389.

Voting the Constitution. General discussion on the floor of the Assembly began on August 21. It continued for exactly one month. In the beginning, the able presentation by M. Coste-Floret of the draft document proved so effective that only the Communists and Radicals remained in opposition. With the President of the Assembly, M. Vincent Auriol, constantly active as a strong force for conciliation, hope for general agreement seemed reasonably bright, when the situation in the Assembly was materially affected by an outside event. One week after the beginning of general discussion in the Assembly, General de Gaulle in a public speech expressed strong hostility to the proposed Constitution. This intervention caused certain curious exchanges of position on the part of elements in the Assembly. The Communists rallied to support of the Constitution, whereas the small groups of the Right (PRL and Independents) joined the Radicals in opposition. In this way, the MRP was thrown into a position of embarrassing isolation. To take steps towards meeting the views of General de Gaulle without breaking with the Socialists seemed impossible. A complete breakdown was avoided only through the vigorous mediation efforts of M. Vincent Auriol. The great compromise that cleared the way for final success took place on September 11. The "big three" were able to agree on a weak Council of the Republic as a second house of Parliament.[33] The Government of the day helped by intervening with an acceptable scheme concerning French imperial structure, that is, concerning what is called the French Union. In spite of another attack by General de Gaulle, a second reading in the Assembly was successfully completed; and a draft Constitution was voted in the early morning of September 28. The vote stood 440 (the "big three") to 106 (Radicals, with their allies, and elements of the Right), with 30 members not voting. Meanwhile, the Assembly had voted, by no means always easily, certain supplementary laws, such for example as those dealing with election of the two houses of Parliament; and analogous acts were passed just before adjournment of the Assembly on October 5. Referendum on the Constitution had been set for October 13.

Decision of the Nation. The campaign period was marked by a decrease in popular interest. The "big three" had shown themselves capable in elections of polling three-fourths of the electorate. The outcome thus seemed a foregone conclusion. On the other hand, General de Gaulle continued his opposition. Moreover, the prevailing electoral law,[34] though not voted in the referendum, was the cause of some opposition to the proposed political system. Finally, a certain amount of general dissatisfaction with political and economic conditions was an adverse factor. In the result, nearly a third of the voters stayed away from the polls. The vote stood in round numbers 9,295,000 to 8,165,000. The approximate percentages, 53 and 47, were, in reverse order, the same as in May. In any case, the voters had given France a Constitution.

[33] Cf. Ch. v, p. 81, *infra,* and Ch. vi, p. 90, *infra.*
[34] Cf. Ch. vi, p. 97, *infra.*

CHAPTER V

THE CONSTITUTION OF OCTOBER 27, 1946

1. INTRODUCTORY

Length. The Constitution of the Fourth Republic belongs to the class of French Constitutions which are long, elaborate, symmetrical, and logical. There is no need to recall that in this respect it is to be contrasted with the Constitution of the Third Republic.[1] It is somewhat longer than some complete French Constitutions, such for example as the Charters of the Restoration; but it is somewhat shorter than the Constitution of April 19, 1946,[2] and it is by no means so long as such Revolutionary Constitutions as those of 1791, 1793, and 1795.

Contents. The provisions of the prevailing Constitution of the French Republic fall into two general divisions. Some eighteen unnumbered initial paragraphs constitute the Preamble. The main body of the document, that is to say, the remainder, is entitled "The Institutions of the Republic." Its 106 Articles are grouped into twelve sections known as Titles. The headings of these Titles are worth viewing in outline; for they give a good general idea of the structure of the basic law of the Fourth Republic. The rubrics of the Titles are as follows:

I. Sovereignty (Arts. 1–4)
II. Parliament (Arts. 5–24)
III. Economic Council (Art. 25)
IV. Treaties (Arts. 26–28)
V. President of the Republic (Arts. 29–44)
VI. Council of Ministers (Arts. 45–55)
VII. Penal Responsibility of Ministers (Arts. 56–59)
VIII. French Union (Arts. 60–82)
IX. High Magisterial Council (Arts. 83–84)
X. Territorial Collectivities (Arts. 85–89)
XI. Amendment (Arts. 90–95)
XII. Transitory Provisions (Arts. 96–106)

[1] Cf. Ch. II, pp. 53–54, *supra.*
[2] The First Constitution contains 134 Articles as against the 106 of the second. Inasmuch as the First Constitution numbers the provisions of the Declaration of Rights, the body of the Second Constitution actually contains the greater number of Articles. On the other hand, the fact that the Preamble of the Constitution of April 19, 1946, is so much longer than the Preamble of the Second Constitution accounts for the greater total length of the former.

2. BASIC PRINCIPLES

INDIVIDUAL RIGHTS

The First Constitution. The student of government who feels a special interest in bills of rights and similar phenomena may find in the post-War constitutional history of France great wealth of material for study. The Constitution of April 19, 1946, contained, it will be recalled,[3] a long initial Declaration of the Rights of Man. Rejection of the Constitution on May 5 was interpreted by certain commentators as being due at least in part to the character of the Declaration. More particularly, adaptations in an extreme direction of the Declaration of 1789 in the matter of the rights of property and in the matter of education were cited as another example of the proposition that the majority in the First National Constituent Assembly was further to the Left than the body of the people in the country.[4] There was therefore some presumption that, in this matter as in others, a slight swing to the Right would occur in the Second National Constituent Assembly.[5]

The Second Constitution. In the Second National Constituent Assembly, the solution of the question of individual rights was in general a function of the political situation that caused the Constitution of October 27 to be an adaptation of the two adaptations which the MRP and Socialist drafts were. Compromise was the order of the day. Nevertheless, the debate in the Committee and in the Assembly was long, sometimes exceedingly bitter, and in some respects distinctly sterile. Controversy could, as in the First Assembly, always be counted on where, as in the matter of property, views which were inspired by the older tendency to regard rights as being absolute came into conflict with more modern and evolutionary views which were inspired by a more socialist and positive concept of government. The same was true where, as in the matter of education, the perennial question of religion was involved. In instances where compromise was arrived at, it took the form either of silence or of broad, abstract, and sometimes obscure generalities. In the result, the final solution was the somewhat brief Preamble, which consists of two parts. In the first place, the French people are said "solemnly to reaffirm the rights and liberties of man and the citizen hallowed by the Declaration of Rights of 1789 and the fundamental principles recognized by the laws of the Republic"; and, in the second place, there is a general proclamation "that every human being without distinction of race, religion, or creed possesses inalienable and sacred rights," to which is added the proclamation of certain connected "political, economic, and social principles particularly necessary to our time." The last-mentioned principles fall, in turn, into several groups. In the economic and social sphere, women are guaranteed equal rights; certain rights of workers, as well as the duty to work,

[3] Cf. Ch. IV, p. 73, *supra.*
[4] Cf. *ibid.,* p. 70, *supra.*
[5] The four draft constitutions that were introduced into the Second National Constituent Assembly (cf. *ibid.,* p. 74, n. 26, *supra*) contained elaborate introductory sections that were concerned with rights and their declaration. The Communist draft confined itself to listing concisely in an early Article (Art. 4) some fifteen subjects of legal guarantees.

are proclaimed; the continued socialization is assumed of a national economy that is recognized for the time being to be partly public and partly private; and the nation is asserted to owe to the individual and to the family certain duties in the material and spiritual realm that are subsumed under the concept of "conditions necessary for their development." The right of asylum in French territory is proclaimed; the principles of an enlightened colonial policy are declared and accepted; and, in the international sphere, war of conquest or "against the liberty of any people" is renounced, whereas "on condition of reciprocity France consents to the limitations of sovereignty necessary to the organization and defence of peace."

PARLIAMENTARY GOVERNMENT

The Basic Constitutional Problem. The central question with respect to the main body of the Constitution of the Fourth Republic is the problem of what kind of government it establishes. The short answer is scarcely surprising. The basis is laid for the parliamentary system of government.

The Nature of the Parliamentary Regime. Parliamentary government, as historically evolved, is of course characterized by a nice balance between the legislature and the political executive. This is arranged by intricate interrelations between principle and practice, between law and convention, which involve subtleties that are difficult, if not impossible, completely to reduce to written constitutional form. In general, parliamentary government may be said to require harmony between the representatives of the people and the principal policy-forming members of the active branch of government. Such harmony is maintained through the reciprocal relationship of the control by parliament of the ministers and the political responsibility of the ministers to parliament. The most familiar practical aspect of this relationship is its sanction in the form of resignation by the ministers when they are made aware that they do not "possess the confidence" of parliament, which is to say that they are not in harmony with parliament.

Variants of the Parliamentary Regime. History suggests that the "classic" ideal of a nice balance between legislature and executive may, in the actual operation of a particular regime, give way to deviations from perfect equilibrium which are relatively so great that a special "variant" of parliamentary government may be said to exist. So far as the government of the Fourth French Republic is concerned, numerous serious commentators in France assert or imply that the variation is so great in that country as to require the conclusion that parliamentary government can scarcely be said in reality to exist under the present Constitution. What is conceived to prevail is, it will be recalled,[6] something that is variously denominated the convention system (*régime conventionnel*), an assembly system (*régime d'assemblée*), or assembly government (*gouvernement d'assemblée*).

Assembly Government. Discussions in France of assembly government are so diverse that a satisfactory statement of what it is, in relation to whether

[6] Cf. Ch. iv, p. 70, *supra*.

it actually exists in certain circumstances, is exceedingly difficult, and perhaps impossible, to formulate. The matter is certainly in some degree, probably in large degree, a question of definition; but definitions in this connection tend to be so broad as to lose much of their value. The common assertion that parliamentary government is characterized by the separation of powers whereas assembly government is characterized by the *confusion* of powers seems to point to a tenable distinction; but the distinction is on examination not very helpful. Precisely the same distinction has been more than once made between presidential government on the American model and parliamentary government, the latter in this instance being said to be characterized by the *confusion* of powers. Moreover, the whole doctrine of the separation of powers, which has been so widely discussed in the history of political thought, is a matter concerning which the writers who have discussed it display the widest differences of view. Again, the employment of example, for instance identification of assembly government with the system of government under the Convention during the Revolution, is at first sight helpful to clarity; but probably more difficulty is raised than is settled. Conditions under the Convention varied considerably; and scholars in France are far from being in agreement as to whether there prevailed, even at a given time, parliamentary government or assembly government. Finally, typical expressions, such as the assertion which holds that ministers under parliamentary government are "autonomous" but responsible to the legislature, whereas under assembly government the ministers are "completely subordinate" to an "omnipotent" legislature, are little if any more helpful. The language tends to be figurative, and distinction to become vague. Possibly a number of fairly specific conditions could be imagined which would individually be consistent with the existence of parliamentary government but which in combination would not; and yet the likelihood is that the combination, when once imagined, would be such that doubt would remain whether in modern conditions it does or could exist. In this respect, political tradition and political habits are, it should be recalled, of more far-reaching importance than constitutional provisions. The fact would seem to be that assembly government is a more useful concept when envisaged, not as a realizable actuality, but as a *tendency*. On this view, the concept becomes more easily applicable to conditions that are dynamic, which are the kind of conditions that prevail in the realm of government. Inasmuch as parliamentary government is a term in a classification that employs as a standard the law-making, law-enforcing relationship, no logical difficulty whatever is involved in stating either as a fact or as an opinion that one of the branches is relatively stronger than the other or that one is stronger than it ought to be. If the statement is made about the law-making body, not only would there seem to be no harm, there may be actual advantage, in referring to the situation as a *tendency* towards assembly government.

The Issue of Regime in France. Students of political science who are acquainted with the elements of English government are aware that the possession of supreme legal power by Parliament, which is certainly in a definite sense "legislative omnipotence," is perfectly consistent with the existence of a strong and stable executive. In France, opponents of assembly government are, if they are at the same time believers in representative democratic government, prepared to admit that the final political authority must belong to the representatives of the people; and so their advocacy of a variant of parliamentary government possessed of a strong executive must be admitted to be less a question of legal power than of political practice. But it is precisely this kind of combination of principle and practice that is, as has been seen, so difficult, if not impossible, to formulate in written constitutions. Hence, it is not strange that in the two French National Constituent Assemblies of 1945–1946 opposing tendencies concerning parliamentary government and assembly government manifested themselves less with respect to the central issue itself than with respect to practical institutional arrangements that are commonly regarded as not in principle basic to the central issue. Two such matters [7] were particularly prominent, namely, the question of the formal structure of the legislature and the question of the formal head of the State. Adoption by the First Constituent Assembly of a unicameral legislature and controversy concerning it, insistence that this solution was in considerable measure responsible for rejection of the First Constitution by the voters, subsequent acceptance of a form of bicameralism by the Second National Constituent Assembly, controversy as to whether there should be a President of the Republic, changes of attitude concerning this question, modification and adaptation of proposals with respect to the office—all these considerations were a function of the basic constitutional issue between Left and Right.

ADMINISTRATIVE STRUCTURE

The Problem of Decentralization. Reference to the contents of the Constitution of the Fourth Republic will reveal that Title X, Territorial Communities, consisting of five short Articles, recognizes, as the Constitution of the Third Republic did not, a problem of regime that involves a standard of classification [8] which is little if any less important than the legislative-executive relationship. In general, the intent of the Constitution—representing presumably the desire of a majority of members in the Second National Constituent Assembly, albeit in some cases possibly little more than a pious hope—was that the highly centralized unitary system which had long prevailed in France should be fundamentally altered. In the body of the Constitution, Communes and Departments and their elected assemblies are recognized to be basic; and organic Acts of Parliament are anticipated which would effect the desired far-reaching changes. Among the last mentioned are such interesting and important matters as the regrouping of territorial communities, the devolution of extensive powers upon the localities, a departure from existing uniformity in respect of institutional organization, and a loosening of control by agents of the central government. There is likewise anticipation that organic legal provisions will effect a

[7] Cf. *ibid.,* p. 73, *supra.*
[8] Cf. Ch. I, p. 36, *supra,* and Ch. VIII, pp. 151–154, *infra.*

greater measure of what is called in France *deconcentration,* that is, the devolution upon agents of central government of greater authority in their respective spheres to make decisions without the necessity of securing approval from their superiors. In all these matters, there has been, it should be noted, practically no disposition up to the present to carry out the principles enunciated in the Constitution.[9]

The Concept of Indivisibility. Among the difficulties which the Anglo-American student of French government encounters in attempting to understand the French administrative system, none is more elusive than the content of the concept phrased in the expression, "the Republic one and indivisible." This somewhat mystical phraseology of the French Revolution has, interestingly enough and no doubt naturally enough, been incorporated into the Constitution of the Fourth Republic. Article 1 begins with the assertion that "France is an indivisible Republic"; and Title X begins (Article 85), as an apparently necessary introduction to recognition of "the existence of territorial communities," with the expression "the French Republic one and indivisible." Whatever the difficulty—or impossibility—of understanding the concept, its great influence must at the least be taken for granted. In any case, comprehension, however partial, of the concept or of its influence can, it is certain, be realized only through study of the details of the system.[10]

OVERSEAS FRANCE

Territorial Structure. Title VIII, The French Union, is in a measure interconnected with Title X. The Union is conceived to consist of European France proper, referred to in the Constitution, as in current discussion, as Metropolitan France, together with various overseas communities. These latter communities being in some instances subdivided into Departments as in Metropolitan France, Title VIII inevitably anticipates to a certain extent Title X. On the other hand, inasmuch as Title X is concerned with Territorial Communities of the French Republic in general, reference is made not only to Communes and Departments, but also to such parts of the French Republic overseas as are not divided into Departments.

Constitutional Importance. Title VIII forms much the longest subdivision of the present Constitution. This in itself is a simple indication of the concern which the French in general feel for imperial and colonial problems and of the importance which the Second National Constituent Assembly attached to these questions. Special students of the subject regard formulation of this part of the Constitution as the most praiseworthy accomplishment of the Assembly. There can be little doubt but that the Second Assembly wrought much better in this respect than did the first. Understanding of the nature of the solutions naturally requires a more detailed study of them.[11]

[9] The voting of a special Act with respect to the status of Algeria is a notable exception. Cf. Ch. vi, p. 118, *infra.*
[10] These are treated in Ch. viii, *infra.*
[11] These are treated in Ch. vi, *infra.*

3. CONSTITUTIONAL AMENDMENT

Basic Changes. The governmental system of the Fourth Republic has by no means remained static. From the beginning, changes began to set in. However, formal amendment of the basic law has been of minor importance. Students of political science will scarcely be surprised to learn that practically all the considerable development that has taken place has been in part the work of supplementary legislation, such for example as acts of Parliament, executive regulations, and rules of the houses of Parliament, and even in greater part the result of practice or custom.

Formal Amendment: Constitutional Provisions. Advocacy of alteration of the text of the Constitution of the Fourth Republic began with the formulation of that document. It has not unnaturally continued ever since. Hence, the prophecy may be confidently made that some change by formal amendment will from time to time be effected. With substantial agreement concerning what is desired, realization is not difficult. The procedure defined in Title XI of the present Constitution is, while in appearance somewhat complex, not calculated seriously to hinder needed change. The principal stipulations in the matter, contained in Article 90, are phrased as follows:

Amendment must be decided upon through a resolution adopted by a majority of the members composing the National Assembly.

The resolution shall specify the object of amendment.

After a period of at least three months, unless [12] the Council of the Republic, the same resolution having been referred to it by the National Assembly, shall have approved by majority vote, it shall be given a second reading for which the procedure shall be the same as for the first.

After this second reading, the National Assembly shall draft a measure to effect amendment of the Constitution. This measure shall be submitted to Parliament and shall be voted by majority, according to the procedure followed in the case of an ordinary statute.

It shall be submitted to referendum unless it shall have been adopted on second reading in the National Assembly by a two-thirds majority or shall have been voted by a three-fifths majority in each of the two assemblies . . .

No constitutional amendment in respect of the existence of the Council of the Republic may be effected without the agreement of said Council or employment of the referendum procedure.

Formal Amendment: Procedure. Analysis of the pertinent constitutional provisions will reveal that the amending process consists essentially [13] of *initiative* and of *ratification,* with respect to each of which several possibilities are envisaged. The first step consists of approval of a resolution stating the *object of amendment.* This resolution must be twice adopted by a majority of the

[12] French commentators find some ambiguity in this provision. As here translated, the meaning would be that favorable action by the Council of the Republic might reduce the period of three months before the second reading. In the original the qualifying clause occurs at the end; and this has caused some French students to hold that favorable action by the Council of the Republic eliminates the second reading. However, this would scarcely seem consistent with the beginning of the next paragraph.

[13] There is, it may be noted, the final formal step of *promulgation* by the President of the Republic within a week. The constitutional provision is not translated here.

membership [14] of the National Assembly. The interval between the two deliberations cannot be less than three months unless meanwhile the Council of the
Republic approves the resolution. The second step consists of final approval of
a *draft amendment*. Such final approval may be secured by a two-thirds vote of
the National Assembly alone,[15] by a three-fifths vote in each of the two houses,
or by popular vote following upon adoption by a simple majority in the National Assembly.

Formal Amendment: Limitations. Title XI contains two Articles which
are given the form of limitations on the amending power. The second, Article 95, is incorporated *verbatim* from the Constitution of the Third Republic.[16]
It is phrased as follows:

The republican form of government may not be subject of proposed amendment.

The first of the limiting provisions, Article 94, has a manifest reference to the
Vichy experience. It is worded as follows:

In case of occupation of all or part of the metropolitan territory by foreign forces, no
amendment proceedings may be initiated or carried out.

The student of political theory will be aware that hair-splitting, and on the
whole sterile, controversy is possible concerning whether a defined constituent
authority may be materially bound by constitutional provisions. If the arguments stick to logic and remain in the juristic sphere, there can in reality be
little doubt but that a conflict of terms is involved in the question, which as a
result poses a dilemma. On the other hand, the historical and moral reasons for
introducing into fundamental law the condemnation of certain possible actions
are important and interesting. In the case of the two examples in the Constitution of the Fourth Republic, comprehension presents no problem.

Formal Amendment: Popular Participation. The Constitution of the
Third Republic, it will be recalled,[17] made formal constitutional amendment
possible without participation by the voters. The Constitution of April 19,
1946, on the contrary, stipulated that final ratification should be submitted to
national referendum. The situation under the prevailing Constitution stands
therefore somewhere between these two cases, being another example of the
compromises effected by the Second National Constituent Assembly. Explicit
or implicit acceptance by the voters is manifestly the basic principle; for where
referendum is not required, the majorities are made so large as to establish a
strong presumption of popular approval. The whole question, it is of impor-

---

[14] This is one of several connections in which the Constitution of the Fourth Republic
establishes a special majority, commonly referred to as "constitutional" majority, to be distinguished from an ordinary majority. The same distinction was employed in the Constitution
of the Third Republic in respect of amendment. This gave rise to a certain amount of controversy. The question is not that of the distinction between a majority (called "absolute" in
French) and a plurality ("relative majority" in French) but that of the basis on which a majority is reckoned. For this purpose, "membership" has now been authoritatively interpreted
(by the National Assembly in 1947) as the total number of seats minus those at the moment
vacant.

[15] The final paragraph of Article 90, here translated, clearly constitutes an exception.
[16] It had been introduced there as an amendment in 1884.
[17] Cf. Ch. II, p. 54, *supra*.

tance and interest to note, is considered in France to involve the relationship between the two principles of "popular sovereignty" and "national sovereignty."

NATIONAL SOVEREIGNTY

Revolutionary Origin. Sovereignty of the nation, if not an exclusively French concept, has received in France a largely unique content. This fact, in turn, is a simple function of French history and tradition, which have given to the concept a particularly rich connotation. Before the French Revolution, the character of the absolute monarchy was such that identification of King and State was a plausible principle. One accomplishment of the Revolution was to secure that the State should be identified not with the King but with the nation. Sovereignty was insisted to be a possession of the nation.

Evolution of the Concept. With the passing of time, an organic view of the nation, which is by no means without mystical overtones, has been widely developed in France. In general, the nation has been conceived to have an existence that transcends the existence of the individuals who enter into its make-up. In this respect, experience both inside and outside France demonstrates that when the question of practical application is raised, some difficulty inevitably arises. A nation, as a distinct person or moral being, may be asserted to exist; but the performance of acts by it is another matter. The nation may doubtless be said to *possess* sovereignty, but how it may *exercise* sovereignty is less clear. This, it is not difficult to understand, is the basis of the distinction between national sovereignty and popular sovereignty. If the people are conceived as being for practical purposes the same as the voters, then the performance of acts, including the exercise of power, becomes feasible.

Constitutional Application. All these matters received full and vigorous —and, it must be confessed, somewhat futile—discussion in the Second National Constituent Assembly. A striking compromise was effected through the following wording of Article 3 of the Constitution:

National sovereignty shall belong to the French People.
Neither any section of the people nor any individual may appropriate its exercise.
The People shall exercise it in the matter of constituent activity through vote of its representatives and through referendum.
In all other matters it shall exercise it through its deputies in the National Assembly . . .

4. THE QUESTION OF UNCONSTITUTIONAL LEGISLATION

THE FRENCH SOLUTION

Constitutional Basis. Inasmuch as the Constitution of the Fourth Republic has established a method of formal amendment which differs from the regular law-making process, inasmuch as, in other words, the *constituent* authority and *statutory* authority are different, the Constitution is to be classified technically as a *rigid* constitution. This, of course, involves inevitably the question what the situation is if an Act of Parliament should be in conflict with the

Constitution. In negative terms, the answer is simple. It is a fact that judicial review does not prevail in France, in the sense that no court is conceived to possess the authority to declare a legislative enactment to be contrary to the Constitution. Nevertheless, conflict is recognized by the provisions of the Constitution to be possible. The solution envisaged is the interesting one of bringing the Constitution into harmony with the statute. For this purpose, a novel institution is established, namely, a Constitutional Committee. The pertinent provisions of the Constitution are phrased as follows:

Article 91.—The Constitutional Committee shall be presided over by the President of the Republic.

It shall consist of the President of the National Assembly, of the President of the Council of the Republic, of seven members chosen at the beginning of each annual session by the National Assembly from outside its membership by proportional representation of the groups, and of three members chosen in like manner by the Council of the Republic.

The Constitutional Committee shall examine whether Acts voted by the National Assembly involve amendment of the Constitution.

Article 92.—Within the period for promulgation of an Act, the Committee shall have cognizance of any request emanating jointly from the President of the Republic and the President of the Council of the Republic, the Council having taken action by a majority of the members composing it.

The Committee shall examine the Act, shall endeavor to bring about an agreement between the National Assembly and the Council of the Republic; and, if it shall not succeed, shall come to a decision within five days after taking cognizance. This period shall be reduced to two days in case of urgency.

It shall be competent to take action only in respect of the possibility of amendment of provisions in Titles I to X of the present Constitution.

The Outlook. The Constitutional Committee has in practice played a very modest role. The chances would seem to be that it will continue to do so. There is no reason to think that the National Assembly will be inclined deliberately and flagrantly to violate the terms of the Constitution. This is as true of the provisions which fall outside the competency of the Constitutional Committee as of those which come within it. For example, the fact that the Constitutional Committee is itself stipulated for in Title XI would theoretically render it liable to abolition by ordinary statute without any possibility that the technical question of constitutionality could be raised by the ordinary procedure; but this would scarcely seem to make such a contingency likely in practice. For one thing, the members of the National Assembly, if sufficiently aroused to contemplate such action in this or other hypothetical cases, would have little difficulty in effecting their will through the process of formal amendment. Furthermore, the actual opportunity for unconstitutional action is, it must be clear upon reflection, less great in the case of a Constitution like the French, which, unlike the Constitution of the United States, is concerned almost wholly with the structure of government and very little with careful distribution of the broad powers of government. But after all, to assume that power will be abused, without distinguishing between its exercise by the representatives of a great people and by less responsible potential despots, is more worthy of the eighteenth than of the twentieth century. So far as individual rights are concerned, exclusion of the provisions of the Preamble from the competency of the Constitutional Committee is here again of more theoretical interest than it is likely to prove of actual importance in practice. The serious student will realize—and, if he does not, he may take it on the authority of repeated assertion by the Supreme Court of the United States—that rights are not absolute. They must at all times be balanced against the public interest. If at the highest level, that is to say, in the case of national legislation, the representatives of the people, not the judges, have the decision, the arrangement would at least seem to be defensible in terms of democratic principle. In any event, the fact is that the framers of the Constitution of France considered judicial review to be a conservative and undemocratic phenomenon. The American student can make his own comparisons. He will find no little evidence in opinions of "conservative" courts for the French view. In instances where progressives and democrats have applauded court protection of individual rights, probably national legislation will be found rarely to be at fault. But protection of individual rights from lesser agencies and agents is a function of the courts in France as well as in other civilized countries. The American student will do well to reduce to a minimum the contrasts which he includes in his conclusions.

C H A P T E R   V I

THE LEGISLATIVE BRANCH OF GOVERNMENT

1. THE STRUCTURE OF PARLIAMENT

CONSTITUTIONAL ISSUE

First National Constituent Assembly. French Republican tradition, it may be recalled, demands a single national assembly.[1] Hence, the Socialists and the Communists in the First National Constituent Assembly were, it would seem, on sound historical ground in refusing to compromise in the matter. On the other hand, other members of the First Assembly saw in unicameralism the principal manifestation of the "legislative omnipotence" to which they were so strongly opposed.[2] Opposition by the once powerful Radical Party was a highly striking aspect of the situation. During the Third Republic, the party claimed with some justice to be the traditional and typical republican party and the real heir of the French Revolution;[3] and it more than once asserted that the convention system (*régime conventionnel*)[4] represented its ideal. However, in the First Assembly, it was, for whatever reason,[5] on the side of the Right with regard to the constitutional issue. "The single assembly," asserted the veteran Radical leader, M. Herriot, "will absorb the executive as well."

Second National Constituent Assembly. Article 5 of the prevailing Constitution is worded as follows:

Parliament[6] shall be composed of a National Assembly and of a Council of the Republic.

This provision, though it gives no real idea of the relations between the two chambers, establishes technically a bicameral Parliament. The simple words in-

[1] Cf. Ch. II, p. 48, *supra*.
[2] Cf. Ch. IV, p. 74, *supra,* and this Ch., pp. 116–117, *infra*.
[3] Cf. Ch. XII, p. 203, *infra*.
[4] Cf. Ch. IV, p. 70, *supra*.
[5] The Senate, from being reluctantly accepted in 1875 by Gambetta and the Radicals as the necessary price of a republic, came to be a not unimportant seat of their power. Thus, support for the Senate was, at least in part, a function of Radical support of the Third Republic. Moreover, during the National Constituent Assembly, the Radicals were attempting to employ somewhat complex political tactics (cf. Ch. XII, p. 204, *infra*).
[6] This word was here introduced into the terms of a French Constitution for the first time.

corporate the compromise solution [7] of the principal problem with which the Second National Constituent Assembly was concerned. After the defeat by the voters of the Constitution of April 19, 1946, one common interpretation of the event was to see in it a popular expression of preference for a bicameral legislature. The Communists and Socialists, it is true, paid little more than lip service to this interpretation; but, in the end, they reluctantly supported the Council of the Republic. This body was provided for in the draft text [8] both of the MRP and of the Republican Party of Liberty; [9] so that to this extent it began with rightist associations. However, those two texts proposed for the Council of the Republic a subordination to the National Assembly considerably greater than that of the Senate to the Chamber of Deputies under the Third Republic; and the provisions concerning the Council of the Republic which are incorporated into the present Constitution give the Council a position not greatly different from that envisaged in the draft texts of the MRP and the PRL.

CONSTITUTIONAL SOLUTION

Bicameralism or Unicameralism. A Radical speaker asserted with some reason during debate in the Second National Constituent Assembly that support of bicameralism by the Committee on the Constitution was pure pretence, inasmuch as its members declared their support of two chambers only to argue throughout on the hypothesis of unicameralism. As a matter of fact, if Parliament under the Fourth Republic is technically bicameral, it displays certain fundamental resemblances to unicameralism. In general, the indirectly chosen Council of the Republic, while it has considerable freedom to engage in debate of, and to suggest amendments to, measures passed by the National Assembly, has only subordinate power of initiative; and, in accordance with the provision [10] that "the National Assembly alone shall vote laws," it has no final authority.[11] M. Paul Coste-Floret, General Reporter of the Constitution, suggested, by way of summary of the matter, that the legislative structure established for the Fourth Republic is one of "incomplete bicameralism" or of "tempered monocameralism."

Associated Bodies. The proposition might be plausibly argued that most of the reasons for regarding the present French Parliament as bicameral would equally be reasons for considering it to be quadricameral.[12] As a matter of fact, among the institutions established by the prevailing Constitution are two Assemblies that possess a consultative character not unlike that of the Council of the Republic.[13] These are the Assembly of the French Union and the Economic Council. The former is representative of what used to be called the French

---

[7] Cf. Ch. IV, p. 76, *supra*, and this Ch., pp. 107–108, *infra*.

[8] Cf. Ch. IV, p. 75, *supra*.

[9] Cf. Ch. XII, p. 208, *infra*.

[10] Art. 13.

[11] Cf. this Ch., pp. 107–108, *infra*.

[12] Or even quinquecameral, if count is made of another associated body, the High Court of Justice, chosen by the National Assembly at the beginning of each legislature. Its jurisdiction is in general that of the Senate under the Third Republic in respect of impeachment trials.

[13] As a matter of fact, both Assemblies, unlike the Council of the Republic, may discuss measures initiated by themselves. Cf. this Ch., p. 105, *infra*.

Empire.[14] The Economic Council, according to the Constitution, "shall examine, with a view to giving its opinion, Government and private members' bills within its competency," another provision adding that "such bills shall be referred to it by the National Assembly before the latter shall debate them." [15] The Council is actually an institution brought over from the Third Republic. Created by executive decree in 1925, it was several times modified by Act of Parliament, such modifications marking steps in the Council's growth in importance. Its composition was, and is, based on a somewhat elaborate system of "professional representation." [16] When these two advisory assemblies were stipulated for in the Constitution of April 19, 1946, M. Herriot referred to them as "useless" and as "encumbrances"; but this was doubtless the exaggeration of a debater who favored the bicameralism of the Third Republic. In any case, the bodies were retained in the second Constitution; and, while less in the public eye than the Council of the Republic, they would seem to have justified their existence.

Basic Position. In the course of debate in the Second National Constituent Assembly, the Council of the Republic came to be called a "chamber of reflection." This is perhaps still the best statement of the matter. In general, there can be no doubt but that the Council has grown in stature since its establishment. This is, of course, a matter of moral authority. Possibly the part of wisdom for the Council would be to remain satisfied with such authority. The fact is, on the contrary, that this has not been so. The Council has been pressing for increased legal power.[17] The chances are that before long it will be in some measure successful in its efforts. Whether its authority will become substantially greater or whether, paradoxically, increase in legal power will affect adversely its moral authority only time can tell.

2. THE COMPOSITION OF PARLIAMENT

THE CHAMBERS AND THEIR MEMBERS

Size. At present, the National Assembly is composed of 627 members. This number, approximately the same as that for the last Chamber of Deputies

---

[14] Cf. *ibid.,* p. 118, *infra.*

[15] Art. 25 (forming Title III). The Council is also an advisory body of the Council of Ministers, that is, of the executive. Cf. Ch. VIII, pp. 140–141, *infra.*

[16] A special statute, required to determine the organization of the Council, was adopted by the Second National Constituent Assembly in October of 1946. V. *J. O.,* 3 octobre 1946, p. 4399. The Act (*loi no. 46–2384 du 27 octobre 1946 relative à la composition et au fonctionnement du Conseil économique*) is to be found in *J. O.,* 28 octobre 1946. Its text, together with relevant articles of the Constitution, supplementary statutory provisions, executive regulations, and the rules of procedure of the Council, is printed in a convenient pamphlet: *J. O., Textes constitutifs du conseil économique et règlement intérieur* (1948).

[17] This is referred to as re-establishment of the "navette" (shuttle). Actually, this would be only partial, and would take the form of giving to the Council of the Republic authority to debate its own measures before sending them to the National Assembly. The Council has in actuality gone so far as to amend its rules to allow its committees to discuss bills before transmittal to the Assembly. This is probably unconstitutional. In any case, the practice has never been employed. A proposed constitutional amendment in 1950 would, if carried through, not greatly affect the *status quo.* Members of the Council, it may be noted, have, by an amendment of an original provision of the rules, bestowed upon themselves the title *Senators.*

under the Third Republic, is established by statutory enactment, namely, by an Act of October 5, 1946. The Council of the Republic consists of 320 members. This number, established by an Act of September 23, 1948, represents the outside limit set by a provision of the present Constitution which stipulates [18] that "the number of members of the Council of the Republic cannot be inferior to 250 or superior to 320."

Terms. The legal term for members of the National Assembly is five years, of the Council of the Republic six. These periods, in accordance with the general principle [19] of the Constitution of the Fourth Republic that such matters shall be left to ordinary law, rest on the basis of statutory provisions. They could, of course, theoretically be changed at any time by Act of Parliament. However, public opinion would scarcely allow a prolongation of the terms of sitting members, unless physical impossibility of holding elections prevailed. On the other hand, public opinion might conceivably impose, as has been much discussed, the passage of an Act reducing the terms, especially that of the National Assembly, with a view to bringing about a kind of self-dissolution. On the whole, this seems not much more likely than dissolution by executive decision.[20]

Renewal. All the members of the National Assembly are chosen at the same time. This integral renewal rests on statute, and so could be changed by Act of Parliament. The contingency is unlikely; for the associations of national sovereignty [21] in France cause especial importance to attach to the periodic testing of public opinion on a nation-wide scale. The Council of the Republic is renewed partially, a provision of Article 5 of the present Constitution stipulating that it "shall be renewable by halves." Details in the matter are regulated by statute. The Departments are divided alphabetically into two lists, and all the Senators in all the Departments in each of the lists, between which are also distributed the overseas representatives, are normally chosen at the same time. Council of the Republic elections furnish a by no means unimportant reflection of public opinion; and, inasmuch as such elections coincide with Assembly elections only once every fifteen years, they furnish, between general elections, interesting information about national trends. In this respect, the same purpose is served on a smaller scale by special elections, made necessary from time to time to fill vacancies in the Council of the Republic.[22]

[18] In Art. 6.

[19] V. *ibid.*: "Duration of the powers of each Assembly, its electoral system, conditions of eligibility, and the system of ineligibilities and incompatibilities shall be determined by statute."

[20] Cf. Ch. vii, p. 134, *infra*, and Ch. xii, p. 209, *infra*. In reality, in order for elections to be held in June of 1951, instead of in the autumn, the term of the first National Assembly was by statute reduced by several months.

[21] Cf. Ch. v, p. 85, *supra*.

[22] So far as vacancies in the National Assembly are concerned, special elections were in effect abolished by provisions of law establishing proportional representation, a vacancy being filled by the seating of the person whose name appeared next in the list. Necessary minor adjustments were made when the electoral system was modified in anticipation of the elections of June, 1951. After the elections, the Gaullists were reported to be considering employment of a technique (reminiscent of Boulanger) which would consist of having their Deputies resign where the result would be special elections with some of the characteristics of a referendum.

Eligibility. Statutory provisions, often dating from a period anterior to the Fourth Republic, regulate in considerable detail the matter of eligibility to the National Assembly and to the Council of the Republic. Fundamentally, the situation is relatively simple. The basic qualification for membership in both houses is eligibility to become a voter. Therefore, women, contrary to the situation under the Third Republic, are eligible. There exists an age requirement of twenty-three for the National Assembly and of thirty-five for the Council of the Republic.

Ineligibility and Incompatibility. A few relatively unimportant classes of persons are disqualified by statutory provisions to sit in Parliament, even though they possess the qualifications of a voter and are above the age limits. Such classes of persons include members of families that have reigned over France, naturalized citizens,[23] soldiers and sailors on active service and persons who have not yet performed their military service, bankrupts, and certain offenders against the election laws. Moreover, certain administrative officials are made ineligible in the communities in which they are stationed, though eligible elsewhere. To be distinguished from ineligibility is what is called "incompatibility." This means that a person may not at the same time be a member of one of the houses of Parliament and hold one of certain kinds of positions. He must choose either membership in the house of Parliament or the other position. Primary examples are determined by provisions of the present Constitution worded as follows:

Art. 20.—No one may belong at the same time to the National Assembly and to the Council of the Republic.

Members of Parliament may not have membership in the Economic Council or in the Assembly of the French Union.

On the other hand, members of Parliament, it should be noted, may be, and frequently are, at the same time members of elective local assemblies.[24] A second class of incompatible positions, established by statute, includes nearly all holders of governmental offices. Among the exceptions in this respect, the most important are Ministers and Secretaries and Under-Secretaries of State. The principle of this "cumulation" has, of course, long been considered a basic aspect of parliamentary government.[25] Finally, certain statutory provisions, which antedate the Fourth Republic, also render incompatible with membership in Parliament the holding of several kinds of offices in commercial organizations subsidized by the State or bound to it through contract to furnish it with supplies. Legislation during the Fourth Republic has added a number of positions in nationalized industries; but these are in reality, it would seem, to be assimilated to governmental offices.

Re-eligibility. Members of both houses of Parliament are re-eligible immediately and indefinitely.

[23] I.e., until they have been naturalized ten years.
[24] Cf. Ch. VIII, p. 146, *infra.*
[25] Cf. Ch. VII, p. 130, *infra.*

PARLIAMENTARY ELECTIONS

Constituencies. The prevailing Constitution stipulates [26] that "the two Chambers shall be elected on a territorial basis." In principle, the Department is the constituency for elections to both houses. In the case of the National Assembly, the 544 members for Metropolitan France are distributed amongst the Departments, roughly in proportion to population. According to further statutory provisions, Departments entitled to as many as nine members may be divided. This gives rise to several exceptions to the rule that the Department is the constituency. One Department (the Seine, including Paris) is subdivided into six constituencies, one Department into three constituencies, and five into two. The number of members to the constituency varies from two (in four Departments) to eleven (in two constituencies of the Seine). So far as the Council of the Republic is concerned, its 246 Metropolitan members are similarly distributed among the Departments. A few Departments return only one Senator; the majority choose two or three; the largest numbers are nine and twenty.

Electorate. The members of the National Assembly are said [27] in the Constitution to be elected by "universal suffrage." This phrase is in effect defined in a previous article, which is worded as follows:

Art. 4.—In the conditions determined by law, all persons of both sexes shall be voters who are French citizens, are of age, and are in possession of their civil and political rights.

In other words, any man or woman is a member of the electorate if registered as possessing the legal qualifications. The details are determined by various provisions of legislative enactment and executive regulation, most of them antedating the Fourth Republic. The electorate, it may be noted, is the same for national and local elections and for referenda. In other words, there is only one voting list. This is prepared in each Commune, and is revised annually. Normally, qualified persons need take no initiative in order to be included on the list; but they are entitled to make formal claims and objections, and detailed arrangements for hearings and appeals exist. The practical necessity of registration results in the fact that to the basic qualifications of citizenship and age, connection with a Commune is added. According to law, a French citizen who is twenty-one years of age may establish the necessary connection with a Commune through domicile, residence, or liability for payment of direct taxes. In these conditions, a name may manifestly find its way to more than one list; but legal provisions forbid seeking or exercising in more than one Commune the privilege of voting.

Woman Suffrage. The employment in the Constitution of the Fourth Republic of the phrase "all persons of both sexes" is a simple recognition of the acceptance of woman suffrage. Thus, the original decision [28] of the Provisional Government of the French Republic and the practice with respect to choice of the two National Constituent Assemblies and to the several referenda became incorporated into constitutional provision. In this undramatic way, France was removed from the short list of countries in which women are not permitted to

[26] In Art. 6.   [27] V. *ibid.*   [28] Cf. Ch. IV, p. 65, *supra.*

vote.[29] As experience has demonstrated usually to be the case, the accomplishment was less the result of rational argumentation than the recognition of the persistent demands of common-sense justice. Likewise, as experience elsewhere might have suggested, the results of woman suffrage in France have not in practice been very far-reaching.

Family Voting. With the suffrage in France extended to women, adults may vote on a scale as wide as the logic of political democracy can well demand. Interestingly enough, the suggestion that the vote should be extended to children, somewhat shocking at first sound, was strongly advocated during the Third Republic, and was urged during the two National Constituent Assemblies. The system proposed was some form of what is called "family voting." In general, the head of the family would cast as many votes as there are dependent members of the family. Though the system is sometimes supported on the doubtful grounds that it is a logical extension of *universal* suffrage, the basic argument made in its favor is that only a representative body elected under such a system can be expected to possess sound fundamental social views. Rejection of the system by both National Constituent Assemblies doubtless reflects good French republican instinct, plural voting being contrary to democratic tradition.

Electoral Colleges for the Council of the Republic. The present Constitution contains a provision worded as follows:

Art. 6.—The Council of the Republic shall be chosen on a territorial basis [30] in the Communes and Departments by indirect universal suffrage.

The system of choice of the first Council of the Republic, regulated by an Act of October 27, 1946, was exceedingly complex. The present system, itself not a model of simplicity, is basically determined by an Act of September 23, 1948, as supplemented primarily by a Decree of September 24, 1948. For the indirect election of the members of the Council of the Republic the electorate is an electoral college in each Metropolitan Department.[31] In such college several elements are contained. In the first place, there are included the members of the National Assembly from the Department and the members of the General Council of the Department.[32] All of these being themselves directly elected by the voters, their vote in the electoral college is two degrees removed from the people. In the second place, an electoral college in a Department contains as

---

[29] Under the Third Republic, though the argument that "woman's place is in the home" was employed in France, conservative circles, interestingly enough, furnished much of the strongest support for votes for women. As in so many things in French politics, religion (cf. Ch. x, p. 177, *infra*) was a consideration of paramount importance. Influence of the priests with women was greatly feared in important nonconservative provincial circles. The Catholic Church strongly advocated woman suffrage. Industrial laboring classes, accustomed to women working on the same plane as men, likewise supported it. This combination succeeded on several occasions in securing acceptance of the principle by the Chamber of Deputies; but the Senate, with its large anticlerical elements, obstinately refused to agree.

[30] As has been noted, the actual constituency is the Department. Some support appeared in the Second National Constituent Assembly for professional, as distinguished from territorial, representation in the Council of the Republic; but this gained no real headway.

[31] In the case of overseas Senators, some five systems exist, naturally resulting in considerable complexity.

[32] Cf. Ch. VIII, p. 146, *infra*.

the most numerous element representatives of the Communes in the Department. The law establishes numerous variations. If a Commune has a population of 9,000 or more,[33] all the members of the Commune Council [34] belong to the electoral college, their relationship to the voters being the same as in the case of members of the National Assembly and of the General Council. If the population of the Commune is less than 9,000, its council chooses from one to fifteen *delegates,* depending on the size of the Commune; and in the case of Communes of more than 45,000, there is, over and above the members of the Council, a delegate for every 5,000 inhabitants or fractions thereof. Delegates, chosen by a highly complex system in the Councils, cast votes in the electoral college removed, it may be seen, by three degrees from the voters. The electoral college meets and votes at the capital city of the Department. The President of a court of the regular judiciary located in the city, with the assistance of other persons determined by law, is in charge of the proceedings.

Polling Dates. French elections, not only national but local, are regularly held on Sunday. This practice is conceived to involve a minimum disarrangement of daily life. The date at which elections for both houses of Parliament are held is determined by executive order within limits set by statutory provisions. Thus, existing law requires that elections to the National Assembly shall be held within a period of sixty days before the normal expiration [35] of the five-year term of that body, and that renewal of one-half the members of the Council of the Republic shall take place within the month of May. Other detailed statutory provisions further restrict the range of executive discretion. The time between issuance of the executive decree and the date of the election is known as the "electoral period." Within this span of several weeks, the official "declaration of candidacy" must be made; and in it the electoral campaign takes place.

Declaration of Candidacy. According to law, only a simple formal declaration of candidacy is required of any person who wishes to seek election in either of the two houses of Parliament.[36] However, the need in practice of organized supporters, more particularly the support of a political party, is, it need scarcely be said, in normal circumstances imperative. This is, of course, especially true under proportional representation; for in practice success in an election normally depends on position of a name on a list, and such determination is made by the party militants.

Proportional Representation. Throughout the Third Republic, electoral reform was an issue of very great importance, actual or potential, in the internal politics of France. The same thing is at least equally true at present. During the Third Republic, three electoral systems were in use. From 1876 to 1885, the single-member constituency [37] prevailed; from 1885 to 1889, the general ticket

[33] Or is located in the Seine.

[34] Cf. Ch. VIII, p. 146,. *infra.*

[35] If dissolution should take place, Art. 52 of the Constitution would require that elections take place at most thirty days after dissolution. Cf. Ch. VII, p. 134, *infra.*

[36] Under the Third Republic, such declaration was required in respect of the Chamber of Deputies but not of the Senate.

[37] The basic constituency was the Arrondissement. Cf. Ch. VIII, p. 139, n. 10, *infra.*

system was employed; from 1889 to 1919, the single-member constituency was again in use; from 1919 to 1927, a modified system of proportional representation was attempted; and after 1927, the system was again that of the single-member constituency. Many theoretical arguments were advanced in favor of each of the three systems; but, in reality, considerations of practical politics were in large measure the determining factors. A matter of the highest importance was—and is—the fact that in France possession of the Ministry of the Interior gives a certain advantage to the government of the day.[38] By the same token, those in power during the Third Republic tended to favor the single-member constituency system. The principal part that with the passing of time was played by the Radical Party [39] in the exercise of power gave rise to the reciprocally related facts that the single-member constituency system became part of the party's tradition as well as the typical system of the Third Republic. After Liberation, these considerations led to the abandonment, naturally rationalized and supported through theoretical arguments, of the single-member constituency system in favor of "something new and reasonable," that is, Proportional Representation.[40] Introduced by the Provisional Government in August of 1945, Proportional Representation, after giving rise to the success of the big three monolithic parties, was confirmed by the First National Constituent Assembly in April of 1946 and by the Second Assembly [41] on October 5, 1946, an Act [42] of the last-mentioned date serving as a basis for election of the first National Assembly, chosen in November. The "new electoral law," which was the basis for the election of the second National Assembly in June, 1951, is, being technically an amendment of the Act of October 5, 1946, comprehensible only in terms of the basic Act and of the system of Proportional Representation established by it. This system was described as one involving a "general ticket, non-runoff system of proportional representation without split or incomplete ticket." This meant that a voter chose one or another full ticket prepared by a party.[43] The proportional feature operated in accordance with provisions couched in the following somewhat forbidding terminology:

Art. 13.—Seats shall be distributed in each constituency among the several lists in accordance with the rule of the largest mean. This rule shall involve allotting seats successively to that list to which division of the number of votes cast for the list by the number of seats that have already been allotted to the list plus one [44] shall give the largest answer.

[38] This Minister, with the passage of time, can, under the centralized administrative system that prevails in France, place agents favorable to his party in strategic positions and bring pressure on such agents to exert the desired influence.

[39] Cf. Ch. XII, p. 203, *infra*.

[40] Cf. Ch. IV, p. 73, *supra*.

[41] The vote, it is worth recalling, was very close (295–245).

[42] The basic Act was several times amended, before being drastically changed in anticipation of the 1951 elections.

[43] The law allowed voters to express a preference with respect to the order of names on the list; but, in the absence of agreement by a majority on a change, the list remained unaltered. There was not a single instance of such change at the 1946 elections of the National Assembly. The same expedient was retained, where applicable, for the 1951 elections.

[44] The list with the highest number of votes got the first seat; for, inasmuch as no seats had been already allotted, the division was by $0 + 1$. The number of votes for that list was then divided by $1 + 1$; and it would at once get the second seat, if the original vote divided

Working of the rule gave rise to certain criticisms directed against the system. Aside from the fact that party managers were given practical mastery [45] over the order of names on their lists, the large parties were, by virtue of absence of any feature in the law for distribution of remainders, afforded a distinct advantage; in other words, national representation of the smaller parties was by no means proportional to the numbers of votes cast for such parties. The most important practical aspect of this situation was, in the eyes of patriotic Frenchmen, the undoubted fact that the system worked to the advantage of the Communists. However, while all other political elements would have been glad if possible to support some system that would deprive the Communists of their favored position, this desire in numerous cases conflicted in different ways with preference for the system that was regarded as most advantageous for it by a given party.[46] Even within a given party, certain leaders, it was said,[47] were lukewarm to the system officially advocated by the party if this system was calculated to be less favorable to them individually. However that may be, the complexity of French politics of electoral reform was, as the elections of 1951 approached, such as to lead some students to pronounce the situation insoluble. The Communists, it need hardly be observed, exploited conditions to the full, in any way calculated to maintain the confusion from which they profit. When Proportional Representation looked as if it might well prevail by default, a compromise solution, highly likely itself to remain the subject of bitter controversy, was found. The "new" law stipulates basically for a general ticket system, combined slates being allowable. If any ticket obtains a majority of votes cast, the entire ticket is elected. The same is true of a combined slate, the seats being distributed among the several lists in accordance with the previous system of Proportional Representation. Moreover, this system not only still applies if no ticket or slate receives a majority; it is integrally retained in certain constituencies, primarily in the Parisian area.

Electoral Campaigns. As time for election approaches, there is no lack of popular interest in any part of the country. Appeal is made to the people through most of the methods employed in other democratic countries.[48] Thus, use is made of the basic and elementary procedure of addressing by mail the individual voters. Statutory provisions arrange that declared candidates may

---

by 2 was greater than the vote of the next highest list. Otherwise, the second seat would go to the second highest list, its vote would then be divided by 2, and so on. In this way, the same result was achieved as by the use of a "quotient."

[45] This made the system attractive to ambitious party militants, who might get their names on a list but who were not necessarily good candidates in a personal campaign.

[46] After the elections to the Second National Constituent Assembly, the Radicals complained that nearly 59,000 voters were necessary for them to secure one seat, whereas the MRP needed only about 35,000. For the National Assembly elections of November of 1946, the corresponding figures were approximately 36,000 and 32,000.

[47] For example, it was at times suggested that M. Herriot, President of the National Assembly, would have a difficult time being re-elected in his old constituency in Lyon in a straight campaign; and it was even whispered that General de Gaulle might prefer to head a list under Proportional Representation rather than engage in a majority contest. Actually, M. Herriot was successful; and the General did not stand for election.

[48] Naturally reference in these respects is more to the National Assembly than to the Council of the Republic.

have printed at public expense envelopes,[49] ballots, election circulars, and post-ers. Dispatch of material by mail is likewise free of charge. Deposits must be made by candidates, the money being returned if a fixed minor fraction [50] of the votes is received. Such candidates as secure the return of their deposits may also be reimbursed for gasoline and for the cost of arranging display of posters. In the second respect, boards are especially erected in each Commune, legal provisions determining the number of such boards and the distribution of space on them. Meetings are organized on a large scale, and speeches are made in great numbers. Members of the Government and other orators of national reputation, most of whom will themselves be candidates somewhere, make speeches in various parts of the country. Less formal discussion is particularly characteristic of French politics. The Café du Commerce in provincial com-munities has become proverbial as a centre of political activity. The electoral systems of the Fourth Republic have undoubtedly tended to cause national issues to be stressed and party programs to be followed more closely by can-didates; but personalities and local interests have naturally continued to play no little part. The newspapers are unusually active. Broadcasting was employed for the first time on a wide scale in 1936. Stations are required by law to dis-tribute on a fair basis time for campaign addresses. No considerable complaint is heard of corrupt practices. Use of money has in general given rise to no special problems—in any event, campaign funds are not regulated by law.

Disputed Elections. A provision of the prevailing Constitution, reminis-cent of the terms of the Constitution of the United States, is worded as follows:

Art. 8.—Each of the two Chambers shall be judge of the eligibility of its members and of the regularity of their election.

On the basis of this provision, the two houses follow the old French practice, dating back to the States-General, of "verifying" [51] after an election the creden-tials of members-elect. Disputed elections are in practice relatively rare.[52] As in the United States, these disputes tend to be decided on political grounds. Scholarly opinion holds that they ought, as in the case of local elections, to be determined in the courts of law.

STATUS OF MEMBERS OF PARLIAMENT

Economic Security. The present Constitution contains a provision worded as follows:

Art. 23.—Members of Parliament shall receive payment fixed on the basis of the salary of a category of civil servants.

[49] Though the reference here is to envelopes for campaign material, use of envelopes is, it should be further noted, an important aspect of secret voting in France. Even under the Third Republic, these latter envelopes were officially furnished; but ballots were printed at the candidates' expense, the voter taking as many as he liked into the polling booth, where he put whatever he pleased into the envelope. Under the present law, the officially printed ballots must be used.

[50] For the National Assembly 5 per cent, for the Council of the Republic 8 per cent.

[51] Cf. this Ch., p. 102, *infra.*

[52] The aftermath of the 1951 elections was exceptional in this respect. According to press accounts, supported by reports in the *Journal officiel* of long-continued wrangling, the number of disputed elections was in excess of a hundred.

By statutory provision, the salary of members of the two houses is assimilated to that of members of the Council of State.[53] The amount is, up to nearly 50 per cent, tax exempt. Members likewise have the benefit of certain railway, postal, and other advantages, including a contributory pension system.

Immunities. Concerning the traditional privileges of members of Parliament, the present Constitution contains the following provisions:

Art. 21.—No member of Parliament may be proceeded against, sought out, arrested, detained, or judged because of opinions or votes given by him in the exercise of his functions.

Art. 22.—No member of Parliament, unless with the authorization of the Chamber of which he is a member, may, during his term of office, be proceeded against or arrested for a felony or misdemeanor, except in case of *flagrante delicto*. The detention or prosecution of a member of Parliament shall be suspended if the Chamber of which he is a member shall require it.

The first of these articles establishes what is called in France *irresponsibility,* the second *inviolability*. The provisions have, generally speaking, very infrequent application in practice. The houses are loath to waive the immunity of a member. However, some of the activities of Communist members have in recent years been so extreme that the National Assembly has reluctantly agreed to prosecution. A standing committee has been established for the express purpose of dealing with suggestions of such legal action.[54]

3. THE ORGANIZATION OF PARLIAMENT

PREPARATION FOR WORK

Sessions. When the houses of Parliament, with their composition determined, are in a position to meet, arrange their organization, and proceed to business, they convene and remain in session in accordance with certain provisions of the Constitution. The principal pertinent stipulations are worded as follows:

Art. 9.—The National Assembly shall automatically convene in annual session on the second Tuesday in January.

The total duration of interruptions of the session may not exceed four months. Interruptions of the session shall be construed to be adjournments in excess of ten days.

The Council of the Republic shall sit at the same time as the National Assembly.

Art. 12.—When the National Assembly shall not be sitting, its officers, controlling the action of the Cabinet, may convene Parliament. They must do so upon the request of one-third of the Deputies or upon that of the President of the Council of Ministers.

Art. 52.—In case of dissolution . . . general elections shall take place at least twenty days and at most thirty days after the dissolution.

The National Assembly shall convene automatically on the third Thursday following its election.

These stipulations, according to French constitutional commentaries, have the effect of abolishing the distinction, which existed under the Third Republic, be-

[53] The amount is approximately 98,000 francs (*c.* $280) per month. For the Council of State, cf. Ch. IX, pp. 164–165, *infra*.

[54] It is a committee of twenty-two, created in February of 1949.

tween ordinary and extraordinary sessions. A strong case may undoubtedly be made for this interpretation; but in practice the government of the day has once or twice called Parliament into session in January previous to the second Tuesday, and, in spite of protests by persons claiming to construe the Constitution in the only possible reasonable way, the expression "extraordinary session" has been officially employed.

Rules. Each of the two houses possesses a set of written Rules, known as a *règlement.* Use of the singular number is an indication that the Rules are regarded as forming, so to say, a miniature code. The principle that a legislative assembly, not being able to get on without Rules, possesses the power to formulate them is so well established in France that the prevailing Constitution merely assumes their existence without expressly authorizing their adoption. It would be almost impossible to exaggerate the importance and influence of what is frequently called the "internal law" of the Chambers. The National Assembly adopted its *règlement* on March 20, 1947, the Council of the Republic on June 5, 1947. Since that time, a certain amount of detailed amendment has been effected in both codes.

Bureau. A provision of the present Constitution is worded as follows:

Art. 11.—Each of the two Chambers shall choose its *bureau* each year at the beginning of the session by proportional representation of the groups.

The word *bureau,* as used in this provision, refers to the body of officers. According to its Rules, each house has at present (1) a President, whose position is in principle that of the presiding officer of any deliberative assembly, (2) several [55] Vice-Presidents, who on occasion act as substitutes for the President, (3) a number [56] of Secretaries, whose not very important position involves for the most part merely the supervision of functionaries who do the actual work, and (4) officials in each house, known as Questors,[57] who are in charge of such matters as the order, cleanliness, comfort, and conveniences of the buildings in which the Chambers are housed. At the opening of a session, before the annual election of officers, a provisional group of officers known as the *bureau d'âge,* the oldest member [58] acting temporarily as President and a number of the youngest members as secretaries, serves, in accordance with the Rules, in each house.

Presiding Officers. The presiding officers of the French Chambers occupy a position somewhere between the English Speaker and his American counterpart. The French President is, in theory, an impartial arbiter of the English type; but there is a certain amount of difference between theory and practice. During the Third Republic, a tendency existed, it is true, for the Presidents to

---

[55] Six in the National Assembly, four in the Council of the Republic.

[56] Fourteen in the National Assembly, eight in the Council of the Republic.

[57] Three in each Chamber.

[58] For the sessions of the first National Assembly, this was in all cases M. Cachin, a Communist. He so abused his position that the Rules were changed to deprive the *président d'âge* of his position as soon as the regular president should be chosen. For the first session of the second National Assembly in July of 1951, the oldest member was from the Right, a M. Pebellier, who caused a slight sensation by advocating amnesty for Marshal Pétain and others regarded as "collaborationists."

be re-elected in spite of political changes; and several Presidents served for considerable periods. The Fourth Republic does not seem likely to develop any pronounced break with this tendency. The Presidents rank high on ceremonial occasions, coming next after the President of the Republic. They are well lodged; and they receive, in addition to the salary of a member of Parliament, relatively generous salaries and allowances.

WORKING ORGANS IN THE HOUSES

Smaller Bodies within the Larger. The French Chambers, like all relatively large deliberative bodies, find it convenient, and indeed imperative, to make use of certain smaller organs consisting of a restricted number of the whole body of members. Particular mention may be made of (1) bureaus, (2) groups, and (3) committees.

(1) *Bureaus.* The bureaus, in the sense of the word here involved, are sections of the two houses, somewhat like sections of a large American college course. There are ten of these bureaus in the National Assembly and six in the Council of the Republic. The Rules determine that they shall be established, in accordance with an old tradition, by lot. Until pressure of business during the Third Republic caused fundamental simplification of French parliamentary procedure, legislative measures were discussed simultaneously in the bureaus, since these sections, because of their smaller size, offered better opportunity than did plenary sittings for fruitful debate. At present, the function of the bureaus is the "verification of powers." [59] After an election, the credentials of the members-elect are distributed alphabetically by Departments [60] among the bureaus, which, having examined election returns through small committees chosen by lot, report to the house. Except in the relatively rare case of disputed elections, the reports are accepted without question.

(2) *Groups.* In each of the houses, members who are affiliated with one another through similar political views form in principle what is known as a *group.*[61] The best examples are the groups that are, like an American caucus, composed of those members of a Chamber who belong to a national political party. However, in spite of the original monolithic, big three parties, to which must now be added the organization of General de Gaulle, and the tendency towards strong organization which they represent, not all the groups correspond to political parties. The existence of numerous groups in the Chambers continues to be a characteristic feature of French parliamentary life. It is of course intimately interconnected with the much discussed multi-party system. [62] At present, the groups number nine [63] in the National Assembly and

[59] Cf. this Ch., p. 99, *supra.*
[60] Those of overseas members are likewise distributed alphabetically by area.
[61] Cf. Ch. xii, p. 191, *infra.* According to the Rules of each Chamber, a group is constituted when it has submitted "a list of members accompanied by a public declaration common to all members, signed by them and serving as a program of political action."
[62] Cf. Ch. x, p. 172, *infra.*
[63] These are as follows: Communist (99); Popular Republican Movement [MRP] (83); Socialist (105); Radical (66); Democratic and Social Resistance Union [UDSR] (14); Independent Republican (43); Republican Centre of Peasant and Social Action and of Independent Democrats (34); African Democratic Assemblage (3); Assemblage of the French People

eight [64] in the Council of the Republic. Under the Third Republic, the groups became in the twentieth century *official,* in the sense that the Rules in each Chamber came to recognize these political bodies through provisions requiring the groups to propose lists of their members, giving the groups a principal part in the choice of committees, imposing functions on the presidents of the groups, and so on. Under the Fourth Republic, the Constitution itself actually refers to the groups; and the Rules of the two houses naturally continue and extend recognition established under the Third Republic. Though a member of a French Chamber is of course not compelled to belong to a political group, no member may belong to more than one of them. Under the Third Republic, members formed within the Chambers various associations, called "study groups," which served as a nucleus of various forces, corresponding in a general way to lobbyists in the United States, that defended particular interests of one kind or another. Under the Fourth Republic, the Rules of both houses specifically forbid such groups. Thus, Article 13 of the *règlement* of the National Assembly, Article 13 of the *règlement* of the Council of the Republic being essentially identical, is worded as follows:

Establishment in the body of the Assembly shall be forbidden of so-called groups "for defence of special, local, or professional interests."

As is well known, the French political groups, according to long-established custom with respect to seating arrangements,[65] take positions, on the floor of the Chambers, that are determined by the complexion of their political views. Sections to the left of the President are occupied by the more "advanced" groups, which constitute the Left. At present, the position at the extreme left is held by the group of the Communist Party. The tendency has been for a new group to appear at the far left, thus forcing towards the right the groups formerly occupying the extreme left position. Similarly, the Right consists of groups with conservative or reactionary tendencies. Left and Right in theory [66] come together at the Centre. Groups of the Centre tend to hold, through a balance of power, a position that is of an importance out of proportion to their size.

(3) *Committees.* The committee system of the French Chambers possesses an importance in French government that can scarcely be exaggerated. In gen-

---

[RPF] (118). Three groups, affiliated with one of the above, raise the total to 12. These are as follows: Independent French (3) with the Republican Centre, Overseas Independent (9) with the MRP; Progressist Republican (4) with the Communist. Individual Deputies, twenty-six in number, are also affiliated with seven of the groups. Nineteen Deputies are unlisted. Details naturally change from time to time.

[64] These are as follows: Assemblage of Republican Lefts [RGR] and Democratic Left (72); Socialist (59); Democratic and Republican Action (57); Independent Republicans (42); Republican Centre of Rural and Social Action (15); PRL (10); MRP (20); Communist (15). One group, the African Democratic Assemblage (3), is affiliated with the Communists. Individual Senators are affiliated with or "administratively attached" to one of the groups in several instances. Details naturally change from time to time.

[65] Cf. Ch. x, pp. 173–174, *infra.* Following the 1951 elections, the RPF protested the seating arrangements, contending that its members were drawn from all shades of opinion and should not be concentrated; but their objection was not sustained.

[66] In practice, the Left groups are so large that they overflow considerably beyond the literal centre axis.

eral, these organisms prepare the work that Parliament is to do.[67] Though they are mentioned in the Constitution of the Fourth Republic, their character, number, size, method of choice, and the like are determined in each house by the Rules.[68] Much the most important of the committees are the General Committees.[69] There are at present nineteen of them in each house. They have identical titles, which indicate their sphere of competence. Simple examples include committees on finance, on foreign affairs, on agriculture, on education, on national defence, and so on. They consist of forty-four members in the National Assembly and of thirty in the Council of the Republic.[70] They are chosen annually by a system of proportional representation in the Chambers. The system was established in 1910 in the Chamber of Deputies and adopted in 1921 by the Senate. According to the present operation of the scheme, the political groups, five days before the day fixed for the election of committee members, draw up and submit to the officers of the Chambers lists of their members and affiliates, which are published. A group is entitled to choose the same proportion of the members of each committee as the membership of the group bears to the size of the Chamber.[71] The groups choose from their membership the members to which they are entitled on each committee. The names are submitted to the officers of the Chambers, who are then in a position to compile the list of members for the several committees. The lists are published; and if within three days objection is not made through petitions signed by at least a certain number of members—fifty in the National Assembly, thirty in the Council of the Republic—the lists are considered to have been approved by the Chambers. According to the Rules, if objection should be thus made, the Chamber involved would proceed to a vote.

[67] Cf. this Ch., pp. 105–106, *infra.*

[68] Cf. *ibid.* The Constitution, after stipulating that the National Assembly shall study bills in its committees, adds that "it shall fix the number, composition, and scope."

[69] Other committees include (1) *special committees,* set up *ad hoc* in connection with some measure, and (2) particular specialized committees, such for example as the Committee on Accounts and the Committee on Petitions. Employment of special committees was once the prevailing system.

[70] The number forty-four in the National Assembly is, it may be observed, a multiple of eleven, the number of bureaus in the Chamber of Deputies under the Third Republic. Under the old procedure, after discussion of a measure in the bureaus, each bureau chose one or more members to serve on a committee for further study of the measure. Use of special committees of eleven was originally the basic system. However, larger committees were on occasion formed; and by the time choice of committees in the bureaus was abandoned, standing committees of forty-four had become established. The National Assembly has retained the number forty-four, although there are now only ten bureaus. Similarly in the Senate there were nine bureaus and committees of thirty-six. The Council of the Republic, it may be seen, has abandoned both numbers.

[71] A provision of Article 15 of the Rules of the National Assembly stipulates that "in order to establish a list of candidates for a General Committee, the groups must contain at least fourteen members." The explanation of this is that division of the number of members of the National Assembly by forty-four gives fourteen, the number of members required for a group to be entitled to one member in a General Committee.

4. THE FUNCTIONS OF PARLIAMENT

THE MAKING OF LAW

Legislation and Related Functions. The French Parliament, in accordance with general democratic practice and especially with the practice of parliamentary government, performs three principal interrelated functions. It makes laws; it administers public finance; and it controls the executive.

Parliamentary Procedure. French legislative procedure is determined by the provisions of the Rules of the two houses,[72] as supplemented by precedent and custom. The general aspects of this procedure are at the present time relatively simple.

Bills and Their Introduction. The Constitution of the Fourth Republic contains the following provisions:

Art. 14.—The President of the Council of Ministers and the members of Parliament shall have the intiative of bills.

Government bills and private members' bills in the National Assembly shall be laid on the table of the latter.

Private members' bills in the Council of the Republic shall be laid on the table of the latter and transmitted without debate to the table of the National Assembly.

These provisions, aside from furnishing an initial indication of the subordination of the Council of the Republic to the National Assembly, accepts an old distinction among public bills under parliamentary government. However, Cabinet measures [73] in France have no priority really comparable to that possessed by Government bills in England. In France, what is known as unlimited individual initiative exists, that is to say, every member may introduce as many measures as he sees fit. In this flood, Cabinet bills and private members' bills for the most part take their chances together. The distinction is largely one of nomenclature, Cabinet measures being called *projects* of law, private members' measures *propositions* of law. Any advantage that the former possess over the latter is one inherent in the position of the Cabinet, given only minor formal recognition by rule. Both kinds of measures must be reduced to the same form, that is to say, they must be in writing, must be composed of one or more articles, must have a succinct title, and must be preceded by a short explanation of the proposal. They are placed before the presiding officer, who theoretically informs the house that the measures have been introduced, and in fact orders them to be numbered, printed, and distributed.

Committee Stage. The present Constitution contains a provision [74] worded as follows:

Art. 15.—The National Assembly shall study in its committees the bills laid before it . . .

[72] Cf. this Ch., p. 101, *supra.*

[73] Under the Third Republic, the power of executive initiative was vested in the President of the Republic, which meant that government bills were introduced by one or another of the Ministers in his name. The present Constitution vests this power in the Prime Minister (cf. Ch. VII, p. 123, *infra*), which means that, though a given Minister is in charge of a bill, it is introduced by the Prime Minister. The difference, it may be seen, is not great.

[74] Cf. this Ch., pp. 103–104, *supra.*

This stipulation "constitutionalizes" an important aspect of modern French procedure, whereby a measure is regularly referred, after introduction, to a standing committee into the sphere of which the measure falls. The general practice is for the committee to place the measure in the charge of a member who is known regularly as its reporter.[75] The reporter gives to the measure the most careful study of which he is capable, whereupon he brings before the committee for examination and discussion a provisional measure that he has prepared. This may well be in much the same form as that in which the measure was introduced; but frequently the original measure undergoes no little alteration. Whatever may be the case, the committee undertakes, in the course of its examination, to discuss in detail the terms of the provisional measure prepared by the reporter. Committee members who feel that they have some competence with respect to the question under discussion present their views. This means primarily, though not exclusively, the president of the committee, who is usually a man of considerable experience, and the reporter, who has acquired knowledge through his special study. Witnesses are frequently heard. The author of the measure under discussion, if he is not a member of the committee, is naturally afforded a special hearing, being given by the Rules in fact the right to attend meetings of the committee. Ministers are afforded the same right by a constitutional provision as well as by a provision of the Rules,[76] though in the absence of such stipulations mutual desire would undoubtedly produce the same result. In the context of parliamentary government, the Minister wishes to have his position understood by the committee, and the committee desires to know the views of the executive. Finally, the committee decides on the measure it proposes to sponsor, the reporter being authorized to prepare the report.[77] This offers to the ambitious members an opportunity to impress the Chamber and the public.[78]

Reports and Order of the Day. A reporter who has completed his report and has been authorized by the committee to present it lays it before the President, who orders it numbered, printed, and distributed. The next step, if the report is to come up for discussion, is for it to become a part of the program of proposed business known as "the order of the day." In each house, the order of the day is prepared by what is called the Conference of Presidents. This Conference, according to the Rules, is composed of the President and Vice-Presidents of the Chamber, of presidents of General Committees, and of the presidents of the political groups. The Cabinet is informed of meetings in order that it may send a representative. The Conference regularly has weekly meetings. Its proposals are submitted to the house for approval, after which the order of

[75] The Rules of the two Chambers require that a reporter shall be chosen for each measure soon (two weeks at most in the National Assembly, one week in the Council of the Republic) after it has been referred.

[76] Cf. Ch. vii, p. 130, *infra*.

[77] On occasion, the reporter is not in agreement with the views of the committee. In such case, he may either defend the measure by giving the committee's position as distinguished from his own; or he may withdraw in favor of another.

[78] E.g. Briand, as a young man, demonstrated his undoubted ability on the occasion when he served as reporter of the measure effecting the separation of Church and State. Cf. Ch. xi, p. 187, *infra*.

the day is printed and posted. Thereupon, it may not be altered except upon the request of the Cabinet or of a committee or on the petition of thirty members.

Debate. When a measure is called up for discussion before one of the houses, it must, in order to be passed, follow certain procedural steps which, though the Rules regulating them are somewhat complex, are in outline simple. The steps are these: (1) general discussion, (2) a vote to pass to the reading of the articles, (3) detailed discussion and voting of the several articles, at which time amendments that have been suggested are considered, and (4) vote on the measure as a whole. As was well said [79] of French procedure during the Third Republic—and the same is true of the Fourth—"In principle, three groups of actors carry on parliamentary debate,—the Government, the Committees, and the mass of Deputies." According to the same suggestion, the situation is symbolized by the physical arrangement of the chambers, where, in front of the seats on which the body of members sit, special benches are marked as reserved respectively for the members of the Cabinet and of the committees. So far as a committee in charge of a measure is concerned, the reporter and president play a principal role in debate. This is true even of a Government measure; for, although one or more Ministers naturally take an important part, it is technically not the measure originally introduced by the Cabinet but that of the committee—or more strictly its report—which is the basis of discussion. Members who desire to speak hand in their names to the President, who, in general, attempts to arrange that speakers for and against a proposed measure shall be heard alternately. Ministers and the reporter and president of the committee may speak whenever they request it, except that any one of them may be followed by an ordinary member.

Agreement of the Houses. When a measure has been passed by the National Assembly, it is sent to the Council of the Republic. In spite of the basic similarity of procedure in the two houses, the Council of the Republic has time limits upon its deliberations. This, as well as other limitations, grows of course out of constitutional provisions which have as their specific aim establishment of a subordinate position for the Council of the Republic. The principal stipulations in this respect are worded as follows:

Art. 20.—The Council of the Republic shall examine, with a view to giving its opinion, Government and private members' bills that shall have been voted at a first reading by the National Assembly.

It shall give its opinion at the latest within the two months following transmittal by the National Assembly [80] . . . When the National Assembly shall have decided upon passage by an urgency procedure, the Council of the Republic shall give its opinion within the same time limit as that established for the debates of the National Assembly by the Rules of the latter. The time limits provided for in the present article shall be suspended during interruptions of the session. They may be extended by decision of the National Assembly.

If the opinion of the Council of the Republic shall be favorable or if it shall not have

[79] Joseph-Barthélemy et Paul Duez, *Traité de droit constitutionnel* (2e éd., Paris, 1933), p. 543.

[80] At this point is a provision establishing a possible special time limit, equal to the time used in the Assembly, in the matter of the discussion of the budget. Cf. this Ch., p. 112, *infra.*

been given within the time limits provided in the preceding paragraph, the act shall be promulgated in the text voted by the National Assembly.

If the opinion is not favorable, the National Assembly shall examine the bill upon a second reading. It shall come to a definitive and sovereign decision solely upon the amendments proposed by the Council of the Republic, accepting or rejecting them in whole or in part. In case of total or partial rejection of these amendments, the vote on second reading of the act shall take place by a recorded vote of the members composing the National Assembly, when the vote on the whole shall have been accomplished by the Council of the Republic in the same conditions.

In practice, procedure has regularly followed the several courses outlined in the constitutional provisions. Where the Council of the Republic accepts the text sent it by the National Assembly, there is of course no problem. Concerning the situation when amendments are suggested by the Council of the Republic, no generalization is possible. Sometimes the Assembly accepts out of hand the Council proposals; sometimes it rejects them in equally forthright manner; often, particularly in the matter of longer texts, it accepts some and rejects others. Some justifiable complaint is made that urgency procedure, which is employed by the National Assembly in large numbers of cases, draws time limits that are too narrow round Council procedure. The Council frequently asks for extension of time, which is often, but not invariably, granted.

THE ADMINISTRATION OF PUBLIC FINANCE

Basic Principles. In France the fundamental democratic principle is well established which demands that ultimate control of the public purse shall rest with the legislative branch of government. The principle had become so definitely accepted by 1875 that the Constitution of the Third Republic implied legislative control of public finance, without containing any explicit stipulation in the matter. The same is true in general of the Constitution of the Fourth Republic, though the number of provisions implying this control is greater. Thus, the Preamble, through acceptance of the Declaration of 1789,[81] gives constitutional status to the revolutionary insistence on financial control by the representatives of the nation; and various provisions in the body of the Constitution clearly imply the same principle.

The Budget: Constitutional Basis. The prevailing Constitution contains the following provisions:

Art. 16.—The National Assembly shall have laid before it the Government budget bill. This measure may contain only strictly financial provisions.

An organic act shall determine the method of promulgation of the budget.[82]

Art. 17.—Deputies of the National Assembly shall possess the initiative in respect of expenditures.

However, no proposal which would have the effect of increasing estimated expenditure or of creating new expenditures may be presented during discussion of the budget, of votes on account, or of supplementary estimates.

[81] Cf. Ch. v, p. 78, *supra.* Art. 14 of the Declaration of 1789 asserts the right of citizens or their representatives to determine need for taxation and freely to consent to it, as well as to control employment of the proceeds.

[82] This budget act has not yet come into existence.

The Budget: Initiative. The clear presumption in constitutional provisions that there shall be one annual budget formulated by the executive merely gives constitutional authorization to a practice long existing in France. Express recognition in the Constitution that initiative in the matter of expenditure shall belong to members of the National Assembly continues a legal situation that prevailed throughout the Third Republic. On the other hand, it represents, it will be recalled, a striking difference from the Act of November 2, 1945.[83] Actually, during discussion of the present Constitution, a sustained effort, invoking explicitly the practice and experience of the English House of Commons, was made to continue a provision confining financial initiative to the executive. The Second National Constituent Assembly was in the end unwilling to go so far; but the second part of Article 17 in practice is no small reinforcement of the executive's financial authority, and the Rules contain provisions buttressing this authority.[84]

The Budget: Contents. The budget is still defined legally in France in terms of a Decree of 1852 as "the act by which are estimated and authorized the annual expenditures and revenues of the State." Actually, the "unity" of the budget has become in recent times in considerable measure a fiction. In practice, there is not one document, but several. Not only are there an "ordinary" and an "extraordinary" budget, these being considered divisions of the "general" budget; there are also "annexed" budgets, which do not differ in principle from the general budget, and more particularly various special budgets of an autonomous character as well as somewhat mysterious, but increasingly important, "expenditures covered by the Treasury." In practice, several bulky volumes of many thousands of pages are involved.

The Budget: Preparation. The budget documents are prepared with much care and difficulty in the Ministry of Finance, headed by the Minister of Finance. In it are to be found the aristocracy of the Civil Service, the Inspectors of Finance.[85] The Ministry's authority with respect to revenue and to estimates of expenditure for the Ministry itself is exclusive. The situation with respect to expenditure by other Ministries is more complicated. The estimates in each Ministry, requested some time before the beginning of the fiscal year on January 1, are required by law to be submitted to a controller of expenditure appointed in the Ministry by the Minister of Finance. These controllers formulate their opinions concerning the estimates; and estimates and opinions are communicated to the Ministry of Finance. An initial part of the great task of the Ministry, based on the ultimate obligation of securing a balance between outlay and income, is that of coordinating the various estimates of expenditure. In this respect, authorities on public finance are in agreement that the Minister is not in a position to exercise all the authority desirable. Controversies that

---

[83] Cf. Ch. IV, p. 68, *supra.*

[84] Likewise, the practice has been developed of establishing "maxima" by statute, with the result that in financial discussions Ministers may invoke the Constitution, statute law, and the Rules to demand of right the elimination of amendments that would increase expenditure or reduce income.

[85] Cf. Ch. VIII, p. 143, *infra.*

arise are in the last analysis decided by the Cabinet.[86] In the end a budget is put in written form, preceded by certain introductory observations, explaining and defending the proposals made.

Finance Procedure: Introduction. In a formal sense, a budget, though of special nature and of paramount importance, does not differ from other government measures. This is to say, it is prepared for, and under the direction of, the Cabinet, and is introduced and considered in Parliament on its responsibility, following in general outlines the procedure employed in the passage of ordinary legislation. Thus, introduction of a budget into the National Assembly is, as in other cases, a pure formality. Once introduced, a budget is ordered to be numbered, printed, and distributed; and it is referred to the General Committee on Finance. In practice, budget proposals are by no means always ready before the beginning of the summer recess. Consequently, the Minister of Finance may have to introduce a dummy measure, this fiction regularizing subsequent consideration by the Committee on Finance of the several parts of the budget as they are furnished to the Committee by the Ministry. As a result, members of the Committee on Finance are required to meet during the hot days of the recess, when other Deputies are enjoying vacations at the seashore or in the country.

Finance Procedure: Commitee on Finance. The Finance Committee is much the most powerful of all the General Committees. Though its primary task consists of dealing with annual budget measures, more bills come before it than before any other committee. Inasmuch as practically all proposed measures of any importance are related in some way, immediate or remote, to public finance, the Committee on Finance is usually called on either to study a measure itself and report on it or to formulate an opinion concerning its financial aspects. In practice, the Committee is in large measure an aggregate of reporters. The fact that a reporter is forthwith named for each of the numerous measures coming before the Committee means that there is no lack of work for individual Committee members. So far as budgetary proposals are concerned, they are divided into various parts, the most typical being the estimates of the several administrative departments and services; and the parts are distributed to special reporters. Moreover, a general reporter performs the function of reviewing the general financial situation, of dealing with the principles common to the several parts of the budgetary measures, and of directing public discussion in each of the houses. The special reporters subject their several parts to careful consideration and vigorous criticism. They formulate their own proposals, and these form the basis of Committee hearings. Witnesses, particularly members of the executive, are heard. The fact that substantial changes by the Committee are not necessarily regarded by the Cabinet as an indication of lack of confidence in it gives to the Committee a wide range of action. Indeed, French students of public finance suggest that legislative preparation of budget

---

[86] As has been seen, the initiative is, according to the Constitution, that of the Prime Minister. The elements of administrative organization that have to do with the budget are in the Ministry of Finance. If there is a Minister of the Budget as well, a division of labor is arranged.

proposals is superimposed upon executive preparation. However that may be, Ministry of Finance proposals are practically certain to undergo a large amount of modification; and the measures finally adopted for submission to the National Assembly are considered, as in the case of ordinary legislation, to be not executive but Committee measures. In reality, the texts, whatever the theory, are combinations of proposals emanating from the two sources. These texts are contained in the various reports made in the name of the Committee, the reports consisting of a number of special reports, several general reports, and numerous supplementary reports. There is no pretense that these reports are confined to the estimates of expenditure and to revenue proposals. A general review is made of the defence forces, of foreign affairs, of agriculture, and so on. Questions of high policy are dealt with and freely criticized. This is, in turn, the basis of fundamental criticism brought by students of public finance against the Committee on Finance and, in lesser degree, by students of government against all the General Committees. A definite tendency exists in the direction of encroachment on the proper sphere both of the executive and of Parliament as a whole, with serious consequences for leadership, responsibility, and stability. In other words, operation of the parliamentary regime is involved. The Committee on Finance has been characterized by many unpleasant names, such as "shipwreckers of ministries"; and the committees as a whole have been more than once called "parliaments within Parliament" and various other similar things.

Financial Debate. Discussion by the National Assembly of budgetary proposals begins when the Committee on Finance is ready with its reports; but the time at which the Committee on Finance is prepared to report is determined in considerable measure by delay on the part of the executive in submitting the budget proposals to the Committee. In practice, the last few weeks of the calendar year are crowded with such discussions in anticipation of the beginning of the fiscal year on January 1. The budgetary proposals are rarely voted on time. This was true even during the more normal times of the Third Republic; and, since the Liberation, conditions have been far from normal. In the result, various expedients are employed; and much budgetary debate takes place in the course of, rather than previous to the opening of, the fiscal year. At any time, such debate regularly includes, as in the case of ordinary bills, general discussion of the whole and detailed consideration of the various parts. Inasmuch as financial proposals inevitably involve, as is well known to students of government, matters of policy, discussion of what are in appearance details of finance regularly takes the form of criticism of governmental policy. Principal roles in debate are naturally played by the Minister of Finance, the President and general reporter of the Committee on Finance, and, in discussion of specialized aspects of proposals, by relevant Ministers and by the special reporters. The reporters, especially the general reporter, are likely to feel that they are at least the equal of Ministers. The result of the rivalry is a certain amount of friction and divided responsibility. The reporters have been called "heirs apparent" of the Ministers.

Amendment of Financial Measures. In connection with those parts of budgetary debates which are concerned with particular items, the matter of amendments is of the highest importance. The provisions of the Constitution, of statutes, and of the Rules of the National Assembly which limit private members' initiative in respect of budgetary measures [87] are in practice applicable principally in the matter of amendment. This means that suggested amendments of budgetary expenditure proposals must be in the direction of reduction. Actually such reductions are moved in considerable numbers by private members,[88] often in the amount of a small sum. In this way, occasions are presented for discussion of government policy.[89] When the debate is concerned with broad lines of policy, the practice is, it would seem, to be commended; but where a reduction is moved merely to afford a member an opportunity to ask a Minister a question of detail or otherwise to deal with a minor point, the practice is undoubtedly more questionable.

Budgetary Proposals before the Council of the Republic. When budgetary acts have been voted by the National Assembly, they are sent to the Council of the Republic. In the latter house, a possible reduction of the two-month period of consideration is set by a special provision of the Constitution. The pertinent stipulation is as follows:

Art. 20.—The Council of the Republic . . . shall give its opinion . . . when the budget bill is involved, within its time for deliberation shortened if occasion shall demand so as not to exceed the time employed by the National Assembly for examination and approval.

Within such time limit, the financial proceedings in the Council of the Republic in practice follow the same lines as in the case of ordinary legislation; and its proposals for alteration, sent to the National Assembly, receive the same kind of treatment upon second reading.

Budgetary Proportions. In France, as in other countries, there has been over a period of time a relatively steady increase in government outlay. The upward curve has naturally been steeper in times of war and of crisis, the latter including in large measure the whole period of the Fourth Republic, than in more normal times. Thus, annual expenditure has reached the neighborhood of 2,500,000 million francs (*c.* $7,143,000,000), more than 30 per cent of the national income. On the side of revenue, nearly 80 per cent of public resources is derived from taxation. The remainder comes from several sources, such as proceeds from government industries and monopolies and income from government property. Loans are naturally employed, especially for capital outlay. So far as taxes are concerned, the French system is proverbially complicated. The number of taxes is almost literally countless. In general, indirect impositions exceed direct. Even so, the French regard themselves as heavily taxed;

---

[87] Cf. this Ch., p. 109, n. 84, *supra.*
[88] Similar proposals likewise emanate from the Committee on Finance both in the National Assembly and in the Council of the Republic.
[89] Cf. this Ch., p. 113, *infra.*

and tax evasion is practiced on a wide scale.[90] Reform in the direction of simplification has made some progress, but much remains to be done.

Audit. The prevailing Constitution contains certain stipulations worded as follows:

> Art. 18.—The National Assembly shall settle the accounts of the nation.
>
> It shall to this end be assisted by the Court of Accounts.
>
> The National Assembly may entrust to the Court of Accounts all inquiries and studies relative to execution in respect of revenue and of public expenditure and relative to the management of the Treasury.

This article, it will be seen, gives constitutional status to the Court of Accounts, [91] a body that has existed since the beginning of the nineteenth century. The Court is composed of competent experts who, through a serious examination of accounts, perform the real function of audit.[92] A report is made to the President of the Republic and distributed to Parliament.[93] On the basis of the findings of the Court, Parliament in principle approves the accounts. However, the practical utility of this potential control is considerably lessened by the fact that final approval by Parliament of the accounts is normally delayed until several years after expenditure of the money involved.[94] On the other hand, statutes, by requiring various reports and authorizing committee investigation of current financial transactions, establish more serious means of control.

CONTROLLING THE EXECUTIVE

Information and Criticism. Control by Parliament over the political executive is, of course, the converse of ministerial responsibility, the characteristic feature of the parliamentary system of government.[95] In order to make its control effective, Parliament, in addition to the oversight it maintains during the processes of legislation and financial administration, employs in its day-to-day proceedings various special expedients for keeping itself informed concerning legislative activities and for subjecting these activities to criticism. Among the special forms of control in France, some of the more characteristic are (1) questions, (2) investigations (*enquêtes*), and (3) interpellations.

(1) *Questions.* Oral questions were of very limited importance during the Third Republic. As a matter of fact, although, with the coming of the Fourth Republic, some hopeful effort was made to render them a more effective instrument, the practice catches hold slowly in France. According to the Rules, one whole sitting each month is reserved for answers to oral questions; and on one

---

[90] This is sometimes explained in France as a survival of the influence of the *ancien régime* and as evidence of a liberal instinct on the part of a Frenchman like his ancestors to regard the tax collector as a symbol of arbitrary absolutism.

[91] Cf. Ch. IX, pp. 165–166, *infra.*

[92] What is called in France *control,* classified as administrative, judicial, and parliamentary, is a special subject, technical and complex. In certain respects, control is highly satisfactory, in others less so.

[93] The first reports under the present Constitution caused considerable sensation because of the revelations made with respect to laxness in the spending of public funds.

[94] So far there has been no settlement during the Fourth Republic.

[95] Cf. Ch. vii, pp. 130–131, *infra.*

day [96] each week at the beginning of the sitting [97] ten oral questions [98] may be set down for answer in the National Assembly. The question is not, as under the Third Republic, "developed" by the questioner in a fifteen-minute speech; rather, the Minister, after the reading of the question, gives his answer, after which the questioner is allowed five minutes for reply. The matter is then closed. In practice, the monthly sitting is not employed; the Minister is frequently not present when a question is called; the question is sometimes a year or more old; and the questioner is frequently not interested in commenting. Much more extensive use is made of written questions, which run to several thousand every year. A member writes out and hands in a short question, which is printed in the official account of the proceedings on a given day. The executive replies without undue delay. At its best, this system elicits official interpretations on difficult questions, particularly those connected with public finance; at its worst, it results in trivial questions prompted chiefly by desire on the part of the questioner to have his name appear in print.

(2) *Enquêtes.* In France as in other countries, the familiar practice of legislative investigation is carried out through the natural instrumentality of a committee. The matter is regulated in part by statute and in part by the Rules of the houses of Parliament. In practice, a committee, whether one of the General Committees [99] or a specially instituted body, is in practice directed to undertake an investigation either of a specific matter or of some general situation. The committee holds hearings; and it may, by special decision of a house, be authorized to compel attendance of witnesses and to hear them under oath. The committee usually makes a report of its findings, concerning which the house makes whatever decision it sees fit. These investigations are scarcely an unqualified success in France. As a rule, the findings are without much importance or the hearings give rise to bitter partisan controversy. Not infrequently, both results occur.

(3) *Interpellations.* Interpellation is a more typically French and a more efficacious form of control than are questions and investigations. A member of the National Assembly [100] is said to "interpellate" a Minister, that is to say, he asks from a Minister an explanation of some action or policy that concerns an executive department, or he seeks from the Prime Minister an explanation of general policy. Of the requests presented in the Assembly, the Conference of Presidents decides which shall be brought before the house, similar requests frequently being grouped together as one. At the appointed time, the presiding officer asks the Minister what date he proposes for discussion. The Minister either agrees to immediate full debate, or he in principle refuses such debate by asking that the interpellation be taken in its regular order on a waiting list.

---

[96] Two under the Third Republic.

[97] The end under the Third Republic.

[98] Five in the Council of the Republic, two under the Third Republic.

[99] A committee must designate a maximum number of its members for such investigation— seven in the National Assembly, four in the Council of the Republic.

[100] The interpellation as such does not exist in the Council of the Republic. However, the Council has established the practice of "oral questions with debate," which do not greatly differ from interpellations.

In the latter case, its turn will never be reached. However, the member or members sponsoring the interpellation are afforded opportunity to "develop" it. The Minister replies, in theory giving reasons for proposing that the interpellation be taken in its regular order. The sponsors may reply to the Minister. Thus, in the result, an abbreviated debate in reality grows out of the very refusal of a debate. Voting on the Minister's proposal to take the interpellation in its order is naturally a test of strength of the Cabinet. If the Minister accepts discussion of the interpellation, debate assumes more extensive proportions. It begins in much the same way as the more restricted debate, but later on general debate ensues.[101] Finally, the debate is brought to an end by a motion that the house "pass to the order of the day." This motion, known as an "order of the day," is sometimes a simple motion to pass to the order of the day; but, more frequently, it is a "qualified order of the day," that is to say, the motion, by means of numerous variations of phraseology, expresses confidence or lack of confidence in the Cabinet. A simple unqualified motive is rarely accepted by the Cabinet, being normally a manifest acknowledgment of weakness. Usually, the Cabinet demands the equivalent of a vote of confidence. In practice, the situation is regularly solved through indirection. Of the several orders of the day that are generally before the house, the Cabinet selects the one it prefers, requesting "priority" for that. On this question, issue is joined between supporters and opponents of the Cabinet. If, as is to be anticipated, priority is voted in accordance with the wishes of the Cabinet, passage of the order of the day becomes a formality. In general, although interpellations employed in moderation serve a useful purpose, students of government are in agreement that the institution is one which easily lends itself to abuse.

5. THE POWER OF PARLIAMENT

BASES OF AUTHORITY

Legal Sovereignty. The stipulation of the Constitution of the Fourth Republic [102] to the effect that "the National Assembly alone shall vote law" is not merely determinant of the fundamental relationship between the two houses of Parliament; it vests, for all practical purposes, final and complete law-making power in the National Assembly. This body, it is true, cannot by its ordinary majority amend the Constitution; and therefore, according to the principles of analytical jurisprudence, legal sovereignty does not technically belong to the National Assembly. However, the distinction between *constituent* authority and *legislative* power is here of minor practical importance; the important thing in practice is that the provisions of the Constitution are not serious limitations on the effective exercise of power. In reality, the National Assembly may enact into law any measure which it considers to be calculated to promote the general

---

[101] The whole matter is regulated in great detail in Ch. xv (Arts. 89–93) of the *règlement* of the National Assembly.

[102] Art. 13. Cf. this Ch., p. 90, *supra*.

welfare. In a practical as distinguished from a technical sense, legal sovereignty rests in the National Assembly.

Legislative and Moral Authority. Inasmuch as the National Assembly is for practical purposes possessed of unlimited legal power, such restraint as it displays is, so to say, self-restraint. The limitations within which it seeks to promote the general welfare are set not by a law superior to the law made by the National Assembly, but by that complexus of forces commonly denominated *public opinion.* In other words, only extra-legal forces afford effective protection to individuals and groups against abuse of power at the hands of the National Assembly. The body of the French people do not consider this an alarming situation. On the contrary, they regard it as being fundamentally democratic. They feel that the primary protection for the individual and for groups is to be found in an arrangement whereby laws are made by the elected representatives of the people, that is, by average men, after full and free discussion and wide publicity. In these conditions, a highly developed sense of moral responsibility is the best guaranty—and the same may be argued to be true even of countries with bills of rights and other formal limitations enshrined in a higher law interpreted by judges—against abuse of power.

PARLIAMENTARY OMNIPOTENCE

Authority of the Cabinet. The fact that the practical legal sovereignty of the National Assembly in France is at all times tacitly assumed has an important result. While a legislative measure is pending, the issue is practically always the simple one of whether it ought or ought not to be law. The issue is almost never confused by any question of whether the National Assembly possesses the legal power to make the law in question. The question is, in a broad sense of the word, always a moral one. In other words, the question is whether the proposal is in the general interest; and public opinion is the final arbiter. Indeed, when the expression "omnipotence of Parliament" is employed in France, the reference, it should be recalled, is not to the fully accepted principle of final and legally unlimited power to make law, but rather to a different practical situation. Parliamentary omnipotence refers to a tendency [103] for the National Assembly in practice to reduce the executive to a position of subordination and dependency in a governmental system the ideal of which is accepted theoretically to be a nice balance between legislature and executive. This tendency is, as has been more than once observed, in considerable if uncertain measure approved by the Left; and steps that have been taken to strengthen the executive and proposals that are made towards the same end collide with approval of assembly government. The point to be noted here is that the greatest amount of reinforcement of the executive which could reasonably be expected would not affect the principle of the ultimate and legally unlimited power of the National Assembly. There would be merely practical restraint during the exercise of power. However, in this respect, an important difficulty consists of the fact that a vicious circle tends to be established. Inasmuch as the execu-

[103] Cf. Ch. IV, p. 74, *supra,* and Ch. V, pp. 79–80, *supra.*

tive is weak, the National Assembly, in order to exercise its disproportionate practical power, tends to organize itself and otherwise to consolidate its position in such a way as to keep the executive in its subordinate position. A principal, though by no means sole, manifestation of this state of affairs is to be seen in connection with the well-known phenomenon of ministerial instability.[104] With frequent changes of Cabinet, the National Assembly tends itself to assume responsibility for continuity and stability. Making use particularly of its committees, it tends to formulate policies that reflect the general wishes of the country; and it succeeds in a measure in translating these policies into a unified and uniform body of legislation.

TERRITORIAL AUTHORITY

Parliament and Local Government. The preponderant practical power of the National Assembly is of very marked importance in connection with the highly centralized character of the French administrative system.[105] Centralization involves, of course, the relationship between national government and local government. In formal logic, no connection exists between this relationship and the relationship of executive and legislature in national government; but, in practice, the relationship between national government and local government cannot but be influenced by the nature of the national government. As a matter of fact, the potential strength of the national executive is magnified through centralization, involving, as it does, administrative control over the minutest affairs in all corners of France; so, as a result, the National Assembly, in its strength, is the more determined, by maintaining the executive in a subordinate position, to prevent it from reaping the advantage of its potential situation. The argument can be, and is, made that a substantial measure of decentralization, with genuine devolution of power from the national government, would so lessen the potential strength of the central executive as possibly to render the National Assembly willing to see the position of the executive reinforced in relation to the legislature. At least equally important would be the benefits that local life would experience. In this respect, a wide devolution of authority by the national government to existing localities, devolution to larger regions that might be created, or devolution on functional lines would merely carry out, as has been noted,[106] an injunction of the present Constitution; but such legislation would not, it must be clear, affect the principle of the ultimate legal authority of the National Assembly.

The French Union: Constitutional Basis. The Constitution of the Third Republic was silent with respect to the French Empire. As a matter of fact, reestablishment of a colonial empire was an accomplishment of the earlier years of the Third Republic. French legislation came to be applied to an area more than forty times as large as France proper.[107] The Constitution of the Fourth

---

104 Cf. Ch. VII, pp. 131–132, *infra.*
105 Cf. Ch. I, p. 36, *supra,* Ch. V, pp. 81–82, *supra,* and Ch. VIII, p. 137, *infra.*
106 Cf. Ch. V, *loc. cit., supra.*
107 The French colonial population, on the other hand, was at the same time only about one-seventh of the Metropolitan population.

Republic, on the other hand, contains within it, so to say, another constitution —a shorter, embryonic constitution of the French Union.[108]

The French Union: Territorial Units. The overseas parts of the French Union are classified as communities which form an integral ("assimilated") part of France and as those which are technically independent ("associated"). The assimilated parts may be subdivided into those which are organized into Departments [109] and those which are not; the associated communities consist either of protectorates ("associated states") [110] or of "associated territories," formerly held under mandate from the League of Nations and at present under trusteeship on behalf of the United Nations. All the assimilated areas, which are represented in Parliament, possess, through French legislation, representative assemblies of their own and administrations headed by representatives of the French central Government. Each of the associated states has, according to the Constitution,[111] a status "resulting from the act which defines its relations with France."

The French Union: Governmental Agencies. The central organs of the French Union are the President of the French Union, who is merely the President of the Republic, a High Council of the French Union, which is subordinate to and advisory to the French Cabinet, and an Assembly of the French Union. The Assembly is at present composed of 240 members, of which half, representing Metropolitan France, are chosen by Parliament (two-thirds by the National Assembly and one-third by the Council of the Republic) and half, representing non-Metropolitan France, are chosen in overseas communities (forty-five by associated states, seventy-five by others). The members possess a status which is in general the same as that of members of Parliament. The Assembly itself is a purely consultative body. Though its advice must be sought in certain matters, this is not true in others; and in no instance is its opinion binding, even to the extent, as in the case of the Council of the Republic, of requiring reconsideration.[112]

The French Union and Parliament. In the matter of the relationship of the National Assembly to French overseas areas, as in its relationship to the local communities that constitute Metropolitan France, less practical importance attaches to the legal principle that the National Assembly may pass any legislation it sees fit than to the concrete question of what legislation it sees fit to pass. As a matter of fact, a large, and from the nature of the case an exceedingly complex, body of legislation is in existence. In general, Acts of Parliament are applicable overseas if they are concerned with criminal regulations, with public liberties, and with political and administrative organization. In other matters, Acts are directly applicable only if they expressly so stipulate. The President of the Republic, that is to say, the Cabinet, possesses authority

[108] Cf. Ch. v, p. 82, *supra.*

[109] I.e., Algeria, Guadeloupe, Guyane, Martinique, and Réunion. The remaining "assimilated" parts—"overseas territories"—constitute a long list.

[110] I.e., Tunisia, Morocco, and Indo-China (where the situation is somewhat uncertain).

[111] Art. 61.

[112] However, unlike the Council of the Republic, it may discuss proposals initiated by itself before transmitting them to the National Assembly. Cf. this Ch., p. 90, n. 13, *supra.*

to extend Acts of Parliament to overseas areas; and, in some instances, he can directly formulate provisions applicable to them. In both instances, the advice of the Assembly of the Union must be asked.

THE FRENCH CONCEPT OF LEGISLATION

The National Assembly and Subordinate Law-Making. The employment in France through administrative orders of a large measure of what is substantially law-making authority is a matter of the highest importance and interest for students of government. This exercise of executive authority is, it must be clear from established principle, completely subject to the legal power of Parliament; and yet its consequence in practice for the actual exercise of legislative authority is very great. French statutes (*lois*), that is, Acts of Parliament, have for a long time been contrasted by students of government with statutes in England and the United States, in the matter of the terms in which they are expressed. In France, the regular practice, it has been asserted, has been for statutes to state only the fundamental principles of law and, therefore, to be couched in general language. In contrast, English and American statutes have been regarded as attempting to regulate in great detail the matters with which they deal. In recent years, however, special students of these matters have testified to a tendency for the two contrasted practices to approach each other. Thus, a somewhat pronounced tendency in the direction of French practice has been developing in England and in the United States; whereas the complaint is being formulated in France that statutes are entering into too much detail. Nevertheless, in all cases, details are often omitted and left to be filled in; and in the event administrative orders are employed. In France, the criticism leaves the impression of being in considerable measure a counsel of perfection. On the whole, the situation in that country is met in realistic fashion. The legislature normally confines itself in the realm of legislation to what it is competent to do—that is, it approves or disapproves general principles in the popular interest. It refrains on the whole from concerning itself with details with which it is not really qualified to deal and which in practice are likely, in any event, to need modification and adaptation that legislatures are too deliberate easily to effect. This does not mean, it should be stressed, that a single agent or agency makes rules, executes them, and settles controversies that may arise in the course of their execution. On the contrary, the doctrine of the separation of powers is applied at a level at which it affords real protection to the individual. The association of consultative and advisory bodies with the executive,[113] taken together with ministerial responsibility, affords substantial protection; and the separation of active administrators and the administrative courts is a highly effective guarantee for the individual.[114]

Decree-Laws. In principle, executive orders may not, of course, violate the law. Thus, an executive decree is valid only within the limits set by provisions of the statute which the decree is issued to execute. However, if, as happens in

[113] Cf. Ch. VIII, pp. 140–141, *infra.*
[114] Cf. Ch. IX, pp. 156–157, *infra.*

exceptional cases, the provisions of the statute, instead of establishing principles of law with respect to the solution of a given problem, merely authorizes the executive to deal with a general situation, including power to alter existing statutes—then, the character of the decree power becomes, though exact distinctions are difficult if not impossible, substantially a different affair. This is roughly the case in France with respect to the striking phenomenon known as "Decree-Laws." Parliament in effect turns over to the executive the task of dealing with a critical general situation and delegates the legal power to solve it. There were some striking examples of such delegation during the period between the two Wars. All these cases, it was frequently asserted, were a kind of admission of the inability of Parliament to cope with an acute situation. They marked, on this view, a substantial decrease in the prestige of political democracy. The grant of authority, it is true, was made only for a limited time, and a period was fixed within which Parliament had to ratify the Decree-Laws. Even so, the critics insisted that each time that Parliament, through expiration of the period of delegation, reassumed its normal position, it was weaker than before, and that parliamentary government itself was thereby seriously threatened. Such criticism was sufficiently influential to cause the framers of the Constitution of the Fourth Republic to attempt to destroy the practice of Decree-Laws. To this end the following provision was introduced into the Constitution:

Art. 13.—The National Assembly alone shall vote law. It may not delegate that right.

Concerning the whole subject, which is certainly complex and difficult, there was during the period of constitution-making, and there has been since, a large amount of elaborate and hair-splitting, but somewhat unequal, discussion. More particularly, legislation in 1948 granting broad powers to the executive gave rise to vigorous controversy inside and outside Parliament. On the view that the constitutional stipulation was specifically intended to prohibit Decree-Laws as they had been known in France during the period between the two Wars and that at least some of the articles of the 1948 legislation were indistinguishable from those of such Decree-Laws, the conclusion is difficult to avoid that Parliament in fact passed some unconstitutional provisions. However, the matter was not brought before the Constitutional Committee.[115] Those commentators appear plausible, or at least their views deserve pondering, who hold that in modern conditions delegation of law-making authority to the executive is inevitable and that therefore the wise approach to the problem is not prohibition but careful regulation.

[115] Cf. Ch. v, pp. 86–87, *supra.*

CHAPTER VII

THE EXECUTIVE BRANCH OF GOVERNMENT

1. THE FORMAL EXECUTIVE

PRESIDENT OF THE REPUBLIC: OFFICE AND OCCUPANT

Third Republic Background. Under the Third Republic, the position of President of the Republic was in general developed according to the classic pattern of the head of State in the parliamentary regime. This position was therefore essentially that of a constitutional monarch under parliamentary government. Perhaps the position was, as suggested by a distinguished President of France, not fully understood by most Frenchmen. Certainly sporadic suggestions that the office be strengthened or that it be abolished did not seem to proceed from great understanding of the real character of the parliamentary system. In reality, the body of the people accepted and approved, rationally or instinctively, the Presidency as it existed.

Constitutional Issue. With the coming of the Fourth Republic, the matter of the position of the President of the Republic, though manifestly in essence a formal question, was from the beginning elevated into a constitutional issue between Left and Right.[1] In the First National Constituent Assembly, the Socialists and Communists, invoking the views of Clemenceau, declared themselves opposed to establishment of the office. This seems scarcely a very logical way to advance the cause of assembly government; but perhaps abolition of the office would have been symbolic, and it was doubtless consistent with the irrational opposition to the Third Republic as responsible for French military defeat. However that may be, the Socialists and Communists, in accepting the President of the Republic later during the First National Constituent Assembly, were not very convincing when they insisted that this acceptance was evidence of their willingness to compromise in order to meet the constitutional views of their opponents. The Right, on the other hand, would not seem to have been on very firm ground in choosing the position of the formal head of State as an issue on which to oppose assembly government. A number of members who favored

---

[1] Cf. Ch. IV, p. 73, *supra.*

a stronger executive, though it is impossible to estimate how many, held the confused view that under a parliamentary system the executive will be strengthened if a certain amount of real power is vested in the head of State. Though it is perfectly true that parliamentary government can exist in principle without a formal head of State, the presence of the classic type of this position, certainly as it existed under the Third Republic, is scarcely connected one way or the other with the actual strength of the executive. The position in its classic form is itself a compromise of a basic historical problem; so that the compromise of the Fourth Republic which came out of the two National Constituent Assemblies is largely lacking in logic and symmetry.

Constitutional Solution. The constitutional provisions dealing with the office of President of the Republic, as distinguished from the powers of the position, are relatively brief and simple. The wording of the principal ones is as follows:

Art. 29.—The President of the Republic shall be elected by Parliament.
He shall be elected for seven years. He shall be re-eligible only once.
Art. 39.—Thirty days at the most, and two weeks at the least, before the expiration of the powers of the President of the Republic, Parliament shall proceed to the election of the new President.
Art. 43.—The position of President of the Republic shall be incompatible with any other public function.
Art. 44.—Members of families having reigned over France shall be ineligible to the Presidency of the Republic.

Election in Practice. The President of the Republic is, as under the Third Republic, chosen by the two houses sitting together.[2] More detailed constitutional provisions deal with possible vacancies and similar matters. In the event of premature end of a Presidential term, a new full term of seven years begins for the next incumbent. There are no "unexpired terms." The first election under the Fourth Republic was uneventful. The voting was secret. M. Vincent Auriol was chosen on the first ballot. Manifestly, rapid agreement on a man helps to give the President of the Republic the imposing position he ought in principle to have.

Republican Dignity. Dignity is given to the position of President of the Republic through certain external trappings. The Elysée Palace in Paris, principal residence of the President of the Republic, is not unworthy of a head of State. Moreover, the President has at his disposal several other residences, of which the best known is the château at Rambouillet, famous for Presidential rabbit-shooting parties. Associated with the Presidency are a Civil and Military Household, direct descendant of two royal institutions. The several members of the Household dispatch such business as devolves upon the President. They examine reports, study proposals, prepare documents, offer advice, and in other ways assist the head of State. The budget of the Presidency is 30,000,000 francs (*c*. $85,000.). Of this by no means imposing sum, the actual salary of the President amounts to only one-tenth.

[2] The meeting is, according to statutory provision, held at Versailles.

PRESIDENT OF THE REPUBLIC: POWERS

From Third to Fourth Republic. Neither the provisions of the Constitution of April 19, 1946, nor those of the prevailing Constitution follow the Constitution of the Third Republic and numerous other European constitutions constructed on the parliamentary model, which, it should be recalled, vest in the head of State all powers commonly regarded as executive in character, with the assurance that they will be exercised only by responsible Ministers. In other words, there is not at present the same clear-cut distinction between the *possession* of power and the *exercise* of power. Thus, the President of the Fourth Republic is not even theoretically vested with the duty of law-enforcement, the direction of military affairs, the initiation of legislation, or the general power of appointment and removal. As a whole, these are powers specifically granted to the Prime Minister.[3] In this respect, the striking argument of the Committee on the Constitution in the Second National Constituent Assembly was that departure from tradition was necessitated by establishment in the Constitution of the position of Prime Minister. The Constitution of the Third Republic, silent with respect to this office, was asserted to be no guide in the matter. Contentions in favor of the more logical arrangement in the Constitution of 1875 were brushed aside with the assertion that "something new and reasonable" was required.

Prevailing Powers. The powers possessed by the President of the Republic are largely formal in character. On the other hand, the distinction between formal and real power is considerably obscured by the constitutional stipulations,[4] basically the same as analogous provisions of the Constitution of the Third Republic, that the President shall be responsible only in case of high treason and that all of his acts shall require counter-signature by the Prime Minister and another Minister. In any case, the list of powers mentioned in the Constitution constitute in appearance a somewhat formidable list. Thus, the President is *ex officio* President of the French Union. He in principle chooses the Prime Minister. He presides over the Council of Ministers, of whose minutes he has charge; and in Council he appoints a number of categories of officials. He likewise presides over the High Magisterial Council, in which he exercises the power of pardon, over the Committee on the Constitution, and over two important defence councils. He is kept informed of international negotiations, and signs and ratifies treaties. He accredits to foreign powers ambassadors and the like; and corresponding officials are accredited to him. He promulgates the laws; he may communicate by message with Parliament; and he may request reconsideration of Acts of Parliament.[5]

Present Position. The present position of the President of France is on the whole not very different from what it was under the Third Republic. As in the earlier period, the personality of the incumbent is a matter of considerable mo-

[3] Cf. this Ch., *infra.*
[4] Art. 42; Art. 38.
[5] This power was never exercised under the Third Republic. It has been employed several times by M. Auriol.

ment. The first holder of the office under the Fourth Republic, M. Vincent Auriol, has put his stamp upon the position; and he has set a high standard. The very fact of depriving the President of even the theoretical possession of certain powers has to some extent, though it is difficult if not impossible to say how much, tended to establish the implication that the President is not without personal decision with respect to the powers actually vested in him. However that may be, there has on the whole been confirmation of the generally held view during the Second National Constituent Assembly that the "moral authority" of the position can be so great as to render the matter of powers of little importance. The tradition of Republican simplicity will always prevent the position from being as highly ceremonial as the similar position under monarchy; but the President of the Republic personifies acceptably the French nation, he exerts a legitimate and useful influence from a position above the conflict of partisan interests, and he is an element in the parliamentary system which, if not in theory absolutely essential, is, in the conditions that have come to exist in France, practically indispensable.

2. THE REAL EXECUTIVE

THE PRIME MINISTER

Policy Forming under Parliamentary Government. The student of political science cannot too often recall that in the European context democratic government is parliamentary government. Hence, there is in France application of the simple but important principle that the policy-forming executive consists of a first and other responsible Ministers. They have in practice both an individual and a collective existence.

Head of Government. Among the Ministers, first consideration naturally belongs to the first, or Prime, Minister. He has for long been known in France as the head of Government, in contradistinction with the head of State. He is officially known as the President of the Council of Ministers. The office existed in law as early as 1815; it existed in fact at the time the Constitution of the Third Republic was formulated; and, though it was not expressly mentioned in that Constitution, it became well established in law and practice during that regime. The position tended during this period to increase in importance. Hence, the framers of the Constitution of the Fourth Republic, having determined to give the office full constitutional status, were able to draw on abundant experience.

Selection: Constitutional Provisions. The French Prime Minister, in accordance with the principles of parliamentary government, may be defined as an individual who may expect the support of a parliamentary majority. In the operation of the system in its classic form, the head of State is of course assumed to be able normally to identify such an individual. However, the Left in the First National Constituent Assembly declared itself unalterably opposed to appointment by the President of the Republic; and, according to the terms of the Constitution of April 19,[6] the head of Government was to be chosen by the National Assembly itself from among names submitted to it, after the usual consultations, by the President of the Republic. The prevailing Constitution contains the following somewhat elaborate provisions:

Art. 45.—At the beginning of each legislature, the President of the Republic, after the usual consultations, shall designate the President of the Council.

The latter shall submit to the National Assembly the program and the policy of the Cabinet he proposes to form.

The President of the Council and the Ministers may be appointed only after the President of the Council shall have been invested with the confidence of the Assembly . . .

It shall be the same in the course of the legislature if there should be a vacancy . . .[7]

Art. 46.—The President of the Council and the Ministers chosen by him shall be appointed by decree of the President of the Republic.

Selection: Practice. The striking thing about the complex constitutional procedure for choice of the head of Government is the extra step involved in the requirement that the Prime Minister present himself alone [8] to the National Assembly before naming his Ministers. This was bitterly criticized by M. Herriot in a series of interventions in debate in the Second National Constituent Assembly; but he was not able to move the Committee on the Constitution or the Assembly. In practice, the criticism has been largely borne out; and criticism has continued. It has not been unknown for the National Assembly to approve the program and policy of a designated Prime Minister, only a day or two later, on the occasion of the interpellation [9] which regularly takes place in the matter, to refuse to accept the composition of the Cabinet. The situation is almost certain to be simplified by formal amendment of the Constitution in the early future.[10]

Selection: Political Considerations. In the regular operation of parliamentary government in France, the majority, it will be recalled, is always composed of a coalition of political groups, the Prime Minister being at most the actual leader of only one group. The existence of numerous groups brings it about that a majority can in theory be one of many combinations; and sometimes several combinations are possible in practice. On the other hand, during a large part of the life of the Fourth Republic, the irreconcilable opposition of the Communists and of certain extreme elements of the Right—especially the RPF—has given rise to a majority of the Third Force,[11] which in simple terms of arithmetic is so limited that extensive maneuvering is precluded. Neverthe-

---

[6] Art. 73.

[7] Exception is made for the case of dissolution. Cf. this Ch., pp. 133–135, *infra.*

[8] In 1950, M. Pleven compared with the plight of St. Sebastian his position on the Ministers' bench unattended by Ministers. In connection with his attempt—subsequently successful—to solve the long ministerial crisis following the elections in June of 1951, M. Pleven was in a striking cartoon shown thinly clad and lightly armed entering the Assembly, depicted as a Roman arena, with parties of the Third Force represented as raging lions and with the bones of his unsuccessful predecessors strewn about under foot.

[9] Cf. Ch. vi, pp. 114–115, *supra.*

[10] The amendment procedure, put in motion in 1950, was expected to be completed in the course of a year or two, in view of acceptance of the change by practically all Deputies except the Communists.

[11] Cf. Ch. xii, p. 191, *infra.*

less, more than one group leader, even from one group, may well be capable of forming a majority combination. Hence, the President of the Republic has no little freedom of choice. In practice, the President must, it is true, be guided by the various elements of the existing situation. Moreover, there are a few rules of the game. Now and then, these rules point unmistakably to the logical choice. Even in such a case, however, the President of the Republic goes through a certain routine of consultations. Indeed, this practice, which became well established during the Third Republic, is, it will be recalled, expressly stipulated in the Constitution of the Fourth Republic. Such consultations are naturally more important when more uncertainty exists. The President regularly requests and receives calls from the President of the National Assembly, the President of the Council of the Republic, the presidents of various political groups, and so on.[12] Finally, on the basis of his consultations and of his analysis of the situation, the President of the Republic arrives at a decision, and invites the man on whom his choice has fallen to become Prime Minister. The person invited usually asks a short time for consideration, which means that he wishes to consult various individuals, particularly leaders of parliamentary groups, with a view to determining whether he can effect a combination that can command support by a majority in the National Assembly. Sometimes he is so discouraged as to decline; more often, he accepts. Then, in constitutional terminology, he is "designated" by the President, after which he seeks "investiture" by the Assembly.

THE MINISTERS

Choice. Under the Third Republic, the President of the Republic was conceived to possess the legal power to appoint both the Prime Minister and the other Ministers by virtue of the constitutional stipulation authorizing him to "appoint all civil and military officers." However, in practice, the President of the Republic appointed the Prime Minister within the limits of discretion determined by the political situation; and the Prime Minister appointed the other Ministers. Under the Fourth Republic, legal theory and actual practice have been brought much closer together. The President of the Republic no longer possesses even the theoretical power to appoint the Ministers other than the Prime Minister. With the exceptions already noted, not only has the general power to "appoint all civil and military officers" been transferred to the President of the Council; the specific power to appoint Ministers is clearly implied in the provisions dealing with the "investiture" of the Prime Minister where mention is made of "the Cabinet he proposes to form."

Creation of Ministries. The French Prime Minister is not limited by law in respect of the number of Ministers and other important political executives he may desire to appoint. In 1920, an Act of Parliament stipulated that Ministries and similar agencies should "be determined only by statute" already

---

[12] In 1950, President Auriol caused a certain amount of comment by assuming the responsibility of delegating to a Socialist leader, M. Guy Mollet, the unusual task of trying to bring together the groups of a majority, to support M. Pleven as Prime Minister.

passed; but this Act was observed frequently in the breach. The principle involved was regarded as being contrary to French tradition; and this tradition was re-established at the outset of the Fourth Republic. France, in common with most Continental European countries, operates on the principle that the executive ought to determine executive structure and distribution of functions.[13] Under parliamentary government, this means that the head of Government shall have the determination. Such determination is, legally speaking, effected in large measure by executive decree, Acts of Parliament being, generally speaking, not required. The theory is that the representatives of the people have, after all, the last word; for they must vote the money necessary for any ministerial organization to exist.

Heads of Departments. The typical Minister is, of course, head of a great Executive Department, or Ministry.[14] As such, he is a Minister "with portfolio." Under the Third Republic, the Prime Minister also usually served as head of a Department. However, in some half dozen cases during that period, the Prime Minister assumed the position of President of the Council without portfolio, the position being thus assimilated to that of the English Prime Minister, free to devote his whole efforts to leadership of the political executive. Indeed, towards the end of the Third Republic, the position of Presidency of the Council was organized by law; and, in 1934, the Hôtel Matignon, former embassy of Austria-Hungary, was acquired as an official residence for the President of the Council and his staff. Under the Fourth Republic, the later development has been regularly followed, only one or two Prime Ministers having exceptionally undertaken to add the burdens of a headship of a Department. Under the Third Republic, there were on a few occasions other Ministers without portfolio; and the same exceptional practice has been followed under the Fourth Republic, the expression "Minister of State" usually being employed. Sometimes such Ministers are charged with a special duty; but in any case their reason for being is fundamentally political, posts being given in this way to certain party figures.

Ministerial Titles. Since the beginning of the Fourth Republic, the smallest number of Ministers that has existed at a given time is twelve, the largest twenty-five. The list of Ministers drawn up by M. Pleven in August of 1951 is as follows:

President of the Council of Ministers
Vice-President of the Council of Ministers, Minister of National Defence
Vice-President of the Council of Ministers, Minister of Finance and Economic Affairs
2 Ministers of State
Deputy Minister of National Defence
Minister of the Budget
Minister of Justice
Minister of Foreign Affairs
Minister of the Interior

[13] The pertinence of this situation for administrative reorganization is manifest. Cf. Ch. VIII, p. 140, *infra.*
[14] Cf. *ibid.*, p. 136, *infra.*

Minister of National Education
Minister of Public Works, Transportation, and Tourist Business
Minister of Industrial Production and Power
Minister of Commerce and Foreign Economic Affairs
Minister of Agriculture
Minister of Overseas France
Minister of Labor and Social Security
Minister of Reconstruction and Town Planning
Minister of Ex-Service Men and War Victims
Minister of Public Health and Population
Minister of Post Offices, Telegraphs, and Telephones
Minister of the Merchant Marine
Minister of Information
Minister of State for the Associated States

LESSER POLICY–FORMING EXECUTIVES

Secretaries and Under-Secretaries of State. Under the Third Republic, the principal political executive officers on the plane next below that of the Ministers were Under-Secretaries of State, a title borrowed from the *ancien régime*. Under the Fourth Republic, Under-Secretaries have been used to a considerable extent; but the employment of Secretaries of State [15] has persistently increased. The numbers have varied within somewhat wide limits. Only the first Prime Minister after the establishment of the Constitution has managed to get on without either. One Prime Minister in 1948 employed nine Secretaries and no Under-Secretaries. The largest combination was contained in a Ministry formed in 1949, which included nine Secretaries and seven Under-Secretaries. The last four Prime Ministers increased the number of Secretaries to about a dozen, but dropped Under-Secretaries altogether. The primary consideration which weighs with the Prime Minister in the matter is political in character. He finds the employment of Secretaries and Under-Secretaries a valuable means of strengthening his position with the political groups. On the other hand, the objective may on occasion be that of placing a capable civil servant in a position of directorship. What may be regarded as a typical Secretary or Under-Secretary is one who is an assistant to the Minister, his title including, as does normally the Minister's, the name of the Ministry. He is a subordinate who relieves the Minister of a certain part of his duties. However, not only do Ministries exist without any such assistant; at times the Secretary or Under-Secretary has a position that involves direction of an important governmental service that is practically autonomous. The list of Secretaries of State drawn up by M. Pleven in August of 1951 is as follows:

Secretary of State: 2 for the Presidency of the Council; for the Armed Forces (War); for the Armed Forces (Navy); for the Armed Forces (Air); for Foreign Affairs; for Finance and Economic Affairs; for Commerce; for Agriculture; for the Interior; for Fine Arts; for Technical Education, Youth, and Sports; for Public Works, Transportation, and Tourist Business.

Ministerial Cabinets. The members of what is known as the Cabinet of a particular Minister ought to be listed among the agents who compose the po-

[15] This title, likewise from the *ancien régime,* was re-established by Vichy.

litical executive.[16] They are chosen freely by the Minister, and they possess his personal confidence.[17]

MINISTERS COLLECTIVELY

Two Organs. French Ministers in their collective capacity form either (1) the Council of Ministers or (2) the Cabinet Council.

Distinction. The difference between the two collective meetings of Ministers is expressed in French practice in several ways. A simple formal distinction consists of the fact that the President of the Republic is present at a meeting of the Council of Ministers but not present at a meeting of the Cabinet Council. However, although the present Constitution stipulates that the President of the Republic shall preside over meetings of the Council of Ministers, for which he has the duty to "take and keep minutes," [18] he is not a member of the Council, in the sense that he has no vote. All the Ministers are members of both Councils. Otherwise, composition is not precisely fixed. The tendency seems to be for Secretaries and Under-Secretaries to be present at Cabinet Councils, but to attend Councils of Ministers only when matters pertaining to their agency are to be discussed. A further expression of the fact that the Council of Ministers is a more formal body than the Cabinet Council is the saying that in the Council of Ministers there is no smoking but that in the Cabinet Council there is. Probably the most fundamental distinction is that the Council of Ministers collectively performs legal functions, its formal decisions having the force of law, whereas the Cabinet Council, though the Cabinet is mentioned in the Constitution, performs no legal functions, being essentially an extra-legal and political body. The Constitution in several places speaks of certain actions that require decision "in Council of Ministers"; and Acts of Parliament frequently employ the same expedient. Where conditions are such that it seems desirable for the Ministers as a whole, rather than a single Minister, to direct the carrying out of provisions of law, an Act of Parliament stipulates that the decisions shall be made "in Council." These decisions are formulated as decrees of the President of the Council,[19] required by the Constitution, as are his other acts, to be countersigned by one or more Ministers. In the more informal meetings of the Cab-

[16] In French studies this institution, establishing a link between Minister and the *bureaus,* is regularly considered in connection with the French civil servants and their departmental organization. It does normally contain a certain number of civil servants. Nevertheless, its members are in actuality members of the political executive. More specifically, they retire with the Minister, when there is a change of Government.

[17] The composition of such a Cabinet may be illustrated by an example. Thus, the Cabinet of the Minister of the Interior, formed in July of 1950, was as follows: one Cabinet Director (Master of Petitions, Council of State; Director of Personnel and of Political Affairs, Ministry of Interior); one Assistant Director (Honorary Paymaster General, Treasury); three Assistant Heads ([1] Administrator, Exchange Office; [2] Sub-Perfect; [3] Civil Administrator, Ministry of Interior); three Attachés (two for National Assembly; one for Council of the Republic); one technical Adviser (Councillor of State); two Special Agents ([1] Sub-Prefect unattached; [2] without titles).

[18] French authorities under the Third Republic were in some uncertainty as to whether the President of the Republic presided. The best view seems to be that he did not.

[19] This power, which is deduced from power faithfully to execute the laws, was vested in the President of the Republic under the Third Republic. The two solutions are for practical purposes the same.

inet Council, discussion and decisions are political in character.[20] Conditions in such meetings are more propitious for political action, though there seems to be no reason why such discussion and decision should not likewise take place on occasion in the Council of Ministers.[21]

MINISTERIAL RESPONSIBILITY

Ministers in Parliament. The close relationship between legislature and executive that is characteristic of the parliamentary system and the nice equilibrium between the law-making and law-enforcing authorities that is the ideal of the system are in practice effected through the existence of the Cabinet. A simple but important manifestation of this is the fact that members of the Cabinet are in practice regularly members of Parliament. In France, the Prime Minister may in theory form his Cabinet by including anyone he likes as a Minister, law stipulating no special requirements; but, in practice, the conditions in which parliamentary government operates favor strongly members of Parliament. In principle, the Ministers are leaders of a parliamentary majority. As leaders, they in greater or lesser degree direct the principal activities of the two houses. They present and support their views and proposals; and they defend their actions. In accordance with this aspect of parliamentary government, the present Constitution in France includes the following stipulations:

Art. 53.—The Ministers shall have entrance into the two Chambers and into their Committees. They must be heard when they request it.[22]

They may be assisted in discussions before the Chambers by commissioners who shall be designated by decree.

The second paragraph means that Ministers may be accompanied in the houses by civil servants,[23] who may even take part in debate.

Ministerial Control by Parliament. The two converse principles of parliamentary government, leadership in Parliament by the Ministers and control by Parliament over the Ministers, define fundamentally *ministerial responsibility* in the special form that it assumes under the parliamentary system. As is well known, the sanction for ministerial responsibility under the parliamentary system is political in character. It takes the form of *resignation*.[24] In France, legal responsibility with legal sanction was demanded in the period before the Revolution; and it was established at the time of the Revolution. Out of this

[20] Nothing of course prevents real decisions from being taken in the Cabinet with respect to matters requiring legal action. In this case, formal confirmation in the Council of Ministers will be taken.

[21] The peculiar regard which is felt for President Auriol has, it is interesting to note, apparently caused Cabinet Councils to be relatively infrequent.

[22] The same situation existed under the Constitution of the Third Republic (though Committees were not mentioned). Similar provisions are to be found in almost countless French and other European constitutions of the nineteenth and twentieth centuries. The English practice, regarded as so important in the development of parliamentary government, has clearly been improved on.

[23] This is also a more convenient practice than that employed in England, where the civil servants must be close at hand but cannot be technically on the floor of the House. In France, as many as twenty or more functionaries (though such number is exceptional) may be named by decree for an important debate. They sit just behind the Ministers' bench.

[24] Fundamentally this is true whether or not dissolution is employed.

responsibility, political responsibility with its political sanction grew gradually and to a large extent imperceptibly. This growth was naturally reflected only imperfectly in the terms of written constitutional documents. Thus, under Charters of the Restoration and the Monarchy of July, the stipulation that "the Ministers shall be responsible" left open the questions what kind of responsibility was intended and to whom the responsibility was. The Constitution of the Third Republic, in stipulating that the responsibility was "to the Chambers," went a step further; but theoretically a non-parliamentary relationship between legislature and executive might, without violation of the letter of the law, have developed. Nevertheless, circumstances, more important than the law at least in this connection, ensured that parliamentary government should be established and developed. Resignation had been frequently practised in France before the time of the Third Republic, especially in the period from 1815 to 1848; and examples actually occurred during the life of the National Assembly that framed the Constitution of the Third Republic. What was well understood was not unnaturally omitted from the incomplete document which the Constitution of the Third Republic was. The framers of the Constitution of the Fourth Republic, on the other hand, went further and undertook to give a complete account of ministerial responsibility and its operation. The pertinent provisions are phrased as follows:

Art. 48.—The Ministers shall be collectively responsible to the National Assembly for the general policy of the Cabinet and individually for their personal acts.

They shall not be responsible to the Council of the Republic.

Art. 49.—The question of confidence may not be put except after discussion in the Council of Ministers, and except by the President of the Council.

Voting on the question of confidence may not intervene except one full day after it has been put in the Assembly. It shall take place by recorded vote.

Confidence in the Cabinet may not be refused except by a majority of the Deputies of the Assembly. Such refusal shall entail the collective resignation of the Cabinet.

Art. 50.—Voting by the National Assembly of a motion of censure shall entail the collective resignation of the Cabinet.

Such vote may not intervene except one full day after introduction of the motion. It shall take place by recorded vote.

A motion of censure may not be adopted except by a majority of the Deputies of the Assembly.

MINISTERIAL INSTABILITY

Short-lived Governments. The provisions of the prevailing Constitution that deal with votes of confidence and of censure indicate the concern which was felt in post-War France for "ministerial stability." These provisions were matched by almost identically worded stipulations in the Constitution of April 19; and both, interestingly enough, bear a fairly close resemblance to the provisions of the Act of November 2.[25] All were aimed at remedying the well-known experience of the Third Republic.[26] During that regime, the average life of Cabinets did not greatly exceed six months. Some lasted literally only one

[25] Cf. Ch. IV, p. 68, *supra.*
[26] Cf. Ch. XI, p. 184, *infra.*

day; others had a life of only a few weeks. Long Ministries were definitely exceptional.

Prevailing Situation. The President of the Committee on the Constitution in the Second National Constituent Assembly, M. André Philip, did not hesitate to assert in debate that the old form of ministerial instability would be "completely eliminated from now on." Unfortunately, the facts of the Fourth Republic have not borne out this optimism. Since the establishment of the present Constitution, there have been some twelve Cabinets.[27] Interestingly enough, the constitutional provisions have in a sense worked as was anticipated. The question of confidence has been put a large number of times, and on every occasion but one the Cabinet has been upheld. A motion of censure has been employed only once, when the Cabinet was also successful. In other words, resignations have taken place in the great majority of cases as the result of less formal manifestations of Cabinet weakness. Thus, the arguments advanced against the withdrawal of General de Gaulle have not prevailed.[28] As in his case, some Prime Ministers have, together with their Cabinets, withdrawn without basing their action on any specific hostile vote of the National Assembly. Others have taken such votes as the occasion for resignation, without putting a formal question of confidence.

Multiparty Majorities. M. André Philip's hopeful assertion about the elimination of ministerial instability was undoubtedly based not so much on the new procedures with respect to confidence and censure as on the assumption that the majority in the National Assembly would regularly consist of a few large, well-disciplined parties. This was, in turn, connected with the much discussed electoral law and the variant of proportional representation established by it.[29] The assumption, it must be confessed, seemed for a time to be borne out when cooperation among the "monolithic" parties resulted in "quasi-unanimity."[30] Even so, the Cabinets were for various reasons short-lived; and, since the exclusion of the Communists in May of 1947, the character of the majority has not been greatly different from typical coalitions under the Third Republic. On the other hand, as has been said, the considerable strength of the opposition, composed of extremes hostile to the regime itself, confines the majority, the Third Force, within such narrow bounds that basically only one combination is possible. In this respect, the picture of rapidly changing Cabinets is in considerable measure misleading.

Basic Stability. There can be no doubt but that much inconvenience attends the fall of a Cabinet. This is true even though the new majority may not be greatly different and the composition of the Cabinet may be to some extent the same. In such instance, however, it is worth underlining that no fundamental change in public opinion will have occurred. Indeed, in this basic

[27] The number would be increased by four if the count should begin with the coming into operation of the Act of November 2, 1945.

[28] Cf. Ch. IV, pp. 71–72, *supra.*

[29] Cf. Ch. VI, pp. 96–98, *supra.*

[30] Cf. Ch. IV, pp. 69–70, *supra.* Predictions in connection with the elections of June of 1951 that a "hexagonal" party structure would result have been largely borne out (cf. Ch. VI, pp. 102–103, n 63, *supra*).

sense, governmental stability is at least as great in France as elsewhere. If only ministerial changes should be reckoned that result from deep-running movements of opinion, the number since the beginning of the Third Republic would not appear inordinately large. In this context, the multi-party system can be and has been defended, justified, and advocated on fundamental grounds. The basic argument goes to the very nature of representative government by majority. By no means all questions, it would seem clear, can be solved satisfactorily by the simple expedient of a vote. Solution of a matter through majority decision is efficacious, experience suggests, only where the matter is of such a character that general agreement exists on the convenience of a decision. A solution which leaves a cohesive, determined, and unreconciled minority is no real solution. Although it is a matchless virtue of political democracy that a minority may freely become a majority, nevertheless relatively sudden swings in the matter of policy from one side to the opposite are likely to have unfortunate results. The argument is that the two-party system lends itself to these very disadvantages,[31] whereas under the multi-party system such swings are very unusual. The existence in connection with an important question of policy of a real, as distinguished from a transitory, majority means something more, the argument runs, than numerical superiority. It is an indication that varied views and interests have been reconciled and that genuine consensus has been realized. The fact that in France solution of fundamental questions must, when the system is at its best, await such a situation results in marked consistency in the development of policy. Such consistent development is a manifestation of what is sometimes called in France "conservatism in the highest and best sense of the word."

DISSOLUTION

Theory and Practice. No serious argument will maintain that the multi-party system approximates to perfection or that ministerial instability as it exists in France is desirable. Reasoned criticism in that country is frequent, and worth-while reform is often advocated. For example, a quasi-unanimity exists, especially among academic writers, with respect to the institution of dissolution. Indeed, nowhere can better academic accounts of the nature of the institution be found than in France. Its essentially democratic character, involving as it does consultation of the voters, is in principle recognized. Its regular employment, it is held, would result in a tendency for Cabinets and changes of popular attitude more nearly to coincide; and such a development would undoubtedly present conditions more favorable to improved leadership. At the same time, opposition from the Left to the institution is persistent, especially among persons in active political life.

Hostile Attitudes. French opposition to dissolution, perhaps the most important power of a parliamentary executive, is an interesting phenomenon. Fear of its abuse in practice is frequently voiced—often no doubt sincerely,

---

[31] It would not be difficult to find in English and American history examples of the unfortunate results of swings in the matter of policy from one side to the opposite.

sometimes probably "for demagogic purposes." The one precedent since the establishment of the Third Republic, namely, dissolution of the Chamber of Deputies by MacMahon in 1877, is invoked as a warning against possible employment of the power with a view to a *coup d'état.*[32] However, there exists perhaps a deeper reason. At bottom, a speaker in the Second National Constituent Assembly was probably not far wrong when he asserted that the majority could not accept dissolution in its classic form because it is "in manifest contradiction with the principles of Assembly Government." Rational justification of hostility is likely to display the mystical overtones of national sovereignty.[33] With this concept a fixed term for the *National* Assembly is felt to be more consistent. This body, viewed in terms of the Revolution as the "Nation Represented," ought on this score to have a life unaffected except by necessary periodic consultations of the nation.

Constitutional Arrangements. Whatever may be the explanation, possibility of dissolution of the National Assembly of the Fourth Republic is so hedged about as to bear little resemblance to the classic form of this institution. The present Constitution dropped a provision of the Constitution of April 19, 1946, whereby the National Assembly could dissolve itself by a two-thirds vote. Inasmuch as the same result can be accomplished by a simple statute reducing the term of the National Assembly,[34] this difference would seem to be of little moment. Otherwise, the provisions of the two Constitutions with respect to dissolution differ only in detail. The stipulations of the prevailing Constitution, which are of no little interest, come immediately after the articles dealing with votes of confidence and of censure, and are worded as follows:

Art. 51.—If, in the course of a given period of eighteen months, two ministerial crises shall take place in the conditions anticipated in Articles 49 and 50, dissolution of the National Assembly may be determined upon in the Council of Ministers, after consultation of the President of the Assembly. Dissolution shall be pronounced in conformity with this determination by decree of the President of the Republic.

The provisions of the foregoing paragraph shall be applicable only upon the expiration of the first eighteen months of the legislature.

Art. 52.—In the case of dissolution, the Cabinet, with the exception of the President of the Council and the Minister of the Interior, shall remain in office for the purpose of dispatching current business.

The President of the Republic shall name as President of the Council the President of the National Assembly. The latter shall nominate the new Minister of the Interior in agreement with the Secretariat of the National Assembly. He shall nominate as Ministers of State members of groups not represented in the Government.[35]

General elections shall take place at least twenty days, at most thirty days, after dissolution.

The National Assembly shall automatically convene on the third Thursday following its election.

[32] Cf. Ch. xi, p. 183, *infra.*
[33] Cf. Ch. v, p. 85, *supra.*
[34] Cf. Ch. vi, p. 93, *supra,* and Ch. xii, p. 209, *infra.*
[35] According to agreement in 1950 by the Third Force concerning formal amendment of the Constitution, this provision will be eliminated. The object is to avoid the necessity of including in the Cabinet temporarily, in the event of dissolution, Ministers from the extremist parties.

These provisions concerning dissolution are in considerable measure self-explanatory. Fear of abuse is manifest in almost every line. The classic concept is largely absent of an appeal to the people with a view to discovering whether the executive is correct in thinking that the legislature is no longer representative of the basic wishes of the voters. The spectre is clearly present of a dictator seeking in a plebiscite ostensible mandate for personal power. Methods of persuasion and of intimidation are anticipated which experience shows distort in practice expression of popular consent; and protection is established against the Minister of the Interior, head of a highly concentrated and centralized administrative machinery.

CHAPTER VIII

ADMINISTRATION: NATIONAL AND LOCAL

1. INTRODUCTORY

POLICY-FORMING AND ADMINISTRATION

Ministerial Direction. In French theory, the political executive gives direction to the governmental process. So far as the individual Ministers are concerned, this direction takes the form, in the case of most of the Ministers, of oversight of a Ministry, or executive department.

Political and Routine Executives. The structure of French Central Executive Departments, or Ministries, is, in general outline, uniform. In each, the policy-forming head, usually a Minister, has associated with him other political officials, relatively few in number. Thus, there may be, as has been noted,[1] a Secretary or Under-Secretary of State, or both; and there is regularly a Cabinet of the individual Minister, as well as of the Secretary or Under-Secretary, where they exist. All these political executives are sometimes referred to as the "executive proper," as distinguishd from the "administration proper." The latter is composed of the many times more numerous group of routine executives, the permanent civil servants. They are currently known in France as "functionaries." In each Department, they perform, in principle under direction by the political executive, the actual task of conducting the public services.

Minister and Civil Servant. The relationship between the Ministers and the functionaries is, as is often said, one of amateurs and experts. The Ministers are men of executive ability who are politically responsible for the decisions that are made. The functionaries furnish the technical knowledge, and dispatch the routine business. From the nature of the case, these government officials, especially those of top rank, may exercise substantial influence on the course of affairs.[2] Nearly all have, with persistence, various means of getting their way. This tends to be true in any country; in France, ministerial instability, together with the high degree of concentration and centralization, ren-

---

[1] Cf. Ch. VII, p. 128, *supra.*
[2] Cf. this Ch., p. 145, *infra.*

ders the tendency peculiarly pronounced. Striking accounts have been penned of conscientious Ministers who have started out with excellent intentions of giving personal attention to the business of the Ministry, only to find that lack of time and of experience, coupled with the large number of affairs demanding consideration, forced them in the end to sign without reading, and hence to be at the mercy of the functionaries. Though such a situation would seem to be in some degree inevitable, the Cabinet of the individual Minister exists precisely for the purpose of lessening the extent of such dependency. A competent Cabinet, composed of friends of the Minister who know his views and policies and who are worthy of his confidence, may do much to avoid the worst results of routine, formalism, and red tape. Even more important are the character and the personality of the Minister himself. These qualities will, according to one phrasing of the matter, enable the head of a great public service "to drive a stream of policy" through it. Men of worth may make, and have made, a genuine imprint on an executive department.

CENTRAL AND LOCAL ADMINISTRATION

The Problem of Centralization. The fact that no simple test exists by which centralized government can in itself be distinguished or differentiated from what is presumably its opposite, *decentralized* government, and the consequent manifest difficulty of definitions in the matter throw doubt not on the accuracy but on the simplicity of the dictum that the administrative structure of France is highly centralized.[3] If, as seems reasonable, the relationship of local government to general government may fairly be said in a given case to be on the whole or on the balance centralized or decentralized, France must certainly be classed as a centralized country.

Local Government as Administration. In France, the expression *local government* is, though not unknown, neither usual nor, on the whole, congenial. French studies employ more naturally the expression *local administration.*[4] The ties between national government and local government are so close that local government is viewed primarily as serving the purpose of supplementing national governmental activities. Aside from legislation, which is regarded as establishment of general principles of law by the representatives of the nation,[5] the practical business of government is viewed as consisting of administration—administration at a national level, at a regional level, and at other lesser local levels. The existence of several kinds of elective local councils is the basis, it is true, for several finely drawn French distinctions;[6] but, nevertheless, local governmental activities are, in general, regarded as being administrative in character.

---

[3] Cf. Ch. I, p. 36, *supra,* and this Ch., pp. 151–154, *infra.*

[4] It may be recalled that even where a relatively decentralized relationship exists, such as in England and in the States of the American Union, local government is not infrequently spoken of as administration, when the emphasis is less on local activity as a manifestation of autonomy on the part of a local community than on the relationship of local government to the general community.

[5] Cf. Ch. v, p. 85, *supra.*

[6] Cf. this Ch., pp. 151–152, *infra.*

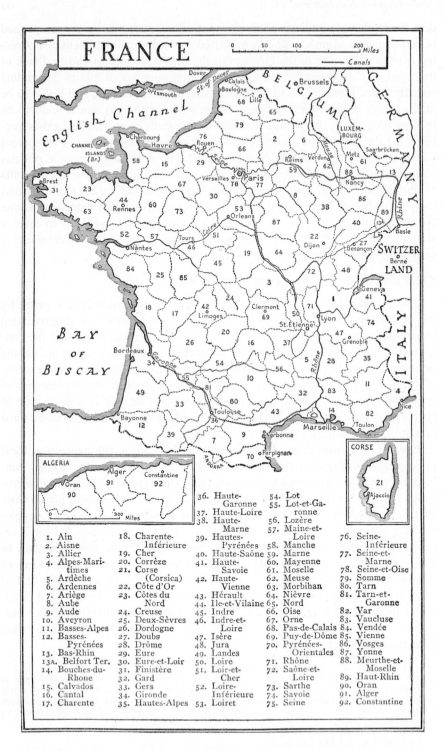

FRANCE

0   50   100   200 Miles
Canals

BELGIUM
GERMANY
LUXEMBOURG
SWITZERLAND
ITALY

English Channel
BAY OF BISCAY

CHANNEL ISLANDS (Br.)

Dover
St. of Dover
Portsmouth
Calais
Boulogne
Brussels
Lille
Cherbourg
Havre
Rouen
Reims
Verdun
Metz
Saarbrücken
Nancy
Versailles
Paris
Orleans
Rennes
Nantes
Tours
Brest
Bordeaux
Bayonne
Toulouse
Narbonne
Perpignan
Dijon
Besançon
Berné
Geneva
Lyon
St. Étienne
Grenoble
Nice
Toulon
Marseille
Limoges
Clermont
Basle
ANDORRA

ALGERIA
Oran 90
Alger 91
Constantine 92
300 Miles

CORSE
Ajaccio
21

1. Ain	18. Charente-	36. Haute-
2. Aisne	Inférieure	Garonne
3. Allier	19. Cher	37. Haute-Loire
4. Alpes-Mari-	20. Corrèze	38. Haute-
times	21. Corse	Marne
5. Ardèche	(Corsica)	39. Hautes-
6. Ardennes	22. Côte d'Or	Pyrénées
7. Ariège	23. Côtes du	40. Haute-Saône
8. Aube	Nord	41. Haute-
9. Aude	24. Creuse	Savoie
10. Aveyron	25. Deux-Sèvres	42. Haute-
11. Basses-Alpes	26. Dordogne	Vienne
12. Basses-	27. Doubs	43. Hérault
Pyrénées	28. Drôme	44. Ile-et-Vilaine
13. Bas-Rhin	29. Eure	45. Indre
13A. Belfort Ter.	30. Eure-et-Loir	46. Indre-et-
14. Bouches-du-	31. Finistère	Loire
Rhone	32. Gard	47. Isère
15. Calvados	33. Gers	48. Jura
16. Cantal	34. Gironde	49. Landes
17. Charente	35. Hautes-Alpes	50. Loire

51. Loir-et-	68. Pas-de-Calais	82. Var
Cher	69. Puy-de-Dôme	83. Vaucluse
52. Loire-	70. Pyrénées-	84. Vendée
Inférieure	Orientales	85. Vienne
53. Loiret	71. Rhône	86. Vosges
54. Lot	72. Saône-et-	87. Yonne
55. Lot-et-Ga-	Loire	88. Meurthe-et-
ronne	73. Sarthe	Moselle
56. Lozère	74. Savoie	89. Haut-Rhin
57. Maine-et-	75. Seine	90. Oran
Loire	76. Seine-	91. Alger
58. Manche	Inférieure	92. Constantine
59. Marne	77. Seine-et-	
60. Mayenne	Marne	
61. Moselle	78. Seine-et-Oise	
62. Meuse	79. Somme	
63. Morbihan	80. Tarn	
64. Nièvre	81. Tarn-et-	
65. Nord	Garonne	
66. Oise		
67. Orne		

AREAS OF LOCAL GOVERNMENT AND ADMINISTRATION

Departments. The principal territorial subdivision of France for governmental purposes is the Department. The total number of metropolitan Departments, including the Territory of Belfort, is ninety.[7] These areas are, in terms
of history, relatively recent, dating from 1789.[8] Though with the passing of
time they have entered to some extent into the customs and habits of the French
people, they remain for the most part artificial and lifeless areas, for which the
people are commonly said to feel little respect and less affection. At the time
of the Revolution, pronounced provincial particularism and definite autonomous aspirations existed; but they were submerged by certain forces making
for unity and uniformity. Indeed, the Departments were set up precisely for the
purpose of destroying local feeling. They were established on the simple principle that any person ought to be able from any point in the area to make a
trip to the capital of the Department and return in the course of a day. Needless to say, conditions in this respect have been greatly altered by improved
means of communication. This fact has for some time past been made the basis
of arguments that France has need of larger governmental subdivisions; but
such suggestions, usually combined with proposals for decentralization, are,
though they emanate from most respectable quarters, unable to make any real
headway against the forces of tradition and bureaucracy.[9]

Communes. There are in France approximately 38,000 Communes. Their
history extends far back into antiquity. They are natural divisions that have
pronounced self-consciousness and possess real vitality. They resist jealously
proposals of absorption; so that their number tends to increase rather than decrease. Paris is the largest of the Communes, all cities large and small being
Communes. The smallest Communes are mere hamlets of a few families. Indeed, a large majority of the whole number of Communes are small areas.
Thus, about 30,000 Communes have populations of less than one thousand.

Other Areas. Other governmental subdivisions [10] are of little importance,
especially in connection with local government. So far as national administration is concerned, use is made of all areas in some connection or other,
grouping being employed on occasion as well.

[7] The area of France is 212,659 square miles. It is thus somewhat smaller than Texas
(265,896 sq. mi.), but by almost the same amount larger than the next largest State, California
(158,297 sq. mi.). The reckoning may easily be made that the average size for the ninety Departments is about 2,360 square miles, almost exactly the area of Delaware (2,370 sq. mi.).
The largest Department in area is the Gironde (4,140 sq. mi.); and, aside from the Seine
(185 sq. mi.), in which Paris is located, and from the Territory of Belfort (235 sq. mi.), the
smallest is the Rhone (1,104 sq. mi.). The Territory of Belfort consists of that small part of
Alsace-Lorraine which, in 1871, was not taken by Germany. When, after World War I, Alsace-
Lorraine was restored to France, the region was divided into three Departments; and the Territory of Belfort retained its identity.

[8] Cf. Ch. II, p. 41, n 7, *supra.*

[9] Cf. Ch. V, pp. 81–82, *supra,* and this Ch., p. 145, *infra.*

[10] There are some 280 Arrondissements, which were for long under the Third Republic
the basic constituency for elections to the Chamber of Deputies. The area remains a relatively
unimportant administrative subdivision, with a Sub-Prefect and a practically functionless council. Paris, Marseille, and Lyon are, though Communes, exceptions in being divided into Arrondissements. There are about 3,000 Cantons. They are employed in a military, an electoral (in
local elections), and in a judicial (cf. Ch. IX, p. 159, *infra*) capacity.

2. NATIONAL ADMINISTRATION

CENTRAL MINISTERIAL STRUCTURE

Administrative Organization. Each of the French central executive departments is composed of a number of *bureaus,* which are the cells of administrative organization. In a bureau are to be found the functionaries having to do with some primary aspect of departmental business. With respect to other constituent elements.there is much variation of detail. In general, the largest subdivisions of a Ministry are *directions,* at the head of which is a director.[11] Directions may be composed entirely of bureaus; but often there are one or more agencies standing between the two, such for example as subdirections, divisions, services, and the like.[12] These, like bureaus, regularly have heads and sometimes assistant heads. Only a few Ministries have General Secretaries, that is to say, single permanent heads corresponding to the well-known English civil servants who hold such positions.[13] Directors in most Ministries meet in council once a week or oftener for the purpose of coordinating departmental work; but this arrangement is not regarded as being highly successful.

Administrative Reorganization. The power of the executive branch of government in France to determine the composition and organization of executive departments [14] would seem in theory to afford genuine advantage as regards logical and effective grouping. In practice, the situation is doubtless better than it would be if organization were regularly effected by Act of Parliament. At the same time, the kind of overlapping, duplication and illogical arrangement that has given rise to the movement for administrative reorganization in the United States is far from unknown in France. Simple evidence of recognition of the need for constant attention to the problem is to be seen in the existence of a Secretary of State who, associated closely with the office of the Prime Minister, is not only concerned with the problems of the Civil Service as a whole,[15] but who also, as his title indicates, is charged with attention to the general matter of administrative reorganization.

Technical Councils. A particularly salient characteristic of the French governmental system in general and of administrative organization in particular is the existence of a multitude of advisory and consultative bodies. Some, such

---

[11] In some instances this official is called a general director.

[12] The Ministry of the Interior may be taken as an example. Aside from certain elements attached to the Minister or his Cabinet, the Ministry consists of eight Directions. Each of three of the Directions has two Sub-Directions, each of the two in one instance being divided into two Bureaus, each in the second into four, and each in the third into three (though one bureau is called by another name). One Direction is composed of six Bureaus, with no intervening Sub-Directions. Another Direction has two Bureaus directly under the Director and also one Sub-Direction composed of six Bureaus. Two Directions have *Services* (though not all so called) directly under the Director, in one instance there being also one Sub-Direction composed of two Bureaus and, in the other, two Sub-Directions containing no Bureaus. Finally, one Direction has another Direction subordinate to it.

[13] The permanent head of the Quai d'Orsay, as the Ministry of Foreign Affairs is currently called, is doubtless the best known exception. A system of General Secretaries was established by Vichy, but as a system it did not long survive the Liberation.

[14] Cf. Ch. VII, pp. 126–127, *supra.*

[15] Cf. *ibid.,* p. 128, *supra,* and this Ch., p. 142, *infra.*

for example as the Union Assembly and the Economic Council are, though primarily associated with Parliament,[16] likewise functionally connected with the executive. Others, including the Council of Ministers itself, together with the highly important Council of State [17] and various others, are attached primarily to the executive as a whole. So far as Ministers and other executive agents are concerned, material on which their decisions are based are in principle prepared in bureaus; but, similarly, councils, to which may be added committees, commissions, offices, and so on, have the general function of furnishing expert views calculated to enlighten Ministers and executive agents on matters concerning which decisions have to be made.[18]

FUNCTIONARIES

Central and Local Agents. In general, French functionaries in a given executive department either serve in a part of the central organization of the Ministry in Paris or they are employed "in the field," that is to say, in the various communities that make up the country, to dispatch there the affairs of the national Government. These two classes of functionaries have, by military analogy, been denominated [19] "non-combatants" and "combatants." In connection with combatants, it should be repeatedly stressed that administration in France is conceived to include local government as a whole; so that, consequently, all organs and agents of local governments are administrative in character, and, even where further classification distinguishes between administrative agents of the national Government and functionaries connected with local government or administration, these latter officials are usually both agents of local government and local agents of the national Government.[20]

Legal Basis. The French public functionaries, that is to say, civil servants of the national Government, possess a general legal "status." This is determined by a statute, for many years previously promised and anticipated, the Act of October 19, 1946,[21] passed by the Second National Constituent Assembly. Its provisions seek to formulate a definition of public functionaries as persons who "being appointed for permanent employment are possessed of a specific position in a grade within the hierarchical structure of a central administration of the State, of exterior services attached to it, or of public establishments of the State"; the provisions attempt to determine the precise legal

---

[16] Cf. Ch. VI, pp. 90–91, *supra.*

[17] Cf. Ch. IX, pp. 164–165, *infra.*

[18] Cf. this Ch., pp. 136–137, *supra.* The importance for the future of this practice, which exists in some degree in all countries, scarcely receives sufficient attention. With the growing complexity of problems, it is a striking means of combining knowledge and responsibility. Acceptance of advice by the Minister or other official with power of decision is of course voluntary; but where the advice is known to exist, especially if seeking it as distinguished from following it is compulsory, the public is in a better position to judge responsibility when a decision has been made.

[19] By M. Hauriou, *Précis de droit administratif et de droit public* (11e éd., Paris, 1927), p. 121. Clearly, this terminology is by no means identical with the use of the terms *staff* and *line* in the United States.

[20] Cf. this Ch., p. 147, *infra.*

[21] The text of the Act (*loi no. 46–2294 du 19 octobre 1946 relative au statut général des fonctionnaires*) is to be found in *J. O.*, 20 octobre 1946, pp. 8910 *et seq.*

position of functionaries as "in a situation determined by statute and order in relation to the Administration"; they propose to effect a general organization, with the Prime Minister at the head, for the purpose of dealing with problems of public service; and they undertake to establish the principles regulating classification, recruitment, discipline, remuneration, responsibility, advancement, retirement, and the like. These provisions are not applicable to the agents of local government; and, even with respect to employees of the central Government, certain classes are not covered, such for example as the agents of the judiciary, of the military services, and of public services and enterprises that possess an industrial or commercial character, including state factories and nationalized concerns. The Act, though designedly general in character, is careful to avoid undue uniformity, anticipating special "statuses" with respect to certain public functions, and otherwise authorizing supplementary executive regulations.[22]

Equality of Opportunity. In principle, the French public service is open to everyone who can meet certain minimum tests set up by law, and who possesses the ability to succeed in established competition. The Act of October 19, 1946, declares men and women to be on the same basis. Its provisions require that a candidate shall have been a French citizen for at least five years, shall be in enjoyment of civil rights, shall be of moral integrity, shall be in good standing with respect to military service, and shall meet certain physical tests.

Classes in the Public Service. Traditionally in France the principle has been accepted that a close correlation ought to exist between the public service and the schools and universities. Acceptance of the principle has in turn resulted in the fact that competitive examinations have fallen, in a very general sense, into classes determined by whether the competition assumes successful completion by the candidate of the primary, the secondary, or the university stage of education. Corresponding groups of public servants have included routine clerical and manipulative workers, more responsible clerical workers, and holders of the highest administrative and professional posts. The Act of October 19, 1946, assumed that executive regulation would determine this matter along accepted lines; and an important Instruction of April 2, 1947,[23] distinguishes these groups, on the basis of whether their typical function is "conception and direction," "application," or "execution." The first of these groups, composed of the highest or "superior" functionaries, is from the nature of the case the most interesting. In the past, a high degree of autonomy had traditionally existed in the several central Ministries with respect to personnel matters; and there was a corresponding lack of unity.[24] An exceedingly impor-

[22] The various regulations in this respect from October of 1946 to the present are naturally scattered through recent numbers of the *Journal officiel.* They are collected in convenient form in several places, e.g., Union générale des fédérations de fonctionnaires, *Annuaire de la Fonction publique, Année 1949–1950.*

[23] The text (*Présidence du Conseil: Instruction no. 1 pour l'application des dispositions du statut général des fonctionnaires*) is to be found in *J. O.,* 2 avril 1947, pp. 3128 *et seq.,* and in collections.

[24] In the past, this was a characteristic feature of French recruitment through competitive examination. Thus, there was no agency corresponding closely to a Civil Service Commission. The several Ministries established separate systems of recruitment and in general formulated

tant Ordinance of October 9, 1945,[25] with a view to effecting a measure of con- solidation in respect of the "superior" functionaries in the various Ministries, established a new corporate group and title, those of Civil Administrators. The Act of October 19, 1946, accepted this creation; so that the new group was definitively added to existing famous corporate groups such as the Inspectors of Finance, officials of the Council of State, those of the Court of Accounts, and those of the Quai d'Orsay (foreign office). Similarly, the Ordinance cre- ated, and the Act accepted, at the next lower level a body of Secretaries of Administration. At the third and lowest level stand, of course, the great body of routine government workers.

Recruitment: The Merit System. The great majority of French func- tionaries are said to be *appointed*,[26] which, according to the concept prevailing in France, means that actual choice is in the hands of one person. The power guaranteed by the Constitution to the Prime Minister "to appoint all civil and military officers" does not in practice prevent statutes and executive regulations from vesting appointment in given instances in Ministers and other executive officials. In any case, regard is had, as a general principle for the "merit sys- tem." There exists only a very small amount of political influence and intrigue. The basic fact is that entrance to the service and improvement of position within it are determined by competition.

Recruitment: Examination. In the past, French Civil Service examina- tions at the highest level commanded the greatest interest; and the same is true at present. Previously, it was for the various superior administrative and profes- sional positions that the typical competitors traditionally were the most bril- liant graduates of the universities and of the famous technical schools [27] main- tained and controlled by the State. The competitive examinations at this level were proverbially of exceedingly great difficulty. Here, as indeed in practically all instances, the practice was to set searching written examinations, supple- mented by oral examinations. The examining authority was normally estab- lished in the department concerned. It was generally made up of officials in the service,[28] to whom were added persons from the outside, particularly from aca- demic life.

---

separate solutions of kindred personnel problems. No Ministry was without a special establish- ment—in a few cases there were more than one—concerned with these problems. On the other hand, the rules of the several services were by no means wholly dissimilar. There was at least a tendency for similar problems to be solved in a similar way. Nevertheless, the several Ministries were, it may be repeated, in principle and practice largely autonomous. All in all, a great variety of examinations existed.

[25] The text (*ordonnance no. 45–2283 du 9 octobre 1945 relative à la formation, au recrute- ment et au statut de certaines catégories de fonctionnaires, et instituant une direction de la fonction publique et un conseil permanent de l'administration civile*) is to be found in *J. O.,* 10 octobre 1945, pp. 6378 *et seq.* It was issued as a reprint (*tirage spécial, J. O.,* no. 397). All the pertinent texts may be found conveniently in Présidence du Gouvernement, *Réforme de la fonction publique* (Paris, 1945).

[26] Cf. this Ch., p. 146, *infra.*

[27] Graduates of the *Facultés de droit* (Law Schools) have been traditionally regarded as the most typical candidates. Prevailing regulations, in addition to listing other *Facultés* of the Universities, mention some thirty technical schools, of which perhaps the best known is the *Ecole polytechnique.*

[28] This is presumably the basis for the criticism which has on occasion been made that the French bureaucracy is "self-perpetuating."

Recruitment: The National School of Administration. It is at the highest level of the French public service that a striking innovation has been introduced under the Fourth Republic. The Ordinance of October 9, 1945, established what is known as the National School of Administration.[29] From this School are to be recruited the famous older bodies of "superior" functionaries and the newer body of Civil Administrators. Admission to the School is determined by keen competition. The competition, in turn, has two aspects, in the sense that recruitment is in part from academic life and in part from functionaries already in the service. In the first instance, the candidates must be less than twenty-six years of age and possessed of a high university degree or of a diploma from one of the great technical schools; in the second, the candidates must be between twenty-six and thirty and must have served at least five years as a national or local functionary. The examining authority has in general the same composition as the traditional agencies in the Ministries. The successful candidates, if they are not already functionaries, become functionaries on probation.[30] Their course extends over three years. In each of the three there is a certain amount of a sort of internship, considered the great innovation of the system. During the first year, the students are associated with some high functionary in some local area of metropolitan France away from Paris, or in North Africa, or in the French zone in Germany. At the end of the year, a fifty-page original study must be presented. The second year is spent at the School in Paris, during which internship involves association with central Ministries and government establishments. During the first two years, the students are distributed, so far as possible according to choice, into four sections—general administration, economic and financial administration, social administration, and foreign service. At the end of the second year there are examinations in each section. On the basis of their standing in these examinations and of their previous performances, the rank of the students in each section is determined. Then, on the basis of rank and section, the student makes his choice of a career among the positions available. Specialized groups for a career or combination of similar careers are established for the studies and internships of the third year. At the end, the student is appointed to a particular position in the particular service to which he is attached.

Unionization. French functionaries are organized on a large scale. Not only public employees who perform functions that are practically identical with those performed by workers in private industry but also officials whose activities are specifically governmental in character have felt, not without reason, that in the absence of organization their interests would be unlikely to receive

[29] The provisions of the ordinance and various other provisions effected other interesting reforms. Thus, on the academic side, Institutes of Political Science in the Universities were stipulated for, one at Paris (the old *Ecole libre* transformed) and one at Strasbourg immediately, others gradually, which would broaden the opportunities for students while they are pursuing their education previous to becoming candidates; and there was created a Centre of Advanced Studies, affording in-service opportunities for functionaries.

[30] This has manifest advantages in terms of economic security. Evidence has been prepared in France tending to show that already substantial democratization has taken place in the public service.

much attention. The development that has resulted in the present situation began before the opening of the twentieth century. Before the end of the Third Republic, organizations were successful in practice in securing certain improvement in working conditions. However, the whole situation was recognized to be unsatisfactory. For one thing, the legal situation was far from clear. There was much controversy among jurists and among special students of the subject.[31] Numerous bills were introduced into Parliament, but none was enacted into law. It remained for the Act of October 19, 1946, to tackle the subject seriously.[32] Here for the first time the legality of unions of functionaries is explicitly recognized.[33] Moreover, the functionaries are given membership in two agencies that are established in each service—a *joint administrative commission,* for dealing with all matters of personnel, and a *joint technical committee,* for dealing with all questions of organization.

Bureaucracy. Various aspects of the French public service and of French public servants have been satirized and even burlesqued. The French themselves have been foremost in criticism of this kind. Red tape, procrastination, and other aspects of "bureaucracy" have become proverbial. The situation is undoubtedly in large measure the result of centralization and of ministerial instability; and for these phenomena the public servants can scarcely be said to be responsible.[34] Neither are they the cause of the French type of individualism, one of the traditional aspects of which is a latent antipathy for government and hence for its agents. As a matter of fact, French functionaries, it may be plausibly argued, are not on the whole abnormally numerous. What is striking is the relatively large fraction of functionaries who are agents of the central Government in comparison with agents of local government.[35] But this is merely to repeat the fact of centralization. In reality, the French public service displays a number of admirable qualities. The superior officials are as a rule genuinely educated persons of real culture, hard-working and devoted to the interests of the country. The criticism, sometimes encountered, that they are all devoid of sense of responsibility and initiative is by no means tenable. The principal functionaries can always be counted on to show intelligent and cooperative interest in movements for salutary reform. The fact cannot be too often repeated that it is primarily to the public servants that are owed continuity and stability in the process of government.

[31] Some jurists went so far as to assert that the special character of all government employees rendered all law dealing with association inapplicable to them and to hold that consequently all organizations of functionaries were illegal. The courts in their decisions by no means accepted this sweeping view. They made a distinction between "associations," which were held valid, and "unions" (*syndicats*), which were forbidden. Ministries of the day tended to have more regard for political considerations than for judicial decisions.

[32] The Vichy regime dealt seriously with the question; but from the nature of the case, its solutions were temporary.

[33] Concerning the controversial question of the right to strike there is silence.

[34] Unless perhaps in the sense that their skepticism concerning reform may somewhat tend to perpetuate the phenomenon.

[35] Consensus concerning statistics in these respects is notoriously difficult to find in France. It would seem that roughly a million functionaries (about 940,000 of them in Metropolitan France) and similar agents are charged on the national budget. There are also some 45,000 agents charged on the particular budgets of National Public Establishments, the employees of nationalized enterprises not being counted. Local agents number slightly more than 400,000.

3. LOCAL GOVERNMENT AND ADMINISTRATION

COUNCILS

Deliberative Character. Agents of local government are classified in France as deliberative agents and executive agents. This classification, though in appearance based on a difference of function, is, practically speaking, closely connected with difference of origin. Thus, agents that are denominated *deliberative* are regularly elective in practice, whereas *executive* agents are appointive.[36] Deliberative agents are in all cases members of councils, these councils being the basic organs of local self-government in France. The councils are called General Councils in the Departments, and Municipal Councils in the Communes. All have the same origin as the National Assembly; that is to say, they are elected by secret, direct, universal suffrage.

Composition and Organization. The councils in the Departments and the Communes are chosen for six years. In the Departments, the single-member constituency system is employed; in the Communes, election at large is, with a few exceptions, the prevailing system. In general, the members are men of considerable experience, ability, and importance. Among them are to be found many members of Parliament, who are willing and even eager to enter the local governmental world, conducting, where necessary, vigorous campaigns to be elected. Once chosen, the councils select their officers, establish their rules, set up their committees, and, at meetings held during relatively short annual sessions, transact the business falling within their somewhat limited spheres of competence. Special mention should be made, so far as Departments are concerned, of the *Department Committee,* "an emanation of the council," created by law for the purpose of representing the council in the intervals between sessions.

Functions. The activities of French local councils are of several kinds. In the first place, councils exercise a certain amount of elective power. Thus, aside from the part played by both kinds of council in elections of national Senators [37] and the choice of their own officers, more especially the choice of the Maires and Deputy Maires by the Municipal Councils, the councils select certain of their members to serve on bodies in which they are entitled to representation. In the second place, local councils formally express their opinion, in the form of advice or of resolutions, in respect of various matters of a public character. In the third place, and more important, decisions of the local council take the form of resolutions having the force of law concerning local affairs proper. These affairs are fewer in the case of the Departments than in the case of the Communes. In the first instance, they fall traditionally into three classes— maintenance of buildings and other property, construction and management of roads and other means of communication, and public welfare. In the case of the Communes, the affairs are numerous and greatly varied, though large and small Communes naturally differ in practice. Examples of communal activities

---

[36] Cf. this Ch., p. 143, *supra.*   [37] Cf. Ch. VI, pp. 95–96, *supra.*

include construction and management of public works, administration of Commune property, and direction of municipal public services. Finally, but by no means least, there is the administration of local finances. This, though some of its technical details involve no little complication, is, in its general outlines, relatively simple. The councils naturally concern themselves with the raising and spending of money. The Departments and Communes are required by law to have budgets. These are prepared by the Prefect and the Maire, or, in practice, by the civil servants. The budgets must, of course, be voted by the councils.[38] In general, control over the budgets by the councils is very effective. The Prefects, Maires, and local financial agents must submit their accounts to the councils; and the councils are required to discuss these accounts promptly. This gives rise to a substantial amount of control by the councils over local executive activity. When the councils have discussed the accounts, higher authorities audit and approve them.

EXECUTIVES

Classification. Aside from the *deliberative* local agents, who form the councils, other agents concerned with government on a local scale, that is, several hundred thousand, are considered to be *executive*. These executive agents fall theoretically into two classes. Some are officials who have been placed by the national Government in a local community for the purpose of attending to national affairs on the spot; some are the agents of the local community, in so far as it governs itself. Some, that is to say, are local agents of government; others are agents of local government.[39] At the same time, this reasonably clear distinction is far from easy to apply in practice, whether the standard of origin or of function is employed. There is no good example of an executive agent popularly elected locally, the nearest approach being the Maire, head of the Commune and presiding officer in its council, who is chosen by the council. In the matter of function—a somewhat better standard of classification—a local official may be defined as one whose public activities are directly related to the sphere of competence of the council of his community. However, there are actually, in terms of this definition, few if any exclusively local French officers. Practically all are also allotted national functions to perform; so that little more can be said than that if their activities are *primarily* local, they are essentially local officials. Moreover, many important local functions are performed by agents whose primary activities are national in character. In the one case as in the other, the agents have both a national and a local side. They play, as is emphasized in French studies, a "dual role." Thus, of the two most important officials in French local government, the Prefect and the Maire, both have a dual role; but the Prefect, it should be noted, is primarily a national, though likewise in spite of recent tendencies still an important local, agent; whereas the Maire is primarily a local official, with numerous national duties.

---

[38] In the Departments, a preliminary examination of the budget is made by the Department Committee.

[39] Cf. this Ch., p. 141, *supra.*

Prefects. There is a Prefect in each Department.[40] These officials are in reality chosen by the Minister of the Interior, though they are said, legally speaking, to be appointed by decree of the President of the Republic. The Minister is not bound by any law that stipulates special qualifications for the office of Prefect as such; but, in practice, the Minister, though definitely influenced by political considerations, usually chooses Prefects from certain classes of subordinate administrative officials. The position is undoubtedly a difficult one, requiring for success a number of somewhat rare qualities. It has been suggested [41] that the principal requirement is that of a man of worth who will serve as a tool of the national Government and yet find the career attractive. By decree of the President of the Republic, that is, by decision of the Minister of the Interior, a Prefect may be dismissed, though this is extremely rare; he may be transferred; and he may be placed on an inactive list on half-pay. Transfers are relatively frequent. An important political change is manifested in the attitude of the Ministry of the Interior; and what is known as a "movement of the Prefects" takes place. In addition to an official mansion and a salary, a Prefect receives a variable allowance for travel, office expenses, and the like. Pension arrangements exist; but the political character of the position, with the resultant uncertainty of tenure, causes such retirement to be a less fixed expectation than in other cases.

Maires. The legal basis for choice of Maires by the Municipal Councils in the Communes is a provision of the Municipal Act of April 5, 1884. Such choice may be regarded as a republican, as distinguished from an imperial or monarchist, system. The imperial system was unrestricted choice of the Maire by the national Government; whereas, under the monarchical system, the Maires were selected by the national Government from among the members of the councils. The existing republican practice clearly represents an advance in the direction of local self-government. However, the national Government may by decree remove a Maire, in which event the Maire is ineligible for the period of a year, unless a new council is elected in the meanwhile. Moreover, the Minister of the Interior may suspend the Maire for three months, and the Prefect may suspend him for one month.[42] Maires receive no regular salary; but legal provisions and fixed practice allow certain payments for expenses. The Maire in a considerable number of instances proceeds to his position through the office of Assistant Maire. Frequently, though by no means always, he makes the position a stage of a political career on the way to higher places. That the position is held in no little esteem is indicated by the fact that members of both houses of Parliament are glad to serve, if they can be elected, as heads of Communes. Indeed, the approximately 38,000 Maires are sometimes said to rule France. They form an Association of Maires, whose procession at their annual meeting is a picturesque event. Although the overwhelming majority of Communes are minute in area and population, the differences that would be expected between

---

[40] In the Department of the Seine, in which Paris is located, there are two Prefects—a Prefect of the Seine and a Prefect of Police.

[41] Cf. M. Hauriou, *op. cit.,* p. 131.

[42] Legal provisions, it should be noted, protect to some extent the Maires in these respects.

the Maire of a small rural community and the Maire of a large industrial city by no means exhaust the variations that occur. In the result, there are noblemen and laborers, demagogues and leading citizens, illiterates and university professors, Communists and reactionaries.

Local Employees. Executive agents of the Departments and Communes consist of the staffs of the Prefects and Maires respectively and of other employees of the Departments and the Communes. Generally speaking, the agents of all the Departments and of the larger Communes constitute in each case a small army. Each Prefect has associated with him a kind of intimate political family which, as in the case of the analogous institution connected with national Ministers, is known as his *cabinet.*[43] All the members are chosen by the Prefect himself. The Cabinet Chief is in reality a kind of private secretary. At the beginning of the Napoleonic era there was established the position of Secretary-General of the Department, an official who was originally not unlike the present-day Cabinet Chief; but, just as the Prefects have tended to become the *political* heads, so the Secretaries-General have become more and more the *administrative* heads of the Departments. Their status is in most respects similar to that of the Prefects. They are chosen, removed, suspended, and pensioned by decree, the real decision belonging to the Minister of the Interior. They are the recognized substitutes for the Prefects, when the latter for any reason are absent or otherwise unable to perform their duties; but primarily they are, as general administrative heads of the Departments under the political guidance of the Prefects, general directors of the staffs of the Prefectures, which are organized into divisions and bureaus with a structure similar to that of the national Ministries.[44] In small Communes, that is to say, in the large majority, the staff of the Maire is not very extensive. Indeed, in the smallest, the complete staff consists of a Secretary, who corresponds in a general way to the Secretary-General of the Department. The position of Secretary in the small Communes has traditionally been held by the local schoolmaster; but this practice, while still common, appears not to be so widespread as formerly. In all cases, the Secretary is chosen freely by the Maire. His salary is an expense imposed by law on the Commune. Political considerations do not often play much part in selection of the Secretary, for the effectiveness with which the Communes are governed depends largely on the ability of this official. In the larger Communes, the Secretary is the general director of a staff that is a formidable establishment. The Act of October 19, 1946, being silent concerning the agents of local government, other legal provisions prevail with respect to them.[45] In the Departments, the status of executive agents is regulated by an Act of 1920, except

[43] Cf. Ch. VII, pp. 128–129, *supra.*

[44] Previous to 1926, there was associated with the Prefect an administrative agency known as the Prefectoral Council. It was a consultative body, though in this capacity it was relatively unimportant; and, much more important, it served as an administrative court, with the Department as the area of jurisdiction. Since 1926, there have been only twenty-two Prefectoral Councils. One is a Council for the Department of the Seine, the others being regional organs. The Councils have practically lost their consultative character, with the result that they are almost wholly judicial tribunals. Cf. Ch. IX, p. 165, *infra.*

[45] An important bill calculated to establish a "status" for employees of the Communes has had rough going in the National Assembly.

where stipulations of other Acts prevail; and, in Communes with a population of more than 5,000, establishment of a merit system is, by an Act of 1919, as amended by subsequent Acts and supplemented by executive orders, required for appointment, promotion, and discipline of Commune agents not covered by other legal provisions. The existing situation in the two kinds of areas is, generally speaking, the same. Salaries are paid, and arrangements for pensions are made. Positions are obtained through competition, which is open to both sexes. Promotion is made through a roster in accordance with definite principles. Suspensions, removal, and discipline are surrounded with various safeguards. Finally, redress may be sought and obtained through the processes of administrative justice.

4. BASIC PRINCIPLES

CONCENTRATION

Executive Unity. It has been customary to attempt graphic emphasis of the concentration and centralization of French administration through reference to its pyramidal structure. However, a little reflection should suggest that considerable caution is desirable in employment of such a figure of speech. The graph can be, and has been, applied to the administrative structure of other countries; so that its value, so far as France is concerned, depends not only on how far it shows resemblances with other examples but also on the extent to which it suggests the elements of uniqueness in the French system. Thus, in the matter of areas and of the relationship of larger areas to lesser areas, division and subdivision almost everywhere render applicable the figure of a pyramid. Again, anywhere that executive unity prevails in respect of the general government, the central administration will appear in graphic representation much the same. In France, if the President of the Republic and the President of the Council be conceived as forming the apex of the pyramid and if the several national Ministries be conceived as the beginning of a symmetrical spread outward and downward, the figure up to that point would seem accurate enough, even if not greatly different from that representing the situation in other countries. So at the next and succeeding levels, those of territorial administrative divisions and subdivisions, the pyramidal figure is almost everywhere applicable when continued downward and outward in further symmetrical manner, with lines running from each of the several national ministerial departments to one or more of its agents in the principal divisions, and so on. In France, however, such a symmetrical pyramid, it should be emphasized, represents a modern development corresponding in general to the addition of social and economic functions of government to the older primary functions associated with the era of *laissez-faire*. As a graph, it must therefore be superposed upon an older pyramid.

Position of the Prefect. The older and basic French administrative structure is characterized by the established position of the Prefect, a position to which nothing closely corresponds in the Anglo-American tradition. The Prefect was intended to represent the national government as a whole; and, hence, from the nature of the case a line running from the Ministry of the Interior to the Prefect ought, in a graphic representation, to be especially pronounced, because the Minister of the Interior appoints the Prefects, and primary national functions performed locally by the Prefects fall within the sphere of, and are under the control of, that Minister. At the same time, lines would have to be drawn also to the Prefect from newer Ministries, to take care of the considerable extent to which the Prefects, as general national agents, are concerned with newer as well as older functions. The fact that a tendency prevails for Prefects to become less powerful agents than formerly, even in respect of national affairs,[46] and that the Ministries in Paris, owing to modern means of communication and other developments, are able to get much of their business done on a local scale through their own agents without recourse to the Prefects, would be shown by the direct lines of the superimposed pyramid. In general, the two graphs, one on top of the other, with almost countless lines, no small number of which criss-cross one another, ought at least to suggest the complexity of the national administrative structure. They would probably also indicate to some extent what is technically called in France the *concentration* of the system. An attempt to represent its *centralization* would complicate the graph still more.[47]

CENTRALIZATION

Logical Complexity. The question of the relationship in France of local government—or administration—to the national governmental system is by no means a simple affair. Some aspects of the matter are in principle the same as in countries like England and the United States which possess a tradition for less highly centralized arrangements. Other aspects, highly interesting and not always easy to explain or to understand, are characteristic of the centralized French system as such.

National Analogy. According to French concepts, *decision* in local government, which is followed by *execution,* is preceded by *deliberation.*[48] Hence, deliberation, in other words, the activities of deliberative bodies, that is to say, the deliberative local councils, is the primary function of local government. French students of the matter readily accept the proposition that local councils share with Parliament the characteristic of being *deliberative.* However, they do

---

[46] Cf. Ch. v, pp. 81–82, *supra.* In respect of the Prefect's position as a local government executive, the prevailing Constitution, it may be recalled, stipulates (Art. 87) that decisions of the Department Councils shall be executed by the Presidents of the Councils. The Prefect is not mentioned by name in the main body of the Constitution, his national functions being said (Art. 88) to devolve on "Delegates of the Government." However, legislation is recognized (Art. 89) to be required; and in its absence, one of the Transitory Provisions (Art. 105), which does mention the Prefect by name, maintains for the most part the *status quo,* with the following interesting *proviso:* "Nevertheless, acts performed by the Prefect, in his capacity as representative of the Department, shall be executed by him under the permanent control of the President of the Department assembly."

[47] Cf. Ch. i, p. 36, and Ch. v, *loc. cit., supra.*

[48] Cf. this Ch., p. 146, *supra.*

not normally draw a comparison between the national legislature and lesser assemblies. More particularly, the view that local councils make law is distinctly distasteful to most French students.

Legal Sources of Local Authority. French agencies of local government, like local agencies in other countries, derive from legal provisions their existence and all the authority they possess. All legal provisions regulating the organization, functions, and authority of French local government—general and special Acts of Parliament, executive and administrative orders, and what is called the "jurisprudence" of the Council of State—form a part of French administrative law. This law is conceived, as is coming to be the case everywhere, as being by definition composed of all rules determining the organization, functions, and authority of administration; and, since local government is *administration,* rules regulating it are a part of administrative law.

"Tutelle Administrative." In the matter of the extent of the authority of French local government, the theoretical principle is exceedingly simple. The law declares that the Department Council shall manage the business of the Department and that the Municipal Council shall regulate the affairs of the Commune. Such a statement of principle, however, not only fails to suggest the difficulty of determining what the business of the Department and what the affairs of the Communes are; it takes no account of the modern tendency, which is especially pronounced in France, for the public as a whole, acting through its national government, to be increasingly concerned with the entire process of government and, accordingly, with local agencies and activities. In the second respect, the tendency manifests itself through the phenomenon of *control.* In the French view, failure for the national government to maintain control in the general interest over local government would have the alarming result of abandoning France to the whims of 90 Department Councils and 38,000 Municipal Councils. This control is, in France, the basic characteristic of local government. It is currently called "administrative guardianship," the expression suggesting that local communities, like children not yet grown up, are not capable of looking out for themselves. Such national control over local government assumes several different forms.

Judicial Control. A certain amount of control over all agents and organs of local government grows out of the familiar principle that they must not exceed their legal authority. Though establishment of the legal provisions that serve as limitations is sometimes itself regarded as a form of control, practical application of the provisions brings the judiciary into play; so that the control is frequently known as *judicial control.* The phenomenon is familiar both in England and America. However, in France, typical control is not so much control by courts—in this case administrative courts—as control by active administrative agents and agencies.

Decision and Execution. The French distinction between deliberative and executive agents is of especial importance in connection with administrative control of local government. Control of deliberative agents, that is to say, of councils, involves control of their decisions. However, in practice, the decisions must, of course, be executed; and executive agents are likewise subject to control.

Control over Councils. From the point of view of administrative control, decisions by local councils fall, generally speaking, into two classes. The first class consists of decisions which require, to be binding, the approval of a higher authority. Disapproval need not have a legal basis; it may be based wholly on grounds of policy, the implication being that the decision is considered unwise in the general interest. However, this control is somewhat softened by the fact that approval is assumed to have been given if disapproval is not expressed within a fixed legal period. The decisions falling into this first class are *enumerated* by law, being less numerous for the Departments than for the Communes. All other decisions fall in the second class, and are known as *definitive* decisions. They may be defined as decisions that become binding if not disallowed on legal grounds by a higher authority within a certain period. They may not be annulled as being merely unwise. Hence, annulment of definitive decisions may be seen to be a case of anticipating judicial action; for, after the end of the legal period within which annulment by administrative authority is possible, an individual affected may seek annulment in the administrative courts.

Effective Control. Real local autonomy is to be measured much less by possible or theoretical control than by actual control. In practice, control in France is pervasive and continuous; and the amount of genuine local self-government is small. This is true in spite of appearance, especially in the matter of the concept of definitive decisions. These decisions, involving by definition a broad residual sphere of power within which local action may be annulled only on legal grounds, would seem to allow considerable freedom from control; and yet at this point the practical importance is to be seen of the distinction between decision and execution. Decision may be free, but execution is subject to control. Especially in connection with the expenditure side of local budgets is the far-reaching potentiality of control of execution manifest. Inasmuch as practically every function of any interest or importance involves the spending of money, an estimate of expenditure must be inserted in the budget; and not only is the sphere of optional expenditure very restricted, but, in the case of the Communes, control involves considerable power of reduction or disallowance, even in connection with optional expenses. Moreover, an anticipated expenditure, if it involves capital outlay, may well necessitate a loan. In such case, not only does liquidation of the loan involve regular budgetary appropriation subject to control, but authority for the council to float a loan is subject to various restrictions. Thus, in the Departments, final decision to proceed by loan may be made by the council only when the loan is to be amortized within a fixed number of years through use of the Department's own revenue. Otherwise, the central Government must give formal consent through administrative action. The situation in the Communes is similar, but the restrictions are more rigid and detailed. Hence, in general, control in the matter of loans goes far towards offsetting freedom of decision in respect of an activity for which a loan is required. Moreover, a free decision, such for example as one to construct a public building, may be subject to other kinds of control in execution. Thus, if land has to be taken through exercise of the right of eminent domain, control of a higher authority exists; and the required bids on the work are likewise subject to control. To all this should be added the existence of a certain amount of what is called in France *control of personnel*. It may be recalled that though Department and Commune Councils are directly elected by universal suffrage, and Maires are elected by the Municipal Councils, the Prefect is appointed by the central Government. Moreover, individual members of councils may be removed. Municipal Councils may be suspended; and though power of suspension does not prevail in the case of General Councils, they as well as Municipal Councils may be dissolved by action of national administrative officials. Such considerations, along with various other aspects of administrative guardianship, form the basis for the traditional judgment that France is the most highly centralized of the great free countries of the world.

CHAPTER IX

THE FRENCH JUDICIARY

1. HISTORICAL PRINCIPLES

TWO SYSTEMS OF COURTS

Ordinary and Administrative Tribunals. The judicial system of France differs in several interesting respects from the judiciaries of countries with legal systems based on the Common Law of England. Not the least striking difference is the possession by France of two separate systems of courts. One of these is the system of ordinary courts; the other is a system of administrative tribunals.[1] In general, most controversies in which the state or an administrative officer is a party are heard in the administrative courts. However, criminal cases have always constituted one large class of exceptions. These, together with civil cases in which the parties are private individuals, form, roughly speaking, the province of the ordinary tribunals. For the purpose of settling doubt in a given instance as to whether a case falls within the jurisdiction of one set of courts or the other, a court, known as the Tribunal of Conflicts, has been set up at the head of both systems.

Court of Conflicts. The Tribunal of Conflicts consists of eight judges and two substitute judges. Six of the judges are chosen three each by the highest court of the ordinary system and the highest administrative court. These six choose the remaining members. The Minister of Justice is *ex officio* president of the Tribunal; but he does not ordinarily serve except in a case where the judges are equally divided. In actual practice, the Tribunal of Conflicts hears only some six or eight cases a year.

Judiciary and Administration. The origin of two systems of courts in France is to be found in the establishment at the time of the French Revolution of a rigid separation between administrative and judicial authorities. The end sought to be accomplished was prevention of interference by the regular judi-

---

[1] This is of course not to say that agencies which are in reality administrative tribunals do not exist in Great Britain and the United States. On the contrary, they do exist and have in recent years become increasingly important; but there is no organized system.

ciary in the work of administration. Following the Revolution, the formidable work of political and social reorganization that was contemplated was currently considered, for historical reasons, to be work that ought to be accomplished by the administrative authorities. According to de Tocqueville, all classes of people looked to the administration as to "a special providence." In 1789, examples of judicial interference with administration were known to everyone, the judiciary in the immediate past having more than once nullified attempted reforms.[2] In the result, various legal provisions were formulated during the period following 1789, with a view to preventing the judiciary from interfering in the work of administration.[3] Finally, the Penal Code provided in several places for punishment of judges who should encroach on administrative functions.

THE SEPARATION OF POWERS IN FRANCE

Montesquieu at Home. Although Revolutionary legislation with respect to interference by the judiciary with administration was based largely on practical experience, it was at the time justified theoretically, as the prevailing situation in France continues to be justified, through appeal to the famous doctrine of the separation of powers. Discussion of the doctrine in France concerns itself on occasion, as discussion of Montesquieu has regularly been concerned in the United States, with the legislative-executive relationship;[4] but, in the home land of Montesquieu, it is a striking fact that the doctrine of the separation of powers has been applied primarily to the relation between the administration and the judiciary. Inasmuch as the addition of administrative courts to ordinary courts grew out of the separation of the judiciary and administration, the doctrine of the separation of powers, the same doctrine which furnishes a theoretical justification in the United States for the non-parliamentary character of American governments, serves in the land of Montesquieu as a solid theoretical basis for two systems of courts.

Judicial Administration. In the period immediately following the Revolution, the imposition of absolute prohibitions on the judiciary resulted in a simple, though unsatisfactory, situation. Administrative agents were freed from all judicial control. For private individuals, the only relief against the administration consisted of appeal to active administrative agents. The elective character of these agents was, according to Revolutionary ideas, sufficient guarantee. In practice, however, the administration possessed a dominant position; and it practiced domination. An inevitable reaction gave rise to various developments which, with the passing of time, gradually improved the position of the individual in his relationship to the process of administration. A first step,

---

[2] Cf. Ch. II, p. 40, *supra.*

[3] Thus, a law passed in August of 1789 contained the following stipulations: "Judicial functions shall be distinct and shall always remain separate from administrative functions. Judges shall not, under penalty of removal, disturb in any manner whatever operations of administrative bodies." Again, a provision of the Constitution of 1791 was phrased as follows: "The tribunals shall not encroach on administrative functions or summon before them administrative officials by reason of the exercise of their functions." So also, the following stipulation was contained in a law enacted in the Year III: "It shall be expressly forbidden for the tribunals to take cognizance of administrative acts of any kind whatever." Other provisions of the same tenor were subsequently enacted.   [4] Cf. Ch. V, p. 80, *infra.*

one of much potential importance, was establishment under Napoleon Bonaparte of councils of jurisconsults.[5] At the national level, the Council of State was set up, and, in the Departments, Prefectoral Councils. Out of these developed the present system of administrative courts. History suggests that where an active administrator follows the practice of seeking the counsel of a group of men who surround him, a tendency will develop for advice concerning controversies falling to the administrator for settlement to become the specialized province of a specialized personnel of specialized ability. This was, as students of comparative government know, the general historical origin everywhere of the judicial branch of government; and it was the particular origin of French administrative courts. In the latter respect, there was evolved in the course of the nineteenth century the distinction that the French now regularly make between *active* administration and *judicial* administration. Certain members of the Council of State and the Prefectoral Councils, though administrative officials, became men of judicial training and character. In other words, they became administrative judges. Active administrators were, by the end of the nineteenth century, as a general rule eliminated from concern with litigation growing out of administration. In turn, to such litigation were extended forms of procedure and protection that had been evolved by the ordinary judiciary. Real guarantees were developed. In the final result, the French citizen has come to feel that the administrative courts consist of true judges and that with them his interests in relationship to the state are in good hands. Simultaneously, through developments that are by no means simple to trace in detail, ideas concerning liability of the state for injury suffered by individuals at the hands of its agents have, partly through legislation, partly through decisions of the Council of State, and partly through the teaching of administrative law, been extended to limits increasingly more liberal and reasonable.

2. THE ORDINARY COURTS AND JUSTICE

HIERARCHY AND STRUCTURE

Horizontal and Vertical Division. The courts of the ordinary system in France are established on certain levels one above the other in the manner familiar everywhere. This hierarchical arrangement, or horizontal division, is supplemented by a vertical division of the ordinary courts into criminal courts and civil courts, the result thus being a double hierarchy. A few specialized courts are likewise regularly listed as parts of the ordinary judicial system.

Judges. In accordance with the view that justice is not safe in the hands of a single judge (*juge unique, juge inique*), French courts have traditionally been collegial bodies. In spite of exceptions at the bottom of the ordinary system in the form of Justices of the Peace and in spite of a few recent experiments,[6]

[5] Cf. Ch. II, pp. 43–44, and Ch. VIII, p. 149, *supra.*
[6] These for the most part take the form of establishment of single magistrates in judicial towns where two or more judges were previously located. This procedure has as an aim, and as a result, some economy; but where a sitting of the Tribunal is required, its composition of course remains collegial. Cf. this Ch., p. 161, *infra.*

plurality remains the rule. The relatively large size of the more important courts and the relatively large number of courts at the two principal levels under the highest court cause the principle of collegiality to result in a large number of judges. This, in turn, is an important consideration in connection with the fact that French judges, according to English and American standards, are very badly paid. On the other hand, no little compensation results from the fact that the bench is much respected by the people and that the judges enjoy high social standing. Moreover, French judges are genuinely independent, in virtue of real security of tenure. In this respect, the Constitution of the Fourth Republic contains the following simple provision:

Art. 84.—The judges shall be irremovable.

In general, members of the ordinary French judiciary, judged by usual standards of impartiality and learning in the law, deserve high rank.

The High Council of the Magistracy. Though the high rank of the ordinary French judiciary was well established before the end of the Third Republic, the Fourth Republic is commonly regarded as having taken a noteworthy step in establishing through the Constitution the body known as the *High Council of the Magistracy.* In this respect the principal provisions are worded as follows:

Art. 83.—The High Council of the Magistracy shall be composed of fourteen members:
The President of the Republic, president;
The Keeper of the Seals, Minister of Justice, vice-president;
Six persons selected for six years by the National Assembly, from outside its membership, by a two-thirds majority, six substitutes being selected in the same manner;
Six persons chosen as follows:
Four magistrates chosen for six years representing each of the categories of magistrates, in the manner provided by law, four substitutes being selected in the same manner;
Two members chosen for six years by the President of the Republic from outside Parliament and the Magistracy but from the body of the judicial professions, two substitutes being chosen in the same manner.
Decisions of the High Council of the Magistracy shall be taken by majority vote. In the event of a tie, the vote of the president shall decide.
Art. 84.—The President of the Republic shall appoint, upon presentation by the High Council of the Magistracy, the magistrates . . .[7]
The High Council of the Magistracy shall, in conformity with law, ensure the discipline of said magistrates, their independence, and the administration of the judicial tribunals . . .[8]

Sitting and Standing Magistracy. In France, the judiciary and the bar, it is of the greatest interest and importance to note, are in general separate and distinct careers. A young man in that country must normally determine in the beginning which career he desires to follow. If he elects the bench, he enters the judiciary early and works his way up the ladder of advancement. Before en-

[7] An exception is here made of judges who form part of the Standing Magistracy.
[8] The provision, quoted a little earlier, on the irremovability of judges comes in at this point.

trance, he must be twenty-five years of age; he must possess a university degree in law; he must serve a period of apprenticeship, in which he gains practical experience through study of actual work at the bar and in the administration of justice; and he must pass a qualifying examination. The positions open to him upon entering his career include, it should be further noted, those of several kinds of state attorneys and their assistants attached to the various courts. Indeed, a young man entering upon the judicial career usually begins by serving in such a position. These officials are known as Judges of the Public Ministry. Together they constitute what is called the "Standing" Judiciary as distinguished from the "Sitting" Judiciary, composed of course of what most people think of as judges, namely, the judges who from the bench hear cases and render decisions. To whichever of the two sides a judge belongs, he wears the same costume and enters a tradition imbued with the same spirit. He can, and does, move from one side to the other, and back again. When he is a Standing Judge, he performs, on behalf of the state or society or the public, important functions. Much the most important of these he performs in criminal cases, when, as representative of society, he prosecutes alleged wrongdoers, who by definition are accused of having violated the peace and dignity of society. In civil cases, the Standing Judges who are attached to the several courts give their considered opinion concerning the questions at issue. Such officials speak after the lawyers representing the parties to the controversy have concluded their arguments. The Standing Judge must be heard, failure in this respect leading to the quashing of a decision. His is conceived to be "the impartial voice of the representative of the law." [9]

THE CIVIL COURTS

Juges de Paix. At the base of the ordinary French judicial system are Justices of the Peace. In principle, there is a Justice of the Peace in each of the 3,000 Cantons. However, the fact that the jurisdiction of a Justice may extend to two or more Cantons, as well as the fact that in more than 150 jurisdictions the functions of a Justice are performed by a judge of the next highest court, reduces the number of posts held by Justices of the Peace to approximately 1,200. The office was established in France through English influence at the time of the Revolution; but the differences [10] between the two kinds of Justice of the Peace are probably greater than the resemblances. The French Justice, unlike his English counterpart, is paid a small salary; and he is required, unless he has had somewhat extended experience as a public official, to possess some knowledge of the law. He has two substitutes, who serve when he is unable to do so.

Justices of the Peace and Civil Justice. Justices of the Peace, in addition to sitting as a court, have certain administrative duties, and perform several special judicial functions. Thus, in the last-mentioned respect, they are com-

---

[9] L. Gensoul, *L'Organisation de la justice* (Paris, 1928), p. 33.

[10] The English Justices of the Peace are, practically speaking, without civil jurisdiction, tribunals known as County Courts administering justice on a local scale in this respect.

petent, in certain cases determined by law, to serve as arbitrators. Note should be made that in general the whole system of French civil justice is supplemented by the possibility of *arbitration*. This is in essence a procedure by which a controversy is, through a contract under seal, submitted by the parties for decision to a private individual.[11] Again, the Justices of the Peace engage in extensive efforts at *conciliation*. By law, no civil process may begin until the parties have appeared before a Justice of the Peace, who instructs them as to their rights in the matter, points out the difficulties and costs of prolonged suits, and attempts to bring about a peaceful settlement of the controversy. This is generally said to be the typical function of Justices of the Peace; and, in fact, they perform a valuable service in this respect. In urban communities, the conciliation procedure, it is true, tends to be a pure formality; but, in the countryside, especially among peasants, a large part of potential litigation is settled without trial. Where conciliation is unsuccessful with respect to a matter falling within the limits of his own jurisdiction,[12] the Justice of the Peace sits as a court to hear the case. In certain kinds of controversies connected with real property, the Justice of the Peace possesses jurisdiction regardless of the money value involved. However, in other controversies connected with real property and in controversies connected with persons and personal property, his jurisdiction extends only to cases involving claims up to 30,000 francs (*c.* $87); but where the amount is less than 10,000 francs, no appeal is possible.[13] In general, the Justices of the Peace, who are men of shrewdness and wisdom, effectively administer substantial justice in a summary and inexpensive fashion.

Industrial Disputes Councils. On the same plane with the Justices of the Peace stand approximately 200 special bodies known as *Conseils de prud'hommes*. They are Industrial Disputes Councils, which may by executive decision be established in industrial and commercial cities for the primary purpose of dealing with controversies growing out of contracts between employers and workers. A *Conseil* consists of an equal number of employers and fellow workers of both sexes.[14] One employer and one employee make up a Conciliation Bureau, before which parties to a controversy must appear in order to allow an effort at settlement without trial. If conciliation is unsuccessful, the case is heard by a General or Trial Bureau, composed of an equal number of employers and workers. In the event of an equal vote, a Justice of the Peace is called in to preside and to cast the deciding vote. The jurisdiction of such a Bureau extends in principle to all controversies growing out of a contract for work and out of various other labor relations and problems. A controversy involving any amount may be brought before a Council; but where 10,000 francs or more are involved, higher courts [15] have concurrent jurisdiction. If the case

---

[11] Justices are stipulated by law to be the arbitrators in certain employer-employee contract matters.

[12] Such conciliation is known as "small" conciliation as distinguished from "large" conciliation, which is concerned with matters falling beyond the jurisdiction of the Justice.

[13] Justices are also said to have a voluntary (*gracieuse*) jurisdiction, which primarily involves presiding over family councils.

[14] The members are elected for six years, one-half being renewed every three years.

[15] These are the Tribunals of First Instance, or where they exist the Commercial Tribunals, to which also appeals that are authorized are taken.

is brought before the Council, no appeal is possible unless 10,000 francs or more are involved.

Tribunals of First Instance. The basic trial courts for civil causes are the *Tribunals of First Instance.* They number approximately 350. The composition of these courts varies in their several jurisdictions according to the average amount of business to be dispatched. The Tribunal sits, if desirable, in sections. In accordance with the French principle that the administration of justice is the function of a plural body, a case is normally heard by three judges—a president and two others. In practice, the President of the Tribunal performs alone a few functions;[16] and the members of the Tribunal, sitting in chambers, dispatch a certain amount of business. Sitting as a court, the Tribunal has appellate jurisdiction in respect of cases appealed from Justices of the Peace and from the Industrial Disputes Councils; and it possesses a general, unlimited original jurisdiction beginning where the jurisdiction of the Justice of the Peace ends. Up to a certain point, the decision of the Tribunal is final; but if the amount at stake exceeds a certain figure, appeal may be taken.

Commercial Tribunals. Special courts known as Commercial Tribunals, numbering about 300, stand on the same plane as the Tribunals of First Instance. Such special courts are by executive decree established in commercial centres. When no such tribunal exists, the special commercial jurisdiction is exercised by the Tribunal of First Instance. The Commercial Tribunals are composed of members elected for two years by business people domiciled in the community. A President of the Tribunal is elected separately from the other members of the court. The Tribunal may sit in sections. Its jurisdiction extends to commercial cases as defined by a special body of commercial law. No appeal may be taken from its decisions unless the amount of money involved exceeds a certain sum.

Courts of Appeal. Competent to hear appeals from the Tribunals of First Instance and the Commercial Tribunals and next in the judicial hierarchy above them are twenty-seven Courts of Appeal.[17] A Court of Appeal is composed of a first president, of section presidents for such sections as are necessary to handle the normal business of the Court, and of the number of judges required to constitute the sections. In practice, five judges usually sit. There is at least one Civil Section. A case that is appealed is heard *de novo,* and the decision either affirms the original determination or formulates another in its place. In certain instances, two or more sections join to perform specific functions. In others, the whole membership deliberates behind closed doors.

Court of Cassation. The highest French court of the ordinary system is the Court of Cassation. It is composed of four sections, among which are divided equally sixty members, not including a first president and four section presidents. Three of the sections form part of the civil side of the judicial hierarchy.

---

[16] Where only one judge is established, he is empowered to perform these functions of the President. Cf. this Ch., p. 157, n 6, *supra.* The large number of courts and judges has given rise to various other attempts at reform. Some improvement has taken place; but local resistance and pressure have been important considerations.

[17] This is the number for Metropolitan France. There exist three Courts for Overseas Departments, and three in North Africa.

The three stand on the same plane,[18] a body (*bureau*) of somewhat complex composition presided over by the First President determining the distribution of work among them. Cases are brought from any court of last resort; and hence they are not, in the strict sense of the word, *appealed* [19] to the Court of Cassation. This supreme court accepts without question the facts determined by the court which has previously heard the case. It concerns itself only with correct application of the law. The relief sought from it is known, as the name of the Court implies, as *cassation*. This word (from *casser* = to break) is equivalent to *quashing*. When the Court, on the basis of law, quashes a decision, it remands the case to another court having the same jurisdiction as that from which the case was brought. At the rehearing, after due allowance for the correct interpretation of the law as decided by the Court of Cassation, the decision may, though of course by no means necessarily, be the same as before. If the case should be heard a second time on a point of law by the Court of Cassation, the Court sits with all sections meeting together. If the Court quashes the decision again, the court to which the case is next remanded must accept the solution of the Court of Cassation.

CRIMINAL JUSTICE

The Penal Hierarchy. On the criminal side, the hierarchy of ordinary courts follows in outline the series of civil courts. The principal exception consists of the introduction of a Court of Assizes for the trial of cases involving serious crimes. Otherwise, the criminal courts, with the names changed in some cases, correspond to the civil courts, other than the special courts. Thus, a Justice of the Peace sits to try minor offenses, the court in this case being known as a Simple Police Tribunal. Minor offenses (known as *contraventions*) are those punishable by a small fine or by short imprisonment. Then, misdemeanors (known as *délits*),[20] with the exception of those connected with the Press, are tried by a Correctional Tribunal, the name given to Tribunals of First Instance when sitting as a criminal court. The Tribunal, as when serving as a civil court, is normally composed of three judges. It sits without a jury. Appeals from the Simple Police Tribunals are taken to the Correctional Tribunals, appeals from the Correctional Tribunals to the Criminal Section of the Courts of Appeal. On a point of law, further relief may be sought in the Criminal Section of the Court of Cassation.

Courts of Assizes. A Court of Assizes is established in each Department. Such a Court is normally set up once every three months; but special sittings may on occasion be held, and in Paris the exception is practically the rule. The judges of the Court consist of a president and two assessors. The President is regularly taken from the Court of Appeal. The assessors are usually taken

---

[18] Before 1947, one of these was a Petitions Section, which had as its task the preliminary examination of civil cases, brought from the Courts of Appeal, with a view to determining whether they deserved hearing and decision at the hands of a Civil Section.

[19] In French law, an appeal implies that a higher court can substitute another decision in place of that pronounced by a lower court.

[20] These are offenses punishable by fines exceeding 6,000 francs or by imprisonment for more than ten days.

from the Tribunal of First Instance in the capital city of the Department; but if this city is also the seat of the Court of Appeal, the assessors may be taken from that Court. The Court of Assizes is the only French court in which a jury is employed. Jurisdiction of the Court extends to misdemeanors in connection with the Press and, in general, to felonies (*crimes*). From a decision of the Court there is, strictly speaking, no appeal. The Criminal Section of the Court of Cassation may merely quash on legal grounds a decision of the Court, and remand the case for further trial.

Criminal Procedure and the Jury. Certain aspects of French criminal procedure are of no little interest. When the police have indicated that a penal offense has been committed, the case, upon receipt of a communication from a prosecuting official of the state, is thoroughly examined by a specially qualified investigating official (*juge d'instruction*). This official in small communities is a judge of the Court of First Instance, who combines the work of investigation with the task of serving as judge; in larger communities, he gives practically all his time to investigation. An investigating judge possesses wide powers. He can order arrests, authorize searches and seizures, summon and question witnesses, and employ experts. He may dismiss a case if he thinks that the evidence does not warrant proceeding with trial. Otherwise, he decides whether the case is one for the Correctional Tribunal or for the Court of Assizes. In the latter event, the case is sent by the investigating judge, through the prosecution, to a section of the Court of Appeal known as the Indictment Section. This Section, composed of at least five judges of the Court of Appeal, performs the same general function as a grand jury. After thorough examination, it decides either to dismiss the case or to send it to the Court of Assizes for trial. The jury that is employed in connection with a Court of Assizes consists of seven regular jurors and four alternates.[21] These members are chosen by a somewhat complex process of list preparations, lot drawings, judicial selection, and prosecution and defence eliminations. The President, both in the Correctional Tribunals and in the Courts of Assizes, directs the trial, developing the case against the accused and questioning him and the witnesses. Counsel address only the President. At the end, the prosecuting officer pleads the case for the state, and counsel for the defence follows. In the Correctional Tribunal, the judges decide guilt or innocence; but, in the Court of Assizes, the judges and jury deliberate together, deciding guilt or innocence and, in the first eventuality, the punishment.

The Civil Party. In connection with the administration of French criminal justice, a striking contrast with Anglo-American practice consists of the fact that in France a private party who desires to seek redress for injury which he feels he has suffered in the course of the events on which a criminal case is based is not compelled to institute proceedings in a distinct civil case, but may as a "civil party" regularly enter a criminal trial. On the basis of the evidence adduced, the matter of damages or other civil right is decided by the court at

---

[21] The alternates substitute, if necessary, for one or more jurors who may in some way become incapacitated, the object being to avoid retrial.

the same time that the question of guilt or innocence is determined by the court
or by the court and jury, as the case may be.

3. ADMINISTRATIVE JUSTICE

THE ADMINISTRATIVE COURTS

General and Specialized Tribunals. The general structure of the regular
system of French administrative courts is exceedingly simple. There is one
highest court, the Council of State; and subordinate to it are a limited number
of Prefectoral Councils. Likewise, there exist certain specialized administrative
courts.

Council of State: Origin. Though an institution known as the Council of
State existed under the *ancien régime,* the present Council of State was in
reality established by Napoleon at the beginning of the Consulate. Since then,
the composition and organization of the Council as a court have naturally
varied from time to time. Changes in these respects have been closely interrelated with stages of development in the modern concept of administrative
justice.

Council of State: Composition. As a court the Council of State is composed of career officials known as the "regular permanent personnel" of the
Council. Its present constitution is as follows:

(a) 1 Vice-President; 5 Section Presidents
(b) 42 Councillors on Regular Service
(c) 45 Masters of Petitions (including General Secretary)
(d) 44 Auditors (20 first class; 24 second class).

Councillors render decisions after due consideration; the Masters and Auditors
prepare business for the consideration and decision of the Councillors; the
General Secretary serves as administrative officer for the Council. Second-Class
Auditors enter upon their positions through the National School of Administration,[22] being in practice a highly trained group. They may serve as such for
a maximum of eight years, after which those who have not been promoted are
appointed to various administrative posts.[23] First-Class Auditors are selected
from the ranks of Second-Class Auditors or from among former Auditors who
have served a minimum of four years in an administrative position. Of the
Masters of Petitions, who must be thirty years of age or more, at least three-
fourths must be taken from the First-Class Auditors. The remaining fourth, if
taken elsewhere than from First-Class Auditors, must be able to show at least
ten years of public service. In all cases, choice is made through executive
decree on recommendation by the ranking members among the Councillors.
For the Councillors there is an age requirement of forty. A provision [24] of

[22] Cf. Ch. VIII, p. 144, *supra.*
[23] Such appointment should be distinguished from situations in which members of the
Council of State obtain leave in order to accept various positions.
[24] Art. 30.

the prevailing Constitution stipulates that they shall be appointed by the President of the Republic in Council of Ministers. At least two-thirds are required by law to be taken from among the Masters of Petitions. Though the other third may be selected without regard for legal requirements, those who do not rise from the ranks of the Masters of Petitions are chosen from among high ranking civil servants.

Council of State: Organization. The working structure of the Council of State is somewhat complex, being the result of a series of careful reforms with the aim of expediting business. The docket of the Council is always highly burdened, and dispatch is imperative. In the first place, there is a Litigation Section, divided into eight subsections. Then, there is a Plenary Litigation Assembly, which is composed of the Vice-President of the Council, the President of the Litigation Section and the vice-presidents of its subsections, and four high administrative officials.[25] In principle, a case is investigated by one of the first four subsections and decided by two of these sitting together. The second four subsections, operating either singly or two at a time, are specialized in certain kinds of "small litigation," such for example as election, tax, and pension cases. The Litigation Section and the Plenary Litigation Assembly confine themselves to cases especially sent to them, usually at the request of the Vice-President of the Council or a section president.

Prefectoral Councils. From the time of the Consulate and Napoleon to 1926, there was a Prefectoral Council in each Department. A decree of 1926 established the present arrangement. There continues to be a Prefectoral Council for the Department of the Seine; but the remaining metropolitan Departments are grouped into twenty-two regions, each with an Interdepartmental Council. The Council of the Seine is composed of a President, two Section Presidents, and ten Councillors. Each of the Interdepartmental Councils consists of a President and three or four Councillors. The members are recruited in principle through the National School of Administration; and promotion is based on merit.

Specialized Courts. Of the several specialized administrative tribunals, typical examples include the Court of Accounts,[26] the Councils of Public Instruction, and the Councils of Military Review. The Court of Accounts is of somewhat numerous personnel and complex organization. Councils of Public Instruction exist on the national, regional, and Department levels; and a Council of Military Review, composed of four members, is established in each Canton.

JURISDICTION OF THE ADMINISTRATIVE COURTS

Specialized Jurisdictions. The jurisdiction of the specialized administrative tribunals is in general sufficiently indicated by their names. The Court of Accounts passes judgment on public accounts, except for those of the Com-

---

[25] This is the only aspect of the matter in which the separation of judicial and active administration is not complete.
[26] Cf. Ch. VI, p. 113, *supra.*

munes and of certain public establishments with revenue below a certain fixed amount. In the exceptional cases, accounts go to a treasury official, and come to the Court of Accounts only on appeal. The Councils of Public Instruction judge controversies that arise in the course of application of the various laws concerning education. The Councils of Military Review hear claims growing out of the operation of the system of military service.

General Jurisdiction: Division. Both kinds of administrative courts of the regular system exercise original jurisdiction. Traditionally, the general principle of distribution of cases has been one of enumeration and residue. The Prefectoral Councils have had original jurisdiction in certain specifically defined classes of cases, the Council of State in the remainder.[27]

General Jurisdiction: Prefectoral Councils. Each Prefectoral Council naturally has jurisdiction only in its own region. It has no final jurisdiction, all its determinations being subject to appeal. At the time of the establishment of the Prefectoral Councils, their fourfold jurisdiction, namely, in cases involving direct taxes, public works, highways, and sale of government property, seemed perfectly consistent with the principle of enumeration. However, the same was not altogether true after 1934, when the jurisdiction of the Councils was so widened that exact enumeration was not easy. Nevertheless, the view was often expressed that nonenumerated original jurisdiction should be given to the Prefectoral Councils, subject to appeal; and legislation proposed in 1950 would go a considerable distance towards meeting this view.[28] In practice, the largest class of cases heard by the Prefectoral Councils remains that of cases connected with direct taxes, thousands being dispatched every year.

General Jurisdiction: Council of State. The Council of State possesses three kinds of jurisdiction. The first of these, its *original jurisdiction,* which traditionally included all cases not specifically allocated by law to the Prefectoral Councils, placed a great burden on the Council of State; and the legislation proposed in 1950 was intended primarily to afford substantial relief in this respect. In the second place, the Council has, with respect to the Prefectoral Councils, *appellate jurisdiction* in the literal French sense; that is to say, it has authority to hear cases on review and, in respect of them, to hand down final decisions, either affirming or altering the decisions of the lower courts. Finally, the jurisdiction of the Council of State includes authority, analogous to that of the Court of Cassation, to *review and quash* decisions handed down by the specialized administrative tribunals, such for example as the Court of Accounts. In such an instance, the case is remanded for rehearing and decision in keeping with the decision of the Council of State.

RELIEF IN ADMINISTRATIVE COURTS

Private and Public Interest. In the increasingly complex conditions of modern life, an individual is correspondingly less likely to be so lucky as to

[27] Legislation introduced by the Government in 1950 with a view to altering this situation by widening the jurisdiction of the Prefectoral Councils is probably somewhat premature.
[28] Cf. previous note.

live out his life, as it used to be said in France as in other countries he could, without contact with the judicial branch of government. He may well be thankful that society, acting through Government, has established impartial arbiters, in the form of courts, to judge between himself and his fellow citizens. However, the individual, who is likewise increasingly likely, possibly through no fault of his own, to come into conflict with agents of Government, finds himself on such occasion in a situation which, though in form similar to that of a private civil suit, is substantially less simple. An impartial arbiter established by society is at least as important in the second instance; but the trouble is that one of the parties is conceived to represent the interests and rights of society itself. In other words, the problem is that of striking a proper balance between the general welfare and individual right. Determination in such matters is the province of what has come to be called "administrative justice." It is recognized to have become so important as to be a subject in itself. Many of its details are technical and complicated, but its general principles may with reasonable effort be understood by the layman.

France and Common-Law Countries. France is well known to have been a pioneer in the matter of administrative justice. In Great Britain and the United States, where a substantially different system has prevailed traditionally,[29] a considerable amount of misapprehension concerning the French system, especially during the formative period, was formerly widespread. In recent years, the developed French system has become better understood; and it is, to no little extent, admired. This, in turn, is in considerable measure the result of the fact that developments in Britain and America, like those previously encountered in France, have given rise to similar problems; and serious study of them has tended to make "administrative law" and "administrative justice" respectable subjects. The student who looks below the surface of things is likely to conclude that the solutions, in spite of some undoubted differences of detail, are fundamentally the same in Common-Law countries as in France. The latter may be considered as in various respects a model.

Excès de Pouvoir. Application of simple concepts of agency and of the principle of *ultra vires* is made in France as well as in Common-Law Countries. In other words, under the French as well as the Anglo-American legal system, any individual who feels that he has an interest in the matter involved may take the position that he is not bound by an attempted exercise of governmental authority, on the ground that there is in reality no legal authority for the act in question or, in other words, that the act is *ultra vires*. In such a situation, an issue is joined; and the courts are called upon to effect settlement. As long as the case is heard and decided by learned and independent judges, no fundamental question would seem to be involved in the matter of what court is employed. Nevertheless, in respect of certain details that are not without importance, the individual would appear to be somewhat better off under the

[29] Anglo-American views have been much influenced by what is called the Rule of Law. The classic treatment of this matter, criticized by various writers in later years and recognized by the author himself to have been too severe towards the French system, is A. V. Dicey, *Introduction to the Study of the Law of the Constitution* (9th ed., London, 1939), Part II.

French system. French procedure is simple and, what is of no little moment, cheap. Under the Anglo-American system, it is as a general rule only where a considerable amount of property is involved that an individual will take the trouble to initiate an expensive and possibly dilatory judicial action in which he may have to go through several courts only to lose in the end and to pay the costs. Moreover, cases in which wealthy parties contest the validity of governmental action are likely to be the very ones in which the public interest would be best served if the judges possessed expert knowledge of modern administration. In these respects, the French system seems to possess solid advantages. Another difference between the French and Anglo-American systems is of less actual consequence. In France, a decision of the Council of State holding that a controverted governmental action, for example an executive order or a local ordinance, is *ultra vires* involves annulment; whereas a similar decision under the Anglo-American system applies only to the question in controversy, the principle being that the court, in applying the law and only what is the law, declines in a given instance to apply what it decides is not the law. Only failure to recognize the strength of precedent under the Anglo-American system would result in stress on the difference in this respect. Much more important is the more general consideration that by no means all governmental actions of doubtful validity are of such a character that the consequences of the actions may be avoided in practice through a decision that the actions are *ultra vires*. Justice will demand not annulment but recompense. This raises the somewhat complicated question of the liability of Government.

Governmental Liability. If a party seeks redress, say in the form of damages, for an injury where the other party is an agent of Government, the basic principle is not highly difficult; it is the exceptions and the modifications which for the most part give rise to the complexity. Strict accuracy would insist that an official, such as a collector of taxes, cannot in his official capacity violate the law which defines his official capacity. Hence, inasmuch as the processes of justice may not be invoked against anyone who has not violated the law, the courts may not take action against a governmental official in his official capacity. Current discussion, it is true, would not hesitate on occasion to assert that a collector of taxes had acted illegally and that a court had in some respect decided against him; but in such a case it is not the collector of revenue, strictly speaking, who is involved, but a private citizen who is also, when he acts within the terms of law defining the position of a collector of taxes, a governmental official. Thus, the concept of *ultra vires* is basically applicable, though in a way clearly different in practice from the way it is applied where annulment of an action affords sufficient relief. If redress—for example payment of damages— is sought, application of the concept of *ultra vires* results in the fact that it must be sought against the person involved, not in his official but in his individual capacity. These strict concepts offer perhaps the best starting point for understanding the practical difficulties involved and the adaptations and exceptions that have been developed. Among the difficulties, two specific disadvantages appear. In the first place, a judgment against a largely propertyless administrative agent in his personal capacity may, as in any civil action, afford little if any substantial relief. In the second place, agents of government may in the course of duty, without exceeding their authority, injure private individuals in ways which, if another private individual were involved, would constitute breaches of law. However, in the Anglo-American system, these disadvantages, growing out of an apparent rigidity of principle, are in actual practice much softened by various considerations. Possibility of relief is specifically arranged by law. Exceptions to general principle are made. Consent to be sued is expressed by Government through law in respect of matters concerning which it is possible to foresee that individuals may have substantially just claims against Government. This has been especially true in the matter of contracts, but it is also true in increasing measure with respect to torts. The point is that, whenever the law so arranges, Government assumes liability for injurious results of the actions of its agents, not alone in the strict sense of the word; and public funds are available when the courts, to which are added more and more frequently "quasi-judicial" agencies, award damages. Under the French system, according to somewhat different principles, at least as wide a measure of protection has for a somewhat longer time been possible.

French Relief: Administrative. In terms of logical classification employed in France, relief against administrative action that may be had from judicial decision is to be distinguished from relief that may result from appealing to the governmental agent or organ concerned (*recours gracieux*) and relief that may result from appealing to a superior of the agent or organ concerned (*recours hiérarchique*). Such nonjudicial relief, it need hardly be recalled, is of course also possible in Common-Law countries, the existence of democracy and a highly developed sense of justice ensuring that it will be available in most cases where circumstances warrant it.

French Relief: Judicial. Under the French system, a case in which satisfactory remedy results from a judicial declaration that an administrative action is *ultra vires* is not essentially different, it will be recalled, from a similar case under the Anglo-American system. Such cases are decided in different courts under the two systems; literal annulment takes place in France, and French procedure possesses solid advantages in respect of simplicity and economy; but no fundamental difference exists. The most characteristic difference appears in connection with *ultra vires* cases in which further relief is desirable and with cases in which injury results from actions that are within the authority of the agents performing them. In respect of both kinds of cases, the French employ a different principle of classification. So long as injury results from an act done in good faith in the course of duty,[30] no distinction is made between an action authorized by law and one not authorized by law. In the one case as in the other, there is said to be an "official wrong" (*faute de service*), and the Government is liable. Decision is, of course, in principle made by administrative

[30] This is a broad concept, the strict concept of "course of duty," as legally defined by provisions determining the exact scope of authority, not being relevant according to French principles.

courts. An official wrong is to be distinguished from a "personal wrong" (*faute personnelle*), a wrong characterized by being "detachable" from the function involved, because, for example, of the bad faith and the evil intent of the person performing the action. Here the liability is personal, and redress must be sought in the ordinary courts.

Liability for Faute de Service. The official wrong, with government responsibility for it, has been the traditionally outstanding aspect of French administrative justice. Two claims have been made, not without considerable reason, for the French system. In the first place, the individual citizen has sometimes been able to secure relief in cases in which, under Anglo-American systems, he would have been without remedy. In the second place—and this is a consideration of much importance in the realm of public administration—an agent of government is not rendered cautious about performing his duty in good faith for fear of inadvertently becoming personally liable.

CHAPTER X

BASIC TENDENCIES IN FRENCH TRADITION

1. INTRODUCTORY

THE STUDY OF THE POLITICAL

Institutions and Politics. French party politics are proverbially complex. This fact causes some persons, even in France, to dismiss the subject as incomprehensible. Special students of comparative government, however, will scarcely be so easily discouraged. Such students will realize that some acquaintance with political doctrine, with political controversy, with political parties, and the like is imperative, if they are to gain any understanding of the French political system. An intelligent study of French institutions, like that of all free institutions, must assume at every point the existence of political considerations. In reality, the two things are, as is well known, closely and reciprocally related. Institutions, it is true, are on the whole specific phenomena, concerning which knowledge is relatively easy to acquire. They are, as it were, manifestations or crystallizations of human thought, emotions, aspirations, and effort, these latter being relatively more difficult to understand than institutions. Consequently, students no doubt naturally tend to begin with, or to place a primary emphasis on, institutions. At the same time, free institutions, it may be repeated, cannot operate in the absence of political considerations; and a study of institutions that neglected to recognize the pervasive influence of such considerations would be an abstract, formalistic, law-book kind of affair.

Politics and the Moral Problem. The fact is that the difficulty of French practical politics may easily be exaggerated. Much of the difficulty, it may be suggested, is not so much inherent in French political life itself as it is in general characteristics of a serious effort to understand the political aspects of government. Basically, the problem is a special form of an old problem of moral philosophy, namely, the problem of how accurate knowledge may be had of what goes on inside people, when the only source of judgment would seem to be that of outward actions. Nevertheless, the study of this difficult problem, as applied to government and politics, may be as interesting as it is important.

More particularly, most students find the study of French practical politics a highly fascinating one.

COMPLEXITY OF FRENCH POLITICS

Political Multiplicity. Probably the simplest—certainly a highly important—manifestation of the somewhat pronounced complexity of practical politics in France is the "multi-party system." The multiplicity of political groups in the French Chambers and of political parties in the country is well known to students.[1] On the more theoretical side, even French authorities frequently speak of the development of a two-party system as an end to be desired and, if possible, to be achieved. On the other hand, the prevailing complexity ought not, it may be repeated, to be exaggerated. Thus, elementary importance attaches to distinguishing official political groups from other kinds of similar groups.[2] At least equally important is the distinction between *group* and *party.*

Parties and Groups. Strictly speaking, the word *party* is in France correctly applied to political organizations in the country at large; whereas the word *group,* in the sense of official *political* group, is in general equivalent to *parliamentary party* in Great Britain and to *caucus* in the United States, referring, that is to say, to a number of members of one or the other of the Chambers bound together more or less closely by certain political affiliations and for certain political purposes. The somewhat greater formal recognition in France of political groups is probably of no special importance;[3] but the fact that there is by no means always correspondence between political organizations in the country and political associations in Parliament is of considerably larger moment. The "monolithic" or "big three" parties,[4] it is true, have well defined corresponding groups both in the National Assembly and in the Council of the Republic, and the same thing is true in a few other instances; but under the Fourth Republic, as was the case under the Third Republic, parties exist to which no groups correspond, and there are several groups to which there are no corresponding parties. In other words, there is no necessary connection, though in certain instances there is close actual connection, between political parties and political groups. On the other hand, in respect of one important aspect of the matter, namely, in respect of a basic question of terminology and all that it involves, consideration of political parties as they exist at large in the country must presuppose the existence of political groups in Par-

---

[1] Cf. Ch. vi, pp. 102–103, *supra.*

[2] Cf. *ibid.*

[3] Mention of groups in the Constitution of the Fourth Republic and in the *règlement* of each of the Chambers clearly goes beyond American practice; but, in the second respect, the Rules of both Houses of Congress assume, without specifically mentioning as do the Standing Orders of the House of Commons in England, the existence of parties; and, if a multi-party system prevailed, parties would probably be explicitly recognized. There is of course frequent mention of parties in Acts of Congress.

[4] Cf. Ch. iv, pp. 67–68, *supra.* Following the elections of 1951, a group of the RPF as such was for the first time established in the National Assembly (cf. Ch. vi, *loc. cit.,* n 63, *supra,* and Ch. xii, p. 209, *infra*).

liament.[5] This is, of course, the matter of the well-known political classifications, Right and Left.

Parties and Political Tendencies. The French writer who is at the present day probably the outstanding authority on party politics in France [6] stresses strongly the importance of distinguishing between political parties as such and what he calls "the inorganic tendencies of the public mind." He feels that the confusion of terms which has traditionally been made in France through application to both of them of the word *party* resulted previously in no great disadvantage; but he insists that at present failure to make the distinction involves the risk of genuinely serious misapprehension. He even goes so far as to apologize for having employed the expression *party politics* in the title of a distinguished book,[7] on the ground of contributing to the perpetuation of confusion. No serious student of comparative government will do anything but applaud employment of a highly influential voice in favor of the importance of making careful distinctions in respect of a peculiarly difficult aspect of political science. Such a student, on the other hand, will be careful, it is to be hoped, to avoid the somewhat common practice of swinging to the opposite extreme and assuming that when one thing can be clearly distinguished from another, there is no connection between them. Actually, political parties and political tendencies stand in the same relationship to each other as political institutions and political thought in general; and this relationship, it can scarcely be too often repeated, is, while admitting of and profiting from accurate distinction, a close reciprocal one. Each, it seems clear, influences the other. Thus, if a political party is conceived of as an organized association of individuals, then, whether the concept is widely interpreted as including all individuals connected however loosely with the association or whether more exclusively as being composed only of the "wheel horses," that is to say, of persons intimately connected with and actually constituting the principal structure of the organization, the elements are after all individuals and as such members of the public, thereby contributing to the thinking of "the public mind," just as they are in turn influenced by certain aspects of such thinking.

2. RIGHT VERSUS LEFT IN FRANCE

DUAL DIVISION

Origin. The simple consideration of the physical position occupied by the several groups in a house of Parliament,[8] whereby these groups sit in a semi-circle in front of the presiding officer, ranging from reactionary on the presi-

---

[5] Cf. Ch. VI, pp. 102–103, *supra,* and this Ch. p. 174, *infra.*

[6] François Goguel, Professor in the Institute of Political Studies of the University of Paris. This and the two following chapters owe much to his books and his articles (especially in the review *Esprit* and in the two editions, 1940 and 1950, of *Encyclopédie politique de la France et du monde*).

[7] *La Politique des partis sous la IIIe République* (Paris, 1948).

[8] Cf. Ch. VI, p. 103, *supra.*

dent's right to the opposite extreme [9] on his left, furnishes the basis for the far-reaching classification of the political parties in the country, together with their political tendencies, as Right or Left. The correspondence of the terms to the particular tendencies was naturally an accident in the beginning; but, once established at the time of the Revolution, the seating arrangement and its political implications have continued to the present day.

Barricades and Clarity. Distinction between parties and tendencies and recognition that the terms *Right* and *Left,* while not unnaturally applied to parties, are, basically considered, really tendencies should be sufficient to suggest the importance of avoiding two extremes—namely, the extreme on the one hand of conceiving that the classification of a given party as Right or Left is a complete explanation of its character, and the extreme on the other hand of assuming that because an "exact" distinction cannot be made between Right and Left, manifestations of the two tendencies are not helpful to understanding. In reality, they are fundamental. Two parties, it is of course true, can be identified as separate organizations, whereas tendencies, because of their nature, are more difficult clearly to define and to distinguish. Moreover, the more complex prevailing conditions are, the more pronounced the difficulty will be. On the other hand, the French Revolution contributed a concept the figurative application of which is of great importance in connection with political affairs. This is the concept of the "barricade." Just as in certain times of stress and strain the barricades are literally set up and people take positions, in large part through clear and simple decision, on one side or the other, so in other crises the barricades tend figuratively to be erected, and people find that issues become so clearly drawn that they feel they can or must definitely take sides one way or the other. Modern French history affords a number of examples of such situations. At these times, Right and Left are identifiable with relatively little difficulty, the elements of difference being on the whole clearly understood. Naturally, when conditions are less critical, distinctions are less clear-cut; and there is talk of the Centre and of other things that shows the problem of definition to be more complex. Moreover, with the passing of time, the complicated character of public life tends to become so pronounced that even acute crisis succeeds only partially in simplifying and clarifying issues. In any case, the Fourth Republic, which has known little else than crisis, has witnessed a pattern in practical politics that varies substantially from that which regularly prevailed in the crises of the Third Republic. Nevertheless, distinction between Right and Left remains, it may be repeated, fundamental; and no understanding of French government and politics is possible without some study of the character of the two tendencies.

Liberalism and Conservatism. The tendency for the Right to be identified with *conservatism* and the Left with *liberalism* is apparently inevitable. The explanation is in large measure to be found in terms of history and of tradition.

---

[9] The English term commonly employed is of course *radical;* but in a study of French politics it is probably better to avoid the word except as a designation of a French phenomenon. Cf Ch. XII, p. 203, *infra.*

Caution and boldness with respect to certain conditions and to proposed changes in them have at a given time in the past constituted fairly definite attitudes towards political affairs, and even today fundamental analysis on the basis of these concepts may be of considerable value; [10] but, with the passing of time, *conservatism* and, probably even more, *liberalism* have become two of the most ill-defined words in political terminology. Certainly, in contemporary usage, Right and Left are less ambiguous terms. In France, the label *conservative* has come to be in considerable measure an opprobrious epithet that would scarcely be adopted voluntarily by a political party, whereas *liberal,* possessing traditionally favorable connotations, has been largely appropriated by parties of reaction. The two terms, as a result of bitter controversies, have not unnaturally changed, and to some extent even exchanged, their earlier meanings.

COMPLICATING FACTORS

Industrial Revolution. The suggestion has been made in France that the simplest distinction between Right and Left is to be found in terms of rejection or acceptance of the French Revolution.[11] According to this view, the distinction is primarily determined by different attitudes towards certain questions which in the beginning were bitterly debated by advocates and opponents of the *ancien régime.* These questions were that of the regime and those of the two great forces, spiritual and physical, that form the bases of any regime, namely, the Church and the Army. They are questions which clearly seem to be essentially political in character. With respect to them, the positions of the Right and the Left have, it may be repeated, by no means remained constant. One clue to the situation is to be found in terms of the effects of the Industrial Revolution. Though the forces set in motion at the time of the French Revolution are still to be felt, they have in a definite sense become of secondary importance as compared with the social and economic problems resulting from the Industrial Revolution. During the later years of the Third Republic, differences between Left and Right were to be understood in terms of each of these Revolutions and, more especially, in terms of both of them in their interrelationships.

World War II. This situation was complex enough; but it has become even more complicated under the Fourth Republic. Certain effects of World War II have been varyingly but profoundly influential.

POLITICAL ISSUES: REGIME

Monarchy versus Republic. One aspect of the traditional distinction between Right and Left has undoubtedly been support by the Right of monarchy and support by the Left of republicanism. At the present time, this difference is not in literal terms highly important. The question of monarchy versus republic is not a very burning issue. Fairly early in the Third Republic, members

---

[10] Cf. this Ch., pp. 179–180, *infra.*
[11] Cf. A. Siegfried, *Tableau des partis en France* (Paris, 1930), pp. 57 *et seq.*

of the Right accepted the Republic without great difficulty.[12] It was this which caused Léon Bourgeois to utter his famous exclamation: "You have accepted the Republic! Do you accept the Revolution?" Even so early, in other words, the primary question of regime had become subordinate in importance to other considerations. The simple fact was that the republican regime was accepted as the established system. Being identified with political democracy, acceptance by the great body of the people was inevitable.

Government for the Few or the Many. After all, a system of government, it seems clear, is not an end in itself. It is important primarily in terms of the end it undertakes to further. Monarchy originally served principally the interests of a relatively small class; it was opposed, just as republicanism was supported, by those who claimed to give principal importance to the interests of the large body of the people. In this respect, the modifying effects of the Industrial Revolution became increasingly significant. During the Third Republic, supporters of interests of the body of the people attempted with greater and greater persistence to employ the potential advantage afforded to them by political democracy to deal in such a way with social and economic problems created by the Industrial Revolution as to further the interests of the body of the people. On the other hand, those who desired to support primarily the interests of the few opposed such use of power. In the numerically unequal contest, the few were able in some measure to offset inferiority of numbers through certain inherited economic and social advantages. Some members of this class trusted to these advantages, or hoped on various grounds, to gain control of the existing regime. Others stressed somewhat more the desirability and possibility of a change. In this respect, by no means all were literally reactionary in the sense of being traditional monarchists. Their principal common characteristic was tenderness for "direct action." Especially during the period between the two Wars, certain elements of the Right developed a fondness for the methods and accomplishments of the dictatorships in Italy, Germany, and Spain.[13]

Democracy and Dictatorship. Thus, by what in political affairs is sometimes called a "pendulum swing," republicanism and political democracy, after having gained the ascendancy in France over monarchy, became in turn subject to opposition and attack at the hands of elements that may be regarded as being in a continuous Right tradition. The issue in its new form was of course not so patently that of monarchy versus republic. In terms of regime, the issue that ultimately developed during the Third Republic was rather that of a Left tendency towards assembly government versus Right advocacy of a strong executive,[14] ranging from loyal support of a more nearly classical type of parliamentary government to treasonable approval of dictatorship. The Vichy regime, marking the temporary success of the more unsavory anti-republican elements,[15] served among other things to arouse movements which

---

[12] Cf. Ch. XI, p. 185, *infra.*   [13] Cf. Ch. XII, p. 207, *infra.*
[14] Cf. Ch. IV, p. 70, *supra.*
[15] Some of these came from the Left; but it seems fair to say that the more numerous and more typical examples were from the Right.

demonstrated that the body of the French are unshakably, even if not enthusiastically, republican, parliamentary, and democratic.

The Present Scene. Under the Fourth Republic, the issue of regime has not, at least so far, assumed a traditional dual pattern. The Third Force, composed of somewhat heterogeneous anti-extremist elements, favor in general the elements of the parliamentary system, characterized by greater or lesser tendencies towards assembly government. The principal forces of the opposition bracket the Third Force on both sides, advocating in each case a different regime. General de Gaulle persistently asserts that France's fundamental problem is that of regime. He himself appears to advocate something close to the American type of presidential government; but some of his ablest lieutenants assert themselves much less ready to support such a regime; [16] and the General's organization is officially on record against it.[17] Just how far these opponents of the Third Force would, in the event of victory, go in the matter of regime, and just how far they would confine themselves to legal methods are, it would seem, uncertain and open questions. Concerning the other enemies of the Third Force, the Communists, there can be little if any uncertainty. Their predilection for ruthless and unscrupulous methods is proved by abundant experience. Their ideal regime is of course that of the USSR; but they talk much of, as they persistently defend in every detail, the "popular democracies" of the Soviet satellites.

POLITICAL ISSUES: CHURCH

Clericalism and Anticlericalism. From the point of view of tradition, the distinction between Right and Left in terms of attitude towards the Church is clear enough. The Right regularly supported the Church, the Left was anticlerical. Throughout the Third Republic—not to go back further—the religious question was an issue—often actual, always potential—of the highest importance in French politics. Concerning the difference between Right and Left, a well-known French professor of the Right wrote in 1939: [18] "Perhaps the surest criterion would still be opinion on the subject of the Churches in the State, of religious liberties, of relations with the Vatican, and so on. Religious questions have been tearing our country for centuries."

Religion and Politics. As a matter of fact, the issue of religion, it seems clear, is a more deep-running problem than a question like that of regime, for example, in the sense that the relation of means and end is not so manifest; but, however simple and accurate a test of membership in the Right or in the Left the attitude towards this issue may have been, it was a formal test in the sense that it offered no basic explanation of why people disagreed on this question. Religious questions are, it may be further suggested, largely independent, as such, of economic and social questions. Hence, although members of the

16 Cf., e.g., R. Aron, *Le Grand schisme* (Paris, 1948), p. 261.
17 V. R. Capitant, *Rapport sur la Revision de la Constitution* (1948), pp. 2–3. This is a document adopted by the National Council of the RPF at its second session during the second National Assizes. Cf. Ch. XII, pp. 208–209, *infra.*
18 Joseph-Barthélemy in *Gouvernement de la France* (3e éd., Paris, 1939), p. 44.

Right have traditionally been in most cases both supporters of the Church and opponents of solutions that have been attempted by the Left in respect of social and economic questions, there is no necessary logical connection between the two attitudes. That a distinction can be made in practice is demonstrated by the fact that some uncompromising supporters of the Church are men of somewhat bold social and economic views. This combination was not widespread in France during the Third Republic, but it did exist.[19]

The Present Scene. As is well known, one of the striking results in France of World War II was emergence at the outset of the Fourth Republic of a Catholic party of Left tendencies, the MRP, a monolithic party and a member of the "big three." [20] For essentially the same reasons which caused this phenomenal growth in the strength of social Catholicism, namely, relationships for the most part established during the Resistance, the age-old phenomenon of anticlericalism has been far less manifest during the Fourth Republic. At the same time, there can be little doubt but that the issue, if sometimes apparently dormant, is never far below the surface of things. The occasion on which it is certain to re-emerge is that of any real discussion of the important matter of education. This matter is sure to assume first-rate proportions sooner or later. A strong committee was set up in 1950 with a view to serious studies and careful recommendations in respect of the question. The student genuinely interested in French politics will do well to be on the lookout for discussion in the country and in Parliament of proposals that may be made. On the basis of tendencies that have already manifested themselves, especially during the long ministerial crisis following the 1951 elections, prophecy may be made with some confidence that the traditional Right-Left pattern will be considerably modified. The traditionally anticlerical party, the Radicals,[21] now commonly regarded as being essentially a party of the Right, can be counted on to join with the Socialists and Communists in defence of the "laic" principle in education; whereas the MRP will part company with the Left to join conservatives and reactionaries of the Right in favor of "free," that is, Catholic schools.

POLITICAL ISSUES: ARMY

Constants and Variables. Originally and traditionally, the Right tended strongly to support the Army, the Left to be antimilitarist. The historical basis for this was an instinctive opposition on the part of the Left to the Army, an opposition based on the not unfounded feeling that the Army had been employed as a bulwark in the protection and furtherance of the interests of the privileged few. On the other hand, a tendency has from time to time manifested itself for the two sides to exchange positions, or, at the least, for the Left to assume a different attitude towards the Army. Such considerations as the democratization of the Army and the tendency for the Left to become po-

[19] Cf. Ch. xii, p. 200, *infra.*
[20] Cf. *ibid.,* and Ch. iv, pp. 67–68, *supra.*
[21] Cf. Ch. iv, p. 66, *supra,* and Ch. xi, p. 186, *infra.*

litically the strong side have caused the Left on occasion to supplant its traditional distrust with a measure of confidence in the possibility that the Army might be made to serve the ends, internal and foreign, which the Left felt to be in the interests of the masses. Thus, early in the Revolutionary period the Left accepted the necessity of employing armed force; and, at times towards the end of the Third Republic, the Left, in spite of pacifist tendencies on the part of some of its elements, favored armed strength against dictatorial tendencies, elements of the Right being correspondingly hostile to opposition of this kind.

The Present Scene. At the present time, the situation is in some respects clearer, in some respects more complicated. France is officially committed to armed preparation against the menace of Communism. The Communists and their sympathizers are solidly opposed to this policy, and the rest of opinion is, at least in a negative sense, unified on the other side; but, within the limits of this general unity, many shades of belief or advocacy exist.

3. POLITICS AND HUMAN NATURE

Facts and Their Interpretation. Distinct and acute traditional differences between Right and Left and survivals and modifications of them are on the whole not difficult to observe. In other words, certain political facts are evident to everyone. On the other hand, great difficulty attaches to formulating the facts in terms that will command general agreement even on the part of men of good will; and there is still greater difficulty and still more likelihood of disagreement, when questions of interpretation are raised. In other words, human reason and human emotions are closely connected not only with political facts but also with the difficulty of understanding them.

The Nature of Man. This is one way of saying, as is often said, that serious efforts to understand fundamental political considerations inevitably lead to examination of human nature. Such examination regularly distinguishes the general animal aspect of man from the aspect which characterizes man specifically as such, distinguishing him from other varieties of animals. In the second respect, many statements of the matter have been attempted; but they practically all tend in some way to stress the moral or ethical character of human nature. The animal and moral sides are naturally related closely in a reciprocal manner; but human nature more nearly realizes its true self in the degree that it transcends the animal elements.

Pessimism and Optimism. Political differences, it would seem, are determined in part by the dual nature of man and in part by attitudes towards it. The basic source of knowledge in this respect is examination of self; but the practice of judging, by extension and analogy, the character of others is apparently inevitable. Some persons stress the animal aspect of man, doubting his capacity to transcend it and to improve himself, in other words, to be good. Reason, according to this emphasis, is essentially ineffective, progress is an illusion, and man not worthy of trust. Others emphasize the rational and moral aspect of human nature, believing in the goodness and perfectibility of man.

The more pessimistic view insists that the masses should be under the control and guidance of the few who are exceptions and on top. The more optimistic view holds that the body of the people should be free to develop their potentialities and that they are "backward" largely because they have been so long subjected to the few, who are exceptional because they are on top, not on top because they are exceptional. Thus, the serious student is almost certain to discover that one thing runs through political history like a thread. At all times, certain people, for whatever reasons more specific than the matter of interest, interpret the general welfare in terms of the interests of the few, and others in terms of the interests of the many.

CHAPTER XI

HISTORICAL SKETCH OF PARTY POLITICS IN FRANCE

1. BEFORE THE THIRD REPUBLIC

GENERAL CONSIDERATIONS

Remote and Recent Origins. If in the history of practical politics in France the matter of sentiment and tendency is stressed, the question of origins may without difficulty be pushed back to the French Revolution, and even beyond. If the matter of organization is emphasized, particularly if substantial rigidity and discipline are insisted upon, parties in France are of relatively recent foundation.[1]

Parties and Parliamentary Government. Students of political science in Europe are not unnaturally inclined to underline the reciprocal influence of the development of political tendencies and the development of parliamentary government. So far as France is concerned, the fact that previous to the Fourth Republic the parliamentary system was twice established in that country, once on the monarchical basis of a highly restricted suffrage and once on a liberal democratic and republican basis, is undoubtedly an important background consideration.[2]

NINETEENTH–CENTURY REGIMES

Monarchy. After the Restoration, the voters were so few in number that members of elected chambers were able largely through personal relations to maintain with their constituents the contact which parties are instrumental in effecting in more modern democratic conditions. As a matter of fact, the law with respect to associations before 1848 made parties illegal. The result was that the concept of parties, as distinguished from groups within the chambers,

---

[1] Acceptance of such emphasis would make the Socialist Party the first real French party. Cf. this Ch., p. 185, *infra,* and Ch. XII, pp. 195–197, *infra.* It is an interesting fact that although democratic parliamentary government was established in France in the 1870's, liberal legislation establishing real right of assembly was not passed until 1901.

[2] Cf. Ch. III, p. 59, *supra.*

carried a distinct overtone of conspiracy, a fact illustrated during long periods by the position of Republicans.[3]

Second Republic. During the brief period of the Second Republic, liberalization of the law encouraged in a measure the development of political association; but, although the Right was successful in establishing the rudiments of a national organization, the growth of numerous clubs and similar organisms on the Left was too scattered for anything like a party to be established on a national scale.

Second Empire. Under the Second Empire, even in its more liberal form, conditions were scarcely propitious for political organization. Elements in opposition during the Liberal Empire, namely, Paris Republicans and Orleanist and Bourbon Monarchists, were scarcely homogeneous enough for unification to be realized; and, for the members of the majority, supporters of the regime, administrative organization, with "official candidates," [4] performed the principal functions of a party.

2. THE THIRD REPUBLIC

Shifting Scene. In the more immediate sense, the political situation at the present day in France evolved out of political developments in the course of the Third Republic. It is this consideration that gives to the period as historical background its importance and interest. During the Third Republic partisan organizations and groupings underwent many vicissitudes. The deep division between Left and Right was never really absent; but the confused surface often presented a chaotic and kaleidoscopic appearance. Groups displaying greater or lesser degrees of organization came and went. Names were changed and even exchanged, until much terminology became unmeaning, except to the initiated and sometimes even to them.

HEROIC PERIOD: 1871–1879

Monarchists and Republicans. At the beginning of the Third Republic, the situation with respect to political parties was relatively simple. Opposition of Monarchists and Republicans represented a fundamental division.[5] The issue served to introduce much clarity into the political scene in France; and this remained the situation until the Republican forces were definitively victorious. It was "the heroic period, with which the name of Gambetta has remained associated." [6] It lasted until 1879.

Republican Successes: The First Legislature. On the occasion of the election in 1876 of the first Parliament under the Constitution of the Third Republic, the Monarchist camp, the Right, was flabbergasted by the fact that the Republicans, the Left, secured more than two-thirds of the seats in the Chamber of Deputies. President MacMahon, a Monarchist, made only half-

---

[3] Cf. *ibid.,* pp. 57–58, *supra.*
[4] Cf. Ch. II, p. 53, *supra.*
[5] Cf. *ibid.,* p. 46, p. 54, *supra.*
[6] Cf. Bourgin, Carrère et Guérin, *Manuel des partis politiques en France* (2e éd., Paris, 1928), p. 9.

hearted efforts to accept the implications of parliamentary government; and the first two ministries that were formed, though ostensibly from the majority, were short-lived. Indeed, MacMahon dismissed the second of these ministries, thereby creating an acute crisis and, in the end, causing his own downfall.

Republican Successes: Seize Mai Incident. The issue between the Republican majority and MacMahon was at bottom religious. It originated in a request from the Pope to the French clergy to bring pressure on the Government in connection with an anticlerical law in Italy. Resulting agitation, which even threatened the equilibrium of international relations in Europe, caused Gambetta, eloquent leader of the Left, to revive as a war cry a formula from the Second Empire: "Clericalism! That is the enemy!" The clergy and the clerical press were undoubtedly unrestrained and violent in their campaigns. MacMahon, though determined to dismiss a Ministry regarded by him as faithless because of its effort to steer a middle course, was unwilling for the religious issue to appear as the immediate cause of dismissal. Hence, he sought and finally found pretexts of a less serious character. Nevertheless, the Republicans vigorously protested the action, which they associated with personal, antiparliamentary government. MacMahon sponsored formation of a Ministry of the Right; and this Ministry, soon seen to be in a hopeless minority, secured dissolution of the Chamber of Deputies. The Right, with the assistance of the administrative machinery of the country and with the aid even of the President of the Republic, conducted a campaign that was not only highly vigorous but also decidedly scurrilous. The Left, on the defensive, maintained remarkable discipline; and the Republicans, though their majority was slightly reduced,[7] scored an undoubted victory. The whole incident was represented by the Republicans as an attempted *coup d'état* on the part of MacMahon; and this attitude entered into the tradition that has in large measure been responsible for the fact that dissolution, though an integral part of parliamentary government in its classic form, has not since 1877 been employed in France.[8] In the event, MacMahon, after considering several expedients including a military *coup,* decided to give in. He sponsored formation of a Left ministry.

Republican Successes: Final Victory. Parliamentary government had triumphed; but the Republican Party, though it had won a notable victory, had yet to consolidate its position. Two of the three institutions of national Government, the Presidency of the Republic and the Senate, still belonged to the Right. After about a year, on the occasion of the partial renewal of the Senate at the beginning of 1879, the Republicans gained a comfortable majority in that body. MacMahon, thus isolated, gave his resignation before the end of the month.

REPUBLICAN DIVISION: OPPORTUNISTS VS. RADICALS: 1879–1893

Right and Left Republicans. The Republicans, after definitive defeat of Monarchy, in 1879, displayed a characteristic that is a not uncommon phe-

---

[7] From the famous 363 to 321.
[8] Cf. Ch. VII, p. 134, *supra.*

nomenon in all political history. They were united when on the defensive, frequently divided when on the offensive. In the second respect, the division between Left and Right, when no longer resting on the uncertain matter of regime,
reappeared in the ranks of the victorious Republicans. The all-important religious question and the only less important military question remained; and
economic and social issues were crowding upon political issues as potential
sources of deep-cut divisions.[9] A second period, extending from 1879 to
World War I, was a "period of Republican division." [10]

Radicalism versus Gradual Reform. The first of several forms taken by
Republican division extended over a period of roughly fifteen years. There was
opposition between an element known as Opportunists and an element known
as Radicals.[11] The division, however, was merely a sort of family altercation
concerning the best methods of accomplishing agreed ends, as was demonstrated by the fact that any serious conditions, especially those conceived to
endanger the regime, brought all elements of Republicans together in a unified
defence. The Opportunists, though not forming a compact majority, succeeded
on the whole in guiding the course of events for approximately half of the
fifteen-year period. Their general policy was to effect gradual piecemeal reform, the real desire of the leaders, especially Gambetta, being to unite the
Left. However, unity was compromised not only by the unbending attitude of
the Radicals but by personal antagonisms among Opportunist leaders. As a
result, a rapid succession of Ministries occurred, a situation that came to be
considered a characteristic feature of parliamentary government in France.[12]
In the course of the fifteen-year period of Opportunist and Radical Opposition,
there were more than fifteen Ministries.

Concentration and Appeasement. About midway in the period 1879–
1893, the Right, in spite of Republican discipline, succeeded in substantially
increasing its representation in the Chamber of Deputies. The two Left factions
became almost exactly equal, each alone having about the same representation
as the Right. Conditions more than ever lent themselves to short-lived ministries. One or the other of two combinations tended to prevail. The first, known
as "Republican Concentration," resulted when the greater part of the two Republican factions could be brought into substantial agreement. The second
combination was that of the "Policy of Appeasement." It was formed through
support afforded by a part of the Conservatives to the more moderate Republicans, on condition of abandonment of anticlerical measures.

Republican Scandals and Crises. During the same period, three events—
the Wilson scandal, the Boulanger episode, and the Panama scandal—had important political repercussions. Such crises are in part the cause and in part the
effect of the intensity of French politics. Wilson, son-in-law of President Grévy,
was shown to have used in numerous ways influence derived from his intimacy
with the President; and the President was forced to resign when Parliament
would have no relations with Ministries sponsored by him, the actual suprem-

---

[9] Cf. Ch. x, p. 175, *supra.*
[10] Cf. Bourgin et al., *loc. cit.*

[11] Cf. Ch. iv, p. 66, *supra* and Ch. xii, p. 203, *infra.*
[12] Cf. Ch. vii, pp. 131–132, *supra.*

acy of Parliament being proved to extend to an insufficiently impartial, formal head of State. Boulanger, beginning as a young general of considerable personal attraction, subsequently declared his intention of abolishing the parliamentary system and otherwise displayed an ambition for personal power; but although he gathered a considerable following, especially from elements of the Right, he showed himself in the end to be a man of little determination, whereas political democracy was proved to be, while not without vulnerability to vigorous sudden attack, strongly and solidly founded. The Panama scandal likewise demonstrated the fundamental vitality of parliamentary republicanism and the basic solidity of a system resting on genuine political democracy; for, although reputations suffered [13] and the regime lost some prestige through the discovery of unsavory relations between high finance, the press, and politicians,[14] democracy proved itself sufficiently flexible to accept as a moral of the affair the desirability of reform rather than of change of regime.

REPUBLICAN DIVISION: MODERATE BLOC VS. LEFT BLOC: 1893–1906

New Forces. Beginning in 1893, the split in the ranks of the Republicans assumed for about a dozen years a different form. Behind this change was the addition of two new elements to the Republican forces. As a result of the proclamation by the Pope of a new policy, a small group appeared on the Right characterized by reconciliation—the "rallying" (*ralliement*)—of Catholicism to the Republic; on the Left, Socialism, after near destruction at the time of the Commune in 1871 and after subsequent sporadic activities and internal difficulties, reappeared on the political scene with substantial minority representation in the Chamber of Deputies.

Blocs. With these conditioning factors, division of Republican forces gave rise to two groupings that came to be known as "blocs." A Moderate Bloc, formed of Catholic Republicans and of the remains of the Opportunists, known as "Progressists," was a sufficiently homogeneous majority to direct, in spite of the familiar succession of Ministries, the general course of events. Its members conceived themselves to be defenders of property and order, thus joining square issue with the Left. In the result, the Radicals, among whom younger members had for a decade asserted that their great party of the French Revolution and of the Republic ought to accept priority of social and economic questions,[15] were pushed in the direction of the Socialists, with whom they gradually coalesced to form the Left Bloc.[16] The two blocs were in the event sharply opposed on such questions as freedom of the press and a sliding-scale income tax; but, with the passage of time, the religious question, though clearly interrelated with other issues, became the outstanding point of deep-running difference. This was clearly manifest during agitation over the famous Dreyfus affair.

"The Affair." Captain Alfred Dreyfus, an Alsatian Jewish artillery staff officer, was accused in 1894 of furnishing documents to Germany, and con-

---

13 Notably that of Clemenceau.
14 Cf. R. Recouly, *La Troisième République* (Paris, 1927), p. 170.
15 Cf. Ch. XII, *loc. cit., infra.*
16 Better known merely as the Bloc.

victed by court-martial. His friends and family, convinced of his innocence, persisted, in spite of difficulties and discouragements, in the attempt to vindicate him. Finally, the false character of the accusation became evident; Dreyfus was pardoned in 1899, and in 1905 reinstated in the Army. The case, beginning as an apparently simple affair of military justice, to which the body of the people at first remained largely indifferent, ended by splitting France into two hostile political camps. All the bitterness, vehemence, and violence inherent in the opposition of Right and Left were brought to the surface in a country where people think and feel intensely. Friendships of long standing were wrecked; emotions were in general heated to an almost unimaginable pitch. On the one side were those Frenchmen who had been traditionally grouped as conservatives—supporters of the Monarchy, of the Church, and of the Army. They launched scurrilous attacks against the Republic and against parliamentary government, democratic phenomena which they disapproved as opposed to caste and privilege. On the other side were supporters of the tradition of the French Revolution and advocates of bold solutions of problems emerging from the Industrial Revolution. They were enraged by the close alliance between Army and Church. The Radicals, traditional enemies of intervention by the clergy in political life, were joined by the Socialists in a bitter anticlericalism. Both were vehemently hostile to an Army regarded as being so officered as to constitute a real menace to democracy. The Right was, as things developed, constrained to argue that the question of Dreyfus's guilt or innocence was of secondary importance. Justice had to yield precedence to considerations of State. The prestige of the Army and the honor of the Church must be defended at all costs. On the other hand, the Left derived strength from consciousness of the justice of its cause. Intellectuals flocked to its side; and foreign countries recognized the rightness of its position.

Republican Defence. Effects of the Dreyfus affair may be felt in France even today. At the time, the most direct consequence was unification of the Left to a point where it could work its will with respect to the Army and the Church. The actions [17] taken were known as "Republican Defence." After the middle of 1899, certain generals and other officers of the Army who were held to be especially dangerous to the Republic were pensioned, relieved, or disgraced; and reorganization was effected that was calculated to break the power of a Monarchist and reactionary clique. Treatment of the Church was if anything even more far-reaching. In the latter days of the Dreyfus affair, certain powerful and rich religious orders, more particularly the Assumptionists [18] and Jesuits, appeared to be giving vigorous support to the agitation of the Right. Governmental investigation disclosed various consequences of the unauthorized presence in France of many religious orders and the illegal existence of

[17] The Prime Minister, Waldeck-Rousseau, formed in June of 1899 his "Ministry of Republican Defence," the longest-lived Ministry of the Third Republic. Waldeck-Rousseau was a jurist of conservative instincts who had been much influenced by the Dreyfus affair. His Ministry had not the appearance of leaning heavily to the Left, though it included in the person of Millerand the first Socialist to hold ministerial office. Cf. Ch. xii, p. 196, *infra.*

[18] This order was soon dissolved as not possessing the authorization required by existing legislation.

monasteries which possessed valuable property, conducted remunerative commerce in liqueurs and other products, and received, contrary to law, bequests
on which no duty was paid. The teaching orders, which were regarded as undermining the republican and democratic ideas of sons of the noble, the wealthy,
and the military classes, were found to be conducting the education of more
pupils than were the state schools. Remedial legislation was passed; and subsequently a somewhat vindictive anticlerical ministry [19] undoubtedly carried out
the legislation more vigorously than had been intended at the time of its passage, but scarcely in the face of disapproval on the part of the existing majority. Later, as was doubtless inevitable, direct conflict with the Pope occurred.[20]
In the event, French sentiment was so aroused that diplomatic relations with
the Vatican were strained to the breaking point. Finally, after much discussion,
legislation was passed in 1905 effecting the separation of Church and State.
The policy of the Republic became that of withdrawing its recognition, declining to pay salaries, and refusing subsidies to all churches. A property settlement, according to which possessions of the Church were allocated to associations of citizens, was, in its principle and its execution, subject of further
protest, resistance, and bitterness.

REPUBLICAN DIVISION: BREAK-UP OF THE BLOC: 1906-1910

Responsible Radicalism. The period of approximately the second five
years of the twentieth century was characterized by the break-up of the Left
Bloc. Several considerations, especially the Bloc's rigorous anti-clericalism,
caused the defection of a certain number of supporters from the right wing;
and on the extreme left the Socialists were, owing to unification of their several
organizations, lost to the Bloc. Elections during the period, it is true, gave
to the Left, especially the Radicals, a position of much strength; but after a
relatively long lease on power, many of the Radicals, under the influence of
experience and responsibility, tended to become more moderate, with the result that they came into conflict, because of measures taken for the purpose
of maintaining order against organized labor under revolutionary influence,
with the Socialists. In these conditions, disintegration of the Bloc became
complete.

Extremes against the Middle. The Radicals, as so often happens to
liberal parties, were caught in a cross-fire from Right and Left. The electoral
system became a burning issue, the Right and the Socialists joining forces in
the matter, the Radicals being split on the issue.

REPUBLICAN DIVISION: REFORMING OF THE BLOC: 1910-1914

Immanence of War. The period between 1910 and the outbreak of
World War I witnessed an obscure situation in Parliament. The period was

---

[19] Headed by Senator Combes, a little old man of seventy, who, after being a student and
teacher of theology, had become strongly hostile to clericalism.

[20] On the occasion of a visit in March of 1904 by President Loubet to the King of Italy,
the Pope protested through diplomatic channels to various countries; and two or three months
later the Pope ordered two French bishops to proceed to Rome for trial.

one of short Ministries, of continued conflicts with organized labor, and of momentous events in the realm of foreign affairs.

Military Service and Income Tax. In the last respect, critical conditions did not prevent the Socialists and some Radicals from joining in vigorous and partially successful opposition to extension of the period of military service; and the Bloc was reformed on the basis of a program containing as its principal item advocacy of the sliding-scale income tax.

WORLD WAR I: 1914–1919

Submergence of Party Politics. The basic political fact of the period of World War I was the formation of the "Sacred Union." Party conflicts and differences were renounced. At the outbreak of the War, the Left possessed a majority in Parliament of unprecedented proportions; but the Right and Socialists were at once included in the ministry.

Left Opposition. After a short interval, political activities, especially those of a personal character, began to reassert themselves, though on a somewhat restricted scale. Parliamentary government, with its characteristic control, began slowly to operate again. Still later, divisions began to appear among the Socialists; and, before the end of the War, a majority had gone into opposition. A few Radicals who favored peace without victory, and even worked for it, were accused of being defeatists and traitors. In the result, the Left suffered. The Right, in general, had warned against Germany and urged a strong military and diplomatic policy; so that events tended to bear out the Right and to discredit the Left.

BETWEEN WORLD WARS: 1919–1939

National Bloc and Left Cartel. After the victory, a National Bloc was formed. It was announced by its founders as a continuation of the Sacred Union, extended into times of peace for "the great work of national reconstruction." It secured a large majority in Parliament. Influenced by post-War psychology, even the Radicals and independent Socialists joined the pact; but they soon abandoned an alliance that seemed to them to develop a definitely reactionary character. As a matter of fact, the Right can scarcely be said to have solved with much success the difficult internal and international problems with which the country was confronted. The opposition formed what came to be known as the Left Cartel, composed primarily of Radicals and Socialists. It inveighed against the record of the National Bloc in respect of unwise loans, unstable currency, high cost of living, unjust taxation, friendliness to vested economic interests, weakness towards clericalism, hostility towards organized labor, and aggressiveness in foreign policy. At the next elections—in 1924— the Left was victorious, and assumed control.

Left Majority and Crisis. In the remainder of the period between the two World Wars, foreign affairs played, from the nature of the case, an especially important role. At the same time, there was, to say the least, little lessening of intensity in internal politics. Economic—and particularly financial—questions bulked especially large. The whole complexus of external and internal forces determined a course of events that followed a somewhat uniform pattern. With the exception of 1928, when Poincaré—known after 1926 as "savior of the franc"—sought and obtained a vote of confidence at the polls, the general elections, namely, those of 1924, 1932, and 1936, resulted in marked successes for the Left—for the Left Cartel in 1924, for another amicable understanding between Socialists and Radicals in 1932, and for the famous Popular Front in 1936. However, after each victory, a Left ministry, with the passing of time, encountered critical difficulty that was in large measure, though not wholly, financial. Thus, there was the crisis of the franc in 1926; there was a famous scandal in 1934, attended by rioting and street fighting; and, after the first year or two of the Popular Front, related internal and international storms led directly to World War II. In such crises, the Left was not slow to accuse elements of the Right of conscious effort and intrigue to discredit the Left at the expense of the general interest. Such crises were regularly followed either by a nonpartisan, coalition Ministry of "national union," with leadership tending to lean to the Right,[21] or by a Ministry of more moderate complexion than the Left majority,[22] receiving relatively wide support for efforts to realize internal and external stability. In such conditions, traditional divisions inevitably became on occasion distinctly less clear-cut. The outstanding example near the outbreak of World War II was the split of practically all political organizations into pacifist and antipacifist wings at the time of the Munich settlement.

Communist Exclusion and Resistance. Probably the most far-reaching political event connected with World War II was the proscription by law of the Communists.[23] As things turned out, the early entrance of the Communists into the underground gave to them a long lead in the matter of clandestine activity. When the Vichy regime later left to the elements of other political organizations that were opposed to collaboration with Vichy no alternative but illegal resistance, non-Communists were largely unprepared for such activity. The ultimate political results of collaboration are by no means easy to appraise. Influence of the Fascist political and militia organizations [24] encouraged by the Nazis in the occupied zone was not great, and the permanent effects appear to be largely negligible. The same was not true of the unoccupied zone. There, Vichy-sponsored organization [25] was more extensive. Participation by elements of the Right was considerable; and the fact that a few notable leaders [26] opposed Vichy from the first and had distinguished records in the Resistance was not sufficient to prevent the Right from being greatly discredited. So far as the

[21] E.g., Poincaré in 1926 and Doumergue in 1934.
[22] E.g., Daladier in 1938.
[23] Cf. Ch. XII, p. 192, *supra.*
[24] The principal political organizations were those of Déat and Doriot; the militia was that of Darnand.
[25] This was primarily the militia known as the Fighters' Legion. Its several leaders had been connected during the Third Republic with the Right.
[26] Notably M. Louis Marin, head of the National Republican Party, principal party of the Right under the Third Republic. Cf. Ch. XII, p. 206, *supra.*

principal non-Communist elements of the Left were concerned, the record of the Socialists was with very little exception highly creditable, that of the Radicals somewhat less so. In the second respect, the unpreparedness of Radical organizations for clandestine activity was an important factor in preventing Radical accomplishments in the Resistance from being as well known as the considerable, though minor, participation of Radicals in collaboration. Resultant loss of prestige at the time by this principal party of the Third Republic has had manifest results under the Fourth Republic; and, though French Radicalism has shown some signs of regaining part of the lost ground, its future would appear to be somewhat uncertain.[27] In the Resistance, the strong position of the Communists was, as perhaps might have been foreseen, in the end a cause of disunity. Even in the carefully elaborated organization of Resistance forces, the Communists were ultimately responsible for a deep split;[28] and final determination of the older and newer political parties to organize themselves along essentially traditional lines was largely caused by the Communists. It is a fair question whether honest men can give Communism the kind of allegiance it demands and whether, when they have had any substantial practical experience with it, they can continue long to believe in the possibility of loyal collaboration with its militants. The widespread and deep desire in the Resistance for union to be retained after Liberation is an undoubted fact. Primary Communist responsibility for failure is equally certain. In this respect, a highly important consideration is the striking part that was played by social Catholicism. Its distinguished record in the Resistance, its loyal cooperation with other elements, its strong sentiment for unity, and the relative lack of interest in politics on the part of its young leaders—all suggested nonparty activity after the Liberation. And yet conflict with the Communists gave rise to a decision almost immediately after the Liberation to form a political party.[29] Somewhat more difficult to estimate is the influence, especially after the Liberation, of the position of General de Gaulle. On the whole, his entrance into politics would seem, rightly or wrongly, to have influenced further the disintegration of Resistance unity and the re-emergence of political parties. Even the MRP, with the founding of which General de Gaulle is said not to have been unconnected, ended by becoming a part of the Third Force, which the General habitually criticizes only slightly less bitterly than he does the Communists. But this projects history into the period of the Fourth Republic.

[27] Cf. *ibid.,* p. 205, *infra.*

[28] The Communist-controlled National Front came in conflict with the non-Communist Movement of National Liberation, the result being stress and strain in both organizations. Cf. Ch. XII, p. 193, *infra.*

[29] Cf. *ibid.,* p. 200, *infra.*

CHAPTER XII

PARTIES IN THE FOURTH REPUBLIC

1. INTRODUCTORY

The present-day picture of political parties in France is by no means without obscure areas. Multiplicity of parties continues to be the source of possible confusion. Just as the number of parties, and even of their major groupings, fails to correspond with the traditional dual division of Left and Right,[1] so the correspondence between party organization in the country and political groups in Parliament continues in a number of cases far from exact.[2] Moreover, the several parties display, as compared one with another, varying degrees of organization and homogeneity. The best organized are the "big three"— the French Communist Party, which is one side of the extremist opposition, and the Socialist Party and the Popular Republican Movement (MRP), which are the most considerable elements of the Third Force.

2. THE COMMUNISTS

THIRD REPUBLIC BACKGROUND

Foundation. The party of Communists in France dates as an organization from the year 1920,[3] when a split in the Socialist Party occurred. At that time a majority of the Socialists voted to become part of the Third (Moscow) International, whereupon a minority, the present Socialist Party, seceded. The majority, which likewise experienced in the first few years some relatively minor secessions, developed into the French Communist Party.

Doctrine. As members of the Moscow International, French Communists accepted unquestioningly, as long as that organization existed (to 1944), lines of policy prescribed by it. In respect of program, they have subscribed to the body of doctrine that owes its formulation primarily to Marx, Lenin, and Stalin. They have stood basically for the overthrow of the capitalist system by revolutionary means. They have advocated class warfare, the dictatorship of the pro-

---

[1] Cf. Ch. x, p. 174, *supra.*
[2] Cf. *ibid.,* p. 172, *supra,* and Ch. vi, pp. 102–103, *supra.*
[3] Cf. this Ch., p. 197, *infra.*

letariat, and the socialization of the means of production, distribution, and exchange.

"Tactic." In terms of tactic, the French Communist Party, it is true, has on occasion followed its own program of action, within the general limits approved by Moscow. Thus, not long after the origin of the Party, the International, it is said, urged it to join the Left Cartel against the Right; but a real working agreement was not effected until the period of preparation for the 1936 elections. Indeed, in the intervening period of approximately ten years, the Communist Party lost ground in every respect except that of building a rigid and ruthless organization of militants. Its very lack of flexibility caused it to be repudiated by Left parties and by organized labor. In 1932 it lost more than a quarter of the number of votes it received in 1928. However, during the period from 1934 to the outbreak of war in 1939, the Party was able to make effective use of the strong organization that had been constructed. It felt strong enough in 1935, influenced by the accession of Hitler to power and by Fascist activities in France at the time of the crisis of 1934, to take the initiative towards formation of the Popular Front,[4] carrying its apparent cooperativeness to the point of proclaiming its willingness to work together with the Catholics. During the electoral campaign of 1936 the Communists behaved with marked restraint. Though they urged the election of their candidates on the first ballot, they consistently advocated and practiced support on the second ballot for Socialist or Radical candidates leading the field after the first ballot. Communist leadership expressed the hope that some day Communism, in a French form, would come to France, but it asserted that it did not consider the Popular Front a means of bringing Communism or even socialization. As a result of the elections of 1936, the number of members of the Communist group in the Chamber of Deputies rose to seventy-two, nearly three times as great as in any previous Chamber.[5] However, Communist support even of Socialist Ministries was lukewarm; and its influence in the Popular Front was not important either in internal or external affairs. In the second respect, the Communists, whatever may be thought of the merits of their opposition to Franco and to Munich, were constrained by their unswerving support of the USSR to make some nimble policy changes in opposing the growth of Nazi strength, defending the Nazi-Soviet pact, denouncing the German invasion of Poland, and approving the presence of Soviet forces in East Poland.

Legal Proscription. In the days following the beginning of war between France and Germany in September of 1939, members of the Communist group in Parliament undertook certain activities, such for example as petitioning for the cessation of war, that were in clear contravention of existing law. As long as Parliament was in session, these members were covered by their parliamentary immunity; but, after prorogation, many of them were arrested in connection with government moves to effect abolition of the Party.[6]

[4] Cf. Ch. XI, p. 189, *supra.*
[5] There were even two Communist Senators.
[6] Cf. Ch. XI, *loc. cit., supra.*

VICHY AND LIBERATION

Communism in Resistance. During the Vichy period—to some extent before, but more especially after, the Nazi attack on Soviet Russia in the summer of 1941—the French Communist Party employed in clandestine activity against the Nazis and their French collaborators its highly developed organization. Its early insistence that both sides in the War were "imperialist" was later modified in view of collaboration by Soviet Russia with Great Britain, the United States, and the other United Nations. In the same way, its attitude towards General de Gaulle changed from one of hostility to one of recognition of his authority and to participation by certain Communists in the French Committee of National Liberation.[7] The same cooperativeness, reminiscent of Popular Front days, was manifest during the Resistance in establishment through Communist initiative of the National Front,[8] into which all elements of the Resistance were welcomed, though the Communists not unnaturally maintained control of it. Finally the Party played a major part in the National Council of Resistance.[9]

Obstacle to Unity. With the coming of the Liberation, the French Communists somewhat surprisingly eschewed, at least in appearance, employing their strong position with a view to realizing revolutionary ends. They were doubtless influenced in this respect by failure of the Resistance to maintain its unity,[10] a non-Communist Movement of National Liberation refusing union with the National Front. In any event, the Party, after undertaking various divisive tactics and opposing General de Gaulle in connection with one referendum at the time of the election of the First National Constituent Assembly, later joined other parties in entering the Ministry of the General.[11] Again, with defeat of the Constitution sponsored by it and the Socialists,[12] it continued its ostensible collaboration, establishing a strong position in several of the public services.

THE FOURTH REPUBLIC

Early Tactics. The Party almost continuously participated in Ministries of the day until May of 1947. Meanwhile, the Communists had increasingly alienated the other factions by such tactics as exploitation of labor unrest in France, encouragement of extremist agitation in overseas areas, and unfailing support of Soviet Russia's hostility to American policy; and when Communist Ministers went so far as to vote against the Government of which they were members, they were excluded.[13]

Communism in Opposition. The Communist Party, though it performs—often with provocative skill—some of the functions of a normal opposition, displays few of the characteristics of a "loyal" opposition. Since establishment of the Cominform in the fall of 1947, French Communists have furnished ample

[7] Cf. Ch. iv, p. 64, *supra.*
[8] Cf. Ch. xi, p. 190, *supra.*
[9] Cf. Ch. iv, *loc. cit., supra.*
[10] Cf. Ch. xi, *loc. cit., supra.*

[11] Cf. Ch. iv, p. 69, *supra.*
[12] Cf. *ibid.,* p. 74, *supra.*
[13] Cf. Ch. vii, p. 125, *supra.*

evidence, if any were needed, that they receive and obey orders inspired by Moscow. The utterances of members are often manifestly prepared for them and delivered so stolidly and stupidly that non-Communists who trouble to twit them exclaim how badly learned are their lessons or, with some reason, compare such utterances to old and worn records, played over and over. The members frequently demonstrate that according to traditional standards they are without moral or intellectual integrity. Their strength lies partly in their unswerving adherence to a rigid doctrine of the rightness of which they apparently possess a profound conviction and partly in their ruthless and persistent conduct of flexible tactics conceived, because of the authoritative source, to be applications of right doctrine. They exploit relentlessly economic difficulties, and they are undoubtedly conscious of the fact that they thereby hinder solution; for they furnish abundant evidence that they are interested in maladjustments and in propaganda effects to which they know improvement would run counter. They untiringly but tiresomely repeat assertions to the effect that French relations with the United States destroy French "sovereignty" and are calculated purposely to wage aggressive war on Soviet Russia; and to criticisms that Communists continually propose expensive policies without ever voting any revenue measures they repeatedly insist that cessation of the war in Indo-China would make available huge resources. In general, their position is increasingly one of isolation; and though they have inside and outside Parliament a small number of fellow-travelers, their proposals of cooperation [14] receive little response from elements which have had the minimum experience necessary to show that the Communists will inevitably resist compromise and insist on domination. Perhaps their most conspicuous failure of this kind is in respect of the CGT (General Confederation of Labor), which fused with the Communist confederation at the time of the Popular Front, came under Communist control during the Resistance, and finally at the end of 1947 was deserted by non-Communist elements.

COMMUNIST ORGANIZATION

Political Geography. Between a third and a half of Communist voters are to be found in the suburbs of Paris and in the regions between Paris and the Belgian border, characterized by a high degree of industrialization and by large-scale agriculture. At the same time, even though this may be regarded as the typical aspect of Communist political geography, the Communists in France draw their strength as well from other regions, especially in the South and Centre of the country, which are of a different economic and social complexion. Here their support is due principally to their being the Party furthest Left, a custom of long standing dictating such support either as an expression of discontented protest or as a kind of affectation or fashion of being "advanced."

[14] This was not only true of the National Front during the Resistance, but is true at present of an organization like the Fighters for Peace and Liberty, which though theoretically independent of the Communists is so dominated by them that non-Communists normally steer clear of it.

Basic Structural Principles. The organization of the French Communist Party, though it has some superficial resemblance to that of other parties in France and in other countries, is in fundamental principle different. One way of phrasing the matter is through the proposition that, whereas authority in other instances proceeds from the bottom up, for the Communists authority proceeds from the top down. This is in general the secret of Communist discipline. It results from the famous, if somewhat curious, Soviet concept of "democratic centralism," according to which those who elect delegates or officers from below become completely subordinate to them. This in turn is supplemented by a principle of organization that allows no contact on the same plane between organized groups, but permits relations through delegates only at a higher plane.

Party Machinery. Primary Communist units are called *basic groups.* They consist of three members. Several of these groups are combined into a *cell.* Cells are organized, according to general principle, in industrial plants and the like; but some exist on a territorial basis in villages or urban districts. Discussion appears to be very free at this level, within the limits automatically imposed by the fact that members consist of carefully selected militants.[15] Cells are under the command of elected officers, primarily a secretary and a treasurer. At the next level, a number of cells are grouped through delegates into *sections,* either on a territorial or plant basis. A section chooses its officers. Sections in turn are grouped through delegates into *federations* on a territorial basis, a Department or smaller community serving as the unit. Federation agencies include a *conference,* meeting once every six months, a *committee* chosen by the conference, and officers chosen by the committee. At the highest level stands the *National Congress,* which is composed of delegates from the federations. It meets once every two years. In it, freedom of discussion, in accordance with the principle that freedom decreases as the cells are left behind, is almost nonexistent. The Congress chooses a permanent *Central Committee,* consisting of a hundred members. The Committee chooses three highly important agencies, the principal of which, though little in the public eye, is the *Committee of Political Control,* the others being the ten-member *Political Bureau* and a *Secretariat* consisting of a General Secretary and three secretaries.

3. THE SOCIALISTS

THIRD REPUBLIC BACKGROUND

Foundation: Early Difficulties. After the defeat of the Commune in 1871 and the consequent destruction or dispersal of the forces of revolutionary Socialism, the vitality of such forces was demonstrated by the resumption as early as 1876 of their activities and by the formation in 1879, on the occasion of a

---

[15] There is evidence that the turnover in respect of nonmilitants is very great, persons other than those forming a solid core being disillusioned by experience.

Congress of Labor Unions held in Marseille, of the Socialist Political Party.[16] This event was followed in a short time by a Parliamentary vote of amnesty for those who had been condemned in connection with the Commune. The reappearance of older revolutionaries soon gave rise, in turn, to a split in the ranks of the Socialists. One branch, with its strength principally in the north of France, was composed of thorough-going Marxists. Its recognized leader was Jules Guesde. After a marked lack of success in the elections of 1881, this faction, which was in a minority, was excluded from the Socialist organization by the majority branch, which was more moderate in its "reformist" and "possibilist" aims. The split illustrates the tendency for advocates of Socialism, who are presumably in agreement on the end to be attained, everywhere and at all times to divide on the basis of means to end. The division is into "revolutionaries" and "evolutionaries." In France, the same division, though personal rivalries were not without their effect, occurred within a few years in the ranks of the majority that had excluded the followers of Guesde. The more revolutionary minority, this time under Allemane, who advocated preparation for a general strike, was again excluded by the less extreme majority, composed of followers of Brousse. Such division and subdivision naturally dissipated greatly Socialist efforts; and yet the rival factions carried on vigorous Socialist propaganda in the industrial areas. This activity, in turn, had an important influence on the industrial side of the labor movement; and the labor unions, legalized by Act of Parliament in 1884, became increasingly Socialist in personnel and program.

Foundation: Jaurès. In anticipation of the elections of 1893, the several Socialist factions effected an organization with political aims. The guiding spirit was Jean Jaurès, who was elected to Parliament in 1892. He is considered the founder of the Parliamentary Socialist Party. He advocated for the elections of 1893 that Socialist candidates should conduct their campaigns on the basis of the political program of the Radicals and the economic program of the Socialists. In the result, about fifty Socialists were elected to the Chamber of Deputies. They consisted for the most part of working-class Socialists; but they also included "bourgeois" members like Jaurès, Millerand, and Viviani. During the next momentous decade,[17] the leadership of Jaurès was, though statesmanlike, not successful in preventing further dissension among the Socialists, especially with respect to Socialist participation [18] in a "bourgeois" ministry and even close cooperation with kindred parties. Guesde and his followers continued to maintain a doctrinaire position, opposing Socialist support of the Bloc and Republican Defence.[19] In the end, Jaurès was compelled to give in to the anti-cooperation elements; and in 1905 unity was effected. This was the real founding of the present Party.

[16] Cf. Ch. XI, p. 185, *supra*. The political side of the modern labor movement in France, it may be observed, grew in a definite sense out of the industrial side of the movement, instead of being a left-wing political development of an existing liberal political party, as was the case, for example, with the British Labor Party.

[17] Cf. Ch. XI, pp. 186–187, *supra*.

[18] The celebrated case was that of participation by Millerand in the Waldeck-Rousseau ministry. Cf. Ch. XI, *loc. cit., supra*.   [19] Cf. *ibid.*

Evolutionary Socialism. The Socialist Party since 1905 has called itself the Unified Socialist Party.[20] Though elements of mild Socialists remained independent of the new organization,[21] the latter itself did not, from its founding to World War I, emphasize class conflict.[22] This abstention, in turn, was almost certainly not unconnected with the phenomenal growth of the Party in the same period, its strength both in terms of voters and members of Parliament being approximately doubled. With the coming of war, the Socialists, in spite of the assassination of Jaurès, loyally supported French resistance to Germany; and for two or three years several of their leaders held important ministerial positions. This fact undoubtedly exercised strong, and even permanent, influence in the direction of evolutionary Socialism. Nevertheless, as early as 1915 certain elements began to reassert the traditional pacifist and international tenets of the Party. This extremist movement gradually gathered strength, being especially influenced by the Russian Revolution. Such elements, after the end of the War, constituted a "bolshevizing" minority. They found themselves directly opposed by elements which desired a complete break with the Communism of Lenin, and in partial disagreement with elements which favored a position that would accept the lessons of Russian experience without subscribing unquestioningly to everything emanating from Russia. In the end, the extremist elements succeeded in rallying a considerable majority of the militants. These, adhering to the Third International and following its instructions to expel certain leaders, founded in 1920 the Communist Party.[23] The minority, refusing to be dominated by Moscow, re-established itself as the French Section of the Workers' (Second) International.

Principle and Practice. The French Socialist Party, between the two World Wars, continued to be plagued with the difficulties growing out of the problem of reconciling doctrine with such action as was suggested by existing conditions. In the latter respect, it felt constrained to re-establish, beginning with the Left Cartel[24] at the time of the 1924 elections, close cooperation with the bourgeoisie in the form of the Radicals. On the other hand, the Socialist Party, by forbidding its leaders to take office, consistently refused until 1936 to accept responsibility. As a result of the elections of 1936, when the Socialist representation in the Chamber of Deputies became for the first time larger than that of the Radicals, or, in other words, the largest in the Chamber, the Unified Socialists modified their doctrinal principle of not accepting office without power, that is, without a majority. With Léon Blum as Prime Minister, they were the principal element in a ministry of the Left, which the Communists, though refusing office, undertook to support. The achievements of this Blum

[20] Frequently referred to officially as the SFIO (French Section of the Workers' International).

[21] Two bodies of such independents subsequently joined to form the Party of Socialist and Republican Union, occupying a position between the Unified Socialists and the Radicals. It formed a minor element of the Popular Front, its group in the Chamber of Deputies consisting of about thirty at the beginning of World War II.

[22] Cf. Ch. XI, p. 185, *supra.*

[23] Cf. this Ch., p. 191, *supra.*

[24] Cf. Ch. XI, p. 188, *supra.*

Ministry were little short of astounding. Rapid reforms, widely recognized as "overdue," were made in respect of labor conditions, social security, monetary policy, the agricultural situation, corruption of the press, the Bank of France, status of Fascist organizations, and so on. Unfortunately, the effects, actual and potential, of the reforms were in considerable measure obscured by the international situation. After a year or two, difficulties both internal and external increasingly caused discouragement and confusion in the ranks of the Party. A little later, the culmination of the situation was the fact that only Blum and a minority of Socialist Deputies opposed the voting of dictatorial power to Pétain at Vichy.

VICHY AND THE LIBERATION

Socialism in the Resistance. The vitality of French Socialism was demonstrated by the highly respectable part played by its adherents during the period of the Resistance.[25] The organization of the Party was rebuilt underground; and it had representation in the National Council of Resistance.[26] Its adherents likewise took part in various other Resistance organizations in France and abroad. The Party's propensity for uncertainty growing out of contradiction between rigid doctrinal principles and actions that often verged on opportunism prevented any firm decisions looking to the future; so that the Liberation found the Socialist policy tending in several not altogether consistent directions.

Socialist Cooperation. Late in 1944, the Socialist Party, at its first post-Liberation national meeting, decided upon a purge [27] and reorganization; but it was unable to effect the sort of close alliance, either with the Communists or the MRP, that had been envisaged during the Resistance. On the other hand, some of its leaders took part in the Provisional Government. The Socialists were not unnaturally disappointed to find their representation in the Constituent Assemblies inferior to that of the Communists and of the MRP; but their key position between the other two "monoliths" gave their constitutional principles disproportionate influence.

FOURTH REPUBLIC

Parliamentary Position. Largely because of conditions over which the Socialists have had little control, the Party has continued to be plagued under the prevailing Constitution by a conflict between doctrine and practice. In the 1946 elections for the National Assembly, it lost some of its forces both on the right and the left. It realized only a slight recovery in the elections of 1951, its popular vote actually declining.

Push towards the Centre. A member of the Socialist Party has been the only President of the Fourth Republic.[28] Likewise, the first Prime Minister was a Socialist; but it was this same Prime Minister who was constrained to exclude

[25] Cf. *ibid.,* p. 190, *supra.*
[26] Cf. Ch. IV, p. 64, *supra.*
[27] This consisted primarily of exclusion of Socialist members of Parliament who had voted for Pétain.
[28] M. Vincent Auriol. Cf. Ch. VII, p. 124, *supra.*

the Communists.[29] This move, in turn, has tended to drive the Socialists away from a position as far left as their doctrine requires; and though resulting strains have caused them to abandon leadership in the form of occupation of the office of premier, they have for the most part supported, and participated in, Ministries of the Third Force.[30]

SOCIALIST ORGANIZATION

Political Geography. The pre-War strength of the Socialist Party was to be found principally in the central belt running from Burgundy westwards. Here under the Fourth Republic the Socialists have suffered serious losses to the Communists. In so far as this setback has been compensated for elsewhere, it has been in general at the expense of the Radicals in the Southwest and, to a lesser extent, in the West, Northwest, and the Northeast. The Party has suffered only slight losses in the South and Southeast.

Party Structure. The organization of the Socialist Party has in most respects remained the same since its founding. It is pyramidal in structure, and does not vary greatly from that of other democratically constructed party arrangements in France and other countries. The basic units are groups of members called *sections.* They are organized (except in Paris, where the *Arrondissement* is used) in the Communes and Cantons. On the next higher plane, sections are federated, with the Department as the federation area, delegates from the sections forming a *Federal Congress.* Delegates from the federations compose the annual *National Congress.* The National Congress, in turn, chooses a *National Council,* which meets several times between Congresses. The Congress likewise selects a *Directing Committee,* which appoints the General Secretary, directs the national central office, and supervises dispatch of current business. In general, the several representative organs are constituted and chosen on the basis of proportional representation, any area being entitled to representation determined by the ratio of its members to the whole and any delegation being made up proportionally of members reflecting the tendencies of various elements. At all levels, decisions are taken by majority vote after discussion. Voting is by "mandate"; that is, each delegation is entitled to vote a number of mandates proportional to the members involved. Decisions are then regarded as being so binding that violation is punished by exclusion from the Party. At the same time, the effects of such rigid disciplinary principle are in practice less restrictive than might be imagined. As is not difficult to understand, questions by no means always arise in Party meetings at the various levels and in Parliament in a form so precise that they have been anticipated by previous decisions so specific that no discretion is left.

[29] An all-Socialist Ministry was formed by Léon Blum (December 17, 1946, to January 22, 1947). It effected the transition from a crisis at the end of the provisional period (fall of Bidault Ministry, November 28, 1946) to a Ministry (M. Ramadier's) resulting from the elections of the National Assembly. M. Ramadier's Ministry with the Communists extended from January 22 to May 9, 1947. His Ministry without the Communists extended from May 9 to October 22, and another Ministry formed by him from October 22 to November 24.

[30] The principal exceptions have been the Bidault Ministry formed without Socialists on February 7, 1950 and the Pleven Ministry of August 11, 1951.

4. THE POPULAR REPUBLICAN MOVEMENT

THIRD REPUBLIC BACKGROUND

Precursors. Although establishment and development of the MRP as one of the "big three" Parties of the Fourth Republic is one of the most striking events of all French political history, the phenomenon was naturally not wholly without historical background. During the latter part of the period of the Third Republic, two antecedents especially are worthy of note. These were the Popular Democratic Party, founded in 1924, and the league known as the Young Republic, established about fifteen years earlier.[31]

Political Complexion. Both forerunners of the MRP were definitely Catholic in inspiration, but both had the aim of breaking with the traditional tie between the Church and reaction. In this the Young Republic was the more successful in maintaining a progressive position. The league, however, was not able to muster so much political strength as the Party; whereas the Popular Democrats, with some twelve to fifteen members in the Chamber of Deputies, were never successful in establishing a position sufficiently unequivocal to avoid being classed as a party of the Right.

VICHY AND LIBERATION

Catholic Resistance. In reality, it was during the Resistance that the MRP was born. To certain men from the Young Republic and from the Popular Democratic Party were added new men, who were often without extensive previous political experience. The latter were by no means always Catholics; but in the course of their activity they found themselves at one with other elements in their respect for religious influence and in their conviction of the rightness of political, social, and economic democracy. Organization of the constituent elements of a political party was decided upon and undertaken as early as 1943; and these were the basis of the National Congress convened in Paris near the end of 1944, at which the organization and the doctrinal and tactical program of the MRP were settled.

MRP Cooperation. After the Liberation, the MRP, apparently influenced both by sentiment and expediency, accepted the leadership of General de Gaulle. Future members of the MRP throughout the Resistance had been so strongly moved by conviction of France's need for a national renascence that they conceived a genuine antagonism for the Third Republic; and when soon after Liberation certain politicians of the old type entered into intrigue against de Gaulle, the Party was confirmed in its support of the General and in its conviction of the need for a break with the previous regime. The Party found itself, except in the matter of anticlericalism, in general accord with the Socialists. This relationship, together with support from elements of the former Right, was an important factor in the striking success of the MRP at the time of the election of the First National Constituent Assembly.[32] The Party at the same time

---

[31] Cf. this Ch., p. 207, *infra.*   [32] Cf. Ch. IV, p. 74, *supra.*

avoided an open break with the Communists; and its leaders entered the Ministry of General de Gaulle.[33]

Gaullist Relations. The relations between the MRP and de Gaulle became somewhat strained after the resignation of the General in January of 1946. The event was not anticipated by members of the Party; and among them some unrest was caused by lack of understanding of the motives of de Gaulle, who in turn was displeased to note the readiness with which the MRP continued to participate in a Ministry based on the "monoliths." However, failure of de Gaulle to associate himself with the Party in opposition to the draft Constitution did not prevent the MRP, after rejection of the extreme Left document, from being returned to the Second National Constituent Assembly with the largest representation of all the parties.[34] An MRP leader, M. Georges Bidault, became head of the Government. The Party avoided the danger of being forced into alliance with the Right only by substantial compromise with the extreme Left in respect of a constitutional system;[35] but the resulting opposition by de Gaulle increased the rift between the General and the Party. Previous MRP voters, at the time of the referendum in October, stayed away in large numbers from the polls, no small number voting in the negative and only a few favorably. Nevertheless, most of these voters rallied again to the Party at the time of the elections of November; and on the basis of an anti-Communist campaign, the MRP secured in the first National Assembly of the Fourth Republic a representation (166) only slightly inferior to that of the Communists.

FOURTH REPUBLIC

In the Third Force. At the beginning of 1947, the MRP, in spite of its attitude towards the Communists, again participated in a three-party Ministry; but when the Communists were excluded, it gave full support to the Third Force, in which it hoped to see realized the kind of progressive union most consistent with its doctrine. However, the almost simultaneous action of General de Gaulle in forming a national organization placed the Party in an exceedingly difficult position. As between separation from the Socialists and from de Gaulle, the break with the General was doubtless inevitable. The result was the loss of some twenty members of the representation in the National Assembly; but the mass of Party militants were beyond doubt favorable to the choice of support for progressive social and economic principles over what many regarded as essentially, or in any case potentially, a traditionally rightist anti-parliamentary movement. To what extent loss of its support on the right[36] will permanently injure the MRP is highly uncertain. However that may be, the elections of 1951 fulfilled predictions with respect to the MRP, its popular vote and its representation in the National Assembly both being cut approximately in half.

[33] Cf. *ibid.*, p. 69, *supra.*
[34] Cf. *ibid.*, p. 74, *supra.*
[35] Cf. *ibid.*, p. 75, *supra.*
[36] Cf. this Ch., p. 202, *infra.*

MRP ORGANIZATION

Political Geography. A large part of the strength of the MRP, having been originally gained at the expense of the older elements of the Right, is to be found in regions where the Right has been traditionally strong, namely, in the East and in the West.[37] The later weakening of the Party has not on the whole been geographic, in the sense that loss of strength has been for the most part equally distributed.

Party Structure. The organization of the MRP in a number of structural respects is similar to that of the Socialists. Thus, local *sections* are grouped at the level of the Departments into *federations,* which in turn are the bases of the annual *Congress.* Between meetings of Congresses, a *National Committee* decides matters of policy, which are carried out by an *Executive Committee.* Beyond this, however, the resemblances with Socialist organization are less close, notably in the matter of the basis of representation in the Congress and in the matter of the composition of the Committees.[38] In the first respect, the mandates of the federations, instead of being directly proportional to membership, are reckoned on the basis of a decreasing ratio for the larger memberships. The object is to avoid excessive regional influence. In the second respect, the National Committee is based less exclusively than is the corresponding Socialist agency on the militants of the Party, the Committee's membership including any MRP Ministers in office, a third of the MRP members of the two houses of Parliament, and ten co-opted members; whereas only a minority [39] of the members of the Executive Committee are representatives of the federations, the majority being composed of Ministers, a dozen members of Parliament, and five Party members chosen by the National Committee on an individual basis. The important place in the Committees allotted to MRP members of Parliament is to be explained by a desire to avoid the kind of conflict between militants and Party groups that frequently characterizes the Socialists. A final difference between the two Party organizations is the much larger part played in the case of the MRP by special auxiliary organs at the regional and national levels, such for example as groupings of youth, of women, of workers, and so on.[40]

5. THE RADICALS

THIRD REPUBLIC BACKGROUND

Basic Principles. The Radical Party, although its influence is somewhat out of proportion to its representation in the National Assembly, is, under the Fourth Republic, a minor element of the Third Force. Under the Third Republic, it was on the whole the most important single party. It belonged to

[37] Most of Lorraine must be excepted.
[38] Note may also be made of the fact that the MRP has not only a General Secretary but also a President.
[39] Eighteen in number.
[40] Cf. this Ch., p. 207, *infra.*

the same international organization as the English Liberals. This correspondence gives a fairly good idea of the character of the French Radicals, though the Party largely escaped the fate of English Liberals, almost ground to pieces between the Labor Party and the Conservatives. The term *radical* was in France an historical survival; [41] and as applied to the Party of that name, it did not possess the meaning and associations attaching to the ordinary use of the expression in the United States. The French Radical Party was officially founded in 1901, but its antecedents went back much further.

Party Characteristics. The Radical Party claimed with some reason direct descent from the French Revolution. In this tradition, it was the typical Republican Party. Its official name was "The Republican Party of Radicals and Socialist Radicals." The name indicates a dual composition that persisted for many years. One wing was in the old political liberal tradition, which laid stress on individualism.[42] The other wing was in the more modern economic and social liberal tradition, advocating employment of democratic processes to bring an increasingly great degree of social justice to the masses. Advocacy in the 1880's by a group of young Radicals of supplementing the political program with a program of social reforms caused the term *Socialist* to be added to the name of the Party.[43] However, the later and younger element was not Marxist or collectivist; and it did not advocate class warfare or revolution. The Party played a leading role in securing a large part of France's most important laic and social legislation. Indeed, it was essentially a "party of government." Having had experience of a long lease on power, its actions were inevitably affected in some measure by determination to possess power, a characteristic frequently labeled "Jacobin" by opponents of the Party. Members of the Party were, with a few notable exceptions, not generally recruited from the upper bourgeoisie. More of its members came from the middle bourgeoisie, and the mass of its membership from the "petite bourgeoisie." Indeed, the Party was said [44] to be "as by instinct" in favor of what is "small" and against what is "big." The Party group in the Chamber of Deputies, as a result of the elections of 1936, consisted of only 116, as against about 160 in the previous Chamber; but it is by no means certain that in more normal times the decline would have been permanent.

VICHY AND LIBERATION

Resistance and Collaboration. During the Vichy period, the substantial loss of prestige suffered by the Radicals [45] was due to several factors. Previous organization of the Party did not lend itself to concerted underground activities; the distinguished records of some Radicals were not only not well known but were also offset by the collaboration of others with Pétain; and identifica-

---

41 It was employed because of the revolutionary connotations, and hence forbidden character, of *republican*.
42 Thus, the Radicals were closely associated with the founding of the important League of the Rights of Men and of the Citizen.
43 Cf. Ch. X, p. 175, *supra*, and Ch. XI, p. 184, *supra*.
44 Cf. A. Siegfried, *op. cit.*, p. 159.
45 Cf. Ch. XI, p. 190, *supra*.

tion of the Party with the Third Republic caused the former to suffer the discredit which was visited upon the regime as responsible for the defeat of France.[46]

Traditional Opportunism. After the Liberation, many Radicals found that they could profit, in spite of the presence of Radical leaders in the Provisional Government of General de Gaulle, from its old practice of political opposition based on the principle of "no enemies on the Left," a practice which brought the militants temporarily close to the Communists. The initial result was considerable success in the local elections of 1945.[47] On the other hand, the policy of opposition in the Consultative Assembly and the decision to recommend a negative vote on the first referendum of October of 1945, while joining the Communists in urging a negative vote on the second question, were rewarded by a serious setback in the elections to the First National Constituent Assembly, Radical representation being only approximately one-third as great as that of each of the "big three." As a result, the Party, understanding that leaning politically to the Left paid few dividends, took up a position more in keeping with its economic and social views, that is, further to the Right. Thus, although Radicals participated in the Ministry of President de Gaulle, they refused, after his resignation, to take part in the following Socialist-led (Gouin) Ministry based on the "big three"; and they opposed its policy and the Constitution formulated by the extreme Left.

RGR. The Radicals found near themselves potential allies in the First National Constituent Assembly. These were the members of the UDSR (Democratic and Socialist Resistance Union). For the elections, members of the Union had been in alliance with the Socialists; but, not being willing to accept the prescribed discipline, they broke with the Socialists and founded a coalition with the Radicals. The alliance adopted the name RGR (Assemblage of Republican Lefts), the term *left,* according to a simple rule of French politics, indicating that their tendency was to the right. The RGR opposed ratification of the first Constitution; and it made a respectable showing in the elections for the Second National Constituent Assembly, the Radicals increasing their representation by some two-thirds. The RGR, with the Radicals gaining from the infusion of new blood and remaining much the most important element in it, likewise opposed the second Constitution. It emerged from the 1946 elections for the National Assembly with its strength almost exactly the same as before. In the elections of 1951, the RGR popular vote slightly declined, but its representation in the National Assembly increased by about 50 per cent.

FOURTH REPUBLIC

Traditional Tactics. The RGR succeeded to its key position in the Third Force as a result of the exclusion in 1947 of the Communists from the "big three" coalition. It has been aided not only by tension between the Socialists and the MRP but also by the experience of older Radicals in negotiation, ma-

---

[46] Cf. Ch. IV, pp. 66–67, *supra.*   [47] Cf. *ibid.,* p. 65, n 3, *supra.*

neuver, and compromise. Much skill has been manifested in the maintenance of a position characterized at one and the same time by both support of and opposition to the government of the day. In the latter respect, the organization in considerable part subscribes to General de Gaulle's strictures on the regime, without being willing to give him full support. The RGR on more than one occasion has furnished a Radical or other Prime Minister,[48] not to mention incumbents of lesser ministerial positions. It has fortified its local positions; and, as a result, it has the largest representation in the Council of the Republic.

Prospects. In spite of its substantially improved parliamentary position, the RGR can scarcely hope to achieve soon in the National Assembly a position comparable with that of the Radicals under the Third Republic. In other words, its future is uncertain; but prophets who are disposed to envisage its disappearance are scarcely likely to be borne out at any early date.

RADICAL ORGANIZATION

Political Geography. Post-War loss of strength by the Radicals has followed no geographical pattern. The Party has suffered fairly evenly in its old strongholds. Partial later recovery, especially in local elections, has left the Radicals in a relatively strong position in considerable portions of the Southwest, in the region to the south of the Parisian area, and in certain parts of the Centre and Southeast.

Party Structure. The RGR, being only an alliance and not in reality a party, has as such no members and almost no organization. In the latter respect, there is merely a committee for the purpose of coordinating the action of the participating parties and of settling controversies that may arise. The Radical Party has a structure which in general outlines is similar to that of the Socialists and MRP; whereas the UDSR has only a skeleton organization, composed for the most part of its members belonging to Parliament and to local councils, of candidates, newspaper men, and the like. The Radicals at the local level are grouped into *committees* in the Communes and Cantons; the Committees are grouped in *federations* in the Departments and likewise at a higher regional level; and there is an annual National Congress. On the national scale there is likewise an *Executive Committee* of several hundred, which at the time of the annual Congress chooses a national directing body, the *Bureau*. In general the Radical Party is less disciplined than the Socialists and MRP, a long-standing tendency prevailing for influence in the Party to be exercised by self-constituted and frequently rival cliques of active members.

6. THE TRADITIONAL RIGHT

THIRD REPUBLIC BACKGROUND

Republican Federation. Under the Third Republic, the principal organization of the Right was the Republican Federation. It was founded in 1903 through fusion—whence the name "Federation"—of three organizations of a

[48] Notably Queuille and Pleven.

conservative or reactionary character. Many of its members were former Monarchists or sons of former Monarchists—whence, in common with many para-
doxes of party labels, the epithet "Republican." Towards the end of the period
of the Third Republic, it assumed the name "National Republican Party." It
persistently maintained a traditionally Right—and anti-Left—position. It
championed the cause of religion, in its program inveighing against the Left
as antireligious. It favored woman suffrage; it opposed the single-member
constituency system of elections, preferring proportional representation; and
it advocated establishment of judicial review. The Party disliked the income
tax and taxes on business, and disapproved any extension of the tax system that
would impose greater obligation on the moneyed classes. Vigorously *laissez-
faire* in economic doctrine, it opposed all socialization and regulation in industry. In foreign policy, the Party was highly nationalistic, feeling that the situation in which France found itself previous to the outbreak of World War II
was due to weaknesses and vacillation attendant on flirtation with pacifism
and collective security.

Democratic Alliance. A somewhat less typical party of the Right was the
Democratic Alliance. It was founded in 1901, and several times reorganized.
It was not a closed party, its members being permitted to belong also to another
party or other political organization. The Democratic Alliance was not greatly
different from the National Republican Party. In general, it was slightly less
to the Right. It claimed that its position was "conservative but not reactionary."
In this context, it was most clearly to be distinguished from the National Republican Party in respect of the religious question. It advocated a position of
neutrality for the State, opposing equally anticlericalism and clericalism. The
Party accepted reluctantly the income tax and taxes on business; but it was
vigorously antisocialist. Its individualist economic views and its foreign policy
did not differ greatly from those of the National Republican Party.

SINCE THE THIRD REPUBLIC

Vichy and the Liberation. Elements of the Right suffered even more
discredit during the Vichy period [49] than the Radicals. After the Liberation,
these elements tended to accept the leadership of de Gaulle, voting in most
instances affirmatively in the two referenda, less because of hostility to the
Third Republic than because of loyalty to the General. They were especially
pleased when he postponed the nationalization that had been advocated in the
Resistance. Nevertheless, they did not approve all the activities of the Provisional Government; and they adopted a position of vigorous opposition after
de Gaulle's resignation, disapproving both Constitutions.

Present Position. After the inauguration of the Fourth Republic under
the prevailing Constitution, the elements of the Right modified to some extent
their uncompromising opposition; and, even before the exclusion of the Communists, a few members accepted ministerial posts. The body of members at

[49] Cf. Ch. XI, pp. 189–190, *supra.*

present seem to feel some attraction towards the RGR, but they are subject to a greater pull in the direction of the new organization of General de Gaulle.

RIGHT ORGANIZATION

Political Geography. Loss of strength by elements of the Right in their traditional strongholds in the East and the West has left them in control of only fragmentary areas of those regions. The principal remnants are to be found in Lorraine and in the south central part of France. At the same time, the Right has gained some strength, largely at the expense of the Radicals, in Burgundy.

Traditional Pattern. During the Third Republic, parties of the Right were distinctly less closely organized and less disciplined than the Communists and Socialists and even the Radicals. Party structure was pyramidal, following in outline the conventional pattern; but it was largely skeletal in character. Membership was not numerous, consisting primarily of elected representatives, candidates, and newspaper men. These were organized into local units, federated at the Department level, and convened annually in a national General Assembly (National Republican Party) or Congress (Democratic Alliance and Popular Democrats). However, youth organizations and other leagues and auxiliary groups were proliferated on the Right, as on the Left; and they probably possessed more vitality and importance than Right parties. Indeed, typical Right organizations, like employer associations, taxpayers' leagues, and other bodies that defended privileged religious, economic, and social interests, performed some of the functions commonly associated with political parties. They thus made lack of party organization on the Right less serious. During the 1930's, certain elements of the Right, influenced by developments in Italy, Germany, and Spain, became violent in their hostility to political democracy and parliamentary government. This hostility was pushed to the point of disloyalty before World War II; and after the defeat it was characteristic of the Vichy regime. Monarchists, beginning as a league at the time of the Dreyfus affair, became, before the end of the Third Republic, a picturesque and ably led Party known as the *Action française,* supported by auxiliary agencies of extremist tendencies; and its scurrility and violence subsequently developed to such a point that it was dissolved by law in 1936.[50] Even more in the public eye during the 1930's was the *Croix de feu.* This was originally an organization of war veterans, the political possibilities of which after its founding in 1927 the forces of reaction were not long in appreciating. Its membership was, particularly following the riots of February of 1934, greatly increased; and it frankly became political in character. The forces were armed and well disciplined, and they demonstrated that they possessed the faculty of rapid mobilization. Their leader, Colonel de la Rocque, turned out, however, to be a man of indecision, of mediocre intelligence, and of limited personal force.[51]

[50] Its well-known leader, Charles Maurras, an intimate adviser of Pétain at Vichy, died in prison in 1951.

[51] He subsequently had a minor position under Vichy.

The organization, together with lesser Fascist groupings, was dissolved in 1936.[52]

PRL. There has been since the Liberation no party of the Right really worthy of the name. The National Republican Federation and the Democratic Alliance have not been reconstituted. Other elements of the Right have attempted various groupings, but no national party has been evolved. The nearest approach to such an organization is the PRL (Republican Party of Liberty), established during the First National Constituent Assembly. It aspires to be the "fourth big party"; but it has not been able to attract more than a minor fraction of the elements of the Right, and its units of organization are not strongly established.

7. THE GAULLISTS

"ASSEMBLAGE OF THE FRENCH PEOPLE"

Political Paradox. The decision of General de Gaulle to found and organize the RPF (Assemblage of the French People) has resulted in at least the appearance of a paradox. The General's impatience with the prevailing regime and his hostility to it have been based in great measure on his criticism of the existing parties. The creation of his own organization certainly involves in some sense the addition of another party. The General and his followers would undoubtedly insist on the difference between the RPF and the other parties, stressing the elevated spirit and high aims of the former. Opponents would underline the similarity of organization and methods, arguing that claims of uniqueness are in reality manifestations of leanings towards support of a "one-party state."

Political Doctrine. When General de Gaulle, after his resignation in January of 1946, emerged from retirement in June to attack the work of the Second National Constituent Assembly,[53] he initiated a series of speeches, interviews, and the like that have continued to stress the need for a renovation of the regime; and though his criticisms of party activities have become increasingly bitter, his proposals for reform of the political system have scarcely become more specific. His insistence on a stronger executive is something to which many persons who are not followers of the General would in principle subscribe. His hints of stronger personal power for the President of the Republic may either be interpreted as an example of the confused view sometimes advanced that under a parliamentary system the executive will be strengthened if a certain amount of real power is vested in the head of the State; [54] or they may be viewed as evidence of preference for the presidential system and, opponents would doubtless say, of aspirations for dictatorial power. In the ranks of the RPF, creation of which was announced in April of 1947, some outstanding members frankly prefer the presidential system, others hold it to be

[52] They were in a measure re-established as the PSF (French Social Party).
[53] Cf. Ch. IV, p. 76, *supra.*
[54] Cf. Ch. VII, pp. 121–122, *supra.*

unsuitable for France.[55] This uncertainty about regime would seem, in spite of the fact that de Gaulle continues to assert the regime to be the primary French issue, to be at least in part the result of the vagueness of the General himself; and it may be doubted whether a very appealing case against a regime which is parliamentary in character with tendencies towards assembly government can be made by the advocates of a regime parliamentary in character with tendencies toward presidential government. A somewhat analogous difficulty may be detected in respect of the RPF's "corporatism." The idea of the association of capital and labor for the purpose of avoiding or curing some of the evils attendant on the employer-employee relationship is defensible as a democratic process if the assumption is that freedom will prevail; but the idea has Fascist connotations that suggest caution and lend themselves to forming the basis of attack by opponents. So far as other RPF themes are concerned, hostility to Communism is far from being their monopoly; whereas approval of American aid with simultaneous insistence on a completely independent foreign policy is in the second respect closely akin to the Communists' position, while in the first more patriotic if less consistent.

Political Tactics. Since its founding the RPF, in accordance with its insistence that it is not just another party, has welcomed adherents from the traditional Parties other than the Communists. This double membership has been forbidden by the Socialists and the MRP, but it has otherwise had a certain amount of success in practice. On the basis of it, the RPF has had signal victories in certain local elections; [56] and it has secured a respectable representation in the Council of the Republic, where its own representatives have joined with sympathizers to constitute an "intergroup," a formation which also existed in the first National Assembly, in which, without direct representation, an intergroup was sponsored by the RPF. At the same time, Gaullists pressed so uncompromisingly for the dissolution of the first National Assembly [57] and General de Gaulle so persistently attacked the Third Force as not much to be preferred to the Communists that sympathy from others than militants clearly tended to diminish rather than to increase. Thus, although the RPF emerged from the 1951 elections with a representation in the National Assembly (about 19 per cent of the total) slightly larger than that of any other single group, its popular vote of only slightly more than 20 per cent—substantially less than that of the Communists—was undoubtedly a great disappointment to General de Gaulle and his friends.

GAULLIST ORGANIZATION

Political Geography. The RPF has almost no strength in the southern half of France. Its geographic strength may be said, without undue oversimplification, to be the result of loss by the MRP to the RPF of much of what had been gained from the Right. In other words, alliance of elements of the Right

[55] Cf. Ch. x, p. 177, *supra.*
[56] This has been particularly true of Paris and of large cities in general. For the national elections of 1951, however, the RPF refused combinations with other parties.
[57] Cf. Ch. vi, p. 92, *supra.*

with the RPF has given to the latter mastery of famous reactionary areas of the West and of a considerable part of those in the East. The RPF also has much strength in certain former Radical strongholds to the south of Paris and in the Loire valley.

RPF Structure. The RPF is an assemblage not of parties as such [58] but of individual members.[59] Organization is marked by a high degree of centralization. Committees of members, with directing staffs (*bureaus*), exist at the local and Department levels; but to some extent there are also cells in various enterprises, roughly speaking on the Communist model. At the national level, the assembly corresponding to the congresses of the traditional parties is called by the RPF the "National Assizes." Their public sessions are confined to speeches and to approval of decisions made by committees in secret sittings. Other national RPF organizations are characterized by the personal pre-eminence of General de Gaulle. A *National Council* of a hundred members is chosen by a *Directing Committee,* which in turn is selected by de Gaulle and has a *General Secretariat* composed of his personal collaborators. The General likewise selects the members of an *Administrative Board,* from which members of Parliament are excluded. This exclusion, which is also practiced in directing agencies at the lower levels, gives some impression that the RPF is an anti-parliamentary organization not unlike the direct action leagues of the pre-War period, an impression which is accentuated, at least in the eyes of opponents of the RPF, by the existence of disciplined bodies of élite shock troops.

8. THE OUTLOOK

The political future of France is, from the nature of things, highly uncertain. Confident prediction is impossible. The international situation is too much a determining factor for this to be otherwise. At the same time, no good reason seems to afford support for the belief that France has lost that vitality which has often surprised and confounded her opponents and critics. Recovery from the effects of the War has been in many respects remarkable. There is after all something not unimpressive about the plodding way things go on in France, in the political as in other aspects of life, in the midst of stress and strain. Although feelings during prolonged crises give rise somewhat naturally to desire for, and advocacy of, dramatic and inspired attacks on problems and shortcomings that are manifest, nevertheless the slower tempo of patience and persistence is perhaps more consistent with genuine moral stamina. If relatively normal conditions should come again to prevail, without intervening catastrophe, then supporters of the middle way may say of France with some satisfaction not only that, like Sieyès, it survived, but that it realized slow but sure progress.

---

[58] In this it differs from the other "Assemblage," the RGR.
[59] Some, as has been indicated, belong to other parties.

BIBLIOGRAPHICAL NOTE
ON THE FRENCH POLITICAL SYSTEM

Some suggestions concerning sources for the study of French government and politics may be had from the footnotes on the preceding pages. An exhaustive list, at this point, of works dealing with various aspects of the subject would almost certainly not be very useful to the student. Most of the outstanding works that are involved are naturally written in French; and, from the nature of the case, they are not everywhere in this country readily available. It is hoped that the suggestions which follow may prove of some value to the student.

1. Primary Materials

(a) *In French*

First place naturally goes to the Constitution of the Fourth Republic. There is no lack of readily available copies of the French text of this document. (Cf. Ch. II, p. 47, n 18, *supra.*) Of English translations, special reference may be made to that which has been issued, as has been also the French text, by the French Press and Information Service (501 Madison Avenue, New York 22).

So far as official publications are concerned, a central position is occupied by the *Journal officiel de la République française.* The student who has occasion may learn without difficulty to make his way through the bound volumes of this publication. He should be acquainted with a few historical facts concerning it.

A periodical, *La Gazette nationale: ou Le Moniteur universel,* was founded on November 24, 1789. It contained, in the form of résumés, information on foreign affairs and the debates in the National Assembly. On February 3, 1790, this journal absorbed the *Bulletin de l'Assemblée nationale;* and debates were reproduced in "dramatic form." At this same time, in anticipation of the binding of the first volume, *post factum* numbers were made up for the period from May 5, 1789, date of the convening of the States-General, to November 24, 1789. The journal was made official in the Year VIII and its title was shortened to the familiar *Moniteur universel* in 1811. It remained, with the exception of the period from July 8, 1814, to February 1, 1815, the official government journal until 1869. It was replaced at that time by the *Journal officiel,* which has continued to the present day. The *Moniteur universel,* having lost its official status, appeared as a conservative newspaper until 1901, at which time it went out of existence.

Publication of the *Journal officiel* (to which title was added *de l'Empire français* until September 5, 1870, since when *de la Republique française* has been added—except for *de l'Etat français* during the Vichy period) was until 1880 entrusted to private enterprise. Since that year, it has been a government undertaking. The volumes are not always bound uniformly, but this presents no great difficulty. The present contents fall into six parts: (1) *Edition des lois et décrets,* which contains the text of statutes, decrees, regulations, circulars, opinions, etc., together with monthly and annual indexes; (2), (3), and (4) *Edition des débats de l'Assemblée nationale, Edition des débats du Conseil de la République,* and *Edition des débats de l'Union française,* all containing stenographic transcripts of proceedings in the respective assemblies, along with indexes, and (2) and (3) containing written questions to Ministers and their answers; (5) *Edition des avis et rapports du Conseil économique,* its contents, to which there is an index, being indicated by its title; and (6) *Edition complète,* which contains, in addition to (1) to (5), parliamentary and administrative documents, together with indexes.

Various other collections of documentary material exist. Special mention may be made of the codes of procedural rules of the chambers, of which new editions appear from time to time. They are:

Le Règlement de l'Assemblée nationale
Le Règlement du Conseil de la République.

(b) *In English*

Translations of various documentary materials, together in some cases with certain "readings," may be found in:

Anderson, F. M., *The Constitutions and Other Select Documents Illustrative of the History of France 1789–1907* (2nd ed., Minneapolis, 1908).

Hill, N. L., Stoke, H. W., and Schneider, C. N., *The Background of European Government* (3rd ed., New York, 1951), Part II.

Laing, L. H., Vernon, M. C., Eldersveld, S., Meisel, J. H., and Pollock, J. K., *Source Book in European Governments* (New York, 1950), France.

2. Secondary Works

(a) *In French*

The subjects treated in the United States in a general work on a political system are on the governmental side dealt with in France in accordance with a division that is somewhat legalistic and rigidly and formally logical. Thus, the student must give his especial attention to Constitutional Law, to Administrative Law, and to Public Finance; and, though he may study them together in outline in some books on Public Law, he will normally tackle them separately in separate works. In respect of Constitutional Law, the outstanding older works, those of Duguit, Esmein, Hauriou, and Joseph-Barthélemy, are, while still of philosophical and historical value, out of date so far as the Fourth Republic is concerned. Of current works, several of the most important are:

Burdeau, Georges, *Manuel de droit constitutionnel* (5e éd., Paris, 1947).

Duverger, Maurice, *Manuel de droit constitutionnel et de science politique* (5e éd., Paris, 1948).

Laferrière, Julien, *Manuel de droit constitutionnel* (2e éd., Paris, 1947).

Pinto, Roger, *Eléments de droit constitutionnel* (Lille, 1948).

Prélot, Marcel, *Précis de droit constitutionnel* (Paris, 1949).

Vedel, G., *Manuel élémentaire de droit constitutionnel* (Paris, 1949).

In respect of Administrative Law, the specialist will wish to examine the older outstanding works, such as those of Barthélemy and of Hauriou; but, for the current scene, it is sufficient to cite:

Waline, Marcel, *Traité élémentaire de droit administratif* (6e éd., Paris, 1951).

In respect of Public Finance, the student should consult:

Trotabas, Louis, *Précis de science et législation financières* (10e éd., Paris, 1951), in which will be found (pp. 25–27) a list of the older as well as of the newer books.

In respect of party politics, special reference may be made to:

Goguel, François, *La Politique des partis sous la IIIe République* (Paris, 1948).

Marabuto, Paul, *Les Partis politiques et les mouvements sociaux sous la IVe République* (Paris, 1948).

Priouret, Roger A., *La République des partis* (Paris, 1947).

All the works listed above could be employed in the preparation of an elaborate and exhaustive bibliography of French books, monographs, and articles in periodicals. However, bibliographical problems are much simplified in France by the existence of:

Grandin, A., *Bibliographie générale des sciences juridiques, politiques, économiques et sociales de 1800 à 1925–1926* (3 vol., Paris, 1926). This work has, in peacetime, been kept up to date by annual supplements (of which there are so far nineteen).

(b) *In English*

Works like those of Bodley, Bryce, Lowell, and Sait are of course considerably out-moded; but, as classics, they are worth reading.

Several excellent studies were made of French government under the Third Republic, of which most permanent value attaches perhaps to:

Thomson, David, *Democracy in France: The Third Republic* (Oxford, 1946).

So far as the Fourth Republic is concerned, no student should fail to read in connection with its founding:

Wright, Gordon, *The Reshaping of French Democracy* (New York, 1948).

Accounts of French government and politics, as of the early years of the present system, are to be found in general textbooks on European government, such as those of Professors Ranney and Carter, Buck and Masland, and a number of others. Special reference should be made to two books which appeared in 1951. They are:

McKay, Donald C., *The United States and France* (Cambridge, 1951).

Earle, Edward Mead (ed.), *Modern France: Problems of the Third and Fourth Republics* (Princeton, 1951).

The Government and Politics of

ITALY

by ARNOLD J. ZURCHER

CHAPTER I

THE MONARCHICAL PARLIAMENTARY PERIOD

THE UNIFICATION OF ITALY

Progress towards Unification. The historian of the nineteenth century will never cease to marvel at the remarkable chain of events which in less than a dozen years transformed the Italian peninsula from a welter of political jurisdictions into a modern national State. In 1859 Italy was still, to use Metternich's phrase, "a geographical expression." The Italian people owed allegiance either to Austria or to one of a half dozen petty ruling houses, only one of which, that of Savoy, sovereign in the Kingdom of Piedmont,[1] was regarded as Italian in character. Yet within less than two years the process of amalgamating this political welter into a single kingdom, under the aegis of Piedmont and the House of Savoy, had already been virtually accomplished. Austria had been compelled to give up Lombardy, and that rich area had voted to join Piedmont; Modena, Parma, Tuscany, and the Emilia had thrown off their former rulers and followed Lombardy's example; Francis II, Bourbon King of the Two Sicilies, had been driven out of Naples, and the entire southern part of the peninsula had imitated the more northerly regions; and on March 17, 1861, before a national Parliament at Turin, Victor Emmanuel II, King of Piedmont, had proclaimed the existence of the Kingdom of Italy. Four more years and the new kingdom, as an ally of Bismarck in his war against Austria, had emerged with Venetia as its share of the victor's spoils; and then in September, 1870, following the withdrawal of the French garrison near Rome, that city had been taken from the Pope by force and proclaimed the capital of an Italian State which embraced the entire peninsula.[2]

Earlier Efforts at National Union. Though achieved with such amazing celerity the unification of Italy was not merely the result of fortuitous events.

[1] Technically the Kingdom of Sardinia. The dukes of Savoy became kings of Sardinia in 1720 upon the acquisition of the Island of Sardinia. Piedmont, however, was the Sardinian King's most important territory and his government was located at Turin, Piedmont's chief city.
[2] On the unification of Italy see Bolton King, *A History of Italian Unity*, 2 vols. (London, 1899) and W. R. Thayer, *The Dawn of Italian Independence*, 2 vols. (Boston, 1893).

In the early part of the sixteenth century, Niccolò Machiavelli, the great Florentine, had pleaded earnestly for the expulsion of the foreign ruler from the peninsula and the consolidation of all its people under a single Italian prince. Generations of patriots since Machiavelli's time had actively sought by one means or another to realize his hope; and Italian literature is studded with the names of those who thereafter contributed patriotic inspiration in prose and poetry. Napoleon Bonaparte, invader and conqueror though he was, brought the French vision of national fraternity to all of Italy between 1796 and 1815. In southern and most of northern Italy, he created nominally independent kingdoms and made common to much of the peninsula the advanced legal and administrative systems which had been perfected in France. The impetus to nationalism thus fostered lost little of its force even after the Congress of Vienna sought in 1815 to undo in Italy and in Europe all that the Corsican had done. Thus long before national unity became a reality, its foundations had been firmly established.

Chief Protagonists of Unification. Chief responsibility for the actual success of the movement for unity is, however, rightly attributed to the four principal actors in the drama. The first of these is Victor Emmanuel II, King of Sardinia-Piedmont and the first King of the united nation. Victor Emmanuel II is esteemed by Italians for the patriotism which prompted him to pledge the fortunes of his dynasty to the great cause, and for the moral and material aid he constantly extended to those actively engaged in furthering that cause.[3] No less important than the King was the nineteenth-century mystic and revolutionary, Giuseppe Mazzini. Through his writings and correspondence, his creation of the famous "Young Italy" movement, and his numerous conspiracies against foreign and, particularly, Austrian rule, Mazzini did much to renew Italian patriotism after 1821 and to instill hatred of foreign control in the Italian youth. Perpetually coupled with his name is that of Giuseppe Garibaldi. His was the contribution of the practical crusader and of the adventurous military filibusterer. It was Garibaldi's motley army of red-shirted volunteers, the legendary "Thousand," which conquered Sicily in 1861 and helped materially to bring about the downfall and expulsion of the Bourbon dynasty in southern Italy. Garibaldi also led in similar, albeit less successful, exploits against the papal power at Rome.[4]

Cavour. But the greatest of all the immediate architects of Italian unity was Victor Emmanuel's Prime Minister, the enlightened liberal statesman, Count Camillo Benso di Cavour. It was Cavour, more than any other man, who molded and directed the forces which made national unity a realizable ideal. He it was who raised parochial Piedmont to a position of influence in the peninsula and among the European chancelleries. It was his reforming zeal and administrative ability which made Piedmont a model kingdom and gave her the military and financial sinews to conduct a war of liberation. His astute diplomacy secured the active aid of France and the latent sympathy of

[3] E. Dicey, *Victor Emmanuel* (New York, 1886).
[4] See G. M. Trevelyan, *Garibaldi and the Making of Italy* (New York, 1911).

England against Austria; and his successful statesmanship attracted to Piedmont's banner almost every Italian faction interested in the national cause. However ripe that cause may have been in the middle of the nineteenth century, without Cavour it might have languished indefinitely.[5]

CHARACTERISTICS AND PROBLEMS OF THE NEW STATE

Some Statistics. Outwardly the nation which had thus been brought into being had the characteristics of a great power. It was the home of a civilization millenniums old; indeed Rome, its capital city, was the mother of the civilization of the West. It contained the seat of the largest of the Christian faiths and many of the world's centers of art and learning. In size, moreover, united Italy compared favorably with the established powers of Europe. The area of the peninsula and the two great islands of Sardinia and Sicily which she occupied was somewhat more than 110,000 square miles; the inhabitants in 1870 numbered approximately 27,000,000.[6] The population was almost purely Italian; indeed the Italy of 1870 fell far short of embracing even all the Italians in Europe, many still remaining under the jurisdiction of Austria, Switzerland, and France. The population was also overwhelmingly Catholic in religious sentiment, only a very small number—less than one half of one per cent of the whole—professing other faiths.

National Diversity. But the new State also had many serious weaknesses. In the first place the population was not nearly so homogeneous as statistics might indicate. Although Italians had possessed a national literary language since the days of Dante, the dialects used by the common folk of the various regions differed greatly. Then, too, northern and southern Italians, owing to diverse racial origins and admixtures, differed remarkably in physical and even in psychological attributes. More remarkable still was the difference in the intellectual level and political capacity of the people of these two areas. Piedmontese, in touch with the currents of nineteenth-century European thought and far advanced commercially and even industrially, were perhaps as enlightened and politically as mature as the French across their borders. So, too, were the inhabitants of Tuscany, the "cradle" of the Renaissance, of the former duchies, and of Lombardy and Venetia. But the people of southern Italy had known little but despotic personal government and economic vassalage for centuries, with results all too plainly revealed in the moral and social outlook of the peasantry. Neapolitans and Sicilians especially were among the most backward peoples in Europe. Illiterate, living for the greater part in the most abject poverty, subjected as late as the middle of the nineteenth century to the benighted and scandalously corrupt Government of the Spanish Bourbons, a Government which Gladstone had once described as the "negation of God," they were fitter subjects for misgovernment than for government. Conditions in Campania, Basilicata, and Sicily were so bad that for more than a genera-

---

[5] On Cavour see W. R. Thayer, *The Life and Times of Cavour,* 2 vols. (Boston, 1911).

[6] The area of continental Italy (1951) is 116,235 square miles. The population (1951) is approximately 46,000,000.

tion the newly united kingdom had to give special attention to the problems of combating brigandage in these areas and of raising the elementary economic, intellectual, and moral levels of the inhabitants. Indeed, in 1951, almost a century after unification it may still be said that the retarded development of the "South" and of the "Islands" continues to be one of the principal problems with which Italian governments must cope.

Local Particularism. Subjects of the new kingdom were also locally minded to an intense degree. Florentines were proud of the fact that they were Tuscans; Venetians could not forget the glories of their ancient republic; and many a Torinese looked with sorrow and anger upon the reduction of his erstwhile sovereign state to mere provinces of a greater kingdom. In the Parliament of a united Italy it was to be uncommonly difficult for the representatives of these and other areas to place national before regional interests and to subordinate local to national patriotism. In many instances, indeed, regionalism was to prove so strong a factor that political parties were organized along purely local lines. It was a condition for which geography was partly responsible. Isolated by mountains and even by the sea, the Italian was foreordained by nature to be somewhat parochial in his political loyalties. But history, too, had played its part. Centuries of political division and the consequent lack of commercial and cultural intercourse had necessarily fostered local patriotism and inhibited the growth of a broadly national and cosmopolitan outlook.

Enmity of the Church. In gaining unity, moreover, Italy had seriously offended the Catholic Church. The creation of a national State had necessarily required the destruction of the Church's temporal power over Rome and central Italy; and the forcible entry into these areas of Italian troops had seemed to the Head of the Church an unforgivable act. After 1870 he secluded himself in the Vatican palace, a self-declared prisoner; for more than a quarter of a century the faithful were admonished to refrain from active collaboration with the authorities of the new State.

Economic Weaknesses. In addition to all this the new nation was poor, at least in those economic resources out of which material might is built. Industry had been barely started in the northern cities. The country lacked capital for industrial development as well as the elementary industrial raw materials such as coal and the basic metals. By far the larger portion of the population was engaged in agriculture, from which returns were considerably below the standard of productivity maintained elsewhere. Except in the valley of the Po River, in Campania, on the Apulian tableland, and in certain Sicilian areas, Italian soil is poorly adapted to agriculture. Much of it is entirely unproductive, being mountain or marshland; much of the remainder is distinctly below par in fertility. Deforestation of mountain slopes in the past has caused serious erosion in many districts and increased the hazard of flood. Allied with nature in reducing agricultural productivity is a notorious system of land tenure. Along the Po and in southern Italy most of the arable land is embraced in huge estates known as the *latifundia*. The peasants work on these estates as sharecroppers or as day laborers; and their economic condition is often as wretched as that of any agricultural laborer in Europe.[7] For such a poor country even nominal taxation was a burden; but taxation in some parts of Italy had been abnormally high for many generations and most of it had been of a direct character. Moreover, the formation of a single national exchequer offered little immediate relief, because the Government of united Italy, besides having to pay its own increasingly burdensome way, had also assumed the debts of the previous political regimes of the peninsula.

Future None Too Promising. In view of these many liabilities the future of the newly united kingdom seemed none too bright in 1870. To be sure, Italy's influence in international affairs mounted rapidly, and her statesmen, as skillful in diplomacy as their ancestors, quickly gained for her an honorable place in the family of nations. But the country was hardly equal to the requirements of the role of great power; and the desire to play such a role itself became something of a major liability in Italian politics. That desire tempted even the country's wiser statesmen to risk more than the national economy or resources warranted. Rasher statesmen, animated by the same desire, brought the nation to the brink of ruin on more than one occasion. Economic weakness and the uneven political and social development of the country were also partly responsible for the relative instability of the internal political institutions. As we shall note in the following pages, the political system of liberal parliamentary Italy never quite achieved the strength and durability that characterized the governments of certain of the older and better established states of Western Europe. The inherent weaknesses of the original political structure contributed, in turn, to the triumph of Fascism sixty years after unification, and partly explain the substitution of republic for monarchy in 1946 after Fascism itself had been formally liquidated.

THE GOVERNMENT OF LIBERAL ITALY

The Albertian Statuto. The political system of united Italy was largely taken over from Piedmont. During his long tenure as Piedmontese Prime Minister, Cavour had succeeded in giving that political system a thoroughly liberal cast. Its legal basis was a written Constitution known as the Fundamental Statute of the Kingdom (*Statuto fondamentale del regno*). This document, modeled along the conservatively liberal lines of the French and Belgian Constitutions of 1830, had been granted by Piedmont's king, Charles Albert, in March, 1848, as a concession to the revolutionary spirit which in that year swept over Piedmont as well as over the rest of Europe. In the jargon of the political scientist, it was an "octroyed" Constitution. Unlike the heads of the other Italian states of the day who had also been compelled to issue written Constitutions, Charles Albert did not suspend or abolish his instrument when the inevitable reaction to revolution set in. Upon Charles Albert's abdication in 1849, moreover, his son and successor, Victor Emmanuel II, gave his promise to continue the *Statuto*. The new King's fidelity to this promise, maintained despite efforts of Austria and legitimist Europe to compel him to break

[7] This land-tenure system is now (1951) undergoing some modification. See pp. 317–319.

it, earned for him the popular title of *"re galantuomo"* (the king who was an honest man). Nominally, at least, Charles Albert's Constitution continued as Italy's basic law until January 1, 1948, when it was superseded by the new republican Constitution.

The Kingship. The nominal center of authority under the *Statuto* was the King. Victor Emmanuel II occupied this office first as King of Sardinia-Piedmont and then as King of united Italy until 1878. His successor, Humbert I, reigned until 1900. He, in turn, was succeeded by his son, Victor Emmanuel III, the end of whose long reign in 1946 virtually spelled the end of the Italian monarchy. Humbert II, his son, became regent for his father in June, 1944, and king in May, 1946, when his father abdicated. Humbert reigned for one month, or until June 13, when the proclamation of the Italian Republic brought the Savoy dynasty to an end.

Owing to the usages developed by Cavour as Prime Minister, the King's position had gradually come to be comparable to the position of the British monarch. The Italian King's constitutional prerogatives were discharged by Ministers whom he appointed and dismissed, not as his personal wishes might dictate but according to the political will of Parliament. It would be a mistake, however, to identify the Italian kingship too closely with the position of constitutional irresponsibility developed for monarchy in Britain toward the close of Victoria's reign. National traditions and an undisciplined and somewhat chaotic party structure frequently made it possible for King Victor Emmanuel II and his successors to modify the course of public policy and control even the personnel and tenure of the ministries.[8] As we shall see later, it was the personal wishes and formal action of King Victor Emmanuel III, and not the wishes of his Ministers or Parliament, which brought Benito Mussolini's Cabinet into power in 1922 and thus paved the way for the Fascist Revolution.[9]

Parliament: Composition of the Deputies. Parliament was bicameral, consisting of a Chamber of Deputies and a Senate. The membership of the first of these two houses was secured through popular elections conducted until 1919, except for a brief interval, in constituencies each returning a single deputy. By the time of World War I the Deputies numbered 535. The franchise was originally rather carefully restricted, being limited by rather high property and direct-tax qualifications. The total eligible to vote in 1870 did not exceed 500,000.[10] Successive liberalizations of the franchise law in 1882 and in 1912 gradually increased the electorate; and by 1919, when a third electoral reform bill was enacted, Italy attained universal manhood suffrage.

Electoral Abuse. The most liberal franchise provisions, however, did little to correct an electoral abuse from which Italy suffered throughout the post-Cavourian period. This was the habit of governmental interference with electoral freedom. By exploiting official prestige, political favors, money, and

[8] For early examples of royal intervention, see King, *op. cit.*, ɪɪ, pp. 233, 253, 334 and 360–361. On the other hand note also the adherence of Victor Emmanuel II to the electoral and popular will in his acceptance of the first Depretis Cabinet in 1876; see p. 229.
[9] See p. 251.   [10] King, *op. cit.*, ɪɪ, p. 307.

sometimes tactics which savored of physical compulsion, national ministers, deputies, and local governmental officials exerted an unblushing control over those privileged to vote. Rare indeed was the ministry which did not yield to the temptation to use these convenient methods of ensuring parliamentary majorities; and rarer still were the occasions when such methods, having been resorted to, failed to return a majority to the chamber favorable to the government of the day. "Working the elections" became a habit which even the most high-minded statesmen were unable to eradicate. Other European states, suffering from the same evil, attempted more or less successfully to combat it towards the end of the nineteenth century; in Italy, however, it persisted well into the twentieth and became a standing reproach to the political morality and capacity of the nation. One of the reasons why the new republican Constitution, adopted in 1948, places such emphasis upon regional and local autonomy is the desire to strengthen the hand of the local authorities and, through them, maintain a check on possible electoral abuses by the prefect or other local representative of Rome officialdom.

The Senate. The Senate, or second Chamber of Parliament, consisted of persons nominally appointed by the King but actually chosen by the Cabinet. The persons appointed had to be selected from some twenty-one categories of Italian subjects. These included important clerics, past presidents of the Chamber of Deputies or deputies themselves, ministers, ambassadors, chief judges, high officials of the public forces, and holders of important positions in the permanent Civil Service; members of the Royal Academy of Sciences and of the Superior Council of Public Instruction; persons who paid at least 3,000 lire annually in direct property or business taxes; and persons who, because of their public services or high individual merit, deserved to be honored by their country. Senatorial tenure was for life. Princes of the royal house became members of the Senate as a matter of right at the age of twenty-one and were given a vote in its deliberations at the age of twenty-five.[11] Although there was no limit to the number of Senators, the total membership of the upper Chamber rarely exceeded 425.

Parliamentary Organization and Procedure. In matters of organization and procedure the two houses strongly resembled the equivalent parliamentary Chambers of France's Third Republic. The King named the president of the Senate while the Chamber elected its own presiding officer. These officials generally acted in a nonpartisan manner. Legislation was introduced both by private members and by the Ministers who had access to both houses. The number of bills from ministerial sources, known as *disegni di legge,* increased in the course of time, the executive thus gaining a distinct advantage in the determination of legislative policy. Both Chambers employed various methods of voting common to European parliaments; but the *Statuto* required that the vote on the final stage of a bill should be by secret ballot.[12] For detailed

---

[11] For the provisions relating to the Senate, see *Statuto,* arts. 33 and 34, W. F. Dodd, *Modern Constitutions* (Chicago, 1909), II, pp. 5 *ff.*

[12] Art. 63.

scrutiny of legislative and other matters, both houses divided themselves by lot into bureaus or *uffici,* nine in the Chamber and seven in the Senate. Members of the *uffici* then selected from their own number *ad hoc* committees to report on legislative projects. In the Senate these committees consisted of one member chosen from each of the seven *uffici,* the procedure requiring that at least four of the *uffici* favor a bill before a committee could be named. As in France this system was gradually supplemented by a standing committee system; and in 1920 the lower Chamber did away with the *uffici* altogether, establishing instead ten permanent commissions chosen directly by the members of the Chamber and reflecting the Chamber's political complexion.[13] In the Senate the *uffici,* chosen by lot, continued until 1939, when Fascist reorganization did away with them.[14]

Relative Powers of the Two Chambers. It was originally intended that the Chamber and the Senate of monarchical Italy should be essentially equal in power.[15] The only derogation from the principle of equality was the provision of Article 10 of the *Statuto,* not uncommon in nineteenth-century constitutions, that taxation or budgetary proposals should be initiated in the first or more popular house. But since the *Statuto* set no limit to the number of Senators whom the Cabinet might appoint, the Senate, like the House of Lords in England, became subject to the threat of ministerial packing whenever it failed to be complaisant in the face of ministerial legislative demands. Cavour used such a threat with effect against the Senate as early as 1855.[16] This subordination to the government of the day, combined with the fact that the Senate lacked popular authority and was at best somewhat artificially constituted, caused its power and prestige to dwindle even before the united kingdom came into being. Although its assent continued to be necessary to all legislation, it consistently gave way to the Cabinet or to the latter's majority in the Deputies on all major issues. By 1870, therefore, the Senate of Italy had already become a kind of honorary political academy, membership in which was regarded as a reward for faithful service to monarchy and State; and the place thus established for it in the constitutional system was not afterward substantially altered until the advent of the new republican Senate in 1948.

Ministers and the Parliamentary System. As already indicated, the Ministers of the Government were appointed by the King in accordance with the political will of Parliament. Usually they were chosen from the membership of the Chambers. Collectively the Ministers formed a Cabinet or Council, presided over by a Prime Minister, officially designated as President of the Council. Except for the prestige attaching to the latter's office and to his political status in the nation at large and a certain primacy in the determina-

---

[13] For a good description of the procedure of the Italian Parliament prior to Mussolini's changes see H. R. Spencer, *The Government and Politics of Italy* (Yonkers, 1932), pp. 156–157 and 181 *ff.*

[14] For the Fascist Parliament see p. 258.

[15] *Statuto,* art. 55, Dodd, *op. cit.,* ii, pp. 5 *ff.*

[16] King, *op. cit.,* ii, p. 20.

tion of official policy which usage accorded him, the Prime Minister was the equal of the other holders of Cabinet portfolios. The Cabinet, thus constituted, administered the affairs of the country as long as it had the confidence of a majority of the Parliament or, to be more exact, of the Chamber of Deputies. The post-Cavourian Italian government was therefore a "responsible" or "parliamentary" government. Cabinets or Councils of Ministers were constructed, reconstructed, and dissolved, and Prime Ministers came and went, much as in other parliamentary systems such as the British or, after the establishment of the Third Republic, the French.

Peculiarities of Italian Parliamentarism. But the Italian parliamentary system of the monarchical period early developed certain marked peculiarities which distinguished it from similar systems elsewhere. The *Statuto* reserved to the King the power of dissolving the Deputies, and this prerogative was freely used by the Ministers, no Chamber, prior to 1914, having been permitted to continue for its entire five-year legal term. Unlike the result of similar tactics in Great Britain, dissolution and a subsequent election in Italy rarely led directly to the overthrow of a ministry, chiefly because ministerial electoral manipulation invariably ensured the return of a favorable parliamentary majority.

Transformism. A second and more important peculiarity of Italian parliamentarism was "transformism" (*trasformismo*). This was the name given to the practice, dominant on the Italian political stage after 1876, of constructing a Cabinet with little reference to the party affiliations of its members. Deputies and Senators entered into ministerial combinations under the aegis of some astute parliamentary strategist or "broker," sacrificing party loyalties and whatever responsibility they owed to their constituents for the desire to hold a portfolio or to aid their political friends. As a result the most diverse elements, drawing support from every political wing of the Chambers, and often subscribing formally at least to utterly opposed political principles and programs, were to be found in intimate collaboration as Ministers of His Majesty's Government of the day.

Transformism Criticized. Many harsh words have been uttered against transformism by critics, particularly by foreign critics. Not the least serious of these strictures is that transformism completely sterilized Italian political life and made the parliamentary system meaningless. The criticisms are not entirely unjustified. As a result of the practice electoral mandates certainly came to mean less than they ordinarily do; and political principles and party labels lost much of their significance. The parties themselves were encouraged to split into an unending series of minor personal factions. High office, including the prime ministership, did not necessarily go to the politicians who had won the confidence and affection of the nation but to those who were adept as parliamentary tacticians. Moreover, it must be admitted that transformism helped to lower the standard of political morality since it encouraged Cabinet architects to use patronage and even more questionable favors in order to win adherents.

A Not Unmitigated Evil. On the other hand it must in all fairness be pointed out that if transformism balkanized the Italian party structure, it merely contributed to a tendency already inherent in that structure. As will be noted later,[17] it was precisely because of the instability of the parties in Parliament that transformism received its initial impetus. Parliamentary Italy, like parliamentary France, was blessed or cursed with a multiple-party system; and if parliamentarism was to be engrafted upon such a system it had to take some form of coalition regime. Transformism was coalition carried to an extreme. Nor can it be denied that transformism was not without certain positive virtues. If it obscured political differences it also encouraged political unity. To some extent it facilitated the formation of Cabinets and thereby reduced the number and duration of those Cabinet crises which have so often plagued parliamentary states on the Continent. Transformism also made possible that constancy of political leadership which was so signal a feature of the Italian government until the end of World War I. If the lengthy tenure as Prime Minister of such men as Depretis, Crispi, and Giolitti gave them the appearance and occasionally the substance of dictatorial power, it also ensured a continuity to the outline and substance of Italian domestic and foreign policy greater than is ordinarily secured in a parliamentary state. If transformism was an evil it was by no means the unmitigated evil which non-Italian historians are wont to assert it was.

Local Government. Local governmental institutions of the liberal monarchical period were largely created *de novo* during the years of national unification, although the influence of the models which Napoleon I had introduced during his occupation of the Italian peninsula is clearly discernible. Chief areas of local government were some seventy-five provinces and 8,000 communes, both of which were autonomous legal corporations enjoying considerable discretionary authority over such matters as elementary education, local police protection, public health, and local public works. In addition to these two areas mention might also be made of the *circondari,* corresponding rather closely to the French *arrondissements.* The *circondari* served as electoral and judicial districts for the national Government.

Prefect and the Provincial Administration. The chief provincial officer under the constitutional monarchy was the Prefect, an official whose creation had been directly inspired by his French compeer. Appointed by the Minister of the Interior and directly accountable to that national official, the Prefect performed the dual role of supervising autonomous local government both in province and commune on behalf of the national authorities and of serving as the chief local law enforcement official for the Crown. The Prefect was also notorious for his political activities on behalf of the national Government, his office being the agency through which ministers and deputies attempted to control the voting in national elections. Assisting the Prefect in his duties was a Prefectoral Council of the Prefect's own appointees and a Provincial Administrative Junta (*Giunta*). The latter, composed of members of the Pre-

[17] See p. 230.

fectoral Council and of representatives of the autonomous governing authorities of the province, exercised important supervisory powers of a financial character over local governmental agencies including those of the commune. In addition it served as the administrative court of first instance, appeals on questions of administrative law going from it to the Council of State at Rome.[18] In each province there was also a general council chosen by the local electorate which after 1914 embraced practically all adult males. Through a permanent committee of its own members and a president whom it elected, the Council discharged the actual powers delegated to the province as an autonomous governmental entity.

Communal Government. Affairs of the commune were in the hands of a communal council, one-half of whose members were chosen by the local "administrative" electorate every triennium for a term of six years. The communal electorate was governed by the same qualifications as controlled the electorate of the province; it was therefore quite democratic in character. Like the provincial council, the communal council chose a permanent committee of its members to act in its behalf in the rather long intervals between its regular sessions. The commune's chief executive official was the Syndic (*Sindaco*). Originally appointed by the Minister of the Interior, the Syndic was, after 1896, elected by the communal council and subjected to its control. The Syndic, however, continued to exercise certain functions assigned to him by the national authorities and thus served in the dual capacity of a national and communal administrative official. His term of office was for four years; but he was subject to suspension during that interval on motion of the Prefect or of one-third of the communal council and he could be removed by the Minister of the Interior.[19]

POLITICAL CONSOLIDATION AND THE RULE OF THE RIGHT
(1861–1875)

The Successors of Cavour. As fate would have it, Italy's great leader, Cavour, died in 1861 before the final stages of unification had been realized, and before the problem of the political organization of the united State had barely been touched. Leadership had therefore to be entrusted to Cavour's former colleagues and lieutenants in the nationalist movement. These, with the possible exception of Baron Bettino Ricasoli of Florence and the able financier, Quintana Sella, were men of a mold inferior to the great Piedmontese. Moreover their efforts to pilot the new State towards political equilibrium were beset by the foreign complications involved in winning Venetia from Austria and in wresting Rome from the Church.

Progress towards Uniform Institutions. Considerable progress was nevertheless made in the decade after Cavour's death in introducing administrative, legal, and economic institutions of national scope. The public debt of

---

[18] For a description of both the administrative and regular judicial systems of the Italian State see pp. 291–296 *ff.*

[19] For a description of Italian local government under the Republic, see pp. 296 *ff.*

the previous political entities was consolidated in 1865; and some measure of uniformity was secured in the various tax systems which had theretofore existed in the peninsula. Legal codes were formulated in 1865 and the education laws of Piedmont were extended to most of the kingdom. Local governmental legislation of a definitive character was also adopted in that year. The various armed forces, those which had belonged to the formerly independent governments as well as irregular volunteer forces such as Garibaldi had organized to conquer Sicily, were absorbed into a common military establishment. Internal customs lines were obliterated except for the municipal octroi duties; and a common tariff schedule, derived from Piedmont, was applied to all the frontiers of the new realm.[20]

Law of Guarantees. Perhaps the major issue of a quasi-domestic character facing Italian statesmen at the end of this period of constitutional consolidation was the so-called "Roman Question," the question as to what to do with the Papacy now that its lands had been absorbed into the Italian State and its temporal power destroyed. As previously indicated the Church's head after 1870 had declared himself a prisoner of the "usurper" and had urged Catholic communicants to abstain from actual participation in the affairs of the new State. Balked alike by papal hostility and by the indifference of the powers of Europe in its efforts to secure a solution of this question by an international conference, Italy's Government finally sought a unilateral solution, and enacted the famous Law of Guarantees of March 21, 1871. In this statute Italy declared the person of the Catholic Pontiff sacred and inviolable and applied the same measure of legal protection to him as she applied to the King. She recognized further that the Pope possessed the attributes and prerogatives of a temporal sovereign, granting extra-territoriality and tax exemption to the Vatican and Lateran palaces and to other ecclesiastical property and guaranteeing that all emissaries to and from the Vatican should enjoy full diplomatic immunity. Catholic theological institutions within Rome were also promised immunity from any interference by State authorities. To reimburse the Church for the loss of revenue from her former possessions, Italy promised to pay into the papal exchequer an annuity of approximately $600,000. Finally Italy renounced in the statute virtually all public control over relations between the Church and Italian citizens which usage and law had formerly sanctioned, attempting thereby to realize Cavour's ideal of "a free Church in a free State." The statute, however, did not conciliate the Papacy. Two months after its enactment, the reigning Pontiff, Pius IX, rejected it and called for the restoration of temporal sovereignty. Subsequently papal interdiction of electoral and other forms of participation by Catholics in the Government of Italy was reaffirmed. As we shall see, not until the first decade of the twentieth century did the Church recede in any particular from this uncompromising position; and the "Roman Question" with all of its ramifications continued to plague Italian statesmen for more than half a century.

[20] For these developments see B. Croce, *History of Italy, 1871–1915,* trans. by C. M. Ady (Oxford, 1929), pp. 30–31; and King, *op. cit.,* II, p. 301.

Politics Within the Right. The dominant political group in the Chamber of Deputies at the time of Cavour's death consisted of the combined factions of the Right. This coalition comprised deputies from all over Italy but chiefly from Piedmont, Lombardy, and the northern areas. It was intensely national and, for the greater part, liberal in its political views. The Prime Ministers coming immediately after Cavour also relied on the Right; under them, however, this coalition began gradually to disintegrate. Regional groups asserted their independence on various major or minor issues or demanded special concessions for their continued support; sometimes they seceded altogether. Bad blood arose between the Piedmontese faction, the backbone of Cavour's old majority, and leading politicians of the extreme Right from other parts of Italy, who were referred to at the time as the *Consorteria.* When, in 1865, the decision was taken by a Cabinet dominated by the *Consorteria,* to remove the national capital from Turin to Florence, the Piedmontese faction vowed a policy of implacable opposition to any government dominated by the *Consorteria.*[21]

Decay of the Right. While being thus weakened by internal bickerings and dissensions, the Right also became increasingly unpopular with the nation at large. Its conservatism on social issues and on such political questions as electoral reform alienated the more progressive elements; its preoccupation with northern industry and agriculture seemed prejudicial to southern agriculture; and its policy of taxation culminating, in 1869, in the imposition of the detested grist tax (a tax on cereals) proved extremely unpopular with the great majority, imperative though the need for revenue was at the time. In the Chamber popular discontent was stressed with increasing vehemence by deputies belonging to the Republican and Radical Parties and by the factions comprising the moderate Left. After unification had been finally achieved in 1870, the Right thereby fulfilling the historic mission set for it by Cavour, it began to appear that shortly the destiny of the nation would be committed to other and quite different hands.

THE RULE OF THE LEFT—DEPRETIS AND CRISPI (1876–1896)

Advent of Depretis. The last Cabinet of the Right was formed by Marco Minghetti, the Romagnuol, in 1873 and it came to an end in the spring of 1876. The new Prime Minister, Agostino Depretis, was a leader of the political Left and a southerner. He was a former Mazzinian and Republican, as were many of his colleagues, such as Baron Nicotera, Zanardelli, Cairoli and Crispi. Few of these men had theretofore held responsible political or administrative posts in the government. At the time of their accession the nation regarded the event as a virtual revolution; and Conservatives spoke fearfully of the danger of the Left to the established institutions and even to the status of the monarchy. Some of the King's counselors of the Right attempted to dissuade him from granting the seals to Depretis, advice which the King,

[21] An authoritative account of these political developments may be secured in King, *op. cit.,* II, pp. 308–309.

mindful of his constitutional position under a parliamentary regime, refused to accept.

Policies of Depretis. Except for two fairly brief intervals Depretis remained Prime Minister and the nation's political leader until 1887. Although his achievements fell short of the expectations of even his more moderate supporters of the Left and although his regime was characterized toward its close by vacillation and "stand-pattism," Depretis' decade of power were years of some progress in the nation's political life. A greater degree of political democracy was introduced by the franchise bill enacted in 1882. The bill halved the tax-paying qualification, introduced a moderate educational requirement, and reduced the minimum voting age from twenty-five to twenty-one. As a result the total voting population rose from somewhat over half a million to more than two millions. The tax on cereals was abolished; and beginnings were made in social legislation. A bill to regulate child labor was passed in 1886, and one of the first compulsory school laws in 1877.

Break-up of Parties and Advent of Transformism. The Depretian period was especially notable for the permanent impression it left upon Italian parliamentary life. The majority which the elections of 1876 had given Depretis soon showed signs of crumbling. Considerable differences manifested themselves among the leaders of the Left on such questions as the suffrage and taxation. On these issues the alleged conservatism of Depretis was attacked by the extreme Left led by Cairoli and by the Republican group led at the time by Bertani. Eventually these two and their followers withdrew their support from the Cabinet. The growing disloyalty and unreliability of his own section of the Chamber caused Depretis to seek alliances with the more moderate factions of the political Right. His efforts proved successful and by 1882 Depretis was ruling over a Cabinet with the united support of the moderate elements of his own Left combined with a large faction which had split off from the Right. Thus was born that system of parliamentary government by coalitions consisting of heterogeneous and often conflicting party groups and factions which we have already denominated as transformism.[22]

Progress under Crispi. Depretis' successor in 1887 was Francesco Crispi. Like Depretis, Crispi was a former Republican who had made his peace with the monarchy. Like Depretis, also, in whose Government he had served as a Minister, Crispi was nominally a member of the political Left, albeit of a more radical faction than his predecessor. Except for the interlude of the premiership of the Marquis di Rudini in 1891 and of the first Giolitti Cabinet in 1892, Crispi's power lasted until 1896. The earlier period of his rule was notable for the energetic character of his foreign and colonial policy. The bonds of the Triple Alliance with Germany and Austria, concluded some years before, were drawn more tightly, and the penetration of Ethiopia, which incidentally was to end in disaster, was begun in earnest. Crispi's "energy" evoked from the European chancelleries more respect for Italy as a power than had theretofore been the case. Important advances were also made in internal affairs. An inde-

[22] See p. 226.

pendent system of administrative courts was set up and a new penal code adopted; local government was made more democratic, first in the larger and then in all the communes by entrusting the election of the Syndic to the communal councils; and the local franchise was broadened.

Bank Scandals. It was during the interval between the end of Crispi's first premiership in 1891 and his re-elevation to that office in 1893 that the Italian people became aware of the unsavory *Banca Romana* scandal. Tanlongo, a director of the *Banca Romana,* was alleged to have circulated more than fifty million lire of duplicate bank notes. A parliamentary committee indicated in 1893 that Tanlongo had for a long time been making unsecured loans to ministers and deputies without expectation of repayment; that he had contributed money to the press to influence and corrupt elections; and that the ministry of the day, over which Giovanni Giolitti was presiding, although apparently aware of these conditions, had not brought them to the attention of the prosecuting authorities or of Parliament. It was a form of corruption of which little had been heard in Italy for over a generation; and the evidence of its existence, like the contemporaneous Panama Canal scandal in France,[23] intensified an already pronounced attitude of popular cynicism toward politicians and parliamentary institutions.

Social Unrest. The second half of Crispi's rule was marked by the beginning of an epidemic of social unrest and labor disturbances which was subsequently to form one of the most formidable problems Italian Cabinets were called upon to solve. The first serious disturbances occurred in Sicily in 1893 where the peasants and the agricultural laborers on the great estates, their accustomed poverty aggravated by a severe depression, formed unions and other associations which demanded reform in the system of land tenure and cooperative marketing and distribution of products. The movement brought sufficiently strong pressure upon the landlords to secure concessions from them; and it was the landlords' demand for governmental protection against the unions, coupled with severe rioting in various parts of the country and conflicts between the peasants and the police, that finally led the central Government to intervene. Although a Sicilian himself and a former Republican, Crispi showed no leniency in putting down the disorders. Military authorities were dispatched to the island. They proclaimed a state of siege and broke up the associations. Military tribunals replaced the civil; and unusually long sentences of imprisonment were meted out to the leaders of the peasants.

Crispi's War on Socialists. Among the condemned were several Socialists. Socialism had come to Italy in the 1880's under the leadership of Andrea Costa, who was elected Deputy from Imola in the Romagna as early as 1882. In 1891 the first Socialist Congress was held at Genoa and a Socialist review, the *Critica Sociale,* was founded at Milan under the editorship of Filippo Turati, destined to become a leader of the Socialist cause for more than a quarter of a century. Allegedly connected as a party with the Sicilian disorders, the Socialists, like the peasant associations, became an object of

[23] See E. M. Sait, *The Government and Politics of France* (Yonkers, 1918), pp. 285–286.

Crispi's repressive policy. From a subservient Parliament he secured legislation paralleling Bismarck's laws against the German Social Democrats; and,
thus armed, his prefects proceeded to disband the popular and Socialist associations in all the principal cities of the North. Legislation was also secured
in July, 1894, to revise the electoral registers; and Socialists as well as other
enemies of the Crispi regime suffered in the subsequent purge of almost a
fourth of the total electorate.

AN INTERVAL OF REACTION (1897–1900)

Fall of Crispi. Crispi fell from power and into complete eclipse in 1896,
owing to the public outcry raised over his Cabinet's alleged responsibility for
the terrible defeat inflicted upon an Italian army in that year by the Negus
Menelik of Ethiopia at Adowa. The reactionary policy against the labor unions
and the Socialists had by no means proved successful. Liberal sentiment
throughout the nation rallied to the defense of many who were deemed to
have been unjustly or harshly treated by the Government. Radicals, Socialists,
and even the moderate Left combined in Parliament and, under the leadership
of the Radical, Cavalotti, boldly defied the majority. Socialist Deputies whose
mandates had been canceled by the Government majority were triumphantly
re-elected in their constituencies despite governmental opposition; and in the
general elections of 1895, despite the purging of the electoral rolls and the
usual pressure of the prefects in favor of Crispi candidates, the Socialist delegation in the Deputies rose from eight to twelve.

More Social Unrest. Failure of the Crispi policy, however, taught nothing
to Crispi's successors. To be sure, the Marquis di Rudini, who became Prime
Minister on the morrow of Crispi's retirement, strove at first for conciliation.
Crispi's anti-Socialist laws were rescinded and amnesty was extended to the
Sicilian political prisoners. The Rudini Government also took important
steps in the direction of social-welfare legislation, providing in 1898 for the
compulsory insurance of workers against accident suffered during the course
of employment, and for bettering existing provisions of old-age pensions and
sick benefits. But when Socialist and labor disturbances broke out once more
in Italy in the spring of 1898, culminating in a virtual insurrection in Milan
on May 6, 1898, the Crispian tactics were once again employed. A state of
siege was proclaimed in Milan and other northern industrial centers. The military was called out and in Milan their indiscriminate shooting and repression
of the civilian population left casualties of more than eighty dead and hundreds wounded. Military tribunals again sentenced leaders of Socialist and
other Leftist groups to long terms of imprisonment; radical newspapers were
suspended; and Socialist, Radical, and Catholic clubs and cooperative societies
were summarily dissolved.

Pelloux and Reaction. Subsequently, in June, 1898, a Cabinet under
General Pelloux, made up chiefly of reactionaries and dominated by the military, came into power. After a few conciliatory gestures, Pelloux, with the apparent approval of King Humbert, inaugurated a period of political reaction

more severe than any the nation experienced between the days of its founding and the Fascist conquest of power in 1922. The advent of the reaction was heralded by a series of measures which General Pelloux introduced into Parliament in June, 1899. Among other things these provided that the right of public meeting should in the future be subject entirely to the discretion of the police or provincial authorities and that a virtually military discipline be imposed upon the Civil Service. They also gravely threatened the existing freedom of the press and proposed to introduce penal settlements for political offenders.

Parliamentary Opposition. The entire parliamentary Left at once coalesced and bitterly fought the proposals, so obviously a violation of the *Statuto* and of the traditional liberties of Italians. To delay Parliament's consideration and final action, the Leftist leaders resorted to a policy of obstructing deliberation, using all the devices known to the astute parliamentary tactician. Premier Pelloux's answer to these tactics was the prorogation of the Deputies and the declaration that the proposed measures should become law by decree of the executive power. Upon its reassembly four days after the prorogation, Parliament, for the time being at least, apparently in a mood to submit to executive dictation, granted the ministers a bill of indemnity, that is, a law which absolved them of liability in case their use of the questionable decrees brought them before a judicial tribunal.

Annulment of the Pelloux Decrees. The decree power of Continental executives has always been of greater scope than a similar power wielded by British or American executives.[24] In Italy, since the invocation of the power by Crispi in the Sicilian revolt, it had been greatly extended, and precedents existed for its application to the legal rights of citizens. Nevertheless, on February 22, 1900, the Court of Cassation at Rome annulled the Pelloux decrees. Nothing daunted, the Prime Minister and his Cabinet renewed their effort to have them incorporated into law. To check obstructionist tactics in the Chamber, the Cabinet proposed new standing orders to take effect immediately and without debate. Most of the opposition thereupon walked out of the Chamber, a form of protest sanctioned by ancient usage and destined to have a fateful parallel a quarter of a century later upon the inauguration of the Fascist reaction.[25] Upon the opposition's withdrawal, the remaining Deputies adopted the new standing orders and the Chamber was again prorogued.

Pelloux Resigns. But the new orders proved of little merit against ever more ingenious obstructionist tactics devised by the opposition when Parliament reconvened in May. As a last resort, Pelloux decided to dissolve the Chamber and appeal to the country, confident that the Cabinet, by exerting the usual electoral pressure, could secure a vindication of its policy. The results, however, were disappointing; although a Government majority was returned, it was a reduced majority. It was, moreover, plain, in view of the

---

[24] Art. 6 of the *Statuto* merely stated that the discretionary decree power for the enforcement of law shall not suspend the law's execution nor grant anyone exemption from the law's operation; otherwise the power was left quite elastic.

[25] See p. 253.

popular acclaim with which Deputies of the Left had been greeted at the polls and elsewhere, that the Pelloux measures were unpopular and that the country wanted none of them. Pelloux accordingly resigned and a ministry of conciliation, headed by the president of the Senate, Giuseppe Saracco, was appointed. A tragic sequel to the whole affair occurred at Milan on July 29, 1900, when the anarchist Bresci shot and killed King Humbert.

THE GIOLITTIAN PERIOD

Subsequent Dominance of Giolitti. The reaction was now promptly liquidated and as soon as the Saracco ministry expired, the new King, Victor Emmanuel III, entrusted power to the Left once more. There it remained until the days of World War I and beyond. The seals were first given to Zanardelli, the veteran Radical, and upon his death to Giovanni Giolitti who, having retrieved his political reputation since the days of the *Banca Romana* scandal, had taken office under Zanardelli as Minister of the Interior. This Cabinet of Giolitti, his second, lasted from 1903 to 1905; his third Cabinet was organized in 1906 and lasted until 1909; his fourth dated from 1911 and lasted until 1914.[26] For the intervals between these terms of office, leadership was supplied by Signori Fortis, Sonnino, and Luzzatti. Each of these was essentially a stopgap for Giolitti whose political leadership was in the ascendant throughout. The span of years from the beginning of the twentieth century to World War I or, if we include Giolitti's fifth Cabinet, until 1921, may therefore quite properly be labeled the· "Giolittian period"; it was dominated by him just as the period between 1876 and 1887 was dominated by Depretis and that between 1888 and 1896, by Crispi.

Civil Progress. The Giolittian period was one of considerable advance in almost all lines of national endeavor. The Italian philosopher and historian, Benedetto Croce, says it constituted the epoch in which the liberal ideal was most fully realized in Italy.[27] Certainly it was at once made clear that the lesson of the reactionary years of the last decade of the nineteenth century had been completely understood. After 1900 the press was free and the Government respected its freedom as well as the freedom of public meeting and association. Proof of the existence of these rights came with the extraordinary growth of popular and radical journals and the organization of numerous Left-wing and extremist political groups.

Labor and the Government. Proof was also to be discerned in the considerate attitude which the Government maintained towards labor. Strikes and disturbances were by no means ended; on the contrary, warfare between capital and labor became more intense, strikes grew in number, and the demands of labor became ever more importunate. Workers on the railways threatened to tie up transportation by a general strike in 1902; in 1903 there was a general strike in the capital; and in September, 1904, a general strike, partly political

[26] Giolitti's fifth and last Cabinet was formed in June, 1920; see p. 247.
[27] *Op. cit.*, p. 214. For this period consult also G. Giolitti, *Memoirs of My Life,* trans. by E. Storer (London, 1923).

in origin, tied up the utilities of Italy's chief cities. The Government acted with firmness to preserve order; in the railway strike it called the strikers to the colors and charged them with desertion when they failed to appear; in the general strike of 1904, it used troops. But there was none of that indiscriminate repression which had culminated in 1898 in the notorious May massacre in Milan; on the contrary, serious efforts at conciliation were made, the Government acting as mediator between strikers and employers, and even contributing public funds on one occasion to meet certain of the strikers' demands.

Welfare Legislation. The new official attitude toward labor was also emphasized by the advance of social legislation of all kinds. Previous acts dealing with child labor, compulsory industrial insurance, health insurance, and old-age pensions were extended and strengthened. Night work was forbidden to women and to children under thirteen, and a weekly rest day was guaranteed all workmen. Provision was made for the municipalization of certain utilities, and loans were offered communes to aid in public health and sanitation programs. Various forms of insurance were made a state monopoly by the third Giolitti Cabinet; and in 1910 the national Government assumed a larger share of the financial responsibility for local elementary education.

Financial Stabilization. Despite the mounting expenditures occasioned by these and other projects, increase in the nation's wealth and more efficient fiscal administration brought the finances of the State into a sounder condition than they had been at any time in its history. The fiscal problem, as frequently reiterated in these pages, had been Italy's bugbear from the very beginning. Heroic and intensely unpopular measures, including the cereals tax, popularly known as the "tax on hunger," had been necessary to secure a balanced budget in the 1870's. Deficits reoccurred between 1885 and 1897; thereafter, however, surpluses once again became the order of the day. A series of able finance ministers, of whom the most noteworthy was probably Luigi Luzzatti, subsequently Prime Minister, so improved Italy's credit position that in 1906 an advantageous conversion of approximately three-fifths of her total indebtedness was carried into effect. The conversion involved reduction of the interest rate on Italian consols from 4 to 3¾ and eventually to 3½ per cent, the reduction netting an annual saving of many millions of lire to the Treasury. Responsibility for the success of the conversion was chiefly Luzzatti's; and the resulting favorable credit position and balanced financial state were maintained until the period of World War I.

Franchise Reform. Further evidence of political maturity was afforded in 1912 when still another franchise reform was adopted. This extended the ballot to Italian males who had reached the age of thirty even though they could not satisfy the existing educational requirement. Voting rights were extended to those who, though less than thirty, could satisfy the existing educational requirements, and to those who had completed their military service. The liberal character of the reform bill resulted largely from the insistence of Giolitti who, returning as Prime Minister for the fourth time in the spring of 1911, had scrapped the reform measure of the preceding Cabinet of Luzzatti which had been considerably more conservative. Franchise reform raised the eligible electorate from something under three millions to something over eight, and placed Italy in the van of the Continental states possessing democratic political institutions.

War with Turkey. Mention must also be made of the first military contest with a European power in which Italy engaged after her unification. This was the war against Turkey, begun in 1911, from which Italy emerged victorious in the following year. The war was a deliberately willed colonial adventure out of which Italy received the areas still under Turkish sovereignty in North Africa, namely, Tripolitania and Cyrenaica. These areas were later combined to form Italian Libya. Their conquest contributed somewhat to allay earlier colonial disappointments and particularly the loss of Tunisia to France in 1881. During the Turkish War, Italy also seized and afterwards held Rhodes and other islands comprising the Dodecanese group in the Aegean. Her formal title to these islands was finally confirmed in 1923. As we shall see, all these conquests had to be relinquished after World War II.

POLITICAL CONDITIONS ON THE EVE OF WORLD WAR I

The Extreme Left and the Socialists. During Giolitti's ascendancy a marked evolution had occurred among the organized political forces of the nation. The Republican Party, a group of some influence since the days of Mazzini, had become relatively insignificant, and its closest ally, the Radical Party, had been considerably weakened. Supplanting these groups on the extreme Left were the Socialists, whose origins in Italy have already been remarked upon. Socialism had greatly increased its parliamentary strength, having seated some seventy-two Deputies in the lower house of Parliament in the elections which followed the extension of the franchise in 1912. Socialism was also able to count upon organized labor for support, having intimate ties with the various Chambers of Labor and other labor organizations. The party had frequently supported the government of the day, particularly in the enactment of social legislation; and in its national congresses a strong moderate wing had more than once manifested a disposition to develop a thoroughly gradualist philosophy. Two leaders of this wing, Turati and Bissolati, had on separate occasions in 1904 and 1911 been asked by Giolitti to enter his Cabinet. Italian Socialism, however, was even more seriously afflicted with doctrinal and tactical controversies than the world body of Socialism; and in 1912 the more radical or "orthodox" elements, aided by Socialists of a Sorelian syndicalist persuasion, seized control of the party, expelled such gradualists as Bissolati, Bonomi, and their followers, and charted for the party a policy of militant noncooperation with middle-class governments. The expelled Socialists thereupon organized an independent reformist Socialist group. One of the leaders of this swing to the Left was Benito Mussolini, later to become the leader of Fascism and the most bitter opponent of Socialism and all its works.[28]

[28] For an account of Socialism up to 1911 see R. Michels, *Storia critica del movimento socialista italiano* (Florence, 1926). For later developments see I. Bonomi, *From Socialism to Fascism,* trans. by J. Murray (London, 1924).

The Left and Political Catholicism. Chief support for the Cabinets prior to World War I continued to come from the so-called "Left." In reality this had become a sort of "Right-Center" composed of numerous personal factions to which the title of "party" could be extended only by courtesy. In this area of the political firmament there had gradually come to exist a sizable group of Catholic Deputies. This group had grown up because of the easing of restrictions which official Catholicism had formerly imposed upon political participation, a policy brought about partly by the more conciliatory attitude of Pope Pius X who had succeeded Leo XIII in 1903, and partly because of the Church's fear of Socialism. The organization of a really formidable Catholic political party was not, however, attempted at this time. That effort, as we shall see, was delayed until 1919.

The Right. The old Right of pre-Depretian days had largely passed from the parliamentary scene. Attenuated in number by the Leftward orientation of political life and suffering from the transformist tactics of Leftist cabinets, it had virtually succumbed as an organized political force. On the extreme Right, however, a new group of so-called "Nationalists" had arisen. Theirs was the intolerant, belligerent nationalism of the early twentieth century which contrasted so markedly with the liberal and popular nationalism of the middle of the nineteenth century, the nationalism that inspired the revolutionary movements of 1848. Professedly accepting Mazzini's myth of the nation, these new Nationalists rejected utterly his international tolerance and democratic republicanism; they also had the profoundest contempt for what they described as the political laxness and ineptitude of the liberal politicians of the day. Hierarchy and authority and the subordination of all classes, particularly of labor, to the national will was their ideal of internal polity; and a vigorous policy, involving imperialist competition and war, characterized their views on international affairs. They greatly idealized the former Prime Minister, Francesco Crispi, discovering in the "energy" which he had displayed both in his domestic and foreign policies their own best traditions.[29] These twentieth-century Nationalists began to appear in the Italian Parliament after 1910. Although their group remained numerically insignificant, it was nonetheless destined to exercise an important, albeit evil, influence upon Italy's future, since from the Nationalist group was to come, after 1922, many of the leaders and much of the ideology of Fascism.

Weaknesses of the Liberal Regime. By 1914 national Italy's political system had thus acquired some semblance of maturity and constitutional equilibrium. Nevertheless the system suffered from certain fundamental weaknesses. In the first place, although the Government had a liberal orientation, liberalism as a political faith was largely unknown to the literature of the day. That faith had been popularized by Cavour and the leaders of the *risorgimento*. In the years since their passing little effort had been put forth to describe its evolution as political doctrine. To many the liberalism of Giolitti's day still meant primarily the liberalism of Cavour's day. Forgetting that political and

[29] E. Corradini, *Il Nazionalismo italiano* (Milan, 1914), especially pp. 5–23 and 126 *ff.*

civil liberty had grown up side by side with a considerable amount of public intervention in economic and cultural affairs, there were those in the Italy of 1914 who still spoke of the liberal State as the regime of *laissez faire* envisioned by the classical economists, and as a system of government indifferent to morality, religion, and social welfare.

Distrust of Politicians. The parliamentary politicians had also acquired a certain reputation for moral insensibility and cold-blooded political practicality which, it must be confessed, was not unmerited. The compromises which transformism encouraged in the construction of cabinets, the wirepulling, log-rolling, patronage dispensation, and cloakroom politics which accompanied such activity, and the contempt and downright dishonesty which so often characterized the attitude of minister, deputy, and prefect toward elections, all lent credence to the hypothesis that liberalism meant moral decay in political life. These practices tarnished liberalism's shield for others than moral absolutists; they encouraged cynicism and political indifference among the masses, and supported the belief, by no means limited to Italy, that government, and particularly parliamentary government, was a game in which the politicians always won.

Liberalism's Dearth of Youth. These conditions helped to drive the youth of the nation out of the ranks of liberalism into the camps of those who professed other faiths. Most of them embraced Socialism; many of them were attracted to the brilliant and more glaring light of twentieth-century Nationalism. Far too few of the intelligent and the ambitious remained to lend their talents to the existing regime. Even when they did remain, too little use was made of them owing to the tendency of the older politicians to monopolize the posts of power. The historian Croce says that Giolitti realized liberalism's dearth of young men, and quite early in his career as Italy's leading politician he tried deliberately to recruit a group of them under his patronage and train them for future responsibilities. Croce adds that fortune did not smile on Giolitti's efforts, death claiming some of the recruits in their prime and apostasy overtaking others.[30]

If these and other weaknesses of the liberal parliamentary regime did not manifest themselves too clearly before 1914, they were to become all too clear in the stress and strain of World War I and the post-War period. In 1919 Don Luigi Sturzo, leader of the Catholic Populist Party, was to sum them up in his oft-quoted phrase, the "crisis of the political class." [31] It might well be added that these weaknesses were not restricted to the later years of the Giolittian period or even to Italy. In the middle of the twentieth century, after two world holocausts, Western civilization, challenged by totalitarian ideologies, was striving to rearticulate its professed ideals of liberalism and democracy and to rekindle enthusiasm for such ideals among a generation that had grown dangerously indifferent to them or at least to the moral and civic responsibilities such ideals impose upon individuals.

[30] *Op. cit.*, p. 216.
[31] See his *Italy and Fascismo,* trans. by B. B. Carter (London, 1926), p. 59.

CHAPTER II

THE MONARCHICAL PARLIAMENTARY REGIME
SUCCUMBS TO FASCISM

ITALY AFTER WORLD WAR I

Democracy's Ebb Tide. As World War I drew to a close, the parliamentary political dispensation was introduced into many new constitutions and re-emphasized in many older documents; and parliamentarism, as the institutional expression of the democratic political faith, acquired an unprecedented vogue. But the vogue was more apparent than real. Comparatively few years were required to convince observers that democracy's post-War gains were illusory: that in large measure they had been artificially propagated by the war aims and wartime propaganda of the victor powers and by the prestige acquired by the domestic institutions of the victor powers. Indeed, as the post-Versailles period unfolded, it became clear that, as far as democracy was concerned, the period was to have an historical significance quite the contrary of what had been anticipated. Instead of advancing the cause of democratic parliamentary institutions, these years were to witness the inauguration of the democratic counter-revolution. Democracy, as a political faith, was to lose much of the dynamism that had sustained it in the nineteenth century; its popular appeal was to decline; and institutional alternatives to parliamentary government, authoritarian in form and spirit and totalitarian in scope, were to become fully elaborated.

Italy Leads the Way to Reaction. Among Western states, the real, as opposed to the apparent, constitutional trend was perhaps best revealed in Italy. Even before the ink had dried on the Treaty of Versailles, the liberal parliamentary regime which Cavour had inaugurated and Giolitti had brought to maturity was encountering such threats to its integrity as only the most courageous and informed leadership could counter successfully. Leadership of that quality, unfortunately, did not exist or did not assert itself. From 1918 to 1922, the Government was conducted by ministries seemingly incapable of preserving a minimum of public order or of giving energy to administration.

As a result the State became a prey to contending political factions; and with its authority at low ebb and its internal defenses seemingly paralyzed, the Italian parliamentary regime fell victim, in October, 1922, to one of the most ingenious of contemporary *coups d'état*—the Fascist March on Rome. Although many of the parliamentary institutions and processes survived even that event for another two years, they rapidly lost whatever vitality and practical significance they still possessed. Eventually, in 1925, the instigators of the *coup,* under the leadership of the renegade Socialist, Benito Mussolini, liquidated the remnants of Giolittian parliamentarism and established one of the more formidable of contemporary dictatorships styling itself the "Fascist regime." Brought to maturity during the next decade by Mussolini and his followers and by their imitators, the German Nazis, Fascism became a full-fledged alternative to democratic parliamentarism and the liberal State not only in Italy but elsewhere in the Western world. To be sure, Fascism in Italy fell victim to its own international ambitions; and the regime which Mussolini had elaborated formally disappeared with Italy's unconditional surrender to the United Nations in World War II. But the model of government and society which Fascism developed is still all too viable. Like Soviet Communism, Fascism continues to provide an alternative to democracy—a gruesome political and economic strait jacket for any people incapable of governing themselves or of preserving their civic freedom.

Aftermath of the War. As already suggested, parliamentary decay in Italy after World War I may conceivably be explained, at least in part, by the local impact of revolutionary forces world-wide in scope. At the same time it is clear that the more tangible and immediate causes of that decay were directly traceable to conditions in the peninsula. Most important of these causes was the War itself. Although Italy emerged from that holocaust a technical victor, it was at great cost. Six hundred thousand of her sons had died in camps and battlefields; a million more had been wounded and many of these permanently incapacitated. Her Venetian provinces had been invaded and Italian territory had provided one of the War's great battlegrounds. Production for normal peacetime needs, both in industry and agriculture, had fallen off, owing to the mobilization of man power and productive enterprise for military purposes. Budgetary deficits of the War years, covered by foreign and domestic loans, had raised the public debt to astronomical proportions. The unsatisfactory state of the national finances and the reduction of the metallic coverage for her currency had greatly lowered the value of the lira. Prices had skyrocketed and the cost of living had soared to levels unheard of before 1915. In addition to all this the conclusion of hostilities had left the nation with the problem of reabsorbing some two million conscripts into peacetime vocations, of liquidating the War economy, and of redirecting much of production into normal peacetime channels. In a measure these difficulties afflicted all belligerents; but for Italy, relatively a poor country, they were particularly serious. To cope with them successfully required a degree of political acumen and leadership which, as the event proved, the Italy of 1918 was unable to muster.

The War Divides the Nation. Besides these liabilities, which can be reduced to statistics, the War produced others which, if less tangible, were nonetheless real. From its inception, World War I had been unpopular with important sections of the nation's political life. Intervention on the side of the Entente had been championed chiefly by nonparliamentary forces, that is, by the Nationalists, military leaders, journalists, certain renegade Socialists, and ardent spirits like the poet D'Annunzio. Parliamentary opinion was strongly antiwar. Giolitti, the veteran political leader, who had been superseded as Prime Minister by Antonio Salandra in May, 1914, had counseled indefinite neutrality, fearful of the exhaustion which might follow a prolonged conflict and confident that the diplomacy of neutrality would pay better national dividends than belligerency. Even as late as May, 1915, after the Salandra Government had already committed Italy's fortunes to the Entente cause in the secret Treaty of London,[1] more than 300 Deputies and Senators left their cards at Giolitti's home to express their support of his peace views.[2] Organized labor and the bulk of the Socialists were even more firmly committed to neutrality. This unfortunate cleavage of opinion over the War persisted throughout the conflict. It undoubtedly contributed to the low estate of Italian morale after a belligerent status had been assumed and helped to bring on the military disaster of Caporetto late in 1917. Even after the national honor had been retrieved at Vittorio Veneto in October, 1918, and Italy and her allies had emerged victorious from the struggle, politicians continued to capitalize the schism engendered by Italian belligerency. Socialists and "neutralists" blamed the politicians of the wartime cabinets and the "interventionists" for the social and economic dislocations which came in the wake of war and victory. Among the masses, afflicted by the economic uncertainties characteristic of the period, such charges provided moral justification for revolutionary claims and disrespect for law and authority. They also provoked the most savage rejoinder and retaliation on the part of the military and "interventionist" leaders who were thus assailed, and deepened the division of the nation.

Instead of reducing the public temperature, the treaties which ended the War increased it. Military leaders, "interventionists," and die-hard Nationalists were outraged at the treatment which Italy received at the Paris Peace Conference. With some justice they alleged that Italy's allies failed to honor the territorial pledges given in the Treaty of London.[3] Their censures were directed at the wartime and post-War governments and most particularly at V. E. Orlando, Prime Minister at the time of the Peace Conference and one of the "Big Four" at Paris, and at his successor, Francesco Nitti. These were charged with diplomatic apathy and with the surrender of Italy's national interests. As a symbol of their discontent and of their contempt for the Govern-

---

[1] Signed on behalf of Italy by Baron Sidney Sonnino, Salandra's Foreign Minister, Apr. 24, 1915.

[2] Cf. G. Giolitti, *Memoirs of My Life* (London, 1923), pp. 386 *ff.*

[3] In the Paris settlements, Italy received only the former Austrian territories of the Trentino and the Istrian peninsula. She was denied Dalmatia which the treaty had promised her. Nor did Italy share in the distribution of colonial spoils.

ment of the day, some of these critics organized a filibustering expedition under the leadership of the poet, D'Annunzio, to occupy Fiume. Though not included in the original Italian territorial demands, this city was ethnically Italian. For months the twentieth-century Garibaldi and his motley followers held the city in defiance of the Italian Government. Theirs was an effective demonstration of the low estate of the Government's prestige and of the impunity with which rebels might defy constituted authority in the peninsula. That demonstration, moreover, was not lost upon the swashbucklers of the Fiume expedition. Some months later they were to provide much of the leadership and inspiration of Fascism's mortal thrust at Italy's parliamentary life.

The War's Effect upon Parliament. To the catalog of influences inimical to Italy's parliamentary life which grew out of the War and its aftermath, one more must be added. This was the atrophy which overtook Parliament's legislative function. Distrusted because of its pacifism, Parliament was seldom convoked during the years 1915–1918; when convoked it was soon prorogued. Italy's legislature was thus denied virtually every normal opportunity to discuss the budget and expenditures and to keep informed on the financial and diplomatic engagements assumed by the Cabinet. The policy of the nation was determined almost exclusively by the ministers without parliamentary consultation; and administration fell into the hands of bureaucratic underlings and army officers. These officials ruled by decree. Allegedly most decrees derived their validity from the statute granting full powers to the Cabinet to conduct hostilities, which Parliament had reluctantly enacted on May 22, 1915.[4] But decrees frequently went considerably beyond the bounds contemplated by the full-powers statute. Nor did the cessation of hostilities witness a revival of Parliament's legislative prerogative. On the contrary, legislation by decree became, as Sturzo well says, "the normal and unchallenged procedure," Parliament frequently enacting full-powers measures which authorized decree legislation in certain civil and penal matters.[5] As late as the summer of 1920, a year and a half after hostilities had ended, when Giolitti assumed the premiership for the fifth and last time, he had made the restoration of the legislative power of Parliament a cardinal point of his platform;[6] even so, before he stepped out of office in 1921 he too had sought a full-powers bill granting the Cabinet the right to reorganize the Civil Service by decree.[7] The simple fact is that, in Italy as elsewhere, the War had accustomed leading politicians to the idea of getting along without parliamentary discussion and debate. They had become habituated to the practice of legislating by decree and found it difficult to restore normal parliamentary authority once the emergency had passed.

Here, then, were some of the major obstacles with which Italian politicians

[4] No. 671, *R. U.* (*Raccolta ufficiale delle leggi e dei decreti*), 1915, III, pp. 2005–2006.
[5] Luigi Sturzo, *Italy and Fascismo*, trans. by B. B. Carter (London, 1926), p. 77.
[6] Giolitti, *op. cit.*, p. 415.
[7] *Ibid.*, p. 446.

had to contend in their effort to restore the constitutional life of the Italian parliamentary State following World War I. If not hopeless, the outlook for restoration was at least precarious. At any rate, it is not surprising that, in the vicissitudes of the immediate post-War political struggle, these obstacles should have turned the scales against survival and helped to ensure the success of the Fascist *coup d'état*.

THE TREND TO THE LEFT (1919–1920)

Formation of Populist Party. As might be expected in view of some of the conditions just described and the universal trend of the period, political life in Italy, following the Armistice of 1918, took a course far to the Left. In January, 1919, a new party, called the Catholic *Popolari* or Catholic Populist Party, was formed under the leadership of Luigi Sturzo, who was both a priest and the Syndic of a Sicilian commune. Although independently organized and possessing no direct connection with the Church, the new party was clearly dominated by clerical influences and represented the culmination of the tendency, noticeable after 1904, toward active participation of the Catholic laity under clerical auspices in the politics of the Italian State. For some months after its formation the Populist Party was only indirectly represented in the Italian Chamber, that body, elected in 1913, having continued, like the Parliaments of other belligerent states, beyond its legal term. But in the elections of November, 1919, the first to be conducted under a system of proportional representation and universal suffrage for all adult males, the Populists secured 100 seats. They thus had nearly a fifth of the voting strength of the Chamber and became that body's second largest party. The Populists were pledged to far-reaching political and social reforms. They demanded woman suffrage, political decentralization and regional self-government, guarantees for the integrity of religious schools, extensive social-welfare and labor reforms, legal protection for small landholders, and the establishment of peasant proprietors on the southern *latifundia*.[8] Although this program was decidedly Leftist and reformist in character, the Populists, restrained by the Church's respect for law and order, were necessarily pledged to secure it by orthodox constitutional means.

Revolutionary Tendencies of the Socialists. No such restraint affected Socialism, the other organized force on the Left which now shared with Catholic Populism a preponderant influence on Italian political life. Opposed to the War, Socialist leaders nevertheless regarded its dissolvent effects upon society as providing them with an excellent opportunity for applying their theories of social and economic transformation. The Socialist Party had been deeply affected by the success of the Bolshevik Revolution in Russia; and although the old right wing led by Turati, Treves, and Modigliani did not think that Bolshevism afforded any precedents for Italian Socialism, the more numerous and therefore preponderant radical wings, led by Lazzari, Gennari,

[8] Cf. Sturzo, *op. cit.*, p. 91.

and Graziadei, wished to profit by the Russian example and apply the same direct and violently revolutionary tactics which had availed Lenin in overcoming Kerensky and establishing the Soviet regime.

They Adopt a Campaign of Direct Action. Hence as soon as the Armistice of 1918 had been concluded and wartime restrictions on political activity had been lifted, Socialism began an earnest campaign to bring the "revolution" to Italy. Strikes and industrial disorder became chronic, public services were tied up, riots multiplied in the streets, and the military and police were insulted and often assaulted. In the agricultural districts along the Po, Socialist leagues and labor leaders acquired a virtual monopoly of the supply of farm labor, dictating to the landowners and agricultural operators under what terms labor might be hired and under what conditions produce might be harvested and marketed. Destruction of the owner's property was the punishment for anyone who refused to abide by the regulations thus set forth. The ostensible purpose of these tactics to improve the economic position of labor but imperfectly veiled the wider aim of overthrowing or greatly modifying the existing capitalist structure of society.

Socialist Electoral Gains. In the national elections of November, 1919, the same in which the Catholic Populists received 100 seats, the Socialists obtained 156, thereby becoming by far the largest single political unit in the Chamber. In collaboration with other groups they might have done much to establish the supremacy of the working classes by law. Dedicated, however, to a policy of direct action, they scorned any form of parliamentary collaboration with "bourgeois" groups, preferring instead to obstruct parliamentary deliberation, and to practice political blackmail upon the various cabinets of the day. In the local elections of the following year they were also immensely successful, no less than 2,000 communes, located chiefly in the North, returning Socialist majorities to their councils. Here Socialism used its power to inaugurate or to strengthen municipally socialized or cooperatively organized services, thereby stimulating the wrath of the private entrepreneur and the taxpayer.

The Factory Seizures. The crisis of Socialism's policy of direct action came with the occupation of various factories by the workmen in September, 1920. On August 30, following the threat of a strike among some of the more specialized workmen of the Romeo foundry in Milan, the owners ordered a lockout. Fearing that lockouts would spread to other industries, leaders of labor counseled all workmen in Milan to remain at their posts on the following day and not leave the factory premises. Thus began what is probably the first "sit-down" strike in modern industrial history. The example thus set spread to other industrial cities of northern Italy and even to certain industrial centers of the South. Relying upon supplies brought to them by sympathizers on the outside, the workmen barricaded themselves in the various plants which they had seized, organized committees of factory management, and in some cases actually operated the plant under their own auspices. The more radical labor and Socialist leaders looked upon the development as the first stage of the "revolution" which would expropriate capital and inaugurate the Soviet State; and the operators frankly feared for the future.

End of Factory Seizures. Had the leaders of the workmen been more resolute, the situation might easily have precipitated a sanguinary civil conflict. But the revolutionary tide had already turned and more moderate elements were in command. In a plebiscite conducted on September 11 to determine whether the strikers should negotiate with the employers or hold out indefinitely, a sizable majority voted for negotiation. Several days later the Government promised to require by law the establishment of workmen's councils in the factories, with the right of representing labor before the management. This, coupled with a slight wage concession, broke the back of the "sit-down" strike; and by the end of September all the occupied factories had been evacuated and a relatively normal situation had been restored.[9]

Decline of Socialist Revolutionary Threat. The end of the factory occupations also marked the end of the Socialist revolutionary threat. To be sure, the party was still a power in Parliament and in the communes; and in Parliament it persisted in its policy of noncollaboration. But its revolutionary fervor was spent, partly because its leaders had not dared to take the final step when the opportunity had presented itself in September, partly because reports filtering back from the party's own emissaries to Russia painted a gloomy picture of the Soviet paradise. Socialism's erstwhile unity as a political organization was now also destroyed. In January, 1921, on orders from the leaders of the Third or Moscow International (Comintern) who were disgusted with the tactics of the Italian right-wing Socialists in the factory occupations, the extreme left wing of the party, led by Graziadei, seceded to form a separate Italian Communist Party. A middle group, calling themselves Maximalists, led by Lazzari, and the right wing of Reformists, led by Turati and Modigliani, continued an uneasy partnership for a little longer. Eventually on October 13, 1922, these too parted company, the Maximalists taking the name of the Italian Socialist Party while the Reformists became the Unitary Socialist Party.

COUNTER–REVOLUTION AND THE EMERGENCE OF FASCISM (1920–1921)

Reaction of the Propertied Classes. But although historians may now conclude that the Socialist revolutionary threat was definitely ended after September, 1920, such knowledge was not vouchsafed to contemporaries. To the Italian middle class—to the industrial magnate, the landed proprietor, and even the small shopkeeper—the factory occupations, far from seeming like the zenith of Socialist revolutionary activity and the beginning of its decline, appeared to be a certain harbinger of a Bolshevist *coup*. An attitude of resistance to Socialism, which had been gradually hardening in the months after World War I, now ripened into resolution. It was an attitude of resistance quite

[9] For a good account of this episode see E. A. Mowrer, *Immortal Italy* (New York, 1922), pp. 306 ff.

as contemptuous of law and duly constituted authority as the Socialists themselves had displayed. All that was needed to give it effect was an organized
movement and a leader. These were quickly forthcoming. The organization
was Fascism; the leader, Benito Mussolini.

  Mussolini: His Early Career. This man, destined within a few years to
become the dictator of Italy and to hold that position until 1943, had had
a most versatile, if not chameleon-like, political career. At quite an early age
he had chosen Socialism as his politics and journalism as his vocation. His
Socialism was of the more intemperate brand, stemming from the revolutionary syndicalism of Sorel; and he had nothing but contempt for the easy-going
moderates of the party. In 1912 he had been one of the leaders in ousting
such moderates as Bissolati and Bonomi from the party and was rewarded
for his intransigence by being made editor of *L'Avanti,* the leading Socialist
journal. The outbreak of World War I, however, found Mussolini preaching
Italian intervention on the side of the Entente, in direct violation of the party's
official stand of neutrality. For his political contumacy he was ousted from
both the party and *L'Avanti.* After a brief term of service at the front he was
invalided home early in 1917 and founded his own newspaper, *Il Popolo
d'Italia,* in Milan. In that organ he championed that peculiar combination of
chauvinism and social revolution which, however incompatible as actual public policies, became the principal formal ingredients of the official doctrine of
Fascism at least in the early stages of that movement.

  Apparently the first step in organizing Fascism took place in March, 1919,
in Milan when Mussolini created his first *Fascio di Combattimento,* or fighting band. Like Mussolini himself, the fifty-odd individuals who became members of this *Fascio* were chiefly renegade Socialists and demobilized soldiers.
Some were veterans of the Fiume expedition and other ventures in "direct
action." In the new movement's first manifesto, Mussolini advocated an ultra-
democratic franchise, various advanced forms of social insurance, an eight-
hour day, worker participation in factory management, and a capital levy. His
Socialist faith, thus indicated, did not falter during the early part of 1920. He
justified seizure of the land by the peasants, and somewhat guardedly supported the workmen in their seizure of the factories.

  He Leads the Reaction against Socialism. Gradually, however, his
Socialism became more tepid. He began to assert that the organized Socialist
Party was going too far, and his denunciations of the Socialist leaders knew no
bounds. By the end of 1920, as Salvemini says,[10] he had ceased to call these
leaders ineffectual revolutionaries and had begun calling them dangerous Bolsheviks. At the same time, Mussolini began vigorously expounding nationalism, the other facet of his post-War political faith. The only practical explanation of this *volte-face* seems to be that Mussolini's *Fasci* were rapidly filling
up with middle-class youth seeking vengeance upon the Socialists; and Mussolini, opportunist *par excellence,* saw that political success lay no longer
along the revolutionary path of Socialism but along the revolutionary path of

[10] *The Fascist Dictatorship in Italy* (New York, 1927), pp. 52–53.

bourgeois anti-Socialism.[11] At all events, by the autumn of 1920 his *Fasci* had become the sword and buckler of the counter-offensive against Socialism. In the principal cities and towns of the North, Fascist squads of young hooligans armed with castor oil, clubs, and more lethal weapons assaulted and sometimes killed Socialists and workmen, and looted and wrecked the headquarters of their political organizations, their cooperatives, and their newspaper offices. The town halls of many of the communes which had been won by the Socialists in the elections of 1920 were occupied, and the Socialist syndics and councilmen forced to resign their posts. The Fascist squads also extended their operations to the countryside, terrorizing the agricultural laborers and their organizers. In many areas violence approached the status of civil war when the attacked Socialists and workers struck back. Almost everywhere, however, the Fascists won, partly because their victims lacked leadership and morale, partly because the Fascists were aided financially and otherwise by middle-class elements and by the but poorly concealed sympathy of the police and military.[12]

POST–WAR PARLIAMENTARISM

The Nitti and Giolitti Cabinets. During this period of civil strife the Italian Government pursued what amounted to a policy of political *laissez faire,* apparently preferring to allow the storm in the country to take its own course and hoping that it would eventually blow itself out. On the fall of Orlando, in June, 1919, following his disappointing performance at the Paris Peace Conference, the seals of office were entrusted to Francesco Nitti. His accomplishments were virtually nil. Torn between the Left and the Right, he found it difficult to maintain the prestige, let alone the authority, of the Government. The Nationalists prevented him from taking effective action on the Fiume question; the Socialists would not permit him to lower the wartime bread subsidy which was ruining the Treasury and aggravating the current inflation. Though augmented by a new force of 25,000 so-called Royal Guards, the police were incapable of maintaining order. Even the universal male suffrage law and the proportional electoral system, which the Nitti Cabinet introduced, represented concession to Socialist pressure rather than the Cabinet's own deliberate policy. After several unsuccessful efforts to relinquish his office Nitti was succeeded, in June, 1920, by Giolitti, the parliamentary wizard of pre-War days. This Government, Giolitti's fifth and last, remained in power until July, 1921, and thus covered the period of the factory occupations and the middle-class revolt against Socialism. Toward both these happenings the new Prime Minister followed Nitti's policy of neutrality, although there is some evidence that his neutrality toward the Fascists was benevolent. Nevertheless, Giolitti did succeed in reasserting, in a measure, the authority of the Government and in carrying out certain important and

---

[11] For Mussolini's early career see his *Autobiography,* trans. by R. W. Child (New York, 1928), pp. 1 *ff.*; see also Herman Finer, *Mussolini's Italy* (New York, 1935), pp. 98 *ff.*

[12] For an account of the middle-class counter-revolution, see Salvemini, *op. cit.,* pp. 46 *ff.*; also Mowrer, *op. cit.,* pp. 344 *ff.*

necessary political decisions. Most important in this connection was the work of Giolitti's Foreign Minister, Count Sforza, in establishing a definitive post-War boundary with Yugoslavia and disposing of the Fiume issue by making that port a free city.[13] A brief naval demonstration on Christmas Day, 1920, quickly disposed of any objections which D'Annunzio and his Nationalist allies might have had to this settlement, and finally terminated the "Fiume occupation."

Elections of 1921. With affairs proceeding in this tolerable fashion, Giolitti, in April, 1921, unwisely decided to dissolve Parliament and order new elections. By combining the parties of the Right, including even Nationalists and Fascists, in single lists under the new proportional electoral law, he hoped to reduce the power of the Socialists and even of the Populists and gain allies for his own parliamentary cohorts. But his strategy miscarried. In the elections held in May the Socialists, including the new independent Communist Party, lost only 21 of their 156 seats in the previous Chamber; at the same time the Populists increased their mandates from 100 to 106. In addition the Fascists, benefiting by their association with Giolitti's lists, secured a delegation of thirty-five Deputies, their first in any Italian Parliament; and, contrary to Giolitti's expectation that he could make them submissive allies, the Fascists assumed an attitude of extreme intransigence on the far right of the Chamber. Victim of his own miscalculation, Giolitti subsequently resigned (June, 1921).

The Problem of Giolitti's Successor. In retrospect it is clear that the retirement of the old liberal leader marked the end of an epoch in Italian parliamentary life. The elections of 1921 had merely confirmed the verdict of the previous elections of 1919, namely, that preponderant power in Italian politics had passed from the old conservative liberal groups to the newer parties on the Left—the Catholic Populists and the various Marxist groups. Because of this shift it was no longer possible for Giolitti and his lieutenants to rely on the old Left for governing majorities as they had for a generation. If a sturdy parliamentary authority was to come into being in post-War Italy it was necessary that one of two possible developments take place: either Giolitti must assimilate the new forces on the Left to what remained of the historical parties and develop a broader coalition; or, what seemed more likely, a new parliamentary broker must arise who would succeed in welding the new political forces into coherent majorities. In any case it was clear that parliamentary life in Italy must pass through a period of radical readjustment, and that anything resembling parliamentary normalcy would be unlikely until the new pattern of partisan coalition and leadership had been elaborated.

Unfortunately this problem of providing a successor to Giolitti proved to be unusually complicated. Protracted negotiations brought a solution no nearer, and it was soon evident that more than a few months must elapse before issues could be adjusted and some of the major differences among lead-

---

[13] The status of "free city" thus imposed upon Fiume proved no more satisfactory than the same status imposed upon Trieste a generation later. In 1924, Fiume was incorporated into the Italian Kingdom. For a description of these diplomatic negotiations, see C. Sforza, *Makers of Modern Europe* (Indianapolis, 1928), pp. 244 ff.

ing personalities could be resolved. The conservative liberal politicians, who still hailed Giolitti as their chief, were understandably loath to face the consequences of political change and give up their former position of primacy. Catholic Populists, that element among the new parliamentary forces which by temper and policy was closest to the older liberal forces, found alliance with them impossible because their leader, Luigi Sturzo, distrusted Giolitti, allegedly because of the latter's anticlericalism, and would agree to no Cabinet which Giolitti might lead. Alone, moreover, the Populists were hardly capable of governing since, numerous as they were, they did not yet possess that virtual preponderance in Parliament which they were to secure a generation later under de Gasperi. Socialism, the other important segment of the new Left, was riven by the usual Marxist doctrinal schisms and afflicted with numerous secessions. As we have seen, moreover, it had frittered away its opportunity to provide serious leadership by espousing a sterile policy of direct action. In Parliament it had indulged in the favorite Marxist tactic of noncollaboration with other parties and general obstructionism, behavior that hardly persuaded observers that Socialism was ready to assume the responsibilities of political leadership. In time, the more moderate elements in the Marxist ranks would claim a place in a governing coalition of broad political scope; but for the immediate future, Socialism was even less prepared to govern or to share in the Government than Populism.

Prolonged Parliamentary Crisis. More than a year elapsed after the fall of Giolitti's last Cabinet before the politicians began to make serious efforts to solve the parliamentary impasse and bring about a durable democratic coalition. In August, 1922, for example, Turati, leader of the Reformist Socialists, went to King Victor Emmanuel with a plan for a concentration Cabinet along the broadest political lines. Given a few more months, the problem of the succession might have been resolved in an orderly manner and Italy vouchsafed another generation of parliamentary rule. But the crisis had already persisted overlong; and "caretaker" Cabinets, in whom authority nominally reposed while the leading political figures jockeyed for short-term advantages, did little more than go through the motions of governing. Their lack of any policy, their failure to enforce order or command respect for law, and their apparent inability to cope with the administrative paralysis that gripped the Italian State, had brought parliamentary government to its nadir in public esteem. Cabinets had become a laughing stock and the butt of bitter satire; people had become weary of political incompetence and official timidity; and many responsible elements in the nation concluded that Parliament and its parties were truly an impossible muddle.[14]

THE FASCIST COUP D'ÉTAT

Mussolini and the Problem of Giolitti's Successor. Evidence that resolution of the parliamentary crisis had been delayed too long and an earnest

---

[14] For a good account of the parliamentary crisis and its historical significance, see F. L. Ferrari, *Le Régime fasciste italien* (Paris, 1928), pp. 36–43.

of the penalty Italy was to suffer for this delay now became apparent in the machinations of Mussolini and his Fascists. Intent upon fishing in troubled waters, as are all opportunists, they began to exploit the parliamentary stalemate and prevailing public dissatisfaction to further their own ends. Mussolini seems to have realized even more clearly than other politicians that the succession to Giolitti was the great issue. Indeed the vacuum in the government, resulting from the decline of the pre-War liberal groups, had intrigued Mussolini from the very first days of his post-War political career; and whether he was fighting the middle class in the name of his own brand of Socialism, or orthodox Socialism in the name of the middle class, his paramount concern had been to fill this vacuum with his own political following. For a short time during the spring and summer of 1922, Mussolini appears to have given thought to achieving his goal through orthodox parliamentary channels. His *Fasci* had been welded into a national Party, the *Partito Nazionale Fascista,* in November, 1921. This organization enabled him to exercise disciplinary control over the thirty-five Deputies who had been elected under the Fascist banner earlier in 1921. Although a decided minority, these Deputies gave him the status of leader of a parliamentary group and a degree of bargaining power among Parliament's other political leaders; and one or two projects embracing Mussolini's participation in a coalition were actually broached early in 1922.

Mussolini, however, wanted dominance, not participation; and it soon became apparent, to him at least, that the policy of "parliamentary legality" would never give him such dominance. After a brief interval, therefore, Mussolini gave up his incipient parliamentarism and had recourse again to the policy in which his movement had been nurtured. This was the policy of direct action, that is, the policy of using private armies, street demonstrations, and mob violence, culminating, as and when the occasion warranted, in insurrection and the *coup d'état.* Although demonstrations against left-wing labor leaders and Socialist politicians continued, Mussolini's primary objective was no longer to extirpate "subversives" but to destroy existing public authority and then seize the Government. In other words, in the late summer of 1922, Mussolini made the classic "about-face" of so many self-appointed vigilantes who, at the outset, use illegal means to protect society and the State against alleged "subversives," but subsequently turn upon the State itself.[15]

The March on Rome. Against this revived policy of direct action the parliamentary State, weakened by the year-old crisis, succumbed with startling suddenness. Mussolini was an astute director of strategy and rarely failed to seize an advantage. He strengthened Fascism's connections with the military, established during the days of the "Fiume expedition" and made stronger still during the period of Fascism's "War on Bolshevism." The resulting fraternization between army chiefs and heads of the Fascist squads and the benevolent and approving attitude of the army towards Fascist violence and law-breaking were nothing short of scandalous. Mussolini also recanted his former repub-

---

[15] For Mussolini's own account of this change of tactics see his *Autobiography,* trans. by R. W. Child (New York, 1928), pp. 164–165.

licanism, thereby recommending himself still more emphatically to the military and making himself *persona grata* with the House of Savoy. Then, on October 27, 1922, came the *coup d'état* in the form of the so-called "March on Rome." From various parts of the peninsula a motley array of several thousand Fascist partisans, most of them armed hooligans making up the so-called Fascist "action squads," converged upon the Eternal City. Their presence at or near Rome was a direct threat to the safety of the Government and constituted nothing less than insurrection. Mussolini, who awaited developments at his newspaper office in Milan, confidently anticipated that this culminating phase of his policy of direct action would bring the faltering Government to its knees and result in the King calling him to the premiership.

The Government Capitulates. Had the Government acted with courage and determination, Mussolini's hopes might well have been foiled even at this late date. Instead there was vacillation and weakness. Some authorities feared that resistance to Fascism would be useless—that victory for Mussolini was certain. Apparently a few within official circles were openly sympathetic to the Fascist leader and the cause he was thought to represent—or they concealed their sympathy with difficulty. The existing Cabinet, headed by the colorless and ineffectual Luigi Facta, demanded on October 27, and again on the following day, that a state of siege be declared and that the Fascist bands or squads be treated as insurrectionaries; but King Victor Emmanuel, fearful of resistance to Mussolini or, as some have suggested, not unsympathetic to Fascist aims, violated constitutional practice and refused to sign the appropriate decree. Instead, on October 29, following the failure of former Prime Minister Salandra to form a Cabinet which would have included the Fascist leader, the King called upon Mussolini himself to form a Government; and on October 30 appointed him Prime Minister.[16] Thus Mussolini made good his *coup d'état:* the liberal parliamentary regime in Italy succumbed to the revolutionary pressure of those who had defied authority with impunity and had exploited the freedoms of the liberal State to secure a political monopoly. To be sure, the parliamentary regime which had thus died in Italy was relatively weak because it was in the throes of readjustment. Even so, the fundamental threat to free government, implicit in Fascism's victorious tactics, should have served as a warning to the supporters of free institutions everywhere and alerted them effectively against the danger of subversion. Instead, the sanguinary events in Italy were merely the preface to a long series of parallel developments in other parts of the world where the story of parliamentary destruction varied but slightly from the pattern which had served the Fascist leader so well.

EPILOGUE

Pseudo-Parliamentarism. Developments in the months immediately following the *coup* were almost anticlimactic. For a time at least Mussolini apparently toyed with the idea of ruling with a semblance of parliamentary legal-

---

[16] For some of these developments, see Sforza, *op. cit.,* pp. 319 *ff.*

ity. His Cabinet, although preponderantly Fascist and Nationalist, included representatives of all other parties save the Marxists. For this Cabinet he sought and obtained Parliament's vote of confidence and a bill which gave him and his ministerial colleagues the power to rule by decree for a year. Although he made it clear that he expected Parliament to withhold criticism and "cooperate" with him, he promised to render it an accounting of his extraordinary powers after a suitable interval. What Mussolini seems to have had in mind was a regime in which he might enjoy the reputation of ruling with the people's representatives without rendering them any accounting save as he chose and on his own terms. Like every actual or potential dictator of history, he sought the approval of public opinion but denied that he was accountable to its forums.

Revival of Opposition. Pseudo-parliamentarism of this type could not last. Among other reasons why it could not was the fact that the vigilantist tradition was much too thoroughly engrained in Mussolini and his followers: having come to power by force and violence, it was inevitable that they continue to rely upon these same resources to keep themselves in power. Moreover the Deputies, though "cooperative" at the outset because they had been cowed by the *coup,* soon retrieved their self-confidence; and, even though represented in the coalition, they began to act in their accustomed manner, openly criticizing the Government's leadership. With increasing vehemence they began also to demand an end to Fascist illegality.

Electoral Changes and the Elections of 1924. Mussolini thereupon sought to make Parliament more tractable by changing its composition in such a manner as to give Fascism a majority. To this end, by cajolery, threats, and appeals to the prejudices of the Conservatives, he forced through Parliament in July, 1923, a new electoral law—the so-called "Acerbo Reform." This provided that any party which received at least 25 per cent of the total vote in a national election would be assigned two-thirds of the seats in the Chamber, the remaining seats to be distributed proportionally among all other parties. This new law was applied to the elections of April 6, 1924; and with the benefit of considerably more than the usual amount of electoral corruption and the peculiar administrative pressure at the polls in which the Fascists were especially competent, the law produced an electoral result which measured up to Mussolini's most optimistic expectations. After the votes had been officially counted two-thirds of the Deputies owed allegiance to the Fascist Party.

Continued Opposition: The Matteotti Affair. Nevertheless, in a short time even such a Parliament became a thorn in the flesh of Mussolini's political ambition. Opposition criticism and censure, though supported now only by a minority, compensated for the relative lack of volume by becoming increasingly bitter and denunciatory. Criticisms were aimed particularly at Fascism's electoral corruption and the illegal activities of its vigilantist squads. Especially scathing was the historic speech of the Socialist Deputy, Giacomo Matteotti, on May 30, 1924, in which he declared that Fascism's majority had been obtained by fraud, intimidation, and violence and that the Party, consequently, had no right to represent the nation. The sequel to this philippic was the kidnapping and murder of its author by a gang of Fascist hooligans who apparently acted with Mussolini's connivance.

From Pseudo-Constitutionalism to Dictatorship. Matteotti's murder laid bare the political depravity of Fascism, its total lack of moral resource, and its inevitable reliance on force and intimidation in order to maintain its political ascendancy. This historic political crime made it clear that the hybrid parliamentary regime with which Mussolini sought to govern after his *coup d'état* was no longer a practical possibility even with the opposition parties reduced to a minority. A public aroused by the murder of the Socialist orator demanded that the malefactors be brought to justice, that Fascist vigilantism cease, and that constitutional order be restored. The entire parliamentary opposition absented itself from the Chambers, figuratively withdrawing to the Aventine Hill, as did the plebeians of ancient Rome, there to await surcease from tyranny. Opposition to Fascism in the press and in the country at large grew by leaps and bounds; and all the elaborate promises made by Mussolini to reform his Cabinet, punish Matteotti's murderers and curb the violence of his black-shirt squads did not serve to appease. By the autumn of 1924, two years after his *coup,* the fraud and violence in which his regime had been born and nurtured had caught up with him. Thereafter he had a clear choice: either give up his primacy in the Government and restore constitutional rule or frankly embrace arbitrary power and force as the basis of existence for his rule. He quickly made the latter choice. In a series of speeches early in 1925, Mussolini openly acknowledged responsibility for the political conditions which led to the murder of Matteotti and virtually declared it to be an historic necessity. At the same time he openly defied political opposition from any source, clamped a complete censorship upon the press, outlawed the "Aventine Opposition," as the seceding Deputies were popularly known, and made it unmistakably clear that he was inaugurating an era of essentially personal, and certainly arbitrary, rule.

CHAPTER III

THE FASCIST INTERLUDE

Once Mussolini had frankly broken with the past and set his course in the direction of personal government, steps were quickly taken to make the instrumentalities of legislation and administration more amenable to Fascist control and to develop uniquely authoritarian instruments of persuasion and coercion. Even so, the process of transforming governmental organs according to peculiarly Fascist principles remained a gradual one. One reason for this lack of zeal in transforming the government was Fascism's desire to retain the aura of respectability and legitimacy implicit in the persistence of such organs as the Kingship and the Senate. Another, more important, reason was Fascism's opportunism. In the early years, at any rate, the Fascist leaders appeared to care relatively little for constitutional forms so long as they were politically in the driver's seat. The Party had no political or constitutional theory of any consequence and no developed conception of the form of the State. Such ideas came gradually in response to some practical need of the Fascist propagandists. Not until 1939, on the eve of World War II, did Mussolini and his sycophants suggest that the Fascist State had achieved a final and, in their opinion, a durable form. By that time, the Fascist State had indeed become a rather formidable structure. In part it was composed of certain institutions inherited from the former regime modified as Fascism required. To these had been added numerous instrumentalities derived from the Fascist Party itself and from the apparatus of public economic control which Fascist doctrinaires had come to call the "Corporate State." Then, too, there were organs such as the secret police and special judicial tribunals and other instrumentalities of coercion peculiar to any contemporary dictatorship. National and social objectives of this apparatus of the regime and its *raison d'être* were identified by an ideology which was also brought together and polished into semicoherent form in the years between the March on Rome and World War II. This chapter will identify Fascism's institutions in greater detail, particularly as they stood on the eve of their abolition in 1943.

ANATOMY OF THE FASCIST DICTATORSHIP

The Dictator's Office. Fascism's most characteristic political instrument was Mussolini's personal dictatorship. His pre-eminence as the political leader *de facto* was matched by a formal constitutional recognition of his primacy throughout the entire political system. Authority of every kind—executive, legislative and administrative—was made to converge upon him or to radiate from him; and traditional nineteenth-century conceptions of separation of public powers and the autonomy of judicial and administrative agencies were entirely disregarded. The dictator's most important office was that of Head of the Government (*il capo del governo*). Under that title he exerted general control over the entire administration, directed and coordinated the activities of the various Ministers of State, settled disputes among them, and countersigned all their important acts. Not content with his formal power over the Ministers, Mussolini frequently assumed several ministerial portfolios himself. On one occasion he assumed as many as seven, although he was usually content with three or four, these including the defense Ministries and the Ministry of the Interior through which he controlled the police and other internal security agencies. The Ministers were indeed his puppets whom he appointed and removed at will. Frequently he would reconstitute the entire Cabinet, shifting individuals from one post to another, appointing some to positions outside the administrative departments or quite arbitrarily retiring still others to private life. This was the Fascist practice of "changing the guard." It resulted normally (though not invariably) from the exercise of the personal discretion or caprice of the dictator and was in no way comparable to the changes of ministries brought about in *bona fide* parliamentary regimes by a dissolution of parliamentary majorities. Mussolini also acted as President of the Council of Ministers, thus serving as the Ministers' conciliar, as well as their administrative, chief. In that role he fixed the agenda for collective discussions, limited the length of such discussions and controlled their tenor, and cast the deciding vote if a vote was cast.

Mussolini Controls Entire Governmental Apparatus. Mussolini's formal authority in the Government was by no means restricted to these traditional executive and administrative areas. As Head of the Government he became the *ex officio* head of a great variety of judicial, administrative, and deliberative tribunals. He played the leading role in the apparatus of the so-called "Corporate State," to be described later,[1] and officially controlled the agenda of the Fascist legislative establishments. As Duce of the Fascist Party, moreover—an office which gradually acquired public status—he exercised decisive authority over the whole Party apparatus including such Party councils as acquired a public character. Among the more important of these was the Fascist Grand Council, made up of Fascist "bigwigs" and the principal organ in the Party hierarchy after the Duce himself. Partly because of its composition and partly, as will be noted later, because it acquired important

[1] See p. 264.

policy-making and constitutional prerogatives in the Government, the Grand Council took precedence over all conciliar governmental agencies.

Absence of Legislative or Other Control. Confirmation of the dictatorial nature of Mussolini's system was to be discerned not so much in the vast scope of authority committed to him as in the complete absence of effective means for holding him accountable for his political acts. The statute which created the office of Head of the Government specifically exempted him from control by Parliament. At the same time the statute abolished the historical parliamentary privileges of voting censure and lack of confidence in a Minister, so characteristic of the *bona fide* parliamentary period in Italy. Even the parliamentary privileges of interrogating and interpellating the Ministers were rendered meaningless by the statutory stipulation that the parliamentary order of the day, or agenda, should contain no matter of which the Head of the Government had not previously approved.

Fascism and the Kingship. Mussolini remained responsible to the King; but this responsibility was purely nominal. In signing the decree making the Fascist leader Prime Minister, Victor Emmanuel III rendered Fascism a signal service. The Fascist Party was clearly indebted to him and apparently the King became the regime's not unwilling pensioner. He helped to legitimate Fascist rule and voluntarily exploited the symbolism and pageantry inherent in the royal office to make Fascist authority more palatable to the masses. Nominally the royal prerogatives, as limited and defined in the Albertian *Statuto,* remained intact; but they were without practical significance in holding Fascism accountable for its acts. In fact, throughout the Fascist period, the direct personal authority of the King in the Government was virtually nil. Victor Emmanuel exercised no personal influence upon affairs unless it suited the Fascist politicians or propagandists to give weight to what he said or did. To be sure, on July 23, 1943, the King signed the decree of the Grand Council which deposed Mussolini; but the King apparently contributed less toward the initiation of this act of deposition than he had toward the earlier act which elevated the dictator. On the whole, the opinion of most Italians that the King and the monarchy suffered from more than a bare taint of Fascism, an opinion implicit in the vote of 1946 to oust the House of Savoy and establish the Republic, was probably in accord with the weight of the evidence.

FASCIST LEGISLATIVE CHAMBERS

Modification of the Chamber of Deputies. To obscure the nakedly autarchic character of its authority, the Fascist regime, like so many dictatorships, historic and contemporary, sought to implement itself with a plethora of conciliar bodies nominally exercising decisive, or at least significant, political powers. Probably the most interesting of these was the Fascist substitute for a *bona fide* parliamentary representative assembly. In the course of achieving such a substitute, the Chamber of Deputies, lower house of the pre-Fascist Parliament, underwent several changes in composition and structure and finally disappeared altogether.

It will be recalled that the Chamber elected under the so-called Acerbo electoral reform [2] was two-thirds Fascist; with the secession of the Aventine minority, these Fascist Deputies continued to serve as a rump Chamber until 1929 and did yeoman service in enacting most of the basic Fascist legislation.[3] For a decade after 1929 the Chamber was the product of a plebiscite in which the electorate, behaving with such unanimity as only authoritarian governments can or wish to secure, formally ratified a slate of 400 Deputies. The slate consisted of tried and true Fascist Party henchmen, actually nominated by the Party chiefs although ostensibly the product of an elaborate nomination procedure in which not only the Fascist Grand Council, but a great variety of local bodies, economic, cultural, and moral, participated. The Chamber resulting from this process was superlatively Fascist; still it did not satisfy the Party doctrinaires who now proceeded to abolish the very name "Chamber of Deputies" and replace it with "Chamber of Fasces and Corporations." This formidable nomenclature was to identify an assembly in which were combined ideas derived from what were alleged to be the major springs of the regime's constitutional thought, namely, the Party and the so-called "Corporate State." [4] The membership of this super-Fascist creation consisted of about 600 National Councillors designated to serve from the membership of the two highest Party councils, that is, the Fascist Grand Council and National Council, and of the National Council of Corporations, supreme body in the machinery of public control which Fascism had erected over the national economy. Terms of the National Councillors coincided with whatever period of service they enjoyed in the constituent body from which they had been chosen. Needless to say, designation of the membership of this new legislative Chamber was made without benefit of elections, even of a plebiscitary nature; Fascism had finally abolished all elections.

The Fascist Senate. As respects the Senate, or upper Chamber, of the pre-authoritarian Parliament, no formal changes in the rules governing recruitment of its membership were made; hence, in a formal sense at least, the Senate, like the monarchy, represented institutional continuity in the governments of Fascist and pre-Fascist Italy. Apparently the Fascists refrained from changing the rules of the Senate's membership partly because sizable groups in that assembly had, from the first, evinced Fascist leanings; partly because the traditional method of selecting Senators from twenty-one categories of candidates, explained earlier,[5] and the Senators' life tenure accorded with Fascism's authoritarian mood. Moreover, since there was no limit to the number of Senators which the Fascist regime might itself appoint, and since the comparatively high death rate among the elderly incumbents caused a fairly rapid turnover in membership, it was not long before the Senate's political complexion became overwhelmingly Fascist. In 1939 the regime had appointed about three-fourths of the 400 members; and except for some half

[2] See p. 252.
[3] For relevant citations on this legislation, consult the first edition of this book, pp. 623 ff.
[4] See p. 264.
[5] See p. 223.

dozen dissidents like Count Carlo Sforza, who was living in exile, the Senate counted no one in its ranks unwilling to profess his solidarity with the regime—at least in public.

Servile Nature of Fascist Parliament. What thus finally emerged as a triumph of Fascist constitutional art was one of the most servile deliberative assemblies that any dictatorship has ever devised. Only those of Hitler's Germany and Stalin's Russia are comparable. For practical purposes, plenary sessions of the two Chambers were abolished and such legislative service as they were called upon to render was performed by the parliamentary commissions. Of these, there were thirteen in the lower Chamber and eight in the Senate. Ministers of the Government submitted legislative measures simultaneously to commissions with parallel jurisdiction in the two Chambers; these were expected to discuss and approve the measures within a thirty-day period and return them to the Head of the Government for approval. In case the commissions failed to approve the legislation—an emphatically hypothetical contingency so long as Mussolini was in power—the Government could always resort to the decree power with which an obliging legislature had armed it in 1926. Legislation by decree was indeed the preferred procedure; and the pseudo-parliamentary apparatus could readily have been abolished with very little effect upon the course of Fascist policy-making. As suggested earlier, that apparatus was continued because it lent a note of constitutional decorum to dictatorship and because it provided positions of some dignity and no little income for deserving Party henchmen.

THE NATIONAL FASCIST PARTY

Party and the Regime. Alongside the traditional apparatus of Government and public administration remodeled, as already noted, to suit the exigencies and aspirations of dictatorship, Fascism built its authoritarian political Party. Officially this was styled the "National Fascist Party." In the course of time the administrative apparatus of this organization, from Duce to the lowest administrative echelon, became so extensive and its bureaucracy so numerous that the Party rivaled the Government and, in fact, became a kind of Government within a Government. Ultimately the courts extended formal recognition to the Party as an organ of public law and identified the Party's officers as public officers. Moreover, several of the principal Party organs were officially identified as a part of the formal governmental apparatus of the State. As noted earlier, the Party's Grand Council actually became the most august of all conciliar public bodies. It became superior in rank and dignity to the Fascist Parliament and was invested with prerogatives relating to foreign affairs, the amendment of the existing *Statuto,* and the enactment of other Fascist constitutional law, the composition and powers of various public bodies, and the succession to the throne and to the dictatorship itself. In short, in Fascist Italy, as among all contemporary one-Party dictatorships, there was such a commingling of governmental and Party offices and functions that any effort to distinguish them in the operating mechanism of the regime would have been artificial.

Services of the Party: (1) *Coordination of the Governmental Apparatus.* Various considerations counseled continuation of the Party during Fascism's early days when, surprisingly enough, proposals to disband it were seriously advanced. These considerations gained weight as experience demonstrated the practical value of such an organization in an authoritarian State. One of these considerations was the possibility of using the Party and its various organs to coordinate and direct the formal governmental apparatus. As Duce, Mussolini was in supreme command of the Party; and since Party henchmen were in charge of virtually every department of the Government, they brought the entire State apparatus under the informal, albeit effective, control of the dictator. The latter was thus enabled to exercise authority over units of Government which, for the sake of appearances or for other good reason, had been kept nominally autonomous or not legally subject to his will. In short, what Mussolini might have been unable to accomplish as Head of the Government, he accomplished most effectively, if somewhat informally, as Duce of the Party. It is thus that the monolithic mass Party of the dictatorships of the twentieth century enables such dictatorships to maintain an efficient, centralized control over a state apparatus which superficially is far more complicated, and apparently provides more autonomy for its various branches, than the Government of a *bona-fide* free society.

(2) *The Party as an Instrument of Political Control in the Provinces.* The Party proved especially helpful in providing the Italian dictator and his principal colleagues at Rome with the means of keeping in direct contact with affairs in the provinces and communes. In each of the latter areas a local *Fascio* usually maintained some sort of headquarters where Party wheelhorses interpreted the will of the leaders to the rank and file of the citizenry and kept close watch on political developments. A still more important link between the center of Government and the outlying areas was provided by the Federal Secretary, or *"federale"* of the Party. His title derived from the fact that he served as the principal administrative officer of the provincial federations of local Party groups. Actually he was the provincial Party boss, the substance of whose power rivaled that which was nominally reposed in the Prefect, the official representative of Rome in the provinces and the Government's own provincial "boss."

(3) *The Party's Identification of the Masses with the Dictatorship.* Another service rendered the dictatorship by the Party was the important one of identifying the self-interest of a maximum number of people with the regime, thereby broadening and strengthening Fascism's popular base. This service was rendered in various ways. The most direct method of identification with the regime was through membership in the Party itself. During the 1930's outstanding Party cards normally approximated two million. For the nation's youth, in which Fascism was especially interested, there were various

levels in the Fascist youth organization, known as *Gioventú Italiana del Littorio* (*GIL*), suitable for boys and girls of various ages from candidates for the nursery school through adolescence. The youth organization trained the regime's future leadership and Party cadres, many thousands of selected young men having been graduated annually from the organization's highest echelon into the Party proper. In addition, there were numerous ancillary or affiliated Party agencies, such as veteran and athletic groups, a galaxy of feminine auxiliaries, and Fascist social-service agencies operating under the Party's direction. Of the latter the best known, and probably the most important, was *Dopolavoro,* the National Leisure Time Organization. In the name of the Party, this sponsored an amazing variety of welfare activities among peasants and industrial workers, thus succeeding, at least in part, in masking the unlovely characteristics of an unfree regime with a reputation for benevolence and good works. Needless to say, whatever the Party instrumentality and its avowed aim, the *raison d'être* was invariably that of identifying the interests of the masses with Fascism and thereby ensuring a greater degree of popular loyalty.

(4) *The Party a Major Instrument for Indoctrinating the Masses.* In thus trying to identify the material interest of the rank and file with the dictatorship, the Party took advantage of every opportunity to indoctrinate and thus rendered still another service to the regime. Through the Party's local agencies, particularly through its communal headquarters and its network of affiliated and auxiliary institutions, spokesmen for Fascism exploited every opportunity to preach its alleged virtues and condemn its opponents. In the time-honored way of politicians everywhere, Fascist experts in winning friends and influencing people arrogated to themselves a reputation for virtue and good works, extolled the movement's alleged interest in the welfare of the common man, pointed with pride to constructive achievements, ignored the material and moral sacrifices which were demanded of the people and the regime's own shortcomings, and exploited every symbol of national patriotism. Fascist politicians, of course, had an advantage over politicians elsewhere in that the Fascist brand had a complete propaganda monopoly and could censor any opinion considered challenging or critical in the slightest degree. If that did not suffice, they could remove the author of the opinion. In other words, there was no open opposition.

(5) *The Party as an Instrument of Coercion.* Finally, without exhausting the catalog of the Party's services, mention may be made of the apparatus it provided for extirpating heresy and applying informal coercion whenever the arts of persuasion failed to secure desired conformity. This was accomplished chiefly through the Party Militia (*Milizia volontaria per le sicurezza nazionale*), a para-military force of about a half million men. This Militia was the dictator's own praetorian guard, bound to him by personal oath of fealty, and bound to do his bidding with unquestioning zeal. Though given the status of a public force in 1923, the Fascist Militia was simply a continuation of the old black-shirt squads whose fondness for direct action, before and after the

March on Rome, symbolized Fascism's reliance on force and violence and its rejection, both as a matter of choice and of necessity, of moral principles and constitutional decorum.

Fascism's Political Theory. As Fascism, in the 1930's, entered its second decade, it developed a theory of the State and society to which Mussolini formally gave his blessing. It thereupon became the aim of the Fascist orators to inculcate the gist of this orthodox theory in the minds of the rank and file. Fascist political theory condemned liberalism and democracy as unsuited to the twentieth century and likely to lead to anarchy and the dissolution of society. It rejected Marxian Socialism allegedly for its all-pervasive materialism and denial of idealistic factors. At the same time, the official doctrine of Fascism praised force and violence because they allegedly stimulated the creative energies of peoples and nations. It recommended the purported virtues of militarism, and declared that war put the "seal of nobility" upon a people. Along with these perverted concepts of personal and national virtue and well-being, Fascist theory emphasized the desirability of an authoritarian, irresponsible government that brought every facet of society under its disciplined control—in other words, a totalitarian dictatorship. And as a logical corollary of this conception of the State and government, the duty of blind obedience to superior authority was enjoined upon the individual. In short, the alpha and omega of the Fascist doctrine, which the Party orators sought to spread among the masses, is well summed up in the slogan, repeated *ad nauseam* by Fascism's disciplined, uncritical cohorts: *"Credere! Obbedire! Combattere!"* (Believe! Obey! Fight!).

DEVELOPMENT OF A TOTALITARIAN STATE

Fascist Totalitarianism. The monolithic mass Party such as Fascism developed and the contribution of such a Party towards the maintenance of a political monopoly constitute one of the more unusual characteristics of dictatorship in our day. Another unusual characteristic, also illustrated by Fascism, is the phenomenon we have come to call "totalitarianism," that is, the extirpation of voluntary or free institutions in the civic, economic, cultural, and moral spheres of society and the substitution therefor of State-directed enterprises. Stated differently and more succinctly, totalitarianism is the extension of the arbitrary discipline of an authoritarian government to social concerns generally. Totalitarian jurisdiction adds immensely to the power and security of a dictatorship because it eliminates open opposition from any quarter, seals off objective information from the citizenry, and allows the fullest opportunity for official propaganda to influence mass opinion and behavior. It also permits the State to exercise a direct and positive influence over the production and distribution of goods and services and places the entire population at the mercy of the government for its livelihood, the government being, for all practical purposes, both entrepreneur and employer.

Fascist Control of the Press. Fascism's totalitarian ambitions developed gradually. At any rate, the realization of those ambitions was a relatively gradual process. First victim of the totalitarian drive were the news- and opinion-disseminating media, control of which always enjoys a high priority in any dictatorship. Between 1924 and 1926, all newspapers and journals hostile to Fascism were effectively muzzled and then transformed from independent institutions into "mouthpieces of the regime." The transformation was accomplished in various ways—by judiciously-coerced changes in management and ownership, by licensing journalists and requiring their membership in Fascist professional associations, by effective use of censorship, and by requiring the dissemination of officially-inspired propaganda.

Control of Other Media. What was done to the press had its counterpart in the case of other institutions which influence or mold thought and opinion. Political censorship of films and stage plays was exercised through special Party boards of review and the representatives of the police and the Prefect's office. The Government itself entered the cinema field and produced and distributed propaganda films. Radio, as its technology developed, remained a governmental monopoly which could be relied upon to put forth only the approved official version of any event, domestic or foreign, and to play up the ideology of the regime in fair weather and foul. Over the entire communications apparatus, moreover, the Fascist Minister of Culture exercised a ubiquitous and intensive discipline.

Decline of Personal Liberty. Elementary personal liberties also became an early victim as Fascism moved to consolidate its authoritarian position. Under the Public Security Act of 1926 and later statutes, the police were permitted to classify private gatherings as public affairs and to prohibit them on various grounds, including possible injury to the dignity of the Government or its officials. Citizens were confined to their communes unless they held identity cards and their freedom of movement was seriously curtailed. Open opponents of the regime and even political suspects were brought before Fascism's Special Tribunal for the Defense of the State and sentenced to death or imprisonment after mere mockeries of judicial trials. Most notorious were the discretionary prerogatives given to the OVRA, or secret police, and to security officers in dealing with those considered politically suspect. Often these were held without trial and subsequently confined for long periods in Fascism's island concentration camps.

Fascism's Campaign Against the Freedom of Education. Education, too, early came under the ministrations of the Fascist exponents of totalitarian "coordination." The more notorious of the measures in this sphere were the transfer of authority over local schools from the commune to the central Government in 1923; the subjection of the teachers to compulsory membership in professional associations sponsored by the Party and their subjection to political surveillance and every conceivable form of informal pressure to compel conformity; and the editing of textbooks by State commissions to make them serve as instruments of Fascist indoctrination. In 1939 a so-called Fascist Charter for the Schools was elaborated. Its provisions only served to emphasize the disappearance of objective teaching from the Italian school system and the complete subjection of teacher and curriculum to the propaganda exigencies of the regime. The whip of Fascist conformity was also felt by the universities, although it was never applied as vigorously as in the case of the lower rungs in the educational ladder. An ironclad oath of loyalty, requiring indoctrination of student charges with Fascist ideology, was decreed for professors in 1931. About a dozen well-known savants refused to take this oath and were dismissed; others, equally well known, resigned. University administrative heads, moreover, were more successfully disciplined than the professors and became almost universally subservient to Fascism.

Assimilation of Economic Society—Labor. Slowest to mature, but ultimately as characteristically totalitarian as any other enterprise of Fascism, was the regime's economic program. The first stage in the dictatorship's efforts to bring the national economy under its direct control related to the labor unions. From its earliest days, Fascism had sought to break up the Socialist and independent trade unions and become the Kingdom's labor broker. Hence, by direct action and monopolistic legislation, it quickly broke the power of the free trade unions and destroyed their organizations. In their stead it set up a complex hierarchy of Fascist trade unions or syndicates. Acting nominally through the upper echelons of this hierarchy of syndicates which, needless to say, were exclusively staffed with Fascist partisans, the regime's so-called "Ministry of Corporations" established "labor agreements" with industry on a national or regional basis and fixed wage scales and conditions of employment. The Fascist syndical organizations, particularly at the lower level, were little more than instrumentalities for disciplining the rank and file of labor. By no stretch of the imagination were they *bona fide* representative agencies of the agricultural or industrial laborer existing to articulate his aims and to protect his interests.

The labor agreements thus formulated were given the protection of law. Disputes concerning the interpretation to be accorded their terms and any other disputes between labor and management, were settled by a special set of labor tribunals whose authority was compulsory; and all forms of economic warfare, including strikes by labor and lockouts by management, were condemned as illegal. In other words, labor was denied both its right to *bona fide* organization and its traditional economic weapons, such as the strike. Legislation outlining this system of labor relations was adopted in April, 1926. Definitive legislation, under the title of the "Fascist Labor Charter," was promulgated with much fanfare a year later.[6]

Fascist Intervention in the Managerial Field. This system of public syndicates, by means of which the Fascist dictatorship exercised direct control over the supply of labor and the terms of its employment, was later supplemented by large-scale intervention in the processes of the market and public direction of economic enterprise. Unlike the Soviets whose Marxist predilections caused them to give a high priority to the public assimilation of economic life, the Fascists temporized in the case of management. Moreover, when they did move into the managerial field, ideological convictions and monopolistic political ambitions seem to have been somewhat less important than certain

[6] For appropriate citations, see the original edition of this book, pp. 677 *ff.*

more practical considerations. Among these were the depression of the 1930's, the burden imposed upon the nation's productive activity by the intensely autarchic economic policies of the regime, and the further burden imposed by the requirements of a State preparing for military adventure. Even so, once steps were taken to expand and intensify political direction of production, exchange, and distribution, an ideological rationalization was quickly provided.

Large-scale Economic Intervention. Really large-scale public intervention on the managerial side of economic life began in 1932 when industry, heavily devoted to specialty and luxury goods and peculiarly dependent upon foreign markets, saw those markets close down and its financial stability threatened. As elsewhere, it turned to the Government for assistance and Mussolini's aides-de-camp acted promptly. Through a variety of special Government agencies, the public credit was extended to private banks and industries in financial straits, various obligations of the private establishments thus assisted being taken as security. The process was not unlike that undertaken in the same year by the Reconstruction Finance Corporation and similar public agencies in the United States except that, relatively at least, public assistance in Italy affected a much wider segment of the economy. In due course, the Italian Government actually became the principal creditor of many companies or the preponderant shareholder.

Control of Credit Agencies. Alongside this proprietary activity there grew up all the now familiar devices of twentieth-century neo-mercantilism and economic nationalism. The Bank of Italy became a Government central bank and through it and other principal banks of the Kingdom, the Government determined the flow of credit; business was compelled to amalgamate or, in lieu of physical unification, its cartelization was compelled. A special Ministry was created in 1937 to control the nation's foreign trade, foreign exchange being allocated only for those imports of which the Ministry approved. Expensive agricultural reclamation projects were set on foot, the object being less to benefit the peasant farmer than to increase production of agricultural staples and make the nation self-sufficient in wheat. All production of such staples as wheat, other cereals, wool, and raw silk were placed under special control committees which purchased the new crop from producers at fixed prices and resold to distributors and processors. Efforts were even made, without regard to comparative cost, to extract certain vital minerals, such as iron, manganese, and tin from uneconomic Italian sources and to promote independence of the rest of the world in the production of fibres. It was all part and parcel of the revived Colbertism of the contemporary world; but Italy under Mussolini proceeded to implement such a policy with an especial zeal.

Creation of the "Corporate State." Having achieved so extensive a degree of State capitalism and governmental direction of production and distribution, the Fascist State thereupon provided a kind of institutional "top dressing." This took the form of the "Corporate State." Reviving ideas about labor-management cooperation which had achieved some prominence at the time in 1926 when the Fascist syndical system was set up, Mussolini's Government, in 1934, established a complicated mechanism of twenty-two corporations, or economic associations, representing as many areas of economic enterprise. On paper, at least, equal representation was given capital and labor on each corporation, additional members being drawn from the Fascist Party, cooperatives, and other bodies. All these representatives, it is probably unnecessary to add, were tried Fascist partisans or non-partisans whose loyalty to the Fascist cause could not have been excelled by an actual partisan. Each corporation was supposed to exercise a considerable degree of influence over the economic area it represented, particularly over such matters as prices, markets, production standards, plant management, and labor relations. Activity of the corporations was, moreover, coordinated through a plenary body known as the National Council of Corporations consisting of all active members of the corporations, 500 in number, a Central Corporative Committee of fifty members, and the Ministry of Corporations in the Cabinet.

The Corporative Mechanism Lacks Significance. But this elaborate mechanism, impliedly self-governing, was in fact a mere façade for the centralized direction and control over industry and agriculture exerted by the Fascist Party, certain of the Party's labor specialists, its favored captains of industry, the bureaucracy of the Ministry of Corporations, and particularly the Head of the Government. At best the corporations served as advisory bodies which could make recommendations affecting public policy. Even at this level of activity, less than half of them ever achieved limited importance. Like so many other Fascist creations, the "Corporate State" was chiefly a paper mechanism. It was but another example, albeit more obvious than others, of the incompatibility between the improvisations of Mussolini's system of personal, irresponsible, oligarchical rule and the paper formulae of a model system which Fascist constitutional theoreticians were forever devising.

Conclusion. This, in brief, is the story of how the Fascist dictatorship's political structure and way of life developed. Most Italians and most of the rest of the world would probably just as soon forget it, for it is a grim story. But the story cannot be ignored. Stretching as it does over more than two decades, it is an important part of the historical record not only for Italy but for mankind. Moreover, it has a special importance partly because of the impact which Italy under Mussolini had upon world events but chiefly because Mussolini's regime, in large measure, originated much of the symbolism and much of the basic apparatus and "political know-how" of contemporary totalitarian dictatorship. This latter may indeed be the knowledge of Mephistopheles; but it is knowledge which no Government, least of all Italy's new Government, can afford to dismiss. That Government, operating again under a regime of freedom, may be politically stronger than the preceding free Italian Government that succumbed to Mussolini. But one of the chief ingredients of its relatively greater strength is the knowledge outlined in this and the immediately preceding chapters, that is, an understanding of the way in which a political monopolist like Mussolini successfully challenged and destroyed a free Government and then developed the contemporary totalitarian dispensation to consolidate his ill-gotten authority.

CHAPTER IV

THE REVIVAL OF FREE INSTITUTIONS

In the period immediately following World War II the outlook for free institutions has been none too promising. Hence Italy's struggle to rid herself of the nightmare of Fascist dictatorship and, in Churchill's phrase, "work her passage home" and rejoin the community of free nations has been particularly challenging. Resolution of some of the major problems that confronted the nation during this transition required the better part of the period from 1943 to 1948; and although at this writing, six years after the close of the second instalment of global hostilities, Italy may still be in a parlous condition, especially as respects her economic position, at least the foundations of a free and stable Government have been laid. Considering the immense obstacles which had to be overcome, this achievement has been truly remarkable. No doubt the benevolent attitude of some of the nations who opposed her in World War II, especially of the United States, aided considerably; but the achievement is to be credited primarily to the high quality of the political leadership upon which Italy has been able to rely since Mussolini's demise and to the immense capacity for sacrifice of the Italian rank and file.

END OF MUSSOLINI'S DICTATORSHIP

Mussolini Resigns—the Badoglio Cabinet. Mussolini fell into eclipse following a fateful session of the Fascist Grand Council held July 24, 1943, when the accumulated hostility toward his regime, and especially toward his alliance with Hitler's Germany, caused open revolt among some of his colleagues. These, under the leadership of Count Dino Grandi, former Italian ambassador to London, and Count Galeazzo Ciano, the dictator's ill-starred son-in-law, prevailed upon a majority of the Grand Council (18 to 7) to adopt a motion which clearly implied a reassertion of the constitutional authority of the monarchy and the rejection of Mussolini's leadership. On the day this vote was taken, Mussolini formally resigned as Head of the Government. His resignation was accepted by King Victor Emmanuel, apparently much to Mussolini's surprise and chagrin, and the King thereupon called upon Marshal Pietro Badoglio to become chief of the Government and to organize a Cabinet.

Mussolini's Italian Social Republic. Mussolini, himself, was placed under arrest. Subsequently German paratroopers rescued him from his place of detention; and until his death at the hands of anti-Fascist Partisans at the village of Dongo, on Lake Como, on April 28, 1945, the Fascist leader remained a hostage of the Germans. During that period he nominally headed a truncated version of Fascism in Northern Italy calling itself the "Italian Social Republic," which continued the alliance with Hitler and sought to revive Fascism under republican and allegedly proletarian auspices. Under German protection, some of the symbols of Mussolini's erstwhile authority were thus restored; but the restoration was distinctly temporary and these institutional remnants of Fascism disappeared as the German military power waned and that of the Allies waxed in the North.

Badoglio's Efforts to Restore Authority. Meanwhile, the Badoglio Government, embodying the legitimate authority of the nation, began the giant task of bringing a semblance of order out of Italy's domestic chaos and of reordering her international position. The armistice ending Italy's active participation in World War II on the side of Hitler's Germany was signed on September 3, 1943, and her unconditional surrender came five days later. Thereafter Italy assumed the status of co-belligerency alongside her former foes and sought to assist them in driving the Germans out of the peninsula. For various reasons that task proved unexpectedly difficult. Even Rome, the capital, fell into German hands for a time after the Italian surrender; and the Badoglio Cabinet's writ ran in only a few provinces in the extreme South. Gradually, however, as Allied forces pushed northward, occupied new territory, and relinquished their control of such redeemed territory to the Italian authorities, the Cabinets of Badoglio and of his successors became the *de facto* as well as the *de jure* authority in the peninsula. Even so, it was not until August, 1944, a year after Mussolini's fall, that Rome again came under Italian jurisdiction; and another nine months elapsed before German, and the remnants of Fascist, resistance in North Italy finally disappeared.

Fascist Institutions Abolished. One of the Badoglio Cabinet's first tasks was the formal liquidation of the more notorious Fascist institutions. This task was undertaken with dispatch, necessary decrees having been announced the day after the new Cabinet came into being. High on the list of proscribed institutions was Fascism's star-chamber court, the notorious Special Tribunal for the Defense of the State. With it went the Grand Council, the Chamber of Fasces and Corporations, and the principal organs of the "Corporate State" including the National Council of the Corporations, the Central Corporative Committee, and the twenty-two corporations themselves. Also into oblivion, along with this governmental apparatus of Fascism, went the machinery of the Fascist Party and the great variety of affiliated agencies, such as the Fascist youth movement and welfare organizations.

Anti-Fascist Purification Measures. More important than ridding the nation of Fascist institutions was the task of ridding it of Fascists. Initial steps in this direction had been taken by the Allied Military Government, which removed most Fascist Prefects, other local officials, and Fascist-inspired teachers whenever Allied forces occupied a particular area. The task of "defascistization" was more systematically organized when it subsequently devolved upon the Italians themselves. Under legislation enacted in July, 1944, and supplemented in November, 1945, provision was made for the dismissal of proven Fascists of long standing from every branch of the civil administration, from State enterprises, and from the professions. Dismissals were effected by local committees organized within a particular service or profession. The ranks of the State security organizations were even more carefully culled to exclude any suspected Fascist. Authorization was also given the Government to take over all property that might have belonged to the Fascist Party or its auxiliary organizations and to confiscate property held by private individuals which allegedly had fallen to them because of their position in the Fascist hierarchy or because of the favor which the regime had shown them.

Prosecution of Fascist Crimes. The more notorious Fascist leaders were imprisoned and charged with various crimes. Among such crimes were those of violating popular liberties and judicial guarantees; of participating in the Fascist *coup d'état,* that is, the March on Rome; of abolishing the basic institutions of the free political system which antedated Mussolini; of dragging the nation into an unwanted war and military disaster; and of traitorously supporting Mussolini's Fascist Social Republic in Northern Italy after Badoglio had become Premier. Special attention was given to certain categories of Fascist criminals, for example, those who had participated in establishing and administering the infamous Special Tribunal. Those accused of crimes enjoyed the normal procedural guarantees to ensure a fair trial and were tried either by a special section of the regular district Assizes or, in unusual cases, by a special high court of justice organized to deal with the prosecution of cases against Fascists. The entire operation of Fascist "purification" was placed under the direction of a special high commissioner, an office held for a time, appropriately enough, by the distinguished anti-Fascist, Count Carlo Sforza, who, in this post, and subsequently as Foreign Minister and leading elder statesman, contributed his immense prestige and unique moral authority to freedom's renascence in his native land.

On the whole, the Italian policy of ridding the nation of Fascists placed its emphasis upon the upper echelons of those who had been responsible and ignored the rank and file, or let them off lightly. The policy also sought, as far as possible, to make legal responsibility personal and not collective and to ensure the application of due process to the trial of those who might be accused. In these respects, Italian purification machinery set a somewhat higher standard than was observed in similar situations elsewhere. Efforts were also made to carry through this process of purification as rapidly as possible in order to restore normal, or nearly normal, conditions in the public services and in the nation's economic life. These efforts, however, were not entirely successful and considerable criticism resulted. Even so, the major part of the task had been accomplished by the summer of 1946.

RESTORATION OF DEMOCRATIC POLITICAL LIFE

Revival of the Parties. As the debris of dictatorship was cleared away, the leadership of free Italy, which had been operating underground or had been in prison or in exile, began to assert itself in the press, on the forum, and, of course, through revived political parties. Six of the latter quickly developed something like a national following even while much Italian territory was still in German hands. On the Left were the Communists and the Socialists. Both were mass parties with a common ideological origin. For the moment, moreover, these two parties were closer together, as respects aims and strategy, than they had ever been in the recent past. Associated with the Left was the so-called Action Party, relatively small but with distinguished leadership and uncompromising in its opposition to both the dictatorship and the Savoy monarchy. In the Center were the Christian Democrats, also a mass party, and destined to become the new Italy's largest political group. The Christian Democrats were the direct successors of the moderate, clerically-minded, pre-Fascist Populists (*Popolari*) whom Don Luigi Sturzo had led in the Parliament elected immediately after World War I. Of about the same orientation politically was another small group calling itself "Labor Democrats," led by the former Premier, Ivanoe Bonomi. It was the successor of the Reformist Socialists who had organized in 1912 following a break with Marxist orthodoxy.[1] The Liberals were the sixth of the revived political groups. They comprised the more conservative elements, remnants of the parties which had furnished the leadership in the Parliaments of pre-Fascist Italy.[2]

Revival of Party Coalition Cabinets. Representatives of these six renascent parties became active politically in the first instance in supporting clandestine anti-Fascist Partisan activity in areas still under German control and in forming *ad hoc* local governments as such areas were liberated. For a relatively considerable period they had no formal connection with the Badoglio Cabinet which consisted largely of career civil servants and military officials. Indeed, despite several reorganizations, the Marshal's Cabinet continued to be "nonpartisan" until April 17, 1944. At that time the renascent parties, having at least temporarily composed certain fundamental differences, joined the Badoglio Cabinet and thereby restored *de facto* representative government in the Kingdom.

Normalization of Cabinet Government. Two months later, following the liberation of Rome, Marshal Badoglio, in accordance with a promise given party leaders, resigned and passed from the active political stage. Thereupon leadership was assumed by the Labor Democrat, Ivanoe Bonomi, whose Cabinet, reconstituted in December, 1944, in turn gave way in June, 1945, to still another coalition headed by Ferruccio Parri, one of the leaders of the Action Party. This new coalition, which included representatives of all the parties, symbolized the liberation of Northern Italy and the entry of politicians from that section into the Government. Parri's Cabinet lasted only six months.

[1] See p. 236.
[2] For a discussion of the parties of Republican Italy, see pp. 301–310.

Afflicted by internal divisions and defections on the Right, it gave way in November, 1945, to the first Cabinet to be led by the chief of the Christian Democrats, Dr. Alcide de Gasperi. With de Gasperi as Prime Minister, parliamentary Government in Italy after World War II emerged from its transitional chrysalis and acquired firm and enduring leadership. At any rate, in 1951, more than five years after de Gasperi created his first Cabinet, he was still Prime Minister. Like Giolitti of old, the Christian Democratic leader bids fair to become the symbol of another major period of Italian political history.

LIQUIDATION OF THE MONARCHY

The Parties Object to the Monarchy. From the first days of the reassertion of party government, the great issue was the so-called "Institutional Question," that is, the status of the monarchy. The significance of this issue had been demonstrated in the spring of 1944 at the time the first six-party coalition under Badoglio was being considered. At a congress at Bari, in Southern Italy, representatives of the six parties formally resolved that the reconstruction of the nation presupposed the abdication of the King. Subsequently, Christian Democrats and Liberals agreed to enter a party coalition if King Victor Emmanuel abdicated in favor of his son, Crown Prince Humbert. Leftist parties, however, persisted in refusing cooperation until the Communists, under the leadership of Palmiro Togliatti, at the moment newly returned from his two decades of exile in Soviet Russia, did an "about-face" and also agreed to join a coalition ministry if the King abdicated in favor of his son. This move of the Communists caused all Leftist parties to veer toward cooperation and the first coalition under Badoglio became possible.

Humbert Becomes Lieutenant-General of the Realm. A few weeks later, when Rome had been liberated from the Germans and when, as we have seen, Badoglio had given way to Bonomi as Prime Minister, King Victor Emmanuel, apparently in fulfillment of his part of the understanding with the parties, retired from formal participation in the Government by making the Crown Prince the Lieutenant-General of the Realm, legally capable of acting for his father in all cases. It was not abdication but had substantially the same effect.

"Institutional" Plebiscite and the End of the Monarchy. All this, however, was merely a stopgap, there having been a general understanding among the parties that, as soon as the peninsula had been cleared of enemy troops, the people were to be consulted in a referendum on the question whether Italy was to continue as a monarchy or become a republic. Hence in March, 1946, Prince Humbert issued a formal call for the plebiscite on the "Institutional Question" and declared that he would abide by the result. The plebiscite was held June 2, 1946, and provided a relatively slim, but nonetheless decisive, majority for a republic. The vote was 12,717,923 for the republic (54.3 per cent) and 10,719,284 for the retention of the monarchy (45.7 per cent).[3] Three weeks before the plebiscite, the King had finally ab-

---

[3] Statistics from the *Statesman's Year Book* (1948), p. 1027.

dicated, in law as well as in fact, and his son had assumed the title of Humbert II. Apparently this development was planned to influence the voting in favor of the monarchy and place Humbert in a better position to claim the throne. Be that as it may, a fortnight after the plebiscite, Humbert, King for one month, formally honored his promise to abide by the people's decision and left Italy for exile in Portugal.[4] With his departure, the Savoy dynasty came to an end in Italy and the nation joined the ranks of the world's republics. All reference to the monarchy disappeared from official processes and State papers and the shield of Savoy was removed from the Italian Tricolor. Some months later, the decision for the republic was formally ensconced and elaborated in the nation's new Constitution, the last Article of which (139) declares that the republican form of government is not subject to constitutional amendment and which elsewhere denies political rights to all members of the House of Savoy.

THE NEW CONSTITUTION AND THE TREATY OF PEACE

Election of the Constituent Assembly. The plebiscite on the "Institutional Question" was held on the same day as the elections to the Constituent Assembly. These elections—the first national ones in Italy in more than a generation—provided the first reliable index of the popular following of the various parties, and determined the political orientation of the nation for the next two years. First in the field when the votes were counted were the Christian Democrats with 207 seats and more than eight million votes. The Socialists, with somewhat more than half as many votes, acquired 115 seats; and the Communists, with a popular following about equal to that of the Socialists, laid claim to 104 seats. The remaining 131 seats were distributed among a variety of parties who, together, accounted for almost six million voters.[5] All told, the Popular Front of Communists and allied Socialists won about 40 per cent of the seats, the moderate Christian Democrats, about 36 per cent; and the remaining parties, moderate and conservative, about 24 per cent.[6] The extreme Left of the Popular Front was thus in a minority; but it was so sizable a minority that it made difficult the assembling of an effective moderate majority coalition. A factor in swelling the total vote for the Constituent Assembly was the enfranchisement of women which had been stipulated in the new electoral law decreed by the Cabinet on March 10, 1946. The women's vote probably also accounted, in part at least, for the fact that the Christian Democrats acquired a plurality over all other parties.

[4] In a legal sense the Republic became a *fait accompli* on the formal announcement of the results of the plebiscite by the Supreme Court of Cassation, June 10, 1946.

[5] See statistics in *Statesman's Year Book* (1947), pp. 1017–1018.

[6] From March to November, 1946, communal elections were also held throughout the country with somewhat similar results. In some 6,941 communes with a population of less than 30,000, the Popular Front won majorities in about one-third and the Christian Democrats in about one-third. In 146 larger communes, in which proportional representation was applied, Christian Democrats won 31 per cent of all seats, and the Popular Front, 38 per cent. In the Rome municipal elections, October 12, 1947, the Popular Front and Action Party obtained 33.4 per cent, while the Christian Democrats won 32.8 per cent, of the seats.

The New Constitution is Drafted. The Assembly thus elected began deliberations on the proposed new Constitution on July 1, 1946, and continued them into the following year. At the outset, a special commission of seventy-five, on which the various parties were given proportional representation, was charged with elaborating a preliminary draft. Working through three subcommittees, this constitutional commission developed a draft project which became the nucleus of the new fundamental statute of the republic.

As might be expected, in the ensuing Assembly debate on the draft project, numerous issues divided the parties. Among these were the issue of interest representation versus the representation of political parties; the lay State as against the State with an established religion; a centralized administration or one with considerable regional and local autonomy; legislative supremacy or a system of constitutional checks and balances; and bicameralism as against unicameralism. Major issues also arose over the question of education, the content of the bill of rights, the status of property, and the type of national economy. The powers to be given the executive, the role of the President as head of the State, the scope of emergency authority, and a host of other topics excited heated and often significant discussion. Apparently reference was frequently made in the deliberations to the experience of other political systems, particularly contemporary ones; and the names of relevant, and sometimes irrelevant, political philosophers and politicians, from Aristotle to the moderns, were much on the tongues of the debaters. In their search for authority to support their particular views, the participants in the debate sometimes exhibited surprising loyalties. In his excellent description of the formation of the new Constitution, Professor Mario Einaudi states that the Communists relied on Washington and Benjamin Franklin for arguments to weaken bicameralism while the Christian Democrats looked to Stalin to strengthen such a concept.[7]

The Constitution is Adopted. In the course of the debate, the draft project of the constitutional commission underwent major changes. Nevertheless, its basic content survived and ultimately became the substance of a document upon which a majority could agree. That the Assembly could achieve such a consensus on so important a matter in the eighteen months during which the constitutional project was pending, is an indication of the political maturity of the Italian people and of the excellence of their political leadership. On December 22, 1947, the final corrected draft of the new Constitution, comprising 139 articles and 18 transitional clauses, was approved by a vote of 453 to 62; and on Christmas Eve, the Provisional President of the Republic, Enrico de Nicola, promulgated it. Six days later, that is, on January 1, 1948, it became the basic law of the new republic, almost exactly one hundred years after Charles Albert had promulgated the fundamental statute that later became the first Constitution of united Italy.

Terms of the Peace Treaty. Only somewhat less important than the Assembly's constitutional function, and a logical supplement thereto, was its

[7] "The Constitution of the Italian Republic," *American Political Science Review*, XLII (August, 1948), p. 662.

responsibility for making peace with the nations with whom Mussolini had gone to war. As we have already noted, Italy signed an armistice and surrendered unconditionally to the United Nations early in September, 1943. Her delegates signed the Treaty of Paris, February 10, 1947. Territorial losses were severe. Frontier rectifications, including cession of two communes, Briga and Tenda, were made in favor of France. Most of Venezia Giulia and one or two Adriatic islands went to Yugoslavia; and Trieste with some of its environs became a free territory and port under the United Nations. Colonial territory was either ceded to another power outright, as in the case of the Dodecanese Islands, which went to Greece, or was turned over to the major powers and the United Nations for disposition at a later date.[8] In addition, Italy was called upon to pay substantial reparations to Ethiopia, Greece, Yugoslavia, and the Soviet Union; to restrict her armed forces within stipulated maximums; and to give up the right to fortify her frontiers. Most Italians considered these terms unnecessarily harsh and there are few who do not believe that they will eventually be altered in Italy's favor. As we shall see,[9] revision in favor of Italy has already been made and more is in prospect. Nevertheless, even if revised somewhat, the Treaty can hardly be regarded as anything but a calamity to nationally conscious Italians. It is the price the nation had to pay for Mussolini's bellicosity and shortsighted diplomacy.

ABATEMENT OF THE COMMUNIST THREAT

Post-War Communist Cooperation. As the outlines of the new republican Constitution emerged from the Constituent Assembly and the nation's international position was being normalized, Italian Communism began to show its true colors. As in France and elsewhere in Western Europe, Communism in Italy enjoyed considerable growth in power and influence after World War II. Partly this upsurgence was due to the prestige world Communism had acquired in the successful Soviet resistance to German Nazism; partly it was due to efforts which Italian Communists had made to resist Fascism and German Nazism in Italy; partly it was due to reasons peculiar to the Marxist movement in Italy. At any rate, the first party coalition under Badoglio in 1944 included Communists, as we have already noted; and representatives of the party continued in governing coalitions until 1946. Thereafter they were relegated to the opposition. By that time it had become clear to patriotic Italians, as to patriots in other lands, that a coalition or united front with the Communists was impossible; that Communist policy was to "collaborate" with other parties in order finally to swallow them up or destroy them.

The Communists' Subversive Threat. Once the political Rubicon had been crossed and the Communists had been read out of polite political society in Italy, the Government was faced with augmented Communist efforts at direct political and economic sabotage. For these efforts Italian Communism

[8] See p. 315.
[9] See p. 313.

had financial means which, though derived from somewhat mysterious and questionable sources, were nonetheless adequate. During the wartime Partisan struggle against the Germans and Italian Fascists, and immediately afterward, the party had also taken a commanding position in the Italian labor movement, the General Italian Confederation of Labor (CGIL); and this was a distinct advantage in the kind of wrecking tactics and subversion in which the party specializes. In addition, the prevailingly low estate of the Italian economy and the hopelessness of much of the population, both industrial workers and peasants, provided fertile soil for exploiting Communism's characteristic incitation to class warfare and fratricidal strife. All told, Italian Communism was well-equipped to make a strong bid for power through "direct action"; and the renascent parliamentary leadership of the country had to muster all its courage and sagacity to counter the threat of a new dictatorship, this time of the red-shirted, rather than the black-shirted, variety.

Reaction of the Government. Fortunately this time, instead of a Facta, there was a Premier at the helm who was willing to act. Moreover he led a mass party organization that matched the discipline and the popular strength of the Communists themselves. De Gasperi also had lieutenants in his own party who realized the importance of maintaining respect for established authority and who not only had well-trained police forces at their command but were not loath to use them. Certain foreign critics have expressed the opinion that some of de Gasperi's lieutenants, particularly his Minister of the Interior, have sometimes used their police forces too hastily and too indiscriminately. Such criticism may be valid; but the fact remains that the de Gasperi Cabinet's ability to vindicate its authority, whenever challenged by Communist-inspired political strikes and demonstrations and sporadic street fighting, was the greatest single factor in overcoming the Communist menace of a *coup d'état* after 1947 and in persuading the Communist leadership to stay within the bounds of "legality." As a result, Communism had to be content with the verdict of the ballot box; and, as we shall see, that verdict, when finally given by the people freely and without constraint, made it clear that Communism would not gain a majority. The best it could hope for was to continue as the Government's disloyal opposition.

TRANSITION TO THE REPUBLIC COMPLETED

Elections of 1948—Defeat of the Communists. Elections for the first Parliament of the Italian Republic were held on April 18 and 19, 1948, four months after the promulgation of the Constitution. With these elections, the transitional phase of Italy's political history after World War II may be said to have been completed. Observers generally considered this first appeal to the electorate under the republican dispensation as one of the most important in the nation's entire history, an opinion which, in retrospect, does not appear to have been an exaggeration.

The most important result was the popular affirmation of the decision, previously taken by the Government, to have no "truck" with Communism or its allies. Despite formidable electioneering, which exploited Communism's favored position in the labor movement, the electoral appeal of the hammer and sickle was no match for that offered by the non-Communist parties. These rallied support by emphasizing patriotism and the symbols of Italian nationhood. They also had the assistance of the Vatican and of the Church throughout the republic. In addition, the patriotic parties' appeal to the voters had been enhanced by the nation's improved economic position, largely the work of Italy's leading economist, Dr. Luigi Einaudi, who was subsequently to become the first constitutionally elected President. To the Italian elector it was clear, moreover, that Marshall-plan aid from the United States, of which Italy stood in need, would continue only if the Communists did not come to power. In addition the Western powers, by announcing, during the campaign's last days, that they favored the return of Trieste to Italian jurisdiction implied that Moscow, and hence Moscow's Italian apologists, the Italian Communist Party, stood in the way of achieving an objective that every patriotic Italian will always strive to achieve. In the electoral reckoning, the Communist-controlled Popular Front won somewhat less than 31 per cent of the seats in the Chamber and somewhat more than 34 per cent of the membership of the Senate. As noted earlier, approximately the same partisan aggregation had won about 40 per cent of the seats in the elections of 1946 for the Constituent Assembly. Communism had by no means been routed; but it had suffered a setback from which it will be difficult to recover.[10]

Victory of the Christian Democrats. Almost as significant as Communism's defeat was Christian Democracy's victory. From the status of a party enjoying the support of somewhat more than a third of the Italian electorate, registered in the elections of 1946, this party now advanced to the position of a virtual majority organization with more than 53 per cent of the seats in the Chamber of Deputies and somewhat more than 43 per cent of the seats in the Senate.[11] This new electoral status of the Christian Democrats meant that Italy, like Britain, had a party strong enough to rule alone, if it

[10] It should be noted that in the communal and provincial elections of May and June, 1951, the vote given Communism and its allies rose from 31 per cent of the total, registered in 1948, to approximately 37 per cent of the total. Despite this fact the non-Communist parties, through electoral alliances and otherwise, managed to expand their hold on the nation's local popular assemblies.

[11] The party had relatively less seats in the Senate because of the mixed elective-appointive system applicable to that body. See p. 280. The seats won by the various parties in the two Chambers in the 1948 elections are listed as follows:

Party	Chamber of Deputies	Senate	
		ELECTIVE SEATS	APPOINTIVE SEATS
Christian Democrats	307	130	21
Popular Democratic Front	182	74	46
Right-wing Socialists	33	12	14
Liberals and Allies	18	9	17
Republicans	9	3	5
Monarchists and Allies	14	4	4
Italian Social Movement	6	1	—
Others	5	4	—
Total	574	237 (344)	107

wished, and provide that initiative in policy, firmness in administration, and authority in leadership which only a Cabinet, relying upon a partisan parliamentary majority, can offer.

Some Dangers in Christian Democratic Hegemony. Potential advantages of this virtual hegemony of the Christian Democrats also have their price. Part of that price is the decline or virtual disappearance of several smaller parties which represented important values in the composite of Italian political theory and tradition. Such declines were registered especially among the old Liberal groups of the Right; but they also occurred among certain Center groups like the Republicans and the Actionists.[12] Then, too, there was danger that, because of their newly achieved pre-eminence, the Christian Democrats, strong supporters of clerical influence in the State, might drift away from the secular political tradition altogether and embrace theocratic conceptions closer to Calvin's Geneva or Dollfuss's Austria than to the liberal parliamentary tradition of Cavour and Mazzini. For many, including a good many Italians, this might represent too high a price for the unquestioned benefit flowing from de Gasperi's having slain, or at least severely wounded, the Communist dragon and for having conferred upon Italy the potential blessing of a disciplined majority-party Government.

Whatever temptation may have existed along these lines, Dr. de Gasperi's actions, on the morrow of the elections, indicate that he has no intention of trying to transform Italy into a purely Christian Democratic commonwealth or even of giving Italy a purely Christian Democratic Cabinet. Instead he sought diligently for a coalition and continued to share his governing responsibilities with Ministers drawn from the right-wing Socialists, the Republicans, and (for a time) the Liberals. Admittedly these coalition allies of Christian Democracy are small and of limited influence in the country. Moreover, in April, 1951, the right-wing Socialists, beckoned by the persistent mirage of Marxian unity, left the Cabinet and later that same year de Gasperi, plagued by revolt within his own party, found it necessary to resign. Commissioned by President Einaudi to form a new Cabinet, his seventh, de Gasperi continued to rely upon a coalition. In this persistent search for support outside the ranks of his own party, the Christian Democratic leader gives every assurance that the nation will not soon be strait-jacketed into Christian Democratic conformity.

Conclusion. Thus in the few years immediately after the fall of Mussolini, Italy had come a long way towards the goal of post-War normality. In that brief period she had purged herself finally of the Mussolinian octopus; liquidated the mesalliance with Hitler; assumed the status of co-belligerency at the side of her former foes among the United Nations; and signed a treaty which, despite grievous sacrifices, restored her to a position of some international dignity. At the same time she had formally abolished her ancient monarchy; fashioned a new republican Constitution; and, despite her economic

[12] See p. 307.

weaknesses and the menace of Communist subversion, she had laid the foundations of a stable parliamentary system. With such accomplishments to her credit in so short a time, the country had reason to face the future with confidence, or at least with equanimity, however difficult the problems that continued to loom on the political horizon.

CHAPTER V

GOVERNMENT OF THE REPUBLIC: POLITICAL ORGANS

If we except the interlude of the Fascist regime, Italy's experience with free, popular political institutions spans more than a century. Inevitably that experience has influenced the content of the new republican Constitution. Those acquainted with the pattern of political institutions of Giolittian Italy will undoubtedly find many a familiar landmark in this republican dispensation. At the same time, even a cursory examination of the new *statuto fondamentale* reveals that its authors had more in mind than merely a return to pre-Mussolinian constitutional normalcy. Quite often, in the case of major governmental and administrative agencies, machinery has been introduced and political ideas have been incorporated which, if not strange to the student of comparative government, are at least relatively unknown in Italian political experience. Hence in the examination of republican Italy's governmental structure, upon which this chapter will embark, we are likely to encounter a blending of the prescriptive and the new; and the total effect of such blending is likely to be a governmental pattern and a political process that depart perceptibly, if not radically, from anything Italians have previously experienced.

LEGISLATIVE INSTITUTIONS

Parliament's Supremacy. In this chapter we shall deal with the political apparatus of Italy's new Government. The dominant organ in that apparatus is Parliament. Conceptions of regional autonomy and such institutions as judicial review of legislation and the popular referendum—all of which have found a place in the new scheme of things—may conceivably reduce the republican Parliament to a position juridically inferior to that which came to be enjoyed by its Giolittian counterpart. Even so, the new Parliament remains supreme in the apparatus of Government. It is the primary symbol of the political sovereignty of the people and the only instrument through which such sovereignty may gain tolerably effective expression. Moreover, since the Constitution-makers have continued the traditional system of ministerial or "responsible" Government, Parliament remains the master of the Ministers. It can make and unmake Cabinets, hold them accountable for policy, and insist that all major political decisions and legislation have its stamp of approval. Clearly any examination of the mechanism of Italy's contemporary governmental system may properly begin with Parliament.

The Chamber of Deputies: Electoral System. In accordance with the precedent established by the Albertian Constitution, the Parliament of the republic is bicameral, consisting of a Chamber of Deputies and a Senate. Members of the first of these bodies, who totaled 574 after the elections of 1948, are chosen under a proportional electoral plan first applied to national elections after World War I and revived for the elections to the Constituent Assembly in 1946. For the election of the deputies, the country is divided into some thirty-one districts (including Valle d'Aosta) each of which returns a fairly large number (in one instance as many as twenty-seven) of deputies to Parliament. The principle of *scrutin d'liste* applies to the voting; that is, the elector casts his ballot for a party list of candidates and not for individual candidates; and each party list elects as many deputies as the total vote for the list contains the electoral quota.[1] Seats won by any party list are distributed among the individual candidates in the order in which their names appear on the list, this order having been fixed in advance by the party high command. However, by a system of so-called preference voting (*voti di preferenza*), individual voters, in casting their ballot for any party list, may single out as many as three names and give them the first three positions on the ballot. If enough voters do this for certain less favored candidates, the voters may conceivably change the order of priority assigned the candidates by the party. In each of the thirty-one electoral districts, the surplus votes of a party's list, that is, votes the total of which does not equal the quota necessary for election, may be cumulated nationally. Such votes are then used to elect candidates which appear on a party's national list.

In the parliamentary elections of 1948, some 348 party lists appeared in the thirty-one electoral districts and bore the names of some 5,623 candidates. In the same elections, twelve parties compiled national lists which included the names of some 302 candidates many of whom also appeared on the district lists. Some forty-four of the successful candidates in these elections apparently had had their names inscribed on one of the twelve national lists; but less than half of these were actually returned to the Chamber of Deputies from such national lists, the majority having been elected from the districts.

The Senate: Efforts to Differentiate from the Chamber. In creating the Senate some effort was made to vary its composition from that of the Chamber of Deputies. At one point in the proceedings of the Constituent Assembly, the Christian Democrats actually sought to have the Senate represent economic groups and thereby give expression to the corporative concepts of public organization which are never far below the ideological surface of parties with a clerical, and especially a Roman Catholic, orientation. As indicated elsewhere, this plan met defeat; and since the Leftist Parties generally desired

[1] According to the Constitution, Art. 56, there shall be one deputy for 800,000 inhabitants.

to make the two Chambers as alike as possible, it is not surprising that the constitutional provisions to differentiate their respective memberships are somewhat less than effective. In the course of time some difference in the prevailing social and economic background and political views of the respective memberships of Chamber and Senate may result from the fact that the Constitution makes a Senator's term six years or one year more than the term of a Deputy, and that the qualifying minimum age for a Deputy is twenty-five whereas it is forty in the Senate. Some differences may possibly result also from the fact that the minimum age for a senatorial elector is twenty-five whereas that for a Chamber elector is twenty-one. On the whole, however, it is unlikely that these special constitutional provisions will contribute much toward making distinctive assemblies out of the two Chambers of Italy's new Parliament.

Method of Choosing Senators. Senators obtain their seats either by appointment or by a somewhat complicated system of popular election. Appointed Senators, all of whom enjoy life tenure, are nominally chosen by the President of the Republic. Those selected must have distinguished themselves in the arts or sciences, in literature, or in some form of social service, a requirement not unlike that which applied to the appointment of Senators under the former Constitution.[2] Presidents of the Republic also become life Senators upon retiring from office. Elective Senators are apportioned among the nineteen Regions into which the country has been divided, roughly according to the ratio of one Senator for 200,000 inhabitants; however, no Region is to have less than six Senators (except Valle d'Aosta which has one) no matter what its population may be. Selection of the Region as the senatorial constituency was expected to enhance the political significance of this new political unit and strengthen the rather artificial idea that the Senate represented territorial interests. Elective Senators may be chosen in the first instance in one of the various electoral districts into which a Region is divided, each district being entitled to elect one Senator; but since the law stipulates that the winning candidate must have at least 65 per cent of the vote of the district, few Senators are actually chosen in this fashion. Indeed, of the elective Senators in the first Parliament, not more than twenty were chosen in senatorial districts. The remainder were elected from the Region at large. For this purpose the vote given the candidates of the same party in each of the Region's indecisive senatorial districts is cumulated for the Region as a whole, the lists of local candidates are consolidated into Regional party lists, and the choice of the required number of Senators is then made under a system of proportional representation.

Elective and Appointive Senators in the First Parliament. Republican Italy's first Senate secured about two-thirds, or 237, of its 344 [3] members by the electoral process just described. The remaining one-third (106) were appointed; but the appointments were made in accordance with a special tran-

[2] See p. 223.
[3] The authorized total is 350 Senators.

sitional provision of the Constitution [4] and not under the presidential power to appoint Senators, previously described. In addition, one Senator in this first Parliament, Enrico de Nicola, held his office by virtue of having been Provisional President of the Republic.[5]

Similar Political Complexion of Senate and Chamber. In general the Senate, thus constituted, reflected the political orientation of the Chamber of Deputies. As indicated elsewhere, the Christian Democrats claimed 53.5 per cent of the membership of the Deputies; in the Senate the same party had 43.2 per cent of the total. Communists and Socialists, making up the Popular Front, had 31.7 per cent of the seats in the Chamber and 32.9 per cent in the Senate. Other parties had comparable minor variations in their respective followings in the two houses. Moreover, the percentage of the vote which each party enjoyed in the senatorial elections rarely varied by as much as one per cent from the share these same parties secured in the Chamber elections.[6] Undoubtedly experience under the new Constitution has been too limited to permit of safe generalizations; but so far as the present situation permits of judgment, it would appear that the political complexion of the two Chambers will not vary greatly in time to come.

Constitutional Equality of the Chambers. That the new Italy should have two legislative Chambers is scarcely remarkable since, as already noted, a similar arrangement existed under the Albertian regime. What is rather remarkable is the fact that the Constitution makes the two Chambers essentially equal in power and prestige, thereby countering the policy, discernible after World War I, of transforming second Chambers into what one writer has appropriately called "secondary Chambers." In contrast to the Council of the Republic, upper house in the Parliament of France's Fourth Republic, Italy's new Senate has all the prerogatives of the lower house. Like the Deputies, the Senate may initiate any legislative or fiscal project and its concurrence is essential to the enactment of any legislative or fiscal project. Moreover, in order to remain in power, a Cabinet must have the confidence of both the Senate and the Chamber of Deputies, a requirement which illustrates in rather dramatic fashion the practical significance of the formal equality of the two Chambers but which, as we shall see later, may also endanger the stability of the Cabinet.

Parliamentary Commissions. Regulations traditional in a representative assembly govern the organization and procedure of each of the two Chambers. In addition to certain special committees, such as those on rules, elections, and treaties, each Chamber has a series of permanent commissions with jurisdiction over specific areas of prospective legislation or administrative action. In the Senate there are eleven such commissions each of which has an average

---

[4] See Clause III of the Transitional and Final Arrangements of the Constitution.
[5] Constitution, Art. 59.

[6]

Party	Per cent of Chamber vote	Per cent of Senate vote
Christian Democrat	48.7	47.9
Popular Front	30.7	31.0
Right-wing Socialists	7.1	7.0

membership of thirty-two.[7] An effort is made to represent the parties proportionally on each commission. The Chamber of Deputies also has eleven permanent commissions which, as respects size, political complexion, and jurisdiction, are virtually identical with comparable bodies in the upper Chamber.
Reflecting the traditional priority of the lower house in financial matters, the
members of the permanent commission on finance and treasury matters in
the Deputies are organized in thirteen subcommissions. Four of these advise
the plenary commission on the financial aspects of proposed legislation brought
before the remaining standing commissions. The other nine serve as liaison
agencies between the finance and treasury commission and the other commissions.[8]

Introduction and Consideration of Measures in Parliament. Legislative measures may be introduced in either Chamber by the respective members, by the Cabinet, by means of a popular initiative petition bearing at least
50,000 signatures, and by certain public bodies. It is scarcely necessary to
add that, in practice, the introduction of measures in Parliament is a prerogative largely monopolized by the Cabinet. Normally bills and other projects are
submitted to one of the permanent commissions which reports the measure
back to the appropriate Chamber after study. Long delay in commission may
be avoided if a measure is declared urgent by the Cabinet. Moreover, in either
Chamber, a measure may be called out of a commission and voted upon by
the Chamber if one-tenth of its membership demand such action or if one-fifth
of the relevant commission or the Cabinet demand it. When either Chamber
in plenary session votes upon a measure, it is customary to vote upon each
article and then upon the measure as a whole. Because of the equality of the
Chambers, anything which one may enact must be adopted in precisely the
same form by the other if it is to become law. No formal procedure exists
for ironing out differences and securing agreement on the terms of a proposed
statute; hence when differences arise, they must be overcome by informal
means or through the intervention of the Minister primarily interested in the
measure.

Executive Veto. To become law of the land, a bill or other project of
law, enacted by the two Chambers, must be formally promulgated by the President of the Republic within one month after he receives it. Apparently promulgation is a discretionary duty,[9] for the Constitution permits the President
to request another vote on the measure by each Chamber if he so desires, and

---

[7] The names of the commissions are as follows: (1) Internal Affairs and Affairs Relating
to the Office of the Prime Minister; (2) Grace and Justice; (3) Foreign Affairs and Colonies;
(4) Defense; (5) Finance and Treasury; (6) Public Instruction and the Arts; (7) Public Works,
Transport, Posts, Telecommunications and the Merchant Marine; (8) Agriculture and Food;
(9) Industry, Domestic and Foreign Commerce, and Tourism; (10) Labor, Emigration and
Social Insurance; (11) Health and Sanitary Matters.

[8] See *Annuario parlamentare* (1949–50), pp. 16–17.

[9] The discretion is defined by Arts. 73 and 74 of the Constitution. It should be added that
if the Chambers each pass a particular measure by an absolute majority and thereby indicate
that the measure is urgent, the President must promulgate the measure within the time the
Chambers have fixed for such action. See Art. 73.

requires promulgation only after they have each reaffirmed their previous decision. Such discretion amounts to a suspensive veto. Since this veto is likely to be exercised by the President only with the concurrence of his "responsible" Ministers, and since the latter normally have political control over the Chambers and their proceedings, it is unlikely that the veto will acquire significance. Certainly it is not likely to acquire the significance that might develop if Italy's Government were not "responsible" but, like that of the United States, operated under a constitutional separation of executive and legislative powers.

Other Parliamentary Powers. Besides the financial and law-making prerogatives normally confided to the contemporary legislature, Italy's Parliament has various others. It may be called upon, for example, to approve certain types of international treaties, especially those which affect internal legislation, impose financial burdens upon the State, or alter national boundaries. Parliament must also decide upon declarations of war, the issuance of pardons and amnesties, and the conduct of public investigations. To exert the latter prerogative, the scope of which is unusually broad, a special investigating committee must be set up. Unlike similar bodies in other national Parliaments, an Italian legislative investigating committee is required by the Constitution to operate like a judicial agency and to observe procedural limitations of a judicial character.

Decree Power and Delegated Legislative Power. Although the legislative power is nominally vested exclusively in Parliament, much of its substance is exercised by executive and administrative officials who issue decrees or norms with the force of law. In Continental European states especially, officials who enforce a statute or similar measure traditionally wield discretionary authority to issue decrees with the force of law, such decrees being considered necessary to carry out the intent of the statute. Power to issue the decree is said to inhere in the statute to be enforced. This kind of ancillary decree power is not to be confused with the actual delegation of legislative power to the executive by means of blanket statutes, an increasingly common practice in the modern State. In such a case the decree power is actually an executive power to make law *de novo,* expressly delegated to the executive by Parliament. Italy's republican Constitution-makers appear to have been somewhat loath to authorize delegation; nevertheless, they assumed it would take place and attempted to set metes and bounds. This intention seems to be accomplished in an Article of the Constitution which declares [10] that Parliament may not delegate its power except according to fixed principles and criteria and only after having established the duration of the delegation and after having defined the purpose of the authority delegated. Finally, there is the phenomenon of emergency decree power, that is, assumption by the executive of power to issue decree laws without statutory or constitutional warrant on plea of overwhelming necessity or public emergency. The Constitution continues to be realistic and recognizes the possibility that emergency decrees will be

[10] Art. 76.

issued. Again, therefore, it attempts to set metes and bounds to executive discretion by asserting that such decrees must be regarded as "provisional" in
nature and by requiring the Cabinet to submit them to Parliament for approval
and conversion into law on the same day they are issued, Parliament to be
called into session for such action within five days if in recess. The Constitution further states [11] that if Parliament does not convert the emergency decrees
into law within sixty days of their issuance, they are to be deemed without
legal effect from the day they were first issued. This latter provision may conceivably have a deterrent effect upon some hapless Minister who may hesitate
to act in a crisis because he fears that Parliament will not support him. But if
an emergency decree is issued, failure of Parliament to convert it into law
can hardly invalidate it in fact; because rights become vested and obligations
are incurred under the terms of the rejected decree which no failure of Parliament to act can erase. Indeed the Constitution, quite inconsistently and somewhat superfluously, itself recognizes that the condition of invalidity is largely
theoretical by declaring that, if legal relationships do arise under decrees not
converted into law, Parliament may regulate those relationships.

Popular Referendum. One of the novelties of the new regime, at least
for Italy, is the attempt to engraft a popular referendum upon the nation's
representative institutions. A half million registered voters, or five of the Regional Councils acting together, may request the abrogation of all, or part, of
any existing law that does not relate to the budget, taxation, or certain other
special topics. The electorate for the Chamber of Deputies is eligible to vote
in the referendum, and a simple majority can secure adoption of a petition in a
poll in which a majority of the eligible electorate participates. In view of the
structure of Italian politics, it does not appear probable that the referendum
will ever acquire much practical significance in the political process of the new
Italy.

Amendment of the Constitution. Both Parliament and the new device
of the referendum are involved in the formal process of amending the republican Constitution which, unlike the Albertian instrument, does not exclude
formal change. Amendments and supplementary constitutional laws are
deemed to have been adopted if passed by each Chamber of Parliament on two
successive occasions, an absolute majority of each Chamber being required on
the second vote. The interval between the two votes must not be more than
three months. If, in the second vote, at least two-thirds of all members of each
Chamber support the amendment or constitutional law, no popular referendum may take place. If the majority on the second vote is less than two-thirds,
then five Regional Councils, a half million registered voters, or one-fifth of
the members of either Chamber may demand a referendum on the enacted
measure within a period of three months after Parliament has passed it a
second time. If in the ensuing popular balloting the measure is not sustained
by at least a majority of those voting, it is deemed to have been lost.[12] Thus

[11] Art. 77.
[12] Constitution, Art. 138.

the referendum has been exploited to provide a popular check on the constituent powers of Parliament.

THE EXECUTIVE AND THE PARLIAMENTARY SYSTEM

The President of the Republic. As indicated in an earlier chapter, kingship in Italy came to an end in the summer of 1946 [13] and was replaced by republican institutions. Of these, the most characteristic is that of the Presidency of the Republic which replaces the Savoy monarchy. To elect the President, the Constitution has set up a special electoral college consisting of members of the two Chambers of Parliament meeting in joint session and three delegates from each of the nineteen Regions (except Valle d'Aosta which has only one delegate) into which the nation is divided. Regional representation may possibly have been designed to reduce the President's dependence on Parliament; principally, however, it seems to have been intended to enhance the political significance of the Regions themselves,[14] since they are new and somewhat artificial units of local government. Professor Luigi Einaudi, the first President to be formally elected for the constitutional term of seven years,[15] was chosen by Parliament on May 11, 1948, without the Regional representatives being present, the Constitution having provided for such an initial election if, as proved to be the case, the Regional delegates were not available.[16] In choosing a President, the electoral college votes by secret ballot. A two-thirds majority is necessary for a choice on any of the first three ballots; but an absolute majority suffices after the third ballot. President Einaudi was elected on the fourth ballot by a vote of 518 to 320 and won over such opponents as former Prime Minister V. E. Orlando and Count Carlo Sforza. Besides his own Liberal supporters, President Einaudi had the backing of the Christian Democrats and of the right-wing Socialists. The President of Italy has a salary equivalent to $21,000 per annum and a drawing account of some $300,000.

Presidential Powers and Political Influence. Besides serving as the head of the State and thus symbolizing the unity of the nation, the President is also given executive prerogatives. The list of such prerogatives is rather formidable. It includes command of the armed forces, ratification of treaties, exchange of diplomats with other States, nomination of the Prime Minister, dissolution of the Chambers, and other equally important functions. Both the phraseology of the Constitution and the opinions of certain commentators might imply that these are personal powers of the President and that, in exercising them, he relies upon his personal discretion in much the same fashion as the American President. Such, however, is not the case; for the Italian President, like the Savoy Kings before him, is a titular executive. He is legally irresponsible unless he commits treason or deliberately violates constitutional provisions. Both the legal and political responsibility for his public acts must be assumed by others who must answer for them before Parliament and the

[13] See p. 270.
[14] See p. 298.
[15] He was preceded by Enrico de Nicola as Provisional President.
[16] Constitution, Transitional Provisions, Clause II.

courts.[17] It must be added that this arrangement, which is the foundation stone of what the British call "responsible" government and of what others call "parliamentary" government or, sometimes, "cabinet" government, does not preclude the exertion of considerable presidential influence upon the course of government, especially since the President must often serve as the official vehicle for executing some power or even for initiating some official action. Measurement of the practical effect upon the governmental process of the moral authority, personal prestige, and political acumen of a titular executive like the Italian President involves constitutional nuances which few writers have identified satisfactorily for any particular country. Probably Walter Bagehot has provided the only outstanding performance in this respect and his examination related only to the British system as that operated a hundred years ago.[18] In the case of an office so recently created as the Italian Presidency, an observer can only conjecture as to its ultimate impact upon the political process.

Prime Minister and Cabinet. A necessary corollary of the President's irresponsibility is the investiture of effective authority and power to determine the major lines of policy in the Cabinet or Council of Ministers, normally a body of some seventeen or eighteen heads of ministerial departments and, occasionally, of one or two Ministers without portfolio, and in the Cabinet's leader, the Prime Minister or President of the Council of Ministers.[19] This corollary is clearly recognized in the Constitution, which explicitly enjoins the Prime Minister to direct the general policy of the Government and holds him "responsible" for that policy. He is also authorized to coordinate the activity of the Ministers and to secure unity in administration. He and the Ministers are formally declared to be "collectively responsible" for the corporate acts of the Cabinet; and the Ministers assume "responsibility" as individuals for the activities of their respective administrative departments. As already noted, selection of the Prime Minister is declared to be a prerogative of the President of the Republic who, in collaboration with the Prime Minister-designate, also nominates the other Ministers. In making such selections, it is under-

---

[17] The Constitution, Art. 49, makes this condition very clear: "No act of the President of the Republic is valid unless countersigned by the Ministers proposing it, who assume responsibility for it. Acts which have the force of legislation and other acts indicated by law are also countersigned by the President of the Council of Ministers."

[18] See his *English Constitution*, revised edition, New York, 1929.

[19] Because of parliamentary usage in English-speaking countries, the word "Cabinet" in this discussion is given the same significance as "Council of Ministers" even though "Cabinet" has no official status as a title in Italian parliamentary law. It should be added that the word is often used in Italy, as in France, to designate collectively certain of the immediate bureaucratic subordinates of a Minister or other important official. Nor is the phrase "Prime Minister" an official designation. Mindful, perhaps, of the monopolistic pretensions of Mussolini who, as already indicated, called himself "Head of the Government," the makers of the republican Constitution contented themselves with the title "President of the Council" for the leader of the Cabinet and avoided the suggestion of his pre-eminence over other Ministers, implied in the less cumbersome and more popular term "Prime Minister." They did this even though the head of the Cabinet is in fact pre-eminent both by reason of his superior political prestige and by reason of the greater significance attaching to his official functions. Again, however, usage, based on British precedent, has sanctioned the use of "Prime Minister" for the leader of Cabinets in all parliamentary States; hence we shall use "Prime Minister" and "President of the Council of Ministers" interchangeably.

stood that the instrument of appointment will subsequently be countersigned either by the outgoing or incoming Prime Minister.

Parliamentary Theory and Practice Contrasted. Although wholly respectable precedent exists for these detailed constitutional prescriptions as to the selection of the Prime Minister and his Cabinet and as to their "responsibility," the prescriptions are, in fact, academic and not particularly informative as to the position of the Cabinet in the governmental structure and its relation to Parliament. As a practical matter, in republican Italy as in other parliamentary States, the Cabinet obtains its political and administrative leadership, and becomes in fact the "Government," because it consists of the leading parliamentary politicians who, in their conduct of affairs, can count upon the support of a majority in Parliament. The Prime Minister is the parliamentary political leader *par excellence.* As head of the Cabinet he is either the head of the party that commands the allegiance of a majority of Parliament or he is the architect of a coalition of politicians from different parties whose followers command a parliamentary majority. His selection as Prime Minister and the appointment of his Cabinet colleagues is determined by this demonstrated capacity to command majority parliamentary support. Moreover, so long as this majority exists, the Prime Minister and his Cabinet can govern effectively. Their "responsibility" to Parliament and the need for formal parliamentary approval of their policies constitute no serious impediment. By the same token, when the majority disappears, the Cabinet disintegrates and the Prime Minister resigns.

Relative Strength of Cabinets in Republican Italy. In view of the formidable strength of the Christian Democratic Party which, in 1951, had the allegiance of more than one-half of the Deputies and almost one-half of the Senators, its leader, Dr. de Gasperi, has had comparatively little difficulty in constructing the parliamentary majorities required to support the Cabinets which he has led. He was Prime Minister of five successive Cabinets in the four-year period between December, 1945, and December, 1949. In January, 1950, he formed his sixth Cabinet consisting of thirteen representatives of his own party, three Republicans, and three right-wing Socialists. As indicated earlier, this coalition disintegrated during the spring of 1951, and in July of that year Dr. de Gasperi tried his hand at forming his seventh Cabinet. Among the rank-and-file leadership of a political organization socially as heterogeneous as Christian Democracy, it is sometimes difficult to enforce discipline or prevent the growth of faction; nevertheless in view of his acknowledged pre-eminence, Dr. de Gasperi, or some successor of equal stature within the party, ought to experience little difficulty in continuing to muster supporting majorities built around a Christian Democratic core. At any rate difficulty should not be experienced during the life of the Chamber elected in 1948, which has a mandate until 1953. Republican Italy's parliamentary system has the political wherewithal, at least for the time being, to operate successfully.

Some Special Features of the Parliamentary System. It should be added that the new Constitution has somewhat complicated the Cabinet's task of discharging its political responsibility to Parliament. Thus within ten days of the formation of a Cabinet, its leader and his ministerial colleagues must present themselves in each Chamber and secure a formal expression of confidence.[20] Two such formal referenda on the issue of parliamentary confidence, before a newly constituted Cabinet has even had time to take stock of its political assets, may well have the effect of shortening its life span, especially if the Cabinet coalition is not too durable to start with. A more formidable complication is involved in the Constitution's requirement that the Cabinet have the confidence of *both* Chambers. This means that the Prime Minister and his colleagues must constantly have supporting majorities in each of the two Chambers and not merely in one as under the current French system; and during the Republic's first years, votes to determine the presence or absence of such majorities have been about as frequent in the Senate as in the Chamber of Deputies. The requirement may lead to trouble if, despite expectations, the Senate should, in the course of time, come to have a radically different political orientation than the Chamber. For the time being the fact that the two Chambers have essentially the same political complexion has obviated embarrassment for the Cabinet. The wisdom implicit in the adage that a man cannot serve two masters simultaneously apparently did not impress the Italian constitutional solons; it is just possible, however, that such wisdom may one day impress those for whom they wrought.

Seemingly as a sort of compensation for these potential hurdles, the Constitution has set up some special protections for the Cabinet whenever it is called upon to test its political leadership or to vindicate its "responsibility" to Parliament. Thus defeat of a Cabinet-inspired measure in either or both Chambers does not require the Cabinet to resign forthwith. In case of such a defeat, the Prime Minister is at least given time to marshal his forces for the voting on the formal motion of confidence which is likely to follow. Such a motion, moreover, cannot be placed on the agenda of either Chamber unless at least one-tenth of the membership have signed the call for the motion. If such support is secured, the motion must lie over for three days when it may be subjected to discussion and a vote. The obstructions thus interposed are designed to allow passions to cool and to make certain that lack of confidence will not be voted until the Cabinet has had every chance to make its position clear and to patch up differences among its parliamentary following.

The Power to Dissolve the Chambers. Finally, to protect its position *vis à vis* Parliament, a Cabinet may threaten dissolution of one or both Chambers and, in extreme cases, carry such a threat into effect. Dissolution is one of the executive prerogatives which the Constitution formally reposes in the President. Before exercising the prerogative, the President is required to confer with the president of each Chamber. Hence a Prime Minister's demand for a dissolution might be delayed. But that the President and his conferees

[20] Unlike the situation in the United Kingdom, Ministers in Italy have the right to attend sessions of either Chamber, whether or not they are members, and may also demand to be heard at any time. See Constitution, Art. 64.

could successfully resist a Prime Minister's determination to put an end to the life of an existing Parliament, or one of its Chambers, is unlikely if the Prime Minister is willing to assume responsibility for the action in accordance with the conditions of the parliamentary system of government. The Constitution stipulates that neither Chamber may be dissolved during the last six months of any President's term. During the period of Italy's first republican Parliament, at least, any Cabinet is likely to have fairly large and relatively well-disciplined majorities in either Chamber. Hence, for the time being, discussion of the prerogative of dissolution is largely academic.

CHAPTER VI

GOVERNMENT OF THE REPUBLIC: ADMINISTRATION, COURTS, AND LOCAL GOVERNMENT

In the preceding chapter we have described the principal political organs of republican Italy's central Government, that is, Parliament, President, Prime Minister, and Cabinet, and have examined the operation of the system of Cabinet responsibility to the Chambers. In the next few pages we shall explore the administrative apparatus of the central Government, the judicial system, and the various levels of local government.

PUBLIC ADMINISTRATION

The Ministries as Administrative Units. As members of the Cabinet, the Ministers are a part of the most important political council of the realm. With the exception of those few who are occasionally appointed as Minister without portfolio, the individual Ministers also serve as heads of the eighteen or more ministerial departments into which the administration of the central Government has been divided in recent years. Within a department, a Minister is usually assisted by at least one undersecretary and sometimes by two or three. Like their chiefs, the undersecretaries are either Deputies or Senators; that is, they are also politicians who enjoy a tenure coextensive with the life of an existing Cabinet. In addition, each Minister has his private entourage which, as previously explained,[1] is known as his "cabinet." The chief permanent career officials of a ministerial department are known as "directors general," one of whom heads each of the major units into which an administrative department is usually divided. Subordinate units of Italy's central administrative organization are variously known as "divisions," "offices," and "services."

Functional Significance of Various Ministries. The welfare responsibilities of the contemporary State and the collectivistic trend in economic life have greatly augmented the activities, and hence the importance, of certain ministerial departments. Especially is this true of such ministries as those of

[1] See footnote 19, p. 286.

Labor and Social Insurance, Public Works, Public Instruction, and of the ministries having to do with industry, agriculture, foreign and domestic commerce, the merchant marine, transport, and communications. Among the more traditional ministries, that of the Interior manages to maintain a position of primary importance for the well-known reasons that it deals with internal security and with local government and administration. An unusual feature of the Italian administrative organization is the distribution of fiscal matters among three separate ministries, one having to do with budgetary matters, another with taxation and ways and means, and still another with money, public debt, credit, State property, the supervision of State financial agencies, and related matters.

Symmetrical Administrative Structure. Proliferation of administrative machinery, universal in our time, has frequently caused governments to develop a set of "independent" bureaus and commissions, that is, administrative agencies operating outside the normal departmental structure. Such, for example, has been the case in the American national Government. Traditional emphasis upon symmetry has discouraged such a trend in the Italian bureaucratic structure. Except for certain public corporations (*Enti, Istituti*), dealing chiefly with credit and related matters, virtually all of the central Government's administrative machinery has found an abode within the framework of one of the various ministries. To achieve this result, some of the ministries have had to serve as a sort of "catch-all." This is especially true of the Prime Minister's Office in which have been lodged a considerable variety of administrative enterprises that are none too homogeneous. In that Office are to be found the Central Statistical Institute, the National Research Council, and other agencies dealing with such disparate matters as tourism, food supply, public sanitation, youth movements, the welfare of disabled veterans, and relations with Italy's new Regional governments.

The Consultative Administration—The Council of State. In the Prime Minister's Office are also to be found most of the auxiliary organs of public administration, sometimes known collectively as the "consultative administration." Among these the most important, and certainly the most distinguished, is the Council of State (*Consiglio dello stato*). Consisting of about seventy-five councilors and divided into six sections,[2] its duties are akin to those of the body with the same name in France. From one of its three "consultative" sections, individual Ministers or ministerial departments must secure the Council's advice and sometimes its consent before a particular decree or regulation may be issued. The fourth, fifth, and sixth sections determine controversies of a jurisdictional nature among the national administrative services and serve as courts of last resort for cases in administrative law which originate in local tribunals throughout Italy, especially among the local prefectoral councils.[3]

---

[2] A special seventh section was added recently for the administration of the Fascist purification laws, but it is temporary.

[3] See p. 298.

Other Consultative Agencies. A second consultative administrative agency, likewise under the wing of the Prime Minister, is the Office of the State Attorney. It represents the Government in civil actions in the courts, renders legal advice, and scrutinizes the form of proposed decrees. Finally, mention must be made of the Court of Accounts (*Corte dei conti*), also attached to the Prime Minister's Office. Its councilors and other personnel, far more numerous than in the case of the Council of State, not only exercise budgetary control over all public agencies, national and local, and audit their accounts, but also serve as a court in cases of claims against the State, particularly pension claims, and pass upon the legitimacy of certain executive decrees.

National Council of Economy and Labor. The republican Constitution calls for the establishment of still another consultative agency which will apparently also be attached to the Premier's office. This is the National Council of Economy and Labor.[4] As its name implies, it is to have fairly broad interests in the economic field and is expected to advise Cabinet and Parliament on economic matters and even initiate economic legislation. Pending proposals to organize this Council call for a sixty-man body drawn from labor, industrial and commercial associations, and the Government, and provide that three-fifths of the membership must concur on the clauses of any economic measure which might be drafted by the Council and presented to the Cabinet. The Council's president would be nominated by the Prime Minister. Cabinet and Parliament have shown no enthusiasm for the proposed Council and give the general impression that it would be a largely useless, and hence superfluous, piece of governmental machinery.

The Civil Service. Personnel policies of the Italian bureaucracy are similar to those which obtain in the French Civil Service. Officials and employees of the State have been classified and graded in five major categories; and, for many years, examinations, oral and written, or some other competitive device, have been employed to select recruits. The new republican Constitution specifically states that admission to the public service shall be competitive unless the law makes an exception.[5] University training of a fairly specialized type is normally regarded as a prerequisite for application for appointment to the highest division in the service, that is, Class A, members of which are appointed to advisory or directorial positions. Thus, for the foreign service, for example, university graduates who have specialized in law, economics, or political science are preferred. Examinations are conducted in each ministerial department under the nominal supervision of the Minister. Preference is shown only for certain military veterans who apply for positions in the lower, nonspecialized brackets. Each of the five classes is distinct and there is normally no transfer from one class to another. Promotions to higher grades in each class are determined by a special council in each ministerial department. Public services in Italy are notoriously overstaffed, Government, like private industry, indulging in this form of concealed unemployment. Currently,

[4] Constitution, Art. 99.
[5] Constitution, Art. 97.

employees and officials attached to the central administration are said to approximate a million persons. State employees, both those engaged in Government service proper and in State economic enterprises, and local-government personnel are affiliated with the Communist-dominated General Italian Confederation of Labor and with the newly formed non-Communist Italian Confederation of Labor Syndicates.

THE JUDICIARY

Restoration of a Free Judiciary. Restoration of a free Government in Italy has been accompanied, logically enough, by the re-establishment of an independent judiciary. As noted earlier, the notorious Special Tribunal, epitome of Mussolini's conception of "political courts" and of Fascism's negation of due process and judicial independence, was about the first Fascist institution to be abolished after the dictator had himself been retired. Against these Fascist conceptions of the status and role of the judiciary, the new republican Constitution takes the firmest possible stand. The judges, it declares, "are subject only to the law." Only "regular judges" may exert the judicial power in accordance with the established principles governing the exercise of such power; and the naming of extraordinary, or special, judges is expressly interdicted.[6]

An Independent Judicial Department. In various clauses of the Constitution unusual emphasis is placed upon the conception of a judicial establishment which is autonomous and hence completely independent of the political departments of the Government. In pursuance of this ideal, the new basic statute has transferred some of the authority over the judiciary, customarily exercised by the Minister of Grace and Justice, to a so-called "Superior Council of the Judiciary" over which the President of the Republic presides.[7] This body consists exclusively (except for its presiding officer) of members of the bench and bar and of university professors of law,[8] and exercises general authority over the appointment and promotion of judges and over their assignment and transfer. On motion of the Minister of Grace and Justice, the Council may take steps to discipline a judge although, in principle, a judge is irremovable. Concern for the ideal of an independent judiciary is manifested in other ways. Judges who must preside in "special" jurisdictions are declared to be quite as independent as those who preside over more routine proceedings; special police are allocated directly to the courts to carry out their orders; prosecutors attached to the various grades of courts are professionally as independent of political influence or pressure as their brethren, the "sitting magistrates"; and the principle is emphasized that a judicial appeal from the acts of public authorities, either to a regular or to an administrative court,

---

[6] Constitution, Arts. 101, 102.

[7] The Council was first established July 14, 1907.

[8] The First President of the Supreme Court of Cassation and its chief prosecutor are members *ex officio;* two-thirds of the elective members are chosen by the judges from among their own number; one-third are chosen by Parliament from among law professors and attorneys who have practiced for at least fifteen years. Elective members have a four-year term and are not immediately re-eligible.

shall always be facilitated. On these issues of judicial autonomy and the independence of judges the policy of the Republic has been to return to the principles first enunciated officially in the judicial reforms of 1907 and 1908 and to expand and develop them. So generously have these principles been articulated in the new constitutional order that Italian jurists consider the judiciary as one of four supreme organs of the State, the others being Parliament, the President, and the Cabinet.[9]

The Lower Courts. In the judicial structure the tribunal of lowest grade is a local office of conciliation or people's court of which there are more than 7,000, one or more being found in every Italian commune. The magistrate (*conciliatore*) of this tribunal, who is not a professional member of the bench, is appointed by the presiding judge of the Court of Appeals of the area. Procedure is of a summary, informal character, and the disputes presented are likely to be of a petty civil nature involving not more than four or five hundred lire. Above the conciliation agencies are the justices of the peace (*preture*). These are to be found in every province, although their number varies greatly from province to province, a populous area like Naples having twenty-four whereas other provinces may have only two or three. Praetors have original jurisdiction in civil cases involving not more than 5,000 lire and in criminal cases involving fines of less than 5,000 lire or imprisonment for a period less than three years. Above these, in the judicial structure, come the so-called Tribunals (*tribunali*) which occupy the first rung in the hierarchy of the courts of higher grade. Every provincial capital and certain other large centers of population contain a Tribunal and their total for the Republic is 146. Appropriate sections of each Tribunal exercise original jurisdiction in practically all civil cases and in all criminal cases except the most serious not tried originally in the courts of summary jurisdiction. The Tribunals also entertain appeals from the praetor's court.

Courts of Appeal. Courts of appeal (*Corti d'appello*) exist in most of the major cities of the peninsula and the islands. Normally the territorial jurisdiction of an Appellate Court includes an entire compartment or Region, the largest territorial area into which Italy is divided for local administration, although a special Region like Valle d'Aosta has no separate Appellate Court, while one or two of the more populous Regions may have two. In all there are twenty-two Appeals Courts and a special section for the Region of Reggio Calabria. Most of the civil appeals from the lower courts go to this tribunal, and some of the civil cases of great importance may be originated in the Appeals Court. Each such court also exercises some supervisory authority over the Tribunals and lesser courts in its area. A special section of the Appellate Court, known as the Court of Assize (*Corte d'assise*) sits at intervals in practically every province. This court, composed of one professional magistrate from the Appeals bench and selected laymen who serve as a jury, is the nation's ranking criminal tribunal exercising original jurisdiction. It tries most

---

[9] See Giuseppe Grassi, "La Magistratura Nella Nuova Costituzione," in *Il Centenario del parlamento,* published by the Secretariat of the Chamber of Deputies, Rome, 1948, p. 429.

capital cases. Appellate judges also serve on the bench of a special Court for Minors which was apparently established during the Fascist period.

Supreme Court of Cassation. In the regular judicial ladder the highest rung is occupied by the Supreme Court of Cassation (*Corte suprema di cassazione*) at Rome. It is comparable to the tribunal of the same name in Paris. It might also be compared with the United States Supreme Court except for the fact that the latter possesses the power to review the question of the constitutionality of legislation and hence may be said to combine the functions of the Court of Cassation and Italy's new Constitutional Court.[10] Various sections of the Court of Cassation, of which there are three for civil cases and an equal number for criminal cases, constitute tribunals of last resort for appeals from the lower courts.[11] Appeal is restricted to cases where procedural or jurisdictional errors are alleged or where a defendant claims there has been an abuse of discretion. An appropriate section of the Court of Cassation may void or uphold judgments or require new trials. Each criminal or civil section usually has approximately twenty judges (Councilors), those with seniority in point of service acting as section presidents. The senior judge is known as the First President of the Court and has certain supervisory powers over the tribunal. At one time there were five courts of cassation in Italy, each the equal of the other; their consolidation into a single court at Rome in 1923 was one of the earlier and more acceptable of the Fascist judicial reforms.

The Constitutional Court. Of potentially great importance as a conservative influence in Italian politics and of outstanding interest to political scientists is the new Constitutional Court (*Corte costituzionale*). Both the formal phraseology of the Constitution [12] and the legislation creating this court unquestionably invest it with power to review and nullify legislation and decrees with the force of law, if they are found to be inconsistent with the court's interpretation of the Constitution. Hence, as Professor Mario Einaudi suggests, the establishment of this tribunal reflects a desire of the Constituent Assembly to place the written Constitution and subsequent constitutional laws "beyond the temptation of legislators." [13] If that desire is realized, the Assembly will not only have placed judicial metes and bounds to the policies of politicians, but it will have broken the tradition of legislative supremacy which, in Italy as in France, has been dominant throughout the democratic era.

In setting up the new Court, serious efforts have been made to secure a qualified, politically independent, magistracy. Terms of the fifteen judges, which will normally be fixed at twelve years, have been arranged to expire at different times so as to permit of partial renewal of the bench.[14] Incumbent judges are not immediately re-eligible upon the expiration of their terms. Candidates for the judgeships must be active or retired magistrates of the highest

---

10 See p. 296.
11 This statement may no longer be quite accurate in view of the jurisdiction of the new Constitutional Court.
12 Constitution, Arts. 134–137 inclusive.
13 *Op. cit.*, p. 674.
14 However the original appointees are each assured a 12-year term, Constitution, Transitional Provisions, Clause III.

regular or administrative courts, law professors, or attorneys who have practiced for at least twenty years. Five of the appointments are made under the authority of the President of the Republic and five by Parliament in joint session. The remaining five judges are appointed by the courts, that is, three by the Supreme Court of Cassation, one by the Council of State, and one by the Court of Accounts. Jurisdiction extends to questions about the constitutionality of national and regional laws and legislative decrees or decree laws and to issues involving the constitutional distribution of powers among the organs of the central Government, between the central Government and a Region, and between Regions.[15] Legislation outlining the exact nature of the Court's authority is quite explicit as to just when and under what circumstances it may take jurisdiction of a case. Apparently this may be done whenever the issue of constitutionality is raised by a presiding magistrate during the course of a judicial proceeding or when it is raised by either party to a proceeding and his action has not been vetoed by the presiding magistrate as irrelevant or unfounded. When augmented with sixteen additional lay members chosen by Parliament, the Court may also try impeachments brought against the President of the Republic or the Ministers. Needless to say, Italian jurists and their brethren abroad will watch the evolution of this unusual tribunal with keen interest.[16]

LOCAL GOVERNMENT AND LOCAL ADMINISTRATION

Local Political and Administrative Areas. Establishment of the Republic has apparently served to augment Italian interest in local government. All of Italy continues to be divided into some 7,757 communes and ninety provinces, each of which is an autonomous local government corporation or quasi-corporation as well as a local territorial unit for the operation of the central Government's administrative services. For electoral and other purely administrative purposes, the Republic has also revived the *circondari,* historic equivalent to the French *arrondissement,*[17] which the Fascists abolished in 1927. In addition to this traditional machinery, the creators of the new Italy have set up the Region, a new level of self-government midway between the province and Rome. In area, the Regions are often roughly coextensive with certain of the historic Regions, the consolidation of which produced united Italy and which, known as compartments, have sometimes served in the past as relatively unimportant judicial and administrative units.

The Commune: Its Government. With slight variations the restored pattern of local government at the communal and provincial levels follows pre-Fascist models.[18] The principal institution of communal government is

[15] Some have suggested that the Court was necessary to protect the autonomy of the newly-established Regions; but this seems to be a rather narrow conception of the true motives animating its creators.

[16] A summary of the legislation affecting the Constitutional Court appears in *Annuario parlamentare,* 1949–50, pp. 255–56. There is also an excellent article on this tribunal by Michele La Torre entitled "Le garanzie costituzionali nella nuova costituzione" in *Il Centenario del parlamento,* Rome, 1948, pp. 439 *ff.*

[17] See p. 226.

[18] See p. 227.

once again the Communal Council (*Consiglio comunale*), members of which are elected for four years under a suffrage law which, as in the case of parliamentary elections, qualifies all adult men and women. In some communes—those with less than 30,000 inhabitants—the membership of the Council varies from fifteen to forty. In communes with more than 30,000 inhabitants, the Council may have as many as eighty members and they are elected by a modified system of proportional representation in which the party with the largest vote may win as many as two-thirds of the seats. Out of its membership, the Council selects the Syndic (*Sindaco*), or chief executive officer of the commune, and the so-called Communal Committee (*Giunta comunale*) which serves at one and the same time as a sort of watch-dog committee for the Communal Council and as an advisory body for the Syndic. As in former times, the Syndic represents the commune before the courts, promulgates local ordinances, negotiates contracts, and supervises the commune's property and administrative services. He is also a local officer of the national Government and, under the jurisdiction of the Prefect, supervises the collection of vital statistics, keeps army and electoral registers, and maintains order and security. The Syndic's chief administrative assistant is the communal secretary. In addition there are the necessary legal advisers and administrative departments and services. Although a great metropolitan commune like Rome, Milan, or Naples technically has the same pattern of municipal government as some small, rural, hilltop commune, the metropolitan commune has a most extensive and extremely complex administrative establishment and provides its residents not only with the normal municipal services but sometimes with a good many others of an economic or cultural character which betray a considerable emphasis upon municipal socialism.

The Province: Its Autonomous Government. Pre-Mussolinian democratic principles have also been reapplied to the autonomous government of the Italian province. The Provincial Council (*Consiglio provinciale*), like its communal counterpart, is elected popularly. A small number of the Council, usually not more than fifteen, known collectively as the Provincial Deputation (*Deputazione provinciale*), acts for its principal when the latter is not in session. The chief executive officer of the autonomous provincial administration is the provincial President (*Presidente*). Alone, or in conjunction with the secretary-general of the province and the Provincial Council or its Deputation, the President supervises the provincial services and the corporation's personnel, local public works, and fiscal activities.

The Prefect and His Powers. As in former years, President and autonomous provincial administration in republican Italy are wholly overshadowed by the Prefect (*Prefetto*) for whom the territory of a province continues to be the normal area of jurisdiction. This official, who has a lengthy and significant history in Italy [19] as in France, is the local emissary of Rome. Specifically, he is the local emissary of the Minister of the Interior and exercises that bureaucratic potentate's vast powers over local affairs. These include authority

[19] For comments on this official in pre-Fascist Italy, see p. 226.

to safeguard the public peace, security, and health and to supervise the conduct of elections; and in exercising such authority, the Prefect necessarily assumes control over local police and related public forces and issues appropriate orders to such local officials as the Syndic of the commune and the President of the province. A corollary prefectoral power, arising out of this supervisory authority, is that of issuing decrees with the force of law. A special council consisting of representatives of the provincial administration and prefectoral appointees provides the local "consultative" administrative agency, that is, an advisory body for the Prefect and a local administrative court.

Other Prefectoral Powers. Coordination of the activities of the field agents of certain other Rome Ministries is another responsibility confided to the Prefect, and he is supposed to serve as a sort of liaison officer for such national agents in their contacts with autonomous local government agencies and officials. Finally, the Prefect has immense powers over local government. He may investigate the administration of the commune and province, review and veto acts of the local government authorities, call them to account, force them to act when the law requires and, in extreme cases, supersede local authority. Prefectoral prerogatives over Italian local government are the substance of a system of "administrative" control which stands in sharp contrast to the traditional American system of impersonal "judicial" control of local government. The authority which continues to be vested in the Prefect reminds all observers that, if local government in Italy is democratic, it is democracy tempered by a form of "bureaucratic centralism." As thus tempered, it provides a blend of the amateur and the official for which perhaps France offers the only counterpart.

The Region. We turn now to the Region, latest creation in the hierarchy of local governmental and administrative arrangements in Italy. Nineteen Regions [20] are named in the Constitution, and provision is made for the creation of additional Regions as well as for the consolidation of existing ones.[21] Each of these areas is to have its own constitution and governmental structure, the latter following the local governmental pattern traditional in modern Italy. Legislative and other discretionary powers, conferred upon a Region by the national Constitution, are to be exercised by the Regional Council (*Consiglio regionale*); and executive and administrative authority are to reside in the Regional Executive Committee (*Giunta*) whose President will act as the formal head of the Region's government and symbolize the Region's juridical personality.

Region and State. The thinking that inspired creation of this new level of government was quite radical and apparently aimed at a national State so decentralized that it would savor of a federal regime. However, by the time the concept of the new Region emerged from the Constituent Assembly, it was something distinctly less significant than a component of a federal system.

[20] According to Art. 131, they are: Piemonte, Valle d'Aosta, Lombardia, Trentino-Alto, Adige, Veneto, Friuli-Venezia Giulia, Liguria, Emilia-Romagna, Toscana, Umbria, Marche, Lazio, Abruzzi e Molise, Campania, Puglia, Basilicata, Calabria, Sicilia, and Sardegna.
[21] Art. 132.

To be sure, the Constitution anticipates that the Region will develop its own sources of revenue and it confers a long list of powers; [22] but the Region is also expected to rely upon the national exchequer for support, and nearly all the powers conferred upon the Region seem to be of a traditionally local character, more likely to conflict with the existing prerogatives of province or commune than with the prerogatives of Parliament. Moreover, since it is anticipated that province, commune, and other existing local agencies will serve as the Region's administrative instrumentalities, the net effect of the creation and empowerment of the Region may well be to reduce the political significance now possessed by province and commune.

Earlier it was pointed out that, through the intervention of the new Constitutional Court,[23] the Regions are assured of a judicial determination of a jurisdictional dispute with the central authorities. Indeed the Constitution [24] has provided elaborate machinery for resolving differences between the central Government and a Regional Council which, in case of failure, relies upon the Court to settle the issue. Nevertheless, in practice, control of regional discretion is likely to assume an administrative rather than a judicial form. Such, at least, is the Italian tradition and the tradition is influential. Moreover, instruments to develop such administrative control of the Region are not lacking in the existing constitutional scheme. Thus Article 124 of the basic law speaks of a "Commissioner of the Government" (*Commissario del governo*) who is to be sent to the Region's capital, there to coordinate the administrative functions of the central Government with those exercised by the regional apparatus. On paper, at least, the Commissioner looks like another, albeit a somewhat glorified, Prefect. Other existing constitutional provisions point up this suggestion of administrative control of the Region by the central authorities. Thus through the instrumentality of the President of the Republic, the Cabinet, acting in conjunction with a parliamentary committee on regional affairs, may dissolve a Regional Council. The reasons for such action may range from the alleged exigencies of national security to allegations that the Regional Council or its Executive Committee have violated the Constitution or the laws. Most of the regional system is still in the blueprint stage; hence it is difficult to determine how much real autonomy will be achieved. Whatever develops, however, is likely to be a far cry from the relatively self-sufficient, politically independent series of local regimes which some of the more particularistic politicians originally thought they had secured.

Regions with Special Autonomy. For the two island areas, Sicily and Sardinia, where a separatist tradition has occasionally reared its head, and for three other areas, Valle d'Aosta, Trentino-Alto Adige, and Friuli-Venezia Giulia, where there are minority and frontier problems, the Constitution has required a special form of regional autonomy.[25] This is to be guaranteed by a special statute for each Region thus identified, each such statute to have the status of a constitutional law juridically on a par with the national Constitu-

22 Arts. 117, 119.
23 See p. 296.
24 Art. 127.
25 Art. 116.

tion. At least four of these statutes, each providing an autonomous governmental system for one of the Regions in question, were enacted in February,
1948. As a result, Sicilians may take some sort of satisfaction in the fact that
their Regional Council is to be known as the "Regional Assembly" and in
other symbolic concessions to local particularist feeling; and other special Regions may feel that their local interests and distinctive cultural traits secure
greater protection under this specialized regional regime. In general, however,
the distinction between special Regions and the regular ones is formal and
juridical.

Outlook for Local Government in Italy. Creation of the Regions and
the concomitant renewal of popular forms of local government at other territorial levels may well herald a sort of local-government risorgimento in contemporary Italy. In turn, this may reduce the hitherto preponderant influence
of national officials in local matters and presumably extirpate, or at least reduce appreciably, the electoral and other abuses which in the past have been
attributed to that influence. All friends of the new republican regime fondly
hope that such will be the case. At the same time, it must be reiterated that the
nineteenth-century tradition of bureaucratic centralization, personified in the
Prefect, is apparently as strong as ever; and it is unlikely that any mere proliferation of local-government mechanics will extirpate that influence. Neither
will the expansion of local-government arrangements, such as is provided by
the Region, stop the steady expansion of the number and variety of national
officials sent to keep the Prefect company at the local level. Besides the more
or less traditional financial, police, and judicial officers, these include health
and education inspectors, agricultural experts, public-works engineers, heads
of a variety of public enterprises, and many others who personify the new
centralism inspired by the twentieth century's collectivism and the centripetal
influences of our technology. Contemporary Italy may indeed achieve a genuine form of local autonomy; but such an achievement is much more likely to
stem from a more broadly diffused sense of political morality and responsibility
at the "grass roots" than from added local governmental and administrative
machinery.

CHAPTER VII

REPUBLICAN ITALY'S POLITICAL PARTIES

Historic Parties Continue. As noted earlier,[1] one of the surprising facts about the restoration of free Government in Italy was the immediate reactivation of most of the historic political parties. Parliamentary politicians, familiar with political labels in the Chamber and Senate of 1919, find many of these labels used in the Chamber and Senate of 1952. Indeed, in a great many cases, contemporary parties trace their origins back to the years which antedate Mussolini. The long night of Fascism did not snuff out their existence. Sometimes, by means of an underground organization or an organization in exile, the free parties of Giolittian Italy continued at least a *pro forma* existence right through the two decades of Fascist ascendancy. Even when a new label is used, it does not necessarily mean a new party but one which has merely changed its name. As we have already pointed out, this is true of the largest of all the contemporary parties, the Christian Democrats, who are simply the *Popolari* of 1919 under a new name.

But if most of the historic parties have continued into post-Mussolinian Italy, it is also true that important shifts have occurred in their relative importance. Of greatest significance in this respect is the changed complexion of the Left already foreshadowed in 1919 as the liberal monarchical period was drawing to a close. The "Old Left," composed of the various liberal groups which provided parliamentary support for Giolitti's Cabinets, though still in existence, is but a shadow of its former self. Power has now shifted irrevocably to parties which, in 1919, had only just come into a position of political strength and had not yet had a real opportunity to exert parliamentary influence.[2] These include the Christian Democrats and the various Marxian groups. Together they account for more than 80 per cent of the parliamentary membership. As Cabinet makers and reservoirs of political leadership, these parties of the "New Left" have apparently permanently eclipsed the old Giolittian Left.

[1] See p. 269.
[2] See p. 248.

THE RIGHT

The Liberal Party. What remains of "Giolittian Liberals" in contemporary Italy serves as the most important, or at least the most distinguished and politically trustworthy, component of the political Right. In 1951 such Liberals and their allies could count upon the political loyalty of some seventeen Senators and eighteen Deputies; and they still exerted a political influence disproportionate to their numbers, Liberal politicians having participated in all governing coalitions from 1944 to 1950. The issue which precipitated the Liberal defection from the sixth de Gasperi Cabinet, in January, 1950, was that over the proposed application of the proportional principle to electoral legislation, the Liberals objecting to the failure of the Christian Democrats to apply that principle as generously and as widely as possible, particularly to local elections. In general, Liberals remain loyal to the ideal of a secular State and frown upon the preferred position given the Roman Catholic Church in the new Constitution and in the policies of the dominant party. The Liberal majority is probably still pro-monarchist in sympathy although the party as a whole has loyally accepted the Republic. Liberals are likely to take a critical view of certain welfare and collectivistic policies of other parties, farther to the Left; generally opposed radical land reform; and remain devoted to the cause of a pluralistic society, a private-enterprise type of economic system, and to customary civil liberties.

The Monarchists. Among numerous smaller partisan aggregations on the Right which have a degree of permanence, mention might be made of the Monarchists, officially styled the "National Monarchist Party." The fall of the Savoy dynasty in 1946 has largely removed the party's *raison d'être;* but it remains loyal to monarchism as a social and political principle and would probably give at least tacit support to any overt movement for a restoration. On most social issues, the party is generally strongly conservative in its views. As the so-called "National Freedom Bloc," it won sixteen seats in the elections to the Constituent Assembly in 1946 and mustered about 5 per cent of the vote. Shorn of some of its allies in the Chamber elections of 1948, it yet managed to win some fourteen seats and enjoyed about 3 per cent of the total vote. Monarchist lists are usually most popular in the southern peninsular area.

Neo-Fascist Movements. Also on the Right, but much more dangerous to the existing order, are the various neo-Fascist movements. One such organization, the so-called "Movement of the Common Man" (*Uomo Qualunque*), had a rather meteoric rise in public favor in 1946 when it won some thirty seats in the Constituent Assembly and ran many successful candidates in local elections including the municipal elections in Rome. Subsequently the Common Man Movement deteriorated, to be succeeded by an even more obviously neo-Fascist group calling itself the Italian Social Movement (*Movimento sociale italiano*). The MSI had six seats in the Chamber in 1951 and in the local elections of that year its lists polled about 4 per cent of the total

national vote.[3] Its political and journalistic leaders, many of them once ranking members of Mussolini's Fascist hierarchy, endorse that fallen leader's
totalitarian ideas, especially his conception of an authoritarian political system
and a monopolistic political party. Its political tacticians also make vigorous
efforts to win acclaim by engaging in combat with the Communists, preferably
in street battles and through direct-action techniques such as Mussolini found
so useful in the early 1920's and which the parliamentary State ultimately
found were so fatal to its own integrity. Since the Constitution expressly forbids the revival of Fascism and since many steps, recounted on an earlier
page,[4] have been taken to purge the nation of the Fascist menace, there is
little excuse for tolerating such a revival as is implicit in the Italian Social
Movement. Legislation developed in 1950 permits the Cabinet to suspend
neo-Fascist organizations and authorizes the courts to disband them and
punish their leaders for publicly advocating Fascist ideology. Among the constitutional parties there is little fear that legislation of this type will jeopardize
the democratic or libertarian character of the present Italian regime.

THE CENTER

Center Parties—The Christian Democrats. Identification of a "Center"
in Italian politics presents certain difficulties, since all parties, save some already mentioned, would undoubtedly consider themselves a part of the "Left"
both for historic reasons and for reasons of party strategy. Any realistic
classification would, nevertheless, place the largest of all the Italian parties,
officially known as the Party of Christian Democracy (*Democrazia cristiana*)
in such a Center position. Its program is a moderate one and its policies appeal to constituents of almost every walk of life and of nearly every level of
society. Indeed, largely because Christian Democracy counts upon the support
of so cosmopolitan and vertical a class structure, clearly defined left and right
wings have emerged within the party. Often these are emphatically opposed
to one another as, for example, in July, 1951, when the jousting of factions
within the party over the Government's fiscal and other policies helped to pre-
cipitate the break-up of de Gasperi's sixth Cabinet. To keep the peace between
these factions, compromise and essentially opportunist concessions to both
radicals and conservatives cannot be avoided by the party policy-makers.
Ideologically, Christian Democracy is oriented in the direction of the philosophy of the Roman Catholic Church's encyclicals on social issues, especially
such seminal ones as *Rerum novarum* and *Quadregessimo anno.* Indeed it is
the Church's views on social justice that provide the ideological cement binding together, in a common political organization, people of the most diverse
interests and social standing. Christian Democracy's Church-inspired social
consciousness is revealed in the party's support of adequate social legislation
and the efficient administration of such legislation. It is also apparent in the

[3] In Sicily the MSI candidates, leagued with Monarchists, polled as much as 8 per cent of
the total vote.
[4] See p. 268.

party's efforts to promote a sturdy, free, trade-union movement (though not necessarily independent of the party itself); to subsidize housing for the urban worker; to break up large estates and vest title to the subdivided tracts in the peasant cultivator; and in the program, recently undertaken, to raise the economic and social level of some of the more backward southern areas. Dr. de Gasperi's followers have also been officially sympathetic to limited programs of industrial nationalization, especially where the industry in question was deemed monopolistic in character; on the other hand, except for certain minority left-wing elements within the party, they have never suggested any hostility to private business.

Christian Democracy's Influence on the New Constitution. Because of sheer strength of numbers, Christian Democracy's role in the Constituent Assembly was considerable, and it was able to influence rather remarkably the foundations of the new Republic. As was noted earlier, Christian Democrats in the Assembly strongly favored corporative political institutions for Italy including political representation of economic and professional interests. In thus voicing their predilection for a corporative system they were merely voicing one of the cherished constitutional ideals of Catholic Parties in Europe generally, most of whom had advocated corporative constitutional principles long before Mussolini bastardized them. Defeated in this effort, the party applied its energies successfully toward incorporation of "regionalism" in the Constitution. The autonomous Region—the new level of local government superior to that of the province—was inspired in part by Christian Democracy's fear of authoritarian and centralized government and in part by the hope that greater local responsibility for public affairs would widen popular participation and responsibility in government generally and thus strengthen democratic competence at every governmental level. As might be expected, the party took advanced ground in developing a favorable constitutional position for the Roman Church, having been largely responsible for the inclusion, in the new republican *statuto fondamentale,* of the essential provisions of the Lateran Agreements.[5] A corollary of this policy respecting Church and State is to be discerned in the party's support of private schools which, of course, mean Church schools. The party advocates public financial support for Church schools equivalent to the support rendered public schools.

Its International Policies. Internationally, Christian Democracy's orientation is wholly toward the West. It takes a position favorable to virtually all policies which seek to strengthen Western Europe and its allies against Soviet Russia and her satellites, including economic cooperation under the European Recovery Plan, the integration of Western Europe both politically and economically, and the implementation of the North Atlantic Pact and Western European defense plans. Like all other constitutional Parties, the Christian Democrats stand four-square in favor of the ultimate return to Italy of Trieste and adjacent territory. Even so, they have consistently sought to foster friendly relations with Tito's Yugoslavia, a policy which became more realis-

[5] See p. 316 for provisions of the Agreements.

tic when Tito and the Cominform fell out in 1948. Allied to the Trieste policy was that of preserving as much as possible of the nation's former colonial domain. Relatively unsuccessful in this, Christian Democratic leaders have not been slow to censure the leadership of certain Western powers, especially of the United Kingdom, for allegedly having frustrated what are regarded as legitimate Italian aspirations.

The Party Continues Coalition Policy. As noted elsewhere, the majority position of de Gasperi's Party in the Chamber of Deputies after the 1948 elections [6] has not tempted it to abandon coalitionism. The Christian Democratic leader has continued to share responsibility with one or two small groups who have served on his Cabinets since he first organized the Government. Apparently the coalition policy is continued because it is thought the Cabinet will acquire greater national authority and support and possibly also because de Gasperi considers his own party, powerful though it may be, insufficiently united and disciplined to wear the mantle of authority alone as is customary with a majority party in the United Kingdom.

Right-Wing Socialists. One of the groups especially favored by Dr. de Gasperi for his governing coalitions, and which may also be considered a part of the Center, is the Socialist right wing led by Giuseppe Saragat. Officially styled the "Socialist Party of Italian Workers," it joined forces, at least transiently, in the elections of 1948 with a minor dissident Socialist following, the resulting coalition adopting the label of "Socialist Unity Party." Historically the *Saragatiani* constitute the more moderate wing of the Italian Socialist Party which was riven asunder in January, 1947, on the issue of Socialist collaboration with Communism and Communist sympathizers. Although their intellectual orientation is Marxist, Saragat's Socialists insist upon achieving the workers' millennium, if it is to be achieved at all, within the framework of the democratic parliamentary State and with the traditional freedoms and civil liberties of the individual unimpaired by the exigencies of any Marxist blueprint. This gradualist "constitutional" Socialism is perhaps their most distinctive ideal—at least it is the ideal, insistence upon which caused Saragat's followers to split with their left-wing brethren and to secede in 1947 from the then unified Italian Socialist Party.

Policies of the Right-Wing Socialists. As befits a relatively small party, Signor Saragat's followers emphatically endorse proportional representation both in local and national elections. As good Marxists they favor a generous dose of nationalization; division of the landed estates in the interest of peasant proprietors; amelioration of the regressive burden of direct taxation of which Italy appears to be so fond; a State-stimulated policy of full employment; a strong trade-union movement and preservation of labor's right to strike except possibly in the case of essential public services; and, of course, a maximum number of social services identified with contemporary State paternalism. This splinter party is Western in its international views, a good friend

[6] The party had 307 seats (53 per cent) in the Chamber and 151 seats (43 per cent) in the Senate.

of the ideal of Western European unity and of Western European cooperation
with America in opposing the spread of international Communism.[7] From
such Western association it would exclude only Franco Spain, and it takes a
firm stand against occasional proposals of the Christian Democrats that the
Caudillo's regime be recognized. The party is also a strong supporter of the
lay State and hence occasionally finds itself opposing de Gasperi's followers
on ecclesiastical matters. But differences of viewpoint on this and other matters have not prevented loyal service on de Gasperi-dominated Cabinets
which was continuous from the time the *Saragatiani* set up shop as a separate
entity. Qualms about associating with clericals did overtake the leadership
of the party toward the end of 1949 and for a time it appeared that the party
might go into opposition; but such qualms were dissipated successfully and
collaboration continued until the spring of 1951. At that time a desire to
merge with the Unitarian Socialist Party required the resignation of the
party's representatives from the de Gasperi Government, and the three existing right-wing Socialist ministers in the Cabinet accordingly withdrew.

With their allies in the elections of 1948 the *Saragatiani* won some thirty-
three seats in the Chamber and were able to claim the loyalty of twenty-six
Senators. Voting strength in those elections hugged the two-million mark and
constituted about 7 per cent of the total vote cast. As we shall see later, the
Saragatiani have lost their partisan identity, at least for the time being, be-
cause they have followed certain other Socialist groups into the so-called
Unitarian Socialist Party. In this new organization, however, the right-wing
Socialists are likely to be the dominant group because they are the most
numerous; and whether they move forward alone or in conjunction with other
Socialist segments, they will continue to exert a major influence in directing
Italian Marxism towards liberal parliamentary ideals and a moderate, albeit
progressive, social policy.

The Republican Party. Examination of Italy's political Center would be
incomplete without some comment on the Republican Party (*Partito repub-
blicano italiano*). Harking back to Mazzini and Garibaldi and the romantic
republican ideals of the mid-nineteenth century, this party has had a long and
honorable history. In 1948 it had the satisfaction of realizing its historic ideal,
namely, the transformation of Italy from a monarchy into a republic and the
proscription of the Savoy dynasty. Italian Republicans remain professedly
anticlerical and supporters of the secular State; and they demonstrate sincere
attachment to civil liberty and to parliamentary traditions. Their interest in
the labor movement is relatively strong and they are usually in the van of the
supporters of social reform through public action. In 1948 the party elected
nine Deputies and polled somewhat more than a half million votes or about
2 per cent of the total cast. Despite its small size it has wielded considerable
influence on policy recently, having participated in all governing coalitions
since 1947. Part of the secret of its strength is to be discovered in its excellent

---

[7] But a majority of the Party has occasionally opposed Saragat and a minority on the
issue of supporting the Atlantic Pact.

leadership. The Republican chief, Randolfo Pacciardi, since his somewhat disillusioning days of association with the Communists in the Spanish Civil War, has acquired stature as republican Italy's Minister of Defense and one of her stalwart defenders of free ideals against Communism.

Minor Center Parties. As noted in an earlier chapter,[8] at least two additional minor Center groups played a role of some importance in the transition from Fascism to the republican parliamentary regime. These were the Labor Democrats, holdover of the Reformist Socialists of an earlier day, and the Action Party. Neither of these parties survived the transitional period in any strength. The Labor Democrats joined with the Liberals in the elections of 1946 and virtually lost their identity. The Actionists, suffering from internal dissension, eventually split into fragments none of which received enough support at the polls to pull much weight in the party struggle for power in Parliament.

THE LEFT

The Italian Socialist Party and the Popular Front. If Signor Saragat's Socialists may be identified with the political Center, virtually all other Socialists in Italy ought to be identified with the political Left. Of these the most important is the left-wing remnant of the erstwhile unified Italian Socialist Party. This remnant continues to use the party's traditional name. Under various leaders, of whom probably the best known outside of Italy is the former Vice Premier, Pietro Nenni, the Italian Socialist Party can still claim the support of some two and one-half million voters and of some fifty Deputies in the Chamber. Nominally the party adheres to the gradualist Marxist principles of other West European Socialist Parties; actually it is a captive of Communism and both tactically and ideologically it behaves as the Communist Party's junior partner. This slavish status originated in a pact for unity of action which the Socialist and Communist Parties signed in October, 1946. It was discontent with the political discipline imposed by this pact that, as was noted earlier, caused the secession of the right-wing Socialists in January, 1947. As a result of the unity pact, the Socialist Party does not even enjoy electoral freedom, invariably joining forces with Communism in common lists in both local and national elections under the label of the "Democratic Popular Front."

Socialists as "Fellow-Travelers." Servitude to Communism is even more manifest in the Socialist Party's policies. In domestic matters, it advocates such Socialist shibboleths as nationalization of industry, abolition of monopolies, national planning, and other orthodox Marxian formulas for social action which Communism likewise endorses. The Party also advocates the lay State, improved educational opportunity for all, land reform, and advanced social-welfare legislation. More obvious evidence of Communist "conditioning" is to be discerned in the Socialist Party's views on constitutional matters and foreign policy. As respects governmental processes and basic civic values,

[8] See p. 269.

orthodox Socialism seems to be quite as "realistic" as any disciplined member of the Cominform. Apparently, for Signor Nenni's partisans, the "administrative discipline" of Communism, polite euphemism for totalitarian dictatorship, holds no terror; nor do personal freedoms, civil liberties, and representative institutions enjoy the priority that is assigned them among the Socialists of the Right. As respects foreign policy, the party advocates, at least in theory, a neutral course for Italy, proposing that the nation join no bloc but cooperate with all "democratic" states. For the greater part, this is simply double-talk, a sort of phraseological veneer to obscure somewhat its hostility to the European Recovery Plan, to the Atlantic Pact, and to any form of Western orientation; and to render more palatable to some of its followers its diplomatic support of that negation of democracy known as a "peoples' democracy." The Socialist Party may be merely an ally of Communism; but the difference between alliance and outright merger is largely academic. The distinction would cease to be even academic if, as in Czechoslovakia not so long ago, Communism in Italy should essay a *coup d'état* and find it necessary to crack the disciplinary whip over Marxians who had been Communists in all but name. For their support of the Cominform, Nenni Socialists were suspended in June, 1948, by the international Socialist movement, then officially known as the Committee for International Socialist Conferences (Comisco); and in May, 1949, the Nenni Socialists were expelled from the international organization.

Minor Socialists of the Left. From what has been said it would appear that the most important fact about Signor Nenni's Socialists is their inability to call their political soul their own. A somewhat similar observation may be made about the odds and ends of Marxist sects and schismatics who, as in the past, continue to infest Italian politics. Chief among these, and the only group that is likely to achieve any prominence in the future, are the Unitarian Socialists (*Partito socialista unitario*) who held their first congress at Florence in December, 1949. Ostensibly this group's purpose was to heal the breach between the Left and the Right in the Socialist world. This aim it sought to achieve by defining a kind of Socialist "third force" which would appeal to both political extremes among the Marxians. In the international arena, Socialists were to refuse to support the policies of the predominantly Christian Democratic Cabinet. Instead they were to be "neutral" and support neither the West nor the East, thus allegedly assuring an "independent" diplomacy for Italy. Although this formula for unity won adherents from among both extremes of Socialism, that is, from among the followers of both Saragat and Nenni, only the former and one or two small independent Marxian groups joined the new organization *en masse.* The agreement which brought the right-wing Socialists into the new combination provided, moreover, for a considerable modification of some of the principles which the Unitarians had originally adopted. Although the right-wing Socialists agreed to end their cooperation with the de Gasperi Government, as the more militant among their new allies had demanded, most of Signor Saragat's followers insisted that a firm stand be taken against any so-called "neutralist" or "third force" policy in international affairs, and they also demanded that their new associates support an anti-Communist policy both in international and domestic matters.

It is possible that this new Socialist grouping may become the nucleus of a reunited "gradualist" Socialist Party which, in time, may even reclaim the followers of Signor Nenni from their docile attachment to Communism. Such a prospect, however, appears remote. Membership in a common political organization has by no means overcome differences in policy among the groups presently associated; and if that membership were to be extended to groups even farther to the Left, it is quite unlikely that even the pretense of organizational unity could be maintained. Moreover, the history of Italian Socialism— a history replete with doctrinal conflicts and organizational schisms—offers little reason for optimism: instead of becoming the great unified political movement of constitutional Socialism, the Unitarian Socialist Party could, in due course, add just another splinter to political Marxism in Italy.

The Italian Communist Party. Farthest left, of course, is the Communist Party of Italy, in point of numbers the largest Communist aggregation in Europe after that of the Soviet Union itself, and among Italian parties, the largest after the Christian Democrats. Up to 1951 it was ably led by its chief strategist and ideologue, Palmiro Togliatti, a former divinity student, and one or two of his lieutenants, well-known in the Cominform world. As already stated, the party went into the opposition in 1947 and has since been Italy's most dangerous fifth column. Officially the Italian party, like Communist aggregations elsewhere, advocates the usual social and economic nostrums dear to the heart of Marxism; but the Communist emphasis is upon the class struggle and upon an uncompromising hostility to the Italian social and constitutional structure. In foreign policy, it rarely deviates from the Kremlin line, however tortuous that line may be, and, under cover of the usual Communist slogan of cooperation with democratic and peace-loving countries, it vindicates a sycophantic devotion to Cominform diplomacy,[9] however aggressive, and a ruthless vilification of every Western power, especially of the United States.

Communism's Political Influence Assayed. In a previous chapter,[10] a detailed description has already been given of the effort made by the Communists and their political stooges, the Italian Socialist Party, to win power by means of an electoral majority in 1948. Decisively beaten in this attempt, they have continued to exert pressure through strikes, sabotage in industry, malicious propaganda, and street demonstrations. Besides resisting every overt Communist threat, the Government has recently struck at Communism's power over the labor unions. Legislation has outlawed strikes for manifestly political motives and has sought to curb Communism's control of organized labor in other ways. As already related, in the elections of 1948, the Communists and their Popular Front allies, the Socialists, won 182 seats in the Chamber, 132 of which were Communist, and polled some eight million votes

---

[9] Signs of Titoist "deviationism" did, however, appear in 1951.
[10] See p. 275.

of which two-thirds were Communist votes. Party statisticians have asserted that card-carrying, dues-paying Communists totaled more than two and one-half million. More recent estimates by somewhat more neutral statisticians indicate that, though the party may have had close to that number in 1948, it lost almost a million members in the next twelve months. Even so, Communism easily maintains its status as Italy's second largest party. Supporters are still to be found in great numbers in the industrial centers of the North and, oddly enough, in recent years particularly, in some of the more depressed agricultural areas of the South. The persistence of its hold on the masses was demonstrated in the local elections of 1951 when the percentage of the total vote going to Communism and its Popular Front allies actually rose above the level of 1948.

THE LABOR MOVEMENT

The Political Nature of Italian Trade Unionism. As in most European countries, organized labor in Italy has a vigorous tradition of political action, so much so that labor unions are often quite frankly recognized as auxiliaries of political parties. They thus differ from American unions which, until the last decade or two, have at least professed to be nonpartisan and more interested in bargaining directly with management for economic benefits than in acting as a political pressure group. Italian labor unions may, therefore, quite properly be considered in a chapter devoted to political parties.

General Italian Confederation of Labor. Trade-union organization was revived in Italy during the halcyon period of cooperation among the parties in June, 1944; and the three mass political organizations, Communist, Socialist, and Christian Democrat, having at that time ostensibly somewhat similar social blueprints, gave their blessing to a common labor organization. This was known as the General Italian Confederation of Labor or CGIL (*Confederazione generale italiana del lavoro*). First in the field and under the broadest possible political auspices, the Confederation quickly gathered under its wing most of the various labor federations and syndicates and became the spokesman of organized labor in Italy, boasting at one time of as many as five million members. From the very beginning, however, the Confederation was weighted in favor of Communism, largely because of the success with which the Communists established and maintained their discipline over the ranks of the Socialist left wing. A professed Communist became Secretary-General of the organization, and the Confederation became one of the most vocal members of the Communist-dominated World Federation of Trade Unions (WFTU). It also became a thorn in the flesh of the Government, used or misused again and again by the Communists in their campaign of direct action.

Secession of the Non-Communists from the Confederation. After 1947, when political cooperation among the mass parties had ceased, anti-Communists in the CGIL gradually withdrew. First to go were the Christian Democratic trade unions who, in October, 1948, organized the Free General Italian Confederation of Workers. Next, during the summer of 1949, the right-wing Socialist labor leaders and those who followed the line of the Republican Party canceled their membership and formed the Italian Workers' Federation. About a year later, Christian Democrat, right-wing Socialist, and Republican labor organizations merged to form the Italian Confederation of Labor Syndicates. This principal labor competitor of the CGIL has about a million and one-half individuals enrolled in its subsidiary syndicates while the CGIL still boasts of a membership of more than four million. The non-Communist syndicates have a much larger percentage of clerical and professional workers, manual workers remaining, by and large, under Communist tutelage.

Outlook for the Italian Labor Movement. Thus the evolution of the Italian labor movement has reflected the evolution of the parties since 1946. The results of this evolution have, however, left the Communists in control of the industrial workers and admittedly provide the Cominform politicians with their most important and most disciplined source of popular support. The Government has attempted to overcome the Communist politician's influence over the manual worker by requiring a union to possess a democratic organization if it is to enjoy legal recognition.[11] The Government also demands *bona fide* elections of the leadership of a union by the rank and file. But the fact remains that the manual worker is still under the control of Italy's fifth column; and until the constitutional parties, through their new, independent, labor confederation succeed in weaning the manual worker away from Communism, their appeal to the Italian masses will continue to encounter an ideological barricade that will be difficult to surmount.

[11] As a matter of fact, the Constitution, Art. 39, states that as a condition of the public registration of a labor union, the union's by-laws must require a democratic organization.

CHAPTER VIII

SOME PROBLEMS AND POLICIES OF
THE REPUBLICAN REGIME

Loyalty to a political system is likely to be inspired, in large measure, by symbolism, tradition, and other considerations that primarily affect the emotions. But more practical considerations, appealing to the reason and self-interest of the citizen, are also involved in this phenomenon of obedience. Unless Government provides for the elementary security of the citizen and experiences at least relative success in solving major social issues and promoting material welfare, loyalty is likely to falter, allegiance to become a mere habit whose sanctions are indifference and inertia, and the citizen to become a prey of self-seeking political charlatans. In this concluding chapter, an effort will be made to identify at least the more important international and domestic problems that have challenged the ingenuity and resourcefulness of the new Italy and to comment upon the degree of success that has attended her effort to solve such problems or at least mitigate their impact where solutions are difficult or have had to be delayed for one reason or another. In so doing, we may gain insight into the quality of her statesmen and an understanding of the extent to which the new regime enjoys the support of the Italian rank and file.

FOREIGN POLICIES

Pro-Western Orientation. Having but recently suffered her greatest military disaster, Italy has understandably given priority to the problem of re-ordering her relations with the rest of the world. As respects the principal issue presented by this problem, namely, whether to orient the nation toward the Russian orbit or toward the West, the parties which have governed Italy since the close of World War II have had little difficulty in making a decision. Overwhelmingly that decision has been in favor of the West. To be sure, there have been political elements outside the Popular Front who have had doubts about too emphatic a Western orientation. They have occasionally cautioned moderation in giving endorsement to Western policies or they have suggested pursuit of that will-o'-the-wisp policy of "neutrality," so characteristic of the indecision and war-weariness of the Europe that came out of the Hitler holocaust. Others, and that includes some of the leaders of the Christian Democratic coalitions, have sometimes been quite bitter about one or more of the Western powers for their allegedly unsympathetic attitude toward Italy's colonial aspirations. Nevertheless the Western, antitotalitarian orientation in foreign policy has been instinctive with most of the governing parties: it is indeed implicit in their political and moral values and in their social outlook and can, therefore, hardly be regarded as a matter of deliberate choice.

Treaty Revision. Identification with the West has also been good politics and has undoubtedly been of advantage to the nation and its interests. Especially has this been true of the demand for revision of the Italian Peace Treaty. Modification of this instrument in Italy's favor has been the touchstone of recent Italian diplomacy, and revisionism influences the views on world questions of every Italian politician. Although the Treaty provisions still seem onerous to most Italians and probably always will, the Western nations have certainly introduced mitigating concessions, often over Soviet Russian protest, and are likely to continue doing so. Thus they have waived certain property rights assured them under the Treaty and, in contrast to Russia, have renounced reparation claims and claims on the Italian fleet. As already noted, prior to the Italian elections in 1948, the United States, the United Kingdom, and France announced they favored the return of Trieste and are now committed to assisting Italy in overcoming Yugoslav objections and Russian resistance to the liquidation of the political monstrosity known as the "Free Territory of Trieste" which these same Western powers had been chiefly instrumental in creating in 1947.

Participation in Movements for European Integration. In pursuit of her pro-Western policy, Italy has identified herself with various efforts to knit the nations of the Western bloc more firmly together. Some of these efforts proved abortive, as for example, the attempt to conclude a customs union with France in 1949. The attendant failure was due primarily to the fact that the economies of the two nations are too nearly alike. Italy also participated loyally in the effort to bring into being some form of formal European unity at Strasbourg in 1949 and 1950. Her delegations were part of a Continental bloc which sought to overcome the objections of the British and other national contingents to conferring respectable prerogatives upon Strasbourg's Council of Europe. Once more, however, her efforts brought little in the way of concrete results although they did demonstrate that Italy had resumed a status of full equality among the nations by whom she had so recently been worsted in war.

Italy and the European Recovery Plan. Distinctly more tangible results, of the greatest national advantage, flowed from Italy's participation, with her European neighbors, in the European Recovery Program. She was among the Western European Governments which submitted estimates to the United States of the assistance required under this Program, and Italy helped to establish the OEEC, the Program's European organ. During each of the first two years of the Program's operation, she received approximately a half billion dollars in gifts from the United States. Material assistance on such a scale, coming just as UNRRA, the post-War rehabilitation agency, was being liquidated, was of incalculable advantage. It reduced inflationary pressure on her economy, helped to bring Italy's international accounts into balance, and greatly stimulated investment within the country.

Western European Defense Enlists Italian Support. As the threat of aggression against the free world mounted during 1949, Italy was invited to become a signatory of the North Atlantic Pact and join the Atlantic community of states in a system of mutual defense. With so many native Communists threatening reprisals if her Government should forge this additional link with the West, there was reason for Italians to hesitate. But if their Government hesitated, it was barely noticeable; for in March, 1949, the nation's Chamber of Deputies gave the North Atlantic Pact a two-to-one majority and the Senate provided endorsement only slightly less emphatic. Since the Italian Peace Treaty severely limits Italy's armed forces, restricting her army to 250,000 men, her air force to 350 planes of all types, and her navy in a comparable manner, there is some doubt as to Italy's ability to become an effective partner in the Atlantic defense community. On the other hand, the will for loyal cooperation appears to exist; and with the matériel and other military assistance that the United States has given her, it is likely that her forces, however limited in quantity, will achieve a high standard of fighting efficiency and morale.[1]

The Broader Aspects of Italian Foreign Policy. On more than one recent occasion Italy has indicated that she would be quite willing to enlarge her diplomatic sphere and play her part in the United Nations. Realization of this ambition has been prevented by the Soviet veto, a veto which has been interposed even though the Soviet, along with the Western powers, virtually promised UN membership when Italy signed the Peace Treaty. Denied membership in the UN proper, she has sought to identify herself with the world organization through some of the specialized agencies, among them the International Labor Organization (of which Italy had been a member before the War), the International Bank and the Fund, UNESCO, and the International Refugee Organization. Italy has also been "realistic" about her relations with certain Russian "satellite" countries, especially Yugoslavia. Prospects of mutual economic advantage argue for friendly relations between these two states; and as Tito's dependence on the Kremlin waned and he developed an independent policy, hopes of an Italo-Yugoslav *rapprochement* improved greatly. Even the continuing issues of Trieste and the Istrian peninsula have failed to dampen these hopes. In its Yugoslav policy as in all others, the aims of Italian diplomacy have been to recapture, at least in part, the position which the na-

[1] In a three-power declaration on September 26, 1951, the United States, the United Kingdom, and France indicated their willingness to remove "restrictions" and "discriminations" in the Peace Treaty which "are wholly overtaken by events or have no justification in the present circumstances or affect Italy's capacity for self-defense." See *New York Times*, Sept. 27, 1951.

tion lost because of military defeat, to promote viable economic relations with other states, and to assure dependable allies in case of attack. Characteristically, despite unusual obstacles, Italian diplomacy has given a good account of itself in seeking to achieve these aims.

LIQUIDATION OF EMPIRE

Fate of Italian Colonies Undecided in Peace Treaty. Probably the most serious and certainly the most enduring effect of Italy's defeat in World War II was the loss of her colonial empire. Italian possession of Mussolini's ill-gotten gains in Ethiopia and Albania did not survive hostilities, since no moral or legal consideration prevented immediate restoration of the legitimate sovereign in these territories once *de facto* Italian control had ended. Such restoration was formally recognized and ratified in the Peace Treaty which Italy signed at Paris February 10, 1947. As noted earlier, the Treaty also disposed of the Dodecanese Islands to Greece. But on the issue of the fate of Italy's African possessions, differences among the victor powers were so great that a decision was impossible. It was accordingly agreed to put the matter over for one year, the four major powers, the United States, the United Kingdom, France, and the Soviet Union to meet once more at the end of that time to dispose of the issue. But the differences remained and, agreement proving impossible, it was finally resolved, on September 15, 1948, to entrust the fate of the former colonies to the General Assembly of the United Nations and abide by its decision. In the meantime, these territories remained under British (and French) administration.

Final Settlement Leaves Italy Little of African Empire. During this two-year interval of indecision among the powers, Italy sought valiantly to preserve some of her stake in her erstwhile African domains. In this policy she was motivated by understandable considerations of national pride and national advantage and by her desire to protect and preserve the interests of Italian citizens who, in the past, had emigrated to these territories. For a time it appeared that the persuasive diplomacy of her primary spokesmen, Dr. de Gasperi and Count Sforza, would succeed in giving Italy a temporary United Nations trusteeship over both the former Italian Somaliland and Tripolitania. But in the end the General Assembly of the United Nations rejected this proposal and voted to make Italy trustee only for Somaliland. This status was to continue for ten years, or until about 1960, at which time Somaliland was to become an independent nation. In making the Somaliland decision, the UN also decided that the former Italian colony of Libya, consisting of Tripolitania, Cyrenaica, and the Fezzan, would become an independent State and assume that status not later than January 1, 1952. Decision as to the fate of Eritrea was held over until the next session of the United Nations General Assembly in 1950 when agreement was reached to federate Eritrea with Ethiopia. The plan called for a customs union with Ethiopia and made that Government responsible for the foreign affairs and defense of the federated area. At the same time the United Nations guaranteed Eritrean local autonomy and sought to provide protection for the economic interests of Italian residents. Such, then, was the fate in 1950 of the fairly considerable overseas empire which Italy had won by costly wars, colonization, and the investment of capital over a period of some sixty years.

CHURCH AND STATE

The Lateran Agreements. The issue which provides an excellent transition from the subject of Italy's foreign policies to a consideration of her domestic policies is that of Church and State, since this issue, especially in Italy, has both foreign and internal ramifications. The so-called "Roman Question," involving both the international position of the Roman Catholic Church with its headquarters in the Vatican and the relation of the Church to Italy, plagued Italian politics for more than half a century. Adjustment of this question, through the conclusion of the Lateran Agreements on February 11, 1929, and the resulting *rapprochement* between the Church and the Italian Government were regarded by Mussolini as among his greatest achievements. Apparently there was some justice in the Fascist leader's claim because, after his demise and the fall of his regime, his successors incorporated the Lateran Agreements into Article 7 of the new republican Constitution. According to the first of these agreements, Italy recognizes the sovereignty of the Papacy over the small area within the City of Rome now known as Vatican City. Within that area the Pope functions as a temporal sovereign, the equal of any other head of State. The agreement confirmed exclusive papal jurisdiction over various ecclesiastical properties within Rome and in the immediate vicinity, including the papal summer residence at *Castel Gandolfo*. Most of the provisions of the former Law of Guarantees [2] respecting the inviolability of the head of the Church and his freedom of communication with the outside world were confirmed. The second agreement was really an integral part of the first since it merely embraced a financial indemnification for the extinction of Papal sovereignty outside of Vatican City and for the physical losses suffered by the Church following the annexation of the Papal States by the Kingdom of Italy. The sum guaranteed by the Italian Government to the Vatican Treasury was approximately one and three-quarters of a billion lire, in cash and Italian consols.

The Concordat. The third agreement, which is a formal concordat, regulates the Church's ecclesiastical functions within Italy. It proclaims Catholicism as the official religion of Italy, regulates the civil position of the Church's clerics, the appointment of its bishops and other ecclesiastical officials, and the juridical status of its religious corporations. It also provides for payment out of public funds for the maintenance of religious activities and exempts Church property from taxation. Of great importance is the Italian Government's undertaking in the Concordat to recognize the civil implications of the marriage sacrament and the rules of canon law affecting marriage. The institution of marriage comes in for special protection in the new Constitution,

[2] See p. 228.

although that document does not, as some desired, formally endorse the Church's view of the indissolubility of the marriage tie. The Concordat also pledges the Government to permit religious instruction by priests in the schools of the Republic and to allow the Church to maintain secular organizations, such as the Catholic Action, under religious auspices.[3] More important still is the Church's right to maintain schools at various levels and secure State financial assistance, a policy which seems to be confirmed in the Constitution [4] and which is certainly espoused by the leading Government party.

Significance of the Policy in the Agreements. Under the Lateran Agreements, modern Italy rejected the liberal Cavour's conception of the lay State and his policy of reducing the Catholic Church (or for that matter any Church) to the status of a purely voluntary organization. Catholicism is Italy's established and official religion. The republican Constitution nevertheless states that all confessions are "equally free under the law," permits them to establish an autonomous organization, and invites them to negotiate what might be called "little concordats" which, in the manner of the Catholic Concordat, presumably would govern the relation of the State and non-Catholic confessions.[5] Relatively the latter are so few in Italy that this provision of the Constitution is probably fated to become somewhat academic.[6] It does nevertheless establish the principle of equality for all religious denominations.

AGRARIAN REFORM

Social and Economic Justification for Redistribution of the Land. Turning now to purely internal issues, we shall consider first the one with an acknowledged priority in Italian politics, namely, agrarian reform. Italy is still primarily an agricultural country, almost one-half of the population depending upon the soil for a livelihood. Hence problems connected with the land loom large on the political horizon. One of the most important of these, age-old in its impact, is the tenure problem. More specifically, it is the desire of the tenant or sharecropper peasant or employed farm laborer to own the land he cultivates. That desire has inspired a political demand of long standing that the large estates, and particularly the southern *latifundia,* be divided up. That Italy could profit by such redistribution of perhaps the bulk of her large-scale holdings is clear. In a recent study of the operation of the European Recovery Program in Italy, a group of American Congressmen pointed out that one two-hundredth of Italy's landowners possess more than a third of the land; and that much arable land, incorporated in great estates and private preserves, is allowed to lie fallow.[7] Such conditions are hardly defensible in a country where the pressure of population is relatively as great as in contemporary Italy and where much of the staple food supply must be imported.

[3] For the text of the Concordat see *Current History,* xxx (July, 1929), pp. 558–566.
[4] Art. 33.
[5] Art. 8.
[6] Non-Catholics comprise less than 0.5 per cent of the population.
[7] "Status and Progress of the European Recovery Program," Report of a Subcommittee to the Committee on Foreign Affairs, House of Representatives, 81st Congress, 2nd Session, Washington, 1950, p. 2; cited hereafter as "Report on European Recovery Program."

The Political Parties and Land Reform. As might be expected, all parties have made political capital out of the land hunger of the Italian peasant; but the Communists, by relying upon their special variety of irresponsible demagogy, have clearly outdistanced all others in exploiting the issue for partisan advantage. Chiefly because of Communist inspiration and leadership (though not in every case), peasants have frequently taken matters into their own hands in the years since World War II and have invaded and occupied the property of absentee landlords. Occasionally bloodshed has resulted from such direct action. As noted earlier, Christian Democrats and their moderate coalition allies have also favored the policy of division. Prime Minister de Gasperi can himself point to a long record of support of peasant demands on the part of his party, a record which antedates Fascism and for which Fascism used to dub the Christian Democrats "White Bolshevists." [8] Occasionally he has lectured obstructionist landlords for their refusal to recognize the "social function of property," a principle which is incorporated in the republican Constitution in an Article of that document that refers particularly to landed property.[9] Of all the parties apparently only the Liberals and some of the Christian Democratic right wing entered serious objections to the land redistribution policy.

The Official Land Reform Program. Nevertheless, despite political and moral pressure and the acceptance of the principle of reform by the Constitution and the Cabinet, actual reform has been slow. Legislation to condemn certain classes of large holdings, provide compensation to former owners, and subdivide the land thus expropriated into small holdings of about fifteen acres was introduced as early as 1947; but it was not until May, 1949, that the specific land reform policy was announced. This will nationalize from 20 to 50 per cent of some 8,000 holdings that exceed 250 acres each, the condemned land costing the state about $170 million. Apparently one of the first actual redistribution projects got under way late in 1950 in the Region of Calabria in southern Italy. Even this initial project was apparently inaugurated sooner than the Government intended and was designed to serve as a sort of token of good faith in the face of Communist pressure.

Incidental Problems Which Delay Reform. Despite this apparent procrastination, there is no reason to doubt the Government's sincerity on the land question. The fact is that any redistribution plans, however well intentioned and however justifiable on politico-moral and economic grounds, must take cognizance of a variety of complicating and limiting factors. Among these is the special legal position toward the land of the tenant farmer and the sharecropper; the danger of splitting up large-scale units now practicing relatively efficient agriculture and thereby making the whole less productive; and the problem of compensating present owners fairly and of financing the new small holder not only as respects the purchase of his plot but also as respects necessary equipment.

[8] Then known as the *"Popolari."*
[9] Art. 44.

Chief Obstacle to Land Reform: Lack of Water. But the consideration of chief importance in slowing down redistribution, as American observers are wont to stress, is the scarcity of water resources and the absence of necessary public works such as roads. Subdivided farm plots without adequate water and without access facilities will neither fortify the national economy nor satisfy the aspirations of the peasants. Clearly these auxiliary requirements must be met before any redistribution program can have meaning. Irrigation projects, at least on a limited scale, were begun well back in the nineteenth century; and it is well known that Mussolini's regime vociferously besought applause, sometimes justifiably, for its integral land-reclamation policy (*bonifica integrale*). This involved marsh drainage, conservation of top soil, water conservation for irrigation and domestic use, and road-building. Once an "integral" plan had been carried out, an area was made ready for "colonization." Such "colonization" schemes actually resulted in the creation of several new communes and at least one new province in the vicinity of Rome. With the help of the European Cooperation Administration, the Republic has continued and expanded this historic reclamation and irrigation policy. In a recent year more than 100 billion lire, 70 billion of which came from Italy's ECA-counterpart fund, were devoted to water and related public-works projects. Encompassed in this program is the planned reclamation of some five million acres in about 100 separate areas, the whole program to provide employment for some half million people.[10] Any land-distribution scheme, if it is to be more than a political gesture, must obviously be keyed to the time-table of this public-works program and be carried forward in stages as various planned improvements are effected.

SOCIAL POLICY

Social Welfare. In line with the paternalistic trend of the contemporary State, Italy's republican Constitution makes much of the Government's duty to safeguard the interests of the individual. In various articles of the new Charter, the Government is enjoined to protect the material welfare of the individual in his relationship toward his family, his profession, his school, his labor union, and other possible associations. Measures are to be taken to protect maternity, infancy, and youth; to safeguard the health of the individual; and to provide material assistance to the indigent, the incapacitated, the unemployed, and others who may become wards of society either transiently or permanently. In short, the Constitution's bill of rights provides a fairly comprehensive blueprint of the welfare state.

The National Insurance Institutes. Actual developments along these lines hardly embrace the scope outlined in the Constitution but they are considerable. As respects social insurance, the republican regime has built up antecedent developments which go back beyond Fascism. Social insurances are administered under the supervision of two national institutes which were originally established in 1883 and 1898 respectively. The first of these agen-

[10] See Report on European Recovery Program, p. 2.

cies, known as the National Institute for Accident Insurance, controls compensation to workmen who develop a disability as a result of their employment. All major industries are covered, including the transportation and construction industries and farm laborers. The second agency, known as the National Institute for Social Insurance, supervises other forms of social insurance. These include pensions for the aged or incapacitated, unemployment insurance, and protection against tuberculosis and other diseases. This agency also has general supervision over a considerable variety of institutes, autonomous funds, and administrations, each of which provides some form of public protection for a special category of persons. Both institutes supervise a great deal of disease-prevention activity and provide for the hospitalization and rehabilitation of incapacitated persons.

Unemployment. Although overpopulation is a relative term, most demographic experts are likely to agree that Italy suffers from that condition. At any rate her economy, under present conditions, seems incapable of absorbing all who wish employment; and almost perennial unemployment therefore exists. It is a problem, moreover, which is not likely to be solved by any or all the measures to which the Government resorts, including unemployment insurance for some categories of workmen, food subsidies, and compulsory inflation of payrolls both in private and public employment, the latter constituting a sort of officially-inspired system of featherbedding. In contrast to Fascism, the present regime has also sought to encourage emigration, Italian laborers having been sent to various European countries on a temporary basis. Official support has also been extended to the resettlement of Italians abroad. For a time serious consideration was given to a plan to use ECA funds to finance Italian emigration; and ships were actually allocated to transport immigrants to other lands. For various reasons, this plan was abandoned. It is unlikely that even emigration will relieve the pressure. The problem is a deep-seated one and at least a part of its solution lies in diversifying and improving the efficiency of Italian production and the expansion of both domestic and foreign markets for Italian goods.

PUBLIC FISCAL POLICIES

The Public Revenue System. Still another domestic problem which affects every department of public activity is the tax problem. Italy has long been notorious for an essentially regressive and inequitable revenue system. Relatively too large a part of the tax burden falls upon those least able to bear it. Fiscal experts likewise charge that too little attention is paid to the ill effects of the tax system upon private enterprise or to the objective of securing a ratio between the cost of collection and the tax yield which would reflect wise policy and efficient administration. Up to the present, moreover, the prospect of overcoming the more serious of these weaknesses has seemed none too bright. A lethargic bureaucratic tradition coupled with a pressing demand for revenue from almost any source to finance current need and a huge public debt have had the effect of inhibiting reform.

Tax Sources and Proposed Reforms. In 1951, the principal revenue sources included: (1) real-estate taxes levied upon income from the use of unimproved land and upon the rental value of buildings and improvements; (2) income taxes levied both upon investment and earned income which featured low exemptions and rather steeply progressive rates and which apparently did not apply to the incomes of public employees or civil servants; (3) inheritance taxes; (4) a variety of business taxes including a general sales tax; (5) customs duties including duties upon exports; and (6) special excises upon the manufacture of liquors, sugar, gas, alcohol, and electric power. In addition appreciable revenue was derived from State monopolies such as those on tobacco, salt, quinine, matches, and from the State lottery. To expand income in times of emergency, the State in the past, and particularly during the Mussolinian period, occasionally made special assessments upon business which amounted to capital levies. It has been estimated that five-sixths of the current revenue of the Italian Government comes from indirect excises, business taxes, and State monopolies and about one-sixth from direct taxes, notably the income tax. Reform of the tax system, proposed in 1951, sought to secure one-third of the revenue from income taxes, one-third from business taxes, and one-third from special consumption taxes and State monopolies. Such a reform, if achieved, would represent real progress in the fiscal field. In some years immediately after World War II, the income of the central Government was less than half the total expenditure. Augmented by such deficits, the public debt has reached astronomical proportions. Although severe budgetary pruning, a deliberate deflationary policy, and assistance in the way of loans and gifts from abroad, particularly from the United States, have wrought a remarkable improvement in the public finances, the improvement is likely to be temporary unless other measures are adopted. Undoubtedly the most important of these is a conscientious effort to place in effect the tax reforms to which allusion has been made.

ECONOMIC POLICY

Qualified Restoration of Economic Freedom. In this survey we come finally to a consideration of the Government's economic policies, particularly as they affect industry, finance, and trade. As noted in an earlier chapter,[11] the Italian state under Mussolini placed the nation's economy in a public strait-jacket. Fascism's syndical system, its so-called "Corporate State," its autarchic economic outlook, and the exigencies of war and preparation for war, all contributed toward a high degree of political regimentation of production and distribution before, and during, World War II. Formal abandonment of the Fascist system has by no means eradicated its economic effects. Republican Italy has tried to revive a measure of economic freedom. Labor unions now have freedom of organization and free collective bargaining has been restored, at least in principle. Private enterprise has been re-endorsed and the productive energies of the nation have been released from the thrall-

[11] Chapter III.

dom of centralized Fascist direction. Even so, the impact of Mussolinian economics remains and the Italian economy continues to have a highly collectivistic cast.

Continuation of State Capitalism. This conclusion is reinforced by the considerable amount of state enterprise which exists in contemporary Italy, much of it a direct legacy of previous regimes and especially of the Fascist regime. Through its control of the stock or other securities of private companies, the Italian Government exercises proprietary rights over the whole of the nation's passenger-shipping, almost all of its ship-building, more than half of its steel plants, three-quarters of its telephone industry, and one-third of the electric power generating industry. In addition, the Government has a majority stock interest in concerns producing aircraft, chemicals, cellulose, and synthetic rubber. As noted elsewhere,[12] proprietary rights such as these fell to the Government, in large part, during the depression years after 1931 when public credit was extended to many private firms threatened with bankruptcy. A variety of special public lending agencies, of which the best known was the Institute for Industrial Reconstruction (IRI), advanced the Government's credit to industry and banks. Subsequently the Government was compelled to "take over" many of the companies whose stock it had purchased or to whom it had lent funds, or at least continue indefinitely the rights of ownership acquired during the depression years; and the IRI became a sort of public holding company through which the Government's proprietary rights could be exercised. The Institute continues to be the instrument through which the Government manages or directs nationalized industry. The Institute also continues to be an important credit reservoir. Indeed, through certain important private banks which the Institute controls and from its own statutory funds, it is the instrument through which most large-scale industrial financing is likely to take place in the Italy of 1951. In other words, directly or indirectly through the IRI, the Italian Government largely controls investment credit in contemporary Italy and directs its use. Currently (1951) the authorized capital funds of IRI total sixty billion lire.[13]

Economic Theory of the Constitution. Continuation of the collectivistic features of Italian economic life encounters no hostility in the new Constitution. To be sure, that document may recognize private enterprise as being consistent with public policy; but the document is equally emphatic in demanding that the private entrepreneur be directed and controlled by the Government toward what are identified as "social ends." Corollary constitutional principles are expressed concerning private property which, though specifically recognized and publicly guaranteed, may always be regulated in such manner as will serve the collective interest. More significant still, as respects the Constitution's economic theory, are its declarations that enterprises or classes of enterprise which have pre-eminent public significance, or create a monopoly, or provide essential services or sources of energy, may be taken from private

[12] See p. 264.
[13] *Annuario parlamentare,* 1949–50, pp. 460–61.

owners with compensation and turned over to the management of the State, public bodies, trade unions, or consumer unions.[14] Hence both existing practice and constitutional theory underscore the conclusion that Italy, like most Western European nations, supports a "mixed" economic system in which the State's managerial role is likely to become more, rather than less, important with the passage of time.

Post-War Economic Difficulties. However the economic system may be characterized, whether collectivistic, mixed, or free, that system had an uphill struggle after World War II. Not until 1949 did it begin to emerge from the post-War doldrums. Inflationary forces, released by the wartime famine in production and the War's destruction, ran rampant in Italy immediately after the armistice and the value of the lira declined at a fantastic rate. Huge Government deficits, the emission of large amounts of currency by various belligerent regimes operating in the peninsula, low production volume in industry which was hampered by excessive labor costs and antiquated machinery, public-works projects that were too often distinguished by a dearth of material and equipment and a plethora of employees, and a drought that helped to bring on at least one unusually poor harvest, all added fire to the prevailing inflation. On her international account, also, Italy had much trouble making ends meet. As in most of Western Europe, dollar exchange was especially short—so much so that Italy could not import the many things necessary to the functioning of her economy, particularly the raw materials and machinery which came from dollar sources.

The European Recovery Plan and Economic Revival. Under the circumstances, protagonists of the European Recovery Program had an unusual opportunity in 1948 to dramatize that Program's possibilities; and with the cooperation of the Italian Government, they did succeed in producing some remarkably favorable results. As material assistance from the United States began to flow into the channels of trade and production, the Italian Government, advised by its leading economist, Dr. Luigi Einaudi (later President of the Republic), began a contraction of bank credit and imposed other deflationary measures. In a very short time the value of the lira became stable; the public budgetary deficit was reduced to the vanishing point; and a trend toward exchange equilibrium with the dollar countries and a favorable balance with sterling exchange areas manifested itself. Moreover, production climbed rapidly. In December, 1949, national income was up to 97 per cent of the 1938 totals. By 1950, production had exceeded pre-War norms both in industry and agriculture.

Continuing Weaknesses. American officials of the Economic Cooperation Administration in Italy subsequently criticized the policy as too deflationary. They claimed it hampered progress in public works, particularly in the agricultural domain, and held up the modernization of plant in industry. Moreover, at least two million employables remained without a job; and, despite the climb beyond pre-War levels, production remained relatively in-

[14] Arts. 41–43 inclusive.

efficient because of continuing labor featherbedding in private and public employment, obsolete plant, and failure to cultivate mass markets either in Italy or overseas. Other critics insist that there is too great a degree of State control over production and distribution and that private producers fear the spur of competition and hanker after national autarchy and cartels. Undoubtedly most of these criticisms are well taken; and despite the Government's record of relative progress and stability, some of the weaknesses to which the critics have pointed are likely to become much more apparent when the stimulus of gifts and loans from abroad begins to taper off. On balance it must be said that nine years after Italy's surrender in World War II, the prospects of stabilizing the nation's economy at high and efficient levels of production are by no means assured. And in that lack of assurance in the economic sphere resides much of the persisting doubt about Italy's capacity to stabilize her democratic political system or to defend herself against potential foreign aggression or internal fifth columns.

BIBLIOGRAPHICAL NOTE
ON THE ITALIAN POLITICAL SYSTEM

Statutory and Administrative Materials

The official publications of the Italian Government are quite extensive. The text of laws, decree laws, decrees and administrative regulations may be found in the *Gazzetta ufficiale della repubblica* (until 1946 *Gazzetta ufficiale del regno d'Italia*), issued every week-day under the jurisdiction of the Ministry of Grace and Justice. The official collection of laws and decrees is known as the *Raccolta ufficiale delle leggi e dei decreti*, a number of volumes of which have been published each year since 1861. The Italian Institute of Legislative Studies, operating under the Ministry of Grace and Justice, publishes articles and summaries of the work of Parliament and the courts and on the development of law in various fields both as respects Italy and foreign countries. A translation of the *Albertian Statuto* may be found in W. F. Dodd, *Modern Constitutions*, 2 Vols. (Chicago, 1909), Vol. II, pp. 5 ff., and in H. L. McBain and Lindsay Rogers, *The New Constitutions of Europe* (New York, 1922), pp. 551 ff. The text of the new republican Constitution, as translated by Howard McGaw Smyth and Kent Roberts Greenfield may be found in the United States Department of State, *Documents and State Papers*, I (April, 1948), pp. 46–63. Useful information of an official character relating to the administration of the Government is to be found in the bulletins of the various ministries and in the publications of the Secretariat General of the Chamber of Deputies and of the Senate.

Statistical Sources

A great variety of publications are issued by the Central Institute of Statistics (*Istituto centrale di statistica*). Among these are the *Annuario statistico italiano*, available annually since 1878; the *Compendio statistico italiano*, annually since 1927; and the *Bollettino mensile di statistica*, monthly since 1926 (with interruptions during World War II). Monthly statistical publications are also available on the subject of prices, foreign trade, and agriculture. Occasional publications of note are *Annali di statistica* and the *Annuario statistico dell'agricoltura italiana*.

Historical Works Relating to the Period of the Liberal Constitutional Monarchy

The period of the *risorgimento* and of the early years of united Italy are traced in the following historical and biographical works: *Memoirs of Francesco Crispi*, trans. by M. Prichard-Agnetti, 3 Vols. (London, 1912–1914); Edward Dicey, *Victor Emmanuel* (New York, 1886); C. S. Forester, *Victor Emmanuel II and the Union of Italy* (New York, 1927); Bolton King, *A History of Italian Unity*, 2 Vols. (London, 1912); Bolton King, *The Life of Mazzini* (London, 1911); W. R. Thayer, *The Dawn of Italian Independence*, 2 Vols. (Boston, 1893); W. R. Thayer, *The Life and Times of Cavour*, 2 Vols. (Boston, 1911); and G. M. Trevelyan, *Garibaldi and the Making of Italy* (New York, 1911). A standard history of liberal Italy down to World War I is B. Croce, *A History of Italy, 1871–1915*, trans. by C. M. Ady (Oxford, 1929). Attention is also called to René Albrecht-Carrié, *Italy from Napoleon to Mussolini* (New York, 1950); M. Hentze,

Pre-Fascist Italy: The Rise and Fall of the Parliamentary Regime (London, 1939); and A. J. Whyte, *The Evolution of Modern Italy, 1789–1919* (Oxford, 1944). The political system of liberal monarchical Italy is briefly treated in Chapter XL of Frederic A. Ogg, *European Governments and Politics,* 2nd ed. (New York, 1939), in Chapter III, Volume I, of A. L. Lowell, *Governments and Parties in Continental Europe,* 2 Vols. (Boston, 1896) and in H. R. Spencer, *Government and Politics of Italy* (Yonkers, 1932). Useful information on the parties and party doctrines of Italy before Mussolini may be gleaned from Enrico Corradini, *Il Nazionalismo italiano* (Milan, 1914); Giovanni Giolitti, *Memoirs of My Life,* trans. by E. Storer (London, 1923); Filippo Meda, *Il Socialismo politico in Italia* (Milan, 1924); Roberto Michels, *Storia critica del movimento socialista italiano* (Florence, 1926); Carlo Sforza, *The Makers of Modern Europe* (Indianapolis, 1928); and Luigi Sturzo, *Italy and Fascismo,* trans. by B. B. Carter (London, 1926).

Descriptions of the Revolutionary Period Leading to Fascism

The decay of the liberal parliamentary monarchy, the Fascist *coup d'état,* and the transition to Mussolini's authoritarian regime have been treated in a number of volumes many of them written by participants in the events recorded. A list is appended herewith. One or two titles, favorable to Fascism, are deliberately included to acquaint the reader with the nature of the Fascist apologia at this stage in the evolution of the dictatorship. William Bolitho, *Italy under Mussolini* (New York, 1926); Ivanoe Bonomi, *From Socialism to Fascism,* trans. by J. Murray (London, 1924); F. L. Ferrari, *Le Régime fasciste italien* (Paris, 1928); Guglielmo Ferrero, *Four Years of Fascism,* trans. by E. W. Dickes (London, 1924); Edwin W. Hullinger, *The New Fascist State* (New York, 1928); E. Lémonon, *L'Italie d'après guerre, 1914–1921* (Paris, 1922); Giacomo Matteotti, *The Fascisti Exposed,* trans. by E. W. Dickes (London, 1924); Edgar A. Mowrer, *Immortal Italy* (New York, 1922); Gaetano Salvemini, *The Fascist Dictatorship in Italy* (New York, 1927); H. W. Schneider, *Making the Fascist State* (New York, 1928); Curzio Suckert (C. Malaparte), *Technique du coup d'état,* trans. into French by J. Bertrand (Paris, 1930); Tommaso Tittoni, *Modern Italy* (New York, 1922); and Luigi Villari, *The Awakening of Italy* (London, 1924), the latter strongly pro-Fascist.

The Fascist Period

A plethora of material exists on the dictatorship. Much of it, even when written by outside observers, is not particularly objective. For the record, the following brief bibliography is suggested. The official compilation of Mussolini's writings is *Scritti e discorsi di B. Mussolini,* ed. by V. Piccoli, 11 Vols. (Milan, 1934–1938). Mussolini's brief pamphlet in English translation entitled *The Doctrine of Fascism* is still regarded as the most authoritative exposition of Fascist ideology. It was incorporated as a preamble to the last official statute of the Fascist Party and the whole was printed in the Official Gazette of the Kingdom (*Gazzetta ufficiale del regno,* May 18, 1938, no. 112, pp. 1848 *ff.*). Other items, most of them highly critical, which may be cited are Max Ascoli and Arthur Feiler, *Fascism for Whom?* (New York, 1938); G. A. Borgese, *Goliath, the March of Fascism* (New York, 1937); H. W. Schneider and S. B. Clough, *Making Fascists* (Chicago, 1929); Herman Finer, *Mussolini's Italy* (New York, 1935); and Gaetano Salvemini, *Under the Axe of Fascism* (New York, 1936). H. A. Steiner, *Government in Fascist Italy* (New York, 1938) and H. W. Schneider, *The Fascist Government of Italy* (New York, 1935), provide brief descriptions of the governmental apparatus. The so-called "Corporate State" and Fascist economics are treated more or less sympathetically in such works as Carl T. Schmidt, *The Corporate State in Action* (New York, 1939); Alberto Pennachio, *The Corporative State* (New York, 1927); William G. Welk, *Fascist Economic Policy* (Cambridge, Mass., 1938); and Paul Einzig, *The Economic Foundations of Fascism* (London, 1933). Some of the more unlovely characteristics of

Fascist terrorism are depicted in H. H. Tiltman, *The Terror in Europe* (New York, 1932); Pietro Nenni, *Ten Years of Tyranny in Italy,* trans. by A. Steele (London, 1932); and F. F. Nitti, *Escape* (New York, 1930).

Period of the Republic

Italy's emergence from defeat and dictatorship and the advent of the Republic are treated in the following: Pietro Badoglio, *Italy in the Second World War* (New York, 1948); Barbara B. Carter, *Italy Speaks* (London, 1947); G. Ciano, *The Ciano Diaries, 1939–43,* trans. by Hugh Gibson (New York, 1946); Benedetto Croce, *Due Anni di vita politica italiana, 1946–1947* (Bari, 1948); T. L. Gardini, *Towards the New Italy* (London, 1944); Muriel Grindrod, *The New Italy* (London, 1947); W. Hilton-Young, *The Italian Left* (New York, 1949); B. Mussolini, *The Fall of Mussolini: His Own Story,* trans. and edited by Max Ascoli (New York, 1948); Carlo Sforza, *Contemporary Italy— Its Intellectual and Moral Origins* (New York, 1944); Luigi Sturzo, *Italy and the Coming World* (New York, 1945); G. Salvemini and G. LaPiana, *What to Do With Italy* (New York, 1943); and Elizabeth Wiskemann, *Italy* (Oxford, 1947). Developments relating to the new republican Constitution are treated in M. Ruini *et al., La Nuova Costituzione Italiana* (Rome, 1947) and in Roberto Lucifredi, *L'Assemblea Costituente* (Milan, 1948). An excellent series of articles on the history of Italian parliamentarism and the meaning of the new Constitution appear in *Il Centenario del parlamento,* published in 1948 by the Secretariat-General of the Chamber of Deputies, Rome.

The Political System of

SWITZERLAND

by ARNOLD J. ZURCHER

CHAPTER I

THE NATION AND ITS POLITICAL IDEALS

A PRELIMINARY SURVEY

Physical Characteristics. The republic of Switzerland, known by the formal title of the Swiss Confederation, is a federal state of twenty-five semi-sovereign cantons and half cantons,[1] with a population numbering about four and one-quarter millions. Its territory, roughly equivalent to that of Holland or Denmark or of the American state of Maryland, is almost inclosed by the frontiers of the three Continental powers, France, Germany, and Italy. Few states have been less favored by nature and physical circumstance. The high Alps and the Jura range across Switzerland's domain and render more than 22 per cent of her area entirely unproductive. Much of the remainder is suitable only for grazing purposes or for woodland; and only some 35 per cent is actually devoted to agricultural production. Nor is the basis for industry much more promising. Mountains and valleys yield no coal or metallic ores, and the broken terrain of the country makes transportation and communication difficult. About the only natural industrial resource of moment is hydro-electric power, of which Switzerland has an abundance.

Despite these adverse physical circumstances, Switzerland has developed an

---

[1] The Swiss cantons and half-cantons in the order of accession to the Confederation are as follows:

1. Uri (1291)
2. Schwyz (1291)
3. Unterwalden (1291), divided into the two independent half-cantons of Upper Walden; Lower Walden
4. Luzern (Lucerne) (1332)
5. Zürich (Zurich) (1351)
6. Glarus (Glaris) (1352)
7. Zug (Zoug) (1352)
8. Bern (Berne) (1353)
9. Solothurn (Soleure) (1481)
10. Fribourg (Freiburg) (1481)
11. Basel (Bâle) (1501), divided into the two independent half-cantons of Basel Country; Basel City
12. Schaffhausen (Schaffhouse) (1501)
13. Appenzell (1513), divided into the two independent half-cantons of Appenzell Exterior Rhodes; Appenzell Interior Rhodes
14. St. Gallen (St. Gall) (1803)
15. Aargau (Argovie) (1803)
16. Thurgau (Thurgovie) (1803)
17. Grisons (Graubünden) (1803)
18. Vaud (Waadt) (1803)
19. Ticino (Tessin) (1803)
20. Valais (Wallis) (1815)
21. Geneva (Genf) (1815)
22. Neuchâtel (Neuenberg) (1815)

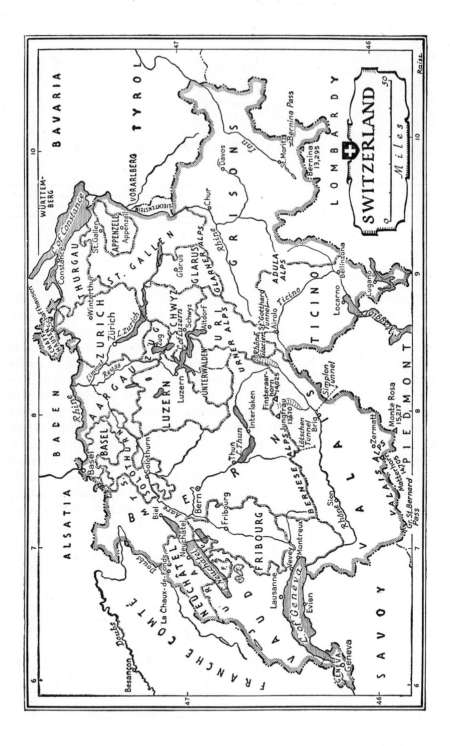

SWITZERLAND

Miles

WÜRTTEM-BERG

BAVARIA

TYROL

VORARLBERG

ALSATIA

BADEN

L. of Constance

Schaffhausen

St. Gallen

THURGAU

APPENZELL
Appenzell

LIECHTENSTEIN

Chur

Rhine

ST. GALLEN

Winterthur

ZURICH

Zürich
L. Zurich

Glarus

GLARUS

GLARNER ALPS

GRISONS

Inn

St. Moritz

Davos

Bernina Pass

Bernina
13,295

LOMBARDY

Limmat

Reuss

ZUG
Zug

SCHWYZ
Schwyz

Luzern

LUZERN

L. of Luzern

Altdorf

UNTERWALDEN

URI

URNER ALPS

Rhone
Glacier

St. Gotthard
Tunnel

Airolo

ADULA
ALPS

Ticino

TICINO

Bellinzona

Locarno

Lugano

AARGAU

Rhine

BASEL
Basel

SOLOTHURN
Solothurn

Biel

Aare

FRANCHE COMTÉ

Besançon

Doubs

Doubs

La Chaux-de-Fonds
Le Locle

NEUCHATEL
Neuchâtel

L. of Neuchâtel

Bern

Fribourg

FRIBOURG

JURA

VAUD

Lausanne

L. of Geneva

Vevey
Montreux

Evian

GENEVA
Geneva

SAVOY

Interlaken

Thun
L. Thun

BERNESE ALPS

Finsteraar-
horn
14,025

Jungfrau
13,670

Lötschen
Tunnel

Brig

Simplon
Tunnel

Sion

Rhone

VALAIS ALPS
Matterhorn
14,705

Zermatt

Monte Rosa
15,217

Gt. St. Bernard
Pass

PIEDMONT

Raist.

economy which is reasonably stable and fairly prosperous. Not quite a fourth of her population is engaged in agriculture or dependent upon it; the vast majority of the remainder makes a living from industry or allied pursuits. Since the country lacks many essential industrial materials, and since her agrarian production will not suffice to feed her own population, the expansion of this economy has required extensive trade with foreign nations. In normal times, Switzerland has a larger *per capita* volume of foreign trade than any other nation in the world. The coal, the metals, and the agricultural staples which she imports are paid for with dairy products, textiles, and highly specialized manufactures, such as watches and precision instruments of various sorts. The normal excess of imports over exports is charged to the revenue from the tourist trade and to the return from external investment and fiscal services.

Demographic Features. A unique and one of the most challenging features of Swiss nationhood is its violation of the nationalistic canons of demographic and cultural unity. The population of Switzerland includes three different language groups, German, French, and Italian. Approximately three million Swiss use the first of these languages; somewhat over 800,000 use the second; and about 225,000 use the third. In addition some 50,000 use a dialect known as Romansch, which has some literary significance. The linguistic groups, moreover, are geographically quite sharply separated from each other by the cantonal boundaries. Thus the Ticino is almost exclusively an Italian-speaking canton; Geneva, Vaud, Neuchâtel, and Valais are almost exclusively French; and all the remaining cantons, except Bern and Fribourg, are almost exclusively German. In Bern the German population predominates over the French in the ratio of five to one; and in Fribourg the French population predominates over the German in the ratio of two to one. Romansch is the prevailing language in the Grisons. It must be added that linguistic interpenetration among the various cantons is becoming a noticeable fact. Moreover, all the languages, including even Romansch,[2] are regarded as official for matters relating to the Confederation Government and administration; and there are few educated Swiss who cannot use two or even three of these languages. Even so, the three major linguistic communities remain quite sharply differentiated geographically and they probably have as many cultural affiliations with their respective linguistic brethren in contiguous Germany, France, Italy, and Austria as they have with each other.

Religious Differences. Another centrifugal factor affecting Switzerland's nationhood is the confessional cleavage. Through Switzerland runs the boundary line of the Reformation, Zwingli and Calvin, with other Swiss, having helped to establish it. It is a line drawn with astonishing intricacy. Avoiding the linguistic boundaries, it divides both the German cantons from each other as well as the French. Among the latter, Vaud, Geneva, and Neuchâtel are predominantly Protestant, whereas Fribourg and Valais espouse the older Christian faith; among the German cantons, Zürich, Bern, Glarus, Thurgau, and

---

[2] Romansch was adopted as a national language in a constitutional referendum held on February 20, 1938.

both of the Basel half-cantons are overwhelmingly Protestant; while Luzern, Zug, the two half-cantons of Unterwalden and the canton of Solothurn are overwhelmingly Catholic. Many of the cantons are themselves fairly evenly divided between the two branches of Christendom. This is notably true of St. Gallen and Aargau. Somewhat less than sixty per cent of the entire population of the Confederation is Protestant and most of the remainder is Catholic.[3]

The Swiss a United Nation. Religious differences have in the past contributed their due share to internecine strife. For three centuries after the Reformation, the cantons fought amongst themselves on numerous occasions.[4] At the end of the sixteenth century, religious strife was the occasion for the partition of the canton of Appenzell into the two half-cantons, respectively, the Interior and Exterior Rhodes.[5] Even as late as 1846, the Catholic cantons of Luzern, Uri, Schwyz, Unterwalden, Zug, Fribourg, and Valais leagued themselves together into the *Sonderbund,* or Separate League, and began a rebellion which the Confederation had to put down by force of arms.[6] At the present time, Catholic Switzerland is almost entirely identified with the aims of a single political party, the so-called Catholic Conservative Party. Linguistic differences have also occasionally caused trouble, or at least aggravated difficulties arising from other causes. Nevertheless, despite these religious and linguistic differences, and the internal discord which they have sometimes occasioned, Swiss legal and moral unity has grown firmer with each passing generation. Today there is no people in Europe among whom a sense of national unity and of patriotic devotion is more firmly fixed than among the Swiss. In a world grown somewhat weary of the too frequent reiteration of the principle of political "self-determination" for racial and linguistic groups, the Swiss offer a splendid example of how statehood and national patriotism can be fostered in utter defiance of such a principle.

NATIONAL AND CONSTITUTIONAL DEVELOPMENT

Origins of Confederation. Switzerland has evolved through the gradual unification of the cantons of which she is today composed. The first step in this process began in 1291 when the inhabitants of the so-called Forest Cantons, Uri, Schwyz, and Unterwalden, made a Perpetual Covenant in which they mutually pledged themselves to protect their existing rights and privileges against their feudal lords.[7] Of these, the most important were the Hapsburg rulers of Austria, themselves of Swiss origin, who, at the time, were serving also

[3] Religious and linguistic data have been taken from recent editions of the *Statesmen's Year-Book* and the *Statistisches Jahrbuch der Schweiz.*

[4] See F. O. Adams and C. D. Cunningham, *The Swiss Confederation* (London, 1894), pp. 170 ff.

[5] W. Oechsli, *History of Switzerland,* trans. by E. and C. Paul (Cambridge, England, 1922), p. 178.

[6] *Ibid.,* pp. 390 ff.

[7] This Covenant is translated and reprinted in J. M. Vincent, *State and Federal Government in Switzerland* (Baltimore, 1891), pp. 191 ff. The history of the formation of the Perpetual Covenant may be found in W. D. McCrackan, "The Real Origin of the Swiss Republic," *Report of the Amer. Hist. Asso.* (1898), pp. 357–362.

as Holy Roman Emperors. An attempt by the Hapsburgs to reassert their feudal authority met with the successful resistance of the three confederated cantons at the Battle of Morgarten in 1315. During the next forty years, five more cantons joined the original three. These accessions included the important cantons of Bern and Zürich. The enlarged Confederation won a second victory over Austria at Sempach, in 1386, and thereby vindicated its *de facto* independence. For two centuries and a half thereafter it maintained a precarious existence, the bonds of unity often threatened by secessionist movements among the member cantons and by inter-cantonal strife. Nevertheless the bonds held. Indeed they became strong enough to enable the Confederation to humble Charles of Burgundy when, toward the end of the fifteenth century, that bold ruler aspired to Swiss conquests. Some of the member cantons and the Confederation as a whole also succeeded in making territorial acquisitions by their military prowess. Such acquisitions were usually treated as subject areas and their respective populations were given a status of civil inferiority.

Character of the Ancient Confederation. The Confederation had achieved its *de facto* independence of the Holy Roman Empire after the Swabian War (1499) although the Empire's nominal suzerainty over the cantons was not extinguished until the Peace of Westphalia (1648). By that time the membership had grown to thirteen cantons, all German-speaking, the latest accession, that of Appenzell, having occurred in 1513. In the management of their internal affairs, the cantons acted as sovereign entities, great variations being exhibited by their respective polities. Some, like Bern, were aristocratic republics; others, like Zürich, were rigid oligarchies; and still others, like the Forest Cantons, were peasant democracies, political power being intrusted in them to direct assemblies of the citizens known as *Landsgemeinden.* The affairs of the Confederation, which included relations with foreign powers, matters relating to peace and war, and inter-cantonal disputes, were managed by a Diet which met at irregular intervals. In this assembly each canton had two representatives, and each territory allied with the cantons, one representative. The leading canton, or *Vorort,* called upon the Diet to assemble. Originally this prerogative of leadership belonged to no particular canton but was exercised by each of the principal ones in turn; in the course of time, however, it became vested, by custom, in the canton of Zürich. Although a certain formal precedence may thus have been accorded to the larger cantons in this assembly, particularly to Bern and Zürich, each of the cantons insisted vigorously upon the substance of its equality with the others and behaved in a manner not unlike that of a sovereign state participating in an international conference.

Revolution and Restoration. As thus constituted, the ancient Confederation persisted until the time of the French Revolution. Then great changes occurred. In 1798 a French army invaded and conquered Switzerland. The invaders destroyed the cantons' historic internal social and political institutions, particularly those of an oligarchic and aristocratic character, altered their territorial extent, and, abolishing the organs of the old Confederation, welded the cantons together into a centralized State with democratic and representative governmental features resembling those of revolutionary France. This regime was known as the Helvetic Republic. The violation of political tradition, occasioned by this sudden and violent change, caused such dissatisfaction among the majority of Swiss citizens that five years later Napoleon, imperial successor to the French Revolutionists, partially restored the old Confederation and the former autonomy of the cantons by his so-called Act of Mediation (1803). With the fall of Napoleon, twelve years later, and the triumph of legitimism all over Europe, the process of restoration was carried still further, an attempt being made in the Pact of 1815 to revive both the Confederate and cantonal institutions of the eighteenth century.[8]

Modern Switzerland Is Created. But the basis of modern Switzerland had been firmly laid between 1798 and 1815; and no amount of restorationist activity could ultimately prevail against what had thus been done. The Act of Mediation had added six new cantons to the thirteen which had formerly existed.[9] These had been created chiefly out of French- and Italian-speaking territories which had been allied with, or considered as subject territories of, the formerly dominant German-speaking cantons. The new cantons were continued in the restorationist settlement of 1815 and three more, Valais, Geneva, and Neuchâtel,[10] all French-speaking, were added. The number of cantons was thus brought to its present total of twenty-two; and Switzerland officially became a tri-lingual country. In time, moreover, the liberal, democratic, and centralizing influences, generated during the period when France controlled Switzerland, began to manifest themselves. After 1830, the power of the aristocracies and oligarchies was permanently destroyed in all the cantons where such power had been revived, and representative institutions of a popular character were universally introduced; and on November 12, 1848, following the brief *Sonderbund* War, already referred to, a new Constitution was adopted for the Confederation as a whole. This Constitution, based largely on the model of the American system of government, supplied a central political system with adequate and effective national authority and definitively transformed Switzerland from a confederation into a federal State. Hence, although Switzerland may retain the word *confederation* in her legal name, she is technically a *federation;* that is, a State with relatively autonomous geographical components and a central government that enforces its will directly upon the individual and his property. A complete revision of the new Constitution, in 1874, further augmented the powers of the central government and laid the legal foundations for the present governmental system of the Swiss State.

SOME BASIC PRINCIPLES

Significance of the Constitution. Switzerland's existing written Constitution is therefore the fundamental law of a federation. Juridically it is presumed to be the sovereign expression of the joint will of the people of the entire Con-

---

[8] This period is well treated in Oechsli, *op. cit.,* pp. 302 *ff.*

[9] The six new cantons were: St. Gallen, the Grisons, Aargau, Thurgau, the Ticino, and Vaud.

[10] Technically Neuchâtel did not become a full-fledged canton of the Confederation until 1850, when the erstwhile sovereignty of the Prussian King was finally extinguished.

federation and of the cantons as juridical entities. Its formal supremacy over both Confederation and cantonal governments is unquestioned. At the same time it must be recognized that the means of protecting that supremacy are juridically imperfect. As will be noted later, the Swiss Federal Tribunal, which is the Confederation's only court,[11] is empowered, in all cases which may come before it, to vindicate the supremacy of the Confederation Constitution and laws as against cantonal constitutions, laws, and administrative acts. The Federal Tribunal thus possesses at least a limited power to protect the Confederation Constitution from acts of the cantons which are held to violate the constitutional clause. On the other hand, neither this, nor any cantonal, court possesses power of constitutional review as against federal legislation. In Swiss political theory, as in the political theory of virtually all Continental democracies, the legislative branch is regarded as the supreme organ of Government; and whatever interpretations it may make of the clauses of the written Constitution are regarded as decisive and binding interpretations. In speaking of the legislative branch of the Confederation Government we must, of course, include not only Parliament but the voters at large who, as will be shown subsequently, exercise legislative power through the referendum.[12] In the last analysis, then, the substantive integrity of the Swiss Constitution may be said to depend upon the self-imposed political discipline of the Swiss legislature and of the Swiss electorate.[13] In practice, the provisions of the Constitution have been generally respected. At least this is one inference to be derived from the fact that since 1848 no less than ninety efforts have been made to change the basic document in accordance with the provisions for its own amendment. Approximately half of these ninety efforts, as we shall note later,[14] have been successful.

Federalism. Certain fundamental principles upon which Swiss political society is based and which explain that society's general structure and purpose, permeate the constitutional document. The first of these principles is federalism. Those who formulated Switzerland's basic law in 1848 and then amended it in 1874 modified the erstwhile sovereignty of the cantons so as to confer adequate authority for national purposes upon the central Government of the Confederation. Besides the traditional control over foreign relations and questions of peace and war, this authority included a variety of prerogatives of an internal character relating to such matters as the currency, communications, commerce, weights and measures, naturalization and expatriation, higher education, conservation of natural resources, and necessary fiscal powers. In addition the Government of the Confederation continued to enjoy its former authority to settle inter-cantonal differences and to protect the integrity of the cantonal Governments against invasion or domestic insurrection. To the can-

---

[11] There is also an administrative court known as the Insurance Tribunal.

[12] See p. 342. Swiss voters also possess the power to amend the Constitution by means of a popular initiative; but this is a constituent and not a legislative power.

[13] For a discussion of this subject see W. E. Rappard, *The Government of Switzerland* (New York, 1936), pp. 49 *ff.*, 90 *ff.*

[14] For the amending process and its results, see pp. 341 *ff.*

tons the federal Constitution reserved all powers not expressly granted to the Confederation, the rule in this respect virtually paralleling the provisions of the Tenth Amendment of the American Constitution.

Growth of Centralized Power. Developments since 1874 have greatly altered the distribution of powers within the Confederation. The central Government's authority has been extended to such subjects as patents; water-power exploitation; the civil and criminal law; the alcoholic beverage traffic; aerial, maritime and surface transportation; banking; social-welfare projects; the protection of the family; the regulation of industry, trade and agriculture; the arms traffic; public hygiene; and the production and marketing of grain. Public ownership has been extended by the Confederation to the nation's telephonic and wireless communications systems and to the railways. Many new sources of Confederation taxation have been created; and a considerable number of subsidies to the cantons have been inaugurated. This vast centralization of power has necessarily exalted the prestige and influence of the Government of the Confederation at the expense of the separate cantons and has convinced many observers that the vitality, if not the formal integrity, of the federal principle of government is in jeopardy.

Federal Status of the Cantons. In spite of these developments, the cantons remain important elements of the Swiss constitutional system. To the cantons still appertain many of the essential prerogatives of government such as the maintenance of domestic peace and order, the care of social dependents, the construction of local public works and highways, the control of elections, the responsibility of providing a system of public education, and the control of local government. It is by being a citizen of a canton that national citizenship is ordinarily acquired; and the laws and regulations of the respective cantons still determine many of the citizen's ordinary civil rights in Switzerland, at least in peace time. The cantons also play an important subsidiary role in affairs which are predominantly the concern of the central Government. Thus although national authority determines the substance of most of the criminal and civil law, the courts which administer that law are almost exclusively cantonal and the procedural aspects of the law are therefore subject to determination by cantonal authority. Similarly the cantons enforce the national legislation relating to weights and measures and pure-food standards. They likewise enforce the Confederation's military regulations, raise certain contingents for the national army, and provide the personal equipment of each soldier. Indeed it is a general principle of Swiss federalism, as of Continental federalism generally, that the execution of the policies of the general Government shall, wherever possible, devolve upon the administrative organs of the federal components. The juridical personality of the cantons is also recognized in the composition of the Confederation's organs of government. Notable in this connection is the principle of equal cantonal representation observed in the second chamber of the Parliament, that is, the Council of States (*Ständerat*). In this body each canton is entitled to two delegates, and each half-canton, to one delegate. Of equal significance is the recognition of the cantons in the process of amending the federal Constitution. No change in that instrument can be considered legally adopted unless approved by a majority of the cantons as well as by a majority of all Swiss voters.

Liberalism. A second important principle of the Swiss political system is liberalism. The Confederation Constitution and most of the extant cantonal instruments were adopted in the latter half of the nineteenth century when the liberal philosophy of government was dominant. Constitutional phraseology consequently stresses that philosophy at every point. The controlling influence of the Constitution is particularly exploited to guarantee all the traditional liberal freedoms such as the freedom of the press, of speech, of association, of petition, and of the courts. Liberal antipathy to martial authority is also expressed in the constitutional provision against a standing army. Equally significant, as evidence of the liberal cast of Switzerland's basic law, is its vigorous assertion of the duty of the State to provide free and compulsory instruction. The constitutional clause on this subject contains the injunction that the public schools shall be open to the adherents of all religious denominations and be so managed as not to infringe upon anyone's liberty of conscience or belief. This secularism in education secures expression in other directions, notably in the exclusion of the Jesuits and affiliated orders, in the prohibition of new convents or religious congregations, in the abolition of ecclesiastical jurisdiction, and in the emphasis upon the civil character of the marriage contract. In some cases the secularism of the Constitution verges upon anticlericalism, a condition explained by the lengthy conflict between the civil and ecclesiastical authorities in Swiss history.

Recent Modifications of Liberalism. Traditionally, Switzerland was strongly addicted to other important tenets of nineteenth-century liberalism, namely, the idea that economic life should be relatively free of political restriction and that the integrity of the institutions of freedom of contract, free enterprise, and private property should be maintained. As in other Western communities, however, these economic tenets of the liberal philosophy have, in recent years, undergone surprising modifications. In some instances they appear to have been virtually erased. Efforts to overcome the baneful effects of the economic depression of the 1930's, the huge drain on the national resources required to maintain the country's neutrality in two World Wars, the pressure of various elements of the population for special favors from the public treasury, and the almost universal drift toward the welfare state and political collectivism have all contributed toward bringing about this change in the philosophic underpinning of the Swiss political and economic systems. As a result, the Swiss economy has become accustomed to political controls of the market and to the heavy tax burdens required to finance an immense public debt, various types of subsidies, current defense needs, and a greatly expanded system of social insurance and social services. Switzerland's economy has also become accustomed in recent years to a rather strictly controlled system of management-labor relations, a system which often extends the terms of a collective labor contract, negotiated by one part of an industry or trade, to embrace other parts even though these have had no hand in the negotiations. Factors other than governmental regulation have also contributed toward undermining the older economic philosophy. One of these factors has been the phenomenon of cartelization, for which Swiss industry appears overfond. By weakening, and often virtually annihilating, competition and augmenting private monopoly power, cartelization has often made meaningless the basic conditions upon which the operation of a free-market economy is premised.

It remains to be seen whether, in thus qualifying or virtually obliterating traditional liberal principles in the economic field, Switzerland can find that alleged "middle ground" between economic freedom and political intervention-ism which the political leaders of so many Western states appear to be seeking and which most of them insist, rather too vociferously, can be achieved and sta-bilized. It also remains to be seen whether, in the search for that middle ground as respects economic freedom, the State can preserve the wider domain of cul-tural, religious, and personal freedom which constitutes the principal heritage of the liberal tradition.

Democracy. Still another principle of Swiss political institutions is democ-racy. This principle has become so thoroughly ingrained in the nation's po-litical life and its governmental processes, and appears to be so ardently sup-ported by the bulk of the population, that *Switzerland* and *democracy* have in recent times become almost synonymous terms. Application of the democratic principle to Swiss political life is to be discovered in the Constitution's formal abolition of all aristocratic and oligarchic privileges and in its guarantee that all citizens shall be equal before the law. Such application is also to be dis-covered in the equal electoral rights of all male (but not female) citizens, twenty years of age or over; in the republican character of all the leading execu-tive offices; and in the representative character of the cantonal and Confedera-tion legislative assemblies.

Instruments of Direct Democracy. But the Swiss preoccupation with democracy as a political principle is most characteristically revealed in the na-tion's extensive reliance upon the instruments of direct popular government. The most ancient of these is the *landsgemeinde,* or open meeting of all the vot-ing citizens. This still obtains in the four miniature half-cantons into which Appenzell and Unterwalden are divided and in the canton of Glarus. In all the remaining cantons and for matters affecting the Confederation as a whole, use is made of the more modern instruments of direct democracy, namely, the popular referendum and the popular initiative. The first of these enables the voters to veto or approve acts of representative assemblies. The initiative, on the other hand, may involve the actual proposal by a portion of the electorate of a law or similar measure which may or may not be approved subsequently by a representative assembly but which, in any case, is usually submitted to a referendum decision of the voters. The remainder of this chapter will relate to the operation of these devices on the national level.

USE OF THE INITIATIVE AND REFERENDUM

Adoption of the Instruments of Direct Democracy. In the Swiss Confederation regime the referendum was made compulsory in 1848 for all proposed changes in the Constitution; [15] and this provision was continued in the constitutional revision of 1874. In that revision, moreover, the referendum was extended on an optional basis to all the principal laws and resolutions of the Federal Assembly (Parliament), and in 1921 the referendum was further extended, on the same basis, to international treaties concluded for an indefinite period or for more than fifteen years. The popular initiative was likewise introduced into the Confederation regime by the Constitution of 1848, that instrument providing that the electorate might initiate proposals for a complete revision of the Constitution. In 1891 this initiative was broadened to include popular initiation of proposals for constitutional amendments. The Government of the Confederation thus provides at present for (1) a popular compulsory referendum on all constitutional changes; (2) a popular initiative for proposing constitutional revisions and amendments; and (3) a popular optional referendum on laws and treaties.

Operation of the Constitutional Referendum. The compulsory constitutional referendum applies to such amendments or total revisions of the Constitution as may be formally proposed by the Federal Assembly. To be approved in a referendum, an amendment must be supported by a majority of the participating electorate of the entire Confederation and by a majority of the cantons. In determining the will of the cantons, each canton is held to possess one vote, and each half-canton, a half of a vote. The vote of the canton or half-canton is then cast, pro or con, in a referendum, in accordance with the decision expressed on the proposed amendment by the popular majority within the canton or half-canton.

For a complete revision of the Constitution, the same course is pursued as in the case of an amendment unless the two houses of the Federal Assembly disagree. If this happens, that is, if one house wishes to revise and the other does not, the procedure becomes more complicated. In such a case a popular referendum is held to determine if the revision sought by one part of Parliament shall be proceeded with. In this referendum, only the popular, and not the cantonal, vote is recorded. If the referendum is favorable to the revision, the members of both houses of the Federal Assembly are deemed to have been automatically re-elected and they are forthwith obligated to submit a draft of a revised Constitution to a referendum of the people and the cantons.

The Constitutional Initiative. The constitutional initiative has simply been engrafted upon the compulsory constitutional referendum. The complete revision of the Constitution, or specific amendments thereto, may be proposed in petitions bearing at least 50,000 voters' signatures. If a complete revision is proposed, the subsequent procedure is identical with that followed when one

---

[15] Provisions for a compulsory referendum on constitutional changes had also been incorporated in the Constitution of the Helvetic Republic of 1798.

house of the Federal Assembly proposes a complete revision and the other house opposes.

If the popular petition proposes merely to amend the Constitution, the procedure pursued thereafter is dependent upon whether the proposed amendment has been formulated in specific, or merely general, terms. If formulated in specific terms, and if the Assembly or one house approves of it, the proposal is at once submitted for popular and cantonal action in the usual manner. If the Assembly disapproves of the proposed specifically formulated amendment, that body may advise the electorate to defeat the proposal or submit a competing proposal for popular and cantonal action along with the proposal which has been popularly initiated. When the popular initiative has merely formulated the proposed amendment in general terms, the Assembly again has two courses of action open to it. If it approves of the policy of the initiative proposal, it must draft an amendment expressing the sense of the initiative proposal and submit it to the people and the cantons for action. On the other hand, if it disapproves of the policy of the popular proposal, it must seek a decision in a popular vote (in which the cantons as such have no voice) on the question as to whether or not the initiative proposal shall be proceeded with. If the popular verdict is favorable, the Assembly must then draft an amendment expressing the sense of the initiative proposal and submit that to a regular vote of the people and the cantons.

Optional Referendum on Laws and Treaties. Unlike the compulsory referendum on constitutional changes, which requires both a popular and a cantonal vote, the optional referendum on laws and treaties requires only a popular vote, a majority of the voters participating being sufficient to decide the issue. The optional referendum may be inaugurated either by 30,000 voters or by eight cantons. Laws or resolutions which are not general in character or which are of an emergency nature cannot be submitted to a referendum. The Federal Assembly is the judge as to what laws or resolutions may thus be excepted; and it has often been charged with using this discretion to prevent popular action upon its measures.[16] It has also been apparent that the practice of transferring legislative discretion to the executive in blanket statutes, so characteristic a phenomenon since 1930, has inhibited the use of the popular referendum since executive decisions and resolutions are not susceptible to popular action even though they may, in fact, add to the body of substantive law. Long-smoldering dissatisfaction with this state of affairs culminated, on September 11, 1949, in the adoption, by narrow majorities and in a poorly attended poll, of the popular initiative to "return to direct democracy." This had the effect of limiting the operation of much of the "emergency" legislation, particularly tax laws, enacted during and after World War II to a period of one year immediately following the date of the adoption of the initiative unless, in the meantime, such legislation or any part of it was ratified and extended by popular vote.

---

[16] See on this subject remarks of Dr. Zellweger in the publication of the Association Juridique Internationale, entitled *Régression des principes de liberté* (Paris, 1938), p. 74.

Undoubtedly this was an unwise decision—probably as unwise a decision as an electorate, otherwise noted for conservatism and sagacity, has taken in recent years. The provocation, however, was great; and lacking the constitutional stewardship of a court of last resort, this seemed to be the only means by which a popular majority in Switzerland could serve notice upon their governors that their acts could no longer be rendered immune from the traditional popular right of veto and that traditional interpretations of the scope of the constitutional power of the Confederation Government could not simply be ignored by the plea of "emergency." The reaffirmation of the idea that a written constitution is a limitation on the power of those who govern is clearly one of the more important implications of the "popular revolt" of September, 1949. For the contemporary breed of democratic politician, who is prone to regard written constitutions as something of a nuisance and who often dismisses the allegation that such documents are intended to limit political discretion as an expression of conservative naïveté, the action of the Swiss electorate, ill-considered and hasty though it may have been, may nonetheless provide a needed lesson.

Experience with Direct Democracy. During the first century of the existence of the modern Swiss Confederation its citizens have attended some 150 plebiscites.[17] Of these, fifty-five were compulsory constitutional referenda; fifty-two were optional referenda on laws (including one international treaty in 1923); thirty-five were constitutional initiatives; and eight were proposals offered by the Federal Assembly as substitutes for popular initiative proposals.[18] The greatest percentage of affirmative popular majorities has been registered in the case of the obligatory constitutional referenda, the record being thirty-eight acceptances and seventeen rejections, or an acceptance ratio of two to one. Apparently the cantonal majorities have coincided in all cases with the popular. In the case of the optional referendum on laws, approximately two laws have been rejected for each one accepted by the voters, a total of thirty-six of the Federal Assembly's measures having been invalidated by the people and only sixteen sustained. Greatest caution has been shown by the electorate in the case of the constitutional initiative, there having been six rejections for every initiative proposal accepted by the voters and the cantons, or a total of thirty rejections and five acceptances. Parliament's substitute for initiative proposals to amend the Constitution were accepted by the voters and the cantons on six of the eight occasions when such substitutes were submitted. Altogether, in the century after 1848, the people of the Confederation accepted proposed laws or constitutional amendments on sixty-five occasions and refused to accept them on eighty-five occasions.

Of the three instruments of direct democracy used by the Confederation, the popular initiative is the most radical. Presumably, therefore, its use is the best index as to the degree of responsibility the Swiss voter brings to his task

[17] From the inauguration of the modern Confederation in 1848 up to, and including, March, 1949.

[18] The statistics on Swiss popular plebiscites have been secured from the *Statistisches Jahrbuch der Schweiz* (1933), pp. 394 *ff.;* (1940), pp. 408 *ff.;* and (1948), pp. 475 *ff.*

of lawmaker. Resort was had to the popular initiative much less frequently in the twenty-six-year period from 1891 to 1918 than in the thirty-year period from 1918 to 1948. In the earlier period, ten popular initiatives were proposed, whereas after 1918 the number of proposals rose to thirty-two, this figure including seven counter-initiative proposals offered by the Assembly. One reason for the increase of proposals in the later period and for an increasingly high mortality rate among such proposals is the apparently growing tendency of pressure groups, minority parties, and special constituencies of various kinds to exploit the initiative. Each of these is tempted to use the device in order to foist its pet nostrum upon the public or to bring to the attention of the voters some extreme measure that enjoys no prospect of being taken up in any other way. Needless to say, few of these measures have any prospect of success.

Among the more extreme initiative proposals rejected by the voters since 1918 was a plan for a capital levy in 1922; a Socialist-inspired "crisis initiative," offered in 1935 to combat the economic depression, which would have given the Government vast powers over the economy; and a proposal offered in the same year by native Fascist groups to revise the entire Constitution and replace many of the nation's democratic institutions with others of an authoritarian cast. A new crop of relatively extreme and unacceptable initiative proposals came to the fore during, and just after, World War II. Among them was a "right-to-work" initiative which rallied 19 per cent of the voters in 1946 and a similar proposal, coupled with plans to reorganize the nation's economy, offered in 1947, which was supported by 31 per cent of the voters. Both of these proposals would have had the Government guarantee "full employment." A plan to increase the membership of the collegial Confederation executive and have its members elected by the people was also advanced as an initiative proposal in 1942. It was coupled with a plan to reorganize the lower house of the Federal Assembly. Both plans met defeat. It should be noted, however, that the high degree of electoral conservatism, implicit in this behavior, has not prevented an occasional victory for supporters of a "radical" or "progressive" initiative proposal. It was such a proposal, for example, that recently amended the Constitution to enable the Confederation to legislate for the welfare of the family unit. Moreover, as already noted, an initiative in September, 1949, virtually invalidated all existing emergency legislation and thereby registered a veritable revolt against the representative Government of the nation.

Direct Democracy Today. Some of the more extreme initiative proposals of the period since World War I and the controversy over the emergency clause in the operation of the referendum may suggest that the Swiss are not as partial to direct democracy as they have been. Undoubtedly many of the nation's more conservative citizens have reservations. They may fear that an age as proficient as ours in manipulating public opinion could very well substitute popular decisions inspired by irresponsible propaganda and pressure tactics for the relatively more responsible decisions assured by the processes of representative government. Doubts such as these, however, probably do not assail the majority of Swiss citizens—at least not in 1951. Whatever the future may hold, the record of the past has been creditable. It is a record which now embraces the experience of a century. By and large, with minor exceptions, it is reassuring to even the most cautious and conservative. It is a record of relatively sustained electoral interest, of discriminating electoral participation, and of electoral decisions that, on the whole, reflect caution and common sense. It is a record in which Switzerland can take pride; and for the exponent of the democratic faith, Switzerland's experience with these instruments of popular government probably represents the most daring and the most successful application of that faith that any nation has made.[19]

[19] For an excellent discussion of direct democracy in Switzerland see William E. Rappard, *The Government of Switzerland* (New York, 1936), pp. 66 *ff.*

CHAPTER II

GOVERNMENTAL STRUCTURE OF CONFEDERATION
AND CANTONS

Switzerland's unusual emphasis upon the use of the instruments of direct democracy is but one of the more novel features of her political system. Other novelties, equally fascinating to the student of comparative government, will appear in the course of this chapter as we extend our study to the structure of the Government of the Confederation and the cantons. Among these novelties will be the special position which the federal tradition has assigned the second chamber of the national Parliament, a position so like that of the American Senate but quite different from that enjoyed by comparable bodies in the majority of European governments; the "vertical" type of federal administrative and judicial structure, as opposed to the "horizontal" type prevalent in America; and, above all, the conventional executive regime which prevails in both the Confederation and the cantons.

FEDERAL LEGISLATIVE AND EXECUTIVE ORGANS

The Federal Assembly: (1) The National Council. The Parliament of the Confederation is bicameral and is known as the Federal Assembly (*Bundesversammlung, Assemblée Fédérale*). Its primary and more popular house is the National Council (*Nationalrat, Conseil National*). It now consists of approximately 196 members, elected for a term of four years, suffrage being universal among males twenty years of age or over. Qualifications for membership in the National Council are the same as those required for voting; however, all clerics, executive and principal administrative servants of the Confederation Government, and members of the second house of the Federal Assembly are specifically excluded. Cantons and half-cantons serve as electoral constituencies, representation being distributed among them in accordance with the ratio of one councilor for every 22,000 inhabitants. Half-cantons whose population does not equal 22,000 are guaranteed at least one councilor. In the cantons which elect three or more national councilors, parties and political groups secure proportional representation. Lists of candidates, equivalent to the number of councilors to be elected, are submitted to the electors by the parties. Each elector may vote as many times as there are councilors to be elected. Normally he distributes his votes among the candidates as they appear on some party list, substituting other names and even voting twice for one candidate, a privilege allowed by the electoral law. This behavior of the elector is important; for it is chiefly the votes cast by the electors for the candidates as individuals that determine the latter's standing when the seats are distributed according to the proportional electoral quota.[1] As in all legislative bodies elected according to a proportional plan, membership is fairly stable. As a rule, at least a fourth of the membership has served for more than a decade and another fourth is likely to have served at least two terms or eight years. As in most parliamentary assemblies, lawyers predominate; but farmers, business men, and cantonal officials also have sizable quotas in the National Council.

The Federal Assembly: (2) The Council of States. The second house of the Federal Assembly is the Council of States (*Ständerat, Conseil des États*). In this body, as previously noted, every canton, no matter what its size or population, is entitled to two delegates, and every half-canton to one delegate. The total membership of the Council of States is thus forty-four. The concept of cantonal sovereignty and personality, still influential in Switzerland, is chiefly responsible for this equality of cantonal membership as, indeed, it is also for the very existence of a second chamber. To this same concept of cantonal sovereignty is to be attributed the circumstance that each canton determines how its delegates to the Council of States are to be elected, what their terms shall be, and what compensation shall be paid them out of the cantonal treasury. At the present time the people in twenty-one cantons or half-cantons elect their State Councilors either by ballot or in their *Landsgemeinde;* in the four remaining cantons State Councilors are elected by the representative legislatures. Terms of the State Councilors vary from one to four years, being longest in those cantons where they are popularly elected and shortest in those cantons where they are elected by the legislature.

Legislative Powers. The makers of the Swiss Constitution did not pay much attention to the orthodox theory of the separation of powers in establishing the Federal Assembly, since they conferred upon it all kinds of authority, legislative, executive, and even judicial. The enactment of laws dealing with Confederation matters are of course within its province. In addition it elects the seven members of the Federal Council who compose the executive department of the Swiss Government; it also elects the commander-in-chief of the army when one is needed, the members of the federal judiciary, and other officials of the Government. It declares war and concludes peace; ratifies treaties; issues amnesties and pardons; authorizes measures to guarantee the integrity of the cantonal Governments and the domestic peace of the Confed-

[1] The Swiss system of proportional representation is described in H. L. McBain and L. Rogers, *New Constitutions of Europe* (New York, 1923), pp. 109–113.

eration; disposes of the army; supervises the activities of the civil service; and even decides administrative disputes and conflicts of jurisdiction between federal officials. Few Parliaments have more miscellaneous duties.

Legislative Organization and Procedure. In exercising its power to elect executive, judicial, and other officials of the Confederation, its power to issue amnesties and pardons, and its authority to settle conflicts of administrative jurisdiction, the Federal Assembly acts as a unitary body, Council of States and National Council sitting together under the chairmanship of the president of the latter house. For all other matters, the two houses of the Assembly sit and act separately; and their concurrence is necessary to any parliamentary decision. Both houses hold an ordinary session annually beginning on the first Monday in December; and they meet in extra session at the request of the executive, or Federal Council, or of one-fourth of the members of the National Council or of five cantons. Each house elects a new president for each annual session, to whom is largely intrusted the determination of the daily order of business. Most of the new business of the two houses comes from the Federal Council, which has the duty of making innumerable reports and the privilege of initiating legislation. The latter privilege also inheres in either house or in members of either house of Parliament and, theoretically, in the individual cantons. A proposal introduced by a private member of Parliament takes the form either of a postulate or of a motion. Both are resolutions which seek to have the executive or Federal Council actually draft a bill on some specific subject and introduce it in Parliament. A postulate, which needs the majority vote of only one house to secure adoption, merely requests the Federal Council to draft legislation on some subject; the Federal Council enjoys discretion in determining whether or not the postulate shall be complied with. A motion, on the other hand, must be sustained by majorities in both houses to become effective and, when voted, requires the Federal Council to draft legislation on a specific subject and introduce it in Parliament. In any case it is clear that, wherever legislative initiative may reside, the Federal Council, or executive, virtually monopolizes the prerogative of drafting bills and formally introducing such bills in Parliament.

In order to use the time of the houses effectively, the respective presidents try to apportion to each of them an equal share of the agenda presented by the Federal Council at the opening of each session. Most of the measures introduced in either house are eventually referred to committees which normally reflect the proportional strength of the various political parties. These committees may present both majority and minority reports to the houses through *rapporteurs.* In case a difference of opinion arises between the houses on a pending measure, the respective committees having charge of it try to iron out the difference. Normally this is not difficult, since neither house is inclined to assume an uncompromising attitude. Of course, since the two houses are coordinate in power, insistence by one of them upon its version of a pending measure, contrary to the will of the other, means that the measure is killed. In accordance with the official position occupied by the various languages used in Switzerland, all parliamentary documents and decisions are published in both French and German, and some also in Italian; and parliamentarians are privileged to address their colleagues in French, German, or Italian.

The Federal Council. The scope and limitations of parliamentary activity at Bern will become clearer if we now turn our attention to the federal executive. As already indicated, this body is known as the Federal Council (*Bundesrat, Conseil Fédéral*) and consists of seven members elected by the Federal Assembly. Constitutional usage prescribes that Zürich and Bern, being among the oldest of the cantons and having the largest population, shall always be represented. A similar right is guaranteed in the same manner to Vaud, largest of the French-speaking cantons. Usage further prescribes that another Romance canton besides Vaud shall always be represented. The legal term of service in the Council is four years.[2] Its prerogatives are manifold. They include the actual conduct of foreign affairs; the supervision of inter-cantonal relations, particularly cantonal concordats; the preservation of internal security, including especially the enforcement of the federal Constitution's guarantee of cantonal political integrity and the federal right of intervention to preserve order in a canton when the latter is unable to do so; the immediate supervision of all Confederation officials, civil and military; the administration of the national finances; and the enforcement of the Confederation's laws and ordinances and federal judicial decisions. Formerly the Federal Council also served as the principal administrative court of last resort; but since 1928 it settles only such appeals against decisions of the Confederation's administrative services as have not been transferred to the agenda of the Federal Tribunal.[3]

Although the detailed administrative responsibilities to which these prerogatives give rise are distributed among seven administrative departments each headed by one of the Federal Councilors, it is the theory of the Constitution that all important executive decisions shall be made by the Federal Council as a body and that the Council shall assume corporate responsibility for such decisions. When acting collegially, four Councilors constitute the minimum number for a quorum; and it would therefore appear that at least three Councilors must concur in every conciliar decision. This theory of a collegial executive does not always square with practice. At any rate, many important executive decisions are made by individual Councilors.[4] By law, moreover, activities which at an earlier date were the responsibility of the entire Council have been passed on to specific Councilors and by them to subordinates.[5]

The President of the Confederation. Annually the Federal Assembly designates a member of the Federal Council to serve as President of the Confederation and a second member to serve as Vice-President. The Constitution expressly forbids the re-election of an incumbent President or Vice-President.

[2] In 1931 the term of Federal Councilor, like that of National Councilor, was extended from three to four years.

[3] For a description of this body, see p. 353.

[4] Cf. J. Dürsteler, *Die Organisation der Exekutiv der schweizerischen Eidgenossenschaft* (Aarau, 1912), p. 298.

[5] R. C. Brooks, *Government and Politics of Switzerland* (Yonkers, 1918), p. 128.

Usage requires that the Vice-President succeed the President and that the two offices rotate among the members of the Federal Council. Although the Presidency of the Confederation is an office of some dignity, it has none but purely formal prerogatives, the principal ones being those of presiding over the deliberations of the Federal Council and serving as the titular head of State both within the country and in the conduct of foreign relations. Such official authority as the President may wield comes to him as a member of the Council and as head of one of the seven administrative departments.[6]

Executive Subordination to the Legislature. Numerous political commentaries remark upon the unique characteristics of the Swiss national executive. Besides its collegial structure, which incidentally distinguishes the executive of almost every level of government in Switzerland, what seems remarkable in the Swiss executive to foreign observers is the position of inferiority which the Constitution assigns it in its relations with the legislature. In Swiss constitutional theory the executive is not an independent or coordinate branch of government as it is, for example, in the American system; the Swiss have made the executive the formal servant of the legislature. This servitorship is implied in the Federal Assembly's election of the Federal Council and in the Assembly's use of the Council as a sort of glorified legislative drafting bureau. Executive servitude is made still more obvious by the Assembly's supervision of the executive province. Because of the wide scope and miscellaneous character of the powers constitutionally committed to the Federal Assembly, that body's previous authorization or subsequent ratification must usually be secured by the Federal Council when it exercises prerogatives relating to the armed forces, to foreign relations, or even to the ordinary conduct of public administration. The Assembly, moreover, resorts to postulates or motions to direct the executive's course in the conduct of the administration in much the same manner as it uses these instruments to direct that the executive draft desired legislation.[7] It is also customary for the Assembly to require detailed written reports on the general conduct of executive business; and it does not hesitate to question the Councilors orally or to interpellate them on the floor of the respective houses. It may be interjected here that Federal Councilors, although excluded from membership in the Assembly, have the privilege of attending all plenary legislative sessions, or committee meetings, and of participating in the debate. The most striking evidence of the subordination of the executive to the legislature in Switzerland is to be discovered in the fact that neither constitutional law nor usage requires the resignation of the Federal Councilors should their policy happen to conflict with that of the Assembly; in such a case the Councilors merely change their policy in order to make it conform with the Assembly's expressed will.

Sources of Executive Influence. Despite what has just been said, it must not be concluded that the Swiss Federal Councilors lack influence on the course of public affairs. The very fact that the Assembly transfers to them

[6] Cf. R. Hübner, *Die Staatsform der Republik* (Bonn, 1919), p. 231.
[7] See p. 348.

most of the legislative initiative, combined with the Councilors' immediate responsibility for the conduct of the Government, gives them many opportunities to determine the tenor and direction of public policy. Nor does the constitutional supremacy of the Federal Assembly greatly hamper such activity on their part. In Switzerland as elsewhere—in Great Britain, for instance—the parliamentary responsibility of the executive serves to justify the exertion of executive discretion almost as often as it serves to check such discretion or to modify it. In this connection it should be recalled that the Swiss Federal Councilors are usually the leading politicians among the parties which dominate the Federal Assembly. This fact necessarily assures the Councilors a certain degree of partisan support in that body even though Swiss tradition frowns upon the exploitation of partisan discipline on behalf of the executive and requires that the Federal Council conduct itself in a nonpartisan manner.

Lengthy Tenure of Federal Councilors. Still another factor which contributes to the practical importance of the Federal Council in the Swiss Government is the individual Councilor's relatively lengthy tenure. Partly because of the Swiss habit of re-electing public servants as long as they wish to serve and partly because of the tradition that Federal Councilors shall not resign for political reasons, their actual term of continuous service usually exceeds by many years that of their ministerial counterparts in other governments. Continuous service for two decades is not uncommon.[8] Occasionally a Federal Councilor will round out three decades or more. One of the more recent illustrations of such a record of service was that of Signor Giuseppe Motta, Councilor from the Ticino, who served from 1911 to 1940. So accustomed are the Swiss to continuing in office their chief executive personnel that the pension system for the Federal Council does not apply to one of its members unless he has served at least ten years. Certainly one consequence of this long period in office is the enhancement of the Councilor's official prestige, administrative skill, and political judgment, and therefore of his practical capacity for political leadership.

Recent Executive Developments. Finally it should be added that Switzerland has not been immune from the contemporary world-wide tendency to strengthen executive power. Efforts to preserve her neutrality and protect her economy during the two World Wars, combined with measures to combat the interbellum economic crisis have necessitated the erection of a veritable emergency regime in the Swiss political system. One characteristic of this regime is the delegation by the Federal Assembly to the Federal Council of "blanket" authority over matters hitherto regulated directly by statute. Thus in the National Defence Act, passed on August 30, 1939, as World War II was beginning, the Federal Assembly instructed the executive to take whatever measures it deemed necessary to preserve the country's security, independence, and neutrality; to safeguard the national credit and economy; and to ensure supplies for the nation. As a result of this important statute, the legal rights and duties of

[8] On this subject see Hübner, *op. cit.,* p. 230; also, W. E. Rappard, *The Government of Switzerland* (New York, 1936), p. 80.

individuals came to be defined primarily by executive decree and decision rather than by statute, at least for the duration of the War. Much of the discretion thus confided to the executive has, moreover, been continued since the close of hostilities in 1945. Occasionally the Federal Council has also issued ordinances (*Notverordnungen*) affecting the body of private law on the mere plea that the public safety and necessity required such action.[9] This is a type of executive power which, though common enough in some Continental political systems, has been relatively unknown in Switzerland. Apparently this system of emergency government by the executive has profoundly irritated the Swiss people. At any rate, on September 11, 1949, as noted earlier in these pages,[10] the electorate adopted a constitutional initiative which looks to the repeal of most of the emergency decree legislation within a year. Despite this reaction, it seems reasonably clear that the legislative significance of the Federal Council has been permanently enhanced and that in Switzerland, as elsewhere among Western democracies, the executive has become, at least *de facto*, the dominant branch of the Government.

THE FEDERAL ADMINISTRATION AND THE JUDICIARY

Administrative Departments. As previously stated, administration of federal affairs is distributed among seven departments, each headed by a Federal Councilor. These departments are as follows: (1) Political Affairs; (2) Military Affairs; (3) Justice and Police; (4) Finance and Customs; (5) Interior; (6) National Economy; and (7) Posts and Railways. As in the case of the American State Department, the jurisdiction of the Swiss Department of Political Affairs embraces some relatively minor domestic responsibilities as well as the foreign affairs of the Confederation. During certain periods in the past, this Department was entrusted to the President of the Confederation; its headship and that of at least one other department thus had to be changed annually since a new President is elected within the Federal Council every year. This custom has been discontinued since World War I; and the Political Department, like the other departments, continues under the same Councilor indefinitely. The miscellaneous federal duties attributed to the Interior Department also permit comparison of that Department with one of the same name in the American Government and sharply distinguishes it from interior departments of centralized Continental governments whose chief duty is the maintenance of internal security. The duties of the remaining Swiss administrative departments are probably self-explanatory. Of great importance among these remaining departments are those of Posts and Railways and of National Economy, the first because the Confederation owns and manages the postal, telephonic, telegraphic, wireless, and railway systems, and the second because of the increasing intervention of the Confederation Government in economic affairs. It should be added that the Railway Administration, although under the jurisdiction of the Department of Posts and Railways, enjoys a con-

[9] On this general subject see Kurt Reber, *Das Notrecht des Staates* (Zürich, 1938).
[10] See p. 342.

siderable degree of autonomy, having among other things, an entirely separate budget. In recent years the duties of some of the departments have become so complex and numerous as to justify an increase in their number; but since their number is constitutionally restricted to that of the membership of the Federal Council, an increase cannot take place unless the roster of the Council is expanded by a constitutional amendment.

Civil Servants and Public Employees. Administration of the Confederation's laws and policies is often entrusted to cantonal officials. Such a "vertical" administrative structure seems desirable not only because it promotes economy but also because it helps to overcome cantonal objection to the growing political centralization in the nation. Because of this federal administrative structure, the personnel of the Confederation's Civil Service and its corps of public employees is less numerous than might be expected, although Switzerland has been no less susceptible to bureaucratic expansion than other states. Until World War II, moreover, roughly three-quarters of those on the Confederation payroll were employed on the publicly owned railway and communications systems or on the state monopolies. Most of the civil servants and employees are appointed by the Federal Councilors in their capacity of department heads. Railway officials and employees are appointed by the autonomous Federal Railway Administration. Appointing authorities fix most of the conditions relating to the appointment, dismissal, promotion, and privileges of a public servant. Citizenship, a good character reference, a satisfactory level of attainment in the country's educational system, and, occasionally, specific training are required of candidates for basic positions in each of the major levels of the various branches of the public service. Appointments are usually made on the basis of competitive examinations. The entire service is comparatively free of nepotistic or political influences and is unusually efficient. The rate of compensation, traditionally low, has risen steadily since 1920; the attractiveness of the service is, moreover, enhanced by security of tenure and a generous pension system. Public employees and civil servants have their own service organizations, which in many instances are affiliated with the Swiss Federation of Trade Unions.

The Federal Judiciary. The judiciary is the most recently developed branch of the Confederation's Government. The Constitution-makers of 1848 had provided for a Federal Tribunal (*Bundesgericht, Tribunal Fédéral*); but the agency actually set up under this name was distinctly rudimentary. It had no fixed location for the transaction of business and lacked qualified professional personnel. A more serious weakness was its lack of authority. Public-law cases, such as disputes between the cantons and between the cantons and the Confederation, that might logically have been submitted to it, went instead to the Federal Council or Assembly. All this was changed, however, in 1874. From the constitutional revision of that year the Federal Tribunal emerged as a full-fledged federal court. A year later its headquarters were formally set up at Lausanne, capital of the Canton of Vaud, the choice of this site apparently having been intended to allay lingering dissatisfaction in Romance Switzerland because the rest of the Confederation Government had been centered at Bern in German Switzerland.

At the present time the Federal Tribunal consists of some twenty-six judges elected for six-year terms by the Federal Assembly. There are also eleven supplementary judges. Biennially, Parliament designates the judge who shall serve as president of the court. The Constitution formally requires Parliament to consider the claims of the three major languages of the country to representation on the federal bench; usage supplements this requirement with similar claims for individual cantons and even for partisan groups. As in the case of Federal Councilors, the judges of the Federal Tribunal are re-elected as long as they wish to serve. This practice, guaranteeing virtually permanent tenure, largely removes the danger to judicial independence which might otherwise inhere in the brevity of the judges' legal term and in the influences which affect their original election. After at least ten years of service on the bench, judges are guaranteed a pension that approximates half their salary in case they retire.

The Tribunal's Jurisdiction. The Federal Tribunal acts as a corporate entity only when it meets to transact business affecting its own establishment or to issue regulations relating to the conduct of judicial business. In dispensing justice it operates in various sections for public, criminal, and civil law, such sections being appointed for two-year intervals. Although the Federal Tribunal is often described as the supreme court of the Swiss nation, its powers do not quite justify such a title. Most of the ordinary criminal and civil law of the land, which is incorporated in federal codes, is administered by the courts of the twenty-five cantons and half-cantons. Over these courts, the Federal Tribunal has only a limited right of review, civil cases involving a relatively large sum being appealable to it, under certain circumstances, from the highest court of the respective cantons. The remainder of the Tribunal's jurisdiction is original in character and rather specialized. It involves cases of civil, criminal, constitutional, and administrative law. Its original civil jurisdiction extends to controversies of a proprietary character between the Confederation and the cantons, between cantons, and between individuals and the Confederation or the cantons. Apparently, under certain circumstances, this original civil jurisdiction also extends to cases between individuals. The Tribunal's original criminal jurisdiction is limited to cases involving treason or insurrection against the Confederation, counterfeiting, violence against national officials, offences against the law of nations, and criminal charges preferred by superior Confederation officials against their subordinates. Apparently this jurisdiction can be expanded by legislation. To hear its criminal cases, the Tribunal holds assizes from time to time in five different centers of the country. In these assizes a section of the Tribunal, consisting of three judges, sits with a jury of twelve men elected from the vicinage; and the concurrence of five-sixths of the jurymen is necessary to convict an accused person. The Tribunal's constitutional authority relates to jurisdictional conflicts between cantonal and Confederation agencies, inter-cantonal public-law conflicts, and cases of alleged violation by the cantons of personal rights secured under the federal or cantonal constitutions, inter-cantonal agreements or treaties. Finally, as a court of administrative law, the Federal Tribunal has, since 1928, been invested with the power to settle disputes regarding the legal competence of public officials.[11]

Lacks Powers of a Constitutional Court. As stated elsewhere, the Swiss Federal Tribunal has no power to ascertain the constitutionality of federal statutes, the Federal Assembly having reserved to itself or to the people the final interpretation of the Confederation's basic statute. The Tribunal's power of constitutional review is thus limited to those cases, described above, where it is called upon to vindicate the rights of citizens under cantonal or federal constitutions against alleged violations by cantonal statutes. It might be added that in view of the Tribunal's limited and unsystematic jurisdiction, it could hardly serve as an effective instrument for reviewing federal legislation judicially, even if such a power inhered in it.

THE CANTONS

Present Significance of the Cantons. As already indicated, the Swiss cantons are no longer the essentially sovereign states which they were prior to 1848. Moreover, the present trend toward the nationalization of political power and political loyalty has undoubtedly reduced their historic individuality. Nevertheless they continue to be highly developed autonomous political communities within the federal state. Each of them still has powers which, in many respects, resemble those of a sovereign government. Each of them, moreover, has a complete governmental apparatus, including a written constitution, legislative, executive, and judicial organs, a fiscal system and a civil service. In addition the cantons control all forms of local self-government. Since the autonomous functions of the cantons and their functional relationship to the Confederation Government have been commented upon elsewhere,[12] it remains for us to describe briefly certain aspects of their political structure.

The Landsgemeinde Cantons. The federal Constitution requires that the political system of each canton shall be republican in form; but this republicanism may be either of a purely democratic or of a representative type. As noted earlier, one canton, that of Glarus, and the four half-cantons into which Appenzell and Unterwalden are divided, still center political authority in their medieval *Landsgemeinde* or annual assembly of all the citizens. In formal constitutional theory, at least, these bodies exercise the legislative power of the canton and elect and supervise the cantonal executive and administrative officials. Hence Glarus and the four half-cantons using the *Landsgemeinde* must be regarded as possessing a government of a purely democratic-republican type.

Representative Cantons. In all other cantons or half-cantons a representative republican form of government prevails. In these, legislative power and the surveillance of the administration is entrusted to unicameral representative

---

[11] As suggested earlier, the Insurance Tribunal, operating at Luzern, might be considered a special federal administrative court.
[12] See p. 338.

assemblies known as Great Councils or Cantonal Councils. These are elected
on the basis of a democratically enfranchised citizenry and proportional representation. The cantons which are not pure democracies have, however, modified their representative character with a large measure of direct democracy
introduced by means of the modern initiative and referendum. Every one of
them is required by the federal Constitution to submit all changes in the cantonal constitution to the people and to allow the people to propose constitutional amendments. Hence every representative canton has a constitutional
initiative and a compulsory constitutional referendum. In addition each representative canton provides for a popular initiative on ordinary legislation and
for a legislative referendum. In some the legislative referendum is optional;
in the majority it is compulsory for all laws of a general character and for certain fiscal measures. The representative Swiss cantons thus have a far greater
admixture of pure democracy in their institutions than the Government of the
Confederation; and between some of them and the so-called *Landsgemeinde*
cantons there is scarcely any difference in the amount of actual responsibility
for law-making placed directly upon the populace.

Cantonal Executives. In harmony with the pluralistic Swiss tradition, the
executive power in all the cantons is vested in a commission. Variously known
as the Governing Council, or the Small Council, or the Council of State, the
commissions consist of from five to eleven members, all of whom are popularly elected. Various political parties are usually represented and sometimes
efforts are deliberately made to give the parties proportional representation.
As in the Federal Council, each member of a cantonal executive commission is
the head of an administrative department of the Government. Collectively the
commission is responsible to the legislature for whose will it must exhibit
the same formal deference that the Federal Council exhibits for the will of the
Federal Assembly. But, like the Federal Council, the cantonal commissions
assume the responsibility for drafting and introducing most of the legislation;
this, in addition to their administrative duties, ensures them substantial powers of leadership.

Cantonal Courts. As we have seen, the only Confederation court is the
Federal Tribunal whose competence is relatively specialized. It follows, therefore, that the administration of justice continues to be primarily a cantonal
responsibility, and that most cases and controversies requiring adjudication go
before cantonal tribunals. In most cantons, justices of the peace or petty magistrates' courts in the communes settle minor civil disputes. More important civil
cases may originate in a cantonal district court and, under certain circumstances, may be appealed to a court of review bearing the name of cantonal,
or higher, court or court of civil justice. In a variety of civil cases, appeals
may be taken to the Federal Tribunal. Considerable use is also made of arbitration and commercial tribunals in settling industrial and trade disputes,
particularly disputes over labor contracts. Original jurisdiction in the case of
offenses against the State is usually distributed among three grades of cantonal courts: petty offenses are handled by police or magistrates' courts; major

misdemeanors and less serious felonies, by the so-called correctional courts; and major felonies, involving long-term imprisonment and loss of civil rights upon conviction, by the criminal court or court of assizes. The death penalty was abolished in Switzerland in 1942, although during World War II, military courts occasionally exacted the penalty for the crime of treason. As in most Continental states, a special section of the trial court, known as an indictment section or court of indictment, determines whether a person is to be held for trial on the basis of information furnished by an examining magistrate and the public prosecutor. All except the petty tribunals in the cantonal judiciary have plural magistracies and the judges may be elected by the people or by the legislature; or they may be appointed by their superiors on the bench. The term of the judicial office varies from three to ten years, the longer term usually applying to the higher magistrates. No Swiss judge may hold office during good behavior, that is, for life; but since reappointment or re-election is habitual, judges have a virtual life term. Juries ranging from six to twelve members exist in some of the courts of assizes.

The Communes. For purposes of local self-government, the cantons are divided into communes of which, in the whole of Switzerland, there are presently some 3,107.[13] A few are comparatively large cities; a few more are large towns or urban communities; but the great majority are rural areas or hamlets. The governmental structure of the commune is not dissimilar to that of the canton, democracy being the guiding principle. Many of the smaller communes vest their affairs in an assembly of the citizens; others, having representative organs consisting of an assembly and an executive council headed by president, mayor, or syndic, have adopted the democratic device of the referendum. Communal powers are extensive and allow for many activities of an economic and cultural character. In a democracy like Switzerland, local government assumes more than ordinary importance since it provides the civic training and sense of community responsibility so essential to success in the management of the affairs of the canton and the nation as a whole.

It should be noted that in most of the cantons there are special communal corporations in addition to the governmental commune just described. These special communes may not, and usually do not, embrace all persons actually resident within the local area. One type of special communal corporation may be ecclesiastical and embrace those belonging to a particular faith. It organizes and finances public worship for the creed in question. Another type might be called the native citizens' commune. It consists of those inhabitants of a particular area who are natives of that area and of such others as claim the area as their place of origin. Only these share in the support of this special commune and receive its benefits, the latter assuming chiefly the form of financial assistance for indigent members.[14]

---

[13] *Statistisches Jahrbuch der Schweiz* (1948).

[14] In all but eight cantons there are also districts (*Amtbezirke, arrondissements*) consisting of the area of several political communes. In charge of the district is a commissioner or prefect who represents the cantonal government locally and supervises certain aspects of the operations of the communes in the district.

CHAPTER III

POLITICAL PARTIES AND THEIR PROGRAMS

EVOLUTION OF SWISS PARTIES

Reliance upon Political Parties. Switzerland follows other democratic states in relying upon a variety of political parties to organize and promote national opinion, to sponsor such opinion in the various organs of government, and to provide those group disciplines and loyalties essential to the successful operation of deliberative and plebiscitary political institutions. As in most other states the political parties are organized spontaneously and find little if any recognition in official documents. About the only recognition formally accorded parties in Switzerland is that discovered in the rules governing the organization and procedure of Confederation and cantonal Parliaments and in the federal and cantonal proportional electoral laws.

Liberal-Radical Ascendancy. In 1848, when the modern Confederation was created, federal affairs were dominated by two groups of politicians whose principal support came from the Protestant German cantons and from Protestant French cantons. These groups subsequently became known respectively as the Liberal Democrats or, more briefly, the Liberals and the Independent Democrats or Radicals.[1] Of these two groups the Liberals were the older. They advocated a traditional nineteenth-century political philosophy that emphasized the *laissez faire* economics of the Manchester School, moral and cultural freedom, and republican political institutions. The younger and more progressive Radicals were inclined towards a liberalism of a more advanced type, which sought to extend political democracy by means of such instruments as the initiative and referendum, and which was willing to temper economic liberty with a certain degree of state intervention. Despite the differences in their views, these two groups had nonetheless collaborated in bringing into being the new federal Constitution; and their respective philosophies had been chiefly responsible for that document's centralistic, libertarian, secular, and democratic fea-

[1] Throughout the remainder of the text these parties will be referred to as Liberals and Radicals.

tures. Opposed to them was a party consisting mainly of those elements which had formed the *Sonderbund* in 1846 and brought on the War of Secession in 1848. Known as the Catholic Conservative People's Party, it represented Catholic Switzerland, was antiliberal, clerical, and even ultramontane in its views, and emphasized cantonal rights. It paid only grudging allegiance to the constitutional settlement of 1848, into the acceptance of which it had been virtually coerced.

Decline of the Liberals. With the Catholic Conservatives in opposition, the Liberal and Radical Parties governed the country from 1848 to 1890. Between them they controlled a large majority in the Federal Assembly and, of course, monopolized all seven places on the Federal Council. During this period of joint ascendancy, the Liberal Party's electoral strength gradually ebbed whereas that of the Radicals increased enormously. In time the Radicals became not only the dominant party in the coalition but by far the largest party in the country; while the Liberals approached the status of a minor political group. The change in their respective strengths was not accurately reflected in the Federal Council because of the practice, already commented upon, of re-electing the members of that body as long as they wished to serve; but as Liberal Councilors retired, their places were invariably taken by Radicals, and toward the end of 1890 the Federal Council's membership came to include only a single representative of the Liberal Party.

Recent Partisan Coalitions. When this Liberal member retired during the following year, a profoundly important political shift took place; for the Federal Assembly proceeded to elect in his stead a representative of the Catholic Conservative Party. Thus forty-three years after the inauguration of the federal Constitution, this party finally gave up the role of official opposition and assumed a share of the responsibility of Government. The executive partnership of Radicals and Conservatives has continued, a second Conservative having been added to the Federal Council in 1919. Their predominance has, however, been challenged in the past quarter century by newer political parties who have demanded, and ultimately have been accorded, representation on the Swiss executive. Thus in 1929, partisan representation on the Federal Council was broadened to include a member of the Farmers' Party, a group which had broken away from the Radicals in 1918. Again in 1943 a member of the Social Democratic Party joined the governing circle of seven, an event of no little significance, since it marked the end of the monopoly which parties representing bourgeois, or middle-class, ideals had exercised over the Swiss executive for almost a century. At the present time (1951), therefore, the Swiss Federal Council consists of three Radicals, two Catholic Conservatives, one member of the Farmers' Party, and one Social Democrat. Politically it is a coalition which might be described as somewhat left of Center albeit more moderate in temper, particularly on social issues, than the governing groups of some contemporary democratic States.

Rise of Marxist Parties. As already indicated, until 1943 the role of chief opposition party in the Swiss legislature had been assumed by the Social

Democrats. This party's representatives first appeared in the National Council in 1891 at just the time the coalition between Conservatives and Radicals was first elaborated. That these two events should have transpired at approximately the same time is probably no coincidence. With Socialism's arrival on the political stage, Catholic Conservative and Radical undoubtedly considered themselves well advised to compromise their differences. Swiss Socialism arose in sympathy with similar movements in other countries inspired by Karl Marx's materialistic interpretation of history and his doctrine of the class struggle. The onset of industrialization and the growth of such manufacturing centers as Zürich, Winterthur, and Basel, so noteworthy a feature of recent Swiss economic history, offered splendid opportunities for the propagation of Socialist doctrines; and the party grew apace. At the end of World War I, it claimed forty-one seats in the National Council. By 1935 it claimed fifty seats, and had wrested from the Radicals the reputation of being the party with the largest popular following in the country. Subsequent splitting off of the more militant Left-wing elements, who leaned toward the Marxism of Russian Communism, gave the ascendancy in the National Council once more to the Radicals, the latter having fifty-two seats to forty-eight for the Social Democrats in the quadrennial elections of 1947. Marxism's left wing first broke with the moderate Social Democrats in 1922, although for two decades it rarely elected more than three or four delegates to the National Council. In 1941 the Confederation Government dissolved the two elements of Marxism's extremist wing, then known respectively as "Communists" and the "Socialist Federation"; but the ban was lifted three years later, and extremist Marxism reformed and consolidated its ranks, assuming the name of "Labor Party." In the 1951 elections, this party chose five delegates to the National Council.

Establishment of Other Parties. Socialism's rise to power in the Swiss National Council was greatly aided by the use of proportional representation in national elections after 1918. This electoral reform may also be held at least partly responsible for the subsequent development of various other parties or electoral groups. Attention has already been directed to one of these, the so-called Farmers' Party,[2] which split off from the Radicals in 1918 largely because of dissatisfaction with Radical agrarian policies. In 1929, when it joined the governing group in the Federal Council, this party claimed thirty-one seats in the National Council. From this high point its strength declined, especially after the elections of 1935; and in 1951 its delegation in the National Council numbered only twenty-three. Other parties represented in the Swiss legislature after the 1951 elections consisted of the Independent Party, newly formed in 1935, with ten seats in the National Council and a loose grouping of cantonal democratic parties, particularly from Zürich and Glarus, which accounted for four seats.[3]

[2] The official name is the Farmers, Artisans, and Middle Class Party.
[3] The standing of the parties in the National Council from 1919 to 1951 is indicated by the following table:

CONTEMPORARY PARTY PROGRAMS

Policies of Catholic Conservatism. The generations of governmental
responsibility and collaboration with other parties have largely dissipated the
Catholic Conservative Party's early antipathy to federalism and to a central
government within the Confederation. Nevertheless it is still strongly pro-
cantonal and particularistic in its approach to national issues: it is still the
Swiss "states'-rights" party. Although it is willing to admit that a degree of
political intervention is warranted by the conditions of modern society, the
party's pronouncements repeatedly include warnings against the dangers of a
centralized bureaucracy. As antidotes for the growing dominance of politics in
modern life, it demands special protection for the family and private property
and the encouragement of private philanthropy and cooperative institutions.
In this connection it also emphasizes its peculiar concern for the welfare of the
Catholic Church, suggesting that the preservation of the Church's prerogatives
and authority, especially in matters affecting morals and education, is the best
safeguard for social peace and discipline. In general it may be said that the
Catholic Conservative Party favors a corporative conception of society as opposed to a conception of state dominance or political totalitarianism.

Certain papal encyclicals of recent years have encouraged the development
of a Christian Socialist wing within the party. This has caused the party to
take a more tolerant view of social legislation and to adopt a more benevolent attitude toward labor. Officially the party recognizes the need for certain
types of industrial reforms benefiting labor and the consumer; it recognizes the
"dignity" of labor and labor's right to a living wage; and it justifies the growth

Party	Number of seats					Per cent of total				
	1919	1931	1943	1947	1951	1919	1931	1943	1947	1951
Radicals	58	52	47	52	51	30.7	27.8	24.2	26.8	26.0
Liberals	9	6	8	7	5	4.8	3.2	4.1	3.6	2.6
Conservatives	41	44	43	44	48	21.7	23.5	22.2	22.7	24.5
Farmers	31	30	22	21	23	16.4	16.0	11.3	10.8	11.7
Social Democrats	41	49	56	48	49	21.7	26.2	28.9	24.7	25.0
Independents	—	—	6	9	10	—	—	3.1	4.7	5.1
Democrats	—	—	—	5	4	—	—	—	2.6	2.0
Communists	—	2	—	7	5	—	1.1	—	3.6	2.6
Others	9	4	12	1	1	4.7	2.2	6.2	0.5	0.5
Totals	189	187	194	194	196	100.0	100.0	100.0	100.0	100.0

The standing of the parties in the Council of States after the
two elections of 1943 and 1947 was as follows:

Party	Number of seats		Per cent of total	
	1943	1947	1943	1947
Radicals	12	12	27.3	27.3
Liberals	2	2	4.5	4.5
Conservatives	19	18	43.2	40.9
Farmers	4	4	9.1	9.1
Social Democrats	5	4	11.4	9.1
Others	2	4	4.5	9.1
Totals	44	44	100.0	100.0

of labor unions and collective bargaining so long as individual workmen are not intimidated or coerced. The party's primary interest, however, continues to be in the middle class of society. Its ideal commonwealth appears to be one in which peasants, artisans, and petty business men dominate; and to protect the interests of such groups it favors setting curbs to competitive individualism and large-scale capitalism. On the whole the aims of Catholic Conservatism are not too well articulated; at any rate they seem somewhat obscure to the un-initiated.[4]

Present Radical Program. As in the past, the Radical Party continues to be the chief sponsor of federal centralization, and it stands solidly behind a strong Confederation government. At the same time it seems to have become somewhat more cautious on this issue of centralization than it used to be, and its official pronouncements of party policy occasionally contain warnings against further violations of cantonal integrity. Moreover, when a new power is added to the jurisdiction of the Confederation, the Radicals are usually ready to have Bern share its administration with the cantons and to subsidize the cantons from the Confederation Treasury for the resulting financial respon-sibilities. Although largely forsaken by its former working-class supporters, who have gone over to Marxism, the Radical Party continues to be a vigorous champion of social-welfare legislation. Nor has the party lost its faith in secularism, in constitutionally guaranteed personal liberties, or in political democracy. Its continued belief in the latter is evidenced by the inclusion in several of its more recent platforms of a plank demanding the popular initia-tive for federal legislation. Liberal capitalism is still regarded as the essential ingredient of the Radical's economic philosophy; but the foundations of that philosophy have been undermined by the party's advocacy of tariff protection, its espousal of a variety of public monopolies, its relative indifference to carteli-zation, and particularly by the protective legislation and subsidy programs for farmers and business men which it has championed ever since the depression of the 1930's. Traditionally the Radicals have been outspoken in their demand for adequate national defense, and they continue to lay great stress upon the need for a military establishment recruited by a system of universal compul-sory service and equipped with the most modern armanents. On issues affect-ing the country's foreign relations, the Radicals, like virtually all other Swiss parties, seek to vindicate and make secure the traditional policy of neutrality.

Program of the Farmers' Party. As indicated earlier, the Farmers' Party, third member of the governing fraternity in the Federal Council, is the result of a secession from the Radical Party in 1918. Like the organization of which it was once a part, the Farmers' Party is a vigorous exponent of adequate na-tional defense and has no philosophical objection against strengthening the government of the Confederation if the national interest seems to require a policy of centralization. On the other hand, as respects social issues, this party is more conservative than the Radicals and less willing to make concessions to

---

[4] Brief abstracts of the programs of contemporary Swiss parties appear in *Political Hand-book of the World*, Walter H. Mallory ed. (1949), pp. 171–172.

the advocates of the welfare state. Despite the fact that its official title suggests that its constituency includes small shopkeepers and other urban elements, the party's supporters are almost wholly agrarian. It is not surprising, therefore, that its primary concern should be the agricultural interest. It seeks to protect this interest in various ways: by advocating federal subventions to agricultural producers; by reserving the domestic market for Swiss agriculture through tariffs and other trade restrictions; by seeking the enactment of farm-mortgage relief legislation; and by having the Government fix "fair" prices for agricultural commodities. Recent legislation has favored this party greatly, many of its aims having been secured in the constitutional amendment of March, 1929, which authorized various forms of public assistance in the production, marketing, and processing of grain and the protection of the domestic agricultural producer against foreign competition.

Socialism's Reorientation. As the second largest political entity in the National Council and the fourth party represented in the Swiss executive, the Social Democratic Party has acquired a position of considerable importance in present-day Switzerland. On the whole, even in the period when this party enjoyed that luxury of relative irresponsibility which is the prerogative of the political opposition, it failed to develop tendencies socially as radical or politically as militant as those of Socialist Parties in certain other countries. Various explanations may be offered for this moderate orientation of Swiss Socialism. Partly it may be ascribed to the Swiss factory worker's retention of much of the conservative social outlook of the peasant and artisan classes from which he has but recently sprung. Partly it may find an explanation in the fact that the collectivistic, and hence neo-Socialistic, policies of the Radicals and other parties have stolen much of the Socialist thunder, thereby making even the orthodox Marxian position appear less revolutionary and less dangerous to the existing social order. Then again, Swiss Socialists follow a moderate course because such a course is inherent in their decision, taken after World War I, to eschew the revolutionary tactics of Russian Marxism and to use parliamentary means to secure their aims. The elementary requirement for success in the parliamentary forum is a popular following at the polls that approximates a majority or at least a plurality; and Swiss Socialists can attain such a following most readily by reaching beyond the factory worker into the ranks of the salaried professional class, such as the civil servants, and even into the ranks of the peasantry. Reconciliation of the interests of so catholic a following has obviously required compromise with orthodox Marxian principles. Of course, still another restraining influence upon Swiss Socialists was their acceptance of a share in the Government in 1943.

Erosion of classical Marxian principles has, however, not caused Swiss Socialists to abjure a collectivistic type of society. They remain committed to a "mixture" of modified capitalism and Socialism. At intervals they recommend more public planning in the economic sphere, the maintenance or reimposition of public controls of the market experienced during World War II, and the nationalizing of so-called monopoly industries and of banks and credit institutions. They would have the State fix minimum wages in every area of enterprise, guarantee full employment, expand every type of social insurance, and allow the Confederation Government virtually to monopolize direct taxation in order to finance these social goals. On several occasions since 1935, the party has resorted to the instruments of direct democracy to secure a popular referendum on some of these proposed economic and social goals. The proposal to have the Government guarantee full employment has been submitted twice. Uniformly these plebiscites have rebuffed the Socialist sponsors. Since joining the Federal Council in 1943, the party has shown increasing concern for political and civil rights. It is one of the most outspoken supporters of woman suffrage in Switzerland and it professedly yields to no party in its solicitude for the integrity of the country's democratic and free institutions. Such staunch defenders of the civil and political rights of the bourgeois State may seem somewhat incongruous to those who recall the historic attitude toward such rights on the part of the movement in which these defenders claim discipleship. But Swiss Socialists had ringside seats in observing Italian and German Fascism, and presumably this experience taught them and their co-nationals not to take such rights for granted. Apparently it was this same experience as observers of Fascism combined with the still more recently acquired understanding of Communist tyranny that has persuaded Swiss Socialists to give up their historic opposition to the military and to join the middle-class parties in voting credits for adequate national defense.

Other Political Groups. Of the parties outside the governing circle, none is particularly important in 1951 either as respects the magnitude of its following or the ideas it advocates. A group calling themselves "Independents" came into being in 1935, during the economic depression, in protest over the cost of living. Its founder-leader has sought to demonstrate how modern large-scale merchandising can lower costs to consumers, and the party is dedicated to the aim of reducing the cost of living for middle-class city dwellers. In 1951 the Independents had ten members in the National Council and their influence was apparently growing, especially in Zürich. The Communist Party, re-established in 1944 as the Swiss Labor Party after having been dissolved in 1940, counted five members in the National Council in 1951. Officially it advocates a nationalization and social-welfare program which, on paper, is not unlike the program of the Social Democrats. Prior to 1940 Switzerland was afflicted with a variety of reactionary or nationalist movements which took their inspiration from German National Socialism or Italian Fascism. The largest of these groups called itself the "National Front." Others were the "Young Conservatives," "New Switzerland," the "National League," and the "Peasant League." These "movements" or "fronts" were chiefly responsible for the popular initiative of September 8, 1935, calling for a total revision of the Swiss Constitution. Had this initiative been successful, some of these reactionary sponsors apparently would have used the opportunity, thus presented, to incorporate their anti-parliamentary and illiberal social ideals into the country's basic statute. Though supported by the Catholic Conservatives and the Liberal Party, the initiative was beaten decisively.[5] In 1940, moreover, the Government proceeded to ban all these reactionary fronts as a security measure; and they have not since been formally revived.

PARTY ORGANIZATION

Geographical Distribution of Partisan Supporters. In view of the centrifugal influences of language, religion, and cantonal loyalty, the constituencies of the major Swiss parties are surprisingly well distributed geographically. This is especially true of the Radicals and Conservatives, each of whom have supporters in nearly every canton. Among loyal Radical cantons are French-speaking Vaud and Geneva, Italian-speaking Ticino, and the German cantons of Solothurn, Luzern, and Schaffhausen. The Radicals also have significant followings in St. Gallen, Urban Basel, Aargau, Zürich, Bern, and Neuchâtel. Catholic Conservatism is strong in the cantons of Fribourg, Valais, Unterwalden, and Appenzell Interior Rhodes. The candidates of this party usually run ahead of the Radicals in Schwyz, Zug, and the Grisons. A student of Swiss history, mindful of the issues of the War of the *Sonderbund* and of the partisan and cantonal alignments of that struggle, would expect to find the strongly Catholic cantons overwhelmingly conservative. Yet the fact is that a century after the *Sonderbund,* Radical candidates often run a close second to Conservatives in many of the predominantly Catholic cantons. The remaining parties have a more restricted geographical following. Socialism is most powerful in Bern, Zürich, Vaud, St. Gallen, and Aargau; does well in Solothurn, Urban Basel, Thurgau, and Neuchâtel; and is increasing its strength in some of the predominantly rural cantons. The focal point of the Farmers' Party is Bern, although several other cantons, among them Zürich, Thurgau, Aargau, Vaud, and Rural Basel also give it appreciable support. Geneva, Vaud, Neuchâtel, and Urban Basel continue to be important centers for the declining Liberal Party.[6]

Local Party Organization. Switzerland's federal traditions, the absorption of her voters in local politics, and the absence of any such truly national electoral contests as are quadrennially required in America to choose a President, have all tended to give the country's partisan organization a highly localized cast. With the exception of the Social Democratic Party which, as elsewhere, has developed a considerable amount of partisan machinery on a centralized basis and has a national dues-paying organization,[7] the principal parties of the Confederation are little more than loosely organized federations of autonomous cantonal parties with similar political tendencies. It is these cantonal parties which provide most of the funds and draft the list of can-

[5] *Statistisches Jahrbuch der Schweiz* (1936), p. 401. For a discussion of the constitutional revision proposal, see *La Lutte au sujet de la Constitution fédérale,* ed. by L'Union syndicale suisse à Berne. See also F. Fleiner, "Ziele und Wege einer Eidgenössischen Verfassungsrevision," *Wirtschaftliche Publikationen der Züricher Handelskammer* (*Heft* 20, 1934). The vote was 511,000 against, and 196,000 for, the proposal. Three cantons voted affirmatively. *Statistisches Jahrbuch der Schweiz* (1948), p. 479.

[6] See *Statistisches Jahrbuch der Schweiz* (1948), pp. 481 ff.

[7] Cf. H. F. Gosnell, *Why Europe Votes* (Chicago, 1930), p. 136.

didates for the quadrennial National Council elections. Often these local parties do not even bear the name of the national party with which they are affiliated. Thus the local unit of the national Catholic Conservative Party is known in Bern as the Catholic Democratic Party; in Zürich, as the Christian Social Party; in Uri, as the Conservative Party; in Urban Basel, as the Catholic Peoples Party; and in Rural Basel, as the Conservative-Christian Social Party. Likewise the local affiliate of the Radical Party is known in Zürich as the Radical-Democratic Party; in Unterwalden, as the Progressive People's Party; and in the Ticino, Fribourg and Vaud, as the Liberal-Radical Party.

National Organization. Of course, as the Confederation has expanded its governmental responsibilities, a national party structure has been built upon these cantonal foundations. The Radicals established the first partisan parliamentary group in 1878, and Catholic Conservatives and Liberals followed suit a few years later. At present all parties, represented in the National Council and Council of States, have an annual party diet and a permanent central committee consisting of members chosen by the party diet or by the individual cantonal units or by both the diet and the cantonal units. The party diet reviews at its sessions the actions of the Federal Assembly and of the Confederation's administrative officials, and may discuss at length the proposals which are likely to come before ensuing sessions of the two houses of Parliament. Except again in the case of the Social Democrats, such resolutions as are drafted by the party diets are not considered binding upon the party's legislative representatives but are designed for their instruction and guidance. Proceedings of the diets are democratic in character and usually afford the rank and file opportunity for debate. From time to time each of the national party organizations issues a statement of principles for the guidance of its leaders and for propaganda among the voters. Essentially partisan newspapers, some of which have a national clientele and a few of which are known outside Switzerland, also exist. Among the major Radical journals are the *Neue Zürcher Zeitung* and the *Nationalzeitung* of Basel. Both of these papers are among the largest and most influential in Switzerland. *Vaterland* of Luzern, *Liberté* of Fribourg and the *Neue Zürcher Nachrichten* are representative organs of Catholic Conservatism, while the views of the old Liberal Party find expression in the *Journal de Genève* and the *Basler Nachrichten* among others. Social Democracy's point of view may be found in the *Berner Tagwacht* and the *Volksrecht* of Zürich. Even the new Independent Party has an organ of respectable circulation in *Die Tat* of Zürich, published by the Party's leader.[8]

---

[8] A still pertinent description of Swiss party methods and organization may be found in R. C. Brooks, *Government and Politics of Switzerland* (Yonkers, 1918), pp. 305–310.

CHAPTER IV

SOME MAJOR ISSUES OF PUBLIC POLICY

PUBLIC POLICY—THE STATE AND ECONOMIC ENTERPRISE

The review of the history and programs of the various political parties in Switzerland which has just been completed has given some indication of the past and present trends of national opinion. On the other hand it has afforded but an imperfect conception of the various public policies to which the Confederation has committed itself. This chapter will accordingly be devoted to a description of some aspects of the Swiss Government's legislative and administrative activities in certain selected areas, namely, economic enterprise, social welfare, foreign relations, and public finance.

Federal Economic Activities—Public Monopolies. Fear of centralized power and nineteenth-century liberal economic doctrines were responsible for the limited nature of the Confederation's original authority over economic affairs. As already noted,[1] however, after 1880 this authority was gradually enlarged by successive constitutional amendments. This augmented economic authority has in certain cases assumed the form of public monopolies or quasi-monopolies in the production and distribution of some commodity or service. A precedent for such ventures had been established even prior to 1874 by the investiture in the Confederation of proprietary powers over the manufacture and sale of gunpowder. The primary purpose of this monopoly was to ensure an adequate supply of powder for national defense, although sale to private consumers has regularly yielded a small profit to the national exchequer. To this monopoly there was added in 1885 a similar authority over the manufacture and sale of various distilled liquors and industrial alcohol. Broadened in 1930 so as to include all forms of distilled and rectified spirits, and the right to tax certain special liqueurs which were still reserved for private manufacture, the alcohol monopoly gives the Confederation complete control over the importation, manufacture, and wholesale trade in products of a high alcoholic content. The principal aims of the monopoly, when first formed, were to combat the evils of alcoholism and intemperance and to improve the quality of dis-

[1] See p. 339.

tilled liquors used for beverage purposes. From the very beginning, however, the revenue derived from the monopoly proved to be a most important consideration. The Confederation was at first required to turn all profits over to the cantons, which were permitted to use all but one-tenth of them for ordinary budgetary expenses. The reserved 10 per cent had to be applied by them to measures for the promotion of temperance. When, however, the monopoly was reorganized after 1930, one-half of the total profits was allocated to the Confederation.

Communications. Another, more orthodox, proprietary enterprise of the Confederation, which has expanded in recent years, is that relating to the communications systems. Besides the postal and telegraph establishments, this monopoly now includes such more recent inventions as the telephone, radio broadcasting, and television. Unlike the situation in the United States, the postal administration in Switzerland has normally shown a surplus. Deficits, however, have appeared recently, that for 1948 having totaled twenty-six million francs. The telegraph and telephone systems continue to show a sizable profit, income having exceeded outgo by as much as fifty-six million francs in 1948.[2]

Bank Note Monopoly and National Bank. According to a constitutional amendment adopted in 1891, the Confederation Government was given still another monopoly. This was the right to issue bank notes, a privilege theretofore reserved to cantonal and private banks. For the purpose of exercising this monopoly the Confederation was authorized to establish a central bank of issue and to control its operations. The first attempt to establish such a bank met with a popular rebuff in a referendum conducted in 1897, the opposition coming chiefly from cantonal and private banks. Not until 1906 did the Confederation succeed in bringing about the desired legislation; and the Swiss National Bank opened its doors at its main offices in Bern and Zürich in 1907. Two-fifths of the stock of this bank may be owned by the cantons and at least one-fifth by private banks. Annual dividends are limited to 4 per cent of the capital stock, profits above the dividend and surplus accounts being distributed to the cantons and federal Government according to a two-to-one ratio. Since its establishment the Bank has been a pronounced success. It has not only provided Switzerland with a uniform and elastic currency but has stabilized the national money market, handled international payments, and provided a convenient instrument for conducting the fiscal operations of the central Government.[3]

The Swiss Federal Railways. The most important of all the economic enterprises over which the Confederation has come to exercise proprietary rights is the railway system. The Swiss railways were made subject to federal purchase following a popular referendum held on February 20, 1898; and

---

[2] *Statistisches Jahrbuch der Schweiz* (1948), pp. 177, 182. For the early history of the federal telephone enterprise see A. N. Holcombe, *Public Ownership of Telephones on the Continent of Europe* (Cambridge, Mass., 1911), chaps. xii–xiv.

[3] For a brief account of the Bank see J. and V. J. Steiger and C. Higy, *Finanzhaushalt der Schweiz* (Bern, 1934), p. 27.

between 1902 and 1909 nationalization of five main lines in the system was carried into effect. Various motives, more or less defensible from an economic standpoint, prompted this action. Among them were: (1) the extension and improvement of railway service in parts of the country where topographical conditions made private extension impossible or at least unprofitable; (2) the reduction of capital cost through the use of public credit; (3) the improvement of railway labor conditions; (4) cheapening of service to shippers; and (5) the removal of the influence of foreign stockholders who, in the case of some of the individual lines, were in a majority. The purchase of the railway system, its extension since 1910, and the electrification of most of the lines represent at once the Confederation Government's greatest physical asset and one of the heaviest financial burdens. In 1950, about a fourth of the consolidated debt of the Confederation, totaling somewhat more than 12,000 million francs, was identified as capital investment in the railways. The loans for which the Government obligated itself at the time the railway system was purchased were to be extinguished within sixty years; this period of amortization was extended in 1920 to 100 years. During the period of Governmental ownership, the facilities of the railways have been considerably expanded; even so, technological advances in railroad transportation have made it possible to reduce the total personnel employed on this enterprise by about 4 per cent in the years between 1913 and 1950. Economic operation, however, has not always saved the system from operating at a loss, annual financial statements exhibiting deficits about as often as they show surpluses. Deficits occurred regularly between 1914 and 1922 and reappeared during the decade of the 1930's because of economic depression and the competition of other forms of transportation. The more recent record, on the other hand, is better, only one year, 1945, having shown a deficit in the decade 1938–1948. Administration of the roads is largely autonomous. Subject to the authority of the Confederation Parliament and executive, supervisory powers over the system are vested in a Federal Council of Administration consisting of fifteen members chosen by Parliament to represent various economic interests. Responsibility for operations rests with a general directorate of three persons at Bern and in three sectional directorates at Lausanne, Luzern, and Zürich.[4]

Agricultural Intervention. Not unlike these various proprietary economic powers is the authority over the nation's agricultural activity which a constitutional amendment confided to the Confederation in March, 1929. According to the terms of this amendment and subsequent implementing legislation enacted in 1932, the Confederation must seek to promote the production of domestic wheat, furnishing farmers with seed adapted to Swiss soil and climatic conditions and granting such subventions or fixing such prices as will ensure profitable production under relatively adverse conditions. The Govern-

---

[4] Cf. A. N. Holcombe, "First Decade of Swiss Federal Railways," *Quar. Jour. Econ.,* xxvi (Feb. 1912), 352. See also Z. Giacometti, "Die Fortbildung des oeffentlichen Rechts der schweizerischen Eidgenossenschaft," *Jahrbuch des oeffentl. Rechts,* xvi (1928), 373; and J. and V. J. Steiger and Higy, *op. cit.* pp. 86 *ff.* For recent financial statistics consult *Statistisches Jahrbuch der Schweiz* (1948), p. 192.

ment is also charged with maintaining a minimum reserve of 80,000 tons of food grains—a sort of national granary for emergencies—accumulating stocks from domestic growers at the favorable prices fixed by law and from foreign sources. To protect its price-fixing prerogative, the Government may monopolize the right to import grain and flour.[5] Difficulties experienced by the Swiss in provisioning the nation during World War I was partly responsible for this grain policy,[6] especially for the provision for a minimum grain reserve; and experience during the second global conflict between 1939 and 1945 has convinced most Swiss that the policy is a wise one. Of course the policy is most uneconomic and partakes of the character of special-interest legislation, aiding those parties who represent the farmer. It is defended as sociologically necessary to check the flight from the land and maintain the economic position of the peasantry. Whatever rationalization may be given for this type of legislation and however justifiable it may appear to be in view of Switzerland's peculiar needs, there is nothing unique about it. On the contrary, parallels exist for it in almost every Western state. Indeed agrarian legislation of the type which Switzerland has enacted is but another phase of the contemporary trend toward economic nationalism and the collective State, a trend which has other facets in Switzerland and which seems to be only slightly less popular there than in most of the other states of Western Europe. Because Swiss soil is, for the greater part, notoriously ill adapted to the production of cereals, this nationalistic agricultural policy will cost the Swiss taxpayer relatively more than a similar policy costs taxpayers elsewhere. In the decade after the policy was adopted it is estimated Swiss farmers received treasury grants totaling approximately a quarter of a billion francs.

Trend Toward a Directed Economy. The trend toward what the French call *"dirigisme,"* to which allusion has been made in the preceding paragraph, is by no means limited to agriculture but has affected the entire front of the Swiss economy. In part this trend may be ascribed to ideological considerations—for example, the collectivistic ideas advanced by Marxian and other groups. But principally, as we noted in an earlier chapter, it is to be ascribed to the impact upon Swiss life of the two global wars and the interbellum economic depression. Thus, in 1914 and again in 1939, the Swiss Parliament passed full-powers acts for the political and economic security of the nation and for the maintenance of its neutrality. Under cover of the broad authority conferred by these statutes, the Swiss executive proceeded to regulate the national economy in great detail, to levy taxes without precedent either as to kind or magnitude, and to subject production, distribution, and consumption to the most thoroughgoing controls. Particularly was this the case during World War II. Not dissimilar responsibilities and powers were assumed by the Confederation Government during the depression years of the 1930's, when rigid public controls were imposed upon foreign-exchange, credit, and

---

[5] For the amendment on the grain monopoly see Constitution, Art. 23.
[6] Cf. W. E. Rappard, *L'Individu et l'état dans l'évolution constitutionnelle de la Suisse* (Zürich, 1936), pp. 497–498.

currency transactions, and the Government began its policy of granting loans and subsidies to various private sectors of the economy at the expense of the taxpayer. Besides the farmer, beneficiaries of this latter policy included the dairy and hotel industries, local transportation companies, livestock breeders, watchmakers, and embroidery manufacturers.

Although much of this interventionist policy was regarded as temporary, the Swiss, like other peoples, have learned that it is difficult to liquidate such a policy, or even to modify it seriously, once it has been introduced. Those who acquire a vested interest in its continuance, be they consumers or producers, insist upon maintaining their advantage. Moreover, experience with such an interventionist policy is itself a major factor in persuading a government to continue it on a permanent basis; for the experience furnishes precedents to justify continuation of the policy even in relatively "normal" times, gives politicians and administrators the "know-how" for managing economic affairs on a national scale, and gives the politician an opportunity to promise specific constituencies such concrete benefits that he is virtually assured of their support at the polls unless a competitor should outdo him in such promises.

At any rate, as noted earlier in these pages,[7] the economic interventionism of the past four decades has laid the foundations for a system of public control of the Swiss national economy which places severe limitations upon the traditional freedom of the market, restricts the contractual freedom of private entrepreneurs and labor organizations in many particulars, subjects production and distribution to considerations which are as often social or sociological as they are economic, and makes the Government a kind of "senior partner" in the conduct of more than one economic undertaking. If this regime cannot be described as a "collective State," it is certainly one far removed from the ideal that animated those who, in 1874, inserted the principle of freedom of trade and industry in the Swiss Constitution.[8] The Swiss appear to have realized this, and have sought to bring their constitutional theory abreast of the current conception of the relation of the state to the economy. The principal contribution toward such a reconciliation was the constitutional amendment which went into effect October 1, 1947. This specifically authorizes the Confederation to legislate in the economic field; correspondingly restricts the freedom of trade and industry originally guaranteed by the Constitution; contemplates special legislation to protect certain sectors of the economy; and even restricts competition by requiring public permission to open certain new enterprises. The Swiss may continue to enjoy a reputation for being an island of private capitalism and economic freedom in the heart of Europe; but the factual foundations of that reputation are becoming increasingly precarious.

PUBLIC WELFARE

Labor Legislation. The interventionist activity of the Confederation Government has also assumed a social form and a great deal of welfare legis-

[7] See p. 339.   [8] Art. 31.

lation is now contained in federal Constitution and statutes. Power to regulate child labor, to limit the hours of labor of adults, and to ensure protection of workmen engaged in dangerous occupations had already been granted the Confederation in the revised Constitution of 1874; and with the concurrence of the people the Federal Assembly enacted a general factory act in 1877. Still broader powers over the field of labor, including such matters as industrial relations and the regulation of unemployment, were authorized by a constitutional amendment in 1908. The original factory act was accordingly revised in 1914 and again in 1920. The net result is a labor code as advanced as any on the Continent. More recently, in order to promote industrial peace, the Confederation has applied so-called "corporative" principles to the relations of capital and labor. Such principles implicitly reject the Marxian idea of the class struggle and stress instead the common interests and solidarity of capital and labor. They have furnished a somewhat questionable justification for the Government's policy of making collective labor agreements compulsory for an entire trade or industry when approved, through collective bargaining, by a majority of the employers and workmen involved. Provision has also been made for the compulsory arbitration of disputes arising out of such labor contracts.

Other Welfare Activities. Other fields of social action have claimed the Confederation's attention. Subsidies for primary education were first made to the cantons in 1903 following a constitutional amendment authorizing such subsidies in 1902. These federal primary-school subsidies were considerably augmented in 1930; and special assistance was extended to the educational system of the Grisons and the Ticino. For more than sixty years the Confederation has also been making financial grants to encourage the arts and handicrafts and to improve agricultural methods. Steps have likewise been taken to combat epidemic and dangerous diseases through the agency of the Confederation Government, constitutional authority for this purpose having been broadened by an amendment adopted in 1913. Measures to combat tuberculosis have been particularly far-reaching, a law passed in 1928 having offered federal aid up to 50 per cent of the cost incurred by cantons, communes, and private institutions in fighting this disease. Mention might also be made, in this connection, of the effort to encourage temperance, implicit in the alcohol monopoly, and of the effort to abolish professional gambling and lotteries undertaken after the passage of a constitutional amendment in 1920.

Insurance against Illness and Accident. Social insurance became an object of national concern in 1890 when the federal Constitution was amended to authorize sickness-and-accident insurance. The first plan for such insurance elaborated by the Federal Assembly was, however, rejected by the people in 1900 chiefly because it did not safeguard the interests of private and cooperative insurance societies. Twelve more years elapsed before a second plan passed safely over the hurdle of the referendum. This plan provides quite different regulations for the two kinds of insurance. Practically all the voluntary sickness insurance societies have been allowed to continue with Confederation subventions. In addition cantons and communes are encouraged to establish compulsory sickness insurance institutes which receive aid from the central Government. Despite the decentralized administration and largely voluntary character of this federally regulated sickness-insurance system, it has been quite effective. In 1950 there were approximately 1,150 cantonal and private sickness-insurance organizations in operation; and the number of persons insured in them amounted to about one-half of the entire Swiss population. Accident insurance was organized as a Confederation monopoly, its administration being vested in the Federal Accident Insurance Institute established at Luzern in 1918. Such insurance was also made compulsory for all employees in public monopolies and for the employees in private establishments with a sizable payroll. Premiums are paid to the Institute by the employee and the employer according to a one-to-three ratio, their respective contributions being generously supplemented by the Confederation exchequer.[9]

Social Security. After World War I efforts were made to extend the social insurance system so as to provide public assistance to widows, orphans, the aged, and the incapacitated. A constitutional amendment with this object in view was elaborated by the Federal Council in July, 1924, and, with certain changes interposed by the Parliament, was accepted by the people and the cantons on December 6, 1925. According to this amendment a pension system of a voluntary or compulsory character was to be provided for the aged and for widows and orphans and subsequently extended to the incapacitated. From tobacco and liquor revenues, the Confederation was to contribute not more than one-half of the cost of such a pension plan; for the plan's administration, moreover, the services of the cantons, communes, and the private insurance companies were to be enlisted. Considerable time was to elapse, however, before a concrete pension and public-assistance plan, based on this new amendment, was to become an actuality. Indeed it was not until the summer of 1947, about a quarter of a century after the adoption of the social-security amendment, that Parliament was able to devise a plan which secured a majority in a popular referendum.[10] The plan, thus adopted, went into effect January 1, 1948. Its primary purpose is to provide an annuity for persons reaching the age of sixty-five. It also provides survivorship benefits for the insured's spouse and minor children. The scheme, essentially compulsory and contributory, embraces virtually every gainfully employed person, citizen or alien. Self-employed persons pay the insurance fund a tax equal to 4 per cent of their income. Wage earners and salaried employees pay 2 per cent of their earnings, their contribution being matched by a payroll tax of like amount levied upon their employers. Both the Confederation and the cantons contribute toward the administrative expense of the insurance system. Apparently the new social-security plan does not embrace benefits for the tem-

[9] Summaries of this insurance plan are to be found in Frankel and Dawson, *Workingman's Insurance in Europe* (New York, 1910), pp. 73 *ff.* and 214 *ff.*

[10] An earlier plan was rejected at the polls in December, 1931; for a discussion of this plan and the reasons for its rejection, see W. E. Rappard, *L'Individu et l'état dans l'évolution constitutionnelle de la Suisse* (Zürich, 1936), p. 500.

porarily unemployed, although provision for such benefits would appear to be a probable future development. Meanwhile unemployment relief remains the primary responsibility of the communes although, by a system of grants-in-aid, both Confederation and cantonal treasuries assume much of the actual financial burden.

SWISS NEUTRALITY AND FOREIGN POLICY

Origins of Neutrality. Just as federalism, democracy, and "progressive" liberalism are the principal tenets of Switzerland's internal policies, so neutrality is the essence of her foreign policy. This faith in neutrality may be said to date from 1515 when, after a century of war and conquest during which the soldiers of the Confederation acquired the name of being the best in Europe, the Swiss were defeated by France at Marignano in Lombardy. Thereafter, although many of the rulers of Europe continued to hire Swiss troops for mercenary service, the Confederation itself generally pursued the policy of remaining behind its own frontiers and of refusing to participate in recurrent coalitions and wars. During the next three centuries this policy of diplomatic abstention and neutrality became a characteristic of Swiss foreign policy. Indeed it became so much of a tradition that even Napoleon paid lip service to it in his Act of Mediation, the Constitution which he drafted in 1803 for a Switzerland which, at the time, was completely at his mercy.

Neutrality a Recognized Policy. In 1815 the powers concluded that a neutral Switzerland would serve the purposes of the broad European settlement which they were attempting to effect in the wake of Napoleon. Consequently on November 20 of that year, the representatives of France, Great Britain, Prussia, Russia, Austria, Sweden, Spain, and Portugal formally affixed their signatures to a document which declared that the maintenance of the inviolability and independence of the Confederation was necessary to the peace and stability of Europe. The document also pledged the signatories to respect and maintain the integrity of the Confederation. Switzerland's own obligation to protect her neutrality has found expression in various clauses of her major public documents since 1815. The present Constitution declares that it shall be the duty of the Federal Assembly to take measures "to protect the nation's independence and neutrality" and the duty of the Federal Council to watch over "the maintenance of independence and neutrality." Another article has formally invalidated the "capitulations" or agreements by which various cantons once furnished mercenary contingents for foreign governments. Still another article of the Constitution prohibited all except a few Confederation officials from receiving foreign pensions, titles, decorations, and similar distinctions. As amended in 1931 this article now interdicts all foreign pensions and distinctions in the case of Confederation officials and extends the prohibition to cantonal officials as well. Finally, as we shall see, the Constitution and the laws have been frequently changed in order that a substantial military force might be developed for the protection of the nation's frontiers.

Neutrality Tested by Experience. Considerably more than a century has elapsed since Swiss neutrality became part of the international law of Europe and of the formal constitutional law of the Confederation. During that time the policy has been tested several times, notably in the Franco-Sardinian War against Austria in 1859, the Franco-Prussian War of 1870, and the two World Wars of the twentieth century. The tests provided by the two World Wars were serious indeed. Throughout almost the whole period of each conflict, Switzerland was surrounded by the warring powers and had no contact with the outside world except over the territory or air space of a belligerent.[11] In 1914, and again in 1939, the Swiss Government formally notified each belligerent of its commitment to respect the nation's neutrality. Thereupon the Swiss Assembly passed the full-powers acts, previously described,[12] which directed the executive to mobilize Swiss forces and the nation's economy, prevent violation of the nation's air space and frontiers, and pursue a policy of at least formal impartiality in dealing with the warring belligerents. During the early months of both global conflicts and particularly of the second, it was freely predicted that one or another belligerent would invade Switzerland and set her neutrality at naught. But except for occasional technical violations of the nation's air space, the hazards of involvement were surmounted and formal neutrality was maintained throughout both conflicts.

Continued Faith in Neutrality. As a policy, neutrality has thus acquired an impressive reputation at least in the eyes of the Swiss people. To them it seems that neutrality, in conjunction with the traditional emphasis upon military preparedness, is mainly responsible for the 136 years of peace which the country has enjoyed since the Napoleonic invasions and for the absence of any serious external threat to Swiss territory or domestic institutions. The Swiss also believe that neutrality fosters internal unity. At any rate, it tends to discourage the three principal linguistic segments of the country from taking sides with their respective linguistic brethren in adjacent states when these go to war with one another. Hence it is hardly surprising that Switzerland continues to make neutrality the keystone of her foreign policy and that she allows no other principle to take precedence over it. When, for example, membership in the League of Nations was broached, the Swiss felt that the departure from full neutrality, inherent in any collective-security arrangement, warranted the solemn plebiscite of a constitutional referendum. This, held in May, 1920, was favorable, and Switzerland formally joined the League a few weeks later. But the Swiss always had reservations about the League, and from the very first demanded and obtained a so-called "neutralized" status.[13] In substance this meant that Switzerland agreed to impose eco-

---

[11] To provision the country, the Government on April 9, 1941, authorized a high-seas merchant fleet. The port of registry was Basel. Ships used the Italian port of Genoa.

[12] See p. 370.

[13] Cf. W. E. Rappard, *L'entrée de la Suisse dans la Société des Nations* (Geneva, 1924). The vote was 416,000 for entry into the League and 323,000 against. Eleven and one-half cantons provided affirmative majorities.

nomic sanctions against states which the League identified as aggressors but was exempted from imposing military sanctions against such aggressor states and from the requirement of permitting the passage over her territory of troops bound on a League mission. Even this conditional responsibility seemed inconsistent with traditional neutrality; and in 1938 Switzerland successfully importuned the Council of the League to declare that Swiss membership implied no obligation to cooperate in the imposition of sanctions of any kind. Switzerland has not yet become a member of the United Nations (1951) and apparently is in no hurry to apply for membership. Even if she does decide to apply, it is unlikely she will join unless the rest of the world proves to be as complaisant as it was in the case of Switzerland's League membership. In other words, because of Switzerland's fondness for the policy of permanent neutrality, the United Nations would undoubtedly be requested to acknowledge that Swiss membership, if granted, should be *sui generis:* the Swiss would wish to enjoy the unusual status of having most of the privileges of membership in a collective-security organization without the more serious responsibilities.

In the light of the recent record and the broader stream of Swiss history it is not too difficult to understand the Swiss citizen's faith in the policy of permanent neutrality and to sympathize with his view. At the same time it must be admitted that, to the non-Swiss, that faith appears increasingly uncritical and unrealistic as mankind moves forward into the second half of the twentieth century. Weapon technology, logistics, strategy—indeed, the whole art and science of war—have reached such a point in their development that it is virtually impossible to contemplate the conduct of military operations on the limited national basis premised in Switzerland's neutrality policy, some states becoming involved as belligerents and others remaining neutral. From a territorial standpoint, war in our day is all too likely to involve continents rather than nations and become global in its ramifications, allowing little possibility for any nation—particularly any small nation like Switzerland—to indulge in the luxury of deciding whether it shall become involved or remain neutral. Those who advance such considerations are likely, moreover, to dismiss the suggestion that it was neutrality that saved Switzerland from invasion during the first two global wars of the century; in their view Switzerland escaped involvement partly because it suited the belligerents' policies to keep her neutral, partly because, unlike the case of Belgium, the military cost of invading and investing the country was disproportionate to the resulting military advantage.

Such arguments against neutrality are difficult to refute. Equally difficult is it to gainsay the proposition that the converse of neutrality, namely, an effective collective-security arrangement, is the only road to national salvation. Even so, it is quite unlikely that the Swiss will soon give up neutrality. If it is unrealistic in the modern world, they will probably persist in being unrealistic, at least until such time as the United Nations or some comparable organization offers greater assurance of effectively safeguarding the integrity of its members than is presently the case or until some major development in world history requires a re-examination of Switzerland's position.

Recent External Relations. Although Switzerland has not become a member of the United Nations, her name is found on the roster of some of the UN's specialized or auxiliary agencies. These include the International Civil Aviation Organization, the Food and Agriculture Organization, and the World Health Organization. Swiss membership has also been continued in the International Labor Organization. Preoccupation with neutrality has, moreover, not prevented the nation's participation in America's European Recovery or Marshall Plan. During 1948, with the overwhelming approval of the Swiss Parliament, the Swiss became a member of the Organization for European Economic Cooperation (OEEC), the Marshall Plan's European agency. In thus subscribing to the Recovery Program, the Swiss made it plain that they themselves wanted no American loans or grants; their cooperation was motivated solely by a desire to assist in restoring a trading area upon the prosperity of which Switzerland's own prosperity ultimately depends.

Considerable success has also attended the nation's efforts to re-establish formal relations with other states. Beginning in 1946 trade and fiscal agreements were made with all the nations with which Switzerland has had important commercial contacts. The Swiss also agreed in 1947 to compromise the issue of German assets allegedly secreted in Switzerland for safekeeping during World War II. The victorious powers asserted that the value of such assets approached the sum of 750 million dollars. The compromise on this issue required Switzerland to surrender to the powers half of whatever German assets might turn up and permitted her to retain the other half to satisfy Swiss claims against Germans. This compromise agreement apparently persuaded the United States to take the related step of releasing a half billion dollars of Swiss credits which had been frozen during the early days of World War II. Even relations with Soviet Russia were normalized. The assassination of a Soviet delegate at the Lausanne Conference in 1923 had resulted in a protracted diplomatic rupture between Bern and the Kremlin. This continued until 1946 when diplomats were exchanged. In March, 1948, moreover, a Soviet-Swiss trade agreement was announced. Under its terms, Swiss machinery and consumer goods are to be exchanged for grain and petroleum, the latter products apparently coming chiefly from Rumania, Soviet Russia's satellite.

The Savoyard Free Zone and Liechtenstein. Switzerland has certain privileges and duties involving her immediate neighbors, France and the Principality of Liechtenstein, that deserve a word of comment. In the case of France, a part of her territory in Upper Savoy has been a free zone for Swiss goods since the post-Napoleonic European settlement of 1815. After World War I France sought to eliminate this zone and move her customs frontier up to her political frontier on Lake Geneva. A treaty accomplishing this purpose was tentatively accepted by the Swiss Government; but on February 18, 1923, in the first popular referendum on a treaty held in modern Switzerland, the

Swiss people rejected the treaty. Thereupon France acted unilaterally to abolish the Savoyard free zone but agreed subsequently to submit the entire question to the Permanent Court at The Hague. In decisions given in 1929 and 1933, that tribunal upheld the historic Swiss right to the zone and France accordingly moved her customs frontier back to the original position.

In the case of Liechtenstein, Switzerland has established a virtual protectorate. Prior to World War I, this diminutive Principality had been included in the Austro-Hungarian postal and customs administration. With the break-up of the dual monarchy, Liechtenstein petitioned for a similar arrangement with Switzerland; and in a convention concluded on November 10, 1920, Switzerland agreed to extend her legislation over the Principality's postal, telephonic, and telegraphic systems and to commit their administration to appropriate Swiss authorities. For reasons which philatelists will appreciate, the Principality continued to issue its own postage stamps. By a treaty with Liechtenstein on March 29, 1923, Switzerland also agreed to take over the Principality's customs and to extend the Swiss customs frontier accordingly. Customs duties between the Principality and Switzerland are abolished. The customs treaty may be automatically renewed at intervals of five years. For the loss of customs revenue the Swiss Government compensates the Principality with an annual grant of 250,000 Swiss francs. Other arrangements between the two states have resulted in the extension of some Swiss security legislation to the Principality and in the assumption, by the Swiss Government, of the responsibility of representing Liechtenstein in foreign capitals.

NATIONAL DEFENSE

Unusual Features of Swiss Military Service. For the defense of their neutrality, the Swiss rely not merely upon the pledges of other states but also upon their own army and military aviation. Like virtually all European states, Switzerland has adopted universal and compulsory military service. Except for certain public officials and those exempted or debarred for physical, mental, or moral reasons, every male Swiss must undergo training for active or auxiliary service, and officially becomes a part of the armed forces for the whole of his active adult life.

There are, however, some important differences between the Swiss system and other systems based upon compulsory service. One of these is the relatively limited period of service with the colors. The call for initial training comes in the nineteenth year and active service lasts about four months. During this time, the infantry neophyte goes to a recruit school for basic training and subsequently qualifies as a full-fledged member of the army's first-line troops, known as the *Auszug* or *Elite.* Following this basic training, he returns to civilian life. Recruits in other branches of service undergo training periods of equal duration. During the next twelve years, or until the soldier reaches the age of thirty-two, he is called to the colors every year for a refresher course lasting twenty days. From his thirty-second until his forty-first year, the soldier belongs to the *Landwehr.* Until 1936, this was considered the first-line reserve; since that date, however, the lower age brackets of the *Landwehr* have been consolidated with the *Elite* to form a larger and more experienced first-line field army. While in the *Landwehr,* the soldier is normally called up once every two years for a refresher course lasting twenty days. Between the ages of forty-one and forty-eight, the Swiss soldier belongs to the *Landsturm,* or second-line reserve; after his forty-eighth year and until his sixtieth, he remains on call for various kinds of auxiliary service. Thus, though the Swiss male may officially be a part of the national military establishment for almost his entire adult life, actual service with the colors during all that time may not amount to one full year unless a national emergency supervenes.[14] It should be added that while the Swiss soldier, enrolled in the *Elite* or *Landwehr,* is off duty, he must maintain membership in a rifle club and present himself regularly for rifle practice.

Hence, though Switzerland may conscript her army, a serious attempt is made to preserve the soldier's "amateur standing." Actual service with the forces is intermittent and relatively brief; and identification with the civilian life of the nation is maintained even by the youngest recruit. When not on active duty, moreover, the Swiss soldier, like a true militiaman in a democracy, continues in possession of the personal arms and equipment originally issued to him by the authorities. He is responsible for keeping such arms and equipment in good condition, available for instant use when called up for a regular period of duty or for an emergency. In keeping with this amateur, nonprofessional military tradition, the Swiss also try to avoid having a professional military staff, fearful that it might develop into a military caste. No person may be appointed to the rank of commander-in-chief except in time of national emergency when the Federal Assembly has decreed general mobilization. The Federal Assembly itself must make the appointment, that appointment lapsing as soon as the emergency has passed. A commander-in-chief has been appointed on six different occasions since 1848.[15] The most recent appointment was that of Colonel Henri Guisan, who held office from September, 1939, to the end of hostilities in World War II. Like the private soldiers, the officers of the Swiss army, from lance corporal to general, are called upon to serve with the colors only intermittently after the initial period of training and study; at other times they engage in ordinary civilian pursuits although they continue the use of the military title. Traditionally the only military officials in the permanent, full-time service of the Confederation were the corps and divisional commanders and noncommissioned officers who instructed the recruits. More recently, in response to the demand created by technological advances in the art of war, the Swiss have had to compromise with their nonprofessional ideals in military matters. To their "standing troops" they have added the personnel of an air corps and an army corps guarding the various Alpine and frontier fortresses.

---

[14] During the six years of World War II, when Swiss forces were at least partially mobilized at all times, it is estimated that a Swiss soldier of the *Elite* and of the first-line ranks of the *Landwehr* was with the colors an average of eighty-six days per annum.

[15] The dates are as folows: 1848, 1849, 1856, 1870, 1914, and 1939.

Dual Political Control. Like other federal States, for example the United States, Switzerland maintains a dual (local and national) political control over military affairs. The cantons continue to exert their special military prerogatives, although it is clear that, as a result of constitutional amendment and the practical exigencies of military administration, the substance of military power is rapidly passing to the Confederation. Within their respective territories, the cantons still enforce many military regulations, keep the military registers, and provide the troops with their personal equipment. They constitute some of the infantry battalions and the battalions of the second-line reserve, or *Landsturm,* and appoint officers for such units, such appointments ranging up to, and including, the rank of lieutenant-colonel. Military powers are exercised by the cantonal authorities under the supervision and with the approval of the Military Department of the federal executive; and, for at least a portion of the expenditure which the cantons incur, they are reimbursed by the Confederation.

Strength of the Confederation's Forces. In a period of national emergency, Switzerland can muster a field and auxiliary force of 800,000 trained men. During the most recent such period, extending from 1939 to 1945, almost 150,000 men were constantly under arms and every Swiss in the public forces underwent an average of three months of active service each year for the six consecutive years. This same emergency period and the years immediately preceding witnessed an extraordinary increase of military expenditures. In addition to expanded operational budgets, funds were needed to build the Alpine redoubt, improve the frontier defense system, expand and modernize the air force, and supply the troops with the latest mechanized and motorized equipment and the most modern weapons. In the fifteen years between 1930 and 1945, the military defense budgets totaled some ten billion francs. This represents a per capita expenditure not much less than that imposed upon the populations of some of the actual belligerents in World War II.

It has already been remarked that this growing emphasis upon an adequate and efficient defensive force has weakened the nonprofessional tradition of the Swiss military system. Even so, that tradition is not dead; true Swiss liberals still regard it as a necessary bastion of a free polity. Only with the greatest reluctance will they permit that tradition to be violated and then only to the extent that military necessity and national survival appear to require. It is possible that the failure of our century to solve the problem of national security through collective means will require our freest States to subordinate all principles of civil government to the ideal of a Spartan barracks; if so, the Swiss State will be among the last to submit to such internal discipline.

PUBLIC FINANCE

Expanded Taxing Powers of the Confederation. Changes in the relative political importance of Confederation and cantonal Governments are clearly reflected in their changed financial position. The fathers of the Confederation were parsimonious in providing the Government at Bern with sources of revenue. Principal sources were the customs receipts and a portion of the special capitation tax, quite unimportant in volume, which is imposed upon those exempted from military service. In addition it was anticipated that the Confederation would secure assistance in balancing its books from the profits of its public monopolies and enterprises. If all these resources proved insufficient, the Constitution stipulated that the cantons were to make contributions to the Confederation exchequer in accordance with their wealth and taxable resources. These arrangements worked well enough for almost two generations, or until about 1914. Then a fiscal revolution began, the ultimate consequences of which cannot yet be measured. Already, however, that revolution has completely transformed the Confederation's financial position *vis à vis* the cantons. The Confederation now monopolizes all the important sources of tax revenue, and the cantons, instead of being the potential benefactors of the Confederation, as originally intended, have been reduced to virtual pensioners of the Confederation Treasury. Indeed, the cantons now rely upon Confederation subventions and a share in the proceeds of Confederation taxes for much of their income.

Steps in This Fiscal Revolution. How this revolution in Swiss public finance came about provides an interesting illustration, not only of the trend toward centralization of power in a federal State, but also of the public fiscal effects of state paternalism and the twentieth century's penchant for total war. The first overt step came with the advent of World War I and the unusual military outlays which that conflict made necessary to place the nation on the alert and protect its neutrality. To finance the expanded outlay, an amendment was added to the Constitution in 1915 which authorized the Confederation to levy an income tax and a tax on property. These having proved insufficient, a war-profits tax was subsequently authorized and also a stamp tax on securities and documents used in legal and commercial transactions. Then, in 1919, the Constitution was again amended to provide for still another special levy on property. Although, with the exception of the stamp tax, these wartime levies were deemed to be temporary in nature and were subsequently repealed, some in 1926 and others in 1932, they established useful (or baneful) precedents; and when the Confederation again found itself short of funds in its efforts to combat the economic depression of the 1930's, some of the former wartime exactions were re-enacted as "crisis taxes." This was done without benefit of formal constitutional amendment. Parliament merely insisted that public necessity and the needs of the budget required and justified steps such as these, thereby furnishing the world with a startling example of the extent to which the emergency powers regime had been substituted for the formal constitutional regime in Switzerland. In addition to these "crisis taxes," the Confederation levied taxes on the manufacture and sale of tobacco and used half the proceeds of the national alcohol monopoly, both of these resources having been granted by appropriate constitutional amendments.

As war came to the world once more in 1939 and the Swiss girded themselves for another period of defense, Confederation expenditures mounted to unprecedented levels and every conceivable revenue source was tapped to reduce the inevitable budget deficits and restrain inflation. To supplement existing levies, the Confederation resorted to a variety of so-called "defense taxes" consisting of expanded income levies on persons and corporations, sales taxes, a so-called excess-profits tax, and a "sacrifice for national defense," in reality a capital levy. For the greater part, these supplementary taxes were levied by decree and were technically authorized by Parliament; but the authority of both Government and Parliament was attributed to the now familiar and almost habitual plea of necessity and national emergency and not to any formal constitutional sanction. It was the continuation of these special levies of World War II and the Government's reiterated refusal, on a technicality, to submit the levies to the test of a popular referendum, that led to the unusual initiative to "return to direct democracy" in September, 1949, already described.[16] At any rate, this was the formal reason for the initiative; the real reason was probably a revolt against the continued high level of taxation resulting from the continuation of these special levies.

Prospects for Continued High Taxation. That the rebellion against the Confederation's tax program, implicit in this action of the electorate, will go far to reduce either the power of the Confederation to tax or the level of such taxation is quite doubtful. As this is written, the rumblings of a drive to gird the free world against another threat of international aggression are already beginning to have their echoes in the Swiss exchequer as in the exchequers of other lands; and a rise in the tax burden is inevitable. Moreover, it is altogether doubtful that the many privileged groups, who now secure largess from the Confederation Treasury, will forego that largess, or that social services, now greatly expanded, will be reduced. To pay for these favors and services, the Confederation will have to tax; and it is hardly likely that either pleas of economy or of lack of constitutional power will or can have much practical effect. Like the electorates of other lands, the Swiss electorate will have to learn that if nations must arm to the teeth and if citizens expect to enjoy public services, someone must pay taxes; and that if any group, like the farmers, expects to enjoy special Treasury favors and subsidies, some other group will have to provide the wherewithal. After all, governments do not normally create wealth and income; they merely redistribute the wealth and income of individuals.

Some Relevant Fiscal Statistics. Relevant budgetary and public-debt statistics provide an excellent footnote for this account of recent Swiss tax policy, and place that account in better perspective. Appropriations for the Confederation Government increased from 126 million francs in 1913 to more than 1,801 million in 1948, a fifteen-fold increase. During the war year, 1944, Confederation outlays reached 2,558 million francs or twenty-one times as much as was expended in 1913. Confederation tax revenues rose from 101 million francs in 1913 to 1,795 million in 1948. Apparently one of the highest revenue yields occurred in 1946 when the Confederation collected 2,220

[16] See p. 342.

million francs. Rare, however, have been the years when revenue equaled outlay, Switzerland's story in this respect being similar to that of virtually all contemporary states. Indeed, since the beginning of World War I in 1914, a balanced budget has been a rarity. It occurred between 1928 and 1932, and equilibrium between revenue and appropriations was attained again in 1946; but it has not been maintained. Chronic deficits have necessarily piled up the public debt, which rose from 78 million francs in 1900 to around 12,000 million francs in 1950. An important fact to be borne in mind about this debt is that one of its principal items is the obligation incurred in the original purchase of the Swiss federal railways and by their improvement and electrification since the date of the purchase. The present consolidated railway debt is somewhere in the neighborhood of 3,000 million francs or about one-fourth of the total public debt. Some of the remainder of the Confederation debt represents investments in public monopolies and property that has a capital value. Thus some portion of the existing debt structure is covered by capital assets which, under favorable conditions, may be expected to produce revenue and provide for autonomous amortization. What remains is nevertheless a very sizable sum. Merely to service it will require a volume of revenue more than twice as great as the whole income of the Confederation before World War I.

RETROSPECT AND PROSPECT

Not even so sketchy a review of governmental practice and public affairs in Switzerland as the foregoing can fail to convey the impression that the Swiss polity changed greatly during the first half of the twentieth century. As we have noted, *laissez-faire* economic policy has, in many instances, given way to political collectivism and state intervention; private capitalism has been limited by the growth of governmental monopolies and by various restrictions on the operation of a free-market economy; and personal freedom, including freedom of contract in economic matters, has often been sacrificed for publicly guaranteed forms of social or economic security. At the same time, the dualistic political relations between Confederation and cantons, once weighted so strongly in favor of the latter, have been modified again and again in the direction of national centralization; and the cantons, although still regarded as autonomous components of a federal State, have, in increasing measure, become the subsidized administrative organs of the Confederation Government. Finally, we have noted that, under the pressure of international and domestic emergencies, the Swiss have become unduly familiar with the instruments of modern "crisis government." In turn this seems to have weakened their traditional respect for constitutional limitations and undermined their belief, hitherto as emphatic as that of any other people, that observance of such limitations is the *sine qua non* of the preservation of liberty and the avoidance of tyranny in a popular government.

That Switzerland has experienced these changes in governmental practice and political belief and that her political capacity and political virtue have suffered as a result can hardly be denied. Every democratic State has experienced such changes in recent years, and in many the effect upon orderly constitutional government and the political morality of the citizenry has been far more serious than in Switzerland. Moreover, both in the case of Switzerland and other democratic States, success in reversing this trend toward decay of free, constitutional government depends as much upon external circumstances as upon any other. Especially does it depend upon the degree of success attending the world's efforts to solve the problem of national security. If that problem cannot be solved—if democratic political societies like Switzerland's are to be called upon to mobilize people and resources every generation for mere survival—then there is no more likelihood that Switzerland will avoid a Spartan-barracks polity than any other country. If, on the other hand, the twentieth century can solve the problem of national security or at least make some tolerably effective efforts in that direction, and if fate be reasonably benign, Switzerland has as good an opportunity of preserving the essential integrity of her existing free, democratic institutions as any European commonwealth. The stalwart patriotism, good sense, and wise leadership which, over the course of six and one-half centuries, have succeeded in welding a congeries of peoples into one of the most admirable of political communities are not likely to fail in preserving what they have evolved if given reasonable opportunity. Certainly that such an opportunity will be made available to the Swiss is fondly to be hoped; for neither the Western World nor the Swiss can afford the decline of a regime that has reconciled democracy and liberty so successfully and that has provided so practical an example of the way in which man may redeem himself from social strife and racial bigotry.

BIBLIOGRAPHICAL NOTE
ON THE SWISS POLITICAL SYSTEM

Statutory, Administrative, and Statistical Materials

The compilation of the statutes and ordinances of the Confederation Government is entitled *Amtliche Sammlung der Bundesgesetze und Verordnungen der schweizerischen Eidgenossenschaft (Recueil des lois et arrêtés fédéraux de la Confédération Suisse)* published since 1848. Official accounts of the activity of the federal legislature, including reports of legislative committees and messages of the Federal Council, are found in the *Bundesblatt der schweizerischen Eidgenossenschaft (Feuille Fédérale de la Confédération Suisse)* published since 1876. Debates in the federal chambers appear in the *Amtliches stenographisches Bulletin der schweizerischen Bundesversammlung (Bulletin sténographique officiel de l'Assemblée fédérale Suisse)* published since 1891. The Swiss Constitution, as amended up to 1935, has been translated and published by W. E. Rappard in Section I of the *Source Book on European Governments,* by W. E. Rappard and others (New York, 1937), pp. 19–54. This volume, which is still of value, also contains other pertinent materials on the Swiss Government including the Bernese Constitution and the programs of the principal political parties. The principal general source of official statistical information is the *Statistisches Jahrbuch der Schweiz (Annuaire statistique de la Suisse)* published by the Confederation Statistical Bureau since 1891 (between 1891 and 1918 it was issued as a volume of *Schweizerische Statistik*). Mention may also be made of the *Statistische Quellenwerke der Schweiz (Statistiques de la Suisse)* volumes of which have been issued since 1930. This publication was preceded by the *Schweizerische statistische Mitteilungen* (1919–1929) which in turn was preceded by the *Schweizerische Statistik* (1863–1918). An excellent unofficial statistical source from 1891 to 1917 is Karl Hilty, ed., *Politisches Jahrbuch der schweizerischen Eidgenossenschaft* (Bern).

Historical Treatises

One of the most extensive historical accounts of the Swiss Confederation is Johannes Dierauer, *Geschichte der schweizerischen Eidgenossenschaft,* 5 vols. (Gotha, 1887–1917). The following briefer works may also prove valuable: Eduard Fueter, *Die Schweiz seit 1848* (Zürich, 1928); Karl Hilty, *Les Constitutions fédérales de la Confédération Suisse* (Neuchâtel, 1891); William Martin, *A History of Switzerland,* trans. by Grace W. Booth (London, 1931); L. F. Meyer, *Der schweizerische Bundesstaat, 1848–1923* (Bern, 1925); W. Oechsli, *A History of Switzerland, 1499–1914,* trans. by E. and C. Paul (Cambridge, Eng., 1922).

Descriptive Constitutional and Political Texts

Among the treatises on the Swiss Constitution W. Burckhardt, *Kommentar der schweizerischen Bundesverfassung vom 29. Mai 1874,* 3rd ed. (Bern, 1931) is a standard work. Also to be mentioned in this connection are W. E. Rappard, *L'Individu et l'état dans l'évolution constitutionnelle de la Suisse* (Zürich, 1936) and *La Constitution fédérale de la Suisse* (Neuchâtel, 1948) and A. Silbernagel, *Suisse; organisation politique, administrative et judiciaire de la Confédération helvétique et de chaque canton* (Paris,

1936). Among the better known works which are devoted in whole or in part to a description of the Swiss political system the following may be consulted with profit: F. O. Adams and C. D. Cunningham, *The Swiss Confederation* (New York, 1884); Robert C. Brooks, *The Government and Politics of Switzerland* (Yonkers, 1918); James (Viscount) Bryce, *Modern Democracies,* 2 vols. (New York, 1921); Raymond L. Buell, *Democratic Governments in Europe* (New York, 1935); H. D. Lloyd, *A Sovereign People,* ed. by J. A. Hobson (New York, 1907); H. Huber, *How Switzerland is Governed* (Zürich, 1947); Bernard Moses, *The Federal Government of Switzerland* (Oakland, 1889); W. E. Rappard, *The Government of Switzerland* (New York, 1936); George Sauser-Hall, *The Political Institutions of Switzerland* (New York, 1946); André Siegfried, *Switzerland: A Democratic Way of Life* (New York, 1950); M. R. Tripp, *The Swiss and United States Federal Constitutional Systems, A Comparative Study* (Paris, 1940); John M. Vincent, *State and Federal Government in Switzerland* (Baltimore, 1891); and Boyd Winchester, *The Swiss Republic* (Philadelphia, 1891).

Specialized Treatises

The following texts deal with specialized phases of Swiss governmental organization or political development: Edgar Bonjour, *Swiss Neutrality* (New York, 1947); Felix Bonjour, *Real Democracy in Operation,* trans. by C. L. Leese (London, 1920); Eduard Bosshart, *Die parlamentarische Kontrolle nach schweizerischem Staatsrecht* (Winterthur, 1926); R. C. Brooks, *Civic Training in Switzerland* (Chicago, 1930); Herman Bunsen, *Die Dynamik der schweizerischen Demokratie* (Breslau, 1937); Johannes Duersteler, *Die Organisation der Exekutiv der schweizerischen Eidgenossenschaft* (Aarau, 1912); Fritz Fleiner, *Unitarismus und Foederalismus in der Schweiz und in den Vereinigten Staaten von Amerika* (Jena, 1931); Fritz Fleiner, *Ziele und Wege einer eidgenössischen Verfassungsrevision* (Zürich, 1934); Carl J. Friedrich and Taylor Cole, *Responsible Bureaucracy* (Cambridge, Mass., 1932); Albert Gossin, *La presse suisse* (Neuchâtel, 1937); J. C. Herold, *The Swiss Without Halos* (New York, 1948); Hans Huber, *Der Kompetenzkonflikt zwischen dem Bund und den Kantonen* (Bern, 1926); Rudolf Hübner, *Die Staatsform der Republik* (Bonn, 1919); Gaston P. A. Jèze, *L'exécutif en temps de guerre* (Paris, 1917); Edgard Milhaud, *La Neutralité suisse et la société des nations* (Geneva, 1919); H. W. Raustein, *Die schweizerischen Halbkantone* (Zürich, 1912); Kurt Reber, *Das Notrecht des Staates* (Zürich, 1938); René de Weck, *La Suisse parmi les nations* (Geneva, 1947); and G. Zschoche, *Das Volk als Souverän und als Gesetzgeber in der Schweiz* (Leipzig, 1931).

The Government and Politics of

GERMANY

by KARL LOEWENSTEIN

THE HOLY ROMAN EMPIRE OF THE GERMANIC NATION (800–1806)

After the Great Migration the leadership of the powerful Frankish kings succeeded in welding together most of the Germanic tribes (*Stämme*) into the Christian universal monarchy of the Franco-Roman Empire as the nucleus and frame of the subsequent Holy Roman Empire of the Germanic Nation. That strange political entity, later called the First Reich, was destined to last down to the age of Napoleon I. But throughout its existence it was hardly more than a loose bundle of the scattered German tribes under their own dynasties, joined together at the most by the spiritual idea of the common Imperial Crown (elective since 911). During the Middle Ages the German Emperor was at the same time the King of Italy (Lombardy) and Roman Emperor as the successor of the Caesars, acquiring his dignity through coronation by the Pope. Completely devoid of centralizing institutions, his power over the Reich was in name only and not in substance.

From tribalism and feudalism there emerged that decisive trait of Germany's political history, namely the spirit and tradition of sectionalism and particularism which, forever averse to centralization, manifested itself throughout German history in incessant and ingenuous experiments of federalization. The subject owed and paid legitimate allegiance to the local ruler only, and the territorial rulers remained factually sovereign on their native lands. While the Emperors futilely spent their strength in the maintenance of their Italian claims and domains and the struggle for supremacy with the Pope—which they ultimately lost—henceforward territorial sovereignty formed the rockbed of political life and organization and became the cause for the lasting political weakness of Germany until recent times. Predominance of selfish dynastic interests intent on aggrandizing their personal domain (*Hausmacht*), conditioned on the dualism between the Imperial Crown and the territorial magnates, was primarily responsible for the hereditary disunity of the German tribes and regions and became the historical root for the ingrained particularist habits of the German people.

THE REFORMATION

These trends were vastly enhanced by the Reformation, another lasting source of internal disruption. The subjects were forced to adopt the religion of

[1] For reasons of space the historical development is presented here merely by way of a summarization. Students interested in a fuller exposition are referred to the first edition, pp. 281–337.

their princes (*cuius regio eius religio*) and religious affiliations of the latter were frequently occasioned by political considerations. The struggle between Protestantism and Catholicism inside Germany, intensified by the intervention of foreign powers, climaxed in the disastrous Thirty Years' War (1618–1648), from which the nation did not recover for generations. The Westphalian Peace (1648), embodying the débacle of the Catholic parties, perpetuated the religious cleavage: Austria, whose dynasty, the Habsburgs, had held the Imperial dignity for several centuries, and most of Southern and Western Germany remained Catholic, while the Northern and Eastern regions, among them Prussia, permanently embraced the new faith. Moreover, the peace settlement internally destroyed the last vestiges of the central power of the Reich and of national unity. While France, England, Spain, and even Russia had attained national unity under a strongly centralized monarchical administration and began among themselves to divide the globe, the map of Germany presented the well-known pattern of multi-colored disunity of hundreds of smaller and larger territorial states, principalities, free cities, and ecclesiastic lands under potentates of every description.

THE RISE OF PRUSSIA

However, after the Westphalian Peace, the Prussian State—a unique creation of energetic and spirited rulers mobilizing the potentialities of an intelligent, hard-working, and disciplined people—rose from a marginal existence to the rank of a European power, primarily through the centralizing instrumentalities of a professional army and a highly trained civil service, both recruited mostly from the landed gentry. In the Seven Years' War (1756–1763) Frederick II held his own against the most formidable coalition of great powers of the time. The result of his successes as a military and civilian leader was the emergence of the supernatural idea of the State, of which he considered himself, and toward which he conducted himself as, the first servant. Half a century later the philosopher Hegel exalted the Prussian State system as the transcendental creation of history. This curious blend of authoritarian rule, devoid of the slightest traces of liberalism and individualism, of enlightened absolutism and the rule of law controlling the relations between subjects and the State, not only set the pattern of German political institutions thereafter but also permanently immunized Prussia and Germany against the ideas of the French Revolution.

THE NAPOLEONIC ERA

However, neither the Frederican state machine nor Austria's feudal paternalism withstood the resurrected power of France. In the wake of his conquests, Napoleon, executor of the mission of the French Revolution, cleared away most of the débris of territorial fragmentation inside Germany (*Kleinstaaterei*). After the sweeping territorial consolidation of 1803 (*Reichsdeputationshauptschluss* of Regensburg) and the formation of the French-sponsored Rhenish Confederation, a block of "sovereign" German satellite states under French hegemony, the First Reich ended by the abdication of the Austrian Emperor as German Emperor (August 6, 1806).

THE GERMAN BUND

Of the three basic ingredients of the French Revolution, to wit: nationalism, social equality, and liberalism, adopting for their realization the techniques of democracy, only the first took root in German soil. Implantation of the other two was resisted by the authoritarian practices of the governments and ruling classes and frustrated by the feudal habits of the people. With the Rhenish Confederation began the chain of experiments with a new form of political organization which German legal writers call *Föderalismus,* implying, in contradistinction to the concept of federalism elsewhere, the combination of several political entities, different in size and actual power, jealously preserving their statehood and sovereignty, yet bound together by some precisely circumscribed common political institutions and, above all, by common political interests. This was the pattern adopted by the new Constitution at the end of the Napoleonic wars, incorporated in the Acts of the Congress of Vienna (1815) and generally integrated with the political system known as the Holy Alliance. The German Federation (*Deutscher Bund*), juridically defined as *Staatenbund* and clearly delineated from the *Bundesstaat* (federal state), was a coalition of at first fifty (later reduced to thirty-five members, all monarchies with the exception of four quasi-republican Free Cities. Its only common organ was the Federal Assembly (*Bundesversammlung*) in Frankfurt on the Main. Since federal statutes and federal executive decisions were binding on the subjects of the member states only if converted into state law, the Bund, deprived of genuine legislative, executive, and judicial power, was a loose federation of sovereign princes rather than a truly federal state. Internally the regime was strictly monarchical and authoritarian; only in Southern Germany, which had come in closer contact with progressive French ideas and practices, some elements of liberalism and parliamentary procedures were introduced into the new constitutions.

THE REVOLUTION OF 1848

Yet progressive sections of the bourgeoisie carried into economic prosperity, by the beginning of industrialization, clamored for their share in political power. But the efforts to attain liberal reforms and democratic institutions, manifesting themselves in the Revolution of 1848, proved abortive in the long run. Setting out vigorously for national unification under a centralized though by no means unitarian Reich government and for liberal and democratic reform, it failed tragically in both. A common parliament, known after its seat as the *Paulskirche* and elected by universal manhood suffrage, wrote, together with a full-fledged Bill of Rights, a democratic and parliamentarian constitution, operating under a constitutionally restricted hereditary monarchy, without, however, finding a solution for the increasing antagonism between Austria and Prussia. Rejected by the governments of both leading states the instrument became a scrap of paper. Finally the dream of German national unity under a democratic political order was rudely dispelled by the bayonets of the reactionary governments.

BISMARCK AND GERMAN NATIONAL UNIFICATION

Yet the aftermath of 1848 marks the end of unbridled feudalism and of the beginning ascendancy of the liberal bourgeoisie in Germany. Its claim to political influence was brutally destroyed by Bismarck. A staunch monarchist and convinced authoritarian, he had been appointed Minister President of Prussia (1862) by King William I (1858–1888) to ward off liberal aspirations and to prepare militarily for the inevitable showdown with Austria, competing with Prussia for hegemony in Germany. The outcome of the famed "constitutional conflict" between his cabinet and the liberal and progressive majority of the Prussian diet determined the political fate of Germany for generations to come. The crisis centered on Bismarck's and his associates' plans for military preparedness and ended with the unconditional surrender of the parliamentary opposition. By three victorious wars of aggression against Denmark (1864), Austria (1866) and finally France (1870), Bismarck vindicated his lawless and unconstitutional regime and thereby implanted into the German mind the notion that might goes before right and that the military establishment must remain beyond the control of parliament. By subsequently unifying Germany north of the river Main in the now truly federal North German Bund (1867–1870) he laid the foundations of the constitutional fabric of the Empire, the Second Reich, constituted on January 18, 1871, when, in the midst of the war against France in which all German states participated, King William of Prussia assumed the title and function of the German Emperor.

IMPERIAL GERMANY (1871–1918)

The Imperial Constitution of April 16, 1871, Bismarck's own creation, established all Germany, without Austria, as a federal state, embracing twenty-five states.[2] Pivot and core of the political institutions was the Federal Council (*Bundesrat*) composed of delegates appointed by the governments of the member states and acting under the latter's instructions. By a skillfully calculated distribution of voting strength—seventeen votes out of a total of fifty-eight—Prussian supremacy was maintained because any amendment of the Constitution could be prevented by fourteen votes; however, the rights of the smaller states were equally protected against majorization by similar voting arithmetic. The federal Government was endowed with jurisdiction in all matters of political and economic importance, with the result that Germany could become in the Imperial period the leading industrial power of Europe. The unitarian elements of the Constitution were the Emperor and the federal parliament, the Reichstag. By force of the constitutional provisions the dignity of

---

[2] Prussia; Bavaria; Saxony; Wuerttemberg; Baden; Hessen; Mecklenburg-Schwerin; Saxony-Weimar; Mecklenburg-Strelitz; Oldenburg; Brunswick; Saxony-Meiningen; Saxony-Altenburg; Saxony-Koburg-Gotha; Anhalt; Schwarzburg-Rudolstadt; Schwarzburg-Sondershausen; Waldeck; Reuss older line; Reuss younger line; Schaumburg-Lippe; Lippe; Luebeck; Bremen; Hamburg.

the Emperor was permanently assigned to the ruling king of Prussia. In this dual function he was always in a position to mobilize the strength and prestige of the hegemonical state Prussia for the purposes of the Imperial office. The Reichstag, on the other hand, though elected by universal manhood suffrage, remained politically powerless. This was due in part to the absence of an organized political opposition which Bismarck, implacable anti-parliamentarian that he was, knew how to forestall; primarily, however, because it was constitutionally deprived of the right and power of control over the government. The Reich Chancellor, heading a rapidly increasing Reich administration and serving simultaneously as the Minister President of Prussia, was appointed and dismissed at the sole discretion of the Emperor. Even if he failed to line up parliamentary majorities for his policies he could retain his office so long as he enjoyed the confidence of the Emperor. Only at the very end of the period (1910) was the Reichstag able to force the resignation of the Reich Chancellor (von Buelow).

This curious system camouflaging intrinsically authoritarian government behind a pseudo-constitutional façade, worked tolerably well while Bismarck, master politician as well as statesman, presided as Reich Chancellor over German destinies, loyally supported by a popularly respected King-Emperor. It was bound to break down under his weak and mediocre successors who lacked the courage to resist the capricious and amateurish interferences of Emperor William II (1888–1918). The result was not only the progressive "Prussianization" of Germany, with the corresponding retrogression of the influence of the more liberal South and West, but also an alarmingly increasing cleavage between the masses of the people and their government. Well-organized political parties, emerging under the impact of universal suffrage, found themselves frustrated by a system of government which could not do without them constitutionally and yet robbed them of any effective influence on the conduct of politics. During the period, the stable pole in the fluctuations of party dynamics was the Catholic Center Party, while the Conservatives and Liberals declined, the former because of their rigid program, the latter on account of internal dissensions and factionalism. When, in the general elections of 1912, the Marxist Socialist Party, which under Bismarck had been unsuccessfully outlawed for twelve years, emerged as the strongest party, the brittleness of the political system became clearly visible. The impending crisis was delayed by the outbreak of World War I in 1914. Readily did the authoritarian constitution lend itself to the military dictatorship of Ludendorff and Hindenburg, which completely eclipsed the weak Emperor and rode roughshod over the peoples' liberties and states' rights. A belated effort of parliamentarization (October, 1918) could not save the Empire. With the military defeat, the Imperial Constitution ignominiously collapsed.

CHAPTER I

REVOLUTION AND CONSTITUTION

THE REVOLUTION OF NOVEMBER, 1918

The events called the German "Revolution of 1918" do decidedly not deserve the name. What actually happened was that the ruling class vanished temporarily and that its visible exponents, the monarchies, both of the Empire and of the states, abdicated without even the application of violent pressure. Only to a very small extent was the Revolution due to the undermining activities of revolutionary parties or individual agitators. After the military breakdown, the people were no longer disposed to accept the traditional authority of the ruling class.

The Revolution of 1918 lasted for exactly one day (November 8). On November 9, 1918, the Reich Chancellor, Prince Max of Baden, offered to the Socialist leader, Friedrich Ebert, the office of Reich Chancellor, and it was accepted. Since the formation of a workable Government was possible only with the collaboration of the radical wing of the Socialist Party, the Independent Socialists [1] (the latter, however, refusing to collaborate with members of the bourgeois parties), a cabinet of three members of the majority group of the Socialists (Majority Socialists) and three Independent Socialists was formed, which called itself at first "Council of the People Commissioners," more frequently Reich Government. Ebert's successful efforts to let the Independents share responsibility in the Government were in the main responsible for staving off the danger of Bolshevization of Germany.

From the start, the German "Revolution" steered a conservative course. The civil service in the Reich and in the states spared, to the regret of many then and later, any "purge," prevented administrative chaos, and accepted the

---

[1] The Independent Socialist Party had grown rapidly from a few dissenters, who had refused to grant war credits to the Government in 1914, to an independent radical group within the Socialist movement. It split from the Socialist Party during 1916 and constituted itself as a separate group in April, 1917. In terms of parliamentary seats it embraced about one-fifth of the party. Politically it was under the influence of Bolshevik tenets and entertained, under the leadership of Liebknecht and Rosa Luxembourg, a militant section which assumed the name of the Roman slave "Spartacus" as a rallying cry.

change in political control without opposition. Ebert managed also to enlist the cooperation of the Supreme Command of the army—Field Marshal von Hindenburg remained in office while Ludendorff had fled to Sweden—for an orderly demobilization.

The conservative trend of the German Revolution expressed itself further in the desire shared by government, parties, and the overwhelming mass of the nation to lay a firm foundation for the new order by calling a Constitutional Convention or National Assembly. In the meantime the Council exercised legislative and executive functions in the Reich; in the states Socialist and Liberal parties, after peaceful dethronement of the dynasties and dissolution of the state diets, assumed governmental powers. A revolutionary Council of Workers, Peasants, and Soldiers constituted itself in Berlin and tried in vain to commit the Reich Government to a policy along Bolshevik lines.[2]

SPARTACUS, FREE CORPS, AND SOVIET REPUBLIC IN BAVARIA

Yet the task of the Reich Government was by no means an enviable one. Hemmed in by the economic consequences of the continuing blockade, it had to overcome separatist tendencies, especially in the West and in Bavaria. But the most difficult task of Ebert and his moderate associates in the Reich Cabinet was that of keeping at bay the growing militancy of the "Spartacus" movement, which aimed openly at the establishment of the dictatorship of the proletariat.

The revolutionary minority of the Independent Socialists (constituted in late December of 1918 as the Communist Party), fascinated by the Russian precedent, forced a showdown. In January, 1919, Spartacus staged an open rebellion in Berlin and ruled the capital for a week. Ebert was placed in the most embarrassing position of having to choose between jeopardizing the peaceful evolution or putting down the revolt by armed force. Dependable troops were not available. Ebert resorted to a device which was to become of momentous importance for the future and, in fact, created the precedent for the militarization of the National Socialist movement. Supported by the army command under General Grœner, he formed corps of volunteers (*"Freikorps"*) taken from the ranks of the old army, mostly officers, students, white-collar workers, and other members of the bourgeois intelligentsia, with which his Socialist lieutenant Gustav Noske put down the revolt in Berlin and in other isolated sections of the country. It may be argued that Ebert had possibly no other choice at that time if he wanted to save the democratic republic, but the fatal precedent was set for Fascism, legalized and organized violence of the reactionary bourgeois classes against labor, and for the new technique of "Free corps" as private military units competing with the regular military power of the government. The radical leaders Rosa Luxembourg and Liebknecht were captured and brutally murdered by nationalist officers. The investigating magistrate let the murderers escape. The incident was followed by a series of the

---

[2] On November 22, 1918, in an agreement between the Reich Cabinet and the "Central Council," the latter recognized the former as legitimate executive of the Reich.

most scandalous political trials, granting immunity from punishment for "patriotic" acts.

Revolutionary unrest continued throughout Germany in the first months of 1919 (in Hamburg, Thuringia, Saxony, Brunswick, and the Ruhr), but was always ruthlessly suppressed by the regular army and the volunteer corps, which became the backbone of German Fascism. The most publicized, though by no means the most dangerous, uprising occurred in Bavaria. The so-called Soviet republic (*Raete-Republik*) in and around Munich in March and April, 1919, was not devoid of carnivalistic features as befits the most easy-going city of Germany, but it grew into a major national catastrophe. After the breakdown of the rebellion, white terror of unprecedented brutality was unleashed against innocent and guilty as the prelude to the establishment, in Bavaria, of the first reactionary government from which henceforward conservative counter-revolution as well as the Hitler movement radiated to all parts of the Reich.

In fairness, it should be stated that the efforts of Ebert and the moderate Socialists prevented Germany from sliding into Russianization which, in view of the bourgeois character of the German nation, could have led only to full-scale civil war. Ebert, like Lincoln, saved the unity of the nation. On the other hand, one cannot fail to overlook the tragic misfortune that circumstances, more than deliberate failures of the Socialist leaders, prevented even the partial fulfillment of the anti-capitalistic yearning of the German masses on which later the Hitler movement was able to capitalize.

THE NATIONAL ASSEMBLY AND ITS WORK

On January 19, 1919, elections for the National Assembly were held. Citizens of both sexes of the age of twenty were entitled to vote on the basis of a still rather crude proportional representation. In evaluating the election results, it is remarkable that, different from French elections after the downfall of the monarchy in 1870, an overwhelming majority of all votes was cast for the parties favoring the democratic Republic.[3] Monarchical restoration had no more chances to the very end of the Weimar Republic. The bourgeois parties outnumbered, from the start, the Socialists of both denominations.[4] The moderate and constitutional Majority Socialists, polling 45 per cent of the total vote, outnumbered the radical wing by five to one.[5] On the whole, the same parties which had composed the Reichstag of the Empire reappeared with partly changed personnel, after having dubbed themselves by democratic labels. Victorious in the election were the middle-of-the-road parties—Socialists, Catholic Center, and Left-wing Liberals (Progressives), now rechristened Democrats—among themselves they held 331 seats, or almost three-fourths of the assembly and became the broad parliamentary and popular basis of political reconstruction, henceforward known as the "Weimar

[3] The parties inclined to monarchical government, namely, the German Nationalist Party (formerly Conservatives) and the German People's Party (formerly the right-wing National Liberals) obtained only 63 from a total of 423 seats.

[4] Sixteen million votes as against fourteen million of the Socialist groups.

[5] 11,509,000 votes to 2,317,000, or 163 deputies to 22.

coalition." These parties had to liquidate the heritage of the Empire, defeat, and economic destruction, and were to bear the brunt of Nationalist attacks when they signed the Peace Treaty and drafted the Constitution. Those responsible for the catastrophe were able to remain in a tactically profitable opposition and to gather strength for the final liquidation of the Republic. Nationalist reaction soon invented the shameless lie, which was to become the principal weapon for Hitler's attacks against the Republic—that Germany was not defeated on the battlefield but "stabbed in the back" by the Socialists and other "November criminals." For the years to come, nationalist propaganda identified the Weimar coalition with the Peace Treaty of Versailles; and the burden of the Treaty weighed down on both the coalition parties and the Constitution it drafted and enacted.

In view of continued unrest in Berlin, the National Assembly was convened, on February 6, 1919, to Goethe's Weimar, the town of glorious cultural past, as a symbolic antidote against Potsdam and the spirit of Prussian militarism. The National Assembly adopted first a preliminary working Constitution.[6] On February 11, 1919, Ebert was elected the first President of the Republic. Moreover, the act, anticipating the final Constitution, introduced formally the parliamentary system under which the Reich Government, appointed by the Reich President, was responsible to the parliament. This provisional solution was superseded by the final Constitution adopted on August 11, 1919.

The main function of the National Assembly, in addition to serving as a regular legislative body of the republic, was to draft and to adopt the new Constitution. Its most tragic task was to authorize the acceptance of and to ratify the Peace Treaty, whose severity shattered all illusions of the German nation that they would not be held responsible for the sins of the monarchy and the old ruling classes.[7] After the adoption of the Constitution, the National Assembly continued as regular Reichstag, and principal pieces of economic and political reconstruction are to be credited to its legislative activity.

As a whole, the National Assembly need not fear comparison with other parliamentary assemblies in modern history. Containing a number of excellent administrators and public officials, distinguished professors and leading lawyers, its work was characterized by speed, consciousness of the magnitude of the task, inventions, and realism (entirely different from the futile idealism of the *Paulskirsche,* to whose spiritual heritage Weimar succeeded), and superior also to the Parliamentary Council in Bonn [8] which, thirty years later (1949), tried to continue the Weimar tradition.

As the "father of the Constitution" figures Hugo Preuss, a Liberal professor of constitutional law and, since November 15, 1918, Reich Minister of the Interior. American constitutional experience together with Swiss and French institutions were incorporated while, on the other hand, the learned author

---

[6] *Gesetz über die vorläufige Reichsgewalt* of February 10, 1919 (RGB. p. 169).

[7] The Peace Treaty was signed, on June 28, 1919, by two members of the government: Bell (Center) and Mueller (Socialist). On July 9, 1919, the Assembly ratified the Treaty by 239 to 116 votes.

[8] See *infra,* pp. 561 *ff.*

clearly realized that Germany, forever delivered to a multiple party system, could not utilize the two-party dynamics of British constitutional tradition.

In historical perspective, the Weimar Constitution, ridiculed by National Socialist propaganda, and underated by Bonn, deserves an unbiased judgment. By no means equaling the singular draftsmanship of the American Constitution, it remains nonetheless a remarkable document of constitutional jurisprudence. The first part, containing the frame of government, ranks high among modern constitutions as to concept, logic in drafting, and political realism. The second part, the Bill of Rights, on the other hand, was a rather unfortunate compromise of liberal and socialistic ideas and postulates; revealing a good deal of the doctrinaire stubbornness of the German mind. The Weimar Constitution was a well-planned democratic house in which the Germans could have lived if they had so wished. Seen as a whole, it was the exemplary embodiment of the rule of law-state of our time, and has duly influenced most of the other democratic constitutions of post-War Europe which have ultimately shared its fate.

CHAPTER II

SYMBOLS AND TERRITORY OF THE REPUBLIC

NAME AND SYMBOLISM

"The German Reich is a Republic." (Art. 1.) [1] In establishing the republican form of government both for the Reich and the states (Art. 17) the monarchical structure of government congenital in German history was officially banned from the German territories. The colors of the Reich were changed from black-white-red to black-red-gold (a rather yellowish gold at that) (Art. 3). This innovation, though historically justified, as black-red-gold had been the flag of the German unification movement in 1848, proved to be a grave psychological error because it rubbed in the military defeat and ran counter to the sentimental memory of the past glory of Bismarck's Second Reich. The new colors were not even popular among the Republicans. From the beginning, the Republic failed in its efforts to emotionalize the values of the republican form of government by appropriate propaganda of symbolism, one of its fundamental shortcomings astutely exploited by Hitler.

TERRITORY OF THE REICH

The member state within the Reich was styled *Land*. After the cession of Alsace-Lorraine to France in the Peace Treaty, no territory under the jurisdiction of the Reich proper existed (*Reichsland*). The "right of self-determination," promised to Germany and badly mauled in Versailles, was given official recognition in the Constitution (Art. 18) for the benefit of the German *Laender*, which were "only casual products of dynastic history." Each *Land* was permitted to join any other *Land*, to dismember itself, or to arrange territorial regroupment or realignment of state boundaries; a rather complicated constitutional process was provided in which the will of the populations involved was to be ascertained through initiative and referendum, and the result accepted

---

[1] For a better understanding of the discussion in the text the reader is strongly recommended to compare references to articles quoted with the actual text of the articles in the Constitution itself. For a suitable translation of the text of the Constitution see the bibliographical note *infra*, p. 656.

by way of a statute with the requirements of constitutional amendment. The machinery of territorial regroupment was utilized, during the period, for eliminating a number of petty states in Central Germany, thus reducing the historical heritage of *Kleinstaaterei.*[2] Nonetheless the *Laender* were very unequal in size and population. At the end of the period, the territory of the Republic consisted of seventeen individual *Laender.*[3]

AUSTRIA

The Constitution considered Austria theoretically a part of the Reich after accession (*Anschluss*) (Art. 61, par. 2). Under pressure of the Allied Powers, the Reich Government, in September, 1919, consented to declare the provision inoperative, without, however, deleting it from the Constitution. When the Cabinet of Dr. Bruening, in 1931, made the ill-advised and untimely attempt to accomplish *Anschluss* by indirection through a customs union, the Allied Powers interfered again, and the plan was outlawed by the Permanent Court of International Justice at the Hague.

TERRITORIAL REFORM (REICHSREFORM)

Efforts for a comprehensive change of the traditional dynastic state boundaries by a territorial rationalization on regional-economic lines continued during the period, particularly with the view of breaking up Prussia, which, in spite of constitutional curbs, still dominated the Reich by the sheer weight of her area and population. A Conference of the *Laender* in 1928 failed to come to a generally acceptable solution of this most knotty problem of German political structure. Even National Socialism was unable to devise a more rational territorial division of the Reich, although the process of simplifying the system of multiple states lines, inaugurated by the Republic, was continued on a limited scale. However, after the collapse of 1945 the division into four zones of occupation occasioned far-reaching changes of the territorial map.

[2] Almost all Thuringian principalities organized themselves in 1919–20 into the new *Land* of Thuringia; Koburg joined Bavaria; Pyrmont (1922) and Waldeck (1928) were incorporated into Prussia.

[3] Prussia, Bavaria, Saxony, Wuerttemberg, Baden, Hessen, Thuringia, Hamburg, Mecklenburg-Schwerin, Oldenburg, Brunswick, Anhalt, Bremen, Lippe, Luebeck, Mecklenburg-Strelitz, Schaumburg-Lippe.

CHAPTER III

THE REICH AND THE LAENDER: THE FEDERAL
STRUCTURE OF THE REICH

FEDERAL POWERS

Of the political institutions provided for by the Constitution, only the Federal Council (now called *Reichsrat*) remained as the recognized exponent of the federalistic structure of the Reich, consisting, like its predecessor, the *Bundesrat,* of delegates dependent on and instructed by the governments of the *Laender.* All other organs of the Republic [1] (Reichstag, Reich President, Reich Government) were national institutions and, as such, instruments of an increasingly intensified process of centralization. Likewise the compass of federal powers of the Reich was considerably extended. While the Bismarckian Constitution still followed the principle that all rights not explicitly conferred upon the Reich are vested in the states and transferable to the Reich only by way of constitutional amendment, the Weimar Constitution from the start endowed the Reich with such far-reaching federal powers that practically state rights existed only at the mercy of the Reich. The catalog of federal powers (Articles 6–13) was virtually all-comprehensive; State legislation not compatible with Reich legislation was automatically invalid (Art. 13: *Reichsrecht bricht Landesrecht*).[2] Federal jurisdiction was either exclusive of state legislation (Art. 6) or in concurrence with that of the *Laender* (Arts. 7–12), with the explicit understanding that federal legislation might be invoked at any time and for any subject enumerated in these articles that the Reich saw fit. In addition, the Reich, in case of need, could issue regulations on various enumerated

---

[1] In terms of American constitutional law the expression "Reich," when used in connection with political matters, corresponds to "Federal" in the United States.

[2] The question of whether or not federal legislation overrides state legislation may lead—and did lead—to controversies which were decided by way of arbitration between the Reich and the *Land* or *Laender* involved. The Supreme Court was designated as the tribunal. (Law of April 8, 1920 [RGB. p. 510]). In taxation matters the Supreme Financial Tribunal had jurisdiction. From 1920–1931 23 such cases were decided by the Supreme Courts. This is the federalistic application of judicial review which is indispensable in any composite state for straightening out differences between the federal government and the states in conformity with the rule of law.

matters binding the whole territory (Art. 12, called *Bedarfsgesetzgebung*). Since this power included public welfare in general and protection of public order and safety, even the police power of the *Laender* was subject to deep and frequent inroads of the federal Government. Finally the Reich could establish standards for state legislation, particularly in the fields of education, religion, population, and settlement, and, most important of all, taxation (Arts. 10, 11, called *Grundsatzgesetzgebung*). Powers of the *Laender* were, on the whole, merely subsidiary to those exercised over all territories by the Reich.

In the actual catalog, the following powers assigned to the federal Government were explicitly enumerated (Art. 6): federal organization as such (constitution, national symbols, federal administration necessary for federal services, federal officials); protection of federal and state territory (including peace and war); foreign relations; army and navy; the right to maintain public order and safety within the Reich, amounting to enactment of extraordinary measures which were to become, in the form of emergency decrees,[3] of vital importance for the political life of the Republic; citizenship, freedom of movement within the Reich, immigration and emigration, extradition; customs and currency; postal services; requirements of as well as restrictions on trade, industry, and crafts; social insurance and social services. These federal powers do not seem considerably broader than under the Bismarckian Constitution; but the Reich could exercise optional jurisdiction on most of the other fields of state activities. Some of the most important were the transfer of state railroads —privately owned railroads had been the exception under the Empire [4]—and the establishment of a comprehensive federal financial administration.[5] These illustrations signify the general trend of Republican Germany toward thorough centralization. The old struggle between state sovereignty and federal necessities of the Reich had become rationalized: the *Laender* governments clearly recognized the need for centralization of an economic and political system going through the common experience of defeat, demobilization, inflation, deflation, and economic depression; and offered their loyal cooperation. Prussian hegemony, now neutralized in the more equitable organization of the Federal Council, was no longer an obstacle. The Federal Council itself, stripped of most of its political influence, transformed itself into an efficient organ of Reich administration. Federal civil service, rid of Prussian control, attracted administrative talent from all over the Reich. The Republic must be credited with having built up a technically competent Reich bureaucracy of its own.

[3] See *infra*, pp. 415 *ff*.

[4] The transfer to the Reich control was accomplished in 1920; thereafter the entire system of Reich railroads formed a self-supporting corporation of public law administered by the Reich, the largest industrial undertaking of the world.

[5] Immediately after the establishment of the Republic, a large-scale financial reform was undertaken, which, by assigning to the Reich its own sources of taxation (income, corporations, etc.) made it independent of subsidies from the states. The latter, through an ingenious system of distribution and allocation of sources and types of taxes, were bound to tap mainly such taxes not claimed by the Reich (real estate, entertainment, liquor and licenses or taxes on trade). Simultaneously, a Supreme Financial Court (*Reichsfinanzhof*) was set up to conform with the standards of due process in taxation matters. Financial centralization was one of the most effective devices for bringing and keeping the *Laender* in line with the policies of the Reich.

Finally, the Reich Government now entered into business in a big way, bringing potash, coal, and various other staple industries and sources of raw materials under its immediate control. Unitarian tendencies were further accentuated by a uniform labor policy all over the Reich. In conformity with the homogeneity of economic interests the legal and judicial system followed a decidedly unitarian trend. To all practical intents and purposes, Germany under the Republic was on the road to a system closely approaching a unitary State.

THE POSITION OF THE LAENDER

As mentioned above, not even territorial sovereignty was left to the *Laender,* since their state boundaries could be changed, by constitutional amendment, even against their will (Art. 18). Furthermore, the internal autonomy of the *Laender* was severely restricted by the provisions (Art. 17) that "every *Land* must have a Republican Constitution," and that "the diet must be elected by all German men and women by way of general, equal, direct, and secret vote in conformity with the principles of proportional representation." This clause, corresponding to the "republican-form-of-government" clause of the American Constitution, enjoined both republican and democratic organization on the *Laender,* and provided for homogeneity in the political structure of Reich and states. Moreover, the article made the parliamentary pattern of government mandatory for the states, while leaving the precise structure of the local diets, whether uni- or bi-cameral, to their own choice. This accounts for the wide variety of types of government and electoral systems existing in the various *Laender,* although the most common pattern was a unicameral organization of the diet, with full parliamentary sovereignty without the counterweight of an independent state president.

Seen as a whole, the Weimar Constitution amounted for the *Laender* to a substantial decline in political influence, power, and independence. Economic as well as cultural life became centered in Berlin; the capitals of the *Laender,* after the disappearance of the dynasties, became largely provincialized. Under local jurisdiction remained only matters directly dependent on local conditions, such as agriculture, religious and educational life, and the sphere connected with local and municipal administration. Deplorable as this result may seem from the viewpoint of cultural diversity in which Germany took pride in the past, it is in keeping with the universal decline of federalism elsewhere in this era.

ENFORCEMENT OF FEDERAL SUPREMACY (*REICHSAUFSICHT* AND *REICHSEXEKUTION*)

The vast and comprehensive powers of the Reich in both legislation and administration were exercised in either of two ways: The Reich established its own administration, in which Reich officials dealt directly with the citizens, as in the case of the Reich taxation and the Reich railroads. More common, however, was a system by which the Reich utilized the existing administrative machinery of the *Laender* for performing Reich services and Reich duties. The

Land authorities thus served as executive organs of the Reich. In the second case, the Reich was entitled to far-reaching powers of supervision of the *Land* authorities (Arts. 14 and 15)—incidentally already a feature of the Bismarck- ian Constitution—called *Reichsaufsicht*. In practice, the controlling and super- vising powers of the Reich occasioned little friction and helped to promote uni- formity and homogeneity in administration. If the *Land* failed to comply with a justified request of the Reich, or if the issue was controversial, the matter was referred to a decision of the Constitutional Tribunal (Art. 19, par. 1). No other modern constitution equaled it in devices meant to make the rule of law a living reality, not only between the citizens themselves and the citizens and the State, but also in the relations between the federal Government and the *Laender* governments and authorities.

If, however, the *Land* stubbornly refused to comply with the decision of the Constitutional Tribunal, or if, in the opinion of the Reich Government, the *Land* failed in the fulfillment of its constitutional duties of maintaining orderly processes of government, the Reich Government, after having exhausted all means of peaceful persuasion, could resort to the *ultima ratio* of applying coer- cion against the recalcitrant *Land* by the process of sanctions known as *Reichs- exekution* (Art. 48). The enforcement procedure was left to the Reich Presi- dent, under political responsibility of the Reich Government, and consisted of all means of indirect or direct pressure, such as financial sanctions, military measures, and even occupation of the *Land* by the armed forces of the Reich. While this procedure, already existing under the North German Confederation and the Bismarckian Reich, was never applied before, the Reich Government, under the Republic, felt compelled no less than four times to marshal the armed forces against a member state. The first three cases occurred in the stormy years of the early Republic (1920, 1923) when in Saxony and Thurin- gia radical governments, partly provoked by reactionary moves (*Kapp Putsch* of March, 1920, and Bavarian Rebellion of 1923), failed to maintain public order within their territories. Although the political wisdom of these acts may be open to doubt, the legitimacy of the procedure was scarcely challenged. The Supreme Court upheld the legality of the measures taken. Contrariwise, the last instance of an allegedly imperative enforcement of federal authority against a *Land* was decidedly *ultra vires* of the Reich Government. It occurred in July, 1932, when the reactionary Cabinet of von Papen ousted, by threat of military coercion, the legal Government of Prussia, composed of Socialists, Democrats, and Centrists. This high-handed act of the Reich against state rights was an open *coup d'état* from above, preluding fatally, as power politics versus legality, the period of lawlessness of the Third Reich.[6]

ARBITRATION BETWEEN REICH AND LAENDER

Relations between Reich and *Laender* were capped, in keeping with the principle of the rule of law, by the institution of the Constitutional Tribunal (*Staatsgerichtshof*), copied from the Bismarckian Constitution but developed

---

[6] For details, see *infra*, pp. 445 *ff*.

into one of the most original and interesting aspects of the Weimar Constitution. Under a federal system of government occasional collisions between state and federal interests and rights are almost unavoidable. Such conflicts call urgently for equitable compromises through some judicial authority of recognized standing; otherwise settlement by power politics instead of by constitutional law would be attempted. Consequently, in place of the Federal Council, which, under the Imperial Constitution, had served this purpose, a genuine judicial and nonpolitical tribunal was now established.[7]

The jurisdiction of the Constitutional Tribunal extended to the following matters: (a) Impeachment of the Reich President, Reich Chancellor, and Reich Ministers (Art. 59). The impeachment procedure was never invoked, and the provision remained a dead letter. (b) Arbitration of constitutional disputes or controversies arising within a *Land,* if no state tribunal for adjustment of such controversies existed.[8] (c) Arbitration of disputes or controversies "affected with public interest" when they arose between different *Laender.* This was the typical issue of federal arbitration serving for the peaceable adjustment of differences between the members of the federal organization. (d) Finally, arbitration of disputes or controversies arising between the federal Government and the member states (unless another Reich tribunal had jurisdiction). The only gap in this all-round system of arbitration was that no arbitration was provided for when organs of the Reich itself disagreed or were deadlocked against each other.

No other institution shows better the principle to solve all possible conflicts within the federal family by means of due process under the rule of law to which the sovereign states had to submit. But, at the same time, the institutionalization of due process as between sovereignties revealed inherent limitations, as power relations, once good will to compromise has been destroyed, are, in the last analysis, unjusticiable. Nonetheless, a very large number of such disputes were solved in a peaceable way. The rulings of the Constitutional Tribunal, without exception, were accepted by all parties.

THE FEDERAL COUNCIL (REICHSRAT)

In keeping with the progressively unitarian structure of the Republic, the Federal Council was a rather hybrid institution, neither a genuine Senate as legislative representation of the *Laender* nor even an effectual clearing house for conflicting interests of the Reich and the member states. Surreptitiously it developed into a federal agency, active both in administration and legislation. Harmonization of state rights with Reich interests was left, on the whole, more to occasional conferences between the Prime Ministers of the *Laender* and the Reich Cabinet in Berlin or to extra-constitutional channels. As a federalistic

[7] Law of June 9, 1921 (RGB. p. 905); the court was technically connected with the Supreme Court, though factually wholly separated therefrom. Its composition reflected the strictly judicial character, the President of the Supreme Court (Chief Justice) acting as Chairman, with six associate justices—three from the ranks of the judges of the Supreme Court and one associate judge each from the Supreme Administrative Courts of Prussia, Bavaria, and Saxony.

[8] In this capacity the Constitutional Tribunal was rarely invoked, since most of the *Laender* established tribunals of their own for the adjustment of such local disputes.

brake on the Reich or shock absorber for *Laender* ambitions, as it was originally intended, the Federal Council was useless and superfluous, because the
Laender, against all expectations, offered on the whole full cooperation with
the Reich. In terms of political power, it lost out to the Reichstag and the Reich
Government.

Within the Federal Council (Art. 61) each *Land* had at least one vote. In
the larger *Laender* each unit of 700,000 inhabitants was entitled to an additional vote (a residue over 350,000 being equivalent to one full vote), thus
substituting for the historical rank of the *Laender* the rather mechanical standard of equality based on population. No *Land* was to hold more than two-fifths
of the total vote. This clause, directed openly against Prussia, served as a curb
on Prussia's natural preponderance in size and population within the Reich.
Here the Republic had learned its lesson from the past. Re-allocation of the
number of votes took place after each official population census. At the end of
the Republic, the *Reichsrat* had sixty-six votes, of which Prussia could hold
no more than twenty-six.[9] Moreover, Prussia's influence within the Federal
Council was weakened by the provision that one-half of the Prussian delegates
were to be controlled, not by the Prussian Government, but by the government
of the provinces into which Prussia's territory was subdivided.[10]

The members of the Federal Council were appointed by the governments of
the *Laender.* As a rule, one delegate held and cast all votes of his *Land.* Thus
the Council in action was a relatively small group of permanent officials who
remained mostly in office even if the political color of the government they
represented changed, because their expert knowledge of administration and
personnel made their services almost indispensable. They acted on instructions
of their governments, but as permanent members of a permanently assembled
body, they were better suited to advise their governments at home than *vice
versa.* The professional homogeneity and *esprit de corps* of a political body
destined to harmonize the conflicting wishes of the Reich and the states explains the evolution of an originally pluralistic organ into a full-fledged agency
of the Reich.

The Federal Council did invaluable work in preparing legislation sponsored
by the Reich Government in the Reichstag. Collaboration was so smooth that
the Federal Council became part of the legislative machinery of the Reich
Government. Practically every bill, from whatever source it originated, was

---

[9] Nine of the midget *Laender* below 700,000 inhabitants (Mecklenburg-Schwerin, Meck-
lenburg-Strelitz, Brunswick, Anhalt, Lippe, Schaumburg-Lippe, Oldenburg, Bremen, and
Luebeck) had one vote each 9
Thuringia, Hessen, and Hamburg two votes each 6
Baden 3
Wuerttemberg 4
Saxony 7
Bavaria 11

Since these 40 votes amount to three-fifths of the total, the maximum of additional votes
Prussia was entitled to was 26.

[10] Provincial votes were not infrequently exercised in contradiction to the policies of the
Prussian Government, particularly in the later years when party differences between the various
Prussian provinces became more acute.

scrutinized and worked over by the Federal Council. In general, the latter had only a suspensive veto (*Einspruch*) against bills originating in the Reichstag which if overruled by a second decision of the Reichstag was subject to referendum (Art. 74). In the overwhelming majority of cases, disagreement between Reichstag and Federal Council was compromised between them through mutual concessions, while differences of opinion between Reich Government and Federal Council rarely occurred. In the field of administration the Federal Council developed into a regular administrative agency of the Reich of distinguished administrative efficiency. In particular, it collaborated in the enactment of federal administrative ordinances if they referred to matters left to the execution of the *Laender* on behalf of the Reich. In the last years of the Republic when emergency powers of the Reich President under Art. 48 superseded the action of the regular organs of legislation [11] the activities and with them the political importance of the Federal Council shrank considerably. In general, however, the Federal Council was one of the most successful institutions of the Weimar Republic.

GERMAN FEDERALISM IN OPERATION 1919–1933

The much debated problem of whether or not the *Laender*, under the Weimar Constitution, were still sovereign states or already in process of transformation into territorial subdivisions of the Reich enjoying merely local autonomy, cannot be answered in terms of the constitutional provisions alone. The Republic came into being as the creation of the entire German Nation, organized in nation-wide parties which transcended state lines. Even in theory, the statehood of the *Laender* was of the most precarious nature. The Reich, by constitutional amendment, could destroy the very existence of the *Laender* against their will. The federal Government could invade practically all jurisdictional areas of the *Laender*. Yet the *Laender* after 1918 were still states, though less so than the states of the American Union. It is here that the imponderables come into play which are reflected less by constitutional arrangements than by the feeling of the people. Though tribal sectionalism was decidedly in retrogression, the South German *Laender* especially—Bavaria most of all—considered themselves states; while Prussia, for the whole period under the influence of the most unitarian party, the Socialists, was much more inclined to subordinate her traditional statehood to the needs of national unity.

It seems almost miraculous that centrifugal tendencies emanating from the *Laender* never seriously endangered the cohesion or existence of the Republic. During the early years, it is true, conflicts occurred between the Reich Government and Bavaria, politically the most backward of the German states, controlled, without interruption, from 1919 to 1933 by the narrow particularism of the Catholic clergy. Bavaria became the happy hunting grounds for political reaction of nationalists, anti-socialists, anti-Semites, and monarchists. In 1922 political assassinations of Republican leaders in which Bavarian officials had their hand, were climaxed in the murder of Walther Rathenau, Reich Minister

---

[11] See *infra*, pp. 415 *ff*.

of Foreign Affairs. Bavaria refused to apply to her territory protective legislation enacted by the Reich, the first act since 1871 of open defiance against the authority of the Reich. Even more serious was a rebellion of the Bavarian government against the Reich in the autumn of 1923, when, at the height of the inflation and coinciding with the collapse of the passive resistance against the Allies in the Ruhr basin, the nationalist reaction, openly protected by the Bavarian government of von Kahr, ripened into concrete plans for civil war against the Reich. At this juncture Adolf Hitler and the National Socialist Party came for the first time into prominence. Hitler, with whom the Bavarian Government was in secret understanding in plotting against the Reich, anticipated the outbreak of the official Bavarian Rebellion by his famous "Beerhallputsch" of November 9, 1923. It was easily crushed by the Bavarian police. The rioters killed by the police became the "blood martyrs" of the Third Reich. Ebert's and Stresemann's moderation compromised matters with Bavaria, who confined herself henceforward to demanding a peaceful revision of the Constitution on more federalistic lines. Strangely reversing its stand, it was the Bavarian Catholic Party which led, at the end of the Republic, resistance against the impending Nazification of the Reich.

The conflicts with Bavaria revealed a danger zone embedded in the Constitution which was to become one of the contributing causes of the ultimate disintegration of Republican Germany. The German Republic not only tried its hand in federalism, but coupled it with the most difficult form of government, namely parliamentarism under multiple party dynamics. The parliamentary system in the Reich was duplicated by parliamentary systems on the local level in each of the *Laender*. Yet party fluctuations and political configurations did not operate in synchronization; frequently they ran counter to each other. National Socialism gained control in some of the *Laender* after 1931 (Thuringia, Oldenburg, Mecklenburg) and used the welcome foothold in power as a political ramrod against the Reich. Likewise, a conflict between the reactionary Nationalist Government of the Reich under the Cabinet of von Papen (1932) and the moderate Weimar coalition of Socialists, Democrats, and Centrists controlling Prussia (lasting without interruption from 1918 to 1932) could not fail to clash. A political order devised under the assumption of good will and compromise between the Reich and the *Laender* was bound to collapse once either the *Land* government or the Reich Government resolved to abandon cooperation. Seen retrospectively, the parallel institutionalization of parliamentarism in both the Reich and the different states became one of the causes of the ultimate breakdown of German democracy when state rights or federal powers were used as vehicles for party interests. Hitler, after the seizure of power, drew only the logical conclusions from his own successful experience in wrecking the Reich by exploiting political autonomy of the *Laender,* when he abolished, in 1934, the *Laender* as political units altogether.

CHAPTER IV

POPULAR SOVEREIGNTY: GERMANY AS A DEMOCRACY

THE PEOPLE AS ORGAN OF THE STATE

From time immemorial Germany had lived under the monarchical form of government. Suddenly in 1918, the dynasties disappeared and the people, without preparation or education, were left to their own devices. Simultaneously with the declaration that Germany had become a Republic, the Constitution stated the principle of popular sovereignty (Art. 1, par. 2): "State authority emanates from the people." In conformity with the principle of democracy, all institutions of the Reich were based either directly or indirectly on the people. As a direct expression of the national popular will, the following institutions were organized: (a) the people themselves (*Reichsvolk*), participating in legislation by initiative and referendum; (b) the Reichstag, the national parliament, elected by universal suffrage; (c) the Reich President, also elected by universal suffrage. Popular sovereignty implied identity of State and Nation. The people were simultaneously subject and object of the government, master and servant of the State.

In the capacity of an organ of the State, the people were organized as electorate or body of voters; universal manhood suffrage had existed since 1871, and its operation offered no difficulties. As a State organ, the people were called upon to act in the following ways: (1) As voters either in the regular election of the legislative body, the Reichstag, held every four years (Arts. 22, 23), or in extraordinary elections held after a dissolution of the Reichstag decreed by the Reich President (Art. 25); (2) as electors in the election (Arts. 41, 43) and the recall of the Reich President before the normal expiration of his term (Art. 43, par. 2); (3) as legislators in the process of direct legislation by the people (Arts. 73–76).

During the lifetime of the Republic the people acted as electorate for the regular election of the legislative body only once, when they elected the Constitutional Assembly (1919). All the seven other parliaments (1920; 1924, May and December; 1928; 1930; 1932, July and November) were dissolved.

Twice the people acted as agency for the election of the Reich President (von Hindenburg, 1925, and re-elected 1932).

DIRECT LEGISLATION BY THE PEOPLE

Direct participation of the people in the legislative process by initiative and referendum, misunderstanding the Swiss precedent, was believed to be an ultra-democratic device, counterbalancing, if necessary, more conservative or tardy action of the representatives. Legislative proposals proper could originate from the people through initiative (*Volksbegehren*). The process was set in motion if one-tenth of the voters requested the introduction of a bill in the Reichstag. This percentage seemed sound because any one of the major parties could easily launch it, while it was difficult for local parties or political cranks to start the ball rolling. If the proposal initiated by the group was accepted by the Reichstag without alteration, it became automatically law. If the Reichstag refused to endorse it, the final decision on the proposal depended on the outcome of a popular referendum. Although this may seem a fairly easy access of the people to legislation, in practice the people were handicapped by two additional provisions: The Reichstag could be overruled only if the majority of voters participated in the referendum (Art. 75). Moreover, if the initiated bill contained a constitutional amendment, the majority of voters had not only to participate in the poll, but also to vote in favor of the bill (Art. 76, par. 1, sentence 2). The result of these additional precautions against the misuse of the device by minorities was that a large party, disfavoring the proposal, could torpedo it simply by nonparticipation.

All these provisions made direct legislation so complicated and difficult that the legislative monopoly of the Reichstag was not in the least affected by it. On the whole, the people were no more enlightened than their representatives. From 1919 to 1933, popular initiative was invoked for not more than eight proposals. Only three reached the first stage of popular registration endorsing the initiative; and only two among them, having found sufficient support of the voters, were submitted to popular referendum. None reached the statute book.[1] By the end of the Republic, the institution, misused by the radical parties of the Left and Right for demagogical purposes, was thoroughly discredited. The experiences of the *Laender,* where initiative and referendum were in much wider use (for the recall of the parliament, etc.), were equally discouraging.

---

[1] Several initiatives were not admitted because they were justly considered as financial measures on which only the Reich President could invoke the referendum procedure (Art. 73, par. 4). Of the three successful initiatives, one (1926) dealt with the expropriation of the formerly ruling dynasties which, supported by legalistic courts, had blackmailed the treasuries of the *Laender* into highly onerous settlements for the latter. The initiative failed in the referendum stage. The second (1928), launched by the Communists against the building of a new "pocket" battleship, failed to obtain the requisite number of voters for the initiative. The third initiative (1929), sponsored by the Nationalists as a protest against the Young Plan settlement of the reparations just got through the initiative, but failed catastrophically in the referendum.

CHAPTER V

THE REICH PRESIDENT

German political tradition, accustomed to monarchy, demanded a strong executive. The American pattern of the popularly elected President who was removed from parliamentary control offered itself conveniently. It was hoped that he would have enough prestige derived from the plebiscitary character of his election to become the stabilizing element in the fluctuations of parliamentary dynamics. On the other hand, in the light of past experiences with the personal regime under the Second Reich, his position was integrated in the parliamentary government by prescribing, in unequivocal terms, that all his acts, including those referring to military matters, were valid only if countersigned by the Reich Chancellor or a Reich Minister (Art. 50). By his countersignature, the Reich Chancellor assumed responsibility before the Reichstag for every act of the Reich President. This arrangement was a curious blend between the powerful American President and the constitutional monarch of the German past.

Eligible to the presidential office was every German citizen [1] who had completed his thirty-fifth year. The term of office was seven years. Re-election was possible, as was recall before expiration of the term, decided by the electorate after the request of two-thirds of the Reichstag.[2] A candidate was duly elected if he polled more than half the votes cast. If no candidate obtained the absolute majority of votes in the first election, a second election was to be held, in which the simple plurality won. The number of candidates for the second election was unlimited, and even new candidates could offer themselves.

During the Weimar Republic, Germany had two presidents. Fritz Ebert, Socialist leader of the Reich Government after the Revolution, was the obvious choice of the National Assembly in February, 1919. After his untimely death

---

[1] Hitler, an Austrian, before running for the Presidency against Hindenburg in 1932, suddenly was made, by political henchmen, citizen of Brunswick and thereby Reich citizen through a fraudulent appointment to a public office which he hever held.

[2] The idea of recalling the Reich President was never seriously entertained, although many people felt that President von Hindenburg had violated his oath of office by supporting "presidential" instead of "parliamentary" cabinets. See *infra*, p. 429.

(February 28, 1925), the first popular election took place (March 29–April 26, 1925), in which, after an inconclusive first election, the old Field Marshal von Hindenburg consented to run in the second election and obtained a majority. In 1932 Hindenburg was re-elected, again only in the second election (March 13–April 10, 1932), Hitler running second by a wide margin.

FUNCTIONS AND POWERS

The functions and powers of the Reich President in practice differed widely from the blueprint in the Constitution. In view of the device of countersignature by the Reich Chancellor, the vast majority of political acts nominally labeled as presidential were in fact instrumentalities for the execution of the policies of the Reich Government. Ebert, with a lifelong experience in politics and trade-union administration, one of the leading parliamentarians of the old Reichstag, accepted advice but let nobody decide for him. While he was in the Presidency, the highest office of the Republic was exercised as intended by the Constitution. When the old Field Marshal was dragged into the office things changed. Nobody expected that complicated legal and economic measures, frequently covering many pages in the Official Bulletin of Statutes, would be understood or even read by an aged general. He had to rely, if not on the Reich Chancellor, on the Secretary of the Presidential Office, Dr. Meissner [3] who served faithfully—as faith goes—three masters, Ebert, Hindenburg, and Hitler. But he relied even more on his son, Oskar, who "had not been provided for in the Constitution," and the irresponsible advisors of the monarchist Junker clique, whose influence on him was as fatal as that of the court clique on the Kaiser. During his second term he was little more than a living corpse.

The principal functions of the Reich President embraced "international representation of the Reich" (Art. 45); but all material decisions had to be left to the Reich Government. The crucial defect of the Bismarckian Constitution was remedied in that military matters, dealt with by the Reich President formally as Commander-in-Chief of the armed forces (Art. 47), were equally brought under responsibility of the Reich Chancellor, i.e., under parliamentary control.[4] The military leaders (most of all Seeckt) and their Cabinet representatives succeeded in keeping the army out of politics and forging it into a neutral instrument of Reich power. But it goes without saying that Hindenburg's prestige with the army generals was greater than that of the Socialist Ebert, although the army loyally served both of them and the Reich.

DISSOLUTION OF THE REICHSTAG

Another important function assigned to the Reich President was that of dissolving the Reichstag (Art. 25). One has to distinguish two different types of

[3] He was acquitted, in 1949, by an American Military Court from the indictment of having committed crimes against humanity.

[4] From the beginning, exercise of military powers was delegated to the Defense Minister (*Wehrminister*), who was factually the subordinate of the Reich Chancellor and under the control of parliament.

dissolution. Under the normal rules of the parliamentary system, the Government in power might dissolve parliament in order to invoke a verdict of the electorate on its policies. If the Government fails to obtain a working majority in the ensuing elections, it resigns. The second type of dissolution, characteristic for the German version of parliamentarism, consisted in this: if the Reich President, differing from the Reich Chancellor, believed that the Reichstag, in which the Government still commanded a majority, no longer represented the will of the majority of the people, by virtue of his independent position in political life, he could compel the resignation of the Government and decree the dissolution of the Reichstag. This use, or rather abuse, of the dissolution power implied in practice that the Reich President, at his discretion, could dismiss the Reich Chancellor whom he disliked, and appoint, in his place, some one in whom he had confidence and to whom he granted dissolution although his predecessor in office had been supported by a parliamentary majority. Hindenburg was induced by irresponsible advisers to use the dissolution power in 1932 in order to secure parliamentary majorities for his presidential Cabinets (von Papen and von Schleicher). This abuse of the dissolution power smashed the parliamentary system of the Republic and paved the way to power for Hitler.

APPOINTMENT AND DISMISSAL OF THE REICH CHANCELLOR

According to the Constitution, "the Reich Chancellor and, at his suggestion, the Reich Ministers are appointed and dismissed by the Reich President" (Art. 53). The assumption behind this rule, copied from the position of the constitutional monarch, was that the Reich President would appoint only a Reich Chancellor and a Cabinet who were assured beforehand of the confidence of the Reichstag or at least had convinced themselves that they would obtain it when installed in office by the President (Art. 54). At an early date in the life of the Republic, however, the Weimar coalition of the Reichstag, composed of Socialists, Centrists, and Democrats, who had enacted the Constitution, was broken. Thereafter no party ever obtained a clear majority. Consequently, the majority supporting the Reich Cabinet by its "confidence" had to be artificially joined together in difficult and prolonged negotiations between the parties. In taking a hand in bringing about a workable Cabinet supported by a workable majority of parties, both Ebert and Hindenburg had an influence in the selection of the Reich Chancellor and the determination of future policies far beyond the expectations of the fathers of the Constitution. While Ebert and Hindenburg (during his first term) conformed to the rules of the parliamentary game, the latter, immediately after his re-election in 1932, claimed the right to dismiss Reich Chancellor Dr. Bruening of whose policies he, or the clique of intriguers behind him, disapproved, although the Reich Chancellor had still the confidence of the majority of the Reichstag. In open violation of the Constitution, he went so far as to appoint Chancellors who never had the slightest chance of gaining the majority support of the Reichstag and at no time enjoyed its confidence. This calamitous perversion of the parliamentary system led, in 1932, to the practice of the so-called "fighting government" (*Kampfregierung*). The "presidial" instead of a "parliamentary" Government was a Cabinet lacking parliamentary support, though backed by the confidence and prestige of the President. It is true that so flagrant a violation both of letter and spirit of the Constitution was occasioned by the difficulty, if not impossibility, of finding a working parliamentary majority for the Government. It is equally true that the fragmentation of party life and the wrecking tactics of National Socialists and Communists alike were responsible for the parliamentary deadlock. But the solution found in the practice of presidential Cabinets was clearly unconstitutional and could be exercised only by equally illegitimate use or misuse of the emergency powers of the President for carrying on the Government. Once the President had been pushed into the legal no-man's-land, it is easy to see that the period of political disintegration of the Reich had begun from which Hitler, in January, 1933, emerged as the "savior of the country."

EMERGENCY POWERS OF THE REICH PRESIDENT UNDER ARTICLE 48

The ominous Article 48 has become perhaps the best known provision of the Weimar Constitution outside of Germany as the symbol of dictatorship. It embodied what has been called "constitutional dictatorship," though its actual application during the last years of the Republic was clearly unconstitutional. Again it should be emphasized that emergency powers nominally emanating from the Reich President were actually emergency powers accorded to the Reich Cabinet, which merely submitted its decrees to the Reich President for signature. Emergency powers for the strictly limited purpose of maintaining public order and safety were a familiar device both of the Imperial Constitution of 1871 and of the pattern of the constitutional monarchy in general. Under the emergency power the Reich Government, under the authority of the Reich President, could take any particular step deemed suitable for meeting the requirements of the emergency situation, or general measures serviceable for restoring normalcy. Moreover, the Constitution permitted deep inroads into the constitutionally guaranteed civil rights by authorizing the Government to suspend, while the emergency situation lasted, one or several of the seven fundamental guarantees of the rule of law, enumerated in Art. 48, par. 2.[5]

After 1930 the emergency powers of the Reich President were stretched far beyond their original intention and scope and utilized, in the most irregular way, for carrying out, under cover of the Reich President's signature, govern-

---

[5] These suspendable rights were the following: inviolability of person (Art. 114), including freedom from arbitrary arrest and detention (*habeas corpus*); inviolability of private residence (Art. 115); privacy of mail and similar communications (Art. 117); freedom of speech (Art. 118), including prohibition of censorship; freedom of association and assembly (Arts. 123, 124); inviolability of private property (Art. 153), including protection against confiscation without adequate compensation. By granting suspension, for an indefinite time, of these fundamental rights destined to protect the citizens from arbitrary government, Hindenburg, in February, 1933, enabled Hitler to enslave the German people. These Emergency Ordinances of the Reich President were repealed only after the collapse of 1945.

mental policies for which no parliamentary support was obtainable. The term of the Constitution: "serious disturbances or threats to public order and safety" was interpreted from the beginning in the much broader sense of coping with political situations in general which *might* ultimately involve dangers to internal peace. Under this extensive interpretation, not only police measures were enacted by way of Article 48, but all measures intended to deal with economic or financial difficulties, labor problems, or revision of civil and criminal law, until the Emergency Decrees or Ordinances finally became a full-sized substitute for legislation when parliamentary support for governmental policies was unobtainable. From 1930 to 1933 emergency decrees of the President were almost exclusively used in the place of regular legislation by the Reichstag.

According to the Constitution, the use of the emergency powers under Article 48 was not without definite constitutional limitations. The strings attached to the power were that the measures taken should be temporary while the emergency situation lasted, and should not infringe on the Constitution itself. In practice, the Reich Government, after 1930, ignored these limitations, at least by indirection, in not a few instances. Furthermore, the Reichstag had to be informed without delay of all measures taken under the extraordinary powers and could demand at any time the repeal of such measures, even against the wish of the Reich Government and the Reich President. In practice, however, this provision remained a dead letter most of the time because the Reichstag, incapable of forming a working majority, was also unable, or unwilling, to revoke the emergency decrees. After 1930 the Reichstag majority, completely stripped of political power, "tolerated" government by emergency decrees of the Cabinet. Thus the Reichstag became an accessory to the crime of assassinating the Republic. In fact, the Enabling Acts of 1933, 1937, and 1939, on which Hitler's dictatorship was based formally, were the inescapable continuation of what Dr. Bruening had inaugurated under the Republic.

CHAPTER VI

THE REICHSTAG

ELECTORAL SYSTEM

Democratization was carried to the limit in the organization of the Reichstag, but it failed calamitously to create the essentials of democratic and parliamentary government, namely, corporate consciousness of the parliament and opportunity for constructive leadership.

The suffrage was universal, equal, direct, and secret, under application of "the principles of proportional representation" (Art. 22). Not a single election in a single district was declared invalid because of dishonest or fraudulent practices. Voting was universal, since men and women of the age of 20 years were entitled to vote. The masses of the younger voters, particularly after the depression had swelled the army of unemployed, naturally voted for the radical parties of the Left and the Right. Nor was the grant of vote to the fair sex an unmixed blessing, since women, against expectation, were more attracted by radical parties than men. Voting was also reasonably equal in that it gave all voters equal voting strength within the confines of proportional representation. That the vote was by no means direct will be seen from the following discussion of the technique devised for proportional representation.

PROPORTIONAL REPRESENTATION

By venturing into the uncharted sea of proportional representation, the Germans forged unwittingly one of the major nails in the coffin of the Republic. For a successful operation of proportional representation, two problems have to be solved: (a) How many seats should the individual parties obtain in accordance with their voting strength as compared with the voting strength of other parties? (b) How are the seats obtained by each party to be distributed among the candidates of each party? Proportional representation has become a crypto-science for mathematicians, statisticians, politicians, psychologists, and demagogues. The common man, at least in Germany, never understood it and rarely cared. The National Assembly, besides the various systems applied by the states, devised an ingenious method for the Reichstag

417

by the so-called "automatic procedure." The number of deputies was not fixed in advance, but varied with the number of votes actually cast in each election. The higher the participation in the election, the higher the number of seats. For each 60,000 votes cast for a party ticket, the party received one seat. A residue of between 30,000 and 60,000 was equivalent to an additional seat. The visible result was that the number of deputies increased with each election, from 421 in 1919 to 647 in 1933; fluctuations faithfully reflect increase or decrease of electoral participation.

As to the problem of how to assign the seats obtained by each party to the candidates of the party, again a rather simple solution was found in that the sequence of candidates arranged before the election by party headquarters, decided the allocation of seats to the candidates (the principle of the "strictly non-variable ticket," *"gebundene Liste"*). The voter had not the slightest influence on the composition of the ticket nor on the sequence of candidates; he had to swallow the ticket hook, line, and sinker. Primaries were unknown. Candidates were selected *in camera* by the party bosses. This allegedly most perfect democratic system was certainly the most soulless imaginable. The election was no longer a contest between personalities, but the automatic endorsement of a party ticket by the voter, at best a competition between lifeless party programs instead of a battle royal between living personalities. The individual voter in this democratically perfect system was only cannon fodder in the lusty warfare of party strategists. Proportional representation, at least under the German technique, disenfranchised the voter mentally and killed, together with his influence, his interest in party politics. Moreover, unimpeachable as the system may have been from the viewpoint of making the parliament a mathematical replica of the party configuration in the electorate, it sacrificed leadership, the living elixir of democracy, for accuracy. The turn-over of parliamentarians was surprisingly small; new men had the greatest difficulty in obtaining admission to the ticket controlled by the party bosses; the machines stood between the aspiring leader and the voter. No wonder that the National Socialists, deriding the system as "pluralism of political parties *(Parteienbundesstaat)*" could profit by the doubtful education of the masses under the Republic and establish an even more automatic, even more dictated, system of appointing the parliamentary personnel by virtue of the military discipline of the masses under the whip of the "Leader."

ORGANIZATION OF THE REICHSTAG

With few exceptions, the organization of the Reichstag offers little which deviates from the Western pattern of parliamentarism. But some of the customary institutions were twisted in a particular way in order to serve the propagandist purposes of the enemies of democracy and to make cooperation between Government and Parliament even more difficult than it was owing to the atomization of party life. Only a few points of organization were regulated by the Constitution itself. Arrangement of business was left to parliamentary autonomy by way of Standing Orders. The Speaker of the assembly was the

Reichstag President, elected by the parliament. On the whole, the Standing Orders, devised for normal times, admitted of too much propagandist and wrecking tactics from the radical parties and condoned promotion of their party interests to such an extent that the Parliament lost much of its prestige by leniency towards its sworn enemies, who utilized parliamentary processes only for destroying it. Likewise, Parliamentary Investigating Committees, a novelty in Germany, failed to promote cooperation between Reichstag and Government. Useful as was the work performed by the Committees in uncovering illegalities and abuses of nationalist circles patronized by authorities, the Government resented their activities and left nothing undone for hampering them.[1] The customary immunities accorded to Reichstag members [2] were equally misused by National Socialists and Communists for propagandistic, subversive, and even treasonable purposes. Liberal democracy, entangled in exaggerated legalism, failed to invoke in time adequate measures of self-defense.

POWERS AND FUNCTIONS OF THE REICHSTAG

In the blueprint of the Constituent Assembly, the Reichstag was to be the center of political dynamics. In reality, however, the Reichstag fell short of the too-sanguine expectations. Its power declined from the beginning, and was finally wholly eclipsed by the Reich Government and the Reich President.

The functions and powers of the Reichstag may be summarized as follows: (1) It was the main legislative organ (Art. 69, par. 2); the Federal Council was reduced to what amounted in practice to merely a suspensive veto.[3] (2) The Reichstag participated in the conduct of government by consenting to the declaration of war and the conclusion of peace (Art. 45, par. 2), and to the conclusion of alliances and treaties. (3) It held the strings of the purse by passing on the budget and other financial transactions of the government (Arts. 85, 86). (4) It controlled the Reich Government by granting or withholding confidence (Art. 54), by interpellations and other means of checking up with governmental activities. (5) It held, at least theoretically, the whip-hand over Reich President and Cabinet by the power of impeachment and removal of the Reich President.

Reviewing the position of the Reichstag during the period, three stages have to be distinguished. During the first, ranging roughly from 1919 to 1923 (to the end of the occupation of the Ruhr and stabilization of the currency), the Reichstag had to cede much of its power to the Reich Government and the Reich President, who steered a difficult course through the aftermath of defeat and the catastrophe of economic collapse in the inflation. Then, from the end of 1923 to 1930, the Reichstag operated normally without interruption, and

---

[1] It is significant that both Dr. Bruening and von Schleicher were felled by the clique around Hindenburg when a Special Investigating Committee of the Reichstag delved into the scandalous misuse of public money by the Junkers in the so-called Eastern Relief (*Osthilfe*).

[2] Arts. 36–38, granting, during the legislative period, freedom from arrest, immunity from judicial and disciplinary investigation on account of actions connected with the parliamentary mandate.

[3] See *supra*, p. 408.

discharged efficiently all functions assigned to it by the Constitution. These years, roughly coinciding with Stresemann's control over the destinies of the Republic, are a striking proof of the potential ability of the German people to handle satisfactorily the complicated parliamentary system. The third period opens with Dr. Bruening in 1930, when the world depression began to press heavily on Germany. The Reichstag lost control and even influence on the conduct of politics by the Reich Government; and was finally superseded, in 1932, by "presidial" cabinets supported exclusively by the Reich President. The fall of the Reichstag must be attributed as much to the inept authoritarianism of Dr. Bruening, who failed miserably in enlisting the cooperation of the Reichstag, as to the self-emasculation of that body, which, paralyzed by party dissensions, "tolerated" the supersession of parliamentary legislation by presidential emergency decrees. Militant democracy was needed, but Dr. Bruening was neither a democrat nor militant. No wonder that the Reichstag, by its own fault, was so much discredited as an institution that Hitler pushed it aside with scorn.

CHAPTER VII

THE PARLIAMENTARY SYSTEM UNDER
THE WEIMAR CONSTITUTION: I

POLITICAL PARTIES

Party dynamics in Republican Germany demonstrate again the tenacity of tradition. With the exception of National Socialists and Communists, the parties operating between 1918 and 1933 were the same as under the Imperial Constitution, without material modifications. Seemingly democratic labels were deceptive. What resulted from political warfare and elections were, on the whole, only minor shifts and fluctuations in party strength. No landslide ever occurred until, with the elections of September, 1930, the National Socialists entered the parliamentary scene, a new mass party, operating under new emotional appeals and under the leadership of the greatest demagogue of our time. The party, revolutionary and reactionary at the same time, destroyed within two years the equilibrium of party life and finally seized government and State.

1. THE CONSERVATIVES

The Conservatives, styling themselves "German National People's Party," stemmed from the Prussian Conservatives who, after the loss of the hereditary domain in Prussia, had spread all over the Reich as a nation-wide party. Never divorcing themselves from their authoritarian past, they were, from the outset, enemies of democracy as well as of the republican form of government. Monarchists without a pretender—the Hohenzollerns having forfeited their claim to the throne by deserting the army—they became, through loud-mouthed patriotism, the center of reaction and opposition against Weimar. They drew their voting strength from the old ruling classes around the army and the civil service, with many adherents also from the higher and middle bourgeoisie and landowners, who feared for their vested rights by Socialist inroads. Any pressure of the victors in the World War on the down-trodden Republic was reflected in an increase in the voting figures for the Nationalists. At no time particularly strong in terms of votes and parliamentary seats,[1] they were influential far beyond their actual strength because no bourgeois government could afford to offend the Nationalists as the "patriotic" party *par excellence*. Only between 1925 and 1927 did they participate with important portfolios in coalition cabinets of non-Socialist composition. In 1930, when Dr. Hugenberg had forced his way to party leadership, the stubborn anti-Socialist prepossessions of that reactionary capitalist led the Nationalists into vehement opposition to Dr. Bruening's bourgeois Government and into the arms of the rising National Socialist movement as allies. The "presidial" cabinets of Hindenburg were supported only by the Nationalists. Hugenberg helped Hitler into the saddle in 1933. It is safe to say that no other party in Germany has so wantonly wasted its considerable capital and has done more harm to the republican and democratic cause. Hugenberg, one of the grave-diggers of Weimar, and his friends received full compensation: Hitler threw them out of the government as soon as their usefulness was spent.

2. THE CONSERVATIVE LIBERALS: THE GERMAN PEOPLE'S PARTY

Next in order from right to left, came the conservative wing of the Liberals, as "German People's Party," the lawful heir to the National Liberals of the Empire; this was the party of Dr. Stresemann, the only statesman of European caliber of the German Republic. A class party without a mass basis, it had its stronghold in big business and industry of the higher, and in the propertied classes of the middle, bourgeoisie, and in the Protestant clergy. It recognized grudgingly the given situation of a republican instead of a monarchical government, but, despite liberal streaks, it never paid more than lip service to democracy. As anti-Socialist as the Nationalist neighbor, the German People's Party was less intransigent in foreign policy, and granted collaboration with the republican parties from an early date. Its real strength, far superior to its actual votes, consisted in the economic power of its members, after Germany, shunning experimentation with Socialism, embraced full-fledged capitalism with its attendant cartels and trusts in full control of economic life. The party participated in almost all cabinets between 1920 and 1931 (second cabinet of Dr. Bruening) within the framework of the so-called "Great Coalition." But the almost incomparable complexity of German party politics may be illustrated by the fact that Dr. Stresemann, the leading figure in all German cabinets from 1923 to his untimely death in 1930, was not always able to carry his own party with him in his efforts to bring Germany back to European cooperation.

3. THE CATHOLIC CENTER PARTY

The most influential and at the same time the most stable party was the Catholic Party, appropriately called "the Center" (*Zentrum*). As a primarily confessional organization, it cut through all layers of the population, embracing Westphalian and Silesian aristocrats as well as the bulk of the peasants in

---

[1] Only in 1924 were the Conservatives the second strongest party of the Reichstag, with 103 deputies out of a total of 493. They fell as low as 37 in July 1932, and recovered to 52 in 1933.

Southern Germany, the Rhineland, and the Catholic parts of Prussia, in addition to the small Catholic bourgeoisie and the Catholic trade unions. Social diversification made the Center an altogether equalitarian and genuinely democratic party. In view of its social structure, the Center could enter an alliance both with the Left, to which it inclined more, at least during the first decade, and with the Right; and thus it occupied the pivotal position. From 1918 to 1932 not a single coalition was formed without the Center, which held important positions in all cabinets of the Republic and provided the Reich with no less than four of the Reich Chancellors (Fehrenbach, Wirth, Marx, and Bruening). Owing to its unshakable entrenchment in the Catholic population, it maintained its strength throughout against the tide of radicalism, never falling below about one-fifth of the total strength of the Reichstag. National Socialism could never make a dent on it, which explains the hatred of the Third Reich for the party of the "black moles." The Center pursued with consistency Catholic aims, stood for the sanctity of home and family life and for giving to the church its due in education and cultural activities. By its policies and leadership, the Center Party rendered invaluable services to the Republic.

4. THE BAVARIAN CATHOLIC PARTY

The Bavarian section of the Center Party split from the main body in 1920 and organized itself as an independent unit (embracing about one-fourth of the total of the Center Party). The Bavarian peasant, frightened by the Soviet experiment in 1919, disagreed with the alliance of the Reich Party with the Socialists. In the years thereafter, Bavaria, dominated by the Catholic People's Party, became the center of reaction as the "cell of order." Serious frictions between Bavaria and the Reich ensued. In addition, the Bavarian Catholics were a professedly monarchist party, in favor of the restoration of the Wittelsbach to the throne of Bavaria. With progressing normalization after 1924, the Bavarian Catholic Party began to collaborate with the Center Party, and became again more or less an appendage of the Center. Under the threat of National Socialism, both sections sank their differences and presented a common front against the enemy of religion and tradition. But the Bavarian government was weaker than it boasted. No other country was subjected to such a relentless process of Nazification as Bavaria.

5. THE LIBERALS: THE GERMAN DEMOCRATIC PARTY

Post-War history all over Europe records the decay of liberal parties. Liberalism is least suited to the new technique of mass democracy. Germany is no exception to the rule. Moreover, German liberalism still suffered from the nineteenth-century failures under Bismarck and the Empire. As a continuation of the former Progressives, the Democratic Party attracted at first the driftwood of the dissatisfied bourgeoisie, stunned by the defeat of 1918. It was the party of the liberal professions and of most people of the Left who refused to endorse the Socialist ticket. Patriotic without nationalism, liberal in economics, the Democrats were the natural brokers between the Socialist laboring class and the bourgeoisie. But the history of the party is a record of decline; the middle classes soon found more congenial political quarters. In due course the party became a group of brilliant officers without an army. A large number of the best brains of the nation were members of the Democratic Party. The party participated, with a few accidental interruptions, in all governments from 1918 to 1931 (second Cabinet of Dr. Bruening); its members held the most important positions as experts (*Fachminister*). In later years it suffered most from the desertion of its members to "economic" parties. At the end of the period it was almost extinct.

6. CONSTITUTIONAL SOCIALISM: THE SOCIAL DEMOCRATIC PARTY

In explaining the position of the Socialist Democratic Party (*Sozialdemokraten;* after the split with the Independent Socialists also called "Majority Socialists"), one has to be on guard against the stultification of contemporary propaganda, which, in assailing "Marxism" in general, no longer cares to distinguish between Socialists and Communists. When the Imperial regime collapsed under the defeat, the Socialist leaders, moderate and well-balanced men, rendered a lasting service by leading the nation from the threatening revolutionary chaos into the legality of constitutional evolution. In doing so they had to steer clear of wild experiments in large-scale socialization or planning, since the bourgeoisie would not have tolerated them. They had to fight on two fronts, against reaction on the Right and radicalism of the Communists on the Left. Together with the Democrats and the Center, they shaped the Weimar Constitution; but in an assembly in which they were outnumbered two to one by the bourgeois partners they had to forego fulfillment of Socialist wishes; the Constitution became a liberal-bourgeois compromise with a few Socialist ingredients.

During the fourteen years of the Weimar Republic, the Socialists participated in the Government only for three and a half years. Socialist Reich Chancellors held office only twice (Scheidemann in 1918–19; Mueller, 1928 to 1930). After Dr. Bruening had formed his first cabinet (March 30, 1930) they no longer participated in the government. There is little in the National Socialist contention that the "Marxists" dominated the republic. On the other hand, the Socialists, together with the other parties of the Weimar coalition, shared power in a considerable number of the *Laender,* as in Prussia (cabinet of Braun from 1925 to 1933), Baden, Hessen, Hamburg, etc. The party paid lip service to official Marxism under the protective coloration of revisionism or evolutionary Socialism, but, on the whole, the structure and policies of the Socialists were deeply permeated with bourgeois spirit, similar to the British Labor Party. As public officials, particularly as Provincial Governors and as County Commissioners (*Landrat*) in Prussia, but also in the civil service, they became as efficient as the old bureaucracy. But their leaders, with very few exceptions bureaucrats, as decent as they were mediocre, were unable to realize that in revolutionary times efficiency in trade-union management is no passkey to statesmanship. Bureaucratic structure and, consequently, lack of courageous leadership are the main entries on the debit side of the Socialist ledger.

Tainted by the concept of "legality," they were unwilling to meet force with force; the Socialist *Reichsbanner,* a defense corps intended as a counter-measure against the militant private army of Hitler, was justly ridiculed by the National Socialists. Fratricidal conflict with the radical wing of Socialism also drained their strength. Every internal or external tension was reflected in an increase of Communist votes at the expense of the moderate and constitutional Socialists. Yet, in spite of all grave mistakes of the leaders and the defects of the party as a whole, the Socialists had established so firm a hold on the laboring classes that their voting strength and membership in the Reichstag rose steadily from the lowest point in 1924 to 1932. As late as in the elections of 1932 (July) they were overtaken by the National Socialists as the strongest party. But after the collapse of 1945 they rapidly regained their commanding position.

7. REVOLUTIONARY SOCIALISM: THE COMMUNISTS

Theoretically, revolutionary Socialism under the Republic was closely patterned on Russian Bolshevism and the idea of the dictatorship of the proletariat. The attitude of the party was consistently negative towards the Republic. In foreign politics more nationalistic than the Nationalists—therefore an easy prey to National Socialist conversion later—they gained strength by exploiting domestic misery caused by inflation and depression. But their tactics helped only the nationalist reaction to build them up as the bogey for the bourgeois classes. The "red menace" scare contributed more than a fair share to the success of National Socialism, which cashed in on the anti-Communist prepossessions of the propertied classes. The increase of the National Socialist votes in the hectic elections after 1930 corresponded to a similar rise of the Communist vote. Practically, however, in spite of election successes after 1930 commensurate to the soaring figures of unemployment under the world depression, the party never had the remotest chance of gaining control of Germany either by infiltration or force. It should be emphasized again that neither at the beginning of the Republic nor at its end did there exist a real danger of a Communist seizure of power. It is safe to state that unity in a Common Front of the two Socialist parties, which between themselves held consistently more than one-third of the total vote, would have prevented the collapse of the Republic and the advent of the Third Reich.

The normalcy of parliamentary life was rudely shattered and finally destroyed by the rise of the National Socialist "movement." Professedly anti-parliamentarian, which strangely enough became one of its strongest attractions for the masses of voters, the National Socialist Party, cleverly catering to the instincts of the bourgeoisie, never was considered "subversive" and was readily admitted to competition for political power through elections. It won the day by its novel and psychologically superior electioneering tactics. Once in power, Hitler smashed the Weimar Republic and with it the parliamentary system.[2]

---

[2] The discussion of the National Socialist Party will be reserved for later; see *infra,* pp. 443 *ff,* 467 *ff.*

CHAPTER VIII

THE PARLIAMENTARY SYSTEM UNDER
THE WEIMAR CONSTITUTION: II

THE REICH GOVERNMENT

THE REICH CHANCELLOR

The Bismarckian Constitution knew of no "cabinet" in the proper sense. The Reich Chancellor was the only recognized Minister who issued binding instructions to the departmental heads as his subordinates. For the monocratic organization of the Reich Government the Weimar Republic substituted the "collegiate" or "conciliar" structure of the Reich Government (*Kollegial-regierung*). "The Reich Government consists of the Reich Chancellor and the Reich Ministers" (Art. 52). Yet, in terms of the Constitution, the Reich Chancellor was more than *primus inter pares;* he was the Prime Minister or the President of the Council of Ministers, the real leader of his group of collaborators in the Cabinet.[1] The Reich Chancellor was to "determine the principal lines of politics for which he is responsible to the Reichstag" (Art. 56). As the leader of the Cabinet, he laid down, either generally or in specific cases, the governmental policies which the Ministers as departmental heads were to translate into practice within their individual departments. But the Bismarckian concept, later copied by Hitler, which made the Ministers the subordinates of their superior, the Reich Chancellor, was abandoned. Resolutions of the Reich Cabinet were carried by majority decisions in which each Minister had one vote.[2] The Reich Chancellor was free in the selection of the Ministers as

---

[1] Functions and conduct of business within the Reich cabinet were more specifically regulated in the "Standing Orders of the Reich Government" (*Gemeinsame Geschaeftsordnung der Reichsregierung*) of May 3, 1924 (*Reichsministerialblatt* 1924, p. 173), one of the most remarkable pieces of documentation for modern constitutional government. Equally important was the Reich Minister Act of March 30, 1930 (RGB., I, 96), which determined in a more precise legal way the position and functions of the Reich Ministers. The Act was in force under Hitler to 1937; its main provisions have been retained under the Third Reich.

[2] However, majority decisions could not overrule the Reich Chancellor when exercising his prerogative of laying down the principles of his policies, nor, in various specified instances, the veto of the Reich Minister of Finances.

his collaborators. The Reich President was bound to appoint the men who were named by his Chancellor. Actually, however, the process of constituting the Cabinet was as much an object for bargaining between the partners of the party coalition to be formed as the designation of the Reich Chancellor himself. On the whole, however, the number of *"ministrables"* was rather limited, and appointments actually made became more or less the obvious choice.[3]

THE MINISTERS

Individual Ministers acted, within the limits of the general program decided on by the Reich Chancellor, independently for their departments under their own and personal responsibility towards the Reichstag (Art. 56, sentence 2). By the natural weight of their functions, the Minister of Foreign Affairs and the Minister of Finances, as everywhere, held the key positions in the Cabinet; while the increasing influence of the Defense Minister was a German peculiarity. The number of ministries, varying according to needs, ran up, in the later years, to ten.[4] As a rule only members of the Reichstag served as Ministers, but it happened not infrequently that outsiders were called as "expert Ministers" (*Fachminister*).[5] The division of work was sound enough to be taken over almost without modification by Hitler.

APPOINTMENT OF REICH CHANCELLOR AND REICH MINISTERS

While the provisions of the Constitution dealing with the powers and organization of the Reich Government were elaborate and, on the whole, reasonable, the rather laconic statement (Art. 53): "The Reich Chancellor and, at his suggestion, the Reich Ministers are appointed and dismissed by the Reich President" holds the crucial misconstruction of the Weimar arrangement, because it is immediately followed by the equally succinct statement (Art. 54): "The Reich Chancellor and the Reich Ministers need for the conduct of office the confidence of the Reichstag. Any one of them must resign should the Reichstag, by explicit resolution, withdraw its confidence." Since exercise of the appointive power of the Reich President was to be more than a mechanical formality, the two requirements of simultaneous confidence of the Reich President and of the Reichstag could produce satisfactory results only if the Reich President and the majority of the Reichstag agreed between themselves and continued to agree on the persons entrusted with the Government. In case of disagreement, an insoluble deadlock occurred, which, when it ultimately happened in fact, destroyed the Constitution, Republic, and democracy.

The explanation lies in the peculiar dynamics of German party life. Multiplicity of parties, of which none could ever get a clear majority at the polls, re-

---

[3] This situation was completely reversed in 1932, when the head of the first anti-parliamentarian cabinet, von Papen, filled the posts of his so-called "Cabinet of Barons" with his henchmen of the Junker class.

[4] Interior, Foreign Affairs, Finances (Treasury), Economics, Justice, Defense, Communications, Postal Services, Agriculture and Nutrition, Labor. The Office of Vice-Chancellor, appearing before 1925, was never of importance. Ministers without portfolio occurred occasionally.

[5] Of the Reich Chancellors, only Cuno, called by Ebert in 1923, and later the heads of the "presidial" cabinets, von Papen and von Schleicher, were not members of the Reichstag.

sulted in the situation that governments could be formed only by an alliance
or coalition of several parties. No such fortunate automatism between the "ins"
and the "outs" existed as under the two-party system, which presents to the
appointing Chief Executive the leader of the victorious party as Prime Minister. Nor would it have helped if the Reich President had called the leader of
the strongest party, since the latter always would have needed the cooperation
of other parties in a coalition. Thus the Reich President had considerable freedom of choice, as in France, in the selection of the man for the Chancellorship.
His only restriction was the prerequisite of the Constitution that the Reich
Chancellor could not govern unless he received and retained the confidence
of the Reichstag.

ACTUAL PRACTICE ADOPTED FOR THE FORMATION OF THE REICH CABINET

How, in actual practice, were the two eventually irreconcilable prerequisites
of presidential and parliamentary confidence towards the Reich Chancellor
handled in the process of constituting the Reich Government? Clearly the practice depended on the initiative and prestige of the Reich President and his interpretation of his constitutional duties on the one hand, and the readiness of
the parties and their leaders to collaborate and to compromise, on the other
hand. In terms of the Constitution, the parties of the Reichstag had no title to
participation in selecting the Chancellor and the Ministers. Practically, however, the parties did so, because only coalition cabinets, to which they had to
grant, or from which they had to withhold, confidence, were feasible. No uniform procedure was followed during the lifetime of the Republic. At times the
coalition parties agreed between themselves on a suitable parliamentary leader
as Chancellor, extending such agreement even specifically to the persons of
the Ministers and the assignment of Cabinet posts. The Reich President merely
deferred to their suggestion. More often the Reich President took the initiative in finding a suitable man and, by negotiations, induced the partners of the
coming coalition to accept his candidate. The actual composition of the Government coalition depended largely on the choice of the future Reich Chancellor. But with increasing bitterness of party life, which made compromise
between the parties on the person of the Chancellor ever more difficult, it was
natural that the influence of the Reich President in the selection of the Chancellor outgrew that of the parties. In later years, when the basis for parliamentary cooperation was narrowed and minority cabinets became the rule, actual
influence shifted definitely from the Reichstag to the Reich President. Once
more Dr. Bruening, whose temperament leaned more to authoritarian than to
democratic government, was responsible for the change in the position of the
Reich President by deliberately creating the popular impression that the Reich
Chancellor is the subordinate of the Reich President and must rely more on the
latter's confidence than upon parliamentary support, which at any time could
be replaced by governing under the emergency decrees of Article 48. The
Reich President, misleadingly labeled the "custodian of the Constitution," re-

ciprocated the loyal services of his Chancellor by dismissing him brutally in May, 1932. In the process of perverting parliamentary government into dictatorial government, the "presidial" or "authoritarian" cabinet is the connecting link.

THE ILLEGAL PRACTICE OF "PRESIDIAL" CABINETS

From these premises grew the lethal constitutional crisis of the Republic, whose seeds were the overlapping and conflicting dualism of a simultaneous confidence of Reichstag and Reich President. Clearly the Reich President should not call into the Chancellorship a man who, he knew or could reasonably expect, in view of his previous contacts with the leading parties, did not and would not possess the confidence of the Reichstag. He might resort to the *ultima ratio* of calling a man to the Chancellorship who, by dissolving the Reichstag, could hope for a majority supporting him. But, once the elections had failed to procure for him the needed confidence of a majority of the Reichstag, to continue him in office was a flagrant violation of the Constitution. And this is just what happened in 1932, when Hindenburg, led by the irresponsible clique of reactionaries and Junkers, dismissed Dr. Bruening, although he was undefeated in the parliament, and appointed von Papen as the head of a "presidial" instead of a "parliamentary" Cabinet—styled by a misnomer "Cabinet of the National Concentration." By an unconstitutional trick, Republican Germany slid back to the practices of the Second Reich, under which Chancellor and Cabinet were the exclusive choice of the Kaiser, irrespective of the wishes of the parties in the Reichstag. Deliberately the Junkers had put back the clock. Von Papen, as Reich Chancellor, was granted permission to dissolve the Reichstag. In the elections of July 31, 1932, the "Cabinet of the Barons" was flatly rejected by all parties, with the exception of a handful of Nationalists. Yet the Reich President, now openly violating his oath, retained him in power and even granted him a second dissolution, which again, in the elections of November 6, 1932, led to an almost unanimous rejection by the electorate and all parties. Only then did von Papen resign; and von Schleicher, again as head of a nonparliamentary, "presidial" Cabinet, succeeded him. The continued practice of "presidial" or "authoritarian" Cabinets, inaugurated under the prestige of the "Wooden Titan" who in fact was only the tool of the antidemocratic reaction, and supplemented by the self-abdication of the Reichstag since 1930, was prelude and precedent to the dictatorial Government of the National Socialists.

THE CABINET AND THE PARTIES

While the preceding discussion dealt mainly with the relations between the Reich Government and the President, it is necessary to explain the equally important position of the Reich Cabinet towards the Reichstag if for no other reason than to make some of the arrangements of the Bonn constitution intelligible.[6] The Constitution itself was emphatic only in stating in unequivocal

---

[6] See *infra*, pp. 567 *ff.*

terms that the Reich Chancellor and the Reich Ministers need individually and collectively the confidence of the Reichstag for the conduct of the Government (Art. 54). A Cabinet had to resign only when struck by a formal and explicit vote of nonconfidence carried by a majority of the Reichstag.[7] If, however, the majority of the Reichstag refused to carry a vote of confidence, initiated by the Government supporters, the Cabinet, as a rule, remained in office because the Constitution required resignation only in case of an outright vote of non-confidence. The subtle distinction between a carried vote of nonconfidence and a rejected vote of confidence helped to circumvent the rules of parliamentarism and to stabilize a Government once in office. At any rate, the practice was deemed justifiable because the cabinets were anyway only coalition governments precariously balanced for a time, or even only minority cabinets, that is, cabinets in which parties commanding only a minority of votes in the Reichstag had formed the Government coalition. This practice led in due course to an even more disingenuous perversion of the parliamentary system in that minority cabinets, very frequent during the whole period, were "tolerated" by parties which felt disinclined to cooperate openly with the Government while they were equally disinclined to join the opposition and bring about the downfall of the Government.[8] However, the device of the nonconfidence vote played no important role in overthrowing cabinets. Cabinets fell because of internal dissensions among the coalition parties and ensuing disintegration, not because of frontal attacks by the opposition. In turn, the opposition itself was as hybrid an institution as the Government coalition. It was composed of the most divergent interests, united only in the hatred of the Government in power. Hence the opposition was not prepared to assume responsibility in case of withdrawal of the Government. Communists and National Socialists, forever unflinchingly in opposition to the governments in power, hated each other even more than the bourgeois cabinets they fought in common and, as a matter of principle, would at no time have participated in a coalition. Their tactics were purely negative, aiming at discrediting and wrecking the parliamentary system as such.

From 1919 to 1933 all Republican governments were coalition cabinets. No party ever obtained a majority of votes and seats. Moreover, periods in which cabinets supported by a majority of the Reichstag were in control were interspersed with rather extended periods in which only minority cabinets could be formed. As to party combinations, three majority coalitions were alternately in power: (a) the "Weimar coalition" of the Socialists, Center, and Democrats (two years and ten months); this combination ended as early as 1922, never to return; (b) the so-called "Great Coalition," an enlargement of the Weimar group to the Right by including the Conservative Liberals (German People's Party), altogether in office for two years; (c) a coalition including the Middle parties and the Right (Nationalists), excluding the Socialists,

---

[7] This happened only three times.
[8] The second Cabinet of Dr. Bruening, lasting from October 1931 to May 1932, was "tolerated" by the largest party, the Socialists, in spite of its professedly anti-Socialist policy.

altogether in control for four years and eight months. These figures demonstrate that politically the Weimar Republic, after a left-of-center start, shifted rapidly to the Right. Minority cabinets rested mostly on the narrow basis of Center, Democrats, and German People's Party, at times supplemented by "nonpolitical expert" Ministers. The "presidial" cabinets of von Papen and von Schleicher in 1932–33 were backed only by the decimated ranks of the Nationalists. Seen as a whole, however, the record of the Weimar Republic, in terms of parliamentary support for the Cabinet in power, was not so bad as the later critics depicted it.

As to duration and longevity of cabinets, the Republic compares none too unfavorably with similar French experience in multiple party government. During the whole period of fourteen years, there were twenty cabinets under eleven Chancellors. A large number of Ministers continued in different cabinets, thus demonstrating a remarkable stability of the cabinet personnel; the *ministrables* consisted mostly of "seasoned" parliamentarians. With very few exceptions, the Ministers as well as the Chancellors were honest and competent men. It was much less "government by amateurs" than later on was complained of. The actual record of the Weimar governments, down to 1932, is much better than their reputation.

PARLIAMENTARISM AND LEADERSHIP

Whatever technical perfection a political system may boast—and the Weimar Constitution had manifest shortcomings—it cannot produce the elixir of good government, namely leadership. If leadership means a vision and the courage to realize the vision in the face of obstacles, the Weimar Republic, with the notable exception of Dr. Stresemann, had not a single leader. Stresemann understood that a defeated nation has no choice between submission and defiance. "Policy of fulfillment" bore its fruits already in Locarno and Thoiry; there was a "silver lining on the horizon." The years which saw him at the wheel (August 1923 to October 1929) were the best of the Republic. The democratic idea began to sink into the nation. Had Stresemann lived or found a successor of his caliber, the Republic would probably have been saved. But his successor was the mediocre Dr. Bruening. The Republic slanted to the Right and into its doom. German political tradition, crippled under a hereditary and irresponsible monarchy, could not adapt itself to the creation of leadership. Moreover, party disunity prevented the rise of a corporate consciousness of the parliament. Neither the Reichstag nor the parties themselves were capable of developing a properly selective process for leadership. Imponderables are beyond the control of a constitution. Hence the German people, or at least a strong minority among them, were swayed off their feet when The Leader appeared who had both a vision and the will power to make it real. The victory of National Socialism should be appraised on the background of the failures of the Weimar Republic.

CHAPTER IX

CONSTITUTIONAL AMENDMENT

THE PROCEDURE OF CONSTITUTIONAL AMENDMENT

Under the Bismarckian Constitution the process of constitutional amendment was more or less identical with that of regular legislation;[1] in practice constitutional amendments were passed like ordinary statutes. The Weimar Constitution likewise refrained from prescribing a special procedure by which the constituent power was divorced from the regular legislative agencies as was the case under the French Third Republic and as is arranged in the United States through a combination of Congress and the legislatures of the individual states. In continuation of the Imperial tradition constitutional amendments under the Weimar Constitution were to be carried out as a rule by way of ordinary legislation and through the regular legislative agencies, that is, the Reichstag and the Federal Council. The only difference from the ordinary legislative process was that a constitutional amendment required, for its acceptance, qualified majorities in both Reichstag and Federal Council (Art. 76, sentences 1–3). In the Reichstag two-thirds of the total membership had to be present, that is, they had to participate in the vote, and of those present at least two-thirds had to vote in favor of the amendment. Thus actually four-ninths of the total membership were sufficient. In the Federal Council the general right to raise "objections" (*"Einspruch"*) against a resolution of the Reichstag (Art. 74) was stiffened in that two-thirds of the members of the Federal Council had to cast a direct vote in favor of the constitutional amendment proposition.

In exceptional cases a constitutional amendment could be initiated also by the people, that is by one-tenth of the electorate; in this case the proposal, unless accepted in its proposed form by the Reichstag, was to be submitted to a referendum of the voters in which the majority of the registered voters had to participate and the majority of the voters participating had to agree with the proposal (Articles 73, par. 3 and 76, sentence 4).

[1] See *supra*, p. 392.

In practice, thus, a qualified minority of one-third of the members of both the Reichstag and the Federal Council could block the passage of any constitutional amendment. This was an ample protection against hasty and ill-considered changes of the fundamental charter by chance majorities in the legislative assemblies, while, on the other hand, a constitutional amendment originating from and sponsored by the people proved practically impossible. Though rather complicated and somewhat cumbrous, the process of constitutional amendment seemed, on the whole, neither too rigid nor too easy. Under normal conditions these arrangements might have proved satisfactory.

THE PRACTICE OF CONSTITUTIONAL AMENDMENT WITHOUT CHANGING THE TEXT OF THE CONSTITUTION

Another aspect of the Weimar Constitution deserves particular attention because here the German version of democratic government bears no resemblance to any other democratic country. Under all democratic constitutions a constitutional amendment implies what it signifies, namely an ostensible and outward alteration of the text of the document proper; a new clause or article, or only a new phrase or new words are inserted into the text, or, as the case may be, are deleted therefrom. Such "explicit" alterations of the constitutional text occurred in Republican Germany not infrequently between 1919 and 1930. On the whole, they involved only such minor corrections in the original text as had become necessary; and none of them changed the fundamental arrangement of the functional structure.

For the bulk of constitutional changes, however, a less precise, a more surreptitious and therefore disingenuous, method was resorted to, a technique inherited from the practice of the Imperial Constitution which lacked a specific amendment procedure. When a clause of the Constitution stood in the way of a legislative proposal intended for a particular legal or political purpose, the Reichstag and the Federal Council, in collaboration with the Reich Government, passed, by way of the constitutional amendment procedure with the required majorities, an appropriate statute which materially deviated from the text of the constitutional charter, though without changing correspondingly also the text of the Constitution itself. This process was called a "statute amending the Constitution" (*Verfassungsaenderndes Reichsgesetz*), its only requirement being the endorsement by the increased majorities. Though strongly objected to by not a few of the responsible constitutional lawyers, this procedure of indirect or "silent" constitutional amendment was applied so frequently that it became almost a routine method incidental to legislation,[2] so much so that in the long run the guileless reader of the constitutional document was unable to realize how much or how little of the original text was still valid without reservation. Judicial review, though belatedly recognized as belonging to the courts of right, was never invoked in practice except within the special jurisdiction of the Constitutional Tribunal. On the other hand, any

---

[2] The exact number of such cases is not known, but the estimate of some sixty instances is conservative.

statute, by using the amendment procedure, could immunize itself from the subsequent blame of unconstitutionality.

Thus the public grew weary of the recurrent controversies as to whether or not a statute had to pass through the process of constitutional amendment, as well as of the political haggling of the parties about it. Even more pernicious was that the people could not fail to notice how parliamentary parties and Government played havoc with the sacrosanctity of the fundamental charter. The practice of circumventing the Constitution by a rather facile procedure which deliberately avoided changes of the constitutional text, dulled the "constitutional consciousness" of the German people since the Constitution was what parliamentary chance majorities thought it was. This attitude contributed, in the last analysis, more than its fair share to the acquiescence of the masses in the usurpation of the constituent powers by the "Fuehrer" after the seizure of powers by National Socialism in 1933.

THE DEADLOCK OF CONSTITUTIONAL AMENDMENT IN PARLIAMENT

It must be obvious that when the elections of 1930 had increased the extremist parties to one-third and more of the total membership of the Parliament, the passage of a constitutional amendment became outright impossible. This fact goes to the very root of political dynamics in Republican Germany. During the latter years of Weimar the responsible sections of the people were almost unanimous in the realization that the framework of 1919 needed improvement in order to adjust it to the political exigencies of crisis government. But any constitutional reform was frustrated by the requirement in the Reichstag of qualified majorities which, by. virtue of the obstructionist tactics of the extremist parties, were unobtainable. In particular, legislation intended to curb the excesses of the radical propaganda of the Right and of the Left could not be carried out because it involved a curtailment of the Bill of Rights. The radical parties against which such measures were directed, naturally refused to lend their support. Under these circumstances the constitutional set-up planned for normal times became obsolete and wholly inadequate. Article 76, constructed primarily and not without skill for the avoidance of deadlocks, was turned into the very gadget for deadlocking the entire constitutional machinery. It was by no means surprising that National Socialism, here as elsewhere benefiting from the errors of exaggerated legalism of the Weimar Constitution, transferred, by one bold stroke, full constituent powers to the "Fuehrer" and his cabinet, thus completely leveling down the distinction between constitutional amendment and ordinary legislation. In another significant point the situation as it existed under the Bismarckian Constitution was restored by the Third Reich.

CHAPTER X

THE BILL OF RIGHTS

GENERAL CHARACTER OF THE BILL OF RIGHTS

As most of the democratic constitutions of the liberal-bourgeois era the Weimar Constitution, next to the frame of government in Part I, contained an elaborate Bill of Rights, styled "Fundamental rights and fundamental duties of the Germans" in Part II (Articles 108–165). The Bill of Rights was to draw a clear line of demarcation between State power and the sphere of the individual. The courts and constitutional jurisprudence were rather tardy in vitalizing its juridical content. It was only after the Weimar Republic had passed its zenith that the importance of fundamental rights of the citizen and their protection by independent courts began to penetrate into the public consciousness. As it happens with liberty in general, the value of inviolate rights of the subject was more cherished when they were in abeyance than at the time when their enjoyment was not yet in jeopardy.

The inclusion of a formal statement on fundamental rights in the Weimar charter was certainly not alien to German civic heritage since both the Constitution of the *Paulskirche* of 1848 and even the Prussian Constitution of 1850 offered indigenous patterns. Moreover, a system of subjective rights of the citizens, protected from unlawful infringement by the administration, had been fully recognized and applied under the Imperial Constitution.

The incorporation of the Bill of Rights in the Weimar Constitution, as it happened to be the case also with other matters of importance, was the result of a compromise between the conflicting political concepts of liberalism, collectivism, and clerical tradition, arrived at only after heated discussion. In its final form the second part of the Constitution was a hybrid assortment of genuine rules of law which were applicable at once and without further implementation by specific statutes, of declaratory statements of policy to be made applicable only by subsequent executory legislation—which, in many cases, failed to materialize—and of principles and postulates of merely programmatic character. This maze of divergent provisions resembled in part a catechism of humanitarian ethics, in part a law book or code on civil liberties.

Yet, in spite of its casuistic and uneven character, the Bill of Rights could have offered to German democracy, had it been self-confident and adequately supported by public opinion, an ample protection of the customary civil liberties. Just because it was characterized by a distinct hue of progressive social justice in which exercise of individual rights was restricted by their possible interference with the welfare of others and of the whole community, it was wholly in keeping with the best of German idealistic tradition. As a document permeated by social though not Socialistic intentions it reflected admirably the post-War pragmatism of a typically liberal bourgeois society based on private property, sanctity of contractual relations, and the optimistic belief in the co-operative qualities of human nature. In its failure, however, to implement social rights by social duties to which only scanty attention was paid, it was strangely out-of-date from the start and it represented, in the last analysis, the mythology of a dying age. Seen retrospectively it is evident that the framers were unaware of the impending revolt of the masses and of the rise of the demagogue for whom fundamental rights were only the instrument for their ultimate destruction.

ACTUAL CONTENT OF THE BILL OF RIGHTS

The motley of rights and duties, programmatic postulates and ethical exhortations, broad institutional guarantees and detailed regulations for specific purposes, was loosely grouped together in five subdivisions. The First Section, devoted to "The Individual," enumerated as individual rights the following: Equality of all Germans before the law (Art. 109), involving, by specific reference, abrogation of privileges of birth or rank; freedom of movement and free choice of domicile within the Reich (Art. 111); freedom of emigration (Art. 112); freedom of the person, in particular freedom from arbitrary arrest (*habeas corpus*) (Art. 114); inviolability of the private home (Art. 115); prohibition of retroactive criminal legislation (Art. 116); privacy of mail and communication (Art. 117); finally, freedom of personal expression and of public opinion "within the general laws"; no censorship was permissible (Art. 118).

The Second Section of the Bill of Rights, inscribed "The Life of the Community," protected family life (marriage, the position of parents in education, children born out of wedlock and youth in general [Articles 119–122]); the right of peaceful assembly (Art. 123) and the unrestricted formation of associations which, if desired, could be incorporated under civil law (Art. 124); freedom to vote and secrecy of the voting procedure (Art. 125); equal access of all qualified persons to public office (Art. 128). This section is concluded with elaborate provisions as to position, function, and exercise of public office, the officials being considered as servants of the community (Articles 129–131). Here civil rights were supplemented by civic duties such as the obligation to serve State and municipality in office and to share in the burdens of the State in accordance with property and income (Articles 132–134).

The Third Section dealt with religious life. Freedom of conscience and religious worship were guaranteed (Articles 135, 136). Churches and State were separated (Art. 137) while State support for religious services was provided for if such assistance was customary (Articles 138–141).

In the Fourth Section (Articles 142–150) art, science, and education were placed under the benevolent protection of the State, which, on the other hand, obligated itself to refrain from any compulsion or from any exercise of its tutelage inconsistent with the tenets of genuine liberalism. In this part, more articulate than in others, the compromise with the Catholic Church was visibly in appearance.

Finally, in its Fifth and last part on "Economic Life" (Articles 151–165) the Bill of Rights tried to square the circle between the liberal concept of private property and private initiative on the one hand, and the more Socialistic or collectivist ideas of utilizing private wealth and national resources for the purposes of the common good, on the other hand. While private property was solemnly recognized (Art. 153) it was at the same time subjected to restrictions by the State deemed necessary for the common welfare; range and limits of such restrictions were not specified. Dispossession of property under eminent domain was permissible though, as a rule, only against adequate compensation. Yet one cannot fail to admit that private property, the mainstay of liberal economics, was less well protected in theory and practice of the Weimar order than one might have assumed within the framework of liberal institutions, and that here the liberal Constitution unconsciously preluded to the later subjugation of private capitalism by the National Socialists, particularly since the provisions surrounding the sanctity of private property were, among those which were suspendable under the emergency conditions of Article 48.

THE REICH ECONOMIC COUNCIL

This last section on economic life referred also, by way of a programmatic promise, to the eventuality of "nationalization" (in Germany called *"Sozialisierung"*) of "suitable private economic enterprises" (Art. 156). In close relation with this ultimate purpose an elaborate system of occupational or economic representation, based on equal participation of management and labor, was envisaged (Art. 165). Of this comprehensive scheme of industrial democracy only two disjointed sections were established by the subsequent legislation of the Republic, namely, at the basis of the economic pyramid, the shop councils of workers and employees in each sizable enterprise (*"Betriebsraete"*), and the Reich Economic Council (*"Reichswirtschaftsrat"*) as its apex. Too sanguine hopes were disappointed. All that the Reich Economic Council achieved—and in fact under given circumstances was able to achieve—was to become a consultative body for the preparation of economic legislation. In view of its limited powers its influence was meager and as an institution it failed completely to integrate itself into the political life of the nation.

LIMITATIONS INHERENT IN THE BILL OF RIGHTS

That the Bill of Rights did not succeed in asserting its claim as a body of inviolate and intangible rights of the people was due, among other causes intimately related to the general submissiveness of the German character, to a particular situation which the Weimar Republic again inherited. In order to be genuinely "fundamental" civil liberties must be guaranteed absolutely, safe not only from arbitrary inroads by the administrative agencies but also from curtailment by parliamentary legislation. In this respect many of the fundamental rights were by no means immune, owing to the specific feature of the German tradition in the technique of drafting. The American citizens' civil liberties are protected unconditionally from Government and administration no less than from the legislatures both Federal and of the states. Contrariwise, the German citizens' rights were secured only conditionally. To most of the fundamental rights the proviso was explicitly added that their exercise was guaranteed only within the limits of the existing or of future statutes. Thus by the Constitution itself the Reichstag was empowered to determine, by way of ordinary legislation, range and limits, content and exercise of civil liberties. This reservation in favor of the legislator reveals, as do other "liberal" constitutions in Europe, the traditional relationship between liberty and authority under which liberty is subjected to the tutelage of authority. State necessity was allowed to override the solemn guarantees of individual rights.

Moreover, the absence of judicial review in Republican Germany tended to militate against the actual enforcement of individual guarantees. By the same token, the misuse of the constitutional amendment procedure for opportunistic or temporary deviations from the fundamental charter was responsible for the continuous process of "hollowing out" [allegedly "inviolate"] rights of the citizen. Most of the "statutes involving a constitutional amendment" were passed by the Reichstag for allowing exceptions from the individual guarantees. Last but not least the authorization granted by the Constitution (Art. 48) to the Reich President to suspend temporarily the seven most important of the fundamental rights in times of emergency, placed the fundamental rights at the mercy of the Government. The *habitat* of the "police state" was stronger than the new gospel of self-determination of the citizens under democratic institutions. During the last two years of the Republic the Bill of Rights had factually ceased to exist by virtue of the constitutional charter itself. Individually and severally the factors mentioned had contributed to such an erosion of civil liberties that in the long run public opinion resigned itself to the fact that their validity was at best conditional and thus precarious. When the National Socialists, in 1933, rudely pushed aside the Bill of Rights, together with the constitutional charter itself, for the people the break with the past was less violent than it might be assumed by one who reads only the letter of the "most democratic constitution of the world" without being aware of how it was operated in reality by allegedly Republican governments.

CHAPTER XI

THE BALANCE SHEET OF THE WEIMAR REPUBLIC

In the official doctrine of National Socialism, the Weimar Republic was scornfully referred to as the "fourteen years of humiliation," or the "interregnum," or simply the "system," signifying political ineptitude, degradation, and corruption. Yet the period between the fall of the Second and the rise of the Third Reich includes, together with obvious frustrations and deplorable shortcomings, a number of achievements.

ACHIEVEMENTS OF THE WEIMAR REPUBLIC

The Treaty of Versailles certainly was a harsh peace, garnished with many senseless humiliations which operated as constant irritants; but it was not a Punic peace, such as Imperial militarism, gone stark mad, tried to impose on Russia and Rumania in Brest-Litovsk and Bucharest (1917–18), not to mention the brutal looting and enslaving of the conquered countries by the master race under the Swastika. The Weimar Republic succeeded in "whittling away" many of the most oppressive clauses of the treaty by the "policy of fulfillment" (*Erfuellungspolitik*). Tangible results of the Locarno Treaty were Germany's unreserved admission to the European community and the League of Nations, the evacuation of the Rhineland five years before the appointed day, and a settlement of the tormenting problem of the reparations in the Dawes (1924) and Young (1926) plans, no longer flagrantly inconsistent with the postulates of economic reason. *Gleichberechtigung* (political equality) was finally obtained and Germany became again, less than a decade after the defeat, a first-rate power in Europe.

Much has been attributed to the continued foreign pressure on the Republic, and with a good deal of truth at that. Continued vexations of the victors in the first years after Versailles harassed the governments willing to fulfill, because they knew that resistance would mean dismemberment of the Reich. But foreign pressure relaxed after 1924, and it was the policy of indirect treaty violations, by Republican governments, such as the toleration of the "Black Reichs-

wehr"[1] and the disingenuous move of Dr. Bruening for "cold *Anschluss*" of
Austria by way of a customs union, which aroused the suspicion even of benevolent foreign governments.

The reparation settlement was instrumental to an influx of foreign loans
which helped, on the one hand, to pay the reparations until a final arrangement had been reached. On the other hand, the foreign loans were used by
Germany for rebuilding and overhauling her industrial plant, which, when
Hitler seized power, was second to none in the world. Thus Hitler's success in
building up Germany's industrial and economic structure for military aggression was due to the efforts of the Republic. Germany had even overcome the
greatest catastrophe which could befall a nation of thrifty and parsimonious
small savers, namely, the inflation of 1922–23. Without the world depression
after 1929, signaled by the crash of the New York stock market and widespread bank failures in Austria and Germany, German financial and economic
structure was as sound as could be expected. Unemployment, it is true, did not
disappear and could not disappear, since it was structural, as an outgrowth of
the unmitigated *laissez faire* system of private capitalism, ineradicable also in
economically better balanced countries with a similar socio-economic structure.

Improved economic and social conditions were mirrored in the high level
of cultural achievements. Although the cultural life of Weimar was denounced
by National Socialism as "degenerate," "effete," and "depraved," its contributions to human enrichment were most respectable. Cultural competition of
State and municipalities of the *Laender* tried not without success to compensate for the loss of dynastic splendor. Cultivation of the arts, assailed by National Socialism as "cultural bolshevism," was progressive, bold in experimentation though occasionally licentious. Democratization of cultural life had
begun in earnest. Finally, the Constitution proper, grave as its structural shortcomings undoubtedly were, accustomed the German people to the security of
due process of law which controlled impartially private as well as public relations. Most important of all, the Weimar Constitution preserved German unity,
acquired at great cost by the preceding generations. Had Weimar not saved
the Reich, the result would have been Balkanization and perhaps the Bolshevization of the heart of Europe.

CAUSES OF THE FAILURE OF THE WEIMAR REPUBLIC

As to the debit side of the Weimar ledger, competent observers agree that
the Republic committed suicide. It has been asserted that a nation accustomed
to monarchy was unsuited to democratic self-government. Yet at no time,
with the possible exception of the last months of Republican agony, had restoration the slightest chance, although the President of the Reich, Hinden-

---

[1] During the whole period of the Republic almost every government connived at the secret
training, by the army, or *Reichswehr*, of forces exceeding the limit set by the Treaty of Versailles,
whereby "cadres" of trained men were maintained even at the time when Republican Germany
was allegedly disarmed completely. Journalists exposing these flagrant violations of the treaty
were sentenced, by reactionary and nationalistic courts, to long terms of prison for treason.
Among them was the Nobel prize-winner Ossietzky.

burg, was a professed monarchist. However, though it may be an overstatement to describe Weimar as a Republic without Republicans, Germany after 1918 progressively became a democracy without democrats. In the elections of 1932, which heralded the impending disintegration, no less than three-fourths of the German people voted for antidemocratic parties of the Right or the Left. But this abnormal turn of the German mind could happen only because the Republic did not have resolute democratic leaders; the very name of democracy was rarely invoked officially. On the other hand, grave errors were committed in allowing the nationalist reaction and the Hitler movement to monopolize patriotism. Moreover, the internecine struggle between Socialists and Communists, both opposed to reaction, jeopardized from the outset the chances of the Republic. The Socialist Party organization had become so tainted by bourgeois mentality that its revolutionary élan was spent before the final test came. Gravely did both Socialist and bourgeois governments sin in allowing the public services to carry on without subjecting the reactionary officials and judges to a purge. Outright sabotage occurred among the judges of the criminal courts who with impunity weighed with different measures the political activities of the Right and of the Left. Finally, the army was permitted to remain a state within the State, and even Left-oriented governments were powerless to bring the army under effective parliamentary control. In spite of the elaborate precautions of the Constitution to forestall resurrection of a super-government of the army, the militaristic machine remained in fact unaffected by political change. Nothing could please the army leaders more than the "stabbing-in-the-back" legend invented by the nationalist propaganda, making the Socialists and pacifists alike a convenient scapegoat for the failures of the General Staff. Had Marshal Foch dictated the peace in Berlin, thus driving home the defeat of the army in the field, perhaps the Germans would have learned their lesson for once. While the army command, backed by the prestige of Hindenburg, brooked no interference from "civilian" governments, it had its hand in almost all matters of purely civilian nature. But perhaps the greatest sin of omission, most directly responsible for the downfall of the Republic, was the inability of Republican governments to understand what political power means and how to use it. Socialists and Liberals alike were entangled in the false concept of legality as an equal opportunity for all political forces to gain access to political power. Naively, the idealists among them believed in the intrinsic value of democracy and its ultimate superiority over authoritarian or dictatorial doctrines, without taking measures for protecting democracy from the *saboteurs*. All German governments, whatever their party tinge, failed to understand the new technique, practiced in a masterly way by Hitler, of the Trojan horse of democratic legality, of utilizing the equalitarian institutions of the Constitution for undermining and destroying the very institutions they were allowed to exploit. German democracy was utterly fair, constitutional, legalistic, but not militant. The same energetic and resolute use of legislative and administrative curbs against political extremism of the Right as they were relentlessly applied against the Left would have nipped the revolu-

tionary movement of the National Socialists in the bud. Abnormal times called
for abnormal means of defense and protection, as was the case in other equally
threatened democracies after 1933. But the bourgeois leaders themselves, fascinated by the "patriotic" ingredients of the National Socialist program, had
lost confidence in the democracy and thus, wittingly or unwittingly, became
instruments for the suicide of the Republic.

CHAPTER XII

NATIONAL SOCIALISM AND THE ESTABLISHMENT OF THE THIRD REICH

HITLER AND THE NATIONAL SOCIALIST PARTY

Forever philosophers of history have argued whether the success of a political leader is attributable to favorable circumstances, or whether his action produces favorable circumstances conditional for his success. In the case of Adolf Hitler and the Third Reich, the answer is: Hitler created the National Socialist movement as an instrument of political power, and through this instrument he created the Third Reich. He made circumstances serve his ends. It was Hitler who as a master molded the sentimental traditions and emotional obsessions of the German bourgeoisie into the most refined and technically perfect system of political power. The National Socialist Party and the Third Reich would never have arisen without Hitler.

The spectacular rise of the *Nationalsozialistische Deutsche Arbeiterpartei* (NSDAP), at first one among the myriad of small political debating conventicles after 1918, was due primarily to entirely novel methods of propaganda and organization. The party—styled a "movement" in order to advertise its fundamental difference from other merely political parties—soon attracted attention far beyond its numerical strength. After the premature and abortive Beerhall putsch of November 9, 1923, Hitler realized that political power could be won only by ballots and through "legal" methods. Henceforward his tactics were concentrated on building up a regular political party which, at the same time, should become the core of a political religion. Yet without the disaster of the world depression, which broke loose in Germany in 1930, he would never have succeeded. In March, 1930, Dr. Bruening took over the Chancellorship. Less than six months later, by a landslide unprecedented in German

---

[1] Limitations of space as well as the shift in interest are the reasons for submitting, in this part, merely a summary review of government and politics of the Third Reich. Readers interested in a detailed analysis of its socio-political structure are referred to the previous editions (pp. 405–558) and to Karl Loewenstein, *Hitler's Germany*, New York, 1939 (fourth edition, 1944).

parliamentary history, the NSDAP rose from 12 to 107 deputies in the Reichstag, from a small faction to the second strongest party.[2]

In its early career, the NSDAP was the political refuge for demobilized professional soldiers unable to adjust themselves to civilian life; for political adventurers, social misfits, and cranks—a strange motley of hooligans, criminals, and idealists, who formed the cadres into which, later on, the masses of voters were to flow. In the landslide of 1930 most of the new recruits endorsing the Swastika came from the lower middle classes, whose economic backbone had been broken by the inflation of 1923 and the deflation thereafter—"respectable" people such as shopkeepers, artisans, clerks and, of course, the unemployed. This stratum was enticed by the Socialist as well as by the anti-Socialist ingredients of Hitler's program. From the outset the party drew its strength from youth. But it was by a stroke of genius that Hitler succeeded, in the following years, in enlisting as well the moral and financial support of influential figures in industry and big business, who were attracted by the hostility of National Socialism towards organized labor and the trade unions. The army, secretly sneering at the uncouth upstart, maintained a benevolent neutrality towards a super-patriotic movement promising freedom from "the shackles of Versailles" and the restoration of military ascendancy.

CAUSES FOR THE TRIUMPH OF THE NATIONAL SOCIALIST PARTY

Hitler's magnetic personality cast its spell on a nation in which "educated" men had heretofore monopolized political leadership of the bourgeois classes. Many were influenced by his oratorical talents. However, the strongest inducement emanated from an entirely novel and unprecedented political technique. It inaugurated the emotional mechanism of mammoth mass meetings and public demonstrations staged with consummate skill, showmanship, and a deep insight into the psychic *lacunae* of the democratic form of government, based on persuasion instead of emotion. His political offerings catered to every taste. Moreover, the party was organized on military lines, carrying violence into the streets and the assemblies of the other parties, fortifying the spirit of its own adherents as well as intimidating its opponents. The brown uniforms of the SA (*Sturmabteilung,* or Assault Guard) and the black military garb of the SS (*Schutzstaffel,* or Elite Guard), tolerated by the Republic in suicidal negligence,[3] became ubiquitous. The NSDAP organized and propagandized with-

[2] The following tabulation shows the increase of votes and seats from 1924 to 1933:

Election	Seats	Votes
May 4, 1924	7 *	(unknown)
December 7, 1924	14	907,000
May 5, 1928	12	810,000
September 14, 1930	107	6,409,000
July 31, 1932	230	13,779,000
November 6, 1932	196	11,737,000
March 5, 1933	288	17,277,000

* On the ticket of the combined "folkish parties," which obtained 32 seats.

[3] Only in 1932 was an anti-uniform ordinance issued by the Cabinet of Dr. Bruening, at the instance of the Minister of the Interior, General Groener; it was rescinded after a few weeks, and Groener lost his position.

out interruption, carrying its meetings and demonstrations into the smallest village and hamlet. Suddenly, in place of the rather idyllic party life of the past, a new militancy and fury swept over the nation, which, unprepared as it was, failed to mobilize resistance to this unprecedented onslaught. The printed as much as the spoken word was used as never before. A novel technique of tabloid emotionalism was invented. Oversimplification, distortion, and outright lies were not answerable by reasoned refutation. In the remarkable passages of his *Mein Kampf* dealing with the elements of political propaganda, Hitler gave all the recipes on which his sensational success was ultimately based. Wrote Hitler: "The German has not the faintest idea of how a nation must be swindled if one wants to have masses of supporters." The most popular weapons in the armory of emotionalism were attacks against Versailles, the "war-guilt lie," the "policy of fulfillment," and, most effective of all, rampant anti-Semitism, for which Germany was ever the most fertile field, focusing resentment on a scapegoat responsible for all evils of state, society, and the individual.

THE BID FOR POWER (1930–1933)

Hitler made various unsuccessful attempts to obtain control of the government by normal political means. In the election for the Reich Presidency (March 13–April 10, 1932) he failed to win, by a wide margin, against Hindenburg.[4] In the elections of July 31, 1932, the National Socialists became the strongest party of the Reichstag (230 out of 608 seats) and raised the claim, justified in parliamentary usage, to the Chancellorship and the formation of the Cabinet. Here began the long series of backstage intrigues, double-crossings, and cheatings which accompanied the last months of the Republic in agony. At long last, on January 30, 1933, under delirious outbreaks of the Nazified masses, the Reich President appointed Hitler to the Chancellorship at the head of a cabinet of "National Concentration," in which the National Socialists and the Nationalists were to share power. The Third Reich had begun.

THE CABINET OF NATIONAL CONCENTRATION

The Cabinet of "National Concentration" under Hitler as Reich Chancellor was appointed and constituted in conformity with the Constitution and the German variety of the parliamentary system. Of its eleven members, only three were National Socialists: namely, Hitler, as Reich Chancellor; Dr. Frick, as Minister of the Interior; and, last but not least, Captain Hermann Goering, as Minister without portfolio and as the man in control of the Prussian police. But these key positions assured them the totality of power from the start.

Once more in keeping with German parliamentarism, the Reich President

[4] First ballot:	Hindenburg	18,651,000 votes	49.6%
	Hitler	11,339,000 "	30.1
Second ballot:	Hindenburg	19,360,000 "	53.0
	Hitler	13,418,000 "	36.8

granted to this Cabinet without a majority in the Reichstag a dissolution in order to let the electorate decide on its tenure of office. The election campaign of 1933 was a startling and breath-taking affair, which nobody who lived through it will easily forget. From the outset, the opposition was arbitrarily curbed in the use of press, assembly, and radio, while organized violence of the National Socialist hooligans against the opposition was encouraged.

On the morning of February 27, 1933, the stunned nation was told that on the preceding evening the Communists and Socialists had fired the Reichstag building and that the vigilance of Goering and his Prussian police had un-covered a widespread Marxist conspiracy. On February 28, 1933, Hindenburg set his signature on an emergency ordinance "for the protection of people and state," [5] which, under Article 48, suspended the seven fundamental liberties: freedom of person, of speech, of press, of assembly, of association, and of privacy of mails; and authorized confiscation of property without compensa-tion and for undetermined purposes. This decree, the Magna Carta of the con-centration camp, established in a nutshell dictatorial government, investing the Government with unlimited powers.

REICHSTAG ELECTIONS OF MARCH 5, 1933

The elections were held on March 5, 1933, without visible violations of elec-toral honesty. In spite of the exploitation of the Reichstag fire and terroriza-tion of the opposition, the Government failed to obtain the hoped-for absolute majority. The National Socialists were, of course, by far the largest party, with 288 out of a total of 647 seats and 43.9 per cent of the total vote.[6] Only in con-junction with the Nationalists, who obtained 32 seats, did the Government have a slender margin above the absolute majority—namely, 340 out of 647 seats, or 51.9 per cent of the total vote.

On the following days all the German states (*Laender*) were "coordinated," by a routine procedure of staged demonstrations by the Nazified mob in the streets, by pressure and individual violence against the members of the Gov-ernment and officials, leading to the establishment of a local dictatorship by a party official, usually the *Gauleiter* (District Leader). No resistance was of-fered. The degenerate bureaucracy of the Socialists gave in; no Socialist martyr

[5] RGB. I, p. 83.
[6] The Nazis drew about one million votes from the Communists, who fell from 100 to 81 seats; they wiped out the "splinter" parties; and attracted at least four millions of the habitual non-voters, which explains the extraordinarily high voting participation of 88.7 per cent. The dis-tribution of votes and seats is shown in the following tabulation of election results:

	Vote	*Percentage*	*Seats Obtained*
NSDAP	17,277,000	43.9	288
Nationalists	3,136,000	8.0	52
Center	4,424,000	11.2	74
Bavarian Catholics	1,076,000	2.7	18
Socialists	7,181,000	18.3	125 *
Communists	4,848,000	12.3	81
Others	1,401,000	3.6	9

* Including 5 Democrats.

died in open battle for the cause. This ignominious surrender left the deepest impression on the masses.

THE ENABLING ACT OF MARCH 24, 1933

During the weeks after their seizure of power, the National Socialists, following blueprints held in readiness, unleashed the first wave of violence and terror. The agencies of public opinion were coordinated (*gleichgeschaltet*); law-enforcement authorities were brought under Nazi control by substituting reliable partisans for Republican officials. The *Rechtsstaat* disappeared. The people, staggered by the hurricane-like fury of events, submitted in apathy.

The Enabling Act (*Ermächtigungsgesetz*) of March 24, 1933, styled an "Act for Relieving the Distress of Nation and Reich," [7] involved in more than one aspect an amendment to the Weimar Constitution formally still in force; the requirements of Article 76 had to be fulfilled. In view of the parliamentary situation, the passage of the bill hinged on the support of the Catholic Center Party; they submitted. The bill was carried by 441 to 94 votes of the Socialists.[8] The vote was taken in an indescribable atmosphere of terrorization and coercion.

The Enabling Act was the pivotal constitutional document of the regime. At first declared in force until April 1, 1937, it was twice, on January 30, 1937, and on January 30, 1939, continued by the Reichstag,[9] and once more prolonged, this time merely by government decree, on May 10, 1943. The Enabling Act embodied the fundamental principle of dictatorship, namely, the abolition of the separation of legislative and executive powers in favor of a concentration of all powers in the hands of the Executive, the Government. Moreover, exercise of all powers and functions by the Government alone was unlimited in time and without any constitutional limitations whatsoever. The governmental machinery set up by the Act introduced a new type of legislation, supplementing and superseding the legislative powers of the Reichstag, the so-called government decrees (*Regierungsgesetz*), issued without further formalities or requirements by the Reich Government (Art. 1). Moreover— and this was in fact the legal key which opened the door for the subsequent complete reconstruction of the constitutional system—"the statutes decreed by the Government may deviate from the Constitution with the reservation that they should not affect the institutions of the Reichstag and the Federal Council" (Art. 2, sentence 1). In addition, it was explicitly stipulated that "the powers of the Reich President are to remain intact" (Art. 2, sentence 2). None of these solemn guarantees were maintained; the Federal Council was abolished in February, 1934; and the office of Reich President, after the death of von Hindenburg (August 1, 1934), was fused with the office of the "Fuehrer" and Reich Chancellor on August 2, 1934.

[7] RGB. I, p. 141.
[8] The 81 Communists and a number (26) of Socialist deputies could not vote because they were either assassinated, imprisoned or in hiding.
[9] RGB. I, p. 105 (1937) and RGB. I, p. 95 (1939).

MEASURES FOR THE PROTECTION OF THE REGIME

After the enactment of the Enabling Act, the fight against "enemies of the State," identified with enemies of the victorious party, could be taken up "legally." By a series of additions to criminal law, acts of actual resistance or of organizing or expressing political opposition were exposed to drastic punishment by Special Tribunals. German nationals beyond the reach of physical violence of the Reich were deprived, by simple administrative act, of their nationality and their property if their activities were deemed harmful to the interests of the regime.[10] Finally, a statute, delicately styled "for the safeguarding of the peace of law," [11] imposed the death penalty on those venturing attacks on State or party officials, and for anti-State propaganda even if committed abroad. Simultaneously with these measures for spreading terror through the statute book, illegal arrests without trial, indefinite detention in police prisons, jails and concentration camps, and an elaborate system of organized violence became integral institutions for the protection of the regime.

DISSOLUTION OF PARTIES AND THE ESTABLISHMENT OF THE ONE-PARTY STATE

Rapidly the old parties were "liquidated." The Communist Party was outlawed in March, 1933; the Socialists were eliminated in June. The Center and the smaller bourgeois parties committed suicide by self-dissolution. The same lot befell, in June, 1933, the National Party, the partner of the Nazis in the Government coalition. After an interlude of only a few months, Hitler had reached "totality of power." The one-party State was finally established by the law "against the formation of political parties." [12] The reconstruction of dissolved, or formation of new, political parties and even attempts at such activities were treated as treason.

COORDINATION (*GLEICHSCHALTUNG*) OF PUBLIC LIFE

The elimination of political opponents from the civil service and public life in general offered a more intricate problem. Many of them, especially judges and higher administrative officials, could not be replaced at once. An elaborate legislation, beginning with the famous law styled by a misnomer "on the restoration of the professional civil service," [13] served to eliminate "Non-Aryans"—as Jews were politely called at that time—from the civil service, including the liberal professions, the educational and State-controlled institutions, and to purge the civil service of undesirable members, Socialists, Liberals, or all persons defined in general terms as "politically unreliable." A very large number were dismissed, in many cases without pension; and the statute continued as a weapon against recalcitrants up to 1937, when its main provisions were included in the codification of the civil service on Nazi lines in

---

[10] Law of July 14, 1933 (RGB. I, p. 480).
[11] Of October 13, 1933 (RGB. I, p. 723).
[12] Law of July 14, 1933 (RGB. I, p. 479).
[13] Law of April 7, 1933 (RGB. I, p. 175).

the Public Official Act.[14] On May 2, offices and property of the trade unions were seized and taken over by the huge Labor organization of the regime, the Labor Front under the leadership of Dr. Ley. By the same devices of pressure, intimidation, coercion, and outright violence, all other fields of public activity, such as press, stage, education, and cultural activities, were brought under Nazi control. The totalitarian State emerged in its full glory, an ordering of society in which all expressions and activities of private life are subordinated to the tyranny of the State and the Party.

THE "PURGE" OF JUNE 1934

The regime was headed for a showdown between the capitalist wing of the party and the "anti-capitalistic yearning" of the rank and file. The economic program of the Government—amateurish and without definite orientation toward the promised new social stratification—had failed to improve the conditions of the masses. The Left wing, embracing the "old fighters," organized in the SA under one of Hitler's oldest friends, Captain Roehm, and the dispossessed lower middle classes felt that Hitler and the party bosses had "betrayed" the revolution.

The "purge" of June 30, 1934, together with the Reichstag fire of 1933, the pogroms of November, 1938, and the July 20, 1944, conspiracy,[15] belongs to the most spectacular events in the internal history of the Third Reich. Under the pretext that a dangerous conspiracy for the overthrow of the Government was imminent, on June 30 and July 1, 1934, a massacre of high-ranking party officials and other enemies of the regime took place, which had no parallel in Europe outside Russia since the Paris Commune of 1871 and was the prelude of the unprecedented mass extermination to come. That an actual plot against Hitler existed was never proved. The revolutionary power of the SA was permanently broken. Hitler and the army command had become close allies, from which sprang in due course his domination of the *Reichswehr,* prerequisite for the future gamble in foreign politics. In his speech before the Reichstag on July 13, 1934, Hitler claimed that he had assumed the powers of the "Supreme Law Lord of the Nation" (*Oberster Gerichtsherr*); freed from all liberalistic concepts of justice, he had saved the State. A Government decree was inscribed in the statute book declaring the acts committed "justified emergency measures." The conscience of the public inside Germany was so dulled that the massacre enhanced his prestige immensely.

DEATH OF HINDENBURG AND THE FUSION OF REICH PRESIDENCY AND CHANCELLORSHIP

On August 1, 1934, at the age of 87, Hindenburg died on his estate in Neudeck, which grim popular humor described as "the one-man concentration camp in Germany." Hitler found the simplest and most logical solution for the succession. The Government merged by the Act "on the Head of the

---

[14] Law of January 26, 1937 (RGB. I, p. 39).
[15] See *infra,* pp. 454 *ff.*

State of the German Reich," [16] the office of the Reich President with that of the Reich Chancellor; all powers hitherto exercised by the President were conferred on the "Fuehrer" and Reich Chancellor. The army, and subsequently all public officials, took the oath of allegiance to the person of Hitler instead of to an abstract document, such as the Constitution. Hitler himself was henceforward the living Constitution. On August 19, 1934, the German people confirmed the succession by a plebiscite.

With the fusion of Reich Chancellorship and Reich Presidency, the Third Reich was constitutionally perfected. Despotism was "normalized" in terms of constitutional law.

[16] Law of August 1, 1934 (RGB. I, p. 747).

CHAPTER XIII

THE GOVERNMENTAL STRUCTURE OF
THE THIRD REICH

POSITION AND FUNCTION OF THE "FUEHRER"

The Weimar Constitution, though at least until 1938 occasionally referred to by the Supreme Court, was never formally repealed; but to all practical intents and purposes, with the advent to power of the Nazi regime, it ceased to exist. In the first years thereafter plans for formulating the governmental system in terms of a constitutional instrument were occasionally hinted at, but they never materialized. By its very nature, dictatorial government defies fixation within the framework of an instrument of government. Even without a fundamental charter, it should be realized that the organization of the Third Reich possessed an all-encompassing and jointless system of constitutional law, if it is understood that what was called "law" was in substance and content mere legalized arbitrariness—legalized by the sole fact that the man whose will was supreme had at the moment the power to enforce his will.

Presented in a nutshell, all powers of the State and the nation were concentrated in the hands of Adolf Hitler as the "Fuehrer" [1] from whom all powers radiated and in whom all powers converged. The Third Reich resembled a pyramid balanced on its apex. Hitler himself justified his being endowed with absolute and supreme powers by his "mission" for the German people, and the achievements before and during the War. His followers, deeply impressed by the rise of an unknown soldier of the World War to heights of the master of Europe, attributed his successes to his supernatural gifts of leadership. His book *Mein Kampf*—the Bible of the Third Reich and, to the end, the political blueprint translated into reality with unrelenting consistency—as well as all his utterances, reflected the unchallengeable, infallible, and apostolic authority of "the greatest German of all times." His authority can be evaluated only in terms of political theology. It was German romanticism and mysticism, en-

---

[1] The term *"Fuehrer,"* an imitation of the Italian "Duce," has idiomatically in German a rather trite, commonplace, and even slightly ludicrous connotation; it is of course alien to German constitutional tradition.

cased in a superior psychological technique, executed by modern technology, and raised to the level of a political religion.

National Socialist doctrine pretended to believe in the existence of a mystical energy emanating from the "Fuehrer" which fused State, movement, and people into one inseparable unit. This ultimate and final source of power, called "Supreme Leadership Power" (*Fuehrergewalt*) was in fact the core of the political theory of the regime, constantly quoted and referred to, the closest approach to constitutional deification of a mortal being. It was, in short, secularized theology. Under this theoretical conception—of fundamental importance in practical politics—there could be no room for the customary pluralism of State functions, elaborated as the separation of powers by Locke, Montesquieu, and modern constitutionalism.

Moreover, the "Fuehrer" integrated the tripartite division in "people" (*Volk*), "movement" (*Bewegung*), and "State" (*Staat*)—one of the basic and recurrent slogans of the doctrine. From this trinity were derived more concretely his powers as symbol and idol of the people, as leader of the National Socialist Party, and as holder of the highest offices of the State and the Government as Reich President and Reich Chancellor. He exercised all powers attributed individually to each of these institutions. Residues of the origin of his functions were visible in the technical arrangement for their discharge, for which he had three different bureaus or staffs; namely, the President's Chancellery, the Reich's Chancellery and finally the Chancellery of the Party, the Headquarters of the NSDAP.

The "Fuehrer," together with his subordinates in the Cabinet, constituted a new political entity, called *Reichsleitung*. It concentrated, in the hands of one group under Hitler, the sum-total of all executive, legislative, administrative, and, if need be, also judicial functions. The powers of the "Fuehrer," therefore, were grouped along the following lines: he exercised all powers which belonged formerly to the President of the Republic, including the Supreme Command of the armed forces; the power to dissolve the Reichstag; the power to appoint and dismiss the Reich Ministers and officials; the power to remodel government agencies and departments (called *Organisationshoheit*). Finally, the power to represent the Reich internationally was extended to the supreme conduct of foreign affairs and occupied from the outset the center of Hitler's personal activities.

In the second place, the "Fuehrer" exercised the new powers derived from the organic acts of the regime itself, such as the appointment and dismissal of the governors of the *Laender* (Reich Regents) and the ministers and public officials serving in the *Laender* as Reich officials. Together with his collaborators in the Cabinet, he issued Government decrees as the main type of legislation in the Third Reich, which could even contain new constitutional law. He controlled, directed, and supervised the entire administration of Reich and *Laender*.

Finally, the "Fuehrer" was endowed with those powers which sprang from the National Socialist mythology, in particular from the function of being the leader of the National Socialist Party. Although the position of the Party in the State was regularized to a large extent by incorporating the Party into the State, a good many of these powers were derived from the mystical or theological implication that the "Fuehrer" was "the bearer of the legal will of the racial community." Since he was, in addition, "addressee of the duty of fealty" (*Treupflicht*), all "racial comrades" were under the moral and legal obligation to be loyal to him and his "mission" for the German people. Since the "Fuehrer" was given to his people by an inscrutable act of Providence, termination of his functions was possible only by voluntary resignation, death, or revolution. According to the Succession Act of August 1, 1934, he could appoint a Deputy-Leader. It was only after the invasion of Poland on September 1, 1939, that Hitler, about to leave for the "front" as the "First Soldier of the Reich," designated Hess and Goering, in this order, as his successors. Goering fell from grace in 1944 and was replaced (though without formal announcement) by Martin Bormann, Deputy Leader of the NSDAP. Hess removed himself by his flight to England (May, 1941). The appointment of Admiral Doenitz in Hitler's "last will" before his suicide (April 30, 1945) was without significance. The Third Reich stood and fell with Hitler.

As to the actual exercise of these absolute powers by Hitler, he was not at all interested in the routine functions of government or matters of civil administration. His capricious living habits rendered him incapable of desk work. His complete ignorance of, and disdain for, economics were largely responsible for the insufficient economic preparation and conduct of the war. Total mobilization was undertaken as late as 1944, when the efficient Goebbels was appointed Mobilization Commissioner. Hitler's main interest, besides hobbies such as architecture, movies, and music, was foreign policy, in accordance with his conviction of his "mission" to make Germany a world power, and military strategy and even tactics. The onslaught on Poland was as perfectly executed as the invasion of Scandinavia was militarily bold and original. He is reliably credited with the brilliantly successful campaigns for the conquest of the Lowlands and France (May–June, 1940) and the initially at least no less grandiose plans for the invasion of the Soviets. In the ultimate failure of the Russian phase of the war he had his share in the responsibility for the Stalingrad disaster.

HITLER AND THE GENERALS

Hitler gained power with the connivance of the *Wehrmacht* generals. Without them he could never have prepared, or embarked, on war. Following on the heels of the old Field Marshal's death, the army took the oath of loyalty to the person of Hitler himself, to whom the powers of the Reich President as Supreme Commander of the armed forces had devolved by the Succession Act. In 1935, by the Law "on the structure of the armed forces," [2] the first open blow against Versailles, and by the subsequent Army Act,[3] Hitler made him-

[2] *Gesetz über den Aufbau der Wehrmacht,* of March 6, 1935 (RGB. I, p. 375).
[3] *Wehrgesetz,* of May 21, 1935 (RGB. I, p. 609).

self Supreme Commander of the Armed Forces (*Oberster Befehlshaber der Wehrmacht*).

To have bent the army command to his will and to have subjugated this most effective instrument of power was the most conspicuous and fatal achievement of Hitler, all the more striking since the army, pillar of German national tradition and unique expression of national corporate spirit, had tenaciously resisted full integration in, and absorption by, National Socialism until 1938. And yet the generals were won over to Hitler's bold strategy. The army leaders had objected to the planned occupation of the demilitarized zone of the Rhineland in March, 1936. The change in the High Command prior to the invasion of Austria (February, 1938) was the prelude to the annexation of Austria (March, 1938), the dismemberment (September, 1938) and the annexation (March, 1939) of Czechoslovakia. The real pay-off for the army came with the brilliantly executed *Blitzkrieg* campaigns against Poland (fall of 1939), Scandinavia (April, 1940) and France and the Lowlands (May–June, 1940). The Nazis had become the masters of Europe. Whatever inhibitions the older crew of "respectable" soldiers may still have entertained were drowned out by the magnificence of the military victories. By that time the galaxy of new Field Marshals had become as subservient to the regime as all the other agencies of the Third Reich. Through Hitler's political, diplomatic, and finally military accomplishments the army had received more than its due in honors, influence, and social prestige.

But it turned out to be a Pyrrhic victory. Hitler, forever distrustful of the army elite of professional technicians, saw to it that Himmler's police organization, needed for the control at home and of the unruly subjugated countries, was steadily built up to a military force (*Waffen SS*) in competition with, and as a counterweight to, the regular armed forces. When, after the turn of military fortune in the Russian campaign, Hitler arrogated to himself the conduct of the war on all fronts, a minority group of the generals began to plan rebellion. After the landing of the Anglo-American forces in Normandy (June, 1944) it exploded in the by now famous conspiracy of July 20, 1944.

The revolt of July, 1944, the second [4] plot with near-success on Hitler's life, has become one of the most controversial incidents of the internal history of the Third Reich, exploited—for understandable reasons—by Germany after the defeat as an allegedly convincing demonstration of large-scale resistance against the regime and supported, for less intelligible reasons, also by American sympathizers with German conservativism. The mass of available evidence allows the definite conclusion that what actually happened was not a widespread resistance movement of the German people worthy of the name, but merely a belated eleventh-hour revolt of a relatively small clique of army officers, public officials, and conservative circles affiliated with them (Goerdeler, von Hassell, Popitz, and others). It had no mass basis and no significance for

---

[4] The first occurred on November 8, 1939, when one Elsler single-handed planted a time bomb in the pillar of the beer hall behind the rostrum where Hitler gave his traditional anniversary address to the "old fighters." Hitler, following a "premonition," suddenly broke off and left; the bomb exploded a few minutes later, wrecked the building, and killed many.

the masses. If successful it hoped to establish an authoritarian government adorned with some pseudo-democratic trimmings, intended, if the Allies permitted, the rescue of the traditional ruling classes.

The plot, prepared as ineptly as it was cowardly executed, failed miserably even though the bomb aimed at Hitler in his Headquarters in Eastern Prussia was a near-miss. The conspiring generals in Berlin, on whom the actual seizure of power depended, were unwilling to break their oath to Hitler though they had not hesitated to break the one they had sworn to the Weimar Constitution. Himmler and his Secret Police had a field day. Several thousands of persons involved or allegedly involved were executed. It can safely be expected that the Hitler legend will draw heavily on this convenient material.

THE REICH CABINET

The members of the Cabinet were without exception the personal confidants of, and subordinated to, the "Fuehrer." They were responsible to him, and to him alone. Interdependence was reflected in the institution of the cosignature (*Mitzeichnung*), by which the individual Minister, in adding his signature to that of Hitler on a Government decree, assumed personal responsibility towards Hitler. The hierarchical order in the Third Reich was reminiscent of the monocratic organization of the government under the Bismarckian Constitution, revealing again the force of traditional trends. On the other hand, the Ministers, described by the National Socialist doctrine as "genuine subleaders," were independent within the fields of their assigned jurisdiction. They acted on their own responsibility, subject only to the ultimate responsibility towards the "Fuehrer." He appointed, dismissed, instructed, and directed them. Cabinet meetings, rare even in the initial years, were wholly abandoned after the outbreak of the war. The irregular private life of the "Fuehrer" did not permit them. Consultation between Hitler and his Ministers took mostly the form of audiences granted in Berlin or at his mountain retreat on the Obersalzberg. In the later years of the regime the functions of the Cabinet Ministers were largely curbed, superseded and duplicated by one or several of the multitudinous Party organizations or groups.

LEGISLATION

Legislation was in the Leadership-State the expression of the will of the Leader who monopolizes the will of the State. It took the form of decrees enacted by the Reich Government (*Regierungsgesetz*) according to the Enabling Act of March 24, 1933. Only the Reich Government legislated. The people did not participate in the process of legislation except when called on by the Government in the plebiscite procedure. The Cabinet drafted legislation by Government decree and submitted it to the "Fuehrer." His decision created the law. The customary distinction between ordinary legislation and constitutional amendment disappeared. By the Reconstruction Act, the second of the "organic" statutes of the new regime,[5] a new Reichstag, elected in No-

[5] *Gesetz über den Neuaufbau des Reichs*, of January 30, 1934 (RGB. I, p. 75).

vember, 1933, on the one-party ticket of the National Socialist Party, unanimously conferred upon the Cabinet the plenitude of the amending power without any limitations. Henceforward the amending process became identical with the ordinary legislative procedure, both being exercised by simple Government decree.

THE REICH CABINET IN OPERATION

In accordance with the specific needs of the regime and the transformation of the Reich into a unitary state,[6] several new Ministries were created; namely, for Propaganda and Public Enlightenment (1933), Air (1933), Church Affairs (1934), and Science and Education (1934). The Ministry of Economics and Agriculture was separated into two offices (1933). During the war there were sixteen Ministries.[7] In addition, the Cabinet embraced Ministers without portfolio.[8] Other high officials participated in deliberations of the Cabinet if their sphere of jurisdiction was involved.[9]

A survey of the Government's personnel reveals the striking fact that in twelve years of power no more than about twenty-five men have held office in sixteen regular departments. The key positions were held at the end of the war by the same men who had obtained them at the beginning, a record equaled by no other contemporary state. All members of the Reich Government were members of the Nazi Party, those originally not belonging to the Party having been appointed "honorary members." Only a few of the Ministers had previous training in government service or administration;[10] all others were men with tested party loyalty instead of expert qualifications for service.

After unconditional surrender, Allied investigations and German reports established the fact that, with the progress of the war, the regime concealed behind its outwardly "monolithic" appearance an indescribable administrative chaos, resulting from the lack of definite jurisdiction; overlapping of functions;

[6] See *infra,* pp. 459 ff.

[7] (1) Interior (Frick); (2) Foreign Affairs (von Ribbentrop); (3) Air (Field Marshal Goering; he was at the same time Minister President of Prussia, in 1936 Commissioner for the Four-Year Plan, and, with the reorganization of the economic apparatus of Germany necessitated in December, 1939, also Supreme Director of War Economics); (4) Finance (von Schwerin-Krosigk); (5) Economics (Funk); (6) Propaganda and Public Enlightenment (Goebbels); (7) Justice (Guertner, later Thierack); (8) Nutrition and Agriculture (Darre); (9) Labor (Seldte); (10) Science and Education (Rust); (11) Church Affairs (Kerrl); (12) Post (Ohnesorge); (13) Communications (Dorpmueller); (14) Defense (General Keitel); (15) Arms and Munitions (Todt, later Speer; the latter Ministry was created in March 1940); (16) Eastern Territories (Rosenberg).

[8] Among these were (1) Hess, Deputy-Leader of the NSDAP; (2) Frank, as Commissioner of Justice for the reform of the legal system in the spirit of National Socialism, and appointed, in September, 1939, Governor-General of Poland; (3) Lammers, as head of the Bureau of the Reich Chancellery; (4) Meissner, as head of the Reich President's Office; (5) Schacht, who remained a titular member of the Reich Cabinet after his demotion from the Economics Ministry and the Presidency of the Reichsbank; finally (6) von Seyss-Inquart, later Commissioner in the Netherlands.

[9] The Leader of the SS and Commander of Police Himmler, after Hitler the most powerful man of the regime; the Reich Labor Leader Ley, controlling the Labor Front; the head of the Foreign Division (*Auslandsorganisation*) Bohle; and the Prussian Minister of Finance, the only Prussian office which until 1943 was not conducted in personal union with the corresponding Reich office.

[10] Von Neurath, Frick, Lammers, Dorpmueller, von Schwerin-Krosigk, Schacht, Guertner, and the generals serving in the Defense Ministry.

red tape; waste of money and energy; jealousy and intrigues between the departments, among themselves, and with the party organizations. All were entangled in a ruthless competition for the favor of the master and in clandestine maneuvers carried on in the antechamber, said more to resemble an oriental court than organized government. Yet there remains the extraordinary fact that the Third Reich, headed by a rank amateur and run largely by administrative dilettantes, not only did not collapse economically or administratively, but prepared for, waged, and almost won a global war, and that its haphazard structure broke down only under the hammer blows of the invading armies from the East and West and from the sky. This phenomenon remains unexplained, though the stamina of the Third Reich may have been due in part to the fact that among Hitler's collaborators there were not a few of exceptional abilities as organizers and executives (Goering, Speer), efficient bureaucrats (Frick, Schwerin-Krosigk, Lammers) and a near-genius of diabolical inventiveness in his spell over the masses (Goebbels).

THE THIRD REICH AS AN "ENNOBLED" DEMOCRACY

According to National Socialist political "philosophy" the Third Reich was a democracy, and an "ennobled" democracy at that, styling itself as a *"volksgeführte Demokratie."* Everything for the people, nothing by the people, and nothing through the people. Reconciliation of the democratic idea and the leadership principle was accomplished by a quaint perversion of the term "democracy" and its adjustment to the semantics of National Socialism. In brief, the people—*Volk*—was something permanent, supernatural, a mystical entity, an "objective existence" faintly reminiscent of Rousseau's "general will." It cannot be seen; it can only be felt or believed. Only the "Fuehrer," by virtue of his supernatural qualities and the intrinsic strength of his "mission," is qualified to express the real or "objective" will of the people. The "Fuehrer" "incarnates" the nation. Hence Germany is a genuine democracy. These harebrained deductions reveal once more National Socialism as a political religion, and the governmental system of the Third Reich as a secularized theology.

ELECTIONS

Consequently, elections arranged by the regime served merely as manifestations of the homogeneity of the "Fuehrer's" and the people's political will. Universal, equal, secret, and direct suffrage as of the Republic was nominally retained. Voters were all Germans of the age of 20 or over, if they were of German or "of racially similar blood." [11] Political pressure of the party introduced compulsory voting. Participation in the poll was exceedingly high, and came close to 100 per cent. Consequently the number of deputies rose from 661 in November, 1933, to 813 in April, 1938 (the last election). Election statistics were of little value. An affirmative vote in the higher brackets of 90 per cent was a foregone conclusion. While, at least in 1933 and 1934, elec-

[11] Law of March 7, 1936 (RGB. I, p. 133).

tion results may not have been overly manipulated, they were sufficiently "doctored" by Dr. Goebbels later to achieve that kind of unanimity which intimidation may have failed to accomplish.

Since the dissolution of all other political parties, the NSDAP had the monopoly of running candidates. The selection was left exclusively to the discretion of the National Party Manager. The voter was presented with a ticket of the Party, headed by Adolf Hitler, and marked it "Yes," as told by party officials "assisting" him at the polling station.

THE REICHSTAG

The Reichstag served merely as a sounding board and rubber stamp of the "Fuehrer." No discussion was demanded, expected, or permitted. An assemblage of party appointees unanimously ratified, by acclamation, in military obedience to the command, the rare bills submitted by him. Committees were abolished together with the Standing Orders. The last meeting occurred in 1942. Legislative activity was even less than the number of meetings would indicate. Only seven acts were passed by the Reichstag.[12] The vast mass of other legislation were enacted by Government decree.

In spite of its rubber-stamp character, the Reichstag was dissolved by Hitler and re-elected no less than four times between 1933 and 1938. Dissolutions and elections were considered acts of "political mobilization" and served the welcome purpose of self-glorification, emotional excitement, and propaganda stagecraft, which are the elixir of a "dynamic" regime.

PLEBISCITES

In addition to elections, the Third Reich practiced also the method of the plebiscite (*Volksbefragung*) proper, as a signification of the "true," "unadulterated," and "ennobled" democracy. Although the Plebiscite Act [13] prescribed that the plebiscite ought to precede the measure, the three plebiscites held merely confirmed measures the Government had taken before.

The first plebiscite (November 12, 1933), in conjunction with an election for the Reichstag, was to endorse the policy of the Government leading to the withdrawal from the League of Nations. The second plebiscite (August 19, 1934) involved the Succession Act and was the only popular vote on an issue of internal policies. The third plebiscite was held on April 10, 1938, both in Austria and Germany, to ratify the preceding annexation of the *Ostmark*. The percentage of favorable votes for the three plebiscites was, respectively: 93.1 per cent, 84.2 per cent, and 99.57 per cent. But even the docile Germans have become aware of the intrinsic value of a vote stripped of its democratic ingredients and offering merely the empty motions through which each voter was compelled to go.

---

[12] Enabling Act of 1933; Continuation Acts of 1937 and 1939; Reconstruction Act of January 30, 1934 (RGB. I, p. 75), and the three so-called Nuremberg Acts of September 16, 1935 (RGB. I, pp. 1146, 1147).
[13] Law of July 14, 1933 (RGB. I, p. 497).

SUPPORT OF THE REGIME BY THE PEOPLE

The problem in how far the people supported the regime—much discussed before and during the war—is of more than posthumous academic interest because, in its individual application, it conditioned the vast procedure known later on as "denazification." [14] It may also cast some light on the question in how far the population in present-day Eastern Germany, whose processes of propaganda and voting techniques resemble the Nazi experience like identical twins, adheres to the Communist regime. On the basis of our post-surrender knowledge of the Nazi terror regime it may be granted that, against the vigilance of the Secret Police, nothing amounting to organized disobedience or outright resistance was possible except with the backing of the *Wehrmacht*. For those who prefer a formula it may be said that perhaps 30 to 40 per cent were sold on the regime—the jobholders, the beneficiaries, the profiteers, and the genuine enthusiasts, the latter particularly and increasingly among the youth. When Hitler, after the victories over the West, was at the height of his triumphs and the war seemed as good as won this percentage cannot but have increased to the point where the vast majority endorsed the regime. Perhaps another 10 to 15 per cent were implacably opposed throughout. This section increased rapidly with the paling of Hitler's star and the impending loss of the war. But to a measurable extent opposition was counterbalanced by the feeling of patriotic solidarity in a nation at war. Aside from these two categories of positive and negative activists, the mass of the people, as everywhere, allowed themselves to be carried along by events. They are the masses that shout "Hosannah!" today and "Crucify him" tomorrow. Consequently, when unconditional surrender came, if one were to believe the Germans, not a single Nazi was left; only a small minority had ever existed, and even those who had been Nazis had been coerced.

REICH AND *LAENDER:* GERMANY'S TRANSFORMATION INTO A UNITARY STATE

THE END OF GERMAN FEDERALISM

Next to the substitution of the totalitarian single-party State for the multiple parliamentary State, perhaps the most conspicuous development under the Third Reich consisted in the transformation of the federal into the unitary and centralized State. Rigid centralization conformed to the necessities of dictatorship, which is bound to dominate the territory without intermediary institutions. The First Act "for coordinating the *Laender* and the Reich" (March, 1933) [15] was aimed mainly at breaking down the existing political differences within the various *Laender*. The political structure of the *Laender* was assimilated to that of the Reich. Most of the *Laender* passed appropriate Enabling Acts, handing over complete powers to the Nazified governments. New elec-

---

[14] See *infra*, pp. 517 *ff*.
[15] Law of March 31, 1933 (RGB. I, p. 153).

tions for the *Laender* diets were no longer permitted. The Second Act "for coordinating the *Laender* and the Reich" (April, 1933) [16] brought the innovation of the Reich Regent (*Reichsstatthalter*), or State Governor, to be appointed by the Reich President, on the advice of the Reich Chancellor. On the whole, he functioned as a sort of state governor appointed by the Reich. The Reich Regents, as subordinates of the "Fuehrer," represented the interests of the Reich, not of the *Laender,* and were to guarantee political unity within the *Land* and political conformity with the Reich.

RECONSTRUCTION ACT OF 1934

In spite of these changes, the dualism between Reich and *Laender* failed to disappear. Regional spirit persisted. Some of the *Laender* preserved to a considerable degree their political identity. Thus the complete elimination of the *Laender* became inevitable, lest the traditional federalism should transcend the framework of the single-party State. This step was taken in the Reconstruction Act of 1934,[17] the second "organic" act of the Third Reich. The sovereign powers of the states were transferred to the Reich, while the governments of the states were reduced to mere agencies of the Reich Government operating on the territory of the *Land*. As a result the *Laender* became only territorial subdivisions of the Reich, and the Reich, to all intents and purposes, a unitary state. The Reich Regents were subordinated to the Minister of the Interior; the governments were converted into bureaus of the Reich; the officials of the *Laender,* including the members of the *Laender* governments, into officials of the Reich. In consonance with these structural changes, the customary institution of federalism, the Federal Council, became obsolete and was formally abolished.[18]

POSITION OF THE REICH REGENTS

The final solution brought the Reich Regents Act of 1935, the third of the "organic" statutes of the Third Reich.[19] It eliminated the last remnants of separate statehood of the *Laender*. The Regent, heretofore subordinated to the Reich Minister of the Interior, was integrated fully as a normal agency into the Reich administration, and was bound to accept instructions from the various Reich Ministers acting within the jurisdiction of their individual departments. On the whole, this move was equivalent to a degradation of the Regent. Appointed and dismissed by the "Fuehrer," he was no longer an official of the *Land* for which he acted. He represented Reich interests towards the *Land,* and not *vice versa*. The Reich Regents functioned as intermediary agents between the central and the local administrations.

Eleven *Laender* of the "old" Reich received a Regent; the division still re-

---

16 Law of April 7, 1933 (RGB. I, p. 173).
17 *Gesetz zum Neuaufbau des Reichs,* of January 30, 1934 (RGB. I, p. 75).
18 Law of February 14, 1934 (RGB. I, p. 89).
19 *Reichsstatthaltergesetz,* of January 30, 1935 (RGB. I, p. 65).

flected much of the dynastic structure of the former states.[20] To these were later added seven Reich Regents acting in Austria and one in the Sudetenland.

The position of the Reich Regents was hybrid and incongruous. But the nominally exalted office of the Regent was created and maintained in order to gratify the ambitions of some of the "old fighters" whose loyalty towards the "Fuehrer" had to be rewarded by an especially fat piece of the spoils. He was the real political boss of the district in most cases by combining his office with the position of the party official, the *Gauleiter*. By the end of the regime the office of the Regent as such had become meaningless.

THE POSITION OF THE LAENDER

For all administrative purposes, what once was Bavaria, Saxony, or Hamburg figured as only one of the territorial subdivisions of the unitary Reich, all of which were equally subjected to the pressure of the one-party State and its strictly centralized administration. Since progressively more functions were transferred to the Reich and the Party, the administrative autonomy of the *Laender* together with their political independence was more and more "hollowed out." Gradually the political institutions of the *Laender* were thrown on the dust heap. First to disappear permanently were the *Laender* diets. Their powers were usurped by the *Laender* governments. As final solution the Reconstruction Act of 1934 transferred also, as a consequence of the disappearance of the legislative powers of the *Laender,* the *Laender* governments into agencies of the Reich, exercising merely powers redelegated by the Reich. *Land* legislation became actually Reich legislation confined to the territory of the *Land,* authorized by the Reich and restricted to purely local affairs. In conformity with the supression of the *Laender* as separate political units, uniform Reich legislation spread rapidly over all fields. This process, perhaps the most beneficial of all reforms undertaken by the regime and largely undone by the Occupation Powers after 1945, was called *Verreichlichung*. Only a few of the more important fields of centralization are mentioned here: civil service, trade and crafts, press, administration of justice, taxation, traffic and communications, local government, police,[21] and even most of the cultural activities. Moreover, all public officials of the *Laender,* appointed and dismissed by the Reich, were Reich officials.

GOVERNMENTS OF THE LAENDER

Yet it is misleading to assume that Germany became a wholly homogeneous and unitarian country like France or Italy (before 1947). Curiously enough,

[20] The "Fuehrer" established Regencies for the following *Laender:* (The city in brackets is the capital). Bavaria (Munich); Saxony (Dresden); Wuerttemberg (Stuttgart); Baden (Karlsruhe); Hessen (Darmstadt); Hamburg (Hamburg); Thuringia (Weimar); Oldenburg and Bremen (Oldenburg); Brunswick and Anhalt (Dessau); Lippe and Schaumburg-Lippe (Detmold); and Mecklenburg (Schwerin).

[21] This important domain was centralized by Edict of the "Fuehrer" of June 17, 1936 (RGB. I, p. 487). Himmler, Chief of the SS and the Gestapo (Secret Police) was head of the entire German police (*Reichssicherheitshauptamt*).

the former *Laender,* though denuded of power and stripped of functions, retained governments of their own (*Landesregierung*), though as organs of the Reich and not of the *Laender.* The "Fuehrer" and Reich Chancellor appointed, dismissed, and instructed them directly; but they were equally bound to accept instructions from the individual Reich Ministers and from the Regent, who might consider them as "his" Government. The main reason for this complicated, wasteful, and overlapping system was the latent fear of the regime that tribal or regional differences, nurtured by "statehood" reminiscences or religious diversities, would reassert themselves.

PRUSSIA

In a class by itself was Prussia. Prussia lost her identity as an individual state even more, if possible, than the other *Laender.* The "Fuehrer" and Reich Chancellor held nominally the office of Regent for Prussia; actually, by delegation, the functions were exercised by the Minister President of Prussia, Goering.[22] Responsible only to Hitler, and taking orders, if any, only from him, he occupied a singularly independent position. In order to avoid duplication in staff and administration, all formerly separate departments of Prussia, with the exception of the Finance Ministry, were in due course absorbed by the corresponding Reich ministries. Thus the Prussian Government became an integral part of the Reich Government, and *vice versa,* and Prussia a sort of jurisdictional province of the Reich. Before 1914 the Reich was controlled by Prussia, while under the regime Prussia was controlled by the Reich,[23] and both by the Nazis.

Furthermore, by increasing the administrative jurisdiction of the Party districts (*Gaue*) and by subdividing the Prussian provinces, the political-administrative unity and even identity of Prussia was completely destroyed, thus antedating by years the subsequent obliteration of Prussia as a state by a decision of the Occupation Powers (1946). On the whole, consciousness of "statehood" and manifestations of regional tribalism, in the past the cornerstones of German political history, were well kept under control and submerged by the tide of the one-party State. It was to be expected that once the pressure of the single-party machine was lifted, state individualities, statehood feelings, states' rights aspirations, would rebound with a vengeance.

REGIONAL PLANNING (REICHSREFORM)

To realize the plan of a regional regrouping of the Reich on geographical, or rather economic, lines (called in Germany *Reichsreform*), in the place of the existing pattern drawn by the accidents of dynastic history, was beyond the powers of even the Third Reich. Minor rectifications of the internal state lines, by exchanging territories among the *Laender* of Prussia, Hamburg, and Oldenburg, were accomplished in the so-called "Little *Reichsreform*" of 1937,

---

[22] Edict of the Fuehrer and Reich Chancellor, of April 23, 1933 (RGB. I, p. 233).
[23] Prussia possessed, in addition, a number of peculiarities, such as the Provincial Governors and the Council of State—the latter a merely ornamental creation of Goering.

by which also the time-honored Free City of Luebeck was wiped from the map and its territory distributed among the neighboring *Laender*.[24] Yet, on the whole, the thorny problem of territorial realignment on economic or regional lines was shelved, perhaps because of underground resistance of local interests, insuperable even for the omnipotence of a totalitarian dictatorship, or perhaps because economic rationalization meant little to a nation bent on preparedness for war. During the war a significant territorial innovation manifested itself in the rise of the *Gau,* the territorial unit of the Party, as administrative district. For the purposes of total mobilization forty-two *Gaue* were created, with vastly increasing jurisdiction, cutting across the traditional boundaries of the *Laender*.

[24] Law of January 26, 1937 (RGB. I, p. 91).

CHAPTER XIV

THE INSTRUMENTALITIES OF POWER

To Hitler who, in his *Mein Kampf,* has presented our age with a basic treatise on the relations of political power and mass psychology, and to his associates, it was an elementary truth that the success and stability of a political system depend less on actual governmental institutions than on the *exercise* of political power. They devised instrumentalities of political control admirably adjusted to the psychological conditions of modern mass-society. The power-generating processes were rooted in the fundamental elements of mass-society, that is, organization and psychological inducement resulting from persuasion, emotion, and coercion. The Third Reich fittingly describing itself as the "state in motion" (*Bewegungsstaat*) stands out as the most accomplished machinery for mass control yet known in history.

THE "FOLKISH DOGMA" AND THE RACIAL MYTH

THE NOTION OF THE PEOPLE (VOLK)

Foremost among the instruments of power was the ideological apparatus built around the concepts of the folkish community (*Volksgemeinschaft*) and the race (*Rasse*). The doctrine drew strength from two plainly mystical sources. One was the notion of the "Fuehrer" as the incarnation of the mission of the German Nation, from which flow the supernatural powers for its fulfillment. The second, closely related, was that the people (*Volk*) are the ultimate source of power and the highest absolute value.

National Socialism introduced into the concept of the people pseudo-biological, pseudo-historical, and pseudo-metaphysical elements, contending that the nature of a nation or people is determined by the totality of its historical, political, and biological experience. Membership in a people is destiny.

THE NOTION OF RACE

The notion of *Volk* developed into mystical collectivism once it was enlarged by the implications of the race, or the "community of descent" (*Abstammungsgemeinschaft*). The ideology of the race or, more concretely, the

464

"community of blood and soil" (*Blut und Boden*), was the *leitmotiv* of the Third Reich from which all practical policies derived their ultimate justification. The myth of the race amounted, in brief, to the assertion that the pure race is the fountainhead of all creative values of life and history. Creative genius is less a quality of brains than of blood. Blood is a metaphysical as well as a merely biological notion, and hence is incapable of rationalization. Again: Race is destiny. The true German Nation is a community tied together indissolubly by bonds of blood. From these premises the National Socialist doctrine [1] evolved a classification of races according to their physical and mental criteria. Races are not only different in blood and soul, but also unequal in value. Among all races, the Aryans [2] alone count; and, among the latter, the Nordics are the most eminent branch. Only the "Aryan" race is creative of cultural values. Aryan and Nordic were the Greeks, the Romans, and finally the Germanic people. Their main spiritual criterion is honor. Creative capacity is innate and is transmitted by blood alone.

The main objective of a race consists in keeping itself free from contamination by alien or inferior blood. It is the supreme task of the State to free the pure race of the Nordics, by a forceful process of elimination, from infection with alien, inferior blood. However, only contamination by the Negro and Jewish races is alien and dangerous; all other admixtures are permissible. The supreme importance of the soil naturally followed. A pure race permeates with its spirit the soil on which it dwells and from which it springs.

It seems hardly necessary to refute the National Socialist race doctrine. Historically it was an outgrowth of crude romanticism. Philosophically it was similar to the class-myth of Marxism, the economic determinism of history, with which it had in common the fact that everything is explained in terms of one denominator. Through its oversimplification, the racial myth had an irresistible psychological appeal to the masses. It was within the grasp of the lowest intellect. It helped to release the subconscious inferiority complex created in the masses by the defeat of 1918. Mr. Everyman discovered that, although economically poor, he was racially pure. The "Aryan" was lifted above at least one section of the people, and the most envied at that—the Jews—as well as over the neighboring "races" whose land he coveted.

PRACTICAL CONSEQUENCES OF THE RACIAL MYTH

(a) *In Foreign Policy.* The practical consequences of the concepts of nation and race were the political postulate of uniting all peoples of German blood and race ("racial comrades") with the mother country. Under this sign

---

[1] The racial myth is not an original discovery of the National Socialists. It appears, in a more spiritual and transcendental manner, in Fichte, the German patriot-philosopher at the time of Napoleon, to reappear, after the exact science of biology in the nineteenth century had little use for it, in the popularized cultural anthropology of the Frenchman Count Gobineau, and of the naturalized German of English descent Houston Stewart Chamberlain, whose book, "The Foundations of the Nineteenth Century," Hitler swallowed hook, line, and sinker. The racial doctrine was fully expounded by its pontiff, Alfred Rosenberg, in his book (1925): "The Mythus of the Twentieth Century."

[2] The term "Aryan" was used before only as a term of linguistics.

the "homecoming" of the Saarlanders, the Austrians, Sudetenlanders, Memel-landers, Danzigers, was accomplished. The "call of the blood" furnished the convincing argument for German aggression.

However, beginning with the rape of Czechoslovakia, the racial myth was replaced by a novel mythology, the need for "living space" (*Lebensraum*), which utilized skillfully popularized political geography (*Geopolitik*) for the purposes of power politics. By virtue of its racial superiority, the German master race was entitled, by history and destiny, to rule supremely over the inferior races of Central and Eastern Europe. Next to the Jews caught in the trap of the Third Reich, the hapless Czechs and the Poles were the first to be-come the laboratory tests in political vivisection. Thus the racial myth served the claims of expanding the living space into "Greater Germany." Living space, as the sequel to race and nation, characterized the second phase of Germany's bid for world power.

(b) *In Internal Policy.* The basic assumption of the holiness of the na-tional soil became the motivation for far-reaching and, on the whole, sound agricultural reforms, leading, through a vast and complex legislation, to the creation of middle-sized farms, permanently assigned to a racially and pro-fessionally qualified farmer's family.[3] Furthermore, the racial myth served for introducing important measures of eugenics and for the improvement of na-tional health. Despite the uncertainty of the underlying biological and anthro-pological theories, commendable measures to promote national hygiene were subsequently enacted.[4] A vicious innovation, however, was a law preventing reproduction by persons afflicted with allegedly hereditary diseases.[5] A health tribunal decided whether a person complained against was to be subjected to sterilization or, from 1935, to castration. These measures could be taken against the will of the person affected. Mental diseases, as well as physical de-fects and deformities, entailed sterilization. The revolting harshness of the law and the excessive arbitrariness of the lower courts evoked much bitterness.[6]

Finally, the folkish dogma and the racial myth were cause, pretext, and jus-tification for the extermination of the Jews. First deprived of their civic and professional rights (1933), thereafter (1935), by the infamous Nuremberg legislation,[7] of their honor and recognition as human beings, subsequently (1938) despoiled of their property and the opportunities to make a living, they were finally liquidated [8] in the gas chambers of the extermination factories

---

[3] *Erbhofgesetz* of September 29, 1933 (RGB. I, p. 685).

[4] *Erbgesundheitsgesetz* of October 18, 1935 (RGB. I, p. 1246).

[5] Law "for the prevention of hereditarily afflicted progeny," of July 14, 1933 (RGB. I, p. 529).

[6] About 200,000 persons were sterilized; about three million earmarked were saved by the later doctors' scarcity. However, during the war the regime killed off the inmates of insane asylums and hospitals to save food, through medical personnel oblivious of the Hippocratic oath.

[7] Act for the Protection of German Blood and German Honor, and Reich Citizen Act, both of September 15, 1935 (RGBl. I, pp. 1146, 1147), followed by an endless stream of "executory ordinances."

[8] The "legal" basis for the "final solution" was a decree of July 1, 1943 (RGB. I, p. 372) which withdrew cases affecting Jews from the courts and assigned them for discretionary action to the Gestapo.

—German Jews as well as those dragged away from their homelands abroad which the Nazis had overrun. Here the National Socialist program was fulfilled to the letter. About four million were destroyed in concentration camps, about two million killed elsewhere, though not without heroic resistance as in the ghetto of Warsaw (1943). Of some 650,000 Jews in Germany less than one-half could save themselves by emigration before 1939. After unconditional surrender only 11,000 had survived this unprecedented gonocide.

THE NATIONAL SOCIALIST PARTY

LEGAL FOUNDATION OF THE ONE–PARTY STATE

The legal bases for the establishment of the one-party State were the Ordinance of the Reich President of February 28, 1933, suspending civil rights, the Enabling Act, authorizing the Government to overrule the Constitution by simple Government decree, and the statute "concerning the formation of political parties" of July, 1933,[9] declaring the NSDAP the only political Party. The legal capstone of the complete amalgamation of State and Party was the statute "on the unity of Party and State" of December, 1933.[10] By this enactment the threefold divisions of State, Party, and people were fused together into one indissoluble unit. The NSDAP, the only permitted political organization as "the bearer of the State idea," became a state within the State. The State machinery was delivered into the hands of the Party hierarchy. The Party members were accorded many privileges exempting them from the common law. On the other hand, they were assigned special duties, violations of which were punishable by special party courts legally recognized as judicial authorities of the State.[11]

ORGANIZATION OF THE NATIONAL SOCIALIST PARTY

(a) **Structural Organization.** In the set-up of the National Socialist Party, the so-called "structural groups" (*Gliederung*) are to be distinguished from the "affiliated associations" (*angeschlossene Verbaende*). The first class could be considered the core and center of the actual controlling machinery. Among the "structural groups" proper—eight in all—were: the SA (Storm Troopers); the SS (Elite Guards), mainly the huge police force of the regime; the National Socialist Motor and Flying Corps; the Hitler Youth; the National Socialist Students' Association; and the Women's Organization. The "affiliated associations," nine in all, embraced the associations of public officials, physicians, lawyers, technicians, teachers, university teachers, and, most important of all in numbers and influence, the German Labor Front, successor of the trade unions. But the truly totalitarian range of the NSDAP emerges from the number and importance of the so-called Party-supervised organizations and those groups which were formed for carrying out Party policies, without for-

[9] *Gesetz über die Neubildung politischer Parteien,* of July 14, 1933 (RGB. I, p. 479).
[10] *Gesetz über die Einheit von Partei und Staat,* of December 1, 1933 (RGB. I, p. 1016).
[11] Ordinance of the Fuehrer, of March 29, 1935 (RGB. I, p. 502).

mally being integrated into the NSDAP. Among the latter were the Chamber of Culture controlling the media of public opinion and mass communications and the vast array of more or less camouflaged organizations for infiltration abroad.

In addition, of course, the Party included the individual party members. Exact membership figures were never published; but the master files discovered after the collapse revealed that, all told, more than nine million people were enrolled in the Party proper as dues-paying members.

The individual Party member, if—as a rule—he had an occupation, was under the double control of the Party and of the Party-controlled professional group to which he belonged. One who was fortunate enough to stay out of the Party was subject to control of the Party officials who ran his professional organization.

The apex of the Party pyramid was the Central Directorate of the NSDAP (*Oberste Reichsleitung*). Its functions were twofold: On the one hand, it took charge of the actual management of Party affairs, such as treasury, membership discipline, racial indoctrination, propaganda. On the other, it constituted a Party cabinet as an authentic counterpart of the Reich Government, duplicating practically all ministries of the latter (for example, foreign affairs, administration of justice, education). This relatively small group of twenty or thirty men of the "inner circle," whose names were next to unknown outside Germany, actually ruled, under the Deputy Leader of the NSDAP, the nation. The Reich Cabinet proper merely executed the policies of the Party directorate to which only a few of the cabinet members ever belonged. The majority, and the most powerful among them, rarely held a State position.

The system became even more complex by the private staffs and departments some of the leaders maintained for themselves, employing a huge and constantly increasing army of jobholders and beneficiaries. These offices, sections, departments, institutions, groups, and organizations were interrelated with and subordinated to one another in the most mysterious ways, constantly shifting according to the game of power politics of the empire builders and favorites of the exalted ruler whose secret of power, perhaps, was the maintenance of crisscross controls and overlapping jurisdictions. One could as well try to describe an antheap as the NSDAP in operation. Yet the amazing fact was that this elaborate chaos worked and it is only fair to say that not a few among the scores of Party bosses were first-rate organizers with business ability and administrative talent.

(b) *Territorial Organization.* The territorial organization took its cue from the military cadres of the army. The "old" territory of the Reich was divided into (after 1942) forty-two Party districts (*Gaue*), increased by the newly established *Gaue* of Austria, of the Sudetenland, and of Bohemia and Moravia. Party organizations of German nationals existed, in more or less secrecy, in all foreign countries where the local authorities were lenient enough to tolerate them. On the highest level of the Party officials, who as a group formed a closely knit hierarchy of Party functionaries (*Amtswalter*), were the Party district leaders (*Gauleiter*), second in influence and power only to the bigwigs at the center and, without exception, trusted Party bosses from the ranks of the "old fighters." On the next lower level followed the regional subdivisions of each *Gau*, called *Kreis*, corresponding to the county and headed by a regional Party leader (*Kreisleiter*). The *Kreis* again was subdivided into the local Party groups (*Ortsgruppe*), which existed in each city, town, village, and hamlet, again staffed by a host of paid Party professionals. In the towns the local group was again split into numerous "cells" and "blocks." The official of the latter, the Blockwarden (*Blockwart*), became the most effective instrument of control, espionage, and denunciation through which the regime held the individual in its grip. Only those familiar with the officiousness, rudeness, and corruption of European janitors can evaluate the totalitarian aspect of this official intrusion into private life.

THE PARTY CONGRESS

In September the Party Congress (*Parteitag*) took place in Nuremberg, the last time in 1938. It served at the same time as a Party convention and an official State ceremony, used by Hitler for important announcements of internal and foreign policy. Huge masses of frenzied participants and spectators —the latter performers no less than the others—created the proper setting for Hitler's pontifical revelations, imbued with a weird and pagan ritualism which few people were able to resist. The stagecraft of the mammoth rallies, the fanaticism of the masses, the banners, marchers, shouters, the circus element and the melodrama woven into it, Hitler's personal performances—miracles of physical endurance—all contributed to the atmosphere of delirious and calculated mass-emotionalism, which may be likened to the religious hysteria of the fanatical Moslem crowds in the forbidden City of Mecca.

"PHILOSOPHY" OF THE PARTY

According to National Socialist doctrine, the Party was an integration of the "trinity of State, movement, and people" into the "movement State" (*Bewegungsstaat*). In order to make these rather cryptic statements more palatable, the doctrine ascribed to the Party four separate though interrelated tasks: (a) The movement educates the people and evokes in them the consciousness of being a political nation with a special mission for which duty and sacrifice are instilled into the masses. (b) The movement conveys to and interprets for the people the proper "world outlook" (*Voelkische Weltanschauung*). (c) The movement devotes itself to the all-important task of selecting and training the future leaders, character being more essential for leadership than professional or bureaucratic knowledge. (d) All three tasks culminate in the fourth and highest: the movement incorporates the political will of the people.

This romantic rigmarole beclouded the simple fact that the one-party system guaranteed the *status quo* of power to the Party elite which, by creating jobs, by arousing mass-emotionalism, and, last but not least, by spreading terror, maintained and increased its hold over the people. Moreover, the Party as such was sovereign and exempt from State control within its own sphere. Party members, in particular "old fighters," were given preferential treatment in obtaining employment and lucrative positions. The Party as a whole and all its officers and members were surrounded by an impregnable legislative armor of protection against attacks and even criticism. The immense Party property, covering whole city quarters, was tax-exempt.

PARTICIPATION OF THE PARTY IN STATE ACTIVITIES

While the Party did not brook interference within its spheres of action, it participated officially in various ways in the actual administration of the State. An ingenious device for the legalization of the spoils system was that of making a Party official the incumbent of a State office. This expedient of "personal union" allowed the penetration of the State by National Socialist spirit and prevented the professional bureaucracy from entrenching itself in the civil service against Party influence. The leading Party boss of the district (*Gauleiter*) was regularly also the leading political official in the government and administration of the *Laender* (Reich Regents, members of the *Laender* governments, Prussian Provincial Governors). Moreover, at the top, leading men of the Party hierarchy occupied key positions in the Reich Government. Such cumulation of offices carried with it also the advantage of accumulated salaries. This, and revenue drawn from universal and unashamed corruption, accounted for the luxury of the new ruling class and its female retinue, all of them a few years ago penniless white-collar workers, retired army officers, or unemployed intellectuals.

Furthermore, the Party participated in the appointive power. The Deputy-Leader of the Party had to pass on all appointments which Hitler had not reserved for himself.[12] No leading official of Reich or *Land* could obtain appointment unless his loyalty was attested by the Party. Similarly, the Party invaded the dominion of communal government. Under the Municipal Government Act of 1935 [13] the mayor (*Buergermeister*) and the associates of the mayor (*Beigeordnete*) were appointed by the Reich Minister of the Interior or, respectively, according to the size of the municipality, by the government of the *Land*. For special interests of the Party, the "Delegate Commissioner of the National Socialist Party" was appointed in each town by the Deputy-Leader of the Party. Local government became as Party-infested as all other phases of public life.

The statute book, of course, does not reveal the extra-legal influence of the party officials on the conduct of civil administration. The Party claimed and exercised the unwritten right to supervise and control the entire administration, and it even usurped administrative activities of the regular officials. The whole fabric of routine administration with which the common man comes most in

---

[12] See Edict of the Fuehrer of September 24, 1935 (REG. I, p. 1203); and also Article 31 of the Public Officials Act, of January 26, 1937 (RGB. I, p. 39).

[13] *Deutsche Gemeindeordnung,* of January 30, 1935 (RGB. I, p. 49).

contact in his workaday life was visibly rotting under the mildew of nepotism and favoritism, through interference of the local Party bosses with orderly processes of administration.

During the war, the Party had its full share in the looting and exploitation of the occupied countries. When at long last in 1943 total mobilization of all resources was undertaken in earnest, it was the Party and not the military or civilian authorities which squeezed the last ounce of resistance against the enemy out of the exhausted people.

However, the impression gained, during the war, from outside that the civil service, under the pressure of the one-party State, had become as atomized as other groups was not verified by the evidence obtained upon unconditional surrender. Vast as were the inroads of Party influence on administration, and subservient to the regime as had become the professional officials, the civil service was, on the whole, able to preserve its identity as a group, and many of its members their personal integrity. After the collapse of 1945, therefore, it was only natural that both professional ability and class solidarity of the civil service reasserted themselves and, in due course, regained the influence and power they had possessed under the Empire and the Republic.

HITLER YOUTH

National Socialism realized at an early date that he who holds the youth holds its future. The Party itself was, from the outset, a movement of young enthusiasts. The Hitler Youth was converted in 1936 into a State institution under Party control and management [14] as a "structural group" (*Gliederung*), headed by the "Reich Youth Leader" (Baldur von Schirach). Beginning at the age of six, boys and girls were conscripted into its various formations, where they remained up to the age of 18.[15] During their tender and most impressionable years, boys and girls were under military training and were educated to a "Spartan life." They were drilled in the world outlook of the Party; taught adulation of the "Fuehrer" and the other Party heroes; and imbued with the racial myth and the tenets of German superiority and mission. Few parents dared to balance Nazi teachings by a more liberal and less mechanical education at home.

But this seemingly most subtle power instrument was blunted. Long before the war the intellectual stultification and militarization of education began to produce negative results among the youth of all classes. During the war the Hitler Youth lost importance. After the war it was found that, on the whole, this infernal device of indoctrination had left few if any indelible traces on the mind of the younger generation. In their attempts at instilling democratic habits into the Germans the Allies, therefore, would have been well-advised to concentrate on the younger generation from the start as was done by the French and the Soviets.

[14] Law on the Hitler Youth, of December 1, 1936 (RGB. I, p. 993).
[15] The subdivisions were between 10 and 14 years, the "Young Folk" (*Jungvolk*) and the "Young Maidens" for boys and girls, respectively; from 14 to 18, the Hitler Youth, for boys, and the Bund of German Girls.

NATIONAL SOCIALIST ADMINISTRATION OF JUSTICE

THE CONCEPT OF LAW

Administration of justice, to subject the German people to the regime, was another instrumentality of political power. The "Fuehrer" was declared the supreme source of law, binding judges and courts. The law was the "order of the 'Fuehrer' " (*Fuehrerbefehl*); and the "order of the 'Fuehrer' " was the law. Law was no longer an impartial concept of justice, but must serve the "folkish ordering of life" (*voelkische Lebensordnung*). Judges and judicial officers were to serve the interests of the regime, or, in the words of one of its most wicked slogans: "Law is what is useful to the German Nation." Concentration of powers in the hands of the "Fuehrer" and the Reich Government was incompatible with independence of justice. When it happened that the courts, still entangled in "liberalistic" concepts of law, questioned the validity of governmental policies conflicting with the existing common law, the Government sternly repressed such residues of independence by withdrawing whole classes of cases from the ordinary courts.[16]

THE SUBJUGATION OF THE BENCH

The legislative step for weeding out the "politically unreliable" members of the judicial profession was taken as early as April, 1933, by a Government decree, paradoxically styled "for the restoration of the professional service," [17] under which "officials who, in view of previous political activities, do not offer the guarantee of defending the national State without reservations, may be dismissed from service." Not only were many known Socialist, democratic, or liberal judges and public prosecutors retired in due course, but the threat of dismissal hung like the sword of Damocles over those remaining in active service.[18] The vacancies were filled with partisans eager for promotion, and later with newcomers who had been subjected to National Socialist indoctrination. It should be noted, however, that not only the Supreme Court (*Reichsgericht*) resisted, to some extent and for some time, complete Nazification; also a sizable number of non-Nazi judges in both the lower and the higher brackets succeeded in staying in office. The Nazi comb was not fine enough to exclude all opponents of the regime from appointment; and the overwhelming majority of the respectable members of the bar neither joined nor professionally supported the regime. It is also fair to point to what has been aptly called "the dual state." [19] in the administration of justice, that is,

[16] This occurred twice in vitally important matters: first, when claims for "illegal acts committed in connection with the National Socialist revolution," were cut off (see law of December 13, 1934, RGB. I, p. 1235); a second time when the courts dared to side with the Protestant Church against the totalitarian State (see law of June 26, 1935, RGB. I, p. 774). Later, the courts had no longer the courage to resist.

[17] *Gesetz zur Wiederherstellung des Berufsbeamtentums,* of April 7, 1933 (RGB. I, p. 175).

[18] Public Officials Act (*Deutsches Beamtengesetz*) of January 26, 1937 (RGB. I, p. 39, see Par. 171), which, after expiration of the statute of April, 1933, took the precaution of continuing the provision for removing "unreliable" judges.

[19] See Ernst Fraenkel, *The Dual State,* New York, 1941.

that, as a rule, in the adjudication of civil cases without political implications, the average judge maintained the standards of objectivity and impartiality. In the later stage of the war, however, the last residues of judicial nonconformity were stamped out by renewed purges, Hitler's assumption of supreme judicial powers (announced in his Reichstag address of April 22, 1942), and the advance instruction issued by the Minister of Justice (Thierack) to the presiding judges as to sentence and punishment to be meted out in all major criminal cases.

CRIMINAL LAW

Criminal law, however, was completely perverted by Nazi techniques and interpretation. Special courts (*Sondergericht*) were created to deal with attacks on the regime and treasonable activities. The dreaded People's Court (*Volksgerichtshof*),[20] permanently established in 1936, was a revolutionary tribunal of the star chamber type. Only two of the five judges were trained in the law; the majority of three were lay assessors appointed from among the Elite Guard and the Party hierarchy. These courts succeeded in terrorizing public opinion by severity of punishments, secrecy of proceedings, and abrogation of the procedural rights of the accused. Only the crimson-red posters eventually announced that the convicted had died under the axe of the executioner.

While comparatively few inroads into the existing system of common civil law, except those motivated by the racial myth, were made by National Socialist ideology, criminal law was completely revolutionized. The liberal concept of the reformatory nature of punishment was superseded by the principles of revenge on the part of the State and the determent of future criminal acts. This applied to political crimes proper, the range of which had been enormously extended under the Third Reich,[21] as well as for common crimes. In the fight against what was called "professional criminals" (*Gewohnheitsverbrecher*), custody in concentration camps as well as sterilization was resorted to. "Preventive custody" (*Schutzhaft*), the term for commitment to a concentration camp, was formally legalized by a law of June, 1935,[22] which also introduced retroactive punishment without law (*nulla poena sine lege*). Punishment could be meted out for an act which the court deemed in conflict with the "healthy sentiment of the people," even if no statute authorizing the punishment had been violated. Justice as an instrumentality of political power was thus degraded to a handmaiden of a political party.

PROFESSIONAL HONOR COURTS

Finally, the so-called Honor Courts were created in connection with the new social stratification of Germany into professional associations or "estates" (*Staende*). These embraced Trade and Industry, Labor, Crafts, Agriculture,

[20] Law of April 24, 1934 (RGB. I, p. 369).
[21] Special mention should be made of the legislation for protecting the "purity of the race," designed to prevent sexual intercourse between Jews and "Jewish mixed offspring," and "Aryans," according to the Nuremberg laws of September 15, 1935 (RGB. I, pp. 1146, 1147).
[22] Law of June 28, 1935 (RGB. I, p. 839).

and Culture in general. The exercise of a profession was considered a public trust. For the sake of a closer control and supervision in the interests of the totalitarian State, all members of the same professional activity were organized by statute into professional associations or guilds, membership in which was mandatory for the exercise of the profession. To each professional group or association an Honor Court was attached, which punished violations of the professional code by its members. Most conspicuous among them were the Social Honor Courts, established in 1934 by the Labor Code, the fundamental statute for organizing capital and labor under the Labor Front and for regulating the relations between the plant owner ("leader of the enterprise") and his workers and employees ("followers").[23] Among other professional Honor Courts may be mentioned those for the press (editors, reporters, and journalists); physicians; attorneys-at-law; business men; artisans; and even huntsmen.

THE END OF THE RULE OF LAW

The organization and administration of justice under the Third Reich may be summed up by the statement that it attained its political ends by completely destroying the rule of law and by abolishing the regularized due process of law. Separation of powers, independence of judges, judicial control of administration, impartiality of the civil service, fundamental human rights, and even the certainty of a written constitution—all these elements of the rule of law were overruled by the monocratic omnipotence of the "Fuehrer" and the National Socialist Party.

THE POLICE

LEGAL POSITION AND ORGANIZATION OF THE POLICE

The instrumentality for maintaining political power through coercion was the police, in particular the Political Police (*Geheime Staatspolizei,* commonly known as the Gestapo). The Gestapo, founded in April, 1933, by Goering, was made an independent department of the Prussian Government in November, 1933.[24] In April, 1934, all police forces of the Reich were centralized under Heinrich Himmler.[25] Finally, the Political Police became an independent supreme Reich authority under the orders and instructions only of Himmler as *"Reichsleiter"* [26] who, during the war when Hitler was preoccupied with military matters, rose to be the most powerful figure of the regime and the undisputed master of its internal affairs. The decree especially empowered the Gestapo to demand information from, and to give orders to, other agencies of the State. Actions taken were beyond judicial or administrative control.

The Secret Police as an organization is to be distinguished from the Elite Guard (SS). It is true that all higher officials of the Political Police were at

[23] Law "for ordering of national labor," of January 20, 1934 (RGB. I, p. 45).
[24] Prussian laws of April 26, 1933 (*Gesetzessammlung,* p. 122) and of November 30, 1933 (*ibid.,* p. 413).
[25] When Himmler succeeded Goering, it was a move of Hitler to check the power of Goering.
[26] Prussian decree of February 10, 1936 (*Gesetzessammlung,* p. 21).

the same time officers of the Elite Guard. But the SS, expanding beyond the tasks of the Political Police, grew into the official army of the regime strictly separated from, and in competition with, the *Reichswehr*. The standards of racial purity were particularly rigid for admission. Subjected to an intensified process of indoctrination and animated by unflinching loyalty to Hitler, the *Waffen SS* constituted the Praetorian Cohort of the regime, serving as body-guard for the "Fuehrer" and party oligarchs and as an army in case of civil war. In the later stages of the war the SS Corps were thrown in wherever military emergencies required it.

On the other hand, the Elite Guard executed the orders and policies of the Political Police, and did in general the dirty work, such as running the concentration camps, policing the conquered territories, and keeping the masses of foreign slave labor at bay. The guiding brain of the Political Police, however, was a bureaucracy with little resemblance to the terror it manipulated. They and many members of the related authority of the SD (*Sicherheitsdienst*) were well educated and academically trained gentlemen with an expert knowledge in the specific fields of their activities. Much of the best talent of the younger generation was attracted by such careers—admittedly an extremely capable group of administrators.

ACTIVITIES OF THE POLITICAL POLICE

Empowered, by the law of February, 1936, "to uncover and combat all tendencies and developments inimical to the State, and to take for this end all measures deemed necessary and expedient," the Gestapo grew into a vast machinery, extending its cobweb over the entire nation, dealing with political, economic, and cultural matters as well as with objectives of penological character. By 1940, it had reached the stage where it resembled more a government than an administrative agency.

As an organization the Gestapo was highly bureaucratized. No layer of the population and no section of the people or the party were immune from its interference, the army generals and the members of the Government not exempted. The State was controlled by the Party, but the Party was controlled by the Gestapo. The Political Police became Germany's innermost core of power.

SCIENTIFIC TERROR

Intimidation by physical violence was the calculated technical device of mass control logically resulting from government by coercion, instead of by consent. Since, at least prior to the war, the regime seemed to have inhibitions to wholesale liquidation of the masses of malcontents and suspects, systematized, cold-blooded, all-pervading terror was applied, geared to the experience that man of today, though ready to die, is deeply afraid of physical suffering. Terror served for the defense of the regime, directed against supporters as well as against opponents, effective through arbitrariness in application, suddenness in performance, varied designs of vengeance, helplessness of the victim, and inescapability of execution. Surrounded by spies and informers, turncoats and stool pigeons, zealots and fanatics, the people lived in an atmosphere of vague though ever-present terror. Physical violence was only the application, in individual cases, of the potential violence to which all were exposed. Scientific terror was as much psychological and preventive as physical and retributive.

The concentration camp became a myth of horrible reality. Since the Mongol storm of the Middle Ages, no such orgy of legalized sadism has despoiled the human race. While in the initial years the regime preferred mortification and humiliation by beating and torturing to killing (though torture frequently resulted in killing), flushed by victory it proceeded to apply the blueprint of its racial mythology against the "inferior" races—Jews, Gypsies, Poles, Slavs, and slaves in general. The concentration camps graduated to the status of death factories; the prisoners of war camps became the mills of death. Of more than fifty concentration camps existing, the most notorious became Dachau, Belsen, Buchenwald, Ravensbrueck, Maidanek, and, that execrable name, Auschwitz. It has been estimated that between 1933 and 1945 about 7.8 million people—Germans and men and women from all countries which the Nazis had befouled—went through the inferno. All told, not more than 600,000 survived. Of those killed only an infinitely small fraction had committed a crime by the standards of civilized justice; all the others died because of their race, religion, political conviction, or because of the private whim of a man in power in a lawless society.

CHAPTER XV

THE FALL OF THE THIRD REICH

GERMANY AND WORLD WAR II

Almost from its inception the Third Reich had strained every muscle on preparedness for the coming war. One by one the alternatives to war, offered with more than generosity by the policy of appeasement, were discarded by Hitler. Following the program he had announced in *Mein Kampf,* he was resolved with unswerving singleness of purpose to obtain a redistribution of the riches of the world in which the lion's share would fall to Germany. After having absorbed, by warlike pressure, Austria (March 12, 1938), the Sudetenland (September 30, 1939) and Bohemia and Moravia (March 15, 1939), and having regained Memel (March 22, 1939) Germany went to war with Britain and France over the reincorporation of Danzig and the destruction of Poland (September, 1939). In 1940 and 1941 Germany attacked, overran, and conquered Denmark and Norway (April, 1940), Luxembourg, Belgium, Holland, and France (May–June, 1940), Greece and Yugoslavia (April– May, 1941). The USSR with whom Hitler had concluded a nonaggression treaty (August 23, 1939) was invaded on June 22, 1941. After Pearl Harbor, Germany declared war on the United States (December, 1941). In due course she found herself at war with practically the entire world. The fortunes of war turned with El Alamein (October, 1943) and Stalingrad (1943). Driven out from North Africa, contained in Italy (1943), and forced by the Red Army to retreat in Russia, Hitler was compressed, after the Normandy landing of the Allies (June, 1944) between the two gigantic pincers of the East and the West. By the end of 1944 the Soviet and the Western armies had reached the German borders and began to invade Germany proper. Escaping capture by the Soviet army closing in on his last refuge, Hitler on April 30, 1945, committed suicide in the underground bunker of the Reich Chancellery in Berlin.

Like most dictatorships in history, Hitler's Third Reich did not fall by its own weight. Faithful to its intrinsic law it ended in war and defeat.

A NOTE ON HITLER

Hitler's personality and the achievements and failures of the Third Reich which he personified, will remain controversial for a long time to come. Although it may be premature for an unbiased appraisal, it seems safe to say that he was less of the God the German state mysticism made the German people believe, and a greater man than Allied war propaganda was willing to admit. Psychopathological traits were present from the beginning, at times to the point of outright insanity, but, at the same time, not being excluded and even conditioned by abnormalcy, there were genuine leadership qualities, and a particular gift, amounting occasionally to a sixth sense, of international manipulation by instinct, all the more surprising in view of his incomprehension of foreign peoples. To these must be added considerable talents in military science (whatever its merits), based on an exceptionally retentive memory, which the *ex post facto* criticism of the military professionals cannot minimize who seek in Hitler's "intervention" an alibi for their own ineptitude. But perhaps his greatest asset was the uncanny and utterly cynical insight into the psycho-emotional structure of modern mass society. His greatest deficiency, however, consisted in the inability to distinguish between personal obsessions or stereotypes and objective realities which induced him to underrate, as it is German habit, absolute values governing the life of the State no less than of the individual. Like all dictators his mental capacities deteriorated sharply with the length of his exercise of absolute power and the pressure of the war. Since he was wholly devoid of morality to support him in reverses of fortune and relied on "intuition" rather than on precepts of rationality, he was, like other psychopaths, unable to adjust himself to changing situations. If what makes the great statesman are vision and moderation, he was possessed by the former and lacked the latter. That the circumstances of his meteoric rise from the depth of the people to Napoleonic heights, his spectacular political, diplomatic, and military successes, together with the mystical fog shrouding his personal habits and his end, will result, in due course, in the emergence of a potent Hitler legend, few historians, conversant with the causation and the ingredients of political mythology, will doubt.

SECTION ONE. *INTRODUCTION*

1918 AND 1945

After her defeat in World War I Germany's international situation conformed to the traditional pattern. Armistice and demobilization were followed
by the acceptance of a peace treaty negotiated among the victors and ratified,
within less than nine months, by German governmental authorities legally
constituted. Germany never lost the status of a sovereign state and remained
a recognized member of the community of nations. Nor was her internal self-
determination ever impaired. Adopting a form of government of their own
choosing, the German people went through the traditional stages of establishing a democratic republic. Throughout they never ceased to possess their own
government. In line with international law the victors refrained from interfering with, or even influencing, her internal affairs. German territory had not
even been scratched by the war. Subsequently the financial obligations imposed by the peace treaty were discharged mainly by default, most of the territorial losses were recouped, and, by her resurgent economic power, Germany
rose again to the rank of a great power.

After Germany's total defeat in World War II—the classical example of
debellatio—her territory was occupied by the military forces of the victorious
United States, the Soviet Union, the United Kingdom, and France. Considerable parts of her Eastern provinces were annexed, without the formality of a
peace treaty, by Poland and the Soviets. As an organized state Germany had
ceased to exist. No indigenous government on the central or state levels survived. The shadow government of Admiral Doenitz, established in Flensburg
(Schleswig-Holstein) as successor or caretaker cabinet under the terms of
what purported to be Hitler's last will, having served its purpose of issuing
credentials of the military representatives for the acts of unconditional surrender, was arrested (May 23, 1945) by British Military Police. Most major
cities had been shattered into heaps of rubble and agglomerations of empty
brick shells. Millions of Displaced Persons, transferred to Germany during
the war as prisoners or slave labor, roamed the countryside in search of food
and tramped the roads towards their own country. Millions of Germans, evacuated from their bombed-out cities or shifted to war factories, tried to regain

their homes. The normal administrative services were obliterated by the devastations of total war. Factories had stopped work. Only the farmers in the villages untouched by war went after their seasonal chores. The leaderless mass of the German people accepted defeat and occupation with an apathy bordering on stupor. Never in the history of man had a nation great and powerful only yesterday, been plunged into so total a moral, economic, and political chaos.

Six years after the cessation of hostilities, no peace treaty has been concluded. Germany is still occupied by the foreign powers. The former Reich is divided into four zones—American, British, French, Soviet—of occupation, and broken politically into two parts, each with its own government hostile to the other. After the collapse the four powers tried to rule all of Germany by a four-power condominium. When it failed, the United States, Britain, and France, combining their zones, continued to control the Western German State and the Soviets the Eastern State. The foreign powers did not only interfere with the internal affairs of the government-less nation, but their intervention amounted to a complete political tutelage over Germany. The fact that a nation of seventy million people was subjected to foreign rule to such an extent and for such an extended period, is likewise without parallel in modern history. Yet within hardly more than five years, owing to her economic potentialities, her geographical situation, the unbroken vitality of her people, and, last but not least, by virtue of the key position she occupies in the conflict between the East and the West, commonly spoken of as the cold war, Germany today is well advanced on the way to becoming again the fulcrum in the power balance of the world.

GERMAN POLITICAL RECONSTRUCTION AND THE INTERPLAY OF WORLD POLITICS

Of the five wars of aggression Germany had undertaken against her neighbors within seventy-five years, two within living memory had resulted in global conflagrations. Germany's aggressiveness and her lust for aggrandizement were ascribed, not without convincing evidence, to the political habits of a people which prostrated itself before military might, and to a form of government under which the authority of the state was beyond the control of the people. In the seemingly endless chain of German rebellions against a peaceful ordering of international society the last one, the Third Reich, appeared to be merely another of the most terrible manifestations of unbridled militarism and irresponsible power politics. For the world at large, therefore, Germany's integration into a peaceful world seemed dependent on the conversion of the German mind to democratic processes and institutions and the evocation of the sense of political responsibility believed to be innate in every civilized people.

Consequently, if Germany was denied, by the occupying powers, the right of internal self-determination, the departure from a basic principle of international law was justified by the fact that her political structure is of vital importance for the peace of the world. The process of assimilating the German *mores* to a democratic pattern of behavior became known in the Western world as "re-education" in the widest sense of moral, intellectual, social, and political reform. How to achieve these objectives by common policies the four powers could not agree. Each of them, therefore, attempted to recreate that part of Germany under its effective control in its own socio-political image. Instead of being, and remaining, united in the joint effort the West and the East at first used Germany as a laboratory of conflicting ideologies and finally tried to gain "their" Germans as allies against the other in the cold war. Rather than being dealt with on its intrinsic merits the German problem became the focal point of power politics between international Communism and the free world, with the inevitable consequence that Germany, having lost the war, is close to winning the peace.

By 1949 the tug-of-war for the soul and body of Germany resulted in the establishment and the coexistence of two entirely separated and mutually exclusive German states, the German Federal Republic (*Deutsche Bundesrepublik*) in the West, consisting of the three occupation zones under American, British, and French control, and the Soviet-controlled German Democratic Republic (*Deutsche Demokratische Republik*) in the Eastern zone. By the pressure and indoctrination of their foreign masters rather than by their own inclination the Germans themselves developed a split personality unable to agree on the fundamentals of a common future.

It is this bewildering interplay of international and national political forces which renders an unbiased evaluation of Germany's reconstruction since 1945 difficult, and which affects even the mere narrative of events. There is, of course, no lack of information which, in ever-increasing volume, flows from official reports, an unrelenting press and radio coverage, the stream of visitors and, more recently, from the Germans themselves who have regained their articulateness. But not only must the German issue be constantly projected against the background of the international power conflict; in addition, political reconstruction is conducted on different levels—Allied, interzonal, intrazonal, and regional—whose correlation and integration enhance the complexity of the task.

The following discussion will start out with the Allied Control Council, the four-power machinery of government and administration in operation from 1945 to 1948. The second avenue of approach will be the action of Military Government (MG) in each of the four zones and its interrelation with the indigenous German authorities created in each zone on the *Land* or zonal levels. Within this section the American experience with MG has a legitimate priority of the limited space available. Lastly, the discussion will proceed to the establishment of the two larger political entities of the Western and the Eastern German states.

CHAPTER XVI

INTERNATIONAL AGREEMENTS ON GERMANY

INTERNATIONAL AGREEMENTS PRIOR TO MILITARY DEFEAT

Upon the entry of the United States into the war President Roosevelt and his military advisors decided to concentrate the war effort on the defeat of Germany as the leading Axis power. Correspondingly, the international agreements concluded prior to unconditional surrender assigned priority to the victory over Germany.

Of the pre-War declarations the Atlantic Charter (August 14, 1941), that ideal blueprint for a better world—never engrossed on official parchment—referred to Germany only in passing. The famous Article Three, proclaiming "the rights of all free people to choose the form of government under which they will live," subsequently by official interpretations was declared inapplicable to Germany insofar as she would not be permitted to return to a Nazi or militaristic governmental structure. The Declaration of the United Nations (January 1, 1942) bound the signatories not to conclude a separate armistice or peace with Germany or another common enemy. However, a joint Allied policy concerning Germany was slow in the making. The Moscow Conference of the three Foreign Ministers (USA, UK, and USSR) (October 30, November 1, 1943) announced no specific decisions on Germany except a forceful condemnation of German atrocities in conformity with the Allied Declaration on War Crimes (London, January 31, 1942). But it established the European Advisory Commission (with the seat in London), one of the silently most constructive tripartite agencies of the entire war period to which the further study and evolution of post-surrender policies devolved. The division of defeated Germany into two, or, with separate British and American areas, three zones of occupation—with an additional inter-Allied area to serve as the seat of the Allied Control Commission in charge of common German policies—originated in the Big Three Conference in Tehran (November, 1943) and was subsequently fully elaborated by the European Advisory Commission. But the Tehran communique failed to make specific references to German reconstruction. During 1944, though public opinion in America and Britain became increasingly engrossed with both the creation of an international peace organization and the future of Germany after defeat, no common peace strategy could evolve among the Allies.

With the final victory over Nazi Germany within reach, however, the Yalta Conference (February 3–11, 1945) announced concrete plans concerning "doomed Nazi Germany." Germany was to be occupied, in separate zones, by the three powers with an invitation tendered to France to join in a zone of her own. The over-all Allied agency was to be the Central Control Commission, consisting of the four Supreme Commanders with headquarters in Berlin. The broad contours of the post-surrender policies are clearly visible in the following statement:

> It is our inflexible purpose to destroy German militarism and Nazism and to insure that Germany will never again be able to disturb the peace of the world.

It was further emphasized:

> It is not our purpose to destroy the people of Germany; but only when Nazism and militarism have been extirpated will there be hope for a decent life for Germans and a place for them in the community of nations.

Dismemberment of Germany was discussed and not ruled out.

THE AMERICAN ATTITUDE TOWARDS GERMANY

Have the American government and public opinion favored a "harsh peace"? It has been argued that the demand for unconditional surrender [1]— inspired by Grant's demand on Lee and its acceptance under the shadow of the courthouse of Appomattox—hardened German resistance to the bitter end; with generous peace terms offered they would have laid down their arms without the costly invasion. Though this can never be proved or disproved it seems unlikely that the gamblers then in control over a nation as gullible as it was disciplined and, to the very end, believing in the promised "miracle weapons," would have voluntarily delivered themselves into the hands of their enemies. No large-scale internal revolution took place or could reasonably be expected. Unconditional surrender of the "invincible" *Wehrmacht,* therefore, was probably the only way to open the path for rebuilding a peace-minded Germany.

From the start American public opinion was utterly optimistic concerning ultimate victory. Since the entry of the United States into the war, "What to do with Germany?" became the primary concern of many qualified experts and even more of the unqualified. The market was flooded with fool-proof solutions, most of them of ephemeral value. Many were inspired by genuine humanitarianism. Re-education and not revenge was the *leitmotiv*. Proposals ranged from the assumption that the Germans, a mentally sick nation, require careful political therapy, to the postulate that a distinction be made between the "good German people" and "their wicked rulers." The conflicting ap-

[1] The term appeared for the first time officially at the Casablanca Conference of Roosevelt and Churchill (January 19, 1942).

proaches could not fail to have repercussions on the theory of the "collective guilt" of the Germans for the Nazi atrocities.

These widespread discussions served the good purpose of drawing attention to the fact that, differently from previous wars, military victory was not enough, that what would happen after the defeat was as important as defeat itself. That Germany, since Bismarck had begun to create the Reich by blood and iron, had staged five wars of aggression, and that France had been invaded three times within three generations, was counterbalanced by the argument that the Germans, a gifted and resourceful nation, could be taught peaceful integration and eventually be cured of their seemingly congenital lust for aggrandizement. That this goal could not be reached without deep intervention in German affairs was taken for granted. But the American public received next to no guidance from its government which, for a long time, did not have a definite policy, let alone that international agreement on such a policy could be attained.

The situation was highlighted by the so-called Morgenthau Plan submitted by the then Secretary of the Treasury to the Quebec Conference of Roosevelt and Churchill (September 11–16, 1944). Much distorted later as the apex of American vindictiveness, it pleaded the internationalization of the Ruhr, the formation of two separate states to the North and the South, and the conversion of an economic structure top-heavy with the production of capital goods to light and consumer goods industries commensurate with a greater emphasis on agriculture. The concept of "pastoralizing" Germany, psychologically and economically unsound, never became official American policy. But it helped to focus attention on the importance of German heavy industry and the need of permanently reducing the war-making potential if a repeat performance of German aggression was to be forestalled. In this sense it influenced the decisions concerning the prohibition of certain industries and limitations imposed on others in the early policy directives of the United States [2] which were to guide MG policies in the period after surrender. Through these directives the concept of drastically limiting the German war-making potential was carried into the Potsdam Declaration of August, 1945, and the various "level of industry" plans resulting therefrom.

INTERNATIONAL AGREEMENTS
AFTER UNCONDITIONAL SURRENDER

Immediately after the unconditional surrender of the armed forces of Germany at Rheims (May 7) and in Berlin (May 8, 1945) the total occupation of the territory of Germany by the Allied armies was completed. By July the withdrawal of the Anglo-American forces from the areas conquered east of the Elbe and from Thuringia was effectuated in conformity with the Allied Agreements in the European Advisory Commission and Yalta. At the same

[2] Command Directive on Germany Prior to Defeat or Surrender, April 28, 1944, and the famous JCS 1067/3, the Directive to Commander-in-Chief of U.S. Forces of Occupation regarding MG in Germany, April 28, 1945.

time the French zone of occupation, carved out from territory heretofore held by American forces, was transferred to the French (July 10, 1945). Before the end of July, Western military and civilian personnel had moved into Berlin.

Of the three Statements issued by the four Powers on June 5, 1945, the first, the "Declaration regarding the defeat of Germany and the assumption of supreme authority with regard to Germany," proclaimed that the governments of the UK, USA, USSR, and France, since "there is no German government capable of accepting responsibility for the maintenance of order, the administration of the country and the compliance with the requirements of the victorious powers," assumed, through their Commanders-in-Chief, supreme authority over Germany. Though annexation was explicitly ruled out, the Powers claimed the right of "determining the boundaries of Germany and of any part thereof and the status of Germany or any area at present being part of Germany." The remainder of the document dealt primarily with the requirements of military surrender and the disposal of the German armed forces and military installations.

By the second Statement of June 5, 1945, "on zones of occupation," Germany with her frontiers as of December 31, 1937 (that is, prior to the *Anschluss* of Austria) was divided into the four zones of occupation,[3] each under a Commander-in-Chief, and a fifth "zone," consisting of the area of Greater Berlin, subdivided into four districts (later, in distinction from the zones, styled sectors) with an interallied governing authority for which the Russian term *Kommandatura* became generally accepted.

The third document of the same day on "control machinery in Germany" dealt with the Control Council (CC), the four-power agency intended to exercise joint control over Germany as a whole. Consisting of the four Commanders-in-Chief its decisions were to be unanimous, the oblique if current formula to denote that each Power could veto proposals of the other three. This arrangement was to remain in force during an unspecified period following unconditional surrender. The CC was to "ensure appropriate uniformity of action among the Commanders-in-Chief in their respective zones of occupation and will reach agreed decisions on the chief questions affecting Germany as a whole."

---

[3] For details on these and other internal territorial changes, see *infra,* pp. 501 ff. The zone division had been decided on in Tehran and was elaborated by the European Advisory Commission. It has been asked why this method of occupation was chosen instead of a joint administration by all four powers over all of Germany. Considering the divergencies of administrative techniques and occupation aims of the East and the West and the difficulties arising in the two joint governing bodies, the CC and the Berlin *Kommandatura,* the decision seems fully justified.

CHAPTER XVII

THE POTSDAM DECLARATION

The last and most vital of all interallied agreements was concluded at the Potsdam meeting of the Big Three—Stalin, Truman, Churchill-Attlee,[1]—contained in the "Report on the Tripartite Conference of Potsdam" (August 2, 1945). Though lacking legal precision in places, the document is more detailed and more carefully drafted than previous international agreements. Subsequently it became, at least for some time, the "bible" of the Western Powers, and Soviet insistence on its terms at a time when the cold war between East and West had rendered it practically invalid, seems to indicate that the Russians likewise considered it workable.

While the Potsdam agreement contained a number of regulations of general importance,[2] its core (in Part III) are the detailed regulations concerning Germany during the period of Allied control, in execution of the Yalta Conference decisions. Political principles are neatly separated from those referring to economics.

POLITICAL PRINCIPLES

The political principles underlying the occupation policies were to be applied by the four Commanders-in-Chief jointly, organized as CC, for matters affecting Germany as a whole, "to ensure a uniform treatment of the German population throughout." As to content they can be summarized conveniently by the famous four "D's," to wit: demilitarization (and disarmament); denazification; democratization; and decentralization (III A [3]–[6]). These occupation aims are substantially interrelated, since democratization is conditioned on the accomplishment of the other three postulates. Understandably, denazification was given prominence; it implied the destruction of the Nazi Party and its affiliated and supervised organizations; dissolution of Nazi in-

---

[1] After the British general elections of July 15, 1945, Churchill's place at the conference table was taken by the leader of the victorious Labor Party, Clement Attlee.

[2] Such as the establishment of the Council of Foreign Ministers (including China) on a permanent basis primarily "to continue the necessary preparatory work for the peace settlements," policy stipulations with regard to Austria, Poland, Rumania, Bulgaria, and Hungary and concerning the international organization.

stitutions and prevention of their revival in whatever form. Militarism and Nazism were used quasi-interchangeably. Denazification, as the negative, and democratization as the positive, aspect of reform were to be applied, without being confined to them, to specifically named fields of public life, such as the judicial system and the laws; elimination of Nazi personnel from leading positions in public office and positions of responsibility in important private undertakings; and in education. War criminals were to be brought to justice. Decentralization of the political structure and development of local responsibility seemingly were conceived as the keys of democratization proper. While local self-government on democratic principles and in particular through elective councils on the regional, provincial, and *Land* levels were "to be restored as rapidly as consistent with military security," for the time being no central German government was to be established. However, certain administratively essential agencies for finance, transport, communications, foreign trade, and industry were definitely envisaged.

ECONOMIC PRINCIPLES

These were basically geared to the elimination of the German war potential. Allied controls over economic life were to operate only to the extent necessary: negatively, for the purposes of demilitarization and the destruction of the war-making potential, positively to assure a production level necessary for the maintenance of German living standards not exceeding the average of those in other European countries (excluding the United Kingdom, with presumably higher, and the Soviet Union, with presumably lower, living standards). During the period of occupation Germany was to be treated as a single economic unit.[3] These basic occupation aims were believed attainable by decentralizing German economy through breaking up the cartels, syndicates, trusts, and other monopolistic arrangements considered instrumental to excessive concentration of economic power, another Potsdam key word revealing the American occupation philosophy. In the reorganization of German economic life, primary emphasis was to be attached to the development of agriculture and other peaceful industries. Due attention was also paid to the reparations issue agreed on in principle at Yalta, with the proviso that those exacted should not affect the minimum required to allow Germany to exist without external assistance. All these provisions were essentially predicated on a country which for generations had existed in economic union and which could not be expected to be broken up in a number of self-supporting and self-contained economic units.

[3] While the requirement of treating Germany as an economic whole may have been politically logical at the time, subsequently doubts arose as to whether this supposition was actually supported by economic facts. A study of the United Nations Economic Commission for Europe (see *New York Times* of January 18, 1950) came to the conclusion that, while the Eastern zone and especially the Berlin industries, were inter-regionally dependent on Western Germany for production and markets, the Western zones before the war were linked closer to Europe than to the Eastern zone. In retrospect it may have been politically advantageous rather to allow the economic control of each zone individually than to insist on the concept of treating "Germany as a whole."

GENERAL EVALUATION OF THE POTSDAM DECLARATION

The Potsdam agreement constituted a pragmatic effort to deal with a unique situation for which the traditional law of nations offered little guidance. Within the context of this document, for the political ideals and economic policies of the three major powers—France, at that time under the leadership of General de Gaulle, was not a participant—common denominators were believed to have been found. Certainly discrepancies were hidden in the semantics used, but there is no proof that an agreement was not honestly intended by all signatories. For the conciliation of subsequently emergent power politics no formula could have been devised in advance.

Nonetheless, the basic fallacies of Potsdam lie, first, in the assumption that, by providing for the technical devices of democracy its moral values automatically would be created. Secondly, the primarily American-inspired equation of political decentralization with political democracy proved tangibly erroneous. Thirdly, the economic solutions attempted fell short of realities by a wide margin. The aim of German self-sufficiency could never have been reached without foreign assistance, particularly considering the influx of the millions of ethnic Germans from Poland, Czechoslovakia, Hungary, and elsewhere into the truncated country that the very same Potsdam agreement legalized (XIII). Thus, politically and economically, the Potsdam agreement was beyond practical realization even if all participants had faithfully adhered to it. That these intrinsic defects subsequently were caught in the maelstrom of the global power conflict between East and West was merely an aggravating factor in the ultimate failure. To the Germans Potsdam was bound to become the Versailles of World War II.

THE LEGAL STATUS OF GERMANY UNDER THE OCCUPATION

Several highly controversial problems connected with the Four-Power rule established under Potsdam require a brief review. They are, first, whether Germany after May, 1945, has remained a state in the accepted sense of international and municipal law. On the answer depend, for example, the continued validity of international treaties to which Germany is a partner, particularly in relation to neutral states; the vital issues of state succession (such as the liability for obligations undertaken before and after unconditional surrender). The second set of problems centers on the character of the jurisdiction exercised by the CC in matters affecting Germany as a whole and of the zonal commanders relative to their respective zones, more specifically whether it can be legally assumed that they are acting in the place of a non-existing central German government, or as international agencies, or as the representatives of their individual governments. These issues are affinite though not identical with the third problem of how far the practice of the occupation conforms to the rights of "belligerent occupation" under the Hague Convention (1907) on the laws and customs of land warfare (Arts. 42–56). By no stretch of legal imagination can the deep inroads into German internal life and organization be squared with the letter and spirit of the Hague regulations which limit such intervention to objectives determined by the safety of the occupation forces and the maintenance of public order and security.

Without entering into a full discussion of these intricate and, for practical reasons, far-reaching controversies,[4] it must be borne in mind that, by virtue of the unique situation of Germany after unconditional surrender, a new departure in international law automatically and imperatively imposed itself. As much as the international law of war of the nineteenth and twentieth centuries had been incapable of dealing with the impact of technological war, the international law of peace is bound to lag behind the realities of peace after a total war.

(1) The Hague regulations on belligerent occupation are applicable to Germany after 1945 only to a limited extent. They fell by the wayside with the official assumption of supreme power in Germany by the Four Powers under Proclamation No. 1 of the CC (August 30, 1945).

(2) Germany has never ceased to be a state in the sense that the German people as a collective national entity have evidenced a desire to abandon their statehood. On the contrary, they considered the dismemberment of their state into disjointed political fragments temporary only, to be terminated in due course by the reconstitution of a full-fledged unified German state. Jurisprudence and legal practice outside Germany reached the identical conclusion that Germany has not lost the quality of a state.[5] Since Germany never ceased to exist as a state the chain of statehood identity was not broken by the Potsdam agreement and the regime established under it.

(3) Internationally, however, Germany lost, at least until the establishment of the Western and Eastern states in 1949,[6] her quality as an independent and sovereign state. She lacked the essential element of being under the jurisdiction of an independent government of her own; nor could she entertain independent relations with the other members of the international community. Since the four governments, by Statements of June 5, 1945, the Potsdam Agreement and the CC Proclamation No. 1 of August 30, 1945, had assumed jointly supreme authority, the CC, with regard to Germany, in "matters affecting Germany as a whole," and the Zone Commanders, acting as delegates of the CC for their respective zones, were in the place of the indigenous German central government with all attributes attendant on such a position. German sovereignty, confiscated by unconditional surrender *pro tempore,* sub-

---

[4] Students interested in these problems are referred to: Hans Kelsen, "The International Legal Status of Germany to Be Established Immediately Upon Termination of the War," 38 (1944), in *American Journal of International Law,* 689; id. "The Legal Status of Germany According To the Declaration of Berlin, *ibid.* 39 (1945) 518; G. Sauser-Hall, "L'occupation de l'Allemagne par les puissances alliées," 3 (1946), *Schweizerisches Jahrbuch für internationales Recht,* 24; and the articles in *Jahrbuch für internationales und ausländisches öffentliches Recht,* vol. 1 (1948), by Rudolf Laun, pp. 9 ff; F. A. Mann, *ibid.* pp. 27 ff; Eberhard Menzel, *ibid.* pp. 43 ff; W. Friedmann, "The Allied Military Government in Germany," London, 1947, pp. 63 ff. See also R. Y. Jennings, in *British Yearbook of International Law,* 1946, pp. 38 ff.

[5] See among others, *R. v. Bottrill, ex parte Kuechenmeister,* 1 (1946), All. E.R. 635; Obergericht Zürich, decision of December 1, 1947 (*Deutsche Rechtszeitschrift,* 1 (1947) 31; Austrian Supreme Court, January 24, 1946 (*Juristische Blätter,* 68 (1946) 142.

[6] See *infra,* pp. 601 ff., 640 ff.

sequently was restored to the Germans in instalments commensurate with their ability and willingness, as judged alone by the occupying powers, to govern themselves democratically. For the Western zones this process was largely completed with the enactment of the Occupation Statute in 1949.[7] Meanwhile the CC and/or the Zone Commanders were the *de facto* and *de jure* German government; their enactments were German, not international, law.

(4) So long as the CC for Germany as a whole, joined under what in international law is known as condominium, and the Zone Commanders in their respective zones acted as a German government and on behalf of the German people, their jurisdiction is considered as a kind of fiduciary exercise of sovereignty (*Treuhänderschaft*) which, as an institution of international law, is *sui generis* and without precedent.

[7] See *infra*, pp. 592 *ff.*

CHAPTER XVIII

QUADRIPARTITE GOVERNMENT IN GERMANY
1945–1949: THE ALLIED CONTROL COUNCIL

ORGANIZATION

The Interallied Control Authority (or Control Council), residing in the repaired building of the former Prussian Court of Appeals (*Kammergericht*) in the American sector of Berlin, began its operation in August, 1945, notifying the German people by Proclamation No. 1 (August 30, 1945) that it had assumed supreme authority in matters affecting Germany as a whole. The CC consisted of the four Commanders-in-Chief.[1] As a rule they met three times monthly for high-level policy discussions and the signing of major enactments. Decisions required unanimity. In actual practice, however, legislative enactments reached the CC only if agreement had been reached in the Coordinating Committee on the next lower level. The quadripartite arrangement was repeated on all levels of the CC organization, with the difference, however, that disagreements among the four national "elements" on the functional levels did not necessarily prevent a matter from being submitted to the Coordinating Committee for final arbitration. The Coordinating Committee, likewise composed of ranking generals, actually was the heart, if not the brains, of the organism, effectively integrating proposals submitted to it rather haphazardly and without advance planning from the functional Directorates on the next lower rung in the hierarchical ladder.[2] The latter were quadripartite panels composed of the Directors of the functional Divisions of each national "element." They and their staffs (civilian and military) were the technical experts

[1] Of the leading personalities successively participating in the CC's work may be mentioned: —USA: Generals Eisenhower, McNarney, Clay; UK: Field Marshal Montgomery, Sir Douglas Sholto, Sir Brian H. Robertson (the latter became temporarily British High Commissioner in 1949); France: Generals Koeltz, Poiret, and Koenig; USSR: Marshals Zhukov and Sokolowsky.

[2] These were, "subject to adjustment in the light of experience": Military; Air; Naval; Transport; Political; Economic; Finance; Reparations, Deliveries and Restitutions; Internal Affairs and Communications; Legal; Prisoners of War and Displaced Persons; Manpower. This divisional arrangement subsequently underwent some streamlining changes and was not altogether uniform in the corresponding internal organization of the four national "elements."

who did the actual work. Chairmanship on all levels rotated monthly. The Co-ordinating Committee and the Directorates were "to advise the CC in carrying out the Council's decisions and to transmit them to the appropriate German organs, and to supervise and control day-to-day activities of the latter" (Statement of June 5, 1945), the latter function, however, being one which from the very start was assumed by the individual Zone Commanders.

THE CONTROL COUNCIL IN ACTION

Generally speaking, the CC was intended to be, and to some extent actually was, the quadripartite substitute for the nonexisting central German government in matters requiring, in its judgment, uniform treatment of Germany as a whole. The range of such functions was circumscribed by the enumeration of the political and economic principles of the Potsdam Declaration without, however, being guided by a definite catalogue of assignments. This rather loose arrangement had the disadvantage that the flow of business depended largely on the initiative an individual national "element" took in bringing a matter up for quadripartite consideration. At no time did the CC operate with a planned and integrated legislative program. Moreover, neither was the CC under an obligation to legislate on any field nor did it possess exclusive jurisdiction even on the fields enumerated by Potsdam. Zonal authorities, unwilling to wait for CC regulations, thus could not be prevented from permanently occupying a field originally assigned to the CC. From this overlapping of jurisdictions of the CC and the zones resulted inevitably the development of a legislative diversity in the four zones which literally beggared description and could not fail to lead ultimately to socio-political patterns that not only were wholly different in the Soviet and the Western zones, but equally so created vast divergencies among the latter. The consequence was that the CC did not govern Germany in an administrative sense; from the start this function devolved to the Zone Commanders.

So much attention has been paid to the fact that the Allies were incapable of establishing even the limited central German authorities envisaged by Potsdam and so much has been made of their disagreements in the CC which ultimately led to its complete breakdown, that the impression was created of an organization constantly divided against itself and unable to take joint action for Germany as a whole. The objective reviewer will register dissent. The relative success of the CC is amply testified to by the wide compass of legislative activities undertaken by it on behalf of all Germany and the number of legislative enactments issued during the almost three years of its operations. Three proclamations, four orders, sixty-one laws, and fifty-seven directives were placed on the statute-book. The total effort cannot fail to command respect when allowance is made for the enormous and unprecedented difficulties confronting it. The legislative work of a quadripartite and tri-lingual body, with constantly shifting personnel and incessant high-level policy conflicts, was applied to a national environment alien to most officials of all four Powers. In every single case political and economic opposites had to be harmonized in advance which explains why in many instances CC legislation had to confine itself to general policy statements, the actualization of which had to be left to the individual zonal authorities. Even though the Potsdam Declaration never was fully legislated into practice, without the CC Germany would have been thrown into irreparable chaos.

The CC was relatively successful on the fields of demilitarization and disarmament in the widest sense, including both the actual destruction of military installations and an attempt at the elimination of the militaristic tradition from the German life. Of considerable political importance here was the formal abolition of the state of Prussia (CC Law of February 28, 1947). Denazification likewise was a legislative target,[3] but could not succeed globally since it failed also zonally. Major results were accomplished in the fields of the democratization of the administration of justice and at least a beginning was made with the elimination of Nazi-tainted laws and legislation, a task of truly formidable proportions considering the contamination of the entire legal system by Nazi ideologies and practices. In the field of private law at least a uniform marriage statute was passed. The CC must be credited also with a complete reform of the entire structure of taxation and finance; with the elaboration of uniform policies in the labor field including labor courts, wages, hours and labor-management relations, and the elimination of the Nazi legislation on agriculture. Wholly disappointing were the quadripartite achievements in the cultural and political fields, clearly reflecting the increasing tensions between the East and the West. It cannot be denied, however, that once the Soviets had realized they could not use the CC for gaining influence in Germany as a whole, they did not hesitate to interpret the wide frame of reference of the CC enactments to suit their own political needs and to embark on the actual Sovietization of their zone.

THE COLLAPSE OF THE CONTROL COUNCIL

In 1948 the CC became the most conspicuous casualty of the East-West conflict. It was found increasingly difficult to find common legislative denominators for the manifest divergencies of socio-political policies in the Western and Eastern zones even though the relations among the officials cooperating in the CC, in itself constituting a seminar in international semantics on an unparalleled scale, had evolved towards a sort of camaraderie not altogether uncommon among professional technicians of different nationalities. After the breakdown of the Moscow Conference of the Foreign Ministers (April, 1947) many of the CC's operations were little more than waste motion and procrastination. In consulting the political chronology it will be easily observed that the actual end of the CC coincided with the announcement of the economic merger of the three Western zones decided on at the London Conference (February, 1948), a move justified by the assumption that the Western efforts to establish the central economic agencies within the context of Potsdam had proved futile. On the balmy spring day of March 20, 1948, Marshal Sokolowsky requested

[3] See Directives Nos. 24 (January 12, 1946) and 38 (October 13, 1946).

from his Western colleagues an explanation of what he termed, not unjustly, the unilateral establishment of a unified Western economic state. When he was denied it, on equally unimpeachable legal grounds, after reading a prepared statement, the Russians walked out.[4] Credence is lent to the impression that the Western powers deliberately seized the opportunity for terminating the CC by the refusal of General Clay, in the chair after April 1, to convene the next scheduled meeting of the CC.

The CC, conceived as a noble experiment in international government, is dead beyond resurrection, even though it is worthy of note that neither the Potsdam Declaration nor the Statement of June 5, 1945, on which the control machinery is based, was formally denounced by either party. Seen retrospectively the failure of the CC confirms the historical experience of all other condominial arrangements. Moreover, even under the assumption of a continued functioning, its operational usefulness necessarily would have decreased in proportion to the increasing volume of German self-determination and the establishment of indigenous German governmental authorities. The disunity of the powers, and not alone the split between the Soviets and the West, could not fail to deprive the CC of much of its prestige almost from the start. While trying, in a fashion, to conform to the CC legislation, the Germans looked more and more to their zonal masters for guidance. At present the CC is merely an ungainly memorial to Allied incompetence. It may be added here that the companion organization in Austria, the Allied CC, in spite of more than occasional difficulties, on the whole worked tolerably well. It may well be asked whether, given a modicum of willingness of all participants and less concern for diplomatic logistics, the quadripartite organization in Germany could not have been made to work.

[4] See on the incident, Delbert Clark, *Again the Goosestep*, Indianapolis, 1949, pp. 284 ff. That the Russians did hardly intend to make more than a gesture of disapproval, by then not unfamiliar, is evidenced by the fact that, acting as the chairman for the month, they called on the next day meetings of three subordinate committees which in turn were not attended by the Western delegates.

CHAPTER XIX

QUADRIPARTITE ACTION ON WAR CRIMES

Another quadripartite action was the trial of the major Nazi leaders in Nuremberg. At the Moscow Conference (October 30, 1943) the Allies, in the "Declaration on German Atrocities," resolved to punish those major war criminals "whose offenses have no particular geographical location" by a joint decision of the Governments of the Allies. Remembering the failure of the Versailles Treaty to bring the German war criminals of World War I to justice, the London Agreement, concluded by the four major powers August 8, 1945, and subsequently adhered to by nineteen other Allied states, provided for an International Military Tribunal to try war crimes whose perpetration was not confined to a patricular area. Its constitution, jurisdiction, and procedure were set forth in an annex later known as the Nuremberg Charter. Each signatory was to make available to the Tribunal for investigation of charges and trial the major war criminals detained by it. The Court was to be composed of one member and one alternate of each of the four major powers. Its decisions required majority vote with at least three affirmative votes for conviction and sentence.

While the procedure, a mixture of Anglo-Saxon and continental principles of criminal justice, did not contain much that was new, the establishment of jurisdiction constituted a revolutionary departure from the customary law of nations. Punishable (Art. 6 of the Charter) were persons who, in the interests of the European Axis states, whether as individuals or as members of organizations, had committed one of the following acts qualified as international crimes: (a) crimes against peace, in particular by planning, preparing, and initiating a war of aggression or a war in violation of international agreements; (b) war crimes proper, referring to criminal acts in violation of the laws and customs of war; specifically mentioned were slave labor, ill-treatment of the population of an occupied territory, deportation, and wanton destruction not necessitated by military considerations; (c) crimes against humanity, including inhuman acts against civilians and persecution on racial, religious, or political grounds regardless of whether or not in violation of the domestic law where perpetrated. The same article, not happily phrased, added actually as a fourth crime the conspiracy to commit one of the preceding acts, a concept clearly influenced by Anglo-Saxon legal thinking.[5] To obviate certain objections of legal theory and practice the Charter further stipulated that neither the official position of the indicted, whether as head of state or in a governmental position, nor the fact that the act had been committed on orders of a superior—the convenient escape from responsibility in military hierarchies—would free from punishment, though such defense might result in mitigating circumstances. Another novelty consisted in the criminal responsibility of certain specified groups or organizations as a whole.

On October 18, 1945, the quadripartite group of chief prosecutors lodged the indictment against twenty-four major Nazi criminals, including political chieftains, military men, diplomats, and economic leaders. As criminal organizations were indicted primarily the Reich Cabinet, General Staff, NSDAP Leadership Corps, SD (Security Service of the Party), SS, SA, and Gestapo. The trial was conducted from November 20, 1945, to August 31, 1946, in the Palace of Justice (court building) of Nuremberg, notorious seat of the Nazi party rallies and one of the most rabidly nazified cities of the Reich. The most prominent among the prosecution staff was Justice Robert Jackson, whose introductory address is credited with having laid the foundations of a new international law. By all equitable standards, the accused, defended by German counsel of their own choosing (mostly anti-Nazi lawyers) and with unimpaired rights of submitting evidence on equal footing with the prosecution, received a fair trial.[6]

Judgment was delivered on September 30 and October 1, 1946. One of the indicted (Gustav Krupp von Bohlen und Halbach) could not be tried for reasons of health, another (Ley) had committed suicide during the trial, one (Bormann) was tried *in absentia*. Of the nine sentenced to death by hanging one (Goering) took his life on the night of the execution; the eight others (the generals Keitel and Jodl, Ribbentrop, Rosenberg, Frick, Frank, Kaltenbrunner, Streicher, and Seyss-Inquart) were hanged (October 16, 1946). Seven were sentenced to imprisonment (Hess, Funk, and Admiral Raeder for life, Admiral Doenitz, von Neurath, von Schirach, and Speer to terms ranging from ten to twenty years). Three were acquitted on all counts (Schacht, von Papen, and Fritsche). Of the indicted organizations the SS, the Leadership Corps, the SD, and the Gestapo were convicted as criminal, the others (including the General Staff, the Reich Cabinet, and the SA) were acquitted. The Soviet judge entered a violent dissent on the acquittals of the indicted persons and

---

[5] The Court subsequently admitted only conspiracy for aggressive war as an independent crime.

[6] The tribunal held 403 open sessions and heard 33 witnesses presented by the prosecution, 61 for the defense, in addition to 19 introduced by the accused. One hundred and forty-three additional witnesses made depositions. One hundred and one witnesses in defense of the indicted organizations were heard by appointed commissioners, while 1,809 affidavits from others were submitted, not to mention the many thousands of other testimonies in their favor. The Tribunal itself heard 22 witnesses in their defense.

organizations. Those sentenced to prison were transferred to a jail in Spandau (in the British sector of Berlin) and are kept under quadripartite custodianship.

The Nuremberg procedure, easily the most spectacular judicial action of our time, has been praised as a revolutionary innovation in the law of nations and no less assailed, in Germany as well as outside, as a flagrant breach of its formally established principles. That the majority of the indicted morally deserved punishment was generally admitted, even though responsible German lawyers, claiming that the Tribunal was merely an instrument of the victorious powers instead of being truly international in character, would have preferred the participation of German judges; but since the Tribunal was clearly a military court Germans had no legitimate place on it. The allegation that, before an Allied court, no fair judgment was obtainable, is easily disproved by the acquittal of three of the accused. If, as was also claimed, the trial had been conducted by an exclusively German court, it may seem likely that at that time von Papen and Schacht would have been convicted; [7] but certainly no German court would have brought itself to convict generals of their sacrosanct *Wehrmacht*.

The more serious objections raised by the defense may be summarized thus: Only states and not individuals are subjects in international law; individuals, therefore, cannot be made responsible for international crimes. The same argument was directed against a trial involving crimes against peace; certain incriminated acts were acts of state and, therefore, not to be impugned to individuals. Crimes against humanity do not exist in the German criminal code nor are they recognized by international law; moreover, their content was too vague to constitute a basis for criminal prosecution. The concept of conspiracy was declared alien to German law, and thus a violation of the principle *nullum crimen sine lege* (no punishment without definite legal norm proscribing an individual act in advance of its commitment). This was said also to vitiate the conviction of the incriminated organizations. Primarily, however, it was alleged that war is still recognized as a legitimate institution of the law of nations and that the Briand-Kellogg Pact of 1928, to which Germany was a signatory, while outlawing war as an instrument of policy, had failed to establish the jurisdiction of a competent tribunal and sanctions, which could not be applied *ex post facto* without breach of the *nulla poena sine lege* principle. Moreover, aggressive war was alleged to be a political and not a legal concept and not accessible to judicial determination.

Not all these arguments can be brushed aside lightly. Nonetheless, the trial and the convictions were well grounded in international law which progresses by practice and precedent as well as by legislation or custom. Practice creates custom. First, international law, in its present stage, is still largely unwritten; it

[7] Subsequently both were indicted under the German denazification law (see *infra*, p. 522), but von Papen's sentence was rescinded on appeal, and Schacht, fleeing to the British zone, succeeded in obtaining an acquittal when tried again in 1950.

possesses the character of common law, and responsibility under it may well be established without codified norms. Secondly, the judges made individuals responsible for actions of the abstract entity called state, thus contributing to the long overdue process of dismantling that obsolete concept of Byzantine origin, state sovereignty. The Court, in rejecting the argument that the representatives of so-called sovereign states cannot be held responsible for the acts of the latter, stated correctly and realistically that criminal acts are committed by human beings and not by abstractions, and that therefore a state which conducts itself outside the realm of international law cannot claim immunity for persons who shelter themselves behind the contention that the state and not the person is liable. The collateral argument that the indicted acted merely as representatives of the state under its orders was briefly rejected by the statement that under the law of nations orders to act criminally are not binding. The crime of aggressive war had been outlawed by the Briand-Kellogg Pact, thus invalidating the alleged violation of the *nulla poena sine lege* principle; this was probably the least convincing of the Court's arguments. Crimes against humanity are outlawed under the existing criminal codes even though no civilized mind could imagine the deliberate enormity of the crimes committed by the Nazis. Concerning the conviction of the organizations the Court declined to subscribe to the principle of guilt by association and conceded to an individual member the rebuttal that he had not known of, or had not participated in, its criminal activities.

For a long time the Nuremberg trial will remain controversial. On the German people it made very little impression. Contrary to the hope that it would serve as a corrective of their cynicism towards the atrocities committed by the regime, it succeeded only in relieving the individual from whatever qualms of collective conscience he may have shared. The average German was satisfied that justice, as the Allies understood it, had been done to the leaders and that he himself should no longer be exposed to moral impositions on his own conscience.

In view of this attitude it is understandable that the Germans to whom CC Law No. 10 (December 20, 1945) had given the legal device of dealing with their own war criminals by their own courts for violation of the principles of humanity, were utterly reluctant to avail themselves of this means of expiation. Relatively few trials were instituted and among them none for genocide. Likewise the sentences were light.[8] Not a single death sentence was handed down.[9]

The vast majority of trials for the commitment of acts of inhumanity were conducted by Allied military tribunals, many of those under American juris-

---

[8] In some of the more sensational indictments for crimes against humanity, the accused were acquitted; for example, a military court judge who had sent hundreds of persons accused of "undermining resistance" to the firing squads, although some of his colleagues, showing greater leniency, had not been exposed to reprisals; another case was that of a judge of a *Sondergericht* who, in 1943, had sentenced a Jew to death for "race defilement" (*Rassenschande*), that is, intercourse with an "Aryan" woman, although the death sentence was not mandatory under the law.

[9] The death penalty was abolished by the Bonn Constitution. No exception for war criminals was made.

diction by American military courts in Nuremberg.[10] Among those the more notorious were against generals (in the British zone alone); ministerial officials (10 persons formerly in the Ministry of Justice and 21 persons of the former Foreign Office); finally industrialists (of the IG Farben, Krupp, and Flick combines). None of them resulted in a death sentence. In other trials of members of the SS, the medical staff of a concentration camp indulging in medical experiments in living persons with lethal results and other sadists of the concentration camps death sentences were given.

The record completed by the end of 1949 [11] reveals that in the United States and British zones, 776 trials were held and in the French zone about 10, while no figures about the Soviet zone are available. In the United States zone, of 1,539 persons convicted, 444 were sentenced to death, but owing to commutations actually only about 250 persons were executed.[12] Of 927 persons tried in the British zone, 665 were found guilty; the number of death sentences actually executed equals that in the American zone. In the case of socially prominent men who could mobilize legal advice and sympathies abroad, appeals and remissions of punishment led to early release.

The final chapter of the war crimes trials in the American zone was written when (January 31, 1951) United States High Commissioner John J. McCloy, guided by the recommendations of a Board of Clemency that had been completed in the summer of 1950, reviewed the sentences of 88 criminals previously convicted by American military tribunals. The action, officially described as an act of mercy though widely interpreted as a move of appeasement of German public opinion in connection with American efforts to stimulate German participation in Western defense, resulted in the commutation of all but five of the remaining death sentences to imprisonment; 36 out of 41 prison terms were reduced to lesser terms; the terms of 32 persons were reduced to time served and they were forthwith released. The most notorious case of clemency was that of Alfred Krupp von Bohlen und Halbach, sentenced by the Nuremberg International Tribunal to twelve years' imprisonment and confiscation of his property; his term was unilaterally reduced to "time served" and the property confiscation rescinded; he immediately returned in triumph to his former position as head of the mammoth armament concern of Krupp, which had served faithfully the Empire, the Republic, and the Third Reich.

Even this excessive leniency failed to satisfy German public opinion, which, aroused by rising nationalism, noisily demanded rescue from the gallows for the five criminals, although all had been convicted of unheard-of assembly line exterminations in concentration camps, or of the helpless popula-

[10] Special Military Tribunals sitting in Nuremberg tried ten cases with 185 persons indicted. Of these, 35 were acquitted; 8, released from trial; 24, executed by hanging; 20, sentenced to life imprisonment; 87, sentenced to limited prison terms; 11, released with time served (as of April 14, 1949). See *Military Government Information Bulletin,* May 31, 1949, p. 6.

[11] See *New York Times* of December 25, 1949, section IV.

[12] The most notorious remission of punishment was the commutation of the death sentence of Ilse Koch, the bestial sex pervert of the Buchenwald concentration camp. In January, 1951, she was sentenced, by a German court, to life imprisonment. Likewise none of the convicted murderers of American prisoners in the Battle of the Bulge (the Malmédy case) was put to death.

tion in the East. After further legal delays they were finally executed (June, 1951).

After the collapse no revolution occurred in Germany. The Germans seemingly are congenitally incapable of violent revolution. Not a single Nazi had to atone with his life for his crimes through the "rightful wrath" of the German people themselves.[13] The lives of fewer than one thousand criminals exacted by Allied courts may seem to weigh lightly in the scales against the death of all told more than sixteen million innocent people caused by the Nazi regime.

---

[13] The only case reported (besides that of Ilse Koch mentioned before) in which a German court meted out retribution against a professional torturer was that of one Heinrich Baab whom a Frankfurt court, in March 1951, sentenced to life for the successful liquidation of the entire Jewish community in Frankfurt; see the gripping narrative of the trial in Kay Boyle, *The Smoking Mountain,* New York 1951, p. 1 ff.

CHAPTER XX

THE FOUR ZONES OF OCCUPATION AND INTRA-ZONAL TERRITORIAL SUBDIVISIONS

THE FOUR ZONES

A glance at the map will reveal that the territorial organization of post-surrender Germany, when compared with the quasi-unitary state of the Nazi period no less than with the federal structure of the Weimar Republic, has undergone substantial modifications. The change of the external boundaries is conditioned by the defeat and collapse which led to the conquest by the Red Army of the eastern parts of Germany. The northern half of Eastern Prussia (with the City of Koenigsberg—now Kaliningrad) was annexed by the USSR while the German territories east of a line running from the Baltic Sea along the Oder and Neisse rivers to the Czechoslovak frontier (including the southern half of Eastern Prussia and the area of the former Free City of Danzig) were placed (Potsdam Declaration IX [b]) "under the administration of Poland." In spite of the statement that the final determination of Poland's western boundaries would be left to the peace settlement, Poland (February, 1947) formally incorporated the area. This act of annexation was not recognized by the Western powers and vehemently protested by the Western Germans, while the Government of the German Democratic Republic (Eastern Germany) formally accepted the existing boundary line as final (Treaty of Goerlitz, July 6, 1950). These Eastern territories, comprising about one-fourth of the total German area (as of 1937) included, next to the industrial area of Upper Silesia, some of the best agricultural land.[1]

[1] In 1939 the split-off region contained 13.7 per cent of the total population and 24.1 per cent of the total area of Germany. It included one-fourth (25.1 per cent) of the total agriculturally used land and about 29 per cent of the total land planted for fodder, fodder grains, rye, potatoes, and sugar. Management was predominantly by large farms producing for the market. However, the productive value of the area is generally exaggerated; the claim that the region actually was not only self-supporting but produced also food for between four and ten million people elsewhere is unsupported by fact. Actually the greatest food producer of Germany was and is the British zone. Return of the Eastern territories could not solve the German food problem, since in normal times at least fifteen million people were dependent on food imports. Nonetheless, the restoration would measurably improve the food situation.

Internally the large-scale map redrawing is due to the division of Germany into the four zones of occupation, with the area of Greater Berlin as a fifth zone; to the elimination of Prussia as a separate state entity; and, within each of the four zones, to a considerable amount of territorial regroupment. Former provinces of Prussia were either raised to the status of a *Land* or incorporated by adjacent *Laender*.

THE AMERICAN ZONE

The following survey presents the territorial situation in Western Germany as of September, 1950, omitting *interim* changes.

AREA AND POPULATION OF THE GERMAN FEDERAL REPUBLIC AND WESTERN BERLIN

(Excluding Displaced Persons in Camps)

	Capital	Sq. Miles	Population
U.S. Zone			
Bavaria	Munich	27,112	9,118,600
Bremen	Bremen	156	568,300
Hessen	Wiesbaden	7,931	4,303,900
Wuerttemberg-Baden	Stuttgart	5,961	3,884,200
Total		41,160	17,875,000
British Zone			
Hamburg	Hamburg	288	1,604,600
Lower Saxony	Hanover	18,226	6,795,100
North Rhine Westphalia	Duesseldorf	13,153	13,125,600
Schleswig-Holstein	Kiel	6,048	2,588,800
Total		37,715	24,114,100
French Zone			
Baden	Freiburg	3,842	1,335,500
Rhineland-Palatinate	Mayence (Mainz)	7,665	2,992,300
Wuerttemberg-Hohenzollern	Tuebingen	4,017	1,241,000
Total		15,524	5,568,800
Federal Republic	Bonn	94,399	47,557,900
Berlin (Western Sectors)		188	2,142,400
Total (Federal Republic plus Western Berlin)		94,587	49,700,300

The American zone consists of the *Laender* Bavaria, Wuerttemberg-Baden, Hessen, and Bremen. The area of *Bavaria* was unchanged except for the assignation of the Palatinate (on the Western bank of the Rhine) to the *Land* Rhineland-Palatinate in the French zone, and other slight boundary changes (acquisition of one district from Thuringia and loss of the Kreis Lindau to the French zone). The formation of the new *Land Wuerttemberg-Baden* was due to the cutting in two of the formerly separate *Laender* Wuerttemberg and Baden by the carving out of the French from the American zone; the new

Land comprises the northern halves of Wuerttemberg and of Baden. *Hessen,* created by Proclamation of American MG of September 19, 1945, and like-wise a new territorial entity, is composed now, after various interim arrange-ments, of the sections of the former *Land* Hessen-Darmstadt located on the right bank of the Rhine and the greater part of the former Prussian province of Hessen-Nassau. The Free City of *Bremen,* an enclave in the British zone, at first was under American jurisdiction, thereafter (December, 1945) incorpo-rated in the British zone, and became, with the port of Bremerhaven, again a separate *Land* in the United States zone (January 1, 1947).

THE BRITISH ZONE

This is subdivided into four *Laender,* namely: the Free City of *Hamburg* (within the boundaries established by Hitler in 1937); *Lower Saxony,* cre-ated on November 1, 1946, as an entirely new *Land* without historical ante-cedent and composed of the former Prussian province of Hanover and the former *Laender* Brunswick (with slight exceptions), Oldenburg, and Schaum-burg-Lippe; a new *Land, North Rhine Westphalia,* put together, by decision of the British MG on January 21, 1947, from the former Prussian province of Westphalia, the northern parts of the Prussian Rhine Province, and the *Land* Lippe-Detmold; and *Schleswig-Holstein,* the former Prussian province of the same name.

THE FRENCH ZONE

Three *Laender* are embraced in this zone, namely: *Rhineland-Palatinate,* composed of the (Bavarian) Palatinate, the southern parts of the former Prus-sian Rhine Province, the areas of Hessen on the left bank of the Rhine, and some small segments of the former Prussian Province of Hessen-Nassau on the right bank; *Baden,* which is the southern part of the former *Land* Baden, split off by the zonal boundary from the northern half; and *Wuerttemberg-Hohenzollern,* which represents the southern half of Wuerttemberg together with the former Prussian *Regierungsbezirk* Hohenzollern.[2]

THE SOVIET ZONE

This has five subdivisions called *Laender,* namely: *Brandenburg,* consisting of the former province of the same name except the parts east of the Oder; *Mecklenburg,* corresponding to the former *Land,* with the western part of the former Prussian province of Pommern and without the city of Stettin (assigned to Poland); *Saxony,* the former *Land* of the same name, enlarged by the west-ern part of the former Prussian *Regierungsbezirk* Liegnitz; *Saxony-Anhalt,* a new and composite state (created by the Soviets on March 3, 1946) com-posed largely of the former Prussian provinces of Halle-Merseburg and Magde-burg, with the former *Land* Anhalt and small sections added of the former *Laender* Brunswick and Thuringia; and *Thuringia,* at first under American occupation and taken over by the Soviets in July, 1945, consisting of the

[2] On the Saar see *infra,* p. 504.

former *Land* of the same name, with some formerly Prussian areas (Erfurt and Schmalkalden) added.[3]

EVALUATION OF TERRITORIAL CHANGES

An appraisal of the zonal divisions from the economic and cultural viewpoints lends itself to the conclusion that some of the economically most valuable parts of Germany, including the Ruhr, the Rhineland, and Hamburg—sometimes considered more British than the British—came under the United Kingdom. In the Soviet zone lie some of the best (Mecklenburg) and some of the poorest (Brandenburg) soil, together with highly industrialized Saxony. The Americans control Bavaria, whose splendid scenery appears to many an inequitable compensation for her lack of economic self-sufficiency and, at least in some areas, a progress-resisting population. However, the other two South German *Laender* in the United States zone are among the economically and culturally most balanced sections of Germany. The French, finally, did not fare badly with a homogeneous population in their zone, where farming and industrial development are well blended.

THE SAAR ISSUE

The *Saar,* an area of about 800 square miles and with a German population of less than one million, was originally included in the French zone. On December 22, 1946, the French closed it off against the remainder of the zone by a customs barrier as a prelude to the establishment of an autonomous state under French political and economic control. At the London Conferences (November, 1947) the British and American governments agreed, with Soviet dissent, to the economic incorporation of the Saar into metropolitan France. This was alleged to have become indirectly ratified through the election (October 10, 1946) of a *Land* parliament that a constitution drawn up, under French inspiration, by a group of notables had provided for.[4] The assembly, by a majority even more overwhelming (48 out of 49 votes) than that which, in the 1935 plebiscite had returned the area to Hitler's Reich, ratified the constitution (November 8, 1947), and thereby agreed to the status of an autonomous state tied to France by currency, customs union, and French supervision of foreign relations and military protection. With the completion of the economic union (April 1, 1948) the French zonal administration no longer ap-

[3] In the following list allowance must be made for shifts and inaccuracies in population statistics.

	Capital	Sq. Kil.	Population
Brandenburg	Potsdam	27,061	2,527,492
Mecklenburg	Schwerin	22,954	2,139,640
Saxony	Dresden	16,910	5,558,566
Saxony-Anhalt	Halle	24,657	4,160,539
Thuringia	Weimar	15,598	2,927,497
Total		107,180	17,313,734
Berlin, Eastern Sector		~ 400	1,170,300
German Democratic Republic Berlin		107,580	18,484,034

[4] It was subsequently alleged that the limited number of copies of the Constitution available at the time of the election prevented the expression of a considered opinion.

plied to the Saar. On the other hand, the West German Government protested against what in actual fact amounted to the political separation of the Saar from Germany, against the admission of the Saar as an associate member to the Council of Europe (1950), and against the conclusion of a treaty (March 3, 1950) by which the French obtained a fifty years' lease on the coal deposits of the area. As it is not uncommon with volatile border populations, the Saarlanders are more guided by economic opportunism than by patriotism.[5]

Seen as a whole, the internal boundary situation appears as the territorial basis of a new regionalism. A *Reichsreform,* comparable in scale only to the regroupment enforced by Napoleon, for which the Weimar Republic had been laboring in vain and which not even Hitler could accomplish, could be imposed only from outside; no indigenous government could have overcome vested economic interests and the tradition of localism. Much as has been accomplished, it may seem doubtful, however, whether the new territorial arrangements conform fully to the requirements of regional rationalization.

The most striking feature is the obliteration of Prussia as a political and administrative entity. Wholly anomalous and, in the long run untenable, is the situation of Berlin, an empty shell without hinterland and an island in the Soviet sea, as deeply split between the East and the West as the rest of Germany. Over the disappearance of the last remnants of dynastic particularism (Oldenburg, the two Lippes, Brunswick, and Anhalt) few Germans will lose sleep. But the territorial consolidation did not progress as far as it may seem desirable.[6] In the West the formation of North Rhine-Westphalia and Lower Saxony was demographically and economically sound; the former, by virtue of the largest population and the greatest economic assets, has begun to succeed to the leadership of Prussia, to the dissatisfaction of Bavaria, the second most populous state. It may appear a definite defect of American planning that Bavaria was not split into the separate sections of Franconia and Bavaria proper. The new *Land* of Wuerttemberg-Baden and the artificially constructed *Land* of Hessen developed within a few years a surprising statehood feeling based on the awareness of the common interests of the people. But none of the dwarf-*Laender* of the French zone has any legitimate claim to its separate existence. Without the arbitrary zonal demarcation the consolidation of all of Wuerttemberg and all of Baden into a single and economically viable Southwestern *Land* (*Südweststaat*), as desired by the majority of the inhabitants, could have been accomplished.[7] In view of the demographic affinities and eco-

[5] A number of minor and provisional border rectifications in favor of the Netherlands and Belgium were authorized by the Paris agreement of March 22, 1949. The area assigned to the Netherlands was incorporated by the latter. Although only a limited number of localities were affected, the unilateral arrangement was of questionable legal validity as well as politically unwise to the extreme, being prejudicial to the peace settlement and weakening the Western claim to a reconsideration of the *fait accompli* of the annexations in the East.

[6] Under the Empire there were twenty-five member states, under Weimar seventeen. At present there are sixteen and, with Berlin, seventeen different *Laender.*

[7] The union of these three segments by mutual agreement is provided for in Art. 118 of the Bonn Constitution, in deviation of the general rule of Art. 29 (prescribing a federal law for internal territorial boundary changes). On September 24, 1950, a consultative referendum was held in the three *Laender* to decide whether (a) a single Southwest State should be established or (b) the formerly separate *Laender* of Wuerttemberg and Baden within their pre-1945

nomic homogeneity of the entire area, such a consolidated South Western State would fit well into the new regionalism. In the Soviet zone, finally, the territorial divisions into five relatively equal and economically cohesive parts was sound.

If the Allies had been less obsessed by the concept of decentralization and had possessed some degree of advance planning, the German collapse would have presented a unique opportunity for setting up within Germany an integrated system of economic regionalism. Contrariwise, the decentralization policy resulted in many parts in stimulating an exaggerated sense of statehood in political entities of an altogether accidental and artificial character.

THE PROBLEM OF THE EXPELLEES [8]

By all practical standards the influx into truncated Germany of close to twelve millions of destitute expellees constitutes the most crucial issue of present-day Germany. This greatest migration of the people in history will dominate the German future for a long time to come.

Expellees in the technical sense [9] are primarily Germans who, during or after the war, were forced to leave their homelands. Partly they are German nationals, such as the Germans driven out from the area east of the Oder-Neisse line after Potsdam, or non-German nationals though of German ethnic descent (*Volksdeutsche*). In their vast majority they came from Poland, the Balticum, Czechoslovakia, and Hungary under the Potsdam decision. Although the Declaration (XIII) explicitly stated that these population transfers should be effected "in an orderly and humane manner" they were dumped into Germany with at most what they could carry on their backs.

The CC, heavily (by about 50 per cent) underestimating the number of expellees to be accommodated under Potsdam, agreed (November 20, 1945) on a rough key for their distribution among the four zones. The British and the Soviets were to share those from east of the Oder-Neisse line, the Americans and the Soviets those from the Sudetenland and elsewhere. The French refused to take any, and only in and after 1948 they admitted a trickle on a highly selective basis. Actually the human flood, spilling over the "green border"

---

boundaries should be restored. The result was 70 per cent in favor of the first solution, but in South Baden a majority voted for the latter alternative which appears the lesser evil to the statehood vanity of some of its politicians. At the time of this writing the matter is not yet definitely settled. The Federal Government, by a law of the Federal Parliament, determined that on September 16, 1951 a referendum be held to decide whether (a) the three *Laender* are to be united as a single *Suedweststaat*, or (b) the formerly existing states of Wuerttemberg and Baden be restored as separate entities. But even thereafter the matter may not come to rest since the federal statute was challenged as unconstitutional.

[8] Figures in this section are taken from the *Deutschland-Jahrbuch*, 1949 (edited by Klaus Mehnert and Heinrich Schulte), Essen, 1949, pp. 249 ff and various MG Reports, for example: "Population Changes, 1947, US Zone Germany," prepared by Civil Administration Division OMGUS (May, 1948).

[9] Expellees are to be distinguished from Displaced Persons. Most of the DP's, forced into Germany as slave labor, and the prisoners of war, were repatriated. Among the DP's still in Germany the largest contingents constitute foreigners who are irrepatriable because of collaboration with the Nazis, and Eastern Jews fleeing from persecution in Poland, since 1945 (who, however, use Germany mainly as a transit station before emigrating abroad). Until now DP's did not live on the German economy.

between the zones, was beyond control. At least 800,000 from the East flocked to the United States zone which also had to accept the majority of the Sudetens. Moreover, the load of the Western zones was further increased by the arrival of German refugees (technically not expellees) from the Soviet zone and the Soviet sector of Berlin escaping from Soviet economic pressure or political persecution.[10] It is reliably estimated that in 1948 of the total population of 65.9 million there were 11.6 million expellees.[11]

The enormity of the issue can be grasped only by its socio-political implications. More people are living in the rump Reich than in 1937, and this in spite of the huge war casualties and the non-returned prisoners. In some of the *Laender* the refugee element constitutes between 30 and 40 per cent of the population.[12] The distribution of this human mass caused unprecedented shifts in the religious composition of entire areas and specific localities, Catholics (about 60 per cent of the non-German expellees) settling in solidly Protestant sections, and *vice versa*. Since the destroyed cities could not shelter them they were shunted to the villages and the small towns. Substantial farmland could not be provided except in the Soviet zone where about 17 per cent of the land made available through the land reform was distributed to refugees. Vast hordes are still unemployed and living in camps.

The German people disliked their unwanted guests and resented their claim to share their own misery. The *Land* governments, grudgingly and only under MG prodding, did what they could, which was little enough. Though the occupation powers at an early date had insisted on all expellees being accorded

[10] However, this is a two-way passage since a sizable number of such refugees later return to their homes because of unemployment in Western Germany.

[11] The following figures reflect approximately the zonal distribution: U.S. Zone, 3.5 million; British Zone, 4.0 million; Soviet Zone, 4.0 million; French Zone, 0.1 million; total, 11.6 million. The following figures for Western Germany alone are taken from the 4th Quarterly "Report on Germany" (July 1–Sept. 30, 1950) of the U.S. High Commissioner, p. 95 (figures include children born since arrival):

October 29, 1946	6,900,000
July 1, 1950	9,139,000

distributed as follows: Former territories east of the Oder-Neisse line, 4,658,793; Czechoslovakia, Hungary, Poland, and other countries, 3,158,232; Soviet Zone and Berlin, 1,322,682. Of the total population (49,700,300) of the Federal Republic as of September 15, 1950, the refugees and expellees constitute 18.3 per cent. The distribution as per cent of the total population is as follows:

Land	Per cent
Schleswig-Holstein	38.2
Lower Saxony	30.5
Bavaria	23.6
Wuerttemberg-Baden	20.6
Hessen	18.6
Hamburg	10.9
North Rhine-Westphalia	12.0
Wuerttemberg-Hohenzollern	10.6
Bremen	9.5
Baden	8.8
Rhineland-Palatinate	4.6

[12] As a remedial measure the *Bundesrat* passed (March 8, 1951) a Resettlement Act, providing, by September, 1951, for the transfer of 200,000 refugees from the most overcrowded *Laender* of Schleswig-Holstein, Bavaria, and Lower Saxony to areas of the Federal Republic which heretofore had received a lower proportion, authorizing also the resettlement of an additional 100,000 after that date.

German nationality rights, the group as a whole was treated as politically second-class citizens. The established parties catered for their votes and carefully neglected them after the elections. Their absorption as a group proved as yet impossible. They are the flotsam and jetsam for the new radicalism of the nationalist Right. Twelve million people do not wish to belong, and are not wanted, where they are, and for them there is no hope of going back from where they came unless in the wake of a victorious war of the West against the East. This is an unexploded time bomb in the midst of Europe.

Yet the picture is not all black. There were exceptions in the attitudes of the hosts and the guests as well from the beginning. Individuals and splinter groups succeeded in establishing themselves economically and socially. The refugees from Silesia and Eastern Prussia, sturdy and inventive frontier people, no less than the Sudetens, in their majority people with professional skills, are beginning to make contributions of recognized value; the "boy-meets-girl" relationship begins to take off some of the edges of the initial hostility. New blood—and not the least valuable in Europe—is being infused into an old stock, new ideas penetrate stagnant tradition. Perhaps future generations of Germans will praise the refugees and expellees as a blessing in disguise.

SOME GENERAL OBSERVATIONS ON ZONAL GOVERNMENT

The unparalleled complexity of Germany's political situation under the occupation may be better understood if visualized as a system of concentric circles of jurisdiction. Of these the most extensive was the quadripartite rule of the CC under the Potsdam Declaration, applicable to all four zones and to Berlin and remaining in existence until 1948. Moving towards the center followed the division of Germany into four separate zones, each under one of the occupation powers exercising control through the Zone Commander and binding all territorial subdivisions comprised by each zone. Within each zone political dynamics moved on two different levels, namely, that of the governmental and administrative agencies of the occupying power proper, and that of indigenous German agencies. These two areas of jurisdiction, never wholly separated, were overlapping and increasingly integrated. With the progressive restoration of self-government to the Germans by each of the four powers—a process in which the Americans and the Soviets set the pace and thereby compelled the other two powers to achieve a sort of loose synchronization—indigenous German authorities gained control over areas relinquished to them by the occupation powers. The chart is further complicated by the fact that, within the American, British, and Soviet zones, German zonal agencies were established (the *Laenderrat* in Stuttgart, the Zonal Advisory Council [*Zonenbeirat*] in Hamburg, and the German Central Administrations [*Zentralverwaltungen*] in Eastern Berlin respectively); [13] and that, with the economic merger of the American and the British zones (beginning in 1947) [14] both bipartite (British-American) as well as German authorities emerged with jurisdiction over both

[13] See *infra*, pp. 534 ff, 541 f, 632 f.
[14] See *infra*, pp. 535 ff.

zones in all economic matters. Finally, in the summer of 1949 the three Western zones were less permitted than urged to constitute themselves as the Western Federal Republic (*Deutsche Bundesrepublik*) while the Eastern zone, in October, 1949, converted itself, under Soviet sponsorship, into the German Democratic Republic (*Deutsche Demokratische Republik*). In the West this latest stage was accompanied by the establishment of a tripartite Allied High Commission [15] without, however, abolishing the separate zonal authorities of the three Western powers. The division into four zones resulted in the development of four altogether different occupation patterns corresponding to the different political aims and administrative techniques of each power. These differences are particularly marked between the Western and the Eastern zones, as outwardly reflected by the coexistence of two different German states. But even in each of the three Western zones the respective occupation power could not fail to leave its impact.

For the American student the main interest naturally lies in the American zone which, therefore, will be treated here more extensively.

[15] See *infra*, pp. 595 ff.

CHAPTER XXI

AMERICAN MILITARY GOVERNMENT

ORGANIZATION

No other aspect of American foreign policy since 1945 has fascinated public opinion more than Military Government (MG) in the American zone of Germany, and this for reasons not difficult to perceive. This was the first large-scale experiment of the United States to control and administer a defeated country,[1] while the old colonial powers, Britain and France, had a superior experience in the rule over foreign peoples. Moreover, the United States was expected to continue world leadership in the drive for the paramount peace goal it had assumed in defeating the Axis. This was visualized as the conversion, by example and guidance, into a peace-loving nation of a people believed to be congenitally belligerent and democracy-resistant. Since the full burden of success or failure in this undertaking fell on MG, its conduct met with a very considerable critical attention.

During the so-called combat stage and for some months thereafter MG functions were exercised by the joint American-British command authority SHAEF (Supreme Headquarters Allied Expeditionary Forces). After its dissolution (July, 1945) General Eisenhower combined the position of Military Governor and Commanding General, with Headquarters in Frankfurt (United States Forces European Theater—USFET). By late 1945, however, the task of MG had begun to shift to Berlin, where the Office of Military Government for Germany (US) [OMGUS], having absorbed the American "element" destined for the work in the CC (styled US Group CC), operated under General Lucius D. Clay as Deputy Military Governor. The coexistence and competition of two MG capitals, in Frankfurt and Berlin, each with its own staff, policies, and empire-builders with ill-defined and overlapping jurisdictions, resulted in

---

[1] After World War I American forces had occupied a part of the Rhineland; the initial (armistice) period of strictly military control was converted, with the adoption of the Versailles treaty by the German National Assembly, by the so-called Rhineland agreement of the Allied and Associated Powers (June 28, 1919), into civilian rule of an Interallied Authority (likewise styled High Commission). This second stage was terminated with the complete evacuation of the area assigned to the United States in 1923. See Ernst Fränkel, *Military Occupation and the Rule of Law*, New York, 1944, for a competent treatment.

friction and duplication, and bears its full share of responsibility for the confusion and indecision which prevailed in the crucial initial stages of the occupation. Fuller efficiency was not obtained until March, 1947, when, after the elimination of USFET, the functions of Commanding General and Military Governor were combined in Berlin Headquarters under General Clay. However, skeleton staffs were retained also in Frankfurt. In 1948 a new shift occurred which, accelerated by the Berlin blockade, retransferred the bulk of MG operations to Frankfurt, where in the well-appointed building of the IG Farben concern adequate office facilities were available. With the installation of the Headquarters organization of the American element of the High Commission in Frankfurt the administration was finally consolidated. These incessant, though perhaps unavoidable, organizational transmutations could not fail to influence adversely AMG's policies and their execution.

The vertical structure of MG corresponded throughout to the regional division within the American zone. In the chain of command, OMGUS was the top and the roof. Under it four *Land* MG's (since the fall of 1949 called *Land* Commissioners) are functioning in the capitals of the four *Laender* (Munich, Stuttgart, Wiesbaden, and Bremen), headed by a *Land* Governor with his staff more or less patterned on the functional divisions at Headquarters. On all levels the multiplicity of these administrative branches—frequently exposed to reorganization and reshuffling—such as civil administration, economics, property control, education and religious affairs, public health, information control (later information service), legal, and others, reflects the variety of functions MG had to perform. In addition, there existed coordinated agencies for military and security (counter-intelligence) purposes.[2] Later, when the operational control was superseded by the largely supervisional activities, the functional organization had to be readjusted again. Military and civilian operations were finally completely separated. Probably the most important of all divisions was Civil Administration in charge of governmental structure, supervision of internal administration, and democratization. The Economics division, at first in the center, lost much of its operational impetus by the appearance of the Economic Cooperation Administration (ECA) under the Marshall plan, an agency (until 1949) outside MG jurisdiction and frequently at odds with it. By 1949 the increased accent on re-education, now more modestly styled "reorientation," raised the importance of the Education and Cultural Affairs division. Although the shaking-down stage was inordinately extensive the organization, in the final analysis, was sufficiently streamlined to provide for an adequate performance.

Subordinated to the *Land* MG offices were the staffs of MG in the regional districts (*Regierungsbezirke*) and in the smaller administrative areas of the counties (*Kreise*) and towns. With the progressive restoration of German self-government these lower echelons were either withdrawn or lost much of their

---

[2] Military security was no problem at all. Drunken GI's made more trouble than the submissive Germans. The much advertised underground (*"Edelweisspiraten"*) existed only in the imagination of reporters.

influence; but the liaison officials in the *Kreise* continued to perform vital services of closer contacts with the German population and were, therefore, retained under the High Commission. Generally, supervision and integration of the local and intermediary offices of the *Land* MG's were only moderately effective. But similar difficulties vitiated also the relations between OMGUS and the *Land* MG offices which in time developed a surprising and not altogether beneficial independence from the central administration of OMGUS. In the long run, the MG operations in the various *Laender* differed curiously from one another almost to the extent of the *Laender* administrations themselves.

PERSONNEL

At its peak in 1946, MG personnel in the U.S. zone never exceeded 6,000. Thereafter, it fell off sharply and, with the change-over to the High Commission (1949) it was reduced to some 1,600. In quality it varied greatly as to periods and functional assignments. In the early stages of direct MG operations by military field and district detachments, some of the army men had been initiated into their administrative tasks by most rudimentary preparations in MG schools in the United States. As practical Americans they did, on the whole, a commendable job of restoring the technical services in an utterly chaotic country. Owing to the lack of psychological equipment they were less fortunate in their contacts with the German people. The problem, affecting of course also the troops, became widely known under the name of fraternization. Initially high-caliber civilian experts were enlisted for service of a year or more at Headquarters. Replacements were more often than not of an inferior quality. Unlike the British and the French who utilized administrative talent of their colonial services, it took the United States a long time to train on the spot a staff competent to deal with the amazing variety of complex issues the occupation continually presented. Moreover, high army officers occupied many key positions. When good, a professional army officer was often very good; when bad, he was, as a rule, terrible. But in fairness it can be stated that, after trial and error, the quality of the MG personnel, if not first-rate, was thoroughly satisfactory. In time an occupational civil service emerged whose members, if frequently frustrated by the complexity of the job, were capable of attending to the administration of a country and people bewilderingly foreign to most of them.[3]

No report on MG in the American zone could ignore or should minimize the work and the personality of General Lucius D. Clay, Deputy Military Governor until March, 1947, and thereafter (until May, 1949) Military Governor and Commander of the European Theater. A Southerner from Georgia by birth and world outlook, an army engineer by profession, a first-rate organizer and executive, and without doubt a leader of men, the American pro-

[3] MG was particularly fortunate in finding as Governors for Wuerttemberg-Baden two exceptionally able men (Colonel Dawson and Mr. Charles M. LaFollette), standing head and shoulders over their colleagues in the other *Laender,* not to mention the individual that was permitted, for four fateful years, to act as the Commandant of the American sector of Berlin.

consul, during the most critical years of the occupation, was not only the center of policy implementation but in many vital instances the originator of the policies, though they nominally stemmed from the Department of the Army in Washington.[4] In spite of his military training he was possessed of a sincere devotion to democratic ideals. It was probably more the guilt of some of his advisors that he was inclined to equate the outward forms of democracy with its substance as a way of life. Of the German people he knew probably not more than his high-level contacts permitted him to learn. When properly briefed and not overly relying on alleged experts in his entourage, his amazingly retentive mind was capable of sensible and often far-sighted solutions. That he would gain the affection of the Germans could hardly be expected; yet he did. Perhaps the assignment exceeded the capabilities of any man.

THE PHASES OF AMERICAN OCCUPATION POLICIES

During the war against a ruthless enemy the American people favored a peace which would make it impossible that, within a foreseeable future, Germany would again come uncomfortably close to world domination. True, the Versailles peace had proved a fertile soil for nationalism and Hitlerism; but its failure was ascribed less to its terms than to German cunning in whittling them away and to Allied disunity. At an early date it was also intended that the occupation should become the primary instrumentality for converting by what was called, rather arrogantly, "re-education" of the Germans into a democratic and peace-loving nation. In this the American people were much more idealistic or naïve than Germany's neighbors who, without illusions, preferred tangible security to the promissory note of democratization.

It is a matter of record that American top level planners, absorbed with the exacting demands of the global war, failed to give early consideration to the post-hostilities phase of MG operations. Existing plans were concerned primarily with military and economic disarmament. Only after the Yalta Conference had permitted a better evaluation of the Soviet attitude did a more comprehensive blueprint of occupation policies emerge in the famous JCS 1067/3.[5]

JCS 1067, admittedly an interim program (though some of its basic tenets were subsequently incorporated into the Potsdam Declaration) was of a mainly negative nature, under the motto: "Germany will not be occupied for the purpose of liberation but as a defeated enemy nation." And: "The principal Allied objective is to prevent Germany from ever again becoming a threat to the peace of the world." Divided into three parts (political, economic, financial), it proceeded from the assumption (fully confirmed by subsequent experience) that

---

[4] The formal responsibility for the occupation was transferred to the Department of State only with the establishment of the High Commission (summer, 1949). Contrariwise, the British and the French counterparts were almost from the beginning responsible to the civilian authorities at home (Foreign Office and Secretariat for Occupied Territories, respectively).

[5] Directive of the Joint Chiefs of Staff sent on April 28, 1945, to General Eisenhower as Commander-in-Chief of the combined allied forces.

the entire fabric of German political, social, economic, cultural, and moral life had become so contaminated by Nazi techniques and ideologies that the only feasible way for a potential political reconstruction in line with democratic standards consisted in first wiping the state clean. This called for the imposition of strictest measures for demilitarization, denazification, arrest of war criminals and ranking Nazis and the confiscation of their property; prohibition of all political activities; closing of courts and educational institutions until they could be reopened with non-Nazi personnel. Similarly the economic controls were directed towards the paramount need for the decentralization of the economic power and permitted only the maintenance of the essential services. There is next to nothing in the lengthy document suggestive of democratization as an occupation aim. It is obvious that the Potsdam Declaration, with its prominent emphasis on re-education and democratization, constitutes a considerable advance over JCS 1067.

MG policies may be roughly divided into five periods:

(1) The *first* stretched to the Potsdam Declaration and beyond. During this stage AMG governed the American zone in the most literal sense of direct administrative operations. JCS 1067 was the American occupation blueprint. But long before its formal abrogation (July 11, 1947) it had become a dead letter. Valiantly MG Regulations, the code of conduct of AMG officials, tried to square the circle between its unrealistic rigor and the requirements of a more progressive occupation policy.

(2) The establishment of the three South German *Laender* (Bavaria, Wuerttemberg-Baden, and [Greater] Hessen) by USFET Proclamation of September 19, 1945, marks the opening of the *second* period. It is coextensive with the creation of workable democratic institutions of German self-government in the various *Laender* and the drafting of democratic constitutions by them, together with the establishment of the German interzonal agency of the *Laenderrat*. During this period MG exercised indirect control by policy instructions addressed to the *Land* governments and close cooperation with them in their implementation.

(3) The *third* stage was preluded by Secretary of State Byrnes' Stuttgart address (September 6, 1946) and formally inaugurated by General Clay's letter (September 30, 1946) on "Relationships between Military and Civil Government subsequent to the adoption of the *Land* constitutions," addressed to the MG offices of the *Laender*. Stating that "US policy requires that the German people be permitted to increasingly govern themselves," it limited the functions of MG thereafter to "observation, inspection, reporting, and advising," with the important proviso, however, that on certain enumerated fields MG will reserve for itself direct intervention in German internal affairs.[6] General Clay's directive also contained the important American *credo* on the democratic and federal form of government to be striven for in German re-

---

[6] Among the reserved fields were: review of German legislation; removal of public officials whose political activities are in violation of the occupation objectives; demilitarization; MG courts; disapproval of (only) such economic, social and political and governmental activities as MG may clearly find in violation of the occupation objectives.

construction.[7] With the beginning of 1947 direct intervention by MG with internal affairs became a rare exception. During this period the formerly existing symbiosis of the American and the German levels of state administration was superseded by a clear separation, the Americans supervising and the Germans doing things themselves. Most governmental and administrative fields were progressively transferred to indigenous German agencies legally constituted by democratic procedures, and, with the merger of the economic administrations of the British and the American zones,[8] an important step towards territorial unification was taken.

(4) As usual, the official policy of Washington lagged behind actual developments. Another directive of July 11, 1947, formally repealing JCS 1067, reflected the decisive turn in American occupation policies as the *fourth* stage. The directive visualized the problem of Germany in the wider frame of European recovery. Visibly recoiling from the negativism of JSC 1067, the redefinition of the occupation objectives denotes the positive encouragement of *bona fide* democratic efforts. For the first time cultural objectives and education are declared the focal points. The occupation, thus, has traveled a long way from the role of the conqueror, to that of policeman, to that of mentor and friend. The practical result was the sprouting of educational programs in all divisions of MG. The new approach was likewise stressed in the relaxation of political and other controls. Self-government was to be promoted with the fullest assumption of legislative, executive, and judicial powers by German authorities. The Germans themselves were to decide on their ultimate form of government in conformity with their tradition, and "no external forms should be imposed." But the American government showed itself opposed to "an excessively centralized government which through a concentration of powers may threaten both the existence of democracy in Germany and the security of the German neighbors and the rest of the world." Consequently, it was strongly suggested that "the most constructive development of German political life would be the establishment throughout Germany of federal German states (*Laender*) and the formation of a central German government with carefully defined and limited powers and functions." An even more drastic change occurred in the economic field. With the target of German economic rehabilitation within the framework of European recovery, the economic restrictions imposed by the Potsdam Declaration were to limit themselves to war industries. The previous injunction against cartels was mitigated. But no previous document had revealed such interest of the American taxpayer in the liberalization of the economic policies of the occupation.

Once again occupation policies and reality did not tally. By 1948 the substance of MG controls had evaporated and even the shadow of supervision had become evanescent. Under the policy of nonintervention direct operational activities of MG ceased completely. The supervisory activities were kept to a minimum. Loss of power and lack of personnel stood in the way of fulfilling

[7] These objectives will be discussed in detail *infra,* pp. 528 ff.
[8] See *infra,* pp. 535 ff.

even the residual functions of reporting, inspection, and observation. With growing self-reliance the eagerness of the German officials to seek advice or even merely to submit information became proportionally less. Anyone who read the German press was better informed about German affairs than high-ranking MG officials. Increasingly since 1948, MG operated in a political and moral vacuum which could not fail to engender a deep sense of frustration among the best of its staff. Under this policy of self-emasculation for the sake of lofty democratic principles, what influence MG still possessed confined itself to persuasion, possibly remonstration, at best, example. None of the other occupation powers deemed it wise to resort to such a degree of abdication from power.

But it is probably unfair to ascribe the petering out of a respectable experiment either to occupation policies or to the personnel trying to make them effective. The reasons lie deeper. After the breakdown of the London Conference of the Foreign Ministers (December, 1947) the Germans, forever sensitive to the realities of power, had become aware that the struggle for democracy was no longer conducted between themselves and the Western powers, but between the East and the West, and that, regardless of what marks they brought home from the school of democracy, they had risen, in this struggle, to quasi-allies of the West.

(5) This period, and with it the military phase of the occupation, came to a fitting climax with the creation of the Western Federal Republic (summer, 1949) and, as the *fifth* stage, the concomitant establishment of the Allied High Commission whose relations to the Western German Government are determined by the principle of strict nonintervention in German affairs with the exception of those specified fields which the Occupation Statute reserves to the jurisdiction of the High Commission.[9] The latest Directive of November 17, 1949, is geared to another high-flung ideal styled "the integration of Germany into a free Europe." "All efforts to help towards the goal of a unified Germany on a democratic and federal basis will be made. But the United States is opposed to the resurgence of ultra-nationalistic or antidemocratic forces which might threaten again the peace of Europe. Within this frame Germany should enjoy the widest possible freedom of self-determination."

[9] See *infra*, pp. 592 ff.

CHAPTER XXII

DENAZIFICATION

Denazification, or the permanent elimination of the Nazi Party and its influence, preceded democratization chronologically in all international agreements. It figured prominently in the Atlantic Charter, Yalta, and JCS 1067. The Potsdam Declaration realized that democratization and denazification were complementary occupation and peace aims. Since the former is impossible of attainment without the latter, it became the key to German political reconstruction. From the start the multi-faceted term *denazification* had a wider scope than the task of merely removing Nazi-tainted personnel from German public, economic, and cultural life. In the words of the Potsdam Declaration, it implied also "[destroying] the National Socialist Party and its affiliated and supervised organizations, to dissolve all Nazi institutions, to insure that they are not revived in any form and to prevent all Nazi and militarist activity and propaganda." In particular, repeal of the Nazi laws, as the most tangible reflection of Nazi institutions, was given a priority in the Yalta and Potsdam documents and in JCS 1067.

DESTRUCTION OF THE PARTY ORGANIZATIONS

The CC complied with these injunctions in full. The Nazi Party and its affiliated and supervised organizations were prohibited and dissolved. Its vast economic assets, especially those of the German Labor Front, monster labor union of the regime, were seized.[1] As an organization the huge octopus of the Nazi Party has been completely destroyed. To date no attempts at reconstituting or reviving the Party have been undertaken. After twelve years of fierce regimentation it is unlikely that the German people would voluntarily submit again to totalitarian control. Nor would it be tolerated by the Allies so long as the occupation continues.

[1] See CC Law No. 2 of October 10, 1945 (Official Gazette of the Control Council No. 1 at 19); Directive No. 50 of April 29, 1947 (OG/CC No. 15 at 275) and others. In the U.S. zone, Law No. 5 (SHEAF—MG Gazette, Issue A at 17) suppressed the Party itself together with fifty-two enumerated offices and subdivisions and eight paramilitary organizations such as the SS, the SA, and the Hitler Youth.

REFORM OF NAZI LEGISLATION

Much more intricate was the elimination of the Nazi legislation.[2] What may be called the political legislation on which the Nazi regime was based was repealed at an early date by the CC as well as by MG enactment in the American zone.[3] Additional statutes of the Nazi period were rescinded later, but not without encountering considerable difficulties as to how to fill the vacuum created by the cancellation. It was relatively easy to qualify an enactment as Nazi-inspired if measuring it by certain standards believed to embody the Nazi tenets, such as discrimination as to race, religious beliefs, or political affiliation. But in most cases repeal called for a democratically oriented substitute legislation. A veritable Pandora's box of legal controversies was opened. Some fifteen thousand laws and enactments required scrutiny. This tremendous task by far exceeded the capacities of the legal experts of the CC as well as the AMG lawyers. After strenuous efforts to infuse democratic principles and the rule of law into some selected areas of civil and criminal law, denazification of law passed by default of the occupation authorities to the meanwhile restored German agencies which, however, were too preoccupied with more urgent legislative tasks of the day ever to undertake a systematic effort to denazify German law.[4] Nonetheless, the bulk of Nazi-tainted or inspired legislation has been eliminated. Nor is it likely that, under present conditions, German legislative authorities would re-enact discriminatory legislation, or that German courts openly would flout the rule of law.

DENAZIFICATION OF PERSONNEL

However, the term *denazification* is commonly understood to refer to the human element, focusing on the removal of Nazi or Nazi-affected personnel from the public, economic, social, and cultural life. It is this aspect which deservedly has attracted the widest attention. The situation was complicated by the injection into the program of the occupation of the concept of militarism justly deemed as responsible for the German catastrophe as Nazism proper. While certain at least suggestive yardsticks could be established of participation in or responsibility for the Nazi regime, the elusive term *militarism* clearly defied precise definition. Moreover, it soon was found that many persons had held influential positions in economic and cultural life who, by accepted standards, were neither members of the Party nor could be proved to have

[2] Students are referred to Karl Loewenstein, "Law and the Legislative Process in Occupied Germany," *Yale Law Journal,* 57 (1948), pp. 724 ff, 994 ff.

[3] Twenty-five specifically named Nazi statutes were repealed by CC Law No. 1 of October 6, 1945 (OG/CC No. 1 at 6. For the American zone see Law No. 1 (SHEAF) of June 1, 1945 (MG Gazette Issue A at 3 and 5).

[4] AMG legislation subsequently confined itself to such matters which the Germans were believed unwilling to tackle themselves or for which the occupation policies required direct action by MG. Among these were, for example, legislation directed against excessive concentration of economic power (Law No. 56) and restitution of property to Nazi victims (Law No. 65). The former remained a scrap of paper because MG did not enforce it; the latter led to a fair degree of restoration of property to "non-Aryans" arbitrarily despoiled. With the installation of German *Land* authorities this source of MG legislation dried up completely.

tangibly benefited from the regime and yet, from the viewpoint of promoting democracy, were as bad or worse than the registered members of the Party. And finally, even assuming that Nazi personnel could have been temporarily eliminated, how could it be prevented from returning to power?

The magnitude of the problem was hardly anticipated by the occupation authorities. The filing cards of the Party, rescued by a lucky accident just when they were about to be converted into paper pulp, revealed that about nine million people at one time or another had been enrolled as members in the NSDAP. If to these are added the memberships in the affiliated and supervised organizations from which practically no person desirous of earning a living could escape, it is no exaggeration to say that at least two-fifths, if not one-half, of the entire German population were directly connected with the Nazi regime. That, under these conditions, the convenient concept of collective guilt found favor need not surprise. But in fairness it should be stated that it was never officially adopted and that at an early date it was completely superseded, if not by the principle of individualization, at least by the setting up of some recognizable standards of major and minor guilt.

Technically the job of denazification proved even more formidable than numerically. It did not seem feasible to charge the Germans themselves with it. Even if more anti-Nazis had been available, one could not establish a minority as judge over the majority. Obviously the task fell to the occupation authorities. Yet having neither the experience nor the manpower for the required individualization, they could hope to cope with the problem only by applying some mechanical standards. These, in turn, were soon discovered to lead to undesirable results in many cases which did not fit into the categories. If conducted democratically, denazification required individualization, considering in each case the widely different motivations for joining the Party, the extent of the person's identification with the Party objectives, and his or her active share in the Nazi regime's guilt.

Such pragmatic standards were applied by two important CC directives, inspired by precedents in the American zone,[5] "for the removal from office and from positions of responsibility of Nazis and persons hostile to Allied purposes" and "for the arrest and punishment of war criminals, Nazis and militarists." The first mentioned of these enactments spelled out no fewer than 136 specific positions, the incumbents of which were subject to mandatory removal, together with twenty-two more in which discretionary removal was indicated. Among these were categories of officials of the NSDAP and its affiliated and supervised organizations (thirty-seven in all), the holders of certain positions in the legal profession, the civil service, and business. The assumption was that since the regime did not tolerate enemies in key positions the holder of such an office must have been an active sympathizer even though not having become an enrolled member of the NSDAP. In the majority of cases the assumption proved correct; but because of their inelasticity, these mechanical standards wrought individual injustice, particu-

[5] Nos. 24 of January 12, 1946, and 38 of October 12, 1946.

larly since in most cases internment (without trial or even proper individual investigation) was mandatory. Such cases of injustice, skillfully played up by the victims, tended to imperil gravely the democratic objectives of the purification procedure.

A seemingly more refined but intrinsically no less faulty method consisted in adjudging the degree of individual guilt by the year of entry into the party (the so-called "vintage" principle), assuming that the earlier a person had joined the Party the greater his share in its guilt. Once again this method failed to be fair because the motivations for the entry into the Party were too complex to be caught in a purely standardized formula.

Whatever the method chosen, the "revolution on paper," by legislation or injunction of the victors, could not be successful unless supported by the sincere willingness of the German people to rid themselves of the Nazi heritage. Such willingness, let alone the feeling of collective guilt or its attenuated form of collective responsibility, did not exist. The naïve distinction of the American planners between the "good German people" and their "wicked rulers" proved unrealistic. No sooner had the Germans awakened from the stupor of defeat than they constituted themselves into a solid front against denazification and, quite understandably, the latter became the first potent rallying point of a defeated nation against the victors. It was exceedingly rare to find a real Nazi, that is, one who admitted he had joined because he had believed in the Nazi tenets. When Party membership could not be concealed a number of standard explanations were offered: membership had been "nominal" only; it had been imposed without knowledge or under duress, since refusal to join would have endangered life, liberty, and property or at least involved the loss of employment. Subjectively in many cases these excuses may have been true; objectively they were not. If one were to believe the Germans, an insignificant minority had compelled, by terrorization, the vast majority to become Nazis. While terror was adduced as the almost universal reason for membership, the vast majority steadfastly refused to admit knowledge of the concentration camps as the instruments of terror. If confronted with the incontrovertible evidence of Nazi outrages, the wholesale degradation and slaughtering, it was alleged that beyond vague rumors they had known nothing thereof and that at any rate they were not responsible. The Nuremberg trials served as a convenient alibi. Whatever scruples of conscience may have existed they were claimed to have been atoned by the hardships after the collapse.

As the picture slowly emerged it was found that opposition to the regime had been strongest among the laboring classes and the Catholics, although in numerous instances loyalty to the Church and to Hitler were not deemed incompatible. Conformity had been greatest among the socially higher classes and the leaders in professional, cultural, and economic life. Moreover, support of the regime revealed a curve closely following the successes of the Nazis before and during the war. The apex may have been reached with the victories in Russia in 1941; it flattened out with military failures after 1942

(Stalingrad). Finally, there existed from the beginning degrees in support of the Nazis. Fanaticism did exist. But membership in the Party did not invariably mean acceptance of all its tenets. Rather was it in many cases an insurance against professional disadvantages and the personal gratification of belonging to the ruling class. Opportunism was rampant among the younger generation, which could enter the professions only through Party membership. Dissatisfaction grew proportionally with the impending loss of the war. But the spirit of organized and mass-supported resistance was conspicuous by its absence, as evidenced by the abortive rebellion of July 20, 1944.[6]

Grave shortcomings on the American side should not be ignored. The initial assumption of collective guilt did not stand the test of experience. The black-and-white approach did not gibe with the extreme complexity of the situation. Of the mind of the Germans the invaders knew next to nothing. Nor was proper use made of the genuine anti-Nazis of whom, in the early stages of the occupation, there were not a few. Moreover, the attitude of MG personnel was by no means consistent. Revolting as were the excesses of the regime to the American mind, they failed to evoke uniformly negative reactions. The late General Patton's equating the Nazis with "just another political party" was by no means exceptional. Immunity against the anti-Semitic poison was not promoted by fraternization. Most important, however, were the practical reasons for a relaxation of the denazification policy. Practically all technical experts and business leaders had been Nazis. Their temporary removal stood in the way of economic reconstruction and recovery which, in turn, were demanded by both the American taxpayer and the belief that only an economically sound Germany would resist the temptations of Communism. There were just not enough non- or anti-Nazis to fill the gaps. Retrospectively it may seem doubtful whether this was true; at least the Soviets proved what could be done without the Nazis. But sooner or later the choice had to be made between the ideological requirements of denazification and economic expediency. Denazification in due course became another casualty of the cold war.

THE TRANSFORMATIONS OF THE DENAZIFICATION POLICY

Denazification may be divided into four stages:

(1) During the *first,* stretching from the invasion to March, 1946, it was undertaken as a direct operational function by MG detachments. The method was screening through the famous *Fragebogen,* an elaborate and, in the light of experience, constantly refined questionnaire as the basis of investigation by Counterintelligence Corps and Special Branch officials, leading to the decision as to mandatory removal from office and employment, arrest, or discretionary re-employment. Perjured information was subject to heavy punishment by MG courts. The early directives left private business wholly unaffected. This gap was hastily filled by MG Law No. 8 (September 26, 1945)

[6] See *supra,* pp. 454 f.

which prohibited the employment of any "more than nominal" member of
the Nazi Party in positions of business "other than ordinary labor."

The directives were indefinite, conflicting, constantly changing, and subject
to interpretation varying from district to district, and gave more or less arbitrary powers to MG officials eager to discharge their reconstruction assignments or accessible to persuasion, particularly if offered by an attractive
female. The unavoidable result was the return of ex-Nazis who were "nice
people" to economic life and the reinfiltration of Nazi professionals and experts deemed indispensable. Yet, whatever were the defects of this system,
this was, at least in the early stages, the only time when a thorough purge
of Nazism from German life was seriously attempted.

Owing to German reactions and also to misgivings among MG officials
the denazification procedure was turned over to the Germans by the famous
Law "on the Liberation from National Socialism and Militarism" (March 5,
1946) with which the *second* denazification phase begins in the American
zone.[7] The statute, one of the most ambitious measures ever undertaken to
penalize past modes of social and political behavior of an entire nation, compelled all adult persons to register. It established five classes or degrees of
identification with the regime, namely: Major Offenders (Class I—aiming
at the real thugs and hooligans); Offenders (Class II—activitists, militarists,
and large-scale profiteers); Lesser Offenders (qualified as probationers—
Class III); Followers (*Mitläufer*—Class IV); and those Exonerated (Class
V). An appendix (patterned on CC Directive No. 24) contained an elaborate
list of positions and offices whose former holders were considered, on re-
buttable presumption, as belonging to Classes I and II. The law stipulated
various sanctions for the different categories; applicable only to Classes I
and II were internment in a labor camp for a maximum period of ten years;
confiscation of property; loss of civic rights (in particular political rights);
exclusion, permanently or for a limited period, from a profession or an economic enterprise (except manual labor). Minor economic or professional
restrictions, periods of probation and fines, were penalties for the other classes.
All cases were to be adjudicated by German Denazification Tribunals (*Spruch-
kammern*) with an appeal to an appellate tribunal. The presiding judge had
to be a trained lawyer, the associate judges were to be nominated by the political parties. The entire procedure was governed by due process of law.

(2) As those among AMG familiar with the German mentality had not
failed to predict, the experiment "to trust" the Germans themselves with
purging turned in due course into a colossal juridical farce. The number of
persons registered (close to thirteen million) made individualization impos-

---

[7] The measure was German-inspired and did not originate with AMG. Its basic principles
were drawn up by ranking members of the Bavarian ministerial bureaucracy who, while realizing that some degree of retribution was desirable, wished to protect the socially acceptable
Nazis. The measure was drafted with American assistance, General Clay being personally responsible for several of its major shortcomings, and was enacted by the *Laenderrat* in Stuttgart
(see *infra,* p. 534) as a joint measure for the entire American zone.

sible; with the manpower available for about 400 courts the procedure would have lasted for decades. Since the trials were conducted in the locality where the accused resided, pressure to be lenient was brought to bear on the board and the public prosecutor (all laymen). The political nominees on the board leaned backwards not to alienate potential voters. Corruption was widespread and without social reprobation. The *Fragebogen* being the main evidence, falsifications were common and remained largely unpunished. Even where the tribunals were willing to administer justice according to the law, they resorted to the practice of downgrading to the Follower class, which resulted merely in a light fine. If charged at all, the vast majority were classified as Followers, which permitted their reinstatement in office, or as fully exonerated. About 85 per cent of those MG had previously removed from office regained it in due course. MG, prodded by dissatisfaction at home, could do next to nothing. General Clay's occasional threat that the procedure would be returned to MG was shrugged off by the Germans who considered it a huge joke on the Americans. The situation had slipped irretrievably out of MG's hands.

(3) During the *third* period, therefore, ranging from the end of 1946 to 1948, the initial program was further whittled away by sweeping amnesties and wholesale exemptions from the law which decreased the denazification load of the courts by 70 per cent. The amnesties of 1946 exempted youth (those born before 1919) and the small fry, that is those of low income who were declared non-chargeable by the prosecutor. The most fatal blow came with the amnesty of October, 1946, by which MG officially permitted downgrading of Class II Offenders to mere Followers of Class IV to whom no further restrictions were attached. From this benefited primarily the worst activists who had succeeded in delaying trial. Ironically, minor Nazis tried earlier had been sent to labor camps while the vast majority of the big criminals jubilantly paid their fines and were fully redeemed. Complete mechanization was reached with the next amendment (October, 1948) permitting denazification by postcard after the fashion of a traffic court (the so-called *B-Verfahren*). This was the final privilege of the remaining untried Nazi thugs and big profiteers, originally charged as Offenders and reclassified as Followers. Moreover, the *Land* governments at any time could request the reopening of closed cases or grant pardons, individually or wholesale.

The Directive of July 11, 1947, fails to mention denazification, obviously because it believed it of no further importance. In January, 1948 MG relinquished the right of approval for downgrading and in August, 1948 all MG control ended. A uniform procedure winding up denazification for the entire Western German state was under consideration by the Bonn parliament early in 1950.

According to the distinctive pattern evolved by the tribunals the vast majority were either exonerated outright, or, at the worst, classified as Followers; among these were practically all people of social standing in the community: nationally known figures such as university professors, captains of industry who had exploited slave labor, editors and writers who had poisoned minds, high officials in civil service who had enforced the cruel Nazi laws. A relatively small number were placed in Classes III and II, and a mere handful in Class I, mostly quite unimportant minor local Nazis and hardly any "big shots" of the NSDAP. However, the procedure was not overly lenient towards a member of the former Party hierarchy provided he was not prominent socially. In a sense the denazification was the revenge of the "respectable" bourgeoisie against the socially unacceptable upstarts and roughnecks thrown up by the Nazi revolution. Those who had been the moral and economic supporters of the regime, who had financed and propagandized and waxed rich by it, were not affected.

The more the procedure was dismantled, the more the former Nazis, organized into powerful pressure groups and exploiting to the limit their impressive voting strength, clamored for its termination, denouncing it as at variance with democratic principles, penalizing a mere political error and undermining recovery and justice. The churches took up the cudgels; the political parties were anxious to disassociate themselves from the entire concept. In fairness, however, it should be noted that a goodly number of Germans and also leading newspapers were articulate in accusing the tribunals of leniency towards the real culprits and harshness towards the little fellow.

THE RESULTS OF DENAZIFICATION

The following figures [8] speak for themselves:

	Percentage	Thousands
Total registered	100.0	13,180.3
Not chargeable cases	73.8	9,738.5
Total chargeable cases	26.2	3,441.8
Chargeable cases completed	26.1	3,432.5
Amnestied without trial	18.9	2,487.3
Trials completed	7.2	945.2
Chargeable cases to be completed	0.1	9.3
Findings: Cases completed	100.0	945.2
Found as amnestied or proceedings quashed	100.0	314.6
Class I Major Offenders	0.1	1.6
Class II Offenders	2.3	21.9
Class III Lesser Offenders	11.1	106.1
Class IV Followers	51.1	482.7
Class V Exonerated	35.4	18.3

Particularly revealing are the figures for Class I which indicate that fewer persons were punished in this category than by MG courts in Dachau, Nuremberg, and elsewhere. The vast majority of the major Nazi criminals have disappeared in the lower classes, by being classified in a lower category from the start, by downgrading, or by escaping trial altogether.

[8] As of the end of May, 1949. See *Germany 1947–1949,* Department of State Publication 3556, European and British Commonwealth Series 9 (March, 1950), p. 111. They are almost complete; only 7,900 cases were still pending on appeal. Appeals as a rule resulted in downgrading.

Equally distressing are the statistics of sanctions imposed: [9]

	Thousands
Sentenced to labor camp	9.6
Fined	569.0
Temporarily ineligible to hold public office	23.0
Restricted in employment	724.2
Sentenced to special labor chores outside prison	30.4
Subject to confiscation of property	25.8

From these figures emerge two incontrovertible facts: (1) The German denazification mills ground rapidly and exceedingly coarse. (2) Denazification, intended as a self-purging operation of a remorseful nation eager to redeem itself before its own and the world's conscience by meting out fair justice to those who had brought ruin to their own people and untold misery to the world, ended as an unmitigated failure.

RENAZIFICATION

(4) The *fourth* stage of denazification actually is that of *renazification*. It means the return to office, to positions of influence and cultural or economic responsibility, of practically all former incumbents regardless of their Nazi past. A person cleared or "deloused" by a denazification board became eligible to any kind of public office. The ministerial bureaucracies in the *Laender* saw to it—the explicit injunction of the law to the contrary notwithstanding—that their former positions and ranks were kept open for them. Interim appointees to such offices were ruthlessly dismissed. On the other hand, officials of the denazification machinery have become pariahs, as much as Germans working in MG offices, and, like these, find it almost impossible to obtain employment upon conclusion of their work. Reinfiltration was particularly strong in the judicial and administrative services where the social solidarity of the bureaucracy successfully resisted any renovation by admission of democratically-minded officials even if professionally qualified. Former membership is no longer an obstacle to a political career or elective office. With active and passive franchise restored to all denazified persons in 1949, ex-Nazis began to enter the parliaments in Bund and *Laender*.[10]

THE REASONS FOR THE FAILURE

The failure of the American denazification policy could have been avoided only if it had not been undertaken at all. It cannot be explained away by

[9] The figures are derived from the same source as above. As to the sanctions imposed: The maximum penalty of ten years in a labor camp was given to only a few convicted. About 400 were sentenced to five to ten years; two-thirds to one to five years; one-third to below one year. In practically all cases, previous periods of internment were deducted. Of 14,000 assigned to Classes I to III in Bavaria, in 1949 only 55 were still in a labor camp. Of those receiving fines 85 per cent had to pay less than 1,000 Reichsmark (which, before the currency reform of June, 1948, amounted to a few cents). Likewise property confiscations were mostly partial only. Work outside a prison consisted in temporary assignment to a work squad for rubble clearing, etc. Ineligibility and employment restrictions were subsequently lifted in almost all cases.

[10] Of the 402 deputies of the first *Bundestag* (federal parliament) 53 or 13 per cent are former Nazis. The percentage is even higher in some of the *Landtage* (*Land* parliaments).

the—rather debatable—assertion that the denazification record of the other powers is worse than ours.[11] The assumption of Yalta, Potsdam, and JCS 1067 that vast masses of vigorous and socially respected people, in possession of the administrative and technical "know-how," could be eliminated for an indefinite period was fantastic to begin with. Perhaps a restricted target, confining denazification to specified classes and occupations essential in the formation of public life, could have been reached; but even this is doubtful. AMG contributed its share to the fiasco by failing to support from the beginning the anti-Nazi and democratic elements which did exist at that time and later by deliberately jettisoning the program to accelerate economic recovery. Under the exigencies of the cold war any enemy of the Communists has become an American ally.

But the main fault lies with the Germans. Like Prohibition, denazification foundered on the rock of public opinion. Dolefully blaming the regime for the loss of the war and the ruins of their cities the Germans—with very minor exceptions—consider participation in it at the most a political error, but by no means as something even remotely morally reprehensible which would call for expiation. What occurred in Germany on an unparalleled scale is the phenomenon—well-known to the psychiatrist—of "repression" (*"Verdrängung"*), by which they forced themselves to forget the past.

[11] In the British zone the procedure was almost identical though somewhat more realistically handled. The French did a better job by individualization. In the Soviet zone the big Nazis disappeared, either fleeing to the West or never being heard of again. The small fry was soon amnestied and fully "redeemed."

CHAPTER XXIII

POLITICAL DEMOCRATIZATION

QUADRIPARTITE POLICIES

Both quadripartite and early American plans were more explicit on denazification, the negative aspect of political reconstruction, than on its positive corollary, namely the necessity of and the methods for filling the gap by democratic institutions and personnel. Yalta and JCS 1067 ignored the issue. Potsdam, however, significantly visualized democratization as a dual objective: On the one hand, democratic institutions on the educational, judicial, and political field were to be established and removed Nazis "shall be replaced by persons, who, by their political and moral qualities, are deemed capable of assisting in developing genuine democratic institutions." On the other hand, the ultimate goal of democratization was to be reached by the "decentralization of the political structure" and the "development of local responsibility," in the assumption that only a decentralized Germany, in which the central state is weak and the territorial units are strong, would be capable of being democratic. This equation or identification of democracy and decentralization was destined to bedevil the occupation powers and the Germans alike.

In the political field proper, Potsdam intended to promote democracy by local self-government through elective councils; admission of all democratic parties with rights of assembly and public discussion. Representative and elective principles were to be introduced into regional, provincial, and state (*Land*) administrations "as rapidly as may be justified by the successful operation of these principles in local self-government." Finally, "subject to the necessity of maintaining military security," freedom of speech, press, and religion and the formation of trade unions were to be permitted.

Subsequently, quadripartite steps were undertaken to implement this program on the fields of judicial reform,[1] and the re-establishment of trade

---

[1] Proclamation No. 3 (October 20, 1945) on the fundamental principles of judicial reform and CC Law No. 3 (October 20, 1945) on the reorganization of the judicial system. However, only in the Western zones was a certain degree of uniformity achieved in line with German

527

unions.[2] Concerning the freedom of public opinion, quadripartite results were most unimpressive, confining themselves primarily to standards to be followed by German politicians and to allowing belatedly and ineffectually the free exchange of printed material between the four zones. In the fields of education and political organization, however, failing quadripartite agreement, each of the four zones developed its own pattern.

THE AMERICAN ZONE

In Western Germany the restoration of formal democracy was accomplished rapidly between the fall of 1945 and the summer of 1949, with at least outwardly notable success. In retrospect the expectation that the Germans could be "taught" democracy merely by establishing democratic institutions may seem rather naïve. These democratic techniques had existed in Germany as far back as under the Second Empire when the Germans had enjoyed manhood suffrage in advance of most other states, not to mention the Weimar Republic which had been praised as the most perfect democracy ever devised on paper. The claim that MG had "trained" the Germans in the use of democratic processes is unfounded. In technically managing democratic processes the Germans had relatively little to learn. Belatedly, it was recognized that democracy does not mean the ability to operate democratic institutions, but that it requires democratically inspired people, party politics, and civil service. The republican democracy of Weimar had perished because it lacked republicans if not democrats.

AMG deserves credit for having translated Potsdam's rather vague recipes for democratization into concrete and well-phrased standards of democratic behavior. Inspired by the best Jeffersonian tradition, they reflected the American democratic *credo* and reached world-wide prominence when submitted as the American political philosophy at the Moscow Conference (March-April, 1947). They deserve *verbatim* reproduction here.[3]

Democracy: All levels of German government in the U.S. zone must be democratic to the extent that:
(a) All political power is recognized as originating with the people and subject to their control;
(b) Those who exercise political power are obliged to regularly renew their mandates by frequent references of their programs and leadership to popular elections;
(c) Popular elections are conducted under competitive conditions in which no less than two effectively competing political parties submit their programs and candidates for public review;
(d) Political parties must be democratic in character and must be recognized as voluntary associations of citizens clearly distinguished from, rather than identified with, the instrumentalities of the government;

tradition, while the Soviets at an early date revolutionized the entire judicial system in order to adjust it to its political ideologies. See Karl Loewenstein, "Reconstruction of the Administration of Justice in American Occupied Germany," *Harvard Law Review,* vol. 61 (1948) pp. 419 ff.

[2] Here the rather general CC Directive No. 31 of June 3, 1946, permitted establishment of local and intrazonal trade unions.

[3] See letter addressed by General Clay as Governor to the Offices of the *Land* M–Governors of September 30, 1946; also see Department of State Publication 3556, p. 155. These principles were first elaborated as guidance for the *Land* governments in drafting their constitutions.

(e) The basic rights of the individual including free speech, freedom of religious preference, the rights of assembly, freedom of political association, and other equally basic rights of free men are recognized and guaranteed;

(f) Control over the instrumentalities of public opinion, such as the radio and the press, must be diffused and kept free from governmental domination;

(g) The rule of law is recognized as the individual's greatest single protection against a capricious and willful expression of governmental power.

This democratic catechism was further strengthened by the requirement that "German governmental systems must provide for a judiciary independent of the legislative and executive arms in general and the police activity in particular." However, no preference was stated for either the American system of the strict separation of powers, or the interdependence of the legislative and executive functions as under the cabinet system. Authoritarian government, however, was clearly excluded.

Furthermore, proceeding from the conviction—which, on the American side became a near-obsession—that only a largely decentralized political structure could comply with democratic standards, the policy statement strongly emphasized the federal solution for the future territorial organization. Subsequently, the American insistence on excessive federalization proved a thornier issue than the fulfillment of democratic requirements proper, and was responsible for many difficulties besetting the path of the new constitution for Western Germany. This program again should be quoted in full:

German governmental structure shall be federal in character (*Bundesstaat*) and the constituent units thereof shall be States (*Staaten*), not *Laender*.[4] The functions of government shall be decentralized within that structure to the maximum degree consistent with the modern economic life. U.S. policy concerning the relationships between levels of government requires

(a) All political power is recognized as originating with the people and subject to their control;

(b) Power shall be granted by the people primarily to the States (*Staaten*) and subsequently only in specifically enumerated and limited instances to a federal government;

(c) All other grants of governmental power by the people shall be made to the States;

(d) All powers not granted by the people shall be reserved for the people;

(e) A substantial number of functions shall be delegated by the States to the local governments. These should include all functions which may be effectively determined and administered by local governments;

(f) Governmental powers may not be delegated to private or quasi-public economic bodies;

(g) Pending the establishment of a federal government, the popularly responsible governments and *Landtage* of the States shall act as the people's agents for the conferring of powers requiring central execution upon such transitional federal or central body or bodies as may be agreed upon by civil government and military governments, or may be directed by the latter.

This equation of democracy and political decentralization, admittedly nurtured by American home experience, is not borne out by England and France, both thoroughly democratic nations in spite of a largely centralized

---

[4] This contrasting of *Staaten* and *Laender* is obviously a rather crude misunderstanding of the German terminology under the Empire and under Weimar.

organization. Moreover, the tacit assumption that a decentralized state is more dictatorship-proof than a more centralized organization is disproved by German experience. Hitler seized power not by capturing first the Reich and thereby dominating the *Laender,* but, on the contrary, by seizing control first of some of the smaller federal units (Brunswick, Thuringia) and using them as the springboard for the assault on the larger states and finally the Reich itself.

CHAPTER XXIV

GOVERNMENT AND POLITICS IN THE AMERICAN ZONE:
THE GERMAN LEVEL

ESTABLISHMENT OF THE *LAND* AUTHORITIES

As early as in the summer of 1945 AMG appointed in each of the three South German *Laender* of Bavaria, Wuerttemberg-Baden, and Hessen a prominent German of known anti-Nazis antecedents and presumed democratic persuasion [1] as Minister President; he, in turn, appointed, with MG approval, his cabinet. These MG-sponsored governments, without democratic mandate, were clearly authoritarian, faintly assisted, during the first half of 1946, by a consultative or advisory council (*Beratende Landesversammlung*) whose members were selected from among the four political parties that MG had licensed, namely the Christian Democratic Union (CDU), in Bavaria called Christian Social Union (CSU); Social Democratic Party (SPD); Liberal Democratic Party (LDP); and the Communists (KPD).[2] *Land* governments acted under instructions and supervision of the *Land* M–Governors who themselves were expected (but did not always comply) to follow the directives of the Theater Commander in Frankfurt and the Deputy M–Governor in Berlin respectively. In all cases the Minister Presidents offered full cooperation and proved equal to their task of leading their territories towards more normal conditions.

If by democratization was understood the holding of elections and the setting up of representative institutions the assignment was accomplished smoothly and rapidly during 1946. But while the acceleration of the procedure appealed to General Clay and some of his advisors, others were deeply alarmed by turning over to the Germans a large measure of responsibility before denazification, undertaken simultaneously, had insured a sufficiently democratic civil service and a political personnel of adequate democratic con-

---

[1] In Bavaria the first appointment had to be revoked since the appointee, Herr Fritz Schäffer, proved intractable. He became later Minister of Finance in the first cabinet of the Bonn government.

[2] For a full discussion of political parties see *infra*, pp. 546 ff.

viction. The policy of "too early and too much" seemed to them a grievous and irretrievable error.

The Germans in the U. S. zone were invited to conduct themselves as good democrats no fewer than six times in 1946. Municipal elections (January 30) were followed by county elections (April 28), city elections (May 28), and those for constitutional conventions or constituent assemblies (June 30), to be rounded out by plebiscites (referenda) on the constitutions drafted by the conventions and elections of the new diets (*Landtage*) in conformity with the constitutions (November 24 and December 1). The plebiscites resulted in sufficient though unimpressive majorities. All elections were perfectly orderly and honest, with a large participation of the electorate, the Germans docilely voting when being ordered. MG felt inordinately proud of this democratic accomplishment. In Bremen, added as the fourth *Land* to the U. S. zone in 1947, the Parliament (*Bürgerschaft*) accepted the constitution on September 15, 1947; it was ratified by the people on October 12, 1947.[3]

THE CONSTITUTIONS IN THE AMERICAN ZONE

Though technically adequate, the constitutions reveal, on the whole, little originality and are far from embodying a revolution in German political thinking. Lack of inventiveness may be ascribed to the parochialism of their draftsmen and the intellectual vacuum in which they were hatched; only the (rejected) French constitution of April 19, 1946, could serve as inspiration. Uniform as they are in proclaiming democratic aspirations, they differ considerably in institutional arrangements. Haunted by the memory of the abuse of executive power under Weimar they focus on the legislative assembly (*Landtag*) elected for four years by the direct, equal, and secret suffrage of all citizens of twenty-one years, under application of a rather unrefined system of proportional representation. "Splinter" parties which fail to receive a certain percentage of the total vote (varying from 5–10 per cent) are not considered in the assignment of seats. Only Bavaria adopted the bicameral system by providing for a second chamber (Senate) of sixty members in a merely advisory capacity, chosen on the basis of professional and corporate groups. All constitutions abstained from installing a state president. Governmental and executive powers are entrusted to a Minister President, chosen by the majority of the *Landtag* for a four-year term. In the selection of his ministers he is given considerable freedom.

The constitutions vary concerning the relationship of the government (Minister President and cabinet) and the Parliament. The position of the Minister President, to some extent patterned on the experience in Switzerland and the United States as understood by the drafters, is in theory stronger in Bavaria

[3] Elections results in the U.S. zone in 1946–47:

	Number of Seats	CDU	SPD	KP	Others
Bavaria	180	109	51	8	12
Wuerttemberg-Baden	100	41	32	10	17
Hessen	90	34	43	7	6
Bremen	100	24	46	10	20

than in the other two South German states. His and his cabinet's resignation may occur either on his own initiative or if "political conditions make a harmonious cooperation between the Minister President and the *Landtag* impossible." In practice this implies always a break-up of the government coalition, with the result that the opposition party would come into power or new elections must be held. Contrariwise, in Wuerttemberg-Baden and in Hessen the rules of genuine parliamentarism prevail under which the withdrawal of the confidence of the assembly forces the government to resign. Unless the new Minister President has been elected within four weeks (Bavaria) or ten days (Hessen) the *Landtag* is automatically dissolved, and new elections are to be held, a sensible precaution against prolonged cabinet crises. In Wuerttemberg-Baden the resignation of the Minister President is effective only if the Parliament agrees on the designation of his successor, a provision later copied by the Bonn Constitution. In addition, in all three *Laender* the *Landtag* may be dissolved by a popular referendum upon popular initiative— or decide self-dissolution by majority (Bavaria). Both contingencies are unlikely to occur. In Wuerttemberg-Baden the government, not having a veto against legislation as in Hessen, in case of disagreement with the *Landtag* may submit the controversial legislation to a referendum.

Otherwise the constitutions contain restatements of and also some improvements on Weimar such as provisions (presumably adequate) for a real independence of the judiciary; impeachment of members of the government before a state tribunal; determination of a controversial constitutional issue by a (relatively) independent state or constitutional court; a reasonably sufficient protection of the democratic order by excluding antidemocratic parties and restricting antidemocratic manifestations of public opinion; judicial review by the highest court; constitutional amendment by properly qualified majorities of the Parliament, and (in Bavaria and Hessen) with subsequent popular ratification; institutions of direct democracy by initiative and referendum on legislation and (in Wuerttemberg-Baden) also on constitutional matters. Under certain conditions the governments are granted emergency powers involving the suspension of enumerated civil liberties; this power, remembering Weimar, is hedged in by certain judicial and parliamentary safeguards to prevent abuse by the government. The constitutions are equipped with bills of rights of the traditional liberal and social pattern, elaborate to the point of verbosity, formulated somewhat more absolutely than is German custom, reflecting a definite clerical flavor in Bavaria and a mild tendency towards economic planning and state Socialism in Bremen and Hessen. In the latter country, the provisions concerning compulsory nationalization of certain natural resources, banks, and insurance companies were approved, by a separate referendum demanded by General Clay, together with the constitution.[4]

---

[4] Subsequently the entering into force of an implementary law enacted by a Socialist majority was vetoed by MG under the pretext that the matter could not be decided by one *Land* alone. So long as the current party coalition of the federal legislature (*Bundestag*) remains there is no chance of socialization in Germany. Laws on the related issues of works councils (*Betriebsräte*) and codetermination (*Mitbestimmungsrecht*) of factory policies by the trade

The constitution of Bremen, on the other hand, follows the tested pattern of Hanseatic city government. It is probably the best and most progressive of all constitutions in the American zone.

In line with German multiple-party habits and under the impact of proportional representation, in all *Laender* coalition governments of the three major parties became indispensable, controlled in Hessen and Bremen by the Socialists, in Bavaria by the Christian Democrats, and operating as a genuine working team in Wuerttemberg-Baden. But the absence of political crises and the remarkable stability of the cabinets—in all cases they were still headed in 1950 by the same Minister Presidents—were less due to the wisdom of the constitutional arrangements than to the fact of military occupation which, at least until 1949, had artificially frozen the party configuration by the licensing system.

ZONAL ORGANIZATION: THE *LAENDERRAT* (REGIONAL COUNCIL)

To dismember and dissolve Germany into independent states appealed only to the French. American thinking from the start focused on a federal organization. At an early date the pressing need for pooling food resources, pending the establishment of the central agencies under Potsdam, made imperative some degree of coordination of the three South German *Laender*. In October, 1945, MG directed the Minister Presidents to establish a Regional Council—*Laenderrat*—in Stuttgart as the mechanism for cooperation in matters transcending the area of a single *Land,* and thus requiring joint regulation.[5] Guided by the Regional Coordinating Office of MG and supported by a permanent secretariat as steering committee, to which, in 1946, a Directorate was added, the Minister Presidents met at least once a month to adopt, by unanimity, measures elaborated and drafted by an able staff of German experts. When approved by MG (OMGUS) they were submitted by each Minister President to his cabinet and thereafter promulgated for the individual *Land* by decree. Adoption by the *Laenderrat* amounted in substance, if not in name, to uniform zonal legislation. Upon election of the *Landtage* under the new constitutions a Parliamentary Council was added (April, 1947) whose twenty-four members, representing parliamentary opinion, gave the institution a touch of democratic legality. The twin pressures of widespread economic distress and the inescapable need for uniformity over so small an area usually produced agreement within the *Laenderrat*. But after the establishment of the *Landtage,* resenting inroads into their legislative sovereignty, difficulties could not fail to appear. Subsequently MG increasingly sided with the *Landtage* under the pretext that "uniformity though desirable was not necessary." Moreover, with the creation of the bizonal organization

---

unions which had been passed into Hessen and Wuerttemberg-Baden were likewise considered too Socialistic to find favor with AMG which vetoed them. However, after the federal Parliament had failed to legislate on the issues for Western Germany as a whole, the ban was lifted by U.S. High Commissioner McCloy (April, 1950).

[5] Bremen was joined to the *Laenderrat* in 1947 more for political than practical reasons.

in economic matters in 1947 [6] the usefulness of the *Laenderrat* became increasingly eroded. Left to it mainly was the restricted area of the so-called *Justizgesetze,* that is, laws dealing with legal matters excluding economic and cultural subjects. By the middle of 1948 the activities of the *Laenderrat* had almost completely dried out and its existence, shadowy and skeletal, was formally terminated in October, 1949, after the Bonn Constitution had become operative.

Nonetheless, the *Laenderrat* deserves more than a passing reference in the evolution of post-War Germany. The number (seventy-five) and importance of uniform zonal enactments are impressive. Undoubtedly the most significant was the Law on the Liberation from Nazism and Militarism of March 5, 1946. Other statutes secured a modicum of legal uniformity at least in Southern Germany. The bulk of legislation dealt with the impact of war and defeat on the economy of the devastated country. But the initiation of an incisive agrarian reform foundered on the resistance of the vested interests.

No less important may seem, however, the psychological results achieved in bringing conquerors and defeated to a better mutual understanding and respect. The *Laenderrat* proved an invaluable training ground for MG officials and Germans alike. The relationship was one of healthy give-and-take. It is to the credit of both that neither did the Germans resent American tutelage nor the Americans impose their opinions. The Germans gained self-confidence to the point where the conservative bureaucracy which staffed the *Laenderrat* was able to minimize efforts of the American mentors to cross-fertilize German legislation with American experience. This tendency was enhanced by the excessive policy of nonintervention in German domestic affairs which General Clay, after he had lost interest in his creation, enjoined on the American staff. Moreover, it seems in retrospect that the American policy-makers missed a major opportunity for developing this emergency structure of voluntary cooperation between the *Laender* into a genuine federal government for South Germany which later, since a similar device of *Land* cooperation had been successfully evolved in the *Zonenbeirat* (Zonal Council) of the British zone, could have become the frame for a grass-roots federal government for Western Germany.

THE BIZONAL INTERLUDE: ECONOMIC MERGER OF THE AMERICAN AND BRITISH ZONES

The division into four zones of occupation split Germany into four independent segments which, like watertight compartments, were wholly isolated from one another. Raw materials had become divorced from processors, manufacturers from markets, food-supplying farm regions from industrialized areas. Consequently, the amount of calories available for feeding the population varied greatly between the four and even within the individual zones. In the American zone a subsistence level could be maintained only by imports from the United States. Moreover, the French and the Soviet occupa-

[6] See the section immediately following.

tion forces lived off the German economy. Without some degree of central coordination there was no hope to improve the living conditions. When it proved impossible, because of French no less than Russian resistance, to establish the minimum of central economic agencies authorized by Potsdam, the rapidly deteriorating economic situation demanded a drastic change of policy.

To a final request of the U. S. in the CC, in the summer of 1946, for economic unification only the British acceded. They were responsible for the highly industrialized Ruhr where food scarcity of near-famine proportions resulted in the decline of coal production. By September, 1946, agreement was reached, formalized and complemented by the Byrnes-Bevin Agreement (December 2, 1946), to merge the British and the American zones as a single economic area with the aim of attaining equal consumers' rations by equitable distribution of pooled resources and pursuing common import policies. Under bipartite agencies (Control Board [BICO] consisting of the two Deputy Governors, Secretariat, and Control Groups) six German-staffed committees of which the most important was the Economic Committee (at Minden, British zone) were expected to manage the economic affairs of the "Bi-zone." The results were moderate at best. The committees were widely dispersed over the two zones without effective coordination. The Germans were unenthusiastic because they did not wish to lend a hand in anything preluding a split of their country; from the start party quarrels between the Socialists and the CDU and LDP interfered. Lacking enforcement powers and devoid of representative character the committees were unable to overcome the economic selfishness of the *Laender*.

The Anglo-American agreement of May 29, 1947, streamlined the government of the combined economic area (*Vereinigtes Wirtschaftsgebiet*) and increased its powers. (1) The Economic Council (*Wirtschaftsrat*) consisted of fifty-two members; they were chosen—as token of their democratic legitimacy—by the *Landtage* of the *Laender* on the basis of the population of each *Land*—the traditional device of German federalism—and in accordance with the party strength in each *Landtag*. The Council exercised, subject to bipartite approval, full legislative powers over the economic life of the combined area. (2) The Executive Committee (*Exekutivausschuss*), composed of eight members (one from each *Land*), served as the coordinating and supervisory agency; in due course it came to wield more power than the pseudo-parliamentary Council. Actual operational functions, however, were assigned to (3) the Directors who acted as the administrative managers of the five departments (Economics, Food, Agriculture and Forestry; Transport; Post and Telecommunications; Finance; Manpower). Of these, two (dealing with the postal affairs and railroads) had jurisdiction exclusive of the *Land* authorities much in the same way as the corresponding Ministries of the defunct Reich. The other Directorates operated through the authorities of the *Laender*. The Directors were responsible to the Council itself and not to the

Executive Committee. All offices were located in Frankfurt and grew into a vast bureaucratic organization. The progress achieved consisted, next to improved coordination, in the fact that the enactments of the Economic Council, upon approval of the Bipartite Board, overrode any German regulation of intrazonal or zonal character and were binding directly on the *Land* authorities; however, they could not abrogate CC legislation.

Once again, the arrangement, lasting from May 29, 1947, to February 9, 1948, fell short of expectations. From the start it was shot through with party politics which, for reasons of "democratization," the occupation powers had deliberately introduced. The Socialists felt, not unjustly, discriminated against by the appointments of CDU and FDP men to the key positions of the Directorates, while the Executive Committee and the Economic Council itself had Socialist majorities. Different standards of denazification in the British and American zones led to constant friction. Moreover, some of the agriculturally privileged *Laender* failed to cooperate in the implementation of the Council's enactments. Open violations occurred; the most notorious was the "potato war" with Bavaria in 1947. The representatives conducted themselves rather as defenders of the states' rights than acting for the common good. To discharge its legislative functions the Council was too small. The legislative output was correspondingly unimpressive (sixteen laws in all) dealing mostly with food distribution. The impasse was due, next to the unwillingness of the Germans to commit themselves to a Western solution of German unity, to the American policy which believed that it could square the circle between economic unification, states' rights, and democratic re-education in a single package.

Another sweeping reform was undertaken early in 1948.[7] Since the German Minister Presidents disagreed among themselves and were only too glad to escape responsibility, the new organization again was imposed by MG. The bizonal structure consisted now of five closely integrated organs, namely: (1) the Economic Council (*Wirtschaftsrat*); (2) Council of States (*Laenderrat*);[8] (3) the Executive Committee (*Verwaltungsrat*); (4) the High Court (*Obergericht*); and (5) the Bank of German *Laender*. Together with the reorganized Import-Export Agency (JEIA) the new setup was intended to give the Germans the maximum of economic self-determination compatible with MG supervision. After the enactment of the *Land* constitutions it was the second sizable installment in the restoration of German sovereignty.

(1) The Economic Council, simply by doubling the number of its delegates, was enlarged to 104 members in order to alleviate the work load and to

[7] By Proclamation Nos. 7 and 8 (February 9, 1948) and (bizonal) Law No. 60 (February 15, 1948), establishing a new bizonal economic organization, the High Court and the Bank of the German *Laender*. The bizonal agreement was subsequently extended several times and remained in force until the establishment of the German Federal Republic and the Allied High Commission respectively. The Bund became the successor in rights and duties of the Combined Economic Area (see Basic Law, Art. 133).

[8] This term is identical with the one used for the loose coordination of the *Laender* in the U.S. zone; see *supra*, p. 534.

permit a greater degree of representativeness.[9] Bowing to the inherent law of federal organization which requires, for economic reasons, adequate centralized powers, the Anglo-Americans were compelled to grant the Economic Council sufficient financial authority by allocating to it exclusively all revenues derived from customs, excise taxes, postal services, communications (railroads and transportation tax), together with an additional claim to the income and corporation taxes assessed uniformly by CC legislation and collected by the *Laender,* as well as sufficient power to enforce the enactments against recalcitrant *Laender.* All Council legislation required bipartite approval.

(2) The newly established Council of States (*Laenderrat*), the innovation of the reform, was a genuine second chamber representing, in line with German federalist tradition, the eight *Laender.* Its sixteen members were the Minister Presidents and other prominent cabinet officials [10] who, thus, for the first time since the collapse, were officially drawn together in a joint organization; this institution was intended to obviate the dangerously increasing tendency of the individual *Land* towards political independence. The main function of the Council of States was to participate in the economic legislation for the combined economic area by approval, amendment, or veto and thereby to assume responsibility for faithful execution. In this the new organization was successful; most of the previous difficulties disappeared.

(3) The Economic Committee (*Verwaltungsrat für das Vereinigte Wirtschaftsgebiet*) was raised to the level of a veritable government on the economic field. Its five departments corresponded to the central agencies authorized by Potsdam, with a chairman without portfolio added. He was also the president of the important Personnel Office, instituted under American prodding to break down the ingrained caste spirit of the German civil service. Chairman and members were responsible to both the Economic Council and the Executive Committee and removable by vote of non-confidence of the former alone; [11] this contingency, however, never occurred.

[9] The *Laender* participation and party strength may be seen from the following tabulation:

British Zone	Hamburg	4	
	Schleswig-Holstein	6	
	North Rhine-Westphalia	32	
	Lower Saxony	16	58
American Zone	Bavaria	24	
	Wuerttemberg-Baden	10	
	Hessen	10	
	Bremen	2	46
			104
Party composition	CDU and CSU	44	
	SPD	40	
	Liberal Democrats	8	
	Communists	6	
	Center Party	4	
	Economic Reconstruction Party	2	104

[10] The party composition was: CDU/CSU, 5; SPD, 9; FDP, 2.
[11] The chairman could be removed only by concurrent vote of both agencies.

(4) The establishment of a bizonal High Court (*Obergericht*) (with the seat in Cologne), consisting of ten professional judges, was intended, by application and interpretation of bizonal legislation, to overcome the reluctance of the *Laender* courts to enforce legislation if deemed inconsistent with the economic interests of the respective *Land*. Actually the Court had little work. The Germans know a federal organization when they see one and are used to submit to its authority.

(5) The Bizonal Bank finally, patterned on the American federal reserve system, reflected the American preference for decentralization of credit and banking operations. It was authorized to issue bank notes, in which capacity it became subsequently the instrumentality of the successful currency reform (June 1940); to set the discount rates; and to determine the amount of reserves to be held by the member banks. The Germans disliked the federalization of the banking system, partly because they are used to centralized control, partly, and here not without justification, because the Board, in which the *Land* governments are represented, could, by a majority of the economically weak *Laender,* determine the monetary policies for the entire area. The banking structure was retained under the Bonn Constitution.

To the bizonal organization belonged also the Joint Export-Import Agency (JEIA), an Anglo-American authority in which, however, the Americans as the bigger suppliers of German economic needs were preponderant. Merged with the formerly separate Joint Foreign Exchange Agency (JFEA), it functioned to promote and control German foreign trade. This institution, with a large staff of American and German experts, may be credited, together with the skill of German management and the work of German labor, with the amazing economic recovery after the currency reform.

The reform on the German level necessitated also streamlining of the Anglo-American Bipartite Control Office (BICO), with the result that on the increasingly important economic field both the American and the British MG organizations were largely superseded by BICO. Frankfurt became the real capital of Western Germany in substance if not in name. Factually independent, however, from BICO remained the Joint Coal Control Board in Essen (Ruhr) which, in 1948, took the place of the previously British-operated North German Coal Control Board. Responsible for the production and distribution of coal, it was operated entirely by Germans, the Management Board of German Coal Mining Industry (*Deutsche Kohlenbergbau-Leitung*). But neither Anglo-Saxon control nor the subsequent establishment of the International Ruhr Authority [12] could prevent the return to power of the coal barons and the steel masters who had dominated the Empire and the Weimar Republic, survived Hitler, and outwitted also military occupation.

GENERAL APPRAISAL OF THE BIZONAL ORGANIZATION

By repeated extensions, the bizonal set-up remained in operation until September 30, 1949, when the West German State succeeded it. All told it

[12] See *infra*, pp. 597 ff.

enacted 117 laws and several hundred implementary ordinances, covering the economic field in the widest sense of the term and including taxation, agriculture, finance and budgetary matters, labor, and general relief of economic distress. Far more than an emergency institution, it laid in many respects the permanent foundations of German economic life. Under the leadership of the Chairman of the important Economic Committee, Dr. Ludwig Erhardt (a Bavarian member of the CDU), all government controls over production and consumption, rationing as well as raw material restrictions, were successively abolished. After the currency reform—for which the Economic Council was not responsible—Germany was converted into a paradise of free enterprise operating under the laws of demand and supply. The system, for which German semanticists have coined the term *"freie soziale Marktwirtschaft"* ("the free and social market economy"), is probably farther removed from state planning than any other present-day economy, Switzerland and the United States not excepted. In this respect the adept pupils surpassed their American teachers.

Looking to the other side of the ledger the Economic Council fell short of the American expectations that it would serve as a political training ground for the Germans. Its parliamentarism was distorted and hybrid. The Socialists, excluded from the key positions by a CDU-oriented bureaucracy, from the start went into a sulking and unconstructive opposition. The Council represented neither the *Land* parliaments nor the people at large, who continued to look to their *Land* governments for political guidance. Knowing little of the Frankfurt organization and cordially disliking what little they knew of it, they blamed Frankfurt (and, of course, the occupation authorities) for all their hardships. The absence of effective political controls and the American insistence on the maximum of noninterference favored the rise and entrenchment of a huge and domineering bureaucracy which ran the show with customary technical efficiency and equally customary disregard for democratic processes and values. A bureaucratic foundation was laid which the Bonn Constitution could not undo. But in fairness it should be stated that, as a stop-gap between a Germany totally fragmented into semi-independent states and the coming into existence of the Federal Republic of Western Germany, the Economic Council has served its purpose.

CHAPTER XXV

POLITICAL DEVELOPMENTS IN THE OTHER WESTERN ZONES

In spite of the unification program of Potsdam the political and administrative patterns in each of the four zones differ widely, strongly reflecting the impact of the political ideologies and techniques of the responsible occupying power.

1. THE BRITISH ZONE

In contrast to the American zone, the British, relying throughout on a staff numerically if not qualitatively superior, approached the democratization of their Germans with caution. More pragmatic and less doctrinaire, they talked less about democracy and cared little for the seemingly insoluble problem of denazification. Only at the end of 1946 did they proceed to the definitive regroupment of the territories under their jurisdiction, resulting in the establishment of the four *Laender* North Rhine-Westphalia, Lower Saxony, Hamburg, and Schleswig-Holstein. On the other hand, they stressed intrazonal coordination under their own management. Central Offices (*Zentralämter*), closely integrated with the corresponding functional departments of British MG, though staffed primarily with Germans, were created (all told, eleven) for certain functional purposes (for example, for the administration of justice, finances, manpower, communications, etc.). As agencies of the occupying power and not coordinated among themselves, they remained beyond the influence of the *Land* governments. To achieve some degree of administrative uniformity informal contacts of the Central Offices with the *Land* Ministries were permitted.

The Zonal Advisory Council (*Zonenbeirat*) was established (February 2, 1946) as a consultative agency of MG in more general matters transcending the area of a single *Land*. It did not, however, result in the coordination of the Central Offices. At first an appointed body of thirty-two members, it was transformed (June 10, 1947) into a quasi-parliamentary institution of thirty-seven members who were delegated into it by the *Land* parliaments (elected shortly before, on April 20, 1947) in accordance with the strength of the political parties of the latter.[1] As a consultative intrazonal institution in matters affecting more than a single Central Office it retained its value long after the Americans had permitted the *Laenderrat* to wither on the vine, although the establishment of the bizonal authorities could not fail to cut deeply into its jurisdiction.

The British were equally tardy in admitting their Germans to self-government. In 1946 elections were permitted only on the local level. Following Hamburg (October 13, 1946) elections for the *Landtage* in the three other *Laender* were held (April 20, 1947). The electoral system conformed to the British principle of majority elections in single-member constituencies, with some modifications of the final result by a proportional assignment of seats from a "reserved" *Land* list (the so-called "mixed system"). However, it cannot be claimed that different electoral methods have resulted in differences of party structure or voting attitudes.

Nor were the British in a hurry to equip their *Laender* with constitutions whereby it may seem a moot point whether their motives were the tradition at home or the realization of the spurious character of such formalizations. The Germans were thereby not in worse position than their compatriots in the other zones. Upon the establishment of the *Laender* British MG issued (December 2, 1946) the "organic" Ordinance No. 57. Applying the well-tried colonial technique of "dyarchy," it heavily curtailed the legislative authority of the governments and parliaments of the *Laender* by reserving to MG full regulatory powers on fields permanently exempted from German jurisdiction (Schedule A); on certain other fields for emergency or transitional reasons (Schedules B and C); while on others the *Laender* had to follow MG instructions (Schedule D). Autonomy of the *Laender* thus was hardly more than nominal; they could only administer policies, but had little share in policy formation.

Only after the establishment of the Bonn Government in the summer of 1949 were constitutions enacted, instead of by specially elected constitutional conventions, by the regular *Landtage*. Schleswig-Holstein came first (January 12, 1950). It was fashioned and carried by the Socialist Party which, under the elections of 1947, possessed an absolute majority with an all-Socialist government. Certain tenets of the Socialist program, such as the limitation of agrarian holdings to 100 hectares (about 247 acres) or to a value of not more than 50,000 DM, and the abolition of denominational schools were written into the constitutions to protect them against amendments by ordinary legislation. The political system adopted corresponds to the German "demo-authoritarian" version of parliamentarism which is rather based on the ascendancy of the Minister President, who can be removed from office, as a rule, only if the *Landtag* simultaneously has agreed on the person of his successor. The proce-

[1] North Rhine-Westphalia, 20; Lower Saxony, 10; Schleswig-Holstein, 4; Hamburg, 3 members.

dure of constitution-making and the validity of the constitution as a whole were violently contested by the CDU opposition, which had boycotted the drafting and refused to vote on it.

Of greater importance is the new constitution of North Rhine-Westphalia, the most populous and economically leading *Land* and the veritable successor of defunct Prussia. The constitution, likewise drafted by the *Landtag* elected in 1947, was ratified by a referendum, together with the election for a new *Landtag* (June 18, 1950).[2] Its most controversial feature was not the constitutional arrangement of powers, but, as everywhere else in present-day Germany, the decision for retaining denominational schools; the Catholic Church and clergy, cutting across party lines, were able to defeat the liberal-Socialist opposition. Otherwise the well-drafted instrument differs from the older constitutions in Western Germany mainly in the exclusion of public officials from eligibility—another current controversy. It provides also for popular initiative and referendum. Its governmental structure conforms to the by now familiar pattern. The Minister President can be removed during the *Landtag's* four-year term only if the latter agrees on the successor or—a novelty—if a popular referendum confirms the rejection of a government bill by the *Landtag;* conversely, if the people side with the government, the *Landtag* is dissolved.

New constitutions, under preparation in Lower Saxony and Hamburg (which operated under a "provisional" instrument) by the regular parliaments, had not been completed at the end of 1950.

2. THE FRENCH ZONE

Knowing, from long experience, the Germans better than any other power, the French went about the administration of their zone in a business-like and unemotional manner, free from any ideological illusions. Supported by a relatively small but, on the whole, first-rate military and civilian staff, they concentrated from the start on the effort to make German youth of all classes—the generation below twenty represents at least one-third of the people—responsive to equalitarian values. In this long-range program they have perhaps a better chance of success than the American belief that the operation of the formal processes of democracy is a guarantee of effective democratic behavior. They were aided by the fact that the people of their zone, affinite to France, are the most "Westernized" among the Germans. Nor were the French inhibited by scruples of "nonintervention in domestic affairs" for the sake of creating democratic responsibility.

Faithful to the basic conviction that any kind of centralization in Germany is incompatible with the security of France, the French did not countenance any zonal organization except informal and strictly functional contacts between the Minister Presidents of their three *Laender*—the Saar had been attached

---

[2] Figures of the referendum:

For the constitution	57.0%
Against the constitution	35.2%
Invalid votes	7.8%

The Government and Politics of GERMANY

economically to metropolitan France at least since November, 1947—under close supervision of the French High Command (MG). Whenever uniform regulations for the whole zone were required, MG agencies attended to them, taking German advice but never delegating powers to a German zonal organization such as the *Laenderrat* or the Zonal Advisory Council in the other two Western zones.

The same distrust cautioned them against a premature transfer of political responsibility to the Germans. No *Land* authorities were tolerated except on the lowest administrative levels. When granting them constitutions could no longer be postponed, popularly elected constitutional conventions were dispensed with and the local assemblies, acting as electoral colleges, were ordered (1946) to create in each *Land* a consultative body to draft constitutions under High Command instructions. They were ratified by referenda (May 18, 1947) with only minorities of the eligible voters participating; the constitutions in Wuerttemberg-Hohenzollern and Baden were accepted by comfortable majorities; in the Rhineland-Palatinate it narrowly escaped defeat. On the same day *Landtage* were elected in which the CDU obtained absolute majorities in the two *Laender* first mentioned and nearly so in the third.

The constitutions, revealing in all cases the preponderant clerical influence, do not require detailed discussion except for the general statement that, on paper, they come closer to the genuine parliamentary system as practiced in France than those either of the American or British zone. However, the appearance of political self-determination is largely deceptive. Ordinance No. 95 of the French High Command (June 9, 1947)—roughly corresponding to the American instructions of September 30, 1946 [3]—made the *Land* governments subject to the orders of the French MG. Certain public fields were entirely removed from German jurisdiction. Proposals on denazification, decartelization, and democratization had to be communicated to the High Command in advance of their introduction in the *Landtag*. Unwilling to allow coordination of even so small a territory, the French prohibited the Germans from legislating "in the fields of economics for which coordination of the *Laender* is required." On the strength of this provision the parliaments could not even discuss matters of economics, food, agriculture, or transport. Moreover, the Germans were held to obtain advance clearance of all legislation coming before the parliaments, and the French not infrequently disallowed even enactments that were passed by the parliaments. To all intents and purposes the *Land* authorities have only a phantom existence befitting the phantom character of these artificially created miniature "states." Yet at least the Catholic-controlled *Land* of Baden developed in short order a statehood feeling which gave it the nuisance value of successfully obstructing the generally desired regroupment of the entire area into an economically and politically viable South Western state.

For similar reasons of retaining maximum control the French resisted any integration of their zone into the bizonal organization. Even after the establishment of the German Federal Republic in 1949 the French occupation

[3] See *supra*, pp. 528 f.

bureaucracy continued to keep the German authorities under a tight and expert control.

Evidently the French plan to stay in their bridgehead on the right bank of the Rhine for an indefinite time. Owing to the French ability to understand their mentality the Germans resent the tutelage of the French administration less than the cold superciliousness of the British or the well-meant if clumsy "re-education" approach of the Americans.

It is a natural law that the occupied nation dislikes the occupiers. Nonetheless, six years of close acquaintance with the four powers have taught the Germans to differentiate. An epigrammatic summary of what the Germans think, perhaps would read like this: The Russians are hated and respected. The British are respected and not liked. The French are respected and, to some extent, liked. The Americans are liked but not respected.

CHAPTER XXVI

POLITICAL PARTIES

PARTY DYNAMICS UNDER THE OCCUPATION

For the successful operation of the democratic process, political parties, as the transformers of the mass will into tangible public policies, are indispensable. In addition, the Western concept of political democracy requires the competition for public office of at least two political parties. Translated into continental political habits party competition implies their unrestricted multiplicity.

PARTY CONTROL BY LICENSING

The Potsdam Agreement provided that "all democratic political parties with rights of assembly and public discussion shall be allowed and encouraged within Germany." The condition that parties be "democratic" required MG controls, exercised more or less identically in all four zones by the technique of individual licensing. In the American zone the procedure implied the submission, by the founders or charter members of a group intending to operate as a political party, of the program, the by-laws, the names of the officials, and a certain number of signatures of supporters. To comply with these requirements was none too difficult, the paper being patient. Party programs everywhere are distinguished by vagueness, and ex-Nazis were careful not to appear as sponsors. The license was granted, upon checking on the political antecedents of the applicants, at first by the MG *Land* authorities and, after trial and error, by the Political Activities Branch of the Civil Administration Division of OMGUS which could not claim to be one of the most effective groups of the MG organization.

The mechanics of licensing were little changed subsequently. MG Regulations, redrafted in March, 1947, found it necessary to enjoin impartiality towards the admitted parties on the personnel charged with the supervision of the political parties. The rule did not efface the anti-Socialist bias of MG officials who would not understand that the SPD is the strongest bulwark of democracy in Germany. Expellee and refugee political parties were disallowed, in the—erroneous—belief that forcing them into other parties would accelerate their assimilation.

All told, the Allies licensed thirty-one different political parties (excluding all duplications).

Licensing became pointless after denazification had ended. Relaxed before the elections to the Bundestag in the summer of 1949, it was finally abandoned in the American zone in November, 1949, and somewhat later in the other Western zones also. During the entire period in the U. S. zone no party-owned press was admitted, unlike the British practice, in the belief that the press should be "neutral," although it would have been more honest to have press organs with generally recognizable party labels instead of exposing the public to the political indoctrination of the private owner or the editorial staff.

THE REBIRTH OF POLITICAL PARTIES

Since July, 1933, when, with the exception of the NSDAP, the Nazi regime had dissolved all existing parties and prohibited their reconstitution, independent parties had ceased to exist. However, the Communists and, to some extent, the Social Democrats had succeeded in maintaining a certain degree of underground cohesion and were able to reconstitute themselves under their former names almost immediately after the Nazi collapse. The bourgeois parties, on the other hand, completely absorbed and digested by the Nazi Leviathan, had to create entirely new party cadres which, however, almost automatically reverted to the traditional pattern, with some relabeling of the old party firm names and some refurbishing of the old programs. No new party denoting a radical departure from previously prevailing political habits was formed until the emergence of expellee parties in 1950.

Considerably before being officially licensed, Christian Democrats and the Liberal groups had established, by unofficial contacts, a loose frame of association. In 1945 in the Soviet zone political parties were permitted as early as June; in the American zone on August 27; in the British zone in October; and in the French zone in December. Early in 1946 the four parties of the CDU, SPD, LDP, and KPD were duly licensed in all zones. At first authorized only on the local level and soon thereafter for an entire *Land,* they reached by unavoidable private contacts the stage of zonal and nation-wide organization. Only the French, averse to any centralization, continued to prohibit integration of the parties licensed in their zone into interzonal groupings. Subsequently, several regional parties were licensed.[1]

THE GERMAN ATTITUDES TOWARDS POLITICAL PARTIES

The appraisal of political parties in post-War Germany must take cognizance of certain peculiarities of political life conditioned by the occupation. In the *first* place, licensing served as a brake on, and in no wise as an encouragement of, party dynamics. Since the press was equally controlled by licensing, the Germans had no outlet for their real or imagined grievances. Criticism of the

[1] See *infra,* p. 557.

occupation powers (including until the break [1948] also the Soviets) was outlawed. No real opposition party could develop, with the result that the so-called "middle-of-the-road" parties, CDU and FDP, became the political refuge of the discontented, and were inflated far beyond their real strength by voters who, for lack of a party corresponding to their actual convictions, temporarily supported others.[2] By being canalized into the four major parties, party life was hybrid and largely artificial. When, therefore, with the abandoning of licensing in 1949, the "freeze" thawed, a large-scale realignment of the electorate was bound to occur.

Second: From the start the Germans were, and remained, extremely wary of committing themselves to any political party. Denazification had taught them that to identify themselves with a party may lead *ex post facto* to undesirable consequences; why should they again run a similar risk? This explains why actual party membership was, and still is, exceedingly low; even in large cities with an electorate of several hundred thousands, the enrolled membership is insignificant. The exception is the SPD where Party loyalty is instilled by the trade unions.[3]

Third: The high percentage of the registered voters casting their ballot is no indication of their interest in political parties, or in politics, for that matter. The docile Germans go to the polls when told. The relatively high voting percentages in the early stage (about 78.5 per cent) were mistaken by the illusionists in AMG as genuine interest in political life; actually they are traditional in Germany and were lower than in the period from 1930 to 1933 (exceeding 80 per cent). Later they declined visibly. This behavior is less apathy than, in addition to the preoccupation with their daily life—food, shelter, job—their deep-rooted distrust of parties as valuable instruments of politics. The indifference amounting to hostility against any and all parties is particularly marked among the youth of practically all classes, with the exception of the Communists. Nor have the records of the parties and parliaments since 1945 contributed much to convince the Germans of their essentiality for political life.

Fourth: Party life in the past, under the Empire and Weimar, let alone the Nazi regime, was controlled by a relatively small and self-appointed oligarchy of party leaders or bosses (the *"Bonzen"*) on whose selfish decisions the voter or the party member had no influence whatsoever. This situation was aggravated by the system of proportional representation under which the voter did not vote for a candidate of his choice but merely for a slate.

Fifth: Practically all parties are embodiments of ideologies (*"Weltanschauung"*), conforming to the philosophic propensities of the German mind. As a rule the voter adheres to a party not because of the pragmatic policies it represents or the personalities representing it, but because the party platform (or what he believes the platform to be) comes closest to his ideological convictions. Since people are rarely given to changes in their basic

---

[2] The disfranchisement of certain Nazi categories was an additional factor of the inarticulateness of the opposition; numerically it did not amount to much (5 per cent at the maximum).

[3] Dues-paying members in 1947 numbered 875,000, including, however, Western Berlin where the Party is organized as a fighting unit against Communism.

philosophies, the parties are relatively stable, a situation enhanced by the proportional system which tends to deprive the popular will of its flexibility.

Finally, there was, and still is, an excessive scarcity of capable and respected party leaders. Of the men of Weimar few survived who had not compromised themselves. Some of them who climbed with beaver-like eagerness on the old party horses, do not command respect. Exiles were disliked because they were exiles. Genuine anti-Fascists and democrats of whom there were some, were not encouraged by the occupation authorities.

ANALYSIS OF POLITICAL PARTIES

The following analysis of political parties [4] describes the first period under MG licensing. Developments in the second period, initiated with the elections for the Federal parliament in the summer of 1949, are largely unpredictable.

(1) *THE RELIGIOUS PARTIES*

(a) *The Christian Democratic Union (Christlich-Demokratische Union [CDU]).* Throughout the period the CDU, together with its Bavarian affiliate, the Christian Social Union, was the numerically strongest and politically most important party. It is basically the heir and successor organization of the Catholic Center Party which, under the Empire and the Weimar Republic, drawing its strength from all classes of Catholicism, had proved to be the stable middle-of-the-road party. In response to the anti-religious policies of the Nazis the CDU broadened its basis to include Protestants, thus gaining support in regions which heretofore had not favored the Center Party. Lately, however, the bidenominational claim of serving as the common bond for all Christians has become more programmatic than real; large sections of the Protestant middle classes and farmers began to turn to other bourgeois parties, evidently because they resented the increasing influence of the Catholic hierarchy and clergy.

Programmatically the CDU focuses on the dignity of man, seeking to solve social, cultural, economic, and political issues by applying the principles of Christian tradition and teaching. Christianity is considered the supreme human value to overcome materialism and the aberrations of Marxism. However, the program of Ahlen (1947), in conformity with the recently streamlined economic theory of the Vatican, recommended a middle course between unbridled private capitalism with its exploitation of the masses, and any kind of state Socialism. While private initiative is to be preserved, excessive concentration of economic power should be overcome by the establishment, for monopolistic industries, of public corporations in which the State, municipalities, and the workers are to participate. Lately these anti-capitalistic overtones have completely disappeared; the party firmly stands behind free enterprise and the private ownership policies of its leading economist, Dr. Ludwig Erhard, who, as head of the Economic Committee of the bizonal organization and subsequently as Economics Minister of the Federal Government, was chiefly re-

[4] Comparison with the Weimar period (see *supra,* pp. 421 ff) is recommended.

sponsible for the re-establishment of unmitigated *laissez faire* capitalism. However, the economic policies of the CDU are by no means homogeneous; a strong left wing (led by Karl Arnold and Jakob Kaiser), not dissimilar to the *Mouvement Républicain Populaire* in France and supported by the Christian elements of the trade unions, favors the more Socialist approach in economics. In the educational field the CDU stands strongly for denominational schools with compulsory religious instruction, an issue which appears disguised as the right of the parents (*Elternrecht*), and not of the State, to decide which type of school their children should attend; in practice this means preference of strictly denominational schools. Politically the CDU favors the federal, as opposed to the unitary, solution. Proportional representation is rejected in favor of the single member majority system.

Sociologically the CDU cuts across all classes. Strongest in the Catholic rural districts and among the Catholic middle classes, it also contains influential elements of the high bourgeoisie and big business. Geographically its strength lies in the French zone, in the Rhineland and Westphalia, and, as the domain of the CSU, in Southern Bavaria. But there are islands also in North Western Germany.

The CDU was the strongest party in the elections of 1946–47 in five *Laender* (North Rhine-Westphalia, Wuerttemberg-Baden, and the three in the French zone). It shared in the coalition governments of all *Laender* except in Protestant Bremen, Hamburg, and Schleswig-Holstein. It held the key positions in the bizonal organization, dominated the Parliamentary Council preparing the Bonn Constitution [5] and obtained the largest number of seats (139 out of 404) in the Bonn Bundestag. The party leader, Dr. Konrad Adenauer, became the first Chancellor of the Western German Republic. However, in the elections of 1950–51, the party fared badly even in its customary strongholds.

(b) *The Christian Social Union (Christlich-Soziale Union [CSU]).* In spite of close similarity of religious, political, and socio-economic tenets the CSU, an organization confined to Bavaria, prefers a working agreement to an alliance with the CDU. It continues and deepens the policies of the former Bavarian People's Party which, after World War I, broke loose from the all-German Center Party and constituted itself as a separate, conservative, and strictly federalistic party of its own.[6] The original intention of its founder, Dr. Joseph Müller, one of the shrewdest of German politicians, to form a genuine Left-wing Catholic party, was soon frustrated by the old-line party bosses who in due course slanted it to the Right and gave it its arch-conservative and even reactionary flavor. It is an outspoken church party, exploiting the parochialism of the backward Bavarian peasant and the equally ignorant petty bourgeoisie in the smaller towns. Its extreme federalism, nurtured by the congenital hatred against anything smacking of Berlin or Prussia, led

---

[5] See *infra*, pp. 563 ff.
[6] The term federalistic (*föderalistisch* in German) is not identical with the word "federal" in English. It denotes the extreme states' rights position, with definite overtones of statehood.

Bavaria as the only *Land* to the rejection of the Bonn Basic Law. The absolute majority the CSU held in the 1946 elections (104 out of 180 seats) was trimmed down, in 1950, to 64 out of 204 seats. But in fairness it must be noted that the CDU, led by Dr. Hans Ehard as Minister President, possesses the art to rule. The Bavarian civil service dominated by the CDU is as efficient as any comparable group.

Owing to the destruction of Prussia as a political entity, internal policies of Bavaria, the second *Land* in population and area, have repercussions quite out of proportion to her relatively weak economic and financial position. Bavaria has become the witches' cauldron of party politics; possibly the Celtic origin of the Southern Bavarians, whose political habits are reminiscent of the Irish, has something to do with it. From the start the CSU was heavily inflated because of the influx of nationalists and rightist elements without a party cubicle of their own choosing. But soon the radical Economic Reconstruction Party and subsequently the Bavarian Party,[7] cut deeply into the ranks of the CSU. Both parties, running only in Bavaria, scored substantial successes at the *Bundestag* elections of 1949 (twelve and seventeen seats respectively). Fighting, thus, on two fronts, against the Socialists and the new parties to the Right, the CDU is headed for an uncertain future. In the *Landtag* election of November, 1950 it was badly trounced and, for the first time in Bavarian history, failed to be the majority party.

(c) *The Center Party (Zentrumspartei).* The Center Party, unlike its famous namesake under the Empire and Weimar, is a distinctly left-of-center party to which, according to its program, Christianity and Catholicism are so self-evident that they defy support by a political party. In social and economic policies it stands close to the Socialists with whom, together in the *Landtag* of North Rhine-Westphalia, they voted unsuccessfully for the nationalization of the basic Ruhr industries in 1948. In cultural and educational questions it sides with the CDU. For the time being, operating primarily in the British zone, the party is supported by the Catholic proletariat and the lower middle classes, without that admixture of rich people and businessmen characteristic of both CDU and CSU. A merger with the CDU was overwhelmingly rejected in January, 1949. Its numerical strength is as yet insignificant. Although it did not fare too well in the elections for the *Landtag* of North Rhine-Westphalia in June, 1950, it may constitute, in the future, a serious competition to the CDU and serve as a bridge between the CDU and the SPD.

(2) THE SOCIALIST PARTIES

(a) *The Social Democratic Party (Sozialdemokratische Partei Deutschlands [SPD]).* The SPD was, from the start, more fortunate than the other parties in that it could count on the traditional loyalty of the older members of the trade unions. Like the Socialist parties elsewhere it is better organized and disciplined than its bourgeois competitors. An efficient party bureaucracy guides the masses of dues-paying members. It is the only German party

[7] See *infra,* p. 557.

holding (since 1946) annual party conventions. As the strongest bulwark of a democratic and social republic in the past it could qualify as the government party *par excellence* of a democratic and social Fourth Reich. Its record towards Nazism and in denazification was impeccable.[8]

The SPD no longer adheres to orthodox Marxism. Ideology and phraseology of the class struggle have disappeared in program and propaganda. This made it possible for considerable sections of the white-collar workers, the middle-class bourgeoisie, and intellectuals to vote for, if not to join, it. In this respect it closely resembles the British Labor Party, though there exists no formal organizational link with the trade unions as in Britain. Nor has the SPD the religious, non-conformist ingredients of its British counterpart. Programmatically [9] the SPD believes, like British Labor, in "the inevitability of gradualism." Economically the primary target is the public ownership or socialization of the monopoly industries, in particular the vast steel and coal trusts of Rhine and Ruhr; but this is not equivalent to nationalization which, in addition to an unmanageable bureaucracy, would facilitate the surrender of the basic industries to any aggressive government. Public ownership is conceived as the establishment of a system of mixed public corporations in which management and labor, cooperatives, the consumer, and the municipalities and the (central or *Land*) governments will be represented. Under a program described as "regulated market economy" unbridled *laissez faire* and total planning are equally rejected. As a step towards the final goal the SPD demands the codetermination of labor in the management policies of the enterprises (*Mitbestimmungsrecht*).[10] On the formulation of the Bonn instrument the Socialist postulates had little influence.

The SPD is on firmer ground in its political program. All parties pay lip service to the principles of democracy. But the SPD is the only one whose democratic convictions are reliable and sincere. Had AMG given more support to the Socialists and indulged in less fawning on the "respectable" people, democratization would be in a better shape today. As a strong advocate of political unity the party rejects all brands of separatism and exaggerated states' rights. In clear recognition of the permanent deficiencies of a country dependent on imports of food and raw materials, the SPD favors the decentralized unitary state, here in conflict with the American insistence on extreme federalism as a guarantee of democracy. In educational matters the SPD, in line with its anticlerical tradition, strictly adheres to the secular solutions. Its agricultural

---

[8] The SPD had voted as a body and as the only party against the Enabling Act of March 24, 1933. No former Nazis are among its present leaders or parliamentary personnel.

[9] The previous party programs of Erfurt (1891) and Heidelberg (1925) are considered obsolete. A new program is under preparation.

[10] In this, as in other aspects of their program, the SPD was consistently opposed by free enterprise and anti-Socialist-minded men in AMG and even disowned by the British MG which, after all, represented a Labor government at home. Implementation by the *Landtag* of the mild socialization provisions of the constitution of Hessen—at first, on General Clay's orders, subjected to a special referendum—was vetoed by AMG. The same fate befell the majority decision in favor of the nationalization of the *Landtag* of North Rhine-Westphalia (1948), which was vetoed by the British under the pretext that the decision should be left to a Western German parliament. On the enactment of the codetermination principle by federal statute see *infra*, pp. 609 f.

policies are still the weakest part of the program. It has, therefore, no appeal for the peasants.

However, under the tight and at times ruthlessly authoritarian leadership of Dr. Kurt Schumacher, the SPD, like the Jacobins of the French Revolution, has become violently nationalistic. For a member of the Second International traditionally devoted to international cooperation, to vote, for example, against the Republic's entry into the Council of Europe may appear paradoxical. The virulent neo-nationalism can, perhaps, be explained by vote-getting tactics and the irresponsibility of an impotent opposition into which the party was forced almost from the beginning. For the occupation powers the SPD was the least tractable of all major parties.

The SPD was, until 1950, the strongest party in five of the eleven *Laender* (Lower-Saxony, Bremen, Hamburg, Schleswig-Holstein, and Hessen) where it held the positions of Minister President. In all other *Laender* it came second in strength. In the *Bundestag* elections of 1949 it came a close second to the CDU (131 seats); had Western Berlin been included, the SPD as the strongest party would have been entitled to form the government. As an all-weather party it is more immune to accidental fluctuations of the electorate than most other parties though it may lack in emotional appeal for the younger generation. Yet, in the South German elections of late 1950 it captured, riding the crest of the anti-rearmament wave, the strongholds of the CDU even in Bavaria and Wuerttemberg-Baden.

The SPD and the Trade Unions. Differently from Britain—where the trade unions constitute the formal backbone of the Labor Party and are no less influential for the policies of the Labor Government than the Labor Party convention—the trade unions in Germany are not affiliated officially with any political party. However, traditionally they are intimately tied up with political parties. The Social Democrats, having the lion's share, controlled the so-called free trade unions (*Freie Gewerkschaften*) of industry, white-collar workers, and civil service; the Catholic Center Party commanded allegiance of the separate Christian trade unions, and even the Liberals had a (very insignificant) trade-union following of their own. After 1945, the SPD gained ascendancy over all trade unions in the Western zones which, reconstituted on the local, *Land,* zonal and bizonal levels at an early date, gradually were amalgamated (October, 1949) into organizations extending over all of Western Germany. By June, 1951, the trade unions reached, with a membership of 5,641,000, the greatest consolidation of power in the history of the German labor movement, and constituted what is probably the most formidable pressure group in Germany. Different from American unionism, the German trade unions, rather than operating as gigantic pressure groups for obtaining higher wages and better work conditions, are political instrumentalities of the SPD. As yet no separate trade unions aligned with other parties have been reconstituted.[11] In wage

---

[11] Of the twenty-seven members of the governing board of the Federation of Free German Trade Unions (*Freier Deutscher Gewerkschaftsbund*) only two are members of the CDU; all others belong to the SPD.

policies the trade union leadership is conservative. Wages had been frozen at first by the occupation powers; thereafter an increase of 15 per cent was permitted; finally, controls were completely lifted (November, 1949). However, strikes for wage increases were frowned on though they occurred sporadically as protests against dismantling, food shortages, or other acute grievances. The trade unions concentrate their energies on rebuilding German industry and regaining the export markets. However, the German trade-union movement is far ahead of the unionism in the United States in its advocacy of codetermination (*Mitbestimmungsrecht*), easily the most controversial issue of German social policies. It is the demand for full and equal partnership of the trade unions with the management in the operation of all factories and plants, including the determination of production quotas, procurement and investment policies, introduction of new working techniques, layoffs and curtailment of operations, and all other matters materially affecting the joint interests of labor and management in the plant. This is the German approach to implementing political by social and economic democracy. It goes beyond the existence of works councils (*Betriebsträte*) for handling labor grievances and protecting the social rights of the workers, which had existed before, under, and after Hitler, intended to culminate in a national Economic Parliament. As a substitute for the continued low wage level it may seem inadequate to American labor, as it does to many German workers. From the long-range viewpoint it may well constitute a persuasive answer to both the Soviet state-controlled labor movement and the effort to depoliticize labor by wage concessions as in the United States. Codetermination for the coal and steel industries was obtained, by the bold strategy of the trade-unions under the leadership of the late Hans Boeckler, in alliance with Chancellor Dr. Adenauer, in the spring of 1951.[12]

Although the overwhelming majority of trade union members—there is nothing resembling the Anglo-Saxon closed-shop concept—are loyal members of the SPD and its most reliable dues-paying group, the trade unions, to some degree, have emancipated themselves from the old-style alliance with the SPD. This is reflected by the decrease of union officials among the SPD deputies in the *Bundestag*.[13] The trade-union leadership also has begun on occasion to bargain with the different parties and even to disagree with the SPD on important issues (such as the Ruhr Authority). It is by no means impossible that sooner or later the trade-union organization will again split into sections affiliated with different parties even though in this case the SPD will retain the loyalty of the majority.

(b) *The Communist Party (Kommunistische Partei Deutschlands [KPD]).* One of the four original parties licensed in the Western zones, the KPD drew its initial strength from its anti-Nazi record and the prestige of

---

[12] See *infra*, pp. 609 f.

[13] Only seventeen out of a total of twenty-two union officials; five are members of other parties. In the parliaments of the *Laender* the trade-union secretaries constitute a much larger element in the SPD.

the Soviet victory.[14] After the merger of the SPD and KPD as the Socialist Unity Party (SED) in the Eastern zone [15] in March–April, 1946, repeated attempts in the Western zone at converting itself into an affiliate of the Soviet-controlled SED were vetoed by the MGs. The Western KPD participated officially in the Soviet-sponsored first "People's Congress" in Berlin (December, 1947). For tactical reasons the KPD officially severed its relations with the SED in the Soviet zone (January 2, 1949); this move, however, neither increased its popularity among the working classes nor changed the allegiance of its strictly disciplined followers to Moscow. Intensified administrative harassment by both the German authorities and MG, in line with the progress of the cold war, resulted in driving the party organization almost completely underground; but it participated in all elections and at this time (beginning of 1951) it has not been officially outlawed even though the Bonn and various *Land* constitutions provide for the prohibition of antidemocratic parties; the reasons for its continued legal existence lie primarily in the hesitancy of creating an ominous precedent.

Programmatically the KPD is believed to endorse the streamlined Stalinism enjoined on all present-day Communist parties. Socialism can be achieved only by the dictatorship of the proletariat, arrived at by political, social, and economic revolution which will entail the destruction of capitalism and the nationalization of all means of production. However, the official party program (June 24, 1949) skillfully toned down these long-range aims by focusing on tangible economic remedies for the distress of the working classes. Major emphasis is placed on a foreign policy program to appeal to all nationally-minded Germans: unity and peace for Germany; withdrawal of all occupation forces; freedom from foreign economic control. Politically the centralized state with supremacy of the popularly elected chamber is favored, pointing up the Soviet concept of "assembly government."

The KPD derives support exclusively from the solid core of fanatics in the industrial proletariat in metropolitan areas and factory towns, strongest in the Ruhr, Mannheim, and Hamburg. But the Communist vote declined continuously from about 10 per cent of the total in 1946–47 to less than 5 per cent in 1949–50; in the *Bundestag* elections the KPD obtained only 15 (out of 402) seats. But these figures do not tell the whole story. It is reliably reported that many Germans voting for other parties found it wise to insure themselves against the day of a Communist seizure of power by taking out clandestinely membership cards in the KPD. Big business not only profits from the illegal trade with the East but also makes substantial contributions to the party chest. While it is true that Communism in Western Germany has dwindled to the size of a splinter party, it can hardly be assumed that a party which, in 1932, polled six million votes, has ceased to be a potential threat.

[14] The early practice of including Communist Ministers in the coalition governments of the three South German *Laender* was terminated when the last was dropped in Wuerttemberg-Baden (May, 1948).

[15] See *infra*, p. 633.

(3) *THE LIBERAL PARTY (FREIE DEMOKRATISCHE PARTEI [FDP])*

The sizable group which goes by the name "Free Democratic Party" is probably the most interesting phenomenon in the structuration of political parties. The Free Democrats are actually Liberals, the genuine Manchester article of full-fledged economic *laissez faire,* representing the German version of the Hoover-Taft business liberalism familiar to the American student as "rugged individualism." But while in most other European countries this variety is almost extinct (England, France, Italy) it flourishes, at least for the time being, in post-War Germany where a concatenation of fortunate conditions— generous American aid to recovery; American predilection for free enterprise; the aversion of the people against rationing and austerity; the impotence of the working classes and the recapture of its dominant position by big business— have combined to restore a liberal paradise and this in a country which, congenitally incapable of matching imports by exports, may have seemed predestined for reasonable economic controls.

The four regional groups believing in *laissez faire* that had sprung up after 1945 coalesced (December, 1948) into the consolidated party organization of the FDP. It is difficult to assign to the party its proper location in the German political spectrum. It is not only the heir of the genuine liberal-democratic tradition of 1848 and 1919, but also the successor of big business and heavy industrial interests formerly organized in the National Liberal Party of the Bismarck period and the German People's Party of Weimar. It means different things to different people, individually and regionally. But it developed definitely into a party of the Right for which democratic values are identical with free enterprise, rejection of all state controls, and unmitigated private capitalism. Compared with economic tenets, the other planks of an intrinsically contradictory platform mean little; but the party is genuinely anti-clerical, fighting for strictly secular education, and, in demanding a more centralized state, approaching the position of the SPD. In denazification its record is about the worst of all political parties.[16]

The FDP is supported primarily by the upper middle classes and other professional sections of the urban bourgeoisie including many white-collar workers, in addition to anti-clericals and conservative Protestants unwilling to vote for the CDU. Together with the CDU it benefited most from the absence of a professedly Right party. The success of the currency reform in 1948 and economic recovery since are largely attributed to the rebirth of private capitalism proclaimed by the FPD. The striking advances in voting strength appear as the payoff, though actually the party's success is predicated on the Marshall Plan aid. Between the elections of 1946–47 and those for the *Bundestag* in 1949 the FDP increased by 80 per cent; it holds, with fifty-two seats, the third rank in

[16] It should be remembered (though not unduly stressed) that two of its leaders, namely the present President of the German Federal Republic, Theodor Heuss, and the Minister President of Wuerttemberg-Baden (since 1945), Reinhold Maier, as deputies of the State Party, voted for the Nazi Enabling Act of March 23, 1933. Of the fifty-odd former Nazis in the *Bundestag* the vast majority belong to the FDP.

the Bonn Parliament. Since 1945 it has participated in the coalition governments in Hessen, Wuerttemberg-Baden, Wuerttemberg-Hohenzollern, Hamburg, and Bremen. But of all bourgeois parties it is the most artificially inflated and the most likely to succumb to nationalist pressure from the Right.

(4) *SPLINTER PARTIES*

Since 1945 a debate has raged in Germany whether the propensity of the Germans to express their ingrained political individualism in as many separate groups as corresponds to their factional differences, could have been arrested if, instead of proportional representation, the principle of straight majority decisions in single membered constituencies had been adopted as the electoral technique. The former undoubtedly favors the multiple party development. Whether the latter as it is claimed would have led to a stable two-party system may be open to doubt; but at any rate it would have either wholly eliminated or at least reduced the frequency of small, for the most part only regionally important, parties which the Germans call splinter parties (*Splitter-Parteien*). Their existence contributed crucially to the instability of governments under Weimar.

(a) *The Economic Reconstruction Party (Wiederaufbaupartei [WAP])*. The party, licensed in 1946, is a strictly regional phenomenon, thriving in the climate of Bavarian emotionalism. Nurtured by sheer demagoguery and opposition for the sake of opposition, it is bossed, not without conflicts, by a Hitler-type intellectual crank, Alfred Loritz. It caters to the underprivileged, particularly among the expellees and refugees, and obtained rural as well as urban support. In the *Bundestag* elections it fared remarkably well (twelve seats). With the emergence of a genuine refugee party, however, it lost heavily (December, 1950).

(b) *The Bavarian Party (Bayernpartei [BP])*. Likewise a product of the Bavarian political hothouse is the BP (licensed in 1948) which is distinguished by its ultra-federalistic program. Actually it aims at a quasi-independent state of Bavaria, linked with the other German *Laender* merely within a loose confederation. Skillfully exploiting the Bavarian aversion against "centralizing" Prussia—even though Bavaria herself since the Napoleonic period was the paragon of administrative centralization—and with a strong appeal to the monarchist tradition and separatism, the BP succeeded in obtaining in the *Bundestag* elections seventeen seats. In the *Landtag* elections (November, 1950) it became the third strongest party.

(c) *The German Party (Deutsche Partei [DP])*. The DP, mostly confined to the British zone, continues the tradition of the German Hanoverian or Guelph Party which, never reconciling itself with the annexation and assimilation of the former Kingdom of Hanover by Bismarck in 1866, had remained a separate party group under the Empire and Weimar. A plebiscite in 1924 to accomplish the establishment of a separate *Land* Hanover, though failing by a substantial margin, demonstrated the tenacity of the Guelph tradition. When the British, realizing that here organically grown territorial aspirations required recognition as a political entity, created the *Land* Lower Saxony, the dream came almost true. The party constituted itself as Lower Saxony *Land* Party (*Niedersächsische Landespartei*) and served also as the receptacle of conservative rightists with no other place to go. To facilitate the expansion to other *Laender* it reorganized itself as the German Party in 1947. Of all German parties it comes closest to being a genuine conservative party on the pattern of the British Tories. It is predominantly a Protestant group, supported by the rural population of all classes, by no means separatist as its Bavarian counterpart, traditionally favoring the reactivation of a strong Reich in which the individual members remain loyal members. It is strongest in Lower Saxony where, in 1947, it gained 28 out of 149 seats, but is also represented in Bremen and Hamburg. In the *Bundestag* it holds 17 seats and was invited to join the Adenauer coalition government which required its support to obtain the necessary majority.[17]

[17] On later party developments see *infra*, pp. 613 ff.

CHAPTER XXVII

DRAFTING THE "BASIC LAW" (BONN CONSTITUTION)

THE LONDON SIX–POWER ACCORD

It is a tragic reflection on the history of our time that the re-establishment of the second German Republic, rather than being guided by its intrinsic merits, became a move in the game of international chess played by the United States and the Soviets. The Moscow Conference of the four Foreign Ministers (March 10–April 25, 1947) was the last serious effort of the powers to square their divergent approaches to solving the German issue with the Potsdam Agreement. It proved abortive. On June 5, 1947, the (then) Secretary of State George C. Marshall announced the grand scheme of American economic assistance to Europe which later on became the celebrated Marshall plan. It included in due course, if not from the beginning, Western Germany as recipient of aid and as equal partner in European economic recovery. After the break-up of another perfunctory attempt at the London Foreign Ministers Conference (November 25–December 10, 1947) the Western powers had convinced themselves that the integration of Germany into Western Europe could be accomplished only on the basis of the partial solution of a Western German rump state. To this end the bizonal economic cooperation initiated in December, 1946, was pushed forward to the point of complete economic fusion of the British and American zones (December 17, 1947). The next logical step was to overcome the heretofore adamant resistance of the French against any kind of German central organization even if limited to the Western zones. This was attempted in two conferences in London to which the Benelux countries (Belgium, the Netherlands, and Luxembourg) were admitted, the first held from February 23 to March 6, 1948, the second from April 20 to June 2, 1948. French apprehensions, justified by the experience of Germany's three wars of aggression and occupations within two generations, were allayed by special promises in the London Accord for controlling the war potential of the Ruhr, the perennial threat to the security and peace of France. Subsequently, after the Anglo-Saxon Powers had tried to circumvent the French by Law No. 75, which played ownership and management of the Ruhr key industries into the hands of their former owners, scantily veiled as "trusteeship," new negotiations with the French led finally to the creation of the International Ruhr Authority (December 28, 1948). The other price to be paid for French consent to Western Germany's unification was the establishment of the Military Security Board (January 19, 1949) for the continued enforcement and supervision of German disarmament and demilitarization.

However, the London Accord did not succeed in persuading the French to agree to a closer integration of their zone with the other Western zones. But they accepted the currency reform (June 20, 1948) for their zone and, in October, 1948, consented to common foreign trade policies by sending a member to the Joint Import-Export Agency. Otherwise they retained the factual independence of their zone until September, 1949, when the Allied High Commission Charter [1] placed all Western Germany under joint Allied control.

On the other hand, the London Accord laid the foundations for the formation of a unified German state. At long last the governments saw fit to take the policy determinations out of the hands of the generals. The document outlined in detail all steps "to give the German people the opportunity to achieve on the basis of a free and democratic form of government the reestablishment of the German unity at present disrupted": a Constituent Assembly, composed of delegates to be chosen by the *Landtage,* was to be convened by the Minister Presidents of the eleven *Laender* to write a constitution, to be finally ratified by the people of the respective *Laender;* various roadblocks of MG approval were properly interposed. Nor was the content of the constitution to be a government of their own choosing, to use the dated language of the Atlantic Charter. It was not to be the constitution of a centralized Reich, but "a federal form of government which adequately protects the rights of the respective states, and which at the same time provides for adequate central authority and which guarantees the rights and freedoms of the individual." But this American-inspired masterpiece of unintentional doubletalk failed completely to spell out what kind of federalism the Allies desired or would countenance. The formula was chosen because the Allies among themselves did not agree.

The London document thus is less a green light for the Germans than an order of the traffic cop to drive ahead and do it fast. The Western German politicians were utterly reluctant to comply with the Allied injunctions, fearing to be branded later as "collaborators" who had accepted a "dictated" constitution, and recoiling from the responsibility of putting, with their own hands, the seal on the final partition of their country. Both the Allies and the Germans realized that the procedure chosen, or imposed, was a far cry from the free and sovereign exercise of the *pouvoir constituant,* universally recognized as the inalienable right of a sovereign democratic people. The constituent power was strangely attenuated by being canalized through the *Land* governments and parliaments, both deriving their popular mandate from elections as

[1] See *infra,* pp. 592 ff.

far back as 1946–47 and no longer corresponding to the will of the people as evidenced by the recent communal elections. Moreover, the final product did not only require the approval of the M–Governors but was also to be limited, as was Weimar by the Treaty of Versailles, by an Occupation Statute in which the occupying powers in advance reserved for themselves largely unspecified powers. The only genuinely democratic feature of the arrangement, namely the ratification of the constitution by the people of the *Laender,* was later dropped at the insistence of the Germans themselves who were apprehensive of the popular reactions for much the same reasons they did not press for a popularly elected Constitutional Convention. To qualify, therefore, the constitution-making procedure as democratic is subject to definite reservations, an argument that was not lost on the Soviets and the Germans in the Eastern zone. On the other hand, it has to be granted that there was hardly any other way open. A national assembly would not have been tolerated by the Allies as signifying "centralization," and the mass of the German people, just emerging from the economic chaos by the bootstraps of the currency reform, cared little for any constitution. And it is a moot point whether the Germans, if left to their own devices, would have written any, or any better, constitution.

THE ESTABLISHMENT OF THE PARLIAMENTARY COUNCIL

The Minister Presidents of the eleven Western German *Laender* [2] convened in Frankfurt (July 1, 1948) and officially acting as the collective representation of the peoples and governments of the *Laender,* were handed by the three M–Governors (Generals Clay, Sir Brian Robertson, and Koenig) three documents implementing the decisions of the Six-Power London Conference. Document I specified that the constituent assembly should be convened on September 1, that the delegates should be selected by the *Landtage* on the basis of one for each 750,000 inhabitants, and that in each *Land* should be selected a number of delegates in proportion of the population of the *Land* to the entire population in Western Germany. The constitution was to be valid when accepted by the people of two-thirds of the *Laender.* In compliance with the regulation, the *Landtage* subsequently arranged that the number of delegates the *Land* was entitled to were distributed among the parties according to their relative strength in the parliaments. Document II directed the Minister Presidents to re-examine the existing state boundaries with the objective of eliminating states which were disproportionally big or small. This request remained a dead letter from the start; the task of the territorial regroupment was too ambitious to be undertaken at that time, if at all. Neither the Bonn Constitution nor later the authorities organized under it were able to tackle this assignment except for prescribing legal procedures for it. Not even the imperatively required regroupment in South Western Germany could be accomplished to date. Document III outlined the relationship between the powers assigned to Western Germany and those the Allies

[2] Of these five each belonged to the CDU–CSU and SPD, one to the FDP.

wished to reserve for themselves while the occupation continued. The problem of the Occupation Statute proved most troublesome for the Germans as well as for the Allies: for the former because they could not reasonably be expected to draft a constitution without knowing where its jurisdiction began and ended, for the latter because they could not agree among themselves. Only after another Foreign Minister Conference was the final text of the Occupation Statute published (April 8, 1949).

The Minister Presidents, meeting at Koblenz (July 8–10), were unwilling to accept unreservedly the proposals of the M–Governors. Some of their inhibitions were of small importance. They refused to call the constitution a constitution, preferring the allegedly less pretentious term "basic law" (*Grundgesetz*). This implied that Western Germany, being rather a fragment of a state than a state (meaning not having full sovereign rights) could not well write a full-fledged "constitution." This did not prevent them from drafting one of the most ambitious and voluminous instruments of its kind in our time. For similar reasons they preferred the name "Parliamentary Council" (*Parlamentarischer Rat*) to the more ominous term "constituent assembly." The Allies did not object. More serious was the German objection against taking the responsibility for a constitution which would intensify the split with the East. This was overcome later by the claim that the constitution should be valid for all Germany. But, afraid of their own courage, they preferred ratification of the completed document by the *Landtage* instead of by the people. In this the Allies yielded. In a joint meeting of the M–Governors with the Minister Presidents in Frankfurt (July 26) face-saving formulas were finally agreed on.

In August the *Landtage* elected the delegates for the Parliamentary Council. When assembled in the university city of Bonn on the Rhine, on September 1, 1948, it consisted of sixty-five members, with five delegates from Western Berlin admitted as guest observers without vote. The Germans had wished to include the Western sectors of Berlin as a full-fledged twelfth state, but the Allies refused, partly because this would have constituted an imprudent provocation of the Soviets—at that time the final outcome of the Berlin blockade could not be foreseen.[3] The Council consisted exclusively of parliamentarians (that is, members of the *Landtage*). Moreover, it is significant that fifty-one among the sixty-five delegates were at the same time civil servants. The Council thus was a convention of bureaucrats and professors without independents or people from outside with fresh ideas. The sociologi-

[3] Number of delegates from the eleven *Laender:*

Baden 2, Bavaria 13, Bremen 1, Hamburg 2, Hessen 6, Lower Saxony 9, North Rhine-Westphalia 17, Rhineland-Palatinate 4, Schleswig-Holstein 4, Wuerttemberg 2, Wuerttemberg-Baden 5   65

Party composition: SPD 27, CDU–CSU 27, FDP 5, Center Party 2, DP 2, KPD 2   65

Since delegates were selected by the *Landtage* on the basis of the elections of 1946–47, some parties which had made their appearance since, were unrepresented; others, most of all the CDU–CSU, were overrepresented for the same reasons.

cal background of the group explains, as it did in the case of the *Paulskirche*,[4] much of the excessive legalism and perfectionism of the completed document. But it came close to the German ideal of political work done by the *Fachmann* (technical expert).

THE DRAFTING OF THE CONSTITUTION BY THE PARLIAMENTARY COUNCIL

TECHNICAL ASPECTS OF THE COUNCIL'S WORK

The Parliamentary Council elected unanimously Dr. Konrad Adenauer, Chief Mayor of Cologne, a prominent Catholic politician under Weimar and the leader of the CDU, to the office of the President of the Assembly.

Legally the Council was nothing else than the collective representation of the eleven *Landtage*. Its function was strictly consultative. Similar to the Philadelphia Convention, it could draft, but not enact, a constitution. Nor had the subsequent adoption by two-thirds of the *Landtage* a truly constituent character. The Constitution derived its validity from the authorization of the occupying powers acting through the M–Governors. The delegates were neither under instructions of their parliaments nor of the *Land* governments; they conducted themselves as free agents, operating, however, most of the time, as representatives of the different political parties.[5]

The Constitution was given four readings (instead of the usual three) in fifty-six plenary sessions.[6] The customary hard work was done in efficient committees. The debates proceeded at first rather leisurely and were animated by the spirit of mutual compromise. Later the Council ran into such rough weather, because of the fundamental conflicts between the leading factions of the more unitarian Socialists and the outspokenly federalistic Christian Democrats and the increasing interference of the M–Governors, that the entire work was in danger of collapse. Inept publicity techniques and the more dramatic events of the Berlin blockade and airlift contributed to, but were not solely responsible for, the complete lack of interest, let alone enthusiasm, that the German people demonstrated for the work of Bonn; the common man had learned by now how little the spurious exercises in constitutional semantics of the elaborate *Land* constitutions meant for the daily life. The only point on which most people felt satisfied was the disappearance of Prussia as a state.

Constitutions, as a rule, do not spring as original creations from the constituent assemblies as Minerva from the head of Jupiter; they are derived, to

---

[4] See *supra*, p. 391.

[5] Prominent members of the Council were, next to Dr. Adenauer, Adolf Suesterhenn (CDU), Minister of Justice of Rhineland-Palatinate; Carlo Schmid (SPD), professor of international law of the University of Tuebingen, the leading constitutionalist of the assembly; Dr. Walther Menzel (SPD), Minister of the Interior of North Rhine-Westphalia; Dr. Thomas Dehler (FDP), President of the Court of Appeals of Bamberg; Max Reiman (KPD). The Berlin delegation of Paul Loebe (former President of the Reichstag under Weimar), Professor Ernst Reuter (Chief Mayor of Western Berlin), Otto Suhr—these three SPD—and Jacob Kaiser (CDU) was distinguished.

[6] Three additional sessions were devoted to the electoral law; see *infra*, pp. 601 f.

a large extent, from previous constitutional thinking. The Council could draw on the experience of the *Land* constitutions. Foreign constitutional experience was mostly ignored, owing to the ingrained German conviction that what is good for other nations, cannot be good for them. Of their own preparatory work for the new Constitution the most important were the so-called *Herrenchiemsee*-Resolutions, elaborated (from August 10 to 24, 1948) by a "constitutional convention" (*Verfassungskonvent*) composed of constitutional experts appointed by, and working under the auspices of, the eleven Minister Presidents; this semiofficial draft showed German nonpartisan constitutional talent at its best, combining political liberalism with a tolerably federalistic approach.[7]

CONSTITUTIONAL CONTROVERSIES

Controversies concerning the content of the Constitution divided the German parties in the Council, the Allies themselves and, currently, the Allies and the Germans. Although there existed disagreement between the Allies and the Germans on such points as the role of the civil service, the independence of the judiciary and judicial review, basically the differences pertained to what kind of federalism the Germans should adopt. This was likewise the principal conflict among the Germans.

German Disagreements. Curiously little conflict arose on the political structure of parliamentary government. Here the two larger parties were in the same boat in agreeing on the necessity of a strong and stable government which, however, should be prevented from becoming "legally" dictatorial. The position of the President and the issue of the dissolution of the lower house were likewise solved with due regard to the experience under Weimar. Deep cleavages, however, developed about the federalist solution. The CDU wished a return to the federal system that had existed at the beginning of the Empire when the federal Government could exercise only the minimum of central powers enumerated by the constitution and was financially dependent on subsidies of the member states. The SPD and the FDP favored a more centralized federal Government, imperatively required by the economy of a highly industrialized country. The division of jurisdiction between the federal and the *Laender* governments and its corollary, the distribution of financial revenues between them, remained controversial throughout. This affected the structure of the second chamber, whether to be an instrument of federal con-

[7] Other preparatory materials included the following: (1) The Resolutions of Ellwangen (April 13, 1948) and Düsseldorf, reflecting the extreme federalist and conservative viewpoints of the Catholic political intelligentsia and officialdom; (2) drafts supporting the SPD ideology of a more centralized structure, namely, *Directives for the Structure of the German Republic,* issued by the SPD in 1947, and *Draft Proposal of a West German Statute* by Walther Menzel; (3) constitutional proposals prepared by the zonal Advisory Council of the British Zone; (4) constitutional plans influenced by, or originating with, the Eastern Zone Socialist Unity Party (*Constitutional Principles of the German Volksrat* [People's Council]) and *Draft Constitution of the German Federal Republic* (reflecting the assembly type of government sponsored in Soviet-controlled states); (5) finally, the Council was acquainted with the *Declaration of Human Rights* under discussion by the United Nations. Most of these materials were conveniently published by OMGUS under the title, *German Constitutional Proposals and Comparison of the Drafts of the Constitution.*

trol as it was traditional in Germany, or a genuine second chamber on American and Swiss patterns, as preferred by the SDP.

Allied Divergent Approaches. Allied disagreements likewise centered primarily on the type of federalism to be recommended to the Germans. They had existed at the time of the Moscow Conference and later, but were believed to have been adjusted by the vague compromise formula of the London Agreement. The French, having resigned themselves that their preference of a loose federation of quasi-independent states was unobtainable, did what they could to limit the powers of the central government. The British, no great believers in written constitutions anyway and naturally inclined to favor the Socialists, would not have objected to the return to the more centralized structure of the Weimar federal system. But the Americans, more dogmatic and energetic than the others and holding the financial whip hand over both the Allies and the Germans, were unable to cut themselves loose from the belief that decentralization equals democratization.

Disagreements Between the Allies and the Germans and MG Intervention. To the first draft, completed by the middle of November, the M–Governors reacted by the *Aide Mémoire* of November 22, 1948, holding that it deviated from Allied interpretation of Document I which, it should be stated in fairness, never had been spelled out to allow the Germans to understand what the Allies, meaning the Americans, meant by federalism. The Germans were advised that the powers of the federal Government should be limited to those explicitly enumerated in the Constitution and that certain functions (education, religious affairs, social welfare, public health, police) must not be included. In the fields of public finance—the establishment of federal agencies or the administration of federal services by the *Laender*—the memorandum threw the full weight of Allied pressure behind the extreme federalist solutions, aiding, thereby, the CDU–CSU. From now onwards the SPD was clearly driven into opposition.

Upon submission of the revised draft (after the third reading) the M–Governors, in a memorandum of March 2, 1949, insisted that, in several instances, their previous interpretation of the London Accord had not been followed by the Germans. On several points they were correct, such as the German noncompliance with the request for curbing the authoritarian influence of the bureaucracy.[8] While the CDU did not quarrel with the Allied insistence on further attenuating the centralization features in question, the SPD felt that more concessions to MG desires were incompatible with the minimum requirements of a workable federal state. The grave deadlock was finally solved by a direct intervention of the Foreign Ministers who, in the meantime (April 8, 1949), had succeeded in Washington in agreeing on the Occupation Statute. Obviously it was felt in Washington that the international

---

[8] The obduracy of the Germans in acceding to the Allied intentions of converting the German bureaucracy from a privileged class into an instrument of public service subordinate to the government had compelled the M–Governors of the British and American zones to enact, on February 21, 1949, Law No. 15 on Bizonal Public Servants, which, among other reforms, excluded officials from serving as deputies in parliamentary bodies.

situation did not justify the foundering of Western German unification on what may appear retrospectively minor jurisdictional squabbles on the financial arrangements. Consequently, the Germans had their way and, on May 8, 1949—which happened to be the anniversary of unconditional surrender— the Basic Law was finally accepted by a majority of 53–12.[9] MG approval was given on May 12, 1949, with a number of reservations which, however, are little more than of a declaratory and face-saving nature.[10]

It may be asked whether, under these circumstances, the constituent will of the Western German people could, or has, expressed itself freely. While it can hardly be denied that, without MG intervention, the final form of federalization would have been slanted more towards the unitarian experience of Weimar and that, if Western Berlin could have been included, the SDP would have become the strongest party with the claim to forming the government, it is equally certain that the Council neither was, nor did it consider itself, the agent of a foreign principal. By no means was the Constitution "dictated." [11] On the other hand, there is no doubt that Allied intervention, not without ulterior motives in spite of the proclaimed political neutrality, strengthened the position of the CDU at the expense of the SPD.

RATIFICATION OF THE BASIC LAW BY THE *LANDTAGE*

Ratification by the *Landtage* took place in due course (May 18–21, 1949). Since all *Laender,* with the exception of Bavaria, accepted the Basic Law with substantial majorities, it entered into force on May 23, 1950.[12] It is, after the Paulskirche Constitution of 1848 and the Weimar Constitution, the third democratic instrument of government of Germany.

[9] The dissenters were: six deputies of CSU, two of the DP, two of the Center Party, and the two KPD members.

[10] They referred to the exercise of the federal police power; the continued exclusion of Berlin from the Constitution; the retention of the present *Laender* boundaries (with the exception of South Western Germany) until the peace treaty; the direct exercise of federal functions in the *Laender.*

[11] For an authoritative German statement see Hermann von Mangoldt, *Das Grundgesetz,* Berlin-Frankfurt 1950, p. 17: "All told, there is nothing to it that the Basic Law is legislation imposed on by the M–Governors."

[12] See the tabulation of the voting results in the *Landtage* in *Germany 1947–1949,* Department of State Publication 3556, p. 282. In Bavaria the rejecting majority (May 20, 1949) was 101–63, the bulk of the CDU voting against ratification because the Basic Law was deemed too unitarian. However, in a second vote, accepting the Constitution as binding for Bavaria because accepted by two-thirds if the *Laender* had ratified it, the majority was 97–6 (SPD and FDP, having voted before in favor, now abstaining). This double vote is a characteristic example of evading responsibility.

CHAPTER XXVIII

ANALYSIS OF THE BONN CONSTITUTION

THE FEDERAL STRUCTURE

Next to a preamble, the Constitution is divided into ten major sections: I Basic Rights (Arts. 1–19); II the *Bund* [1] and the *Laender* (Arts. 20–37); III The Federal Parliament (*Bundestag*) (Arts. 38–49); IV The Federal Council (*Bundesrat* [Arts. 50–53]); V The Federal President (Arts. 54–61); VI The Federal Government (*Bundesregierung* [Arts. 62–69]); VII Federal Legislation (Arts. 70–82); VIII Execution of Federal Legislation and Federal Administration (Arts. 83–91); IX The Administration of Justice (Arts. 92–104); X Financial Matters (Arts. 105–115). As concluding section follows XI Transitional and Concluding Provisions (Arts. 116–146), dealing primarily with the task of liquidating the disastrous heritage of the Nazi period and the legal and administrative fragmentation resulting from the occupation. This section is touched on in the following discussion only when occasion arises.

THE TERRITORIAL BASIS

In modern constitutional experience the federal structure of a state is primarily evidenced by the line of demarcation drawn between the jurisdiction of the central (federal) authority and the member states in matters of general and fiscal legislation and administration, on the one hand, and the protection of states' rights against federal encroachment, on the other. Next to the jurisdictional distribution of federal and state powers it is the participation of the states in the formation of the will of the federal state which matters most; usually this function is performed by the upper house or second chamber, which under Bonn is called the Federal Council (*Bundesrat*). In both respects the Bonn Constitution follows the Weimar precedent much more

[1] The official translation (see State Department Publication 3556, pp. 285 ff) uses for *Bund* the inaccurate term "federation"; in constitutional theory a federation is an association of states which, while delegating some powers to a central authority, retain their full identity as sovereign states. To avoid terminological confusion the term *Bund* is used here.

closely than German and Allied preoccupation with "true" federalism had suggested. On the whole, the federal clock has been put back by minutes only and not by hours.

However, what distinguishes Bonn sharply from Weimar is that a transformation of the territorial basis had occurred before the Constitution was written. Prussia, whose overwhelming power had dominated all previous federal solutions, had been extinguished as a state. A regroupment of the member units had taken place by *fiat* of the occupation powers which resulted in a large-scale map redrawing. None of the eleven *Laender* composing the *Bund* is so preponderant in size or population as to require a special protection of the smaller units. The territorial division of Western Germany, once the artificial dwarf units in the French zone have disappeared by consolidation into a single South Western state,[2] may seem as well balanced as can reasonably be expected in a people so assiduously preserving its tribal and historical individualities. Nonetheless, Article 29 provides for an eventual territorial regroupment within the federal area "in consideration of regional unity, historical and cultural interrelations, economic rationality and social structure," to be accomplished, within three years, by federal legislation on the basis of initiative and/or referendum. Although such territorial regroupment is mandatory under the Constitution, it is likely that vested interests will do their best to frustrate it.[3]

FEDERAL AND LAND LEGISLATION

As in the United States and most other federal states, sovereignty ("the exercise of state powers") and the presumption of legislative priority lie primarily with the *Laender* (Arts. 30, 70). Since the federal fields of legislation are strictly enumerated (Arts. 73, 105, par. 1) the *Laender* have the residual powers. In line with the Weimar Constitution the legislative powers are split into three categories, namely: those exercised by the *Bund* exclusively; those exercised concurrently with the *Laender;* and those fields in which the *Bund* may set general standards (*Rahmengesetzgebung*) to be observed by *Land* legislation. To keep the federal Government on a meager diet was the basic therapy for a healthy federalism prescribed by the American doctors. Reading only the list of exclusive federal powers (Arts. 73 and 105, par. 1) one is inclined to believe that this aim is accomplished; the catalogue contains the bare minimum of what a central government may justly claim (mainly foreign affairs; citizenship, weights and measures, coinage and money; communications—in Germany always under federal authority—and, in the financial field, customs and fiscal monopolies).[4] But turning to the fields in which the federal Government has concurrent legislative powers, one is

---

[2] See Art. 118.

[3] On the problems of territorial regroupment in general see the report (*Vorberichte*) published in 1950 by the Frankfurt Institute for the Advancement of Public Affairs.

[4] In addition, no fewer than fifteen individual legislative matters to implement the Constitution are assigned to the federal Government by the Constitution itself (for example, the proposed law on political parties).

bound to admit that, to all intents and purposes, the legislative appetite of the federal Government may assume legally huge proportions. Concurrent legislation is permissible (Arts. 74 and 105, par. 2) if it is "needed," and needed it is (Art. 72)

if a matter cannot be effectively regulated by the legislation of an individual *Land;* if . . . a *Land* law could prejudice the interests of other *Laender* or of the *Laender* as a whole; if the preservation of legal or economic unity demands it.[5]

The catalogue of concurrent legislative powers is very extensive, covering no fewer than twenty-four different fields (among them, for example, all matters of economics; labor law and social insurance; the entire civil, criminal, and procedural law; socialization and decartelization; agriculture; automotive traffic; public health); there is hardly any aspect of economic life on which the *Bund* may not legislate. Unless, therefore, the institutions to safeguard states' rights are effective there is actually no limit to the unitarian trend through expanding federal jurisdiction. This cannot be objected to if one realizes that a modern industrialized state, constituting a single market, cannot effectively function without uniform regulations of the economic and social life.

Federal law overrides *Land* law (Art. 31). Moreover, the *Bund* may, by constitutional amendment (Art. 76), arrogate to itself powers at present attributed to the *Laender*.

FEDERAL AND LAND ADMINISTRATION

However, the federalistic approach prevailed on the administrative field. The range of federal administration suffered considerable restrictions in comparison with Weimar, where many important services were under direct federal management. Now the *Bund* administers only foreign affairs, federal finances and certain fields of communications (railroads, mails, etc.). In all other fields administration of federal functions (not to mention those left to the *Laender* otherwise) are assigned to the *Laender* (Arts. 83 ff). This is of specific importance in fiscal and taxation matters where the *Bund* has direct administration (assessment and collection) concerning only certain enumerated taxes.[6] In general, administration of these federal matters is conducted by the *Laender* authorities under their own responsibility, with the *Bund* maintaining merely the right of supervision (Art. 84, par. 3).

The same principle of federal legislation and *Land* administration governs the administration of justice. Only on the highest level of the various legal fields (civil and criminal law; constitutional conflicts concerning the *Bund;* administrative, social, labor, fiscal law [Arts. 93 ff]) does the *Bund* maintain supreme courts of its own, while all lower courts are *Laender* courts administering both federal and *Land* law.

[5] This provision was a bone of contention between the M–Governors and the Germans, the former believing that it constituted an open invitation for centralizing abuses, the latter justly claiming it in order to overcome the diversification of law and economics caused by the divergent occupation policies.

[6] See Art. 106.

As a result of this reduction of federal services the federal bureaucracy has been reduced numerically, without, however, suffering any loss of power because law-making, in the German environment, is a function primarily devolving on the civil service, the formalization through legislative enactment by the Parliament notwithstanding to the contrary.

THE DISTRIBUTION OF FINANCIAL POWERS BETWEEN BUND AND LAENDER

In every federal system the fiscal relations are the touchstone of genuine federalism. Here the Basic Law follows the same pattern of camouflaged centralization which, while paying lip service to the states' rights concept, opens the legal path towards a more unitarian structure. The guiding principle is that *Bund* and *Laender* should be fiscally (*"Haushaltswirtschaft"*) self-contained and mutually independent (Art. 109). In such cases the most obvious solution is that certain sources of revenue be assigned to each of them for exclusive use. But the economically integrated state of our time hardly ever permits a clear line of demarcation, partly because, in the federal state, the central authority requires more revenues, partly because the federal Government has to see to it that economically weaker member units, by grants-in-aid, receive a proper share from the wealth of the richer states; in Germany this situation is known as *Finanzausgleich* (equalization of financial burdens). In post-War Germany the financial responsibilities of the *Bund* are further increased by the decision (Art. 120) that the burdens of the lost war (for example, occupation costs; [7] expenses for expellees and refugees; compensation for war damages; support of indigent people who lost their property through the war, etc. [equalization of burden or *Lastenausgleich*]), are to be borne by the *Bund*.

Consequently, from the start, the fiscal balance (Arts. 105–115) was slanted in favor of the *Bund*. While the *Laender* cannot claim any share in revenues assigned exclusively to the latter (customs and financial monopolies, such as liquor and matches, Art. 105, par. 1) the *Bund* may dip, by way of a concurrent claim, deeply into the revenue wells basically assigned to the *Laender* (excise taxes, for example: beer, tobacco, sugar, coffee [Art. 105, par. 2]) and the taxes on business transactions (for example, corporations, insurance, transportations, etc.). In particular, what is the backbone of public finance and, in any federal state, the most unitarian element, namely taxes on income, succession, and property, may be claimed by the *Bund* if needed for federal purposes. A final distribution of the respective share of *Bund* and *Laender* in the revenues subject to concurrent legislation is to be made before the end of 1952 (Art. 107). Thus, the *Bund* need not fear to be stymied by lack of revenues.

On the other hand, the federalistic principle again prevails in the financial administration (collection of taxes, etc.) in that in particular all direct taxes

[7] This was another subject disputed among the Allies and the Germans, the French wishing to make the *Laender* responsible for them.

are subject to *Land* administration. Nonetheless, an eventual extension of direct federal services and a progressive erosion of the presumed fiscal autonomy of the *Laender,* in line with the experience of the Empire and of Weimar, may in the long run seem unavoidable. Realities will not fail to dispel the federalistic fog that surrounded the drafting of the Constitution.

THE POSITION OF THE LAENDER

Rights and duties of the *Laender* are somewhat better spelled out under Bonn than they were under Weimar. Among the provisions stipulated to be "permanent," that is, not even alterable by constitutional amendment, are the federal structure of the *Bund* and the participation of the *Laender* in legislation (Art. 79, par. 3). The *Laender* are guaranteed their "constitutional order" which must correspond to the principles of the "republican, democratic and social state based on the rule of law" (Art. 28). This may become as much a club the *Bund* may wield against a *Land* deviating from the path of democratic virtue as a protection. *Land* interests must be observed in the appointments for federal service (Art. 36). The duties arising from the membership in a federal state are more implicit than articulated. But in the important aspect of federal compulsion (*Bundesexekution*) the powers of the federal authority are weakened (Art. 37). If a *Land* fails to fulfill its legal obligation towards the *Bund,* the federal Government may take "the necessary measures" to enforce compliance of the recalcitrant *Land* with its obligations, and, in this case, all *Laender* have to follow federal instructions. But, since the approval of the *Bundesrat* is required,[8] federal enforcement is much attenuated and may, in practice, consist more of political and financial pressures than of police or military action. The provision has its corollary in the right and the duty of the *Bund* (Art. 91) to repel, by armed force (which, in the absence of a federal police, implies the use of the *Land* police forces) any threat to the existence of the "free democratic basic order in the *Bund* as a whole or in an individual *Land.*" If the *Land* so threatened is unwilling, or incapable, of action—a reminiscence of the Weimar situation—the *Bund* may take over the police forces of any other *Land* to combat the danger. This is another aspect of what is known in German constitutional law as enforcement of federal authority, or *Bundesexekution.*

THE BUNDESRAT

Next to the imponderables of the spirit of mutual loyalty and cooperation the protection of states' rights in a federal system depends on the powers and position of the organ destined for the participation of the member units in the policy-making, legislative, and administrative functions of the federal state. Under Bonn, this is the *Bundesrat* (Arts. 50–53). Its *composition* is governed by the time-honored German tradition of "federalistic arithmetics." Instead of the usual equal representation of the member units, each *Land*

---

[8] Under Art. 48, par. 5 of the Weimar Constitution, federal compulsion was ordered by the Reich President, that is, the Reich Government, on their exclusive responsibility.

is assigned the number of votes proportionate to its importance roughly measured by the population figures (Art. 51). Each *Land* is entitled to at least three votes; those with more than two million inhabitants, to four; with more than six million, to five (Art. 51). The total membership is forty-seven.[9]

The delegates from Berlin participate in a merely consultative capacity (Art. 144, par. 2). The delegates are appointed and dismissed by the *Land* governments and must be members of them in ministerial capacity (Art. 51, par. 1). They act under instructions from their governments, with the result that changes in party control in an individual *Land* are reflected in changes of the party structure of the *Bundesrat*. Although this is not prescribed by the Constitution, the assembly is in permanent session. The presiding officer, elected for one year, is the acting president of the *Bund* in case the incumbent is prevented from exercising his functions (Art. 57). Close contacts with the federal Government are maintained; a Minister of the federal cabinet is charged with attending to *Bundesrat* affairs.

As to its *functions,* the *Bundesrat* is not a full-fledged second chamber equal in rights with the *Bundestag,* the popularly elected "lower" house.[10] With regard to legislation, the *Bundesrat* is seized with all government bills prior to their submission to the *Bundestag*. It also may initiate legislation (Art. 76). However, there is an ingenuous distinction—one of the few original features of the Constitution—as to the content of legislation and the action of the *Bundesrat* attendant thereon. "Federalistic" legislation (*"Föderativgesetze"*), pertaining to matters in which the *Laender* interests are directly involved, is separated from legislation which affects the *Bund* as a whole. For a bill of the first category, positive approval of the *Bundesrat* is required; otherwise it cannot become law. The joint arbitration committee of delegates from both houses (Art. 77)—another interesting innovation—may only propose, but cannot enforce agreement between the two bodies. For this type of legislation, therefore, the *Bundesrat* is an equal partner of the *Bundestag* and the protection of states' rights is absolute and watertight. All told, there are eleven such cases of "federalistic" legislation mentioned by (though widely dispersed over) the whole document: for example, territorial changes; constitutional amendment; claims of the federal Government for a share in income and corporation taxes; establishment of new federal agencies. In all other legislative matters of a non-"federalistic" nature the absolute veto of the *Bundesrat* is toned down to a delaying action (*Einspruch*) or suspensive veto (Art. 77) compelling the *Bundestag* to a second decision, with the proviso, however, that an objection of the *Bundesrat* carried by a two-thirds majority can be finally overridden by the *Bundestag* only by the same qualified majority.

[9] Bremen, Baden, Hamburg, Wuerttemberg-Hohenzollern, 3 each   12
　Berlin, Hessen, Rhineland-Palatinate, Schleswig-Holstein, Wuerttemberg-Baden, 4 each 20
　Bavaria, Lower Saxony, Rhineland-Westphalia, 5 each   15
[10] This issue was much in dispute in the Parliamentary Council and also among the Allies. The SPD and the FDP favored a genuine second chamber on American or Swiss patterns; the CDU preferred to continue the tradition of an organ in which the ministerial bureaucracy assisted the representatives of the *Land* governments.

The *Bundesrat* is distinguished also from the normal type of a second chamber in a federal state by its participation in *executive functions* of the *Bund* in matters not necessarily resulting from the "federalistic" nature of such actions. In these specified cases, again strewn over the entire document,[11] the *Bundesrat* transcends its position as a watchdog over the protection of states' rights against federal encroachment and functions as a genuine second chamber. Important examples are: Impeachment of the federal president (Art. 61, par. 1); consent to the federal Government's invocation of the "legislative emergency situation" (Art. 81, par. 1);[12] appointment of one-half of the members of the federal Constitutional Tribunal (Art. 94, par. 1). These additional powers contribute to raising the political stature of the agency which, however, is hardly needed because, unless previous experience is contradicted, the *Bundesrat,* by virtue of the administrative talent of the ministerial bureaucracy assembled in it, is bound to rise to the same importance it had in the legislative and administrative environment of Weimar.

Taken as a whole, the actual federal arrangements may seem to conform outwardly to the American hypothesis that federalization equals democratization. But if centralization-minded parties gain control of the *Bundestag* and the *Bundesrat,* the Constitution would prove no unsurmountable obstacle to a completely unitarian state in substance if not in form. In the last analysis, the German constitutional lawyers have outmanoeuvred the American ideologues.

[11] See the (partial) enumeration in Friedrich Giese, *Grundgesetz für die Bundesrepublik Deutschland,* Frankfurt, 1949, p. 73, no. 6.

[12] See *infra,* pp. 578 f.

CHAPTER XXIX

THE FORM OF GOVERNMENT

GENERAL OBSERVATIONS

The mechanics of what is commonly spoken of as the "parliamentary form of government" are based on the interdependence and coordination of a popularly elected parliament and a government which attains and maintains office by virtue of the confidence of the former. In case the government has lost parliamentary support a new government is installed by the parliament, or, under certain conditions, after the dissolution of the parliament, by a verdict of the electorate through a general election. A "neutral" head of state (president, king) is injected into the procedure as the steering wheel. However, the parliamentary system being a generic and by no means homogeneous term, various applications have evolved. If the government is actually subordinated to the assembly the resultant relationship is parliamentary supremacy (existing, for example, in the French Third and Fourth Republics). It may even lead to full-fledged assembly government (*Gouvernement conventionnel*)—preferred by the Soviets. If involving actual dominance of the cabinet over the assembly (as in Great Britain) it becomes cabinet government.[1]

Under the Bonn Constitution the organs operating parliamentary dynamics are the popularly elected federal Parliament (*Bundestag*), the federal Government (*Bundesregierung*), led by the federal Chancellor (*Bundeskanzler*) and the federal President (*Bundespräsident*). The federal Council (*Bundesrat*) has no share in the parliamentary mechanism. Parliamentarism, thus, in Germany, is based on the unicameral concept as is the case in France (under the Constitution of 1946), different from Italy (under the Constitution of 1947).

While outwardly conforming to the form of parliamentary government, the solution adopted by Bonn is neither parliamentary supremacy nor cabinet

---

[1] For a general discussion of the various forms of parliamentarism see Karl Loewenstein, "The Presidency Outside the United States," The Journal of Politics, Vol. 11 (1949) pp. 447 ff, 462 ff.

government. From the former it is differentiated by the dominant position of the Chancellor, in line with the German tradition of the "Chancellor principle"; from the cabinet system, to which it bears a superficial resemblance, it is removed by the lack of effective control of the Parliament over the Government. For this version—or perversion—of parliamentarism by which the Germans have enriched political theory, the term "demo-authoritarian" may seem appropriate.

The German constitutional lawyers were driven to this original system by the experience under Weimar (and other contemporary applications of parliamentary governments as understood by them). They preferred a stable leadership, by which continuous political crises through changes of government could be avoided, to political elasticity and democratic responsibility. The M–Governors and their liaison officers who devoted so much energy on instilling "true" federalism, paid no attention to the deviation from "true" parliamentarism.

THE FEDERAL PARLIAMENT (*BUNDESTAG*)

The federal Parliament (Arts. 38–49) is elected for a four-year term (unless previously dissolved). Elections must be general, direct, equal, free, and secret (Art. 38). But, unlike Weimar, proportional representation is not constitutionally enjoined, the electoral procedure being left to a special electoral law. Nor is the number of deputies determined in the Constitution.[2] Nonetheless, in view of the party character of the electoral mandate the declaratory statement (Art. 38) that the deputies are "representatives of the entire nation, not bound by instructions and only subject to their conscience" is no less hypocritical than its Weimar counterpart. The Parliament enjoys the customary autonomy (to determine beginning and termination of sessions; its Standing Orders; the validity of the elections, subject to a final decision of the federal Constitutional Tribunal). It has the usual rights of establishing investigating committees (Art. 44), which, as an effective method of parliamentary control of the government, have never been popular in Germany; it is protected, in the interval between sessions, by a permanent supervisory committee (Art. 45). The deputies enjoy the traditional immunities and privileges (freedom of speech; from arrest and prosecution; from searches and seizures, etc. [Arts. 46, 47]).

The functions of the *Bundestag* lie primarily in the legislative field. It has the right of legislative initiative (together with the federal Government and the federal Council [Art. 76, par. 1]). It sanctions the laws, in conformity with the unicameral structure (Art. 77, par. 1).[3] In addition, the Parliament approves, by way of legislation, certain governmental acts (for example, confirmation or rejection of treaties with a foreign state [Art. 59, par. 2]; the budget [Arts. 110, par. 2 and 111, par. 1]; and shares in the appointment

---

[2] On the election law under which the first *Bundestag* was elected, see *infra*, pp. 601 f.

[3] See, however, the participation of the federal Council in "federalistic" matters, discussed *supra*, p. 572.

of the judges of the federal Constitutional Tribunal [Art. 94, par. 1]). However, the Constitution is significantly taciturn about its political rights and duties in the control of the government, an omission which, in view of the verbosity of the document, may be more than a Freudian "repression."

THE FEDERAL GOVERNMENT (BUNDESREGIERUNG)

COLLEGIATE CHARACTER AND CHANCELLOR PRINCIPLE

The federal Government (Arts. 62–69), basically a collegiate organ, consists of the federal Chancellor and the federal Ministers (Art. 62). But within the group the Chancellor, by virtue of the "Chancellor principle," occupies the dominant position because he "determines the policy directives and assumes the responsibility for them" (Art. 65, par. 1). He also has the exclusive decision on the persons of his collaborators, the Ministers, who, upon his proposal, are appointed by the federal President (Art. 64, par. 1) [4] which, of course, does not exclude the ministerial positions from being subject to bargaining among the parties which participate in a government coalition. Equally important is that the Ministers may be dismissed on the request of the Chancellor. Various provisions serve for maintaining unity among the cabinet members, but nothing illustrates the subordinate position of the Ministers more than the fact that, in the absence of collective cabinet responsibility, a vote of nonconfidence can be directed against the Chancellor only and not against individual members of his cabinet.

The *functions* of the federal Government, vast as they are on the policy-making, legislative, and executive-administrative fields, do not require much discussion here. In the legislative field, next to the right to initiate legislation, probably the most important power is the right to draft and issue ordinances (*Verordnung*), implementing federal laws (Art. 80, par. 1). As to administrative powers, the federal Government directs the federal administrative services and supervises *Land* administration charged with the execution of federal tasks.

APPOINTMENT OF THE FEDERAL CHANCELLOR

The federal Chancellor reaches office through election, without discussion, by the *Bundestag,* upon the proposal of the President (Art. 63). Under the two-party system the selection of the head of the state automatically is confined to the (or a) leader of the strongest party. Since German political *mores,* aggravated by proportional representation, invariably create a multiplicity of parties, none of which would be sufficient to form a majority by itself, the federal President is necessarily accorded a good deal of discretion in proposing for the office of the Chancellor not necessarily the leader of the numerically strongest party, but a person who offers the best guarantee of forming a stable government coalition of several parties.

The candidate proposed by the President is elected if receiving the major-

---

[4] There is nothing in the Constitution which compels the President to appoint the Ministers chosen by the Chancellor. But if he refuses he runs the risk of losing his Chancellor.

ity of the votes of the legal members of the *Bundestag* (Arts. 63, par. 2, 121). In case the presidential candidate fails to be elected the *Bundestag,* within a fortnight, may elect a Chancellor of its own choosing. In case this second attempt results in his election by the majority of the legal members, the President is bound to appoint him. If, however, the second attempt falls short of the required absolute majority, a third ballot occurs in which the candidate receiving the mere plurality of votes is elected. In this case, however, the President is free either to appoint the person, or to order a dissolution of the *Bundestag* in order to obtain, through new elections, a more workable composition of the federal Parliament. The latter contingency, however, is most unlikely since the elections which resulted in the political stalemate were held, as a rule, only recently, and under the "freezing" of electoral opinion through proportional representation, a reversal is hardly to be expected. On the whole, the procedure seems sufficiently elastic and spaced to allow for the successful election of a person commanding a parliamentary majority.

THE ISSUE OF PARLIAMENTARY RESPONSIBILITY

THE VOTE OF CONFIDENCE

While most of the arrangements discussed before do not reveal any striking deviation from the customary techniques of the modern state, the Bonn Constitution is decidedly original in the formalization and rationalization of parliamentary responsibility which constitutes the acid test of parliamentarism. Significantly one searches in vain for an unequivocal statement that the Chancellor (and his Ministers) require the confidence of the *Bundestag* for the conduct of their office. Perhaps this was implied. Nor is it stated anywhere that the members of the government must be members of the assembly, thus leaving the door ajar for slipping in the familiar nonpolitical expert as Minister (*Fachminister*).

Over the interminable discussions of the issue in the Parliamentary Council hovered the spectre of the Weimar Republic plagued by continual cabinet crises, occasioned by unstable coalitions, governmental majorities cracking up and reforming, and the inability of a parliamentary majority hostile to the government in power to agree on the person of the new governmental leader. To square the vicious circle between instability of the government, the archvice of parliamentarism as the Germans allege, and authoritarian government, the Bonn Constitution adopted a solution which sacrifices the substance of effective parliamentary control over the government for a strong government which, if not wholly irremovable during the four years lifetime of the *Bundestag,* is extremely difficult to get rid of. The Constitution thus approximates the position of the federal Chancellor to that of the American President under the separation of powers, without, however, being able to create what makes the American system tick, namely the power of public opinion without which even the most forceful American president cannot govern.

Once elected by the *Bundestag* the government is presumed to retain its confidence until it is explicitly withdrawn by the parliament through a vote of nonconfidence. Abuses of this institution by overfrequency and the incidence of "snap" decisions are discouraged in most recent constitutions by what has become known as "the rationalization of political power." Under the rules of the parliamentary system confidence can be challenged in two ways: Either by accepting a vote of nonconfidence submitted by the opposition, or by rejecting a vote of confidence when requested by the government. Either method is available to the *Bundestag* (Arts. 67, 68), but the device is hedged in by such difficulties and slanted so much in favor of the government as to blunt completely this most effective weapon of making parliamentary responsibility real. If the parliament wishes to oust the Chancellor, the vote of nonconfidence must not only be carried by an absolute majority (which is sensible), but the parliament must at the same time have agreed on the person of his successor (the so-called "constructive vote of nonconfidence").[5] Thereafter the President, requested to dismiss the Chancellor, has to comply and to appoint the person chosen as successor. Such a fundamental shift of parties within the *Bundestag* would be possible only if the government coalition were to fall apart, and even then it would be most unlikely that agreement on the successor could be attainable. The motivations behind this arrangement were partly the desire for having a strong, that is, stable, government, partly to avoid the experience of Weimar when mutually hostile parties of the Left and the Right combined for overthrowing a government without being able, or willing, to form a government majority themselves. The vote of nonconfidence, thus, is so attenuated that, in practice, the acting Chancellor is immunized against any effort to force his resignation. And what will happen if the hostile majority which could not agree on the successor rejects government bills or the budget? This conflict, not subject to a constitutional solution, cannot but lead into the no-man's-land of an authoritarian dictatorship.

However, the Chancellor himself may request a positive vote of confidence (Art. 68). If carried by an absolute majority, he, of course, remains in office. This is the normal procedure of parliamentary responsibility. However, if he fails to receive an absolute majority two solutions are available: The President has the option of either dissolving the *Bundestag* (within twenty-one days) [6] or to abstain from dissolution, with the paradoxical result that the government, though it no longer commands the confidence of the parliament, remains in power indefinitely.

THE "LEGISLATIVE EMERGENCY SITUATION"

But the cards are even more heavily stacked against parliamentary responsibility. It is obvious that the opposition in the parliament, even though it may not have succeeded in forcing the resignation of the Chancellor by absolute majority, has sufficient parliamentary strength to obstruct his legislation.

[5] This arrangement has precedents in the *Land* constitutions of Wuerttemberg-Baden and, implicitly, of Bavaria.

[6] If, in the meantime, the Parliament should, with absolute majority, agree on the successor, the dissolution order is rescinded; this, however, is most unlikely to occur.

In this case the federal Government may resort to another innovation of the rules of parliamentarism contributed by German ingenuity. At the request of the Chancellor the President must issue the declaration of the "legislative emergency situation" (*Gesetzgebungsnotstand*) (Art. 81, par. 1) which is nothing but the disguised revival of some features of the notorious Article 48 of the Weimar Constitution.[7] In this case a specific bill rejected by the parliament or, for the duration of six months, any bill, is sanctioned by government decree instead of by the parliament. There are some important curbs on the abuse of the legislative emergency powers, namely: consent of the federal Council for each bill; limitation of the duration to six months; the fact that, during the term of office of an individual Chancellor, the decree powers can be granted only once, and that the Basic Law itself cannot be touched by such emergency decrees. But obviously six months of constitutional dictatorship may amply suffice for a Chancellor and a President supporting him to completely subvert the Constitution. In spite of the shadow of Weimar, the switch to the authoritarian track is open again.

THE DISSOLUTION OF THE BUNDESTAG

Dissolution, consequently, has lost much of its function as the regulatory democratic device under authentic parliamentarism where the verdict of the electorate decides a conflict between the government and the parliament. Of this function it is largely stripped under Bonn. Dissolution is provided for in only two rather remote contingencies: In the case that, on the third ballot, the federal Parliament has elected a Chancellor, though without absolute majority, the President may either appoint him or dissolve the assembly (Art. 67, par. 4); here dissolution is most unlikely because of the immediately preceding general election. The second chance occurs when the Chancellor fails to obtain the absolute majority of the parliament on his own request for a vote of confidence (Art. 68, par. 1). In this case he will rather govern with the legislative emergency powers than advise the President to dissolve. In either case dissolution is purely optional. Moreover, so long as elections are conducted under proportional representation the dissolution has lost much of its plebiscitary character. Though it does not prevent genuine landslides normally the party fluctuations are not easily reflected under this system.

THE FEDERAL PRESIDENT

The experience under Weimar discouraged endowment of the head of the State with real powers; instead of a strong President, a strong Chancellor was created. Consequently, since a President anointed by the democratic oil is more powerful than one deriving his mandate from a parliamentary assembly, the President (Arts. 54–61) is elected for a five-year term (and with reeligibility for one term) by a body called *Bundesversammlung* (Federal Convention). One of the quaintest exhibits in the curiosity shop of Bonn, it is composed of the members of the *Bundestag* and the same number of *ad hoc* electors, elected by the *Landtage* under proportional representation, with the

[7] See *supra*, pp. 415 f.

underlying motivation that party shifts that had occurred in the *Laender* since the last election of the *Bundestag* should be considered. Actually the arrangement merely results in a duplication of the party structure of the *Bundestag.*[8] The President is elected by absolute majority on the first two ballots, and by plurality on the third and last ballot.

The federal President possesses the typical representative, state-integrating, and ceremonial functions of the head of a republican state. He is impeachable (Art. 61), a merely academic provision. All his official actions require the countersignature of the Chancellor (or a Minister with jurisdiction [Art. 58]). Though far less powerful than the Reich President under Weimar, he is not quite the soulless rubber stamp he appears in terms of the Constitution. He is explicitly (Art. 58) freed from the requirement of countersignature in the appointment and dismissal of the federal Chancellor, and in the exercise of his discretion concerning dissolution in case, on the third ballot, the Chancellor was elected with a plurality only. By deciding for dissolution he may become a counterweight of some importance to the Chancellor. But where he is really more than a pawn of party dynamics is when he proposes the candidate for the chancellorship, even though he must conform to the realities of the party configuration created by the general election. If, however, Chancellor and President belong to the same party and are willing to gang up on the parliament they constitute an almost unbeatable combination.[9]

CONCLUSIONS: THE DEMO–AUTHORITARIAN FORM OF GOVERNMENT

Outwardly the form of political government of the German federal Republic, according to the intentions of the Basic Law, is a representative democracy in which the federal Parliament is the political center. But the democratic structure is seriously weakened by the ascendancy of the federal Government, which conforms to the German ideal of a government strong enough to rule without parliamentary or popular interference. If to this feature is added the complete absence of the devices of direct democratic participation through initiative and referendum,[10] the erosion of the function of dissolution, the system of proportional representation which places the party hierarchy at the wheel without much back-seat driving of the electorate, the picture that evolves is that of a relatively small parliamentary clique governing the people and, in turn, governed by the strong Chancellor. If it is further complemented by the rule of a politically irresponsible and self-perpetuating bureaucracy the description of the form of government as demo-authoritarian may not seem inappropriate.

[8] That this assumption did not fully materialize on the occasion of the election of the first federal President in September, 1949, was largely due to the arbitrariness of the election methods chosen by the individual *Land* parliaments; see *infra*, p. 605.

[9] Since each of the two leading parties of the CDU–CSU and SPD had reasons to hope that it would become the strongest party and since each was led by an ambitious politician (Dr. Adenauer and Dr. Schumacher respectively) the *dolus eventualis* of authoritarian government cannot be said to have been wholly absent concerning the peculiar form of parliamentary government that was finally agreed on.

[10] Exceptions exist only for the procedure of territorial regroupment (Art. 29).

CHAPTER XXX

FUNDAMENTAL RIGHTS AND THE PROTECTION
OF THE DEMOCRATIC ORDER

FUNDAMENTAL RIGHTS: LEGAL CHARACTER

In American planning for German democratic re-education, fundamental rights were given a high priority even though the record demonstrated that Weimar sinned on the side of giving civil liberties too much protection and by no means too little, at least for a State caught between the twin pressures from the Right and the Left. In many respects the fundamental rights (*Grundrechte*) (Arts. 1–19) of the Bonn Constitution clarify previous controversies about the extent and application of fundamental rights; in others they are antidotal to certain defects that had appeared under Weimar. For democratic emphasis they are placed at the beginning of the document; but visualized in their entirety, they constitute a visible retreat from the pioneering courage of the socio-economic and cultural program of Weimar. Instead, the catalogue of fundamental rights, introduced (Art. 1) by the statement that "human dignity is inviolate and that to respect and protect it is the obligation of the State," confines itself to the libertarian rights of freedom from state encroachment typical of the nineteenth century. The duty of the State to do its share for social betterment of its people is hardly ever mentioned. The reticence of the Parliamentary Council to attempt solutions, or even to commit the Constitution to a program, of social justice as it is understood in progressive societies of today, may be explained by the disagreement of the parties responsible for the Constitution which, incidentally, was duplicated by divergencies among the Allies.

By limiting the bill of rights to the traditional content of a liberal-bourgeois society, the Constitution was able to declare (Art. 1, par. 3) that all enumerated fundamental rights are self-executing, automatically binding on legislation, administration, and judiciary. What this means for the individual becomes evident by the reference to the general validity of the rule of law (*Rechtsstaat* [Art. 19, par. 4]) which stipulates that "should anybody's rights be infringed by the public authority he may seek judicial redress." Many German lawyers consider this clause the Magna Charta of the German people rounding out an all-inclusive protection of fundamental rights by the ordinary and administrative courts.[1] Some progress was also made in making a number of basic rights absolutely binding and not qualifying their validity by the ominous clause that they are valid only "within the limits of the law," that is, subjecting the extent of application to the discretion of the ordinary legislator, and thereby vitiating their inviolate character. Among the basic rights guaranteed unconditionally are: equality before the law (Art. 3), explicitly pertaining to the equality of the sexes and using the internationally known formula of nondiscrimination for reasons of sex, race, language, ancestry, faith, religious, and political opinions; inviolability of life and limb (Art 2, par. 2), implemented by the abolition of capital punishment (Art. 102); freedom of religion and conscience (Art. 4), with the corollary that nobody can be forced against his will to bear arms; the provision reflects the sincerity of German anti-militarism after the defeat. Other rights, however, are guaranteed conditionally only and may be restricted by law as to their exercise or are valid only "within the limits of the law." Among these are freedom of individual opinion, implemented by the right to free information (Art. 5), and freedom of association (Art. 9), limited by the prohibition of associations conflicting with the penal law, or directed against the constitutional order, or the idea of international understanding. The inviolability of the home (Art. 13) is subject to restrictions such as caused by housing shortage.[2] The protection of an accused person against police and judicial arbitrariness (what in Anglo-Saxon countries is understood by habeas corpus) is contained, instead of in the bill of rights, in the context of the administration of justice (Arts. 103 and 104); the apposite provisions of the code of criminal procedure are restated and substantially strengthened.

SOCIO-ECONOMIC AND CULTURAL RIGHTS

Concerning property and education Bonn evolved cautious compromise formulae of a generally conservative character. The guarantees of private property, the right of inheritance and the procedure of eminent domain, with adequate compensation (Art. 14) are almost *verbatim* restatements of the corresponding sections of Weimar (Art. 153). But the ordinary legislator is authorized to transfer, by special statute, natural resources and the means of production to public ownership for the purpose of nationalization (*Vergesellschaftung* [Art. 15]), with judicial redress in case the adequacy of the mandatory compensation is in dispute. On the other hand, existing situations

[1] The right of *amparo* in Latin America guarantees a similar protection.

[2] Moreover, it is generally prescribed (Art. 19) that any restriction of a fundamental right by a law, or on the basis of a law, requires an explicit reference to the article of the Constitution which is affected thereby, remedying one of the flagrant defects in legislative technique besetting the Weimar period. Another answer to the legalistic hairsplitting under Weimar, hardly intelligible to non-German lawyers, consists in the prohibition of such (permissible) constitutional limitations of a basic right which "affect its 'essential' substance" (*Wesensgehalt* [Art. 19, par. 2]).

in the field of religion and education were "frozen" in the Constitution. For the relations of State and Church the regulations of the Weimar Constitution are incorporated in full into the Bonn Basic Law (Art. 140), the only case of the "reconstitutionalization" of the former Constitution. The principle of the separation of Church and State is confirmed without thereby gaining more reality than it had under the Empire or Weimar.[3] Religious affairs are basically left to the *Laender*. But a basic right is created in that the parents may determine the religious education of their children (Art. 7, par. 2).[4] In all public schools religious education is part of the regular curriculum (Art. 7, par. 3). The entire educational system remains under the supervision of the State (Art. 7, par. 1). It is left for the *Laender* to determine whether public schools (primary and secondary) are to be denominational ("confessional") or strictly secular;[5] the parents thus do not have the right to decide what type of school the State should establish as requested by the CDU, against the successful opposition of the SDP and FDP, in the Parliamentary Council.[6]

PROTECTION AGAINST SUBVERSIVE ACTIVITIES

Considering certain peculiarities of the German political philosophy and technique, civil liberties under Bonn appear, on the whole, sufficient to provide the climate in which a liberal society may live. But remembering that the Weimar democracy had committed suicide by allowing its enemies to exploit with impunity the very same civil liberties for their destruction, the Bonn Constitution makes a commendable effort to protect the democratic order against antidemocratic abuses.

(1) The constitutional order of the *Laender* must correspond to the republican, democratic, and social principles of the State under the rule of law (*Rechtsstaat*) embodied by the Basic Law itself. In turn, the continued existence of this constitutional order is guaranteed to the *Laender* by the *Bund* (Art. 28).

(2) In contrast with most other constitutions, political parties are recognized explicitly by the Basic Law as "participating in the formation of the

[3] The Concordat of 1933 between the Holy See and Hitler remains in force (Art. 123, par. 2).

[4] For religious education the Weimar law of July 15, 1921 (RGB., p. 939) is still valid. The upshot is that parents may, or may not, send their children to religious schools and that children having reached fourteen years of age may determine for themselves what to do.

[5] For the former type the Germans evolved the satisfactory system of the *"Simultanschule"* in which children of all faiths attend the same school in a local district, but break up into separate classes for "simultaneous" instruction in their respective religious faiths. This system, however, is violently objected to by the Catholic clergy, which insists on strictly parochial schools, separating the students completely as to religious denominations.

[6] Equal opportunities in education for all classes is one of the keys to the democratization of public life in Germany. This was striven for from the beginning by the French and British MG's. The prevailing educational system intensifies the cleavage between "upper" and "lower" classes by allowing students of the wealthier families to transfer, after four years only of common schooling on the elementary level, to secondary schools (*Gymnasium*) or "reformed" high schools, graduation from which constitutes the only access to universities and other institutions of higher learning. To remedy this defect the British encouraged the system of the "unity" school (*Einheitsschule*) which, for six years, must be attended by all students, in order to mitigate the existing rigid class stratification. In Southern Germany the main line of division is still that between denominational and secular schools. In the Soviet zone a single type of elementary school of eight grades has become mandatory.

political will of the people" (Art. 21). They may be freely formed. But just as associations subversive of the constitutional order are prohibited under the ordinary law (Art. 9, par. 2), so political parties, a higher kind of association, are illegal under the Constitution if, "as judged by their programs or the conduct of their adherents, they aim at impairing or destroying the basic system of a free and democratic organization of the state, or endanger the existence of the federal German Republic" (Art. 21, par. 2). The decision on the illegality is left to the federal Constitutional Tribunal.

(3) Persons (possibly also groups or associations of persons) who "abuse" certain enumerated liberties [7] in order to fight against the free and democratic basic structure cannot claim ("forfeit") the protection of these basic rights for themselves when their activities are countered by the reaction of the attacked public order (Art. 18). Again, the decision as to whether and to what extent the liberties are "forfeited" is left, on motion of the federal or a *Land* government, to the federal Constitutional Tribunal.[8] While the wisdom of this incisive restriction of civil liberties of their enemies may not be in doubt—had such a provision existed under Weimar it might have helped to stem the Nazi tide in time [9]—it may in practice be difficult to draw a line between antidemocratic subversion and the legitimate advocacy of reform.

(4) Another protection of the democratic order is the provision (Art. 98, par. 2) that a federal judge, who, "in office or as a private person, violates the principles of the Basic Law or the constitutional order of the *Land*," may be transferred to another office or be retired; in case of a "deliberate violation" he may be dismissed. The procedure (*"Richteranklage"*), initiated by the *Bundestag,* requires a decision by a two-thirds majority of the federal Constitutional Tribunal. The provision was inspired by the experience with the judiciary under Weimar, which in many cases failed the democratic Constitution by excessive leniency towards, or open sympathy with, its enemies. Elsewhere one would think that a judge violating the Constitution would be dismissed and punished. The mildness of the penalty is indicative of the German anxiety to protect judicial independence and by no means of a distrust in the political reliability of the "denazified" judicial personnel.

(5) To prevent the rise of authoritarian, or "monolithic" political parties operating under the Fuehrer-principle, the internal organization of political

[7] These are: freedoms of opinion (including that of the press), of teaching, of association, and of assembly; the secrecy of mails and other communications; the protection of property; political asylum (the latter, Art. 16, par. 2, an innovation).

[8] This provision, aiming at the protection of the democratic-constitutional order, has nothing to do with the suspension of certain basic rights under the emergency situation of Article 48 of the Weimar Constitution, which pertained to the much less definite situation when the public security and order were believed to be endangered. In actual application Article 48 was anti-democratic and the main instrument to foist authoritarian government on a democratic order. Nor has Article 143 of the Basic Law any direct relationship to the protection of the democratic order; it is merely a temporary substitute for the sanctions against sedition and insurrection (in Germany called high treason) of the former criminal code (Sections 81 ff) which CC Law No. 11 of January 30, 1946, for convincing reasons, had struck off the statute book.

[9] See Karl Loewenstein, "Legislative Control of Political Extremism in European Democracy," 38 *Columbia Law Review* (1938), pp. 591 ff, 725 ff; *same,* "Political Reconstruction," New York, 1946, pp. 126 ff.

parties must conform to democratic principles. They must also account publicly for the sources of their financial means (Art. 21, par. 1). To the inclusion of these provisions American inspiration and German experience with the NSDAP have equally contributed.

(6) These provisions, primarily intended to prevent undermining of the democratic order by antidemocratic conduct in legal disguise that had slain Weimar, should be considered in conjunction with many other regulations implicitly protecting the democratic order against authoritarian or totalitarian perversion. Under this heading come, among other features, the election of the federal President by the Parliament instead of by the people, since, in European and Latin American experience, the plebiscitary head of the State is apt to be more dangerous to political freedom than one who owes his office to his fellow parliamentarians; the protection of the free and democratic basic order of the *Bund* or the *Laender* by calling on the police forces of several or all *Laender* (Art. 91); the inviolability of the principles contained in the section on Basic Rights (Art. 1–20) even by constitutional amendment (Art. 79, par. 3) and the seemingly redundant provision (Art. 20, par. 3) that the legislator is bound by the constitutional order. These safeguards may be serviceable in dealing with temporary antidemocratic fluctuations in the party dynamics. But fundamentally the preservation of the democratic order does not rest on the injunctions of the instrument of government but on the will of the people to abide by its principles and the willingness of the government and the bureaucracy to conduct themselves democratically. This to achieve merely by legalistic formulae or constitutional arrangements can hardly be expected.

THE FEDERAL CONSTITUTIONAL TRIBUNAL

Another significant aspect of the Bonn Constitution is the effort to commit possibly all political conflicts to a judicial decision as if they were merely legal disputes. This effort may be called the "judicialization of political dynamics." It is less due to the deep-rooted respect of the judicial function customary in the Anglo-Saxon countries than the result of the German tradition of normative positivism. For centuries the German legal mind has been trained in the precision and logic of the Pandectist (Roman) law which submits all controversies to ascertainable rules of law, and has become accustomed to codified law which does not admit the existence of gaps to be filled by the judge. Consequently, it is tempted to believe that political controversies, if reduced to legal disputes about rights and duties and submitted to judicial determination, would lose the character of power conflicts and could be peaceably resolved like any other legal controversy. The Bonn Constitution, therefore, is unique in the way it tries to apply judicial brakes to the imponderable dynamics of political power.

The administration of justice occupies a distinguished place in the Bonn Constitution (Arts. 92–104). Two "highest courts" are provided for. (a) The Supreme Federal Court (*Oberstes Bundesgericht*) (Art. 95) is the successor of the *Reichsgericht,* though with a more limited jurisdiction. It serves for the restoration and preservation of the legal unity within the federal State which has heavily suffered under the political fragmentation of the post-surrender situation.[10] Selection and appointment of the judges is entrusted to the federal Ministry of Justice in conjunction with a committee, half of whose members are elected by the *Bundestag,* the other half appointed by the *Land* Ministers of Justice. The position of the federal judges is to be regulated by a special federal law (Art. 98, par. 1). The judges are independent and subject only to the law (Art. 97, par. 1).[11] (b) The federal Constitutional Tribunal (*Bundesverfassungsgericht* [Art. 92]), wholly separated from the nonpolitical federal Supreme Court, extends its jurisdiction to three different fields of action, namely, the relations between the federal State and the *Laender;* conflicts arising in the operation of the federal State as such; and other occasions where a judicial solution of political controversies is called for.

Obviously no federal structure can dispense with an agency that delineates in case of controversy the spheres of federal and state action. Here the federal Constitutional Tribunal has jurisdiction on "differences of opinions" or "doubts" (which, evidently, need not yet be "disputes" or "controversies") on the formal or substantive compatibility of federal law and *Land* law with the Constitution—the typical case of judicial review of the constitutionality of legislation—and the compatibility of *Land* law with federal law; in this case federal law overrides *Land* law (Art. 31). The Tribunal will decide only on motion of the political authorities, that is, the federal Government, a *Land* government, or one-third of the members of the *Bundestag.* However, this procedure is likely to be initiated under exceptional circumstances only. Normally the constitutionality of a law is challenged before a court of law. If, in this case (Art. 100), the court is of the opinion that a law which is essential for its decision is unconstitutional, the lawsuit is suspended and, in case of doubt about a federal law, the decision of the federal Constitutional Tribunal is requested.[12] The Bonn Constitution thus officially introduced judicial review of the constitutionality of (federal and *Land*) law which the Weimar period had theoretically admitted though practically never exercised. The German system which, in the interest of an accelerated decision and a uniform interpretation of the Basic Law, concentrates judicial review

---

[10] The determination of what, after the entry into force of the Constitution, becomes federal law or *Land* law, is among the most complex matters of the entire instrument. Generally, existing law that under the Constitution belongs to federal jurisdiction, becomes federal law; all other laws become *Land* law. Not affected are the laws of the MG's, the CC laws, and the law on the Liberation from National Socialism and Militarism of March 5, 1946. But these principles are so perforated by exemptions and special regulations (Arts. 123–133) that German constitutional jurisprudence is having a veritable field day.

[11] The independence of the judiciary, an important element of the American democratic *credo* which failed to materialize in Germany in the past, was largely misunderstood by MG. Sociological factors, in particular the status of the judges as civil servants and the class mentality resultant therefrom, were responsible for the failure rather than faulty technical arrangements.

[12] In case the court is confronted with an allegedly unconstitutional *Land* law the Constitutional Court of the respective *Land* is seized with the decision. All seven *Laender* in the American and French zones are equipped with a Constitutional Court (*Staatsgerichtshof*) of their own.

in a single court, may be compared with the traditional practice of unlimited and dispersed judicial review in the United States.

Exigencies of the federal structure determine also the jurisdiction of the federal Constitutional Tribunal in disputes covering the rights and duties of the *Bund* and the *Laender* (in particular with reference to the execution of federal laws by the latter and the supervision of the administration of federal matters by the former) and in differences between several *Laender*. These provisions may not seem to deviate in any way from what is customary in other federal states.

The federal Constitutional Tribunal, however, becomes a pivotal political organ with the assignment to decide "on the interpretation of the Basic Law on occasion of controversies concerning the extent of the rights and duties of any one of the highest federal organs." [13] While in the United States political questions wisely are considered nonjusticiable and left to the political branches of the government—in other European states the situation of *"actes de gouvernment"* (France, Italy) and "acts of state" (Britain) is similar— the Bonn Constitution aims at the judicialization of all potential political conflicts on the premise that political power can be rationalized to the extent of subjecting it to objective standards of positive law. A similar assumption was disastrously disproved in the conflict between Prussia and the Reich Government of von Papen in 1932.

Finally, in numerous instances the Basic Law assigns to the federal Constitutional Tribunal the function of solving specific legal or political controversies. In addition to the cases of deciding on antidemocratic activities mentioned before [14] the following deserve mention: Decision, on motion of the *Bundestag* or the federal Council, on the impeachment of the federal President (Art. 61); decision on whether a rule of international law is a valid federal law and binding on individuals (Art. 100, par. 2); decision as to whether existing law belongs to the federal or *Land* jurisdiction (Art. 126).

Such vast competences concerning legal, quasi-legal and outright political disputes require judges singularly combining legal and political abilities. To find such supermen the Constitution merely stipulates (Art. 94) that the members of the federal Constitutional Tribunal shall consist partly of federal judges and partly of others, half of whom are elected each by the *Bundestag* and the federal Council, leaving the details to a special statute.

The latter was enacted by the *Bundestag* on March 12, 1951. [15] The Tribunal is divided into two chambers (Senates) of twelve judges each: they must be forty years of age and qualified for a judicial career or the higher administrative service (accessible only to full-fledged lawyers). Under the

---

[13] The phrasing of this clause is so sweeping as to include not only the federal President, the federal Government, the *Bundestag* and the federal Council, but also collective groups and minorities of these federal organs, perhaps also political parties since "the people" likewise are a "highest federal organ." Because the federal Constitutional Tribunal itself qualifies as a "highest federal organ" it may even decide in controversies to which it is itself a party!

[14] See *supra*, pp. 584 ff.

[15] BGB 1951, p. 243. See also Wilhelm Römer, *Das Gesetz über das Bundesverfassungs-gericht*, JZ 1951, 193 ff.

Basic Law the Tribunal is charged with no less than fifteen different categories of controversies. These types of cases are distributed once and for all among the two Senates. The judges, therefore, of the two branches cannot substitute for one another. A plenary session of all twenty-four judges is called for only if a Senate, on a legal point, wishes to deviate from the established jurisprudence of the other one. Dissenting opinion, it was decided after a protracted discussion, are not to be made public.

One half of the judges are to consist of members of the federal judiciary; six of these are to be elected by the *Bundestag,* the other six by the federal organ, the *Bundesrat* (Section 3). The other twelve judges are to be designated by the *Bundestag* by way of a panel of twelve of its members set up by proportional representation (Section 6) and ultimately elected by it with a two-thirds majority (Section 7). A current list of eligible candidates is kept by the Ministry of Justice, proposals for which may originate with a recognized political party represented in the *Bundestag,* the federal Government, and the *Land* governments (Section 8). Obviously, the two classes of judges are assigned to the Senates indiscriminately, that is, without regard to whether they are "professionals" or "politically appointed." All serve for an eight-year term, with re-eligibility. Their remuneration is commensurate with the importance the Basic Law attaches to the Tribunal.

Although the statute emphasizes (Section 3) that all judges "must be distinguished by a special knowledge of public law and experience in public life" it slants eligibility towards a professional legal career. Considering the narrowness of the professional legal training in Germany today, which no efforts of "re-education" on the part of the Allies could measurably alleviate, the composition of the Tribunal by no means guarantees that it will be able to deal successfully with politically loaded questions by the legal approach alone. And the ultimate success of the institution will necessarily depend on the quality of the judges charged with its functions.[16]

Other recent constitutions (Italy, France) likewise introduced similar institutions for constitutional arbitration. None, however, went as far as Bonn in the attempt at rationalizing the dynamics of political power. Diffident of the ability or willingness of the political leaders and parties to peaceably compromise their differences in the give-and-take of the political battle royal, the Germans are transferring responsibility to an allegedly nonpolitical organ whose power of effective arbitration of political conflicts, in turn, depends on the willingness of the contestants to abide by the decision. The excessive judicialization of political power is a unique feature of German democracy.

---

[16] When, after protracted negotiations between the parties and the governments, the twenty-four judges were finally elected (September, 1951) it was found that on the panel there are now no fewer than ten (acting or former) public officials, eight judges, five professors, and one practising attorney-at-law. Only five of the total have experience in political office.

CHAPTER XXXI

ADDITIONAL FEATURES OF THE BONN CONSTITUTION

THE ROLE OF THE PEOPLE

The Constitution is curiously indifferent to, and distrustful of, the people. It is true that the people are declared sovereign (Art. 20, par. 2);[1] but in the exercise of sovereignty is is confined to the elections of the *Bundestag* normally occurring every four years, with the—very remote—contingency of popular intervention in case of the dissolution of the *Bundestag*. The devices of direct democracy—initiative and referendum—are withheld from the people,[2] admittedly because of their inconclusive success under Weimar. The result, hardly unintentional, is that the actual exercise of political power is monopolized by the political parties,[3] or rather, under the impact of proportional representation, by the party oligarchies on whose hoped-for competitive cooperation the political equilibrium is dependent. In the long run the fact that the Constitution has played all dynamic political power into the hands of the party bosses and a largely irresponsible bureaucracy, cannot fail to result in an atrophy of political interest of the people which can be offset only by the development of a strong and independent public opinion.

CONSTITUTIONAL AMENDMENT

Constitutional amendment (Art. 9) requires approval of the amending legislation by two-thirds of the members of both the *Bundestag* and the federal Council. Not permissible, and therefore illegal, are amendments affecting the federal structure as such, the basic principle of the participation of the *Laender* in the legislative process, and "the principles laid down in Arts. 1 and 20." Article 1 contains a more ethical than legal statement on the in-

---

[1] *"Alle Staatsgewalt geht vom Volke aus"* ("All public authority is derived from the people").
[2] The two cases envisaged by the Constitution (Arts. 29 and 118) refer to the procedure of regional regroupment.
[3] Here again the trait of rationalizing political power is visible in that "the internal organization of the political parties must conform to democratic principles" (as had been demanded by the American democratic *credo* [see *supra*, pp. 528 f]); they are charged to account publicly for the sources of their financial means.

violability of human dignity while the more specific Article 20 establishes Western Germany "as a democratic, social, and federal State," thus purportedly excluding transformation into a unitary organization, a dictatorship, or, possibly, a monarchy. Such "unalterable" guarantees have rarely preserved their character as a privileged sanctuary when exposed to serious political pressure, inviting either their revolutionary overthrow or freezing desirable constitutional evolution. But for normal times they may be serviceable as a warning sign beyond which the legislator may not drive. Constitutional amendment is permissible only if the text of the Constitution is explicitly and simultaneously amended. This sensible provision is intended to terminate once and for all the nefarious practice of "silent" (or clandestine) amendments merely by qualified majorities of the legislature that had been the usage under the Empire and Weimar and contributed much to depriving the Constitution of its sanctity.[4]

FUNDAMENTAL LIMITATIONS ON THE CONSTITUTION

The Basic Law, solemnly renouncing nationalism and militarism, outlaws war, that is, "actions which could disturb the peaceful relations among nations, and are undertaken with such intent, in particular those preparing aggressive war" (Art. 6). Moreover, the *Bund* is willing to limit its sovereignty in the interest of a system of mutual collective security (Art. 24).[5] Furthermore, the principle of obligatory international arbitration is adhered to (Art. 24, par. 3). The general rules of international law are declared to be federal law, to have precedence over the latter, and to be immediately binding (Art. 25).

Validity and application of the Basic Law are limited territorially and as to time. It is provisional in every sense. The Preamble declares that it was created by the people of the enumerated eleven *Laender* (Berlin not included), but acting also on behalf of those Germans "to whom participation was denied." Territorial application, however, was explicitly extended also to Greater Berlin (Art. 23) as a twelfth *Land* (Art. 144, par. 2) which has the right to send representatives to the *Bundestag* and the federal Council.[6] The validity thus is limited "for the time being" (*vorläufig*) to these twelve *Laender*. For other parts of Germany (meaning the Eastern zone) it enters into force upon their accession (Art. 23). Much of the Eastern thunder could have been stolen had the Basic Law been extended to Germany as a whole from the beginning. A further time limit is set by the provision (Art. 146) that it loses

---

[4] See Karl Loewenstein, *Erscheinungsformen der Verfassungsänderung,* Tuebingen, 1932. See also, on the requirement of mentioning explicitly the article of the Constitution in the case where an infringement of the provisions on fundamental rights by ordinary legislation is permissible, *supra,* pp. 433 f.

[5] This offer to participate in international (regional, all-European or intercontinental) peace organizations, however, is carefully kept optional.

[6] The text of this provision is at variance with political reality. The M–Governors, in approving the Basic Law (Letter of May 12, 1949) explicitly excluded the Western sectors of Berlin from the *Bund,* permitting only a small number of representatives designated as observers to attend the meetings of the legislative bodies.

its validity on the day a constitution, accepted, in free decision, by the German people, will enter into force.

Last but not least, the Basic Law is limited by the Occupation Statute and the Ruhr Statute, even though, for understandable reasons, the latter are nowhere mentioned in the document. Eventually it may also be subject to limitations on German sovereignty imposed by the Peace Treaty.

A TENTATIVE APPRAISAL

For a critical review of the Bonn Constitution the Weimar experience necessarily will serve as basis of comparison and evaluation. In many respects Bonn is the answer to Weimar, trying to remedy some of its structural defects and putting roadblocks into the path of the future man on horseback. In others it is a weaker repetition of Weimar's more positive achievements. But in both content and form Bonn falls short of Weimar. Devoid of popular appeal in style or epigrammatical phrasing, it is predominantly a lawyer's Constitution which, striving for perfectionism and completeness, leaves nothing to chance. In sharp contrast to the boldness of the democratic approach of Weimar it is anxious to safeguard governmental powers at the expense of living democratic forces. Confidence in the people is supplanted by the belief of the professionals that political power can be tamed by legalistic formulae. Its federalism is hybrid and artificial. The democratic beliefs of its framers cannot be doubted. But its form of government is slanted towards authoritarian solutions though sanctioned by the popular will. Vital socio-economic issues are carefully side-stepped. In spite of its ostentatious liberalism the Bonn Constitution is perhaps the least progressive of all post-War instruments of government. Much of this, it is true, may be explained, if not condoned, by the peculiar circumstances of its creation: the compromises required by party conflicts; the pressure of the occupation powers; the fear of being responsible for an irreparable break with the East, and, most of all, the lack of a popular mandate. There was no umbilical cord carrying the popular bloodstream into the document. Yet in spite of these inhibitions the Bonn Constitution is a typical link in the historical chain of German constitutional experiments stretching from the Napoleonic period to the present.

No constitution can be evaluated on paper alone. It has to prove its usefulness when exposed to the wear and tear of internal and foreign politics. Constitutions designed for an emergency only have weathered many a storm; others, planned to last, have gone with the wind. Whether the attempted institutionalization of the democratic procedures will help Germany to become a democratic nation, only time can tell.

CHAPTER XXXII

MODIFICATIONS OF ALLIED CONTROL IN
WESTERN GERMANY

With the creation, under Allied authority, of the Western German Constitution a substantial installment of the sovereignty forfeited by unconditional surrender was returned to the Germans. It required the corresponding transformation and relaxation of the exercise of Allied controls. The revised control machinery operates under an organic law of its own, the Occupation Statute, issued by Proclamation of the three M–Governors (released April 8, 1949). Controls are institutionalized in three separate organs, the Allied High Commission (HICOG); the International Authority for the Ruhr (IAR); and the Military Security Board.

THE OCCUPATION STATUTE

The broad outlines of the Occupation Statute had been communicated to the Minister Presidents at the time when they were instructed to proceed to the drafting of the Constitution.[1] But the final test was delayed by deep-reaching dissensions among the Allies, of which the Germans were not unaware. Objections were not confined to the French. An American proposal for establishing an arbitration tribunal to adjust differences in interpretation between the Allies and the Germans on which the Germans should have a seat, was finally dropped; had it materialized the Germans easily could have paralyzed the machinery of the occupation. Controversial also were the questions whether occupation costs should be borne by the *Laender,* as desired by the French, or by the *Bund* as preferred by the two other powers,[2] and the method of arriving at decision within the Control Authority—whether

---

[1] Document III of the Instructions of the M–Governors to German Minister Presidents of July 1, 1948. The Minister Presidents raised various objections (Koblenz meeting, July 7, 1948) as did the Parliamentary Council (memorandum of December 10, 1948). But there is no evidence that the absence of a definite text of the Occupation Statute substantially handicapped the work of the Council.

[2] The issue was divorced from the Occupation Statute and settled in the Basic Law (Art. 120) to the effect that the *Bund* is the collective debtor.

by unanimity, which would have favored the Germans, or by majority. The final disentanglement of these knotty problems came only through the Foreign Ministers themselves in April of 1949 when, with the simultaneous conclusion of the North Atlantic Defense Treaty, French security apprehensions were sufficiently allayed. The text that was finally arrived at—it is rumored that there were more than twenty revisions—is inconsistently drafted and so vague as to make it a political rather than a legal document.

The Occupation Statute is not a bilateral treaty; it is the unilateral declaration of a voluntary change in policy. Nor is it a peace treaty or a substitute for it. It is merely a redefinition of the relationship between the new government of Western Germany and the occupying powers, and, in this sense, it substitutes in Western Germany a three-power regime for the four-power rule of Potsdam which, however, never was formally denounced or abolished either by the East or the West.[3]

According to the text "the German people shall enjoy self-government to the maximum possible degree consistent with the occupation." The federal State and the *Laender* are to have full legislative, executive, and judicial powers "subject only to the limitations of this instrument." However, "in order to accomplish the purposes of the occupation" the Allies reserved for themselves powers on enumerated fields, thus limiting German sovereignty much in the same way, though to a much larger degree, as the Weimar Constitution was limited by the Versailles Treaty. Unfortunately the powers found it unnecessary to define or redefine what they meant by the elastic term "purposes of the occupation" which, as the Germans justly complained, never since Potsdam had been precisely defined by any official document. Among the powers reserved for the Allies are the following: (a) Disarmament and demilitarization (including prohibitions and restrictions on industry); (b) controls in regard to the Ruhr, restitution, decartelization, and deconcentration (the economic counterparts of political democratization); nondiscrimination in trade matters, foreign interests in and claims against Germany; (c) foreign affairs (including international agreements and control over foreign trade and exchange), probably the most important restriction of the entire series; (d) displaced persons and the admission of refugees; (e) prestige and security of the Allied forces (including dependents, employees,[4] and representatives); satisfaction of occupation costs. Most of these restrictions on German self-determination, pertaining to the fact of the occupation, can hardly be objected to so long as the occupation lasts and German economy is dependent on American assistance. Moreover, "control over internal action" will be exercised "only to the minimum extent necessary to ensure use of funds, food and other supplies in such manner as to reduce to a minimum the need for external assistance to Germany."

[3] Major pieces of CC legislation, however, subsequently were officially invalidated by HICOG legislation.
[4] The value of this provision is questionable in view of the fact that the German personnel working for MG are increasingly being treated as outcasts, traitors, and collaborators without the Allies being willing or in a position to help them.

However, another set of reserved powers cutting deeply into the internal self-determination make sense only if the Allies had the will and the intention actually to exercise them. The injunction that "any amendment of the Basic Law requires the express approval of the occupation authorities" seems to be motivated by the rather naïve fear that otherwise the Germans would proceed at once to install an authoritarian regime by constitutional amendment, or that the laboriously fashioned federal structure would be nullified by constitutional processes. *Land* constitutions (referring to the still constitutionless situation in the British zone) and all amendments of *Land* constitutions likewise come under HICOG review. Of an intensely practical importance, however, is the requirement that all other legislation must be submitted to the occupation authorities. Legislation is effective unless disapproved within twenty-one days. Legislative review of the occupation powers in its totality thus is retained, with the proviso that federal and *Land* legislation will be disallowed only if inconsistent with the Basic Law, the *Land* constitutions, the directives of the occupation powers or the Occupation Statute itself, or "unless it constitutes a grave threat to the basic purposes of the occupation." Disallowance pertains also to "any agreements between the federal State and foreign governments." It is obvious that, if the occupation authorities claim for themselves the right of reviewing all legislation as to its compatibility with the federal and *Land* constitutions, they establish an agency competitive with the indigenous German constitutional tribunals and courts. The duplication of the procedure may seem superfluous, not only because it imposes an enormous amount of work on the occupation lawyers, but also because the potential sabotage of the "purposes of the occupation" hardly ever would be cloaked in an open legislative action.

To many observers it would have appeared that the Allies had gone too far in abdicating effective control, had not a general clause been hung as a Damocles sword over the erstwhile enemy whose democratization and denazification were inconclusive at best. While the occupation authorities expressed the hope that they will not have occasion to take action in fields other than those reserved to them, they reserved the right "to resume on the whole or in part the exercise of full authority if they consider that to do so is essential to security or to preserve democratic government in Germany or in pursuance of the international obligations of their governments." The restoration of limited sovereignty (and this even only during good behavior) is intended as a temporary solution, to be reviewed "in the light of the experience with its operation" within twelve to eighteen months. This was under way, in consideration also of German requests for relaxation and reform, in the fall of 1950, the final result evidently being dependent on the progressive efforts of integrating Germany into the community of Western European nations.[5]

---

[5] On the relations between the Allies and the German authorities under the Occupation Statute, see *infra*, pp. 618 ff.

ORGANIZATION OF TRIPARTITE CONTROL

THE TRIZONAL FUSION

Likewise on April 8, 1949, the Foreign Ministers of the three Western powers agreed on the "Basic Principles of Trizonal Fusion" to prepare the merger of the three zones and the establishment of the tripartite control machinery. The Allied Control Authority (High Commission) consists of one High Commissioner for each power. Unanimity is required for approval of amendments of the federal Constitution. In all other matters decisions are by majority, with the sole exception of the reserved powers of control over foreign trade and exchange; if a decision here would lead to an increase in United States financial support, a weighted vote comes into operation which in substance ensures the predominance of the United States in economic matters. In certain critical issues a High Commissioner who is overruled may appeal to his government; however, this contingency seemingly has never occurred. The HICOG must exercise its powers uniformly in accordance with tripartite policies and directives. The *Land* High Commissioners appointed in each *Land* are responsible to HICOG as a body but are nationals of the power which controls the zone. The other powers send observers to each *Land* Commissioner "for information and consultation." The plan entertained at first that controls of the *Land* administrations should be conducted throughout by tripartite teams, was abandoned as unworkable. "Channels of control" run between HICOG and the federal Government and between the *Land* Commissioners and the *Land* governments, thus excluding controls on the lower levels of administration.

In actual practice the uniformity of tripartite policies in the zones did not materialize. The *Land* Commissioners follow instructions of their own High Commissioner and report to him. The functions of the "observers" remain irrelevant. The individual High Commissioner knows little, and cares less, of what is going on in other *Laender* or zones. The flavor of the administration remains what it was before, American, British, or French. The British and the French are much too realistic to abandon established practices of control in favor of the well-meant generality of uniform tripartite policies. Consequently the separate patterns of zonal administration that had existed under MG were not assimilated. In particular, even on fields of non-reserved powers (for example, licensing of political parties) the influence of the occupying power varies, being greatest in the French, least effective in the American zone. The much heralded fusion of policies took place only on the highest level which faces the federal Government.

THE CHARTER OF THE HIGH COMMISSION

According to the Charter of the Allied High Commission (June 20, 1949) the three High Commissioners, acting as "the Council," are the legal successors of the M–Governors. The military establishment of the occupation forces, though at the disposal of the Council, is completely divorced from the civilian administration. Thus, the process of civilianization that had been under way in the MG's since 1948 was finally completed. Headquarters of HICOG are at the seat of the federal Government in Bonn where a small area is set aside, an extraterritorial "concession" in miniature, for its exclusive jurisdiction.[6] Correspondingly, the area in Bonn where the federal Government is located was vacated from occupation forces.

For the internal organization of HICOG the experience with quadripartite and bizonal cooperation was utilized. The Council itself, with chairmanship rotating monthly among the three proconsuls, has organizational autonomy. Committees with tripartite membership initially established were: Political Affairs (with the subcommittee of Information and Cultural Affairs); Foreign Trade and Exchange; Economics (with subordinated committees for decartelization, the Coal Control and the Steel Control Groups); Finance; Legal; and the Military Security Board. By 1951 there existed thirty-one committees, subcommittees, and boards within the organization of HICOG in Bonn. The organization is duplicated on the *Land* level where the *Land* Commissioner is responsible "on matters of tripartite concern" directly to HICOG and constitutes the exclusive channel of communication and liaison between HICOG and the *Land* governments. In conformity with the elevation of the German authorities to full-fledged governments, definite channels of communication were established, formal decisions of HICOG to be addressed in writing to the federal Chancellor, lesser decisions to a Minister, and *Land* matters (through the *Land* Commissioner) to the Minister President.

General Lucius D. Clay resigned his position as M–Governor officially on May 3, 1949. To the position of the American High Commissioner (established by Executive Order, June 6, 1949) Mr. John J. McCloy, a lawyer and administrator with a distinguished career in public service, was appointed (May 18, 1949). As French High Commissioner, in succession to the M–Governor General Koenig, was chosen M. André François-Poncet, a career diplomat and one of the leading experts on German affairs. For the British the M–Governor General Sir Brian H. Robertson continued at first as High Commissioner, later (June, 1950) succeeded by a career diplomat, Sir Ivone Kirkpatrick. The Occupation Statute with the Allied High Commission was proclaimed in force on September 21, 1949, after the authorities provided for by the Basic Law had duly been constituted. On the same day OMGUS and AMG went out of existence.

ORGANIZATION OF HICOG IN THE AMERICAN ZONE

The seat of the American element of HICOG is in Frankfurt in the building of the I. G. Farben corporation.[7] The American High Commissioner reports to the Department of State and no longer to the Department of the

---

[6] U.S. Headquarters were established in Bad Godesberg, near Bonn. Whether unfettered access on "corridors" through the British zone to this "island" has been agreed on is unknown.

[7] British and French headquarters are located in Hamburg and Mainz respectively, where the French moved most of their offices from Baden-Baden in 1950.

Army or Defense. The organization chart reveals the shift of emphasis from the previous policy of control and supervision pursued under the various MG directives, to that of observation, advice, and assistance if requested by the Germans. The High Commissioner serves also as chief of the Economic Cooperation Administration mission in Germany. The center of the organization is now occupied by the Office of Political Affairs. The place of the formerly powerful Civil Administration Division has been taken by a skeletal and relatively unimportant Internal Governmental and Political Affairs Division. The Legal Division (Office of the General Counsel) which, under General Clay, had been one of the weakest spots in the administration, increased in importance (taking charge of the enormous task of legislative review) and efficiency, hardly surprising when the boss himself is a lawyer. In the Office of Public Affairs, the Division for Education and Cultural Relations, on which the French from the beginning had placed major responsibilities, gained influence, though probably it was too late to accomplish much.

The transition from MG to civilian administration under the High Commissioner was anything but smooth. It should be noted that Mr. McCloy had to integrate into an organizational pattern his responsibilities as a member of the Allied High Commission, as the chief of the U.S. organization in the American zone, and as the ECA representative for Germany, while developing simultaneously his relations to the Ruhr Authority, to the High Command of the U. S. forces, and to the Berlin Western Sector. The American personnel was cut drastically (from about 2,200 to 1,600); much firing and hiring was done, since understandably the High Commissioner wished to choose his own staffs.[8] On the whole, the quality of the personnel has deteriorated noticeably, though by the middle of 1950 at least an effective office routine had been secured. Cooperation and coordination between the Divisions and with the *Land* Commissioners leave much to be desired. In general the best among the staff feel frustrated by the lack of real powers, the impotence of coping with undesirable developments among the Germans, and the waste motion so characteristic of American public administration.

THE INTERNATIONAL RUHR AUTHORITY

The Ruhr,[9] with its coal and iron deposits, its mines, plants and factories, its integrated labor force and accumulated management skill, is the economic heart of Germany, the greatest industrial concentration of Continental Europe, and the core of the East-West conflict over Germany. Its post-War importance may be visualized from three inextricably interlocked angles. First: How can Germany be prevented from using her resources again, as

[8] Fortunately, the valuable elements of the resident officers in the local districts (*Kreise*) were retained and strengthened. All of them must speak and understand German and must be married and living with their families, for reasons not altogether flattering to former incumbents without such qualifications.

[9] The circumference of the area located entirely in the *Land* North Rhine-Westphalia, is defined by the Annex to the Ruhr Statute, as comprising thirteen city and twenty-three rural districts of the *Regierungsbezirke* of Duesseldorf, Muenster, and Arnsberg.

under the Empire and Hitler, for aggressive war? For the French, the Ruhr in the hands of the nationalistic tycoons of heavy industry is the eternal dagger pointed at their security. When they realized, after the Moscow Conference of 1947, that their initial goal of internationalizing the Rhine and the Ruhr was unobtainable from their Allies they insisted at least on international control of ownership and management. Here the Socialists and other far-sighted Germans agreed, but they wished to forestall abuse of the economic potential by the steel masters and coal barons by public ownership or nationalization of the Ruhr industry. This, in turn, was anathema to the Americans, though not to the British. Second: How can the natural wealth be made accessible to all of Europe without the Germans, for selfish reasons, being able to discriminate against others? Here the solution was proposed to make the entire area, by internationalization, serve all-European interests; this was strongly opposed by the Germans who wished to retain exclusive control over their most precious asset, particularly since they had lost the two other industrial regions, the Saar to the French, and Upper Silesia to the Poles. Moreover, if the Ruhr was to be "Europeanized," why not the Saar, the Belgian Borinage, or other industrial areas? Third: How can the Soviets be prevented from sharing control and benefits of the Ruhr? This is the intrinsic reason why the Potsdam Agreement, providing for the economic unity of Germany as a whole, proved politically and economically untenable to the Western Powers and remains essential for the Soviets.

The London Six-Power Accord (June 2, 1948), confronted with these conflicting claims and realizing that without the Ruhr European recovery could not be accomplished, decided on the integration of the three Western zones into the European Recovery Program. Instead of internationalizing the Ruhr the establishment of an International Authority should make a contribution of the area to European cooperation possible. But the vital issue of ownership was sidestepped. On the eve of negotiations with the stalling French, the Anglo-Saxon powers, with less than delicate timing (Armistice Day, November 11, 1948), sprang on their ally MG Law No. 75 which ordered the dissolution of the huge trusts and combines—the Ruhr industry is the textbook model of "vertical economic concentration"—and their regroupment in smaller units, under the management of German trustees [10] and under MG supervision. The final decision on the ownership was to be left to "a freely elected German government." To all practical intents and purposes this amounted to a return to power of the former owners and management. Negotiations with the justly indignant French led to their admission to the bizonal coal and steel control groups without waiting for the final trizonal fusion arrangement and the immediate setting-up of the Military Security Board (agreed also in the Six-Power Accord [June 2, 1948]). Subsequently the Ruhr Statute (agreed to on December 19, 1948) was signed in London (April 28, 1949) by the three Western powers and the Benelux

[10] The twelve trustees, chosen from management and trade unions, were finally selected in 1950 after the customary denazification troubles.

states. The International Authority was finally constituted in the summer of 1949 in Duesseldorf.

The objective of the International Authority for the Ruhr was to ensure that "the resources of the Ruhr shall not in the future be used for the purpose of aggression but shall be used in the interests of peace." Voting rights in the Council were assigned to the United States, Britain, France, Germany (three votes each) and to the three Benelux states (one vote each). For an interim period the German votes were to be cast jointly by the occupation authorities. Germany at first sent only an observer. The basic functions of the Authority consist in the division of coal, coke, and steel from the Ruhr "as between German consumption and export" and the elimination of unfair trade practices and discrimination. In order to fulfill these functions the Authority may examine transport, price and trade practices, quotas, tariffs, and other governmental measures or commercial arrangements instituted or permitted by the German authorities. This supervision is intended to prevent underselling by Germany. Allocation of coal, coke, and steel was to be integrated with the European cooperation requirements. A minimum amount of coal, coke, and finished and semi-finished steel had to be made available for export. The American hand is found in the provision that no excessive concentration of industry will be tolerated. The Authority was also charged to prevent production in excess of the steel quota permitted by the level of industry plan (fixed at 11.1 million tons a year).

Whether the arrangement was found useful at the time of its devising may be doubted. The Ruhr Authority was still-born from the start.[11] Although no direct organizational relationship exists between the Authority and HICOG, the former's functions are largely dependent on the latter's decisions. For the period of occupation the right of control and internal allocation belongs to HICOG, which exercises them through its Coal and Steel Control Groups. Actually, thus, the International Ruhr Authority is primarily a consultative and study group without any effective power. Deliberately left without adequate funds, its control operations are entirely dependent on German information and German personnel. As a result of the "Treaty on the European Coal and Steel Community," better known as the Schuman plan (signed by the Foreign Ministers of the six participating powers on April 19, 1951), the Ruhr Authority, in spite of its limited powers a thorn in the flesh of German heavy industry, will terminate its existence as soon as the Schuman plan organization has begun to operate.

The net result of this complex and irritating narrative is that in the vital Ruhr issue the clock has been put back, with American connivance, to before 1945. The managerial board of the trustees, where management and labor are

[11] External allocations subsequently became unnecessary since supply and demand had been brought to an approximate balance. When, in December, 1950, coal scarcity reappeared because of increased industrial demands, the Germans, as could have been expected, became obstinately opposed to the export of coal which they pretended to need at home. Dissatisfaction with the Authority's rulings concerning the export quotas for coal led, in the summer of 1951, to the resignation of the German member, Vice Chancellor Bluecher.

patriotically united against the Allies, is merely a screen for the former owners and their managerial elite whose corporate skill allegedly could not be dispensed with in European reconstruction. Decartelization has come to nothing. The breaking up of the cartels into smaller self-sustaining and competitive units was of course wholly impossible. Socialization or nationalization became academic issues, considering the party structure of the Bonn Parliament and the sullen submissiveness of the labor force confronted with the alliance between German and American big business, which has large investments in the industry. The coal and steel magnates emerged as the victors from this battle royal. Next to the failure of denazification, the re-establishment of the *status quo ante* in the Ruhr is the major defeat of the Allied occupation policies.[12]

THE MILITARY SECURITY BOARD

Another limitation of German sovereignty consists in the establishment of the Military Security Board, agreed on in the Six-Power Accord (June 2, 1948). It has the over-all responsibility for security in Germany, charged also with the task of supervision in the Ruhr. Its primary function is the maintenance of German disarmament and demilitarization, particularly with regard to the prohibited and limited industries and the restrictions on scientific research. Of its activities little is known. But the main protection against an illegal revival of the German military potential is the presence of the occupation forces. This statement, however, is a historical one referring to the situation that existed prior to the German rearmament at the behest of the Allies.

[12] For the remarkable inside story of the failure of German decartelization see James Stewart Martin, *All Honorable Men,* Boston, 1950.

C H A P T E R   X X X I I I

SETTING UP THE MACHINERY OF GOVERNMENT

THE ELECTORAL LAW

Different from Weimar, the Bonn Basic Law refrained from making a uniform electoral system mandatory by constitutional injunction. The Parliamentary Council arrogated to itself the right of drafting an electoral law for the first elections for the *Bundestag*. Heavily weighted in favor of proportional representation it was rejected, under American pressure, by the M–Governors, who would have preferred to leave the matter to the *Laender,* acting under a uniform directive. When the untractable Council nonetheless passed (May 10, 1949) a version little dissimilar to the previous one, the M–Governors, losing patience, amended the text themselves and instructed the Minister Presidents to promulgate it in their respective *Land* (June 14, 1949). Likewise, since the Germans obstinately refused to accede to the Allied request concerning the exclusion of public officials from the *Bundestag,* the M–Governors cut the Gordian knot and enacted a MG Law [1] according to which public officials and employees, if elected, must, upon acceptance of the mandate, resign their official position.

The law for the elections of the first *Bundestag* as it finally emerged is a curious mixture of certain aspects of proportional representation and of the technique of straight majority elections in single-membered constituencies, patterned largely on the experience with similar statutes in the British zone. The basic idea was to allow the voter a choice between individual personalities rather than make him blindly support a party list submitted by the party hierarchy under proportional representation. Of the 400 seats, a certain number corresponding roughly to the population was assigned to each *Land*. Within each *Land* the seats were to be distributed "in an approximate proportion" of 60:40 per cent between the electoral districts electing the deputy in straight majority contest, and supplementary *Land* nomination lists based on

[1] In the U.S. zone MG Law No. 20 of June 2, 1949.

the proportional system. In each electoral district the candidate is definitely elected who has received the plurality of votes. Thereafter, in each *Land* the votes cast for each individual party are added up and the number of seats assigned to each party are calculated according to the proportion of the total votes cast. Next, from the number of seats so obtained the number of mandates is deducted which each party has received in the electoral districts by straight majorities. Finally, the remainder of seats are filled according to the lists submitted by each party. However, if a party has obtained more seats in the direct election in the constituencies, they remain assigned to it even if they exceed the total of mandates a party is entitled to under proportional distribution.[2] Parties with less than 5 per cent of the total vote cast in each *Land* are entitled to share in the pool under proportional distribution of seats only if they have won at least one electoral seat in an electoral district.[3]

The blending of straight majority contests and proportional representation constituted a partial victory of those Germans (and the few AMG officials conversant with recent German history) who justly considered proportional representation a perversion of the democratic idea, in spite of its literal congruity with it, because it had promoted the splitting-up of the electoral will into multiple parties which the German urge for political individualization encouraged anyway. The election of personalities instead of the soulless endorsement of a party-manufactured list was considered indispensable for kindling the voters' interest in elections and for breaking up the hold of the irresponsible party bosses and their bureaucracies on the selection of candidates.[4] When put to the practical test in the elections the mixed system fell short of expectations. If 60 per cent of orange juice is added to 40 per cent of sulphuric acid the mixture will taste accordingly. The voters continued to vote for parties and party lists instead of personalities. But at least the wall of proportional representation had been breached.

THE CHOICE OF THE FEDERAL CAPITAL

The Parliamentary Council, once again transcending its competence, selected Bonn as the future capital. That the badly destroyed university town on the left bank of the Rhine was chosen over the competitive protest of Frankfurt, was the first major political controversy among the Germans. Frankfurt, objectively much better suited as the traffic center of Western Germany and with available metropolitan facilities for accommodating the large staffs of the bizonal administration, was rejected by Dr. Adenauer and the majority of the Council; Bonn, his home town, was in North Rhine-Westphalia, the most pow-

---

[2] This latter provision explains why the first *Bundestag* had 402 deputies instead of the number of 400 fixed in the electoral law.

[3] The law contained also regulations for the election of the first federal Convention charged with the election of the federal President, see *infra,* p. 605.

[4] Credit for bringing the issue before the German public goes to the German Electoral Association (*Deutsche Wählergesellschaft*), founded 1947 in Frankfurt, in which prominent people of all walks of life actively participated. Of the parties, the CDU favored majority elections; the SPD, entangled in obsolete party doctrines, held on to proportional representation; the minor parties which naturally could gain most from proportional representation, wished to retain it.

erful *Land,* and, as his detractors allege, in the shadow of the cathedral of Cologne and the coal and iron stacks of the Ruhr.[5]

THE ELECTIONS FOR THE FIRST *BUNDESTAG*

The Minister Presidents upon whom, after disbandment of the Parliamentary Council (May 23, 1949) the task of keeping things moving had reverted, determined August 14, 1949, as the date for the elections of the first *Bundestag.*

The election campaign, starting late, aroused little enthusiasm. The mass of the people was indifferent towards the Constitution of which they knew little. By no stretch of imagination, therefore, can the vote be taken as a plebiscite on the Constitution. Suspicion towards any and all political parties was unabated. Chauvinistic gibes at the occupation powers—in which the Socialists outdid all other parties except the Communists—seemed to be the foremost vote-catching device. The election itself was traditionally orderly and wholly free from corruption or pressure.

Election results are shown in the following tabulation: [6]

Eligible voters	31,179,422	
Voters participating	24,495,613	78.5%
Valid votes cast	23,732,398	
Invalid votes cast	763,215	

Party	Vote	Per Cent	Total of Seats	Seats Obtained Districts	Seats Obtained Land Lists
CDU–CSU	7,359,084	31.0	139	115	24
SPD	6,934,975	29.2	131	96	35
FDP	2,829,920	11.9	52	12	40
KPD	1,361,708	5.7	15	—	15
BP	986,478	4.2	17	11	6
DP	939,934	4.0	17	5	12
DRP	429,031	1.8	5	—	5
WAV	681,888	2.9	12	—	12
ZP	727,505	3.1	10	—	10
Others	340,228	1.4	1	—	1
Independents	1,141,647	4.8	3	3	—
Total	23,732,398	100.0	402		

These first democratic elections on a nation-wide scale since 1932 were variously interpreted as a victory of the "moderate" parties, as alarming signs of rising nationalism, or as a convincing repudiation of Communism. They require a closer scrutiny than may be obtained by the mere comparison of seats and percentages.

(1) The voting percentage (78.5) does not indicate particular interest except when contrasted with the traditionally low figures in this country. Partici-

---

[5] On November 4, 1949, the *Bundestag,* by 200–176 votes, rejected a motion of the SPD to move the seat of the federal capital from Bonn to Frankfurt. Previously the Parliament, on the initiative of the CDU–CSU, by the narrow margin of 197–185, had accepted an amendment of the Standing Orders permitting, at the request of seventy members, a secret vote (except on matters of legislation), obviously intended to allow the SPD members from North Rhine-Westphalia to vote against their party on the transfer of the federal capital.

[6] The figures are taken from Department of State Publication 3556, p. 319.

pation was lower than for the Weimar Constituent Assembly in 1919 (82.7). Disfranchised Nazis account for a fraction of one per cent only. The increase of votes over the *Landtag* elections of 1946–47 (more than 6.3 million) came from the returned prisoners of war, readmitted Nazis, expellees, etc.

(2) No single party received a majority, nor did anything approximating a two-party system materialize. No government was possible without a party coalition.

(3) The blending of straight majority contests with elections on *Land* lists did not disabuse the voter from the habit of voting for the party ticket, instead of "personalities." The power of the party machines, so greatly enhanced by proportional representation, has not been dented, let alone broken.

(4) No fewer than eighty seats (one-fifth of the total) went to small and very small groups. Majority elections throughout would have eliminated all parties obtaining seats only through the *Land* lists (for example, the Center Party and the Communists),[7] but would in all likelihood have also reduced the number of seats going to parties which obtained the bulk of their mandates from the *Land* lists (for example, the FDP). Only the CDU–CSU and the SDP received more seats in straight elections than through proportional representation.[8] However, the conclusion that, with majority elections throughout, the two-party system, based on the CDU and the SPD, would have emerged with, perhaps, a small Liberal party and a handful of seats otherwise scattered, is altogether unwarranted. Local election agreements, all pointed against the Socialists, may well have resulted in the maintenance of the multiple party structure. This explains why the SPD feels that proportional representation is its best protection.

(5) The election result is distorted by the absence of refugee parties which had not been licensed in time. Since this element constitutes about one-fifth of the total population, refugee parties may be counted on obtaining between sixty to eighty seats in coming elections, with corresponding deflation of other parties now harboring them.

(6) The sharp decline of the Communists (from 9.4 to 5.7 per cent is self-explanatory. It was marked also in traditional citadels like the Ruhr and Hamburg. Unemployment rather than Eastern propaganda may reverse the trend.

(7) But also the two major parties of the CDU and SPD slipped considerably (from 37.7 to 31.0 per cent and from 35.0 to 29.2 per cent respectively), and this in spite of a relative gain in the total of votes. Evidently the expected process of deflation has begun.

(8) The real victor, practically the only party rising in percentage (from 9.3 to 11.9) were the Liberals (FDP). But appearances are deceptive. The FDP, in the German party spectrum farthest to the Right, was preferred by

[7] The Communists and all regionally scattered parties were at a disadvantage owing to the provision that they could participate in the *Land* pool only if obtaining at least 5 per cent in the *Land*. Consequently, the Communists required about 90,000 votes for each seat, as compared with about 55,000 for the major parties.

[8] The case of the Bavarian Party which likewise obtained eleven of its seventeen seats in the districts is a special one because the party is concentrated in Southern Bavaria as a serious competitor of the CSU.

many former Nazis. Neo-Fascism was not yet organized. With the formation of genuine nationalistic parties the FDP is bound to decline. Nazi negativists explain also the relatively large percentage of invalid votes (3.1 per cent).

(9) By all reasonable standards, the Germans have gone Right, not Left. They voted for order, not for democracy. The result may be evaluated as a victory of the Americans over the British, of free enterprise over Socialism. But the margin of the socially heterogeneous CDU is a slim one indeed. The triumph of the moderate bourgeoisie, therefore, is not devoid of hybrid elements. Masses of displaced voters have not yet found their proper cubicles. The party configuration is still far from jellied or stable.

THE ESTABLISHMENT OF THE FEDERAL ORGANS

THE ELECTION OF THE FEDERAL PRESIDENT

The Constitutional Convention for the election of the federal President assembled in Bonn on September 12, 1949. It was composed of 804 electors, consisting of the deputies elected to the *Bundestag* and the same number of delegates designated by the *Landtage*. Since the latter were free to determine the method of selection, the electors were chosen in some *Laender* in conformity with the strength of the political parties as evidenced by the *Bundestag* elections (as in Bavaria), in others in line with the existing party configuration. The procedure revealed its intrinsic absurdity from the start.[9]

The coalition parties had agreed in advance on the candidature of Dr. Theodor Heuss (FDP), sixty-five, native of Wuerttemberg, a former professor of political science, publicist, and convinced anti-Nazi. As a surprise move the SPD presented as competitor its leader, Dr. Kurt Schumacher. The first ballot proved inconclusive, none of the candidates securing the required majority of 403.[10] In the second ballot Dr. Heuss was elected by the unimpressive majority of 416 votes (Dr. Schumacher receiving 312). Thus, the election of the first magistrate of the federal Republic, intended to be "above the parties," was strictly party-engineered.[11]

[9] The least that one would have expected was uniformity of procedures among the *Laender*. The following tabulation demonstrates that the method favored the CDU and SPD, while the FDP was as heavily under-represented as the KPD was over-represented.

Seats in Bundestag		Landtage Electors	Total
CDU–CSU	139	140	279
SPD	131	148	279
FDP	52	36	88
KPD	15	25	40
Others	65	53	118
	402	402	804

[10] Dr. Heuss received 377, Dr. Schumacher 311 votes.

[11] The iron hold of the party hierarchy on the constitutional machinery was revealed with brutality by the election of the first President of the federal Council (September 7, 1949). In the intention of the Basic Law the President of the federal Council should be independent from the federal Government. What actually happened was that Dr. Adenauer, supinely overriding the autonomy of the federal Council, struck a bargain with the Bavarian CSU to join the coalition, in return for designating the Bavarian Minister President, Dr. Hans Ehard, as President of the federal Council. The Socialists, controlling five *Land* governments, not having

ELECTION OF THE FEDERAL CHANCELLOR AND FORMATION OF THE CABINET

The dust of the election had not yet settled when the party leaders began negotiations on the formation of the government coalition. Some leaders would have favored the so-called "Great Coalition," consisting of the CDU–CSU, the SPD, and the FDP that had steered Weimar through the difficult initial stages. But the SPD leadership justly declined, since the election was clearly indicative of a popular mandate for the free market economy instead of Socialism. Consequently, the SPD constituted itself as the official opposition party. Dr. Adenauer, the leader of the CDU, in search of a majority, arranged a combination of his party with the FDP (139 and 52 seats), but was compelled to add also the 17 votes of the DP, pulling together, all told, 208 votes, which amounted to hardly more than the bare majority, 202).

That the newly elected federal President, Dr. Heuss, would propose as federal Chancellor Dr. Adenauer, was agreed by antecedent negotiations among the coalition leaders. He was elected (September 15, 1949) with the barest legal minimum of 202 votes (of 393 members present).[12]

The Basic Law requires neither a vote of confidence nor a formal endorsement of the government's program by the *Bundestag*. Under this curious demo-authoritarian instrument of government he is handed, by the election, a blank check. Nor was the President or anyone else entitled to know in advance the distribution of the cabinet portfolios among the parties, or the persons considered for them, although this must have been under discussion among the coalition parties. The President merely confirmed the list of Ministers submitted to him by the Chancellor (September 20, 1949).

Thirteen ministries were established, eight of the "classical" type (Interior, Justice, Finance, Economics, Food and Agriculture, Labor, Transport, Posts and Telecommunications) and five related to specific conditions (Refugee (*Flüchtling*) Affairs, Housing, European Recovery Program, All-German Affairs, and Federal Council Affairs).[13] No Ministry of Foreign Affairs being permissible under the Occupation Statute, the Chancellor took personal charge of them. Of the Ministers, eight belonged to the CDU (among them no fewer than three assigned to the Bavarian CSU); three to the FDP and two to the

---

been consulted, revolted, supported by the powerful *Land* North Rhine-Westphalia whose Minister President, Karl Arnold (CDU), is Adenauer's competitor within the CDU. The result was that Arnold was elected (by ten out of eleven *Laender,* only Bavaria voting against). The upshot of this finagling was that the President of the federal Council, which is an organ of federalism, from the start was subordinated to the power squeeze of the federal Government. Political realities proved stronger than paper federalism. See *Archiv des öffentlichen Rechts,* vol. 75 (1949), pp. 332 ff.

[12] As the vote was secret the composition of the majority is unknown. It is even doubtful whether the election was legal, since three invalid votes were counted for Dr. Adenauer.

[13] The Ministry of All-German Affairs attends to matters concerning the Eastern zone. The Federal Council Affairs Ministry is anomalous since matters pertaining to the federalist structure belong to the Ministry of the Interior. ERP was split from Economics. Several of these offices were created to satisfy the wish of certain party politicians.

DP. The key men, next to the Chancellor, Dr. Adenauer, were Dr. Ludwig Erhardt (Economics), the creator of the free-market economy; Fritz Schaeffer (Finance); and Dr. Gustav Heinemann (Interior). Several Ministers are not members of the *Bundestag.*

All federal legislative and executive organs duly constituted, the German Federal Republic was launched on what may be expected to be a stormy career.

CHAPTER XXXIV

POLITICAL DEVELOPMENTS ON THE GERMAN LEVEL [1]

THE FEDERAL GOVERNMENT

The time elapsed since the Basic Law has begun to operate is too short and the conditions in Germany are too extraordinary to allow any but the most tentative review of its practical value. But certainly it did not fail its drafters in providing Germany with a strong government, strong to the point of being immune to the influences of the President, the Parliament and the people.

The federal President, Dr. Heuss, keeping strictly within constitutional limits of integrating and symbolizing the Republic, has won the respect of the parties —and even, with certain reservations, the loyalty of the public—by his informality, knowledge of the nature of man, and a refreshing sense of humor.

The federal Chancellor, Dr. Adenauer, made the fullest possible use of his constitutional attribute of "determining the directions of politics" (Art. 65, par. 1) while the collateral duty of "being responsible for them" remained nominal at best. Cabinet meetings are being held, as a rule, twice a week. In foreign affairs (for which Section III of the Chancellory served as administrative basis) he claimed and maintained the monopoly of action and decision. The relations with the Allies, represented by the High Commissioners, he conducted single-handed and at times, it is contended, without consultation with his cabinet, let alone the *Bundestag,* relying, if at all, on personal and irresponsible advisors. Equally impervious to outside control in his recruitment of the personnel for the federal ministerial bureaucracy, he admitted to key positions prominent former Nazi collaborators. He did not hesitate to intervene in the autonomy of the *Laender,* when, after the June, 1950, elections in North Rhine-Westphalia, he forced the *Land* CDU to dissolve the previous government coalition with the SPD and to coordinate the political complexion of the *Land* government with that of the federal Republic.

The only cabinet crisis (if such it was) occurred (September, 1950) when the Minister of Interior, Dr. Heinemann, resigned in protest over the sub-

---

[1] In the following discussion events are covered to January 31, 1951, inclusive.

ordination of the newly created Security Police to the Chancellery instead of to his Ministry. But the underlying cause of the break was the wish of the Minister, who is also the president of the Evangelical Synod, to dissociate himself from the plan of rearmament to which the Protestant Church is opposed.

However, the technique of quasi-authoritarian action, combined with an unusual astuteness in political manoeuvring, stood the Chancellor in good stead in accomplishing what may be the most important internal development of the Bonn Republic, namely, the passage of the Codetermination Act of May 21, 1951. Codetermination, as mentioned before, is the cornerstone in the program of the Socialists, as the first stage of economic democracy in Germany, and may well become of paramount importance in view of Germany's senior partnership in the Schuman plan also for Western Europe as a whole.

Codetermination had been introduced, by an Ordinance of the British occupation authorities for their zone early in 1947, for those "decartelized" plants of the steel industry that, with German "trusteeship," were under the jurisdiction of their Northern Iron and Steel Control Board. The measure distributed the statutory number of eleven members of the Board of Supervisors (*Aufsichtsrat*) between capital (management) and labor (trade unions and plant community) on the principle of "parity of social partners," with the key position of the "eleventh" man assigned to the trustee administration. On the three-membered Board of Directors (*Direktorium*) a trade-union member held the position of "director of labor," in addition to one management or business representative and one for "personnel and labor matters." The system governed plants producing 85 per cent of the iron and steel capacity of Western Germany; it did not extend to coal mining. Its success, equally attested to by management and labor, contributed its full share, by assuring labor peace and giving labor a voice in management policies, to the amazing economic recovery of the Ruhr and the Rhineland.

When, in line with the relaxation of the occupation controls, this important segment of Germany's economic potential was to revert, at the end of 1950, to exclusive German control, Dr. Ludwig Erhardt, diehard liberal Minister of Economics, imprudently announced the impending cancellation of codetermination as inconsistent with German law. The issue had been tossed around in the *Bundestag* for a year and more. The trade unions, taking up the gauntlet, countered with the threat of a strike on February 1, 1951, affirmative action on which was carried by 92.8 per cent of the 800,000 workers in a referendum, unless the Bonn Government formally obligated itself to submit appropriate legislation to the *Bundestag* for the retention of codetermination in the steel industry and its extension to coal mining.

At this point Dr. Adenauer, who before had refused to accede to a strike threat considered "political," reversed himself in support of labor's demands, realizing that otherwise he would jeopardize recovery and also, as a shrewd politician, determined to take the wind out of the propaganda sails of the Socialist competition. Personally presiding over labor-management negotiations, he not only succeeded in overcoming the resistance of the latter (January 27, 1951) but also the parliamentary obstacles to the bill drafted by his Government. In the final vote (April 10, 1951) in the *Bundestag* he was deserted by two of his coalition partners, the FDP and the German Party—among the former the chairman, Vice Chancellor Bluecher, voted against his own party—and the passage was secured by a strange *ad hoc* combination of the reluctant Christian Democrats and the jubilant Social Democrats. A special feature of foreign intervention was also present in the violent protests of emissaries of the American Association of Manufacturers.

In its final form the application of codetermination is limited to plants with more than 1,000 employees; the Socialists had demanded a minimum of 300. Of the eleven members of the Board of Supervisors five are elected by the stockholders, meaning, in practice, capital and management. Of the five labor members three will be designated by the trade unions, two are to belong to the plant community (white-collar and manual labor). For the selection of the "eleventh" man, the "independent" member, holding the key position with regard to potential deadlocks between the two equal groups, a complex arbitration procedure was established, with eventual injection of the local district court, and resulting in a slight edge in favor of the stockholders.

In taking responsibility for this legislation and in successfully steering it through the cliffs of parliamentary opposition, Dr. Adenauer has shown more than average leadership capacity and demonstrated, a portent for the future, the chances of cooperation between the middle-of-the-road parties, the Christian Democrats and the Socialists. Moreover, in identifying himself, a staunch conservative heretofore leaning heavily on big business, with this truly revolutionary legislation he helped to inaugurate what may become the entering wedge of a peaceful social revolution in Germany. On the other hand, labor prepares the extension of codetermination to other segments of industry, particularly the production of chemicals, considering it the first stage of ultimate nationalization. Incidentally, codetermination for all branches of production exists already, through *Land* legislation and against long resistance of the United States Government, in Wuerttemberg-Baden and Hessen.

No one will deny Dr. Adenauer recognition of his consummate political skill in holding the precarious government coalition together, none will doubt his professing (and probably believing in) Europeanism, and none will minimize the ability of the German Talleyrand to exploit to the limit Germany's improved bargaining position towards the Allies which contributed much to whittling away many of the restrictions under the Occupation Statute. But under the existing conditions his rule is quasi-authoritarian and democratic in the remote sense only that a popularly elected Parliament has raised him to power. What may be, however, more fatal in the long run is the suspicion, borne out by much substantial evidence, of the influence exercised over his policies by the magnates of German heavy industry in the Rhineland and the Ruhr who again have taken their place on the industrial thrones of the powerfully recuperating German economy.

THE FEDERAL LEGISLATIVE BODIES

THE BUNDESTAG

Within the period under review the *Bundestag* failed to gain the political weight assigned to it by the Basic Law. At first sessions were held once a week only, later more frequently. Towards the federal Government the assembly was too submissive to exercise efficiently its constitutional role as controlling organ. This was partly due to the structure of the Constitution which makes a vote of nonconfidence dependent on the selection of a successor in case it is carried; substitute methods of control were not developed. Relations with the federal Government were maintained, if at all, through the party leaders; the Chancellor presented himself rarely to the chamber which serves primarily as the technical agency for legislation. Only once the Government encountered a palace revolution of the *Bundestag* when, in view of the universal protest of the parties (including his own), the Chancellor was compelled to continue flour subsidies in connection with a sudden rise of the price for bread (July 14, 1950).

In terms of party dynamics, the *Bundestag* was as strictly controlled by the Government coalition as is the British House of Commons by the Government party. Parliamentary discipline (*Fraktionszwang*) is traditional in Germany; cross-voting occurs rarely, and defections from the party line are practically unknown. The exclusion of the opposition from constructive collaboration— let alone codetermination of policies—is watertight. Advance understandings or compromises with the opposition are uncommon. Consequently, the opposition of the Socialists (and other parties) was unconstructive to the point of futility.[2] The situation improved, however, when, after the electoral victories of the Socialists in the *Laender* late in 1950, the Chancellor became more inclined towards cooperation.

THE FEDERAL COUNCIL

As an organ for the protection of states' rights the federal Council proved of little importance; the *Laender* do not seem apprehensive of federal encroachment. The authorization of concurrent legislation (Art. 76, par. 1) was fully used without much objection on the part of the *Laender*.[3] The interparliamentary conciliation committee for adjusting differences between the two houses was invoked only four times and led always to agreement. There was as yet no need for resorting to the veto (*Einspruch*). On the other hand, the fed-

[2] The situation was drastically highlighted by an incident (November, 1949): Dr. Schumacher, in the heat of a night debate on the Petersberg Accord, made a slighting remark about the Chancellor which, in any other parliamentary milieu, would have been settled by an apology. Instead the offender was excluded, by disciplinary sanction of the submissive *Bundestag* majority, from the plenary sessions for twenty days which would have eliminated the leader of the opposition for about half a year. Only outside persuasion brought rescission of the penalty.

[3] Only in a single case, the proposal for a federal hunting law, did the federal Council seriously contest the federal jurisdiction.

eral Council, as under the Empire and Weimar, regained its position as a group of administrative technicians indispensable for legislation, and thus in time may become a counterweight of the federal ministerial bureaucracy. The body was free from serious political conflicts. Contrary to expectations, voting along party lines rarely developed. What happened instead—and this could have been foreseen if not by the textbook federalists of MG—was that whenever occasion arose, the "have-not" *Laender* (Bavaria, Schleswig-Holstein, and some of the *Laender* in the French zone) "ganged up" against the "haves" (primarily North Rhine-Westphalia, Wuerttemberg-Baden, Hamburg), with Hessen and Lower Saxony joining lustily, to pressurize them in favor of their deficient economies, and this regardless of the party flavor of the individual *Land*. In terms of federal planning this implies that, however federalistic a constitution may be on paper, its character is determined by the power of the purse—or, in Germany, the equalization of financial burdens (*Finanzausgleich*).

THE LEGISLATIVE PROCESS

The legislative process was slow in hitting its stride. This is not surprising. The federal Government had its hands full—Bonn is about as hectic as Washington—in setting up the administrative machinery and preparing legislation. The *Bundestag* exercised its right to initiate legislation fully.[4] The ministerial bureaucracy has no longer a drafting monopoly. However, government bills submitted to it were discussed and eventually amended, but never rejected by the *Bundestag*. The efforts to teach the legislators the American technique of a legislative drafting service and a legislative reference bureau have yielded no dividends as yet, the ministerial bureaucracy believing itself fully capable of drafting a statute as it should be drafted. The legislative process is traditionally cumbrous but not worse than elsewhere. Public hearings were not introduced, again because the ministerial bureaucracy does not believe it needs outside advice. The net result, as under Weimar, is that the legislative process, monopolized by the Government officials and the party experts, is divorced from public opinion.

As to substance, most of the legislation pertained to implementing the constitutional apparatus; in this the federal authorities have reasonably well succeeded. The output of legislation was relatively unimpressive (89 statutes to September 30, 1950). But, in line with German practice, the daily chores in economics, finance, labor, and agriculture were undertaken by legal ordinances (several hundred) on the basis of legislative delegation. The main legislative achievements were laws for the restoration of uniformity (*Vereinheitlichung*) in the fields of civil and criminal law and procedure with which the whims and fancies of the three occupation powers in eleven states had played unconscionable havoc. Here the establishment of the federal Supreme

---

[4] As of December 15, 1950, Government-initiated were 140 bills; those originating with the *Bundestag* amounted to 90. Frequently the bills overlapped dealing with the same subject. In this case the competent committee usually established a joint version (Information obtained from the Ministry of Justice in Bonn).

Court (*Oberstes Bundesgericht* [October 6, 1950]) in Karlsruhe was a major achievement.[5] Politically the most significant legislation was the Law on the federal Constitutional Tribunal (March 12, 1951),[6] by which the various jurisdictional functions of this court, considered the legal capstone of the German *Rechtsstaat,* were duly implemented. The Constitutional Court was inaugurated, likewise in Karlsruhe, on September 29, 1951. On the other hand, none of the major internal problems, such as integration of the expellees, unemployment, equalization of burdens of the lost war, socialization, the regulation of the status and organization of political parties, and housing, was undertaken, or, if attempted, reasonably solved. The policies of the federal Republic, living in the climate of orthodox liberalism, averse to planning and controls and remote from the welfare state, are anything but progressive or fired by imagination.

THE PEOPLE AND THEIR GOVERNMENT

The emerging governmental pattern is unmistakably demo-authoritarian. It is the Chancellor who monopolizes the determination and the conduct of policies, and the ministerial bureaucracy subordinated to him which implements his and the cabinet's decisions. Even though it might be unfair to qualify the *Bundestag* a mere rubber stamp of the federal Government, the political role of the Parliament is decidedly of lesser importance than in democratically more advanced nations. Much of this is intentionally due to constitutional arrangements, but the real cause lies in the impotence of public opinion. The Germans must be credited with having succeeded in establishing a wide-awake, articulate, and, on the whole, independent press. But public opinion has no constitutional means for carrying its influence into the offices of a self-assured bureaucracy, or into the conclaves of the party oligarchy which, isolated from the voters by the party machine and with elections seemingly far off, may ride roughshod over the wishes of the constituents. If to this are added the lack of political "sex appeal" of the Chancellor and the absence of popular leaders in Parliament, it may go far to explain why what the common people derisively call "Bonn"—Chancellor, *Bundestag,* and parties—have failed to ingratiate themselves with the people. Bonn operates in a political vacuum.

PARTY DYNAMICS

The federal structure permits "staggering" of elections on the federal and the *Land* levels. The latter, therefore, serve as a manometer of political opinion much in the manner of the by-elections in Britain.[7] New *Landtage* were elected in 1950–51 in such key states as North Rhine-Westphalia, Schleswig-Holstein, Hessen, Wuerttemberg-Baden, Bavaria, Western Berlin, and Lower Saxony. Taken singly and jointly they confirm the conclusion derived from the first *Bundestag* elections that the party lines artificially frozen by the licensing sys-

[5] At present it is divided into four "Senates" or chambers and composed of twenty-nine judges (including the president).

[6] See *supra,* pp. 585 ff.

[7] By-elections are now possible also for the *Bundestag* if a district seat becomes vacant.

tem at long last are thawing up without as yet being canalized into fixed cadres.[8]

In the elections in North Rhine-Westphalia, considered the most important of the series, the leading parties of the CDU and SPD remained almost station-

[8] *Landtag* elections 1950–51:

North Rhine-Westphalia
June 18, 1950
Electoral participation: 72.5%

	1950	1947
CDU	93	91
SPD	68	64
FDP	26	12
ZP	16	20
KPD	12	28
	215	215

Schleswig-Holstein
July 9, 1950

	1950	1947
SPD	19	43
BHE	15	—
CDU	16	22
FDP	8	—
DP	7	—
SSW	4	4
	69	69

SSW: Southern Schleswig Association, a representation of the Danish minority.

BHE: Federation of the Homeless and Dispossessed, the expellee party.

The Socialist defeat is all the more remarkable since the electoral law, approximating the straight majority system as in England, favored them.

Hessen
November 19, 1951
Electoral participation: 64.9%

	1950	1946
SPD	49	38
CDU	12	28
FDP	13	14
KPD	—	10
BHE	8	—
	82	80

In line with a new electoral law (accepted by referendum July 9, 1950) 48 seats were filled by straight majority elections, 32 by *Land* lists on a proportional basis.

Wuerttemberg-Baden
November 19, 1950
Electoral participation: 57.5%

	1950	1946
SPD	34	32
CDU	28	39
FDP	22	19
KDP	—	10
BHE	16	—
	100	100

Bavaria
November 26, 1950
Electoral participation: 80%

	1950	1946
CSU	64	104
SPD	63	54
BP	39	—
BHE	26	—
FDP	12	9
WAV	—	13
KPD	—	—
	204	180

The number of seats obtained does not gibe with the fact that the SPD, with 28 per cent of the votes cast, surpassed the CSU, with 27.4 per cent.

Lower Saxony
May 6, 1951
Electoral participation: 76%

	1950	1947
SPD	64	65
CDU	34	30
DP	(34)	27
FDP	12	13
ZP	4	6
KPD	2	8
BHE	22	—
SRP	16	—
Others	4	—
	158	149

ary (the SPD slightly gaining); the FDP, helped by election cartels with the CDU and the rightist German Party, gained heavily. But neo-Fascism did not appear on a major scale. On the other hand, the Communists declined heavily (from 14 to 5.5 per cent). On the whole, the *Land* where the factories are humming and the expellees constitute a mere 12 per cent of the total, showed itself disinclined towards radicalism of the Right or the Left. Although both partners in the CDU-Socialist coalition which had guided the country successfully since 1947, had held their own in the elections it broke under the pressure of the federal Chancellor Adenauer who wished to exclude the Socialists from power in his own *Land* as he had done in the federal Parliament.

However, in Schleswig-Holstein, with the largest refugee percentage (38.2), an entirely new pattern appeared. The Socialists who before had had an absolute majority, were soundly beaten (though still remaining the strongest party) by the "Federation of Homeless and Dispossessed," a rightist group drawing its strength from the expellees; the latter, together with the CDU, formed the new government which has the distinction of being the first *Land* government with a majority (four out of six) of authentic Nazis, among them the Minister President.

The pattern was repeated, late in 1950, with even more paradoxical results, in the three South German *Laender* in the American zone. Here likewise a new class party composed of expellees consolidated itself, cutting deeply into both the inflated FDP and the CDU–CSU. The Communists, failing to obtain the legal minimum of 5 per cent of the total vote, are no longer represented in the *Landtage*. But even more startling was the triumph of the Socialists over the Catholics, for generations the entrenched majority party in Wuerttemberg-Baden and "black" Bavaria. In Hessen the Socialists won the absolute majority, reducing the CDU almost to the status of a splinter party, and they became the strongest party in the two other *Laender*. The Socialist victory was due primarily to the opposition to rearmament in whatever form which attracted the young people even of the bourgeoisie. This does not mean that the majority desires Socialism; it was rather the registration of an angry protest against the callous indifference of the Bonn regime toward the deteriorating economic situation of labor and the salaried middle classes under a free-market economy dominated by cartels which make the rich richer and the poor poorer. Since the SPD by now has become about the most nationalist party of all, the shock of these local elections was felt in London, Paris, and Washington.

THE REBIRTH OF NATIONALISM

Moreover, other alarming signs of reviving nationalism are not missing. With the abandonment of licensing in the American zone, a host of neo-Fascist newspapers, some of them managed by the experienced crew trained under Goebbels, sprang up almost overnight, stepping up the tempo of anti-occupation propaganda.[9] Coincidentally, the increasing number of acquittals, by

[9] One of the favorite targets are the high occupation costs which amount to a substantial part of the federal budget. It is true that the occupation personnel are living in comparative luxury

"denazified" courts, of persons indicted for atrocities and crimes committed under the Nazi regime revealed the lack of democratic standards in the administration of justice. Anti-Semitism unmistakably is rising. Anti-Americanism is second only to anti-Communism.

The danger threatening the tender fabric of the Bonn democracy from nationalism and neo-Fascism was highlighted by the *Landtag* election in Lower Saxony (May 6, 1951), among a population customarily stolid and unemotional. A new party, admittedly patterned on Nazi organization and tenets, the Social Reich Party which at the elections for the *Bundestag* in 1949 had been wholly insignificant, obtained, at the first try, no fewer than 11 per cent of the vote and sixteen seats (of 158) in the Diet. The group is led by a former Nazi, Dr. Fritz Dorls, and by the former Major-General Remer, who, at that time a young major in the Berlin garrison, had been primarily responsible for crushing the generals' conspiracy of July 20, 1944. True to style, the party had equipped itself with a guard-like para-military organization, the *Reichsfront,* engaging in such violent pressure tactics that the Bonn Government, on the eve of the election, had seen fit to prohibit it. The organizational core of the party is the *Brüderschaft,* functioning, until 1949, underground as a secret society of former SS (and army) officers aiming at the resurrection of the German *Wehrmacht* and the restoration of its "honor."

Potentially neo-Nazi, by the same token, is the German Right Party (*Deutsche Rechtspartei*)—a name cleverly ambiguous denoting the rightist persuasion as well as "justice" for Germany. With five deputies in the Bonn Parliament it absorbed, in January, 1950, the equally nationalist National Democratic Party, active primarily in Hessen. Professing a virulent nationalistic program, it flies the old banner of black, white, and red, and though paying lip service to current anti-Communism, it is suspected of potentially turning to National Bolshevism to establish the Fourth Reich in alliance with the Soviets.

These, by themselves alarming developments, should be projected against the background of the consolidation of the various refugee and expellee organizations into a nation-wide party which labels itself characteristically the Union of Homeless and Dispossessed (*Bund der Heimatlosen und Entrechteten*), under the leadership of Waldemar Kraft, a former ranking SS man and recently Deputy Prime Minister of Schleswig-Holstein, Germany's political devil's kitchen. The new party obtained in the *Landtag* elections in 1950–51 more than 15 per cent of the total vote and found access to the governments of several *Laender* (among them, since January 1951, Bavaria). While officially aiming at the improvement of the lot of the expellees, the party strongly favors their return to the lost homelands in the East for which admittedly there is no other way than either a compromise with the Soviets or a victorious war of the West against the East.

and some of them "never had it so good." But many of the 445,000 Germans employed by the occupation powers (in the American zone alone 140,000) would otherwise be unemployed. Moreover, the occupation forces are protecting the Germans, who are still living to the extent of about 30 per cent on American subsidies, against Soviet aggression.

For the time being these various groups, whose total voting strength amounts close to 30 per cent of the German electorate, have not yet succeeded in crystallizing themselves into a unified and nation-wide successor movement to the defunct Nazi Party. They are still competing among themselves. As yet no magnetic leader personality has arisen, or is in sight, capable of amalgamating them into a militant unity. Wealthy sympathizers providing them with the means for a large-scale nationalist propaganda are missing. Nor must it be ignored that the governments and public opinion at large are on the alert and disinclined towards political adventures. So long as the factories are humming and the farmers are selling at what prices they like, there is no immediate danger of a repetition of what happened in 1930–33.

Yet the match will be put to the fuse of the time bomb planted in the heart of Europe if and when a German Government officially turns to remilitarization, from which the nationalist parties necessarily will derive an immense impetus. The organization of a well-nigh irresistible pressure group, consisting of the former officers of the *Wehrmacht* and the *Waffen* SS and of the millions of other war veterans, is clearly in the making. Once these forces, all nurtured by nationalist emotionalism, will have coalesced the moderate parties can hardly expect to retain their present control. This is the challenge that will constitute the acid test of the Bonn Constitution.

CHAPTER XXXV

POLITICAL DEVELOPMENTS ON THE ALLIED LEVEL

EXERCISE OF POWERS UNDER THE OCCUPATION STATUTE

LEGISLATION OF THE ALLIED HIGH COMMISSION

That the powers assigned to the High Commissioners under the Occupation Statute were used sparingly was due less to the conviction that the Germans had successfully graduated from the elementary course in democracy than to policy decisions of their governments preparing Germany for her potential role as an ally against the East. HICOG legislation,[1] pursuant to an engagement undertaken in the Occupation Statute, repealed at first MG rules (including CC legislation) in the three zones no longer consistent with the increased powers of the German authorities in the nonreserved fields. Likewise the narrowed range of judicial powers and the offenses against the interests of the occupation powers required redefinition. Otherwise even on the field of reserved powers Allied legislative activities were limited.[2] However, concerning economic deconcentration and decartelization the American High Commissioner impressed on his colleagues the need of a more energetic program than back-stage American and German big business intervention had permitted his predecessor to pursue. Ambitious blueprints for the liquidation and dissolution of the chemical octopus of the I. G. Farben, of the industrial giants in the coal, iron, and steel industries, and of the former Reich monopoly in motion picture production (UFA) were placed on the books [3] without leading to any tangible results

[1] Until October 19, 1950 (HICOG Gazette No. 37) thirty-nine laws, in addition to a considerable number of other enactments (directives, regulations, and decisions) had been promulgated.

[2] Here laws on the prohibition of research and experimentation in atomic energy and on displaced persons were passed. Under the heading of security the new regulations on restrictions of industrial and military production reflected the increasing relaxation of Allied controls.

[3] Law No. 35 (July 5, 1950) on the dispersion of the assets of I. G. Farben included no fewer than 169 different plants located in the Western zone. Law No. 27 (May 16, 1950) on the reorganization of the German coal, iron, and steel industries decreed the "deconcentration" of 92 cartels and combines, among them such by-words of European industrial giantism as *Vereinigte Stahlwerke, Friedrich Krupp, Mannesmann, Kloeckner, Hoesch, Otto Wolff, Gutehoffnungshuette,* and the *Thyssen* and *Stinnes* groups.

in view of the open hostility of the industrial magnates and the lukewarm support by the federal Government influenced by heavy industry.[4] In a single instance only did HICOG feel impelled to invoke the general clause of the Occupation Statute permitting intervention in nonreserved fields "in the interest of the security and the prestige of the Occupation" when the sudden resurgence of the ultra-nationalistic press abused the freedom of public expression.[5] On the whole, the extreme reticence of the Allies even in the reserved fields was in line with the new policy of complete nonintervention in German domestic affairs.[6]

LEGISLATIVE REVIEW

It is, therefore, all the more surprising that HICOG undertook currently to review the entire body of legislation (including executory ordinances) of the federal State and of eleven (or, with Berlin, twelve) *Laender* as to their constitutionality under German law and their compatibility with the "purposes of the occupation." In retrospect it may well be doubted whether the actual result justified the considerable labor of scrutinizing close to one thousand individual pieces of legislation. That the Legal Division of HICOG, operating under a rigid time table and with an elaborate procedure, assumed the function of the federal Constitutional Tribunal (in process of organization) may seem superfluous. Moreover, the dragnet usually caught only small fish. On matters of real importance (*Land* constitutions, various press laws of the *Laender*) HICOG found it the better part of wisdom merely to convey its doubts to the competent German authorities. But even under the assumption that antidemocratic tendencies should be nipped in the bud, the actual success did not warrant the irritation such controls necessarily provoked among the Germans.[7] In very few cases the objection was sustained. As a rule the German authorities were given the opportunity of amendment or merely to promise redress. What fatally minimized Allied intervention was the fact that in the few cases which mattered, HICOG beat an undignified retreat when meeting serious German resistance. Of the two federal laws being disallowed, an income and corporation tax law was objected to because, favoring, as is habitual in a Tory economy, the upper-income brackets, it failed to provide for additional rev-

---

[4] However, in 1950 certain cartels in the abrasive industry were prosecuted and fined.

[5] Law No. 5 (September 21, 1949) on Press, Radio, Information, and Entertainment. The American High Commissioner invoked the clause when, in the summer of 1951, he tried unsuccessfully to stop court proceedings in Berlin against one Dr. Kemritz whom, as a former spy for the United States, he wished to protect. He met with a stinging rebuff by the Berlin authorities.

[6] It is interesting to note, however, that under HICOG in each of the three zones the administrative pattern continued that had existed before and that even matters which obviously required uniformity (such as restitution, judicial organization, etc.) were treated differently. For example in the U.S. zone a hunting and fishing ordinance privileging occupation personnel aroused more indignation among the German public than all decartelization measures taken together.

[7] All told, until September 30, 1950, five federal and twenty-two *Land* enactments were formally objected to. Various procedures of disallowance were applied: outright disapproval (a rare exception); provisional disapproval (the rule); cancellation or even amendment of individual articles (clearly beyond the competence of HICOG). In one case the promulgation of a *Land* enactment was made dependent on federal approval which was granted.

enue to stabilize the budget; this, as Mr. McCloy justly felt, would increase the burden of the American taxpayer. After the Finance Minister (who at first had threatened to resign) promised redress the objection was withdrawn (April 28, 1950).

But the controversy around the federal Civil Service Law revealed the discrepancy between American principles and German application to such an extent that it requires a discussion here.

Realizing that the authoritarian concept of the civil service as a class or caste elevated above the mass of the subjects constituted one of the major obstacles to a genuine democratization of public life, AMG in 1946 had stimulated the enactment, in the *Laender* of the U.S. zone, of a pattern of civil-service laws which was believed to go far in eliminating some of the more objectionable features of the bureaucratic tradition. To assure a uniform and more satisfactory selection of public officials by the Government, a Central Personnel Office was established in each *Land* of the U.S. zone. Reforms were strongly resisted by the ministerial bureaucracy. In particular, impartial examinations for appointment and promotion were required to make public office more accessible to qualified outsiders and to break down the monopoly of the lawyers in the higher administrative positions. Another aspect of the American-sponsored reform was the elimination of public officials from legislative bodies; this habit of a civil servant (judge, ministerial official, etc.) merely to take a leave of absence when accepting the parliamentary mandate, had been the cancer of German parliamentarism and a flagrant violation of the principle of the separation of the executive from the legislative powers.[8]

There is hardly any issue on which the German public, which hates being lorded over by the officialdom and yet is utterly submissive to them, is so unreservedly behind an American reform. But the federal ministerial bureaucrats enacted a (provisional) Civil Service Law which, while adopting many of the technically commendable features of the Nazi Civil Service Act of 1937, arrogantly disregarded the wishes of public opinion and American advices. HICOG vetoed the law provisionally but yielded when the federal Government issued a promissory note of future implementation (which was not honored). The conflict, a major one, ended with a singularly stinging defeat of the Americans.

Of the twenty-two pieces of *Land* legislation disallowed,[9] several regulations were believed to be seriously at variance with the occupation purposes; and objections referred to the exercise of regulatory powers by nongovernmental groups (organization of handicraft, licensing of certain professions), the treatment of Nazi victims, the status of the Jewish community, and *Land* police

[8] In the absence of German action U.S. and U.K. MG's enacted the MG Law No. 15 (March 15, 1949) which embodied the requisite reform with respect to the officials of the bizonal administration. The law remained in force pending appropriate federal legislation. See also *supra*, p. 601 for Law No. 20 (June 2, 1949) concerning the election of the first *Bundesrat* where the same controversy had arisen. For similar reasons objections were raised by HICOG (in 1950) against a new election law in Wuerttemberg-Baden.

[9] The list is headed by Schleswig-Holstein with eight.

[10] Objected to were a Bavarian ordinance concerning the import of chicken and a Hamburg city ordinance reducing the entertainment tax in movies!

power. In other instances HICOG shot with cannon balls at sparrows.[10] Since the major occupation goals in denazification and decartelization had not been reached, insistence on American ideals in petty cases did not add to Allied prestige.

THE "REORIENTATION" PROGRAM

With the establishment of the Bonn Government, Allied operational activities had been terminated and supervision reduced to a minimum. Efforts, therefore, to democratize Germany "by indirection" were intensified. By stimulating "grass roots" democratic habits it is believed that, given time and patience, the German people will learn that democracy does not consist merely of formalized institutions and procedures, but in the individual's attitude towards life. This had been the French policy from the beginning and the Americans at long last were converted to this approach.

Unofficial town meetings, forums, and discussion groups, intended to increase the citizen's interest in the affairs of his community and to make him more critical towards his authorities, are becoming quite popular in the American zone. The effort, however, of creating civil liberties' associations on American lines, though strongly supported by the press, has met as yet with indifferent success. The traditional hold of the police is difficult to curb.[11] The abolition, by MG law in 1949, of all licensing requirements in business and commerce was enthusiastically welcomed by the people. On the other hand, what seemed to the American officials a correlated reform, namely the prohibition of compulsory membership in certain trade and professional associations which exercise quasi-governmental supervision over their members, tended to ignore the merits of professional autonomy which contributes to efficiency and the maintenance of ethical standards. In the field of education the Americans strove to break the monopoly of the propertied classes by insisting on free tuition and free textbooks, but encountered the strong resistance of the higher school administrators who alleged that a foreign pattern was being forced on them. The Universities have reverted fully, under a "denazified" professorial staff, to the pre-Hitler system.[12] The program of interesting women in local and political affairs did not make much headway against the ingrained belief that woman's place in society is circumscribed by the three "K's" (*Kinder, Küche, Kirche*). Youth organizations on a nonpartisan basis evoked little more than a polite response. German youth has been sport-minded for a long time even without the blessing of baseball.

In promoting civic responsibility the American administration could not fail to develop a split personality. On the one hand, the High Commissioner exercised himself to treat the German Government as equals; on the other hand, his staff on the lower levels did not hestitate to kindle the spirit of rebellion among the people against their bureaucracy. Although as yet no visible

[11] For example, of 50,033 searches in private dwellings in Bavaria in 1948, no fewer than 42,288 were conducted without judicial warrant.

[12] However, in the introduction of political science into the curriculum at least a promising beginning has been made.

dent has been made in the traditional submissiveness of the public, more optimistic observers feel that at least the seeds of civic self-assertion have been
planted in the German mind.

But the more conspicuous method of teaching Germans democracy is embodied in the cultural exchange program of which the Exchanges Division—unusually deficient in quantity and quality of personnel—is in charge. By the end
of 1950 about 3,000 Germans of good will of all walks of life (journalists;
publishers; professional people; technical experts; government, municipal, and
trade-union officials; legislators, etc.), in addition to students obtaining instruction for a year in an American institution, were brought for a limited
period, at Uncle Sam's expense, to the United States, expected to observe
American techniques of democracy and to stimulate, upon their return, reform
of indigenous habits. Though currently beset with difficulties as to the selection
of the visitors and the curriculum they are exposed to in the States, the plan is
one of the most constructive efforts of German reorientation.[13] The other
powers have undertaken similar programs, the French emphasizing education,
the British, local government.

To teach the Germans democracy "by indirection" may seem, on the whole,
a thoroughly worth-while undertaking considering that otherwise Allied activities largely have dried up. But at least the American personnel seems inclined
to accept the present readiness of the Germans to let the reorientation program be tried out on them, as an indication of lasting success. Other observers
fear that, with the Allied abdication from actual power, their moral influence
will be limited at best. Yet, historical experience such as the French impact
on Western and Southern Germany in the Napoleonic period encourages the
hope that the symbiosis of Western democratic and German authoritarian
habits may not have been entirely in vain.

THE DISMANTLING OF THE OCCUPATION STATUTE

As was to be expected, the Occupation Statute was under fire from the start.
The Allies, with the pressure of the cold war constantly increasing, offered
little resistance to the erosion and attrition tactics of the Chancellor, who
played his cards well. The first major relaxation of the occupation controls,
agreed on in the Paris Conference of the three Foreign Ministers (November
9–10, 1949) was formalized in the so-called Petersberg Accord, negotiated by
the High Commissioners with the Chancellor (November 15–22, 1949). The
settlement was forced on the Allies by the establishment of an Eastern German
state (October, 1949). It went far to restore sovereignty in foreign affairs by
granting German participation in international organizations, and permitting
the acceptance of the invitation to join the Council of Europe as an associate
member. Subsequently, the *Bundestag* (July 8, 1950) adopted the Charter of
the Council of Europe. A German delegation, selected in accordance with the

---

[13] The exchange of persons program for the fiscal year 1951 calls for the dispatch to the
U.S.A. of 2651 persons. On the entire issue see Henry P. Pilgert, *The Exchange of Persons
Program in Western Germany*, Office of the U.S. High Commissioner for Germany, 1951.

party strength in the *Bundestag,* participated in the second meeting of the Consultative Assembly in Strasbourg (August, 1950). Western Germany became a full-fledged member of the Office of European Economic Cooperation (accomplished already on October 21, 1949) and joined the European Payments Union (September 15, 1950). In June, 1950, a German delegation began negotiations, with full equality, on the Schuman plan for the pooling of the steel, iron, and coal industries of six European states. The "Treaty on the European Coal and Steel Community" subsequently was signed by the Foreign Ministers in Paris (April 19, 1951). When it will have entered into full operation, after ratification by the six national parliaments, it will provide for a single market area within the six participating states and thus come close to the fulfillment of the old dream of German heavy industry to combine the surplus of Ruhr coke with that of Lorraine iron ore under a joint management (High Authority). Germany, as the senior partner in this first concrete step towards the unification of Western Europe, will derive tangible benefits contributing to her economic hegemony of the Continent.

The Petersberg Accord authorized the establishment of consular and commercial representations abroad, which, during 1950, were progressively installed, first in London, Paris, and New York, subsequently in most Western and Latin American countries. The Office of Foreign Affairs in the federal Chancellery was built up gradually into a Foreign Ministry, staffed largely, as was to be expected, by former career officials who had faithfully served the Nazis. Likewise, controls on economic production were substantially relaxed. The list of plants to be dismantled under the Potsdam and subsequent agreements was again and drastically cut.[14] Eleven of the largest synthetic oil and rubber plants and seven similarly important steel production centers were removed from the list. Furthermore, exceeding the steel production limit of 11.1 million tons a year was permitted, and restrictions on the tonnage of cargo ship construction were lifted. In consideration of these concessions the Allies obtained from Chancellor Adenauer the delegation of the German members to the Ruhr Authority, and, together with the promise "to eradicate all traces of Nazism from German life and institutions," the solemn declaration "to maintain the demilitarization of the federal territory and to endeavor,

---

[14] No full discussion of the dismantling issue can be submitted here. Dismantling of war production plants was intended to serve as reparations to compensate for the devastation of Allied industry by German looting—from France alone the Nazis had carted to Germany more than 80,000 machines—and thus to contribute to European reconstruction and to reduce the German war-making potential. As early as in March, 1946, dismantled plants going as reparations to the Soviets were stopped by General Clay. After the Moscow Conference (March-April, 1947) a new reparations plan was announced, according to which 682 plants in the bi-zone, in addition to 172 plants in the French zone, were to be removed, which would have left Germany with a plant capacity at least equal to that of 1936. Yielding to the organized pressure of American and German big business, a Committee, appointed under Congress instructions by ECA Administrator Paul G. Hoffman, recommended in 1948 that 140 of the 858 plants, earmarked for dismantling in 1947, should be retained in Germany to serve for European reconstruction. This program again was stalled, the British being accused, and in some cases not without justification, of using the dismantling program for throttling German competition. In the fall of 1949, Mr. McCloy announced that the entire dismantling program was wrong. The Petersberg Accord was the final payoff. See Albert Z. Carr, *Truman, Stalin and Peace,* Garden City, 1950, pp. 187 ff.

by all means in [his] powers to prevent the recreation of armed forces of any kind."

Thus encouraged, the Germans renewed their agitation against still existing curbs of their sovereignty under the Occupation Statute. They were fully aware of the bargaining power that had accrued to them within the power equilibrium between the West and the East. Relations between the High Commissioners and the self-willed Chancellor—the only person in authority with whom they maintained direct and frequent contact—became at times strained. The German people likewise, goaded on by a vehement press campaign, and riding the crest of economic prosperity, became restive and obstreperous to such an extent that Mr. McCloy, on two occasions (in Stuttgart, February 6, 1950, and in Duesseldorf, June 16, 1950) had to lecture them on occupation morals. While gratitude for the continued American economic help remained conspicuous by its absence, the Germans vented with increasing bitterness their grievances, alleged and real, such as dismantling, decartelization, occupation costs, the Saar and Ruhr issues, imprudent frontier rectifications broached by the Belgians and the Dutch, not to mention security and unification. With growing resistance against Allied-sponsored internal reforms the very word democracy became obnoxious. The neuralgic spots at home—rising unemployment, housing shortage, the expellee situation—were not ascribed to faulty economic policies constantly increasing the cleavage between the rich and the poor, but to factors allegedly beyond German control. Allied unpopularity was mitigated only by the fear of Communist expansion.

These accumulated pressures resulted in further concessions by the London Foreign Ministers' Conference (May 14, 1950). An Interallied machinery for the reform of the Occupation Statute was set up. In the meantime reserved powers were "to be exercised only in essential elements of security and fundamental democratic issues of real importance." Likewise the technically and politically knotty problem of the termination of the state of war was declared under continuous advisement.

The next, and probably the penultimate, step in the dismantling of the Occupation Statute was taken by the New York Conference of the Foreign Ministers (September 19, 1950). The Allies declared themselves to be inspired by "the spirit of a new relationship . . . with the Federal Republic." Western Germany (including the Western sectors of Berlin) were given a full-fledged security guarantee. The Allies "will treat any attack on the federal Republic or Berlin from any quarter as an attack on themselves." A federal police "on a *Land* basis, but which would enable the federal Government to use it to meet fully the emergencies of the present situation" was established, a move which, stripped of its political semantics, may constitute the entering wedge of German remilitarization. This military establishment was likewise attached to the federal Chancellery as the potential nucleus of a Ministry of Defense or War. A complete revision of the Occupation Statute was promised to mark the new phase of mutual relationships in which major extensions of federal authority were to be embodied. Existing internal controls were to be reduced and legislative review to be modified. The Agreement on Limited and Prohibited Industries was to be revised, limitations on cargo ship tonnage and steel production were completely lifted. HICOG's authority remains only in the fields of security, restitution, and deconcentration, but even here, as Mr. McCloy announced later (October 8, 1950), only in consultation with the German authorities.

The check issued by the New York Conference of the Foreign Ministers in September, 1950, was finally honored by the "First Instrument of Revision of the Occupation Statute," promulgated by the High Commissioners on March 7, 1951. The delay was primarily caused by the stalling of the federal Government and particularly the Foreign Relations Committee of the Parliament on the future regulation of Germany's external debts on which the revision was dependent. By letter to HICOG of March 6, 1951, the Germans undertook liability for prewar external debts, well aware that in case of need they could easily be manipulated by "standstill" agreements in the manner of Schacht. But only after long negotiations they also recognized their obligations arising from the foreign assistance given to Germany since May 8, 1945.[15] Details will be worked out in an over-all settlement, with due consideration to Germany's capacity to pay and with arbitration procedures.

The principal points of revision of the Occupation Statute are the following: A Foreign Ministry was authorized, for which office Dr. Adenauer designated himself. German ambassadors to foreign countries (except those in the Soviet orbit) were appointed and the foreign missions heretofore conducting business with HICOG were accredited with the Bonn Government. Foreign trade and exchange control was completely passed on to the Germans. As to German internal affairs, what limited controls still existed were almost all abolished. The Allies renounced all rights of supervision of internal German affairs. Review of German legislation likewise fell by the wayside. Only amendments of the Basic Law were still subject to express approval. However, in view of the rising tide of nationalism and neo-Nazism the Allies were well advised in retaining the right of annulment of any enactment (federal or *Land*) "which, in their opinion, is inconsistent with the (revised) Occupation Statute, or Allied legislation . . . or if it constitutes a grave threat to the basic policies of the occupation." The reserved power relating to "respect for the Basic Law and the *Land* constitutions," hybrid anyway because of its patent unenforceability, were terminated when the Constitutional Tribunal, deemed sufficient to uphold civil liberties by German efforts, has begun to operate.

[15] According to careful American calculations the direct and indirect benefits derived by Germany from the United States alone amounted to the sum of more than four billion within six years, of which $3,602,000,000 were direct contributions to the German economy. The total occupation costs, for several years one of the most insistent complaints of the German public and government, ran up to $1,411,000,000 according to the German and American compilations. From this sum the Army felt entitled to deduct $483,000,000 for salaries paid to German personnel and returnable mandatory expenses, leaving net occupation costs of $927,000,000. Taking into account various other American outlays one arrives, as net American contribution to Germany, at the generous amount of $3,257,000,000. For the foregoing figures see the *New York Times* of June 16, 1951.

In the economic field, Allied controls no longer exist except those relating to decartelization, where it is planned, at least on paper, to complete the deconcentration program of the steel, coal, and motion picture industries, the bank monopolies, and I. G. Farben. Again these powers will lapse if and when a German decartelization law satisfactory to the Allies (meaning the Americans) has been enacted. The relaxation of the (diluted) deconcentration program under HICOG Law No. 27 had been wrested before by the Germans from the Allies as partial prize for their consent to the Schuman plan. A new Agreement on Industrial Controls confirmed the previously granted complete removal of controls and restrictions on the production of steel, ship-building, and the chemical industries, in particular authorizing also the making of synthetic gasoline and rubber. In an annex to the Revision Instrument, the method by which the occupation authorities will exercise the powers still retained, likewise was amended with benefits to the Germans. The "Little Occupation Statute" for Western Berlin was revised accordingly. Termination of the state of war, under advisement for a long time, was formally proclaimed by most of the Allied powers during 1951. With the United States it became effective October 18, 1951.

A mixed German-Allied commission of experts has started the study of how to transform the occupation regime into a system of contractual relations, substituting for HICOG an Allied Council of Ambassadors. This may well dispense with the necessity of concluding a formal peace treaty unless the miracle will have happened of an East-West agreement on German unification. In September, 1951, negotiations between the High Commissioners and the German Government on the final replacement of the Occupation Statute by a contractual arranged were started.

As planned at the time of this writing (October, 1951) Western Germany, in exchange for a promised share in Western defense, will be granted the full restoration of the rights of a sovereign state, with the exception of Allied powers reserved concerning the issue of unification with the Eastern part; the protection of Berlin; the final determination of her boundaries; and the assumption of discretionary emergency powers in case of an acute danger to German democracy (evidently implying threats from Communism as well as from Neo-Nazism).

Thus, what the New York Conference mildly had styled "the progressive return of Germany to partnership in Western Europe," has been accomplished. It is nothing less than the last paid-up installment of the sovereignty confiscated by unconditional surrender. The enemy of yesterday has become the ally of today. Discussions between military experts began in February on the technical aspects of German rearmament. In the Paris negotiations on a European army (since February 15, 1951) the Germans participated as full-fledged partners.

A notable experiment of converting a nation steeped in authoritarianism and militarism has come to its conclusion. The final judgment must be left to history.

CHAPTER XXXVI

THE BERLIN DILEMMA

FOUR–POWER CONTROL

The situation in Berlin—variously called "democracy's show window to the East," "the last outpost of democracy behind the Iron Curtain," or "the free island in the Red Sea,"—is, by all standards, the most dramatic and dramatized single incident in the East-West conflict. But Berlin is more than a political symbol; Germany's former capital was also one of her industrial centers, the seat of her financial power, the cultural and scientific brains of the nation, with a brash and bright people second to none in vitality, endurance, and—a rare thing in Germany—a sense of tolerant humor. After the collapse the sprawling metropolis was found devastated to an extent staggering imagination. Crippled Berlin was crippling Germany as a whole.

It has been contended that the Allies should have seized Berlin before the Soviets laid siege to it in April, 1945. But not only was the Russian occupation agreed on by the European Advisory Commission and confirmed at Yalta; the conquest might have cost the Allies no fewer lives than the fanatical Nazi defenders exacted from the Red Army.

The Four-Power Statement on Berlin of June 4, 1945, provided for the rule of Greater Berlin the same kind of condominium that had been established for Germany as a whole. Quadripartite control was to be exercised by an Interallied Governing Authority called (Russian style) *Kommandatura*, consisting, under the general direction of the Control Council, of the four Commandants, with the chairmanship in monthly rotation. Each of them had jurisdiction over one of the four areas called, in distinction from the zones, sectors,[1] each of which, in turn, was subject to the respective zone

[1] The population figures (census of 1946) are taken from *Deutschland-Jahrbuch*, p. 8.

U.S. sector	985,000	210 sq. kil.
British sector	602,500	170 sq. kil.
French sector	421,400	100 sq. kil.
Soviet sector	1,170,300	400 sq. kil.
	3,179,200	

The U.S. and British sectors included the wealthier suburban and residential communities, with, however, important industrial sections; the Soviets controlled more of the workers' districts.

Commander much in the same way as were the individual *Laender* in the
four zones. Each power organized a special Berlin District M–Government.
The provisions of the Potsdam Agreement were applicable also to Berlin as
a whole.

Communications between the West and Western Berlin consisted of a
single-track railroad, an Autobahn leading to the British zone (about 120
miles) and an elaborate system of canals for barge traffic, in addition to two
formally agreed air lanes (to the British and U.S. zones respectively).[2]

THE POLITICAL SITUATION (1945–1948)

The Western Allies took over their sectors only on and after July 12, 1945.
The Soviets thus had a headstart in setting up the city administration and
indoctrinating the population. They activated the leading political parties
(Communists, Social Democrats, Christian Democrats, and Democratic Liberals) as early as June, 1945, among a population politically more alert than
elsewhere in Germany. When the Soviet-controlled city government (*Magistrat*) continued its efforts to hold sway over the city wards in the Western
sectors, quarrels were bound to arise. They broke into the open when the
Central Committees of both the KP and the SPD decided to merge the two
parties as the Socialist Unity Party (SED) March, 1946. However, the fusion
was rejected (March 31, 1946) by a referendum of the rank and file of the
members of the SPD in all Berlin.[3] The result of this split was that the SED
became the fusion party in the entire Soviet zone including Eastern Berlin
where the SPD was outlawed, while the SED was not licensed in the Western
sectors and zones.

A (provisional) city charter (*Stadtverfassung*) was elaborated by the *Kommandatura* (August 13, 1946), largely drawn from the previous Prussian laws
of 1851 and 1920 (as amended in 1931), under which the twenty administrative subdivisions (*Bezirke*) were under the over-all control of the City
Assembly and its executive organ, the *Magistrat*. All legislation of the City
Assembly and all ordinances and instructions of the *Magistrat* were subject
to unanimous approval by the *Kommandatura*.

When, in the first city-wide elections (October 20, 1946) the SPD won a
near-absolute majority over the SED [4] the Soviet Commandant resorted to
the blocking technique which prevented, in 1947, the assumption of office by

---

[2] At the time of the establishment of the Four-Power Occupation, the military had overlooked making a written agreement on overland communications.

[3] Eighty-two per cent (of the 71 per cent participating in the vote) were against the merger.

[4] The following tabulation presents the election results of 1946 and 1948. Figures are taken
from Department of State Publication 3556, p. 169.

	All Berlin		*Western Sectors*			
	October 20, 1946		*October 20, 1946*		*December 5, 1948*	
	numbers	per cent	numbers	per cent	numbers	per cent
Total	2,051,891	100.	1,302,972	100.	1,330,820	100.
SPD	999,170	48.7	674,220	51.7	858,100	64.5
CDU	454,202	22.1	316,206	24.2	258,496	19.4
SED	405,992	19.8	179,114	13.8	—	—
LDP	192,527	9.4	133,432	10.3	214,224	16.1

the duly elected Chief Mayor, Ernst Reuter. But the city authorities were unable to forestall the communization of the services and personnel in the Soviet sector. A new constitution, approved by the Assembly (April 28, 1948) with four-fifths over the votes of the SED, was still objected to by the Soviet representative in the *Kommandatura* when the latter, in the wake of the break-up of the Control Council, was deliberately and without General Clay's authorization exploded by the American member (May 13, 1948).[5] The Soviets formally withdrew from the *Kommandatura* (July 1, 1948). The split of the city administration into two competing governments, duplicating the situation in Germany as a whole, was under way and the stage was set for the most spectacular *tour de force* of the cold war to date.

THE BLOCKADE

The Berlin blockade, cutting off all communications on land and water, lasted from June 26, 1948, to the end of May, 1949. Two million people could escape starvation only by being supplied with food, fuel, and all essentials of life by planes. In organizing and successfully running the famous air lift (*Luftbrücke*) American and British logistics, together with the unparalleled courage of the Western Berliners, defeated the Soviet plan of squeezing out the Allies from Berlin by exposing the two million people in Western Berlin to starvation.[6] The Soviet action was the answer to the decision of the Western powers at the London Conference (February–June, 1948) to establish a separate Western German State which, in Soviet opinion, violated the Potsdam Agreement and forfeited the right of the Allies to remain in Berlin. Since each party had honored the Potsdam Agreement more by breach than by observance the Soviet claim may seem specious. The actual cause of the blockade was the introduction, without Soviet consent, of the Western currency reform (June 21, 1948) countered by Marshal Sokolowsky with the Eastern mark in the Soviet zone and Eastern Berlin and its extension also to the Western sectors. The Soviets feared that otherwise the people in Western Germany would dump their worthless and invalidated Reichsmark into Berlin and the Eastern zone. Since the Allies thereupon introduced in the Western sectors a special brand of the Western mark, with three currencies in circulation, life for the Berliners became miserable. By July 2, 1948, the blockade became fully effective. Western countermeasures in due course stopped all freight reaching the entire Eastern zone by land, water, or air.

The embarrassed Allies tried in vain to obtain the lifting of the blockade by negotiations, at first through the generals on the spot in Berlin, thereafter twice (August 2 and 30, 1948) directly with Stalin in Moscow. The crucial

---

[5] There is hardly a more damning reflection on the quality of some of the American military leaders in Germany than the self-revealing story told by Frank L. Howley, *Berlin Command*, New York, 1950.

[6] The average need in food and fuel and other essentials amounted to about 10,000 tons daily. Within 462 days (June 26, 1948 to September 30, 1949) 277,264 flights brought 2,343,308.5 tons to the beleaguered city. The record day was April 16, 1949, with 1,398 flights and 12,941 tons.

issue was a mutually exchangeable currency in all zones, the Allies insisting on, and the Soviets rejecting, supervision of the printing of the Eastern mark. On American initiative the conflict came finally before the United Nations General Assembly (September, 1949) which appointed, under the chairmanship of the Argentine Foreign Minister Bramuglia, a committee of neutral experts to work out a fair solution. In retrospect it seems certain that the Bramuglia Committee reached a compromise acceptable to all parties, with only minor points still in dispute. But in the meantime General Clay, wholly in his element, had organized the airlift so successfully that the Western powers were able to see the thing through. A particularly mild winter spared the Berliners the worst cold, though otherwise life for them became extremely uncomfortable. Finally, in the New York Agreement (May 4, 1949) and upon the promise of another quadripartite Foreign Ministers' Conference (held abortively in London, May 23–June 20, 1949) the Soviets lifted the blockade (May 12, 1949) and gradually restored normal traffic conditions.

Spectacular as the airlift was from the viewpoint of the American policy of "containing Communism" under the Truman Doctrine and much as the blockade demonstrated the resolve of the Berliners to resist Soviet pressure, later historians may well doubt whether the military diplomacy may not have seriously disrupted whatever chances there may have existed for a compromise solution of the German problem as a whole.

THE TWO BERLINS

While the Battle of Berlin was in full swing, the municipal government and administration of Berlin developed the same split personality that began to exist in Germany as a whole. The parties in the city administration representing the Western sectors, unwilling to conduct business under organized mob violence, moved (September 6, 1948) to the British sector (Charlottenburg) and established a separate city administration for Western Berlin on the basis of the constitution voted before (April 28, 1948). Elections for the city assembly were held, but only in the Western sectors, in the midst of the blockade, on December 5, 1948.[7] But the act was rather a political demonstration, as a plebiscite against the Soviets, than an electoral procedure, reflecting actual party strength. The SPD gained, with 64.5 per cent, a majority never before obtained by any party in an honest German election. The *Magistrat* of the Soviet sector declared the elections invalid and established (November 30, 1948) an Eastern sector puppet city government. From now on, two entirely independent city administrations, each body claiming for itself exclusive legitimacy, existed side by side, extending to all public services, police, finances, justice, education. The London Foreign Ministers' Conference (June 20, 1949) devised a soothing formula for the quadripartite attitudes towards Berlin as a whole "with a view to normalizing as far as possible the life of the city." Although it was at times subject to strain, on the whole the routine of a *modus vivendi* was maintained, as it could not be otherwise in so closely

[7] For results, see *supra*, p. 628, note 4.

knit an organism as this modern metropolis. The Whitsuntide (1950) meeting of the Free German Youth—the Soviet substitute for the Hitler Youth—which anxious American officials had feared would turn into a violent coup for seizing the Western sectors by the Communists, failed to disturb the peace.

The relations between the Western Allies and the city government were transformed in 1949 in accordance to what took place in Western Germany. The Statement of Principles (May 14, 1949) or the "Little Occupation Statute" of the three Commandants released Western Berlin from political tutelage. The constitution of 1948, adjusted to the Basic Law and the new relationship with the Allies, was approved by the Allied Commandants (August 29, 1950). Although the aspirations of Western Berlin to become the twelfth *Land* under the Bonn Basic Law were not fulfilled, it was raised to the rank of a *Land*. Consequently, the city assembly became a chamber of deputies and the *Magistrat* the city senate. Otherwise the new constitution which entered into force on October 1, 1950, is patterned on the Bonn Basic Law. Subsequent elections,[8] held in the Western sectors under the new constitution, resulted in a normalization of the political situation. CDU and LDP gained considerably at the expense of the SPD which no longer holds an absolute majority. Only 127 of the 200 seats were filled; the remainder were left open until the Eastern sector may join. Ernst Reuter was again, though after some difficulties, elected Chief Mayor of Western Berlin.

But such outward trimmings of statehood are illusory; Western Berlin remains unviable as a *Land* for geographical, political, and economic reasons. The economic predicament was not caused, though it was aggravated, by the blockade. It continued after the blockade and this in spite of substantial support by the Bonn Government, American subsidies, and counterpart money released by the ECA. Many of the industrial assets (including heavy industry) have migrated to the West. Unemployment remains excessively high and has become structural.[9] The enclave of Western Berlin, whose economic arteries with the outside world are precariously kept open by the good will of a hostile government, cannot maintain itself indefinitely.

[8] *Western Berlin Elections:*

	December 3, 1950 Seats	1950 %	1948 %
SDP	61	44.7	64.5
CDU	34	24.6	19.4
LDP	32	23.0	16.1
Others	–	7.7	–
	127	100.0	100.0

[9] As of September 30, 1950, there were close to 300,000 unemployed, amounting to 25 per cent of the total labor force (average in Western Germany at the same date: 5.7 per cent). The index of production was only 32 per cent (index of 1936 = 100), as compared with 115 in Western Germany and (estimated) 80 per cent in Eastern Germany.

CHAPTER XXXVII

THE SOVIET ZONE AND THE ESTABLISHMENT OF
THE GERMAN DEMOCRATIC REPUBLIC

SOVIET MILITARY ADMINISTRATION

The Soviet Military Administration (SMA), with Headquarters in Berlin-Karlshorst, was established (June 9, 1945) by Marshal Zhukow, as Commander-in-Chief of the Soviet forces. He was assisted by deputies for military and civilian affairs. Of importance was the Economic Planning Division. SMA branch offices were set up in the capitals of the five territorial units of the Soviet zone.[1] Details concerning the relations of the Soviets to German authorities were never published, but SMA operational action went farther and lasted longer than in the other zones. No formal policy guiding the occupation was ever announced. But in retrospect it is fairly obvious that the Russians brought with them a definite plan to mold their zone in their image, and that they aimed at communization, if not Sovietization, consistently and without allowing themselves to be deflected either by Potsdam or by the Germans. It is also safe to assume that Marshal Zhukow (and, since the spring of 1948, his successor Marshal Sokolowsky) did not conduct himself as independent proconsul but was subject, even in relatively minor details, to Moscow's orders. After the orgy of looting and raping that the Germans had experienced in the early stages of the occupation, they did not expect the exemplary discipline exhibited by Soviet personnel afterwards. Absolutely no fraternization was permitted. Nor were the Germans slow in realizing that the Soviet staff caught on fast and proved themselves capable administrators.

GERMAN CENTRAL (ZONAL) AGENCIES

From the very beginning rigid centralization prevailed in the Soviet zone. Evidently the Potsdam postulate of the "decentralization of the political structure" was a concept alien to Soviet thinking.

On July 7, 1945, the SMA organized the Central Administrative Authori-

[1] See the description of the *Laender* (or provinces), *supra*, p. 503.

ties (*Zentralverwaltungen*) in Berlin, each under a German president and staffed largely with first-rate former Prussian administrative technicians. Until 1946, fifteen of them covered all administrative fields. At first serving merely as advisory agencies of SMA they acquired, by the end of 1946, immediate jurisdiction over the *Laender,* leading finally (February 2, 1947) to a formal agreement through which the zonal authorities obtained the right of co-ordinating all economic activities of the five territorial subdivisions. This agreement was duly ratified by the *Land* parliaments (April, 1947). Integrating zonal authorities, therefore, existed almost from the start.

Simultaneously (June 4, 1947) with the bizonal organization in the West came the creation of the Permanent Economic Commission (*Ständige Wirtschaftskommission*) which, again synchronized with the corresponding bizonal structure (September 2, 1948), received unrestricted authority for supervising and instructing on all economic fields in the entire Soviet zone. Of its twenty-five members, seventeen, acting as directors of the various economic fields, were appointed by SMA; the remainder represented the five *Laender* and the corporate groups of the Trade Union Association (FDGB)— the Soviets saw to it that organized labor in its communized reincarnation shared whenever feasible in governmental functions—and the Farmers' Mutual Aid Association. Some of the former Central Administrative Authorities, however, such as the important Legal Administration (*Justizverwaltung*) remained separate. This centralized organization, obviously required by planning, differed sharply from the federalist effort in the West; perhaps the federal element is traceable in the arrangement that the central authorities, not having a *Land* staff of their own, used the administrative machinery of the *Laender.* Most of the incisive economic reforms—nationalization of banking and insurance, the agrarian reforms, socialization of production—thus could be accomplished efficiently and uniformly by the SMA. The economic, legal, and political diversity the Allies had prided themselves on having created in their zones, never evolved in the East. Nor was there any touch of self-government in the Western sense. SMA intervened at its discretion in the *Land* administrations through individual instructions addressed to *Land* governments or through general orders issued on its behalf by the German central authorities.

POLITICAL PARTIES

THE SOCIALIST UNITY PARTY (SED)

From the start the Red Army and the SMA favored heavily the Communists whose indigenous ranks were strengthened by Moscow-trained refugee leaders, notwithstanding the fact that during the early period the same other three parties (SPD, CDU, and LDP) were permitted to operate as in the West. With the merger of the two Socialist parties of the KPD and SPD in March–April, 1946, the SED became dominant. It is, perhaps, not altogether fair to qualify the fusion as a shotgun marriage. For a long time, and since the Weimar Republic, the union of the working-class parties had been favored by many leaders to whom Fascism and capitalism were the common enemy; opportunism to side with the victors and personal vanity likewise came into play. But the hope to keep the steering wheel of the new party in the hands of the SPD leaders was soon dispelled.

In its program of orthodox Stalinism, technique of mass control, and organization the SED is patterned closely on the Communist Party of Soviet Russia. It is highly centralized, rigidly disciplined, and obviously acts on Moscow's directions. It is directed by a ten-member Politburo (a committee of the Executive Committee); power at state level is in the hands of the party secretary. The hierarchical chain of command reaches down to the county and local units and into the whole fabric of social life. Although purges have occurred lately in order to elevate the ideological level and to weed out the nonactivists or opportunists, the SED still has a membership of 1.7 million or close to 10 per cent of the total population. Membership in many cases may not be voluntary; yet the number of genuine believers should not be minimized. While the compulsory element and the totalitarian pressure cannot be ignored, reliable reports indicate that, in the same way as under the Nazis, those social strata which benefited directly from the land reform or the privileges accorded to the working population, or those hardest hit by economic insecurity, are convinced members of the new social order.

However, what gives the SED its effectively totalitarian character is the complete penetration into, and control over, the "democratic" mass organizations which, similar to the Nazi-affiliated organizations, actually mobilized the entire population within SED-dominated cadres. Of such collective satellite groups—nine in all [2]—the most influential are the trade unions in which practically all workers are enrolled, and the Free German Youth which, as was confirmed by objective observers of the Youth Rally (Whitsuntide, 1950), has succeeded, within less than five years, in indoctrinating substantial sections of the new generation in enthusiasm for the new religion. The mass organizations are charged with important functions in social, economic, and cultural life and also entitled to nominate candidates for what the regime calls elections.

THE BOURGEOIS PARTIES

Eastern Germany has become a single-party State in substance though not in name. To allow the illusion of the multiple-party state the CDU and LDP were kept in existence as the representation of the bourgeois and the religious elements.[3] But they were exposed to relentless pressure and, by purges,

[2] Free German Trade Union Association (FDGB); Free German Youth; Democratic Women's Federation; Consumers' Cooperatives; Farmers' Mutual Aid Association; Cultural League; Association of Political Persecutees; Democratic Farmers' Union; National Democratic Party. This last is a numerically insignificant group which, posing as a separate political party, aims at making inroads into the middle-class bourgeoisie, catering also to the small-fry former Nazis.

[3] Denazification interested the Soviets little. The Nazi leaders, unless they fled to the West, disappeared. The small fry ("nominal and nonactive Fascists") were amnestied and "redeemed" (SMA Order of August 17, 1947). Denazification was terminated officially on February 22, 1948. But it is to the credit of the SED that no ex-Nazi has been admitted to a position of influence in public life.

resignations, and expulsions, were deprived of effective leadership. By 1948 the last bourgeois *Land* Minister President had been ousted. With the establishment of the German Democratic Republic (October, 1949)[4] the co-ordination with the SED has become almost complete. Party officials have to sign loyalty declarations. Open criticism of official measures is no longer tolerated. Nor do these parties have press or propaganda media of their own. Relations with their sister organizations in Western Germany became more and more tenuous and were finally (October, 1950) officially discontinued by the latter.

LAND GOVERNMENTS AND ELECTIONS

At first the *Laender* of the Soviet zone were governed by SMA-appointed *Land* presidents, with *Land* directors subordinated to them, and the appropriate lower level officials empowered to issue ordinances under SMA approval. In 1946 consultative assemblies were added on all administrative levels, to which the licensed parties and certain collective organizations were permitted to make nominations. Elections for the local (*Kreis* and city) assemblies took place in 1946 and only after the SED had sufficiently consolidated its control. Finally, elections for the *Landtage* were held in the entire Soviet zone (October 20, 1946).[5] The *Landtage* drafted constitutions and passed them without popular ratification (December, 1947–February, 1948).

LAND CONSTITUTIONS

Constitution-making in the Soviet zone conformed outwardly to the democratic pattern; actually, however, it was based on an SED proposal "for a future German constitution" (published November 19, 1946). Furthermore, a committee formed in advance by the three official parties—with SED predominance—served for the elimination of disputes in public and press and presented to the people a unified front of the political parties (the "block" system).[6] This explains the similarity of the constitutions to the point of identity even in phrasing. The instruments are concise, "functional," without verbosity, and with definite ideological overtones.

The form of government chosen belongs to the type of representative government known in constitutional theory as assembly government (the

[4] See *infra*, pp. 640 ff.
[5] Tabulation of election results:

Land	SED	CDU	LDP	Mutual Farmers' Aid
Saxony	49.3%	24.7%	24.7%	3.3%
Saxony-Anhalt	45.8	29.9	29.9	2.2
Thuringia	49.3	18.8	28.6	3.3
Brandenburg	43.64	30.4	20.5	5.5
Mecklenburg	49.6	34.1	12.5	3.8
Votes in the zone	4,556,691	2,292,329	2,328,064	256,213
Percentage in the zone	47.7	24.3	24.7	3.3

In these elections (generally considered fairly honest), the SED obtained the bare absolute majority only with the affiliated Farmers' Mutual Aid Association.
[6] See *infra*, p. 643.

gouvernement conventionnel of the Jacobins),[7] under which a nominally sovereign, popularly elected legislative assembly serves merely as the rostrum on which the strong executive is mounted, streamlined by the existence of a single (or dominant) political party. This political arrangement is favored by the Soviets in their own country and in the satellite states. The constitutions of the Soviet zone uniformly center on the parliament (*Landtag*), a unicameral body vested with legislative powers and charged with the control of the government, the supervision of the administration and even the appointment of the judiciary. The separation of powers is deliberately discarded for the omnipotence of the legislative. There is no specific state president. The *Landtag* is elected by universal suffrage under proportional representation, in practice nullified by the advance assignment of candidates to the parties participating in the "block." The Presidium of the *Landtag,* a Soviet invention, being much more than the usual business organization of the legislative body, actually is the inner circle of the *Landtag,* controlling and supervising the cabinet. Executive power is exercised by the Minister President, elected by, and theoretically responsible to, the *Landtag.* The cabinet or an individual Minister must resign when losing the confidence of the parliament, a contingency which is unlikely to happen. The judiciary, consisting of professional and lay judges—the latter again an interesting Soviet-inspired innovation intended to break down the caste mentality of the professional judiciary—are nominally but not actually independent since they are appointed (with various techniques of nomination) by the *Landtage* and removable by them. Judicial review of the constitutionality of legislation is entrusted either to the parliament itself (Saxony) or to a committee of the *Landtag* to which members of the bench and law professors (Thuringia, Saxony-Anhalt) are added.

The economic program stresses social justice. While the economic freedom of the individual is recognized, planning is considered essential. Private monopolies are outlawed; certain classes of enterprises are subject to socialization through referendum. Agricultural holdings are limited to a fixed maximum size. Education is uniform in strictly secular schools (*Einheitsschule*). Paper guarantees of civil liberties are much the same as in the West, though more summarized than articulated.

THE "BLOCK" SYSTEM

Government, under these formally democratic and parliamentarian constitutions, is conducted by a political technique that has become known as the "block" system. This ingenuous "democratic" *quid pro quo,* raised to the dignity of a full-fledged political theory,[8] provides the convenient method for maintaining the semblance of the multiple-party structure while entrenching the rule of the SED. In order to substitute unanimity among the political parties for the legitimate opposition, all decisions are harmonized in advance

[7] See Karl Loewenstein, "The Presidency Outside the United States," *The Journal of Politics,* vol. 11 (1949), pp. 447 ff, 470 ff.

[8] See Alfons Steiniger, *Das Blocksystem,* Berlin, 1949.

jointly by a committee of all parties, allegedly to attain a compromise by mutual concessions and to eliminate opposition by "voluntary self-restraint," actually to attain unanimity by SED blackmail behind closed doors. Dissensions, therefore, are never "irreconcilable" and do not become manifest to the public. Once the party leaders have been brought to submission to the SED decisions, the rank and file is expected to follow. The "block" technique, thus, replaces the freely moving dynamics of coalition governments in the Western zones by a° system closely approximating the single-party state without abolishing the façade of the multiple-party state. It is not confined to parliamentary activities but also carries the principle of unanimity into the mass organizations. It proved equally useful for the creation of the Eastern state through similarly constituted "People's Congresses."

THE SOCIO–ECONOMIC PATTERN

The unchallengeable control of the Communist SED made possible radical Sovietization of the socio-economic pattern. As lever was used the widely popular seizure of properties belonging to the former Reich, the NSDAP and its affiliated organizations, and property abandoned by absentee owners. Confiscation was extended to firms which had received war contracts or employed slave labor.[9] Larger enterprises, particularly of the heavy industries, were transferred to public ownership of the *Laender,* smaller ones to the counties, municipalities, and cooperatives. The process was progressively stepped up until at present all enterprises with more than fifteen to twenty employees and producing about 70 per cent of Soviet zone manufactured goods are publicly owned and managed. Private monopolies became state monopolies. Simultaneously all the larger concerns, among them those most cartelized, were directly taken over by the Soviets (1946) and subsequently organized as large combines on the pattern of the Soviet state trusts, under Russian management. Most of the output (to 80 per cent) has gone to Russia for reparations which few will grudge the country which the Nazis so utterly and wantonly devastated. A considerable number of these later were returned to *Land* ownership. The process of socialization by now is beginning to affect also the small businessmen, artisans, and the retailers who are crowded out by the consumers' cooperatives.

On the other hand, the agrarian reform was conducted more rapidly and drastically without leading to full-scale collectivization. Private property of small plots of land was retained and even vastly extended by the confiscation of the large estates without compensation to the owners, and their distribution among landless tenants, agricultural workers, and refugees. Here the law of Saxony of September, 1945, served as the model. All "Junker" estates and all other holdings of over 100 hectares were expropriated.[10] Key organizations

---

[9] The transfer of ownership was accomplished by action of the *Landtage;* only in Saxony a plebiscite was held (June 30, 1946) in which 77 per cent of the votes cast favored public ownership. There is little doubt that the result reflected the real will of the people.

[10] Church property was exempted; but the local committees, assisted by uncertain titles, took some of it over anyway.

in the redistribution of land were the local Farmers' Committees for Mutual Aid. In a single sweep 33.1 per cent of the agricultural and forest land in the Soviet zone (over 2½ million hectares) were transferred to a total of 321,291 new owners, to the *Laender* for research or experimental farms, and to municipalities; the average size of the farms is between seven and nine hectares.[11]

Whatever may be said against Soviet policies in Eastern Germany, the transformation of a country in which before two-thirds of agricultural land were held by large and overlarge estates, into one of small farmers amounts to a revolution of the first magnitude. It ended, once and for all, the socio-political influence of the Prussian Junker class whose medieval feudalism no previous German government had been able to break.

[11] See Harold O. Lewis, *New Constitutions in Occupied Germany*, Washington, 1948, pp. 45 ff.

CHAPTER XXXVIII

THE GERMAN DEMOCRATIC REPUBLIC (DEUTSCHE DEMOKRATISCHE REPUBLIK)

ORIGIN OF THE EASTERN GERMAN STATE

PEOPLE'S CONGRESS AND PEOPLE'S COUNCIL

While, in the play-by-play report on diplomatic events, the Soviets usually made a move to counter one of the Allies, in the demand for all-German unity under a common constitution the Eastern Germans, spearheaded by the SED, clearly took the lead. As early as in November, 1947, the SED called on all German parties to convene a general convention to Berlin. Those in the Western zones, except the Communists, declined. The first meeting of the People's Congress (*Deutscher Volkskongress für Einheit und gerechten Frieden*) in Berlin (December 6–7, 1947), though staged by the SED and presided over by the leading Communist, Wilhelm Pieck, was by no means an all-SED affair.[1] The SED saw to it that the principle of party equality was maintained. Leading politicians of the CDU and LDP were chosen to the presiding board. At a second meeting (March 18, 1948), after the London decisions on the formation of a Western State had been announced, it was decided to submit the question of German unification to the entire German people by initiative and referendum. But the Western powers, through General Clay (April 17, 1948), rejected the proposal and prohibited all propaganda for the People's Congress in the West.

Simultaneously the People's Council (*Volksrat*), an executive committee appointed by the Congress, prepared the draft of an all-German Constitution, using a proposal (published August 8, 1948) by Otto Grotewohl, a former SPD leader and one of the moving spirits for the formation of the SED. The draft was unanimously adopted by the fifth meeting of the People's Council (October 22, 1948), declaring itself "the sole legitimate representation

---

[1] Of the 1,729 delegates, 978 came from the Eastern zone, 464 from the West, 253 from all sectors of Berlin. LDP and CDU of the Eastern zone were strongly represented; of the Western bourgeois parties only observers attended.

of the German people," and unleashed an enormous propaganda discussion (Soviet style) which, be it noted, offered a striking contrast with the indifference the Western German manifested towards "their" Constitution.[2] In its sixth meeting (March 18–19, 1949) the People's Council again unanimously accepted the final draft, with some amendments, and transmitted it to the People's Congress for ratification. An initiative, begun in April, 1949, and conducted by house-to-house solicitation, resulted in more than 13 million signatures, sufficient under the Weimar Constitution which was declared applicable for this purpose. On May 15, 1949, a vote took place to confirm the mandate of the newly constituted People's Congress, together with a referendum to decide for or against the Constitution "for the German Democratic Republic." With 98.2 per cent of the voters participating, the official outcome was announced as 66.1 in favor and 33.9 against. In Eastern Berlin the relation was 58.1 per cent for and 41.9 per cent against. Considering the weight of the official propaganda machine, the result may seem hardly impressive, though the polling seemed technically unobjectionable. The new People's Congress ratified the Constitution by 2087–1 votes (May 30, 1949). However, the Soviets delayed its effective date until all diplomatic measures to prevent the formation of the Western State had been exhausted.

THE ESTABLISHMENT OF THE GERMAN DEMOCRATIC REPUBLIC

The new People's Council, elected by the People's Congress, convened in Berlin on October 7, 1949.[3] The Council solemnly announced the formation of the new State, declared the Constitution in force, but postponed popular elections for the lower house (*Volkskammer*) until October 15, 1950, obviously in view of the alarming degree of nonconformity exhibited in the referendum on the Constitution. Meanwhile it acted as the provisional People's Chamber. The federal organ provided for by the Constitution, the Chamber of the *Laender,* was elected by the *Landtage* of the five *Laender* on October 10, 1949.[4]

[2] The discussion was conducted in 9,000 public meetings; 15,000 resolutions were adopted and 500 proposals for amendment submitted.

[3] Of its 400 seats, 70 were reserved for nonvoting Western German delegates (about whose claim to the mandate nothing is known); of the remainder of 330 seats, distributed among the parties according to a prearranged key, only 90 were taken by the SED and the same number by the LDP and CDU (45 each); but the SED controlled the 150 votes of two smaller puppet parties and of the collective mass organizations.

[4] It is composed of thirty-four members as follows:

	Total	SED	LDP	CDU	Farmers' Mutual Aid
Saxony	11	6	3	2	–
Saxony-Anhalt	8	4	2	2	–
Thuringia	6	3	2	1	–
Brandenburg	5	3	1	1	–
Mecklenburg	4	1	1	1	1
	34	17	9	7	1

Political arithmetic, thus, gave the SED only a slight edge over the bourgeois parties. By law of November 8, 1950 (GB. 1950, p. 1135), the number of representatives in the Chamber of the *Laender* was raised from thirty-four to fifty, whereby the smaller *Laender* (e.g., Mecklenburg and Saxony) were more favored. The "observers" from the "capital of Berlin," now called "representatives with consultative vote," were increased from seven to thirteen.

On October 11, 1949, a joint meeting of the People's Chamber and the Chamber of the *Laender* elected unanimously Wilhelm Pieck, seventy-four, veteran Moscow-trained Communist chief,[5] to the Presidency. In accordance with the Constitution (Art. 92) the SED, as the strongest party, designated Otto Grotewohl, former SPD politician, to the position of Minister President. He is assisted by three Deputy Minister Presidents, one each assigned to the SED, LDP, and CDU. The SED man is Walter Ulbricht, considered by many, as Secretary General of the SED, to be the real power, camouflaged by the façade of the two "moderates," Pieck and Grotewohl. In the coalition cabinet of eighteen Ministers the ratio of the SED to the bourgeois parties is 11–7. Among the Ministries are those for Education and Foreign Affairs, which do not exist in the West. The People's Chamber accepted, without formal vote of confidence, the Government program (October 12, 1950). The Eastern sector of Berlin was not represented in the assembly. The Soviets, however, officially withdrew their Headquarters and control points from the area and subsequently (June, 1950) civilianized their administration.

The new State was recognized internationally by all members of the Soviet block and Red China. The United States as well as Dr. Adenauer denied the legality of the new State and Government. It may seem idle to compare the exercise of the *pouvoir constituant* of the Western and the Eastern German States. However, it may be noted that in neither case did a popularly elected assembly draft and accept the instrument of government. If the Western Allies claim that "their" Germans at least elected by an honest vote the new legislative body, the Soviets will counter that "their" Germans at least ratified a Constitution drawn up indirectly (as in the case of the Parliamentary Council) by an (apparently) honest referendum.

THE CONSTITUTION OF THE GERMAN DEMOCRATIC REPUBLIC

The Eastern German Constitution, usually dismissed in the United States as a totalitarian tool without value, deserves close study if for no other reason than that it institutionalizes, in ultra-democratic disguise, the exercise of political power by the "State" party in a fully Westernized environment. It claims, according to the intention of Otto Grotewohl, its spiritual father, to be uninfluenced by foreign patterns and commensurate with German tradition and needs. It proclaims the principles of democracy, federalism, and socialism. To the Weimar Constitution it is even closer than the Bonn Basic Law; in this it follows the policy consistently pursued by the Soviets since Potsdam. But the Weimar blueprint is converted, with an almost diabolical subtlety, to that type of parliamentary supremacy or assembly government which is favored by other "People's Democracies" in the Soviet orbit.

THE PATTERN OF GOVERNMENT

The People's Chamber (*Volkskammer*) is the center of political power, the "highest organ of the State" and the "bearer of State power" (Art. 60).

[5] From his name the jocular appellation of Eastern Germany as "Pieckistan" is derived.

The Parliament is elected by the free, secret, direct, and equal vote of all eligible citizens above eighteen years of age, under application of proportional representation. That there is no room for the qualms besetting the West in refining proportional representation and excluding splinter parties, is evidenced by the provision—drawn from Soviet experience—that only such political parties are admitted to participation in the elections (and to the nomination of candidates) which (Art. 13, par. 2), "according to their by-laws strive for the democratic content of the political and social life of the entire Republic and whose organization extends over the entire state territory," the latter provision excluding regional parties. The democratic mass organizations have equal rank with the political parties proper. In the absence of a judicial decision it must be assumed that the determination of a party's nondemocratic character and its exclusion is decided by the Government. The Presidium, in which each party (*Fraktion*) is represented, is less power-inflated than in other constitutions under Soviet inspiration.

In conformity with assembly government, the People's Chamber, as the virtual core of political power, is not subject to any checks and balances or to constitutional limitations from outside. As on the *Land* level, the separation of powers is abandoned. Dissolution is possible only by self-disbandment and in the exceptional case of a vote of nonconfidence against a new Government. The *Volkskammer* alone is charged with the formation, control, and dismissal of the Government. Here the Constitution institutionalizes officially the technique of the "block" system. The strongest party designates the Minister President. He in turn forms the cabinet of Ministers. An innovation is the fact that a coalition government is mandatory in which all parties with a minimum number of forty members are represented in relation to their strength, unless a party wishes to exclude itself (Art. 92). This principle of unanimity in the Government to which unanimity in the Parliament corresponds nullifies the right of opposition, which is the essence of Western parliamentarism. By all practical standards, the paramount control of the SED is legalized. Nonetheless, different from the Bonn Constitution, and again in conformity with assembly government, the cabinet and each of its members require the confidence of the *Volkskammer* for the conduct of office (Art. 94). The overthrow of the cabinet as a whole is possible only— here in imitation of the Bonn Constitution—by way of a "constructive" vote of nonconfidence which requires simultaneously (Art. 95) the designation and approval of the Minister President's successor by the *Volkskammer*. If the designated successor is not confirmed by the *Volkskammer* the latter's dissolution is mandatory. To all practical intents and purposes, however, the Minister President is irremovable, and thus instrumental in the transformation of assembly government into the rule of the strong executive as is characteristic for this form of government. The elimination of the controlling party from power is feasible only by revolution.

The Constitution, like Weimar, but here different from other versions of assembly government, provides also for a president, elected, without strings attached, by simple majority of both houses (*Volkskammer* and Chamber of *Laender*). The election is a foregone conclusion. He may be retired by a two-thirds majority of both houses. Although his constitutional rights are strictly ceremonial and not even state-integrating, the election of the party leader, Wilhelm Pieck, may indicate that the incumbent will not content himself with the role of a figurehead and may become a counterweight to the Minister President.

THE FEDERAL STRUCTURE

If for the frame of government the contours of Weimar were preserved at least outwardly, they are openly discarded in what purports to be the federal structure. The Constitution is definitely slanted so far towards centralization that, quite unlike Bonn, no serious obstacle would prevent an outright unitary government. This merely confirms the situation existing in present-day Eastern Germany, which is largely a centralized State with little if any statehood individuality visible among the five *Laender*. That the constitution of the *Laender* must conform to that of the Democratic Republic (Art. 109) is not different from the regulation under Bonn. But the Chamber of the *Laender* (*Laenderkammer* [Art. 71]) which is destined to represent the territorial subdivisions, bears no resemblance to the type of a federal Council customary in Germany. The delegates for the Chamber of the *Laender*—each *Land* being entitled to one for each 500,000 inhabitants—are appointed by the *Landtage* (and not, as in the West, by the *Land* governments) proportionate to the strength of the parties represented therein; they do not conduct themselves, or vote, under instructions of the *Land* governments as in the West. While not explicitly mentioned it is implied that the "block" technique will result in the same kind of "unanimity" that prevails in the *Volkskammer*. If the measure of federalism consists in the actual power of the second chamber the German Democratic Republic is factually a unitary State. The Chamber of the *Laender* is endowed merely with a suspensive veto which may be overridden by a simple majority of the *Volkskammer* (Art. 84). In case of constitutional amendment the veto (which is not identical with consent) must be carried by a two-thirds majority, an additional restriction on the power of the Chamber of the *Laender* because it facilitates constitutional amendments desired by the *Volkskammer*.

The deliberate weakening of the federalistic elements is further evidenced in the assignment and distribution of legislative powers. The range of exclusive federal jurisdiction is not much wider than under Weimar (Art. 112) though it includes the entire field of substantive and adjective law which is known to be one of the most centralizing features in any political order. But since there is no enumeration of the fields of concurrent legislation, the presumption of legislative jurisdiction operates in favor of the federal State, no "residual powers" clause protecting the intangible spheres of states. This pertains also to the field of taxation where the right to raise revenue (*Abgabenhoheit*) is located in the federal Government. The complex system of overlapping financial jurisdictions, so much belabored in the West, is avoided.

Nor can the right of the *Laender* to administer the federal services, insofar as no immediate federal administration is provided for, be taken as a token of *Land* self-government because of the incisive powers of supervision accorded to the federal State in all fields in which the latter claims jurisdiction (Art. 116). In practice this implies an unlimited right of coordination of the *Laender* by the federal Government which may exercise it by issuing instructions to the *Land* governments or even by sending enforcement officers directly to the *Land* administrative authorities. Controversies that may arise here are to be adjusted not by an independent federal tribunal but by the *Volkskammer* itself. It requires merely an opinion of its Constitutional Committee, enlarged by three members of the Chamber of the *Laender*.

This shape of things allows the conclusion that the German Democratic Republic, rather than classifiable as a federal State, is a unitary State with some degree of decentralization. This solution may not only conform to the requirements of Socialist planning, but seems intrinsically appropriate for a territory with relatively insignificant residues of a genuine separateness of its component parts. In this sense the state of Prussia, so assiduously written off by the CC and the West, has been revived.

THE BILL OF RIGHTS AND CONSTITUTIONAL GUARANTEES

In the formulation of the classic civil liberties, an elaborate bill of rights follows closely, often to the point of literal identity, the pattern of Weimar. All rights are immediately applicable and binding law. Freedom of religion is guaranteed (Arts. 41 ff). Education is strictly secular and without the clerical flavor it has in the West. Religious instruction is left to the denominational groups (Art. 40). All schools are tuition-free (Art. 39). But what distinguishes this bill of rights from its Western counterpart is the emphasis on social—if not Socialist—justice formalized in a carefully phrased section on the Economic Order (Arts. 19–29). It supplements the right to work (Art. 15), recreation, annual leave with pay and social insurance (Art. 16) and codetermination "in the regulation of industrial production, wages, and working conditions" (Art. 17). The aim of economic life is "to guarantee to all an existence compatible with the dignity of man" (Art. 19). This to attain is the purpose of economic planning through the State (*öffentliche Wirtschaftsplanung* [Art. 21]). Freedom of enterprise for the individual "within the scope of the above aims and tasks" (Art. 19, par. 3) and private property, "whose scope and limitations are determined by the law," are guaranteed (Art. 22). But private monopolies are abolished and prohibited, and private estates of more than 100 hectares are subject to redistribution by land reform without compensation (Art. 24, par. 5). Private enterprises suitable to public ownership may be so transferred (Art. 27). Nationalization is mandatory for mineral resources, economically usable natural power, the mining, iron, steel, and electric power industries (Art. 25).

Most of these arrangements would grace any socially progressive state provided they were surrounded by the rule of law, and the latter, in turn, were grounded in the protection of constitutional guarantees through an independent judiciary. Here the Constitution, by Western standards, is utterly defective. The sovereignty of the legislature under assembly government is incompatible with either the judicial protection of rights by a constitutional tribunal or judicial review of the constitutionality of its legislative acts. To safeguard the citizen "against unlawful administrative measures" is left to "the control exercised by the legislature" and administrative courts (Art. 138); both guarantees are precarious in view of the State Party control of the *Volkskammer* and the political limitations on administrative justice in the Soviet orbit. Instead of judicial review by independent courts the final decision lies with the *Volkskammer,* acting upon an "opinion" of its Constitutional Committee (Art. 66) in which the parties are represented by the "block" technique, with three members of the Supreme Court and three professors of public law thrown in for good measure. The administration of justice (Arts. 126–138) is no longer the monopoly of professional judges with tenure. Specially trained men and women (*Volksrichter*) increasingly have supplanted the university-educated professionals. All judges of superior courts are elected (those of the Supreme Court by the *Volkskammer,* those in the *Laender* by the *Landtage* [Arts. 130, 131]), while the lower court magistrates are appointed by the *Land* governments (Art. 131, par. 3). But all judges are subject to recall or dismissal by the federal or the *Land* parliaments respectively (Art. 132). Independence of judiciary and tenure, thus, are related to "ideological reliability," the provision (Art. 127) to the contrary notwithstanding that the judges, "in the exercise of their functions, are independent and subject only to the Constitution and the laws." If the weak protection of constitutional guarantees is visualized within the context of a repressive state machinery, exercising rigid control over nonconformists and conformists alike,[6] it is obvious that, once again, its application to the Teutonic People's Republic confirms the historical experience that parliamentary supremacy under assembly government lends itself most readily to its perversion into authoritarian government. The absence of any checks and balances on the omnipotence of the Parliament, which make the Constitution a relatively simple document compared with the complexity of the Bonn instrument, is cleverly turned into the unchallengeable dominance of the assembly by the State Party, the SED, while preserving the illusion of "democratic unanimity" by building the "block" technique into the Constitution. The present sociopolitical organization of the Soviet zone, embodied in the federal no less

[6] Four such organizations exist. The State Security Service (secret police) and the State Control Commission (charged with supervision of economic life and planning), are both attached to the Minister President's office. The Personnel Administration (under the Ministry of the Interior), keeps tab on public employees and officials; all offices are staffed with reliable SED adherents. The SED itself is policed and disciplined by the Control Commission of the SED. At least during the early years of the Soviet occupation, internment or concentration camps were widely resorted to, more recently possibly replaced by assignment to work in the uranium mines.

than in the *Land* constitutions, is grounded in Rousseau's concept of the omnipotent general will rather than applying Montesquieu's technique of the separated and coordinated powers. It occupies the twilight zone between the bourgeois-liberal and the Socialist-collectivized state. It is the Teutonic version of the "People's Democracy" familiar in the Soviet orbit.

POLITICAL DEVELOPMENTS SINCE 1949

Reliable information on the internal political life of the German Democratic Republic is scant. Its legislative activities have been of minor importance, with the possible exception of the establishment of the Supreme Court (December 8, 1949), the federal Government evidently believing that the tightly coordinated *Landtage* of the *Laender* would effectively attend to routine legislation. Agitation for German unity, on Eastern terms, has continued. Internal purges and show trials of bourgeois economic saboteurs, probably in many instances not without factual basis, have been staged. The prices of food and consumers' goods were sharply cut (June, 1950), possibly to offset the effect of the steady deterioration of the Eastern German mark (exchange rate of about eight Eastern marks to one Western mark). A five-year plan, announced to raise the present production rate by 90 per cent, went into operation on January 1, 1951. But the principal event was preparing and staging the elections for the *Volkskammer* (October 15, 1950), with the simultaneous election of the five *Landtage*. In true Soviet satellite style, a National Front ticket was to be voted on which contained, under a carefully prearranged key, a common slate for all political parties and the mass organizations entitled to parliamentary representation. Seventy per cent of the seats were assigned to the SED and its affiliated organizations, 30 per cent to the bourgeois parties. The foreordained results of this by now familiar blend of an election for the determination of the legislative personnel and a plebiscite to record popular ratification of the regime's policies, frequently carried out by open vote and bringing 95 per cent of the voters to the polls, would have been envied by Goebbels.[7] The new *Volkskammer* reaffirmed Wilhelm Pieck as President and Otto Grotewohl as Minister President. For the time being neither the elimination of the appearance of a multiparty state nor far-reaching constitutional changes seem to be planned. Organizational measures for integrating the German "People's Democracy" into the Soviet-dominated area may have been carried as far as it is desired.

The elections of October, 1950, were followed by an incisive reform of the governmental structure.[8] The number of cabinet members was enlarged

---

[7] The consolidated figures for the election of the *Landtage* are as follows:

Registered voters	12,325,168
Votes cast	12,144,597
For national ticket	12,097,105
Against national ticket	34,060

98.5% were in favor; 0.28% against.

[8] Law on the Government of the German Democratic Republic of November 8, 1950 (GB. 1950, p. 1135).

from eighteen to twenty-three, increasing the number of Deputy Minister Presidents from three to five and the Ministers proper from fourteen to seventeen. The changes affected primarily the socio-economic offices. In line with Soviet practice, the Ministry of Industry was split into the independent Ministries of Heavy Industry, Machine Construction, and Light Industry, while the Ministry of Labor and Health was divided into two independent branches. On the other hand, instead of the Ministry of Planning a special Planning Commission was attached to the Council of Ministers. An even more important innovation, inspired by Soviet techniques, was the establishment of the Central Commission for State Control charged with the supervision of the execution of the Government's decisions. Both Commissions are directly attached to the Minister President. Their chairmen participate with full rights in the cabinet meetings. The result of this reform, altogether unorthodox in Western governmental practice, is the loss of political influence suffered by the "technical" Ministries. The balance of political power visibly is being shifted to the Minister President and the two commission chairmen, who thus constitute an inner circle or super-government within the Government.

To all intents and purposes, the most discussed of all internal measures to date of the Eastern German regime was the notorious "Law for the Protection of Peace." [9] A political measure intended "against the aggressive policies of the imperialist Governments of the United States, Britain, and France," it outlawed, in conformity with the resolutions of various Communist-sponsored "peace congresses," propaganda for war; incitement to hatred on racial grounds, or against foreign peoples; participation in military foreign formations (e.g., the French Foreign Legion); propaganda in favor of a restored German militarism; glorification of atomic weapons. The sanctions are severe, including, "for agents of foreign aggressive or war-mongering states," the death penalty.

About the relations between the Soviet Government and the new State no reliable information is available. The SMA was converted into the Soviet Control Commission whose complete civilianization was announced in June, 1950. Overt Soviet controls are—next to the diplomatic representation after the formal recognition—the continued presence of obviously large forces of the Red Army. But the covert influence of the Soviet Communist Party on the SED may seem even more decisive. Economically Eastern Germany has become a member of the Council for Mutual Economic Assistance known as the Molotov Plan (September 29, 1950).

THE ATTITUDE OF THE PEOPLE

The memory of how difficult it was to appraise correctly the attitude of the people towards the Nazi regime, which freely admitted foreign visitors, will caution against any judgment on how the people in Eastern Germany stand *vis à vis* the new order. Persons and ideas still circulating freely between the Eastern and the Western halves of Germany indicate there is no iron curtain. Value judgments are much conditioned by the social position of the persons reporting

[9] Law of December 15, 1950 (GB. 1950, p. 1199).

and the persons interviewed. This much is certain: the general living standards are much lower than before the war and decidedly lower than in the West, perhaps less so for the working population. Class differences are beginning to diminish, perhaps with the exception of the privileged group of SED officials and certain technicians. Food seems adequate, consumers' goods are slowly increasing after the Soviets reduced their reparations claims from current production. Indoctrination by propaganda is making headway particularly among youth. This was convincingly demonstrated to all objective observers by the Youth Rallies in Berlin in the summer of 1950 and 1951. There is no unemployment, and the refugees were better absorbed than in the West. Administrative services are only tolerably efficient. Economically, the factory worker and the small farmer are perhaps better cared for than their Western cousins. But the heavy pall of legal and personal insecurity hangs over a people which, before the Nazis, were accustomed to the rule of law. Competent observers estimate that between 15 per cent and 20 per cent of the people are positively in favor of the regime while the vast majority, though submissive, would be willing to turn against it if and when occasion arises. But a substantial minority may be equally unwilling to be again exposed to the economic vicissitudes of the free enterprise system of Western German capitalism.

GERMANY'S KEY POSITION IN THE EAST–WEST CONFLICT

It took the Germans longer than other European peoples to become a united nation. Their proudest patriotic memories stem from the creation of the Reich by Bismarck and Prussia which became the foundation on which they rose to a world power. Understandably they must consider the present split into two unequal and foreign-dominated parts anomalous, absurd, and outrageous. Moreover, economically the two parts had belonged together like piston and cylinder.

But German disunion is more than a German problem. It is the core of the East-West conflict which, stripped of its global complexities, is the battle for the body and soul of Germany. To both the Soviets and the West a united Germany included in the power orbit of the other, constitutes a grave danger unmitigated by the inconclusive results of the effort to convert the Germans into a peace-loving nation. A united Germany allied with the West would form an unsurmountable barrier to Soviet expansion in Europe and, considering the age-old *Drang nach Osten,* a serious threat to the Soviet State itself. A united Germany allied with the East would tip the scales in the balance of power so much in favor of the Soviets that Western Europe and, with it, the Western world would no longer be secure. The political combination of the Soviets and Germany is well-nigh unbeatable. On the other hand, Germany split into two parts is no less dangerous because either half, aiming at unification and thereby trying to impose its socio-economic pattern on the other, might easily drag the world into World War III. From whatever angle German unity or disunity is approached it is fraught with foreseeable dangers and incalculable risks.

THE GERMAN ATTITUDE TOWARDS UNIFICATION

Seen from the outside the German desire for unity seems uniform and universal. Propaganda for unity from whatever quarter has wide popular acclaim. On closer inspection, however, the issue is far more complex than the official manifestations on both sides make it appear. It is true that family bonds stretch between the East to the West regardless of state boundaries. Saxony and Thuringia belong to Germany as much as Franconia or Baden. But aside from such emotional factors, to Southern Germany the Eastern part has little economic, and next to no sentimental, interest. The loss of Berlin and the disappearance

649

of Prussia is considered more often than not a blessing in disguise. Moreover, it should not be lost sight of that Western Germany today is predominantly a Catholic State; with Eastern Germany the Protestant element would be restored to domination, a powerful argument against unification for certain social and political strata. Contrariwise, to the Rhineland, the Ruhr, and other parts of former Prussia, the loss of the East is a festering wound, less for emotional than for economic reasons. Big business and heavy industry are well aware that sooner or later foreign assistance will terminate and they will have to compete with foreign industrial interests under adverse conditions while Germany's opportunities naturally gravitate towards the underdeveloped East. Even under present conditions the clandestine and illegal trade with the East is substantial.

On the other hand, to the Eastern Germans to be cut off from the West is more than a festering wound; it is a lethal amputation. The split has lowered their living standards to the level of the East to which, as non-Slavs, they do not wish to belong. There is also Berlin, and Berlin believes itself, rightly or wrongly, the capital of all Germany. If, therefore, it might not seem impossible for the Western part to exist without the East, the latter, lest it abandon itself, never can reconcile itself to the split from the West. In spite of the lip service paid in both parts uniformly, it is undeniable that propaganda for reunification rings truer in the East than the West.

THE INTERNATIONAL DEBATE ON REUNIFICATION

For a long time the Germans themselves took no part in the debate on unification. Only once, on June 6, 1947, following the conclusion of the first East-West zonal trade agreement (January 18, 1947), the Minister Presidents of all *Laender* of the four zones convened in Munich for a joint discussion. But the Western members—those from the French zone were permitted to attend as observers only—were forbidden by their MG masters to talk about anything except economics. The Minister Presidents from the East at once opened up with the demand to discuss the establishment of common governmental agencies; when rebuffed by their Western colleagues, they walked out. Subsequently, until after the establishment of the two separate States, the Germans remained silent and suffering listeners to the disharmonious dialogue conducted among the former Allies. But consulting the chronology will lead to the conclusion that while the West always set the pace in the various steps towards the two separate States, on the issue of unification the Soviets, echoed by their Germans, insistently took the lead. The Soviet position was throughout, as evidenced, for example, by their spokesman at the Moscow and London Conferences of 1947, that Germany be unified under a common Constitution; that thereafter a peace treaty be concluded; and that, within a year, all occupation forces be withdrawn. The underlying assumption was that, meanwhile, the SED would have captured the governmental machinery and the all-German Government could be counted on to be "friendly," in terms of Soviet semantics, to the East. Into this trap the Western powers refused to walk.

Only after the creation of the Western and the Eastern States did the Germans themselves enter the Great Debate. On March 22, 1950, Dr. Adenauer proposed a unification procedure by demanding elections, to be held in all Germany under the standard principles of democracy, for a constituent assembly which should draw up an all-German Constitution to be ratified by an all-German referendum. The electoral law should be elaborated by the four powers, which also would jointly supervise the election. The proposal was informally rejected by Otto Grotewohl on behalf of Eastern Germany. Undaunted, the three Foreign Ministers (U.S.A., U.K., and France) at their Paris meeting issued (May 26, 1950) a detailed statement of Western conditions of unification which, had it been accepted by the Soviets, would have become the "little" Potsdam Agreement of 1950: A freely elected German Government, based on freedom of action throughout Germany of all democratic political parties; restoration of the rule of law in all Germany; prohibition of all paramilitary forces including the political secret police; assurance of economic unity through action of a German Government on such matters as a common currency, and through quadripartite action on such matters as reparations from current production; return of all industrial enterprises acquired since unconditional surrender by or on behalf of a foreign power unless approved by quadripartite action and only in case it was in the interests of Germany; establishment of a four-power Supervisory Commission with only such reserved powers as not to prevent a German Government from functioning effectively. All these conditions were of course pointed at existing abuses in the Soviet zone; but the cancellation of the Eastern land reform was not among them. Upon fulfillment the path would be open to a joint peace treaty, the Western Allies formally declaring themselves opposed to a separate treaty.

On May 26, 1950, the three Western High Commissioners addressed in a letter to General Chuikow, their opposite number as chairman of the Soviet High Commission, the request for assuming the four-power responsibility for framing the electoral law under which the all-German elections were to be conducted.

None of these proposals found favor with the Soviets or their German understudies, and understandably so because free elections would have exploded the SED rule, and the return of the Sovietized industries would have robbed the Soviets of those reparations which they extracted from their zone after they had been frustrated in obtaining the ten billion dollars they believed themselves entitled to under Yalta and Potsdam. It is hardly believable, therefore, that the Western statesmen wished to do more than state these demands for the record. But an answer came with the Resolution of the Prague Conference of the Foreign Ministers of the Molotov block (October 21, 1950). A National Assembly should be convoked in which the Western and the Eastern German States were to be represented by an equal number of delegates. This was rejected by the Western German Government and the Allies, who felt that the East, with only one-third of the total population could not claim representation equal to the West with two-thirds.

On November 3, 1950, the Soviets addressed to the Western powers a formal request for a new four-power conference confining itself to the German issue. At the same time Otto Grotewohl invited Dr. Adenauer to a joint German discussion of unification. The Chancellor, justly believing himself to be supported by the Western Allies with whom at that time he had begun to negotiate about German participation in the Western European army, at first was utterly reluctant to answer at all. Public opinion, fearful of the Soviet reaction to rearmament and hoping against hope to achieve the status of neutrality in an eventual Soviet-American war, forced his hand. But his reply (January 15, 1951) was uncompromisingly hostile. Western Germany "can enter into discussion of unification only with those who are willing unconditionally to recognize and guarantee a regime based on the acceptance of a form of government that respects liberty, the protection of human rights and the maintenance of peace." Lashing out at the military forces of the East he claimed that Western rearmament does not constitute a threat to peace.

However, during his good will visit to Germany (January 20, 1951) General Eisenhower, Supreme Commander of the North Atlantic treaty defense system, convinced himself—and subsequently the Pentagon—of the deep-seated and widespread resistance among Germans of all walks of life against participation in the Western defense effort except—if at all—on the footing of complete equality. A shift in tactics seemed advisable to the West which could not fail to affect the reunification issue. Replying to the latest Soviet note (December 30, 1950) the Western powers agreed to the Soviet proposal for a preliminary discussion by the deputies of the respective Foreign Ministries of the agenda of a four-power conference on the condition that it would extend, beyond the German issue as demanded by the Soviets, to all possible causes of the present world tension.

Consequently, the deputies met in Paris from March 5 to June 21, 1951, without however, in seventy-four meetings of repetitious monotony, being able to agree even on the agenda. The outward reason for the failure was the Soviet insistence on inclusion of the North Atlantic Treaty, considered by them a prime cause of East-West tensions, while the West refused its official inclusion. But the futile conference revealed—what had been evident to Germany's neighbors from the start—that the real core of the East-West conflict is and remains Germany, which, in view of the dominant position she holds on the Continent, has again become the fulcrum of the balance of power, whether united or split in two.

Alarmed by the increasing willingness of Western Germany to rearm on behalf of the West, the Eastern German Government, in the summer of 1951, intensified the unification propaganda. Adroitly equating unification and peace, or rearmament and the threat of war, it evoked so wide and sympathetic a response in Western Germany that Dr. Adenauer was compelled, by the pressure of public opinion, to modify his heretofore wholly negative attitude towards unification in which he felt himself strongly supported by the American Government. As the next move he had a law drafted (October, 1951) outlining in fourteen points the detailed conditions under which Western Germany would agree to the election of an all-German constituent assembly. Prominently among these figured the supervision, by the United Nations, of the conditions for, and the holding of, such elections. To this neither the Eastern regime nor their Soviet masters seemed willing to agree. But by that time the Germans convinced themselves that integration of Western Germany into the Western defense alliance and unification are incompatible, and, further, that, in view of the enduring disagreement among their protectors, German unity is a problem that can be solved only by the Germans themselves.

THE IMPASSE OF GERMAN UNIFICATION

How this stalemate can be broken and whether it can be broken at all, is beyond prophesy at this time. Neither the Western nor the Eastern German Government can agree to a settlement on the terms of the other without committing political suicide. The overwhelming mass of the Western Germans reject unification at the price of Communization that the group around Pastor Niemoeller and the National Bolshevik partisans seem willing to concede. Nor would the working classes in the East be prepared to accept the precarious economic liberty under capitalism in exchange for the modicum of social security without liberty in the East. If at all feasible, reunification would seem conditioned on a gradual approximation of the conflicting socio-economic systems now prevailing. The longer the split lasts the more difficult the compromise will become. Perhaps, in this age of world revolution, the world has to accustom itself to the existence of two Germanys instead of one.

BIBLIOGRAPHICAL NOTE

ON THE GERMAN POLITICAL SYSTEM

1. Official Publications and Periodicals

The texts of federal (*Reich*) statutes, ordinances, decrees, and similar enactments are found in the *Official Bulletin of Laws—Reichsgesetzblatt* (abridged: *RGB.*)—divided, under the Weimar Republic, into Part I, dealing with matters of internal law, and Part II, containing the statutory material referring to international relations. In addition, the member states (*Laender*) publish *Official Bulletins* of their own for local matters affecting their territories only. Upon the establishment of the Western German State (*Deutsche Bundesrepublik*) in 1949, the collection of federal laws was continued as the *Bundesgesetzblatt*.

Decisions of the Supreme Court (*Reichsgericht*) were published until 1945 in two series of official reports dealing with civil and criminal law respectively (*Entscheidungen des Reichsgerichts in Zivilsachen und in Strafsachen*). A similar collection of the decisions of the *Oberstes Bundesgericht* has been under way since 1950.

For a more intimate knowledge of the governmental practice and the theory behind political institutions, the *Law Journals,* under the Empire and the Republic deservedly famed for their systematic approach and penetrating analyses, are indispensable.

The most distinguished were the *Juristische Wochenschrift* and the *Deutsche Juristenzeitung.* Under the Nazis these monumental legal documentations lost much of their scientific value. After the two publications mentioned had been discontinued by the Nazis, the *Deutsche Justiz,* the official organ of the Ministry of Justice, and *Deutsches Recht,* under the auspices of the Academy for German Law, a Nazi creation, took their place.

After 1945 the *Law Journals* were revived. Among the best ones were *Süddeutsche Juristenzeitung* and *Deutsche Rechtzeitschrift,* combined in 1950 under the title *Juristenzeitung.* For matters of administration see *Die öffentliche Verwaltung.*

Of other periodicals the *Archiv des öffentlichen Rechts* as well as the *Zeitschrift für die gesammte Staatswissenschaft,* both journals of established reputation already under the Empire, contain invaluable material; the former deals more with constitutional law proper, while the latter comes closer to the political science periodicals in this country and in England.

Another important source of information is the *Jahrbuch des öffentlichen Rechts,* also already founded under the Empire; the most eminent professors of law—what political science the Germans cultivate forms a part of public law—contributed to it until 1938 yearly surveys on the constitutional and political developments of the Reich and the *Laender.* Of these the comprehensive studies of Fr. Pötzsch-Heffter in volumes XIII (1925), XVII (1929), and XXI (1933–34) are first-rate. The *Jahrbuch* is in process of publication under a new management (1951).

2. German Treatises and Commentaries Considered as Authoritative

(a) *For the period of Imperial Germany:*

P. Laband, *Staatsrecht des deutschen Reiches,* 4 volumes, Tübingen-Leipzig, 1901; a useful abridged version in one volume was published as 5th edition in Tübingen, 1909.

G. Meyer & G. Anschütz, *Lehrbuch des deutschen Staatsrechts,* 7th edition, Munich and Leipzig, 1919.

(b) *For the period of the Weimar Republic:*

G. Anschütz, *Die Verfassung des deutschen Reichs,* 4th edition, Berlin, 1933.
G. Anschütz & R. Thoma, *Handbuch des deutschen Staatsrechts,* 2 volumes, Tübingen, 1930–32.

3. German History and Politics to 1871 (Foundation of the Empire)

G. P. Gooch, *Germany and the French Revolution,* London, 1920.
R. Aris, *History of Political Thought in Germany from 1789 to 1815,* London, 1936.
H. Lichtenberger, *Germany and Its Evolution in Modern Times,* New York, 1913.
Ralph H. Bowen, *German Theories of the Corporative State,* New York, 1947.
C. G. Robertson, *Bismarck,* London, 1915.
Erich Eyck, *Bismarck and the German Empire,* New York, 1950.
A. J. P. Taylor, *The Course of German History,* New York, 1946.
An outstanding German book is Fr. Meinecke, *Weltbürgertum und Nationalstaat,* Berlin, 1908, 7th edition, 1928.

4. The Empire under the Bismarckian Constitution and World War I

Veit Valentin, *The German People,* New York, 1946.
There is still no up-to-date treatment in English of the German Empire. Thorstein Veblen, *Imperial Germany and the Industrial Revolution* (first published in 1915) remains unsurpassed for its sociological insight.
B. E. Howard, *The German Empire,* New York, 1906.
F. K. Krüger, *Government and Politics of Germany,* New York, 1915.
Th. Wolff, *The Eve of 1914,* New York, 1936.
A. Mendelssohn Bartholdy, *The War and German Society,* New Haven, 1937.
A. Rosenberg, *The Birth of the German Republic, 1871–1918,* London, 1931.
English translations of the text of the Imperial Constitution of 1871 are found in W. F. Dodd, *Modern Constitutions,* volume I, Chicago-London, 1909, and in W. F. Wright, *The Constitutions of the States at War, 1914–1918,* Washington, 1919.

5. The Revolution of 1918 and the Weimar Constitution

F. Blachly & M. Oatman, *The Government and Administration of Germany,* Baltimore, 1928.
H. Finer, *Theory and Practice of Modern Government,* 2 volumes, London, 1932.
H. Quigley and R. T. Clark, *Republican Germany,* London, 1928.
James T. Shotwell, *What Germany Forgot,* New York, 1940.
J. W. Angell, *The Recovery of Germany,* New Haven, 1929.
H. G. Daniels, *The Rise of the German Republic,* London, 1927.
Paul Kosok, *Modern Germany,* Chicago, 1933.
G. P. Gooch, *Germany,* London, 1925.
E. Luehr, *The New German Republic,* New York, 1929.
J. Mattern, *Principles of Constitutional Jurisprudence of the German National Republic,* Baltimore, 1928.
R. E. Emerson, *State and Sovereignty in Modern Germany,* London, 1928.
H. G. Heneman, *The Growth of Executive Power in Germany,* Minneapolis, 1934.
L. Rogers (and others), "Aspects of German Political Institutions," *Political Science Quarterly,* vol. 47 (1932), pp. 321 ff; 576 ff.
N. Reich, *Labor Relations in Republican Germany,* New York, 1938.
Antonia Vallentin-Luchaire, *Stresemann,* New York, 1931.
J. H. Wheeler-Bennett, *Hindenburg, the Wooden Titan,* London, 1936.
J. K. Pollock, *German Election Administration,* New York, 1934.

F. M. Watkins, *The Failure of Constitutional Emergency Powers under the German Republic,* Cambridge, 1939.

Sigmund Neumann, *Die deutschen Parteien,* Berlin, 1932.

T. E. Jessop, *The Versailles Treaty, Was It Just?* London, 1942.

W. M. Knight-Patterson, *Germany from Defeat to Conquest,* London, 1945.

S. W. Halperin, *Germany Tried Democracy,* New York, 1946.

Godfrey Scheele, *The Weimar Republic,* London, 1946.

M. J. Bonn, *Wandering Scholar,* New York, 1948.

Leo Grebler & Wilhelm Winkler, *The Cost of the War to Germany and Austria-Hungary* in *Economic and Social History of the First World War,* Carnegie Endowment for International Peace (James T. Shotwell, editor), New Haven, 1940.

Arnold Brecht, *Prelude to Silence,* New York, 1944.

Books on Weimar by German authors with "hindsight":

Ferdinand Friedensburg, *Die Weimar Republik,* Berlin, 1946.

Willibald Apelt, *Geschichte der Weimarer Verfassung,* Munich, 1946.

English translations of the text of the Weimar Constitution are found, among others, in Blachly & Oatman, *op. cit.,* pp. 642 ff; H. L. McBain & L. Rogers, *The New Constitutions of Europe,* New York, 1922; M. W. Graham, *New Governments of Central Europe,* New York, 1926. See also A. Headlam-Morley, *The New Democratic Constitutions of Europe,* London, 1926, and A. J. Zurcher, *The Experiment with Democracy in Central Europe,* New York, 1933.

6. The Third Reich

Every student of Nazi Germany should thoroughly acquaint himself with the bible of the Third Reich, Adolf Hitler's *Mein Kampf,* Munich, 1925–26, two volumes (with many later editions, partly expurgated and polished). The German standard edition contains the two volumes in one. Two unabridged English editions are available, one published by Reynal and Hitchcock, New York, 1939, with explanatory (and rather superfluous) notes by the editors, the other published by Stackpole Sons, New York, 1939. No translation, however, can convey the atmosphere of this remarkable book; written in the crudest of German styles, it contains, next to semi-delirious divagations of a half-baked and thoroughly uneducated mind, passages of uncanny insight into the mass mind and social psychology which will retain their interest for a long time to come.

The *Program of the National Socialist Party (the Twenty-five Points of 1920)* is found in English translation, among others, in Lichtenberger, Schuman, Hill and Stoke, Rappard (for quotations see *infra*).

The most valuable and, as yet, almost untapped source of information on the socio-political structure and the actual management of the Third Reich are the eight volumes of documentary materials published by the Office of the United States Chief of Counsel for the Prosecution of Axis Criminality under the title, *Nazi Conspiracy and Aggression,* Washington, 1946.

The Germans themselves are still inarticulate about their past experiences, and next to nothing of critical value on the Third Reich has been published by them.

(1) The following books deal with the intellectual background and the spiritual ingredients of the National Socialist "world outlook."

(a) *Among the Nazi sources the most important are:*

Joseph Göbbels, *My Part in Germany's Fight,* London, 1935.

Hermann Göring, *Germany Reborn,* London, 1934.

Alfred Rosenberg, *Der Mythus des XX. Jahrhunderts,* 4th edition, Munich, 1932.

A. Möller van der Bruck, *Das Dritte Reich,* Berlin, 1923 (English translation, New York, 1934).

H. St. Chamberlain, *Die Grundlagen des 19. Jahrhunderts,* Munich, 1899 (many later editions).

(b) *By opponents of the Nazi regime (written prior to the collapse)*:

H. Rauschning, *The Revolution of Nihilism,* New York, 1939.
H. Rauschning, *The Voice of Destruction,* New York, 1940.
A. Kolnai, *The War Against the West,* New York, 1938.
Edmond Vermeil, *Doctrinaires de la révolution Allemande,* Paris, 1938.
R. D. Butler, *The Roots of National Socialism,* New York, 1942.
W. M. McGovern, *From Luther to Hitler,* Boston, 1941.
Peter Viereck, *Metapolitics,* New York, 1941.
Sigmund Neumann, *Permanent Revolution,* New York, 1942.

(2) The following biographies of Hitler and histories of the Nazi movement by anti-Nazis seem somewhat pale in retrospect:

K. Heiden, *A History of National Socialism,* London, 1931.
K. Heiden, *Adolf Hitler,* 2 volumes, Zürich, 1936–37 (in German).
R. Olden, *Hitler,* London, 1936.

(3) For the period of transition from Weimar to Hitler:

R. T. Clark, *The Fall of the German Republic,* London, 1935.
E. A. Mowrer, *Germany Puts the Clock Back,* new edition, New York, 1939.
C. B. Hoover, *Germany Enters the Third Reich,* New York, 1933.
Douglas Reed, *The Burning of the Reichstag,* New York, 1934.

(4) Of the literature on the constitutional jurisprudence of the Third Reich by Nazi dogmatists (expressing the official "doctrine" of National Socialism), only the following are considered leading works:

E. R. Huber, *Verfassung,* Hamburg, 1937.
Th. Maunz, *Verwaltung,* Hamburg, 1937.
O. Köllreutter, *Deutsches Verfassungsrecht,* 3rd edition, Berlin, 1938.
O. Köllreutter, *Deutsches Verwaltungsrecht,* 2nd edition, Berlin, 1937.
O. Meissner & G. Kaisenberg, *Staats- und Verwaltungsrecht im dritten Reich,* Berlin, 1935.

(5) On National Socialist law and legal institutions, as seen by foreigners:

Ernst Fraenkel, *The Dual State,* New York, 1941.
R. Bonnard, *Le droit et l'état dans la doctrine National Socialiste,* Paris, 1936.
H. Mankiewicz, *Le National Socialisme Allemand, ses doctrines et leurs réalisations,* Paris, 1937.
K. Loewenstein, "Dictatorship and the German Constitution" (1933–1937), *University of Chicago Law Review,* vol. 4 (1937), pp. 537 ff.
Raphael Lemkin, *Axis Rule in Occupied Europe,* Washington, 1944.

(6) Descriptions of Nazi Germany, its institutions and intellectual environment, by foreign observers are legion:

Stephen H. Roberts, *The House That Hitler Built,* New York, 1937.
H. Lichtenberger, *The Third Reich,* New York, 1937.
F. L. Schuman, *The Nazi Dictatorship,* 2nd edition, New York, 1936.
J. K. Pollock, *The Government of Greater Germany,* New York, 1938.
F. A. Ogg, *European Governments and Politics,* 2nd edition, New York, 1939, pp. 605–800.

By formerly German authors of anti-Nazi attitude:

F. M. Marx, *Government in the Third Reich,* 2nd edition, New York, 1937.
Albert C. Grzesinski, *Inside Germany,* New York, 1939.
Karl Loewenstein, *Hitler's Germany,* New York, 1939 (revised edition, 1940).
Franz L. Neumann, *Behemoth: The Structure and Practice of National Socialism,* New York, 1942.

(7) On National Socialist economics:

M. Ascoli & A. Feiler, *Fascism for Whom?* New York, 1938.
V. Trivanovitch, *Economic Developments of Germany under National Socialism,* New York, 1937.
G. Reimann, *The Vampire Economy,* New York, 1939.
W. F. Bruck, *Social and Economic History of Germany from Wilhelm II to Hitler,* New York, 1938.
C. W. Guillebaud, *Economic History of Germany, 1933–1938,* London, 1939.
Otto Nathan & Milton Fried, *The Nazi Economic System: Germany's Mobilization for War,* Durham, 1943.
Frieda Wunderlich, *German Labor Courts,* Chapel Hill, 1948.
L. Hamburger, *How Nazi Germany Controlled Business,* Washington, 1943.
Douglas Miller, *You Can't Do Business with Hitler,* Boston, 1941.
The Fate of Small Business in Nazi Germany, 78th Congress, Senate Committee Print No. 14, Washington, 1943.
Frank Munk, *The Legacy of Nazism,* New York, 1943.
Herbert Rosinski, *German Industrial Mobilization,* New York, 1946.

(8) Among numerous eye-witness reports these deserve mention:

Andre François-Poncet, *The Fateful Years 1931–1939,* New York, 1949.
William Edward Dodd, *Ambassador Dodd's Diaries 1933–1938,* New York, 1941.
William Lawrence Shirer, *Berlin Diary,* New York, 1941.
Howard K. Smith, *Last Train from Berlin,* New York, 1942.

The Nazi "elite" among themselves describe pungently:
Ernest A. Pope, *Munich Playground,* New York, 1941.
Bella Fromm, *Blood and Banquets,* New York, 1943.

(9) On Nazi terror and persecution and the political police:

Balticus, "The Two G's: Gestapo and GPU," *Foreign Affairs,* vol. 17 (1939), pp. 489 ff.
Eva Lips, *Savage Symphony,* New York, 1938.
G. Segar, *A Nation Terrorized,* Chicago, 1935.
K. Billinger, *Fatherland,* New York, 1935.
W. Langhoff, *Die Moorsoldaten,* Zürich, 1933.
Eugen Kogon, *Der SS Staat, Frankfurt,* 1946 (in English under the title, *The Theory and Practice of Hell,* New York, 1950).
S. Payne Best, *The Venlo Incident,* London, 1950.

(10) On the Jewish problem:

M. Lowenthal, *The Jews in Germany,* New York, 1936.
J. G. McDonald, *Letter of Resignation and Petition,* addressed to the XVIIth Plenary Assembly of the League of Nations.
Nazi Germany's War Against the Jews, American Jewish Congress, New York, 1947.
G. Jacoby, *The Racial State,* New York, 1945.

(11) On education, religion, and the cultural situation under National Socialism:

A. S. Duncan-Jones, *The Struggle for Religious Freedom in Germany,* London, 1938.
A. Frey, *Cross and Swastika,* New York, 1938.
J. Neuhäusler, *Kreuz und Hakenkreuz,* 2 volumes, Munich, 1946.
N. Micklem, *National Socialism and the Roman Catholic Church,* New York, 1939.
H. L. Childs, *The Nazi Primer,* New York, 1938.
B. von Schirach, *Die Hitler-Jugend, Idee und Gestalt,* Berlin, 1934.
E. Y. Hartshorne, *The German Universities under National Socialism,* Cambridge, Mass., 1937.

H. Bigot, *La chambre de culture Allemande dans le régime totalitaire du IIIe Reich*, Paris, 1937.
Max Weinreich, *Hitler's Professors*, New York, 1946.
Howard Becker, *German Youth, Bound or Free?* New York, 1946.
Frederic Lilge, *The Abuse of Learning*, New York, 1948.

(12) On special subjects dealing mostly with governmental institutions:

A. J. Zurcher, "The Hitler Referenda," *American Political Science Review*, vol. 29 (1935), pp. 91 ff.
J. K. Pollock & A. V. Boerner, *The German Civil Service Act*, Chicago, 1938.
R. H. Wells, "The Liquidation of the German Länder," *American Political Science Review*, vol. 30 (1936), pp. 350 ff.
A. V. Boerner, "The Position of the NSDAP in the German Constitutional Order," *American Political Science Review*, vol. 32 (1938), pp. 1059 ff.
H. Rosinski, *The German Army*, New York, 1940.
John H. Herz, "German Administration under the Nazi Regime," *American Political Science Review*, vol. 40 (1946), pp. 682 ff.

(13) On the 20th of July, 1944, conspiracy:

Allen W. Dulles, *Germany's Underground*, New York, 1947.
Hans Rothfels, *The German Opposition to Hitler*, Hinsdale, Ill., 1948.
Hans Bernd Gisevius, *To the Bitter End*, Boston, 1947.
Ulrich Von Hassell, *The Von Hassell Diaries 1938–1944*, Garden City, 1947.
Rudolf Pechel, *Deutscher Widerstand*, Zürich, 1947.
Wolfgang H. Kraus & Gabriel A. Almond in: Gabriel A. Almond (and associates), *The Struggle for Democracy in Germany*, Chapel Hill, 1949, pp. 33 ff, 64 ff.

(14) On Hitler's influence on the conduct of the war:

Franz Halder, *Hitler as War Lord*, London, 1950.
B. H. Liddell Hart, *The German Generals Talk*, New York, 1948.
Hans Speidel, *Invasion 1944*, Chicago, 1950.
Milton Schulman, *Defeat in the West*, New York, 1948.
Felix Gilbert, *Hitler Directs the War*, New York, 1950.

(15) On Hitler's and the Third Reich's end:

H. R. Trevor-Roper, *The Last Days of Hitler*, New York, 1947.
Gerhardt Boldt, *Die letzten Tage der Reichskanzlei*, Hamburg-Stuttgart, 1947.

(16) For German descriptions of the situation of the Third Reich see also:

Erich Kordt, *Wahn und Wirklichkeit*, Stuttgart, 1949.
Friedrich Meinecke, *The German Catastrophe*, New York, 1950.

In a more metaphysical vein, visualizing the German disaster in the context of European disintegration:

Alfred Weber, *Abschied von der bisherigen Geschichte*, Heidelberg, 1946.
Karl Jaspers, *Die Schuldfrage, Heidelberg, 1946* (English edition: *The Question of German Guilt*, New York, 1947).

(17) Frequently more illuminating on daily life under Nazi rule than books devoted to the description of political institutions are the reports of visiting newspapermen and non-professional observers, some of them in novelistic form:

Nora Waln, *Reaching for the Stars*, Boston, 1939.
Margaret Kent, *I Married a German*, New York, 1938.
G. E. R. Gedye, *Betrayal in Central Europe*, New York, 1939.
Ch. W. Domville-Fife, *This Is Germany*, London, 1939.
Martha Dodd, *Through Embassy Eyes*, New York, 1939.

(18) English translations of some important pieces of National Socialist legislation are found in:

J. K. Pollock and J. H. Heneman, *The Hitler Decrees,* 2nd edition, Ann Arbor, 1934.

W. E. Rappard (and others), *Source Book on European Governments,* New York, 1937.

N. J. Hill and H. W. Stoke, *The Background of European Governments,* new edition, New York, 1939, pp. 373–468.

W. C. Langsam, *Documents and Readings in the History of Europe since 1918,* New York, 1939, pp. 646–738.

National Socialism, Department of State Publication 1864, Washington, 1943.

7. *Germany since 1945*

(1) Official publications:

There is hardly any other segment of recent political history that has been accompanied by as much official reporting, information, and analysis as American Military Government in Germany. The (at first monthly, later quarterly) Reports of the Military Governor, together with the Reports of the various Divisions of AMG (for example, Civil Administration, Law, Education, Economics) constitute the most comprehensive self-portrayal of MG activities in every imaginable field. But the factual value of this material exceeds its interpretative qualities. Understandably, successes in reconstruction were more stressed than failures, and, in a military hierarchy, critical attitudes of the lower echelons were discouraged when their findings were digested in the final Reports at the highest level. Nonetheless, for the study of any specific aspect of the occupation these sources are indispensable.

Since the establishment of the High Commission the Office of the United States High Commissioner issues (less detailed) survey reports every quarter (beginning September 21, 1949) with excellent statistical material.

Most of the essential documents are found in Department of State Publication 2783, European Series 23 (published August, 1947) and Publication 3556, European and British Commonwealth Series 9 (released March, 1950). See also the Chronological Tables on Germany, 1947–1949, prepared by the Civil Administration Division of OMGUS.

The texts (in both German and English) of the German *Laender* constitutions (excluding those of the British zone) are conveniently collected in an issue published by the Civil Administration Division in 1947. The official (though in places debatable) translation of the *Basic Law of the Federal Republic of Germany* is found in Publication 3556, pp. 283 ff.

(a) *Legislative material:*

For the *Control Council:* Official Gazette of the Control Council (in three languages [Nos. 1–18]); for *AMG:* Military Government Gazette *Germany,* United States Area of Control (the issues are lettered A–O); for *HICOG:* Official Gazette of the Allied High Commission for Germany (in three languages); the Gazette contains also the legislative material currently enacted for an individual zone of occupation only.

(b) *German legislation:*

For *federal legislation* of Western Germany consult the *Bundesgesetzblatt;* for *Eastern Germany,* the corresponding *Gesetzblatt.* For the *combined economic area: Gesetz- und Verordnungsblatt der Verwaltung des Vereinigten Wirtschaftsgebiets* (Nos. 1–32, August 21, 1947 to August 30, 1949). In addition, each *Land* has its individual Law Bulletin or Gazette.

For selected pieces of documentary material see also J. K. Pollock, J. H. Meisel, and H. L. Bretton, *Germany under Occupation,* Ann Arbor, rev. edition, 1949.

Excellent materials on all aspects of German reconstruction are found in the (unofficial) *Deutschland-Jahrbuch 1949,* edited by Klaus Mehnert and Heinrich Schulte, Essen, 1949.

(2) General books concerning Germany after the collapse:

Henry J. Morgenthau, Jr., *Germany Is Our Problem*, New York, 1945. The study of the original will rectify to some extent the subsequent distortion of the famous "Morgenthau Plan."

Louis Nizer, *What To Do With Germany*, New York, 1944.

Richard N. Bricker, *Is Germany Incurable?* New York, 1943. Of significance for the medical and psychiatric interpretation.

Ferdinand A. Hermens, *The Tyrant's War and the People's Peace*, Chicago, 1944. The thesis of the "good German people" and their "wicked rulers."

Arnold Brecht, *Federalism and Regionalism in Germany*, New York, 1945. A balanced, competent appraisal of the federalist forces and requirements of German reorganization.

Robert E. Dickinson, *The Regions of Germany*, London, 1945. Valuable analysis of geographical conditions.

Friedrich W. Foerster, *Europe and the German Question*, New York, 1940. A pessimistic forecast of an implacable anti-Nazi who is a good European.

James Stern, *The Hidden Damage*, New York, 1947. Perhaps the most stirring eyewitness report on what moral injury the Nazi regime has inflicted on the German character.

James P. Warburg, *Germany, Bridge or Battleground?* New York, 1947. Analyzes objectively the position of Germany between the East and the West.

Pro-German discussions:

Gustov Stolper, *German Realities*, New York, 1948.

Karl Brandt, *Germany, Key to Peace*, Clarement, 1949.

(3) Comprehensive reviews of American and Allied policies after 1945:

Lucius D. Clay, *Decision in Germany*, Garden City, 1950. The story of the official policy on Germany and its execution authoritatively told by the former Military Governor. A leading book written by a leader, amply documented, but in places understandably more an apologia than an objective report and not without factual inaccuracies.

Gabriel Almond (and Associates), *The Struggle for Democracy in Germany*, Chapel Hill, 1949. A symposium of monographs with valuable bibliographical notes. Eugene N. Anderson's chapter, "Freedom and Authoritarianism in German History," is among the best discussions of this subject.

The Annals of the American Academy of Political and Social Science, *Postwar Reconstruction in Western Germany* (November, 1948), containing informative articles by German experts; *Military Government* (January, 1950), with contributions by persons familiar with occupation activities.

Of the numerous reports by experienced newspapermen covering the German scene the following are among the most brilliant and critical:

Delbert Clark, *Again the Goosestep*, New York, 1949.

Drew Middleton, *The Struggle for Germany*, New York, 1949.

Russell Hill, *The Struggle for Germany*, New York, 1949.

Arthur Settel (editor), *This Is Germany*, New York, 1950.

(4) On Military Government:

The following list includes also books which, beyond dealing with MG organization proper, evaluate MG's activities.

Hajo Holborn, *American Military Government; its Origins and Policies*, Washington, 1947. Primarily the diplomatic and intergovernmental history.

Harold Zink, *American Military Government in Germany*, New York, 1947. Valuable for the early stages of MG developments, but overemphasizing its technical aspects.

Carl J. Friedrich (and Associates), *American Experiences in Military Government in World War II,* New York, 1948.

W. Friedmann, *The Allied Military Government of Germany,* London, 1947. Deals primarily with British organization and experience.

Richard W. van Wagenen, "Cooperation and Controversy among the Occupying Powers in Berlin," *Journal of Politics,* vol. 10 (1948), pp. 73 ff. By a former American member of the Allied Secretariat.

The specialist in American Military Government courts is Eli N. Nobleman. For some of his evaluations see *Federal Bar Journal,* vol. 8 (1946), pp. 70 ff; *ibid.,* vol. 9 (1947), pp. 212 ff.

(5) Individual aspects of the occupation policies:

(a) *The Nuremberg Trials:*

Victor H. Bernstein, *Final Judgment,* New York, 1947.

Robert M. Jackson, *The Nuremberg Trial,* New York, 1947. The author was Chief Prosecutor and one of the intellectual promotors of the new international law created by the trials.

Telford Taylor, *Nuremberg Trials, War Crimes and International Law,* New York, 1949.

G. M. Gilbert, *Nuremberg Diary,* New York, 1947. A psychiatrist's observations on the behavior of the indicted.

Quincy Wright, "The Law of the Nuremberg Trial," *American Journal of International Law,* vol. 41 (1947), pp. 38 ff.

Franz B. Schick, *The Nuremberg Trial and the International Law of the Future, ibid.,* pp. 770 ff.

Sheldon Glueck, *The Nuremberg Trials and Aggressive War,* New York, 1946. Probably the most balanced discussion of a most controversial subject.

Hans Ehard, "The Nuremberg Trial against the Major War Criminals and International Law," *American Journal of International Law,* vol. 43 (1949), pp. 223 ff. The German viewpoint, presented by the Minister President of Bavaria.

Carl Haensel, *Das Gericht vertagt sich,* Hamburg, 1950. By one of the German counsels for the defendants.

Montgomery Belgion, *Victors' Justice,* New York, 1949. Violently anti-American and pro-German attack against Nuremberg's principles and proceedings.

(b) *On expellees:*

The issue, to all intents and purposes the most crucial of German internal developments, is unduly neglected in American literature.

Millionen ohne Heimat, published Frankfurt, 1950, by the *Institut zur Förderung öffentlicher Angelegenheiten* (with an extensive bibliography by Werner Möhring).

(c) *On denazification:*

Though the most discussed reconstruction issue, denazification still awaits a comprehensive and fully documented study. About the best discussion available is:

John H. Herz, "The Fiasco of Denazification in Germany," *Political Science Quarterly,* vol. 63 (1948), pp. 569 ff.

Elmer Plischke, "Denazification Law and Procedure," *American Journal of International Law,* vol. 41 (1947), pp. 807 ff.

(d) *On legal reconstruction:*

Karl Loewenstein, "Reconstruction of the Administration of Justice in American-Occupied Germany, *Harvard Law Review,* vol. 61 (1948), pp. 419 ff.

Karl Loewenstein, "Law and the Legislative Process in Occupied Germany," *Yale Law Journal,* vol. 57 (1948), pp. 724 ff; 994 ff.

Walter Hallstein, *Die Wiederherstellung des Privatrechts,* Tübingen, 1946.

(e) *On economic policies of the occupation:*

B. U. Ratchford and W. D. Ross, *Berlin Reparations Assignment,* Chapel Hill, 1947. The sad story of the fate of the level-of-industry agreement in the Control Council, told by two American officials participating in the negotiations.

Howard Watson Armbruster, *Treason's Peace,* New York, 1947. How American Military Government, divided against itself, failed to break the power of the I. G. Farben trust.

K. Koranyi, *The Ruhr Area,* Washington, 1949.

James Stewart Martin, *All Honorable Men,* Boston, 1950. The former Chief of the Decartelization Branch of OMGUS reveals the nullification of the Allied decartelization policy by an alliance of American and German big business interests with whom General Clay sided.

Freda Utley, *The High Cost of Vengeance,* New York, 1949. A violent indictment of the Allied dismantling policy.

(f) *On education and cultural affairs:*

M. M. Knappen, *And Call It Peace,* Chicago, 1947. Aspirations and failures of AMG policies in education and religious affairs, by a former official of OMGUS.

Helen Liddell, *Education in Occupied Germany,* New York, 1949.

Thomas Carr Howe, *Salt Mines and Castles,* Indianapolis, 1946. The successful recovery of the art treasures absconded by the Nazis.

(6) German Government and constitutions:

There is as yet no major critical study of the evolution of constitutional government in Germany since 1945.

(a) *On the Laenderrat:*

Heinz Guradze, "The Länderrat, Landmark in German Reconstruction," *Western Political Quarterly,* vol. 3 (1950), pp. 190 ff. The entire legislation of the *Laenderrat* was published (Ruth Picht-Hempken, editor) under the title: *Sammlung der Länderratsgesetze,* Düsseldorf, 1950.

(b) *On the German Land constitutions:*

Harold O. Lewis, *New Constitutions in Occupied Germany,* Washington, 1948 (dealing also with those in the Soviet zone).

Early developments are summarized by Karl Loewenstein, "Political Reconstruction in Germany, Zonal and Interzonal," in: James K. Pollock, *Change and Crisis in European Government,* New York, 1947, pp. 29 ff; and James K. Pollock, *Germany under Military Occupation, ibid.,* pp. 45 ff.

Robert G. Neumann, "New Constitutions in Germany," *American Political Science Review,* vol. 42 (1948), pp. 448 ff and William Fleming, "German Post-War Constitutions," *Current History,* vol. 14 (1948), pp. 219 ff and 289 ff are little more than summarizations.

Claude-Albert Colliard, "L'Organisation des Pouvoirs Publics dans les Constitutions des 'Pays Allemands,'" *Revue du Droit Public,* vol. 64 (1948), pp. 452 ff (a first-rate functional study).

(c) *On the Bonn Constitution:*

Arnold Brecht, "The New German Constitution," *Social Research,* vol. 16 (1949), pp. 425 ff. A thoroughly informed, solid, and critical analysis.

Carl J. Friedrich, "Rebuilding the German Constitution," *American Political Science Review,* vol. 63 (1949), pp. 461 ff, 704 ff. Superficial and opinionated.

Ferdinand A. Hermens, *Mehrheits-oder Verhältniswahlrecht?* Berlin-Munich, 1949.

(d) *The elaborate treatises and commentaries on the constitutions in which German jurisprudence excelled under the Empire and Weimar, are slow in coming. There are some on individual Land constitutions. For the Bonn Constitution see:*

Hermann von Mangoldt, *Das Bonner Grundgesetz,* Berlin-Frankfort, 1950 (in process of publication).

Friedrich Giese, *Grundgesetz für die Bundesrepublik Deutschland,* Frankfurt, 1949.

Hans Naviasky, *Die Grundgedanken des Grundgesetzes für die Bundesrepublik Deutschland,* Stuttgart and Köln, 1950; a strictly legalistic discussion, without interest in the functional approach.

Werner Weber, *Weimarer Verfassung und Bonner Grundgesetz,* Göttingen, 1949.

(7) On the Soviet zone:

Reliable information is hardly available. The best seems:

Franz L. Neumann, "German Democracy 1950," *International Conciliation,* no. 461 (May, 1950).

Gordon Schaffer, *Russian Zone of Germany,* New York, 1948, finds as much to praise as Werner Knop, *Prowling in the Forbidden Zone,* New York, 1949, is unable to find anything good.

Alfons Steiniger, *Das Block-System,* Berlin, 1949. A clever defense of the technique to achieve parliamentary "unanimity."

The Government and Politics of the

USSR

by MICHAEL T. FLORINSKY

CHAPTER I

IMPERIAL RUSSIA [1]

HISTORICAL BACKGROUND OF ABSOLUTISM

Beginning of the Russian State. The early history of the Russian State contains many elements of uncertainty. The Grand Duchy of Kiev, the cradle of the future empire, made its appearance on the Dnieper in the second half of the ninth century and up to the middle of the twelfth exercised a vague quasi-patriarchal jurisdiction over a number of principalities and city-states scattered along the rivers of the Russian plain. In the second quarter of the thirteenth century Russia was conquered by the Mongols, who moved irresistibly westward from the uplands of Central Asia. The "Tartar yoke," as this period is traditionally known in Russian history, lasted for over two centuries. Although the effective control of the Mongol khans over their Russian domain was practically suspended by the middle of the fifteenth century and was actually terminated somewhat earlier than 1480, that year is usually given as the date of Russia's liberation from foreign rule. It was chiefly because of the disintegration of the Mongol Empire that Russia was finally able to regain her status as an independent state.

Unification under Moscow. From the early part of the fourteenth century the Grand Dukes of Moscow became the central figures in the painful and tortuous process of the unification of the country, which was divided into a number of small quasi-independent principalities. They leaned heavily on the assistance of the Mongol rulers whose favors they courted; they also found powerful support for their dynastic ambitions in the landed aristocracy, the *boyars,* and in the Church, which had accumulated immense landholdings. The landowners were the first to suffer from internal strife among the princes, and naturally gravitated toward the new political center, Moscow. The emergence of the Muscovite absolutism may be traced to the last years of the rule of Vasili II of Moscow (1425–1462) who, after a protracted and bloody

[1] The dates in Chapters I and II are given according to the old Russian calendar which in the twentieth century is thirteen days behind the Western calendar. In subsequent chapters the Western calendar has been used.

struggle with other princes, succeeded in establishing Moscow's political supremacy.

Influence of the Church. The creation of a national Russian State was favored by the *de facto* emancipation of the Russian Church from its dependence on Byzantium. Christianity came to Russia from Constantinople at the end of the tenth century. Until the middle of the fifteenth century Russia was considered as a metropolitanate, ruled in ecclesiastical matters by the Patriarch of Constantinople, who consecrated the Russian metropolitan. The breach between the Russian and the Byzantine Churches occurred after the Ferrara-Florence Council (1438–1439) when the Greek Church accepted the union with Rome. Moscow refused to bow to this decision and, although the Greek Church eventually repudiated the union, the Russian metropolitans from 1448 on, while nominally elected and consecrated by a council of Russian bishops, were actually appointed by the Moscow Grand Dukes and later by the Tsars. With the establishment of the Russian Patriarchate in 1589 the Russian Church became officially autocephalous. While Mongol influences also contributed to the growth of autocracy, Byzantine tradition had an important part in framing Muscovite absolutism, for the Church invariably fought for the preservation of the unity of the Russian metropolitanate and proclaimed the divine origin of the secular power.

Muscovite Absolutism. In the second half of the fifteenth century Muscovite absolutism had definitely come into existence. Political authority over a unified country was concentrated in the hands of the Moscow Grand Dukes who ruthlessly exterminated whatever independence the landed nobility had enjoyed in the past. The Mongol rule was gone. The Russian Church, for all practical purposes independent of Constantinople (which fell under the Turkish domination in 1453), became an obedient tool of the occupants of the Moscow throne. In 1547 Ivan IV the Dread officially assumed the title of Tsar, a title loosely used by his predecessors. The revolutionary era, beginning early in the seventeenth century and known as the Time of Troubles, failed to produce any important change in the political structure of the Russian State, and the founder of the Romanov dynasty, Tsar Michael, who came to the throne in 1613, was clothed with all the traditional powers of autocracy. But at the beginning of the eighteenth century came the reforms of Peter the Great, reforms that were from many points of view a definite breach with the past. However, while they introduced a number of institutions that survived until the Revolution of 1917, they did nothing to detract from the authority of the Crown whose prestige was further enhanced by Peter's assumption of the more resounding title of Emperor (1721). Nor were any important modifications in the structure of the central Government introduced by Peter's successors in the eighteenth century. The complexity of the administration was growing with the rapid expansion of the national territory and the continuous appearance of new problems demanding solution, problems that were dealt with according to the light of St. Petersburg chanceries, which usually meant very badly indeed. The unflattering description of the Russian Government as a despotism tempered by anarchy, that is, by inefficiency and lack of co-ordination between the various organs of administration, was a fairly accurate statement of the conditions prevailing at the beginning of the nineteenth century.

THE REFORMS OF SPERANSKY AND OF ALEXANDER II

Alexander I. Emperor Alexander I (1801–1825) had little admiration for the Russian form of government which he regarded as despotism; he was continually scheming for the introduction of a constitutional monarchy, to him the only "true monarchy." Of the several projects of constitutional reform prepared during his reign, however, only one had any influence upon the organization of the Russian Government. M. M. Speransky, who enjoyed the confidence of the Emperor, was entrusted in 1808 with the task of drafting a comprehensive plan of reorganization. The ablest statesman Russia ever had, Speransky produced in 1809 a detailed report which is considered by the Russian constitutional lawyers to be one of the outstanding documents of its kind. The plan of Speransky, based on the strict separation of powers—legislative, judicial, and executive—provided for a remarkably logical structure of institutions to be freely chosen by the population, although Speransky did not contemplate the emancipation of the serfs, who were therefore to remain unenfranchised. The Emperor stood at the head of the entire governmental structure and was to be assisted by an advisory body, the State Council, which was to consider every measure, whether legislative, judicial, or administrative, before it was submitted to the head of the Government. The executive branch of the Government was to be reorganized by putting each ministry under a minister responsible for the work of his department; by delimiting carefully the functions of each ministry; and by removing excessive centralization within the departments themselves, thus relieving the ministers of a mass of routine work so that they might devote their time to the more important problems.

The State Council and the Ministries. The new State Council actually came into existence on January 1, 1810, and the ministries established in 1802 were reorganized on June 1, 1811. The major part of the contemplated reform, however, was abandoned. The resumption of the war against Napoleon and Speransky's sudden disgrace in March, 1812, brought the process of reorganization to an abrupt end. Modest as were the changes accomplished, they were not without effect upon the constitutional machinery of Russia. The Manifesto of January 1, 1810, became the source of Article 47 [2] of the Fundamental Laws which proclaimed that "the Russian Empire is governed on the firm foundation of the laws . . . emanating from the Autocratic Power (the Crown)." This article was construed to mean that every bill was to be submitted to the deliberation of the State Council and that once enacted into law it was to be binding on the monarch so long as it was not repealed. Nothing, however, prevented the Emperor from changing the laws. He nominated the members of the State Council and was under no obligation to follow the

[2] Article 84 in the revised edition of 1906; reference to autocratic power was dropped.

advice tendered by the assembly. Therefore no effective limitation of autocracy was imposed by the constitutional changes of 1810. The reorganization of the ministries was of greater practical importance. It brought into existence that modernized Russian bureaucracy which very largely and not entirely without success governed the Empire in the name of the Tsar until the regime was engulfed in the Revolution of 1917.

Nicholas I. The reign of Nicholas I (1825–1855), which opened with the ruthless suppression of the well-intentioned but poorly organized and badly executed revolutionary uprising of a group of aristocrats and liberals known as the Decembrists, was a period of extreme reaction, a regime sternly administered by the unimaginative methods of the drill sergeant. Yet it was not entirely barren of results from the point of view of the organization of government. Speransky returned to active political life and undertook the gigantic task of codifying the Russian laws, which had never been brought together since the publication of the Code (*Ulozhenie*) of 1649, a collection that was inadequate even at the time it was issued. Speransky's difficult enterprise was completed in 1833 with the publication of (1) the "Full Collection of the Laws of the Russian Empire" which contained all the legislative enactments from those embodied in the Code of 1649 to those issued in the reign of Alexander I, and (2) "The Code (*Svod*) of Laws of the Russian Empire," a systematic collection in fifteen volumes of the laws still in operation. Arrangements were also made for the later amendment and revision of these collections. For the first time in the history of the country it became possible to ascertain what actually were the laws governing the Empire.

Reforms of Alexander II. During the long rule of Nicholas I there was growing recognition of the fact that far-reaching reforms could not be indefinitely postponed, and the necessity of a change was admitted by the Emperor himself. Reform was not undertaken, however, until the reign of his successor, Alexander II (1855–1881), and was then at least in part due to the rude shock of Russia's crushing defeat in the Crimean War. The so-called Great Reforms of Alexander II, "The Tsar Liberator," comprised the emancipation of the peasants (February 19, 1861), the reorganization of the *zemstvo* or institutions of local government (1864), the modernization of the judiciary (1864), the revision of the structure of municipal government (1870), the introduction of conscription to be borne equally by all social groups (1874) and to include the nobility, who since the eighteenth century had been exempted from compulsory military service. Measures were also taken for the unification of the budget, which for the first time was made public (1862). The universities, all of them State institutions, received a considerable degree of autonomy in their inner organization (1863). Although these reforms were of paramount importance and opened to Russia the road toward progress and development on which the other European nations had preceded her, they did nothing to limit the autocratic powers of the Crown. The persistent demands of the various social groups, especially of the nobility, who were more likely to gain a hearing, for the creation of an elective representative assembly were invariably rejected. It became clear that the Great Reforms had stopped short of the establishment of a constitutional monarchy. The wide-spread feeling of disappointment and discontent stimulated the activities of the underground revolutionary organizations and a number of terroristic attempts culminated on March 1, 1881, in the murder of Alexander II.

The Loris-Melikov "Constitution." His successor, Alexander III (1881–1894), had little liking for constitutional reforms. On the morning of the fatal day of March 1, Alexander II had approved the project of Count M. T. Loris-Melikov for the creation of a purely advisory committee consisting of members nominated by the Crown and those elected by the institutions of local government. The committee was to examine the bills which were then to be submitted to the State Council. The committee's decisions, however, were to be binding on neither the State Council nor the Emperor. For reasons that it is difficult to comprehend this modest "concession" to public opinion is often referred to as the "Loris-Melikov Constitution." It was shelved after Alexander II's murder and Alexander III proclaimed on his accession to the throne his unreserved devotion to the immovable principles of autocracy. To them he remained faithful throughout his reign.

THE CONSTITUTIONAL CHANGES OF 1905 AND 1906

Nicholas II. Nicholas II (1894–1917), the son of Alexander III, fully shared his father's aversion to a constitutional monarchy. The hopes for reform which were revived after the death of Alexander III were immediately shattered by Nicholas' contemptuous reference to them as "senseless dreams." Under him the regime of political reaction was, if possible, further intensified. Police measures multiplied and increased in severity, stimulating the activities of the revolutionary organizations and the discontent of the liberal groups. In 1904–1905 Russia was defeated in the Russo-Japanese War and the revolutionary movement made rapid progress, reaching its zenith in the autumn of 1905. The country was in a state of turmoil. The peasants burned down the manor houses and plundered large estates. The army in Manchuria displayed a rebellious spirit. The strike movement was rapidly spreading among the industrial workers. The liberal groups were clamoring for constitutional reforms. The Emperor attempted to weather the storm by announcing on August 6, 1905, the impending election of a newly-created assembly, the State Duma, which, however, was to function in a purely advisory capacity. This gesture failed to produce the desired effect. Revolutionary disturbances continued to grow in volume. A general strike took place in October and Soviets or Councils of Workers' Deputies sprang up in the capital and in other cities. Further concessions from the Government were imperative.

Manifesto of October 17, 1905. The Imperial Manifesto of October 17, 1905, granted to the population the fundamental civil liberties—freedom from arbitrary arrest, freedom of opinion, of the press, of assembly, and of organization. The Manifesto also promised the extension of the franchise for the election to the State Duma and announced the "immutable rule that no law shall become effective without the approval of the State Duma and that the elected representatives of the people shall be given the opportunity to participate effectively in the control over the activities of the officers appointed by Us (the Crown) to insure the conformity of such activities with the law." The promised extension of the franchise was enacted on December 11, 1905. In the meantime the revolutionary movement had subsided somewhat and the Government, headed by Count S. J. Witte, retreated from its previous position. The Manifesto of February 20, 1906, revised the charter of the State Council "to bring it in line with the principles announced in the Manifesto of October 17, 1905." In fact, however, it violated if not the letter at least the spirit of the October Manifesto by laying down the rule that legislative bills must be approved not only by the Duma but also by the State Council. The old Fundamental Laws were revised, amended, and reissued on April 23, 1906. These revised statutes are regarded by some authorities as forming the Russian Constitution, although the term *constitution* was never officially used.

THE MONARCH

The Constitutional Monarchy. While the changes of 1905–1906 imposed definite limitations on the legislative powers of the Crown the Emperor continued to occupy a central position in the constitutional machinery of the State. According to Article 4 of the Fundamental Laws, "To the Emperor of all the Russias belongs the supreme autocratic power. To obey his commands not merely from fear but according to the dictates of one's conscience is ordained by God himself." The term "autocratic power," which appeared not only in Article 4 but also in Article 6, and even more the expression "unlimited Autocrat" in Article 222 gave much trouble to the Russian constitutional lawyers who, however, displayed great ingenuity in attempting to reconcile the irreconcilable: autocracy with constitutional monarchy. The most satisfactory explanation would seem to be that the use of the term "autocratic" and "Autocrat" was due to faulty drafting, of which the Fundamental Laws offer many instances.

The Crown and the Legislature. The participation of the Crown in the legislative process was safeguarded by the provision that "no bill shall acquire the force of a law without the approval of the State Duma and the State Council and the sanction of the Emperor." The latter had the exclusive right to initiate bills affecting the Fundamental Laws. To the Emperor also belonged the right to convoke and prorogue the legislative chambers and to dissolve them, with the sole limitation that they should be convoked every year. The Emperor had the right of legislative veto, a prerogative that Nicholas II used only twice. Half of the members of the upper chamber, the State Council, and its president were appointed by the Emperor.

The Crown and the Executive. The control of the executive branch of government was in the hands of the Emperor. He was empowered to issue decrees dealing with administrative matters, provided that such decrees were not in contravention of the law. He appointed the higher government officials, and the ministers who formed the Government were responsible to him alone. As the titular head of the administrative machine the Emperor held wide powers over the government officials upon whom he conferred distinctions or to whom he meted out punishment. It was the Emperor's exclusive right to proclaim a "state of emergency," when civic guarantees were suspended and the discretionary powers of the administrative officers were greatly increased. A "state of emergency" was the normal regime in the Russia of 1905–1914. The Emperor was also the head of the military forces. The conduct of foreign relations, the declaration of war and the conclusion of peace, the negotiation of treaties and diplomatic relations in general were among his prerogatives. Justice was administered in his name and he enjoyed the right of pardon or revision of sentences. The Emperor was the official head of the Russian Church which was governed through the Holy Synod. The Emperor himself must be a member of the Greek Orthodox Church, of which he was the official protector. The throne passed by inheritance, according to the principle of primogeniture, in the male line of the Romanov family and, in case of its extinction, in the female line.

THE STATE COUNCIL

Structure of the State Council. The State Council was the upper house of the Russian Parliament. Half of its members were elected by certain social groups and institutions and the other half were appointed by the Crown. The law divided the State Council, very "inelegantly" according to one authority, into the "State Council" (a legislative body) and the "Departments and Special Boards of the State Council," a confusing terminology where "State Council" appeared both as the whole and as a part. The "Departments and Special Boards," purely administrative agencies, consisted exclusively of the appointed members of the Council and had nothing to do with its legislative work. The functions of the two component elements of the State Council were entirely different and the law made no provision for the integration of these activities.

Appointed Members of the State Council. The appointed members of the State Council were divided into active members, that is, those participating in the work of the Council, and inactive members who did not take part in the deliberations of that body but merely enjoyed an honorary title. The number of appointed active members was not to exceed that of the elected members (one hundred). The Government adopted the practice, the legality of which has been rightly questioned, of issuing on January 1 of each year a list of active members. This procedure effectively destroyed the permanency of tenure granted to the appointed members by the law which provided that they could not be removed from office except at their own request. The transfer to the inactive list was for all practical purposes equivalent to dismissal, and in the hands of the executive was a powerful weapon for exercising pressure upon the appointed members of the upper chamber. Until the outbreak of the War of 1914 the Crown seldom used its power to transfer members of the

Council from the active to the inactive list. During the War, however, such transfers became numerous. Assuming a distinctly punitive character, they undermined whatever little prestige the State Council might have enjoyed.

Elected Members of the State Council. The elected members of the State Council were chosen separately by each of the following six groups: the clergy (six members), the *zemstvo* or institutions of local government (fifty-six members), the nobility (eighteen members), the Academy of Science and the universities (six members), commerce and industry (twelve members), the Diet of Finland (two members). The election of the representatives from the clergy was largely nominal, the actual selection of the members of the upper chamber being determined either by the local bishops or by the Holy Synod. The representatives from the *zemstvo* were elected directly, all the others indirectly, that is, in two stages. For instance, the universities and the Academy of Science chose delegates who assembled in the capital and elected from among their number six members of the State Council. Particularly high property and other qualifications were required of *zemstvo* members, thus ensuring representation from the well-to-do classes. The members from the *zemstvo* were elected for three years; all the others for a full term of nine years. One-third of the members from each group, however, were replaced every three years, the names of those to be retired being determined by lot. The elected members of the State Council could not be considered as representing the country at large, either from a social or from a geographic standpoint. More than three-quarters of their number belonged to the wealthy landed proprietors of the central provinces, a group that also supplied a large majority of the appointed members of the Council. As a safeguard against progressive, not to mention radical, legislation, the upper chamber of the Russian Parliament left nothing to be desired, but it had no claim to either a democratic or a representative character.

THE STATE DUMA

Franchise and the Law of June 3, 1907. The lower house of the Russian Parliament, the State Duma, which came into existence by virtue of the Manifesto of October 17, 1905, and subsequent legislation, was, unlike the State Council, a purely elective chamber. The relatively broad franchise provided by the Act of December 11, 1905, resulted in the election of an assembly with definitely liberal and even radical tendencies. The First Duma was dissolved after a few stormy weeks (June, 1906). The Second Duma, which met in the spring of 1907, proved to be even less manageable and was dissolved on June 3. On the same date the Government, headed by P. A. Stolypin, promulgated a law that greatly curtailed the franchise and made it possible for the authorities to manipulate the elections so as to achieve their political aims. The Act of June 3, 1907, was a violation of the Fundamental Laws which specifically provided that the election law could not be changed without the sanction of the legislative chambers. The Government, undoubtedly aware of the illegality of the measure it took, could find no better legal argument to justify it than to declare that the Tsar was using his "historic powers" and that he was accountable to God for the fate of the Russian realm. This Act controlled the elections to the Third and Fourth (which proved to be the last) Dumas. It introduced a form of election procedure that has often been described as the most involved and complex in the world. The resulting suffrage was not universal; nor was it direct or equal. Without going into the bewildering details of this ingenious puzzle of election procedure it may be noted that the electorate was divided into four main groups which were to choose separately their representatives to the electoral college that finally elected the deputies. These four groups were the landowners (other than peasants), the urban population, the peasants, and the industrial workers. There were further subdivisions within the groups of landowners and the urban population, and property qualifications played an important part in determining the right to vote. Direct elections, that is, voting for the deputies themselves, were held in only five cities (St. Petersburg, Moscow, Kiev, Odessa, and Riga). Everywhere else elections were indirect and were completed in two, three (industrial workers), or even four (peasants) stages. The three- and four-stage elections were unknown in the law of any other country. The final choice of the deputies was decided at a general meeting of the electors in each province. The law provided that the electoral college must first choose one deputy from each of the groups into which the electorate was subdivided. The election of a deputy from among the industrial workers, however, was mandatory in only six industrial provinces (St. Petersburg, Moscow, Vladmir, Ekaterinoslav, Kostroma, and Kharkov). The rest of the quota of deputies for each province could be selected from among the members of the electoral college, irrespective of their belonging to one or another group. Since the landowning interests as a rule controlled the electoral college, these interests really decided who was to represent the industrial workers and the peasantry in the Duma. Under these conditions radical elements had little chance to send their spokesmen to the lower chamber. The Law of June 3, 1907, moreover, conferred upon the Minister of the Interior wide discretionary powers permitting him to split the electorate into small electoral districts on the basis of residence, property qualifications, or race. Each of these districts chose its own electors. The Government thus enjoyed practically unlimited opportunities for influencing the final outcome of the ballot, a privilege of which it made extensive use in the elections to the Third and Fourth Dumas. One consequence of these manipulations was the truly amazing increase in the number of priests among the deputies in the Third and Fourth Dumas and the noteworthy shift in their political allegiance. For a majority of the Russian clergy were obedient tools in the hands of their ecclesiastical superiors, who themselves were tools of the Government. The First Duma had six priests, of whom four were either liberals or radicals; the Second Duma had thirteen ecclesiastics, including two bishops, of whom eight were liberals or radicals. The Third Duma had forty-five and the Fourth forty-six ecclesiastics none of whom belonged to the radical or liberal parties, while the vast majority sided with either the Right or the extreme Right.

Unrepresentative Character of the Duma. Determination of the number of deputies to be sent to the Duma by the basic electoral districts (the provinces) was arbitrary and capricious, the outlying territories receiving usually a smaller representation. Women were denied the franchise. It has been computed that in the election to the Third Duma (1907) not more than 15 per cent of the population were entitled to vote. The secrecy of the ballot, a familiar feature of democratic elections, was maintained through every stage of the complex and undemocratic electoral procedure.

Preponderance of Conservative Elements. Little can be said in defense of the Russian electoral system except that it achieved the purpose for which it was designed. The Third and the Fourth Dumas were just as conservative and almost as uniformly docile as their two predecessors were recalcitrant. Although there were still a number of liberals and a sprinkling of radicals, including the Bolsheviks, the control of the legislative assembly was in the hands of the conservative parties.

THE POWERS OF THE LEGISLATIVE ASSEMBLIES

Immunity of the Deputies. The powers of the legislative chambers, like the election procedure, were subject to a number of ingenious restrictions. In its internal organization the Duma was autonomous and elected its own officers, while the President of the State Council was appointed by the Crown. The freedom of speech and opinion granted to the deputies by Article 14 of the Statute of the State Duma and by Article 26 of the Statute of the State Council received in practice a restrictive interpretation, which considerably curtailed the traditional immunity enjoyed by the deputies in Western democracies. There are instances on record of members of the Duma being compelled to face legal prosecution for statements made from the rostrum of the legislative chamber. Freedom from arrest, without the consent of the house, another traditional prerogative of the members of parliament, was guaranteed only during the sessions and even this protection was withheld if a deputy was apprehended during the commission of the criminal act or "the day after." The members of both houses, moreover, could be brought before the Supreme Criminal Court to answer for breaches of the law committed by them in connection with the performance of their duties. The consent of the Emperor was required to institute such prosecutions.

Legislative Initiative. Individual members of the legislature did not enjoy the right of legislative initiative. A legislative bill could be introduced (1) by not less than thirty deputies, (2) by the committees of the Duma, and (3) by the Government, while the initiative in the revision of the Fundamental Laws was a prerogative of the Crown. Of the 2,197 bills that became law during the lifetime of the Third Duma—the only one that completed its full term of five years under peacetime conditions—two were initiated by the

State Council and thirty-four by the Duma. Government initiative was thus the normal source of the law.

Budget Powers. The control of the public purse has always been one of the cherished rights of parliament and the most effective method of preventing the abuses of the executive. The powers of the Russian legislative chambers in dealing with the budget were, however, distinctly limited. The Rules of March 8, 1906, which determined the rights of the State Council and the State Duma in budgetary matters, were modeled on the provisions of the Japanese Constitution. According to this legislation the budget was divided into three parts. (1) Appropriations of the Ministry of the Imperial Court, of the two branches of His Majesty's Chancery, and provisions for the maintenance of the Imperial family were exempt from control by the legislature and could not be discussed. (2) A long list of appropriations and revenues based on laws, statutes, and imperial orders were subject to the examination by the legislature in the matter of their legality, but they could not be either increased or reduced. (3) There were certain appropriations that could be both discussed and altered by the chambers. In the draft budget for 1913 the "iron-clad" appropriations (groups one and two) accounted for 1,048 million rubles, while the portion of the budget within the control of the legislative chambers represented 2,158 million rubles. In case the budget was not passed by the beginning of the fiscal year the Government departments continued to receive, by virtue of an order issued by the Council of Ministers, monthly appropriations within the limits of the budget for the previous year. Extraordinary appropriations necessitated by an emergency such as war or preparation for war were granted by an order of the Council of Ministers. The provisions of the Russian law dealing with the budget have been considered by many authorities to be a most flagrant departure from accepted constitutional practice.

Control Over the Executive. The State Council and the State Duma exercised no effective control over the executive, although they enjoyed the right of addressing to the Government questions and interpellations. The ministers, however, could refuse to give the information requested in a question on the ground that this would be inexpedient and contrary to the public interest. If the explanation presented by a member of the Government was deemed unsatisfactory by a two-thirds majority of the house the matter was submitted by the President of the State Council to the Emperor, with whom rested the decision as to whether any action should be taken against the minister who had incurred the displeasure of the chamber. It would be unwise to disregard altogether the effects of criticism voiced in the Duma in connection with the discussion of an interpellation (the State Council almost never made use of this right), for the members of the Government were naturally anxious to avoid an open conflict with the legislative chamber. Nevertheless the ministers were responsible to the Emperor alone and on occasion displayed open contempt for a legislative assembly that could do nothing to remove them from office.

ARTICLE 87

Emergency Legislation. A much-discussed feature of the Russian constitutional setup was Article 87 of the Fundamental Laws:

> During the recess of the State Duma, if exceptional circumstances call for a measure that requires legislative decision, the Council of Ministers shall report on it directly to the Emperor. Such measure, however, shall not introduce any change in the Fundamental Laws, or in the statutes of the State Council or the State Duma, or in the provisions concerning elections to the Council or the Duma. The operation of such a measure shall cease if the respective minister . . . shall not have submitted to the Duma within two months following the resumption of the session of the Duma a legislative bill corresponding to the measure adopted, or if it is rejected by the State Duma or the State Council.

Abuse of Emergency Powers. The provisions of Article 87, which had its counterpart in a number of European constitutions, were clear and were designed to meet an emergency that might occur when the legislature was not in session. Unfortunately it became the practice of the Government to make a wide use of the powers granted to the Crown by Article 87 in disregard of its spirit and intent. A vast mass of legislation was enacted by virtue of Article 87, and although these measures were eventually submitted to the legislative chambers, because of the fact that they had been in operation, sometimes for a protracted period, the Duma was confronted with a *fait accompli* that made the repeal or even revision of such laws extremely difficult. How broad was the interpretation put by the Government on the expression "exceptional circumstances" will appear from one or two examples. Article 87 was invoked to change the title of the chief administrative officer in the Akmolinsk and Semiplatinsk Regions from "military governor" to "governor." It was used again to promulgate the Decree of November 9, 1906, which completely changed the structure of agricultural Russia, a measure of paramount importance that should certainly have been discussed by the legislative bodies. The most flagrant case of abuse of Article 87 occurred in March, 1911, when the State Council rejected a bill providing for institutions of local self-government in the Polish provinces of Russia. The bill, which was anything but radical and was approved by the Duma, was vetoed by the upper chamber on the ground that it did not sufficiently safeguard the interests of the landed nobility. Stolypin, President of the Council of Ministers, prorogued the State Duma and the State Council for three days and promulgated the measure under Article 87. It would have been difficult to display greater disregard for the principle announced in Article 84 of the Fundamental Laws that "the Russian Empire is governed on the firm foundation of the laws."

THE ROLE OF PARLIAMENT

Summary. To sum up, it must be said that the procedure of electing the members of the State Duma (to say nothing of those of the State Council) was highly imperfect, the franchise was restricted, the powers of the two chambers in legislative and budgetary matters were very limited, and their control over the executive practically nil. Nevertheless the constitutional changes of 1905–1906 may be rightly regarded as an important landmark in the political history of the country. They were the first timid step in the direction of a constitutional form of government. Further progress on the same lines might have brought Russia along the path traversed by the Western European nations. The Government of Nicholas II, however, like that of the Muscovite Tsars of the sixteenth and seventeenth centuries, almost invariably looked backward and not forward for inspiration and guidance. The humble beginnings of a democratic regime offered the Russian masses their first opportunity to take some part in the conduct of public affairs, to get their first taste of political education. Crippled by the unconstitutional Election Law of June 3, 1907, and closely supervised by a hostile and contemptuous bureaucracy, the State Duma was fated not to reach the status of a representative popular assembly. Its lack of real roots in the country was convincingly demonstrated during the revolutionary year 1917.

THE COUNCIL OF MINISTERS

Origins of the Council of Ministers. The executive branch of the Government was headed by the Emperor and the actual work of administration was carried on by a huge army of officials under the supervision of central departments usually known as ministries. The heads of the central departments were members of the Council of Ministers, a body that first came into existence sometime between 1857–1861, but ceased to meet after 1882. It was revived on a new basis by the Imperial Decree of October 19, 1905, that is, two days after the Manifesto of October 17 promised Russia a constitutional regime. According to the preamble to the Decree of October 19 the ministers and other heads of central departments were directly subordinated to the Crown; it was through the departments over which they presided that the Crown carried on the administration of the country. The central departments were therefore integral parts of the administrative machinery and they all pursued the same object. The Council of Ministers was created to ensure unity in the policies of the Government and to coordinate the activities of the heads of the various departments. Such coordination, the Decree pointed out, was made imperative by the creation of the State Duma.

The President of the Council of Ministers. The Council of Ministers, as has already been noted, was in no way responsible to the legislature and its inner unity was safeguarded by the authority of its President, who was given important duties as the representative of the Council. The ministers retained their right to report directly to the Emperor, but such reports were first submitted by the President to the deliberation of the Council. The law, however, provided that the foregoing rule applied only to reports of "general interest"—an expression that is at best ambiguous—while reports not deemed of "general interest" might be presented to the Emperor by the respective ministers without consulting the Council or its President. Moreover, matters dealing with the Ministry of the Imperial Court, national defense, and foreign affairs were submitted by the ministers concerned to the Council by special Imperial command, but this procedure was also followed in cases where the ministers considered this necessary, or if the question under discussion involved other departments. The right of the Council of Ministers to suggest candidates for higher offices did not extend to appointments under the Ministry of the Imperial Court or to appointments in the army, navy, or diplomatic service. The result of these exemptions was that even the purely formal unification of administrative activities that the Decree of October 19 attempted to achieve was largely illusory, since several important branches of the administration were exempt from the control of the Council of Ministers. In practice the collective or joint character of the Council of Ministers remained fictitious and the dismissal of some of the ministers, including the President of the Council, did not lead to the resignation of the entire Government. In administrative matters the Emperor remained the supreme authority.

OTHER ORGANS OF CENTRAL ADMINISTRATION

Central Administrative Agencies Acting in an Advisory Capacity or Independent from the Council of Ministers. While the ministries and the Council of Ministers were the chief organs of the central administration there survived side by side with them several other institutions that belonged to the same group. Such were the "Departments and Special Boards of the State Council" (to be distinguished from the State Council, as the upper chamber of the Russian Parliament) which dealt with certain financial and other questions; the Army Council and the Admiralty Council, which advised the Emperor on military and naval matters; the Board of Guardians (*Openkunskii Soviet*), which managed the charitable and educational institutions of the "Department of the Empress Marie"; the Finance Committee, which discussed measures and policies bearing on credit and monetary matters. These organs functioned side by side with the Council of Ministers and either acted in a merely advisory capacity or performed definite administrative duties, sometimes even infringing on the rights of the legislature. Their very existence was something of an anachronism, which must be explained by historical reasons, and it further detracted from that coordination of administrative policies which was the primary object of the establishment of the Council of Ministers.

The Holy Synod. The administration of the Orthodox Church was in the hands of the Holy Synod, an ecclesiastical council created by Peter I in 1721, and it was dominated by a lay officer, the Procurator. The control of the Orthodox Church by the secular power, which was the result of a long process of historical development, found its expression in Article 65 of the Fundamental Laws. This Article declared that "in church administration the Autocratic Power acts through the Holy Synod by It established." The creation of the Holy Synod by an act of the secular authority, the secularization of the church properties by Catherine II, and the Decree of 1803 which provided that ecclesiastical dignitaries were to be appointed to the membership of the

Holy Synod only temporarily, thus depriving them of any security of tenure and often of the very opportunity to familiarize themselves with the business they had to transact—were all important steps in depriving the Church of the last vestiges of independence. The nineteenth century saw the rapid ascendancy of the Procurator of the Holy Synod who in 1904 was raised to the rank of a minister. Although officially entrusted with the task of safeguarding the legality of the decisions of the Holy Synod, the Procurator became in fact the autocratic master of the Church and responsible to the Emperor alone. Under these conditions the Holy Synod, in spite of the ecclesiastical robes of its members, was hardly more than a purely bureaucratic institution, a tool in the hands of the Government.

THE SENATE AND THE JUDICIARY

Evolution of the Senate. The governmental structure of Imperial Russia included a department, the "Governing Senate," whose place in the constitutional scheme it is not easy to determine. When the Senate was established by Peter I in 1711 it was a central governmental agency which dealt with legislative, administrative, and judicial questions. During the two centuries of its history the Senate gradually lost its legislative and most of its administrative functions while retaining those of judicial control. After the reform of the judiciary in 1864 the Senate was comprised of separate "departments" which were the higher court of appeal in both criminal and civil cases. In the twentieth century, although the principal functions of the Senate were those of a Supreme Court, including the publication and the interpretation of the laws, it also exercised a general supervision over the administrative machine. The senators, whose number was undetermined, were appointed by the Emperor. The Senate never met as a body, its work being carried on separately by eight "departments" of which five were judicial and three administrative, although the latter, too, were largely concerned with judicial questions. Some of the "departments" held joint sessions, but the purely administrative functions of the Senate were relatively unimportant.

Modernization of the Judiciary in 1864. The thorough modernization of the Russian judiciary, which goes back to 1864, was one of the most successful and important of the "Great Reforms" of Alexander II. In the process of reorganization a system of law courts independent of the administration was established, and the judges were granted permanency of tenure and freedom in the exercise of their duties. The more important criminal cases were to be tried by jury. The equality of all before the law was officially proclaimed and the special courts dealing with crimes committed by members of various social groups were, with a few minor exceptions, abolished. The uniform structure of the judiciary provided for three stages in legal procedure. The courts of the first and second instance dealt with the case as a whole, while the higher court of appeal concerned itself merely with questions of law. Minor infringements of the law were dealt with by the individual justices of the peace, as the court of first instance, and by the conference (*sezd*) of the justices of the peace, as the second. The more important cases came before the district court (*okruzhnoi sud*) and the court of the second instance (*sudebnaya palata*). Two "departments" of the Senate were the higher court of appeal. The proceedings of the courts were public, the parties were granted equality, and the bar or association of attorneys received legal recognition. The conduct of preliminary investigations was brought under the control of the courts and the public prosecutor.

Departures from the Principles of the Reform of 1864. It is generally admitted that the reform of 1864 was successful in improving the administration of justice; unfortunately, however, its smooth operation was handicapped by later measures devised in a spirit incompatible with the ideas of the reform of 1864. The most important change was introduced by the Law of June 12, 1889, which transferred a large number of minor offenses committed by the peasants from the jurisdiction of the elected and irremovable justices of the peace to that of an appointed administrative officer, the *zemski nachalnik*. The strong agitation for the repeal of this law did not bear fruit until 1913 when an act passed by the State Duma and the State Council restored to the justices of the peace jurisdiction over the offenses committed by the peasants. The outbreak of the War, however, prevented the carrying out of the new provision. There were other departures from the spirit of the Statute of 1864. The possibility of governmental pressure on the courts was provided by a law of 1885 which permitted the removal of judges for offenses other than misconduct in office, and by a law of 1887 which gave to judges power to order the hearing *in camera* of cases that might endanger public order, morality, religion, or the State. In spite of these departures from the principles of the Act of 1864 the administration of justice in Russia, according to authoritative opinion, was maintained on a high level.

ADMINISTRATIVE CENTRALIZATION

"The Russian State Is One and Indivisible." The control of the institutions of the central Government extended over the entire territory of the Empire, with the notable exception of Finland. Article 1 of the Fundamental Laws of April 23, 1906, declared that "the Russian State is one and indivisible." The term "indivisible" did not mean that no part of the national territory could be transferred to the sovereignty of another state, but merely that after the passing of the laws of 1906 such cession could take place only on the initiative of the Emperor and with the approval of the State Duma and the State Council. The first part of Article 1—"The Russian State is one" —conveyed no clear legal meaning. It was the enunciation not of a principle of constitutional law but of a program of administrative policy, the acceptance of centralization in preference to local autonomy.

Russification. The uniformity of the administrative institutions over the entire territory of the country and the "Russification" of the regions inhabited by peoples of non-Russian blood and language was with but few exceptions the official policy of the Russian Empire. In a country like the United States, where the federal principle is written into the Constitution and where the question of States' rights *versus* those of the Federal Government continues to be very much alive, it is hardly necessary to argue that uniformity among the administrative organs and the supremacy of the central government over every manifestation of the nation's life is not a necessary condition of national unity. The principle of autonomy, which was occasionally admitted in Imperial Russia, played its part in facilitating the extension of her territory. The Ukraine, the Baltic Provinces (Latvia, Estonia, and Lithuania), Bessarabia, Russian Poland—all had enjoyed at times a varying degree of national autonomy which in every case eventually disappeared. The process of administrative unification, typical of pre-Revolutionary Russia, extended to Russia's vast Asiatic possessions. It did not, however, apply to the semi-independent Asiatic principalities of Khiva and Bukhara, which since 1873 had been under the protectorate of the Russian Crown.

Curiously, the provision that "the Russian State is one and indivisible" was first introduced in the Fundamental Laws of 1906, only twelve years before the dismemberment of the Empire.

THE GRAND DUCHY OF FINLAND

Legal Position of Finland. The Grand Duchy of Finland occupied a peculiar position in the constitutional framework of the Empire. Article 2 of the Fundamental Laws of April 23, 1906, provided that "The Grand Duchy of Finland, forming an indivisible part of the Russian State, is governed in its internal affairs by special institutions based on special legislation." According to Article 26, "With the Imperial Throne of all the Russians are inseparable the thrones of the Kingdom of Poland and of the Grand Duchy of Finland." The territory of Finland was acquired by Russia from Sweden in three stages, in 1721, 1743, and 1809, and the creation of the Grand Duchy of Finland as an integral part of the Russian Empire goes back to the latter date. The exact nature of the legal relationship between Finland and Russia was obscure and controversial. From 1809 to 1863 Finland might be described as a part of the Russian State, governed by its own laws and having its own administrative and judicial institutions retained from the time when it was under the sovereignty of Sweden. As a rule the laws and institutions of the Russian Empire did not extend to Finland and the powers of the Crown in this part of its domain were limited, at least in principle, by the special legislation in force in the Grand Duchy. The chief representative of the Crown in Finland was the Governor-General who was also commander-in-chief of the troops quartered in Finland and president of the Finnish Senate, the highest administrative and judicial organ of the Grand Duchy. The Governor-General, who was appointed by the Emperor, was invariably a Russian. After 1826 there was also resident in St. Petersburg a Secretary of State for Finland, an office filled with but rare exceptions by natives of the Grand Duchy. It was through this Secretary of State and not through the Russian Ministers that questions affecting Finland were submitted to the Emperor.

The Finnish Diet. A Finnish Diet was called into being by Alexander I in 1809, but it did not reassemble until 1863 when new elections were held according to the old Swedish law retained by Finland. Emperor Alexander II, who himself opened the Diet, promised to maintain in Finland "The principles of constitutional monarchy inherent in the habits of the Finnish people." From 1863 on the Diet met regularly. Its powers were defined by the Statute of April 3, 1869. This Act imposed definite limitations on the prerogatives of the monarch by providing that certain legislation, including the Fundamental Laws of Finland, could not be changed without the consent of the Diet. Finland, which was already endowed with its own executive and judiciary, thus had its separate legislature. The Russian Emperor, who was also Grand Duke of Finland, was an autocrat in Russia (until 1905–1906) but a constitutional monarch in Finland. The Grand Duchy, however, had no army and the conduct of its foreign relations was in the hands of the Emperor and the Russian Ministry of Foreign Affairs. The constitutional position of Finland was drastically changed by the Imperial Manifesto of February 3, 1899, which provided that the Crown might legislate for Finland in matters of "Imperial interest" after merely consulting the Diet, whose advice, however, was not binding. The Grand Duchy rejected the Manifesto as an infringement of its constitutional liberties. There followed a period of severe friction which ended in the suspension of the Act of 1899 by the Manifesto of October 22, 1905, restoring the legal situation that existed before 1899. The revolutionary pressure was, of course, responsible for this revision of policies. On July 7, 1906, the Diet was reorganized. The new Finnish Constitution introduced universal suffrage and abolished the former representation by separate "estates" (the nobility, clergy, burghers, and peasants).

Law of June 17, 1910. The Law of June 17, 1910, duly passed by the State Duma and the State Council, once more changed the situation. It provided that legislation binding on Finland should be enacted through the general channels (that is, the State Duma and the State Council) "if its effects are not limited to the internal affairs of that region." The Finnish Diet was called to pass on such legislation in a purely advisory capacity. The Act of June 17, 1910, supplied a list of questions affecting Finland to be dealt with by the Russian legislature. The list contained such items as the contribution of Finland to the Imperial budget and taxation required to raise this revenue, regulations concerning military service, the determination of the curricula of Finnish schools, the associations, and the right of assembly, etc. Legislation on purely domestic affairs was left to the Finnish Diet. This Act was a clear breach of the Finnish Constitution according to which the powers of the Diet could not be modified without its own consent. The Russian Government neglected to comply with this requirement because it knew that the Diet would refuse to renounce its constitutional rights. After the passage of the Law of June 17, 1910, Finland still retained its autonomy, although the latter was undoubtedly curtailed. Whether this law was merely a first step toward that administrative assimilation which had engulfed the autonomous institutions of the other border provinces of Russia is a question that must remain unanswered. The Revolution of 1917 made Finland an independent State.

THE SOCIAL STRUCTURE

"Social Classes" and "Estates." In order to understand the character of the provincial administration of Imperial Russia it is essential to gain at least some knowledge of the country's social structure. In approaching this question one must, first, dismiss the familiar notion expressed in the Declaration of Independence that all men are born equal. Secondly, it must be emphasized that the term "social" is not used here in its customary meaning. The division of the population into social classes, which bears on the organization of provincial administration, had often in Russia no direct connection with the professional, business, or economic interests of the members of these classes. It would be more exact to speak of "estates," meaning by that groups of subjects of the Russian Crown who differed from the rest of the population in certain hereditary rights and duties. This definition, however, was no longer fully applicable in the second half of the nineteenth century and became even more misleading after 1905–1906, when a number of limitations attached to the lower "estates" were removed. Some of the "estates" had lost their hereditary character long before the reforms of 1905–1906 and had no corporate organization. Thus there gradually came into existence a large group of people who did not belong to any "estate" and yet enjoyed civil rights. On the other hand, some of the "estates," retaining both their hereditary characteristics and their corporate organization, continued to perform important functions. The "estate" structure of Russia since the middle of the nineteenth century has been aptly described as a "crumbling temple" (*"donjon"* might have been a better term) whose shattered yet sturdy remnants were gradually submerged by the rising tide of democracy.

Their Origin. Social stratification crystallized in terms of hereditary rights and duties is a phenomenon familiar in the history of all European countries. In Western Europe the formation of "estates" was usually the result of organic development, and their institutions became important political factors that effectively limited the powers of the Crown. In Russia the origin of the "estate" structure, which goes back to the middle of the seventeenth century, was different. It was the direct outcome of the policies of the Muscovite Government, which assigned definite duties to separate groups of the population and made the members of some of these groups jointly responsible for the performance of the obligations that rested upon their respective groups. An important remodeling of the social framework took place in the second half of the eighteenth century, during the reign of Catherine II, when a definite attempt was made to organize the "estates" on the basis of corporate self-government and to entrust to them a number of administrative and judicial functions. The institutions created by Catherine, although they subsequently suffered important modifications, continued to form the foundation of Russian provincial government until the revolution.

The Four "Estates." According to the legislation in force before 1917 the population of the country was divided into four categories: (1) *dvoriane,* a term which in the absence of an adequate English equivalent is usually translated as nobles or gentry; (2) the clergy; (3) urban inhabitants or burghers; and (4) rural inhabitants, or the peasantry. The burghers, again, were subdivided into four groups. Although the law referred to the foregoing classes as "estates" (*soslovie*), this description in a number of cases was nothing but an anachronism. Membership in some of the "estates" was no longer hereditary and such "estates" had themselves no corporate organization (for example, the clergy and certain subdivisions of the burghers group). The rights and duties of the corporate organizations of the "estates," with the exception of those of the nobles and of the peasants, were of little practical significance. The Decree of October 5, 1906, was an important landmark on the road toward legal equality. It extended to all the subjects of the Russian Crown (with the exception of nomadic tribes such as the Samoyeds, Kalmiks, etc., and the Jews) two important rights formerly enjoyed only by the nobles and the upper group of the burghers: the right to choose their place of residence and to move freely about the country, and the right to enter government service.

The Nobility. Political and social influence and much of the wealth of the country was in the hands of the nobility. Yet the Russian *dvorianstvo* had a number of characteristics not usually associated with an aristocracy. To begin with, there were two kinds of *dvorianstvo*—hereditary and personal. The latter was not transferable to the children of a "personal noble"—a term as awkward as the notion for which it stands. Nobility was acquired by descent from a noble father, and also, under certain conditions, through government service. With the enactment of the "Table of Ranks" by Peter I (1722) all civil servants were divided into fourteen classes—*chin*—arranged in a hierarchical order.[3] Membership in these classes was in the nature of an honorary title and had no direct connection with the office held. Every civil servant that reached class nine became a "personable noble," while class four brought with it hereditary nobility. Promotion from class to class was automatic according to the length of service. "Personal nobility" went also with every decoration, while until 1900 hereditary nobility was conferred upon the recipient of the order of St. Vladimir, fourth class, a decoration given to every civil servant after thirty-five years of service. In 1900 this rule was changed and hereditary nobility was conferred only on the recipients of the higher decorations. Similar regulations applying to the officers in the army and navy were even more liberal. Government service thus became the most usual method of filling the ranks of the nobility since honorary titles (*chin*) and decorations were a part of the bureaucratic routine. Even before the Decree of October 5, 1906, admittance into government service was open to all university graduates irrespective of their social origin. It will thus appear that the Russian *dvorianstvo* can hardly be described as an aristocracy. It comprised a number of families of ancient lineage, some of them titled, but also

[3] In 1834 classes eleven and thirteen were abolished.

many "hereditary nobles," as well as the "personal nobles," who were people of humble origin and modest standing. From the point of view of their social and economic status, the majority of the *dvoriane* were much nearer to what is usually known as the middle and the lower middle class than they were to the aristocracy. The corporate institutions of the nobility will be briefly discussed in connection with local government, but it may be noted here that they were organized on a purely provincial basis and that there was no official national organ through which the voice of the highest "estate" in the realm could be heard.

Social Leveling. The legal status of the other "estates" presents little of practical interest, especially since the legislation of the beginning of the twentieth century removed many of the disabilities that were the fate of the unprivileged groups in the past. In the case of the peasants, however, the process of emancipation continued to be particularly painful and slow.

THE JEWS

Legal Disabilities of the Jews. The position of the Jews deserves special attention. The Jews, as a rule, were not permitted to reside outside a specified area which comprised the provinces of western and southwestern Russia. This restriction, however, did not apply to the following categories of Jews: (1) well-to-do merchants who belonged to the first of the two guilds into which all the merchant class was divided; (2) university graduates and holders of higher degrees; (3) dentists, druggists, junior medical officers, and midwives; (4) university students and those studying for the professions listed under section three. The Jews were prohibited (after 1882) from acquiring or leasing land in rural districts, even in the provinces where they were permitted to reside. Government service was open to only those Jews who had graduated from the universities with high honors or to the holders of higher degrees. The admittance of Jewish students to schools and universities was limited by a quota. A curious provision of the law forbade Jewish women to shave their heads. All these restrictions naturally invited abuse and offered almost unlimited opportunities for graft which the police officers seldom overlooked. In sharp contrast with recent German and Italian legislation, Russian legal discrimination against the Jews was based on religious and not on racial grounds. The restrictions just mentioned applied only to Rabbinical Jews and did not affect the Karaites. The acceptance by a Jew of membership in a Christian church automatically removed all disabilities.

The Pogroms. Of great political consequence to Russian Jewry were the pogroms. The first great wave of pogroms swept southwestern Russia in 1881, following the murder of Alexander II in which a Jewish woman, Jessie Helfman, was involved. Few pogroms occurred between 1882 and 1903, when anti-Semitism in its most ruthless and aggressive form came again to the fore. At the end of October, 1905, on the morrow of the publication of the Manifesto granting Russia the rudiments of a constitutional regime, hundreds of pogroms took place throughout the land. They were organized by ultra-nationalistic groups and were condoned and, in some instances, instigated by the police. The pogroms were primarily responsible for the mass migration of Russian Jewry to the United States and, on a much smaller scale, to Palestine. The early Jewish refugees from Russia to the Holy Land were the ideological forerunners of the Zionist movement which, however, did not take shape until 1897.

LOCAL GOVERNMENT

Administrative Territorial Subdivisions. For the purposes of general administration the territory of the Empire was divided into seventy provinces (*gubernia*) and several regions (*oblast, okrug*), the latter denomination being applied to some of the border territories. The division into provinces goes back to 1710, but the actual scheme of administrative subdivision still largely in force on the eve of the Revolution was introduced in 1781. This scheme was an arbitrary one and had but the slightest connection with the historical territorial units that were gradually absorbed by the Russian State. The provinces were subdivided into counties (*uezd*) whose number per province varied from four to fifteen. It was originally intended that a county should comprise a population of some twenty to thirty thousands. In addition to the basic division into provinces and counties, there were ten more divisions for specific purposes, such as the army, the administration of justice, transportation, the church, post, and telegraph. The territorial units comprised in the special subdivisions were usually much larger than a province, although this was not always true of the dioceses.

Dual Nature of Local Administration. Provincial government was administered by two sets of officials: those appointed by the Crown and those deriving their powers from local self-government. By and large, the former dealt chiefly with police and fiscal matters, that is, they represented primarily the interests of the State, while self-government institutions concerned themselves with schools, public health, roads, relief, anti-fire measures, the advancement of agriculture, commerce and industry, that is, with what may be described as social and economic policies.

The Governor. The chief representative of the Crown in the provinces was the governor, who was appointed by the Emperor on the nomination, in theory, of the Council of Ministers, but in practice, of the Minister of the Interior. The governor was originally (1764) designed to be the actual head of the province and the coordinating organ of the provincial administration. Gradually he lost this function and became more and more an official of the Ministry of the Interior concerned chiefly with matters within the jurisdiction of that department. The governor, however, retained wide powers of control and supervision, especially over the personnel of the provincial administration. He appointed the provincial officers of the agencies under the Ministry of the Interior and he confirmed the election of a number of officers chosen by the institutions of local government. He had discretionary powers over the appointments made by the *zemstvos* and the municipalities to offices that were not filled by election. It was his duty to ascertain that administrative officers were "desirable" from the standpoint of their political views. The governor had extensive police powers, although the political police (*gendarmes*) remained outside his control. These police powers were as broad as they were ill-defined, and in the hands of a zealous and ambitious administrator could and did actually become in many instances the instruments of a capricious and arbitrary rule.

The Governor-General. In Moscow and some of the border regions there also existed the office of governor-general. The powers of this high official, who was a personal appointee of the Emperor, were determined by an archaic instruction of 1853 which was never revised and brought in line with subsequent legislation. The position of the governor-general was that of an intermediate organ between the central and the provincial government. His chief functions were those of political control and political supervision over the local administration. His powers were extremely broad and, although most of them were never exercised, they offered practically unlimited opportunities for drastic interference with local administration and private interests.

Agencies of Crown Administration. It was the original intention of the law that the governor should normally exercise his functions not directly but through some special administrative organ thus providing a certain guarantee against arbitrary policies. Practice, however, differed from theory. The central organ of provincial administration, the Provincial Office (*Gubernskoe Pravlenie*), degenerated into the governor's chancery which obediently took his orders. The Financial Board (*Kazennaia Palata*), which dealt with bookkeeping and the collection of taxes, enjoyed a somewhat greater independence. The Provincial Excise Administration (*Gubernskoe Aktsiznoe Upravlenie*) was in charge of the State Liquor Monopoly. The Control Board (*Kontrolnaia Palata*) exercised the functions of financial control, and unlike the other institutions just mentioned, was not subordinated to the governor. There was also a special administration which managed State properties. All these organs were purely bureaucratic in their composition.

Provincial Self-Government. The law provided that provincial government should comprise, side by side with appointed administrative organs, also the institutions of local self-government, the provincial *zemstvo.* The new *zemstvo* institutions were created by the Law of 1864, which was amended in 1890. The latter legislation increased the dependence of the *zemstvo* on the officers of the Crown and changed the franchise in such a manner as to assure the preponderance of the landed nobility. In addition to the functions already mentioned the *zemstvo* had certain duties in connection with the fiscal administration, for instance the assessment of taxes. The organs of the provincial *zemstvo* were the *zemstvo* assembly (*zemskoe sobranie*) and the *zemstvo* board (*zemskaia uprava*). The membership of the provincial *zemstvo* assembly consisted of two categories: (1) delegates elected for three years by the county (*uezd*) *zemstvo* assemblies from among their own number; and (2) members *ex officio* (county marshals of the nobility, a representative of the clergy, the chairman and members of the Provincial Office, the chairman and members of the county *zemstvo* boards). The provincial marshal of the nobility was by virtue of his office chairman of the provincial *zemstvo* assembly which met once a year. The executive organ of the assembly, the provincial *zemstvo* board, was elected by the provincial *zemstvo* assembly and consisted of a chairman and two members. The decisions of the provincial *zemstvo* assembly could be suspended by the governor or by the Minister of the Interior on the ground that they were either illegal or contrary to public policy. In the latter case the governor had the power to substitute his own decision for that of the assembly.

Corporations of the Nobility. The nobility (*dvorianstvo*) had an active part in the provincial government. In thirty-nine provinces of European Russia the nobility formed corporations which had their own organ, the provincial assembly of the nobility. The assembly met every three years and all the hereditary nobles of the province (but not the "personal nobles") were eligible to attend, although only those who possessed specified property and educational qualifications were entitled to vote. The most important function of the assembly was the election of the provincial and county marshals of the nobility. Other elected officers had no political significance. The assembly, as a whole, chose two candidates for the office of the provincial marshal of the nobility. The names of the nominees were submitted to the Emperor who made the final selection. The members of the assembly for each county severally elected their respective county marshals of the nobility who were confirmed in office by the governor. The provincial marshal of the nobility was an important figure in the provincial government and was *ex officio* a member of the various boards appointed to deal with judicial and administrative problems. The assembly held the discretionary power of excluding undeserving members from the ranks of the nobility of the province, thus effectively preventing political opponents from being eligible for membership in the institutions of local self-government or in the State Duma. After 1906 the provincial assemblies of the nobility chose delegates who gathered in St. Petersburg and elected from their own number eighteen members of the State Council.

County Government. Although the subdivision of the provinces into counties goes back to the eighteenth century no definite county administration existed until the second half of the nineteenth. Even during the latter period such administration was haphazard and casual in its composition. The central figure of the county government was the county marshal of the nobility. He was invariably the chairman of the various boards, which consisted of local officials such as the chief of the police, the tax inspector, and others. The second branch of the county government was the county *zemstvo* which consisted of the county *zemstvo* assembly and the county *zemstvo* board. The assembly was composed of elected delegates and local officials, who were its members *ex officio*. The *zemstvo* franchise was based on property and personal qualifications (age, citizenship, length of residence). The electorate was divided into three groups, each choosing a specified number of delegates. These groups were the nobles (both "hereditary" and "personal"), the peasants, and all others. Under the law the nobles, who formed only a small proportion of the electorate, were entitled to a larger representation than were the other two groups. The county marshal of the nobility was *ex officio* chairman of the county *zemstvo* assembly. The assembly was elected for three years and met once a year. Its decisions, like those of the provincial *zemstvo* assembly, were subject to the approval of the governor.

Township Government. At the base of the administrative pyramid were the townships (*volost*) which comprised one or more village communities (*selskoe obshchestvo*). The townships and the village communities had their assemblies of householders and their elected officers who, however, represented only one social class—the peasantry. The township officials, who had the unenviable duty of enforcing the performance by the peasants of their obligations toward the State, were themselves, like the entire peasant population, under the strict and vigilant control of the administrative officers of whom the most dreaded was the *zemski machalnik,* an appointed official armed with broad administrative and judicial powers. In spite of its elective character the township administration was hardly an organ of peasant self-government. It was more in the nature of an agency for the performance of an onerous duty.

Municipal Government. A word must be added about municipal self-government which was established by the Law of 1870 and revised by the Law of 1892. The latter legislation extended the powers of the governor over municipal institutions. The municipal government consisted of the municipal assembly (*gorodskaia duma*) and its executive, the municipal board (*gorodskaia uprava*). The municipal franchise was restricted and based on property qualifications. The functions of the municipalities and their relations with the governor were similar to those of the *zemstvo.*

An Appraisal. It is truly remarkable that in spite of the imperfections of their legal structure and the limited means at their disposal, the institutions of local self-government succeeded in achieving as much as they did. The *zemstvo* particularly distinguished itself by building up an extensive network of schools, hospitals, charitable institutions, experimental farms, and so on. The success of this work was due in no small degree to the fact that the *zemstvo*—strange as this may appear—was traditionally considered as the stronghold of liberalism and the leader in social reform. Its reputation attracted to its banners a large number of men and women eager to contribute to the enlightenment of the masses. Not a few of the *zemstvo* employees—teachers, doctors, nurses, agricultural experts, engineers—were strongly tinged with radicalism, a dangerous thing in Imperial Russia. The reputedly revolutionary character of the *zemstvo* staff added to the frictions between the institutions of local self-government and the administration, frictions that multiplied with the expansion of the scope of *zemstvo* work and were inherent in the very structure of Russia's local government.

THE REGIME IN ACTION

Constitutional Dualism. The antagonism that existed between the Crown officers and the institutions of local self-government permeated the entire political and social life of the country. The regime established by the legislation of 1905–1906 was imperfect and introduced a kind of constitutional dualism by limiting the legislative powers of the Crown while leaving the executive powers intact in the hands of the Emperor. A legislative assembly that had no control over the executive and no effective control over the budget was merely the shadow of a real parliament. But even these modest concessions were wrested from Nicholas II only in a moment of weakness when his throne seemed ready to topple over under the onslaught of the revolutionary storm of 1905. The Tsar never became reconciled to the curtailment of his powers and resented such limitation as a bitter humiliation. At the end of 1913 he made an attempt to revise the Fundamental Laws of 1906 and to reduce the State Duma and the State Council to the position of purely advisory bodies, a status which, in his opinion, was "in accordance with the Russian tradition." Although this attempt was abandoned in its initial stage it helps to explain the liberties taken by the Government with the constitutional prerogatives of the legislature, the abuse of Article 87, and the violation of the law in the revision of the franchise by the Act of June 3, 1907. Refusing to avail itself of the guidance of public opinion, which was naturally and rightly suspicious, the Government relied on measures of coercion and police supervision.

P. A. Stolypin. P. A. Stolypin, President of the Council of Ministers in 1906–1911, succeeded in bringing about domestic "appeasement," not so much by the wisdom of his policies as by putting most of the country under a "state of emergency" regime in which civil liberties were suspended and administrative officers received wide quasi-judicial powers. Courts-martial were busy and a great many people were deported to remote parts of the country without even a trial. The Police Department was like a huge spider web. It had agents everywhere and succeeded in having one of them elected to the State Duma where he served with distinction as the leader of the Social Democratic Party. Stolypin himself perished at the hand of one of his own *agents provocateurs* who murdered him at a gala performance in the opera house in Kiev.

Political Parties. An important source of the weakness of the State Duma was the recency of the political parties and their lack of tradition and experience. Prior to 1905 no legally recognized parties existed in Russia; the Russian Social-Democratic Labor Party, founded in 1898, and other revolutionary groups were underground organizations. In the brief interval between the Manifesto of October, 1905, and the convening of the First Duma in April, 1906, a large number of parties came into being. Not less than twenty-six parties and eighteen national groups were represented in the First Duma and quite a few failed to secure a single seat. Some of the deputies, especially among the leaders of the Constitutional Democratic Party, which formed the

Left wing of the liberal opposition, were men of culture and intellectual distinction, but they still had to learn the subtle art of compromise, of give-and-take, which is essential to the working of a parliamentary government. The multiplicity of the parties and the intransigent attitude of their leaders were other obstacles on the road that might have led to the establishment of a parliamentary regime.

The Four State Dumas. The boisterous activities of the First and Second Dumas proved their undoing and brought about the restrictive franchise of the Law of June 3, 1907. The Third and the Fourth Dumas were meek, conservative, and docile. Only during the Great War, appalled by the decay of the Government and sensing the rapidly approaching doom of the regime, did the Duma rise for a few brief months to a position of national leadership. Party life under these conditions was colorless and relatively unimportant. The First Duma was largely dominated by the Constitutional Democratic Party which united the best elements of Russian liberalism. Its success was partly due to the boycott of the election by the Socialists. Their policies were revised during the election to the Second Duma with the result that the Social Democratic Party (which included both the Bolsheviks and the Mensheviks) elected sixty-seven deputies and the Labor Group, which also had revolutionary tendencies, one hundred and twenty. The electoral Law of June 3, 1907, produced the Third Duma, which had only fourteen Social Democrats, fourteen members of the Labor Group, and fifty-three deputies belonging to the Constitutional Democratic Party. The vast majority of the chamber consisted of conservatives of various hues. The Fourth Duma was just as reactionary.[4]

Conflict between the Government and Liberal Opinion. The Government's hostile attitude toward the Duma and toward the institutions of local self-government was even more in evidence in its relations with the labor organizations. The few trade unions that managed to gain a foothold in the short-lived liberal era of 1905 were soon wiped out of existence by governors exercising their "emergency powers." The Minister of the Interior, admitting in 1915 that abuses in this direction were frequent, explained them by the fact that "the generals and governors prefer to close down the organizations they dislike rather than to look after them and be responsible for them."

The Bureaucracy. The real backbone of the regime was the bureaucracy, which had built up a fairly high tradition of public service and in its higher levels was reasonably honest. A bureaucracy, however, is always slow, unadaptable, and often arrogant. It finds it difficult to meet emergencies and hates to face problems, however urgent, which disturb its complacency and the inflexible routine of its stuffy offices.

The Land Reform of 1906–1910 and Compulsory Primary Education. With all its weaknesses, the political regime of Imperial Russia should be given credit for two important reforms that were introduced shortly before World War I. One of them was the land reform of Stolypin, which made a by no means unsuccessful attempt to remove the many legal and economic dis-

[4] See below, p. 700, n 3.

abilities from which the peasants had been suffering since the days of the Emancipation of 1861. The legislation of 1906–1910 had for its purpose the freeing of the peasants from their former dependence on the antiquated communal land tenure (*obshchina*) and establishing them as independent farmers. The reform was severely criticised, and with some justification, on the ground that it favored the well-to-do peasants at the expense of their less fortunate neighbors. The completion of the reform was prevented by the outbreak of the War. The second important and welcome departure from past policies was the Law of May 3, 1908, which provided for the gradual introduction of compulsory primary education for all children. The plan, if carried out according to schedule, was to be completed by 1922.

Inherent Contradictions of the Regime. The many inherent contradictions and latent antagonisms that were working for the disruption of the social and political texture of the Russian Empire were aggravated, on the one hand, by religious and racial intolerance displayed by both the Church and the Government, and, on the other, by the deep cleavage between the thin layer of the educated classes and the masses of the largely illiterate peasantry. The poverty in which the majority of the people lived, coupled with the inability of many of them even to read, effectively excluded the masses from participation in cultural life. The great leveling influence of a popular daily press was absent. Organized sports such as prize fighting or baseball, which in the United States have a general appeal irrespective of a man's social or financial position, were nonexistent. The divorce between the educated groups and the masses was a fundamental weakness of Russia's social structure, a weakness that prevented the nation from finding a common language at the time of the great emergency.

CHAPTER II

THE WAR AND THE PROVISIONAL GOVERNMENT

THE DECAY OF THE GOVERNMENT

Illusions of the Early Days of the War. Prior to the War of 1914–1918 the many weaknesses of Russia's political and social structure were more or less successfully hidden behind the majestic façade of imperial pomp and circumstance. The boundless expanse of the country and its seemingly inexhaustible natural resources and reserves of man power suggested almost invincible strength. The defeat of Russia at the hands of the Japanese in 1904–1905 no doubt augured ill, but it could be explained away on the ground that the Russo-Japanese War was fought in a distant province, connected with the center of the Empire by three thousand miles of a single-track railway and that, moreover, the Far Eastern venture never ranked as a national enterprise. The War against Germany, Austria-Hungary, and their allies was in a different class and seemed to appeal to the imagination of the nation. The response to the mobilization order was most encouraging, indeed enthusiastic. Even the liberals and not a few of the radicals rallied to the support of the Government, not only because it was widely believed that the Central Powers had perpetrated an abominable outrage on little Serbia and, later, on Belgium, but also because Russia's participation in the struggle on the side of the great Western democracies—England and France—was interpreted as a promising sign for the future. The extravagant hopes fixed by many Allied statesmen and authors on the irresistible efficiency of the Russian "steam-roller" proved as ill founded and deceptive as were the illusions of the Russian liberals about the approaching era of democracy. National resources are of little assistance unless they are properly exploited and transported where they are really needed, and man power that is inadequately trained, ill-equipped, and without experienced leaders is merely cannon fodder for a better prepared enemy, even though the latter be numerically inferior. The cooperation between the Government and the liberal elements so ardently hoped for by many Russians had once more failed to materialize, and with the progress of the War the entire governmental machinery rapidly disintegrated.

695

Elements Which Contributed to the Downfall of the Government. This process was accelerated by certain external developments. The mobilization of 1914, followed by the calling of new classes, which increased the size of the army and the reserve to over fifteen million men (1917), not only created a shortage of labor but brought with it the bewildering problem of equipping and provisioning this huge military force. The blockade of the Baltic Sea and the closing of the Western land frontier and the Dardanelles very nearly isolated Russia from the rest of the world, the only remaining routes being via the White Sea, the Pacific Ocean, or the Scandinavian countries. The railroads, which had already proved inadequate to meet the requirements of the growing pre-War traffic, were unable to cope with the new and heavy burden imposed upon them by the needs of the army. The financial difficulties of the Treasury, inherent in wartime conditions, were aggravated by an ill-advised venture into Prohibition, the Government suspending the operation of the State Monopoly of Liquor which provided more than a quarter of the State revenue. The effects of this measure were exactly like those of the Eighteenth Amendment in this country: drunkenness continued and the illicit sale of liquor flourished at the expense of both legitimate business and the State Treasury. Military reverses not only cooled the enthusiasm of the first days of the War but also brought in their wake hundreds of thousands of refugees, some of whom were forcibly evacuated by the Russian command while others had fled from the advancing enemy.

Inadequacy of Leadership. To deal adequately with these and many other war problems would have required all the energies of the nation under a firm and enlightened leadership. This the Imperial Government proved incapable of providing. It had entered on a process of inner disintegration that culminated in the overthrow of the monarchy.

THE EMPEROR AND THE EMPRESS

Role of the Tsar before the War. The process of disintegration was probably nowhere more pronounced than at the very fountain of power, the Imperial throne. Although under the constitutional arrangements the Emperor enjoyed practically unlimited control over the executive branch of the Government, the influence of Nicholas II was little felt in public affairs before the outbreak of the War. The Emperor was to a large extent merely the nominal head of the Government, which was conducted in his name by the bureaucracy. Even the prerogative of appointing the Ministers of the Crown was in practice less important than one might imagine, since they were usually chosen from among the men qualified for the office by their previous experience and their position in the bureaucratic hierarchy. During the War this practice came to an end.

The Question of High Command. Nicholas II was a man of weak and obstinate character and mediocre ability. A devout son of the Russian Church and a firm believer in the mystical tradition of Muscovite absolutism, he considered it his duty to lead in person the Russian army of which he was the titular head. Nevertheless at the outbreak of the War he appointed the Grand Duke Nicholas Nikolaevich Commander-in-Chief. The Grand Duke knew little about the science of warfare but he was tall and handsome and displayed at times toward the senior officers the same kind of ruthless brutality that was only too frequently the fate of the common soldier. This was probably the source of his popularity with the rank and file of the army, a popularity that was particularly resented by the Tsar's ambitious and restless consort, the Empress Alexandra Fedorovna. A German by birth, the Tsarina was brought up in London at the court of her grandmother, Queen Victoria, and even more than Nicholas II was devoted to the principles of Russian autocracy. A neurotic and unbalanced woman, she was under the influence of the well-known adventurer, Gregory Rasputin, an uneducated, coarse, and licentious peasant. To the Empress, however, he was the "man of God" and "our friend" sent by Providence itself to watch over the autocrat of all the Russias, and the heir to the throne, the sickly boy Alexis. The Empress, instigated by Rasputin, who had a personal grudge against the Grand Duke Nicholas Nikolaevich, used all her influence with the Tsar to persuade him to assume the command of the army. At the end of August, 1915, the Grand Duke was sent to the Caucasus and the Tsar became Commander-in-Chief. The Empress greeted his decision as "a glorious page in your reign and in Russian History."

The Empress at the Helm. The departure of the Emperor for the army headquarters left the Government in Petrograd [1] without a head. With the full approval of her husband the Empress assumed a most active part in the conduct of public affairs with Rasputin as her spiritual guide and trusted adviser. Rasputin's association with the Imperial family had been a scandal even before the War but not until 1915 did the "man of God" become an important factor in national affairs. In 1916 Rasputin was practically the undisputed master of the country, a situation that would have been utterly incredible had it not been established beyond doubt by the letters of the Emperor and the Empress, letters which have since been published. No appointment to any high office could take place without Rasputin's approval. The effect of this state of affairs upon the Government and upon the prestige of the Imperial regime was disastrous. The innumerable warnings of the impending catastrophe that came to Nicholas II from all sides met with rebuke and reprisals. In December, 1916, Rasputin was murdered at the house of Prince Yusupov by a conservative member of the State Duma, Purishkevich, with the Grand Duke Dimitry Pavlovich taking an active part in the plot. The destruction of the evil genius of the dynasty was received with a general feeling of relief, but it failed to clear the political atmosphere, and a few weeks later the regime of which Rasputin had become the symbol was swept away by the Revolution.

[1] The name of the capital was changed from St. Petersburg to Petrograd at the beginning of the War.

THE BREAKDOWN OF THE BUREAUCRATIC SYSTEM

Weakening of the Central Government. The bureaucratic machine, that mainstay of Imperial Russia, suffered during the War one blow after another until it fell into a state of collapse. Its traditional position of unchallengeable supremacy was undermined by attacks from three sides: the military command, the Crown, and progressive opinion expressed through the State Duma and various wartime organizations.

Ascendancy of the Military. A "Law on the Administration of the Army in Time of War," hastily passed in July, 1914, on the eve of the mobilization, drastically curtailed the powers of the civilian authorities within a wide "military zone" comprising the "army in the field" and adjoining territories. With the retreat of the Russian troops in 1915 the "military zone" was extended to a large portion of the Empire, including the city of Petrograd. Within this zone the officers of the civilian administration were to take their orders from the military command, which was given power to dismiss civil servants as well as officials employed by the institutions of self-government. The law made no reference to the Council of Ministers and its President and the relations between these organs and the military authorities were not defined. The result was that the army headquarters displayed utter disregard for the civilian administration, from the Council of Ministers down. According to a statement made in August, 1915, by the Minister of the Interior, Prince N. B. Shcherbatov, "even in Petrograd . . . the Minister of the Interior is a mere 'man in the street' who is permitted to act only so far as this does not interfere with the fanciful orders of the military authorities." And he added that the provinces adjoining the front "present a revolting picture of anarchy, lawlessness, and paralysis of power," conditions which he rightly ascribed to the erratic display of energy by the uniformed "hordes of heroes of the rear."

The Tsar's Displeasure and the Rule of Rasputin. Like the military leaders, the monarch himself turned against his official advisers. It will be recalled that the confidence of the sovereign was the very source from which the Council of Ministers derived its authority. It soon appeared, however, that the Emperor did not trust the Ministers he had appointed. At the outbreak of the war the Council of Ministers was headed by the senile I. L. Goremykin, a man of seventy-five, reactionary to the bone and one of the worst products of the Russian bureaucracy. Changes in the composition of the Government in the early part of 1915 resulted in the formation of a Cabinet which, for a Russian Imperial Government, contained an unusually large number of men who were able, liberal-minded, and eager to cooperate with the State Duma and the newly created wartime organizations. Most of these Ministers were naturally at odds with the President of the Council, who was a friend of Rasputin and who firmly believed, in his own words, that "the will of the Tsar must be obeyed like the Gospel." The decision of the Tsar to assume in person the command of the army was reached without consulting the Council of Ministers and was received by the members of this body with consternation. Over the objections of Goremykin the majority of the Ministers jointly urged the Emperor to reconsider his decision which they felt would prove fatal to the regime. This unprecedented *démarche* had no practical consequences but it "shocked and horrified" the Emperor and his consort. Events proved that the apprehensions of the Ministers had been only too well justified. The departure of the Tsar for the army headquarters opened an era of personal rule by the Empress and Rasputin. In spite of the Ministers' emphatic declaration that the dissensions prevailing in their midst were intolerable and would be fatal to the welfare of the country, a statement amounting to a collective resignation, their plea had no immediate consequence. However, gradually and one by one those members of the Government who had the temerity to speak frankly to their sovereign were dropped and were replaced by men chosen by the Empress and Rasputin. Changes became very frequent as some of the newcomers succeeded in maintaining themselves in office for only a few weeks. Rasputin's blessing was in many instances the only qualification for office. Purishkevich, the arch-conservative member of the State Duma who murdered Rasputin, aptly described this sinister procession of nonentities and adventurers as the "ministerial leap-frog." The appointment of new Ministers was accompanied by the reshuffling of their subordinates, the whole of the bureaucratic pyramid losing its traditional stability.

Awakening of Public Opinion. The gradual awakening of public opinion to the fact that Russia's military reverses were due to its unpreparedness and to the inability of the authorities to organize the country for the conduct of the War, brought forth a strong movement for the creation of a "government enjoying the confidence of the nation." In spite of the Tsar's profound dislike of any manifestation of public opinion he was forced to bow to the criticisms directed against Goremykin, who was dismissed in January, 1916. The succeeding President of the Council of Ministers was Boris Sturmer, a septuagenarian and a bureaucrat of a type even more objectionable than his predecessor. The attacks on him became so violent that he was forced to resign in November, 1916. Sturmer was followed by A. F. Trepov, who lasted for barely five weeks. Then came Prince N. D. Golitsin, the last President of the Council of Ministers of Imperial Russia. He had neither political experience nor political ambition and accepted the burden of office only because he was ordered to do so by the Emperor. The helm of the Russian ship of State was in the unsteady hands of this elderly courtier when the revolutionary storm broke.

A "Government Hanging in the Air." S. D. Sazonov, Minister of Foreign Affairs, described accurately the position of the Council of Ministers when he said in the summer of 1915 that the "Government was hanging in the air." Its authority was openly challenged by the army commanders, it was treated in the most unceremonious fashion by the monarch from whom it derived its powers, and it was rejected as utterly unrepresentative and inadequate by progressive opinion, which demanded a "government enjoying public confidence."

THE RISE OF THE DUMA

Patriotic Attitude of the State Duma. The State Duma gradually became the center of organized opposition. Convoked for a brief one-day session immediately after the declaration of war it solemnly proclaimed its desire to cooperate with the Government in the conduct of the War to a victorious end. The only dissenting voice came from the Social Democratic Party represented by fourteen deputies. After voting military appropriations (the Social Democrats withdrew without taking part in the balloting) the Duma adjourned until January, 1915. The brevity of parliamentary sessions during the War and the general nature of wartime conditions tended to curtail still further the already limited powers of the legislature. Under the Russian law the bulk of war expenditure was outside the control of the Duma and the State Council. Legislation under Article 87 [2] received wide application. No less than 384 measures were made law by virtue of this article during the premiership of Goremykin (January 30, 1914–January 20, 1916). Yet the prestige of the Duma continued to increase. After adjournment in the summer of 1914 the members of the lower chamber residing in the capital constituted themselves a provisional committee for the relief of war sufferers. The committee met regularly and in addition to carrying on its humanitarian work became a kind of unofficial political center which closely watched the development of the political situation. Russia's unpreparedness for war and the disastrous reverses suffered by the army were the focal point of discussion. Official optimism voiced early in 1915 by the spokesmen of the Government—Goremykin and General Sukhomlinov, Minister of War, who was soon to be tried for high treason—were at variance with information that reached the Duma from every side. Nevertheless the three-day session of the legislature in January, 1915, stood firmly by the principle of "safeguarding the moral unity of the country as the best guarantee of victory." But behind this serene façade there began the struggle for the convocation of a business session of the Duma so that it could take an active part in the conduct of the War. The Government made some concessions by replacing four Ministers, among them Sukhomlinov, by men more acceptable to public opinion, but showed no desire to meet the other wishes of the Duma.

The Progressive Bloc. In the summer of 1915 there came into existence a parliamentary combination, the Progressive Bloc, which comprised about two-thirds of the members of the Duma, the deputies from both the extreme Left and the extreme Right refraining from participation.[3] A group of the more liberal-minded members of the State Council led by the former Prime Minister, Count V. N. Kokovtsov, joined the Progressive Bloc. The program of this parliamentary group was modest. The principal demand was for a

[2] See above, p. 678.
[3] The Fourth Duma had 422 members who may be divided into four groups: (1) Conservatives: Right, 65 deputies; Nationalists, 125; "Octobrists," 98; (2) Liberals: Progressivists, 48; Constitutional-Democrats, 59; (3) Radicals: Labor Group (led by Kerensky), 10; Social-Democrats, 14; (4) National minorities—Poles, White Russians, Moslems—21. Seven deputies had no party allegiance.

"government enjoying the confidence of the nation," a vague formula which did not mean a cabinet responsible to Parliament but merely one consisting of men whom public opinion would trust. There was nothing revolutionary about the other demands: greater tolerance toward national minorities, especially the Poles and the Jews whom the military command treated with extreme harshness; religious and political amnesty, including the liberation of all persons who had been deported without a trial; real freedom for the trade unions and other labor organizations. A number of ministers favored the program and even took a hand in organizing the Progressive Bloc, but Goremykin believed that a combination comprising members of the two chambers was illegal and that the demands of the Bloc were outrageous. The Emperor and the Empress shared his view.

Criticism of the Government in the State Duma. The session of the Duma in the late summer of 1915 proved stormy. The program of "national unity" was submitted to a severe test and after six eventful weeks the Duma was suddenly prorogued. The breach between the legislature and the Government was now complete and was further widened by the ministerial changes that followed the departure of the Tsar for the army Headquarters. Sturmer, the new President of the Council of Ministers, attempted to exact from the leaders of the Duma a promise that the name of Rasputin would not be mentioned in the debates, for the grotesque and sinister figure of the illiterate *muzhik* (peasant) overshadowed the political scene and dwarfed all other issues, including that of the War. Although the assurance was not given, the Duma was convoked in February, 1916, and for the first time in its history was visited by the Tsar, who received an enthusiastic reception. The visit had been inspired by Rasputin and the Empress, who seem to have been motivated by a mystical belief in the irresistible fascination emanating from the Tsar's person. The charm failed to work and after the first emotional outbreak had died away the Duma proved more hostile and less manageable than ever. The situation reached a climax in November, 1916, when Professor P. N. Miliukov, leader of the Constitutional Democratic Party, delivered a speech in which he discussed the dark forces behind the throne and insinuated that not only the Prime Minister, Sturmer, but also the Empress was guilty of collusion with the enemy. Miliukov ended each peroration of his indictment of the Imperial regime with the question: "Is this stupidity or treason?" His own answer to the question was not clear and opinion in the country was divided. Miliukov's speech and others in the same vein, some of them delivered by conservative deputies, had immense repercussions throughout the country. Strict censorship and the appearance of newspapers with a blank space where columns containing parliamentary reports and editorials usually appeared only excited general curiosity. The prohibited speeches were circulated in millions of mimeographed copies and were avidly read everywhere, even in the trenches and in the peasant cottages. It has been established since that Miliukov's charges, so far as they concerned treasonable relations of the Empress and Sturmer with Germany, were spurious and were based on foreign newspaper gossip. In 1916 and 1917, however, the accusations produced a powerful impression and finally stigmatized the Empress as the *Nemka* (German), a name by which she was almost invariably referred to in the army and among the common people.

Sturmer's Resignation. The demonstration in the Duma forced Sturmer to resign but failed to clear the political atmosphere. His successor, Trepov, was not permitted to speak when he attempted to read the declaration of his Government from the rostrum of the Duma. The Duma was prorogued until February, 1917, and reassembled for its final session a few days before the outbreak of the revolution.

Leadership of the State Duma. It is no exaggeration to say that from the middle of 1915 until the end of February, 1917, the State Duma was the real center of the political life of the nation and the acknowledged leader of the liberal and progressive elements. In its opposition to the Government the Duma acted in close cooperation with the war organizations that had been created in order to meet the needs of the army.

THE WARTIME ORGANIZATIONS

The All-Russian Union of Zemstvos. The first semi-official wartime organization to make its appearance was the All-Russian Union of *Zemstvos,* an association of local self-government institutions for the relief of the sick and wounded. A similar organization functioned during the Russo-Japanese War and the nucleus of an intra-*zemstvos* union had been retained to act as a coordinating organ in case of national emergencies such as famines or epidemics. The All-Russian Union of *Zemstvos* for the Relief of Sick and Wounded Soldiers, to give the association its full name, came into existence immediately after the declaration of war and was joined by all the provincial *zemstvos* except the notoriously reactionary *zemstvo* of Kursk. Prince George E. Lvov, the future head of the Provisional Government, became president of the Union, an office which he had held during the Japanese War.

The All-Russian Union of Towns and the Zemgor. A few days later the organs of municipal self-government followed a similar course and organized themselves into the All-Russian Union of Towns whose purpose was analogous to that of the Union of *Zemstvos.* Operating with funds they raised themselves, but chiefly with grants obtained from the Treasury, the two Unions built up a comprehensive network of hospitals, medical supply stores, and canteens. During the early months of the War the Unions were concerned almost exclusively with the relief of war sufferers, but as the unpreparedness of the country became more and more apparent they extended their activities into other fields, especially the organization of supplies for the army and the provisioning of the civilian population. To coordinate this work the two Unions created in 1915 a joint committee "for the supply of the army," known by the abbreviated name of *Zemgor.* This committee concerned itself with such matters as the placing of the orders of the Ministry of War and rendering assistance in their execution; the establishment of new factories and other enterprises; the evacuation of industrial enterprises from the areas menaced by the enemy; and the direct supply of the needs of the front. In the performance of their difficult task the leaders and employees of the two Unions displayed considerable ability and great devotion to duty, although of course there were exceptions to this rule, as is inevitable in a large organization working under the trying conditions of a national emergency.

"*Mobilization of Industry.*" The same reasons that forced the Unions of *Zemstvos* and of Towns to turn from the relief of the sick and wounded to the organization of supplies and the manufacturing of munitions brought into being two sets of new organs that were a departure from Russia's bureaucratic tradition. These new organs were the War Industries Committees and the five Special Councils for national defense, transport, fuel, food supply, and refugees. The appearance of these organizations was a consequence of a profound change in the attitude of public opinion, a change that took place in the spring of 1915. The earlier somewhat naïve belief in the virtue of the principle "business as usual" gave way to the realization of the fact that only a concerted national effort could bring the War to a successful end. "The mobilization of industry" became the new slogan, but it was also recognized that the object in view could not be achieved by the traditional bureaucratic methods, which, however, could not be completely discarded. Hence a solution that had all the earmarks of a compromise.

The War Industries Committees. The War Industries Committees, which came into being in the middle of 1915, consisted of representatives of industry, commerce, the Government, the Unions of *Zemstvos* and of Towns, and labor. The Central War Industries Committee had its headquarters in Petrograd while twenty-eight provincial War Industries Committees were operating in different parts of the country by the end of 1915. Their object was to organize industry for the purpose of national defense. The mobilization of industry, however, was envisaged as a voluntary action of business carried out with the approval of the Government but not by its orders or under its control. It was self-mobilization rather than mobilization of industry, and the initiative, too, came from business circles. An almost revolutionary departure from tradition was the inclusion in the War Industries Committee of representatives of labor. The issue of participation in the work of the War Industries Committees split the Social Democratic Party, which largely controlled labor organizations. The Menshevik wing favored participation by labor while the Bolsheviks,[4] led by Lenin, opposed it on the ground that labor should not be involved in the conduct of an imperialistic war. After some friction the Lenin faction was defeated and in the spring of 1916 labor was represented on the majority of the War Industries Committees by duly elected delegates. The Government showed its appreciation of labor's patriotic attitude in a characteristic fashion. With the connivance of the authorities an agent of the secret police, Abrosimov, succeeded in having himself elected as labor delegate to the Central War Industries Committee and all the labor members of that organization were finally arrested early in 1917.

---

[4] See below, pp. 720 ff.

The Special Councils. The second set of wartime institutions—the five Special Councils on national defense, transportation, fuel, food supply, and refugees—originated with the State Duma and were duly established by law in August, 1915. They consisted of representatives of the Government, the State Duma, the State Council, the Unions of the *Zemstvos* and of Towns, and the Central War Industries Committees. The object of the Councils was the coordination of policies within the sphere of their respective jurisdictions. There was undoubtedly a great deal of overlapping in the work of the Unions of *Zemstvos* and of Towns, the War Industries Committees, and the Special Councils, and the methods these bodies used were perhaps not always the best. Nevertheless it is generally admitted that they vastly improved the technical preparedness of the army and that the troops were better equipped and armed at the end of 1916 than they had ever been before.

Political Activities of Wartime Organizations. The Unions of the *Zemstvos* and of Towns and the War Industries Committees, moreover, played an important political role. Like the Progressive Bloc, they adopted the slogan of a "government enjoying the confidence of the nation," an elastic formula to which they gave at times an interpretation more radical than the official version. They not infrequently passed purely political resolutions criticizing the Government in no uncertain terms and their influence was all the stronger since the network of the institutions they controlled covered the entire country, including the army in the field. The reactionary bureaucrats of the Goremykin and Sturmer type were continuously at odds with the two Unions and the War Industries Committees, and the Empress detested them, especially A. I. Guchkov, a former President of the Third Duma and Chairman of the Central War Industries Committee. This, of course, did not make cooperation any easier between business and the representatives of self-government, on the one hand, and the Government on the other.

POLITICAL CONDITIONS ON THE EVE OF THE REVOLUTION

Reports of the Police Department. By the end of 1916 the political situation had reached a stage where the inevitability of an explosion was almost universally realized. The ubiquitous political police, which was probably the only department of the Imperial Government that did its work really well, has left reports describing the state of public opinion with a wealth of detail and forecasting the course of the approaching revolution with almost uncanny precision. The Crown had utterly disgraced itself by the infamous rule of the Tsarina and Rasputin. The Government was the very opposite of a cabinet "enjoying the confidence of the nation" and the whole structure of the bureaucratic State had reached an advanced stage of decadence. Warnings of the impending doom came to Nicholas II from the members of the Imperial Family, the conservative members of the State Council, the reactionary "Council of the United Nobility," the State Duma and its President, the Unions of *Zemstvos* and of Towns, the War Industries Committee, and innumerable other organizations. They failed, however, to influence in the least a man who was as obstinate as he was weak.

Deeper Causes of the Impending Breakdown. Behind the breakdown of the machinery of government there were other and more powerful forces which were working for the Revolution. The War had imposed severe hardships on the country. The disorganization of the service of supply resulted in a shortage of many primary necessities, especially in the cities, in spite of the vast national resources. The army, which was poorly led and poorly equipped (the improvements of 1916 notwithstanding), had suffered terrible reverses and heavy losses. With no idea what it was fighting for, demoralized, disillusioned, and tired, it had an almost irresistible desire to lay down its arms and go home.

The Revolutionary Parties. The revolutionary parties, the Social Democrats and the Social Revolutionaries, who have since claimed credit for the overthrow of the Imperial regime, had in reality little to do with it. Their organizations were practically wiped out of existence in the wave of police repressions that swept Russia on the very eve of the War, a blow from which they did not recover until 1917. They did, of course, carry on some propaganda, but on such a humble scale that it would be unreasonable to ascribe to it an important part in the downfall of the Empire. All the revolutionary leaders were far away from the capital. Lenin was in Switzerland, Stalin in distant Siberia, Trotsky was dividing his time between his office near Union Square, New York City, and his home in the Bronx. The Imperial regime was not really overthrown: it collapsed as a result of its own inner weakness and flagrant ineptitude.

THE FALL OF THE EMPIRE AND THE ESTABLISHMENT OF THE PROVISIONAL GOVERNMENT

The Revolution of February–March, 1917. Although the imminence of the Revolution was freely discussed in Russia at the end of 1916 and early in 1917, the fall of the Empire came in a manner that no one had anticipated. Seemingly minor popular disturbances caused by the shortage of foodstuffs broke out in Petrograd and on February 23, 1917, some seventy or eighty thousand workers went on strike. Their number rapidly increased in the days immediately following. Violent street demonstrations took place, and on February 27 the troops of the Petrograd garrison began to go over to the side of the revolutionary populace. The Government, headed by the helpless Prince Golitsin and with the mentally unbalanced Protopopov in the responsible office of Minister of the Interior, was unable to offer any real resistance. On February 27 the State Duma, which had just reassembled, although prorogued, remained informally in session and elected a Provisional Committee which received the loosely worded mandate "to restore order and to deal with institutions and individuals." The Provisional Committee formed a Provisional Government headed by the then very popular Prince G. E. Lvov,

President of the Union of *Zemstvos*. Two emissaries of the Provisional Committee of the Duma were dispatched to the Imperial Headquarters of the
army but met the Emperor at Pskov where his train had been held. They
had no difficulty in obtaining the abdication of Nicholas II, who maintained
throughout the eventful days of March, as well as during the trying months
to follow, truly remarkable composure. The Emperor signed his abdication
on March 2 but, contrary to the expectation of the leaders of the Duma,
renounced the throne not only on his own behalf, but also on that of his son
and heir, the Grand Duke Alexis. The Tsar nominated his brother, the Grand
Duke Michael, to be his successor. By March 3, when the Duma emissaries
returned to the capital, the situation had taken such a turn that the maintenance of the monarchy appeared no longer possible. The Grand Duke
Michael, accordingly, signed a document in which he declined to accept the
Crown and he entrusted the decision as to Russia's future form of government to a Constituent Assembly to be elected by popular vote. In the meantime the supreme authority was to rest with the Provisional Government. It
was a development for which the liberal leaders of Russia were not prepared.
The difficulties of the task confronting the Provisional Government were
aggravated by the fact that its authority was contested from the very beginning by another revolutionary body that came into being on February 27.
This body was the Petrograd Soviet (Council) of Soldiers' and Workmen's
Deputies.

   The Soviet of Soldiers' and Workmen's Deputies. The Soviet of
Soldiers' and Workmen's Deputies was patterned after a revolutionary institution of the same name that had functioned in the capital in 1905 with Leon
Trotsky as one of its leaders. The Soviet consisted of delegates representing
the garrison and the industrial workers of Petrograd. The deputies of the State
Duma, Kerensky (Labor Group) and Chkheidze (Social-Democrat), were,
respectively, vice-president and president of the Executive Committee of the
Soviet. Soviets were rapidly established all over Russia and similar organizations were created in the army. The brief period of the Provisional Government (March–October, 1917) was characterized by a continuous struggle
between the Provisional Government and the Soviets, with the latter steadily
gaining the ascendancy. It must be noted that the overthrow of the Imperial
Government was the work of the revolutionary soldiery and populace of
Petrograd. The rest of the country and the army took no direct part in the
Revolution but merely accepted it as an accomplished fact, some with enthusiasm, others not without apprehension and fear, but all with the recognition of its inevitability.

   Evolution of the Provisional Government. The Provisional Government suffered in the course of its brief career six important changes in its
composition, the evolution being continuously toward the Left. The Provisional Government of March consisted of the flower of Russian liberalism
and was the embodiment of that "government enjoying the confidence of the

nation" which the Progressive Bloc was striving to achieve. Its only radical member was Kerensky, who accepted the portfolio of Minister of Justice with the special permission of the Soviet. One of the major changes in the composition of the Provisional Government occurred in July when Prince Lvov resigned and was succeeded by Kerensky. Further changes took place later, each of them marking the gains of the more radical elements.

Evolution of the Soviet. The Petrograd Soviet went through a similar evolution, that is, its composition was becoming more radical, but at all times the policies of the Soviet were more revolutionary than those of the Provisional Government, and this was one cause of the Soviets' final success.

SUBSTITUTES OF PARLIAMENT AND THE CONSTITUENT ASSEMBLY

Eclipse of the State Duma and the New Representative Assemblies. The Provisional Government was aware of its weakness and its lack of real support. Prince Lvov, while officially displaying the greatest optimism, privately admitted as early as April, 1917, that he and his colleagues were "tossed about like *debris* on a stormy sea." The State Duma, which was distinctly an institution of the Imperial regime, went into eclipse after the revolution, although its members for a while continued to meet in private sessions. The Provisional Government, itself a child of the Duma, made a timid attempt to restore some of the Duma's authority by calling in April a joint session of the members of all the four Dumas. This gathering, however, had no political influence. Three more attempts were made to find a substitute for Parliament in the vain hope of creating a representative body on which the Provisional Government might rely in its struggle against the encroachments of the Soviets. The Moscow State Conference was called in August. It had some two thousand members representing the four Dumas, the Soviets, institutions of local self-government, cooperative societies, trade unions, industrialists, merchants, landowners, universities, and national minorities. In September came the Democratic Conference which, although almost as large as the Moscow State Conference, consisted chiefly of representatives of the Soviets and of the institutions of local self-government, which had been reorganized on a more democratic basis. An offshoot of the Democratic Conference was the creation of the Provisional Council of the Republic (Russia was proclaimed a republic on September 1), which consisted of some 550 members representing sixty-one political and social groups. The Council was an advisory body which met on October 7, less than three weeks before the Bolshevik *coup d'état*. All these substitutes for a real representative popular assembly failed to achieve their purpose and did nothing to stop the rising wave of Bolshevism.

The Constituent Assembly. In the meantime the Provisional Government appointed a special committee to prepare for the elections to the Constituent Assembly. The electoral law embodied the principles of universal and equal suffrage without distinction as to sex, direct elections, the secret ballot, and proportional representation. It was a welcome departure from the tortuous procedure of the prerevolutionary days. In the election which took place, under the Soviet regime, in the middle of November, 1917, the overwhelming majority of the votes went to the Socialists. The Socialist Revolutionary Party, which traditionally represented the interests of the peasantry, obtained 16.5 million votes, the Bolsheviks 9 million votes, while the other parties trailed far behind. The Constituent Assembly was permitted to meet in January but in view of its anti-Bolshevik majority it was dissolved the next day by the Soviet Government. The event passed almost unnoticed. In a country so remote from parliamentary tradition as Russia an elective assembly meant very little. The mere enactment of an electoral law, however liberal, is not sufficient to transform a backward, illiterate country into a democracy.

THE SOCIAL REVOLUTION

Ascendancy of New Social Groups and New Administrative Agencies.
The downfall of the Imperial Government was only the first stage of the Russian Revolution. The chief element in its further development was the ascendancy of new social groups which rapidly crowded out the former ruling class—the landlords and the bureaucracy—from their position of leadership and finally destroyed them altogether. The institutions of central government either disappeared at once (the Crown, the State Council, the Council of Ministers) or slipped more gradually into oblivion (the State Duma). They were replaced by organs of a purely revolutionary origin such as the Provisional Government and the various substitutes for parliament. The whole administrative machinery was subjected to a drastic process of democratization which was carried out either by hasty legislation or, more frequently, by the spontaneous action of the new social forces. The country was soon covered with a complex network of various committees and councils whose legal origins and functions were by no means clear but which all claimed wide jurisdiction and practically unlimited rights to participate in the conduct of public affairs. But, although the institutions of the Imperial regime were rapidly wiped out of existence, the social groups that had dominated them attempted for a time to play a part in political life.

Program of the Provisional Government. The Provisional Government, it will be remembered, was formed by the Provisional Committee of the Duma which was itself the product of the inequitable election Law of June 3, 1907. Prince Lvov and his colleagues, and later Kerensky, still carried on the traditions of an era that already belonged to the past. The Provisional Government espoused the theory that the revolution was caused primarily by widespread dissatisfaction with the manner in which the war was being conducted. The Government called for the continuation of the War to a victorious end and insisted on the fulfillment of Russia's obligations toward her Allies. Although they were willing to make important concessions on the land questions—especially in the later months of the rule of the Provisional Government—they maintained that all such decisions belonged to the Constituent Assembly and that order and existing conditions should be maintained in the meantime. The new Russia that they visualized was a political democracy within the framework of economic institutions based on individual ownership and freedom of business enterprise.

Aspirations of the Masses. This program was at variance with the aspirations of the masses. Far from wishing to continue the War to a victorious end the rank and file of the army ardently desired immediate peace. To the Russian peasantry, who constituted the overwhelming majority of the population, freedom did not mean the introduction of parliamentary institutions about which they knew nothing, but the immediate division among themselves of the large landed estates in which they saw the real reason for their misery. The peasant-soldier in the trenches and the peasant-worker in the factory had no thought except to hurry back to his native village so as to participate in the impending redistribution of land. This desire, which had existed among the rural population since the days of the emancipation of 1861, has been aptly described by a penetrating historian, Baron Boris Nolde, as "latent socialism without a doctrine." The long-suppressed aspirations of the peasantry now coming to the surface with extraordinary violence were fanned into flame by the propaganda carried on both in the army and behind the lines. Of this propaganda the Soviets, headed by the All-Russian Executive Committee of the Soviet, became the center. The declamations of the members of the Provisional Government about national honor and Russia's international obligations were naturally powerless to stem the tidal wave of this great spontaneous popular movement. The peasants took the law into their own hands and proceeded to divide the landed estates among themselves. The soldiers, not to miss their share of the spoils, deserted the army by thousands and by the autumn of 1917 Russia was in the throes of a violent agrarian revolution.

Divorce between the Educated Classes and the Masses. In this great national emergency the aloofness of the educated classes from the masses bore its evil fruit. As a contemporary document put it, the upper classes and the common people did not speak the same language and could not understand one another. To Russian liberals and to moderate Socialists immediate peace was treason to the cause of the Allies and to democracy, and the seizure of land by the peasants was lawlessness; to the masses, both measures were legitimate and long overdue. In the uneven contest it was naturally the masses that were bound to win.

THE ADVENT OF BOLSHEVISM

Lenin. There was among the intellectuals one group that was free from the inhibitions that paralyzed any constructive action on the part of the liberals. This group consisted of the extreme revolutionaries, especially the Bolshevik wing of the Social Democratic Party led by Lenin.[5] The revolutionary parties, however, played no important part in the overthrow of Tsardom and the

[5] See below, pp. 720 ff.

representation of the Bolsheviks in the Petrograd Soviet in March was quite insignificant. Lenin did not reach Petrograd until April, but on his arrival he threw himself at once into the struggle which to him meant the establishment not of a democratic republic but of a Socialist Soviet State. This attitude was at first opposed by a number of the Social Democratic leaders, including Stalin, but it rapidly gained wide support in revolutionary circles, among whose leading spirits was Leon Trotsky.

Fall of the Provisional Government. The Bolsheviks had at first no powerful party organization, their financial resources were scant, their following insignificant. But the slogans they adopted were the correct expression of the wishes of the masses. Lenin demanded both the immediate end of the War and the immediate transfer of all land to the peasants, inviting the populace to "plunder what had been plundered," that is, to abolish all private wealth. This program was summed up in the brief sentence, "All powers to the Soviets." Lenin's recognition of the decisive influence of the peasantry and his harnessing of the forces of the agrarian revolution to the service of the social revolution has been since recognized as one of the most striking manifestations of his revolutionary genius. He was not really leading the masses but was rather riding the crest of the revolutionary wave. His following increased by leaps and bounds. There was, it is true, an unsuccessful Bolshevik uprising in July, 1917. During this revolt Lenin fled to Finland where he remained in hiding. But time was working for him. In the early autumn the Bolsheviks obtained a majority in the Soviets of Moscow and Petrograd. A fresh Bolshevik uprising in October met with as little resistance as had the movement in March that overthrew the Empire. The Provisional Government of Kerensky found no more people to defend it than had the Imperial Government, although some fighting took place in Petrograd, Moscow, and other cities. On October 26 the Provisional Government had ceased to exist and the Bolsheviks became the masters of Russia.

CHAPTER III

THE NATURE OF THE SOVIET STATE

THE MARXIAN SCHEME

Basic Elements of Marxism. Viewed in retrospect the downfall of the Imperial regime and the overthrow of the Provisional Government appear as two stages of the same historical process. It was only with the establishment of the Soviet rule that the revolution assumed a distinctly social character. This transformation was due to the fact that the Bolsheviks who succeeded the Provisional Government believed in the doctrine of revolutionary Socialism founded on the writings of Karl Marx (1818–1883) and Friedrich Engels (1820–1895).

A basic element in the Marxian theory is the economic interpretation of history which teaches that the political, social, religious, and other institutions of any given historical era are determined by economic factors, by the "mode of production." Starting with this fundamental proposition and operating with a theory of value derived from the classical economists and with a dialectical method that was an adaptation of that of Hegel purged of its idealist assumptions, Marx and Engels submitted the capitalistic system to a searching analysis. They reached the conclusion that the history of the human race must be told in terms of class struggle. Under capitalism the two classes confronting one another are the employers and the workers, the exploiters and the exploited. In spite of the seemingly impregnable position of the exploiters, the mechanics of capitalism and its inner contradictions prepare the way for the inevitable downfall of the capitalistic system. Its doom must take the form of a violent proletarian revolution which will lead mankind through the transition stage of the dictatorship of the proletariat to the Communist commonwealth of the future.

Vladimir Lenin, applying the Marxian analysis to the era of monopolistic capitalism and imperialism, argued that bloody wars are inevitable among the imperialistic nations for the possession of their colonial empires and the defense of their overseas investments, international wars that will merge into civil wars and colonial uprisings followed by revolutions and the eventual establishment of Communism. The inescapable downfall of capitalism necessarily raises the question as to how it will come about and by what form of political and social organization it will be succeeded. The clearest and most comprehensive statement of this all-important problem will be found in a celebrated little volume *The State and the Revolution* written by Lenin in August, 1917.

COMMUNIST THEORY OF THE STATE

Dictatorship of the Ruling Class. According to the Communist doctrine the State is the product of the class struggle, it is the instrument by which the exploiters keep the exploited, that is, the masses of the toilers, in subjugation and obedience. It is always, in the phrase of Engels, "a force for suppression," the dictatorship of the ruling class (which under capitalism is the bourgeoisie) and it cannot be anything else. The fact that many of the modern capitalist States appear in the guise of democracies changes nothing in their nature but merely puts in the hands of the ruling class somewhat different and more refined tools for achieving the same object. Nevertheless the democratic form of government presents important advantages from the point of view of the proletariat: it preserves all the inner contradictions inherent in capitalism and at the same time offers the workers the opportunity to organize for the coming struggle. It is idle to expect that the capitalists who run the bourgeois State will ever voluntarily relinquish their privileged position, and the downfall of capitalism can be brought about only by the forcible overthrow of the oppressors. Although history itself is working for the ultimate triumph of Communism, a successful revolution at any given moment needs the resolute and enlightened leadership of a well-organized and disciplined revolutionary party. Of all the social groups the industrial proletariat alone is prepared by the very conditions under which it lives and works, by its discipline and *esprit de corps,* to assume the leadership in the impending struggle. This is the task that Lenin and his followers fulfilled with such conspicuous success in October–November, 1917.

"Withering Away" of the State. The State, having its origin and justification in the class struggle, can exist only so long as there are classes. Classes under capitalism are the product of economic inequality and especially of the private ownership of the means of production. The final aim of the proletarian revolution is the creation of a classless community and the first step in this direction, a step that must be taken immediately after the overthrow of the rule of the bourgeoisie, is the nationalization of all means of production. A direct transition from capitalism to Communism is held to be impossible. "The proletariat needs a State . . . ," writes Lenin, but "according to Marx, the proletariat, firstly, needs merely a State that withers away, that is, it is so organized that it must begin at once to wither away and cannot fail to wither away; and, secondly, the toilers need a 'State' 'that is the organized and ruling class of the proletariat.' " In other words, the dictatorship of the capitalists will be succeeded by the dictatorship of the proletariat, and the

latter will "wither away" to make room for the Communist commonwealth which will be classless and therefore will not be a State. The revolutionary party to which Lenin assigned so important a role in bringing about the downfall of capitalism is to maintain its unchallengeable leadership during the transition period of the dictatorship of the proletariat.

Abolition of the Army and of the Bureaucracy. Lenin had the deepest contempt for utopias in general and for the utopian Socialists in particular. He was at his best when dealing with concrete revolutionary situations and only seldom did he allow himself to forecast future developments except in the broadest terms, such as, for instance, the expression of his unfaltering belief in the inevitability of the proletarian revolution. It must be a source of some embarrassment to his successors that, in discussing the mysterious process of the "withering away" of the State, Lenin has approached the question in terms which, for him, were unusually precise and concrete.[1] He maintained that "the toilers need a State merely for the suppression of the resistance of the exploiters," and since the latter formed a small minority the breaking down of their resistance appeared to him as a matter "relatively easy, simple and natural." It was not sufficient, according to Lenin, for the victorious proletariat to take over the machinery of government, it must be broken and destroyed altogether, for the bureaucracy was a dangerous inheritance from the bourgeois regime. The proletarian State once established will "immediately begin to wither away because in a society free from class contradictions the State is both unnecessary and impossible." Lenin outlined a number of steps by which this "withering away" was to be brought about. First among them was, in the phrase of Marx, "the abolition of the permanent army and its replacement by the armed people," that is, a popular militia. No less important was the second step, the abolition of the bureaucracy. "Capitalist culture," Lenin wrote, "has created large-scale production, factories, railways, the post, telegraph and telephone service, and so on, and on *this basis* the immense majority of the functions of the old 'State authority' have been so simplified and can be reduced to such elementary operations as registration, bookkeeping, and control, that the performance of these functions will be perfectly accessible to all literate people, that it will be perfectly feasible to perform these functions for the 'wage of a workingman,' that one can (and must) deprive these functions of even a shadow of something privileged, 'authoritarian.' " Civil servants therefore will be mere "supervisors and bookkeepers," positions in government service will be filled by election and the tenure of any office, without exception, will be revocable at any time. Lenin, indeed, demanded the "immediate introduction" of a system under which *"all* should fulfil the functions of control and supervision, *all* should be 'bureaucrats' for a time and therefore *no one* could become a 'bureaucrat.' " The elective representative institutions of the bourgeois democracy will be retained but "parliamentarianism, as a system, that is, the separation of the

[1] It must be understood that in the Soviet Union the correctness of Lenin's views is never questioned. Just as Mussolini was in Fascist Italy, Lenin in the USSR is "always right."

legislative from the executive power, and the immunities of the deputies" will be abolished. The proletarian representative assemblies, according to Lenin, must be a place for work, not for idle talk.

Maintenance of Order in the New Society. Lenin refused to commit himself to any definite forecast as to how long it will take for the State to "wither away." He merely stated that it was to be a natural and gradual process. With the disappearance of exploitation by the capitalists, those formerly exploited will get accustomed to observing, without any outside compulsion, the ordinary rules of a civilized community. The breaches of these rules were themselves the consequence of exploitation and of the misery and poverty of the masses. With the destruction of capitalism all the social evils it has brought in its wake will disappear. Human nature will be changed. In a classless society, to repeat, the State, that instrument of coercion, will be both unnecessary and impossible.

SOCIALISM AND COMMUNISM

Socialism. The transition to Communism is to be achieved in two stages. The preliminary stage, usually known as Socialism but described by Marx as "the first stage of Communism," is characterized by the nationalization of all means of production and, consequently, by the termination of "the exploitation of man by man," held by the Socialists to be inherent in capitalism. But the right of private ownership, except in so far as it applies to means of production, will be retained. The Socialist principle that "he who does not work does not eat" will be put into effect; that is, there will be no unearned incomes. Individual earnings will be determined by the application of another Socialist principle: "for an equal amount of labor an equal amount of the produce." Although the State as an instrument of class oppression will disappear, for there will be no more classes, it will still function in order to enforce the rights of private property in chattels and goods other than means of production. Complete equality will not yet be established. Communism will still be a thing of the future.

Communism. Neither Marx nor Lenin has given a definite answer to the question as to how long it will take for Socialism to evolve into Communism and what form the organization of the future Communist society will take. They have merely asserted that Communism will be characterized by the liberation of man from slavery to the division of labor; by the disappearance of the antagonism between mental and physical labor; by the lifting of labor from the position of a tool for making a living to that of a principal necessity of life; by the many-sided development of the individual, the resulting expansion of the productive forces, and the increase of social wealth. When these developments have taken place it will be possible to put into effect the principle of Communism: "from each according to his abilities, to each according to his needs." Only then will the State finally wither away and mankind enjoy real freedom, for freedom and the State are declared to be incompatible.

Lenin stated that "we do not know and we cannot know" how and when Communism is to be realized.

It is officially claimed that in the late 1930's the USSR reached the stage of Socialism and was advancing toward Communism. The fact that the State, nevertheless, has shown no sign of withering away has led Stalin (as it will appear later in this Chapter) to make important amendments to the theories expounded by Lenin in *The State and the Revolution*.

THE QUESTION OF NATIONALITIES

Importance of the Question of Nationalities. Although the revolution, the civil war, and Russia's absence from the Paris Peace Conference of 1919 resulted in the severance from the former Russian Empire of a number of important territories (Finland, Russian Poland, Bessarabia, the former Baltic Provinces—Latvia, Lithuania, and Estonia), the Soviet Union continued to control a vast area comprising about one-sixth of the land surface of the globe and inhabited by peoples speaking many languages and belonging to many races. The attitude of the Communists toward the national question thus acquires considerable practical importance. Marx, according to Lenin, advocated administrative centralization rather than the federal principle. This centralization, however, was qualified by Lenin as "democratic" and "proletarian" and it did not preclude a wide degree of local autonomy. The "unity of the nation" was to find its expression in the voluntary cooperation of the organs of the regional and local government with the central administration in achieving the common objectives of the proletarian State, chiefly in fighting the resistance of the former capitalists.

The program of the Russian Communist Party adopted in 1919 provided that on the question of nationality the Party must strive for close cooperation with the proletarians of other nations in the struggle for the overthrow of the landed proprietors and the bourgeoisie. In order to overcome the suspicion of the oppressed nations toward the proletariat of the State that used to oppress them the program proclaimed the complete equality of all national groups and the recognition of the right of the colonies and other national territories to secede. At the same time the Party favored the creation of a federation of Soviet Republics as a "transition stage toward complete unity." Particular care should be taken, they believed, to safeguard the cultural rights and to encourage the schools, literature, and the use of the local languages.

Stalin explained in 1920 that the attitude of the Communist Party toward the right of secession was determined "by the concrete factors of the international situation, by the interests of the revolution." The chief consideration was the strengthening of Russia and the weakening of imperialism. "This is why the Communists fight for the secession of the colonies from the Entente," wrote Stalin, "but they must at the same time fight against the severance of the border regions from Russia." He argued that the independence of Russia's former territories would be purely nominal, that they would inevitably become mere tools in the hands of the imperialistic powers. This interpretation of the right of secession renders practically inoperative the relevant articles of the successive Soviet constitutions granting the national groups within the Union the right to decide freely their own fate.[2]

"SOCIALISM IN A SINGLE COUNTRY"

World Revolution. Another brief excursion into the wilderness of Communist theory is essential in order to understand the general trend of Soviet policies since about 1925. It has already been noted that Marxian Socialism, as interpreted by Lenin, is primarily a doctrine of revolution. According to this theory the Socialist revolution should have occurred in one of the more advanced industrial countries, such as the United States, Great Britain, Germany, or France. In order to be successful, that is, to bring about the establishment of Socialism, a national revolution was not by itself considered sufficient. The creation of the Socialist commonwealth required the concerted effort of at least several advanced countries. The process, as envisaged by Lenin, was the merging of the national revolutions into a world revolution. The establishment of a Socialist system in a single country was not seriously considered and the idea was usually rejected as un-Marxian and utopian. The fact that the first proletarian revolution occurred in Imperial Russia, a backward agricultural country, was something of a shock to the more orthodox Marxists. They found solace, however, in the belief prevailing in Russian revolutionary circles after October, 1917, that the example of Russia would be followed in the near future by other European countries and, before long, by the United States. The policy of the Russian revolutionary Government was thus clear and in harmony with Communist theories: it was aimed at the advancement of world revolution. Conditions throughout the world during the last phase of the War and immediately thereafter seemed to favor the Communist cause. Fatigue, disillusionment, economic distress, were undermining the social structure of every country. Political revolutions had occurred in Germany and in Austria-Hungary. Hungary was for a few months in 1919 under a Communist dictatorship, and Soviets made their appearance in Bavaria. The revolutionary movement, however, collapsed in its incipient stage and Europe, not to mention the New World, refused to follow the example of Russia. The "scientific" scheme of Marx and Lenin found itself grievously at variance with the course of historical events.

Stalin vs. Trotsky. If the survival of the Russian Soviet Government in the midst of a capitalistic environment was a pleasant surprise to the rulers of Moscow, the failure of the world revolution was both a disappointment and an embarrassment. The situation was complicated by the death of Lenin in January, 1924. The removal of the acknowledged leader was followed by a bitter struggle within the Communist Party. The two principal claimants to Lenin's mantle were Leon Trotsky, the creator of the Red Army, and Joseph

[2] Stalin, J. V., *Marksism i natsionalnyi vopros* (*Marxism and the National Question*), collection of articles and speeches (Moscow, 1937), pp. 224–225. See below, p. 741.

Stalin, the Secretary-General of the Communist Party. Although the personal element was not absent from the controversy, the contest centered on a fundamental problem of Communism. Trotsky, a brilliant writer and a master of Marxian dialectics, was a strong supporter of the idea of world revolution; its promotion was to him not only the chief but the sole object of the Soviet Union. Stalin, who as late as April, 1924, expressed in print the view that the victory of Socialism in one country only was impossible, suddenly reversed himself.[3] He now advanced the doctrine that "Socialism in a single country" was quite feasible, provided the country in question had a large territory, a large population, and abundant natural resources. This, however, was not yet the "final victory," for there remained the danger of intervention by the capitalist nations. The discussion that ensued kept the Communist bodies busy for four or five years and ended in the defeat of Trotsky. He was deprived of his various offices, expelled from the Party, deported first to Central Asia and in 1929 to Turkey, and was finally murdered in Mexico in 1940.

Importance of the Doctrine. The official acceptance of Stalin's doctrine of "Socialism in a single country" was an important turning point in the history of the Soviet Union. World revolution, of course, could not be and was not renounced, but for a time it ceased to be an active factor in Soviet policies. In the field of international relations Moscow sought cooperation with the capitalist nations; at home it embarked on a vast scheme of economic reconstruction embodied in the Five-Year Plans. Stalin attached the greatest importance to his doctrine. In his report to the Fifteenth Congress of the Communist Party (October–November, 1926), as well as on other occasions, he voiced the conviction that without full assurance that Socialism could be built within the frontiers of the Union the industrialization program would have been futile. Reduced to its simplest expression it may be said that the issue was one of internationalism versus nationalism. It was nationalism that won the day and for nearly two decades remained the cornerstone of Soviet domestic and foreign policy.

REVISION OF THE THEORY OF THE STATE

Soviet Socialism. The building of Socialism in the USSR raised certain disturbing questions of Marxian theory. According to the official view the elimination of private ownership of the means of production resulted in the abolition of classes. Simultaneously the State should have begun to wither away because, to quote Lenin again, "in a society free from class contradictions the State [always the dictatorship of the ruling class] is both unnecessary and impossible." It will be remembered that the disappearance of the standing army and the elimination of the bureaucracy were the principal manifestations of the withering away of the State, as envisaged by Lenin. The evolution of the Soviet Government, however, follows a course very different

[3] See Michael T. Florinsky, *World Revolution and the U.S.S.R.* (Macmillan, New York, 1933), pp. 155 ff.

from the one visualized by the founders of "scientific" Socialism. The professional army, far from disappearing, has been vastly increased, enjoys a privileged status, is flattered and admired. Communist leaders, from Stalin down, eagerly assume military titles and parade in army uniforms bedecked with medals. The bureaucracy, instead of being superseded by a kind of universal temporary service of all citizens, has never been more firmly entrenched. It has invaded every field of activity and hordes of State and Party officials, according to authoritative Soviet statements, display in an exaggerated form the most objectionable characteristics of their colleagues in the capitalist countries. The long and powerful arm of the State guides the Soviet citizen through his daily routine, regulates the conditions under which he lives and works, measures out his "living space," confers upon him decorations and honorary titles if he is diligent and docile, or, with the assistance of the ubiquitous police and of an elastic and comprehensive penal code, chastises him if he is recalcitrant, unappreciative, inefficient, or, perhaps, unable to keep pace with the speed-up of industrialization. Intellectual pursuits, the press, the schools, the arts, and science are rigidly controlled by an omnipotent bureaucracy whose chief qualification is unfaltering adherence to the "party line." Whatever may be the benefits conferred upon Russia by the Soviet system the evolution of its administrative structure has nothing in common with the process outlined by Lenin in *The State and the Revolution*.

Stalin's Report to the Eighteenth Congress of the Party. The contradiction between theory and practice is so flagrant that it could not be indefinitely ignored even in a country that has learned the lesson never to ask those in power embarrassing questions. Stalin has provided in his report to the Eighteenth Congress of the Communist Party (March, 1939) an authoritative explanation of the reasons why Soviet Communism differs in many essentials from the pattern set by Marx and Lenin. Elaborating and amplifying the views he had expressed on several previous occasions, he admitted that not a few of his followers found it difficult to reconcile actual conditions in the USSR with the Communist ideal. The argument advanced by Stalin to set at rest the minds of the doubting Thomases is the direct offspring of his doctrine of "Socialism in a single country." He explained that the contradiction between the Socialist commonwealth envisaged by Marx and Lenin and the Soviet State as it actually exists is due to the capitalist environment and especially to the activities of foreign spies. He pointed out that Engels never discussed the position of a lone Socialist State among hostile capitalist nations. Engels, Stalin argued, either was concerned with the inner process of development of the future Socialist State, irrespective of the international situation, or proceeded on the assumption that Socialism would be victorious in all or in the majority of the capitalist nations. Lenin, of course, could not be suspected of such negligence or lack of foresight. Stalin therefore produced the ingenious theory that Lenin's failure to discuss the behavior of the State in a single Socialist country was due merely to the fact that the writing of *The State and the Revolution* was interrupted by the events of the autumn of

1917. What Lenin intended to say (although he gave no indication of such intention) was now being said by Stalin. The pupil has written the final chapter of the master's great work. According to Stalin, the history of the Soviet Union is divided into two stages. The first stage lasted from the advent of the Bolsheviks to power to the liquidation of the exploiting classes. During this period the State performed two principal functions: suppression of the dispossessed classes at home, and defense against foreign aggression. The third function, the administration of economic and cultural activities, was still relatively unimportant. The second stage is the period from the liquidation of the capitalist elements to the final triumph of Socialist economy and the adoption of the new Constitution. The character of the State has changed. In Stalin's words:

> The function of military suppression at home has been dropped, has withered away because exploitation has been abolished, there are no more exploiters and there is no one to suppress. Instead of the function of suppression the State has assumed the new function of protecting Socialist property against thieves and embezzlers of the people's wealth. The function of military defense from foreign aggression has been fully preserved and, therefore, there are maintained the Red Army, the Navy, as well as the penal agencies and intelligence service necessary to catch and punish the spies, assassins and "wreckers" sent into our country by foreign intelligence services. The function of economic organization and the cultural-educational activities of the State agencies have been maintained and have been fully developed. Now the principal domestic task of our State consists in the peaceful work of economic organization and cultural and educational activities. As to our army, penal agencies and the intelligence service, the point of their weapon is no longer directed inside the country, but outside it, against our enemies. As you see we have now an entirely novel Socialist State, unprecedented in history, a State that differs considerably in both its form and functions from the Socialist State of the first period.

> But progress cannot be stopped here. We are moving further, forward, toward Communism. Shall we maintain the State also under Communism?

> Yes, it will be maintained unless the capitalist environment has been liquidated, unless the danger of military aggression from the outside has been removed. It is evident that the forms of our State will be altered again according to the modification of the domestic and foreign situation.

> No, it will not be maintained and will wither away if the capitalist environment has been removed, if its place has been taken by a Socialist environment.

Stalin's Doctrine Appraised. The Soviet press has unanimously acclaimed Stalin's perhaps not very fortunate venture into theoretical analysis as a "priceless contribution to the treasure-house of Marxism-Leninism." It is difficult to agree with this evaluation even if one has reservations about the contents of the "treasure-house." Far from expounding the doctrines of *The State and the Revolution* Stalin has, in fact, drastically revised them. Lenin wrote that the proletarian State "is so organized that it must begin at once to wither away and cannot fail to wither away"; according to an official Soviet commentator, "Stalin has conclusively proved that the withering away of the State will be accomplished not through the weakening of the State power but through the maximum increase of its strength." [4] Stalin's Socialist-minded

[4] E. I. Soldatenko, *Ob otchetnom doklade tovarishcha J. V. Stalina na XVIII sezde partii* (*On the Report by Comrade J. V. Stalin to the Eighteenth Congress of the Party*), verbatim

critics have long held that the industrialization of the USSR is a kind of inverted Marxism. The Marxian doctrine speaks of the establishment of Socialism through the dictatorship of the proletariat *because* the country has reached an advanced stage of capitalist development, while the Soviet Union is being industrialized *because* it is governed by a proletarian dictatorship. The decisive part in shaping the destinies of the Socialist commonwealth assigned by Stalin to "spies, assassins, and wreckers" sent to Russia by "foreign intelligence services" fits ill into the majestic picture of the interplay of great economic and social forces which forms the essence of the Marxian analysis. Stalin has, indeed, written a new chapter in Lenin's *The State and the Revolution*. The chapter, however, amounts to the rewriting of the book itself.

Its Practical Significance. The characteristic crudeness and humble theoretical level of Stalin's doctrine had the practical advantage of bringing it within the grasp of the rank and file of the Party. It effectively silenced any expression of doubts as to the compatibility of Soviet realities with the teaching of Marx and Lenin. The withering away of the State was relegated to a distant and uncertain future. In the meantime the bureaucracy, the army, and the police received the pleasing assurance that their services will be required so long as the capitalist environment exists. Since the abolition of these three pillars of the regime was never within the realm of practical possibility, it may well be argued that things remained pretty much as they were before and that the revision of the doctrine of the State was of no practical consequence. This conclusion, however, would be unwarranted. The combined effects of the theory of "Socialism in a single country" and that of the survival of the State until the disappearance of the capitalist environment gave the Communist doctrine a degree of integration which heretofore was lacking, even though world revolution has always been the ultimate object of revolutionary Marxism. Stalin has definitely linked the elimination of capitalist environment to the solution of two major issues, one foreign and one domestic: security (prevention of aggression by a capitalist nation) and the establishment of the Communist commonwealth (withering away of the State), thus centering Soviet policies on one concrete goal. The foregoing reasoning may appear abstract and far-fetched, yet it offers a clue to an understanding of the course pursued by Moscow during the closing stage of World War II and since 1945.

HISTORY OF THE COMMUNIST PARTY OF THE SOVIET UNION

Origins of the Communist Party. The party of the revolutionary proletariat occupies an important place in the revolutionary program of Marx and Lenin. As one would expect, therefore, the All-Union Communist Party of

report of a lecture delivered before the All-Union Society for the Propagation of Political and Scientific Knowledge (Moscow, 1949), p. 34. The Society (*Vsesoiuznoe Obshchestvo po Rasprostraneniiu Politicheskikh i Nauchnikh Znanii*) is, next to the radio and the press, the most active propaganda agency in the Soviet Union. Its publications conform strictly to the "party line" and have a wide circulation. The second printing of Soldatenko's pamphlet was issued in 215,000 copies.

the Bolsheviks ($VKP_{(b)}$) is the mainspring of the Soviet regime. Its present name is of recent origin. The beginning of the organization goes back to 1898 when the First Congress of the Russian Social Democratic Labor Party was held in Minsk, Russia. The Congress was attended by merely nine members, and Lenin, who was in exile in Siberia, was not among them. The Second Congress of the Party, which was held in 1903 in Brussels, met with difficulties with the police and was transferred to London. This assembly was marked by a cleavage arising from a minor dispute over questions of organization. The majority group, led by Lenin and Plekhanov, formed the faction of the Bolsheviks (literally "majority") while their opponents became known as the Mensheviks (literally "minority"). It was only gradually that the seemingly unimportant friction within the Social Democratic Party developed into a real parting of the ways, the Bolsheviks generally supporting the more radical policies. The Second Congress approved the Party's program and charter, both of which survived until the revolution of 1917. The program and the subsequent activities of the Party were directed chiefly toward the overthrow of the Imperial regime and the improvement of the position of the working class. The program referred to the proletarian revolution but little serious thought was given to an event that appeared to the majority of the members as remote, and to some as even improbable. The activities of the Party were divided between revolutionary propaganda, including the publication of newspapers which led a precarious existence and had an extremely modest circulation, and internal strife and disputes accompanied by much bitterness and mutual excommunications. Until 1917 there was nothing to indicate that the Social Democratic Party was destined to rule the former Russian Empire. In 1918, after the advent of the Bolsheviks to power, the Bolshevik faction of the Social Democratic Party took the name of the Russian Communist Party of the Bolsheviks. In December, 1922, Russia became the Union of Soviet Socialist Republics and in 1925 the Party once more changed its name to that of the All-Union Communist Party of the Bolsheviks. Until 1943 it was officially described as a section of the Third (Communist) International.[5]

In 1919 the Eighth Congress of the Party approved the new program which gives an outline of the impending doom of capitalism and imperialism and provides for measures of practical policy devised in agreement with Lenin's analysis of the period of transition from capitalism to Communism. The 1919 program is no longer considered adequate. The Eighteenth Congress of the Party appointed on March 20, 1939, a commission of twenty-seven members under the chairmanship of Stalin to draft a new program for submission to the next party congress. As these lines go to press twelve years later (December, 1951) the Nineteenth Congress has not yet met and nothing is known about the work of the commission.

[5] See below, pp. 857 ff.

ORGANIZATION OF THE COMMUNIST PARTY

The Party's Character and Aims. The organization of the All-Union Communist Party has been altered several times, the more important earlier changes being introduced in 1922 and 1925. Since 1934 the constitution of the Party has been determined by the charter unanimously approved by the Seventeenth Congress in February, 1934, and amended by the Eighteenth Congress in March, 1939. The charter described the Party as "the organized vanguard of the proletariat of the USSR, the highest form of class organization. The Party leads the proletariat, the toiling peasantry and all toiling masses in the struggle for the dictatorship of the proletariat, for the victory of Socialism. The Party is the leader of all the organs of the proletarian dictatorship and assures the successful building up of the Socialist society.[6] The Party is a united fighting organization bound by conscious, iron, proletarian discipline. The Party is strong through its unity, its singleness of will and a singleness of action incompatible with deviation from the program, with breach of party discipline, or with the formation of factions inside the Party." All members are pledged to work actively and unselfishly for the achievement of the aims stated in the program and in the charter.

Admission to the Party under the 1934 Charter. Admission to the Party is based exclusively on the ground of personal merit. Prior to 1939 the requirements for admission, which were made more stringent by the charter of 1934, varied with the standing of the applicants, who were divided into four groups: (1) industrial workers of five years' standing; (2) industrial workers of less than five years' standing, agricultural laborers, the Red Army men who were formerly workers or collective farmers, and "technicians"; (3) collective farmers, members of peasant handicraft cooperative organizations and teachers in elementary schools; (4) other employees. Each applicant was to be sponsored by from three to five Party members of five years' standing. In the case of group four the sponsors were to be Party members of ten years' standing. Former members of other political parties might be admitted only with the approval of the Central Committee of the Party. The credentials of each applicant were checked by the local and higher Party organizations, and the standing of the applicant determined which of the higher Party organs should give the final sanction. Applicants under twenty years of age were admitted solely through membership in the *Komsomol* or Union of Communist Youth. The sponsors were held responsible for the candidates they recommended and if the latter proved unworthy the

---

[6] This part of the preamble to the charter was revised in 1939 and reads as follows: "The All-Union Communist Party of the Bolsheviks, being a section of the Communist International, is the organized vanguard of the working class of the USSR, the highest form of class organization. The Party is guided in its work by Marxist-Leninist theory. The Party leads the working class, the peasantry, the intellectuals, that is all the Soviet people, in the struggle for the strengthening of the dictatorship of the working class, for the strengthening and development of the Socialist order, for the victory of Communism. The Party is the leading nucleus of all organizations of toilers, both social and State, and ensures the successful construction of Communist society."

sponsors were liable to disciplinary measures including expulsion from the Party.

Candidates. Admission to full membership is preceded by a period of probation, the prospective members being known as candidates. Prior to 1939 the probation period was one year for applicants in group one, two years for those in groups two, three, and four, and three years for the former members of other parties. The requirements for admission as a candidate are similar to those for admission as a Party member. The candidates participate, with a consultative vote, in the work of the Party organs to which they are attached. They pay monthly dues ranging from twenty rubles for those earning less than one hundred rubles per month to 3 per cent of their wages for those receiving five hundred rubles or more.

After 1934 there were also "sympathizers' groups" which were attached to primary Party organs. The "sympathizers" were described as non-Party men and women who, although they had proved their devotion to the Party, were not yet sufficiently prepared to join it. It was their duty to attend the open meetings of the Party organs, they had the right of consultative vote, and they had to strive for the fulfillment of the decisions of the Party. The "sympathizers' groups" were abolished in 1939.

Primary Party Organs. The Party organization embodies the principle of "democratic centralization" and comprises an extensive network of territorial agencies. The basic units of this complex structure are the primary Party organs, formerly known as Communist "cells." A primary Party organ is established in every industrial or commercial enterprise, factory, collective farm, State farm, machine tractor station, army unit, office, and so on, provided there are three Party members. If an enterprise, farm, or office has less than three Party members the primary Party organ is formed by candidates and members of the *Komsomol* under the leadership of the higher Party organ.[7] The duties of the primary Party organs are agitation for the fulfillment of Party slogans; propaganda among prospective members and their political education; cooperation with the higher Party organs; mobilization of the workers for the fulfillment of the plan and the strengthening of labor discipline; struggle against indifference and abuses and for the improvement of the position of labor; "active participation in the economic and political life of the country." The duties of the primary Party organs were extended in 1939.

Higher Party Organs. On the foundation of the primary Party organs is built the pyramid of higher Party organs with a steadily expanding territorial jurisdiction. Each town and county (*raion*) has its Party conference that meets at least once a year, its committee, its bureau consisting of five to seven members, and its secretary. Until 1939 the secretary of a town committee had

---

[7] The number of primary Party organs in March, 1939, according to Stalin's report to the Eighteenth Congress, was 113,060, that is, only a small percentage of the industrial enterprises and collective farms had primary Party organs. Party organization was particularly weak in agriculture. A. Andreev informed the Eighteenth Congress that of the total number of 243,000 collective farms with a population of 75.6 million only 12,000 farms had regular primary Party organs with an aggregate membership of 153,000. Over 100,000 farms had no substitute *Komsomol* primary Party organs.

to be a Party member of ten years' standing; the secretary of a county committee, a member of seven years' standing. Above the town and county Party organs are those of the major territorial subdivisions of the Soviet Union: the constituent republics, the territories (*krai*), and the provinces (*oblast*). Each of these has its own Party conference (or congress of the national Communist Party of the constituent republic) which meets at least once every eighteen months; its committee of not more than eleven members; and two secretaries who until 1939 had to be Party members of twelve years' standing. The All-Union Congress of the Party with its Central Committee crowns the Party organization. The whole structure is based on the principle of hierarchy, the lower institutions being responsible to the higher ones and subject to their supervision. The officers elected by the lower organs are confirmed in office by the higher ones.

   The All-Union Congress and the Central Committee of the Party.
In theory the supreme authority of the Party is the All-Union Congress which is scheduled to meet at least once every three years. This rule, however, is loosely observed in practice. The Sixteenth Congress met in June, 1930; the Seventeenth, in January, 1934; the Eighteenth Congress, in March, 1939. None has been convened since, to the end of 1951 when these lines go to press. As the congresses are much too numerous [8] and their sessions too short to make possible the exercise of actual control over the work of the Party, they invariably vote unanimously for the resolutions submitted by the leaders. One of the functions of the congress is to elect the Central Committee which consists of some seventy members and approximately the same number of alternates. The Central Committee, which, again in theory, carries on the work of the Party between the congresses, actually meets at considerable intervals. It is generally believed that the Party is run by three agencies appointed by the Central Committee: (1) the Secretariat headed by Stalin as Secretary General, (2) the Political Bureau, and (3) the Organization Bureau. The functions of these two bureaus, which are reported to have about ten members each, are not clearly defined. Another important agency is the Committee of Party Control which was, before 1939, elected by the congress and delegated to watch over the discipline and conduct of Party agencies and members. The Central Committee, moreover, shares with the republican, territorial, and provincial committees the work of supervising a large number of special Party institutions which deal with practically every aspect of national life (agriculture, industry, transportation, planning, finance, commerce, culture, and so on). It would seem, indeed, that far from "withering away" the State bureaucracy that Lenin so deeply hated has been duplicated under the Soviet regime by a no less formidable Party bureaucracy.

---

   [8] The Sixteenth Congress had 2,159 members of whom 1,268 had a "decisive" and the balance a "consultative" vote; the Seventeenth Congress had 1,961 members of whom 1,225 had a "decisive" vote; the Eighteenth Congress had 2,040 members of whom 1,574 had a "decisive" vote. The Central Committee of the Party convokes from time to time Party conferences which have several hundred members. Conferences were abolished by the Seventeenth Congress in 1934 but were restored by the Eighteenth Congress in 1939.

The Party and the Soviet Constitution. Until the adoption of the new Constitution, the Party had no official standing under the Soviet law. Article 126 of the Constitution, however, recognized the Party as an organization of "the most active and politically conscious citizens" and its agencies as "the leading nucleus of all organizations . . . both social and State," while Article 141 states that the Party is entitled to nominate candidates for elective assemblies. Although the Constitution confers no legislative powers on the Communist Party, the more important decrees, which have the force of law, are issued jointly by the Council of Ministers and the Central Committee of the Party. The powers of the Central Committee to participate in legislation are derived either from an extensive interpretation of Article 126 or, more likely, from the extra-constitutional position held by the Party in the Soviet State.

"THE INTRA–PARTY DEMOCRACY"

Rights and Duties of the Members. It is the duty of Party members to carry out the decisions of the Party, to conform with the "general line" of Party policies after they have been duly approved. But, according to the charter, it is the inalienable right of each Party member to participate freely in the determination of these policies. This is what is meant by "intra-Party democracy" which is declared to be the very foundation of "Bolshevik self-criticism" and "conscious discipline." Indeed, the whole history of the Party both before and after the revolution of 1917 is an almost uninterrupted series of inner clashes over questions of policy. Under the regime of Stalin, however, "intra-Party democracy" has been subjected to drastic restrictions. A broad discussion of Party policy is now permitted only under the following conditions: (1) that the necessity of such discussion be recognized by at least several (the exact number is not stated) republican or territorial Party organizations; (2) that there be no "sufficiently strong" majority in the Central Committee on fundamental questions of policy; (3) that when there is such a majority, the Central Committee nevertheless considers the discussion desirable. The Central Committee thus has effective means of stifling any discussion of policy it may dislike and since the membership of the Central Committee is actually decided by the Party leaders headed by Stalin and only formally voted upon by the congress the practical significance of "intra-Party democracy" seems to be slight indeed. The official reason for these stringent restrictions is to preserve the inner unity of the Party and "to prevent all attempts of a small minority to force its will upon the vast majority." The Central Committee, moreover, has the power to subject recalcitrant members to measures of Party discipline including expulsion. Similar penalties may be imposed upon the members of the Central Committee, subject, however, to a two-thirds vote of the Central Committee itself.

Mass Purges and the Trials of the 1930's. From time to time, at the decision of the Central Committee, the membership of the Party is submitted to a thorough examination from the point of view of ideological orthodoxy, devotion to the cause of Communism, and personal character and behavior. Such purges invariably lead to the expulsion of a large number of members and candidates and to the demotion of others. Major purges took place in 1921, 1926, 1927, 1929, and 1933. The murder in December, 1934, of S. M. Kirov, a member of the Political Bureau and a close political friend of Stalin, was the starting point of a new era of purging that lasted through 1938. The purge that followed Kirov's murder differed from those preceding it. It was no longer a question of cleansing the Party of undeserving members but of exterminating altogether the vast majority of the old Bolshevik leaders. Sensational trials were staged in the Hall of Columns of the former Nobles' Club in Moscow. The list of the accused read like the *Who's Who* of the Russian revolution and included former members of the Soviet Government, leaders of the Third International, army commanders, ambassadors, two chiefs of the security police, and many others.[9] The crimes of which they were accused included murder and attempt at committing murder, high treason, plotting with the Fascist powers and "wrecking." Leon Trotsky, who vehemently protested from his place of exile abroad, was the alleged instigator of a conspiracy that seemingly had endless ramifications. A great many other Communist leaders, among them holders of high offices, were removed in a less spectacular manner. Their dismissal was briefly noted in the back page of a Soviet newspaper and in numerous cases even this formality was omitted: they simply dropped out and their ultimate fate remains a matter of conjecture. The purge extended to every sphere of Soviet life and was carried out with ruthless thoroughness even in the remotest corners of the land, in the army and navy, in factories, and on the farms. It has been officially admitted that not a few of the "purgers" were guilty of excess of zeal and that they were sometimes motivated by base personal considerations or vindictiveness. This led to the second phase of the stupendous drama—the "purging of the purgers." It is truly amazing that the Communist Party survived the ordeal.

Confessions. Notable features of the trials were the confessions in which the defendants not only admitted their crimes but vied in claiming for their actions the basest and most despicable motives. The confessions, which followed one another with monotonous uniformity, were the chief evidence against the alleged conspirators. The behavior in court of the accused men was unique and unprecedented, although it has been duplicated since in the countries which came under Soviet domination after World War II. The eagerness with which Hungarians, Czechs, Slovaks, and others, including a few stray Western Europeans and Americans caught in the nets of Communist prosecution, confessed their alleged crimes should dispose, once and for all, of the theory (popular in the 1930's and derived chiefly from a hasty perusal of the novels of Dostoyevsky) that the baffling conduct of the defendants at the Moscow trials was due to some unfathomable peculiarities of the Russian character. A scrutiny

---

[9] For a telling but incomplete list of the accused and a record of their fate see Paul Scheffer, "From Lenin to Stalin," in *Foreign Affairs,* April, 1938. Also Joseph Barnes, "The Great Bolshevik Cleansing," in *Foreign Affairs,* April, 1939.

of the methods of the Communist police might have produced a less absurd theory although no one has yet succeeded in explaining adequately the behavior of the accused men. It is often claimed that Communism will change human nature. The Moscow confessions, and their counterpart in Eastern Europe, suggest that in this instance at least the claim is justified.

Rewriting History. The hasty rewriting of the history of the Russian revolution was a by-product of the great purge. For instance, the official history of the All-Union Communist Party, ascribed to Stalin and published at the end of 1938, either does not mention the fallen leaders who only recently shared with Stalin the applause of the crowds, or represents them as villains and near-monsters. This vilification not only extends to the closing chapter of the career of the victims of the purge but it includes the earlier period when they struggled against the Imperial regime or held high offices under the Soviets. No enemy of Communism could have devised a more bitter indictment of the Russian revolutionary movement.

Stalin on "Cutting Off" Errant Members. Stalin's conversion to the method of destroying his opponents within the Party is relatively recent. "We know that the policy of 'cutting off' [errant members] is fraught with danger to the Party. . . ," he declared before the Fourteenth Congress of the Party in December, 1925. "Today we cut off one, tomorrow—another, the day after tomorrow—a third. But, by then, what will be left of the Party?" Stalin has since changed his mind but the question he asked in 1925 has lost none of its pertinence.

AMENDMENT OF THE COMMUNIST PARTY CHARTER, 1939

Reasons for the Amendment. The effect the great purge must have had upon the morale of the rank and file of the Communist Party presumably inspired the Amendment to the Party charter approved by the Eighteenth Congress of the Party in March, 1939, although the official reason given was the rapid transformation of the Soviet Union into a Socialist classless society. The purpose of the Amendment would seem to have been the rejuvenation of the Party and the promotion of added security and encouragement for the younger generation of Communists brought up in the school of Stalin.

Rules for Admission, 1939. The Amendment did away with the former division into four classes of applicants for membership. All applicants (except former members of other political parties for whom the rules laid down in the charter of 1934 remain in force) are required to be endorsed by three Party members of three years' standing who have known the applicants as co-workers for at least one year. Admission of new members is made effective after the approval of the decision of the primary Party organ by the Party committee of the county or of the city. The advancement of candidates to full membership is facilitated by the rule that they must qualify for promotion by signifying their consent to submit to Party discipline and to the other requirements of the charter and by "accepting" the Party program which, however, they need not understand: the Party itself will take care of the education of its new members in the tenets of revolutionary Marxism after their admission.

Rights of the Members Defined. The Amendment defines in greater detail the rights of the Party members, although it adds little to what was contained in the charter. The members are specifically entitled: (1) to criticize at Party gatherings any member of the Party; (2) to vote in Party elections and to hold Party office; (3) to be heard when their personal conduct is being investigated; (4) to ask information or to make representations to any Party agency, including the Central Committee. That such a clarification of members' rights should be necessary is in itself a telling comment on the practical working of "intra-Party democracy."

Abolition of Mass Purges. More significant is the abolition of periodical mass purges, although the Party retains the right to cleanse its ranks of undeserving members "as a matter of routine." Special care, it is pointed out, should be taken to desist from expelling members for minor offenses. Candidates are entitled to promotion to full membership after one year, except former members of other political parties, for whom the rules of the charter of 1934 remain in force. The Amendment emphasizes the use of the secret ballot in Party elections and provides that voting shall be for individual candidates and not for entire lists of candidates, an illegal practice never sanctioned by the charter, although it appears to have been widely used.

Changes in the Administrative Structure of the Party. The structure of administrative Party agencies attached to the Central Committee is somewhat altered, and strong emphasis is put on propaganda and educational activities. The Committee of Party Control is elected not by the Party congress, as in the past, but by the Central Committee, under whose direction it works. The Amendment provides for All-Union party conferences of representatives of local Party organizations to be held at least once a year, thus reviving a practice that had been discontinued in 1934. The method of electing representatives to the conferences is to be determined by the Central Committee, and the decisions of the conferences are subject to the approval of that Committee. The conferences have the right to replace the members of the Central Committee to the extent of one-fifth of its membership, the new members being chosen from among the alternate members of the Central Committee [10] whose place is taken by new alternate members elected by the conference. Decisions of the conferences dealing with the replacement of members of the Central Committee need not be sanctioned by the latter.

Qualifications for Holding Party Offices, 1939. The length of Party affiliation required for qualifying for the office of secretary in the Communist organizations of the constituent republics, territories, and provinces has been diminished from twelve years to five, for those in the cities, from ten to three, and for those in the counties, from seven to three. One-year Party membership is now a sufficient qualification for the secretaries of the primary Party organs (the former requirement was two and three years). The Amendment provides for the creation of Party organizations in the regions (*okrug*) not mentioned in the charter.

[10] See above, p. 724.

Strengthening of Primary Party Organs. The already predominant position of the primary Party organs was further strengthened by the provision that the primary Party organs in "the productive enterprises, including the State farms, and collective farms and machine tractor stations . . . receive the power to control the work of the administration of such enterprises" for which they are held responsible. In the People's Commissariats (Ministries), where for technical reasons such control is not feasible, the primary Party organs "must single out the defects in the operation of the institution, take note of the defects in the work of the commissariat and of individual employees and forward pertinent materials and considerations to the Central Committee of the Party and to the leaders of the commissariat." Every primary Party organ having at least fifteen members elects an executive bureau of three to seven members.

The Komsomol and "Sympathizers." The age limit for admission to the Party has been lowered from twenty to eighteen years and special facilities are given to the members of the *Komsomol* or Organization of Communist Youth. The participation of the *Komsomol* in the political and economic life of the country is to be increased and it is to exercise the functions of Party control, especially in those industrial enterprises and collective farms which have no primary Party organs. On the other hand the "sympathizers' groups" have been discontinued. The reason for this decision is that the "sympathizers" did not live up to expectation: of the total number of candidates admitted to the Party in the two years preceding the Eighteenth Congress only 21 per cent came from this group.

Except for the by no means unimportant changes mentioned above, the constitution of the Communist Party remains what it has been since 1934. The Eighteenth Congress and the Soviet press dutifully acclaimed the Amendment as a new charter of Communist liberties. That the Amendment would inject new blood into the Party was clear: whether it would succeed in promoting "intra-Party democracy" was less certain. The report presented by A. Zhdanov, a member of the Political Bureau, to the Eighteenth Congress unfolded a shocking picture of abuse of power and a "heartlessly bureaucratic" attitude taken by the Party chieftains toward the rank and file. Scattered information from Soviet sources (examples of which will be found below) indicate that the situation was not improved in later years.

THE NUMERICAL STRENGTH OF THE PARTY

Size of the Membership. In view of the position occupied by the Communist Party its numerical strength is of considerable interest. The unfortunately incomplete and contradictory data on this question are summarized on page 730.

The figures given throw an interesting light on the magnitude of the purge. Admission to the Party was closed from 1933 to November 1, 1936. According to announcement in the *Pravda* of February 4, 1939, the Party has admitted "in the last two years" 180,000 members and 471,000 candidates. Be-

MEMBERSHIP OF THE ALL–UNION COMMUNIST PARTY (FORMERLY THE BOLSHEVIK WING OF THE RUSSIAN SOCIAL–DEMOCRATIC PARTY) [11]

Year	Members	Candidates	Total
		(IN THOUSANDS)	
Beginning 1905	—	—	8.4
Beginning 1917	—	—	23.6
April, 1917	—	—	40.0
August, 1917	—	—	200.0
Beginning 1918	—	—	115.0
Beginning 1920	—	—	431.4
March, 1920	—	—	611.9
January, 1922	410.4	117.9	528.3
January, 1923	381.4	117.7	499.1
January, 1924	350.0	122.0	472.0
January, 1925	420.6	351.4	772.0
January, 1926	638.3	439.8	1,078.1
January, 1927	774.8	372.3	1,147.1
January, 1928	913.2	391.2	1,304.4
January, 1929	1,089.6	442.7	1,532.3
January, 1930	1,182.3	492.6	1,674.9
January, 1934	1,874.5	935.3	2,809.8
March 1, 1939	1,588.9	888.8	2,477.7

tween 1934 and March 1, 1939, the number of members declined by 286,000 and that of the candidates by 46,000. The purge therefore involved the expulsion of some 466,000 members, or almost 25 per cent of their total number in 1934, and of 516,000 candidates, or well over 50 per cent of their total number in the same year. Even when allowance is made for mortality among the Communists these figures indicate that approximately one member out of four and one candidate out of two were expelled between 1934 and the beginning of 1939. According to Stalin's much quoted dictum "to the rank and file of the Party members to remain within the fold of the Party or to be expelled is a question of life and death." Stalin compared expulsion from the Party to execution by the firing squad for army men. Many of the expulsions have been rescinded since and members and candidates reinstated. It was disclosed at the Eighteenth Congress that a very large percentage of the expulsions were made on the ground of lack of interest in Party activities. Official spokesmen have admitted that the effects of the purge on the morale of the Party members have been disastrous. Nevertheless, the authority of Stalin remained unshaken.

Rejuvenation of the Party. The rejuvenation of the Party accomplished by the purge is suggested by the composition of the Eighteenth Congress. Half of the delegates (49.5 per cent) receiving a "decisive" vote were thirty-five years old or younger, another 32 per cent were in the age group thirty-six to

[11] The figures for the period before 1930 are from an article by A. Bubnov which appeared first in Volume xi of the *Large Soviet Encyclopedia* and was issued separately in 1931. The figures for 1930 and 1934 are from the official *History of the Communist Party of the Soviet Union* published in 1938; the 1939 figures are those of the Eighteenth Congress. There is some discrepancy in the figures that appear in the *Encyclopedia* and the *History* and the data used by Bubnov do not always agree. The contradiction may be explained either by the difference in the methods of computation or, more likely, by the fact admitted by the official *History* that "a state of intolerable chaos in registering Communists" existed in 1933 in a number of local Party agencies. It may be surmised that these conditions were not limited to the year 1933.

forty, that is, an overwhelming majority of the delegates had received their training under the regime of Stalin. The congress elected a new Central Committee of seventy-one members and sixty-eight alternates. Only sixteen members of the new Committee were members of the last one, which was elected in 1934.

Its Social Structure. Information on the social structure of the Party is out-of-date. On January 1, 1930, the membership was distributed as follows: industrial workers, 65.3 per cent; peasants, 20.2 per cent; employees, 13.4 per cent; others, 1.1 per cent. In the First to the Fifteenth Party Congresses (1898–December, 1927) not a single peasant was elected to the Central Committee as either a member or an alternate, although in 1927 the peasants formed 19 per cent of the entire membership and in 1924 as much as 28.8 per cent. In 1929, 51.1 per cent of the commanders (officers) of the Red Army were Communists. Women, on January 1, 1930, accounted for 14 per cent of the membership. More recent data are not available. At the Eighteenth Congress 13.3 per cent of the full-fledged delegates elected on the principle of proportional representation came from Moscow and 9.1 per cent from Leningrad. The two capitals therefore remain the stronghold of the Party. Out of 1,574 full-fledged delegates to the Eighteenth Congress only sixty-three were employed in agriculture, while the army, the navy, and the police (People's Commissariat of the Interior) sent 283 representatives.[12]

Membership During and After the War. Figures of Party membership are released on the occasion of Party congresses. The last congress was held in March, 1939, and no official later data are available. It would seem, however, that membership increased considerably in the 1940's—to 3.5 million in 1940 and to 6 million in 1946.[13] These figures include, presumably, both members and candidates.

The Leading Position of the Party. The population of the Soviet Union in 1939 was 170 millions.[14] Of this number less than 2.5 millions, or about 1.5 per cent, belonged to the Communist Party. If the 1946 figure of Party membership quoted above is correct, Communists in that year represented about 3 per cent of the population, which is said to have increased, as a result of annexations, to 193 millions. The proportion of Party members, although larger than before the War, remained small. The influence of the Party in the affairs of State, however, has no relation to its numerical strength. Every public office of any importance in the USSR is filled by Communists. Although according to the official view the Soviet Union has left behind the stage of the dictatorship of the proletariat and is now in the stage of Socialism, the domineering position of the Party has been fully preserved.

[12] The Party bureaucracy was represented by 659 delegates; industry, 230; Soviet administration and the trade unions, 162; transportation, 110; the *Komsomol*, 27; art and science, 35.

[13] *The American Review on the Soviet Union,* February, 1946, pp. 69–70, quoting the *Daily Worker.*

[14] Soviet population statistics are in a state of hopeless confusion. The census of 1937 (the first comprehensive Russian census since 1897), although acclaimed at the time as a model of its kind, was abruptly canceled on the ground that it violated the elementary rules of census-taking. The second Five-Year Plan estimated the population in 1937 as 180.7 millions. According to the census of January 17, 1939, it was 170,467,000.

CHAPTER IV

THE CONSTITUTIONAL AND ADMINISTRATIVE
STRUCTURE

DIVISION OF SOVIET HISTORY INTO PERIODS

The Introductory Period. It is both customary and convenient to divide Soviet history prior to World War II into four periods, although the line of demarcation between them is by no means always clearly drawn. The first or introductory period, lasting from the advent of the Bolsheviks (October–November, 1917) until the middle of 1918, was characterized by the confident expectation in Moscow that world revolution would soon be an accomplished fact. Outside Russia, however, opinion as to the probable course of events was lacking in unanimity; some anticipated the spread of Communism while others expected the inevitable and speedy downfall of the Soviet rule. In February, 1918, the Moscow Government was forced to sign with the Central Powers the extremely harsh Treaty of Brest-Litovsk. The domestic policies of the Soviets were not yet clearly defined. Trotsky has well described the early decrees as the announcement of a Party doctrine "in the language of power," rather than measures of practical policy. Land, banks, foreign trade, and some separate branches of industry and individual enterprises were nationalized. The Bolsheviks had no concrete land program and borrowed from the Socialist Revolutionary Party its program of "socialization" of land. "Socialization" extended to the entire national territory the traditional peasant form of land tenure (communal tenure or *obshehina*), proclaimed the right of every citizen to a land allotment provided he was willing to work on it, and decreed the periodical redistribution of all agricultural land among the farmers in order to maintain equality in the size of the allotments. This utopian scheme was of course never actually applied but it gave an appearance of legal sanction to the occupation of landed estates and their division among the local peasants, a process that had already begun spontaneously in the summer and early autumn of 1917.

War Communism. The second period, known as War Communism, lasted from the middle of 1918 until the spring of 1921. This was a period of civil war and foreign intervention. The so-called White Armies organized by anti-Bolshevik Russians were openly supported by foreign powers. First the Germans and later British, French, United States, and Japanese troops occupied various sections of Russian territory. The blockade of Russia was organized by her former Allies. War with Poland broke out. Hard pressed from every direction the Soviet Government embarked on a policy of wholesale nationalization of industry and drastic regimentation of agriculture. Rigid centralization, militarization of labor, requisition of agricultural produce, and an attempted elimination of the money economy which was to be replaced by State-organized barter were among the chief features of this period. Although most of these measures remained a dead letter, many left-wing leaders saw in them the embodiment of true Communism. The extreme economic disorganization and the ruthless exploitation of the peasantry led to violent agrarian uprisings against the Soviets and to mutinies in the army. In the meantime the White Armies collapsed one after another, war with Poland was terminated, the blockade was lifted, and foreign troops returned home. War Communism was abruptly abandoned.

The New Economic Policy. The next period, known as that of the New Economic Policy or the period of restoration—that is, a return to pre-War economic levels—lasted from the spring of 1921 to about 1927. In the international field it was characterized by the reluctant admission of the somewhat disturbing fact that the Soviet Union and the capitalist countries must continue to exist side by side. In April, 1922, the Soviet Government was officially recognized by Germany (Treaty of Rapallo) and in 1924 by Great Britain, Italy, and France. Recognition by the United States was delayed until 1933. A welcome relaxation manifested itself in domestic policies. The strict regimentation of War Communism was discarded, currency was stabilized, and the peasants were again free to dispose of most of the produce of their farms. A limited degree of economic freedom was conceded in other spheres, especially in distribution. It was generally although erroneously believed abroad that the Communist experiment was over and that Russia was returning to "normal" conditions, that is, to an economy based on private enterprise. Toward the end of the period of the New Economic Policy the situation had greatly improved. At the same time the Party definitely accepted Stalin's theory concerning the possibility of building a Socialist system in a single country.

The Period of Socialist Reconstruction. About 1927 began the fourth period of Soviet history which lasted until the outbreak of World War II. It was the period of Socialist reconstruction characterized by a gigantic drive for rebuilding the country on a Socialist basis. The main features of this era were, in the international field, the entry of the USSR into the League of Nations (1934),[1] and, in the domestic field, the first, second, and third Five-

[1] The decision to join the Geneva organization required a compromise with Communist principles. The 1919 program of the Russian Communist Party, which is still in force, described the League of Nations as "an international organization of the capitalists for the systematic exploitation of all the peoples of the earth and whose immediate efforts are directed to the suppression of the revolutionary movement in every country."

Year Plans, that is, the introduction of planned economy, industrialization, collectivization of farming, and the adoption of the 1936 Constitution. The last much-publicized event coincided with the great purge.

The First War Period, August 1939–June 1941. World War II constitutes two sharply differentiated periods in Soviet history. From the conclusion of the Hitler-Stalin pact of friendship in August, 1939, to the German attack on the Soviet Union in June, 1941, Moscow was a partner, if not an ally, of Berlin. In terms of territorial aggrandizement this partnership was not unprofitable. The partition of Poland engineered by the Soviet and the German Governments, the Soviet-Finnish War, and the predatory moves directed against the Baltic States and Rumania netted the Soviet Union large slices of Poland and Finland, Latvia, Lithuania, Estonia, Bessarabia, and Northern Bukovina. In December, 1939, following the Soviet attack on Finland, the USSR was expelled from the League of Nations. The domestic policies of 1939–1941 were characterized by the expansion of the rearmament program, the tightening of administrative controls, and drastic measures for the regimentation of industrial labor and collective farmers.

The Second War Period, June 1941–1945. With Hitler's attack on Russia in June, 1941, the Soviet Union shifted overnight from the German orbit into that of the Western powers. As it became clear that the invading German legions had met their doom in the roadless vastness of the Russian steppes, the reserve with which the Soviet Union was treated at first by her new allies gave place to boundless admiration and enthusiasm. The Communist International, a thorn in the flesh of the capitalist Governments of the United States and Great Britain, was opportunely dissolved in May, 1943, a tactical move which—quite unwarrantedly—was interpreted in the Western countries as the abandonment by the Kremlin of the idea of world revolution. From the standpoint of territorial expansion, partnership with the Western democracies proved no less profitable to the Soviet Union than cooperation with Berlin. As a result of the War and post-War arrangements, and the altruistic declarations of the Atlantic Charter notwithstanding, Russia not only retained her territorial acquisitions of 1939–1940 but added to them the Ukrainian districts formerly held by Czechoslovakia, East Prussia with the ancient city of Koenigsberg, the southern portion of Sakhalin, and the Kurile Islands. The internal policies of this period were dominated by the stupendous war effort.

The Post-War Period, 1945–1950. The end of hostilities found the Soviet Union at the pinnacle of her popularity with the Western democracies. The honeymoon, however, was brief. The sway of the Red Army and the Allies' incautious commitments stemming from the agreements of Teheran, Yalta, and Potsdam brought under Soviet control a string of States in East and South Europe as well as vast territories in the Far East. As was to be expected, all countries within the Soviet sphere of influence established, within a few months after Soviet occupation, Communist dictatorships on the Soviet model and, with the lone exception of Yugoslavia, meekly submitted to the dictation of the Kremlin. Although the United Nations, of which the Soviet Union is one of the most active members, provided Communist propaganda with a sounding board far beyond the most daring hopes of the Communist International, that unlamented institution was revived in 1947 in the guise of the Cominform. Conflicts between the Soviet Union and her war partners multiplied and increased in violence. There is practically no major issue on which Moscow would not be hopelessly at odds with Washington, London, and Paris. In the autumn of 1951 the principal results of this unhappy state of affairs were the Atlantic Pact directed against the Soviet Union, the re-armament of Western Europe largely at the expense of the United States, and the Korean War which Hanson Baldwin has so well described as the Soviet War by proxy. By comparison with the sinister and spectacular international activities of the Kremlin, Soviet post-War domestic policies are singularly drab and unimaginative. The fourth Five-Year Plan (1946–1950) deals pri-marily with the vital but prosaic and laborious task of repairing the devasta-tion inflicted upon Russia by the German invasion. The methods by which this is being achieved are the same as before the War, even when their in-adequacy had been conclusively proved by past experience. No new idea and no new leader of any stature have emerged from the great upheaval. The striking contrast between the spreading of Soviet influence throughout the world, on the one hand, and what may be called the inner sterility of Communism, on the other, is perhaps the most arresting feature of the post-War history of the USSR.

EARLY CONSTITUTIONS

The Constitutions of 1918 and 1924. The Constitution of 1936 had two predecessors. The first Constitution was adopted by the Fifth Congress of the Soviets on July 10, 1918.[2] It sanctioned much of the Soviet form of govern-ment that came into existence more or less spontaneously after the downfall of the monarchy in March, 1917. The State it established was the Russian Socialist Federated Soviet Republic (RSFSR) whose territory was consid-erably smaller than that of the future Soviet Union, since at that time many parts of the country were still held by anti-Communist forces. The Constitu-tion of 1918 and its preamble, "The Declaration of the Rights of the Work-ing and Exploited People," were imbued with the militant spirit of the new-born dictatorship of the proletariat. This character was retained in the second Constitution which was adopted by the Second All-Union Congress of the Soviets in 1924, after the First All-Union Congress in December, 1922, estab-lished the Union of Soviet Socialist Republics (USSR). The Union originally was formed by four constituent republics: the RSFSR, the Ukraine, White Russia, and Transcaucasia. The Uzbek and the Turkmen constituent repub-lics were carved out in 1924, and the Tadzhik constituent republic in 1929, raising the total number of constituent republics to seven. The Constitution of

---

[2] The numbering of the Congresses of the Soviets was started anew with the formation of the Soviet Union in December, 1922.

1924 provided for a federal form of government. The administrative structure consisted of a pyramid of Soviets (councils) whose territorial jurisdiction was gradually broadened. At the bottom of the pyramid were the village Soviets, then came the county (*raion*) and city Soviets; above them were the Soviets of the territories (*krai*), provinces (*oblast*), and the constituent republics; at the very top of the pyramid was the All-Union Congress of the Soviets, in theory the supreme organ of the Union.

Franchise and Elections under the Constitutions of 1918 and 1924. The whole of this structure, as has already been pointed out, was permeated with the militant spirit of the proletarian dictatorship. The following categories of citizens were disfranchised: persons employing hired labor for the purpose of extracting profit; persons living on income not derived from work; private traders, monks and ministers of religion; former police officers and members of the former royal family; lunatics and persons condemned for disgraceful crimes. Moreover, the number of deputies sent to the All-Union Soviet and to the Soviets of the constituent republics was one deputy for each 25,000 city electors and one for every 125,000 of the rural population. This allotment gave a definite preponderance to the urban proletariat. The Soviet structure under the first two Constitutions was based on the principle of indirect elections, that is, the deputies to the Soviets ranking above those of the town and the village were chosen not by the electorate but by the lower Soviets. Voting was carried on by the show of hands instead of by the secret ballot customary in bourgeois democracies. The distribution of the right to vote was somewhat capricious and by no means easy to comprehend, based as it was on a combination of the territorial principle with that of the "unit of production," that is, some of the electors voted as residents of a certain district, others as employees in a factory or similar establishment.

Rejection of the Principle of Separation of Powers. The two earlier Constitutions, moreover, openly denied the principle of separation of powers, the traditional segregation of the legislative, the executive, and the judiciary. In theory, all State power was vested in the All-Union Congress of the Soviets and was exercised through the agencies appointed by that body. The functions of the Soviets, which met at long and irregular intervals, were largely perfunctory and the actual business of government was carried on by the officers and agencies they appointed, under the control of the Communist Party, which was not even mentioned in the Constitutions of 1918 and 1924.

The All-Union Congress of the Soviets and Its Organs. The All-Union Congress of the Soviets was a large assembly of over two thousand members and was to convene, under the Constitution of 1924, at least once a year; an amendment adopted in 1927 provided that the Congress should meet at least once every two years. Actually the Congress met, most of the time, at longer intervals than those prescribed by the law.[3] The chief functions of the

[3] From the formation of the USSR in December, 1922, to the adoption of the new Constitution in December, 1936, the All-Union Congress of the Soviets met eight times: First Congress, December 30, 1922 (a one-day session); Second Congress, January 26–February 2, 1924; Third Congress, May 13–20, 1925; Fourth Congress, April 18–26, 1927; Fifth Congress,

Congress consisted in approving the political declarations of the leaders and in electing the Central Executive Committee which exercised all legislative and executive powers when the Congress was not in session. The list of candidates for the Central Executive Committee was submitted to the Congress by the leaders and was invariably unanimously approved. The Central Executive Committee consisted of two chambers: the Council of the Union, which had several hundred members apportioned on the basis of population, and the Council of Nationalities, a smaller assembly made up of five representatives from each constituent and autonomous republic, and one representative from each autonomous region. At a joint session the two chambers elected a Presidium of twenty-seven members which the Constitution of 1924 described as "the highest legislative, executive, and administrative organ in the USSR." Originally the Central Executive Committee was to convene at least three times a year, but in 1931 this requirement was changed to at least three times between the regular sessions of the Congresses of the Soviets. "In practice," as Towster notes, "the meetings of the Central Executive Committee became progressively rare." The intervals between the plenary sessions of the Central Executive Committee ranged from two to thirteen months and in the years of the Committee's existence (1923–1937), the sessions occupied 139 days.[4] The brunt of the work of the Congresses of the Soviet devolved, not upon the Central Executive Committee, but upon its Presidium.

Other Governmental Agencies under the Earlier Constitutions. The Central Executive Committee appointed the principal executive organ of the federal Government, the Council of People's Commissars of the USSR, whose functions will be discussed in connection with the Constitution of 1936. Each constituent republic had its own constitution duplicating on a small scale the administrative machinery of the federal Government. The administrative structure of the Soviet Union has been subjected to an almost uninterrupted remodeling, a condition that not only is distressing to the student but must also add greatly to the difficulties of the planning bodies.

THE BASIC PRINCIPLES OF THE CONSTITUTION OF 1936

Drafting of the Constitution. The decision to adopt a new Constitution was announced at the Seventh All-Union Congress of the Soviets in February, 1935, and when the draft of the Constitution was published in June, 1936, it became virtually mandatory for everyone to join in the discussion. According to official data 527,000 meetings attended by 36.5 million people were held for this purpose. Some 154,000 amendments were offered, but only forty-three changes were made, practically all of them in phraseology.[5] The Eighth All-Union Congress of the Soviets after a ten-day discussion unanimously ap-

---

May 20–28, 1929; Sixth Congress, March 8–17, 1931; Seventh Congress, January 28–February 6, 1935; and Eighth and last Congress, November 25–December 5, 1936.

[4] Julian Towster, *Political Power in the USSR, 1917–1947 (Oxford University Press,* New York, 1948), pp. 229–230.

[5] The only amendment of some formal significance which was approved was the substitution of direct for indirect elections in choosing the Council of Nationalities.

proved the text of the Constitution on December 5, 1936, which was proclaimed a national holiday.

Basic Principles of the New Society. Chapter I of the Constitution outlines the basic features of the new society. It defines the USSR as "a Socialist State of workers and peasants" (Article 1). The political foundation of the Union "consists of Soviets of working people's deputies, which grew up and became strong as a result of the overthrow of the power of the landlords and capitalists and the winning of the dictatorship of the proletariat" (Article 2). All political power "belongs to the working people of town and country" as represented by the Soviets (Article 3). The economic foundation of the Union "consists of the Socialist economic system and the Socialist ownership of the tools and means of production" achieved through the liquidation of capitalism and the "abolition of exploitation of man by man" (Article 4). "Socialist property" takes the form of either State property or "co-operative collective property" (Article 5). All land, natural resources, waters, forests, industrial enterprises, means of transportation, and "the basic housing facilities in cities and industrial localities are State property, that is, the wealth of the whole people" (Article 6). Articles 7 and 8 deal with collective farms and will be discussed in Chapter VII.[6] Article 9 authorizes "small-scale private enterprise of individual peasants and handicraftsmen based on their personal labor, provided there is no exploitation of the labor of others." Private property is recognized but is kept within narrow limits. "The right of personal property of citizens in their income from work and in their savings, in their dwelling houses and auxiliary husbandry, in household articles and utensils, and in articles for personal use and comfort, as well as the right of inheritance of personal property of citizens, is protected by law" (Article 10). The two closing articles of Chapter I are the most characteristic. Article 11 declares that "the economic life of the USSR is determined and directed by a State plan of national economy" and sets out the three objects of planning: increase in public wealth, steady improvement in the material and cultural standards of the working people, and the strengthening of the independence of the USSR and its capacity for defense. Article 12 states that "Work in the USSR is a duty and a matter of honor for every able-bodied citizen, on the principle: 'He who does not work, shall not eat.' In the USSR the principle of Socialism is realized: 'From each according to his ability, to each according to his work.'" The latter dictum gives official sanction to the piecework system of wage payments which has been in use in the Soviet Union for a number of years and is an essential feature of Soviet planned economy.

The Constituent Republics. Under the Constitution of 1936, as under its predecessor, the USSR remains "a federal State, formed on the basis of the voluntary association" of Soviet Socialist (constituent) Republics (SSR). In 1936 the number of constituent republics was increased to eleven by adding to the seven constituent republics mentioned above [7] the newly formed repub-

---

[6] See below, pp. 816–817.
[7] See above, p. 735.

lics of Kazakh and Kirghiz and by splitting the Transcaucasian republic, which ceased to exist, into three republics: Armenia, Georgia, and Azerbaidzhan. The territorial gains secured by the Soviet Union during the period of her cooperation with National Socialist Germany led to the creation in 1940 of five new constituent republics: Karelo-Finnish, Moldavian, Lithuanian, Latvian, and Estonian. The number of constituent republics was thus increased to sixteen and has been maintained at that figure during the post-War period, the territories acquired by Moscow at the end of World War II being incorporated into the existing constituent republics.[8]

Powers of the Federal Government. The powers of the federal Government are extraordinarily comprehensive and broad. Article 14 of the Constitution, as amended by three decrees issued by the Presidium of the Supreme Soviet in 1944,[9] assigns to the jurisdiction of "the highest organs of State authority and organs of Government" of the USSR the following activities: representation of the USSR in international relations, conclusion and abrogation of treaties, and "the establishment of the general character of the relations between the constituent republics and the foreign states"; declaration of war and conclusion of peace; admission of new republics into the Union; enforcement of the federal Constitution and insurance of the conformity of the constitutions of the constituent republics with the federal Constitution; confirmation of changes of boundaries between the constituent republics and of the formation of new territories, provinces, and autonomous republics within the constituent republics; organization of national defense, direction of all armed forces of the Union, and "determination of the basic principles of the organization of the military formations of the constituent republics"; administration of the monopoly of foreign trade; protection of the security of the State, that is, administration of the police; establishment of national economic plans; confirmation of the federal budget and of those taxes and revenues which are apportioned between the federal budget, on the one hand, and the republican and local budgets, on the other; administration of banks and industrial, agricultural, and commercial enterprises of All-Union importance; administration of transport and communications; control of the monetary and credit system; organization of State insurance; issue of State loans; determination of basic principles for the use of land and the exploitation of natural resources; determination of basic principles in the field of education and public health; organization of a unified system of cost (economic) accounting; [10]

[8] East Prussia (now province of Kaliningrad; Koenigsberg was renamed Kaliningrad on June 30, 1946); portions of the territory ceded by Finland in 1940 and 1944 and not included in the new Karelo-Finnish SSR; Southern Sakhalin and the Kurile Islands annexed from Japan; and the Tuvinian autonomous province (formerly the republic of Tannu Tuva, in Outer Mongolia, annexed by the USSR in 1945) were incorporated into the RSFSR. The former Polish territories taken over by the Soviet Union in 1939 were divided between the Ukrainian SSR and the White Russian (Belorussian) SSR. Parts of Bessarabia (those not included in the Moldavian SSR) and Northern Bukovina, both ceded by Rumania in 1940, and the Trans-Carpathian Ukraine, ceded by Czechoslovakia in 1945, were incorporated into the Ukrainian SSR.

[9] The three decrees, which will be discussed presently, became effective at once: Article 14 of the Constitution was amended accordingly by the Supreme Soviet in February, 1947.

[10] See below, pp. 789, 792.

determination of the principles of labor legislation; legislation concerning the judiciary and civil and criminal codes; legislation concerning citizenship and the status of foreigners; determination of the basic principles bearing on marriage and the family; the right of amnesty.

Amendments Limiting the Powers of the Federal Government, 1944. Prior to 1944 foreign relations and defense belonged exclusively to the province of the federal Government. On February 1, 1944, however, the Presidium of the Supreme Soviet issued two decrees which, respectively, empowered the constituent republics (1) to enter into direct relations with foreign States and to conclude international agreements, and (2) to organize separate "military formations." Accordingly, the People's Commissariats (now Ministries) of Foreign Affairs and Defense, hitherto All-Union Commissariats, were reorganized as Union-Republic Commissariats.[11] In legal theory the amendments of February, 1944, represented the delegation to constituent republics of important powers formerly vested in the federal Government, and may be interpreted as a move toward decentralization. Such an interpretation, however, is not in agreement with the facts. The February decrees did not reflect the organic trend of Soviet constitutional development but were, presumably, due to external causes. In 1944 the Kremlin was engaged in laborious negotiations concerning the number of constituent republics that would be entitled to representation in the future United Nations. It may be surmised that the conferring upon the constituent republics of two essential attributes of statehood was designed to strengthen the hand of Moscow in these negotiations. The practical consequences of the enhanced status of the constituent republics would seem to confirm the foregoing interpretation. Ukraine and White Russia were duly admitted to membership in the United Nations, where their representatives obediently echo the views of the delegation of the USSR.[12] Otherwise the constituent republics have taken no part in international affairs and what their foreign ministers and foreign offices do is one of the Soviet Union's standing mysteries. There is also no evidence of the reorganization of Soviet armed forces on the republican basis.

Amendment Extending the Powers of the Federal Government, 1944. The view that the amendments of February, 1944, were due to extraneous considerations and were not indicative of any reversal in the centripetal trend of Soviet constitutional development is confirmed by the almost simultaneous extension of the powers of the federal Government over an important

[11] See below, p. 746.

[12] The reasons why of the sixteen constituent republics Ukraine and White Russia were singled out for the honor to represent the USSR in the United Nations is, of necessity, a matter for conjecture. Molotov's statement that the two republics were entitled to separate representation because of the gallant part they played in the War is not very helpful. Surely it was not his intention to imply that the other invaded Soviet republics, including the RSFSR, did not contribute their full share to the struggle against Germany. The real reason for the choice of Ukraine and White Russia would seem to be that the Polish territories annexed by the Soviet Union were incorporated into these two republics. In 1944 and 1945 American and British opinion was still aroused about the fate of the eastern provinces of Poland. Had the Polish issue been raised at Lake Success, as it seemed probable at the time, the presence of Ukraine and White Russia among the founding members of the United Nations would have been a distinct advantage from the Soviet point of view.

field of domestic legislation. From the beginning of the Soviet rule, family relationships and kindred matters (marriage, divorce, abortion, and so on) were within the purview of the governments of the constituent republics, although gradually federal influence made itself felt, especially since 1936. On July 8, 1944, however, the Presidium of the Supreme Soviet issued a decree which introduced far-reaching changes in the legislation dealing with the family and directed the constituent republics to make corresponding changes in the republican codes. In February, 1947, as has already been noted, Article 14 of the federal Constitution was amended and the "determination of the basic principles bearing on marriage and family" became a function of the federal Government.

Actual Scope of Republican Government. The powers of the federal Government listed in Article 14 are broad, comprehensive, and ill-defined, especially if it is borne in mind that the economic plan, the framing and administration of which are federal functions, comprises practically every aspect of the country's life and offers unlimited opportunities for interference with the organs of government of the constituent republics. Moreover, such phrases as "establishment of the general character" and "determination of the basic principles," which occur repeatedly in Article 14, are given in practice a broad interpretation which amounts to dictation by the federal authorities. It will be seen below (Chapters VI and VII) that minute rules regulating the organization of industry and farming, wages, conditions of labor, length of the working day, and so on, emanate from the central agencies of the All-Union Communist Party and the organs of the federal Government. The provision of Article 15 that outside the limits set by Article 14 "each constituent republic shall exercise State power independently" is therefore of small practical value, except that it safeguards the right to "cultural autonomy" (which, however, must conform with Communist ideology) and the use of local languages, a no doubt meritorious departure from the policy of Russification pursued by the Imperial Government. The right of the constituent republics "freely to secede from the USSR" guaranteed by Article 17 is also of questionable significance. This provision must be interpreted in the light of Stalin's dictum quoted above.[13] During the purge of 1937–1938 there were references in the press to leaders of national minorities who were accused of plotting to bring about the secession of some territory from the Union. Such activities have invariably been interpreted by Soviet courts as treasonable and counterrevolutionary. During World War II several national groups which had allegedly favored the invaders were deprived of their autonomous status. The Volga-German Autonomous Soviet Socialist Republic was dissolved in 1941, and the Kalmyk, Chechen-Ingush, and Crimean Autonomous Soviet Socialist Republics, and the Karachaev autonomous province were dissolved in 1943–1945. Members of the native communities in these areas (but not of other ethnic groups such as Russians and Ukrainians) were "resettled elsewhere," that is, deported and scattered through, it is believed, the inhospitable vastness

[13] See above, pp. 715–716.

of Siberia and the Kazakh steppes.[14] In the regions affected, geographical names of local origin were replaced by Russian names so as to eradicate any trace of the national minorities that had failed in their loyalty to the Soviet regime.[15] It would seem, therefore, that the exercise of the right of secession and national autonomy, such as is understood in the Western world, is precluded by the structure of the Soviet State and by the Communist doctrine that governs it.

The Smaller Administrative Subdivisions. The Constitution provides for the following administrative subdivisions below the rank of constituent republics: Autonomous Soviet Socialist Republics, territories (*krai*), provinces (*oblast*), autonomous provinces, regions (*okrug*), counties (*raion*), cities and towns, and rural localities (villages). In December, 1936, when the Constitution was adopted, the RSFSR consisted of seventeen Autonomous Soviet Socialist Republics, five territories, nineteen provinces, and six autonomous provinces.[16] The Ukrainian, Azerbaidzhan, Georgian, Uzbek, Tadzhik, and Kazakh SSR had a substantially smaller number of administrative subdivisions, while the constituent republics of Armenia, White Russia, Turkmen, and Kirghiz had none. The territorial administrative structure of the Soviet Union, however, is subject to incessant remodeling. According to a by no means unsympathetic American observer, "in no other country have there been so many and so extensive changes in internal boundaries. A map showing the administrative regions of the country is likely to be out of date as soon as it is published." The reason for the inclusion in the Constitution of a list of administrative subdivisions was said to be the desire to give the territorial administrative structure greater stability and clarity.[17] Nevertheless the redrafting of the administrative map continued with undiminished vigor after 1936. Articles 22–29 of the Constitution, which list the administrative subdivisions of each constituent republic, have been frequently amended by the Supreme Soviet. In June, 1949, the RSFSR consisted of twelve Autonomous Soviet Socialist Republics, five territories, forty-eight provinces, and six autonomous provinces; the White Russian SSR, of twelve provinces; the Turk-

[14] *The New York Times,* November 30, 1945. "During the great patriotic War," according to the official statement submitted to the Supreme Soviet in June, 1946, ". . . many Chechens and Crimean Tartars . . . voluntarily and together with the German army waged an armed struggle against units of the Red Army. . . . In connection with this the Chechens and Crimean Tartars were resettled in other districts of the Soviet Union." The population of the former Chechen-Ingush and Crimean republics was estimated at 1.5 million. The actual number of those deported from these and other regions that lost their autonomous status was not disclosed but presumably it ran into hundreds of thousands if not millions. Cf. *The New York Times,* June 27, 1946.

[15] The latter action might have been inspired by the punitive measures taken by Catherine II after the defeat of the peasant rebellion led by Emilian Pugachev (1773–1774). Pugachev's native village was renamed and moved to the opposite bank of the Don, and the name of Yalik Cossacks, who participated in the insurrection, was changed to that of Ural Cossacks.

[16] The lower administrative subdivisions—counties, cities, towns, and villages—are not listed in the Constitution.

[17] J. A. Morrison, "The Evolution of the Territorial-Administrative System of the U.S.S.R.," in *The American Quarterly on the Soviet Union,* October, 1938, pp. 25, 38. Mr. Morrison ascribes the frequency of changes, perhaps not very convincingly, to "the requirements of a dynamic economy." A decree of the Central Executive Committee and of the Council of People's Commissars of April 28, 1936, prohibited changes in inner boundaries from September 1, 1936, to January 15, 1937, as a measure preliminary to the abortive census of January 6, 1937.

men SSR, of four provinces; the Kirghiz SSR, of six provinces; while the Armenian SSR still had none.

Legally the sixteen constituent republics enjoy the same status, although only the Ukrainian and White Russian SSR are represented in the United Nations. The RSFSR, however, is by far the most important member of the unequal partnership. The size of its territory and population, its economic resources, its cultural tradition, and its predominance in the Communist Party (even though Stalin is a Georgian) create for it a position that cannot be challenged by the tiny Caucasian and Asiatic republics brought into existence by the whims of Moscow. The RSFSR therefore dominates the life of the Union. The resulting situation is not incompatible with Communist doctrine since the program of the Party provides that the federation of Soviet republics is merely the "transition stage towards complete unity."

STRUCTURE OF THE FEDERAL GOVERNMENT

The Supreme Soviet of the USSR. The Constitution of 1936 retained much of the existing institutional and administrative framework but submitted it to important modifications. In theory, the highest organ of the Union is the Supreme Soviet of the USSR (Article 30) which exercises the powers vested in the federal Government by Article 14, except those specifically delegated by the Constitution to other organs of the federal Government (Article 31). The legislative power "is exercised exclusively by the Supreme Soviet of the USSR" (Article 32), which is elected for four years (Article 36) and consists of two chambers: the Council (Soviet) of the Union and the Council (Soviet) of Nationalities (Article 33). The Council of the Union is elected by the citizens of the Union by electoral districts on the basis of one deputy for every 300,000 of the population (Article 34). The Council of Nationalities is elected by the citizens of the Union by constituent and autonomous republics, autonomous provinces (*oblast*), and national regions (*okrug*) on the basis of twenty-five deputies from each constituent republic, eleven deputies from each autonomous republic, five deputies from each autonomous province, and one deputy from each national region (Article 35). The Council of the Union and the Council of Nationalities enjoy equal rights (Article 37), including the right to initiate legislation (Article 38), and elect each a president and four vice-presidents (Articles 42 and 43).[18] A bill before it becomes law must be approved by both chambers by a simple majority (Article 39). The Supreme Soviet, sitting as a body, elects its Presidium consisting of a chairman, sixteen vice-chairmen, a secretary, and fifteen members (Article 48).[19] The competence of the Presidium is defined in Article 49. The Presid-

---

[18] The number of vice-presidents was increased from two to four by an amendment adopted by the Supreme Soviet on June 17, 1950.

[19] Article 48 originally provided for a Presidium consisting of a chairman, eleven vice-chairmen (one for each of the then existing constituent republics), a secretary, and twenty-four members. An amendment adopted by the Supreme Soviet in August, 1940, increased the number of vice-chairmen to sixteen to bring it in line with the greater number of constituent republics. The resulting enlarged Presidium of forty-two was regarded as unwieldy and in March, 1946, Article 48 was again amended reducing the number of members (other than the chairman, vice-chairmen, and the secretary) from twenty-four to fifteen.

ium convenes twice a year (Article 45) the sessions of the Supreme Soviet; dissolves the Supreme Soviet in case of the failure of the two chambers to agree, and orders new elections; [20] holds referendums on its own initiative or on that of one of the constituent republics; revokes the decisions and decrees of the Council of Ministers (formerly Council of People's Commissars) of the USSR and of the constituent republics if they violate the law; in the interval between the sessions of the Supreme Soviet, and on the recommendation of the President of the Council of Ministers of the USSR, removes from office and appoints Ministers of the USSR, subject to subsequent confirmation by the Supreme Soviet; institutes decorations (orders and medals) and honorary titles; bestows decorations and honorary titles; exercises the right of pardon; institutes military titles, diplomatic ranks, and other special titles; appoints and dismisses the high military command; in the interval between the sessions of the Supreme Soviet, declares war in case of an attack on the Soviet Union or in order to fulfill international obligations; orders mobilization; ratifies and abrogates international treaties; [21] appoints and recalls ambassadors; receives the credentials and letters of recall of foreign representatives; proclaims martial law.

Immunity of Deputies and New Elections. The members of the Supreme Soviet are free from arrest without the consent of that body or, if the Supreme Soviet is not in session, without the consent of the Presidium (Article 52). The Presidium continues in office after the expiration of the term of the Supreme Soviet until the election of the new Presidium (Article 53). New elections must be held within two months after dissolution (Article 54) and the Supreme Soviet must be convened within three months after the elections (Article 55). [22]

The Council of Ministers of the USSR. The Supreme Soviet, at a joint session of its two chambers, appoints the Council of Ministers of the USSR, the highest executive and administrative organ of the Union (Articles 56 and 64). The name of Council of People's Commissars, which the 1936 Constitution applied to the body officially known today as the Council of Ministers, came into use immediately after the establishment of the Soviet regime in 1917 and was maintained for nearly three decades. In March, 1946, however, the Constitution was amended: the title of People's Commissar, which has a revolutionary ring, was discarded in favor of the conventional bourgeois title of Minister; the Council of People's Commissars became the Council of Ministers; and corresponding changes were made in the constitutions of constituent republics. The reason for the abandonment of the traditional terminology was not made clear. Presumably it should not be regarded as the repudiation by the Soviet leaders of their revolutionary heritage but rather as a

[20] The procedure to be followed in case of a disagreement between the two chambers is dealt with in Article 47; such disagreements have never arisen nor could they possibly arise under the Soviet system.

[21] Law of August 19, 1938.

[22] The Constitution originally provided that the Supreme Soviet must be convened not later than one month after the elections; the interval was extended to three months by an amendment adopted in February, 1947.

tactical move designed to strengthen the hand of the Soviet Government in negotiation with the capitalist countries by eliminating a minor cause for irritation and suspicion. The Council of Ministers is responsible to the Supreme Soviet or, when the Supreme Soviet is not in session, to its Presidium (Article 65); it issues decisions and decrees which are based on the existing laws (Article 66) and are binding throughout the Unions (Article 67). The authority of the Council of Ministers extends to the following fields (Article 68): coordination and direction of the work of federal departments; administration of the national economic plan, the State budget, and the credit and monetary system; maintenance of public order, protection of the interests of the State, and safeguarding of the rights of citizens; general guidance in the field of international relations; determination of the contingents of men drafted for military service and direction of the organization of armed forces; appointment of special committees and other agencies to deal with economic, cultural, and military matters.[23] The Council of Ministers of the USSR is empowered to annul the decisions and decrees of the Councils of Ministers of the constituent republics and of the Ministers of the USSR (Article 69). The composition of the Council of Ministers has been altered several times since 1936. In June, 1950, the Council of Ministers consisted of a Chairman, a Deputy Chairman, the Chairman of the State Planning Committee, the Chairman of the State Committee on Supplying the Technical and Matériel Needs of National Economy, the Chairman of the State Committee on Promoting Advanced Technology in National Economy, the Chairman of the State Committee on Construction, the Chairman of the Arts Committee, and the Ministers of the USSR (Article 70).[24] In 1917, on the morrow of the Bolshevik revolution, the Council of People's Commissars had thirteen members and under the 1936 Constitution, twenty-five. Because of the increase in number of People's Commissariats (later Ministries) the membership of the Council rose rapidly to well over sixty in the 1940's. Under the reorganization amendment of June 17, 1950, the Council of Ministers had fifty-eight members.

The Ministers of the USSR. The Ministers (formerly People's Commissars) of the USSR head the federal departments, the Ministries of the USSR. The Ministers direct the work of their respective administrations (Article 72) and may issue orders and instructions dealing with matters within their competence, provided that such orders are based on laws or on

[23] The foregoing list differs from the one given in the 1936 text of the Constitution; Article 68 was amended in February, 1947.

[24] The State Planning Commission, or Gosplan, was reorganized as the State Planning Committee by a decree of the Presidium of the Supreme Soviet of January 9, 1948. The State Committee on Supplying the Technical and Matériel Needs of National Economy and the State Committee on Promoting Advanced Technology in National Economy were established by decrees of the Presidium of the Supreme Soviet of January 9, 1948, and the State Committee on Construction by a decree of May 9, 1950. The four agencies listed above are described as State Committees of the Council of Ministers. Article 70 of the Constitution was amended accordingly on June 17, 1950, but the texts of the decrees of January 9, 1948, and May 9, 1950, were not published in *Vedomosti Verkhovnago Soveta* (organ of the Presidium of the Supreme Soviet), *Izvestia, Pravda,* or, as far as it could be ascertained, anywhere else. The nature of the changes introduced by this legislation and the reasons for the mystery in which it is shrouded remain obscure.

decrees of the Council of Ministers of the USSR (Article 73). The Ministers must answer, orally or in writing, within three days the interpellations addressed to them by the members of the Supreme Soviet (Article 71). The position of Chairman of the Council of Ministers (Council of People's Commissars) is one of the highest offices in the Soviet Union. From 1917 to the autumn of 1951 the Council had four Chairmen: Lenin (1917–1924), Rykov (1924–1930), Molotov (1930–1941), and Stalin (since May, 1941), all of them leading figures in the Communist Party, though Rykov eventually fell from grace, was tried on charges of high treason in 1938, and was executed. The rank and file of the Ministers, however, are men of much smaller political stature and, with the exception of the Foreign Minister, are little known at home or abroad. Elevation to ministerial rank is not due to the pressure of political or parliamentary groups (for none exists in the Soviet Union except the Communist Party) but is rather in the nature of the recognition of personal qualifications for the job or, more likely, of a reward bestowed upon deserving Party functionaries. Changes among ministers are frequent, but are barely noted in the press, and are seldom explained.

Two Kinds of Ministries of the USSR. There are two kinds of Ministries of the USSR: (1) the All-Union Ministries which operate through the entire territory of the Union directly or through organs they appoint; and (2) the Union-Republic Ministries which as a rule act through corresponding ministries of the constituent republics and administer directly only "a definite and limited number" of enterprises according to a list confirmed by the Presidium of the Supreme Soviet (Articles 74–76). The distinction between the two groups of ministries of the USSR would seem to be that those in group one are concerned with what are regarded as purely federal matters, while those in group two deal with questions assigned to the joint jurisdiction of the federal Government and the governments of the constituent republics. The distinction is tenuous, and in the course of the evolution of the Soviet administrative structure a number of ministries have been shifted from one group to another. In 1917 there were twelve People's Commissariats; the 1936 Constitution provided for eighteen, but the number was increased to forty-one by March, 1941, and to fifty-eight (Ministries) by February, 1947; it was reduced to forty-nine by June, 1949, and stood at fifty-one in June, 1950.

The All-Union and the Union-Republic Ministries of the USSR. The Constitution of 1936 provided for eight All-Union and ten Union-Republic Ministries (People's Commissariats) of the USSR, but in June, 1950, there were thirty All-Union and twenty-one Union-Republic Ministries (Articles 77 and 78, as amended on June 17, 1950). The All-Union Ministries were: Aircraft Industry, Automobile and Tractor Industry, Foreign Trade, Army and Navy, Armament, Geological Survey, Town Development, State Food and Material Reserves, Agricultural Stocks, Machine and Instrument-Making Industry, Metallurgical Industry, Merchant Marine, Oil Industry, Communications Equipment Industry, Railways, Inland Water Transport, Communications, Agricultural Machinery Industry, Machine-Tool Industry, Building and Road-Building Machinery Industry, Construction of Machine-Building Works, Construction of Heavy Industry Works, Shipbuilding, Transport Machinery Industry, Labor Reserves, Heavy Machine-Building Industry, Coal Industry, Chemical Industry, Electrical Industry, and Electric Power Stations. The Union-Republic Ministries were: Interior, Armed Forces, Higher Education, State Control, State Security, Public Health, Foreign Affairs, Cinematography, Light Industry, Forestry, Timber and Paper Industry, Meat and Dairy Industry, Food Industry, Building Materials Industry, Fish Industry, Agriculture, State Farms, Trade, Finance, Cotton Industry, and Justice.

Complexity and Instability of the Administrative Structure. The foregoing list indicates the complexity of the administrative structure. Its amazing instability, however, is not fully reflected in the changing number of ministries as recorded in the consecutive amendments of the pertinent articles of the Constitution. The formation of some ministries is offset by the abolition of others, and such changes do not affect the summary number of ministries at the time of the constitutional amendments. Some of the ministries exist for only a few months, others are abolished and established again. For instance, the Ministry of Technical Crops was formed in November, 1945, but was absorbed by the Ministry of Agriculture in February, 1947. The Ministry of State Farms, established in 1936, was dissolved in March, 1946, only to be revived in February, 1947. It is difficult to detect any guiding principle in these incessant shifts. Prior to 1948 the tendency would seem to have been in the direction of greater specialization based on what was known as the territorial-productive principle. For instance, the People's Commissariat of Fuel Industry, formed in January, 1939, was split eight months later, in October, 1939, into two People's Commissariats: Coal Industry and Oil Industry. In January and March, 1946, respectively, the People's Commissariats of Coal Industry and Oil Industry were each divided into two People's Commissariats—one for the Eastern and one for the Western Regions. Similarly in May, 1946, the Ministry of Fish Industry (established in 1939) was split into two Ministries—one for the Eastern and one for the Western Regions. In 1948, however, both specialization and the territorial-productive principle lost their popularity with the Soviet leaders. In December of that year the Eastern and Western Regions Ministries just mentioned were merged into a single Ministry for each of the three industries. Other administrative amalgamations, as has already been stated, resulted in the reduction of the number of ministries from fifty-eight in February, 1947, to forty-nine in June, 1949, but two more were added to the list by June, 1950. The relentless remodeling of the administrative structure must inevitably lead to a great deal of confusion and is hardly conducive to the smooth working of the machinery of federal Government.[25]

[25] A useful summary of constitutional amendments will be found in Lionel H. Laing and associates, *Source Book in European Government* (William Sloane, New York, 1950), annotations to the Constitution of 1936, pp. 234–262.

REPUBLICAN AND LOCAL GOVERNMENT

Government of Constituent Republics. The structure of the government of the constituent republics duplicates, with some modifications, that of the federal Government. Article 16 of the Constitution provides that the constitutions of the constituent republics, while taking into account local peculiarities, shall be drawn up "in full conformity with the Constitution of the USSR." The highest organ of State power in a constituent republic is its Supreme Soviet elected by the citizens of the republic for four years (Articles 57 and 58). Under the republican constitutions adopted in 1937 and in 1940 (for the constituent republics established on the territories annexed by the Soviet Union at the beginning of World War II) the Supreme Soviet is a unicameral body. It elects its Presidium (Article 61) and appoints the Council of Ministers (formerly People's Commissars) of the constituent republic (Article 63) which is the republic's highest executive and administrative organ (Article 64). A constituent republic has two kinds of ministries: the Union-Republic and the Republican Ministries (Article 68). The former correspond to the Union-Republic Ministries of the USSR [26] and are subordinated to both these federal departments and the Council of Ministers of the constituent republic (Article 87). The Republican Ministries are directly subordinated to the Council of Ministers of the constituent republic (Article 88). Not all the Union-Republic Ministries listed in Article 78 of the federal Constitution are organized in every constituent republic, and there are slight variations, from republic to republic, in the number of Republican Ministries.[27] It would be tedious and largely useless to record these minute differences. The nature of Republican Ministries may be gauged from the following list provided by the constitution of the RSFSR (as amended in March 1948): automotive transport, housing, communal (municipal) economy, local industry, local fuel industry, education, and social security. Within the framework of the federal Constitution the Supreme Soviet, Presidium, Council of Ministers, and Ministries of each constituent republic exercise functions which are, broadly speaking, similar to those of the corresponding federal organs. It will be remembered, however, that the limitations imposed by the federal Constitution on the constituent republics are many and far-reaching. Again, like the federal Government, the governments of the constituent republics exercise a high degree of control over the institutions and officials of the smaller territorial subdivisions under their respective jurisdictions: Autonomous Soviet Socialist Republics, territories (*krai*), provinces (*oblast*), autonomous provinces, regions (*okrug*), and counties (*raion*). Local autonomy, therefore, is kept within narrow limits.

[26] See above, p. 746.

[27] Prior to the amendment of February, 1947, the ministries of the constituent republics were listed in Article 83 of the federal Constitution which defines the composition of the Council of Ministers of the constituent republics. In 1947 this practice was discontinued and Article 83 refers merely to "Ministers," without enumerating them. This amendment gives greater flexibility to the administrative structure of the constituent republics; some of the specialized ministries listed in the Constitution would be obviously superfluous in the less industrialized republics.

Government of Autonomous Republics. Each Autonomous Soviet Socialist Republic (ASSR) has a constitution "drawn up in full conformity with the constitution of the constituent republic" of which it is a part, a Supreme Soviet elected for four years, a Presidium, and a Council of Ministers (Articles 89–93). The powers exercised by the government of an autonomous republic are similar to those of the government of a constituent republic, but its sphere of action is further restricted. There were twenty-two autonomous republics on October 1, 1938, including seventeen in the RSFSR. By January 1, 1947, the number of autonomous republics dropped to sixteen: twelve in the RSFSR, two in the Georgian SSR, and one each in the Uzbek and the Azerbaidzhan SSR.

Government of Smaller Territorial Units. The administration of territories, provinces, autonomous provinces, regions, counties, cities and towns, and rural localities is carried on by a Soviet of working-people's deputies elected, for a term of two years, by the population of the respective subdivisions. The Soviet supervises the administrative officers whom it appoints, maintains public order, ensures observance of the law and protection of the rights of citizens, directs local economic and cultural activities, and administers local finance. Each Soviet elects an executive committee and has the power to issue orders dealing with matters within its jurisdiction as defined by the federal and republican constitutions. "Small localities" are administered by an elected chairman, deputy chairman, and secretary (Articles 94–101).[28]

THE JUDICIARY

Legal Framework. Prior to 1936 the structure of the judiciary was determined by a federal law of 1924 and by republican legislation based thereon. The Constitution of 1936 and "The Law on the Judiciary of the USSR, the Constituent Republics, and the Autonomous Republics" enacted by the Supreme Soviet in August, 1938, introduced important changes in the system of law courts and redefined and extended the powers of the legal officers of the State.

The Procurator-General. According to the 1936 Constitution the principal legal officer of the Union is the Procurator-General of the USSR who is appointed by the Supreme Soviet of the USSR for a term of seven years.[29] The Procurator-General is vested with the "supreme supervisory power to ensure the strict observance of the law" by officials, institutions, and citizens throughout the Union. He appoints for a term of five years the procurators

---

[28] On October 1, 1938, there were nine autonomous provinces, thirty regions (eleven of them were classified as "national" and nineteen as "administrative"), seventy-four territories and provinces, 3,464 counties, and 808 cities and towns. On January 1, 1947, there were nine autonomous provinces (including six in the RSFSR), ten national regions (all of them in the RSFSR), 4,250 counties (including 2,541 in the RSFSR and 750 in Ukraine), 1,377 cities and towns (including 716 in the RSFSR and 258 in Ukraine), and 1,979 "settlements of an urban type" (including 1,019 in the RSFSR and 451 in Ukraine).

[29] The title of this official was changed from Procurator to Procurator-General by a law of March 19, 1946; the Constitution was accordingly amended in February, 1947.

of the constituent republics, autonomous republics, territories, and provinces; the procurators of the constituent republics, in turn, appoint for a term of five years the procurators of regions, districts, and cities and towns, subject to confirmation by the Procurator-General (Articles 113–116). The procurators and members of their staff "perform their functions independently of any local organs whatsoever, being subordinated directly to the Procurator-General" (Article 117). Law enforcement therefore is the responsibility of the Procurator-General, an officer of the federal Government.

Basic Principles; Judges and Assessors. The reform of the judiciary introduced by the 1936 Constitution and by the Law of August, 1938, embodies the principles of equality of all before the law; uniformity of civil and criminal procedure throughout the Union; independence of judges who are subject only to the law; use of local languages in the courts; right of defendants, except in specified cases, to be represented by counsel; publicity of court procedure, except when otherwise provided by the law; elective character of the judiciary. Every court consists of judges and "people's assessors," or associate judges. Judges serve as regular members of the court during the term for which they are elected; assessors are chosen in the same manner and for the same term as judges but serve, in turn, no more than ten days per year unless the extension of this period is necessitated by the duration of a case. The assessors receive during their term on the bench emoluments equal to those they earn in their usual employment.[30] Every citizen of the Union entitled to vote may be elected either a judge or an assessor of any court. No educational or other qualifications are required. Cases in every court are heard by a "judicial college" consisting of one judge and two assessors, except when the law provides that the "judicial college" must consist of three judges.[31] The judges and assessors may be removed only by being recalled by the bodies that elected them or by a decision of the courts. Criminal action against the judges and assessors of the lower courts may be initiated only by the procurator of the appropriate administrative subdivision, with the sanction of the Presidium of the constituent republic; criminal action against the judges and assessors of the Supreme Court of the USSR and of the three "special" courts (military, railway transportation, and water transportation) may be initiated only by the Procurator-General with the sanction of the Presidium of the USSR.

The People's Courts. The lower or People's Courts are elected for a period of three years by the voters of a county (*raion*) by direct secret ballot. The candidates are nominated by the Communist Party, trade unions, cooperative societies, youth organizations, cultural organizations, as well as by workers in an industrial organization, army units, collective farmers, and employees and workers of the State farms. The number of judges and assessors

---

[30] An ordinance of May 9, 1939, of the People's Commissar for Justice provided, however, that the remuneration of assessors shall not be less than that of judges.

[31] This rule was frequently disregarded and both civil and criminal cases were decided by individual judges. The practice was specifically prohibited by a decree of the People's Commissar for Justice ratified by the Council of People's Commissars on July 28, 1939.

of the People's Courts is determined by the Council of Ministers of the constituent republics after consultation with the republican Ministry of Justice. The People's Courts exercise jurisdiction over both criminal and civil cases. Their criminal jurisdiction extends to such offenses as murder, rape, assault, robbery, theft, abuse of power or neglect of duty by officials, failure to perform obligations imposed by the State, and minor offenses. The jurisdiction of the People's Courts in civil cases extends to actions involving property rights, violation of labor regulations, and so on.

The Higher Courts. Above the People's Courts are the territorial, provincial, and regional courts, and the courts of the autonomous regions. The members of these courts are elected by the respective Soviets of the working people's deputies for a term of five years. Their jurisdiction as courts of first instance embraces the more serious offenses such as counter-revolutionary activities, theft of Socialist property, and civil actions involving State or public institutions. The autonomous and the constituent republics have their own Supreme Courts elected by their respective Supreme Soviets for five-year terms. The presidents and judges of the three "special courts"—military, railway transportation, and water transportation—are elected for five-year terms by the Supreme Soviet of the USSR, while the assessors of these courts are elected for similar terms by the Soviets of working people's deputies of the territories and provinces and by the Supreme Soviets of the constituent and autonomous republics. The military courts deal chiefly with military offenses and the other two "special" courts with crimes involving the "breach of labor discipline and other offenses disorganizing the normal working of transportation." The Supreme Court of the USSR, the highest tribunal of the land, is elected by the Supreme Soviet of the USSR for a term of five years.

Jurisdiction of the Higher Courts. The higher courts, that is, those above the People's Courts, supervise the activities of the lower courts and perform the functions of both a court of first instance and of a court of appeal from the decisions of the lower courts. The law does not state clearly what types of cases are tried by the Supreme Courts of the autonomous and constituent republics and of the USSR as courts of first instance. It merely provides that they act in this capacity in cases "assigned to their jurisdiction by the law." What this provision means remains uncertain, especially because the most serious offenses under the Soviet law—counter-revolutionary activities and crimes against Socialist property—are within the jurisdiction of the territorial, provincial, and regional courts. Presumably the higher courts deal with those offenses included in the foregoing categories that are considered particularly grave. When the higher courts act as courts of appeal the "judicial college" consists of only three judges, that is, the assessors are not included. The same rule applies to the Supreme Court of the USSR when it hears appeals from the decisions of either the Supreme Courts of the constituent republics or the three "special courts."

The Supreme Court of the USSR. The number of judges and assessors of the Supreme Court of the USSR is not specified in the law. The Supreme

Court elected by the Supreme Soviet in August, 1938, had forty-five judges
and twenty assessors, and its successor elected in March, 1946 (the term of
members of the Court were extended during the War), sixty-eight judges
and twenty-five assessors. The larger number of judges, as compared with
that of assessors, emphasizes the rôle of the Supreme Court as a court of
appeal rather than a court of first instance. Unlike the Supreme Court of
the United States, the Supreme Court of the USSR has no power to pass on
the constitutionality of laws enacted by the Supreme Soviet of the USSR,
nor has it ever questioned any of the innumerable decrees and ordinances
emanating from the Council of Ministers of the USSR. According to the Soviet doctrine the law and the judiciary are always the tools of the ruling class.
The independence of judges (Article 112 of the federal Constitution) must be
interpreted in the light of this theory which precludes the possibility of a conflict between the courts, on the one hand, and the legislative and the executive branches of government, on the other.

Purpose of the Judiciary Defined. The general purpose of Soviet courts,
as defined by the Law of August, 1938, is "to educate the citizens of the
USSR in the spirit of devotion to the fatherland (*rodina*) and to the cause
of Socialism, in the spirit of an exact and unfaltering performance of Soviet
laws, careful attitude toward Socialist property, labor discipline, honest ful-
filment of State and public duties, respect toward the rules of the Socialist
commonwealth." N. Rychkov, Commissar for Justice, admitted in his speech
before the Supreme Soviets in August, 1938, that the administration of justice
in the Soviet Union was suffering from grievous imperfections, but he expressed his conviction that these defects would be overcome because, he said,
"we are led by our great Communist Party, its Central Committee, and our
wise, great, our own (*rodnoi*) and beloved Comrade Stalin." [32]

Law Courts, 1948. Rychkov's incantation proved of no avail. When ten
years later, in February, 1948, he was succeeded as Minister of Justice by
K. Gorshenin, former Procurator-General and a jurist of stern metal, Soviet
judicial mores, as depicted in the new Minister's first report, were grim: low
quality of work of the courts, disregard of the rules of procedure, misinter-
pretation of substantive provisions, ignorance of the judges, negligence in the
execution of judgments, stifling bureaucratism in the relations between higher
and lower courts. Among the verdicts reversed by the Supreme Court of the
USSR was the conviction of a deaf mute who was not given the benefit of an
interpreter familiar with the sign language, and that of a defendant who had
not been shown the full indictment and did not know what were the charges
brought against him.[33] The fact that such cases could have arisen suggests
that the administration of justice, at least in some instances, has sunk to a

---

[32] Among the measures taken by his department for the improvement of the standards of
the judiciary, Rychkov mentioned the establishment of six-months courses for the training of
judges for the People's Courts. A six-months legal training appears hardly adequate for jurists
who have to deal with offenses as grave as robbery and murder.

[33] J. N. Hazard, "Political, Administrative, and Judicial Structure in the U.S.S.R. Since the
War," *Annals of the American Academy of Political and Social Science,* May, 1949, pp. 17–18.

level that prevailed in Russian courts prior to the reform of the judiciary in 1864. Remedial measures demanded by Gorshenin—increase in the number of law students, better legal training, and better law books—were reinforced by a decree of July 15, 1948, on the disciplinary responsibility of judges enacted by the Presidium of the Supreme Soviet. The decree provided for disciplinary action (warning, reprimand, severe reprimand) in case of breach of labor discipline, negligence, or conduct unbecoming a Soviet judge. Judges guilty of violation of the law were to be indicted.

FRANCHISE AND ELECTIONS

Universal Suffrage and Direct Secret Ballot. The 1936 Constitution introduced seemingly revolutionary changes in the electoral system. Disfranchisement of specified groups of citizens, indirect elections, and larger representation of the urban than that of the rural population were dropped. Every citizen who has reached the age of eighteen, irrespective of sex, race, nationality, religion, educational qualifications, residence, social origin, property status, and previous activities, is entitled to vote, except the insane and those under sentence involving the loss of electoral rights (Article 135).[34] Deputies to every assembly described above, from the village Soviet to the Supreme Soviet of the USSR, are chosen "on the basis of universal, equal, and direct suffrage, by secret ballot" (Article 134). Members of the armed forces are entitled to vote and may be elected to office (Article 138). Candidates for election are nominated by electoral districts by the following "organizations and associations of working people": the Communist Party, trade unions, cooperative societies, youth organizations, and cultural societies (Article 141).

THE SOVIET BILL OF RIGHTS

Rights of the Citizens. Chapter x of the federal Constitution deals with what may be termed the Soviet Bill of Rights. Soviet citizens have "the right to work," "the right to rest and leisure," "the right to social security," and "the right to education." "The right to work, that is, the right to guaranteed employment" and payment for the work done "in accordance with its quantity and quality," is safeguarded by "the socialist organization of the national economy, the steady growth of the productive forces of Soviet society, and the abolition of unemployment" (Article 118). "The right to rest and leisure" is ensured by the eight-hour day for factory and office workers (the seven- and the six-hour day in the more arduous, and the four-hour day in the particularly arduous employments), annual vacations with full pay, and facilities for recreation such as sanatoria, rest homes, and clubs (Article 119).[35] "The right to social security"—"to maintenance in old age and . . .

[34] The age requirement for the deputies to the Supreme Soviet of the USSR was originally eighteen but was raised to twenty-three by a decree of October 10, 1945. The Constitution was amended accordingly in February, 1947.

[35] The Constitution originally stipulated the seven-hour day "for the overwhelming majority of the workers." The eight-hour day was introduced by a decree of June 26, 1940, and the Constitution was amended accordingly in February, 1947. See below, pp. 801 ff.

in case of sickness or disability"—is secured "by the extensive development of social insurance of factory and office workers at State expense," free medical service, and "a wide network of health resorts for the use of the working people" (Article 120). "The right to education" is ensured by "universal compulsory elementary education; by free education up to and including the seventh grade; by State scholarships for students of higher schools who excel in their studies"; by the use of native languages in the schools; and by the organization of professional training in factories, State farms, machine tractor stations, and collective farms (Article 121).[36] Citizens enjoy complete equality irrespective of sex, race, and nationality (Articles 122 and 123). The status of women is enhanced by "State protection of the interests of mother and child, State aid to mothers of large families and unmarried mothers,[37] maternity leaves with full pay, and the provision of a wide network of maternity homes, nurseries, and kindergartens" (Article 122). Freedom of conscience is safeguarded by the separation of the Church from the State and the school system, and freedom of religious and antireligious propaganda (Article 124). The patriotic attitude of the Church during World War II has led to an improvement in the relations between the State and the Church and a marked slowing down of antireligious propaganda. Freedom of speech, the press, assembly, and "street processions and demonstrations" is ensured by "placing at the disposal of the working people and their organizations printing presses, stocks of paper, public buildings, the streets, communication facilities, and other material requisites for the exercise of these rights." These freedoms, however, must be exercised "in conformity with the interests of the working people, and in order to strengthen the Socialist system" (Article 125). Refusal by the Government to place at the disposal of a group of citizens the foregoing "material requisites" obviously precludes the exercise of the rights listed in Article 125. Citizens are guaranteed inviolability of person, home, and privacy of correspondence. No one may be arrested except by decision of a court or with the sanction of a procurator (Articles 127 and 128). In practice these enlightened provisions impose no restraint on the extra-judicial powers of the security police (to be discussed presently) which functions in close cooperation with the office of the Procurator-General.

Leading Position of the Communist Party. Soviet citizens, "in conformity with the interests of the working people, and in order to develop the organizational initiative and political activity of the masses," have the right to organize trade unions, cooperative societies, youth organizations, sport and defense organizations, and cultural, technical, and scientific societies. Moreover, "the most active and politically conscious citizens . . . unite in the Communist Party . . . , which is the vanguard of the working people in

[36] Article 121 originally provided for free education, "including higher education." Tuition fees in the upper grades of the secondary schools and in all higher schools were introduced by a decree of October 2, 1940. The Constitution was amended accordingly in February, 1947. See below, p. 804.

[37] The original text of Article 122 contained no reference to mothers of large families and unmarried mothers. State aid for both groups of mothers was provided by a decree of July 8, 1944. The Constitution was amended accordingly in February, 1947. See below, pp. 841–842.

their struggle to strengthen and develop the Socialist system and is the nucleus (leading core) of all organizations of the working people, both social and State" (Article 126). This provision is the mainspring of the political system of the USSR.

Duties of the Citizens. Citizens have the duty "to abide by the Constitution . . . , to observe the laws, to maintain labor discipline, honestly to perform public obligations, to respect the rules of the Socialist community," and "to safeguard and strengthen public Socialist property as the sacred and inviolable foundation of the Soviet system, as the source of wealth and might of the motherland (*rodina*), as the source of the prosperity and cultural life of all the working people." Those guilty of crimes against public Socialist property are branded as "enemies of the people" (Articles 130–131). Service in the armed forces is an "honorable duty" and defense of the country is "the sacred duty of every citizen." Treason—that is, violation of the oath of allegiance, desertion to the enemy, impairing the military might of the State, espionage—"is punishable with all the severity of the law as the most heinous crime" (Articles 132–133).

Right of Asylum and Exit. The Soviet Union "grants the right of asylum to foreign citizens persecuted for defending the interests of the working people, or for scientific activities, or for struggling for national liberation" (Article 129). This provision was given a restrictive interpretation. Moscow is, indeed, the haven of notable revolutionaries, but the Kremlin has manifested no desire to open Soviet frontiers to the hundreds of thousands of victims of racial and political persecution in Central and Eastern Europe, or to refugees from Spain, in spite of the fact that the USSR controls vast, sparsely populated areas and is avowedly short of skilled labor. While clamoring for the repatriation of Soviet citizens who had fled to Central Europe during the War, the Soviet Government has stubbornly denied exit permits to members of the national minorities, notably the Poles and the Jews, desiring to settle abroad.[38] Soviet citizens are not permitted to visit foreign lands, except on official business. The Constitution makes no reference to this fundamental right enjoyed as a matter of course by the nationals of every country outside the Soviet orbit.

CONSTITUTION OF 1936 COMPARED WITH ITS PREDECESSORS

Principal Changes. The 1936 Constitution differs in some seemingly essential respects from the earlier constitutions. Four of the more important changes will be noted here. (1) The powers of the federal Government were extended and made more comprehensive, as evidenced by the requirement that the constitutions of the constituent and autonomous republics should conform with the federal Constitution, and by the institution of federal controls over the alteration of internal administrative boundaries, the judi-

[38] The once powerful flow of Jewish immigrants from Russia to Palestine has practically dried up since the establishment of the Soviet rule. I am reliably informed that in spite of the manifest desire of many Soviet Jews to emigrate to Israel only five applicants were successful: a cripple and two very aged couples.

ciary, security police, preparation of civil and criminal codes, and so on.[39] (2) The 1936 Constitution made some concessions to the principle of separation of powers by differentiating sharply between the functions of the legislative, the executive, and the judiciary. It will be remembered that, according to the Constitution, "the legislative power . . . is exercised exclusively by the Supreme Soviet" (Article 32), the Council of Ministers is "the highest executive and administrative organ" (Article 64), and "judges are independent and subject only to the law" (Article 112). Practice, however, did not conform to the rules laid down in the Constitution. The independence of the judiciary remained a fiction incompatible with the basic Soviet doctrine that courts are always the tool of the ruling class. The bulk of legislation emanates not from the Supreme Soviet but from the Council of Ministers, which frequently issues decrees jointly with the Central Committee of the Communist Party, a procedure for which there is no constitutional foundation unless one chooses to put an unreasonably broad interpretation on the provisions of Article 126 dealing with the position of the Communist Party. Executive decrees have at times the force of constitutional amendments.[40] (3) Chapter x of the Constitution of 1936 containing the Soviet Bill of Rights had no counterpart in the earlier constitutions. (4) The introduction of universal, equal, and direct suffrage, and secret ballot, brought the Soviet electoral system in line with those of the bourgeois democracies.

Stalin on Proletarian Dictatorship. A superficial examination of the Constitution may well create the impression that the Soviet Government is evolving in the direction of a democratic welfare state in the Western meaning of the term. Stalin, however, whose name the Constitution bears, took a different view. In his address to the Eighth Congress of the Soviets on November 25, 1936, Stalin said: "I must admit that the draft of the new Constitution actually leaves in force the regime of the dictatorship of the working class as well as it preserves unchanged the present leading position of the Communist Party." The question naturally arises: How is it possible to reconcile two seemingly irreconcilable systems—democracy based on universal suffrage and secret ballot, and the dictatorship of the working class exercised through the numerically small Communist Party? A glance at the mechanics of Soviet elections and the procedure of the Soviet Parliament may help to solve the riddle.

---

[39] The trend toward greater centralization and unification of government is emphasized by Soviet writers. See, for instance, I. Levin in *Bolshaia Sovetskaia Entsiklopediia* (*Large Soviet Encyclopedia*), supplementary volume on the USSR (Moscow, 1948), pp. 40–41.

[40] For instance, the already mentioned decree of the Council of People's Commissars of October 2, 1940, on tuition fees in secondary and higher schools. The decree became effective at once but the Constitution was not amended until 1947. Article 146 of the Constitution provides that "the Constitution of the USSR may be amended only by decision of the Supreme Soviet of the USSR adopted by a majority of not less than two-thirds of the votes of each of its chambers."

SOVIET DEMOCRACY IN ACTION

Elections, 1937 and 1938. Elections to the Supreme Soviet of the USSR in December, 1937, and to the republican Supreme Soviets in June, 1938, set a pattern which has been strictly adhered to ever since. The federal election was preceded by an appeal of the Central Committee of the Communist Party for a demonstration of national unity, and the candidates ran on the platform of an "election bloc of Party and non-Party people." A similar device was used in the election of June, 1938. Since the "non-Party people" have no organizations of their own that would not be controlled by the "leading nucleus" of the Communist Party it may be surmised that the bloc was somewhat one-sided. While the victory of the Communist Party was a forgone conclusion the possibility of a contest among several candidates was not precluded. Stalin, in a much-publicized interview with Roy Howard in March, 1936, prognosticated a lively electoral struggle over the personal merits of the candidates. For once, he proved wrong. In both elections the name of only one candidate appeared on the ballot in each electoral district, although several candidates had been nominated by the various organizations during the preliminary discussion. Miss Rose Somerville, who had spent most of the years 1935–1937 in Russia studying Soviet Government, rightly remarked that to bring about the withdrawal in each district of all candidates but one, "some machinery must have been in operation which is not revealed by the public record." Miss Somerville was right when she ventured the opinion that "some influence, probably the Communist Party, made the several nominees aware of the desirability of avoiding public contest," although she was probably wrong in believing that this influence was at work in some districts only.[41] In both elections the nomination of candidates was by showing of hands, the secret ballot being used in the final voting. The "non-Party people," being officially in a bloc with the Communists, candidates opposing the one sponsored by the local Communist organization were effectively excluded, for any such opposition would have indicated that its supporters were neither Communist nor "non-Party"; that is, that they were inimical to the Soviet regime, a category in which few would care to put themselves.

Their Results. Candidates need not reside in the district in which they come up for election. No registration of voters is required, the lists being prepared by local Soviets. Everyone is urged to vote, and the authorities keep a record of those who do and do not. Election day is a national holiday, and the voters troop in to deposit a secret ballot on which they had registered their approval or disapproval of the sole candidate. Of the 94 million eligible voters in the federal election of 1937, over 91 million, or 96.8 per cent, went to the polls, and of this number 89.8 million, or 98.6 per cent, voted for the candidates. This record was improved upon in some of the republics in the election of June, 1938, the percentage of both voters participating in the elec-

---

[41] Rose Somerville, "The New Soviet Elections," in *The American Quarterly on the Soviet Union*, October, 1938, pp. 71–72.

tion and those endorsing the candidates running as high as 99 per cent. Communists (Party members and candidates) accounted for 81 per cent of the deputies to the Council of the Union, and 71 per cent of the deputies to the Council of Nationalities. The balance was made up of "non-Party Bolsheviks." The composition of the republican Supreme Soviets did not differ substantially from that of the Supreme Soviet of the USSR. The "Stalin elections" were acclaimed in the Soviet Union as a great success and a tribute to the leader.

Elections, 1939. Elections to local Soviets held in December, 1939, followed a pattern by then well established. Each election district had a sole candidate sponsored by a "bloc of Party and non-Party Stalinites." Of the 93.5 million eligible voters 92.8 million went to the polls. The percentage of votes cast for the candidates varied from 99.7 to 96.7 of the total vote. About one-third of the 1,281,000 delegates to 68,190 Soviets of various types elected on this occasion were members or candidates of the Communist Party, and two-thirds were "non-Party Stalinites." The only novel feature in the 1939 election was the failure to elect Soviets in 134 localities. In nine cases this was due to the death of the candidate or to inclement weather, and in the remaining 125 cases, according to an official but not very helpful statement, "the candidates did not receive the absolute majority of votes."

Wartime Government. The German invasion played havoc with the institutions of Soviet Government, but led to no important constitutional changes. On June 30, 1941, a week after the Germans crossed the Russian border, there was created (by a joint decree of the Presidium of the Supreme Soviet, the Central Committee of the Communist Party, and the Council of People's Commissars) the State Defense Committee vested with practically unlimited powers. The Committee had five members (it was somewhat enlarged later), was headed by Stalin, and included the key men of the regime: Molotov; Marshal K. Voroshilov; the Secretary of the Central Committee of the Party, G. Malenkov; and the People's Commissar of the Interior and head of the security police, L. Beria. The State Defense Committee served well its purpose of unifying and dramatizing the war effort, but it added nothing to the powers actually wielded by Stalin and those at the top of the Communist oligarchy. No elections took place during the War, the mandates of the deputies were extended from year to year by the Presidium of the Supreme Soviet, and the Supreme Soviet itself was in a state of suspended animation and held but four brief perfunctory sessions: one in 1942 and in 1944, and two in 1945; that is, three of them when the War was practically over. The eclipse of the Soviet parliament, "primarily . . . a ratifying and propagating body," [42] was of no consequence, especially since the Presidium continued to carry on its routine duties. On September 5, 1945, with the termination of the War, the State Defense Committee was abolished by a decree of the Presidium of the Supreme Soviet, and the institutions created by the 1936 Constitution gradually emerged from their wartime eclipse. The fact that

[42] Towster, *op. cit.,* p. 263.

the Supreme Soviet and other elective assemblies took no real part in the organization of the war effort is a telling comment on the place they actually hold in the Soviet system.

Elections, 1946–1950. Several elections were held since the War: elections to the Supreme Soviet of the USSR in February, 1946, and March, 1950; elections to the republican Supreme Soviets in February, 1947; and local elections in December, 1947, and January, 1948. The procedure and results in every case duplicated those of the pre-War period. Uniformly there was in each electoral district but one candidate nominated by a "bloc of Communists and non-Party people." Of the 101.7 million eligible voters in the 1946 federal election 101.5 million, or 99.7 per cent, went to the polls and 99.2 per cent voted for the candidates. The percentage of Communists (Party members and candidates) among the delegates of the Council of the Union was 77.5, and among the delegates of the Council of Nationalities 84.5; that of women, was 17 and 24.5 respectively. The 1947 republican elections ran true to form and present no special interest. The 1947–1948 local elections differed in some respects from those of 1939. As a consequence of the remodeling and consolidation of the network of local Soviets the number of deputies elected was 766,600, that is, substantially less than in 1939 in spite of the annexation by the USSR of vast territories. The percentage of Communists was much lower among the delegates chosen in the newly acquired republics (11 per cent in Lithuania, 13 per cent in Moldavia, 18 per cent in Latvia) than in the long-established republics (about 50 per cent). As in 1939 in a small number of districts (102), local Soviets were not elected because the candidates had not received the absolute majority of the votes cast.[43] Finally, in the federal election of March, 1950, 99.98 per cent of the eligible voters (111 million) actually voted and 99.73 per cent cast their ballots for the candidates. Election managers have good reasons to be worried: the margin for improving on the record of unanimity is getting distressingly narrow.

Soviet Parliament. Except for the war years the Supreme Soviet of the USSR has met regularly at least twice a year as required by the Constitution. Its sessions, however, are brief, and seldom last longer than a week. Like elections, they follow an immutable and dreary routine: long program speeches by the leaders, blank endorsement of constitutional amendments and decrees of the Presidium which have been in effect for months or even years, brief speeches by back-benchers pleading some local cause, enthusiastic demonstrations every time that Stalin's name is mentioned (and this means frequently), and practically no independent legislative work. Again, like elections, the motions of the deputies would seem to be regulated by some influence "which is not revealed by the public record." For instance, the budget speech of the Minister of Finance is invariably followed by proposals of the budget commissions of the two chambers (which are supposed to function separately) to increase the tax bill by exactly the same amount;

[43] Hazard, *op. cit.,* p. 12.

these amendments of the budget are invariably accepted by the Minister amidst thunderous applause. Unanimity characteristic of Soviet elections is, if possible, even more in evidence in the Supreme Soviet. At the opening session of the new Parliament in January, 1938, a picturesque group of visiting Kazakhs from Central Asia added color to the proceedings not only by their cerise, flowing robes but also by thrusting up their hands whenever a vote was taken.[44] No one interfered with them: a few more hands merely emphasized the unanimity of the vote. From the unwritten rule of unanimity the Soviet Parliament has never departed.

The "chief purpose" of the Supreme Soviet, writes Towster, "appears to be, periodically or as the occasion demands, to lend the voice of approval of a representative assembly to governmental policy.[45] This statement sums up well the functions of the Soviet Parliament, even though the Supreme Soviet is clearly not a "representative" assembly in any accepted meaning of the term.

PROTECTION OF THE REGIME

The Security Police. The Soviet Government does not rely entirely on indoctrination and the Communist Party to keep everyone in line. The security police—known successively as CHEKA (1918–1922), OGPU (1922–1934), NKVD (1934–1943), NKVD or NKGB (1943–1946), and MVD or MGB (since 1946)—is one of the main pillars of the regime.[46] It comprises both a uniformed force and a body of undercover agents and, unlike the intelligence and security service of the Western countries, combines the police and the judicial functions. Its ubiquitous agents, free from the restraint of the law, are vested with extra-judicial powers which allow them not only to deport citizens suspected of disloyalty to the regime to the penal labor camps that dot the bleak wilderness of Russia's northern and eastern regions, but also to impose death sentences after a trial in *camera* or without the formality of a trial. No official information on these sinister activities is available but the number of their victims is said to be very large. An official British statement put the number of persons subject in the Soviet Union "to some kind of forced labor" at about 10 million or one-tenth of the work-

---

[44] Harold Denny in *The New York Times*, January 14, 1938.

[45] Towster, *op. cit.*, p. 263.

[46] These euphonious names, which make the Russian shudder, are combinations of initials of the agencies that, in turn, controlled the security police. The CHEKA and OGPU were separate administrations subordinated directly to the Council of People's Commissars. In 1934 the OGPU was incorporated in the People's Commissariat of the Interior (*Narodnyi Kommissariat Vnutrennikh Del*) which in 1946 became the Ministry of the Interior (*Ministerstvo Vnutrennikh Del*). In February, 1941, the Commissariat of the Interior was split into two Commissariats—Interior and State Security (NKGB). They were reunited five months later, in July, 1941, and separated again in April, 1943, but the decree dealing with the latter change was never published. (Hazard, *op. cit.*, p. 14, note 33). It would seem that in 1944–1945 the NKVD still controlled the penal labor camps while the other functions of the security police were within the competence of the People's Commissariat of State Security, which in 1946 became the Ministry of State Security (*Ministerstvo Gosudarstvennoi Bezopasnosti*), or MGB. The exact present status of the security police is not known but the appellation MVD is still in common use (see, for instance, Towster, *op. cit.*, p. 384). Throughout these transformations the security police has preserved unimpaired its powers and its identity.

ing population.[47] This and similar estimates are brushed aside by Moscow as mere propaganda. While the size of the population of the labor camps cannot be ascertained with any degree of precision, information from Soviet sources throws much light on the methods and nature of the work of the security police. The trial in March, 1938, of H. Yagoda, head of the NKVD since 1934, and, a year later, that of his successor N. Yezhov, disclosed an almost unbelievable picture of corruption, crime, personal rule, and abuse of power. Both Yagoda and Yezhov were executed, but the security police under its new chief, L. Beria (who, like Stalin, is a Georgian), lost none of its authority. Pains were taken to make it clear that the reform of the judiciary outlined in this chapter did not infringe on the prerogatives of the NKVD. Rychkov, Commissar for Justice, reminded the Supreme Soviet in August, 1938, that agencies other than the courts watch over the security of the State. "This honorable and glorious duty is gallantly performed by the organs of the Commissariat of the Interior under the leadership of the Stalinite Commissar Yezhov," Rychkov declared amid the loud applause with which Soviet democracy never fails to greet any reference to the security police. The tribute to Yezhov was untimely but otherwise Rychkov's statement still holds good.

Counter-Revolutionary Activities. The extra-judicial powers of the security police are supplemented by a formidable array of legal provisions dealing with counter-revolutionary and anti-State activities. No other part of the Criminal Code, adopted in 1927, has been so thoroughly amended and revised as that devoted to the protection of the regime. A counter-revolutionary activity is defined as any action directed to "the overthrow, undermining, or weakening" of the USSR and its constituent parts, or of its "basic economic, political, or national institutions" (Article 58 ^{1}, edition 1937). In addition to treason, armed uprising, and other criminal activities punishable under the law of any country, the Code considers as counter-revolutionary the "undermining of State industry, transportation, commerce, monetary circulation and credit, as well as cooperative societies" (Article 58 ^{7}). The intentional nonfulfillment by a person of his "definite duties" or negligence in fulfilling them, with the intent of weakening the Soviet power or disorganizing the State machinery, belongs to the same class of criminal offenses (Article 58 ^{14}). The penalty varies from imprisonment to execution by a firing squad and confiscation of all property.

Crimes against the Administrative Order. The Code also recognizes a special class of crimes against "the administrative order." These are defined as "any action which, while not aimed at the overthrow of the Soviet Government . . . leads nevertheless to the disorganization of the regular functioning of the organs of the Government and interference with their work, violation of the law, or *other activities which weaken the power and authority of* the State" (Article 59 ^{1}). It is obviously impossible to reconcile these legal

---

[47] Statement by Corley Smith, British delegate to the Economic and Social Council of the United Nations. *The New York Times,* July 23, 1949.

rules with the doctrine of the "withering away" of the State as expounded by Lenin. The loose wording of the provisions just quoted and of many others is susceptible of the widest interpretation. The articles of the Criminal Code have frequently been invoked when the economic and administrative institutions have failed to work satisfactorily.[48]

Post-War Legislation. During and immediately after the War questions of security were dealt with largely by military authorities. Beginning in 1947, however, the Presidium of the Supreme Soviet enacted several measures for the protection of the safety of the State and State property. Disclosure of State secrets ("provided such action does not constitute treason or espionage") or loss of documents containing secret information, became punishable by confinement in a labor camp for a term of six to twenty years (decree of June 4, 1947). The Council of Ministers supplied a comprehensive list of information classified as secret. The list included, in addition to information bearing directly on national defense, information designated as secret by the Council of Ministers concerning industry, agriculture, trade, transport, monetary circulation, financial plans, and other economic activities; also information on "discoveries, inventions, technical improvements, research and experimental work in all spheres of science, technology, and national economy until they are completed and permission has been obtained for publication"; and information on "negotiations, relations, and agreements of the USSR with foreign States, and all other measures in the field of foreign policy and foreign trade which are not contained in officially published data." Another decree of June 4, 1947, imposed heavy penalties (five to twenty-five years in a labor camp, with or without confiscation of property) for embezzlement of State or public (collective farm and cooperative) property. Withholding of information concerning acts of embezzlement committed or about to be committed is punishable by loss of freedom for two to three years, or deportation for five to seven years. A decree of December 16, 1947, imposed Draconian restrictions on the relations of Soviet agencies and officials with agencies and officials of foreign States. The Ministry of Foreign Affairs and, "within the limits of its authority," the Ministry of Foreign Trade were alone permitted to deal with foreign representatives, including members of diplomatic missions. Any request addressed by a foreign representative to a Soviet official must be referred to the Ministry of Foreign Affairs or the Ministry of Foreign Trade. Postal and telegraph employees, clerks selling railway and theatre tickets, waiters, shop attendants, and the like were magnanimously allowed to deal directly with foreigners "within the limits, however, of the usual functions performed by such . . . persons." A foreign ambassador may still buy a newspaper or a meal without Vishynsky's special dispensation, but he must not engage in unnecessary conversation with the news-vendor or waiter. The truly medieval decree of February 15, 1947, pro-

---

[48] The Criminal Code is being revised. In view of recent trends in Soviet legislation (examples of which will be found below) it is not likely that the sections dealing with offenses against the State and State property will lose anything of their severity.

hibiting marriages between Soviet citizens and foreigners was another manifestation of the determination to erect an impregnable barrier between the
USSR and the outside world.

Capital Punishment Abolished and Restored. In the midst of these
bizarre activities the Presidium of the Supreme Soviet announced the glad
news of the abolition of the death penalty. A decree of May 26, 1947, made
confinement in a labor camp for twenty-five years the highest penalty in
peacetime. Two reasons were given for the abolition of capital punishment:
(1) "The historic victory of the Soviet people . . . has demonstrated . . .
the exceptional loyalty of the entire population to the Soviet motherland
(*rodina*) and the Soviet Government"; and (2) the fact that since the end of
the War "the cause of peace may be considered as secure for a long time, in
spite of the attempts of aggressive elements to provoke war." Restraint on
freedom in dealing with opponents, however, is repugnant to the men in the
Kremlin. On January 12, 1950, the Presidium of the Supreme Soviet reversed itself and reimposed capital punishment for "traitors, spies, and saboteurs," a loosely worded provision which may be invoked in the case of practically any offender against the laws and regulations of the ubiquitous and
omnipotent State. The revival of the death penalty was due, according to the
decree, to requests received from national republics, trade unions, peasant
organizations, and cultural leaders. If this statement is to be taken at its face
value it would suggest that the number of traitors, spies, and saboteurs must
be large indeed to create a nationwide outcry for the restoration of capital
punishment. But unanimity, as we have seen, is never wanting in the USSR
when the Government needs it.

Ban on Legislation. A development of the gravest concern to the students
of Russian affairs is the systematic blocking of all channels of information.
The volume of legislation enacted by the Supreme Soviet is surprisingly small.
The *"Vedomosti* (Monitor) of the Supreme Soviet," organ of the Presidium,
contains little except decrees dealing with the establishment of new medals
and decorations, and endless lists of recipients of rewards ranging from Stalin,
cabinet ministers, scientists, ballet dancers, famous composers, factory directors and collective farm presidents down to miners, industrial workers, farmers, and milkmaids. The actual business of government is carried on by decrees of the Council of Ministers of the USSR. These decrees are addressed
primarily to local administrative agents whose educational and intellectual
levels are not too high. They are often couched in a homely and picturesque
language, are illustrated by examples drawn from actual life, and, taken as a
whole, provide a revealing picture of Soviet conditions. Ministerial decrees
were published in the official *"Sobranie* [Collection] of Decisions and Ordinances of the Government [changed to Council of Ministers in April, 1946]
of the USSR," which appeared at irregular intervals several times a year.
Since the War this invaluable source of information showed a tendency to dry
up; the issues of *Sobranie* became shorter and rarer, and much of its dwin-
dling space was taken up by appointments and dismissals of officials while

vital decrees were omitted. In August, 1949, *Sobranie* was discontinued, and the unhappy student of Russian affairs is forced to rummage for gleanings of factual information in the stale columns of *Izvestia* and *Pravda* and those of the few Soviet periodicals that are worth reading.[49] The predicament of Soviet citizens is even graver. It is an old legal maxim that no one can plead ignorance of the law. According to the Constitution, observance of the law is a citizen's primary duty and the decrees of the Council of Ministers are as binding as the laws enacted by the Supreme Soviet. But how can they be observed if they are not published? To this puzzling question I have no answer.

The Citizen and the State. In 1932 Pavel Morozov, a Russian peasant boy, denounced his father for siding with the opponents of collectivization and was murdered by his irate parent and other alleged *kulaks.* This gruesome piece of family history, according to *Pioneer Pravda,* was to be immortalized by erecting a memorial to young Morozov in the Moscow Red Square.[50] The memorial, if it was actually built, conveys better than the lifeless sessions of hand-picked deputies of the Supreme Soviet the essence of Soviet democracy.

[49] The decline and fall of *Sobranie* may be gathered from the following figures: 1940—32 issues, 818 enactments, 1,084 pages; 1942—11 issues, 199 enactments, 200 pages; 1946–14 issues, 283 enactments, 256 pages; 1948—8 issues, 93 enactments, 227 pages; and 1949 (January–August 18)—11 issues, 91 enactments, 272 pages. A minor Soviet official whom I asked why a publication containing so much valuable information should be discontinued exclaimed spontaneously: "Ah, *that* must be the reason," an explanation to which I have nothing to add.

[50] Quoted by Harold Denny in *The New York Times,* November 15, 1938.

CHAPTER V

ECONOMIC PLANNING

PLANNING VS. "ANARCHY OF PRODUCTION"

Anarchy of Production. "Anarchy of production," according to the Marxian analysis, is inherent in an economic and political system based on the private ownership of the means of production. The striving of the capitalists for higher profits leads them into cut-throat competition, with its accompanying evils of periodical overexpansion followed by violent economic depression which throws millions of people out of work, ruins the smaller capitalists, and forces them into the ranks of the proletariat. This sinister rhythm of capitalistic development, the Marxian Socialists maintain, becomes more pronounced with the growth of the capitalist society, the depressions are more frequent and severe, while the misery they inflict upon the working class is continuously intensified. Finally the economic crises, by paving the way to the inevitable Socialist revolution, spell the doom of the capitalism that generated them.

Economic Planning a Necessity under Socialism. The Socialist and, later, the Communist society must be free from the violent fluctuations which, admittedly, are the curse of an economic organization resting on private ownership and private initiative. The cure consists in a comprehensive economic plan prepared by an enlightened body of experts and statesmen possessed of a real knowledge of the country's resources and requirements, a plan that will map out the course of the nation over a protracted period. The necessity of such a plan in a Socialist society is almost self-evident. Under capitalism the economic life is regulated more or less automatically, although no doubt imperfectly, by the relatively free interplay of complex economic forces, the interaction of supply and demand made possible by the mechanics of competition and prices, and the movement (not without considerable friction) of capital and labor from one branch of production into another. In a Socialist economy private competition is nonexistent. The State is the sole producer and distributor of commodities (with but few exceptions), it determines the volume of production of every kind of goods and the prices to be charged for them. Capital, of course, cannot be moved by private initiative from one branch of production to another for the obvious reason that all economic activities are financed by the State and there is no private ownership of the means of production. Having thus eliminated the mechanics of capitalist economy the Socialist State must put something in its place. The solution offered by the Soviet Union—and there seems to be no other—is economic planning. The necessity of such planning was recognized by the Bolshevik leaders from the very beginning of their rule. The program of the Russian Communist Party, adopted in March, 1919, proclaimed that one of the most pressing problems of the day was "the maximum unification of all economic activities of the country in a comprehensive State plan." It was, however, almost ten years before planned economy was actually put into operation. War Communism, with its rigid centralization and the drastic attempt by the State to control every phase of the economic life, was, in a sense, a venture into planned economy although it concerned itself merely with immediate and pressing needs. These economic measures were taken, moreover, under the most unfavorable economic and political conditions and were abandoned early in 1921. The New Economic Policy, with the relative freedom it offered the peasant-farmers and the small traders and artisans, was lacking in some of the essentials of a Socialist economy. It was only with the official inauguration of the first Five-Year Plan in October, 1928, that the Soviet Union definitely entered the stage of economic planning.

Prerequisites and Objectives of Planning. The Soviet economists claim, it would seem on good ground, that there are certain prerequisites essential to the success of any economic plan. The first of these is the nationalization of all means of production and the elimination of all private interests, since such interests are inherently inimical to the smooth working of the mechanism of planning. No less essential is the second condition—unified leadership, which in the Soviet Union is provided by the Communist Party. The Soviet plan, however, is not merely a technical device for the administration of economic activities. It has also definite social and political objectives which received their most authoritative expression in Article 11 of the new Constitution. These objectives, it will be recalled, are: (1) increase in public wealth; (2) steady improvement in the material and cultural standards of the working people; and (3) the strengthening of the independence of the Soviet Union and of its capacity for defense.

THE PLANNING AGENCIES

Early Attempts at Planning. The central planning agency of the Soviet Union is the State Planning Commission of the USSR, or the Gosplan, which was created in February, 1921, as a commission of the Council of Labor and Defense.[1] It was some time, however, before the Gosplan became the actual

---

[1] The Council of Labor and Defense was formed in April, 1920, was given the status of a permanent commission of the Council of People's Commissars (December, 1920), and dealt primarily with the coordination of defense and economic activities.

central planning body. The Supreme Economic Council, established in December, 1917, had somewhat similar functions, some of which it retained until its abolition in 1932. The first comprehensive attempt at planning was made in April, 1921, when a special commission for the electrification of Russia was appointed at the suggestion of Lenin. The commission had the task of preparing a general plan for the development of electric power stations and the use of electric current, a plan that was to be put into effect over a number of years. Lenin attached the greatest importance to this venture, and the plan for electrification was later incorporated in the Five-Year Plan. In 1925 were published the first so-called "control figures" which were a program of economic development for the year 1925–1926.[2] In 1926 the Soviet Union embarked on a more ambitious program which finally became the first Five-Year Plan. Officially put into operation on October 1, 1928, to run for five years, it was declared completed in four years and three months, that is, on December 31, 1932.

The Gosplan. The State Planning Commission, like all other Soviet institutions, has undergone frequent structural changes. From a commission of some forty members it has grown into a vast administration subdivided (under the decree of April 13, 1940) into forty-five specialized agencies, each comprising several sections, and employing thousands of people, including an army of statisticians. The members of the Gosplan are appointed by the Council of Ministers (People's Commissars), of which its Chairman is a member. In April, 1935, the membership of the governing body of the Gosplan was reduced to seventy, less than half its previous number. The reorganization of February, 1938, confirmed the status of the Gosplan as a permanent commission directly subordinated to the Council of People's Commissars, thus giving legal recognition to a situation that has apparently prevailed for some time.[3] Under the 1938 setup the governing body of the Gosplan consisted of Chairman, a board of eleven members, and a council of ninety members.[4] The principal activities of the Gosplan are twofold: (1) the coordination of the vast mass of factual information which reaches it from every corner of the country, and the preparation of a unified plan according to the general directions issued by the Communist Party and the Council of Ministers; and (2) the checking of the performance by subordinate institutions of their assignments under the plan.

Other Planning Agencies. The Gosplan of the USSR is assisted in the carrying out of its task by a complex network of planning institutions which may be broadly divided into two groups: those arranged on the horizontal or

[2] For the purposes of planning, the year was originally reckoned from October to October. Since 1933, it is made to coincide with the calendar year.

[3] The Council of Labor and Defense was abolished and most of its work was taken up, in November, 1937, by a newly appointed Economic Council, another permanent commission of the Council of People's Commissars.

[4] By a decree of January 9, 1948, of the Presidium of the Supreme Soviet the State Planning Commission was reorganized as the State Planning Committee of the Council of Ministers. As far as could be ascertained the text of this decree was never published (see above, p. 745, note 24), but there is no reason to believe that the 1948 reorganization affected substantially the status or functions of the Gosplan.

territorial principle, and those arranged on the vertical or functional principle. The territorial group of planning institutions consists of planning commissions of the constituent republics and other territorial subdivisions. Every locality of any importance has its own planning bodies arranged in hierarchical order and directly subordinated to the planning institutions of the territorial sub-divisions of which they form a part. A similar administrative scheme is fol-lowed in the functional group of planning institutions. This group consists of planning agencies attached to each ministry (People's Commissariat) of the USSR, the State Bank, the Union of Cooperative Societies, and so on. The ministries of the constituent republics have, again, their own planning agen-cies and so it goes all along the line down to the factories and collective farms which, too, participate in the preparation of the plan. It is self-evident that this extraordinarily complex administrative structure of the planning agencies must lead to a great deal of duplication, for the territorial and functional plan-ning bodies necessarily deal with the same problems although, perhaps, from a somewhat different standpoint. It is the duty of the higher planning bodies to iron out as well as they can the differences that must necessarily arise until the Gosplan of the USSR finally produces a comprehensive plan for the Union. The plan is then submitted for the approval of both the Communist Party and the Soviet Government and is put into operation.

The Procedure. The general direction as to the contents of the plan come from the Communist Party and the Soviet Government. It is the duty of the Gosplan to embody these in concrete proposals, supported by a formidable array of statistical data, and to provide a definite assignment for the various branches of economic activity. The preliminary plan is then submitted to the lower planning agencies which transmit the proposed assignments further down the line to the planning bodies under their jurisdiction. Every factory and every collective farm is thus given an opportunity to become acquainted with the proposed plan before it has been finally adopted. Discussions are organized and frequently counter-plans are made by the local bodies. These counter-plans invariably suggest an increase in the original assignment. There seems to be no instance on record of doubts expressed by a factory that the proposed quota could be filled, even though failures to complete the assign-ments are common. With the same unfailing unanimity that has been already noted in Soviet elections industrial workers and farmers, on the invitation of the local Communists, clamor for more exacting assignments and larger quotas.[5] The plan thus revised then moves up through the hierarchy of plan-ning agencies until the many local suggestions reach the Gosplan. Its statis-ticians are kept busy revising the original draft of the plan, although the final assignment would seem to be determined rather by the "general line" of the Party than by the expression of official optimism that comes from the rank and file of the Soviet citizens.

[5] The regulations issued by the Council of People's Commissars on December 17, 1930, and reproduced in the official collection of labor legislation published in 1938, include "passive, indifferent, or negligent attitude" toward the counterplan among the punishable offences against labor discipline.

THE FIRST, SECOND, THIRD, AND FOURTH FIVE-YEAR PLANS

The Four Five-Year Plans. The first Five-Year Plan was published in three bulky volumes comprising, with the appendices, nearly 1,600 pages; the second, in two volumes of a slightly smaller format containing over 1,300 pages; the third, in one volume of less than 250 pages; and the fourth, in a pamphlet of 95 pages. The official summary of fulfillment of the first Five-Year Plan, issued in 1933, was a booklet of 275 pages, and the summary of fulfillment of the second Five-Year Plan, published in 1939, is an even smaller booklet of 157 pages. No comparable factual survey of the results of the third Five-Year Plan is available, although its achievements are, of course, invariably extolled by the Moscow leaders. Basic factual information on Soviet planning, which was never adequate, has therefore been becoming increasingly meager. There is, moreover, no close coordination between the issuance of a plan and the time when it is put into operation. The third Five-Year Plan, for instance, was inaugurated in January, 1938, but until 1939, when the full text was published, its contents were known merely from brief official summaries. Each of the four Five-Year Plans is divided into two main parts: Part I deals with the proposed development of the various branches of national activity over the entire territory of the Union; Part II concerns itself with the apportionment of planned assignments among the principal administrative subdivisions. The difficulties arising from the frequent shifting of internal boundaries and the confusion this introduces in regional planning are duly noted in the introductions to Part II of the first and second Five-Year Plans.

Their Scope. "The Five-Year Plan for the Development of National Economy," to give the plan its full name, is really an understatement of the scope of the gigantic venture. Each of the successive plans contains not only a comprehensive program of economic development but also an exhaustive schedule of social, cultural, and educational activities. The chief emphasis of the plan, however, is on the economic aspects, a policy that is in harmony with the Marxian theory according to which the economic factors—the "modes of production"—determine the character of the social, cultural, and political "superstructure." As an effort at mapping out the future course of the nation the Soviet plans are rightly regarded as a unique and stupendous enterprise without precedent in the annals of any country. To give some idea of the immensity of the undertaking a brief enumeration of the topics covered by the plan will have to suffice. Each of the plans deals, in a varying degree of thoroughness, with the development of industry: machine-building, electric power stations, fuel, mining, chemistry, timber, industries producing consumers' goods, food industries, cooperative associations of producers. Then come agriculture, transportation, post, telegraph, and telephone. Special sections treat the questions of labor, wages, standards of living, cost of production, quality of goods, distribution, and per capita consumption. The discussion of cultural activities includes the expansion of the school system, the training of teachers, the printing of books and newspapers, while the social policies extend to housing, measures for the improvement of public health, and social insurance. The section on finance provides a comprehensive survey of sources from which the stupendous outlay necessitated by the plan is to be met. The first Five-Year Plan had a special brief chapter on foreign trade which, however, was omitted from the subsequent plans.

Under each of the foregoing headings (and the list given is not exhaustive) the plan sets definite goals to be achieved within the following five years and outlines, not always very clearly, by what methods the results desired are to be obtained. The plan maps out the amount of capital to be invested in the various fields, the percentage by which the production of each branch of industry is to be increased, and—also in percentages—the increase in the productivity of labor, the reduction in prices, the increase in monetary and real wages, the reduction of illiteracy, and so on.

The Political and Social Objectives of the First, Second, and Third Five-Year Plans. Each of the consecutive plans is considered as a definite stage along the road leading the Soviet Union toward Communism. The objectives of the first Five-Year Plan, as outlined in a resolution of the Fifteenth Congress of the Communist Party in December, 1927, were the industrialization of the USSR, the reorganization of the rural community on a Socialist basis, the overcoming of the capitalist and the strengthening of the Socialist elements in the economic organization of the country. These goals were declared to have been achieved by January 1, 1933, when the second Five-Year Plan was inaugurated. "The basic political aim of the second Five-Year Plan," according to the resolution of the Seventeenth Conference of the Communist Party, "is the final liquidation of the capitalist elements and of classes in general, the complete elimination of causes that lead to class distinctions and exploitation, and the overcoming of the survival of capitalism in the economic organization and in the minds of men, and the transformation of the entire working population into conscious and active builders of the classless society." V. Molotov, then chairman of the Council of People's Commissars, stated early in 1939 that the chief objective of the second Five-Year Plan— "the elimination of the causes of exploitation of man by man"—had been achieved.[6] He maintained that "the Socialist society of the USSR consists now of two classes friendly to one another—the workers and the peasants—the dividing line between these classes as well as between them and the intellectuals is being effaced, is gradually disappearing." He explained that Soviet intellectuals were actually the peasants and workers of yesterday. The social transformation of society, based on the socialization of industry and the collectivization of farming, is leading the Soviet Union into a new era inaugurated by the third Five-Year Plan. The goal, according to Molotov, is "the completion of the building up of a classless Socialist society and the gradual transition from Socialism to Communism, a period when the determining factor

[6] V. Molotov, preliminary report (theses) on the third Five-Year Plan submitted to the Eighteenth Congress of the Communist Party in *Pravda,* January 30, 1939.

is the Communist education of the toilers, the overcoming of the survival of capitalism in the minds of men—builders of Communism."

Their Economic Program. Such is the political and social program of the first three plans. Their economic program, which displays an even greater uniformity, may be reduced to three principal objectives: (1) rapid industrialization with special emphasis on the building up of the heavy industries that produce the means of production, (2) collectivization of farming, and (3) sustained effort to reduce costs and to increase the productivity of labor.

The Philosophy and Objectives of the Fourth Five-Year Plan. The general approach of the fourth Five-Year Plan, which is officially styled "The Law on the Five-Year Plan for the Reconstruction and Development of the National Economy of the USSR in 1946–1950," differs somewhat from that of its predecessors. The preamble of the new plan proclaims that "as a result of the heroic efforts of the peoples of the Soviet Union and of its gallant Red Army there was achieved a victory of world-wide historic significance—the annihilation of Hitler's Germany and the defeat of Japanese imperialism. The USSR has ended the War by winning a complete victory over the enemy— this is the true significance [*glavnyi itog*] of the War. The victory of the USSR means, first, that victory was won by the Soviet social system, that the Soviet social system has successfully withstood the trials of the war conflagration and has proved its viability. The victory of the USSR means, secondly, that victory was won by the Soviet constitutional system, that the multi-national Soviet State has withstood all the trials of war and has proved its viability. The victory of the USSR means, thirdly, that victory was won by the Soviet armed forces, by the Red Army, that the Red Army has heroically withstood the hardships of war, that it has smashed the armies of our enemies, and that it has emerged victorious from the War. Such a victory of world-wide significance could be achieved only on the foundation of the preliminary preparation of the entire country for active defense. The preparation of this gigantic enterprise required the execution of the three Five-Year Plans for the development of the national economy of the USSR." This interpretation of the true significance of World War II, an interpretation which is not likely to commend itself to Russia's wartime partners, is followed by the endorsement of the policy laid down by the Eighteenth Congress of the Communist Party in 1939, namely, that the gradual transition from Socialism to Communism poses before the peoples of the Soviet Union the problem, first, of reaching, and then of exceeding, the per capita production levels of the capitalist countries. The basic objectives of the plan are "the restoration of the devastated regions, the restoration of the pre-War production levels in industry and agriculture, and then the achievement of much higher levels."

UNCERTAINTIES OF SOVIET PLANNING

Inadequacy of Soviet Statistics. An attempt to obtain a clear picture of the working of Soviet planning unfortunately meets with insurmountable obstacles. Chief among them is the absence of basic statistical data, a state of affairs that is certainly surprising in a country where much energy is being spent in filling out innumerable forms dealing with innumerable subjects. Since 1929 the Soviet Government has discontinued the publication of the index of the cost of living, thus making impossible the determination of the trend of real wages. All computations in the State budget are made at current prices while the State Planning Commission uses alternately current prices and the prices of 1926–1927. For instance, the third and fourth Five-Year Plans give estimates sometimes in terms of current prices and sometimes in those of the "constant" 1926–1927 prices. In the absence of a general index of prices the two sets of figures are not comparable and if the State Planning Commission has worked out a method for comparing them it has never been disclosed.[7] The confusion is further increased by the steady outpouring by official agencies of statistical data grievously at variance with other data, equally official. It is extremely rare that cognizance is taken of the flagrant discrepancies; and they are almost never rectified or explained. "Bolshevik self-criticism," that is, the practice of denouncing the failure to carry out certain policies (but never denunciation of the policies themselves), is the duty of every Communist. Such criticism is freely indulged in by the Soviet leaders who zealously castigate the departments under their jurisdiction for having lagged in performing their assignments under the plan, only to conclude a bitter indictment with the triumphant proclamation that the plan has been over-fulfilled in spite of everything. One or two instances of this distressing practice will be noted below.

Inconsistencies of the State Planning Commission. The State Planning Commission, which is merely a subordinate agency of the Council of Ministers, displays at times puzzling inconsistencies. The first Five-Year Plan, to take a striking example, was prepared in two drafts, the maximum and the minimum, the former setting up a much higher goal of achievement than the latter. It was intended to use the maximum draft only if the general conditions were particularly favorable. According to the official summary of the fulfillment of the first Five-Year Plan issued by the State Planning Commission in 1933, the actual situation in 1928–1932 was even less favorable than had originally been considered necessary for carrying out the provisions of the minimum draft: adverse climatic conditions (and also, no doubt, the forcible drive for collectivization) reduced the 1931 harvest to a starvation level; the world-wide depression and the catastrophic decline in prices, especially those of agricultural produce, completely upset the export and import program of the plan; expenditure or armaments increased far beyond the estimates. Nevertheless the maximum draft not only was put into effect but was completed within four years and three months, thus reducing by nine months the full term of five years. If the official explanation of this amazing development is to be accepted, the people of the Soviet Union displayed a greater zest for planning than did the State Planning Commission and the Government.

---

[7] For a useful summary of the complexities of Soviet statistics see Maurice Dobb, *Soviet Economic Development Since 1917* (New York, 1948), pp. 261–267.

The Plan Is Not a Blueprint. In spite of the vagaries of the planning agencies, the inadequate and fragmentary nature of the available information, and the impenetrable veil of mystery that envelops certain essential phases of the planning procedure, official reports afford sufficient data for a general appraisal of the working of the first and second Five-Year Plans. It is important to realize that the plan is not a blueprint, that its various elements are but loosely coordinated, and that there is nothing permanent in their interrelationship. The Five-Year Plan is much more in the nature of a slogan, of a drive toward the attainment of a definite objective, than a detailed program of practical policies. The Five-Year Plan is being continuously modified by yearly plans which, again, are subdivided into quarterly plans and even into plans for shorter periods. The departures from the original plan in the process of subsequent revisions are sometimes so great as to be almost revolutionary. The truly remarkable flexibility of Soviet planned economy may be best explained by using concrete examples. The striking disparities between the original assignments and the actual performance under the first and the second Five-Year Plans can be traced to three principal causes: changes in the policies of the Communist Party and of the Soviet Government, the state of the world market and the international political situation, and the failure of Soviet enterprises to perform their assignments.[8]

OVERFULFILLMENT AND UNDERFULFILLMENT

Revision of the Program of Collectivization. The most striking example of the revision of the plan by the Communist Party and the Government occurred with reference to the agricultural program under the first Five-Year Plan. The plan set as its goal the increase of the area under crops in the so-called "socialized sector," that is, on land occupied by the State farms and the collective farms,[9] from 2.7 per cent of the total area under crops (in 1928) to 17.5 per cent (in 1932). The part of "socialized agriculture" in the supply of marketable grain in 1932 as determined by the plan was to be 43 per cent. As a result of the ruthless drive for collectivization, however, this assignment of the plan was vastly exceeded. In 1932, 78 per cent of the area under crops was in the hands of the State and the collective farms, and they together produced 84 per cent of the entire marketable supply of grain. The significance of this change of program cannot be exaggerated. It affected scores of millions

---

[8] The execution of the third Five-Year Plan was interrupted by the outbreak of World War II, and, as these lines are written in 1950, the fourth Five-Year Plan has not yet run its course. Scattered information on the fulfillment of the third and fourth plans indicates, however, that discrepancies between assignments and performance remained as great as they were under the earlier plans. Soviet leaders, unlike some of their admirers abroad, claim no finality for the Five-Year Plans. "To us, the Bolsheviks, the Five-Year Plan is not something complete and ordained once for all," Stalin told the Sixteenth Congress of the Communist Party in 1930. "To us the Five-Year Plan, like any other plan, is but a plan, adopted as a first approximation, one that must be refined, amended, and improved in the light of local experience, in the light of experience gained in carrying out the plan. No Five-Year Plan can foresee all the possibilities that are hidden in the womb of our system and which are disclosed only in the course of work itself, in applying the plan in the factory, the enterprise, the collective farm, the State farm, the region, and so on."

[9] See below, pp. 815 ff.

among the rural population and made imperative a fundamental revision of
the entire plan for heavy industry, since collectivization of agriculture, as will
be shown in Chapter VII, is based on the use of modern agricultural machinery. This, again, demanded a far-reaching readjustment of the plan regarding
transportation, production of metal ore and coal, supply of skilled labor,
financing, etc. It is not surprising that the official summary of the performance
of the first Five-Year Plan points out the creation of a number of important
industrial works, some of them among the most ambitious of Soviet ventures,
for which no provision was made in the plan. It thus appears that the Soviet
Government, if and when it is considered desirable, does not hesitate to revise
the plan for political or other reasons.

Abandonment of the Program for the Expansion of Foreign Trade.
It is much more usual, however, that the plan has to be amended as a result
of conditions over which the Soviet Government has no control. The first Five-
Year Plan, for instance, was based on recognition of the necessity of closer
economic ties between the Soviet Union and the outside world. The plan outlined a broad policy providing for concessions to foreign capital and expansion of Russian exports, which were to be increased two and one-half times
between 1928 and 1932. The world-wide depression made a clean sweep of
these optimistic and fanciful schemes. Foreign capital showed little enthusiasm
for the opportunities offered by the Communist State. Russian exports, which
had been valued at 791 million rubles in 1927–1928 and had increased to
1,036 million rubles in 1930, toppled down to 575 million rubles in 1932 and
declined still further in the following years.[10] Although the physical volume of
Soviet exports actually increased, their value, because of the fall in world
prices, remained far below the planned estimates. These conditions necessitated a drastic revision of the import plan which played an essential part in the
process of industrialization. Far from being immune from the effects of the
world depression, Soviet foreign trade reacted to it in a manner in no way different from that of the foreign trade of the capitalist nations. One of the consequences of the failure of the import-export program of the first Five-Year
Plan was the speeding up of the construction of machine-building plants in the
Soviet Union so that its independence of the capitalistic countries might be
increased. Another consequence was the omission of any reference to foreign
trade in the second, third, and fourth Five-Year Plans, an omission that may
be interpreted as tacit acceptance of the fact that international exchanges do
not lend themselves readily to planning of the Soviet brand.

Fulfillment Under the First Five-Year Plan. By far the most important
reason for the revision of the plan was the failure of various branches of the
national economy to fulfill their assignments. The resulting instability affected
the performance not only of the Five-Year Plan but also of plans for shorter
periods. Generalized and comprehensive figures of performance often obscure
the actual situation. For instance, the fulfillment by industry of its assignments
for 1932, the last year of the first Five-Year Plan, was officially stated to be

[10] The average annual Russian exports in 1909–1913 were 1,501 million rubles.

96.4 per cent. This summary figure was composed of divergent elements: the performance of the fuel industry was 99.8 per cent of the assignment; of the metal industry, 127.2 per cent; of the timber industry, 86.3 per cent; of the cotton (textile) industry, 54.2 per cent. Even more noteworthy were the truly remarkable deviations from the plan within the metal industry group in the same year. The performance in the machine-building and metal goods industries was 181.2 per cent of the assignment; pig iron, 62.0 per cent; steel, 56.7 per cent; steel-rolling, 53.7 per cent; iron ore, 62.9 per cent. It is difficult to find a plausible explanation of this extraordinary state of affairs with the machine-building industry over-fulfilling its quota by a large percentage while the production of pig iron, steel, and ore lagged sadly behind.

Fulfillment under the Second Five-Year Plan. The record of performance of the second Five-Year Plan was not vastly different from that of the first. The value of industrial production in 1937, the final year of the plan, was officially stated to have exceeded the target by 3 per cent (95,500 million rubles and 92,700 million rubles, respectively, in prices of 1926–1927; the corresponding figure of production for 1932 was 43,300 million rubles). Fulfillment by separate branches of industry of their assignments remained, however, uneven. The figures of actual and planned production in 1937, as percentage of 1932, were as follows: steel, 299 (actual) and 289 (planned); pig iron, 235 and 260; iron ore, 230 and 282; coal, 199 and 237; oil, 137 and 210; cotton fabrics, 128 and 187; woolen fabrics, 122 and 239; shoes, 218 and 219. It will be noted that, while steel exceeded its quota and the shoe industry very nearly reached the goal, several important industries (iron ore, oil, coal, textiles) failed to do so by a substantial margin.

Official Criticism of Fulfillment Reports. The deceptive nature of summary figures of fulfillment has been officially admitted. The Minister of Finance, A. G. Zverev, in his report to the Supreme Soviet on the 1949 budget (March, 1949), said that "not infrequently leaders of economic agencies violate the State plan in so far as it bears on the quality and the assortment of goods, by overfulfilling production quotas for the less essential articles but underfulfilling the plan for commodities of primary importance." For instance, in 1948 an agency of the Ministry of Heavy Machine-Building fulfilled its production plan, taken as a whole, 110.9 per cent while the output of some of the basic commodities manufactured by that agency was merely 61 per cent, 57 per cent, and 29 per cent of the assignments. A similar situation prevailed, according to Zverev, in the Ministry of Electrical Industry, where the summary figure of production in 1948 was 115 per cent but in several crucial lines of production it was 83 per cent, 71 per cent, and 54 per cent of the planned quotas. The enterprises of the Chief Administration of Perfumery (under the Food Ministry of the USSR) "continue to turn out articles for which there is little demand and do not produce in sufficient quantities goods needed by the population." Zverev stated that "the Council of Ministers has condemned the practice of fulfilling the plan of production as a whole by overproducing unessential commodities and at the same time underfulfilling the plan for the more important articles and the assortment. The plan of production will be regarded as fulfilled if it meets the planned assignments not only from the standpoint of volume but also those of the prescribed assortment and quality of goods." The foregoing stern rebuke notwithstanding, Soviet spokesmen (including Zverev himself) continue to use summary figures of production as conclusive evidence of the triumphant progress of planned economy. The conclusion would seem to be not unwarranted that the close coordination of the component parts of the plan—if it can be achieved at all—is still a thing of the future.

Productivity of Labor and Reduction of Costs. The increase in the productivity of labor, with the resulting reduction in the costs of production and in prices, thus far has proved one of the most unmanageable elements in Soviet planned economy. The whole plan of industrialization is based on the assumption of increased productivity of labor. Soviet leaders never tire of quoting Lenin's dictum that "the productivity of labor is, in the last resort, the most important, the most essential condition for the victory of the new social order." The maximum draft of the first Five-Year Plan called for an increase of 110 per cent (and the minimum draft, of 85 per cent) in the productivity of labor. The actual average increase, according to the Gosplan, was 41 per cent, a most impressive achievement but nevertheless far below the assignment. As a result of the drastic intensification of the industrialization program and of the failure to reach the labor productivity goals the number of wage-earners (workers and employees) which was to increase under the first Five-Year Plan from 11.3 million (1926–1927) to 15.8 million (1932), or by 39 per cent, actually reached the much higher figure of 22.8 million; that is, it showed an increase of over 100 per cent. Instead of the anticipated unemployment the Soviet authorities were faced in 1932 with a shortage of labor.[11] The unplanned absorption of an additional seven million workers (most of them came, presumably, from the farms) necessitated far-reaching revisions of the other parts of the plan (finance, housing, and so on). If the employment provisions of the first Five-Year Plan were too conservative, those of the second Five-Year Plan proved unduly liberal: the actual number of wage-earners in 1937 was 27 million, or nearly two million less than the planned assignment (28.9 million). Nevertheless, the aggregate amount paid in wages and salaries in 1937 was greatly in excess of the planned proposals. According to the plan, the outlay under this heading was to increase from 32.7 billion rubles in 1932 to 50.7 billion in 1937; it actually reached 82.2 billion rubles. The average annual wage (workers and employees) rose from 1,427 rubles in 1932 to 3,047 rubles in 1937, instead of to 1,755 rubles as provided by the plan. The unplanned increase in wages was presumably due, at least in part, to the failure of industry as a whole to cut down the cost of production to the full extent demanded by the plan. For this failure the Gosplan blamed the forest industry

[11] The number of unemployed in 1927–1928 was officially given as 1.1 million. The maximum draft of the first Five-Year Plan provided for the reduction of unemployment to 400,000 (and the minimum draft, to 800,000) by 1932–1933.

and the light industry producing consumers' goods. "We still have a lot of mismanagement, much excess expenditure, outrageously large losses of raw materials, much waste of fuel and electric power, disgracefully long stoppages of machinery," Molotov told the Eighteenth Congress of the Communist Party in 1939. "That means that in many cases no real struggle is being carried on to reduce the cost of manufactured goods, no real fight is being made to reduce construction costs." The admitted failure of industry to reduce costs to the extent required by the plan is not easily reconcilable with the official claim that the productivity of labor under the second Five-Year Plan increased by 82 per cent instead of the 63 per cent that the plan demanded.[12] The rationing of consumption which was in force from 1929 to 1935, its by-product the multiple-price system (differentiation in prices according to the type of the distributing agency from which the purchase was made), and the absence of an index of prices and of the cost of living make it impossible to determine whether higher monetary wages have brought about higher real wages.

The Plan as a Slogan Rather Than a Program of Practical Policy. The foregoing examples, which it would be easy to multiply, indicate that there is little in the Soviet plan in the nature of a blueprint whose component parts are carefully coordinated. The character of the Five-Year Plans as drives toward the achievement of definite political, social, and economic objectives is emphasized by the enthusiastic reception given by the Soviet press to frequent announcements that this or that branch of the national economy has exceeded its quota. If the elements of the plan were properly coordinated, overfulfillment would be no less disturbing and unwelcome than underfulfillment, which is invariably and bitterly denounced. Strange as this may appear at first sight, the practical usefulness of a Five-Year Plan would seem to be slight, except as a slogan. This explains the equanimity with which the Soviet leaders have accepted the delay of the Gosplan in producing the third Five-Year Plan, a delay which was partly due to alleged "wrecking" activities within the Gosplan and the purge of that body.[13] This may also explain why the size of the plan, as a printed document, has shrunk from 1,600 pages—small as it was in view of the vastness of the enterprise—to less than one hundred pages. The fourth Five-Year Plan was completed at the end of 1950. As these pages go to print in December, 1951, the fifth Five-Year Plan has not been made available, but the absence of a plan does not seem to affect the functioning of Soviet economic agencies. Attempts at charting in advance, with any degree of precision, the course of Soviet economy have proved only too often a source of embarrassment.

[12] According to the official summary of fulfillment of the second Five-Year Plan heavy industry reduced costs in 1933–1937 by 27 per cent. Kaganovich, the Commissar of Heavy Industry, stated, however, that "the enterprises of the People's Commissariat of Heavy Industry not only failed to reduce costs in 1937, but, on the contrary, increased them" (*Industriia,* January 29, 1938). It is difficult to see how the Gosplan and the Commissar of Heavy Industry could both be right.

[13] In this report to the Eighteenth Congress of the Communist Party Stalin spoke scornfully of some of the planned assignments proposed by the members of the Gosplan as "sheer fantasy, if not worse."

THE COST OF INDUSTRIALIZATION

Capital Investment. According to official statements capital investment in the socialized sector of the economy under the first Five-Year Plan was 52.5 billion rubles, exceeding the planned estimates by 12 per cent. Capital investment under the second Five-Year Plan was 137.5 billion rubles (the plan called for an outlay under this heading of 133.4 billion rubles), and the third Five-Year Plan stipulated a further investment of 181 billion rubles.[14] The fourth Five-Year Plan (1946–1950) provides for "centralized capital investment" of 250.3 billion rubles.[15] To these huge amounts must be added the rapidly mounting expenditure on administration, armaments, social services, education, and other items of the State budget. It is of interest to ascertain from what sources these large sums are obtained.

The Tax Reform of 1930. The inauguration of the first Five-Year Plan was followed by an important tax reform which revolutionized Soviet finance. A joint resolution of the Central Executive Committee and of the Council of People's Commissars of September 2, 1930, instituted the turnover tax and laid down new rules for the taxing of the profits of State enterprises. According to K. N. Plotnikov, a Soviet authority on public finance, the reform consolidated in the turnover tax and the profit tax ("withholding from profits" renders better the notion conveyed by the Russian term *otchislenie*) sixty-one taxes, rates, and other charges levied formerly by the central and local government: fifty-four were consolidated in the turnover tax and seven in the profit tax. The two taxes are regarded as complementary, but the turnover tax is by far the most important source of revenue and accounts for the remarkable growth of the Soviet budget since 1930.[16]

Turnover Tax Chief Source of Revenue. The table on pages 780–781 shows that the turnover tax, immediately after its introduction, became the principal single source of Soviet revenue, and has remained so for two decades. Its share in Soviet State finance was particularly important in 1935–1937, de-

[14] The figure of 137.5 billion is given in the official summary of fulfillment of the second Five-Year Plan published by the Gosplan in 1939. Speaking before the Eighteenth Congress of the Communist Party in March of the same year (two weeks before the Gosplan summary went to press) Molotov quoted 115 billion rubles as the volume of capital investment under the second Five-Year Plan. The notorious looseness of Soviet terminology, however, allows the charitable interpretation that the items referred to by the Gosplan and by Molotov were not identical.

[15] These figures are in current prices; for instance, capital investment under the second Five-Year Plan is given in 1933 prices, and that under the fourth Five-Year Plan in the "budget" (*smetnyia*) prices of 1945. The investment figures, therefore, are not comparable.

[16] In the opening years of the Soviet regime the financial situation was hopelessly confused. The almost complete absence of the necessary data and the catastrophic depreciation of the ruble (due to the social upheaval, the civil war, foreign intervention, breakdown of railways, sharp decline of production, and the abortive, short-lived attempt at creating a moneyless economy) made budget estimates, such as they were, largely meaningless. According to Plotnikov, budget expenditure in 1920, expressed in terms of "commodity ruble," amounted to merely 4.4 per cent of the corresponding figure for 1913. Budget deficit in 1920 exceeded one million million rubles. By a series of measures enacted in 1921–1924 the ruble, a purely internal currency, was stabilized, the use of the printing press to cover budget deficits (a prevalent practice in 1918–1923) was specifically prohibited as from July 1, 1924, and the methods of computing the budget were gradually improved. State revenue was estimated at 2.0 billion rubles in 1923–1924, at 4.2 billion in 1925–1926, at 8.8 billion in 1928–1929, and at 13.9 billion in 1929–1930.

clined somewhat in 1938–1941, fell even more sharply during the War years 1942–1945, regained in 1946–1948 much of the ground lost during the War, and displayed a new tendency to decrease in 1950 and probably in 1949 (for which no figure of actual yield is available). All other sources of revenue are dwarfed by the turnover tax. Under the second Five-Year Plan (1932–1937), 67.4 per cent of the State revenue came from the turnover tax; 6.3 per cent from withholding from profits; 1.9 per cent from the income tax and other direct taxes paid by enterprises and organizations; 4.8 per cent from direct "taxes and other charges levied on the population" (individual income tax, agricultural tax, housing and cultural development tax in urban and rural localities, local rates); 8.5 per cent from receipts on account of social insurance; 6.3 per cent from State loans; and 4.8 per cent from other sources. The budgetary picture remained essentially unchanged after World War II. In 1947 the turnover tax was scheduled to produce 62.3 per cent of the total revenue; withholding from profits 4.9 per cent (18.7 billion rubles); direct taxes 7.2 per cent (27.7 billion rubles); and State loans 5.6 per cent (21.4 billion rubles). In 1950 the turnover tax was expected to yield 55.2 per cent (239.1 billion rubles) of the total revenue; withholding from profits 9.2 per cent (40.0 billion rubles); direct taxes 8.3 per cent (36.4 billion rubles); and State loans 7.4 per cent (31.8 billion rubles).[17]

Turnover Tax Levied on Necessities. It is thus clear that industrialization is financed by the turnover tax, a general sales tax levied on the turnover of all State-owned enterprises and usually computed in percentages of the retail price. The yield of the tax depends on three factors: the volume of production, the price of goods, and the tax rate. In the Soviet Union all three of these are controlled by the State. It is often stated that the turnover tax is levied primarily on luxuries. Nothing could be more misleading than this assertion, as the huge receipts from the tax should suggest even to students who never take the trouble to consult the actual rates of the tax published in Soviet decrees. Since the Soviet Union is a country of very low incomes it is self-evident that a tax on luxuries could never have produced the huge sums collected by the Moscow Treasury.[18] The budget of the USSR tells a very different story. In

[17] Information on Soviet public finance, particularly on the budget, is notoriously fragmentary and incomplete. Prior to the adoption of the Constitution of 1936 the Government published every year a budgetary statement which outlined in some detail the main sources of revenue and the allocation of expenditure. With the establishment of the new Soviet parliament this practice was discontinued. The *Law on the State Budget* (*Zakon o gosudarstvennom biudzhete*), passed annually by the Supreme Soviet, is a brief, perfunctory document containing no information except the summary figures of revenue and expenditure and their allocation among the federal budget and the budgets of the administrative subdivisions of the Union. The principal sources of information are the budget reports submitted every year to the Supreme Soviet by Zverev, Minister (formerly People's Commissar) of Finance, reports which are only too often confused, contradictory, and grievously incomplete. Zverev invariably mentions numerous agencies which have failed to meet their share of taxes and have caused serious losses to the Treasury; yet the budget is always closed with a surplus. No questions about flagrant discrepancies and glaring omissions have ever been raised in the Supreme Soviet.

[18] The grossest ignorance of Soviet taxation is displayed by Sidney and Beatrice Webb in their much admired but notoriously misleading, monumental work, *Soviet Communism: A New Civilization?* (New York, 1936). "The indirect taxation . . . ," write the Webbs, centers on "undesirable luxuries and upon expenditure not much incurred by the masses of the people." (P. 117.)

TOTAL REVENUE AND REVENUE

	Oct.–Dec. 1930	1931	1932	1933	1934	1935	1936	1937	1938
Total revenue in billion rubles	5.3	25.2	38.0	46.4	58.4	75.0	94.4	109.3	127.5
Yield of turnover tax in billion rubles	2.4	11.7	19.6	27.0	37.6	52.0	65.8	75.9	80.4
Turnover tax as percentage of total revenue	45.9	46.2	51.5	58.0	64.4	69.6	69.7	69.2	63.1

1937 [19] the bulk of the revenue from the turnover tax was derived from the following agencies: Committee for the Purchasing of Agricultural Products (later People's Commissariat and now Ministry of Agricultural Stocks), an institution to which the peasants compulsorily surrender a definite share of their grain at extremely low prices [20]—24.1 billion rubles; People's Commissariat of Food Industry—20.4 billion rubles; the Liquor Administration—6.2 billion rubles; the State Trade Administration and the cooperative societies—4.5 billion rubles; the People's Commissariat of Light Industry, that is, industries producing consumers' goods—11.4 billion rubles. Taxation of foodstuffs alone provided about two-thirds of the yield of the turnover tax and accounted for more than half of the entire revenue of the Soviet Union.

Its Rates. The rates of the turnover tax are extremely high and subject to frequent changes. The rates on bread and flour, which are approximately 70 to 80 per cent, account for the enormous revenue of the People's Commissariat (Ministry) of Agricultural Stocks. The following rates were effective in 1937: meat, from 61 to 82 per cent; salt, 66 to 83 per cent; cigarettes, 75 to 90 per cent; cheap tobacco, 68 to 75 per cent; cottons, 44 to 65 per cent; hose, 15 to 65 per cent; knitted underwear, 25 to 55 per cent; rubber overshoes, 33 per cent; sewing machines, 39 per cent; leather footwear, 17 to 35 per cent; powder, shaving cream, and toothpaste, 68 per cent; soap, 34 to 59 per cent. The rates of the turnover tax were maintained at a high level during the War and the post-War period, although a downward revision is suggested by the three consecutive reductions of retail prices (December 14, 1947; February 28, 1949; and March 1, 1950), the failure to reach—by a wide margin—the turnover tax assignment in 1948 (estimated yield, 280.1 billion rubles; actual yield, 247.5 billion rubles), and the decline of both the total revenue and receipts from the turnover tax in the 1950 budget.[21]

[19] More recent data are not available.

[20] See below, pp. 821 ff.

[21] The following are some of the rates of the turnover tax, as percentage of retail prices, enacted in 1939, 1940, 1941, 1942, and 1946. In 1939: fish and fish products, 5 to 36 per cent; bicycles for adults, 58 per cent; bicycles for children and young persons, 20 to 38 per cent; denatured alcohol, 53 per cent; clocks, including alarm-clocks, 25 to 40 per cent; "artistic" clocks, 7 per cent; playing cards, 55 to 82 per cent; gramophones and gramophone needles, 10 to 60 per cent; potatoes (when the retail price is 0.50 ruble per kilogram) 232 to 348 rubles per ton in Moscow and 194 to 325 rubles in Leningrad (when the retail price is higher or lower than 0.50 ruble per kilogram the rates of the tax are adjusted accordingly). In 1940:

FROM THE TURNOVER TAX *

1939	1940	1941	1942	1943	1944	1945	1946	1947	1948	1949	1950
156.0	180.2	216.2 †	165.0	210.0	268.7	302.0	325.4	386.2	410.5	437.0	433.2 ‡
96.9	105.9	124.5 †	66.4	71.1	94.9	123.1	191.0	239.9	247.5	261.9 ‡	239.1 ‡
62.1	58.7	57.9	40.2	33.8	35.3	40.8	58.7	62.2	60.3	59.9	55.2

* Figures in this table refer to the "union" (*soiuznyi*) budget which comprises the federal budget, the budgets of the constituent republics, and, since 1938, the budgets of the smaller territorial subdivisions. The 1930–1948 figures and the 1949 total revenue figure are those of actual receipts. Contrary to the established practice the Minister of Finance, A. G. Zverev, did not state in his report on the 1950 budget the actual receipts from the turnover tax in 1949. Prior to World War II (and again in 1945) revenue from the turnover tax usually exceeded the estimates, but the trend was reversed in 1946. The estimated and actual yields of the turnover tax were, respectively, 200.1 billion rubles and 191.1 billion in 1946; 254.7 billion and 239.9 billion in 1947; and 280.1 billion and 247.5 billion in 1948 (when the turnover tax was expected to produce 65.8 per cent of the total revenue but actually yielded 60.3 per cent). It is probable that the actual yield of the turnover tax in 1949 was below the estimate. The failure of the turnover tax to reach its goals was reflected in total revenue lower than was anticipated in 1946, 1947, 1948, and 1949. The policy of price reduction embarked upon at the end of 1947 is, presumably, responsible, at least in part, for the difficulties experienced by the authorities in collecting the prescribed amount of the tax, and for the scaling down of the estimated receipts from that source from 280.1 billion rubles, or 65.8 per cent of the total revenue in 1948, to 239.1 billion, or 55.2 per cent, in 1950. It may be significant that the estimated revenue in 1950 was set, for the first time in Soviet history (exclusive of the War year 1942), at a lower level than in the preceding year.
† Budgetary estimates; the figure of the actual revenue in 1941 is not available but was, presumably, lower than planned. The actual yield of the turnover tax in 1941, according to Plotnikov, was 93.2 billion rubles.
‡ Budgetary estimates.

What It Means to the Consumers. In order to realize what the turnover tax means to the consumers one must keep in mind that its rates are usually computed as a percentage of the retail price. For instance, the tax on sugar in 1936 was 85 per cent, and a kilogram (2.2 lbs.) of sugar sold at a fixed price

confectionery, 10 to 57 per cent (cocoa and chocolate—powder, bars, and bonbons—paid the top rate of 57 per cent); canned fish, 10 to 40 per cent; canned dairy products, 35 to 40 per cent; canned meat, 10 to 64 per cent; canned vegetables, 10 to 25 per cent; matches, 45 per cent; shellac varnish, 66 per cent; fresh beef, 67 to 71 per cent; mutton, pork, veal, 62 to 67 per cent; horse and camel meat, 10 per cent (rabbit meat was exempt from the tax); sausage, 50 to 69 per cent; sugar, 73 per cent; kerosene, 71.7 per cent; potatoes, 25 to 62 per cent, according to price (potatoes which were sold at 0.35 ruble or less per kilogram were exempt); salt (ground), 60 to 80 per cent; electric bulbs, 25 to 50 per cent; gramophone disks, 40 to 60 per cent (except for one variety which was taxed at 5 per cent); butter, 50 to 66 per cent; cheese, 10 to 69 per cent; ice cream, 17 to 32 per cent; milk, 15 to 43 per cent; cream, 40 to 65 per cent; animal fats, 20 to 68 per cent; rubber overshoes, 60 per cent. In 1941: footwear, 5 to 56 per cent; aluminum hardware, 30 to 56 per cent; metal barrels, 5 to 35 per cent; saddlery, 3 to 37 per cent; silver and gold wrist watches, 70 per cent. In 1942: vegetables—fresh, salted, or dried—5 to 13 per cent. In 1946: hardware, 10 to 70 per cent; cutlery, 40 per cent; felt boots, 16 to 27 per cent, according to size.
The rates of the turnover tax for the War years 1943–1945 and the post-War period 1947–1950 do not seem to be available. The rates are enacted by decrees of the Council of Ministers and until recently were published in the official "Collection [Sobranie] of Decisions and Decrees of the Council of Ministers." Only four decrees dealing with the rates of the turnover tax appeared in that publication in 1946 and none in 1947, 1948, and the first eight months of 1949, when the publication of the "Collection" was discontinued (see above, p. 763).

of 4.20 rubles. Of this amount 3.57 rubles went to the Treasury and the balance of 0.63 ruble was to cover the cost of production and the "planned profit" of the refinery. It has been estimated that of the total receipts from retail trade 62.1 per cent in 1936 and 58.6 per cent in 1937 were collected by the Treasury in the guise of the turnover tax.

Inequality of Incomes. It is generally accepted that an indirect tax on articles of general consumption, particularly on foodstuffs, is unfair to the low-income groups who spend a large portion of their income on the bare necessities, an argument that would not apply to the Soviet Union if it had done away with the inequality of incomes. This, however, is not the case. The principle, "from each according to his ability, to each according to his work," has been enshrined in the Soviet Constitution, and the inequality of income, albeit less pronounced than in the capitalist countries, is considerable. The decree of November 1, 1937, increased the minimum wage of workers in industry and transportation to 110 rubles a month. It is extremely likely that the earnings of a large group of farmers were below even this very modest level. The average annual earnings of industrial workers in 1938 were, according to Stalin's report to the Eighteenth Congress of the Communist Party, 3,447 rubles, or 289 rubles per month. The decree of August 29, 1938, prohibited the payment of salaries above 2,000 rubles per month, except with the special permission of the Council of People's Commissars of the USSR. The officials in receipt of the higher salaries moreover enjoy valuable privileges such as obtaining better living accommodations and sometimes being permitted even such luxuries as the use of a car. Their standard of living is very different from that of the workers in the lower wage brackets who, with the peasants, represent the bulk of the population. And it is the latter group that contributes in proportion to its earnings the larger share of the yield of the turnover tax.[22] The inequality of incomes fostered by an elaborate system of "incentive" wages has been fully preserved in the post-War period.

Reasons for the Turnover Tax. It may appear strange that the Soviet Government should make use of the devious artifice of the turnover tax, instead of selling goods at remunerative prices and turning over the profits to the Treasury, since the State is the owner of all industrial enterprises. In the discussion of the financial reform of 1930 the latter course, that is, exclusive reliance on withholding from profits as a method of mobilizing the financial

---

[22] It is characteristic of the attitude of the Soviet legislature that the Supreme Soviet of the USSR voted, in August, 1938, to increase (in excess of the estimate) the turnover tax by 591.5 million rubles. Yet the actual yield of the tax in 1938 was some 2.9 billion rubles short of the estimates. This unfortunate experience did not damp the zeal of Soviet legislators. In May, 1939, they again voted an increase of the turnover tax for the current year, this time by 410.8 million rubles. Demands for a heavier turnover tax have become, indeed, a permanent feature of the debate on the budget in the Supreme Soviet. Nevertheless numerous instances of failure on the part of enterprises and whole ministries to meet their turnover tax quotas are noted in the press and in every budgetary statement of the Minister of Finance. Zverev, in his report on the 1948 budget, complained that "some of the leaders of economic agencies are entering the path of concealing the taxable turnover of their enterprises. In 1947 the municipal trading organization (*gortorg*) of Samarkand, in the Uzbek Soviet Socialist Republic, concealed the taxable turnover produced by the sale of oil products and [unlawfully] withheld 600,000 rubles."

resources of the nation, had many supporters among the leaders of Soviet finance. According to Soviet economists the explanation of the decision made in 1930 is that the turnover tax is a more reliable and flexible source of revenue, one more adaptable to the requirements of a planned economy, than withholding from profits of State enterprises. Receipts from the turnover tax are not affected by the cost of production, a factor which determines profits and which thus far has only too often eluded Government control. The turnover tax being payable immediately on the production of goods provides an effective method of checking upon the performance of economic agencies, assures the Treasury of an uninterrupted flow of revenue, and eliminates delays inherent in the determination of profits. The table on pages 780–781 shows that within three months after the introduction of the turnover tax its proceeds accounted for nearly 46 per cent of the total revenue, probably a record for any tax in obtaining speedy results. It is also argued that since the turnover tax is a major element in the formation of prices, skilful manipulation of the rates makes it possible to siphon surplus purchasing power, bring supply and demand into a state of equilibrium, and eliminate inflationary pressure. The latter claim is not supported by the financial history of the Soviet Union. Finally, it is held that the taking over by the Treasury of all profits of State enterprises would have weakened the incentive to higher production and lower cost, and would have undermined the principle of cost accounting (*khozrazchet*), that life nerve of the Soviet economic structure.[23] Since the turnover tax is never discussed in the Soviet press it is probable that the majority of the citizens are just as little aware of its existence as were Sidney and Beatrice Webb. Except in wartime, it has served well its purpose as a source of seemingly inexhaustible revenue.

Withholding from Profits. The rates of the turnover tax are flat rates computed on the basis of the average cost of production for every branch of industry and applied indiscriminately to all goods of a specified class. The cost of production, however, varies widely from enterprise to enterprise.[24] Tax rates based on average cost obviously discriminate against some enterprises and favor others. Withholding from profits takes care of this situation. The share of profits contributed to the Treasury by each enterprise is determined by the supervising authorities and is supposed to take into account the actual cost of production and other pertinent factors affecting the work of the enterprise. Although officially withholding from profits ranks second among the sources of Soviet revenue, its actual contribution to the budget, as has already been stated, has been small but has recently shown a tendency to increase. In 1947 withholding from profits was estimated to yield 18.7 billion rubles, or 4.8 per cent of the total revenue; in 1950 it was expected to rise to 40.0 billion rubles, or 9.2 per cent of the total. It may or may not be significant that in 1950, and

[23] See below, pp. 789, 792.
[24] The Minister of Finance, in his report on the 1947 budget, mentioned the fact that costs in one factory producing electrical appliances were five times as high as in another. He explained the difference by the very high ratio of defective production (47.3 per cent) in the former factory.

probably in 1949, receipts from the turnover tax declined both in absolute amount and in percentage of the total revenue.

THE BALANCE-SHEET

Criticism of Planning. The considerations presented above should not necessarily be interpreted as a condemnation of Soviet planning. It is, however, certain beyond reasonable doubt that the planned order is still in an experimental stage, that it is lacking in precision and definiteness, that the process of industrialization has been extremely costly, and that the compulsory contribution by the poorer groups has been somewhat larger in proportion to their income than that of those with larger incomes. These criticisms, however, must appear captious and trivial to those who share the views of the Soviet leaders that the USSR is about to enter the stage of Communism, to be transformed into the classless and stateless community of the future. Nor should the fact be disregarded that while many parts of the plan have gone by default or have been drastically amended, its general objectives were never lost sight of and some of them have been definitely achieved.

Its Achievements. Private ownership of the means of production has disappeared, and the collectivization of farming is an accomplished fact. The industrialization of the country has made immense progress while the volume of industrial production has increased many fold. In 1937, according to Molotov, 80 per cent of industrial production in Russia came from enterprises established under the first and the second Five-Year Plans. The Chairman of the Council of People's Commissars pointed out with justifiable pride that 90 per cent of all the tractors employed in Soviet agriculture were of domestic manufacture while only a few years before none were made in Russia. This is certainly no mean achievement, even though one may believe not only that it might have been less costly to purchase the tractors abroad, for instance in the United States, but also that the American, British, and German machines are vastly superior to those manufactured in the Soviet Union. The fact remains that the Soviet Government has decided to industrialize Russia and that it has nearly accomplished this purpose within a surprisingly short time.

A Mixed Performance. The volume of production which, it is claimed, increased between 1929 and 1937 by as much as 300 or 400 per cent and which, in spite of the ravages of the War, continues to increase rapidly under the fourth Five-Year Plan does not, however, tell the whole story. There are other elements in the industrial situation that are far less pleasing. The cost of production remains high and the quality is grievously unsatisfactory. Shortage of the most common goods even in Moscow is continuously reported in the Soviet press. The productivity of labor, official statements to the contrary notwithstanding, is extremely low and the Government has to use extraordinary measures to enforce labor discipline, which appears to be sadly lacking. The absence of adequate information, for which the Soviet Government itself is to blame, makes it impossible to reach a definite conclusion about the trend of real wages but it is abundantly clear that even if the standard of living has improved—and this is often and rightly questioned—it continues to remain far below the accepted minimum in any other modern industrial country.[25]

Difficulties Inherent in Planning. There is no indication yet that Soviet planned economy has found a solution of many of the difficulties that beset the capitalist world. Communist economics has failed so far to produce an adequate substitute for private initiative and the mechanism of prices, and some of the fundamental aspects of planning are still enveloped in an impenetrable veil of mystery.[26] The elimination of private enterprise has inevitably led to the enthronement of a huge bureaucracy and the creation of red tape entanglements which the Soviet leaders are the first to lament. The office holders, both the lax and the overzealous, are publicly castigated, demoted, exiled to remote regions, and their place is taken by others. But the question naturally arises: is the failure of the huge government machine to work properly due merely to the dishonesty, negligence, or inefficiency of this or that official, or is it inherent in the system itself? It is probably not unfair to say that while Soviet planned economy has eliminated some of the frictions existing under capitalism it is confronted with new and even more formidable difficulties for which no solution is in sight.

Comparison with the Capitalist Countries. What the Soviet Government has accomplished so far (leaving aside its political objectives) is to have traveled in record time a section of the long road toward industrialization on which it was preceded by other countries. Time, however, is an essential element in every human endeavor, especially when the endeavor involves a revolutionary change in ways of living of some two hundred million human beings. Viewing the situation from a purely economic standpoint it appears that the great capitalist countries—the United States, Great Britain, Germany, and France—were in 1939 far ahead of the Soviet Union in all the essential fields of production, a fact willingly admitted by Stalin and Molotov in their reports to the Eighteenth Congress of the Communist Party in March, 1939. In spite of the dislocation caused by war this statement still holds true in 1950 except perhaps in the case of Germany whose eclipse, however, is due to political causes. It took those countries, no doubt, a much longer time to reach the position they occupy today, but the process of industrialization in those countries was also far less painful than it was under the dictatorship of the proletariat. The Soviet Union is determined to eclipse the record of the capitalist nations within the next few years. This desire for speed, the reasons for which

[25] The hazards involved in determining the trend of real wages in the absence of an index of the cost of living may be illustrated by the following example. Molotov stated at the Eighteenth Congress of the Communist Party in March, 1939, that under the second Five-Year Plan, that is, from 1932 to 1937, the real wages of workers had increased by 101 per cent. A careful analysis of the available data by Professor S. N. Prokopovich, a foremost authority on the subject, led him to the avowedly tentative conclusion that far from increasing, the real wages of industrial workers during this period actually declined by some 45 per cent. Professor Prokopovich, however, believes that in 1927–1928 real wages in industry considerably exceeded the pre-War level. S. N. Prokopovich (Prokopovicz), editor, *Quarterly Bulletin of Soviet-Russian Economics* (Geneva), Nos. 1–2, November, 1939.

[26] Maurice Dobb, an economist sympathetic to the Soviet point of view, rightly notes (*op. cit.*, p. 334) that "it is apparently true that so far little has emerged (at least in published form) in the way of . . . generalised principles" of planning.

are not obvious, has undoubtedly added much to the difficulties of the Soviet leaders and to the hardships the process of industrialization imposes upon the people. The Soviet experiment has proved so far that a Socialist economy can exist, but it still remains to be proved that it is more equitable and more efficient than an organization based on private property and private initiative.

CHAPTER VI

THE STATE IN BUSINESS: I

ELIMINATION OF PRIVATE BUSINESS ENTERPRISE

At the end of 1937, the closing year of the second Five-Year Plan, 98.7 per cent of all the means of production in the Soviet Union were officially stated to be "Socialist property," that is, they were controlled either by the State or by the collective farms. Of the gross production of industry, 99.8 per cent came from State-owned enterprises, 98.6 per cent of agricultural production was supplied by State farms or by collective farms, while commerce—except for the *kolkhoz* (collective farms) market [1]—was in the hands of Socialist distributing agencies. This elimination of private business enterprise is the most striking and the most significant feature of the Soviet economic organization. Under the political regime of the dictatorship of the proletariat the expropriation of the proprietary classes was a relatively simple, if painful, process. Economic planning is avowedly the means for the achievement of a definite aim and not an objective in itself. In the final analysis the ability of the Communist leaders to operate smoothly and efficiently the complex mechanism of a great and rapidly industrialized modern State is the crucial test of the regime, and the success or failure of the economic controls will determine in the long run the ultimate fate of the Soviet experiment.

AGENCIES FOR THE MANAGEMENT OF INDUSTRY

The Early Period. From the advent of the Bolsheviks to power up to the outbreak of World War II, the policy of the Soviet Government toward industry has gone through a number of important transformations which have been reflected in the administrative structure of the agencies in charge of industrial activities. It will be recalled that between November, 1917, and the summer of 1918 only a relatively few branches of industry and some of the larger enterprises in other branches were taken over by the Government. The decree on Workers' Control of November 14, 1917, created (or rather sanctioned) the existence in industry of a regime of uneasy dualism, the management of

[1] See below, p. 819.

industrial enterprises being divided between the owners, on the one hand, and the committees of workers, on the other. The committees of workers were organized spontaneously in many enterprises when the Provisional Government was still in office, that is, before the decree of November 14. It is uncertain whether the regime of Workers' Control was meant to be a program of lasting cooperation between capital and labor, or merely a manoeuvre for the "encirclement of capitalism." It was brought to an end by the decree of June 28, 1918, which ordered the wholesale nationalization of industrial enterprises and ushered in the period of War Communism. The following months, until the inauguration of the New Economic Policy in March, 1921, were characterized by a policy of rigid centralization, industrial enterprises being deprived, at least in theory, of all independence. The whole business of the country was administered from above by the Supreme Economic Council acting through purely bureaucratic agencies known as *glavki* and *tsentri* (Chief Administrations and Central Boards). This method, admittedly, was not a success. By 1921 the production of large-scale industry fell to 17 per cent of its pre-War level, a decline for which the general conditions prevailing during the Civil War were largely responsible.

The Trusts. The period of the New Economic Policy, with its sharp reaction against the methods of War Communism, brought into existence a new type of management of industrial activities through agencies known as trusts. A trust consisted of a number of industrial enterprises, such as factories, plants, mines, etc., grouped together under a board appointed by the Supreme Economic Council after consultation with the trade unions. The position of the members of the board of a trust was analogous to that of the trustees of a public corporation under the American or English law. The trust received from the State definite properties which consisted of the physical equipment of enterprises that were members of the trust, buildings, machinery, stocks of fuel and raw materials, as well as appropriations from the budget. The board of the trust appointed the managers of the enterprises, entered into collective labor agreements with the trade unions, and supervised the work of the enterprises under its jurisdiction, while it was itself responsible to the Supreme Economic Council. Relative independence from the State was the chief feature distinguishing the trusts from the agencies of War Communism. Within the provisions of their respective charters, the trusts enjoyed freedom of action. As the Congress of the Soviets in 1922 put it, "the struggle between Communist and individualistic economies is now being transferred to economic ground, the market; here nationalized industry controlled by the proletarian State must, following the competitive methods of the market, assert its unchallengeable superiority." The trusts were therefore to conduct their business on the "commercial principle," that is, they were to be run for profit. According to the territorial scope of their activities the trusts were divided into three classes: national trusts, republican trusts, and local trusts.

The Syndicates. The trustification of industry proceeded rapidly since the enterprises were anxious to escape the strait-jacket of War Communism controls. It proved, however, more difficult than had been imagined by Communist leaders to assert the "unchallengeable superiority" of nationalized industry. The trusts often found themselves in competition with one another and this led to the creation of syndicates which performed many functions similar to those of syndicates in the capitalist world, with the important difference, however, that Soviet syndicates did not enjoy the power to limit the volume of production and had to accept the maximum prices determined by the Supreme Economic Council. The first syndicate (textile) was organized in February, 1922.

The Principle of "Economic (or Cost) Accounting." The relative economic freedom enjoyed by the trusts proved short-lived. As planned economy was gradually encroaching on the New Economic Policy, the trusts found themselves in a rapidly increasing dependence on the higher government agencies—the Supreme Economic Council, the People's Commissariats, the State Planning Commission. The Law ("model charter") of June 29, 1927, which redefined the position of the trusts, substituted for the "commercial principle," that is, business for profit, the principle of "economic (or cost) accounting" by which was meant the duty of the trusts to strive for the fulfillment of the provisions of the plan. The degree of compliance with the plan was made the yardstick by which the efficiency of any economic agency was to be measured. The interpretation of this principle, which became one of the pillars of Soviet planned economy, was somewhat illogical, since the overfulfillment of planned assignments was considered as a desirable goal, while failures to fill the quotas were sternly discouraged. Another important change introduced by the Law of June, 1927, was the increased independence of the enterprises from the trusts. In the earlier legislation the trust, and not the enterprise, was considered the basic unit of industrial organization. The Fifteenth Congress of the Communist Party, held in December, 1927, voiced some sharp criticism of the stifling influence which the excessive centralization that developed inside the trusts had upon local initiative; it also emphasized the necessity of increasing both the rights and the responsibilities of the enterprises.

Policy of Decentralization. The emancipation of the enterprises from the trust, a process inaugurated by the Law of 1927, was further advanced by the resolution of the Communist Party of December 5, 1929, and by subsequent legislation. The resolution proclaimed that "the enterprise is the basic unit of industrial organization" and must be independent within the provisions of the plan. The directors of the enterprise must be given full authority and must accept full responsibility for the fulfillment by the enterprise of its assignment under the plan. The resolution of December, 1929, moreover, introduced other important changes in the management of industry. The work of the departments of the Supreme Economic Council was declared to be unsatisfactory. New organs of industrial control, the "combines" (*obedinenie*), took over the functions of the syndicates and of some of the departments of the Supreme Economic Council. The "combines" consisted of groups of trusts and industrial enterprises united under an appointed board. The functions of the "combines" comprised "the planning of production, planning of capital investment, technical guidance, organization of sales and supply, control of commercial and financial activities, questions of labor, training of workers, appointment and dismissal of the higher personnel." There were three types of "combines": those uniting trusts and enterprises working on a national scale; those uniting enterprises and trusts working on a national, republican, and local scale; and those uniting enterprises and trusts working on a republican and local scale. The chief duty of the "combines" was the technical guidance of the trusts and enterprises in matters of production. They were to exercise their powers according to the "functional principle." The functions of the trusts, under the 1929 plan, were greatly curtailed. The Supreme Economic Council, which lost some of its powers, was to concentrate on general planning and coordination, and on controlling the work of the "combines" whose boards it appointed.

Reorganization on the Basis of Greater Specialization. The "combines" were duly organized, but the "functional" principle on which the 1929 plan was based proved unworkable. It led, once more, to extreme centralization, the "combines" extending their authority to a very large number of enterprises, sometimes hundreds of them, scattered over the territory of the Union. Stalin denounced the resulting organization of industry in a speech delivered on June 23, 1931, and he demanded its reconstruction on the basis of greater specialization. There followed a hasty remodeling of the administrative structure. The large "combines" were split into smaller units and in January, 1931, the Supreme Economic Council itself ceased to exist and was replaced by three People's Commissariats—that of Heavy Industry, of Light Industry, and of the Timber Industry. The move in the direction of greater specialization was accompanied by a number of measures increasing both the powers and the responsibilities of the higher personnel and substituting responsible officers for industrial boards.

The "Territorial-Productive" Principle. The anticipated improvement, however, failed to materialize and the Seventeenth Congress of the Communist Party in January, 1934, decided to liquidate all agencies based on the "functional" principle and to replace them with new ones organized on the "territorial-productive" principle. The participation of local, regional, and republican bodies in the management of industry was increased. "Combines" were abolished, the number of trusts was reduced, and the ties of the enterprises with the central departments were strengthened. The purpose of the reform was the elimination of bureaucratism and the substitution for it of personal contact and guidance. The plan also provided for the abolition of executive boards in all institutions in charge of industry. Their place was taken by appointed officers. At the same time advisory councils were created in the Commissariats. The councils, which were to meet twice a month, were composed of representatives from the factories, a measure that had for its purpose to keep the heads of the departments in close touch with local conditions.

General Scheme of Industrial Controls. The resulting structure of the industrial administration is approximately as follows. The highest administrative organ for each branch of industry is the Ministry (People's Commissariat) of the USSR. It has a number of departments organized on the "territorial-productive principle," a somewhat mysterious formula which would seem to mean that a department is concerned not with an entire industry, but only with an enterprise engaged in a definite line of production and located in a specified territory of limited area. Such departments have full powers in dealing with the production of the trusts and enterprises. They provide for them guidance on technical and financial questions and they control the sales of goods produced and the supply of raw materials. Ministries have also special councils which deal with technical and scientific questions. The lower links in the chain of administrative agencies are the trusts and the enterprises. The smaller enterprises are controlled by the Ministries of the constituent republics and other subordinate organs. This scheme of industrial administration has been retained since the War.[2]

Problem of the Management of Industry Still Unsolved. It will thus appear that the substitution of Socialist controls for private enterprise proved by no means so easy and simple as Lenin had imagined it to be in 1917. The continuous remodeling of the administration of Soviet industries, a process that has been merely outlined above, suggests that recent trends are in the direction of greater differentiation and specialization.[3] It would be rash to conclude, however, that the riddle of industrial management in a Socialist State has been solved. The truly amazing instability of the administrative structure that directs the industrialization of the country merely indicates that the Soviet Government is proceeding by the time-honored method of trial and error. It is unfortunate for the Soviet citizens that this method is always costly, especially in a Socialist State where the Government controls all the economic activities of the nation.

PRICES AND EFFICIENCY

Difficulties Resulting from the Abolition of Private Enterprise. The fundamental difficulty of industrial management in a Socialist society lies much deeper than is suggested by the verbose and confused discussion in the Soviet press of the relative merits of the "territorial-productive" and the "functional" principle of organization. The root of the trouble is the necessity of discovering an adequate substitute for the mechanism of prices and of creating the stimulus toward business efficiency that is supplied under capitalism by the

[2] The recent tendency, however, has been in the direction of stricter controls. A statute (*polozhenie*) confirmed by the Council of Ministers on January 15, 1949, directed that funds belonging to State, cooperative, and public institutions should be kept at the State Bank or another bank designated by the authorities. The amount of cash an institution was permitted to retain was to be determined by the State Bank and was to be limited to its immediate needs. The object of the statute was to prevent the institutions from using their funds in a manner of which the Government did not approve. In case of infringement of the regulations the State Bank (or the bank with which the institution is requested to keep its funds) may (1) prohibit the delinquent institution to use its cash receipts for a period up to three months, and (2) deny, in part, payments on account of current expenditure to which the institution would otherwise have been entitled. The unauthorized use of funds, moreover, became a criminal offense. The statute of January 15, 1949, did not apply to collective farms.

[3] See above, pp. 746–747.

competition of private interests. Nothing is more distasteful to a Communist than capitalist competition, yet its absence in the Soviet Union has created new and formidable problems which still await solution. It would be easy to fill pages with quotations from pronouncements of authoritative Soviet bodies and leaders denouncing the laxity, inefficiency, waste, and bureaucratic procrastination that infect every department of the country's economic life. The efforts of the Soviet Government are directed toward the eradication of these conditions.[4]

Price Policy. The prices of practically all goods in the USSR are fixed by the State. The method by which prices are computed is not disclosed, but presumably they are based on the "unchangeable prices of 1926–1927," that is, the price level in the last year of the New Economic Policy. Under Soviet conditions planned prices are largely in the nature of a bookkeeping device. They nevertheless play an extremely important part in the actual management of industry, especially in the attempts to reduce costs. Every industrial enterprise and every trust receives under the plan a definite assignment which specifies the volume of goods to be produced, the price and quality of the goods, and the cost of production. The last consists of the cost of raw materials and fuel supplied at fixed prices, labor costs, taxes, and other expenses incidental to the working of the enterprise. The planned cost of production of an enterprise is presumably arrived at by reducing its actual cost in the preceding year by the percentage prescribed in the plan. Every trust and every enterprise has its own balance sheet and is rated according to the principle of "economic (or cost) accounting"; that is, its actual performance is checked against the assignment of the plan. If the enterprise succeeds in producing the volume of goods demanded by the plan and maintains its costs within the prescribed limits without deterioration in the quality of the goods, the income and the outgo of the enterprise are so balanced as to produce a "planned profit."

Its Revision in 1936. It was customary in the early years of planned economy to price raw and building materials, machinery and equipment, below cost as a general measure for the encouragement of industrialization. The deficit was made good by budgetary appropriations. In 1936 this policy

---

[4] For instance, a decree of the Council of People's Commissars of April 5, 1940, stated that the organization of supply in the "economic" People's Commissariats was grievously defective. The chief flaw, according to the decree, was the multiplicity of supply agencies and their "enormous, totally unjustifiable staff." Twenty-six People's Commissariats of the USSR alone maintained 3,550 supply agencies employing 81,000 officials at the annual cost of 332 million rubles, while other economic organs (*otraslevye glavki*) maintained 1,370 supply agencies with a personnel of 23,000 and a payroll of 106 million rubles. The resulting situation was described by the decree as "wholly inexcusable," especially since the supply agencies "indulged freely in spurious purchases from one another, ignored State prices," and carried on other illegal activities. The decree ordered the immediate liquidation of the superfluous agencies. A decade later, in March, 1949, the Minister of Finance Zverev noted in his report to the Supreme Soviet that, although much had been accomplished in reorganizing administrative services and reducing their cost, a great deal remained to be done. "Our administrative apparatus," said Zverev, "has many unnecessary links and subdivisions, inflated personnel and waste of funds on administrative purposes." And he quoted as an example of wastefulness and inefficiency the supply and sale organs of the various ministries which have "many superfluous agencies maintained at a heavy cost to the State."

was abandoned as both uneconomic and demoralizing, and it became the aim of the Soviet Government to make every branch of industry self-supporting. The method adopted consists of fixing the price of every commodity at a figure corresponding to the average cost of production. The losses of some of the enterprises, under this plan, are to be compensated by the gains of others in the same industry. In other words, the less efficient enterprises, which under capitalism would be forced out of business, continue to carry on at the expense of the more efficient enterprises producing similar goods. Various methods are being devised, however, to make all the enterprises self-supporting within the provisions of the plan.

The Minister of Finance Zverev stated in the Supreme Soviet in March, 1949, that, in pursuance of a resolution adopted by the Central Committee of the Communist Party, budget appropriations for enterprises engaged in industry and transport were being "liquidated largely (*v osnovnom*) in 1949 and completely in 1950." What will happen under the new regime to enterprises with costs above the average was not explained.

The "Director's Fund." The creation of direct incentives for the workers and managerial staff of an enterprise to strive for the fulfillment and over-fulfillment of the plan is the theme around which revolves much of Soviet labor legislation. One device used to attain this object is the "director's fund." Introduced by a decree of April 19, 1936, the "director's fund" seems not to have been in use during the War but was reinstated in 1946 and 1947.[5] The object of the fund, as defined by a decree of the Council of Ministers "On the Director's Fund in Industrial Enterprises" of December 5, 1946, is "to strengthen the initiative and responsibility of directors of industrial enterprises in the fulfillment of production programs, reduction of costs, and fulfillment of the plan for profits." The source of the fund is profits or, in enterprises which under the plan are not working for profits, savings resulting from the reduction of costs. All industries are arranged, for the purpose of the fund, into two groups. Group I comprises heavy industries, building materials, rubber, paper, and textiles; group II includes food industries, most of the industries producing consumers' goods, as well as the enterprises working on a republican and local scale. The "director's fund" consists of (1) contributions from "planned profits" (or planned reduction of costs), and (2) contributions from "surplus profits" (or surplus reduction of costs), that is, profits (or reduction of costs) in excess of those planned. In enterprises of group I the "director's fund" benefits to the extent of 4 per cent of the "planned profits" and 50 per cent of the "surplus profits." However, "as an exception," the "director's fund" in specified industries in group I (metallurgy, coal, oil, certain branches of mining, cement, some of the chemical industries, and a few others) retains 10 per cent of the "planned profits" and 75 per cent of the "surplus profits." The "director's fund" of enterprises in group II retains

---

[5] The pre-War and post-War "director's funds" are similar in basic structure and objectives, although they differ in some not unessential details. Nevertheless the post-War decrees speak of "establishing" the funds, a terminology which, presumably, implies that they did not exist at the time.

2 per cent of the "planned profits" and 25 per cent of the "surplus profits."
The greater incentive provided for the heavy industries, as compared with
those producing consumers' goods, indicates that the primary concern of the
Government remains the same as it was in the 1930's—the building up of
industries regarded as essential from the point of view of industrialization,
collectivization (agricultural machines), and rearmament.[6] The size of the
"director's fund" in 1947 was limited to 5 per cent of the annual amount paid
by the enterprise in salaries and wages. Half of the proceeds of the funds are
spent on the expansion of production, construction, and housing, and the
balance on amenities for the employees of the enterprise (expansion of "subsidiary farming" and vegetable gardens, rest homes, dining rooms, clubs,
facilities for games and sports) and bonuses to individual employees.[7]

Position of Enterprises Unable to Fulfill Assignments. The ingenious
device of the "director's fund" extends to the enterprise the principle of
Article 12 of the Soviet Constitution: "From each according to his ability,
to each according to his work." It does nothing, however, to relieve the plight
of those enterprises—and their number appears to be large—that prove unable
to fulfill their assignments. Their directors and Communist leaders are likely
to find themselves in the concentration camps in the Arctic region or in
Siberia, or, if they are lucky, to be merely demoted. But since the enterprises
are to continue in business their deficit in some form or other must be made
good by appropriations from the budget. And this would seem to mean that
the burden of taxation is likely to continue to increase.

Grave Consequences of the Absence of Adequate Price Policy. The
price structure is probably one of the weakest points in Communist economics.
It injects in the planned order an element of uncertainty and arbitrariness the
importance of which cannot be exaggerated.

WAGES AND LABOR DISCIPLINE

Struggle for Higher Efficiency of Labor. Hardly less thorny has thus far
been the problem of increasing the productivity of labor which, according to
the Communists, is the cornerstone of the entire economic structure.[8] Greater
productivity of labor is essential for the reduction of costs, the lowering of
prices, the raising of the standards of living. Productivity of labor depends
on the efficient organization of production, the adequate supply of skilled

---

[6] Under the 1936 legislation, however, the ratio of contributions to the fund was the same
for all industries: 4 per cent of the "planned profits" and 50 per cent of the "surplus profits."

[7] By a decree of the Council of Ministers of June 27, 1947, "director's funds" similar to
those in industrial enterprises were established in public utility enterprises (street cars, buses,
trucking concerns, water transportation of local destination, electricity, gas, water, sewerage,
street cleaning, and illumination) and in the so-called communal enterprises (public baths,
laundries, barbershops, hotels, and even pawnshops), and by a decree of the Council of Ministers
of September 29, 1947, in railway enterprises and the Moscow subway. "Director's funds," as
it will appear later, were also organized in the State farms and machine tractor stations. It
will readily be seen that the administration of the funds must present in some instances truly
baffling difficulties.

[8] The importance of industrial labor in the population of the Soviet Union is increasing.
The number of workers and employees engaged in industry was 11.3 million in 1928, 22.8 million in 1932, 28 million in 1938, and, according to the fourth Five-Year Plan, was to reach
33.5 million in 1950.

workers, the maintenance of labor discipline, and, last but not least, on providing the workers with the proper incentive to do their jobs well. The Soviet Government has given much attention to the training of engineers and skilled labor and to the study of methods of mass production. Nothing is more admired in the Soviet Union than Henry Ford and his assembly line. But the training of highly qualified engineers and skilled mechanics is necessarily a slow process, especially in a country newly converted to methods of advanced industrialization. Mammoth machine-building plants have only too often proved disappointing, a failure that was no doubt due to the novelty of the problems raised, the lack of experience and of skilled labor, and the record-breaking speed with which agricultural Russia is being transformed into a kind of gigantic Pittsburgh.

Labor Discipline. Labor discipline has been one of the Government's chief concerns. A factor that greatly interfered with the productivity of labor was the continuous wandering of the workingmen from one job to another, the so-called "fluidity" of labor which assumed alarming proportions about 1930. The Labor Code (Article 46) specifically provides that a worker who has not entered into a contract for a definite term shall be free to leave his employment after serving the prescribed notice (one to seven days).[9] This provision was presumably not always observed, since the Supreme Court of the USSR found it necessary to rule at least twice (September 8 and November 14, 1936) that Article 46 was still in force and needed no further interpretation. Various measures to induce workers to stick to their jobs have been tried. Workers who remained in the same enterprise for over two years were given longer vacations and the whole structure of social insurance was so reshaped as to confer special benefits on the employees in proportion to the length of their service with an enterprise. The extra privileges thus acquired extended to bonuses, pensions, opportunities for staying at rest homes and sanatoria, and so on. Other and sterner measures were applied to those workers who failed to appreciate the benefits mentioned. The decree of March 4, 1933, providing that the reason for each change of employment and the date thereof should be entered on a special labor card issued to every worker, made it a criminal offense for the director of an enterprise to hire workers not in possession of such a document. On the other hand, the communication of secret information about the character and political views of an employee was specifically prohibited and made a criminal offense by a decree of September 23, 1930. A decree of October 17, 1937, provided for the summary eviction of workers who voluntarily gave up their jobs or were dismissed for a breach of labor discipline or were convicted of a crime. The persons so evicted were not entitled to the allocation of "living space" elsewhere.[10] Unemployment insurance was discontinued in October, 1930, and

[9] The decree of December 28, 1938, requires one month's advance notice from every worker or employee who desires to relinquish his employment.

[10] The cities, towns, and new industrial centers in the Soviet Union are suffering from an acute, perennial housing shortage. Every employed person is entitled to a definite "living space" the size of which varies with the locality. Most of the dwelling houses are controlled by government-owned enterprises or by the municipalities. An evicted person finds it practically impossible to obtain living quarters.

the workers receive no benefit during the time they are looking for new employment.

Wage Policy, 1919–1930. Although the program of the Russian Communist Party (1919) stated specifically that equalization of wages was a remote ideal and not an immediate objective, a tendency toward the leveling of earnings manifested itself during the early years of the Soviet regime and lingered until the late 1920's. In 1920–1921 the Government adopted, allegedly at the request of the fourth All-Russian Congress of Trade Unions, a unified schedule of wages and salaries which provided for seventeen grades of pay covering all wage-earners and salaried employees. Wages of workers engaged in production were confined to the nine lower grades, those of clerical employees to grades below and including thirteen, while the salaries of technicians and the managerial staff were put in the upper grades fourteen to seventeen. The top wage of a skilled worker was three and a half times as high as that of an unskilled worker, and earnings in grade seventeen were eight times as high as in grade one. Since the increment in wages from grade to grade was uneven (for instance, it was 25 per cent between grades one and two, and 10.5 per cent between grades seven and eight), the entire schedule came under severe criticism. It was revised in 1927–1928 but the amendments merely accentuated what came to be regarded as an excessive leveling tendency. Increments between the upper grades were smaller than those between the lower grades, and piecework was discouraged. "In a number of enterprises," Stalin said scornfully in 1928, "our wage schedules are so arranged that the difference between skilled and unskilled labor, between heavy and light labor, has almost disappeared." He argued that this unsound wage policy discouraged the workers from improving their qualifications and had an adverse effect upon the productivity of labor.

Piecework. In 1931 the wage schedule was again revised, this time in such a manner as to increase substantially the rates in industries to which the Government wished to attract labor—coal, oil, electric power, metallurgy, machine-building. *Obezlichka* (literally "facelessness"), or work that cannot be traced to its performer, and *urovnilovka* (literally "leveling"), or equalization of earnings—two picturesque terms coined, with total disregard for grammar, by Stalin—were exorcized in a nation-wide campaign as the implacable enemies of labor productivity. Strong emphasis was put on piecework, a method that has traditionally been combated by the trade unions in the capitalist countries.[11] In the Soviet Union it found its place in the Constitution (Article 12) which proclaimed the principle "to each according to his work" as one of the pillars of the socialist order.

Nominal and Real Wages. Monetary wages increased rapidly. The average annual earnings of workers and employees rose from 708 rubles in 1928 to 1,427 rubles in 1932, 3,093 rubles in 1937, and 4,100 rubles in 1940; according to the fourth Five-Year Plan they should have reached 6,000 in

---

[11] Piecework accounted for 57 per cent of the total number of man-hours earned in 1928; for 64 per cent in 1932; and for about 75 per cent in 1938.

1950. In the absence of indices of prices and of the cost of living these average figures covering both workers and employees (a confused and misleading notion) mean little and cannot be translated, with any degree of certainty, in terms of real wages. It is clear, however, that the incentive of higher earnings cannot be effective unless the wage-earner has some assurance that additional remuneration will actually contribute to his welfare. This assurance was lacking in the Soviet Union in the late 1920's and in the early 1930's. With the introduction of planned economy the Government found it necessary to control distribution, first of foodstuffs and later of manufactured goods, by instituting rationing. The ration cards entitled their holders to purchase, usually in a "closed" shop attached to the enterprise or institution in which they were employed, a limited amount of each commodity at prices considerably below those charged in Government-owned "commercial shops" (where no ration cards were required) or on the *kolkhoz* and the black market. So long as this system existed, monetary wages meant relatively little since real wages were determined by the assortment of goods available in the "closed" shop and by the prices at which they were sold, which varied within a wide range. Walter Duranty, then Moscow correspondent of *The New York Times*, wrote in 1934 that the average monthly wage of a Russian industrial worker will buy in Moscow "on the open market no more than $3 will buy in America." [12] The resulting uncertainty as to the purchasing value of the ruble encouraged the "fluidity" of labor, the workers moving from factory to factory in search for a place of employment that would give them, through its "closed" shop, better value for their money. The abolition of rationing, first applied to bread in January, 1935, was completed by the end of that year. From that date until the outbreak of the Soviet-German War all commodities were sold at State-fixed prices to whoever could afford to buy them. The abolition of rationing and of the multiple price system restored the equilibrium between monetary and real wages and was an important element in the drive for the higher productivity of labor. Rationing was reintroduced during the War but was again abolished in December, 1947.

Other Measures of Encouragement. Various methods have been employed to spur labor to greater exertion and to increase productivity. The seven-hour working day was adopted in 1927 and was made effective in most industries in 1928. The "continuous" six-day or even five-day week (five or four workdays followed by a day of rest), designed to intensify the use of industrial equipment by employing three consecutive seven-hour shifts, was introduced in the early 1930's. There came into being an elaborate system of bonuses and premiums which are paid to those workers who exceed the "norm," or standard performance prescribed for every type of work.

Workers' "Spontaneous" Movement for Higher Productivity. A number of much-publicized devices to increase labor productivity originated, in

---

[12] *The New York Times*, February 4, 1934. The uncertainty of the purchasing power of the ruble during this period was probably in part responsible for discontinuance of the publication of the index of the cost of living.

theory, in the workers' irrepressible enthusiasm for the building up of Socialism. The beginnings of this movement are officially traced back to an article
"How to Organize Emulation," written by Lenin two months after the Bolshevik revolution but first published in 1929. Its earliest practical manifestation, according to tradition, was a *subbotnik*—voluntary work on Saturday—
organized by a group of Moscow railwaymen in April, 1919. Lenin acclaimed
the innovation as a major revolutionary event, but the movement soon came
to nothing and little was heard of it until the end of 1928 when, following an
appeal of the Central Committee of the Communist Party for the mobilization
of all the creative resources of the working class, the first "shock brigade"
was formed. A "shock brigade" consists of exemplary workers (*udarnik*) who
undertake to fulfill their "norms," strictly observe labor discipline, eliminate
truancy, take excellent care of machines and tools, and ensure the uninterrupted flow of production. In January, 1929, *Komsomolskaia Pravda,* organ
of the Organization of Communist Youth, launched a proposal for the organization of "Socialist emulation" (or competition—*sorevnovanie*) among the
enterprises, and *Pravda* published, for the first time, Lenin's article mentioned
above. The hint was dutifully taken up by a few factories and at the end of
April, 1929, the Sixteenth Conference of the Communist Party appealed to
the workers and farmers to use their best endeavor toward the promotion
of "Socialist emulation." The "spontaneous" movement was born. "Emulation is the Communist method of building Socialism on the foundation of
the maximum active participation (*aktivnost*) of the multi-million mass of
the toilers . . . ," Stalin said in May, 1929. "Socialist emulation and [capi-
talist] competition (*konkurentsiia*) are two totally different principles. The
principle of competition: defeat and death for some, victory and domination
for others. The principle of Socialist emulation: comradely assistance to those
who lag behind by those who are in the front ranks, in order to achieve
higher standards for all." "The most remarkable aspect of emulation," Stalin
told the Sixteenth Congress of the Communist Party in June, 1930, "is that
it changes the attitude of men toward labor, for it transforms labor from a
shameful and heavy burden, as it was formerly looked upon, into a deed of
honor, a deed of glory, a deed of valor and heroism." In less exalted language
"Socialist emulation" may be said to consist of contracts concluded between
enterprises, shops, groups of workers, and individual workers pledging the
parties to exceed their production quotas, eliminate defective production, cut
down costs, maintain high levels of labor discipline, reduce absenteeism, improve technical qualifications, and train and rehabilitate indolent and inefficient workers. By the middle of 1931, 71 per cent of all industrial workers
were enrolled in "shock brigades" or participated in "Socialist emulation." [13]
Another feature of the movement is the practice of enterprises to demand the

---

[13] According to official data for 1944, participation in "Socialist emulation" in separate
branches of industry was as follows: oil, 82 per cent of the total number of workers employed;
aircraft, 81 per cent; armament, 85 per cent; tanks, 81 per cent; munitions, 81 per cent; auto-
mobiles, 86 per cent; electrical appliances, 83 per cent; cotton textiles, 91 per cent; rubber, 83
per cent; shoes, 87 per cent.

upward revision of planned assignments, the so-called counter-plan which has already been mentioned in an earlier chapter. Finally, in May, 1932, came the "excellence movement" (*otlichnichestvo*) which takes the form of pledges by workers to improve their technical qualifications and to transmit their superior knowledge to their fellow workers.

The Stakhanov Movement. In the night of August 31, 1935, the Ukrainian miner Alexis Stakhanov won national and international fame by knocking down, with the assistance of two timberers, 102 tons of coal (fourteen times the standard "norm") in a six-hour shift. His remarkable achievement, which, it must be assumed, was contrived not without the assistance of the authorities, was given more than the usual amount of publicity and became the starting point of the Stakhanov movement or drive for more efficient methods of work devised by the workers themselves. Stakhanov's example was emulated throughout the country, and soon practically every branch of industry and agriculture boasted of the breath-taking records of their own Stakhanovites. Improvement of productive processes is, of course, eminently desirable but it is by no means certain that the spectacular methods of the Stakhanov movement succeeded in bringing about a real and lasting change for the better. Maurice Dobb, who holds, quite wrongly in my opinion, that Stakhanov's performance "came as a definite surprise to the management" and "quickly found imitators in other industries almost before it had time to be publicized," admits that "the movement was not without weaknesses and exaggerations; and in certain directions it even became something of a mania."[14] The Communist Party, the real instigator and sponsor of the movement, came to realize that record-breaking performances by individual workers were a disorganizing factor inimical to the even flow of production and, in the last analysis, to labor efficiency. A statement issued by the Central Committee of the Communist Party on December 28, 1937, roundly condemned the practice of high individual records and urged that the movement should be reorganized as a mass movement. How this could be done without discarding the very principles of Stakhanovism remains uncertain.[15] Meanwhile the rec-

---

[14] Dobb, *op. cit.*, pp. 429, 430, 432.

[15] Although by the middle of 1936 between a third and a half of the workers in the major industries were Stakhanovites, conditions in at least some branches of industry were not improved. A decree of March 11, 1939, issued by the Economic Council, an agency of the Council of People's Commissars, reveals an instructive picture of the conditions prevailing in the building industry. "The Economic Council . . .," says the decree, "hereby declares that compliance with the instructions of the Party and of the Government concerning the improvement in the organization of labor in the building industry continues to be unsatisfactory with the result that in a number of building projects the prescribed 'norms' remain unfulfilled. Workers employed on building projects not infrequently work only five or six hours per day; the balance of their time is wasted chiefly because the ground is not prepared, building materials are not delivered on time, and coordination among various operations is lacking. The Economic Council of the Council of People's Commissars considers as intolerable a situation when individual directors of building projects, instead of striving for the improvement in the organization of labor, the liquidation of enforced idleness, and the increase of the amount of work performed (*uplotnenie*), have entered the road of covering up the deficiencies by illegal payments for work not actually done (*namazki*) thus artificially raising wages and concealing the inadequate organization of labor at a heavy cost to the State." The decree quotes an instance when the illicit overpayment of wages in 1938 was as high as 101 per cent. The Economic Council ordered the discontinuance of the illegal practice and directed the Procurator-General to institute legal proceedings against the guilty officials.

ords of the Stakhanovites were used as the reason for the upward revision of the "norms." A general upward revision affecting every branch of economic activity was ordered on December 25, 1935, and revisions increasing the "norms" in separate industries followed from time to time.[16] Since the standard wage is conditional on the fulfillment of the "norm" (which applies to both quantity and quality), those who fall below the "norm" receive less than the standard wage. It has been officially stated that the increase in "norms" has brought about a rise in earnings, but it is not made clear how this result could be achieved by paying the workers the same rates for doing more work.

Decorations and Titles. The Soviet Government confers upon diligent workers medals, decorations, and, as the highest reward, the somewhat awkward title of "Hero of Socialist Labor." The number of medals greatly increased during the War and post-War period and there are now few activities that would not carry the promise of a badge of some kind. Prior to 1948 the holders of decorations were entitled to monthly payments (10 to 50 rubles), exemption from certain taxes, reduction of rent, free use of street cars, preferential treatment with reference to social insurance, pensions, and so on. "Heroes of Socialist Labor" could not be evicted unless provided with adequate "living space" elsewhere and means for moving to new lodgings. The passport regulations of September 10, 1940, entitled the holders of decorations to a "permanent" passport, that is, one that need not be renewed.[17] By a decree issued in November, 1947, most of these privileges were revoked as of January 1, 1948, presumably because of the vast increase in the number of men and women holding decorations. Nevertheless, the material advantages attached to some awards have been retained and tend to become more substantial. A decree of June 10, 1946, remitted the tuition fees of the "Heroes of Socialist Labor" and "Heroes of the Soviet Union" (whose number is relatively small) enrolled in secondary and higher schools and provided scholarships of 400 rubles per month for the students of that group attending colleges and higher technical schools.

Punitive Measures. Soviet legislation supplies a long list of involved and often repetitious measures for the enforcement of labor discipline and the discouragement of laxity and negligence. Only a few of them can be noted here. A decree of November 15, 1932, provided that a one-day absence from work without good reason should be punishable by dismissal accompanied by eviction and the cancellation of the ration card. The "malicious breach of labor discipline" brought immediate dismissal as well as criminal prosecution (decree of December 17, 1930). At the end of 1938 the drive for labor discipline was renewed with much force. A regulation was adopted stipu-

[16] For instance, by a decree of January 5, 1939, the "norms" in the machine-building industry were increased by 25 per cent while the standard piecework rates were decreased by 14 per cent.

[17] Every Soviet citizen who has reached the age of sixteen and resides in an urban or other designated area must carry a passport which is valid for five years. The passport must be registered with the police if its bearer stays away, for longer than twenty-four hours, from the locality where he is domiciled.

lating that from January 15, 1939, every worker should be provided with a "labor booklet" containing a full record of his professional career, including statements of the reasons why he had left his previous place of employment, a measure designed further to discourage the migration of labor. A decree of December 28, 1938, provided that a worker who was late three times in one month or four times in two consecutive months must be dismissed; that vacations should be given only to the workers who had been employed for eleven consecutive months in the same institution; and that the amount of social insurance received in case of temporary disability should depend on the length of employment. Benefits to expectant mothers were drastically reduced to cut down abuses, which were reported to have been frequent. On January 8, 1939, the Government issued an order to dismiss in the future any worker more than twenty minutes late on any working day. A number of spectacular and much-publicized trials were staged in Moscow early in 1939. The defendants, workers who had committed offences against labor discipline and the supervisors and managers who had tolerated these infringements, were branded as enemies of the people and received heavy sentences.

LABOR LEGISLATION, 1940 AND AFTER

Position of Foremen. In 1940 the Kremlin embarked on a legislative program which wrought revolutionary changes in the position of labor. On May 27 came the decree of the Council of People's Commissars and the Central Committee of the Communist Party establishing foremen as responsible and authoritative leaders of the men under their supervision. The powers of foremen included the hiring and dismissal of workers, the assignment of workers to various jobs, the imposition of disciplinary punishments, and the granting of monetary rewards. Foremen were made responsible for the maintenance of tools and machines, for the enforcement of labor discipline, and for the efficient and smooth organization of production. Their wages (550 to 1,100 rubles a month in the machine-building industry with which the decree dealt specifically) were substantially above the average earnings of workers and employees (342 rubles in 1940). Moreover, foremen who performed their duties to the satisfaction of the authorities were entitled to bonuses irrespective of whether the shop, as a whole, had or had not fulfilled its assignments.

The Eight-Hour Day and the Immobilization of Labor. The May ordinance was merely a straw in the wind. On June 26, 1940, the Presidium of the Supreme Soviet issued a decree which opened a new chapter in the history of Soviet labor. The eight-hour day was substituted for the seven-hour day which is guaranteed by Article 119 of the Constitution. In dangerous and unhealthful occupations, formerly on the six-hour-day basis, the seven-hour day became the rule.[18] The eight-hour day was set for young people of sixteen to eighteen who had formerly been permitted to work six hours. The "con-

---

[18] These occupations were listed in separate decrees. In a few industries the six-hour day was retained.

tinuous" six- or five-day week was replaced by the conventional seven-day week, with Sunday as the general day of rest. Workers and employees were prohibited—and herein lies the real importance of the decree of June 26— from relinquishing their jobs and seeking other employment without a release from the director of the factory where they were employed. The decree speci- fied two instances when such release must be granted: (1) if the applicant is medically certified to be unfit for his job and there is no suitable employ- ment for him in the enterprise, or when he is awarded an old-age pension and wishes to retire; and (2) if he has been admitted as a student in a sec- ondary or higher school. Abandonment of a job in contravention of the fore- going rules became an offense which is tried by a People's Court and is punishable by imprisonment for two to four months. Truancy is also dealt with by People's Courts, and the maximum penalty is six months of "correc- tive labor" and a fine of 25 per cent of the convicted worker's earnings. A sentence of "corrective labor" for a term not exceeding six months is served "as a rule" (Corrective-Labor Code, Article 9) in the enterprise where the worker is employed. The decree of June 26 provided that dismissal, the former penalty for truancy, is no longer applicable and, presumably, the convicted worker, if he is sent to a penal institution, is returned after serving his sentence to the enterprise where he was formerly employed. Directors failing to institute criminal proceedings against the violators of the decree, or hiring workers not properly discharged, are themselves liable to criminal prosecution. The decree applied to "all State, cooperative, and public enter- prises and institutions," that is, practically to every enterprise and public agency in the Soviet Union.[19] According to the preamble, the decree was issued "at the request of the All-Union Central Council of Trade Unions." [20] Another decree of June 26, 1940, provided that the existing monthly wages should be retained and piecework rates scaled down in order to keep monthly earnings on the former level, in spite of longer hours. The two decrees be- came effective at once.

The Higher Technical Personnel. The Principles of the June legislation were extended to the labor aristocracy—engineers, technicians, foremen, and

---

[19] The operation of the two decrees of June 26 was extended to the machine tractor sta- tions, principal government agencies in the rural areas (decree of July 17); to cooperative associations of artisans, even though some of their members engaged in trade merely as a part- time occupation and carried on the work in their own cottages (decree of July 22); and to the wood-working shops of the Department of Forestry (decree of July 24). A somewhat different treatment was reserved for the few enterprises leased to concessionaires and other "private interests." The first decree of June 26 was applied to such enterprises only in those provisions dealing with longer hours and the seven-day week, but it was ordered that the wages of workers employed in these enterprises should be proportionally raised (decree of August 16).

[20] "Model regulations" for the enforcement of the provisions of the decree of June 26 were prepared by the All-Union Central Council of Trade Unions and confirmed by the Coun- cil of People's Commissars on January 18, 1941. The regulations laid down minute rules of labor discipline, directed the workers, among other things, "to execute speedily and precisely the orders of the administration," and supplied an impressive list of penalties (including transfer to a lower paid job for a period up to three months) which the administration might impose, at its discretion, upon the workers. The "model regulations" bore the signature of N. Shvernik, secretary of the All-Union Central Council of Trade Unions.

highly skilled workers and employees. Their individual labor contracts were abrogated, and the People's Commissars were given the power to assign them, in the public interest, to any enterprise, however remote (decree of October 19). Directors, engineers, and heads of technical departments became personally responsible for the quality of goods produced and any lowering of the prescribed standards was made an offense punishable by imprisonment for a term of five to eight years (decree of July 10).

Overtime and Revolutionary Holidays. Overtime and night work, formerly prohibited for young people, were permitted for all who had reached the age of sixteen (decree of July 12). The number of revolutionary holidays was reduced to five per annum and it was specifically provided that work on Saturdays must not be shortened (decree of July 27).

Enforcement of Labor Regulations. Good care is taken to prevent excessive leniency on the part of the People's Courts which try labor cases. A People's Court usually consists of an elected judge and two elected "assessors" who have equal rights with the judge in reaching a verdict. The labor cases growing out of the violation of the decree of June 26, however, are tried *without* the participation of the assessors (decree of August 10) and judges have been sternly warned that laxity on their part in dealing with breaches of labor discipline will make them subject to summary disciplinary action (decree of July 24).

The State Labor Reserve. The immobilization of employed persons was followed by the compulsory training of young workers. A decree of the Presidium of the Supreme Soviet of October 2, 1940, called for the annual draft of 800,000 to 1,000,000 boys to be trained in trades and crafts. Boys fourteen to fifteen are sent to trade schools and railway schools which offer a two-year course; boys sixteen to seventeen to factory training schools where instruction is limited to six months. The graduates of these schools constitute the State Labor Reserves.[21] They are under the obligation to work for four years wherever they are assigned, and are paid the same wage as the other workers. On the expiration of the four-year term they are usually drafted into the army. Labor conscription applies to both the rural and the urban population. The collective farms contribute two recruits for each one hundred members of either sex aged fourteen to fifty-five. In cities and towns the draft is administered by local Soviets according to quotas issued annually by the Government. The students in the factory training schools need not have had any previous school training, but those sent to trade schools and railway schools are selected from boys who have completed four years in elementary schools. Students in the trade and railway schools receive, in addition to professional instruction, preliminary military training. During the War, labor conscription for the factory training schools was extended to girls aged sixteen

[21] The Central Administration of Labor Reserves, an agency of the Council of People's Commissars, was established by a decree of October 2, 1940. In May, 1946, it was reorganized as the Ministry of Labor Reserves.

to eighteen, and the age limit for boys drafted into these schools was lowered
to fifteen.

Tuition Fees in Secondary and Higher Schools. It was probably no
mere coincidence that on the same day, October 2, 1940, when the State
Labor Reserves were created, the Council of People's Commissars issued a
decree introducing tuition fees in the upper grades of the secondary schools
and in all higher schools. It will be remembered that free education, including higher education, was guaranteed by Article 121 of the Constitution.
This provision had been generally regarded as one of the real achievements
of the Soviet State. The decree of October 2 imposed tuition fees of 150 to
200 rubles per year in the three upper grades of the secondary schools and
of 300 to 500 rubles in the higher schools. The decree was made retroactive
to September 1, 1940; students who failed to pay their fees by November 1
were dropped.[22] The official reasons for curtailment of free education were
"the higher level of income of the toilers and the increasingly heavy burden"
of school expenditure. Since the average monthly earnings of workers and
employees in 1940 were 342 rubles and minimum wages slightly over 100
rubles, while incomes of the majority of the farmers were presumably below
this modest level, it would seem that higher education—except in the case of
exceptionally gifted children—became the preserve of those in the higher
income brackets. The Soviet press, characteristically, refrained from any
comment on this momentous change.

Reasons for the Legislation of 1940. The basic and obvious reason for
the labor legislation of 1940 was the failure of the earlier policies to achieve
their objectives—efficiency, high labor productivity, and stability of employment.[23] Another reason which was given much prominence at the time was
the rapidly worsening international situation and the danger of an attack on
the Soviet Union. It was ostensibly on this ground that the Central Council
of Trade Unions lent its full support to the Government. An editorial in
Izvestia characterized the Labor Reserves decree as "a new measure for the
strengthening of the economic and military power of the Soviet Union." The
defense argument appealed to many foreign students of Russian affairs who
still persist in treating the 1940 legislation as purely war measures.[24]

---

[22] Scholarships are granted exclusively on the basis of merit (decree of October 2) and
in the higher schools they are awarded only to those students whose records show two-thirds
of "excellent" marks and the balance not below "good." Students taking correspondence courses
(decree of October 2) or evening courses (decree of November 1) pay half of the regular fee.
Instruction under the State Labor Reserves decree is free and students receive the whole, or part,
of their maintenance from the State.

[23] I had advanced this interpretation shortly after the 1940 measures were enacted. See
M. T. Florinsky, "Stalin's New Deal for Labor," *Political Science Quarterly,* March, 1941.

[24] The reluctance to see the legislation of 1940 in its true light reflects the wartime attitude
of Anglo-American opinion towards Russia. In 1940–1941, as the tide of German victories
mounted, anti-Soviet feelings provoked by the Stalin–Hitler pact of August, 1939, and the
Soviet attack on Finland subsided markedly and gave place to an intense desire to win over
the Kremlin to the side of the Western Powers. While prior to Pearl Harbor the United States
was technically nonbelligerent, the exchange of American destroyers for British bases in the
Western Atlantic (September, 1940) and the Lend-Lease Act (March, 1941), although represented at the time as measures to keep this country out of the War, made American participation practically a certainty. When in June, 1941, Hitler invaded Russia, and the Soviet Union,

War and Post-War Labor Policies. Unfortunately for this interpretation, as these lines are being written five years after the end of the War and the dismemberment of Germany, the 1940 legislation is still in force. A wartime decree introducing obligatory overtime of one to three hours daily [25] was repealed in July, 1945, but the eight-hour day and the attachment of workers to their jobs remained. A decree of the Presidium of the Supreme Soviet of June 19, 1947, broadened the basis of labor conscription by extending the draft to boys aged fourteen to nineteen and to girls aged fifteen to eighteen. The fourth Five-Year Plan provided for the training under the State Labor Reserves scheme of 4.5 million young workers. In 1950 the number of students graduating from trade schools, railway schools, and factory training schools was to reach 1.2 million. The immobilization of industrial labor has, in a sense, its counterpart in agriculture in the obligatory participation of collective farmers in communal works ("obligatory labor days"), an obligation first introduced in May, 1939.[26] The elaborate system of incentives notwithstanding, and long before Hitler invaded Russia, the Kremlin was driven to resort to compulsion both on the farm and in the factory. Administrative direction of labor is fully consonant with the methods of Soviet planning, at least in its present stage, and this is why the 1940 legislation has remained in force for a decade and is still the law of the land. It is difficult, therefore, to agree with Maurice Dobb when he writes in 1948, three years after Hitler perished amid the smoldering ruins of the Chancellery and of the Third Reich, that the decrees of 1940 were merely measures "of preparations . . . to resist Hitler's attack," or with Baykov when he argues (in 1947) that these regulations "are not the result of the normal evolution of the labor system." [27] On the contrary, high labor turnover which was the primary cause for the decree of June 26, 1940, is inherent in a situation where demand for labor exceeds supply, and wages and conditions of work vary widely from industry to industry and from enterprise to enterprise. In the Soviet Union of the 1940's immobilization of labor becomes "abnormal" and illogical only if one assumes (as Baykov does) that synthetic propaganda devices such as "shock brigades," "Socialist emulation" and Stakhanovism are genuine mass popular movements, which there are many reasons to believe they are not.

The Outlook. The foregoing account should not lead to the conclusion that the draft and authoritative direction of labor are inherent in Communist society even though today they dominate the Soviet scene. The attitude of the Kremlin toward the 1940 legislation is not uniform. The Labor Reserves

---

much against the wishes of its leaders, became a full-fledged member of the anti-German coalition, enthusiasm for the USSR knew no bounds. Any critical appraisal of Soviet conditions came to be looked upon not only as a mark of intellectual inferiority but also as something unpatriotic and almost subversive. Emotional bias breeds dangerous illusions which refuse to be dispelled by harsh and unpalatable facts.

[25] Decree of the Presidium of the Supreme Soviet promulgated on June 27, 1941, less than a week after Germany attacked Russia.

[26] See below, p. 825.

[27] Dobb, *op. cit.*, p. 448; Baykov, *The Development of the Soviet Economic System* (New York, 1947), p. 352.

program, as has already been noted, is being expanded. Articles 119 ("right to rest and leisure") and 121 ("right to education") of the Constitution were amended in February, 1947, to bring them in line with the new policy of the Government and of the Party.[28] Presumably it is not intended to abandon these measures in the near future. Immobilization of labor, however, is in a different class. As far as I know, Article 46 of the Labor Code which guarantees the right of the workers to change employment has not been abrogated. Soviet economists, one may surmise, are under orders not to discuss this matter. A lengthy survey of labor legislation by B. Markus in the 1948 supplementary volume on the USSR of the Large Soviet Encyclopedia makes a cursory reference to the substitution of the eight-hour for the seven-hour day but ignores the momentous provisions dealing with the attachment of workers to their jobs. The reason for this reticence is probably the conflict between Soviet practice and Communist theory in accordance with which (to quote Lenin) each worker considers himself "part and parcel of the great army of free labor." Freedom of employment remains nevertheless the ultimate objective. Its attainment, however, depends on the establishment of a Communist society and the withering away of the State which, according to Stalin's doctrine, can be achieved only by eliminating the capitalist environment. And the leading capitalist country today—and therefore, in Communist theory, the arch-enemy of the USSR—is the United States.

TRADE UNIONS

Soviet Labor Theory. The functions of the trade unions under the dictatorship of the proletariat differ considerably from those of labor organizations in the capitalist countries. The position and activities of Soviet unions are determined by the theory that the USSR is a State of peasants and workers and that therefore the interests of labor and its employer, the State, are identical.[29] Strikes, organized labor's chief weapon, are not prohibited by law and a few minor strikes occurred in the 1920's. They are, however, incompatible with Soviet labor theory and are inimical to the smooth working of the planned economy. Any incipient attempt at direct action by labor is, therefore, nipped in the bud as a counter-revolutionary activity instigated by the enemies of the regime.

Organization. Soviet trade unions are industrial unions, that is, they include all persons employed in the same industry irrespective of craft and grade, from unskilled workers to engineers and managerial personnel. The basic unit of trade union organization is the factory (shop) committee (*fabkom*) or local committee (*mestkom*), elected by the members employed in an enterprise. On this foundation rests a pyramid of trade union agencies which follows the lines of the administrative structure of the Soviet Union. The highest organs are the biennial Congress of Trade Unions and the Central

---

[28] See above, pp. 753–754.

[29] A similar theory underlay the organization of the *Arbeitsfront* in National-Socialist Germany and, in a somewhat modified form, that of the syndical structure in Mussolini's Corporate State.

Council it elects. The Council, a large body of some 200 members, appoints a Presidium and a Secretariat, the actual managers of the trade union movement. In theory the trade union organization embodies the principles of democracy, each higher organ being freely elected by the lower one, but in practice the elections are controlled by the Communist Party.[30] The trade union organization, like most other Soviet agencies, has undergone many structural changes. In 1930 there were 23 trade unions; but as they were thought to be too large and unwieldy, their number was increased, by splitting the existing unions, to 45 in 1931, to 154 in 1934, to 168 in 1939, and to 176 in 1944. At the end of 1945 the Central Council of Trade Unions, revising itself, decreed the amalgamation of kindred unions in accordance with the "production" principle, a move designed to bring the trade union organization in line with the new setup of the Ministries in charge of economic affairs. As a consequence of this decision the number of trade unions declined to 67 in 1949. The trade union revenue which in 1946 was 2 billion rubles is derived from membership fees levied at the rate of one per cent of the members' earnings.

Membership. Trade union membership is voluntary but carries certain valuable advantages: sickness and disability benefits payable to members are twice as large as those payable to nonmembers; members may obtain loans and grants from mutual assistance funds maintained by the unions as well as grants from special appropriations provided in the trade union budget; members and their families enjoy priorities in such matters as the use of rest homes, sanatoria, and recreational and cultural facilities. In spite of these privileges and strong political pressure, trade union membership, although very large, is not all-inclusive. In the 1940's about one-sixth of the persons eligible for membership (members of producers' cooperative associations, including collective farmers, and individual peasants and handicraftsmen are not eligible) remained outside the fold of the trade union movement.[31]

Functions. Lenin defined trade unions as "an organization of the governing, domineering, ruling class, of a class that enforces the dictatorship of the proletariat, of a class that exercises the function of State compulsion. But it is not a State organization, . . . it is a school, a school of government, husbandry, a school of Communism." But what is "a school of Communism"? Lenin did not explain, perhaps because the answer to him was self-evident, but he stated that "trade unions are becoming the principal creators of the new society because the creators of the new society can only be the multimillion masses." During the first decade of Soviet rule the question of the

[30] In April, 1949, the tenth All-Union Congress of Trade Unions was convened after an interval of seventeen years. The Congress adopted a new statute which, however, retained practically unchanged the existing structure of trade union organization. It elected a new Central Council of 175 members and 57 alternates. The full text of the new statute is published in Isaac Deutscher, *Soviet Trade Unions* (London, 1950), pp. 141–152.

[31] The growth of trade unionism will be seen from the following figures: June, 1917, 1.5 million members; 1918, 2.5 million; 1919, 3.6 million; 1920, 4.3 million; 1921, 6.5 million; 1926, 9.5 million; 1928, 11.0 million; 1933, 17.1 million. During the War, of the 30 million eligible workers and employees, 25 million were members of the unions; in 1947 the union membership was approximately 27 million, and in 1948, 28.5 million.

rôle of the trade unions under Socialism was the cause of several controversies within the Party. Immediately after the revolution and in the early 1920's there was a sharp conflict over the rôle of trade unionism. The so-called "workers' opposition" held that the management of industry should be entrusted to the trade unions, while an influential group led by Trotsky denied the trade unions any independent part and advocated their absorption by the State. Both these extreme views were rejected and a compromise solution was worked out on the basis of Lenin's ambiguous formula. The resulting dual position of the trade unions as representatives of workers' interests, on the one hand, and as agencies for increasing productivity and for carrying out planned assignments, on the other, provoked confusion and friction and led in the late 1920's to the re-examination of the whole question by Party leaders. The debate revolved around the familiar question of the place of trade unionism within the framework of a Socialist State. Michael Tomsky, the veteran President of the Central Council of Trade Unions, came under severe criticism for his allegedly excessive zeal in defending trade union autonomy and for favoring the leveling of wages which Stalin had so sternly condemned (see above, p. 796). Tomsky was dismissed in 1929; he then committed suicide and has since been denounced as a traitor. He was succeeded, as President of the Central Council of Trade Unions by N. M. Shvernik, who proceeded to purge the trade unions of all elements suspected of sharing the aberrations of his predecessor. It was under Shvernik's ruthless leadership, which lasted until 1944, when he became first deputy Chairman (and later Chairman) of the Presidium of the Supreme Soviet, that the relations between the State and the trade unions were definitely crystallized.[32] The main functions of the trade unions in the USSR may be briefly summarized as follows. The unions represent labor in various government agencies. The Central Council of Trade Unions drafts labor legislation which is then submitted to the Government. It will be remembered that the decree of June 26, 1940, increasing the working day from seven to eight hours and immobilizing workers at their jobs, was ostensibly enacted at the request of the Central Council of Trade Unions. In 1933 the People's Commissariat of Labor was abolished and its duties—enforcement of labor legislation and administration of social insurance (other than health insurance and the majority of old-age pensions)—were transferred to the Central Council of Trade Unions. The trade unions negotiate collective labor agreements although the necessity for such agreements is not obvious since wages, hours, and conditions of work are not left to the free decision of the parties but are regulated by the State. It appears that in practice trade unions have often neglected to negotiate labor agreements and that for a while they were discarded altogether.[33] Trade unions provide for the educational, recreational, and cultural

[32] Shvernik was succeeded as President of the Central Council of Trade Unions by V. V. Kuznetsov.

[33] Deutscher's statement that "in February, 1933, collective agreements were formally abolished by governmental decree" and were not revived until 1947 (*op. cit.*, p. 125) is misleading and incomplete. According to a Soviet text on labor law published by the People's Commis-

needs of the workers; strive to improve housing conditions; administer safety measures; and, above all, cooperate with the management and the Communist Party in promoting labor discipline, "Socialist emulation," Stakhanovism, and the fulfillment and overfulfillment of the plan. In other words, the principal function of trade unionism is the fostering of the general objectives of the Socialist State. The chief emphasis in recent years has been on their work in promoting high productivity, efficiency, and labor discipline.

Conditions in the Trade Unions, 1937. It is perhaps not surprising that the trade unions have shown a lack of enthusiasm for a policy which, whatever may be its benefits in the future, imposes no small hardship on their members at present. A resolution adopted by the sixth plenary session of the Central Council of Trade Unions in 1937 presents a bitter indictment of the conditions prevailing in the labor organizations. According to the resolution the trade unions have been invaded by the "enemies of the people" and the labor leaders have displayed "intolerable political blindness, tardiness and levity" in detecting the criminal activities of the "wreckers." The intra-trade union "democracy" has been neglected and all questions have been decided by the presidents and secretaries without consulting the members.

The general meetings of the trade unions are summoned but seldom, they are poorly organized, are unbusinesslike and merely "formal-declarative" in their character. The decisions are frequently not carried out, there is no control over their execution. . . . The administration of social insurance is carried on by bureaucratic methods, the members of the trade unions do not participate in this work, have no control over the distribution and use of the social insurance funds. This situation has made it possible for all sorts of swindlers, chiselers, and enemies of the people to invade the administration of social insurance, to use the funds improperly, to squander and embezzle millions of rubles. . . . The trade unions have frequently paid no attention to the complaints of the workers, employees, engineers and technicians who pointed out criminal violations of labor legislation, and the non-observance of safety measures. . . . The trade unions have greatly weakened the drive for mass production, have failed to lead in the organization of "Socialist emulation" and the Stakhanov movement. . . . The Presidium of the All-Union Central Council of Trade Unions is proceeding by purely bureaucratic methods, is invariably late in deciding the most pressing questions of the trade union movement. . . . The majority of the members of the central committees of the trade unions are not familiar with the conditions in the enterprises, they do not know and do not try to learn what are the interests of the membership, show no desire to discuss the questions vital to the workers.

The resolution outlined a program directed to the improvement of the work of the trade unions and the democratization of their methods (new elections of trade union organs from below, secret ballot, voting for individual candidates instead of lists of candidates, responsibility of the elected officers to the bodies that elected them).

---

sariat of Justice, "the collective agreements concluded in 1933 were extended for 1934." In 1935, however, collective agreements were concluded in only four branches of economic activity and the sixth plenary session of the Central Council of Trade Unions directed (May 15, 1937) the trade unions "to resume the practice of negotiating labor agreements." [*Sovetskoe Trudovoe Pravo* (*Soviet Labor Law*) (Moscow, 1938), p. 32.] In Soviet texts on labor law published in the middle of 1947 collective agreements are not mentioned. Presumably, they were discontinued during the War; but Kuznetsov announced at the Tenth Congress that collective bargaining was resumed, on Stalin's order, in 1947.

Conditions in the Trade Unions, 1938. The seventh plenary session of the All-Union Council of Trade Unions held in September, 1938, passed a resolution dealing with the execution of the program of the sixth plenary session. This resolution offers a typical example of official optimism and "self-criticism" which an outside observer finds it difficult to reconcile. The resolution noted improvement in the work of the trade unions but then declared that "the trade unions have failed to carry into effect the most important decisions of the sixth plenary session," especially those dealing with the daily needs of the workers and the betterment of production. The conditions of workers' dining rooms, of housing, supply organizations, hospitals, day nurseries, kindergartens, etc., were reported to be highly unsatisfactory, with little progress shown in the field of labor protection and the promotion of safety. It was stated that bureaucratic procrastination and the personal rule of trade union presidents and secretaries had not been eradicated, and the resolution noted instances of "aloofness of the trade union leadership from the masses," of "a bureaucratic, heartless attitude toward the vital needs and requirements of the membership."

Conditions in the Trade Unions, 1939. The resolutions of the eighth plenary session of the All-Union Council of Trade Unions held in April, 1939, dealt largely with the promotion of efficiency and the strengthening of labor discipline. It is the duty of the trade unions, a resolution declared, to see to it that every worker performs his "norm." The plenary session noted that "Socialist emulation" continued to be organized "from above," "by purely bureaucratic methods"; that the organization of labor in a number of enterprises was highly unsatisfactory; that trade unions displayed a regrettable laxity in enforcing the rules laid down in the decree of December 28, 1938; [34] that they took little interest in settling questions of wages and in advancing the welfare of the workers.

The trade unions are fully equipped to meet the cultural needs of the toilers and to provide them with recreation facilities (6,000 clubs, and "palaces of culture," 15,000 libraries, 100,000 "red corners," 1,800 radio sets, over 10,000 moving picture installations). These facilities, however, are only too often insufficiently used. A number of clubs, "palaces of culture," and "red corners" are not properly taken care of, premises are uncomfortable, the necessary cultural atmosphere is lacking. For instance, the "Palace of Culture" of the Union of Southern Railroads, in Kharkov, instead of being a model cultural institution and a favorite place for recreation, is sadly neglected and untidy.

The eighth plenary session reiterated the resolution of the sixth plenary session prohibiting the voting in trade union elections for lists instead of individual candidates. It is characteristic of Soviet conditions that the resolutions strongly emphasized the necessity of studying Stalin's report to the Eighteenth Congress of the Communist Party and the *History of the Communist Party of the Soviet Union* [35] as the best method for improving the educational levels of the workers.

[34] See above, p. 801.
[35] See below, p. 844.

Trade Unions After World War II. World War II had inevitably a profoundly disorganizing effect upon the work of Soviet trade unions and inflicted heavy damages upon their cultural institutions. The number of trade union clubs and "palaces of culture" is officially said to have declined from the pre-War figure of 6,000 to 5,000 in 1946, and that of libraries from 15,000 to 3,000 (the disproportion in the ratio of destruction is surprising and inexplicable). War damages were to be fully repaired by the end of the fourth Five-Year Plan. Trade union policies and conditions in the trade unions after the War remained—as far as can be judged from the meager information available—as they were before the German invasion. The fifteenth plenary session of the Central Council of Trade Unions held in 1946 reiterated the all too familiar thesis that "the principal object of the trade unions is to organize the multi-million masses of workers, technicians and employees for the struggle for the fulfillment and overfulfillment of the plan . . . on the basis of 'Socialist emulation.'" This uninspiring program was followed by the customary references to the proposed improvements in the other services administered by the unions. That there is room for improvement is indicated by information scattered through the Soviet press. For instance on August 7, 1946, three months after the Council's plenary session, the trade union newspaper *Trud* launched a vigorous attack on the conditions prevailing in some of the enterprises in the Don Basin. According to *Trud,* wages in these enterprises were never paid on time, and in one instance workers were not paid for six months; bookkeeping and accounting were in a state of lamentable disorder; much waste of time was caused by the failure to supply the workers with proper tools; housing accommodations, both private and those provided by the administration, were so inadequate that workers had to sleep in corridors or were quartered in tents and lodgings lacking in elementary comforts. The special correspondent of *Trud* found no trace of educational or cultural work, "not a single library, newspaper or table game in any hostel." Local trade union and Soviet authorities, according to *Trud,* were fully aware of these intolerable conditions but limited themselves to passing lengthy resolutions on which no action was taken. The legitimate complaints of the workers were invariably defeated by the "heartless, bureaucratic attitude" of trade union officialdom, an ever-recurrent theme in organized labor's self-criticism. It is not suggested that the conditions described in *Trud* are necessarily typical of the USSR, but that such conditions could have arisen at all in important enterprises in a major industrial region is a telling comment on Soviet trade unionism.

Reasons for the Apathy of Organized Labor. The avowed apathy of organized labor in the Soviet Union is probably best explained by the subordinate position held by the trade unions among the agencies that share in the administration of industry. There are three of them in every industrial enterprise: (1) the appointed director who is personally responsible for the conduct of the enterprise; (2) the primary organ of the Communist Party whose duty it is to provide effective leadership in all "social, political, and economic activities of the enterprise" and to ensure their conformity with the policies of the Party; and (3) the shop or factory committee elected by the workers affiliated with the trade unions.[36] The trade union leaders usually refrain from interfering with the local Communist organizations or with the decisions of the director who is either a Party member or a "non-Party Bolshevik," unless the desirability of criticism is hinted from above. The principal function of organized labor is to drive its members toward higher efficiency, a distasteful task for which, one may surmise, trade unions have as little enthusiasm under Socialism as they do under a system of private enterprise. The rapid increase in the number of industrial workers and the steady influx of men and women to whom the tradition of trade unionism, which has hardly any roots in Russia, is alien are other factors that help to an understanding of the inherent weakness of Soviet labor organizations.

Soviet Trade Unions and the International Labor Movement. The foregoing account indicates that Soviet trade unions have little in common with trade unionism as it is understood in Western Europe and in the United States. For this reason the pre-War International Federation of Trade Unions has repeatedly declined to admit Soviet trade unions to membership. After the German attack on Russia, when a tide of unreasoned emotional admiration for the USSR swept the Western world, Soviet labor organizations succeeded in establishing fraternal relations with the British and French trade unions and the American Congress of Industrial Organizations. At a session of the Anglo-Soviet trade union committee in 1942 the representatives of the Soviet Central Council of Trade Unions proposed the formation of a world-wide federation of trade unions. The proposal was well received, and at an international trade union congress held in London in February, 1945, the World Federation of Trade Unions was born. Its charter was formally approved at an international congress which met in Paris in September of the same year. The International Federation of Trade Unions was disbanded and the trade unions of the USSR, Great Britain, France, and other countries joined the World Federation. The United States was represented by the Congress of Industrial Organizations but the American Federation of Labor refused to be associated with Soviet and other Communist-dominated trade unions. The attempt at integrating Soviet trade unionism in the international labor movement proved short-lived. In 1949, exasperated by obstructive Communist tactics and ceaseless attacks on the Marshall Plan, capitalism, and so on, British trade unions, the Congress of Industrial Organizations, and other non-Communist labor groups withdrew from the World Federation and formed the International Confederation of Free Trade Unions, while the World Federation continued to function under purely Communist leadership. It did not take long for the trade unions of the Western world to learn the lesson that their objectives and methods were incompatible with those of Soviet labor organizations.

[36] Decree of September 5, 1929, reprinted in the collection of labor legislation published in 1938.

CHAPTER VII

EVOLUTION OF AGRICULTURAL POLICIES

Results of the Agrarian Revolution of 1917–1918. The evolution of Soviet agrarian policy has been relatively simple. Private ownership in land was abolished by a decree issued by the Soviet Government immediately after it rose to power. Having no agrarian program of their own the Bolsheviks borrowed from the Socialist Revolutionary Party its program of socialization of land. This plan was soon to give place to an attempt to apply the rigid centralized control of agriculture inaugurated during the period of War Communism. While the latter policy with its ruthless requisitions of grain and exploitation of the peasantry led to violent uprisings, the former achieved its political objectives: the large landed estates of the Church and the nobility were divided among the peasants, thus fulfilling the secular dream of the down-trodden Russian farmer. The immense driving force of the agrarian revolution had been effectively harnessed in the service of the newly born Socialist State. The economic and social aspects of the agrarian revolution were far less satisfactory from the Marxian point of view. The majority of the former private landed estates were parceled out among the peasants and were administered by the methods of the antiquated and primitive Russian land commune, or *obshchina*. This form of tenure vested control of the land of a village in the general assembly of house elders who divided agricultural land among the households either on the basis of the labor power of the household or on that of the number of people deriving maintenance from it. The inherent drawback of this form of tenure is the intermixture of strips [1] which leads to compulsory rotation of crops (usually the primitive free-field system) and makes extremely difficult the adoption of better methods of cultivation. The equalitarian principle on which *obshchina* is based requires the periodical redistribution of land among the members of the community and this, again, weakens the

---

[1] Land being of unequal quality the entire holding of a village was divided into fields and the fields into strips of which each household received its allotted number. In certain cases the number of strips farmed by a householder ran as high as 30 or 40.

stimulus to take proper care of the land, since there is no assurance that any particular strip will not pass into other hands at the next redistribution. It was toward the abolition of this perverse form of tenure that the land reform of Stolypin was directed.[2] By 1920 the old-fashioned communal land tenure was restored in the entire territory of the country. A certain leveling in the size of peasant holdings took place as a result of the revolutionary redistribution of land, and, as a Soviet economist put it, the whole of Russia became "the petty bourgeois realm of small peasants." Under the New Economic Policy the farmers were left more or less alone and were permitted to sell a large portion of their produce in the open market. The Government, true to the Marxian doctrine of class struggle, divided the farmers into "poor" peasants, "medium" peasants, and the *kulaks*[3] or well-to-do peasants. The "poor" and the "medium" peasants were regarded as supporters of Socialism, while the *kulaks* were classed among its enemies. This distinction, however, did not become of vital importance until the great drive for collectivization in 1929. The rural community being inherently conservative, the more enterprising farmers managed to hold their own and even to improve their economic status so long as they were free to sell much of their produce in the market.

Socialist Reconstruction of Farming. The idea of reconstructing agriculture along Socialist lines, however, was never abandoned by the Soviet leaders. Beginning in 1918 attempts in this direction were made with the establishment of the *sovkhoz* or State-owned agricultural enterprises, and the organization of the farmers into *kolkhoz* or collective farms, on a cooperative basis. Two important advantages are claimed for large-scale Socialist agricultural enterprises. They make possible the use of intensive methods of farming and the employment of improved machinery, such as tractors and combines. They tend to minimize the psychological differences between industrial workers and farmers and especially to reverse the "petty bourgeois" attitude of the latter. The failure of the early attempts to establish State and collective farms has since been explained by the lack of the necessary prerequisite—agricultural machines. The policy to be followed toward the farmers was a source of much dissension within the Communist Party in 1924–1928. The first Five-Year Plan provided for a comprehensive program of collectivization which, it will be recalled, was greatly exceeded.[4] The very unsatisfactory results of the State grain collection in 1928 probably had something to do with the speeding up of collectivization. The *kulaks* were held responsible for the failure of the collection program and they were "liquidated as a class," that is, they were deported to remote regions and put to work in the lumber camps and on the construction projects of the dreaded OGPU. The actual number of the deportees has not been disclosed but it is believed to have been somewhere between

[2] See above, pp. 693–694.

[3] *Kulak* means "fist" in Russian and was colloquially applied before the revolution to well-to-do peasants who exploited their weaker neighbors. A *kulak* was usually the keeper of the village inn and the village money-lender. No definition of a *kulak* was provided by Soviet law, except that a farmer employing hired labor must be classed as a *kulak*. The village Soviets were given wide powers to determine for themselves who were the *kulaks*.

[4] See above, p. 773.

four and five millions. After application of this coercive measure the collectivization of farming proceeded without much opposition, although not without considerable friction. By the end of the second Five-Year Plan almost 100 per cent of the arable land was in the hands of the State farms or collective farms.

STATE FARMS

Organization of the State Farms. The *sovkhoz* or State farm is a large State-owned and State-managed agricultural enterprise cultivated by hired labor. In establishing State farms the Government had two objects in view: (1) to increase agricultural production by using better methods of husbandry and by extending the area under crops; and (2) to create model agricultural centers which would provide the peasant farmers with an object lesson in the advantages of large-scale farming and thus lead them along the path of Socialism. The State farms, which specialize in various branches of agriculture and animal husbandry, were in the earlier days fondly spoken of as "grain factories," "meat factories," etc. Little progress was made with the organization of State farms until 1928 when a comprehensive and ambitious program for their development was adopted. The Soviet leaders were suffering at the time from what is today scornfully described in the USSR as "gigantomania," that is, the naïve belief that the larger the size of an enterprise the greater are its advantages. In 1930 the average area of a State grain-farm reached the imposing figure of 116,000 hectares.[5] The structure of the agencies in charge of the State farms has been altered several times, but since 1936 they have been under the control of the federal People's Commissariat (Ministry) State Farms and of the corresponding People's Commissariat (Ministries) of the constituent republics. A State farm is managed by an appointed director clothed with full authority. Labor is paid on a piecework basis. Each laborer is permitted to keep, as his private property, one cow, one calf or goat, and one pig, but he is specifically debarred from owning draft animals—horses, oxen, camels (decree of September 30, 1938). The decree of February 7, 1937, provided for the establishment on the State farms of a "director's fund" similar to those of the industrial enterprises. As in industry the "director's funds" were presumably discontinued during the War but were formally reinstated by a decree of May 10, 1947. The object of the fund is "to strengthen the initiative and responsibility of the directors of the State farms in carrying out production programs, obtaining higher yields of crops and livestock, and reducing costs." The fund retains 5 per cent of the "planned profits" and 50 per cent of profits in excess of those specified in the plan. Half of the proceeds of the "director's fund" must be allocated to "expansion of production and construction and renovation of buildings, additional to the capital investments provided by the plan," and the balance to the improvement of "cultural and social amenities" for the staff of the farm and bonuses to individual employees. Personal incentive is thus created for the directors and employees to strive for the fulfillment

[5] One hectare = 2.47 acres.

of planned assignments, higher efficiency, and lower costs. In 1946 and 1947 the proceeds of the "director's fund" were not to exceed 5 per cent of the planned outlay on wages, but the Minister had the power to raise the limit to 10 per cent of the farm's planned expenditure on wages.

A Disappointing Experiment. The practical management by the State of huge agricultural enterprises presented difficulties which were both unforeseen and disappointing. The yield of crops on the State farms was consistently below the average for the country as a whole and the mortality among the livestock just as consistently high. There were frequent changes in the higher personnel and labor was in a state of flux. Stalin admitted in his speech to the Seventeenth Congress of the Communist Party in 1934 that there was a "great discrepancy" between the results obtained and the vast investment engulfed by the State farms. Beginning with 1935 the Government proceeded to disband many of the State farms, transferring the land to the collective farms. The sown area of the State grain farms declined from 16 million hectares, or 12.1 per cent of the total sown area in 1936, to 12.1 million hectares, or 8.9 per cent, in 1938. That is, it was reduced by 25 per cent. Another important development was the breaking up of the State farms into smaller units. The whole experiment belied expectations and admittedly failed to achieve its objectives.

Relative Unimportance of State Farms. The State farms hold a relatively unimportant place in Soviet agriculture. In 1928 they numbered 1,400 and employed 317,000 people; the corresponding figures were 4,337 and 1.9 million in 1932, and 3,992 and 1.3 million in 1938. The State farms would seem to have retained their subordinate position in the post-War Soviet Union. The fourth Five-Year Plan devotes to them one brief uninformative paragraph which sets in most general terms the goals for 1950.

COLLECTIVE FARMS AND THE "MODEL CHARTER"

Progress of Collectivization. The *kolkhoz* or collective farm is the prevailing form of agricultural enterprise in the Soviet Union. In 1938 the sown area of the collective farms amounted to 99.5 per cent of the total sown area. Collectivization, like everything else in the USSR, was carried on at record-breaking speed. On July 1, 1927, there were fewer than 15,000 collective farms with a membership constituting less than 1 per cent of the peasant population. By April 1, 1936, the number of collective farms had increased to 243,600 and included 89 per cent of the total number of peasant households. By the end of 1938, 18.8 million peasant households, or 93.5 per cent of the total number, were members of the collective farms. According to the census of January, 1939, members of collective farms (and their families) numbered 75.6 million, or 44.6 per cent of the total population.

What Is a Collective Farm? A collective farm is, in theory, a voluntary cooperative association for the cultivation of land. The legal status and organization of the collective farms and the basic rights and duties of their members are determined by the "Model Charter" of the Agricultural *Artel* [6] of February 17, 1935, and by Articles 7 and 8 of the Constitution. Each collective farm has its own "freely" adopted charter which invariably follows closely the "Model Charter." Although the land occupied by the collective farms is "public Socialist property" the farms have the use of land in perpetuity, that is, forever. This right is confirmed by Article 8 of the Constitution. Land cannot be sold or leased. The land, buildings, livestock and implements of a collective farm are divided into two categories. Agricultural land, buildings used for communal purposes, agricultural machines and the more important implements, draft animals, and stocks of seeds constitute the "public Socialist property" of the collective farm. Members of a collective farm, however, retain under their individual control their homesteads with an adjoining plot the size of which varies from one-quarter to one hectare, small implements, and some livestock (usually one cow, two calves, one or two sows, up to ten sheep or goats, an unlimited number of poultry and rabbits, and up to twenty beehives). These items constitute the individual property of the collective farmer. The distinction between the two kinds of property is sanctioned by Article 7 of the Constitution.

Membership. Membership in a collective farm is open to all citizens, both male and female, who have reached the age of sixteen. The descendants of disfranchised persons and *kulaks* and members of their families, who formerly were not eligible, have, since 1936, been permitted to join collective farms, provided they are in good standing with the Government. Each member pays an admission fee which varies from 20 to 40 rubles. From one-quarter to one-half of the property he brings to the collective farm (animals, implements, buildings, etc.)—for he is usually a former local individual farmer—is added to the "indivisible fund" of the farm, while the balance is credited to him as his contribution to the share capital. The property absorbed in the "indivisible fund" is not returned to the member if he leaves the farm.

Administration. The administration of a collective farm is based, in theory, on equality and democracy. The chief administrative body is the general assembly of the members which elects the president, the executive board, and the control committee. The president, who can be and in practice often is an outsider,[7] is the chief executive officer of the farm. He is assisted by the executive board of five to nine members (according to the size of the farm) which is elected for two years and must meet at least twice a month. The con-

[6] The Law of February 14, 1919, and the Land Code of December 1, 1922, which superseded it, recognized three types of collective farms: the commune, the *artel*, and the association for the joint cultivation of land. The difference between them is in the degree of collectivism which is strongest in the commune and weakest in the association. In 1933, 96 per cent of the collective farms were of the *artel* type which is officially recognized as the most suitable at the present stage of development. This study deals exclusively with the farms of the *artel* type.

[7] It is customary for the local Communist and Soviet leaders to propose to the general assembly the candidate for the presidency. The motion is invariably carried, the candidate—if he is not already a member of the farm—is admitted to membership, and is then duly elected by the general assembly to the presidency.

trol committee is required to keep a close check on the financial and economic activities of the executive officers and especially to ensure the fulfillment of the plan and of the obligations of the farm toward the State. In view of the great importance attached to these functions the members of the control committee must be confirmed in office, after election by the general assembly, by the Presidium of the Executive Committee of the local Soviet.

Organization of Labor. Cultivation of the collectivized sector of the farm is carried on jointly by the members who are organized into brigades under a brigade leader or brigadier, an official appointed by the executive board of the farm from among the members. His appointment should be for a period of not less than two years and he cannot be removed before the expiration of his term except when he has proved unfit for the job. On the grain farms brigades are organized for the full period of the rotation of crops, are supplied with animals and implements, and are put in charge of a definite area of land. The brigades, usually forty to sixty strong, are sometimes subdivided into smaller units, the "links" (*zveno*) which have their "link leaders." Brigadiers and link leaders assign their men to various tasks and are responsible for the work of their respective units. The collective farmers are paid in kind and also in money, their earnings being computed on the basis of "labor days." The labor day is an abstract unit which comprises the elements of physical exertion, skill, and the "social usefulness" of the work. The Government issued in 1933 elaborate lists in which various types of agricultural work were evaluated in terms of labor days. A decree of February 28, 1933, divided all types of farm work into seven classes. A day's work in the highest class (president of a collective farm, tractor driver) was worth two labor days, while a day's work in the lowest class was counted as only one-half of a labor day. Each collective farm is free to devise its own scale of payments in labor days, but official models are invariably followed. In determining whether a labor day has been actually earned both the quality and the volume of the work must be taken into account. There is an elaborate system of bonuses for the brigades, links, and individual laborers who exceed the standard requirement, and of deductions for those who fail. The brigadiers and link leaders share in both and have good reasons to drive their men hard and fast. The work of each member of a brigade is entered in terms of labor days at least once a week in his personal booklet by the brigadier or the link leader. At the end of the year the net earnings of the farm (that is, the residue of the gross revenue after meeting the statutory obligations imposed on the farm by the Charter), both in kind and cash, are distributed to the members on the basis of labor days credited to them. This scheme of organization of labor and distribution of farm income has been in force since the early 1930's but, as will appear later, it has been elaborated upon and made more exacting by subsequent legislation.[8]

[8] The organization of labor into brigades is also prevalent on State farms, in industry, trade, banking—indeed, in every field of endeavor where this is deemed feasible. Even economists and historians are herded into brigades and toil under the watchful eye of a brigadier.

The Kolkhoz Market. A portion of the produce retained by a collective farm after meeting its statutory obligations (to be discussed presently) is sold on the free market which is a major source of *kolkhoz* revenue, and the balance is distributed in kind to the members on the basis of labor days. Direct sales of agricultural commodities by collective farms and their members to consumers were formerly prohibited but were legalized by decrees of the Council of People's Commissars and of the Central Committee of the Communist Party of May 6, May 10, and May 20, 1932, which established (or, rather, recognized the existence of) the so-called *kolkhoz* market. The dispensation applied to the collective portion of the farm revenue as well as to the produce obtained by the members on the basis of labor days and that of their homestead allotments. Prices on the *kolkhoz* market, unlike practically all other prices in the Soviet Union, are not directly regulated by the State; it is the only surviving competitive market of some importance in the USSR. As long as similar commodities are available in State and cooperative shops at fixed prices, disparity between free and controlled prices is not likely to be great. In times of shortages, however—during the period of rationing in 1929–1935 and again during World War II—the free *kolkhoz* market prices were many times higher than the controlled prices and became a source of substantial revenue for the farming community. According to official computations, 1940 sales on the *kolkhoz* market represented 19.1 per cent of the total commercial turnover.

Strictness of Administrative and Judicial Controls. The assignment of a collective farmer to any particular kind of work, a matter of the greatest importance from the point of view of his earnings, is entirely in the hands of the administration of the farm. Negligence, laxity, or refusal to work brings summary punishment which varies from reprimands, fines, transfers to a lower pay group, or suspension from work to expulsion from the farm. If refusal to work is deemed to have been inspired by counter-revolutionary motives it falls under Article 58 of the Criminal Code. In case of conviction the sentence may be anything from six months' imprisonment to death by shooting. Capital punishment was also the highest penalty for collective farmers convicted of crimes against "Socialist property." The death penalty, it will be remembered, was abolished in May, 1947, but was restored in January, 1950, "for traitors to the homeland, spies, and saboteurs." The more serious offenses mentioned above are likely to come within the purview of the January decree, although "confinement in corrective labor camps for twenty-five years," provided in 1947 as the maximum penalty, should be a sufficient deterrent to recalcitrant farmers.

MACHINE TRACTOR STATIONS

Mechanization of Agriculture. Mechanization of agriculture has always been considered by the Soviet leaders as one of the primary conditions of successful collectivization of farming, even though Stalin in a speech delivered on December 27, 1929, advanced the idea that the mere pooling of rudimentary peasant implements and draft animals would result in a great increase in productivity and expansion of acreage under crops. In 1927 Soviet agriculture had fewer than 25,000 tractors of which 37 per cent were owned by the collective farms, 19 per cent by the State farms, 26 per cent by individual farmers, and 18 per cent by agricultural cooperative associations. All tractors were of foreign make, the majority manufactured in the United States. In 1938 the number of tractors had increased to 483,500, while the number of combines increased from 25,000 in 1933 to 153,500 in 1938. Much of this equipment was destroyed during the German invasion. The fourth Five-Year Plan provided for a minimum of 325,000 tractors and other agricultural machines to be built in 1946–1950 at a cost of 4.5 billion rubles (in prices of 1926–1927). The Soviet Union, moreover, no longer buys her agricultural machines abroad; they are all produced in Russian factories.

Functions of the Machine Tractor Stations. Since 1930 the ownership of tractors, combines, and other large agricultural machinery has been concentrated in the hands of the State and in the late 1930's practically all of them belonged either to State farms or to the machine tractor stations (MTS), the latter having by far the larger share. The machine tractor stations are the most important government agency for the control and direction of collective farms. Each station is headed by a director who has two groups of assistants: (1) engineers, mechanics, and agronomists whose duty it is to look after the mechanical equipment of the station, to assist the officials of the collective farms in drawing production plans, to carry out on the fields of the collective farms the work provided by the contracts entered into by the station and the farms, and to ensure the fulfillment and overfulfillment of the planned assignments of the farms which are serviced by the station; and (2) political officers who are the Party's "eye, ear, and arm" and concern themselves with the political education of the farming population and with the elimination of the enemies of collectivization and of the regime. Early in 1933, when mass collectivization was still a novel phenomenon and opposition to it was strong, the political function was entrusted to specially organized "political sections" of the machine tractor stations, but these were disbanded at the end of 1934 and their duties were taken over by a new official—the assistant director of the station in charge of political work who is subordinated directly to the local agency of the Communist Party. It is the intention of the Soviet Government that every collective farm shall be served by a machine tractor station. The number of stations jumped from 158 in 1930 to 6,350 in 1938. The third Five-Year Plan appropriated 5.2 billion rubles for the development of the network of the machine tractor stations. Nearly 3,000 stations were destroyed during the German invasion but, according to official reports, all resumed operation after the German retreat, even before the end of the War. The fourth Five-Year Plan provided for the establishment of 950 new stations by the end of 1950.

Their Relations with the Collective Farms. The collective farms are under obligation to avail themselves of the services of the machine tractor stations. They enter with the local station into contracts the terms of which are regulated by law, and, in return for the work done by the station, surrender to it a specified portion of their agricultural produce and also make payments in cash.

Their Financial Status. Until 1938 the machine tractor stations appear to have enjoyed a degree of financial autonomy within the framework of the plan. The decree of February 5, 1938, however, declared that their financial organization had been defective, had resulted in the "freezing" of State funds, and had encouraged squandering and laxity. From January 1, 1938, the stations have been financed exclusively from budget appropriations. The payments (both in kind and in cash) received by the stations from the collective farms are handed over to the Government.[9] For the timely collection of these payments the director of the farm is held personally responsible. The decree of February 5, 1938 (supplemented by the decrees of January 13, 1939, March 8, 1940, and May 9, 1942) established a complex system of bonuses for the stations' employees as rewards for efficiency, fulfillment and overfulfillment of the plan, and reduction of costs. A further step in the same direction was the creation at the machine tractor stations of "director's funds" (decree of September 29, 1947) similar to, but even more difficult to administer than, the "director's funds" of industrial enterprises and State farms. Bonuses paid to an employee of the station in the course of a year should not exceed his average earnings over a period of two months.

TAXATION OF AGRICULTURE

Compulsory Deliveries in Kind. Farmers pay a variety of levies and taxes which provide the bulk of Soviet revenue. One of them, payment in kind for the services of the machine tractor stations, has been noted above. The most important and onerous levy, however, is the obligation to surrender a portion of agricultural produce to the State at prices far below those paid by the consumers. Until 1933 the amount of agricultural commodities to be delivered was determined by "contracts" between the farmers and the State (the so-called "centralized purchases"). The volume of obligatory sales and the price being fixed by the Government, the transaction amounted to requisition and destroyed incentive to higher production. By a decree of January 13, 1933, this method was superseded by a levy which took the form of a specified amount of grain (potatoes, sunflower seed) per hectare of the sown area, or of a specified amount of meat, wool, and dairy products per head of cattle, sheep, camels, and hogs. The new method had the advantage of fixing in ad-

---

[9] In his report to the Supreme Soviet on August 10, 1938, the People's Commissar for Finance, Zverev, stated that "the absence of [financial] control had as its consequence heavy losses suffered in 1937 by the machine tractor stations and the State farms." In his report to the same body on May 25, 1939, Zverev again deplored the inefficiency of the leaders of the machine tractor stations. Their laxity, according to the Commissar for Finance, necessitated in 1938 outlays in excess of budgetary appropriations running into several hundred million rubles. It was announced, nevertheless, that the machine tractor stations contributed 1.4 billion rubles to the State budget in 1938, and the anticipated receipts from this source were put at 2.3 billion rubles in 1939 and 2.6 billion rubles in 1940.

vance the obligations of the farmers, thus giving them the incentive to produce more since they were permitted to dispose of the balance of their produce
at far more remunerative prices than those paid for compulsory deliveries.[10]
Compulsory deliveries applied to grain, sunflower, potatoes, meat, milk, and
wool. The "centralized purchases" or "contract" method was retained for the
so-called "technical crops"—cotton, flax, hemp, sugar beet, tobacco, and so
on. Under this arrangement the entire produce of the acreage contracted for
by the State is surrendered to the Government at low fixed prices. Compulsory
deliveries and "centralized purchases" are a primary charge on the produce of
a collective farm; failure to make the deliveries on the prescribed date is a
criminal offense for which the administration of the collective farm bears the
responsibility. Commodities of the same kind as those subject to compulsory
deliveries and "centralized purchases" are also sold to State and cooperative
purchasing agencies under a program of the so-called "decentralized purchases." "Decentralized purchase" prices are higher than compulsory delivery and "centralized purchase" prices but lower than retail and *kolkhoz* market prices. In theory "decentralized purchases" are the result of voluntary
agreements between the collective farms and the purchasing agencies. However, since the plan determines in advance the volume of "decentralized purchases" and each region and collective farm is allocated a quota thereof, the
"voluntary" character of these transactions is obviously fictitious. Experience
was soon to show that the 1933 rules governing compulsory deliveries were
a serious obstacle to the progress of Soviet agriculture. The basis of assessment
was accordingly revised in 1940.

Fiscal Burden of the Farmers. The actual burden imposed upon the
farmers by the deliveries in kind will be gathered from the fact already mentioned that in 1937 the revenue of the Committee (now Ministry) of Agricultural Stocks, which is the purchasing agency, was 24.1 billion rubles, while
another 20.4 billion rubles were earned by the People's Commissariat of Food
Industry, that is, 46 per cent of the total State revenue came from these two
sources. The bulk of the deliveries in kind was supplied by the collective farms
and their members. The provision of Article 8 of the Constitution that collective farms shall enjoy the use of their land "without payment" is, therefore,
only formally true: officially they pay no rent, but for all practical purposes
compulsory deliveries at nominal prices are equivalent to rent, a rent that is
much higher than anything known in the capitalist countries. It is only fair
to add that the financial sacrifices made by the farmers do not contribute to
the revenue of capitalist landowners, but are invested in the vast program of
economic development sponsored by the State.

Other Taxes. In addition to the deliveries in kind the farmers pay several
taxes in money. The more important among them are the agricultural tax,
the tax on the housing and cultural development in rural areas, and the in-

---

[10] Compulsory delivery prices receive little publicity and none have appeared in print for
a number of years. In 1932 *kolkhoz* market prices were twenty (beef), thirty (oats), and even
ninety (wheat and wheat flour, which are not strictly comparable) times as high as those paid
for compulsory deliveries. Alexander Baykov, *op. cit.,* pp. 241 note, and 244 note.

come tax on collective farms. The yield of these taxes is relatively small but their rates in some instances are stiff. Taxation in all its forms is blatantly discriminatory and is used as a method of fostering collectivization. The tax burden of individual farmers has been consistently heavier than that of the collective farmers, and in the case of the *kulaks* it has been definitely confiscatory.[11]

COLLECTIVE FARMS, 1938–1942

Difficulties of Collectivization. In view of the profound changes wrought by collectivization in the ways of life and customs of the Russian village, the conservative instincts of the farming community, the arbitrary and dictatorial nature of the regime established by the "Model Charter," the uncertainty of the advantages it conferred upon the peasantry, and the novelty and magnitude of the experiment, it would be unreasonable to expect that opposition to collectivization would end with the "liquidation of the *kulaks* as a class" in the early 1930's and that new and unforeseen difficulties would not arise. Tangible evidence of the attitude of the peasantry was provided by the wholesale slaughter of domestic animals by prospective farmers, prior to joining a collective farm. The consequences of the depletion of the herd were of utmost gravity to Russian agriculture.[12] In spite of the vast expenditure on mechanization there was no immediate and striking increase in the yield of crops.[13] Stalin admitted in his address before the Seventeenth Congress of the Communist Party in 1934 that tractors and combines had been hopelessly mishandled, but this was ascribed to failures to carry out official policies.

[11] The Law of August 21, 1938, may serve as an illustration. It provided for a tax on horses owned by the individual farmers. The rate of the tax varies, according to the locality, from 275 rubles to 500 rubles on the first horse, and from 450 to 800 rubles each on all other horses. The payment of the tax was due on October 15, 1938, and every individual farmer who owned a horse on August 21 was liable to the tax even if he had disposed of his horse at once. But if he joined a collective farm before October 15 the payment was waived. The reasons for this characteristic piece of legislation, according to the preamble to the law, were the complaints of unnamed collective farmers that individual farmers used their horses for "speculative purposes." The explanation may not seem convincing yet the tax largely achieved its object. The number of "horses and households" liable to the tax declined from 356,600 in 1938 to 89,500 in 1940, that is, by about three quarters. Curiously the yield of the tax (including "fines and overpayment," whatever this may mean) during the same period was merely halved (109.7 million rubles in 1938 and 54.5 million in 1940) [K. N. Plotnikov, *Biudzhet sotsialistcheskago gosudarnstsva (Budget of the Socialist State)*, Moscow, 1948, p. 190]. How individual farmers can survive at all is truly a mystery.

[12] The effects upon the livestock of the drive for collectivization which started in 1929 and the degree of recovery achieved by 1938 will appear from the following official figures:

	1916	1928	1933	1938
		(IN MILLIONS)		
Horses	35.8	33.5	16.6	17.5
Long-horned cattle	60.6	70.5	38.4	63.2
Sheep and goats	121.2	146.7	50.2	102.5
Pigs	20.9	26.0	12.1	30.6

[13] Stalin stated in his report to the Eighteenth Congress of the Communist Party that the total yield of grain in 1938 was 118.6 per cent of the yield in 1913, while the area under grain increased in 1938 to 108.5 per cent of the 1913 figure. The improvement in the yield of grain crops therefore was anything but striking and the advantages claimed for the collective farms remain to be proved. It must also be remembered that the size of the population has increased since 1913.

Soviet pronouncements proclaim that collectivization is an unqualified success and that the Russian farming community is the most prosperous, carefree, and democratic in the world. Documents emanating from the Communist Party and the Moscow Government, however, tell a different story.

Official Criticism, 1938. On April 19, 1938, the Council of People's Commissars and the Central Committee of the Communist Party issued jointly a decree which disclosed an amazing picture of the conditions prevailing on the collective farms. The "Model Charter" specifically provided that no member of a collective farm could be expelled except by a decision of the general assembly attended by at least two-thirds of the members. The decree pointed out that this rule had been frequently disregarded. Members had been expelled in large numbers and for no good reason.

> Practice has proved that the executive boards and the presidents of the collective farms . . . are the chief perpetrators of illegal actions. . . . The leading county (*raion*) Party and Soviet officials . . . display a heartless bureaucratic attitude toward the fate of the collective farmers, ignore the appeals of those who were illegally expelled, take no measures against officials guilty of violating the rights of the collective farmers. . . . Even more, these higher Party and Soviet officials themselves push the presidents and the executive boards of the collective farms into the road of illegal expulsion of the members under the banner of cleansing the collective farms of socially-alien and class-inimical elements.

The decree rightly stated that such policies "foster discontent and bitterness among the expelled farmers, and make the members uncertain of their position on the farm." The decree also provided that the regulations of the "Model Charter" must be observed, that members must not be expelled for minor offenses, and it made the infringement of this rule a criminal offense. Subsequent developments indicate that this and similar measures had little success in curbing the zeal of local bosses and in restoring the shattered morale of the collective farmers. The amendment of the Communist Party charter which was adopted in 1939 extended the authority of the primary party organs and of the Organization of Communist Youth in the administration of the collective farms. There are good reasons to believe that this provision merely aggravated the conditions that the decree of April 19, 1938, so rightly deplored.

Official Criticism, 1939. Another and perhaps even more important aspect of the situation was discussed in a revealing decree, "On Measures for the Protection from Spoliation (*razbazarivanie*) of the Publicly-Controlled Land of the Collective Farms," issued jointly by the Council of People's Commissars and the Central Committee of the Communist Party on May 27, 1939. According to the decree, collective farmers had frequently expanded their individual allotments far in excess of the norms stipulated by the "Model Charter" (see above, p. 817).

"As a result of this practice directed against the collective farms and the State," said the decree, "the interests of the communal economy of the collective farms based on joint cultivation of land are being sacrificed to the interests of the property-minded, anti-social (*rvachi*) elements who use collective farms for speculation and personal enrichment." The decree complained that in a number of collective farms the individual allotments of the members had become for all practical purposes their private property over which the administration of the farm exercised no control. Abuses were facilitated by the hopeless state of confusion and disorder prevailing on such farms: parcels of land under individual and collective management were frequently intermixed; there were no clear boundaries, no proper supervision and registration. "The homestead allotments," according to the decree, "thus lose their subsidiary character and occasionally prove to be the chief source of revenue of the collective farmers. The collective farms therefore have a fairly considerable number of fictitious members who do not participate in the collective work of the farm, or only pretend to participate in it, but who actually devote most of their time to their individual allotments." These conditions, the decree maintained, "inevitably slow down the increase in the productivity of labor on the collectivized section of the farm, disorganize the honest collective farmers, and thus obstruct the further growth of the farms' revenue and the improvement in the standard of living." The responsibility for the violation of the provisions of the "Model Charter," according to the decree, rests largely with the local Soviet and Party officials.

Compulsory Labor Days. The decree provided a long list of measures designed to bring to an end the illegal practices. Allotments in excess of the norms established by the "Model Charter" were to be returned to the collective farms by November 15, 1939. Responsible local officials were to be removed from office, expelled from the Party and committed for trial. While the annual earnings of the large majority of the collective farmers, according to the decree, were from 200 to 600 labor days, in a number of cases the figure was as low as 20 or 30 labor days. The decree "advised" the collective farms to adopt the rule that every able-bodied member who had earned less than a definite number of labor days per year (the figure suggested varied from 60 to 100 according to the locality) should be expelled.

The introduction of compulsory labor days (for the "advice" of the Communist Party and the Government is, *de factor,* mandatory) revolutionized the theory, although not necessarily the practice, of the organization of labor on the collecitve farms. The fiction, which heretofore had been studiously maintained, of voluntary participation of the members in communal work was dropped and work on the socialized sector of the farm became a legal obligation enforceable by severe penalties. Compulsory labor days, however, were not introduced at once in all collective farms and compliance with the decree of May, 1939, was fostered by linking the farmers' earnings with the minimum requirement of labor days. In February, 1940, the yearly minimum of 60 labor days was made obligatory for the collective farmers of the Uzbek Soviet Socialist Republic, except on cotton- and tobacco-growing farms.[14] In May of that year the requirement (100, 80, and 60 labor days, according

---

[14] Decree of the Central Committee of the Communist Party and of the Council of People's Commissars of the USSR of February 21, 1940, confirming the joint decision of the corresponding bodies in the Uzbek Republic.

to the locality) was extended to the collective farms engaged in fishing (co-operative associations of fishermen are rated as collective farms).[15] A decree of December, 1940, established a new scale of bonuses in kind but stipulated that it should apply only to those collective farmers who had earned, between March 1 and November 10, a minimum of 120 labor days on farms growing sugar beet, flax, hemp, and cotton, and a minimum of 100 labor days on all other farms. For collective farmers enrolled in cattle-breeding brigades the minimum required to qualify for bonuses was 220 labor days per annum.[16] By a decree of April 13, 1942, the yearly number of obligatory labor days was raised to 150 for the cotton-growing farms and to 120 for all other farms, except those situated in regions listed in the decree where the minimum requirement was set at 100 labor days. A specified number of labor days must be earned by prescribed dates (prior to May 15, May 15 to September 1, and so on, the dates varying according to locality and the type of the farm). Members aged twelve to sixteen of the families of collective farmers are requested to work at least 50 labor days per annum. The administration of the collective farm was to provide these juvenile workers with labor booklets and to keep a separate record of their performance. Failure by able-bodied farmers to meet the labor day quota is an offense which is tried by People's Courts and is punishable by "corrective labor" for a term of no more than six months. Sentences are served on collective farms which withhold 25 per cent of the earnings of the convicted persons. The decree "invited" the collective farms to adopt the rule that their members, both male and female, who had not fulfilled the required minimum of labor days during the year should be expelled and deprived of their homestead allotments, that is, the imposition of the maximum penalty within the power of the general assembly.[17]

Revised Basis for Assessment of Compulsory Deliveries. The tightening of the screw of administrative control and direction so typical of the mechanics of Soviet democracy made itself felt in still another area of vital interest to the farming community. A joint resolution of the Central Committee of the Communist Party and of the Council of People's Commissars, undated but released to the press on April 8, 1940, proclaimed that the existing system of compulsory deliveries based on planned sowings and the size of the herd worked against the expansion of the cultivated area and the progress of animal husbandry, and was inimical to the interests of diligent farmers who were compelled to supply a disproportionally large share of the commodities levied by the State; it had therefore outlived its usefulness and was to be discarded. Beginning with 1940, quotas of compulsory deliveries were to be determined by the aggregate acreage of arable land held by agricultural enterprises. The

[15] Decree of the Council of People's Commissars of May 16, 1940.

[16] Decree of the Central Committee of the Communist Party and of the Council of People's Commissars of December 31, 1940. Collective farmers who had failed to earn the full number of labor days stipulated in the decree but had to their credit a smaller number of labor days not below a specified limit (90, 75, and 170, respectively, for the three groups of collective farmers mentioned above) were eligible for bonuses of half the full amount.

[17] Decree of the Central Committee of the Communist Party and of the Council of People's Commissars of April 13, 1942,

Government sets the amount of each commodity to be levied per hectare of arable land; the actual assessment is computed by multiplying this figure by the acreage of arable land held by collective farms, their members (homestead allotments), and individual farmers.[18] The new method of assessment applied to grain, rice, potatoes, vegetables (cabbage, beets, carrots, onions, cucumbers, and tomatoes), oleiferous seed, grass seed, hay, milk, hides, skins, eggs, and meat.[19] The resolution of April, 1940, was implemented by several decrees issued in 1940 and 1941. Under this legislation the assessment of individual farmers is higher than that of collective farmers, and in most cases the assessment of collective farms not serviced by the machine tractor stations is 15 per cent higher than that of the farms which avail themselves of the services of the stations. Local authorities were given certain leeway in determining the quotas of agricultural enterprises, provided the aggregate amount of deliveries for the territorial subdivision was not diminished. The revision of the method of assessment pursued two distinct yet closely interrelated purposes: (1) to secure the agricultural commodities needed by the State, and (2) to force the farmers to expand their acreage under crops, to diversify the rotation of crops (even though substitution of one agricultural commodity for another was allowed at fixed ratios), and to increase the size of the herd.

Incentives. The success of the intensification of Government intervention in the affairs of the collective farms depended on the ability to secure a degree of cooperation on the part of the collective farmers and, especially, on the part of the *kolkhoz* administration whose unenviable duty it is to enforce the rules devised by the Kremlin. We know already that in 1939 both were notoriously wanting (see above, p. 824). Ingenious regulations designed to give to the rank and file of the collective farmers and to farm officials—presidents, brigadiers, and link leaders—an immediate and tangible interest in the execution of official policies were enacted and received resounding publicity. The principles of this legislation are simple and familiar: elimination of *obezlichka* (work that cannot be traced to its performer) and *urovnilovka* (equality of remuneration), or, in less picturesque and more concrete terms, the implementation of the dictum laid down in Article 12 of the Constitution: "to each according to his work." But if the principles are trite and simple the adminis-

[18] According to the official definition "arable land" includes ploughland, vegetable gardens, and, in some instances, orchards, meadows, pastures, and wasteland scheduled for improvement under the plan.

[19] A similar regime was applied earlier to wool under the terms of a decree issued by the Central Committee of the Communist Party and the Council of People's Commissars on January 30, 1940. Another decree of the Party and the Council of People's Commissars of April 4, 1942, extended compulsory deliveries to tobacco (which was formerly collected under the program of "centralized purchases"; see above, p. 822) but the method of assessment adopted was different from that used for other agricultural commodities. The decree of April 4 set the quotas of tobacco to be delivered by the tobacco-growing republics and regions of the Union; these quotas were reapportioned by local authorities among the smaller administrative subdivisions, and finally among the collective farms, collective farmers (homestead allotments), and individual farmers. Overfulfillment of the quota by 10 per cent brought a price increase of 50 per cent for the total amount delivered, and overfulfillment by 25 per cent a price increase of 200 per cent.

trative and regulatory policies built round them are not, as will appear even from a cursory summary of pertinent legislation.

Earnings Linked to Productivity. The earliest and most important enactment in this field is the decree "On Additional Remuneration of Labor of Collective Farmers for Increasing the Yield of Crops and Animal Husbandry" of December 31, 1940, issued by the Council of People's Commissars and the Central Committee of the Communist Party.[20] The decree noted that while some of the brigades and links had achieved a high level of production the record of many others working under similar conditions remained unsatisfactory. The chief reason for the unevenness of the performance, according to the decree, was the unsound method of remuneration based exclusively on the number of labor days earned by each farmer, without taking into account the quality of the work and the results achieved.[21] The decree directed that beginning in 1941 collective farmers who had exceeded the standard norm of production should either retain a specified share (one-fifth for vegetable, one-fourth for grain, one-third for sunflower) of the produce in excess of the norm, or receive a cash bonus computed as percentage of the value of the produce in excess of the norm (cotton, sugar beet). A similar principle applied to workers engaged in animal husbandry. For instance, a milkmaid, if she exceeds the assignment, receives 15 per cent of the "surplus" milk, and a farmer in charge of rabbit hutches receives 25 per cent of the animals six months old bred in excess of the norm. The decree seemingly overlooked no commodity produced on a farm. Its provisions applied to the staple crops and the main produce of animal husbandry as well as to chickens, geese, turkeys, down, honey, and wax. The foregoing bonuses in kind and cash payments are in addition to the earnings of the collective farmers on the basis of labor days. The share of each in "additional" payments is equal to his share in the aggregate number of labor days earned by the link or the brigade. The decree emphasized the importance of subdividing the brigades into links, a practice that appeared to have been neglected on many collective farms. The link leader received a monthly bonus of 2 to 3 per cent of the number of labor days earned by his link, and the brigadier a bonus equivalent to one and a half times the average "additional" earnings of the members of his brigade. The emoluments of *kolkhoz* presidents (including both the labor day allowance and the cash payment) are increased, roughly, in proportion to the overfulfillment of the plan. If overfulfillment is less than 11 per cent, the earn-

[20] The decree of December 31, 1940, applied to Ukraine but its provisions were extended, with some minor modifications, to the other parts of the Union by decrees issued by the Government and the Party on January 31 and February 15 (three decrees under that date), 1941, and May 9, 1942. This last decree dealt specifically with "additional remuneration" of the employees of the machine tractor stations and of the collective farmers assisting them.

[21] The decree quotes the following example. On the collective farm *"Vtoraia Piatiletka"* ("The Second Five-Year Plan") the link led by S. Voitiuk harvested 136 centners (one centner = 220 lbs.) per hectare and earned 370 labor days. On a similar acreage (2.5 hectares) the link led by A. Skrypnik harvested 211.5 centners per hectare and earned 350 labor days. Because of the equal distribution of the produce per labor day the earnings of the Skrypnik link which had raised 56 per cent more sugar beet per hectare than the Voitiuk link were actually smaller than those of the latter.

ings of the president are increased by 15 per cent; if overfulfillment is 11 to 25 per cent, by 25 per cent; if overfulfillment is over 25 per cent, by 40 per cent. The percentage of fulfillment, and the consequent increase in the president's emolument, are computed separately for (1) grain crops, (2) "technical crops" and vegetables, and (3) animal husbandry. It would seem therefore that if there is a 25 per cent overfulfillment in each of these three groups of commodities, the bonus of the president amounts to 120 per cent of his basic earnings.

Emoluments of Kolkhoz Presidents. The Government took particular care to improve the financial status of *kolkhoz* presidents. In addition to the bonuses just mentioned they receive regular monthly emoluments of two kinds: (1) an allowance of labor days which varies, according to the size of the sown area of the farm, from forty-five labor days if the sown area is less than 100 hectares, to ninety labor days if it is over 1,500 hectares; and (2) a cash payment which varies, according to the gross receipts of the farm, from 25 rubles if the receipts are less than 10,000 rubles, to 400 rubles if they exceed 1,000,000 rubles. The monthly labor day allowance increases with the length of service on the same farm, a provision designed to discourage the turnover or so-called "fluidity" of farm presidents which has been extraordinarily great. The increase is 5 per cent after two years of service; 10 per cent after three years; and 15 per cent after five years.[22] The regulations just described added greatly to the status of *kolkhoz* presidents. Their emoluments, especially on the larger farms, are far above the earnings of the rank and file of the collective farmers. The position of *kolkhoz* presidents is comparable to that of the better-paid Government officials, and they should be regarded as representatives of the State rather than of farmers who obediently elect them to office.

A Tentative Appraisal. The complexities of *kolkhoz* administration were greatly increased by the legislation of the late 1930's and early 1940's. The maze of minute rules aimed at keeping track of the yield of every few hectares under staple crops, of every patch of onions, cabbage, and cucumbers, of every steer, cow, sow, barn-yard fowl, rabbit, and beehive, and at rewarding every ploughman, gardener, shepherd, and milkmaid, as well as their betters —link leaders, brigadiers, *kolkhoz* presidents, tractor drivers, and other officials of the machine tractor stations—strictly in accordance with the results obtained would have taxed the resourcefulness and endurance of expert agronomists and statisticians. Link leaders and brigadiers, fountains of the basic data, are not, however, trained specialists. Bookkeepers and accountants, who are deservedly among the highest paid officials of the collective farms, toil hurriedly to meet immutable deadlines over the mass of imperfect data that pour incessantly into their dingy offices. Official optimism to the contrary

[22] The rules governing the emoluments of *kolkhoz* presidents were first introduced in the eastern regions by a decree of the Council of People's Commissars and the Central Committee of the Communist Party of April 21, 1940, but were extended to the other parts of the Union by similar decrees of July 26, August 24, September 11, October 4, November 4, December 20, and December 31, 1940.

notwithstanding, it is doubtful whether the objectives of the regulations have been attained, or indeed, whether they are attainable within the foreseeable future. It is certain, however, that the whole system invites evasion, malfeasance, and favoritism and generates innumerable grievances, real and imaginary. Scattered official reports of a factual nature (as distinct from equally official propaganda statements) offer little ground for optimism, but they throw some light on the actual conditions in the countryside. It was officially stated that in 1940 only one-seventh (and in one instance—that of the Tartar Autonomous Soviet Socialist Republic—only 4 per cent) of rural homesteads, including those of the collective farmers, had orchards.[23] In August, 1940, the Government and the Party sternly "warned Party, Soviet, and agricultural organs of the inadmissibility of repeating last year's mistakes when in a number of republics, regions, and districts, because of the careless attitude of the leaders of local organization, harvesting was unduly prolonged and resulted in heavy losses." Preliminary reports indicate, according to the statement, that the 1939 mistakes were being repeated in a number of regions. In several regions enumerated in the statement "many Party and Soviet leaders found themselves [in 1939] prisoners of the anti-State tendencies of separate collective farms and collective farmers, with the result that the plan of compulsory deliveries of grain was underfulfilled and there were large arrears on account of compulsory deliveries and payments in kind for the work done [by the machine tractor stations]."[24] This statement was repeated almost verbatim in 1942, nearly two years after the supposedly remedial legislation outlined above had been enacted. The Government and the Party again "warned Soviet and Party organizations of the inadmissibility of repeating last year's mistakes when in a number of districts, regions, and republics, as a consequence of inadequate preparation, harvesting was unduly prolonged which led to serious losses, the nonobservance of dates established by law for deliveries, and the worsening of the quality of the grain delivered to the collecting agencies."[25] This pathetic appeal, accompanied by the usual crop of promises of bonuses and threats of penalties, was issued at the time when the Soviet Union was engaged in a life-and-death struggle with the invading German troops. It is not, perhaps, unreasonable to conclude that the legislation of the late 1930's and the early 1940's not only failed to improve conditions on the collective farms but probably made them worse.

FARM LEGISLATION AFTER WORLD WAR II

The Ravages of War. The eastward sweep of German armies over more than one thousand miles of the fertile south-Russian plains, the stubborn resistance of Soviet troops, and the "scorched earth" policy proclaimed by Stalin

[23] Decree of the Council of People's Commissars and of the Central Committee of the Communist Party of February 21, 1940.
[24] Resolution of the Council of People's Commissars and of the Central Committee of the Communist Party, undated but released to the press on August 1, 1940.
[25] Resolution of the Council of People's Commissars and of the Central Committee of the Communist Party of July 11, 1942.

inflicted frightful losses on Soviet agriculture. Some 70,000 villages, 98,000 collective farms (roughly two-fifths of the total number), nearly 1,900 State farms (about half of the total), and 2,900 machine tractor stations (slightly less than half of the total) were burned or destroyed. The invaded territory comprised 71 million hectares under crops and was the chief producer of sugar beet and sunflower, the principal oleiferous plant. The official claim that 85,000 collective farms, 1,800 State farms, and some 3,000 motor tractor stations were restored and resumed operation before the War was over is not easily reconcilable with the equally official statements that the Germans destroyed or removed 7 million horses, 17 million heads of cattle, 20 million hogs, 27 million sheep and goats, 110 million fowl, 137,000 tractors, 49,000 combines, and a vast amount of other agricultural machinery. These staggering losses could hardly have been made good, even in part, within a few months, especially since both manpower and industrial capacity were still being diverted to the gigantic war effort. Agricultural enterprises in the devastated regions in 1945 were surely no more than a mere shadow of their former not too vigorous self.

The Drought of 1946. The plight of farming was aggravated by the drought of 1946, said to be the most severe and widespread since 1891, the year of the great famine, and much worse than the drought of 1921, when the American Relief Mission headed by Herbert Hoover saved so many Russians from starvation.

Official Criticism of Collective Farms, 1946. Soviet agrarian policy was an element in the dire predicament of the farming community. The War revealed that after nearly two decades of collectivization the peasants were longing to escape the strait-jacket of the *kolkhoz,* and that Party and Soviet officials were unwilling or unable to control the situation. A decree of the Council of Ministers and of the Central Committee of the Communist Party of September 19, 1946, stated that "information covering a number of regions" had disclosed "serious violations" of the "Model Charter." Illicit practices were listed under three main headings: wrongful allocation of labor days; spoliation of the publicly controlled land of the farm and other *kolkhoz* property; and disregard for the rules of *kolkhoz* democracy. The irregular allocation of labor days caused an inflated administrative personnel harboring numerous antisocial elements (*rvachi*) and idlers (*darmoedy*) who lived in ease at the expense of genuine collective farmers, with the result that on many farms there developed an acute shortage of labor for work in the fields. Disregard for the rules of the "Model Charter" has produced a situation where some of the collective farmers receive far more than their legitimate share of the revenue of the farm, while others get considerably less. In numerous cases farm revenue is distributed by presidents irrespective of the labor day earnings of the members. Collective farms are frequently compelled by local authorities to provide for officials unconnected with the farm and to render services which are not a part of their lawful obligations (deliveries of fire wood and building materials, construction work, haulage, and so on).

Many farms have on their payrolls barbers, shoemakers, tailors, and other artisans who cater to the private needs of the members and should be paid by them. This wastage of labor days, according to the decree, "leads to the depreciation of the labor day, depletes the revenue distributed on the basis of labor days, and therefore weakens the interest of the farmers in collective endeavor." The decree complained that the warning sounded by the Government and the Party in May, 1939 (see above, p. 824), went unheeded and that "spoliation of the publicly controlled land of the farms has assumed the character of a mass phenomenon." It complained further of two more abuses: (1) enlargement of homestead allotments either by direct seizure of land by the members or by unlawful grants made by *kolkhoz* presidents and executive boards; and (2) appropriation of *kolkhoz* land, with the connivance of *kolkhoz* administration and local Soviet authorities, by local Soviets, government agricultural agencies, and "various organizations and persons" under the guise of creating "subsidiary farms" (*podsobnoe khoziastvo*) and vegetable gardens for workers and employees who are not collective farmers.[26] Other *kolkhoz* properties (cattle, grain, seed, fodder, meat, milk, butter, honey, vegetables, fruit) were disposed of in contravention of the rules. "Some Party and Soviet officials and officers of government agricultural agencies," according to the decree, "instead of protecting the publicly owned properties, that foundation of the *kolkhoz* order, flagrantly violate Soviet laws and, abusing their official position, unlawfully dispose of *kolkhoz* property and revenue, both in kind and cash, by forcing the presidents and executive boards of the collective farms to supply them, freely or at nominal prices, with articles of equipment, cattle, and produce belonging to the farms." The decree held that these abuses undermined the morale of *kolkhoz* leaders and encouraged them to tread the path of wrongdoing. Official agencies, moreover, neglected to pay the collective farms for goods delivered and services rendered, thus depriving them of legitimate revenue. *Kolkhoz* democracy fared no better than *kolkhoz* finance. On many collective farms, according to the decree, general assemblies were not convoked, members were denied participation in the affairs of the farm which were administered exclusively by the executive boards or the presidents. Elections of officials were no longer held and the tenure of those in office was extended beyond the prescribed term. "The situation has reached such extremes," said the decree, "that *kolkhoz* presidents are appointed and dismissed by Party and Soviet organs without even notifying the collective farms."

Its Effects. The decree ordered the elimination of abuses and strict adherence to the "Model Charter." Land of which the collective farms were unlawfully deprived was to be restored to them by November 15, 1946; general assemblies were to meet and election of officials to be held not later

[26] This practice was encouraged during the War by authorizing local authorities to grant permission to "industrial enterprises, agencies, organizations, and army units" to cultivate the waste land of the collective farms (Decree of the Council of People's Commissars and of the Central Committee of the Communist Party of April 7, 1942, revoked by the decree of September 19, 1946).

than February 15, 1947; spoliators of *kolkhoz* property and those responsible for other abuses were to be tried as "lawbreakers and enemies of collectivization"; finally, the decree provided for a Council on the Affairs of the Collective Farms, a new supervisory agency attached to the Council of Ministers.[27] There followed a brisk and searching investigation of the collective farms. By January 1, 1947, 140,000 head of cattle, 15 million rubles in cash, and 4.7 million hectares of land (including 521,000 hectares improperly acquired by *kolkhoz* members) were restored to the collective farms. Four hundred and fifty-six thousand "superfluous" *kolkhoz* officials and 182,000 persons unconnected with the farms were removed from *kolkhoz* payrolls. Those guilty of abuses were dismissed, tried, and given appropriate punishments. Their number has not been disclosed but, judging by the magnitude of the figures just quoted, the 1946 campaign for the restoration of the true principles of collectivization amounted to a major purge.

Farm Legislation, 1947. In February, 1947, a plenary session of the Central Committee of the Communist Party examined the agricultural situation and adopted a lengthy resolution "On Measures for the Advancement of Agriculture in the Postwar Period." The resolution revised upwards the production goals set by the fourth Five-Year Plan, outlined various measures of farm relief, and dealt with the perennial question of incentives and labor organization on the collective farms. The latter part of the resolution was implemented by a decree of the Council of Ministers issued shortly after the plenary session.[28] Acclaimed by Soviet leaders and the press as a major landmark on the road toward Communism, the farm legislation of 1947 strikes an outside observer as singularly stale and unimaginative. It stemmed from the "Model Charter" of 1935 which, according to a Soviet economist (A. Karavaev), "rests upon the granite foundation of scientific Communism." In 1947, as on previous occasions, the many admitted failings of the collective farms were explained away by reference to the laxity and wrongdoing of local officials and to the persistence of *obezlichka* and *urovnilovka* (see above, p. 827), that is, lack of proper coordination between earnings and the work actually done. Since the "Stalin" principles of collectivization enunciated in the 1930's were regarded as sacrosanct and immutable, and since little confidence was put in the willingness of the peasants to abide by them, the Party and the Government inevitably fell back on the familiar method of all-pervasive direction and control reinforced by bounties and penalties.

---

[27] The Council on the Affairs of the Collective Farms was appointed on October 8, 1946. Of its thirty-eight members twenty were *kolkhoz* presidents, two *kolkhoz* officials (including one woman link leader), one director of a motor tractor station, and the balance high Party and Government officials. The Council drew up its own statute which was confirmed by the Council of Ministers on October 22, 1946. The object of the new council is the promotion of collectivization in accordance with the principles of the "Model Charter" and the detection of violations of *kolkhoz* legislation. Although primarily an advisory agency to the Council of Ministers, the Council on the Affairs of the Collective Farms is vested with certain administrative and even judicial powers (imposition of summary penalties for breaches of *kolkhoz* rules).

[28] The decree entitled "On Measures for the Improvement of the Organization, the Increase of Productivity, and the Betterment of the Methods of Remunerating Labor on the Collective Farms" was given wide publicity but did not appear in the official collection of decrees and decisions of the Government.

Indeed, many of the 1947 rules were but a recapitulation of those issued previously, although some went further along the beaten path. Strong emphasis was laid upon the permanent character of the brigades—the requirement that land, equipment, and animals assigned to a brigade should remain under its care for a period long enough to show results (full rotation of crops, in the case of field brigades) and that the personnel of a brigade should be kept together and should not be assigned to other tasks. *Kolkhoz* authorities were enjoined to do everything in their power to enhance the status and authority of the brigadier, who is regarded as the central figure in the drive for higher productivity. The subdivision of brigades into links was to receive wider application, and link leaders were given greater responsibilities and greater authority over the members of their links than heretofore. *Kolkhoz* executive boards were directed to check monthly on the participation of all able-bodied members in the collective work of the farm and to take appropriate measures against the laggards. Similar supervision was to be exercised by local Soviet authorities whose duty it became to ensure that every collective farmer earned the prescribed number of labor days. To prevent the wastage of labor days each *kolkhoz* was requested to prepare, simultaneously with the production plan, a plan of expenditure of labor days—a formidable assignment which is to be carried out in cooperation with, and under the direction of, local authorities. The "norms," or standard amount of work required to qualify for the basic pay, were raised by from 10 to 43 per cent, according to the type of work. All farm work was arranged in nine classes (instead of the seven classes provided in 1933), the rate of pay for the fulfillment of the "norm" rising gradually from 0.5 to 2.5 labor days. The new classification, unlike that of 1933, is supposed to cover every task performed on the farm. The linking of earnings to the yield of crops and animals which was applied to "additional" pay in 1940–1941 (see above, p. 828) was extended to the basic pay by increasing or reducing the number of labor days earned by each strictly in accordance with the results achieved.[29] Similar rules applied to the labor day allowance of *kolkhoz* presidents and to earnings of brigadiers; in both cases emoluments vary according to what may be termed the productivity index of the farm or brigade. *Kolkhoz* officials continue to receive the "additional" remuneration provided in 1940 for yields in excess of planned goals, and bonuses for length of service are paid not only to *kolkhoz* presidents but also to accountants, brigadiers, and heads of the animal husbandry division of the farm.

[29] If a brigade or link fulfills its assignment and obtains the prescribed yield per hectare it is credited with the full number of labor days earned. If, however, the yield per hectare exceeds (or falls short of) the goal, the number of labor days earned is increased (or reduced) by one per cent for each per cent of over- (or under-) fulfillment. Deduction in case of under-fulfillment is limited, however, to 25 per cent of the nominal earnings. The earnings of collective farmers engaged in animal husbandry are determined by the yield and condition (weight) of the animals under their care and the breeding of stock. A barn-maid, for instance, serves from eight to fourteen cows. For each 100 litres (175 pints) of milk yielded by the cows under her care she earns from 1.2 to 1.8 labor days during the pasture season and 2.2 to 3.2 labor days during the barn season. A new-born calf earns for her 7 labor days and if the creature lives to be 15 to 20 days old, 12 labor days.

Farm Legislation, 1948. The 1946 and 1947 decrees did not bring about the anticipated improvement. In the autumn of 1948 the Government issued a decree again directing the collective farms to purge their payrolls of "superfluous" officials. Commenting on the decree *Pravda* complained that in certain regions the number of administrative officers had actually increased since 1946. The decree established statutory limits for the number of labor days that may be assigned for the remuneration of administrative personnel. The limits vary from 3 per cent for farms with an annual payroll of 100,000 labor days to 8 per cent for farms with a payroll of 20,000 labor days. Strict control is to be exercised over the allocation of labor days to administrative officials, who, moreover, must participate in field work.[30]

Titles and Decorations. The foregoing regulations appeal to the self-interest of the collective farmers, but the Soviet Government is aware that man does not live by bread alone. The Kremlin has long followed the practice of conferring titles and decorations upon deserving workers. Opportunities for earning such rewards by farmers and farm and machine tractor station officials were broadened and made more explicit by a decree of the Presidium of the Supreme Soviet of March 29, 1947, implemented by several decrees issued by the Council of Ministers in 1947, 1948, and 1949. Under these regulations a specified yield per hectare entitles the producer to this or that reward. If official reports are to be trusted, Russian farmers are crazy about medals, badges, and honorary titles, odd as this may seem to their opposite numbers in western Europe, the American Middle West, and New England.

Recovery and the Collective Farms. The power of agriculture to recover from even the severest ordeal is immense and unfathomable. The Minister of Finance, Zverev, stated in his report to the Supreme Soviet in June, 1950, that the grain harvest in 1949 reached 7.6 billion puds (one pud = 36 lbs.) and was higher than in 1940, and that the number of "productive" cattle owned by the collective farms was substantially above the pre-War level. In spite of the studied vagueness of these remarks there is no reason to doubt that they correspond to reality. The process of recovery was presumably facilitated by various measures which, being of a technical nature and not bearing directly on the administrative methods of the Soviet Government, were not discussed in this chapter.[31] It is far less probable that the 1947 *kolkhoz* legislation succeeded in remedying the conditions so graphically depicted in the decrees of 1938, 1939, and 1946. The regulations enacted by the Party and the Government in 1947 were, to repeat, merely an elaboration of a pattern of administrative controls that past experience has shown to be singularly unworkable. Unqualified success is, nevertheless, claimed by official spokesmen.

---

[30] The *New York Times*, October 19, 1948. The 1948 decree, like its predecessor, did not appear in the official collection of decrees and decisions of the Government.

[31] The most important among them were, perhaps, the resolution of the Council of Ministers and of the Central Committee of the Communist Party of October 20, 1948, on land reclamation and amelioration, and "The Three-Year Plan for the Development of Animal Husbandry on Collective and State Farms (1949–1951)" issued by the Government and the Party on April 18, 1949. In his report on the 1950 budget Zverev referred to the former measure as "the Stalin plan to reform [*preobrazovaniia*] nature."

In 1947, 1,931 farmers and farm officials were awarded the title of "Hero of Socialist Labor," 4,300 the order of Lenin, 12,500 the order of the Red Banner of Labor, and some 40,000 medals for "Labor Valor" and for "Labor Excellence." These awards may be interpreted as evidence that the farmers are behind the Government. Yet in the same year, according to a Soviet economist (A. Karavaev), "a considerable portion" of the collective farmers failed to earn the prescribed number of labor days and in some regions laggards represented 20 to 25 per cent of the total number of able-bodied farmers. Sporadic denunciations of violations of the "Model Charter" were as frequent and bitter in the late 1940's as they were a decade earlier.

Farm Legislation, 1950. In April, 1950, the Communist Party and the Soviet Government launched a vigorous campaign for the amalgamation of the smaller collective farms into larger units. The acreage of a farm, according to the prevalent view, should not be less than 1,200 hectares. The process of amalgamation is said to be proceeding rapidly. By the end of 1950 the number of collective farms in White Russia (Belorussia) declined from just under 10,000 to slightly over 3,250, and in Ukraine from over 26,000 to below 14,500. It is expected that the total number of collective farms in the USSR will be reduced from some 250,000 to about 100,000 or 110,000. The reasons for the new drive are complex but understandable in the light of past experience. It is claimed that the consolidated farms will have the advantage of large-scale enterprises and will allow the more efficient use of modern agricultural machinery. Amalgamations are expected to cut down *kolkhoz* bureaucracy which is said to account for some 30 per cent of the total manpower, and to release three to four million workers for employment in industry. It is believed that the reduction in the number of farms and the increase in their size will facilitate the task of control by State and Party officials. The status of the farm president will be further enhanced. Amalgamations are to be followed by the resettlement of the collective farmers. *The Economist* quotes the following description of the "agro-town" of the future: "Two thousand beautiful houses along asphalted streets and avenues with lawns. Two thousand two-, three-, and four-storey houses with electricity, radio, water supplies and bathrooms. A central square with a statue of Stalin. Next to each house a fruit garden." If this vision is ever realized it will mean a revolutionary change in the position of the collective farmers. Many of them will be removed from the land they and their forefathers had once owned. Household allotments will presumably disappear and be replaced by "fruit gardens," thus eliminating the opportunity for abuses of which the decrees of 1939 and 1946 so bitterly complained. *The Economist* rightly notes that the 1950 farm program would seem to be inspired by the desire "to reduce the collective farmer to the level of the agricultural labourer working in State farms." [32] However, only fifteen years ago many state farms, because of their poor performance were reorganized as collective farms. Soviet agriculture, indeed, appears to be moving in a vicious circle.

[32] *The Economist* (London), January 27, 1951, pp. 202-203.

THE RESULTS OF COLLECTIVIZATION

The Balance. The time has not yet arrived for a final appraisal of Soviet collectivization. The experiment is too novel and many of its essential features are not yet sufficiently known to offer ground for a clear-cut verdict. It may be plausibly argued that the substitution of large-scale mechanized farming for the tiny holdings, scattered strips, and primitive implements of pre-revolutionary Russia is a definite and important step forward. Those critics of Communism who are bent on idealizing the conditions of the Russian village under the Tsars will do well to read Ivan Bunin's remarkable stories, "The Village" and "The Dry Valley." It is just as difficult, however, to condone the methods by which collectivization was brought about. The "liquidation of the *kulaks* as a class" is one of the most horrible persecutions in recent history, except perhaps the treatment of the Jews in National Socialist Germany. The basic difficulty in agriculture is the same that we have observed in large-scale industry: lack of organizing experience and of technical skill, stifling bureaucratic methods, and the vagaries of "planned economy." Of course it takes time to turn a Russian peasant lad, who has never seen a car, into a tractor driver. Stalin declared, and his statement has become one of the nation's slogans, that it is the purpose of the Soviet Government to make every farmer "well-to-do" (*zazhitochnym*). Whether the standards of living of the peasantry are higher or lower than they were before the drive for collectivization is a controversial question to which no definite answer can be given, but it is certain that they are strikingly below those in western European countries and in the United States.[33] It may be argued with some justice that the defects just mentioned are merely "pangs of growth," that the Soviet experiment is still young and that, provided the organization of agriculture it has created is fundamentally sound, it will in due course prove its superiority over individual capitalist farming.

Is Collective Farming Superior to Individual Farming? This brings up the most difficult question of all: is a collective farm inherently superior to an average capitalist individual farm? The former has the advantage of a larger size and, if and when the Soviet mechanics and agronomists master the technique of intensive agricultural methods, it will probably have a better equipment. That day, however, is still remote. In the meantime the farm managers and brigadiers are struggling under the threat of heavy penalties for failure to meet the often exorbitant demands of the plan, and they are snowed under by a mass of reports, some of them very complex and most of them highly "urgent." The rank and file of the collective farmers are completely in the hands of local bosses on whose pleasure depends their livelihood, and sometimes their freedom and even their lives, for it will be remembered that prior to May, 1947, serious offenses against "Socialist property" were punishable by death and that the decree of January, 1950, restoring

---

[33] A careful statistical analysis of available data has led a recent American student to the conclusion that the productivity of farm labor and the standards of living of both the farmers and the urban population were not higher in 1938 than they were in 1928. See Naum Jasny, *The Socialized Agriculture of the USSR* (Stanford, 1949).

capital punishment may be invoked against recalcitrant farmers. Great as may be the technical advantages of large-scale mechanized agriculture, the whole structure of collective farms appears to be fundamentally vicious. Whether farming can develop and prosper under a regime so arbitrary, capricious, and ruthless remains highly uncertain.

TRADE, BANKING, TRANSPORTATION, PUBLIC UTILITIES AND HOUSING

Foreign and Domestic Trade. State agencies for the administration of the main economic activities other than industry and agriculture must be mentioned, however briefly. The State monopoly of foreign trade, which was established in April, 1918, and has been maintained ever since, exercises exclusive control over all commercial transactions with foreign countries and is administered by the All-Union Ministry of Foreign Trade. The monopoly is properly regarded as one of the pillars of Soviet planned economy.[34] The history of domestic trade is more eventful. By the end of 1918 all private commercial establishments were nationalized, while the stores owned by the consumers' cooperative societies were taken over by the State (decree of March 16, 1919) and became the sole distributive agency. Under the New Economic Policy, restrictions on trade were loosened, consumers' cooperative societies recovered a degree of autonomy, and much of the retail trade was in the hands of small merchants, the so-called *nepmen*. With the advent of planned economy in the late 1920's private traders were squeezed out, consumers' cooperative societies lost most of their precarious independence, and a network of State-owned stores was gradually built. Under the regime of planned economy Soviet domestic commerce may be said to consist of two sectors: the controlled sector which comprises State-owned and cooperative stores, and the uncontrolled sector which is the *kolkhoz* (collective farm) market.[35] Soviet consumers' societies, like Soviet trade unions, have little in common with their namesakes in the Western world, their position being akin to that of a government agency. In 1935, cooperative stores in towns and cities were closed and the activities of consumers' societies were confined to rural districts. After the War, however, consumers' societies were directed to resume operation in urban areas (decree of November 9, 1946). General supervision over domestic trade is exercised by the Union-Republic Ministry of Trade.

Banking and Transportation. All private banks were nationalized in December, 1917, and their assets and functions were taken over by newly organized State-owned institutions of credit. The Soviet Union has a number of banks. The center of the financial system is the State Bank, which is a bank

---

[34] Although the State is the only importer, the Soviet Union has a high customs tariff which is frequently revised. One object of the tariff is, presumably, to discourage enterprises which are run on the principle of "cost accounting" from purchasing machines and other supplies from abroad. The monopoly, of course, can achieve the same result by vetoing imports considered undesirable. For the general trend of Soviet foreign trade see above, p. 774.

[35] See above, p. 819.

of issue. The main functions of the other banks are the floating of Government loans and the financing, partly through budget appropriations, of the State-owned and cooperative enterprises. In connection with the latter function the banks exercise what is known as "control by the ruble," that is, funds to which an enterprise is entitled are made available only after it has produced evidence of the fulfillment of its assignments under the plan. There is an extensive network of State savings banks which was reorganized in November, 1948. Railways, shipping, the post, the telegraph, and the telephone are all under State management.

Public Utilities and Housing. Public utilities—electric power, gas, water, street cars and buses—as well as most of the dwelling houses are administered by the municipalities (city and town Soviets). The cooperative societies for the building of dwelling houses, the last refuge of private investments (except for Government bonds), were liquidated in 1937 and their properties were taken over by the municipalities and Government agencies. Individual citizens, however, may own houses (although not the sites on which they are built), a right guaranteed by Article 10 of the Constitution. The sale and purchase of dwelling houses is permitted under certain restrictive conditions.[36] A decree of the Presidium of the Supreme Soviet of August 26, 1948 (implemented by a decree of the Council of Ministers of the same date), encouraged the building of individual dwelling houses by directing local authorities to allocate building sites for this purpose. The size of the site varies from 300 to 1,200 square meters, land is granted in perpetuity, and the owner pays the rent "prescribed by the law." The houses are one or two stories high and may contain from one to five rooms. Bathrooms are not mentioned. The dwelling houses are described as the personal property (*lichnaia sobstvennost*) of those who build them.

Bureaucratic Nature of Controls. The administrative organs in charge of these varied activities are bureaucratic in their nature, that is, officials are appointed from above. The trade unions have the same functions as in industry— to strive for the fulfillment and overfulfillment of the plan, for labor discipline, and for higher productivity. The methods of encouragement are everywhere the same: premiums, bonuses, piecework wages, organization of workers into brigades, "Socialist emulation," fostering of the Stakhanov movement. There is everywhere an elaborate system of penalties for those who lag behind and keep out of step. It will be remembered that the law on the Judiciary of August, 1938, established two special courts to deal with breaches of labor discipline and with disorganization of work on the railroads and in water transport.

[36] Article 182 of the Civil Code of the RSFSR provides that the family group (married couple and children under age) may own only one dwelling house, and only one sale of a house is permitted every three years. The corresponding article of the Ukrainian Civil Code provides that the family group may own as many as three houses.

SOCIALISM VS. PRIVATE ENTERPRISE

Tentative Conclusion. It will appear from this cursory survey that Soviet Socialism was established, not by proving in the process of market competition the "unchallengeable superiority" of nationalized industry over private enterprise,[37] but by the simpler method of Government fiat. The same is even more true of agriculture. The private entrepreneur is gone, but whether his disappearance has brought about the end of "the exploitation of man by man" is necessarily a matter of opinion. The rule of the huge and unwieldy bureaucracy, backed by an all-powerful Party, is stern, harsh, and often erratic. Its mistakes have been many and costly. The Soviet Union has undoubtedly succeeded in revolutionizing agriculture and in building up in a remarkably short time a huge machinery of production. The cost of the ambitious venture in terms of money and human suffering has been extraordinarily high. The uncertainties and difficulties confronting the managers of business under Socialism are at least as formidable as those under capitalism. There is no indication that the solution of these difficulties is in sight. The position of labor does not compare favorably with that of the workers in the United States, Great Britain, or France. The incentives to work, although similar to those in the capitalist countries—greater reward for those who do better work—are reinforced by a formidable array of penalties for those who fail and are therefore deemed inimical to the regime. Even when full allowance is made for the relatively short time the Soviet experiment has been in operation there is nothing in the record to justify its claim to superiority over a system based on private initiative and private enterprise.

[37] See above, p. 788.

CHAPTER VIII

SOVIET DEMOCRACY IN RELATION TO THE CITIZEN AND TO THE WORLD

THE WELFARE STATE

Betterment of Economic and Cultural Standards. The betterment of the economic and cultural standards of the masses is the avowed paramount aim of Socialism and Communism. In the USSR the Communist Party and the State control and direct not only social security, public health, and the schools but also all manifestations of spiritual and cultural life. These activities will be briefly surveyed in the following pages.

Social Security. The social security program includes a variety of measures which, because of the Soviet administrative setup and budget procedure, may be conveniently divided into three groups. Sickness and disability insurance, maternity benefits, facilities for recreation ("parks of culture and rest," rest homes, sanatoria) and sports, and some of the disability and old-age pensions come under the heading of "social insurance" (*sotsialnoe strakhovanie*) and are administered (since 1933 when the People's Commissariat of Labor was abolished) by the All-Union Central Council of Trade Unions and its agencies. The rehabilitation of disabled persons and the majority of old-age, disability, and other pensions (including pensions of war veterans) are classified as measures of "social security" or relief (*sotsialnoe obezpechenie*) and are administered by the republican Ministries of Social Security of the constituent and autonomous republics. Aid to mothers of more than two children comes within the category of "social security," but appears as a separate item in the federal budget. All wage-earners, but not the members of collective farms and other cooperative associations, are included in the social insurance schemes which are noncontributory, that is, the entire cost is borne by the enterprises or by the public treasury. Sickness and disability benefits vary according to the length of continuous employment in the same enterprise from 100 per cent of the earnings (for those employed over six years) to 50 per cent (for those employed less than two years). Benefits payable to non-trade unionists are half as much as those payable to trade union members.[1] Unemployment insurance was abolished in 1930 when the USSR developed a shortage of labor. Expenditure on social insurance, which is an item in the federal budget, increased from 1.1 billion rubles in 1928–1929 to 5.2 billion in 1937, and to 7.4 billion in 1940; it declined to 5.0 billion in 1945, but rose to 9.3 billion in 1947 and to 18.1 billion in 1950. The growth of budget appropriations for social security (in the narrow meaning of the term, as indicated above) was even more striking: 107 million rubles in 1928–1929; 1.3 billion in 1937; 1.0 billion (a decline) in 1940; 17.7 billion in 1945; and 22.4 billion in 1950. War pensions were responsible for the manifold increase of expenditure under this heading in the last decade. Aid to mothers of large families was first introduced in 1936, but was greatly extended by a decree of the Presidium of the Supreme Soviet of July 8, 1944. Under this enactment the birth of a third child entitled the mother to a bonus of 400 rubles, and the birth of a fourth child to a bonus of 1,300 rubles and a monthly allowance of 80 rubles. There was a progressive scale of benefits: every child in excess of ten brought a bonus of 5,000 rubles and a monthly allowance of 300 rubles. Allowances are payable until the child has reached the age of five. Unmarried mothers received a monthly allowance of 100 rubles for the first child, 150 rubles for the second, and 200 rubles for three or more children. The same decree established the "Medal of Motherhood" (two classes, for mothers of five and six children), the decoration "Glory of Motherhood" (three classes, for mothers of seven, eight and nine children), and the title "Mother Heroine" (for matrons who "have given birth to and reared" ten children). A decree of November 25, 1947, however, cut all the pecuniary benefits payable to mothers by half, on the ground that the purchasing power of the ruble had risen. Budget expenditure on aid to mothers was 956 million rubles in 1937, 2.1 billion in 1945, and 5.9 billion in 1947, but declined (after the benefits were cut by half) to 4.0 billion in 1950.[2] To complete the picture it may be added that appropriations for the Ministry of Public Health rose from 661 million rubles in 1928 to 8.6 billion in 1937, to 11.1 billion in 1945, and to 22.0 billion in 1950.

The Social Security Program Appraised. The mounting cost of the social security program suggests higher standards of welfare. It would be hazardous, however, to assume that larger expenditure reflects with any degree of accuracy the actual improvement in social services. The absence of an index of prices makes a comparison of monetary outlays in various years largely meaningless. Basic information on the essential features of the social security system is lacking. The number of people drawing old-age (or any other) pensions is not disclosed although it was reported that in 1937 it was merely 125,-000 in a population of some 170 million.[3] The minimum monthly rates of dis-

---

[1] Decree of December 28, 1938, issued jointly by the Council of People's Commissars, the Central Committee of the Communist Party, and the All-Union Central Council of Trade Unions.

[2] The decree of November 25, 1947, estimated the annual cost of aid to mothers, after the reduction of benefits, at about 3 billion rubles.

[3] Harold Denny in *The New York Times,* August 8, 1937.

ability and old-age pensions provided by the decree of December 28, 1938, which is still in force, are almost ridiculously low: 25 to 50 rubles for pensioners having no dependents, and 25 to 75 rubles for those with two or more dependents. The minimum rates of pensions payable to dependents of a deceased wage-earner are 30 to 40 rubles per month, and those payable to dependents of a veteran of World War I as low as 7.5 to 22.5 rubles. Disabled veterans of World War II fare better: their pensions are either a specified percentage of their pre-War earnings (100, 75, or 50 per cent, according to the degree of disability) or 75 to 150 rubles per month. A decree of January 28, 1946, increased the monthly pensions of totally disabled ("group I") veterans to 300 rubles (250 rubles if they are "connected with farming"), provided disability was incurred in active service at the front; in all other cases (accident, sickness) pensions of totally disabled veterans are lower by 20 per cent than the foregoing rates. The upper limit of pensions payable to members of the academic profession is 300 rubles a month, but distinguished scientists, writers, composers, and others, as well as their families, are sometimes granted higher pensions by Government decrees. The figures quoted above should be compared with those of the average monthly earnings of workers and employees which were 287 rubles in 1938 and 500 rubles in 1950. To turn to another field, 64,000 vacancies in sanatoria and 120,000 in rest homes were to be available in 1950,[4] a number hardly adequate to accommodate 33.5 million workers, to say nothing of their families. Viewed from the standpoint of the benefits received by the citizens, the social security program is singularly unimpressive. This may well explain why practically no factual information on social security is made available.

EDUCATION

Literacy and Growth of the School System. A study of Soviet school policies presents difficulties of a different order from those raised by the social security system. The expansion of the network of schools and the increase in the size of the student body were steady until 1940, although both appear to have suffered a setback during the War and post-War years. The percentage of literacy (for both males and females aged nine and over) rose from 24.0 in 1897, when the first Russian census was taken, to 81.2 in 1939.[5] On the eve of World War II most of the illiterates belonged, presumably, to the older generation (59.1 per cent in the age group 50 and over).[6] The fact that the Imperial Government enacted, as far back as 1908, a law aiming at compulsory

---

[4] These figures refer to rest homes and sanatoria managed by the Central Council of Trade Unions and are quoted by N. Rytikov in *Bolshaia Sovetskaia Entsiklopediia* (*Large Soviet Encyclopedia*), supplementary volume on the USSR (1948), p. 1150. The fourth Five-Year Plan sets for 1950 the much higher goal of 250,000 vacancies in sanatoria and 200,000 in rest homes. Whether the two sets of figures refer to the same group of institutions is uncertain.

[5] If the lower age limit of literacy is put at seven, as was customary in Russian prerevolutionary school statistics, the picture would have been less favorable.

[6] The 1940 decree on State Labor Reserves, however, provided that boys (sixteen to seventeen) drafted in the factory training schools need not have any previous school training (see above, p. 803). Presumably the number of boys in that age group who never went to school was not negligible.

school attendance, by 1922, of all children aged eight to eleven detracts nothing from the achievements of the Soviets. According to Stalin's report to the Eighteenth Congress of the Communist Party, 20,600 schools were built in 1933–1938, and the number of students increased from 23.8 million in 1933–1934 to 33.9 million in 1938–1939. In 1950, if the assignments of the fourth Five-Year Plan are carried out, the Soviet Union was to have 193,000 primary and secondary schools with 31.8 million students; the number of students in technical secondary schools was to reach 1,280,000, and those in higher schools 674,000. The total number of students in 1950, as estimated by the plan, was to be 33,754,000, or some 150,000 less than in 1938–1939.[7] The retrogression was presumably due to the ravages of war. It is not clear how under these conditions "compulsory school attendance for all children aged seven" could be made effective in 1950, as provided by the fourth Five-Year Plan, especially since the population of the USSR increased from 170 million in 1939 to some 200 million in 1950. Expenditure on schools rose from 21.0 billion rubles in 1939 to 59.5 billion in 1950; that is, it nearly trebled while school facilities expanded but slightly, if at all. A sizable portion of post-War school appropriations, however, was presumably spent on rebuilding the schools destroyed during the War.

Standards of Teaching. Advancement of education cannot be measured entirely in terms of the number of schools and the size of the student body. The standards of instruction are obviously a matter of paramount importance. The level of teaching of pure sciences is an unknown quantity, but there is ample evidence of the dire predicament of the social sciences. What became of the once honorable tradition of Russian learning may be gathered by glancing at the *History of the Communist Party of the Soviet Union* (1938), which has been officially ascribed to Stalin and is available in an English translation. Extolled by Soviet commentators as a revelation and an unfailing guide to Marxism-Leninism, the *History* is a dull, clumsy, and pedestrian compilation packed with gross distortions of familiar facts. Nevertheless, courses in the *History* are an immutable feature of school curricula, and Stalin's dogmatic platitudes and untruths are relentlessly hammered in in classrooms and innumerable study groups organized by the Party, trade unions, and so on. The *History,* indeed, is compulsory reading and a compulsory "source of inspiration" for every Soviet citizen, from farm hands and army privates to cabinet ministers and fellows of the Academy of Science.[8] Education under such auspices is not an unmixed blessing.

[7] It seems likely that the students trained under the State Labor Reserves scheme (about one million) were not included in these figures. Zverev, the Minister of Finance, stated in the Supreme Soviet in June, 1950, that in 1950 the number of students in primary and secondary schools, including technical schools, was to reach 37.9 million, and that of students in the higher schools (including students enrolled for correspondence courses), 1,194,000; that is, his estimates, although not strictly comparable, were higher than those of the fourth Five-Year Plan.

[8] By 1949 nearly 36 million copies of the *History* were printed. It was translated into sixty-six languages.

NATIONAL CULTURES

Local Languages. The official policy of the Soviet Government is to encourage local languages and national cultures. In 1938, newspapers and magazines appeared in some 70 languages, and books in nearly 100.[9] A scrutiny of available figures discloses that, of the 40,000 individual titles (books and, presumably, pamphlets), 1,800 journals, and 8,500 newspapers published in 1938, the Russian language accounted for 33,300 individual titles, 1,400 journals, and 6,400 newspapers. In twenty-eight of the ninety-three languages listed, less than ten titles in each language were published in 1938, and in seven languages only one title.[10] The lone title was not named, but one may surmise that it was the *Communist Manifesto* or an article by either Lenin or Stalin. Does official recognition of languages which provides so abundant a literature really contribute to the cultural advancement of national minorities?

Cultural Autonomy and Russian Nationalism. Much encouragement is given to the cultures of national minorities (literature, art, music, dancing, theatre, handicrafts), provided they do not conflict with Communist orthodoxy and resurgent Russian nationalism. Nationalism in its crudest form— glorification of army leaders and debatable historical figures (Ivan the Terrible, Peter I) and insistence on Russia's alleged superiority over other nations in every field of endeavor—made its appearance in the middle 1930's, probably as a by-product of Stalin's doctrine of "Socialism in one country" and of the worsening international situation. Nationalist exaltation reached a high pitch during the early part of the War when Soviet military fortunes were at low ebb. On November 6, 1941, as the German troops were nearing Moscow, Stalin closed a dramatic appeal to the nation by evoking "the manly images of our great ancestors—Alexander Nevsky, Dimitry Donskoy, Kuzma Minin, Dimitry Pozharsky, Alexander Suvorov, and Michael Kutuzov," a moot galaxy of princes and generals (except Minin), two of them unwisely canonized by the Russian Church. With the easing of the war situation the saints and princes lost some of their popularity in official circles, but the generals retained their high status: Stalin was now one of them. After 1945 nationalism was gradually remodeled as "Soviet patriotism," a philosophy which emphasizes primarily devotion to the Soviet Communist regime while still asserting Russia's past unperishable glories. The resurgence of Russian nationalism tends to narrow down the already limited scope assigned to cultural autonomies of national minorities. One example to illustrate this point will have to suffice. The Communist Party of Tartary, being somewhat short of national heroes, encouraged local talents to pay tribute to Khan Ugedei, son of Genghis Khan and ruler

---

[9] The *History of the Communist Party* asserts that in Imperial Russia "it was prohibited to publish newspapers and books in the languages of national minorities." This widely quoted statement is incorrect. A yearbook of Russian periodicals published in 1912 lists 2,167 newspapers and journals which appeared in thirty-three languages. See I. V. Volfson, editor, *Gazetnyi mir* (*The Newspaper World*), St. Petersburg, 1912.

[10] *Tsyfry o pechati v SSSR* (*Figures of Publications in the USSR*), published by the All-Union Book Chamber (*Vsesoiuznaia Knizhnaia Palata*), Moscow, 1939, pp. 4, 24–26.

in the thirteenth century of what is today the Tartar ASSR. Among the variations on this seemingly innocuous theme was an opera which was acclaimed by Soviet critics as a superb example of the national genius of Tartary. On second thought, however, the Kremlin decided that Tartar nationalism had gone too far. The matter was judged of sufficient importance to warrant a public rebuttal by the Central Committee of the All-Union Communist Party. A widely publicized decision of the Central Committee branded Ugedei as a reactionary feudal lord (so were, of course, Alexander Nevsky and Dimitry Donskoy) and leader of predatory raids into Russian territory. Admiration for Ugedei was held to be evidence of narrow sectional nationalism incompatible with Soviet ideology. Tributes to Ugedei were withdrawn from circulation, and the opera glorifying the hapless Khan was pronounced devoid of artistic merit and was dropped from the repertory. The Soviet writer who relates this curious episode states that "Comrade Stalin has given the classic formula for the advancement of culture and art of the peoples of the Soviet Union: culture national in form but Socialist in content, this is the path which will eventually lead to the creation of a universal Socialist culture." [11] Whether a work of art has merit is determined by its conformity with Stalin's rule.

INTELLECTUAL FREEDOM AND THE "PARTY LINE"

"Socialist Realism." The disgruntled Tartar authors and composers may find solace in the thought that, from the standpoint of freedom of creative self-expression, their Russian brethren fare no better than they do. Conformity with the "Party line," capricious yet rigid, is mandatory for every one in the USSR and prevails in every field of creative endeavor, from genetics and linguistics to literature, art, music, the theatre, architecture, and cinematography. There are few Soviet intellectuals of any prominence who, at some time or other, would not have found themselves on the horns of the dilemma: either to bow to Party dictation and recant their "errors," or to be deprived of the possibility of continuing their work. "Socialist realism," which is mandatory, is opposed to the deadly sin of "formalism," or "art for art's sake." The true contents of Soviet art, according to one authority, are "ideological chastity— Soviet patriotism, defense of the motherland, happiness of the free life of toil, love for the great leader Stalin"; [12] or, in more prosaic terms, art is the mouthpiece of Soviet propaganda. It does not necessarily follow that no creative work of real value is done in the USSR. To take a familiar example, Serge Prokofieff, whose professional career began in the prerevolutionary days, is among the leading contemporary composers, as is probably the much younger Dimitry Shostakovich. It would be easy to name Soviet scientists, artists, and writers prominent in their respective fields. Yet the fact remains that Communist orthodoxy, which extends to both the contents and the form or man-

---

[11] A Solodovnikov, *"Za vysokuiu ideinost sovetskago iskusstva"* ("For a High Ideological Level in Soviet Art"), in *Bolshevik*, Moscow, October, 1944, pp. 55–57.

[12] *Bolshaia Sovetskaia Entsiklopediia* (*Large Soviet Encyclopedia*), supplementary volume on the USSR (1948), p. 1570. The statement quoted refers to choral music, but it is equally applicable to any other field of creative work.

ner of works of art, is destructive of creative self-expression. The ravages wrought by "Socialist realism" are particularly evident in literature and painting. Since the death of Maxim Gorky (1936) Russian literature has produced no author of comparable stature. It is not, however, the absence of great masters—no political or social system can produce them at will—but the uniform mediocrity of the general level that gives the measure of the decadence of Russian letters. As to painting, an art in which the Russians had never excelled, it has sunk to a new low level.[13] But even in music, whose evasive medium tends to elude control, Communist orthodoxy has produced curious and unexpected results. Instrumental music, by its very nature, is susceptible to a variety of interpretations, some of which may prove embarrassing or even fatal to the composer. Vocal music obviates this danger, unless there is a serious ideological slip as in Tartary; hence the plethora of choral compositions and the truly amazing number of operas. Lenin believed that "cultural revolution" would inexorably follow political revolution. Contrary to his expectations the outstanding characteristic of Russian art after thirty years of Soviet rule is its stale and aggressive conservatism.

The Press. Little need be said about the press. For all the ruthlessness and stupidity of Imperial censorship, prior to the Revolution all shades of opinion —reactionary, conservative, liberal, social-democratic, and revolutionary— were represented by newspapers and journals. Even *Pravda* was openly and legally published in St. Petersburg, although it had frequent difficulties with the authorities and was finally suspended. No censorship is really needed in the USSR (although preliminary censorship is exercised by *Glavlit*) because only Communist papers are permitted to appear. After one has glanced at the insipid and ponderous pages of *Pravda* or *Izvestia* it would be a waste of time to read the other 8,500 papers: they all say the same thing.

The Stalin Prizes. In 1939 the Government established Stalin Prizes to commemorate the sixtieth anniversary of the leader. The prizes are conferred annually for the highest achievements in the field of literature, art, science, technology, and inventions, and the amount of individual awards ranged in 1948–1949 from 20,000 to 200,000 rubles. The list of "Stalin laureates," whose number in 1949 reached the imposing figure of 3,544, contains few familiar names. Many of the awards went to specialists in the technical branches of knowledge whose contributions cannot be assessed by a layman. With few exceptions (Fadeev, Sholokhov, Ehrenburg, Alexis Tolstoy) "laureates" in the division of *belles lettres* are unknown abroad. The roster of prize-winning composers, headed by Prokofieff and Shostakovich, is more impressive. The poorest showing is, probably, in the division of social sciences. For instance, the *History of Diplomacy* edited by V. P. Potemkin (three vol-

---

[13] Roger Marvell, art critic of a left-wing English journal, wrote of an exhibition of Soviet graphic art at Burlington House, London: "Those who believe . . . in the importance of environment would expect from the U.S.S.R. an art remarkably unlike our own. And what in fact we get is an art like that of our most academic and genteel practitioners, an art that, coming from anywhere else, would be labeled dismally bourgeois." *New Statesman and Nation,* February 10, 1945.

umes, 1941 and 1945), a third-rate textbook according to Western standards, was awarded two first prizes of 200,000 rubles each: in 1941, for volume I, and in 1945, for volumes II and III.

THE CHURCH

The Church and the State. Communism is an avowed enemy of religion. The inevitable predicament in which the Russian Orthodox Church found itself after the Bolshevik Revolution was aggravated by the close ties between the Church and the fallen regime and by the uncompromising anti-Communist attitude of Patriarch Tichon, the titular head of the Church. Tichon died in 1926, and in 1927 the Acting Patriarch Sergius, Metropolitan of Moscow, issued jointly with the Synod (the governing body of the Church) a declaration of loyalty to the Soviet regime, but these advances met with no response. Antireligious propaganda was freely carried on by agencies sponsored by the Government while the activities of the Church were barely tolerated, closely watched, and narrowly circumscribed. A new chapter in the relations between the Church and the State was opened with the German invasion of the USSR. From the first day of the War, Sergius, and in a lesser degree the bishops and the clergy, displayed militant patriotism. The Acting Patriarch exhorted the faithful to rally to the defense of the Soviet Union; unfrocked the clerics and excommunicated the laymen who collaborated with the enemy in the occupied territories; and organized, financed, and dispatched to the front a tank column and an air squadron named, respectively, after Dimitry Donskoy and Alexander Nevsky, the two warrior-saints evoked by Stalin in his address of November, 1941. Sergius, in his numerous messages, addressed Stalin in such terms as "divinely appointed leader of our armed and cultural forces" and invoked the blessing of the Lord upon his "great deeds" (message of November 7, 1942). These efforts brought their reward. Antireligious propaganda was toned down, antireligious publications were suspended on the convenient pretext of shortage of paper, and in November, 1942, Nicholas, Metropolitan of Kiev, was appointed a member of a committee of ten to investigate the crimes of Fascist invaders, a body that showed no undue attachment to the Christian principles of mercy and forgiveness. At the end of August, 1943, the Acting Patriarch and the Metropolitans of Leningrad and Kiev were received by Stalin and Molotov, and early in September Sergius was elected Patriarch by a council of Russian bishops. In October, 1943, the Council of People's Commissars established a five-man Council on the Affairs of the Orthodox Church, headed by a Communist official. The Church thus gained a degree of official recognition, the benefits of which were not slow in showing themselves. Since 1943, the Patriarchate of Moscow has been publishing a journal, a theological seminary for the training of priests was opened in 1944, and although no religion is taught in the schools, religious propaganda and religious instruction of children would seem to be permitted. Decorations and medals were conferred upon ecclesiastical dignitaries and clerics for their participation in the war efforts, especially in the guerrilla warfare.

Patriarch Alexis. Sergius died in May, 1944. Alexis, Metropolitan of Leningrad, was elected Patriarch of Moscow and All Russia by a large council attended by representatives of the Russian clergy and laymen and those of Orthodox Churches and communities abroad (January–February, 1945). Alexis continued the policy of cooperation with the Government inaugurated by his predecessor. Soviet victories were celebrated at solemn masses, and the part allegedly played in them by Stalin, "beloved supreme leader of our people, and of our own army" (message of May 2, 1945), was extolled by the Patriarch in appropriate messages. In agreement with the Kremlin, Alexis vehemently denounced the Vatican for its attempt to intervene on behalf of German war criminals, and Russian ecclesiastical dignitaries were active in the Near East and, especially, in southeastern Europe, lending to Soviet officials the support of the Church in the process of implanting Communist dictatorship in the guise of "people's democracies." The Moscow Patriarchate was also instrumental in the destruction of the Uniat Church which follows the Greek Orthodox rites but recognizes the supremacy of the Holy See, and which severed its relations with the Russian Church at the end of the sixteenth century. The majority of the Uniats live in the districts annexed by the Soviet Union from Poland. Early in 1946, after the Uniat Metropolitan and four bishops were arrested by Soviet authorities on charges of collaboration, the Uniat Church "spontaneously" repudiated the Pope and returned to the fold of Moscow. This development meant, of course, the elimination, or an attempt at the elimination, of Roman Catholic influence in what the Kremlin regards as an important area.

An Appraisal. There is no reason to believe that Soviet leaders have renounced the antireligious doctrines of revolutionary Marxism.[14] The position of the Kremlin is clear: it is using the Church, as it had used its Western democratic allies, as tools for the implementation of the grand strategy of Communism—the elimination of the capitalist environment and the consolidation of Soviet rule both at home and over the countries which came under its sway. It is far less certain whether the Church acted wisely in assuming the part of a minor partner in the execution of Communist designs. The concessions secured by the Patriarchate are niggardly and revocable at will, but the loss of moral authority is great. To put War and post-War developments in their proper setting it is well to remember that intolerance toward dissenters and other religious denominations, militant anti-Catholicism, aggressive nationalism, and subservience to the State are all part and parcel of the tradition of the Russian Church. The one, but vital, difference between the prerevolutionary and the present position of the Church is that the Imperial regime was the patron of Orthodoxy while Communism is its deadly enemy.

---

[14] "These measures [those enacted after the outbreak of the War] do not violate the basic decree of the Soviet power on the separation of the Church from the State and the Schools, and they in no way indicate that the Communist Party and the Soviet State have changed their attitude towards religion and religious prejudices which still command considerable following among the population." A. Kolosov in *Bolshaia Sovetskaia Entsiklopediia* (*Large Soviet Encyclopedia*), Supplementary volume on the USSR (1948), p. 1780.

SOVIET DEMOCRACY

Is the Soviet Union a Dictatorship? Stalin was on solid ground when he told the Eighteenth Congress of the Communist Party that the Soviet Union was "an entirely novel Socialist State, unprecedented in history." But what is this novel State? The USSR is commonly referred to as a dictatorship; this practically self-evident interpretation, however, is not generally accepted. In their monumental study of Soviet Communism published shortly before the 1936 Constitution was adopted, Sidney and Beatrice Webb maintained that the Soviet Union was "the very opposite of a dictatorship." [15] They based this conclusion on an examination of Soviet statutes in which they found nothing to justify the dictatorial powers of Stalin either in the State or in the Party. The Party, too, they argued, cannot be an instrument of the dictatorship because it has no standing in law, a situation which has since been altered by Article 126 of the Constitution, although this article added nothing to the supremacy the Party had enjoyed from the early days of the Bolshevik regime. The Webbs' grievous misrepresentation of Soviet political institutions was due, in part, to their applying to the USSR British constitutional standards. They appear to have overlooked the fact that, while England, in the apt phrase of the eminent Anglo-Russian jurist and historian Sir Paul Vinogradoff, is a country governed by "the rule of law and the manly spirit of freedom," both these elements are as alien to Soviet administrative practice as they are to Russia's historical tradition.[16]

The Official Point of View. The Moscow leaders themselves are anything but helpful in clarifying the nature of the Soviet State. According to the Communist view the USSR is both a dictatorship of the proletariat and a democracy. Stalin's statement to the effect that the Constitution preserves intact the dictatorship of the working class and the leading position of the Communist Party has already been quoted.[17] Yet he insisted in his report to the Eighteenth Congress of the Party that "no one dares to question that our Constitution is the most democratic in the world." The contradiction of these two assertions, which are invariably coupled in Soviet pronouncements, suggests that the term "democracy" has in the USSR a meaning that differs from the one accepted in the United States and in the democratic countries of Western Europe.

The One-Party State. The backbone of the political structure of the Soviet Union is the Communist Party. The one-party State, the Soviet's contribution to political theory and to the practice of government, has been duplicated in Fascist Italy, National-Socialist Germany, and in the "people's democracies" established after the War in the countries under Soviet dominion. The

---

[15] Sidney and Beatrice Webb, *op. cit.,* p. 434.

[16] The Webbs were handicapped by their inability to use the Russian language and also, presumably, by their determination to find in the Soviet Union the promised land of the Fabian dream. They made "the frank admission" that they did not understand what was meant by the phrase "dictatorship of the proletariat" (pp. 440–441) and they quoted, seemingly with approval, the statement that "in the OGPU corrective camps they teach not only reading and writing, but also political wisdom" (p. 590).

[17] See above, p. 756.

Party controls all the activities of the nation and is itself bound together by unfaltering adherence to the "Party line" and absolute obedience to the leader.

Stalin's Position. Stalin's dictatorial powers rest on his uncanny control of the Party machine and his total ruthlessness in exterminating potential opposition. The turning point in his political fortunes (and in the history of the Soviet Union and of the world) was his appointment as Secretary-General of the Central Committee of the Communist Party on April 3, 1922. This office, which he has never relinquished, assured Stalin the extraordinary position he has held for nearly thirty years. It was not until May, 1941, when he unexpectedly became Chairman of the Council of People's Commissars, that Stalin divested himself of the quasi-anonymity of *une eminence grise*. Other public offices and titles followed one another in rapid succession: chairman of the State Defense Committee (June, 1941), People's Commissar for Defense (July, 1941), Marshal of the Soviet Union (March, 1943), Generalissimo (June, 1945). Since the autumn of 1941 Stalin has been officially referred to as Supreme Commander-in-Chief of the Soviet armies, but Soviet sources, including Stalin's official biography which lists his offices, decorations, and titles ("Hero of Socialist Labor," "Hero of the Soviet Union"), shed no light as to when he was appointed to this position. These spectacular developments in Stalin's career added nothing to the power that was his in the days when he shunned public office, but they wrought a revolutionary change in his appearance: the unadorned tunic he invariably wore at public functions gave place to a snug, ornate uniform with rows of medals. Otherwise things remained as they were before.

The Stalin Cult. No other public figure in the Western world is the object of adulation such as surrounds Stalin. He is invariably referred to as "the genius," "the leader of the peoples" (always in the plural), "the beloved," "our own" (*rodnoi*). His opinions are never questioned; his pronouncements, however trite and pedestrian, are treated as revelations. He is protected from even a suspicion of criticism by the controlled press and by the denial to Soviet citizens of the right to travel abroad. Every official must see to it that the rules of the Stalin cult shall be strictly observed. André Gide, the French novelist, visited the Soviet Union in 1936 as a guest of the Government. He delivered the valedictory at Maxim Gorky's funeral in the Moscow Red Square. While traveling in the Caucasus Gide passed through Gori, Stalin's birthplace, and as a matter of courtesy decided to send him a message of greeting. The telegraph employee refused to accept his wire because he addressed Stalin as "you." This, Gide was told, could not be done. Stalin must be addressed as "you, leader of the workers" or "you, master of the peoples" or something to this effect.[18] Since 1936 the ritual has been revised in the sense that Stalin must be addressed in more intimate terms of personal endearment. To love Stalin and to give vent to the feeling of affection is the duty of every Soviet citizen. The obligation is even more stringent in the case of Party members. Never was Stalin more enthusiastically acclaimed than at the Party congress in March,

[18] André Gide, *Return from the U.S.S.R.* (New York, 1937), pp. 45–46.

1939. The body of men and women who shouted themselves hoarse in proclaiming Comrade Stalin's imperishable glory (one of the delegates referred to him as "eternal," a fortunate inspiration that threw the Communist assembly into a paroxysm of delirious ovations) had only recently lost most of their leaders and an extraordinarily high percentage of their own number as a result of the purge. Innumerable instances of shocking abuses and mistreatment of the rank and file of the Party were cynically displayed in the report presented to the congress by Zhdanov. Yet not a single voice was raised to criticize the man who had ordered the purge and who alone had the power to stop it.

An Illustration. The following list of accomplishments ascribed to Stalin by a widely circulated publication may serve as a fair sample of Soviet hierolatry: "creator of scientific history of Bolshevism," "the greatest scientist of all time," "the greatest military genius of all time and all peoples," builder of "the scientific foundation of Soviet foreign policy," author "whose work constitutes an era in the history of science." Moreover, "the genius of the great Stalin inspires every branch of knowledge. Stalin's directions are the guiding star that leads the work of our outstanding scientists. Stalin's personal concern (*zabota*) with the advancement (literally, blossoming) of scientific and technical thought has brought remarkable results." [19] The front pages of Soviet papers are filled with "spontaneous" tributes to Stalin coming from individuals and groups in every station in life. "All my thoughts, all my feelings, are directed toward Comrade Stalin," V. L. Komarov, president of the Academy of Science, declared on the occasion of his seventy-fifth anniversary. "Joseph Vissarionovich—our friend, teacher, and leader—helps every man and woman to live and to create. Every one has many tales of what he owes in his life to the genius of Stalin"—(*Pravda,* October 15, 1945). It will be noted that restraint and understatement are not characteristics of Soviet tributes to the leader. It is a wonder that this sort of thing could be kept going for over two decades.[20]

What Is Political Democracy? The monopolistic position of the Party in the Soviet State and the complete control of the Party by Stalin give a very definite and grim meaning to the phrase "dictatorship of the proletariat," which the Webbs found it impossible to comprehend. Nevertheless, the Soviet leaders have a certain formal justification for describing the USSR as a democracy since the Constitution has introduced universal suffrage and the direct secret ballot. How this dual system works in practice has already been explained.

[19] S. F. Kaftanov, *Vydaiushchaiasiia rol laureatov stalinskoi premii v razvitii nauki i tekhniki v SSSR* (*The Outstanding Place of Stalin-Prize Laureates in the Development of Science and Technology in the USSR*), verbatim report of a lecture delivered before the All-Union Society for the Propagation of Political and Scientific Knowledge (Moscow, 1949), pp. 5–6.

[20] Bad example is contagious. According to Joseph E. Davies, United States Ambassador to Moscow in 1936–1938, Stalin "gives the impression of a strong mind which is composed and wise. His brown eyes are exceedingly kind and gentle. A child would like to sit in his lap and a dog would sidle up to him." (Joseph E. Davies, *Mission to Moscow,* New York, 1941, pp. 356–357.) These lines were written by Mr. Davies in the midst of the great purge. Presumably not without the approval of the Department of State, *Mission to Moscow* was made into a film in which Mr. Davies, impersonated by a most engaging actor, modestly assumed the rôle of savior of the world.

Universal suffrage and direct secret ballot, however, are merely the tools of democracy in the sense that the term is used outside the totalitarian countries. The essence of political democracy is the right to hold and express freely views that do not agree with those of the group in power. Organized opposition is a vital element of a modern democratic system, an element that is indispensable to the efficient and orderly conduct of the business of government. Great Britain has officially recognized the importance of the dissenting minority by providing a salary for the leader of "His Majesty's Opposition" in the House of Commons. The one-party State is the antithesis of political democracy in the accepted meaning of the term.

The One-Party State and the Old-Fashioned Autocracies. The methods of the one-party State are just as different from those of the old-fashioned autocracies, such as Imperial Russia, Royal Spain, or, perhaps some of the South and Central American republics, as they are from democratic procedure. It will be recalled that in Imperial Russia the franchise was limited, the powers of the State Duma were parsimoniously measured out and frequently infringed by the Government. The official slogan was "do not get together" (*ne skopliatsa*), that is, public gatherings were looked upon with suspicion as a potential source of danger to the regime. Under the Soviet rule, on the contrary, "to get together" has become a duty; the masses are not only permitted but are forcibly encouraged to vote, and the elective assemblies enjoy in theory the widest powers. On every conceivable occasion the tramping of millions of feet resounds in the streets of Moscow, just as it did in those of Rome and Berlin in the days of Mussolini and Hitler. Nevertheless the assembled multitudes and their accredited representatives are far more obedient and docile than are public opinion and parliament under any other form of government. The apparent paradox may be explained by paraphrasing the German adage: *"Und der König absolut wenn er unsern Willen tut"*—the king has absolute power if he does what we want him to do. The reverse is true of the modern one-party State: the people have absolute power provided they do as they are told by the leader through the instrumentality of the Party. This is the real meaning of democracy in the one-party State, whether Soviet, Fascist, or National Socialist. On the other hand, through its rule by Government fiat, the Soviet regime is the continuation of a tradition that has been the curse of Russian history since the unification of the country under the Grand Dukes of Moscow and, perhaps, even earlier.

THE TEST OF WAR

Victory. War is the supreme test of the stability of a political regime. The Soviet Union withstood the strain and stress of unexampled defeats and the exaltation of victory, the dictatorship of Stalin and the Communist Party emerged unimpaired from the ordeal, and pre-War administrative and economic policies remained practically unchanged. As a consequence of the War the USSR has expanded its territory, extended its dominion over a number of formerly independent States, and for a year or two after the end of hostilities held an extraordinary high place in the council of nations. Soviet historiography does not understate the part played by the USSR in victory and, indeed, interprets the defeat of Germany and Japan as conclusive evidence of the superiority of the Soviet system. The participation of the Western allies in the struggle is seldom mentioned, except to emphasize that delays in establishing a "second front" in Europe were responsible for the German advance into Russia.

Disaffection. There is, however, another side to the picture which is never mentioned in the Soviet Union and has received little attention abroad: the poor showing of the Red Army in the early stages of the War [21] and the powerful movement of disaffection among both troops and the population of the occupied territories, a movement that appeared to threaten the very foundation of the Communist rule.[22] During the first four months of the Soviet-German War, according to German data quoted by Nicolaevsky, 3.9 million Soviet soldiers surrendered to the enemy and by the spring of 1942 the number of Russian prisoners in German camps had risen to 5.5 or 6 million, a probably unprecedented record in the history of any war. Not less notable was the large proportion of prisoners who expressed the desire to bear arms against the Soviets. In one camp nearly half of the inmates (over 12,000 out of 26,000) signed a petition to this effect. It would be unwarranted to draw broad conclusions from fragmentary data, but the fact of widespread disaffection among the Soviet troops may be regarded as established.[23] Army units recruited among Russian *émigrés,* prisoners of war, and members of national minorities (Ukrainians, Armenians, and so on) were organized by the German command. By the autumn of 1942, according to Nicolaevsky, the number of men enrolled in, or affiliated with, these formations ran into "hundreds of thousands." By far

[21] According to Hopkins, at a dinner in Teheran (1943) Stalin "said that in the winter war against Finland the Soviet Army had shown itself to be very poorly organized and had done very badly; that as a result of the Finnish War the entire Soviet army had been reorganized; but even so, when the Germans attacked in 1941, it could not be said that the Red Army was a first-class fighting force. That during the war with Germany, the Red Army had become steadily better. . . ." R. E. Sherwood, *Roosevelt and Hopkins* (Harper & Brothers, New York, 1948), p. 790.

[22] This section is largely based on a study by B. I. Nicolaevsky, *Porazhencheskoe dvizhenie 1941–1945 godov i General A. A. Vlasov* ("The Defeatist Movement of the Years 1941–1945 and General A. A. Vlasov"), in *Novyi Zhurnal (The New Review),* New York, 1948, vol. XVIII, pp. 209–234, and vol. XIX, pp. 211–247, and two articles by George Fischer, "The New Soviet Emigration," and "General Vlasov's Official Biography," in *The Russian Review,* New York, 1949, vol. 8, No. 1, pp. 6–19, and vol. 8, No. 4, pp. 284–311. Both Nicolaevsky and Fischer visited Russian "displaced-person" camps in Europe and interviewed their inmates. Nicolaevsky, a careful historian and journalist, has also drawn on Russian newspapers published during the War in occupied Europe, on the records of the Nuremberg trials, and on the archives of Alfred Rosenberg, German Minister for the Eastern Territories in 1941–1945. The documentation is avowedly incomplete and much of it appears to have been deliberately destroyed by Soviet authorities.

[23] This conclusion is corroborated by Stalin's frantic appeals to the Allies and by the state of dismay, bordering on despair, that prevailed in the Kremlin. On July 31, 1941, Stalin told Hopkins that "he would welcome the American troops on any part of the Russian front under the complete command of the American Army" (Sherwood, *op. cit.,* p. 343). In a message to Churchill of September 4, 1941, Stalin spoke of the "mortal menace" facing the Soviet Union. He asked the impossible: establishment of a "second front" in the Balkans or in France before the end of the year, delivery of 30,000 tons of aluminum by the beginning of October, and a monthly minimum aid of 400 airplanes and 500 tanks. "Without these two forms of help," Stalin wrote, "the Soviet Union will either suffer a defeat or be weakened to

the largest number of volunteers were prisoners of war. A plan for the amalgamation of the scattered Russian units into a "Russian Liberation Army" is said to have been approved by Field Marshal von Brauchitsch in November, 1941, but its execution was delayed by lack of agreement among the German authorities. It was not until the end of 1944, when the fortunes of war turned definitely against Hitler, that the Russian Liberation Army came into existence, and even then it did not include all Russian military formations. The army was commanded by A. A. Vlasov, a former lieutenant-general of the Red Army. Vlasov (1900–1945) was son of a peasant, a veteran of the Russian civil war, a member of the Communist Party, and an outstanding officer of the Soviet general staff. He took a prominent part in the defense of Moscow in 1941, but was made prisoner by the Germans a year later and almost immediately threw himself into the work of organizing an anti-Soviet Russian army under German auspices. According to Fischer, the Vlasov movement claimed a following of about 300,000, but its combatant effectives did not exceed one division which, moreover, took little active part in fighting. The disproportion between the number of Soviet nationals and Russian *émigrés* in occupied Europe (estimates vary from 8 to 15 million), on the one hand, and the actual size of the Russian Liberation Army, on the other, is partly (but not entirely) explained by the difficulties in obtaining equipment and the half-heartedness of the German command about the whole matter.

Repatriation. The tribulations of Russian nationals in occupied Europe did not end with the termination of the War. Under the terms of the Yalta agreement (February, 1945) the displaced nationals of the signatory powers were to be repatriated. The strict enforcement of this provision by Allied commanders led to suicides, disorders among the displaced persons, and mass flights of Russian inmates of the camps. Forced repatriation was discontinued in the American zone in 1946 and in the British zone in the spring of 1947. The number of Soviet nationals turned over to the Soviets, and the fate that befell them, are not known. Vlasov and the other leaders of the Russian Liberation Army ranked high in the Soviet list of "war criminals." They were handed to the Red Army, tried, and hanged in Moscow.

Significance of the Movement. It may be significant that in the human flotsam that gathered under Vlasov's banner were many ranking Red Army

---

such an extent that it will lose for a long period any capacity to render assistance to its Allies. . . ." (W. S. Churchill, *The Grand Alliance*, Houghton Mifflin, Boston, 1950, pp. 455–456.) A few days later, as an alternative for the "second front," Stalin advanced a different plan. "It seems to me," he wrote to Churchill on September 15, "that Great Britain could without risk land in Archangel twenty-five or thirty divisions, or transfer them across Iran to the southern regions of the USSR." Commenting on this proposal Churchill writes: "It was almost incredible that the head of the Russian Government with all the advice of their military experts could have committed himself to such absurdities. It seemed hopeless to argue with a man thinking in terms of utter unreality" (*ibid.*, pp. 462–463). The pressing requests for a "second front" and the dispatch of American and British troops to the USSR are characteristic of the limitations of Stalin's vision. Thinking in the familiar terms of masses of Russian soldiers plodding wearily through the mud and slosh of their roadless plains "the greatest military genius of all time and all peoples" was incapable of grasping the self-evident and immense difficulties involved in a major amphibious operation.

officers and men formerly holding responsible positions in the Communist Party and Soviet administration. The success of the Soviet Government in checking disaffection and in restoring the morale of the army may, perhaps, be explained by the utter ruthlessness of the Germans in the occupied territories, and by the equally ruthless measures employed by the Kremlin to restore order and obedience. It is also arguable that the generous flow of Lend-Lease (over $11 billion) helped to strengthen the hold of the Moscow Government by relieving shortages and by providing tangible proof of the close cooperation between Soviet Communism and the Western democracies. The fact that in 1943–1945 three autonomous republics and an autonomous region were wiped off the map and their population "resettled elsewhere" [24] is additional evidence that the disaffection movement was a factor of considerable magnitude and that the Government suppressed it with an iron hand.

MARXISM AND THE SOVIET REVOLUTION

Internal Developments. The Soviet revolution raises a host of nice problems of Marxian analysis. Some of them have already been mentioned. By a curious paradox the triumph of revolution in Russia and its subsequent course demonstrate the fallibility of the Marxian prognosis and, indeed, may be construed as its negation. Contrary to the expectations of Marx, based on his "scientific" analysis of the capitalist society, the revolution took place not in an advanced industrial State, but in the backward agricultural Empire of the Tsars, a country for which Marx had the greatest contempt. The establishment of the dictatorship of the proletariat was not brought about by the inexorable contradictions at work in a capitalist society; on the contrary, the Soviet Union has been industrialized because it is governed by a proletarian dictatorship. The State has not withered away, the army is huge, and the bureaucracy omnipresent and omnipotent.

Foreign Relations. The international doctrines of Marx, Lenin, and Stalin fit ill into the realities of the situation. The Soviet Union, especially since the acceptance of Stalin's theory of "Socialism in one country," has been in a dual position: on the one hand, it is the leader of the international proletariat in the struggle against capitalism; on the other hand, it is heir to the Empire of the Tsars and a great national and nationalistic power. These two elements have been often in conflict, but it would seem that from the middle of the 1920's to about 1943, when the defeat of Germany appeared imminent, national considerations (determination to build up the "Socialist homeland" which required peace and the cooperation of capitalist countries, and later the exigencies of the defense of the Union) were uppermost in Soviet foreign policy, the advancement of world revolution having been relegated to the background. Fascism, especially its German brand, had been invariably represented by Stalin and his lieutenants as the last stage of "decaying capitalism," and the chief aim of capitalism, of course, is the destruction of the Soviet Union. Yet Stalin aligned himself for a time with Hitler, and later was forced

[24] See above, p. 741.

into an alliance with the capitalist Western democracies, an alliance that was instrumental in saving the Soviet Union from a "mortal menace" and probable defeat. The emergence of Communist dictatorships ("people's democracies") in a number of countries in Eastern and Southeastern Europe, again, was the result not of the inner contradictions within the capitalist societies of Rumania, Yugoslavia, Czechoslovakia, *et al.,* but of the relentless pressure of the Red Army which was imposed upon these unhappy countries not without the connivance of the Western capitalist powers, a situation that neither Marx nor Lenin had foreseen.

Theory and Realities. It is not easy to force these bewildering and conflicting developments into the strait jacket of a dogmatic scheme. This may well explain why the commission for the revision of the program of the Communist Party of the Soviet Union, appointed in 1939, has given no sign of life. Whatever the qualms of the pundits of Marxism, practical-minded Communists have no ground for alarm. If Socialism means the elimination of private enterprise and public ownership of means of production, the Soviet Union is definitely a Socialist State.[25] Communist influence throughout the world has immensely increased and the destruction of the capitalist environment, on which, according to Stalin, depend both the security and the future of the Communist commonwealth, is making steady progress both in Europe and in the East. What, from the Western point of view, was a fantastic nightmare a decade ago is a reality today. The theoretical predicament of Communism is due not to the course of world events but to the insistence, contrary to all evidence, on the infallibility of the Marxian dogma.

SOVIET DEMOCRACY AND THE WORLD

The Comintern. The ebb and flow of the interest taken by the Kremlin in the promotion of world revolution, and the consequent fluctuations in Soviet foreign policy, are epitomized by the history of the Third (Communist) International, or Comintern. The Third International, a world-wide alliance of the Communist parties, was established in Moscow in March, 1919.[26] Its charter provided that "The Communist International has for its purpose the struggle by all available means, including armed force, for the overthrow of the international bourgeosie and the creation of an international Soviet republic as a transition stage to the complete abolition of the State." A manifesto issued by the Second Congress of the International amplified the foregoing statement by adding that the "international proletariat will not lay down its sword until Soviet Russia has become a link in the federation of the Soviet republics of the world." Officially there was no connection between the Soviet Government and the International, but the latter was entirely dominated by Soviet leaders,

[25] Since Tito's break with Moscow, the Yugoslav Communist Party has looked upon the Soviet system as a poor specimen of Socialism. In 1950 the Yugoslav Party reached "the very important decision" that the Russian Soviet system is not Socialism.

[26] The First International was organized by Marx and Engels and functioned from 1864 to 1872; the Second International was established in 1889 but was eventually repudiated by the Communists as lacking in revolutionary spirit, and became extinct after World War I.

had its headquarters in Moscow, and was, presumably, financed by the Soviets. No wonder, therefore, that the activities of the International closely reflected those of the Soviet Government. True to its charter and in agreement with the early militant attitude of Moscow, the International in the beginning held its congresses yearly in 1919, 1920, 1921, and 1922. The Fifth Congress met in 1924, the Sixth in 1928, and the Seventh and last, after several delays, in 1935. The decline of the interest taken by the Soviet leaders in world revolution is indicated by the growth of the intervals between the congresses. Moreover, the Sixth Congress, held in 1928, produced the International's new program which was largely the work of Stalin and Bukharin, who was later executed during the great purge. The program, while retaining the inflammatory phraseology of Marx's *Communist Manifesto,* introduced some important modifications in the revolutionary doctrine. The most significant among them was the strong emphasis on the duty of the world proletariat to defend the Soviet Union against the capitalist nations. Although the International never repudiated the revolutionary theories of its founders, its character has suffered an unmistakable change: from the militant leader of the revolutionary world proletariat it became primarily an institution for the defense of the Soviet Union against capitalist "aggression." Moreover, the practical influence of the International both in Russia and abroad was negligible. The "general staff of the world revolution" led in Moscow the obscure and uneventful existence of a minor government department. Yet the very presence of the headquarters of the International in Moscow and its close although unofficial association with the Soviet Government not only indicated the dual nature of the Soviet State (as a national power and the leader of world revolution) but were also a source of embarrassment in matters of foreign policy.

Litvinov's Pledges. The provisions of the charter of the International quoted above were obviously incompatible with some of the obligations entered into by the Soviet Government. For instance, Litvinov gave President Roosevelt on November 16, 1933, the pledge that it would be the fixed policy of the Soviet Government "not to permit the formation or residence on its territory of any organization or group—and to prevent the activity on its territory of any organization or group, or of representatives or officials of any organization or group—which has as an aim the overthrow of, or the preparation for the overthrow of, or bringing about by force of a change in, the political or social order of the whole or any part of the United States, its territories or possessions." This pledge was clearly inconsistent with the existence in Moscow of an organization such as the Comintern. The State Department, however, showed good judgment in not insisting on the fulfillment of a promise incompatible with the Communist doctrine and inserted in the agreement, presumably, to pacify a section of Congressional opinion. What seemed impossible under peacetime conditions became feasible during the War. As Lend-Lease supplies poured into the USSR and momentous international decisions bearing on the future of the world were in the making, the Kremlin, proceeding on the principle that *Paris vaut bien une messe,* ordered the Comintern to dissolve itself. The act of dissolution (May 22, 1943), a verbose, long-drawn-out and awkward document which few took the trouble to read, made it plain that the abolition of the Comintern was a purely organizational matter and in no way signified the repudiation of world revolution.[27] Western statesmen, newspaper editors, and news commentators inclined to take the opposite view. Enthusiasm for Soviet resistance ran high, and it was a pleasing thought that the great Eastern Ally had at last renounced its revolutionary eccentricities and had returned to the fold of "normalcy."

The Cominform. It was a rude awakening when on October 5, 1947, Moscow announced that at a conference held in Poland at the end of September the international organization of Communist parties had been revived. There is an essential difference in the position of the Comintern and that of the Cominform, as the new organization came to be known: in the 1920's and the 1930's the chances of international Communism were practically nil; this statement is no longer true in a world shattered by the War.

Coexistence with the Capitalist Nations. After the exhuberance of the early months of the revolution had subsided and the unwillingness of other countries to follow Russia along the path of revolution had become patent, the Soviet Union settled down to a protracted period of peaceful coexistence with the capitalist world. There were, of course, frictions and disturbing incidents, but Moscow did nothing to threaten even remotely international peace. Russian Communism remained strictly a domestic product. Prior to 1939 not a single country embraced the Communist creed. The Soviets withdrew into their shell and played but a minor part in international affairs. The fact that the USSR was not represented in Munich on the fateful day of September 29, 1938, was symbolic of Russia's eclipse as a great European power.

The Stalin-Hitler Pact. The Stalin-Hitler Pact of friendship and non-aggression (August 23, 1939) marked the dramatic reappearance of the Soviet Union on the stage of world politics. The Kremlin had negotiated simultaneously with Germany and with England and France, but the English and the French Governments did not go far enough in meeting Soviet wishes; there were particular difficulties about the border States which, suspecting what was in store for them, refused to allow the "temporary" occupation of their territory by the Red Army. It was easy for Hitler to outbid London and Paris. The

[27] The resolution of the Presidium of the Executive Committee of the Communist International of May 22, 1943, said in part: "The whole development of events in the last quarter of a century and the experience accumulated by the Communist International convincingly showed that the organizational form of uniting workers, chosen by the first congress of the Communist International, answered conditions of the first stages of the working-class movement, but it has been outgrown by the growth of this movement and by the complications of its problems in separate countries and has even become a drag on the further strengthening of the national working-class parties. . . . Guided by the judgment of the founders of Marxism and Leninism, Communists have never been supporters of the conservation of organizational forms that have outlived themselves. They have always subordinated forms of organization of the working-class movement, and methods of working of such organization, to the fundamental political interests of the working-class movement as a whole, to the peculiarities in the concrete historical situation and to problems immediately resulting from this situation. . . . The Communist International, as the directing center of the international working-class movement, is to be dissolved, thus freeing the sections of the Communist International from the obligations arising from the statutes and resolutions of the congresses of the Communist International. . . ."

Soviet-German agreements sanctioned the annexation by the Soviet Union of Eastern Poland, Latvia, Estonia, Lithuania, and Bessarabia and gave Moscow a free hand in Finland. What were the motives behind Stalin's decision to side with Hitler? They were probably mixed: lack of confidence in the Western powers; fear of Germany; quest for security in the traditional meaning of the term; nationalistic ambitions to recover the territories lost by Russia in 1917–1918; desire to spread the Communist gospel in the annexed territories; security, in the Communist meaning of the term, by eliminating capitalist environment. Moreover, the Soviet-German pact made war in Europe a certainty and wars, according to Lenin, lead to revolutions. The German invasion was a terrible price to pay for the machinations and miscalculations of the Kremlin, yet at the end of the War which was fought under the banner of freedom and democracy the Soviet Union relinquished none of its ill-acquired gains and, indeed, expanded them. It is arguable, however, that since Hitler was clearly determined to fight the Soviets it might have been sound national policy for Moscow to let Western Europe bear the brunt of the German onslaught and to postpone Soviet participation until the German war machine had lost some of its driving power and cooperation of the Western nations was definitely assured. On the other hand, according to von Ribbentrop, deliveries under the Soviet-German trade agreements "were carried out by the Soviets according to schedule until the last day before the rupture," [28] and Soviet historiography, which credits Stalin with unfailing foresight, makes one exception to this rule: according to the official view the German attack was both unprovoked and unforeseen.

Post-War Policies. The motives of Soviet post-War policies conform more closely than those of the earlier period to a definite pattern directed at the achievement of the central goal set by Stalin—the elimination of capitalist environment. By capitalist environment I mean not the "predatory" rule of "monopoly capital" or "Wall Street" but the sum total of the political, economic, and social institutions which form the common heritage of the Western world and which we call Western civilization. The Soviets strive to attain their objective through a variety of means: outright annexations; military occupations which led to the establishment of "people's democracies"; removal of capital equipment by way of reparations, a policy which not only undermined the capitalist structure of Germany but had profound and disastrous repercussions on the economic conditions of other countries; trials of "war criminals" and denazification which have shattered the social structure of the former totalitarian countries where affiliation, often nominal, with the ruling party was mandatory for everyone in any position of prominence; the veto power of the permanent members of the Security Council of the United Nations which reduced the international organization to impotence; finally, "war by proxy" in Korea. The passionate advocacy of many of these policies in the United States and in Western Europe (dismantling of German plants, trials of war criminals, denazification, the veto power) detracts nothing from the fact that in the final

[28] *The New York Times,* June 23, 1941.

analysis these measures serve well the main object of Soviet Communism—the elimination of capitalist environment. Fomentation of disaffection in the colonial empires and of extreme nationalism among the "under-developed" or "backward" peoples is another formidable weapon in the arsenal of Moscow.

Lenin Again. Nearly fifty years ago, in the course of a seemingly futile controversy with the Mensheviks over the desirability of cooperation with the liberal bourgeois groups in the struggle against autocracy, Lenin laid down the rule that the revolutionary proletariat may use the bourgeoisie as a tool but should never support it as an ally. This is the principle applied by the Kremlin in its relations with the Western powers. Another principle traceable to Lenin may be helpful in understanding the essence of Soviet democracy. *Iskra* (*The Spark*), a paper founded by Lenin in 1900, carried on its front page the proud device: "From the spark—the conflagration." In 1900 the Russian Social-Democratic Party, precursor of the Communist Party, was a mere spark but from it came the conflagration which consumed the Empire and is spreading throughout the world. From their experience the Soviet leaders have learned the lesson that sparks lead to conflagrations, and they take no chances. The stamping out of sparks, that is, the destruction of any potential opposition, is the only branch of administration in which the Kremlin has achieved unrivaled efficiency. A firm grasp of this principle which has been extended to "people's democracies" is essential to a comprehension of the mechanics of Soviet democracy.

Theory and Practical Policies. It may be argued that in the interpretations offered in these pages undue prominence is given to Communist dogma. Scholasticism is repugnant to the Western tradition. "Marxism-Leninism," says the journal of the Central Committee of the Communist Party, "is a scientific world-theory of the Bolsheviks which guides the Party in all its practical activities." [29] One is tempted to discount such statements, but an examination of Soviet policies discloses their conformity with the "Party line." The Soviet system is, intrinsically, a godless theocracy governed by an order whose members are bound together by a mesh of closely interwoven personal interests and are committed to the Marxian revelation as interpreted by Lenin and Stalin.

[29] *Bolshevik,* September, 1944, p. 1.

BIBLIOGRAPHICAL NOTE
ON THE USSR

SUGGESTED READINGS

The number of authoritative books on Russia available in the English language is surprisingly small. Those who desire to obtain a broader understanding of Russia should familiarize themselves with the Russian classics—Griboedov, Gogol, Turgenev, Dostoevsky, Chekhov, Tolstoy, Gorky, Bunin—whose works have been translated into English. The books listed below deal more directly with Russian government and politics.

Part I. Russia Before the Bolshevik Revolution

Badayev, A., *The Bolsheviks in the Tsarist Duma* (New York, International Publishers, 1929). An account of the activities of the Russian Social-Democratic Party under the Imperial regime by a former Bolshevik member of the Duma.

Chamberlin, W. H., *The Russian Revolution, 1917–1921* (New York, Macmillan, two volumes, 1935). A good history of the revolution.

Curtiss, J. S., *Church and State in Russia: The Last Years of the Empire, 1900–1917* (New York, Columbia University Press, 1940). A sound and reliable survey of position of the Russian Church under the Empire.

Florinsky, M. T., *The End of the Russian Empire* (New Haven, Yale University Press, 1931). A historical explanation of the fall of the monarchy.

Gronsky, P. P., and Astrov, N. J., *The War and the Russian Government* (New Haven, Yale University Press, 1929). A useful discussion of the central and municipal government.

Kerensky, A., *The Catastrophe* (New York, Appleton, 1927). Kerensky's own story of the revolution of 1917.

Kokovtsov, Count V. N., *Out of My Past* (Stanford, Stanford University Press, 1935). Illuminating memoirs of the former Prime Minister and Minister of Finance of Imperial Russia.

Michelson, A. M., Apostol, P. N., and Bernatzky, M. W., *Russian Public Finance during the War* (New Haven, Yale University Press, 1928). A reliable account covering the War and the pre-War period.

Miller, Margaret S., *The Economic Development of Russia, 1905–1914* (London, P. S. King and Son, Ltd., 1926). A dependable historical survey.

Pares, Sir Bernard, *The Fall of the Russian Monarchy* (New York, Alfred A. Knopf, 1939). An attempt to explain the revolution by the influence of the Empress and Rasputin.

Polner, T. J., and others, *Russian Local Government during the War and the All-Russian Union of Zemstvos* (New Haven, Yale University Press, 1930). A useful study of the development and achievements of local government.

Robinson, G. T., *Rural Russia under the Old Regime* (New York, Longmans, Green and Company, 1932). A good account of rural conditions prior to the revolution.

Trotsky, L., *The History of the Russian Revolution* (New York, Simon and Schuster, three volumes, 1932). Trotsky's revolutionary classic.

Zagorsky, S. O., *State Control of Industry in Russia during the War* (New Haven, Yale University Press, 128). A careful and penetrating study.

Part II. The USSR

Arakelian, A., *Industrial Management in the U.S.S.R.* (Washington, Public Affairs Press, 1950). Translation of a study published by the Soviet Academy of Sciences in 1947.

Arnold, A. Z., *Banks, Credit, and Money in Soviet Russia* (New York, Columbia University Press, 1937). A well-documented and sound discussion of monetary and financial policies.

Baykov, A., *Soviet Foreign Trade* (Princeton, Princeton University Press, 1946). A factual and statistical study.

Baykov, A., *The Development of the Soviet Economic System* (New York, Cambridge University Press, 1947). A well-documented and thorough but uncritical and dull survey of Soviet economic conditions prior to World War II.

Bergson, A., "The Fourth Five Year Plan," *Political Science Quarterly,* June, 1947. A useful statistical summary.

Berman, H. J., *Justice in Russia* (Cambridge, Harvard University Press, 1950). Dr. Berman provides some useful information on the Soviet judicial system. Unfortunately he is unduly impressed by the "paternal" character of Soviet justice.

Bienstock, G., Schwartz, S. M., and Yugow, A., *Management in Russian Industry and Agriculture* (New York, Oxford University Press, 1944). A reasonable and accurate discussion of problems of management.

Bogolepov, M. I., *The Soviet Financial System* (London, Lindsay Drummond, Ltd., 1945). A useful study by a Soviet authority.

Carr, E. H., *The Bolshevik Revolution, 1917–1923,* vol. I (New York, Macmillan, 1951). A lucid but highly imaginative and personal account of the formative years of the Soviet rule interpreted exclusively in terms of the Bolshevik Party.

Central Committee of the All-Union Communist Party, *History of the Communist Party of the Soviet Union* (New York, International Publishers, 1939). History of the Soviet Communist Party ascribed officially to Stalin.

Chamberlin, W. H., *Collectivism: A False Utopia* (New York, Macmillan, 1937).

Chamberlin, W. H., *The Russian Enigma* (New York, Scribner's, 1943). Two highly critical accounts by the former Moscow correspondent of the *Christian Science Monitor.*

Chamberlin, W. H., *The Soviet Planned Economic Order* (Boston, World Peace Foundation, 1931). Useful discussion of the early stages of planning.

Citrin, Sir Walter, *I Search for Truth in Russia* (New York, E. P. Dutton, 1937).

Citrin, Sir Walter, *In Russia Now* (London, R. Hale, Ltd., 1942). Personal narratives by the former President of the International Federation of Trade Unions who was particularly interested in labor questions.

Dallin, *The Real Soviet Russia* (New Haven, Yale University Press, 1944). A grim picture by a Russian *émigré* historian.

Deutscher, I., *Soviet Trade Unions* (London, Royal Institute of International Affairs, 1950). A common-sense appraisal of Soviet trade unions which, unfortunately, contains several important errors and omissions of essential facts.

Deutscher, I., *Stalin: A Political Biography* (New York, Oxford University Press, 1949). An up-to-date but not very profound interpretation of Soviet history and the Communist leader.

Dobb, M., *Soviet Economic Development since 1917* (New York, International Publishers, 1948). An evaluation of Soviet economic developments from the orthodox Socialist point of view.

Florinsky, M. T., *World Revolution and the U.S.S.R.* (New York, Macmillan, 1933). A study of the evolution of Communist theory and its repercussions.

Grinko, G. T., *The Five Year Plan* (New York, International Publishers, 1930). Official summary by a former Soviet Commissar.

Gsovski, V., *Soviet Civil Law* (Ann Arbor, University of Michigan Law School, two volumes, 1948–1949). A survey of the development of Soviet civil law and a collection of the principal enactments.

Harper, S., and Thompson, R., *The Government of the Soviet Union* (New York, Van Nostrand, 1949). A reasonable study of the Soviet Government.

Hubbard, L. E., *Soviet Money and Finance* (London, Macmillan, 1936).

Hubbard, L. E., *Soviet Trade and Distribution* (London, Macmillan, 1938).

Hubbard, L. E., *The Economics of Soviet Agriculture* (London, Macmillan, 1939).

Hubbard, L. E., *Soviet Labor and Industry* (London, Macmillan, 1942). Four concise, informative, and readable volumes which throw much light on Soviet economic development and policies.

Jasny, N., *The Socialist Agriculture of the U.S.S.R.: Plans and Performance* (Stanford, Stanford University Press, 1949). A monumental, critical statistical study of Soviet agriculture.

The Land of Socialism Today and Tomorrow. Reports and Speeches of the Eighteenth Congress of the Communist Party of the Soviet Union, March 10–21, 1939 (Moscow, Foreign Languages Publishing House, 1939). A most valuable official collection.

Lenin, V. I., *The State and the Revolution* (various editions). Lenin's celebrated discussion of the future of the Socialist commonwealth.

Littlepage, J. D., and Bess, D., *In Search of Soviet Gold* (New York, Harcourt, Brace, 1938). The fascinating story of an American engineer who spent ten years in the service of the Soviets.

Lozovsky, A. *Handbook of Soviet Trade Unions* (Moscow, Cooperative Publishing Society of Foreign Workers in the U.S.S.R., 1937). An official Soviet account.

Petrov, V., *My Retreat from Russia* (New Haven, Yale University Press, 1950). Personal narrative of a former inmate of a Soviet labor camp.

Popov, N., *Outline History of the Communist Party* (New York, International Publishers, 1934). An early official version of the history of the Soviet Communist Party.

Rappard, W. E., Sharp, W. R., and others, *Source Book on European Governments* (New York, Van Nostrand, 1937). Some useful basic documents.

Schwartz, H., *Russia's Soviet Economy* (New York, Prentice-Hall, 1950). A useful array of up-to-date facts and figures.

Smith, W. B., *My Three Years in Moscow* (Philadelphia, Lippincott, 1950). A sound, reliable, and well-documented account by the United States ambassador to Moscow in 1946–1949.

Souvarine, B., *Stalin, A Critical Survey of Bolshevism* (New York, Longmans, Green, 1939). A good history of the Bolshevik movement by the founder of the French Communist Party. The bibliography which appears in the French edition has been omitted in the English version.

Stalin, J. V., *Problems of Leninism* (Moscow, Foreign Languages Publishing House, 1940). A collection of Stalin's writings.

Strong, Anne L., *The New Soviet Constitution* (New York, Henry Holt, 1937). A good translation of the 1936 Constitution and a useful but uncritical survey of earlier constitutional developments.

Timasheff, N. S., *The Great Retreat* (New York, E. P. Dutton, 1946). Some useful information on the social conditions in the USSR which, unhappily, Professor Timasheff interprets as a retreat from Communism.

Towster, J., *Political Power in the U.S.S.R., 1917–1947* (New York, Oxford University Press, 1948). A good account of the structure of the Soviet Government. Some of the author's conclusions, however, are based on slight evidence or would seem to be contrary to the evidence he himself produces.

Trotsky, L., *The Revolution Betrayed* (Garden City, N. Y., Doubleday, Doran, 1937). A bitter indictment of Stalin's rule.

Trotsky, L., *Stalin: An Appraisal of the Man and His Influence* (New York, Harper and Brothers, 1946). A political biography the completion of which was interrupted by Trotsky's murder.

USSR, Council of People's Commissars, State Planning Commission, *The Soviet Union Looks Ahead: The Five-Year Plan for Economic Construction* (New York, Liveright, 1930). An official Soviet statement.

USSR, Council of People's Commissars, State Planning Commission, *Socialist Construction in the U.S.S.R.* (Moscow, Soyuzorgouchet, 1936). Another official Soviet statement.

USSR, Council of People's Commissars, State Planning Commission, *Summary of the Fulfillment of the Five-Year Plan* (New York, International Publishers, 1934). Official record of the fulfillment of the first Five-Year Plan.

Volin, L., *A Survey of Soviet Russian Agriculture* (Washington, D.C., Government Printing Office, 1951). A valuable up-to-date study prepared under the auspices of the United States Department of Agriculture.

Webb, S. and B., *Soviet Communism: A New Civilization?* (New York, Scribner's, 1936). An elaborate but highly imaginative and untrustworthy account of the social structure, government, and planning in the USSR prior to the adoption of the 1936 Constitution.

Werner, M. R., editor, *Stalin's Kampf* (New York, Harcourt, Brace, 1937). A useful, annotated collection of Stalin's writings.

LIST OF PRINCIPAL SOURCES

Books, Pamphlets, and Articles

Aksenenok, G. A., *Pravo gosudarstvennoi sobstvennosti na zemliu v SSSR (Law of State Ownership of Land in the U.S.S.R.)*, edited by Professor N. D. Kazantsev (Moscow, 1950).

Aleksandrov, G. F., and others, *Iossif Vissarionovich Stalin (J. V. Stalin)*, a short biography, second edition (Moscow, 1948).

Aleksandrov, N. G., and Moskalenko, G. K., *Sovetskoe trudovoe pravo (Soviet Labor Law)* (Moscow, 1947).

Andrianov, V., *"Za dalneishee uluchshenie organizatsii i oplaty truda v kolkhozakh"* "For Further Improvement in the Organization and Remuneration of Labor on the Collective Farms") in *Bolshevik,* No. 12 (Moscow, 1948).

Arkhipov, K. A., editor, *Deistvuiushchee zakonodatelstvo po sovetskomu upravleniiu (Soviet Administrative Law)*, arranged by Kuchkel, A. V., and Orlov, R. P. (Moscow, 1926).

Astrakhanov, S., and Brodovich, S., *Administrativnoe zakonodatelstvo (Administrative Legislation)* (Moscow, 1936).

Berdniakov, A. I., and Eidelman, B. I., editors, *Narodnoe khoziaistvo SSSR (National Economy of the USSR)*, collection of articles published in Soviet journals (Moscow, 1948).

Bergson, A., *The Structure of Soviet Wages* (Cambridge, 1944).

Bolshaia Sovetskaia Entsiklopediia (Large Soviet Encyclopedia), especially the supplementary volume on the USSR (Moscow, 1948).

Bubnov, A., *VKP* (b) *(The All-Union Party of the Bolsheviks)* (Moscow, 1934).

Bulletins on Soviet Economic Development, Department of Economics and Institutions of the USSR, University of Birmingham, Nos. 1–4 (Birmingham, 1949–1950).

Davydov, N. V., and Poliansky, N. N., *Sudebnaia reforma* (*Reform of the Judiciary*), two volumes (Moscow, 1915).

Diachenko, V., editor, *Biudzhetnaia sistema SSSR* (*The Budget System of the USSR*) (Moscow, 1937).

Gorshenin, K. P., Orlov, R. P., and Karasev, Ya. A., editors, *Sovetskoe trudovoe pravo* (*Soviet Labor Legislation*) (Moscow, 1938).

Gosplan SSSR, *Piatiletnii plan narodno-khoziaistvennago stroitelstva SSSR* (State Planning Commission, *The Five-Year Plan for the Development of the USSR,* three volumes, third edition (Moscow, 930).

Gosplan SSSR, *Itogi vypolneniia pervago piatiletniago plana razvitiia narodnago khoziaistva SSSR* (State Planning Commission, *Summary of Fulfillment of the First Five-Year Plan for the Development of the National Economy of the USSR*) (Moscow, 1933).

Gosplan SSSR, *Vtoroi piatiletnii plan razvitiia narodnago khoziaistva SSSR, 1933–1937* (State Planning Commission, *The Second Five-Year Plan for the Development of the National Economy of the USSR, 1933–1937*), two volumes (Moscow, 1934).

Gosplan SSSR, *Dvadtsat let sovetskoi vlasti* (State Planning Commission, *Twenty Years of Soviet Power*), a statistical handbook (Moscow, 1938).

Gosplan SSSR, *Itogi vypolneniia vtorogo piatiletniago plana razvitiia narodnago khoziaista SSSR* (State Planning Commission, *Summary of Fulfillment of the Second Five-Year Plan for the Development of the National Economy of the USSR*) (Moscow, 1939).

Gosplan SSSR, *Tretii piatiletnii plan razvitiia narodnago khoziaistva SSSR, 1938–1942* (State Planning Commission, *The Third Five-Year Plan for the Development of the National Economy of the USSR, 1938–1942*) (Moscow, 1939).

Grazhdanskii kodeks (*Civil Code*) (Moscow, 1937).

Karavaev, A., *"O dalneishem ukreplenii selskokhoziaistvennoi arteli"* ("On the Further Strengthening of the Agricultural Artel"), in *Bolshevik,* No. 8 (Moscow, 1948).

Kiselev, Ya. L., and Malkin, S. E., *Sbornik vazhneishikh postanovlenii po trudu* (*Collection of Labor Laws*) (Moscow, 1938).

Kleinman, A. F. *Sovetskii grazhdanskii protsess* (*Procedure in Soviet Civil Courts*) (Moscow, 1938).

Knorin, V., editor, *Kratkaia istoriia VKP* (b) (*Short History of the Communist Party of the Soviet Union*) (Moscow, 1934).

Konstitutsiia SSSR (*Constitution of the USSR*), various editions amended through June, 1950.

Konstitutsiia RSFSR (*Constitution of the RSFSR*), amended through March, 1948 (Moscow, 1948).

Korkunov, N. M., *Russkoe gosudarstvennoe pravo* (*Russian Constitutional Law*), two volumes, seventh edition (Moscow, 1909).

Lazarevskii, N. J., *Lektsii po russkomu gosudarstvennomu pravu* (*Lectures on Russian Constitutional Law*), two volumes, second edition (St. Petersburg, 1910).

Lazarevskii, N. J., *Russkoe gosudarstvennoe pravo* (*Russian Constitutional Law*), vol. I, second edition (St. Petersburg, 1913).

Malenkov, G. M., *O zadachakh partiinikh organizatsii v oblasti promyshlennosti i transporta* (*On the Tasks of Party Agencies in Industry and Transport*), report to the Eighteenth Conference of the Communist Party, February 15, 1941 (Moscow, 1941).

Marx-Engels-Lenin Institute, *Vladimir I. Lenin, A Political Biography* (New York, 1943).

Mikolenko, Ya. F., and Nikitin, A. N., *Kolkhoznoe pravo* (*Legislation on Collective Farms*) (Moscow, 1939).

Miliukov, P. N., *Istoriia vtoroi russkoi revoliutsii* (*History of the Second Russian Revolution*), Vol. I, parts 1–3 (Sofia, 1921, 1922, and 1924).

Nastolnyi kalendar kolkhoznika (*The Collective Farmer's Yearbook*) (Moscow, 1937).

Nolde, Baron B. E., *Ocherki russkago gosudarstvennago prave* (*Studies in Russian Constitutional Law*) (St. Petersburg, 1911).

Plotnikov, K. N., *Biudzhet sotsialisticheskago gosudarstva* (*Budget of the Socialist State*) (Moscow, 1948).

Popov, P., and Tirzbanurt, T., *Okhrana truda—zadacha professionalnikh soiuzov* (*Protection of Labor—A Task of the Trade Unions*) (Moscow, 1939).

Postanovleniia sedmogo plenuma VTsSPS (*Decisions of the Seventh Plenary Session of the All-Union Council of Trade Unions*) (Moscow, 1938).

Postanovleniia vosmogo plenuma VTsSPS (*Decisions of the Eighth Plenary Session of the All-Union Central Council of Trade Unions*) (Moscow, 1939).

Presidium Verkhovnago Soveta SSSR, Informatsionno-statisticheskii otdel. *SSSR: Administrativno-territorialnoe delenie soiuznikh respublik na 1 oktiabria 1938 goda* (Presidium of the Supreme Soviet of the USSR, Bureau of Information and Statistics. *The U.S.S.R.: The Administrative-Territorial Subdivisions of the Constituent Republics on October 1, 1938*) (Moscow, 1938).

Programma i ustav Vsesoiuznoi Kommunisticheskoi Partii Bolshevikov (*The Program and the Charter of the All-Union Communist Party of the Bolsheviks*) (Moscow, 1938).

Prokopovicz (Prokopovich), S. N., *Russlands Volkswirtschaft unter den Sowjets* (Zürich, 1944).

Prokopovicz, S. N., *Vierter Fünfjahrplan der Sowjetunion, 1946–1950* (Zürich, 1948).

Rosenblum, D. S., *Zemelnoe pravo RSFSR* (*Land Law of the RSFSR*) (Moscow, 1929).

Rovinsky, N. N., *Financy SSSR za XXX let, 1917–1947* (*Thirty Years of Public Finance of the USSR, 1917–1947*) (Moscow, 1947).

Rovinsky, N. N., *Gosudarstvennyi biudzhet SSSR* (*State Budget of the USSR*) (Moscow, 1944).

Rychkov, N., *O proekte polozheniia o sudoustroistve SSSR, soiuznikh i avtonomnikh respublik* (*Report on the Bill Dealing with the Judiciary of the U.S.S.R., and That of the Constituent and Autonomous Republics*) (Moscow, 1938).

Shvernik, N., *O rabote profsoiuzov v sviazi s resheniiami vosemnadtsatago sezda VKP* (b) (*On the Work of the Trade Unions in Connection with the Decisions of the Eighteenth Congress of the Communist Party of the Soviet Union*) (Moscow, 1939).

Stalin, J. V., *Marksism i natsionalnyi vopros* (*Marxism and the Question of Nationalities*) (Moscow, 1937).

Stalin, J. V., *Sochineniia* (*Collected Works*), vols. I–XII (Moscow, 1946–1949).

Stalin, J. V., *Voprosy leninisma* (*Questions of Leninism*), eleventh edition (Moscow, 1945).

Sverdlov, G. M., *Sovetskoe zakonodatelstvo o brake i seme* (*Soviet Legislation on Marriage and the Family*) (Moscow, 1949).

Ugolovno-protsessualnyi kodeks (*Code of Criminal Procedure*) (Moscow, 1937).

Ugolovnyi kodeks (*Criminal Code*) (Moscow, 1937).

Vsesoiuznaia knizhnaia palata, *Tsifry o pechati* (The All-Union Book Chamber, *Figures of Publications*) (Moscow, 1939).

Vyshinsky, A. Ya., editor, *Sovetskoe gosudarstvennoe pravo* (*Soviet Constitutional Law*) (Moscow, 1938).

Vyshinsky, A. Ya., *Spravochnik sovetskago rabotnika* (*Soviet Worker's Manual*) (Moscow, 1939).

Vyshinsky, A. Ya., editor, *Sezdy sovetov SSSR v postanovleniiakh i rezoliutsiiakh* (*Congresses of the Soviets of the USSR in Decisions and Resolutions*) (Moscow, 1939).

Zakon o piatiletnem plane vozstanovleniia i razvitiia narodnago khoziaistva SSSR na 1946–1950 gg. (*Law on the Five-Year Plan for the Restoration and Development of the National Economy of the USSR in 1946–1950*) (Moscow, 1946).

Zverev, A. G., Reports on the State budget of the USSR (entitled *Gosudarstvennyi biudzet* or *O gosudarstvennom biudzehete*) submitted annually by the People's Commissar (later Minister) of Finance to the Supreme Soviet in 1938–1941 and 1945–1950 (Moscow, printed separately in the respective years).

Periodicals

Biuleten finansovago i khoziaistvennago zakonodatelstva (Moscow).
Bolshevik (Moscow).
Ekonomicheskaia zhizn (Moscow).
Izvestia (Moscow).
Plan (Moscow).
Planovoe khoziaistvo (Moscow).
Pravda (Moscow).
Sobranie postanovlenii i rasporiazenii pravitelstva SSSR (Moscow).
Sobranie postanovlenii i rasporiazhenii soveta ministrov SSSR (Moscow).
Sobranie zakonov i rasporiazhenii raboche-krestianskago pravitelstva SSSR (Moscow).
Sotsialisticheskaia rekonstruktsiia selskogo khoziaistva (Moscow).
Trud (Moscow).
Vedomosti Verkhovnago Soveta (Moscow).

INDEX